For Henry Shapiro,
scholar, colleague, and friend,
— and one who collects good books!

Jim Finny

THE CORRESPONDENCE

OF

ROBERT DODSLEY

The publishers are grateful to the Division of Research Programs of the National Endowment for the Humanities, a federal agency which supports the study of such fields as history, philosophy, literature, and languages, and which kindly provided a grant towards the costs of production of this book.

CAMBRIDGE STUDIES IN
PUBLISHING AND PRINTING HISTORY

TITLES PUBLISHED

*The Provincial Book Trade in
Eighteenth-Century England*
by John Feather
Lewis Carroll and the House of Macmillan
edited by Morton N. Cohen and Anita Gandolfo
The Correspondence of Robert Dodsley, 1733–1764
edited by James E. Tierney

TITLES FORTHCOMING

Book Production and Publishing in Britain, 1375–1475
edited by Derek Pearsall and Jeremy Griffiths
The Making of Johnson's Dictionary, 1746–1773
by Allen Reddick
Caxton's Early Printing
by Paul Needham

Portrait of Robert Dodsley (1760/1) by Joshua Reynolds
(reproduced by permission of the Governors of Dulwich Gallery)

THE CORRESPONDENCE
OF
ROBERT DODSLEY
1733–1764

EDITED BY

JAMES E. TIERNEY

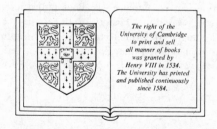

The right of the
University of Cambridge
to print and sell
all manner of books
was granted by
Henry VIII in 1534.
The University has printed
and published continuously
since 1584.

CAMBRIDGE UNIVERSITY PRESS

CAMBRIDGE

NEW YORK   NEW ROCHELLE

MELBOURNE   SYDNEY

Published by the Press Syndicate of the University of Cambridge
The Pitt Building, Trumpington Street, Cambridge CB2 1RP
32 East 57th Street, New York, NY 10022, USA
10 Stamford Road, Oakleigh, Melbourne 3166, Australia

© Cambridge University Press 1988

First published 1988

Printed in Great Britain at
the University Press, Cambridge

British Library cataloguing in publication data
Dodsley, Robert
The correspondence of Robert Dodsley, 1733–
1764. – (Cambridge studies in publishing
and printing history).
1. Dodsley, Robert   2. Booksellers and
bookselling – England – Biography
1. Title   II. Tierney, James A.
381′.45002′0924   Z325.D6/

Library of Congress cataloguing in publication data
Dodsley, Robert, 1703–1764.
The correspondence of Robert Dodsley, 1733–1764.
(Cambridge studies in publishing and printing history)
Includes index.
1. Dodsley, Robert, 1703–1764 – Correspondence.
2. Booksellers and bookselling – Great Britain –
Correspondence.   3. Publishers and publishing – Great
Britain – Correspondence.   4. Authors, English – 18th
century – Correspondence.   5. Book industries and trade –
England – London – History– 18th century.   6. London
(England) – Intellectual life – 18th century.
1. Tierney, James E.   II. Title.   III. Series.
Z325.D68A4   1987   070.5′092′4 [B]   87-14645

ISBN 0 521 25925 8

This work is dedicated to a master Monotype operator, who began it, and to his devoted wife who counted it into existence.

But it must be remembered, that life consists not of a series of illustrious actions, or elegant enjoyments; the greater part of our time passes in compliance with necessities, in the perform-ance of daily duties . . . The true state of every nation is the state of common life . . . they whose aggregate constitutes the people, are found in the streets, and the village, in the shops and farms; and from them collectively considered, must the measure of general prosperity be taken.

SAMUEL JOHNSON
A Journey to the Western Islands of Scotland

CONTENTS

Preface   *page* xiii

Acknowledgements   xvii

Notes on the text   xxi

Cue-titles   xxiii

Chronological list of Robert Dodsley's correspondence   xxvi

Alphabetical list of correspondents   xxxvi

Introduction   I

LETTERS

  A   Letters, 1733–1764   65

  B   Public letters   494

Appendixes

  A   Robert Dodsley's Will   503

  B   1 Abstracts of Robert Dodsley's publishing   506
          agreements, receipts, and bills

      2 Copyrights registered at the Stationers'   530
          Company

      3 Dodsley's purchases of copyrights and stock   531
          at booksellers' sales

  C   Provenance of autograph letters and citations to   534
      major printed versions

  D   Untraced correspondence of Robert Dodsley   546

  E   Correspondence and documents of James Dodsley   555

Index   568

PREFACE

When approaching a major city from a distance, a traveler takes his first impression from the great buildings and structures that dominate its skyline. But if his itinerary carries him around the city and not into it, he leaves with no idea of the many forces energizing that metropolis – the people, systems, institutions, and industries that make it what it is. In somewhat the same way, time obscures our view of history. An age looms out of the past on the strength of a few dozen names that Fortune has made great. But if one settles for this "gentleman's acquaintance," he fails to recognize or to understand those vital, pervading forces that really made daily life go forward in that age, those shoulders on which the great ones stand.

The present work focuses on one major force in eighteenth-century London life whose name and work time has obscured: Robert Dodsley (1703–64), poet, playwright, and bookseller. Actually, the twentieth century has not entirely forgotten Dodsley. Since he served as literary midwife for so many contemporary writers, modern biographers and bibliographers cannot refuse him a place in their pages. Probably it was an awareness of Dodsley's ubiquity in eighteenth-century letters (perhaps assisted by Boswell's recommendation that the bookseller's life be written) that prompted Ralph Straus, in 1910, to write the first, and only, biography of Dodsley. Yet, despite Straus's thorough and lively portrait, his subject gradually receded into the shade as the revival of interest in eighteenth-century studies showed a preference for more "literary" topics. Now the biography, regrettably, serves more often as an obscure mine of information for scholarly notes to other men's works.

Consequently it might surprise even some of those acquainted with the age, that Dodsley was more than just a bookseller, that he was a poet and playwright, as well. In fact, it was in the latter capacities that he got his start in the literary world, as the present collection will demonstrate. For the moment, however, perhaps it will be sufficient to call attention to the nine and a half columns his creative achievements claim in the *British Museum General Catalogue of Printed Books*, or the nineteen pages in the *National Union Catalogue*. That his reputation was still holding sixty years after his death is suggested by the thirty-seven pages his verses occupy, alongside other poets of his age, in Chalmers's standard *Works of the English Poets* (1812). Yet it might prove even more striking to recall that Dodsley had three plays running on the London stage within a single month during 1738, one of them performed every season until 1775.

But times and tastes change. Although his own age honored him with the laurel, posterity has not been so generous, and perhaps justly so. To his credit, Dodsley strove to clothe his verses and domestic scenes in simple style, consciously rejecting the traditional tumid dress awkwardly heaped on middle-class subjects, then taking their place in literature. But this honest, practical assessment of both life and poetry placed restraints on whatever emotive potential he had. At its best, Dodsley's poetry is sensitive, clever, and rhythmical, sometimes even charming. But his verses rarely soar or thrill. And, for us, the themes and perspective that motivate his dramas seem transparent, sometimes even naive.

But as a literate and literary bookseller, who recognized, advised, and patronized genius, Dodsley was not outdone in his century. For this service alone, he justly claims a major place in the history of English culture. Some sense of his contribution is captured in his editing of the twelve-volume *Select Collection of Old Plays* and the six-volume *Collection of Poems by Several Hands*, doubtless his most remembered works. In these, he preserved not only the fullest collection, to date, of early English drama but also the most complete reflection of contemporary poetic taste. Among his hundreds of publications are listed the first major works of many of the age's fashionable and enduring authors, including such names as Edmund Burke, Thomas Gray, Samuel Johnson (who called "Doddy" his "patron"), and Laurence Sterne. To these he added original publications by Alexander Pope, Tobias Smollett, Jonathan Swift, and Edward Young. The extent of his influence was perhaps best captured many years ago by the late Wilmarth Lewis. When founding a social club of distinguished eighteenth-century scholars at Yale, Lewis chose to call it: "Dodsley's Collection."

Some comment should be made regarding the title "bookseller" as applied to Dodsley in his work. Those unfamiliar with the eighteenth-century booktrade are probably unaware that the meanings of "bookseller" and "publisher" have changed considerably during the last two centuries. Today, a bookseller is normally one who keeps a shop where the books of many publishers are displayed and sold. The eighteenth-century bookseller, however, did much more than sell books. Much of his time was spent soliciting, reading, and negotiating the purchase of manuscripts, which he then proceeded to print, publish, advertise, and circulate. In short, an eighteenth-century bookseller functioned much like the modern publisher, except that he also sold books in a retail shop. On the other hand, the eighteenth-century publisher operated on a lower rung of the trade ladder. He rarely purchased copyrights, published primarily pamphlets or short works, frequently served as a distributor for booksellers' wares, and sometimes published works for booksellers to which the latter chose not to put their names. Dodsley, then, operated in much the same way as a modern "publisher." However, because his age called such a tradesmen a "bookseller," that title has been used here.

In addition to the body of correspondence that makes up the substance of this work, several other kinds of related material are found in the appendixes. Appendix A provides a copy of Dodsley's will, as probated in London eleven days after his death. Appendix B stands as an important ancillary to the correspondence. It is comprised of abstracts of Dodsley's publishing agreements with authors, receipts for payments to authors, receipts for copyright purchases, customer book bills, records of copyright registrations at Stationers' Hall, and records of purchases at book auction sales. In many ways, these materials not only complement Dodsley's correspondence but also afford insights to the operation of his business. Appendix C supplies the provenance of surviving holograph letters printed in the collection, at least what has been discovered. Appendix D lists all untraced Dodsley correspondence, either alluded to in contemporary statements or listed in auction house or autograph dealer catalogues. Finally, Appendix E lists the James Dodsley correspondence discovered in the course of the present work, as well as the younger Dodsley's publishing agreements and receipts. Several instances amount to corrections for library catalogues and printed sources where Robert Dodsley is incorrectly cited as either sender or recipient. Their presence in this appendix should clarify their absence from the body of the text.

At the outset, the present work was undertaken as primarily a literary project, an attempt to provide a minor chapter in eighteenth-century literary history. Dodsley's correspondence was used as the link between an extensive list of authors, both major and minor, whose works and inter-relationships constituted the principal interest. In time, a body of new data for the literary historian began to emerge, both from the corpus of unpublished letters and from the annotation they prompted. The work had uncovered much information relevant to contemporary critical opinion in both poetry and drama, the reception of works, anonymous authorship, revisions of works, and author biography. In addition, new perspectives surfaced regarding authors' political and religious persuasions, their personal and literary liaisons and contentions, and the processes by which they secured the publication and circulation of their works. These and related matters continue to fill the following pages.

However, with the more recent encouragement of Cambridge's editors, the project gradually grew beyond these primarily literary concerns to take in the practical aspect of Dodsley's bookselling business, including his relations with the trade. Such a direction was appropriate, for a new scholarly interest in the history of the book had already begun to blossom. These past dozen years, for instance, have seen the inception of the *Eighteenth-Century Short-Title Catalogue*, as well as the founding of such periodicals as *Publishing History*, *Journal of Newspaper and Periodical History*, and *Bibliography Newsletter*. Most recently the study of book history has been significantly encouraged by the filming of the Stationers Company records, Chadwyck-Healey's filming of British and American publishers' archives, and now by this new series on publishing history undertaken by Cambridge University Press. Indeed it would have been unfortunate to have published a work on a major bookseller like Dodsley that did not take into account the practical aspects of his business.

On the other hand, the additional perspective caused further delay in the work's publication, for it introduced a brace of unexpected problems. An editor who blithely sails into a publisher's world soon encounters treacherous waters of perplexing diversity and scope. As David W. Davies once shrewdly observed: "The innocent enthusiast who attempts to follow the activities of a publisher as he moves in the various milieux will constantly find himself in strange regions he knows nothing about. He will probably wish he never entered them, and his learned readers will probably wish so, too" (*The World of the Elzeviers 1580–1712* (1954) p. v). And indeed the attempt to introduce this new material led into strange regions.

Booksellers' use of the eighteenth-century franking system, the inferences to be drawn from booksellers' imprints, contemporary price structures for printing and paper, copyright laws and law suits, distinctions between true editions and simple reprintings, booksellers' modes of payment to authors, the implications of shared printing, the divisions of labor within the book trade and the terms of their relationship – these and other labyrinthian matters drove this editor to harry the experts with unremitting conversations and correspondence. Sometimes, only extensive calculations or collations of masses of bibliographical data supplied an answer, or a hint of one. But a concern for completeness, or definitiveness, was not always rewarded. Perhaps the sagest advice came from one beleaguered, but much respected, correspondent who counseled: "You wish (as we all do) to know what actually once happened, when all you have to go on are bits of the record. There comes a point when one has to be content with half truth (or a guess at it)."

It is hoped that the work does not frequently disappoint students of the eighteenth-century book trade, especially those who have encouraged its completion. At the least, it stands as the fullest collection of Dodsley correspondence and publishing records in print, and perhaps the fullest of any eighteenth-century bookseller available. As such, it should prove of value to the ongoing study of a fascinating aspect of English culture.

ACKNOWLEDGEMENTS

Many pleasures have come of this work over seventeen years. Not the least has been this eleventh-hour opportunity to reflect on the hundreds of persons, institutions, and agencies who have generously furnished or enhanced its stores, or whose advice and support have brought it to fruition. To all, I am deeply indebted and would like to take this occasion to express my sincere appreciation.

Many to whom I am obliged for specific information have been acknowledged in the text. Here I am pleased to recognize the valuable contributions and assistance of others, many of whom go unmentioned elsewhere. If, in the process, I have neglected some generous benefactor, I deeply regret the oversight. How difficult is full payment when so much is owed.

First of all, I would like to acknowledge with special thanks the following who have graciously permitted the printing of manuscript materials from their collections:

Her Majesty, Queen Elizabeth II
Lord John Crichton-Stuart, 6th Marquess of Bute
Lord Henry Frederick Thynne, 6th Marquess of Bath
Birmingham Public Libraries
Lawrence G. Blackmon, Stamford, Connecticut
The Curators, Bodleian Library, Oxford
   Department of Western Manuscripts
   The John Johnson Collection
Department of Rare Books and Manuscripts, Boston Public Library
Department of Manuscripts, The British Library
The Bancroft Library, University of California, Berkeley
Research Center, Colonial Williamsburg Foundation
Department of Special Collections, Norlin Library, University of Colorado
Typographic Manuscript Collection, Rare Book and Manuscript Library, Columbia University
Edinburgh University Library
The Folger Shakespeare Library, Washington, D.C.
The Houghton Library and The Harvard College Library, Harvard University
Historical Society of Pennsylvania, Philadelphia
The Henry E. Huntington Library, San Marino, California
Mrs Mary Hyde, Somerville, New Jersey
Raymond Dexter Havens Collections, Special Collections Division, The Milton S. Eisenhower Library, The Johns Hopkins University
Kenneth Spencer Research Library, University of Kansas
Leicester Record Office
The Lewis Walpole Library, Farmington, Connecticutt

xvii

Methodist Archives and Research Centre, John Rylands University Library of
    Manchester
Robin Myers, London
The Trustees of the National Library of Scotland
New College Library, University of Edinburgh
Henry W. and Albert A. Berg Collection, The New York Public Library. Astor,
    Lenox and Tilden Foundations
The Poetry / Rare Books Collection of the University Libraries, State University
    of New York at Buffalo
Principal Archivist, Nottinghamshire Record Office
The James Marshall and Marie Louise Osborn Collection, Beinecke Library,
    Yale
The Pierpont Morgan Library, New York
Robert H. Taylor, The Robert H. Taylor Collection, Princeton University
    Library
The Royal College of Surgeons of England
The Royal Society of Arts
The Honourable Michael Shenstone, Canadian Ambassador to Austria,
    Vienna, Austria
Somerset Record Office
Humanities Research Center, University of Texas at Austin
Trinity College Library, Oxford
Victoria and Albert Museum
World Methodist Council Museum, Lake Junaluska, North Carolina
For fellowships and grants that afforded the necessary free time, travel, and
assistance to carry on the work, I am obliged to the American Council of Learned
Societies, the American Philosophical Society, the Bibliographical Society of
America, the Henry E. Huntington Library, the National Endowment for the
Humanities, and especially to the University of Missouri–St Louis for generous
funding through every stage of the project.
    The assistance of librarians is a *sine qua non* for a work of this kind. My largest debt
is due the staff of the British Library where most of the research was carried forward
over the years. Librarians and assistants in the Department of Manuscripts, the
North Reading Room, and the Main Reading Room, as well as the staff of the
Eighteenth-Century Short-Title Catalogue, were of inestimable value. Particularly I
would like to thank Michael Crump, Richard J. Gouldon, Charles W. Hind, Mary
Hurworth, and David Paisey, all of whom carefully and patiently dealt with my
queries.
    Likewise, for major assistance with collections under their care, I owe many
thanks to Alfred Andrews, former archivist at the Birmingham Public Libraries;
D. Molly Barratt, Bodleian Library; D. G. C. Allan, Royal Society of Arts; Derek
M. Shorrocks, Somerset County Archivist; Laetitia Yeandel and Nancy Klein
Maguire, The Folger Shakespeare Library; Martha Mahard, Harvard College
Library; Rodney Dennis and Elizabeth Anne Falsey, The Houghton Library,
Harvard; and Beth Riley, formerly of the James M. Osborn Collection, Yale.

For special services, I am also obliged to the following librarians: Susan Bellingham and Charlotte Stewart, McMaster University; Herbert Cahoon and Thomas Lange, The Pierpont Morgan Library; Gene K. Rinkel, University of Illinois at Urbana; Joan Sinar, Derbyshire County Archivist; Linda Stanley, The Historical Society of Pennsylvania; and Peter Van Wingen, the Library of Congress. Likewise I owe many thanks for assistance to the Washington University library staff, including Kenneth Nabors, Terry Keegan, Holly Hall, and, while at UMSL, William Wibbing. At my own university the list of creditors is long, but I would like to mention Mary Doran, Barbara Lehocky, Frank Persche, and, formerly of UMSL, Sally VanAusdal.

To the following collector-scholars, I am obviously doubly indebted. Mrs Mary Hyde of Somerville, New Jersey, shared several pieces from her famed Johnson collection and carefully fielded my queries. Robin Myers's advice on the book trade and her hospitality in London brightened many a rainy day in that city. I much regret that the late Wilmarth S. Lewis and James M. Osborn have not lived to see in print the many contributions they made to this work. The same beneficent spirit has characterized their curators, Stephen Parks at Yale and Catherine Jestin at Farmington, to whom I am obliged for many favors.

The list of scholars who generously responded to my queries is long. When consisting of a single letter or other response, that help has been acknowledged in the notes. But, for extensive or periodic advice, I would like to mention Frank Baker, Duke University; Martin and Ruthe Battestin, University of Virginia; OM Brack, Arizona State University; Francis Burns, Newman College, Birmingham; the late James L. Clifford, Columbia University; Carl W. Conrad, Washington University; Donald D. Eddy, Cornell University; A. C. Elias, of Philadelphia; David Fairer, University of Leeds; J. D. Fleeman, Oxford University; David Foxon, Oxford University; Bertrand Goldgar, Lawrence University; Donald Greene, Professor Emeritus, University of Southern California; Robert Halsband, Professor Emeritus, University of Illinois; Nicholas Lyons, Brigg, Lincolnshire; Keith Maslen, University of Otago; Donald F. McKenzie, Victoria University of Wellington; T. O. McLoughlin, University of Rhodesia; Henry J. Pettit, Professor Emeritus, University of Colorado; Clarence Tracy, Professor Emeritus, Acadia University; and Michael Treadwell, Trent University.

Three scholars deserve particular mention. Michael Shugrue, CUNY-Staten Island, first encouraged and guided my study of Dodsley many years ago at New York University. John C. Riely, Boston University (formerly of Wilmarth Lewis's Walpole team at Yale), and James Woolley, Lafayette College, generously contributed advice throughout the duration of the project.

In addition, I am obliged for favors and advice to N. John Hall, CUNY Graduate School; John Edward Hardy, University of Illinois at Chicago; Michael Harris, University of London; Curt Hartog, Washington University; Gerald Hodgetts, King's College, London; Gae Holladay, University of California at Santa Barbara; John Mulryan, St Bonaventure University; Pierrette Murray, St Louis; Leo Sides, London; Hazel Simpson, London; Henry L. Snyder, University of California-Riverside; Edward Sullivan, University of Illinois, Urbana; David

M. Vieth, Southern Illinois University at Carbondale; and Roy Wolper, Temple
University.

Whether for reading, refereeing, research errands, or computer assistance, I
am obliged to the following colleagues at the University of Missouri–St Louis:
B. Bernard Cohen; Charles T. Dougherty, Professor Emeritus; Robert M. Gordon;
Charles H. Larson; Eugene B. Murray; Jane Williamson; and Peter Wolfe.

Among these attributes, a special place of acknowledgement is reserved for the
late Violet B. Lancaster, sister to Dodsley's biographer, Ralph Straus. Generous
access to Straus's private library marked the beginning of treasured parlor visits
with this grand lady. Her daughters, Heather and Elizabeth, special London
friends, lent early assistance with Dodsley queries and typing chores.

For research into their records or other assistance, I am thankful to the following
autograph dealers: Ifan Kyrle Fletcher, Maggs Brothers; Winifred Myers,
Pickering and Chatto; and Sotheby's, all of London; and Richard Hatchwell, of
Chippenham. For similar research, I owe thanks to the Bank of England; Barclays
Bank, Gosling's Branch; Drummonds Bank; and C. Hoare & Co., Bankers.

For research and secretarial assistance, I was fortunate to have the extraordi-
narily capable services of Joleen Hourihan, David Reis, Mary Lacey, Shirley
Gieble, Kathy Ryan, Regis Propst, and Dorothy Hogue. More recently, Carole
Jerome, in St Louis, and Alison Shell, in London, have done yeoman's service.

Although not of a scholarly character, the support of family and friends has
played a significant role in the course of this work. For understanding, support, and
hospitality, I am grateful to Akhtar Awan, Betty Bostetter, Robin Myers, and
Kathy Williams. My brother, Jack, and sisters, Helen and Kathy, and their
spouses, freely and faithfully supplied both encouragement and material support.
There is little need to elaborate on my mother and father's contribution: to them
the work is dedicated. My wife Susan has played several roles – researcher,
corrector of prose, deadline-watcher, and patient "computer widow" – by all of
which the work was successfully brought to a close.

Finally, I am most grateful to my Cambridge University Press editors. Terry
Belanger and David McKitterick have contributed their wisdom on the history of
the book; Kevin Taylor has graciously borne missed deadlines; and Caroline Hull
has honed the manuscript into publishable shape. To Terry Belanger, I owe many
thanks for bringing the manuscript to the attention of Cambridge.

NOTES ON THE TEXT

a) *Style*. The texts of the letters follow the original manuscripts as closely as possible, in all matters of variant spelling, capitalization, punctuation, superscripts, abbreviations, and elisions. The only exception to this rule is that internal long "ʃ" has been rendered as a modern "s." For a discussion of the advantages of a diplomatic over a normalized text, see Introduction B, section 2.

b) *Heading*. The initial heading, designating the recipient or author of each letter, has been supplied by the editor.

c) *Date*. In all cases where a letter was dated by its author, the date has been reproduced in its original form. Those letters left undated by their authors have been assigned dates by the editor, and these appear in square brackets. In those cases where authors wrote dates at the end of their text, these have been moved to the head of the letter.

References in the notes to dating by the "Letter Book Principle" indicate that a draft letter appears in Robert Dodsley's Letter Book, a pre-bound volume, now in the Birmingham Public Library, in which the bookseller wrote drafts of many letters, from 1756 to 1759. The integrity of the original binding, together with various instances where a fully dated "sent" version of a letter corroborates an assigned date, supports the assumption that the order of drafts in the Letter Book is chronological. For further details on methods used for letter dating, see Introduction B, section 3.

d) *Salutation and complimentary close*. These are line-for-line reproductions of the originals.

e) *Postscript*. Postscripts are placed flush left on the page, with no attempt to duplicate the arrangement of the original.

f) *Cover address, etc.* Cover addresses, frankings, and endorsements duplicate the originals, except that they are printed in a single line, their original line divisions designated by slash marks. Only those endorsements which appear in a contemporary hand are printed.

g) *Postmark*. Although all postmarks found on manuscripts are represented, the contemporary configuration of dates, e.g. $\frac{12}{NO}$, has not been reproduced: day and month are simply placed side by side, as "12 NO." The date is followed by the post town, when available.

h) *Brackets*. Material enclosed within square brackets in the text usually attempts to reconstruct the text or to assign dates, and has been supplied by the editor. Arrow brackets enclose deciphered material which the author originally crossed out. Although frequently trivial, the latter often reveals the workings of the author's mind in the process of composition. Slanted brackets represent the few cases of author brackets within the text. Parentheses belong to the authors of the letters.

To avoid excessive clutter resulting from the use of multiple kinds of brackets, as well as to afford intelligible continuity in the text of those letters heavy with author cross-outs, letter writers' marginal notes clearly marked for inclusion within the text have often been silently introduced. In most cases, writers' second thoughts are easily perceived from the material crossed out, which is enclosed within arrow brackets.

i)   *Drafts.* Where holograph draft letters constitute sole surviving texts, these are printed. However, in at least eleven cases, both the draft and the "sent" letter have been discovered. In most of these instances, the "sent" letter alone has been printed, and the draft letter, together with its significant variants, alluded to in the notes. In a few cases, however, in order to show Dodsley's "thinking on paper," both texts have been included.

j)   *Source.* The text of each letter is followed either by the designation "*MS*," where the source is a manuscript (sent letter, draft, or copy), or by "*Source*," where the text has been taken from a printed source. In each case, a full citation is supplied.

k)   *Provenance.* The provenance of the letters, in so far as this can be determined, together with a record of their previous publication, can be found in Appendix C.

l)   *Citations to contemporary works.* Where possible, bibliographical details have been derived from original copies of contemporary works. When such copies have not been located, citations have been taken from contemporary newspaper and periodical advertisements and reviews. For foreign works for which neither of the above methods succeeded, the editor has relied upon national library and union catalogues. Occasional discrepancies in bibliographical style occur where a work, or a particular edition of a work, seems no longer extant.

With regard to Dodsley's own *Collection of Poems by Several Hands*, all references are to the first edition of each volume. See Introduction B, section 4, for a full discussion of this matter.

m)   *Biographical data.* Biographical sketches for each of Dodsley's correspondents follow a simple rule: for well-known figures whose story has been frequently recounted in standard works, only those details pertinent to the subject's relationship with Dodsley are noted; for lesser-known and obscure persons, biographical detail, culled from various sources, has been included with notes on the subject's relationship with Dodsley. In all cases, such biographical data appear in the first note accompanying the initial letter exchanged with Dodsley. Occasionally, subsequent letters carry additional information, where that information is regarded as being of more significance to the later letter.

Biographical data have been derived from the following sources, unless otherwise cited: *Alumni Cantabrigienses*, *Alumni Oxonienses*, *Dictionary of National Biography*, Cokayne's *Complete Baronetage* and *Complete Peerage*, LeNeve's *Fasti Ecclesiae Anglicanae* (rev. T. D. Hardy), Scott's *Fasti Ecclesiae Scoticanae*, the *Gentleman's Magazine* obituaries and biographical accounts, Sedgwick's and Namier & Brooke's histories of Parliament, Musgrave's *Obituary Prior to 1800*, Plomer's *Dictionary of Printers and Booksellers*, and *The Victoria History of the Counties of England*. Full citations to these works appear in the list of Cue-titles.

CUE-TITLES

Alum Cant	Venn, John and J. A. Venn, *Alumni Cantabrigienses*. Part I to 1751 (4 vols. Cambridge, 1922–7; Part II 1752–1900, ed. J. A. Venn (6 vols. Cambridge, 1940–54).
Alum Ox	Foster, Joseph, *Alumni Oxonienses: The Members of the University of Oxford, 1715–1886* (4 vols. London, 1887–9).
BL. Add. MS.	Additional Manuscripts, British Library
Boswell, *Life*	Boswell, James, *Boswell's Life of Johnson*, ed. George Birkbeck Hill; rev. L. F. Powell (6 vols. Oxford: Clarendon Press, 1934; repr. 1971)
Brooks	*The Correspondence of Thomas Percy & William Shenstone*, ed. Cleanth Brooks. *The Percy Letters* (Vol. 7. New Haven: Yale University Press, 1977)
Collection	Dodsley, Robert, comp. *A Collection of Poems by Several Hands* (6 vols. London, 1748–58)
Complete Baronetage	Cokayne, George E., comp. *The Complete Baronetage* (6 vols. Exeter, 1900–9)
Complete Peerage	Cokayne, George E., comp. *The Complete Peerage*, rev. Vicary Gibbs et al. (13 vols. London, 1910–59)
Courtney	William Prideaux Courtney, *Dodsley's Collection of Poetry: Its Contents and Contributors* (London: Arthur L. Humphreys, 1910)
CR	*Critical Review*, London, 1756–1817 (Monthly)
DA	*Daily Advertiser*, London, 1730–98 (Daily)
DNB	Stephen, Leslie and Sidney Lee, eds. *Dictionary of National Biography* (63 vols. London, 1885–1900)
DP	*Daily Post*, London, 1719–46 (Daily)
Fasti Ecclesiae Anglicanae	LeNeve, John, comp. *Fasti Ecclesiae Anglicanae 1300–1541*; rev. and expanded to 1850 by T. D. Hardy (3 vols. London, 1854)
Fasti Ecclesiae Scoticanae	Scott, H., comp. *Fasti Ecclesiae Scoticanae*, rev. (9 vols. Edinburgh: Oliver and Boyd, 1915–)
GA	*General Advertiser*, London, 1734–52 (Daily)
GEP	*General Evening Post*, London, 1733–71 (Thrice weekly)

GM	*Gentleman's Magazine*, London, 1731–1900+ (Monthly)
JD	James Dodsley, brother of Robert and his successor at Tully's Head
LC	*London Chronicle*, London, 1757–1823 (Thrice weekly)
LEP	*London Evening Post*, London, 1727–1806 (Thrice weekly)
LM	*London Magazine*, London, 1732–85 (Monthly)
London Stage	Van Lennep, W. B., E. L. Avery, A. H. Scouten, G. W. Stone, and C. B. Hogan, *The London Stage, 1660–1800, A Calendar of Plays, Entertainments, and Afterpieces* (11 vols. Carbondale, Ill.: Southern Illinois University Press, 1960–9)
Mallam	Mallam, Duncan, ed. *Letters of William Shenstone* (Minneapolis: University of Minnesota Press, 1939)
MR	*Monthly Review*, London, 1749–1845 (Monthly)
Musgrave	Musgrave, Sir William, comp. *Obituary Prior to 1800*, ed. Sir George G. Armytage (6 vols. London: Harleian Society, 1899–1901)
Namier and Brooke	Namier, Sir Lewis and John Brooke, *The History of Parliament: The House of Commons, 1754–1790* (3 vols. London: H. M. Stationery Office for The History of Parliament Trust, 1964)
PA	*Public Advertiser*, London, 1752–94 (Daily)
Plomer	Plomer, H. R., G. H. Bushnell, E. R. McCDix, comps. *A Dictionary of the Printers and Booksellers Who Were at Work in England Scotland and Ireland from 1726–1775* (Oxford, 1932; rpt. London: The Bibliographical Society, 1968)
RD	Robert Dodsley
Robert Dodsley Letter Book	Holograph volume of Dodsley draft letters, Birmingham Public Libraries
Scots Peerage	Paul, Sir James Balfour, *The Scots Peerage* (9 vols. Edinburgh, 1904–14)
Sedgwick	Sedgwick, Romney, *The History of Parliament: The House of Commons 1715–1754* (2 vols. New York: Oxford University Press for The History of Parliament Trust, 1970)
Stationers' Company	*Index of Titles and Proprietors of Books Entered in the Book of Registry of the Stationers' Company from 28th April 1710 to 30th December 1773.*
Straus	Straus, Ralph, *Robert Dodsley, Poet, Publisher &*

	Playwright (London and New York: John Lane, 1910)
Victoria County History	*The Victoria History of the Counties of England* (Oxford: Institute of Historical Research, London, 1901–)
WEP	*Whitehall Evening Post*, London, 1746–1801 (Thrice weekly)
Williams	Williams, Marjorie, ed. *The Letters of William Shenstone* (Oxford: Blackwell, 1939)

ROBERT DODSLEY'S CORRESPONDENCE

A. LETTERS, 1733–1764

1733–1745

from Alexander Pope 5 February 1733
to Alexander Pope 8 May [1734]
to [Mr Wright of Mansfield] [1735–6]
from Alexander Pope 20 August [1737]
to [Thomas Hooke?] [1738]
from Charles Balguy 14 June [1741]
from John Brown [*c.* 25] September 1743
from John Brown 8 October 1743
from John Brown 24 December 1743
from Roger Comberbach 20 February 1744
from Christopher Pitt [*ante* 1 March 1744]
from Christopher Pitt 6 April [1744?]
from Christopher Pitt [*post* 30 May] 1744
from Christopher Pitt [1 June–9 August 1744?]
from Christopher Pitt 4 July [1744]
from Frances Seymour, Countess Hertford 9 August [1744]
from Thomas Sheridan [15 or 22 August 1744?]
to Solomon Mendes [8 November 1744]
from John Wesley 12 December 1744
from John Wesley 8 February 1745
from John Brown 18 February 1745
from John Brown 14 March [1745]
to Thomas Warton, the younger 16 March [1745]
to George Selwyn 12 September 1745
from John Brown 5 October 1745
from John Brown 17 October 1745
from Glocester Ridley 2 December 1745
from John Gilbert Cooper 18 December 1745

1746–1747

from John Brown 15 February 1746
from John Brown 5 March [1746]
from John Gilbert Cooper 12 March 1746
from William Warburton [6 or 7 April 1746]

from John Gilbert Cooper 7 April 1746
from John Gilbert Cooper 23 April 1746
from John Gilbert Cooper 28 May 1746
from Samuel Johnson [June 1746?]
from Jacob Calton 15 June 1746
from John Gilbert Cooper 7 July 1746
from John Gilbert Cooper 26 July 1746
from Christopher Smart 6 August 1746
from William Whitehead 21 August 1746
from John Brown 27 October 1746
from John Brown 8 November [1746]
from John Gilbert Cooper 15 November 1746
from Samuel Johnson 26 December 1746
from William Melmoth 26 December 1746
from William Melmoth [26 December 1746 or 2 January 1747]
to   Thomas Warton, the younger 29 January [1747]
from Lucy Pitt 9 February 1747
from John Gilbert Cooper 11 February 1747
from John Gilbert Cooper 18 February 1747
from Lucy Pitt 18 February 1747
from William Mason 31 May 1747
from Christopher Smart [*post* 30 May 1747]
from William Mason [*post* 31 May; *ante* 16 August 1747]
from William Mason 16 August 1747
from Lucy Pitt 8 October 1747
to   William Shenstone 8 October [1747]
from Edward Young 16 October [1747]
to   William Shenstone 17 October [1747]
from John Gilbert Cooper 14 November 1747

1748–1749

from Christopher Smart 7 January 1748
from Christopher Smart 12 January 1748
from John Gilbert Cooper 8 February 1748
from Christopher Smart 9 February 1748
from David Fordyce 11 February 1748
from James Massey 10 March 1748
to   William Shenstone 24 March [1748]
from Henrietta St John Knight, Lady Luxborough [*post* 3 May] 1748
to   William Shenstone 17 May [1748]
from Matthew Pilkington 1 October 1748
to   Joseph Spence 22 October 1748
from John Gilbert Cooper 5 December 1748

from John Gilbert Cooper 16 January 1749
from John Gilbert Cooper 15 February 1749
from John Barr 19 April [17]49
from William Melmoth 1 June 1749
from John Gilbert Cooper 23 September 1749
to   John Gilbert Cooper 2 December [1749]
from John Gilbert Cooper 9 December 1749
to   John Gilbert Cooper 9 December 1749
to   John Gilbert Cooper 19 December [1749]
from John Gilbert Cooper 23 December 1749
to   John Gilbert Cooper 26 December [1749]

                            1750–1753

to   Thomas Birch 24 February 1750
from John Gilbert Cooper [25 or 26 February 1750]
from John Gilbert Cooper 22 October 1750
to   Joseph Spence [19 June 1751]
from John Gilbert Cooper 26 August 1751
from William Warburton 28 September 1751
from John Gilbert Cooper 13 November 1751
from John Gilbert Cooper 23 November 1751
from John Gilbert Cooper 19 January [1752]
from John Baskerville 2 October 1752
from John Baskerville 19 October 1752
from Robert Lowth 16 January 1753
from Thomas Gray 12 February [1753]
from Robert Lowth 24 February 1753
from Robert Lowth [late February] 1753
from Robert Lowth 7 March 1753
from Theodore, Baron de Neuhoff 8 March [17]53
from Robert Lowth 13 March 1753
from Robert Lowth 15 March [1753]
from Benjamin Victor August 1753
to   William Shenstone 29 September [1753]
to   Joseph Warton 29 September 175[3]
from John Berckenhout 28 October [17]53
from Horace Walpole 4 November 1753
to   William Shenstone 10 November 1753
from Benjamin Victor 12 November 1753
to   Joseph Warton [*post* 19 November 1753]
to   William Shenstone [*c.* 28 November [17]53]
from John Berckenhout 10 December 1753
to   Solomon Mendes [December 1753 or early 1754]

1754–1755

from John Mason 7 January [1754]
to   William Shenstone 12 January [1754]
from John Baskerville 16 January 1754
from Matthew Pilkington 26 January 1754
to   William Shenstone [23 February 1754]
from John Berckenhout 26 February 1754
to   William Shenstone 27 August [1754]
from John Gilbert Cooper 21 September 1754
from John Gilbert Cooper 7 October 1754
from John Gilbert Cooper 14 October 1754
from David Hume 14 October 1754
to   [George, Lord Lyttelton] 16 October 1754
from James Dodsley to William Shenstone 22 October [1754]
from Joseph Spence 25 October 1754
from Richard Graves 26 October 1754
to   William Shenstone 29 October [1754]
to   [George, Lord Lyttelton] [October–December 1754]
to   Joseph Warton 8 November [1754]
to   William Shenstone 19 November [1754]
to   William Shenstone 30 November [1754]
to   William Shenstone 16 December [1754]
to   William Shenstone 31 December [1754]
to   William Shenstone [18 January 1755]
to   Joseph Warton 18 January 1755
to   Thomas Warton, the younger 20 January 1755
to   William Shenstone [24 January 1755]
to   William Shenstone 15 February 1755
from William Shenstone 4 March 1755
from John Gilbert Cooper [5] March [1755]
from Thomas Lisle [*c.* 18 March 1755]
from John Gilbert Cooper [20 March 1755]
from William Shenstone 23 March 1755
to   William Shenstone 25 March 1755
to   William Shenstone 29 March 1755
from William Whitehead 1 April 1755
from Richard Jago [early April 1755]
to   William Shenstone 3 May 1755
from Charles Bisset 9 May 1755
to   William Shenstone 27 June [1755]
to   William Shenstone 28 July [1755]
from Edward Young 10 August 1755
to   William Shenstone 28 August [1755]

to   [William Shipley] Secretary of the Society for the Encouragement of
Arts, Manufactures and Commerce 1 October [1755]
to   William Shenstone 8 November [1755]
from John Pixell 3 December 1755
from William Warburton 26 December 1755

1756

to   William Warburton 6 January [1756] (also, fragmentary version)
from Thomas Blackwell 15 January 1756
to   William Shenstone 9 February 1756
from William Mason 3 March [1756]
to   Thomas Warton, the younger 11 March [1756]
to   Jacob, Lord Viscount Folkestone, President of the Society for the
Encouragement of Arts, Manufactures and Commerce [*c.* 17 March 1756]
to   Joseph Warton 8 April 1756
to   William Shenstone 17 April [1756]
from Thomas Blacklock 3 May 1756
from Richard Berenger 31 May [1756]
from Richard Berenger 10 June 1756
to   William Shenstone 12 June [1756]
to   William Shenstone 28 June 1756
to   William Shenstone 28 August [1756]
from Thomas Lisle 2 September 1756
from Richard Graves [*c.* 3 September 1756]
from John Hawkesworth 14 September 1756
from John Scott Hylton 16 September 1756
to   John Scott Hylton 28 September [1756]
to   Mary Godolphin Osborne, Duchess of Leeds 28 September 1756
from Richard Graves 30 September 1756
to   William Shenstone 5 October [1756]
to   Edward Young 7 October [1756]
from David Garrick [14 October 1756]
to   David Garrick 18 October [1756]
from David Garrick 18 October 1756
from John Ogilvie 12 December 1756
to   William Shenstone 13 December [1756]
to   Society for the Encouragement of Arts, Manufactures, and Commerce 14
December [1756]
to   William Melmoth 16 December [1756]
from John Baskerville 20 December 1756
to   William Shenstone 21 December [1756]
to   Richard Graves 30 December [1756]

1757

from Richard Graves 7 January 1757
to   William Shenstone 11 January 1757
to   William Strahan 14 January 1757
from John Scott Hylton 20 January 1757
to   William Strahan 24 January 1757
to   William Melmoth 27 January [1757]
to   John Baskerville 10 February [1757]
to   William Shenstone 17 February [1757]
from Richard Graves 22 February 1757
to   Miss Nelly Wright 24 February [1757]
from John Perry 7 March 1757
to   William Shenstone 11 March 1757
to   [James?] Cawthorn 2 April [1757]
to   John Baskerville 7 April [1757]
to   William Shenstone 11 April [1757]
to   William Shenstone 21 April 1757
to   John Smith, Lord Clanricarde 25 April [1757]
to   William Shenstone 26 April [1757]
to   William Shenstone [30 April 1757]
to   Miss Nelly Wright 3 May [1757]
from John Dyer 12 May 1757
to   David Garrick 17 June [1757]
to   George Box [*c.* 21 June 1757]
from Thomas Blacklock 27 June 1757
to   William Shenstone 13 July [1757]
to   Thomas Blacklock 16 July [1757]
to   Nicholas Herbert 20 July [1757]
from Robert Lowth 9 August 1757
to   Miss Nelly Wright 30 August [1757]
from Robert Lowth [September 1757]
from David Garrick 15 September 1757
to   William Shenstone 20 September [1757]
from Richard Graves 10 October 1757
from Robert Lowth 17 October 1757
from John Hoadly 18 October 1757
to   Richard Graves 24 October [1757]
from Richard Jago 25 October 1757
to   John Hoadly 26 October [1757]
to   Moses Mendes 26 October [1757]
to   George Faulkner 28 October [1757]
to   Richard Jago 29 October [1757]
to   William Shenstone 29 October 1757

to   Elizabeth Montagu [late 1757?]
from Richard Jago 3 November 1757
from Robert Lowth 3 November 1757
to   Thomas Gataker 4 November [1757]
to   Robert Lowth [*post* 4 November, *ante* 3 December 1757]
from John Pixell 7 November 1757
from Richard Jago 21 November 1757
to   David Garrick [November 1757] (with additional draft)
to   William Shenstone 3 December [1757]
to   John Hoadly 5 December [1757]
from John Scott Hylton 6 December 1757
to   William Shenstone 18[–20?] December [1757]
to   Philip Dormer Stanhope, 4th Earl of Chesterfield 19 December [1757]
from William Shenstone 21 December 1757
from Philip Dormer Stanhope, 4th Earl of Chesterfield 22 December 1757
to   William Shenstone 27 December [1757]
to   Thomas Percy [December 1757–10 March 1758]

1758

from Richard Berenger 1 January 1758
from Thomas Blacklock [early January 1758]
to   William Shenstone 5 January 1758
to   Philip Dormer Stanhope, 4th Earl of Chesterfield 5 January 1758
to   Anonymous [5–6 January 1758]
to   John Rich 6 January [1758]
to   Richard Berenger 10 January 1758
to   William Shenstone 16 January 1758
to   [Thomas?] Thackray 16 January [1758]
to   William Shenstone 21 January [1758]
to   William Shenstone 2 February [1758]
from Richard Graves 3 February 1758
from John Scott Hylton 4 February 1758
from Thomas Cheyney 6 February 1758
from John Scott Hylton 9[–13] February 1758
from John Hoadly 11 February 1758
from Robert Lowth 12 February 1758
from John Scott Hylton 16 February 1758
to   [Thomas?] Thackray 18 February [1758]
to   [John Scott Hylton] 20 February [1758]
from John Scott Hylton 24[–5] February 175[8]
from Robert Lowth 24 February 1758
to   Joseph Warton 27 February [1758]
from John Scott Hylton 2[–4] March 1758
from Robert Lowth 5 March 1758

from John Hoadly 8 March 1758
from Thomas Lisle [13 March 1758]
to   William Shenstone 15 March [1758]
from Thomas Blacklock 19 March 1758
to   William Shenstone 30 March [1758]
to   [John Brown] [2–6 April 1758]
from John Scott Hylton 22 April 1758
from Richard Graves 25 April 1758
to   William Shenstone 23 May 1758
to   Sir Charles Hanbury Williams 23 May 1758
from Robert Lowth 9 June 1758
to   William Shenstone 13 June [1758]
to   William Shenstone 22 August [1758]
from Thomas Blacklock 23 August 1758
from Sir James Stonhouse 24 August 1758
from George Tymms [*post* 24 August, *ante* 9 September 1758]
to   Sir Charles Hanbury Williams 31 August [1758]
from William Whitehead 2 September 1758
from George Tymms 9 September 1758
from John Scott Hylton 14 September 1758
from George Tymms [*ante* 18 September 1758]
to   William Shenstone 19 September [1758]
to   Arthur Charles Stanhope 19 September [1758]
to   William Shenstone 10 October [1758]
to   William Shenstone 14 October [1758]
from George Tymms 14 October 1758
to   William Shenstone 24 October [1758]
to   William Shenstone 4 November [1758]
from Richard Bentley 20 November 1758 (with note from Horace Walpole)
from David Garrick [3 December 1758]
to   John Stuart, 3rd Earl of Bute 5 December 1758
to   David Garrick 5 December [1758]
from David Garrick [6 December 1758]
to   William Shenstone 9 December [1758]
from John Hawkesworth 10 December 1758
to   William Strahan 12 December [1758]
to   William Shenstone 16 December [1758]
from Richard Graves 20 December 1758
from Richard Jago [1758?]

1759

to   William Shenstone 20 January 1759
to   William Shenstone 8 February [1759]
to   William Shenstone 20 February [1759]

from John Scott Hylton 21 February 1759
from Thomas Blacklock 4 March 1759
from Richard Jameson 4 March 1759
to   William Shenstone 15 March [1759]
to   William Shenstone 19 March [1759]
from Richard Graves 27 March 17[59]
to   William Shenstone 27 March [1759]
from William Shenstone 31 March 1759
to   William Shenstone 3 April [1759]
from [George Steevens] 9 April [1759]
from John Pixell 20 April [1759]
from Laurence Sterne 23 May 1759
from William Melmoth 28 July 1759
from Edmund Burke [*c.* 6 September 1759]
from Laurence Sterne [*c.* 5 October 1759]
to   William Shenstone 12 October 1759
from Richard Graves 15 October 1759
from Philip Parsons 29 October 1759
from William Melmoth 20 November 1759
from John Hawkesworth [mid-November 1759]
to   William Shenstone 1[–4] December 1759

1760–1761

to   William Shenstone 4 January 1760
from Thomas Blacklock 4 February 1760
to   William Shenstone [*post* 18 February, *ante* 21 April 1760]
to   William Shenstone 17 June [1760]
from Robert Lowth 19 June 1760
to   William Shenstone 24 June [1760]
from William Melmoth 3 July 1760
from William Melmoth 29 August 1760
from William Melmoth 9 October 1760
to   William Shenstone 30 December [1760]
from Robert Lowth 9 January [1761]
to   William Shenstone 12 February [1761]
from John Scott Hylton 18[–20] February 1761
to   William Shenstone [March or April 1761]
to   Elizabeth Cartwright 1 May [1761]
to   William Shenstone 25 June [1761]
to   [Elizabeth Cartwright] 27 September [1761]

1762–1764

from Richard Graves 10 January 1762
from George Steevens January [1762?]

from William Shenstone [11 February 1762]
from Robert Lowth 5 March 1762
from William Melmoth 13 March 1762
to   Elizabeth Cartwright 26 July 1762
from Joseph Baretti 13 September 1762
to   William Shenstone 18 September [1762]
from William Shenstone 20 November 1762
to   Elizabeth Cartwright [January 1763]
to   Samuel Cartwright 12 April 1763
from Richard Graves 25 April 1763
from Richard Graves [*post* 25 April, *ante* 21 May 1763]
from Richard Graves 21 May 1763
from Richard Graves 20 June 1763
to   Elizabeth Cartwright 3 August 1763
to   Elizabeth Cartwright 25 August 1763
to   Elizabeth Cartwright 10 November 1763
from [Elizabeth Cartwright] 24 November [17]63
to   Elizabeth Cartwright 15 December [1763]
from Richard Graves [*c.* 6 January 1764]
to   Elizabeth Cartwright 2 February [1764]
from John Hoadly 15 February 1764
from Richard Graves 30 March [1764]
from Richard Graves 9 April 1764
from John Pixell 16 April 1764
to   Elizabeth Cartwright 28 April 1764
from Joseph Spence to Elizabeth Cartwright 12 June 1764
from John Scott Hylton 24 June 1764
from Joseph Spence to Elizabeth Cartwright 24 July 1764
from Richard Graves 30 August 1764
from Richard Graves to James Dodsley 1 October 1764

B. PUBLIC LETTERS

from Sir Charles Hanbury Williams February, 1743
to   the *London Chronicle* 24–7 December 1757

CORRESPONDENTS OF ROBERT DODSLEY

To	From	
1	0	Anonymous
0	1	Balguy, Charles (1708–67)
0	1	Baretti, Joseph (1719–89)
0	1	Barr, John (*c.* 1709–78)
2	4	Baskerville, John (1706–75)
0	1	Bentley, Richard (1708–82)
0	3	Berckenhout, John (1730–91?)
1	3	Berenger, Richard (d. 1782)
1	0	Birch, Thomas (1705–66)
0	1	Bisset, Charles (1717–91)
1	7	Blacklock, Thomas (1721–91)
0	1	Blackwell, Thomas (1701–57)
1	11	Brown, John, of Carlisle (1715–66)
0	1	Burke, Edmund (1729–97)
0	1	Calton, Jacob, of Kelsey, Lincs.
10	1	Cartwright, Elizabeth (1737–1811)
1	0	Cartwright, Samuel (1701–92)
1	0	Cawthorn, [James?] (1719–61)
0	1	Cheyney, Thomas (1694–1760)
0	1	Comberbach, Roger (d. 1757)
4	29	Cooper, John Gilbert (1723–69)
0	1	Dyer, John (1700?–57)
1	0	Faulkner, George (1699?–1775)
0	1	Fordyce, David (1711–51)
4	5	Garrick, David (1717–79)
1	0	Gataker, Thomas (d. 1768)
2	21	Graves, Richard (1715–1804)
0	1	Gray, Thomas (1716–71)
0	3	Hawkesworth, John (1720–73)
1	0	Herbert, Nicholas (1706–75)
2	4	Hoadly, John (1711–76)

To	From	
1	0	Hooke, Thomas (1693–1772)
0	1	Hume, David (1711–76)
2	13	Hylton, John Scott (d. 1793)
1	5	Jago, Richard (1715–81)
0	1	Jameson, Richard
0	2	Johnson, Samuel (1709–84)
0	1	Knight, Henrietta St. John, Lady Luxborough (d. 1756)
0	3	Lisle, Thomas (1709–67)
1	17	Lowth, Robert (1710–87)
2	0	Lyttelton, George, Lord (1709–73)
0	1	Mason, John (1706–63)
0	4	Mason, William (1724–97)
0	1	Massey, James
2	9	Melmoth, William (1710–99)
1	0	Mendes, Moses (d. 1758)
2	0	Mendes, Solomon (d. 1762?)
1	0	Montagu, Elizabeth (1720–1800)
0	1	Neuhoff, Baron de, King Theodore of Corsica 1694–1756
0	1	Ogilvie, John (1733–1813)
1	0	Osborne, Mary Godophin, Duchess of Leeds (1723–64)
0	1	Parsons, Philip (1729–1812)
1	0	Percy, Thomas (1729–1811)
0	1	Perry, John (*c.* 1713–80)
0	2	Pilkington, Matthew (1705–65)
0	5	Pitt, Christopher (1699–1748)
0	3	Pitt, Lucy
0	4	Pixell, John (1725–84)
1	2	Pope, Alexander (1688–1744)
1	0	Rich, John (1682–1760)
0	1	Ridley, Glocester (1702–74)
1	0	Selwyn, George (1719–91)
0	1	Seymour, Frances, Countess Hertford (1699–1754)
81	6	Shenstone, William (1714–63)

o	1	Sheridan, Thomas (1719–88)	1	o	Stuart, John, 3rd Earl of Bute (1713–92)
o	5	Smart, Christopher (1722–71)	2	o	Thackray, [Thomas?]
1	o	Smith, John, 11th Earl of Clanricarde (1720–82)	o	4	Tymms, George (1699–1781)
4	o	Society for the Encouragement of Arts, Manufactures, and Commerce (Royal Society of Arts)	o	2	Victor, Benjamin (d. 1778)
			o	1	Walpole, Horace, 4th Earl of Orford (1717–97)
			1	3	Warburton, William (1698–1779)
			6	o	Warton, Joseph (1722–1800)
2	1	Spence, Joseph (1699–1768)	4	o	Warton, Thomas (1728–90)
1	o	Stanhope, Arthur Charles (1716–70)	o	2	Wesley, John (1703–91)
			o	3	Whitehead, William (1715–85)
2	1	Stanhope, Philip Dormer, 4th Earl of Chesterfield (1694–1773)	2	o	Williams, Sir Charles Hanbury (1708–59)
o	2	Steevens, George (1736–1800)	3	o	Wright, Nelly
			1	o	Wright, Mr
o	2	Sterne, Laurence (1713–68)	1	2	Young, Edward (1683–1765)
o	1	Stonhouse, Sir James (1716–95)			
3	o	Strahan, William (1715–85)			

In addition, the following six letters are included:
James Dodsley to William Shenstone
Joseph Spence to Elizabeth Cartwright (2)
Richard Graves to James Dodsley
Public letters (2)

INTRODUCTION

A. ROBERT DODSLEY'S LIFE AND CAREER

1. Life, writings and associates

Writing to Thomas Percy in 1761, William Shenstone took obvious delight in recounting an anecdote arising from Lady Gough's recent visit. Apparently the Lady had taken the liberty of peeking into a letter from Dodsley that lay open on the table. Confusing the bookseller with the deistical pamphleteer Henry Dodwell (d. 1784), she soon thereafter sent Shenstone the advice that he should "break off all correspondence with that Dodwell; for that she had heard he was an infidel." Since then, Shenstone hastens to tell Percy, she has "accused our Friend Dodsley of no Less than Blasphemy; by reason that he in his verses makes so free with silvan Gods & rural deities."[1]

One smiles at the Lady's ingenuousness, but not with complete confidence, for even those familiar with eighteenth-century London society have difficulty distinguishing among those notables whose surnames approximated Dodsley's. Lurking in the shadows of the century's annals are several who occasionally make a show on the stage to complete the historian's cast of characters. The clergyman and author William Dodd (1729–77), for instance, by forging a four thousand pound bond in the name of the 5th Earl of Chesterfield, earned considerable notice on the way to a public execution in 1777. Two other controversial clerical authors swell the chorus of notable "Dods": the active dissenting lecturer and hymn-writer from Northampton, Philip Doddridge (1702–51), and the forementioned Henry Dodwell's more traditional brother, William Dodwell (1709–85), Archdeacon of Berkshire. Perhaps the best known of the "Dods" at the time was George Bubb Doddington, Baron Melcombe, a popular wit, political pamphleteer, and patron of literature. But more obviously blurring the picture within Dodsley's own trade were Anne and Benjamin Dodd. Not only did the careers of these two London booksellers overlap Dodsley's, but their names were occasionally joined with his in imprints.

It is not entirely surprising, then, that even modern scholars occasionally blunder when referring to Dodsley, especially confusing him with his younger brother and successor, James Dodsley. A. S. Collins, in his standard *Authorship in the Days of Johnson* (1928), claims that "where Dodsley gave 220 guineas for Young's *Night Thoughts* in 1742, he gave Percy in 1765 300 Guineas for his *Reliques*."[2] R. W. Chapman prints among Samuel Johnson's *Letters* (1952) one piece to Dodsley whose date he estimates to be sometime in September or October 1765.[3] Neither

---

[1] *The Letters of William Shenstone*, ed. Marjorie Williams (Oxford: Blackwell, 1939), p. 601. Lady Gough was sister to Sir Henry Gough of nearby Edgbaston.
[2] London: George Routledge & Sons, p. 34.   [3] Oxford: Clarendon Press, I, 182.

Collins nor Chapman seems to realize that he is confounding the two brothers: Robert had died in 1764. The same error abounds in library catalogues, sometimes marring even those of our most sophisticated research libraries.

Robert Dodsley, bookseller, poet, and playwright, was born the eldest son of a Mansfield schoolmaster on 13 February 1703. He was descended from an old Midland family whose origins can be traced to the thirteenth century.[4] Of his four brothers and two sisters, only the youngest, James, would approach Robert's stature in eighteenth-century society. Joining Robert as a partner, he later succeeded to the business, which he carried on until 1797. John, who took up the family tradition as a farmer and maltster, remained in the Mansfield area, as it seems did Lucy.[5] Isaac travelled to Bath to become Ralph Allen's gardener, and Alvory to London where, Straus suggests, he might have run a Westminster pamphlet shop.[6] Alice, having married Francis Dyer and moved to London, tended the ailing Robert during his retirement at her home in Bruton Street.

Like the early history of many notables, Dodsley's is difficult to chart; he seems not to have saved much (if there was anything to save) from the period of his migration from Mansfield to London. From various sources, we know that he had been apprenticed to a Mansfield stocking weaver, but doubtless the education Robert, Sr., had expended on his first-born chafed under the restrictions of the menial trade, and he soon departed the city – under what conditions it is not known.

The road to London was not direct, nor without distress. His anxieties were exacerbated by an ambition and an awareness much beyond his humble origins. He records in an early essay, *Miseries of Poverty*: "The miseries of a thinking man are intolerably aggravated by the quick sense he has of them . . . every uncomfortable circumstance depresses his spirits; the contempt with which the world looks upon him in a mean and despicable habit, the rude illiterate company he is forced to associate with, and the many insults, inconveniences, and restraints which he undergoes . . . are themes which afford him a great many melancholy reflections." These frustrated psychological energies initially drove him to seek relief as a footman, first at the house of the epicure and humorist Charles Dartiquenave, then probably for Sir Richard Howe of Gloucester and Notts., and finally at the Whitehall residence of the Hon. Jane Lowther, where he seems to have remained at least until 1732. Here, no doubt, he met many titled persons and literary celebrities of the Lady's acquaintance; and here he had access to a library. Most importantly for his career, he parlayed his experience in these services, with the assistance of the Muse, into verses that captured the fancy of some influential visitors. (He was obviously aware that the Wiltshire farmer, Stephen Duck, was currently being lionized in London as the "Thresher Poet.")

[4] Because Ralph Straus's biography seems to have exhausted available evidence on Dodsley's pre-London days, the following account relies on Straus for that period.

[5] Perhaps some estrangement or favoritism was at work when John inherited his father's Mansfield property in 1750, property that would have been rightfully Robert's.

[6] Straus (p. 9) does not reveal the source of his suggestion. Perhaps his notion of Alvory's pamphlet shop stems from the imprint to *Memoirs of Field Marshal Leopold Count Daun* (1757): "London printed for R. Withy and J. Ryall; and sold by A. Dodsley."

By some unknown means, the young footman gained access to Daniel Defoe. Defoe read, revised, and added some front and back material to Dodsley's poem *Servitude* (1729), and then saw to this first publication of the footman's works. His acceptance among influential circles by 1732 is confirmed by the appearance of his *A Muse in Livery, or the Footman's Miscellany.* This anonymous collection of one hundred and fifty pages of verse was prefaced by a subscription list of over two hundred names, many of them from among the peerage. Within a few months, a second edition appeared, this time printed as "By R. Dodsley, now a Footman to a Person of Quality at Whitehall." It is difficult to imagine that his bookseller's shop at the sign of Tully's Head was less than three years away. But now he was ready to meet the revered Alexander Pope, and here begins the present collection of letters.

Pope's pleasure with Dodsley's little satiric play, *The Toy-shop*, is recorded in a letter of 5 February 1733, where Pope promises to recommend it to John Rich, the manager of Lincoln's Inn Fields. Two years would intervene before the production, during which Dodsley turned out three poems after the manner of his benefactor: *Epistle to Mr. Pope, Occasion'd by his Essay on Man* (1734), *The Modern Reasoners* (1734), and *Beauty, or the Art of Charming* (1735). Again, his patron was obviously pleased, for all were issued by Pope's current publisher, Lawton Gilliver.

On 3 February 1735, Rich produced *The Toy-shop* at his new theater in Covent Garden. It scored an immediate success both on and off the stage. Eleven editions were called for within the first two years, and it passed through a number of translations. Despite its lack of plot, its gentle satire of contemporary extravagances so pleased audiences that it enjoyed a considerable run as an afterpiece and was frequently revived at both major theatres over the next two decades. Most importantly, however, it provided Dodsley with the financial resources (together with a hundred pound contribution from Pope) to open his bookseller's shop within months of the play's debut.

As might be expected, Pope's patronage was crucial to the new business from the outset. Switching some of his trade from Gilliver to Dodsley, Pope would publish at least seven works from Tully's Head by 1739, including his *Letters* and the second volume of his *Works*, though in the former "RD" was joined by Knapton, Gilliver, and Brindley.[7] Likewise, the appearance of Pope's works from Dodsley's shop doubtless brought the new bookseller's name to the attention of other authors, as well as inevitably inserting him into the mainstream of the trade. In 1737, he published Richard Glover's *Leonidas*, a poem of epic proportions that, to some critics, rivaled Milton's *Paradise Lost*. More significantly at this time, it was to Dodsley that the then little-known Samuel Johnson brought his poem *London* (1738), which became a milestone in the careers of both author and publisher.

One misfortune during these years, Dodsley would not forget in the future management of his business. His publishing of Paul Whitehead's satiric poem *Manners* in early February 1739, enraged certain members of the House of Lords, particularly Thomas Sherlock, Bishop of Salisbury, who caused the bookseller to be summoned before that body. When the poem was judged a scurrilous reflection on

---

[7] The problem of copyright ownership is taken up in the notes to Pope's first letter and in Appendix B, section 2.

certain members, Dodsley was committed to prison in Butcher Row. There he stayed for a week until his friend and neighbor Benjamin Victor used his influence with one of the offended parties, Lord Essex, to secure his release on 20 February.[8] By absconding, Whitehead had escaped prosecution.

The ease and success of Dodsley's transition from footman poet to London businessman, quite extraordinary in itself, says something about his versatile talents. But, amidst it all, he did not forget his first love, writing. *The Toy-shop* was followed by *The King and Miller of Mansfield*, a melodrama first acted at Drury Lane on 29 January 1737. With Colley Cibber playing the King, the play captured the fancy of London audiences, ran for many nights (including a command performance at the order of the Prince of Wales), and was acted every season thereafter until 1775. Although its sequel, *Sir John Cockle at Court* (1738), lasted but two performances, the young playwright must have been elated to realize that his first three plays (*The Toy-shop* being revived) were being acted on London stages within a single month, during February and March 1738. Still a fourth play, *The Blind Beggar of Bethnal Green*, with Kitty Clive in the lead, was performed at Drury Lane in 1741, but this sentimental afterpiece proved equally ineffective.[9]

Other works continued to flow from his pen through the early 1740s, including *Rex et Pontifex* (1745), a "new Species of pantomime," for which Dodsley failed to find a producer. Most likely a realization of his waning ability to entertain the town prompted him, by the middle of the decade, to turn his attention to the publication of other men's plays.

His love of the theater, together with an ever-present patriotism, at some point had set him to collecting old English plays. The first fruit of this new endeavor appeared in 1745 as *A Select Collection of Old Plays* (10 vols.), followed by two more volumes in 1746 (though all were dated 1744). Dodsley's purpose in gathering these sixty-one plays, ranging back to the year 1547, is expressed in the preface to the volumes: "My first End was to snatch some of the best pieces of our old Dramatic Writers from total Neglect and Oblivion."[10] And, for some, Dodsley is best remembered for this service. Apparently he had collected well over six hundred plays in these days, many of which would pass into the famed collection that David Garrick formed over the next three decades.[11]

---

[8] *Journal of the House of Lords*, 12, 19, 20 February 1739.

[9] None the less, Richard Bevis, tracing the development of the sentimental comedy, thinks this "earliest of the sentimental afterpieces was also the best" – *The Laughing Tradition. Stage Comedy in Garrick's Day*. (Athens, Geo.: University of Georgia Press, 1980), p. 105.

[10] I, xxxv–xxxvii.

[11] Dodsley mentions (Vol. I, p. 2) that the "Harleian Collection of old Plays, consisting of between 6 and 700 . . . are now in my Possession." In *The Garrick Collection of Old English Plays* (London: The British Library, 1982), George M. Kahrl and Dorothy Anderson trace some of the origins of Dodsley's collection and identify volumes that passed into Garrick's. Reportedly, Garrick had written in his copy of Gerard Langbaine's *The Lives and Characters of the English Dramatic Poets* (1699) the following: "All the Plays marked thus X in this Catalogue I bought of Dodsley." Garrick's note was recorded by Saunders in his sale catalogue of Garrick's library in 1823 (lot 1269). Garrick's copy of Laingbaine was offered again the same year by Thomas Thorpe (item 14360), but it has since disappeared.

Dodsley's bookselling business hit full stride by the mid-1740s. Through the first half of the decade, he had been issuing, either by himself or in collaboration, well over a dozen titles a year, a figure that reached nineteen in 1744 and twenty-nine in 1745. In an age when authors were at the mercy of crass, "dealing" booksellers, Dodsley had leavened his negotiations with a literary sensitivity, apparently fulfilling Pope's prediction: "Dodsley . . . as he has more Sense, so will have more Honesty, than most of that Profession."[12] Besides issuing some of Pope's works, he had inserted himself in the ongoing Bathurst edition of Swift through a purchase of original Swift manuscripts from Thomas Sheridan, the younger. To these, he joined a number of first works from the decade's rising stars: William Shenstone's *The Judgment of Hercules* (1741), William Whitehead's *The Danger of Writing Verse* (1741), John Brown's *Honour* (1743), Mark Akenside's *The Pleasures of Imagination* (1744), Joseph Warton's *The Enthusiast* (1744), Thomas Warton's *Five Pastoral Eclogues* (1745), Thomas Gray's *Ode on a Distant Prospect of Eton College* (1747), and William Mason's *Musaeus* (1747). At the same time, a number of established authors turned to Dodsley's services, including John Dalton, DD, Stephen Duck, George, Lord Lyttelton, Joseph Spence, Gilbert West, and, probably the best remembered, Edward Young, who would issue the first six of his *Night Thoughts* from Tully's Head. This predominantly literary cast reflects Dodsley's own interests, as well as illustrating that, in the first decade of business, Dodsley's shop had become synonymous with *belles lettres*.

Surrounded with such figures, and no doubt inundated with the petitions of so many more, it is not surprising that Dodsley should conceive of a project with which his name has been linked ever since. With something of the foresight that gave birth to the *Select Collection of Old Plays*, Dodsley decided "to preserve to the public those poetical performances, which seemed to merit a longer remembrance than what would probably be secured to them by the Manner wherein they were originally published." So read the Advertisement to *A Collection of Poems by Several Hands*, whose first three volumes appeared on 14 January 1748. There Dodsley re-printed many of his earlier successes but also included a number of original pieces, as well as many older favorites. Together with the three concluding volumes issued in the 1750s, the *Collection* has sometimes been regarded as an index to mid-eighteenth century taste.[13] And to some degree, this is true. Of course, some notables are missing – Swift and Young, for instance – but such were probably excluded either because their works were readily available in numerous editions or because copyright ownership prevented their inclusion. Indeed the volumes contain a good deal of trivial material (probably imposed upon the bookseller by friends and acquaintances). On the other hand, it is difficult to find half a dozen notable, practising poets who are not represented.

In the same year that he published the *Collection*, the enterprising Dodsley

12 Letter to William Duncombe on 6 May 1735. *Correspondence of Alexander Pope*, ed. George Sherburn (Oxford: Clarendon Press, 1956), III, 454.
13 R. W. Chapman, "Dodsley's *Collection of Poems by Several Hands*," *Oxford Bibliographical Society: Proceedings and Papers*, III, iii (1933), 269. Donald Eddy qualifies the view in "Dodsley's *Collection of Poems by Several Hands* (Six Volumes), 1958. Index of Authors." *PBSA*, 60 (1966), 11–12.

launched another work of broad significance, in terms of public utility. As one who struggled to gain a rudimentary education, Dodsley never forgot the needs of schoolboys, especially the less privileged who were forced to earn their education at home. Accordingly, on 7 April 1748, he issued the two-volume *Preceptor: Containing a General Course of Education*. The introduction was written by Samuel Johnson, whose other contribution to the work, "The Vision of Theodore, the Hermit of Teneriffe," Johnson later thought was entitled to the "Palm over all he ever wrote."[14] Boswell himself regarded the *Preceptor* as "one of the most valuable books for the improvement of young minds that has appeared in any language."[15] The volumes covered a broad range of topics, offering lessons on mathematics, architecture, geography (125 pages), rhetoric, drawing, logic (195 pages), ethics (140 pages), trade and commerce (82 pages), law and government, to mention only a handful. The products of several authors, the pieces were selected and edited by Dodsley, who even secured a special license from George II to protect his copyright. The whole work was conducted in an atmosphere of deism, pragmatism, and common sense. Something particularly "Dodsley" surfaces in the estimate of trade and commerce: "the only effectual means of banishing idleness, indigence, and ill humours." The work passed through at least four editions during the bookseller's lifetime, spawned a number of imitators, and was used even by young scholars at Rutgers University during the century.[16]

Besides Pope, undoubtedly the most popular authors that Dodsley saw through the press in the 1740s – in terms of numbers of works and editions – were Mark Akenside and Edward Young. Three editions of Akenside's *Pleasures of Imagination* (1744) were called for in the first year, the same year the author published *An Epistle to Curio*. Two editions of *Odes on Several Subjects* were printed in 1745, as were two editions of *An Ode to the Right Honourable the Earl of Huntingdon* in 1748. Akenside served his bookseller in another capacity during 1746–7, when he took on the compiling and editing of Dodsley's fortnightly *Museum: or, Literary and Historical Register*, to be considered below.

But among Dodsley's poets in this decade, no one matched Edward Young for productivity and popularity. Within three years, Dodsley had paid Young more than 230 pounds (see Appendix B) for the copyright to the first six "Nights" of the poet's *The Complaint; or Night Thoughts on Life, Death and Immortality*. The "Nights" were issued individually but on no regular schedule from 1742 to 1743. "Night the First" passed through two editions in the first two months, followed by the next three "Nights," all of which were then published under one cover through two editions. The next two "Nights" followed in order, and then appeared a collected edition of all six, which, by 1749, had enjoyed eight editions. It is not clear why Dodsley refused to purchase "Nights" VII–IX when offered by Young in a letter of October 1747 (q.v.). Perhaps the bookseller thought he had expended enough on

[14] Thomas Percy letter to William Shenstone on 12 March 1760. *Correspondence of Thomas Percy and William Shenstone*, ed. Cleanth Brooks (New Haven and London: Yale University Press, 1977), p. 57.
[15] Boswell, *Life*, I, 192.
[16] Dale Randall, "Dodsley's *Preceptor* – A Window into the 18th Century." *Rutgers University Library Journal*, XXII (1958), 10–22.

the work or that the public had begun to have enough of Young's weighty *Complaint*. Whatever the reason for it, the refusal did not dampen their relationship. In 1751, Dodsley joined with Andrew Millar, who had bought the remaining "Nights," to issue a complete edition of all nine "Nights," a work they continued to issue through the 1750s. Finally, in 1753, Dodsley would be publishing Young's tragedy *The Brothers*, and, two years later, his *Centaur Not Fabulous*.

In 1741, Dodsley struck out in a new direction. He attempted to capitalize on the phenomenal growth in the periodical market, particularly on the popularity of the relatively new form, the magazine. Since Edward Cave had begun the *Gentleman's Magazine* ten years earlier, his imitators had proliferated. The more elaborate monthly had already taken its toll on such specialized periodicals as essay sheets, journals, and reviews, leaving itself and the newspaper as the most prosperous undertakings in the field. Apparently Dodsley attempted to beat Cave at his own game by publishing a weekly three-penny pamphlet that combined high-quality essays with fresher news than Cave was able to offer in his monthly. The *Public Register: or the Weekly Magazine* got off to an encouraging start on 3 January 1741, but apparently by the fourteenth number it had begun to make inroads on the territory closely guarded by Cave and his chief rivals. When it was reported to the authorities that the *Register* carried news, Dodsley was forced to pay the stamp tax or discontinue the news. He chose the latter, and the circulation began to drop. Three numbers later, he paid the tax, restored the news, but cut the size of the magazine. However, even then, the forces working against him proved too strong, and he concluded the periodical with the twenty-fourth number, adding the complaint: "the additional expense I was obliged to in stamping it, and the ungenerous usage I have met with from one of the proprietors of a certain monthly pamphlet, who has prevail'd with most of the common newspapers not to advertise it, compel me for the present to discontinue it."[17]

Five years later, however, having firmly secured himself in the trade and now with Tully's Head bustling with fashionable literary talent, Dodsley made another run at the periodical market. On 20 January 1746, he signed an agreement with Mark Akenside to conduct the fortnightly *Museum: or, Literary and Historical Register* (see Appendix B), whose first issue appeared on the following 29 March. The periodical's regular forty pages were divided into four well-defined sections: essays, poetry, literary memoirs, and historical memoirs. Besides the work of Akenside, through the course of its thirty-nine numbers, the *Museum* included contributions from such as William Collins, the late Lord Hervey, Soame Jenyns, Samuel Johnson, Robert Lowth, George, Lord Lyttelton, Joseph Spence, Horace Walpole, Joseph and Thomas Warton, and the future poet laureate William Whitehead. Although its predominantly literary character hardly posed a marketing threat to the more general pitch of the *Gentleman's*, once again Cave smugly congratulated himself when the *Museum* was discontinued in September 1747. The Preface to the

---

[17] At the time, newspapers were largely controlled by share-holding booksellers, who could effectively squelch competition from new publications simply by refusing to advertise them. For a thorough consideration of the subject, see Michael Harris, "The Management of the London Newspaper Press during the Eighteenth Century," *Publishing History*, 4 (1978), pp. 95–112.

collected edition of the *Gentleman's* for that year delighted in the fact that this "super-excellent Magazine [*Museum*], which was entirely to extirpate all others . . . a work of genius and learning" had expired. Accompanying verses roundly chastised the pretentions of the *Museum*'s projectors. Why Dodsley discontinued the *Museum* at this time is not known. Perhaps it had been designed for only a stated number of issues, as would be his next periodical, *The World*. But it is true that, by 1747, Dodsley had already engaged himself in another large, time-consuming project, his three-volume *Collection of Poems by Several Hands*, which would appear the following March.[18]

A major addition at Tully's Head during the 1740s should be mentioned before leaving the decade. One piece of evidence suggests that, sometime before 3 June 1742, Dodsley's brother James had come to work for him. On that day James witnessed an agreement Dodsley signed with Henry Baker for the purchase of *The Microscope Made Easy* (see Appendix B). Unfortunately this single document is all that we have to link the younger Dodsley with Tully's Head during the 1740s, for his name does not appear with Robert's in an imprint until 1753. But since he was
? admitted as a member of the Stationers' Company in 1754 (albeit by redemption), it is likely that he served some time with Robert during the previous decade. The extremely low profile James kept at Tully's Head – even after 1754 – is perplexing, however. Although numerous letters he exchanged with authors after Robert's death are extant, only one brief piece predating 1764 has turned up.[19] Likewise, despite James's intimate involvement with the business during the 1750s, Robert does not mention his brother in the letters printed here until 20 July 1757, when writing to Nicholas Herbert; that is, less than two years before he surrendered the business to James. But no evidence survives to explain this curious omission.

Dodsley opened the 1750s with a work of his own pen that proved immensely popular. *The Oeconomy of Human Life. Translated from an Indian Manuscript, written by an Ancient Bramin* earned some of its success because it was commonly thought to have been the work of Lord Chesterfield, an opinion that endured as late as Tedder's entry on Dodsley in the *Dictionary of National Biography*.[20] Some of this confusion arose because the book was published anonymously from the shop of Mary Cooper (who, curiously, issued a sequel not by Dodsley) and because the volume was purportedly written as a "Letter from an English Gentleman, now residing in China, to the Earl of ****." Essentially, the book consisted of more than a hundred pages of moral aphorisms, conveyed in something of a biblical air but with an ease and neutrality that made it accessible and agreeable to all. The

---

[18] Recognizing the book value of bound editions of periodicals, many shrewd publishers set a predetermined number of issues as their goal, after which they would discontinue publication and re-issue the periodical in collected editions, thereby realizing a second profit on their intial outlay. If the original periodical had enjoyed popular authors, book publication was almost assured of success. For more on the *Museum* and its contributors, see my article "The *Museum*, the Super-Excellent Magazine." *SEL*, 13 (1973), pp. 503–15.

[19] See James's letter to Shenstone on 22 October 1754.

[20] Considering all available evidence, as well as opposing opinions, Straus (pp. 169–80) argues convincingly for Dodsley's authorship. *The British Library Catalogue of Printed Books* credits Dodsley with the work.

Oeconomy passed through at least ten editions during Dodsley's lifetime and was translated into French, German, Italian, Latin, and Spanish within the first five years of its publication. It was truly, as Straus calls it, a "minor literary success of the century" (p. 180).

Another of Dodsley's own compositions, issued in 1753, did not enjoy the same reception; in fact, it turned out to be quite a disappointment to him. *Agriculture* had been planned as the first book of a three-part work to be entitled *Public Virtue*. But the eighty-eight pages of tedious blank verse, despite its concern with the increasingly popular subject of landscape gardening, did not sell, and Dodsley abandoned the entire project.

Towards the end of 1754, the bookseller became involved with a work, which, because of its delicate nature, found him vacillating on the decision to put the Tully's Head imprint to it. From the very start, he had been anxious about Joseph Warton's treatment of Pope in Warton's proposed *Essay on the Writings and Genius of Mr. Pope*. In the forefront of the new trend in poetry, Warton had some negative things to say about Dodsley's old benefactor. But besides worrying about the inevitable charge of ingratitude, Dodsley had been fidgeting lest the door be closed on a lucrative business opportunity. William Warburton, Pope's executor, had inherited the poet's manuscripts and had issued the "authoritive" edition of Pope's *Works* in 1751. For some time, Dodsley had hoped to buy into the edition, but as late as 1754 Warburton had refused him. While still continuing to hope, he knew that Warton's *Essay* would not assist his case with Warburton. The full story is told in the Dodsley–Warburton exchange in late December 1755, and consequently it is not rehearsed here. It will be adequate to say that, despite the apparent finality of that exchange, Dodsley engaged Mary Cooper to put her name to the *Essay* when it appeared in March of 1756. Only the "Second Edition, corrected" (1762) carried the names "R. and J. Dodsley."[21]

In his letter to Warton on 18 January 1755, Dodsley revealed another distraction he had endured over the past month, an event that hurt him deeply. His wife of twenty-three years, Catherine Iserloo, had died on 12 December. Little is known of "Kitty," except the passing references to her in Dodsley's correspondence, more frequent during her last years when she was seeking relief at Bath. She had certainly claimed a major place in Dodsley's early verses, however, inspiring the young footman's muse on many an occasion. His *Wish* offers but one example:

> A wife, young, virtuous, fair and kind,
>   If such a one there be;
> Yes, one there is 'mongst Womankind
>   O Kitty! thou art she.
> With her, ye gods, with her but make me blest,
> Of all your blessings – that would be the best.

Shortly after, another "lady" of Dodsley's acquaintance would cause him additional sorrow, although she would ultimately prove a source of great joy and triumph. Sometime in the mid-1750s, he had been at work on a tragedy, whose

[21] It is interesting that the title was revised to read: *An Essay on the Genius and Writings of Mr. Pope*. James Dodsley published the much-delayed second volume in 1782.

subject, Cleone, he had borrowed from the legend of St Genevieve. Rounded into shape by 1756, *Cleone* was submitted to Garrick for Drury Lane, but the theater manager refused it. Again and again, Dodsley revised the play with the help and encouragement of his friends, but Garrick would not have it. Finally, with the patronage of Lord Chesterfield, Dodsley ventured the play at John Rich's then unfashionable Covent Garden theater. Dodsley's friends, including Samuel Johnson, rallied round him, and soon the Town was split into factions over the anticipated performance. Garrick had privately condemned the play to Dodsley's leading actress, George Anne Bellamy, and, to insure his judgment, had scheduled Susannah Centlivre's *Busy Body* (with himself playing the lead for the first time) to run against *Cleone*'s opening night. Tension mounted when the performance of *Cleone* was delayed for a few nights, and Garrick likewise delayed his production of *The Busy Body*. Finally both opened on 2 December 1758, and the rivalry spawned a host of partisan newspaper accounts. The story of Dodsley's enormous success and Garrick's chagrin is reflected in Dodsley's letters to Shenstone immediately following the play's debut and in his bitter exchange with Garrick at the same time, a feud from which the two former friends never seemed to recover.

Some defense of Garrick is in order, however. Although *Cleone* enjoyed a long run, was graced with the presence of the Prince and Princess of Wales, passed through two editions and four thousand copies within two weeks, and generally turned the tide of fashion at Covent Garden, the tragedy has perhaps appropriately not outlived its time. The echoes of Shakespeare are too evident, some of its happenings extremely improbable, and the sentimental tug irksome. In his letter to Shenstone on 20 January, Dodsley reports that both men and women wept aloud at Cleone's woes. And Samuel Johnson says the same of its author: "Doddy . . . went every night to the stage-side, and cryed at the distress of poor Cleone."[22] But although faithful to his patron, Johnson had serious reservations about the tragedy, as Boswell later records. When Bennet Langton had finished reading aloud a particular act to him, Johnson urged: "Come let's have some more, let's go into the slaughter-house again, Lanky. But I am afraid there is more blood than brains."[23]

On the other hand, whatever might be said of *Cleone*, few plays have been written with a more studied attempt to achieve a particular effect. Dodsley's tireless revising in the face of Garrick's repeated rejections might suggest the wearisome author who has written his "masterpiece" and will not let the world rest until his prodigy is recognized. And thus it may be. But there is more to it than that, as is revealed in a little-known commonplace book of Dodsley's now in the Bancroft Library.[24] This loosely constructed essay on tragedy, running fifty folios and studded with quotations from seventeenth and eighteenth-century critics, demonstrates how extensively the playwright had read and reflected on the subject when preparing *Cleone*. The culmination of his effort is expressed in a letter to James Cawthorne twenty months before *Cleone* was produced. Writing in response to Cawthorne's criticism of the play (now missing), Dodsley offers his own perceptions on the proper nature of domestic tragedy, the form he was championing. There, among other things, he says he has been "so great an enemy to that tumidity of style

[22] Boswell, *Life*, I, 326.   [23] Ibid., IV, 20.
[24] Originally Phillipps MS 20112, but now in the Bancroft Library, University of California at Berkeley.

so often made use of in tragedy." He claims "a domestic distress like this, should be as far remov'd from all pomp of expression as elegance will permit." Similarly his versification has purposely avoided "a smooth & flowing harmony of numbers (which I have always look'd upon in Rowe as a fault)," and instead has striven for "a natural ease and simplicity of language, as might flow . . . from the lips of the Speaker." And indeed that is how the play reads; one might even call it forward-looking, for its simplicity of expression is well wedded to the domestic scene. Regrettably, however, Dodsley could not resist the melodrama that his age demanded.

The same preoccupation with dramatic theory was no doubt responsible for Dodsley's *Melpomene: or The Regions of Terror and Pity*, a 25-stanza ode he published in September 1757 while still pining over the unproduced *Cleone*. Issued anonymously from Mary Cooper's shop, the ode was well received, even the chary Thomas Gray confessing a liking for it.[25] Sometime in November, responding to Robert Lowth's kind words, Dodsley explained his motivation: "To confess the truth, I have long been an admirer of the fair Melpomene [muse of tragedy], of late had made my addresses to her with some assiduity, and . . . I thought my self in a fair way of gaining her good graces. But the King of her Country [Garrick], being inform'd by the said Cleone of my design on his favorite Melpomene forbad my entrance into his Dominions on pain of Damnation, deem'd my humble spirit audacious and presuming, and dismiss'd poor Cleone from his presence with visible marks of unkindness and disgrace. Piqued at this repulse, I publish'd my Ode on Terror and Pity, to show ye World my pretensions, and to let the Tyrant see, tho' he scorn'd my offers, that the Lady had not disdain'd to admit me into some of her secret Misteries." So were Dodsley's spirits born up for the ensuing year until the opening of *Cleone*.

But Dodsley's reputation and influence had been expanding by still another work that was going forward at the same time as was *Cleone*. The reception of his *Collection of Poems by Several Hands* (1748; three editions by 1752), together with his ever increasing stores of poetry, prompted him to consider a fourth volume sometime in 1753. Although initially planned for the winter of 1754, its progress suffered several delays, not the least cause being the death of his wife in December 1754. Finally it appeared on 18 March 1755, together with a fourth edition of the first three volumes.

As the author of *Tristram Shandy* would at one point happily complain – "the more I write, the more I shall have to write"[26] – so Dodsley, the more he published, the more he was obliged to publish. Within little more than a year after the appearance of the fourth volume of the *Collection*, he wrote to Shenstone that he now intended to add two more volumes to the work.[27] But again numerous delays,

---

[25] Letter to William Mason on 28 September 1757. *Correspondence of Thomas Gray*, ed. Paget Toynbee and Leonard Whibley (Oxford: Clarendon Press, 1935), II, 530.

[26] Vol. IV, Chap. XIII.

[27] Perhaps a caution should be urged here. If one were to rely strictly on Dodsley's extant correspondence, it would seem that the production of Volumes V and VI of the *Collection* pivotted on Shenstone's participation, but this impression results merely from the disproportion of their correspondence in relation to the total number of extant letters from the period.

especially caused by the ailing Shenstone in the closing months, held up the publication for almost two full years. When they appeared on 18 March 1758, twenty-nine of Shenstone's poems opened Volume V, and ten of Akenside's did the same for Volume VI. Slightly represented are a dozen names that have survived the age, such as Fielding, Gray, Hawkesworth, Percy, Pope, and Thomas Warton, but for the most part Dodsley did indeed preserve for many poetical performances "a longer remembrance than would probably be secured to them [otherwise]." None the less, the volumes passed through six more editions in the century and prompted other editors to issue supplements in various forms.[28]

For eighteenth-century booktradesmen, the profits and reputation to be earned from the publication of a successful periodical proved irresistibly fascinating; and Dodsley was no exception. Not quite five and a half years after the *Museum* had been concluded, he contracted with Edward Moore for the conduct of a weekly essay journal to be called *The World*.[29] The periodical was designed and carried on as a lively, light-hearted satire on contemporary customs and foibles, somewhat in the mode of the *Spectator* papers. But, because its authors were various, it enjoyed little of its predecessor's consistency of style. The first issue of the *World*, on 4 January 1753, scored an immediate success. Shortly after its inception, Dodsley was printing 2,500 copies of each Thursday number of the periodical, which ran for 209 numbers through 30 December 1756.

Moore, carrying on the work under the pseudonym "Adam FitzAdam," had the advantage of Dodsley's corps of fashionable authors to support his weekly effort. Among those who took a turn at filling *The World*'s columns were Lords Bath, Chesterfield, and Hailes, John, Earl of Cork, Sir Charles Hanbury Williams, Richard Owen Cambridge (twenty-one numbers), Soame Jenyns, Joseph Warton, William Whitehead, and Horace Walpole. It was in *The World* (Nos. 100 and 101) that Chesterfield, a rather frequent contributor (twenty-four numbers), printed the praises of Samuel Johnson's *Dictionary* that provoked the irate lexicographer's famous letter to his would-be patron.

A little over a year after *The World* had concluded, Dodsley was back in the periodical market, but this time with a more substantial and enduring project. In April 1758, he and his brother James signed an agreement with another rising star, Edmund Burke, to write and compile the *Annual Register*. The first number appeared thirteen months later as a 400-page volume. A comprehensive work, the *Annual Register* chronicled the major events of the previous year, offered literary, historical, and topographical essays, carried numerous poems, and reviewed what Burke regarded as the best books published during that period. Once more, Dodsley had designed another triumph. The first number alone was reprinted nine times by the end of the century, and its successors enjoyed similar reprintings. Although Burke's political fortunes allowed him to drop out of the project

---

[28] See Harold Forster, *Supplements to Dodsley's Collection of Poems* (Oxford: Oxford Bibliographical Society, 1980).

[29] Moore, patronized by Dodsley's friend George Lyttelton, had gained some reputation in his own right for his *Fables for the Female Sex* (1744) and for a few plays during the late 1740s.

sometime in the mid-1760s, James Dodsley continued to publish the work, under the direction of other compilers, until his death in 1797.[30] Another evidence of Dodsley's commercial genius in filling a public need, the *Annual Register* ran well into the present century.

Dodsley also became involved in the publication of three newspapers during his career, although, in the case of two of them, he merely functioned as shareholder. As early as 5 May 1747, he had purchased a one-fifteenth share in the thrice-weekly *London Evening Post*, at the time the most influential London paper in the provinces.[31] By his own testimony, however, it is clear that he had nothing to do with its actual publication, despite the fact that he had regularly used the paper for placing poems as well as for advertising his books.[32]

It is probably no coincidence that after competing with Cave's *Gentleman's Magazine* on two occasions, Dodsley should purchase a major share in the *Gentleman's* chief rival, the *London Magazine*. On 9 December 1748, he bought a quarter share for 350 pounds, probably his largest purchase up to that date. Again, he seems to have had little say in the magazine's production, except perhaps to insert an occasional poem.[33]

The *London Chronicle*, however, found him at the headwaters. He undertook this thrice-weekly evening newspaper with William Strahan, who served as the paper's printer. With an introduction by Samuel Johnson, the first number was issued on New Year's Day 1757, and was well received. When printing his *Life of Johnson* (1791), James Boswell noted that the paper "still subsists" and that when he had been abroad, he found it to have "a more extensive circulation upon the Continent than any of the English newspapers."[34] It is sometimes thought that Dodsley sold his share of the paper shortly after the eleventh number because Strahan had continued, against his protest, to admit scurrilous material to the paper, principally articles reprinted from *The Test* and *The Con-Test*.[35] Although Dodsley wrote to Strahan on 24 January, expressing this determination, he seems not to have carried out his threat. The evidence occurs in another letter to Strahan, almost two years later, where the successful playwright is urging that the attacks on Garrick for his conduct toward *Cleone* be discontinued in "our paper."[36]

The last major project in Dodsley's career involved the compilation, writing, and editing of 159 fables that would appear on 23 February 1761 as *Select Fables of Esop and Other Fabulists. In Three Books.* The reception was extraordinary. The

[30] Scholarship has been at great pains to determine exactly when Burke's conduct of the *Annual Register* concluded. For a survey of the principal opinions and some new evidence, see my article "Edmund Burke, John Hawkesworth, the *Annual Register*, and the *Gentleman's Magazine*." *Huntington Library Quarterly*, 42 (1978), pp. 57–72.

[31] See G. A. Cranfield, "II. The 'London Evening Post' and the Jew Bill of 1753." *Historical Journal*, 8 (1965), p. 17. ✒ [32] See his letter to [?George, Lord Lyttelton] in late 1754.

[33] Dodsley's name should be added to those Donald F. McKenzie identifies as partners in the *London Magazine*. See *The Ledger of Charles Akers* (Oxford: Oxford Bibliographical Society, 1978), pp. 8–11.

[34] *Life*, I, 317–18.

[35] Besides Straus (p. 99), J. A. Cochrane also believes that Dodsley sold his share in the *London Chronicle* at this time. See the latter's *Dr. Johnson's Printer. The Life of William Strahan* (Cambridge: Harvard University Press, 1964), p. 104. [36] See Dodsley's letter on 12 December 1758.

Monthly Review (March) called it "ingenious . . . elegant . . . and very useful . . . a
classical performance."[37] The *Critical Review* praised Dodsley as the "best prose-
writer of apologues of this or any country."[38] The work saw several editions during
Dodsley's lifetime and continued a favorite through the rest of the century. Part of
its success might be attributed to Dodsley's wise printing of two separate editions,
one on fine paper printed by Baskerville and another cheaper edition for the use of
schools.

The three books presented, respectively, the fables of Aesop, fables by modern
authors, and those written by Dodsley and his friends. Although no complete list of
authors and their contributions has been possible, some are able to be identified.
Various pieces of evidence show Richard Graves, Robert Lowth, William
Melmoth, Thomas Percy, Joseph Spence, even James Dodsley, to have had a hand.
Shenstone translated Antoine Houdart de la Motte's *Discours sur la fable*[39] (upon
which Dodsley relied for his Preface) and provided the elaborate table of
contents.[40] Besides writing most of the original fables, Dodsley made a major
contribution in his extended Preface, where, as the *Critical Review* says, he set down
the "best rules for writing apologues." Indeed the Preface borrows much topical,
argumentative, and organizational support from Dodsley's predecessor, la Motte.
But much is new, enough to credit the author with an originality that, at times,
pushes beyond the Frenchman's penetration.[41]

The stature of Dodsley's business in the English booktrade during the 1750s can
be measured by the number of major literary personalities who chose to associate
themselves with Tully's Head. Many have already been considered, but a
particular handful, for whom he served as either advisor or patron, deserves special
mention.

Because no correspondence between the two survives, Dodsley's publishing
relationship with François Marie Arouet de Voltaire must be pieced together from
limited evidence. Also obscuring our perspective on the relationship was the
London trade's custom of issuing works of Continental authors (in the orginal or in
translation) without the author's permission. Although Voltaire did not personally
court Dodsley's services but had commissioned his English friend, Sir Everard
Fawkener, to find an appropriate publisher, it seems that once Dodsley had begun
to issue Voltaire's works, he enjoyed the Frenchman's cooperation thereafter.
Fawkener had sought Dodsley's advice regarding a London edition of Voltaire's *Le
siècle de Louis XIV* in early August 1751. Although Dodsley had thought it improper
to offer the author proposals, he did agree to sell the work from his shop if Voltaire
would supply the copies, including a title page indicating that the work had been
printed in London expressly for him, Dodsley. Such a procedure would give the
impression that Dodsley held the copyright, thereby forestalling piracies and faulty
editions. All of this Fawkener conveyed to Voltaire in a letter of 13 August.[42]

---

[37] March 1761, pp. 150–6.   [38] February 1761, pp. 122–7.
[39] *Fables nouvelles dediquées au roy par M. de la Motte . . .avec un discours sur la fable* (Paris, 1719).
[40] See Hylton's letter on 18 February 1761.
[41] See Robert Dodsley, *An Essay on Fable*. Introduction by Jeanne Welcher and Richard Dircks.
      Augustan Reprint Society. No. 112. (Los Angeles: William Andrews Clark Memorial Library,
      1965).   [42] *Voltaire's Correspondence*, ed. Theodore Besterman (Geneva, 1956), XX, 20–1.

Dodsley's publishing of the work in the original on 11 April 1752, followed by three more editions by June and a translation in July, would suggest that Voltaire had agreed with the arrangements. However, the evidence proves otherwise. First of all, an impersonal reference to Dodsley in Voltaire's letter to Fawkener on the following 22 August indicates that the author had no prior knowledge of these editions: "I have been informed that a London bookseller named Dodsley has printed by subscription the age of Louis XIV in two fine volumes."[43] Equally significant, entries in William Bowyer's ledgers on 30 April, 15 June, and 30 June 1752, show that the first two duodecimo editions and the following quarto edition – all in the original French – had been printed in London with imprints tailored to suggest a French origin: "Londre, chez R. Dodsley. 1752." Voltaire goes on, in that letter, to say that Dodsley should have known that a first edition is but a trial run and that he should have waited for improvements, which he now promises to send Fawkener for Dodsley in two months' time. And indeed, in 1753, appeared from Tully's Head a "new edition, revised, and considerably augmented, by the Author." Regrettably no evidence exists to show whether or not the other three pieces by Voltaire that Dodsley published over the next seven years were issued with the author's cooperation, but then there is no reason to think that they were not.

Another eighteenth-century luminary, the future statesman Edmund Burke, began his rise to fame through his association with Dodsley. The young Irishman, deprived of a paternal allowance because he had neglected his studies at Middle Temple, turned to his pen for a living in 1756. The first of his works, *A Vindication of Natural Society*, Dodsley apparently decided to farm out to Mary Cooper in order to preserve its anonymity. Its true origin was evident the following year, however, when the second edition appeared under Dodsley's imprint. That same year, Dodsley issued Burke's best known work, *A Philosophical Enquiry into the Origin of our Ideas of the Sublime and the Beautiful*, as well as the two-volume *An Account of the European Settlements in America*, though the latter is thought to be principally the work of his kinsman, William Burke. Burke's last production for Dodsley began in April 1758, when – ever in financial distress – he signed an agreement to conduct the bookseller's new periodical project, the *Annual Register*, for the yearly sum of one hundred pounds. But that story has already been told. Dodsley's ability to single out genius perhaps is no better illustrated than in the case of Burke. Responding to an inquiry from Shenstone, Dodsley wrote on 20 January 1759: "That Mr. Burke who writes so ingeniously, is an Irish Gentleman, bred to the Law, but having ye grace not to follow it, will soon I should think make a very great figure in the literary World."

Still another author destined to become a major figure applied for Dodsley's services at this time. Yet an unknown curate at York Cathedral, Laurence Sterne offered Dodsley his first volume of *The Life and Opinions of Tristram Shandy, Gent.* in a letter of 23 May 1759. The London bookseller had been suggested to Sterne by John Hinxman, Dodsley's former apprentice, who had recently set himself up in the trade at York. Dodsley balked at the purchase of this maverick work, preferring

---

[43] Ibid., XXI, 35–6.

to have it printed at York and sent down to London for sale at his shop. Unfortunately Dodsley's side of the correspondence is missing, and so it is impossible to know the specific arrangements with Sterne. However, although the Tully's Head imprint does not appear on the initial edition of the first two volumes in 1760, apparently some agreement had been struck, for James Dodsley (now having succeeded his brother) purchased the copyright to the volumes on 8 March for 250 pounds. At the same time, Dodsley was promised the copy of the next two volumes for 380 pounds. Accordingly, the second edition of the first two volumes, as well as the first of Volumes III and IV, were issued from Tully's Head within the year. Likewise, in May 1760, James Dodsley also purchased the copyright to Sterne's *The Sermons of Mr. Yorick* and published the two-volume work the same month.

Of course the initial volumes of *Tristram* were enormously popular. In May, Sterne came to London to enjoy his fame in person and was appropriately lionized by the town. His meeting with the Dodsleys, capped by the signing of the agreement for the next two volumes of *Tristram*, occasioned a classic Shandean remark. Emerging from Tully's Head, Sterne announced to his friends Croft and Chomley that "he was mortgaging his brains to Dodsley."[44] Within the year, however, Sterne had decided to claim more of the profit from future volumes by retaining the copyright and seeing to the printing himself. Accordingly, in December 1761, Volume V and the following began to be issued by two newcomers to the trade, Thomas Becket and Peter De Hondt.

Dodsley's three chief friends and supporters during the 1750s were Samuel Johnson, William Shenstone, and Joseph Spence. They were integral to both his social and business activities. Although Dodsley's payment for Johnson's *London* had been meager, apparently the bookseller's person, as well as his shop's flow of literary worthies, had proven very agreeable to Johnson. He was frequently to be found in company at Tully's Head and returned again and again with his manuscripts. In 1749, Dodsley issued the ill-fated *Irene* but, more importantly, the memorable *Vanity of Human Wishes*. In 1747, in collaboration with five other booksellers, Dodsley signed an agreement with Johnson for the work that would make the author famous, *A Dictionary of the English Language*. Finally, the month Dodsley retired, he issued, along with William Johnston and William Strahan, Johnson's novel, *The Prince of Abissinia* (*Rasselas*).[45]

It is difficult to imagine that Johnson harbored any special appreciation of Dodsley's own literary productions, but he was ever faithful to the man who had given him his start. When, in 1758, Dodsley decided to pit his tragedy *Cleone* at Covent Garden against all of Garrick's forces at Drury Lane, Johnson was on hand: "I went the first night, and supported it as well as I might; for Doddy, you know, is my patron, and I would not desert him."[46] Johnson had not forgotten that not only had Dodsley seen through the press his first major works, but had been the chief instigator of the work that had made Johnson famous. Writing to Charles Burney the month of the *Dictionary's* publication, he revealed, "It was by his [Dodsley's]

[44] *The Whitefoord Papers*, ed. W. A. S. Hewins (Oxford: Clarendon Press, 1898), p. 227.
[45] See Gwin J. Kolb, "*Rasselas*: Purchase Price, Proprietors, and Printings." *Studies in Bibliography*, 15 (1962), pp. 256–9.   [46] Boswell, *Life*, I, 326.

recommendation that I was employed in the work."⁴⁷ The scarcity of their extant correspondence is to be regretted but perhaps is explained by their frequent meetings. As the present letters show, Tully's Head was a regular gathering place of Johnson's friends and acquaintances, and Johnson himself used to say, as Joseph Warton recalled, "The true Noctes Atticae are revived at honest Dodsley's house."⁴⁸

As contributor to Dodsley's undertakings during the later 1750s, probably no one played a greater role than William Shenstone (1714–63). Although Dodsley had published the poet's work as early as 1741, Shenstone's contributions to Volumes IV–VI of the *Collection of Poems by Several Hands* turned a publisher–author relationship into a friendship that lasted until Shenstone's death. Dodsley closed Volume IV in 1755 with seventeen of Shenstone's poems, and when it came time for Volumes V and VI, he opened the former with another twenty-four of his friend's pieces, adding six more to Volume VI. As already evident, Dodsley likewise revered the Birmingham poet's critical abilities. Not only did he submit his own writings to Shenstone for correction, but he printed many poems belonging to Shenstone's acquaintances largely upon his friend's recommendation.⁴⁹

The deepening of their relationship during the production of the last volume of the *Collection* can be charted by the ever-increasing tone of familiarity that marks their letters and by the parcels Dodsley was regularly shipping off to Birmingham. Various *objets d'art* to enhance Shenstone's estate, the Leasowes – busts of Virgil and Horace, bronzed piping fauns, even swans and pigeons – made the route by Frimen's Wagon from London. But Dodsley's special delights were his summer jaunts to the Leasowes. He would head north, sometimes with Joseph Spence but always with some manuscript in tow about which he wanted Shenstone's advice. In June 1756, he wrote that he was carting with him "an unfortunate melancholy creature" (the rejected *Cleone*) who needed Shenstone's loving care. The next summer, he tells his host he is bringing along his ode *Melpomene* (1757) for further correction. And distressed with Shenstone's delay in submitting his own poems for the *Collection*, he says in the same letter that he will corrupt Shenstone's housekeeper so as "to join with me in robbing your Bureau of every scrap of Poetry in it." In 1760, when preparing his edition of Aesop's fables, he seems to have spent the entire period from July to October at Shenstone's, reading and revising the text with his friend's help. During these visits, too, he had the opportunity of meeting Shenstone's friends, several of whose poems he had published earlier in his *Collection*. It was no surprise, then, that Shenstone appointed Dodsley as one of his executors, or that Dodsley issued an edition of Shenstone's *Works* shortly after his friend's death.

Soon after Alexander Pope died in 1744, his protégé Joseph Spence (1699–1768) turned to Dodsley as bookseller and friend. Spence's most respected work during his lifetime, *Polymetis*, appeared from Tully's Head in 1747, and Dodsley printed eight of Spence's narrative essays in his fortnightly *Museum* at about the same time. These were followed by a series of works running into the 1750s, some of which were

---

⁴⁷ Chapman, *Letters*, I, 69.   ⁴⁸ *The Works of Alexander Pope*, ed. Joseph Warton (London, 1797).
⁴⁹ Those of Richard Graves, John Scott Hylton, Richard Jago, Lady Luxborough, Thomas Percy, John Pixell, and Anthony Whistler are documented in the correspondence printed here.

signed with the pseudonym "Sir Harry Beaumont." Something of the relationship of the two men is revealed as early as 1748 when Dodsley, longing for the delights of Spence's rural retreat (Spence had retired to his living at Byfleet after earning fifteen hundred pounds from his *Polymetis*), wrote to his friend: "If I did not love you, I should certainly envy." Occasional hints in Dodsley's correspondence also suggest that Spence was a preferred reader of manuscripts at Tully's Head: no doubt he had a hand in the selection of poems for Dodsley's *Collection*. One of their most evident collaborations occurred in 1754 when they introduced English readers to the blind Scots poet Thomas Blacklock. For Dodsley's edition of Blacklock's poems – encouraged by the poet's friend David Hume – Spence provided a prefatory biographical account.

But the fullness of their relationship emerges during their summer treks north, especially their last. In 1753, Spence had gained a prebend at Durham, which the pair visited on two occasions, passing through Shenstone's Leasowes on the way. Upon his return from the first visit in August of 1758, Dodsley wrote Shenstone a lengthy letter in which he described in detail the enchantment of Durham, claiming that "it is one of the most romantic places I ever saw." In this light, one is tempted to speculate on the gout-ridden Dodsley's motivation in undertaking a second trip to Durham with Spence in 1764, a trip from which he would not return. Spence's account of Dodsley's painful walks about Finculo Abbey in those last days was conveyed in his letters to Elizabeth Cartwright, and is printed here. Worn out, Dodsley died at Durham on 23 September, aged sixty-one, and was buried in the Durham Cathedral churchyard. There Spence had the following inscribed on a large brown stone covering his grave:

> If you have any respect
> For uncommon industry and merit
> Regard this place
> In which are interred the remains
> of
> Mr Robert Dodsley
> Who as an author raised himself
> Much above what could have been expected
> From one in his rank of life
> And without a learned education.
> Who as a man was scarce exceeded by any
> In integrity of heart
> And purity of manners and conversation.
> He left this world for a better
> September 23rd 1764
> In the 61st year of his age.

In life, Dodsley exhibited the social virtues and customs, the political and religious inclinations, of many an enlightened middle-class London businessman. His thrifty but fair-dealing ways built a steady and respected name both among his authors and within the trade. The industry and imagination that bred such distinguished accomplishments were leavened with a modesty that never seemed to forget its origins. His cautious and pragmatic approach to business did not stifle an innovative spirit that gave birth to a number of novel publications. In an age still dominated by the poetry of Pope, he had the foresight and courage to sponsor a new poetic spirit, as exhibited in the works of Collins, Smart, and the Wartons.

Little evidence exists to afford a consistent sense of Dodsley's religious persuasion, but it does seem that, like many of his well-bred, fashionable friends, he found deism most compatible. Although he was christened and married in the established church, the subject of formal religion is peculiarly absent from his correspondence, even from his private letters. He listed among his friends many authors from the clerical ranks, but their profession seemed to exercise little effect on the relationship. Dodsley's most notable reference to formal religion is strikingly antagonistic to one of its fundamental rites. Writing to Solomon Mendes in November 1744, he reflects: "My wife and I are going this evening to the solemn foolery of a christening. 'Tis very wisely done, to tye us down so early to believe, what otherwise, perhaps, might never enter into our heads. I think it would be a good way of promoting the sciences, to have godfathers and godmothers at our birth, to promise and vow for this, that he shall be a poet; for that, that he shall be a mathematician: at least, there is as much sense in one as the other."

The anti-sacramental character of the remark fits the deistic persuasion that marked many of Dodsley's current associates, as it did some of his own publications. Of course it is dangerous to rely on a bookseller's list of publications, especially such a diverse one as Dodsley's, to frame some picture of his religion. On the other hand, a few works of this period projected by Dodsley himself and over which he exercised close control clearly evidence a taste for deism. Many of the essays in his fortnightly *Museum*, for instance, take their themes from the Earl of Shaftesbury and make explicit references to his *Characteristics*, the principal statement of the deistic creed. Likewise, Dodsley's *Preceptor* (1748), a comprehensive instruction for students covering a broad range of subjects, certainly had place for some commentary on formal religion, but instead it maintained a distinctly deistic air throughout. Like all patriotic Protestant Englishmen, though, he was strongly anti-papist, as evident from the virulent titles issued from Tully's Head during the Jacobite Rebellion in 1745.

Although Dodsley shrewdly avoided mixing politics with business, his early sympathies lay with the Opposition, as is clear from the Leicester House personalities who turn up among his friends and authors. Through Pope, a friend of the Prince of Wales (figurehead of the Opposition), Dodsley had probably become acquainted with the Prince's favorite, George (later Lord) Lyttelton, a number of whose works would emanate from Dodsley's in the 1740s. Another leader of the Opposition, the Earl of Chesterfield, would become a regular contributor to Dodsley's publications and, of course, would prove instrumental in securing the performance of *Cleone*. It is probably not insignificant that Dodsley's play *The Toy-shop* was once performed (in 1735) at the command of the Prince and Princess of Wales.

To some extent Dodsley's allegiance to the government followed the fortunes of Lyttelton's career. In 1754, when Lyttelton had become a Privy Councillor, Dodsley's anonymous letter late in the year (probably addressed to the Lord) reveals his support of the current government. It was probably also Lyttelton who, as a lord of the Treasury, had secured Dodsley the franking privilege that the bookseller availed himself of during the years 1753 to 1755. In July 1757, however, when the Scottish poet Thomas Blacklock requested Dodsley's intercession to help him gain a post through Lyttelton's political influence, Dodsley regretfully replied that the Baron was not only out of town but now also out of power. Two last political favors suggest that Dodsley had won the respect of John Stuart, 3rd Earl of Bute, who had become the dominant influence in the Court of the more recent Prince of Wales. A letter to Bute in early December 1758 asking support for his *Cleone* resulted in the Prince's attendance three days later. In 1762, Dodsley was instrumental in acquiring Bute's permission to allow Baskerville to dedicate his new edition of Horace to the now Secretary of State.

Finally, in an age when mercantilism became synonymous with patriotism in the minds of industrious tradesmen, Dodsley regarded himself as being in the front ranks of patriots. As an early member of the Society for the Encouragement of Arts, Manufactures, and Commerce (now the Royal Society of Arts), Dodsley not only worked assiduously to expand the young Society's mission, but also served on many committees to effect the production of native English paper that would relieve the country's dependence on a supply from the Continent. His concept of the Society's role in the nation's progress is no better illustrated than in the letters he wrote to its membership regarding its name and its need to take Letters under its wing. On 14 December 1756, he wrote to propose that the members consider the name "The Philopatrian Society of London," a name that "most happily includes the very Motive and bond of our Association, namely the Love of our Country; and as every man either is or ought to be a Lover of his Country, and as most men wish at least to be thought so . . . so honourable and engaging a Name may induce many to associate with us in these good designs." It was no idle gesture that, in 1757 when Dodsley challenged Garrick to act *Cleone* at Drury Lane, the playwright offered to donate the third night's profits to the work of the Society.[50]

2. Business at Tully's Head

The exact site and date on which Dodsley first opened the doors of Tully's Head are not known. The imprint on Volume II of Pope's *Works* (1735) shows his address to have been Pall Mall, but his name does not appear in the Westminster Rate Books until 1738. Straus suggests that he might have occupied one of the smaller houses on the same cul-de-sac where Tully's Head was to be found three years later. Whatever the original location, in 1738 Dodsley took over Sir William Yonge's former quarters, a large house at the end of a passageway almost directly opposite Marlborough House and running up toward King Street.[51]

The earliest reference to the opening of Tully's Head occurs on 6 May 1735, when Pope mentions in a letter to William Duncombe on that date that Dodsley "has just set up as a bookseller."[52] Since the shop was opened with proceeds from the production of Dodsley's *The Toy-shop*, which had made its debut in early

---

[50] For Dodsley's role in the Society, see my article "Robert Dodsley: First Printer and Stationer to the Society." *Journal of the Royal Society of Arts* (July and August, 1983), pp. 480–3, 563–6.
[51] Straus, p. 38.   [52] See note 12.

February of this year, it can be reasonably assumed that Tully's Head began business sometime in March or April 1735.

Both the timing and location of Tully's Head proved opportune. The 1730s witnessed a falling-off of enterprising booksellers with strong literary interests. Retirement, death, or bankruptcy claimed such familiar trade names as Jacob Tonson the elder, Bernard Lintot, and James Knapton. With the ranks thinned, an energetic and literate newcomer like Dodsley, especially with Pope's support, had a fine chance to make his mark.

Probably because he had no roots in the trade, Dodsley did not attempt to invade the City proper with his new business. Perhaps he made virtue of necessity by locating in Pall Mall, but what might have seemed initially a compromise soon proved advantageous. By setting up in Pall Mall, Dodsley placed himself within fashionable St James's and within easy reach of the government offices in Whitehall. The St James's coffee house, made famous by Steele's *Tatler* papers and still frequented by devoted Whigs, was near at hand in St James's Street. In the same street, the Cocoa Tree and Ozinda's still thrived, as well as the most fashionable of all, White's Chocolate-house, the modish meeting place for both town and Court. Immediately at the door of Tully's Head, the Smyrna coffee house served up the latest political rumours and news from abroad. In short, although remote from the center of the trade, Tully's Head was neighbor to the haunts of the alert and the literate. And, except for a few pamphlet shops in Pall Mall and James Brindley in New Bond Street, Dodsley had no serious competitors in the immediate area.

Present evidence shows that Dodsley's name, during his twenty-five years at Tully's Head, appeared in imprints as publisher ("Printed for") for first editions of at least 468 titles.[53] Assuming that this total is not complete, that perhaps he should be

---

[53] A truly complete listing of Dodsley's publications could have been compiled only by a contemporary bibliographer who had periodic access to the shelves at Tully's Head. Much has gone astray in the interim. Present resources and systems are inadequate for accomplishing the task. The figures used here are derived from two major resources, which the editor has supplemented with his own research. As expected, the British Library enjoys the fullest holdings of works in whose imprints Dodsley's name figures. The timely completion of the first stage of the *Eighteenth-Century Short-Title Catalogue* has made available bibliographical descriptions (including imprints) of these titles in a Blaise-Line print-out.

This listing was collated with the second resource, Straus's 73-page bibliography of Dodsley's titles, found at the rear of his biography of the bookseller. It was discovered that Straus, although having overlooked a good number of appropriate British Library volumes, had listed one hundred and forty-two titles not found in the Blaise-Line print-out. These additions were possible because Straus had not only examined BL volumes but had also consulted eighteenth-century newspaper advertisements, which normally included mention of publishers' and sellers' names. He had identified works that had not made their way into the British Library, perhaps not even into the twentieth century.

These additional listings in Straus were not, however, entered into the master list indiscriminately. Each entry was verified by recourse to the original newspaper or periodical advertisement. Although Straus was discovered to have erred occasionally, the instances were surprisingly few. Most of his errors involved listing Dodsley as publisher of a work when he had served simply as seller.

To this master list compiled from Blaise-Line and Straus, were added entries discovered by the editor himself in the course of reviewing newspaper and periodical advertisements, bookdealer catalogues, and a wealth of secondary material over many years. In short, although admittedly incomplete, the present figures represent the fullest accounting of Dodsley's publications, to date.

credited with another thirty or so, we can see that he was publishing approximately twenty new titles per year; or, one nearly every two and a half weeks.

Not all of these 468 titles show Dodsley's name as the sole publisher. "Printed for R. Dodsley in Pall-mall" appears in 233 imprints. Beginning in 1753, when James Dodsley's name becomes linked with Robert's in the imprint, another 124 titles are issued as "Printed for R. and J. Dodsley in Pall-mall." The other 111 titles find Dodsley's name joined, in sixty-five instances, with one or more booksellers; and "R. and J. Dodsley" collaborating with other booksellers in the remaining forty-six cases.

But the foregoing publications do not exhaust the occasions when the Dodsley name appears in imprints. In at least another 135 instances, Robert's, or Robert's joined with his brother's, is listed in the imprint as "seller" ("And sold by"). Since "sellers," when listed, were customarily multiple, it is probably not surprising that Robert's name is found by itself as seller for only two publications, and, when joined with James's, for only another ten. He is listed with other sellers in seventy-five cases, and in an additional forty-eight titles when joined by James.

In toto, then, the Dodsley name is found, either as publisher or seller, in at least 603 titles issued during the period 1735–59. But it should be noted, at this point, that the number of publications for which Dodsley was actually responsible might be considerably larger if we could identify all of those he published surreptitiously; those, for instance, to which he persuaded the publisher Mary Cooper to put her name. At least two major instances of such publications have come to light in the course of this correspondence. The pre-publication preparations of both John Gilbert Cooper's *Cursory Remarks on Mr. Warburton's New Edition of Mr. Pope's Works* (1751) and Joseph Warton's *Essay on the Writings and Genius of Mr. Pope* (1756) can be traced in Dodsley's correspondence with the authors, but, in the end, the bookseller preferred not to put his name to the works. The extensive collaboration between Dodsley and Mary Cooper – to be taken up later – suggests that there were probably many other pieces consigned to this mode of publication.

To afford an overview of the foregoing figures, the table opposite will be useful.

Dodsley's reputation as a publisher of *belles lettres* is certainly justified by an analysis of his record. Tables 1 and 2 (pp. 26, 28) present a complete breakdown, both by literary type and by content, of all works in whose imprints Dodsley's name appears during the period 1735–59, whether as publisher or as seller. Although the roles of publisher and seller differ in an essential way – the latter sharing none of the financial risk – they are purposely merged here to give an overall picture of the kind of publication with which Dodsley chose to be associated.

First, a few cautions are necessary regarding the manner and make-up of the two tables. Only first editions are used, except in those cases where a later edition constituted Dodsley's first edition of the work. A certain degree of overlap was inevitable, for some works fit a number of categories. For instance, in Table 1, Pope's *Works* are properly classified under both "Collection of Works" and "Poetry"; and Dodsley's own *Trifles* is a "collection" that includes both "poetry" and "drama." The number (208) listed under "Prose" can be misleading; it must be understood that this field embraces a number of sub-classifications. "Transla-

	1730s	1740s	1750s	Total
Publisher				
("Printed for")				
RD	40	142	51	233
RD *et al.*	7	27	31	65
R&JD	—	—	124	124
R&JD *et al.*	—	—	46	46
Total	47	169	252	468
Seller				
("And sold by")				
RD	—	2	—	2
RD *et al.*	5	41	29	75
R&JD	—	—	10	10
R&JD *et al.*	—	—	48	48
Total	5	43	87	135
Grand total				603

tions" (49) is itself swollen by entries of poetry, as is also "Collections" (37). Similar duplication occurs in Table 2, where such a piece as *The Principles and Practices of a Popish Government* meets the requirements for both "Politics" and "Religion." The effect of this overlap is to increase the number of entries beyond the actual number of publications in which Dodsley was involved. Hence the resulting totals must be looked upon solely as indicative of Dodsley's interests, not as representative of the quantity of imprints in which his name appeared.

Conversely, the subject totals in Table 2 fall short of the number of publications in which Dodsley was involved, principally because some works – e.g. collections, biographies, memoirs – defy classification by a clearly defined subject. Furthermore, to avoid extending the list beyond manageable proportions, only those subjects were included whose total entries numbered at least five. Consequently another nineteen subjects – e.g. drawing, cookery, music, sculpture – are not represented in the table. Also, because some works could not be traced, their subjects could not be included.

Finally, classifying such a large number of entries inevitably involved some arbitrary decisions. The reader should understand the categories in the broadest sense.

Nevertheless, despite their limitations, the tables afford a fairly faithful account of the nature and scope of Dodsley's publishing interests. Table 1 makes it quite clear that Dodsley was principally a publisher of poetry. The 238 items in that category far outnumber all other categories. (For the category "Prose," see above.) The number under "Translations" (49) reveals Dodsley's penchant for both classical and imported works. (The latter is supported by the twenty entries under the heading "Foreign Language.") The next largest and clearly distinct categories "Sermons" (34) and "Drama" (33) are perhaps indicative of nothing more than Dodsley's addressing the main-stream market, although his particular interest in

Table 1. Types of works for which Dodsley acted as either publisher or seller

Type of work	1735	1736	1737	1738	1739	1740	1741	1742	1743	1744	1745	1746	1747	1748	1749	1750	1751	1752	1753	1754	1755	1756	1757	1758	1759	Totals
Auto/biographies/Memoirs/Diaries	1	1		1	3					1	1	1		2	2	2	2	2	1	1	1	1		1	2	21
Collection of Works	1		1	1	1		1		1	1	2	2	3	3	3	2	1	1	3	1	3	1	2	3	2	37
Dialogue (Question/Answer)		1	2	1	2		1	2	1	1	2	2		2		3		1					2		1	10
Drama	1	1	2	2	2		1	1	1	1	2		2	1	3	1	1		5	2		1	5	2		33
Fable/Fairy Tale						1	1	1	1	1				2					2	1		1	2	1		6
Fiction				1						2	2	1		1	3	2			1	4		2	1	1	1	23
Foreign Language						1	1	1	1		2		1		2	1	3		1		4			2	1	20
Handbook/Calendar/Memorandum Books				1						1			3	3				3	2	4					2	8
History			1			1			1		1			1	1	1	4	4	1		3	6			1	17
Lectures/Speeches								2	1			1			1			1	1		3		1			6
Letters	2	1	1	1	2					1	1	1		3	1	3	11	1	1	1	1	1	2	1	1	11
Poetry	2	4	7	12	12	9	8	8	12	13	17	11	6	3	3	3	11	7	13	13	14	11	12	13	12	238
Prose: Essay/Dissertation/Tract	5	2	5	5	2	7	7	1	4	5	10	6	11	6	9	9	4	6	20	13	19	19	15	21	15	208
Sermons				1	1	2	1	1		1	1	2	2	1	1	1	3		2	2	3	1	2	2	2	34
Translations	1	1		1	1	2	2	2	2	4	3	2	1	1	3	1	3	3	9	3	3	3	1	2	3	49
Travel books										2					1						1	1				6
Total																										727

drama has already been cited. Despite the mid-century's increasing taste for fiction, Dodsley's conservative stance is reflected in the mere twenty-three pieces he published over his 24-year career. Finally, the number of works of a biographical character – twenty-one – is somewhat surprising; one might have expected more of a friend of Johnson.

Dodsley's commitment to Augustan poetry looms in Table 2. By far the largest subject entry concerns either the reissuing of Greek and Latin authors or the publication of imitations by Dodsley's fellow Englishmen. Dodsley himself published the works of no fewer than twelve classical authors, and he served as agent for the sale of another half dozen. Included among the ancients are Aesop, Caesar, Callimachus, Cicero, Epictetus, Herodotus, Horace, Lucan, Martial, Persius, Pindar, Plato, Pliny, Polybius, Sallust, Tacitus, Theophrastus, and Virgil. The long list of imitations he published shows Dodsley's concurrence with the mid-century's love affair with Horace. Whereas three imitations of Juvenal take the runner-up position, the twenty-one inspired by Horace far oustrip all others.

As might be expected in an age where religion and its concerns permeated every aspect of life, the subjects of theology, morality, church government, and so on, claimed a major place in the printed word. In Table 2, works treating of formal religion, God, the Bible, and the clergy represent the next highest category among Dodsley's publications, with fifty-seven entries. Closely related, the large entry under "Morality/Ethics" helps to confirm the ongoing popularity of literature stressing theology and virtue. Although himself a man inclined to virtue, Dodsley certainly did not ignore the market's needs.

Also, as a middle-class businessman, Dodsley necessarily had political interests. Although he cautiously avoided offense in his publications, the number of entries (38) in the "Government/Politics" category shows that, far from being just a literary publisher, he sponsored many works on theoretical and practical politics, both domestic and foreign. His early alignment with the Opposition at Leicester House echoes in his publication of Baron Paget's *Some Reflections upon the Administration of Government* (1740); his vehement antagonism to the papacy expressed in such works published during the '45 as John Downes' *A Popish Prince the Pest of a Protestant People* (1745); his ongoing concern for current administrations implied in such as the anonymous *Free Thoughts, and Bold Truths . . . a politico-critical Essay* (1755). All emanate from a keen patriotism evident in such titles as Boucher Cleeve's *Scheme for preventing a further Increase of the National Debt* (1756), Leonard Howard's *The Good Government of a Country its great Object* (1753), and Dodsley's own *Public Virtue* (1753). Also significant in this regard are the number of works Dodsley published that treated of military affairs, including personnel, sieges, and strategies.

Perhaps most striking, in light of his reputation for poetry, emerge the numbers of works Dodsley issued on the subject of science, particularly on medicine. William Cheselden's *Anatomy of the Human Body* (1741), Henry Baker's *The Microscope Made Easy* (1742), Robert Douglas's *Essay Concerning the Generation of Heat in Animals* (1747), Thomas Gataker's *Observations on the Venereal Complaint* (1755), and Robert Whytt's *Physiological Essays* (1756) are but a few that ranged through his career at Tully's Head.

Table 2. Subjects of works for which Dodsley acted as either publisher or seller

Subjects of works	1735	1736	1737	1738	1739	1740	1741	1742	1743	1744	1745	1746	1747	1748	1749	1750	1751	1752	1753	1754	1755	1756	1757	1758	1759	Totals
America																					2	1	3		1	7
Architecture						1	1	1	1													1	1		1	7
Classics and Imitation of			5	6	4	2		2	1	2	1	2	2	2	9	3	3	3	9	6	4	4	4	6	7	87
Commerce/Trade/Economics/Agriculture						1		2			1	5	3	2	1	1	1		2					2	1	22
Domestic/Marriage										1	1	1	1							3						7
Drama							1		1	1		1													1	5
Education/Learning (Youth)									1	1	1	1	1	3					2		1	3				14
Entertainment/Resort														1	3			1			1					6
Geography/Topography					2					2		2														6
Government/Politics (Practice/Theory)					2					2	3	6	1	1		2	2		5	1	5	6			2	38
History			1				2			2			2			1	1		2	4			1		2	18
Literary Criticism									1	1			1		1				1						1	6
Mechanical/Physical Arts				1			2							1								2				6
Monarchy/Nobility (Domestic/Foreign)	1	2			2			2		2	2		2	2		2	2	3	3				1	3		29
Morality/Ethics										1	1	1	2	2	2	2			4	2	3		1	2	1	24
Patriotism			2								3	7	1							6						19
Philosophy/Esthetics				3		2	2			1	1	1			2				1	6	1	3		3	3	29
Physicians/Surgeons/Health										1		1		1		1			2	1	2		2			11
Poetry										1	1	1	4				1		3	2	2	2	2	2	1	22
Pre-1700 Works	1	1		1		2		1	1				4			1					1				1	14
Religion/God/Bible/Clergy				1				1		3	8	8	3	2	2	4	2		7	1	5	4	2	2	2	57
Science/Medicine/Math									3	3	1	5	2		1	1			2		6	5	1	1		31
Self-help/Personal Improvement														2						2			2			6
Society/Criticism				3					1	1	1	1		1		1		1	1	1	1	1	1		1	16
Social Reform							1		1		1				1									1		5
Theater/Entertainment																					2			2	2	6
War/Peace/Military								2		3	3	4	2	2						1		3	4	4	4	32
Women				1	1			2		2		1		2								2	2			13
Total																										545

Probably because of trade monopolies, Dodsley's list of credits in pre-1700 English authors is comparatively slim. He appears as seller in the imprints to the *Canterbury Tales* (1740), Michael Drayton's *Works* (1737), and Jonson's *Eastward Ho* (1751), and he was sole publisher of an edition of Raleigh's *Works* (1750), Massinger's *New Way to Pay Old Debts* (1748), and Norton and Sackville's *Gorboduc* (1736). To these must be added his own twelve-volume *Select Collection of Old Plays*. But that was all. His menu of Continental classics was somewhat broader. The offerings included the principal works of Boccaccio, Cervantes, Erasmus, Fénelon, Gelli, Tasso, and Vida. Credits in contemporary European literature extend to many subjects and authors, including such as Baretti, Crébillon, Riccoboni, and Voltaire.

Much of Dodsley's success in the trade can be attributed to a happy combination of skills: an ability to detect new talent and a keen sense of the market. He recognized gifted beginners, and he knew what would sell. As a prime result, many of the works he took in tow saw multiple editions, the bread and butter of a publisher's business. Works of major authors that would be issued again and again have already been mentioned. But there were others (though now little known) which also proved popular with contemporary readers. In fact, at least 113 works with Dodsley's name in the imprint – twenty-four per cent of all he published – passed through multiple editions during his lifetime. At least forty-five of these reached three or more editions, and ten of them reached five. Among his best sellers were Samuel Johnson's *London,* George, Lord Lyttelton's *Observations on the Conversion and Apostleship of St. Paul,* William Mason's *Caractacus,* Gilbert West's *Observations on the History and Evidence of the Ressurection of Jesus Christ* (five editions each); Mark Akenside's *Pleasures of Imagination,* Nathaniel Cotton's *Visions in Verse,* Sir Thomas Fitzoborne's (i.e., William Melmoth's) two-volume *Letters on Several Subjects* (six editions each); John Dalton's adaptation of Milton's *Comus* (seven editions); Thomas Gray's *Elegy Written in a Country Church Yard* (eleven editions); and Edward Young's *Complaint, or Night Thoughts* (twelve editions).

Evidence of press runs is not abundant. Occasionally, Dodsley mentions specific figures in his correspondence with authors, but the ledgers of Wiliam Bowyer and William Strahan prove a more rewarding source. Similar data can be gleaned from publishing agreements, although the latter reflect only "intended" runs. None the less, despite the incompleteness of the record, it is possible to make some generalizations about Dodsley's press runs, and naturally they reflect the usual quantities in which printers offered copies: 250, 500, 750, 1,000, 1,500, 2,000, 3,000, etc. Normally, for a poem or a pamphlet by an unknown author, or for a work of limited appeal, Dodsley printed 500 copies; or if he had some special expectations for it, 750. Editions or translations of the Classics regularly merited 750 copies. Printing a thousand suggested a particular faith in a work, usually stemming from an author's reputation or the currency of the topic. Printing 1,500 or 2,000 copies was reserved for those authors or works that had already proven themselves with the public and for which there continued a high demand.

These estimates can be illustrated with specific cases. The smallest run recorded to Dodsley – 250 copies – was given *The Memoirs and Letters of Ulick, Marquis of Clanricarde* (1757). The expensiveness of the edition (it sold for £1.11.6) and perhaps Dodsley's uneasiness with the text (see his letter to John Smith, current Earl of Clanricarde) probably account for its size. An almost unknown author at the time, Edmund Burke settled for a run of but 500 copies in the case of his *Vindication of Natural Society* (1757), as did the aspiring John Gilbert Cooper for his *Life of Socrates* (1749), and the established Henry Brooke for his slight *Songs in Jack the Gyant Queller* (1749). The same run was accorded William Hatchett's pamphlet *Fortune's Tricks in Forty-Six* (1747).

Gilbert West's translation of *The Odes of Pindar* was issued in 750 copies, both in its first and second editions. But more saleable translations like William Duncan's *Caesar's Commentaries* (1753) and Christopher Pitt's *Aeneid* (1740) saw 1,000 copies. Similar printings were bestowed on such substantial undertakings as *The Microscope Made Easy*, by Henry Baker (1742) and *Poems on Several Occasions* by the established poet and chaplain to George II, Edward Cobden. Volume I of William Melmoth's ("Sir Thomas Fitzoborne's") *Letters on Several Subjects*, in each of its first three editions (1748–9), received 1,000 copies, and its popularity dictated 1,500 copies for Volume II (1749).

The most generous printings, however, were reserved for works with the largest anticipated sales. Dodsley's edition of Pope's *Works*, Volume III, Part I (*Dunciad*, 1743) was printed in 2,000 copies. The bookseller's long-awaited Volume 4 (1755) of his *Collection of Poems by Several Hands* (as well as the reissue of the first three volumes) appeared in 1,500 copies. The largest single issue of any of Dodsley's works appropriately honored Tully's Head's patron. In 1753, he printed 3,000 copies of the first edition of William Melmoth's translation, *The Letters of Marcus Tullius Cicero to Several of his Friends*.

A fairly good sense of Dodsley's treatment of authors can be derived from the material supplied in Appendix B: the catalogue of extant publishing agreements, receipts acknowledging payment, and references to purchases found in other printed sources. For the most part, the agreements were drawn up in legal language, merely signed by the agreeing parties, and witnessed by acquaintances or by those at hand. Each agreement normally specified the date of the signing, the proposed title of the work, its length, the number of copies to be printed, and the size of the volume. If it was a commissioned work, these details were usually followed by the specification of a delivery date or a schedule for the submission of the manuscript. Whether it concerned an outright purchase of an existing manuscript or a commissioned work, the agreement usually set forth a payment schedule. (No payment in full was ever made at the time of signing.) Finally, most contracts carried some arrangement for additional payment should a work go into a second or later edition.

Payments varied in size, nature, and scheduling, depending upon the character of the work and the reputation of the author. Pamphlet-size poems usually brought their authors ten to fifteen guineas, while recently acted plays almost regularly earned a hundred pounds. Translations, especially of Latin authors, paid well, usually 150 to 200 pounds. Substantial works in science and medicine paid likewise.

The most common agreement, whether for a solicited or unsolicited manuscript, called for an outright purchase of the copyright. Obviously Dodsley would offer less for an unsolicited manuscript, especially if the work of an unknown author. So Samuel Johnson was given ten guineas for his *London* in 1738 and fifteen guineas for *The Vanity of Human Wishes* eleven years later. In 1757, Dodsley paid the already esteemed Thomas Gray forty guineas for his two odes, "The Progress of Poetry" and "The Bard." In the same year, the newcomer Edmund Burke received twenty guineas for his original *Philosophical Enquiry*, whereas two years earlier the popular Edward Young had been given 200 pounds for *The Centaur Not Fabulous*.

Another mode of payment, though less common, involved payment by the sheet. Invariably only authors of commissioned works of some length were paid in this manner. The payment varied from one to two guineas per sheet. Henry Baker found himself at both ends of the range for his *Microscope Made Easy* (1742) and *The Natural History of the Polype* (1743). Tobias Smollett was paid one and a half guineas by Dodsley, Rivington, and Strahan for his *Compendium of Authentic and Entertaining Voyages* (1756). Usually such agreements also specified a particular length for the proposed work. So Smollett's was to run approximately one hundred sheets, while John Campbell's uncompleted *Geography, Natural History and Antiquities of England and Wales* was required to be no less than sixty nor more than eighty sheets. Sometimes a forfeiture was stipulated for the author's failure to meet a deadline, as in Campbell's case.

Another form of payment came in the way of books. Both of Baker's agreements called for the additional payment of twenty copies of the work prior to publication. Robert Paltock's payment of twenty-one pounds for the *Life of Peter Wilkens* (1751) was supplemented with a dozen printed copies of the work. Frequently authors used these volumes as presentation copies, but on other occasions merely sold them for additional profit. An uncommon arrangement was struck by Dodsley's frequent author John Gilbert Cooper. Cooper regularly left his full payment "on account" at Tully's Head and, from time to time, would order books from Dodsley to be charged against his account.

The record shows two deviations from the usual modes of payment. In 1743, Dodsley agreed with William Whitehead to risk the costs of paper, printing, and advertising for the publication of the author's *Ann Boleyn to Henry the Eighth*. After expenses were deducted, the two were to share equally in profits from sales. In 1753, Dodsley signed an agreement with Sarah Fielding whereby he purchased half of the copyright to *The Cry* (1754) for fifty pounds and held himself responsible to the author for the profits deriving from the other half.

The scheduling of payments for commissioned works varied, but some general patterns can be detected. Although no author seems to have been paid in full at the signing of an agreement, occasionally Dodsley made small advances at that point. Both of Baker's contracts show an advance of a token five shillings. In 1754, Dodsley advanced Archibald Campbell fifteen guineas for eight books of a proposed 24-book epic *Alcides*, a work Campbell did not complete. (How the agreement was resolved is not known.) One exception shows William Melmoth to have been paid a hundred pounds at the time of signing for his translation of Cicero's *Letters* (1753).

Dodsley was more likely to agree to pre-publication payment when it was carried out by installment. Campbell himself was to receive five guineas per book as they were produced. William Duncan received two payments of twenty guineas each before the publication of his translation of Caesar's *Commentaries* (1753). Those commissioned to produce lengthy works were sometimes paid by the sheet as the work was produced, apparently to encourage the project's completion. In two cases, the plan proved futile, for the works seem not to have been completed. For Thomas Salmon's *Tradesman's Dictionary*, Dodsley agreed in 1749 to pay a guinea per sheet as prepared; for John Campbell's *Geography, Natural History and Antiquities of England and Wales*, a year earlier, the bookseller had committed himself to a guinea per sheet as the work went forward. The failure of the latter perhaps is explained by a somewhat unusual stipulation in the contract requiring Campbell to deliver the whole book in ten months or to forfeit fifty pounds.

The most common payment schedule, both for commissioned and unsolicited works, called for a flat partial payment either upon delivery of the manuscript or at publication, the remainder to be paid some months after publication. (This arrangement eased the cash flow for the bookseller and allowed him to be processing several works concurrently.) The two payments were usually of equal amounts (half payments) and were completed normally three to six months after publication. One exception to this schedule is doubtless explained by the size of the payment – the largest recorded by Dodsley for a single work. For Cicero's *Letters*, Dodsley contracted to pay William Melmoth six hundred pounds in three installments: one hundred at both the signing and the publication, and four hundred twelve months after publication. Perhaps the sale was not as brisk as expected, for Melmoth did not receive full payment until more than two years after publication.

Occasionally Dodsley would purchase the copyright of a work that had been in print for some time. Although most of such instances involved his own publications, he did occasionally purchase such old standards as William Cheselden's *Anatomy of the Human Body* (1713). Handsome sums were usually laid out in such agreements, for they frequently included (as did Cheselden's for two hundred guineas) the author's surrender of the plates for the work, as well as all unsold copies. (Including the latter in the purchase, of course, protected the bookseller's investment.) In the case of the posthumous purchase of Christopher Pitt's translation of Virgil's *Aeneid* – the first edition of which Dodsley himself had published in 1740 – the bookseller paid fifty guineas for the copyright but an additional sixty-two pounds, ten shillings, for the five hundred remaining copies. Similar purchases included Colley Cibber's *Apology* (1740) in 1750 for fifty guineas, Nathaniel Cotton's *Visions in Verse* (1751) in 1757 for fifty pounds, and Joseph Spence's *Polymetis* (1747) for the generous sum of two hundred pounds.

Frequently agreements carried some provision for payment covering future editions – an early form of royalty. For *Caesar's Commentaries*, Duncan agreed to accept an additional ten shillings and sixpence per sheet for a second edition. Baker claimed an additional guinea per sheet for all copies sold after the first printing (1,000 copies) had been exhausted. For a second edition of *A Vindication*, Edmund

Burke bargained for a sum identical to the original payment (six guineas) but then settled for only half of the original payment (twenty guineas) for a third edition of *Philosophical Enquiry.* Some authors were accorded additional sums for alterations required in later editions, although these were perhaps not part of the original agreements. So Francis Coventry sold Dodsley the copyright of *The History of Pompey the Little* (1751) for fifty guineas but earned thirty additional pounds in the same year for alterations in the third edition.

A different kind of right in future editions was negotiated with others. In the case of Gray's *Odes,* Johnson's *Vanity,* and Whitehead's *On Nobility* (1744), each author, although essentially selling Dodsley the complete copyright, reserved the right of one future impression. Such a clause afforded an author access to his work should he decide, at some future date, to issue a collected edition.

Payments to editors of periodicals were made on a considerably different basis. For conducting the fortnightly *Museum: or, Literary and Historical Register* (1746–7), Dodsley agreed to pay Mark Akenside fifty pounds semi-annually. Edmund Burke's contract for producing the *Annual Register* (1758–), although implicitly intended to be continuous, specified payment for only the first issue. Burke was to be paid fifty pounds by Michaelmas and another fifty by Lady Day, the proposed date of publication. Edward Moore's agreement for conducting the weekly *World* (1753–6) differed radically. He was due not only three guineas upon publication of each 1½-sheet issue but also half of the copyright and profits from any future collected edition. So successful was the *World* (by one report 2,500 copies per issue) that Dodsley was able to pay Moore four hundred pounds for the latter's share when the periodical concluded in 1756.

Two interesting additional stipulations turn up in these agreements with editors of periodicals. Each contract contained a provision stating that if either of the parties – the bookseller or editor – should decide to discontinue his efforts, due notice should be provided, and the other party should be allowed to continue the periodical, either with a new editor or with a new bookseller. Secondly, both the *Museum* and *Annual Register* agreements required Dodsley to supply whatever books or pamphlets were necessary to carry on the endeavor, thereby saving the editor trouble and expense.

Overall, Dodsley's agreements with authors are typical of their times.[54] Judging from surviving records, one can see that his payments reflect current standards: they were neither niggardly nor overly generous. New authors were encouraged, but not with the larger sums paid to established names. Decisions on the size of offers were based on an estimate of saleability and anticipated income. As did other booksellers, Dodsley had to calculate not only the price of a manuscript but also expenditures for printing and advertising, costs that he risked before the first copy was sold.

Although offering but two examples, Harry Ransom claims that, in 1738, ten guineas was a "round sum for a poem of good length."[55] On the basis of the

---

[54] See A. S. Collins, *Authorship in the Days of Johnson* (London: Robert Holden, 1927), passim; Harry Ransom, "The Rewards of Authorship in the Eighteenth Century." *Studies in English,* 17 (1938), pp. 47–66.   [55] p. 53.

examples he offers – Johnson's *London* and Paul Whitehead's *State Dunces* (1733) –
one understands "good length" to mean at least sixteen pages of printed text and
probably no more than forty-five (although we are left to guess the latter from
Ransom's rather loose introduction of Young's *Night Thoughts*). As one whose
publications were largely of this sort, perhaps Dodsley himself offers the best index
to the current purchase price for such pieces. From 1738 through the 1740s,
Dodsley's extant agreements reflect six poems of this kind, for all of which his
payments ranged from ten to fifteen guineas.[56]

For a full-length play, the average purchase price in Dodsley's time, A. S. Collins
informs us, was one hundred pounds.[57] Once again, Dodsley's payments reflect the
contemporary standard. He paid exactly one hundred pounds for Whitehead's
Roman Father (1750) and *Creusa* (1754), Henry Jones's *Earl of Essex* (1753),
MacNamara Morgan's *Philoclea* (1754), and Johnson's *Irene* (1749). The only
exceptions involved Young's *Brothers* (1753), for which Dodsley paid 147 pounds;
Susannah Cibber's afterpiece *The Oracle* (1752), fifty pounds; and Kitty Clive's
farce *The Rehearsal* (1753), twenty-one pounds.

Dodsley's offers for fiction certainly fell short of those laid out by his
contemporary and sometime collaborator Andrew Millar, the bookseller whom
Samuel Johnson claimed "raised the price of literature."[58] His payments for novels
– at least as revealed in the three surviving agreements involving fiction – in no way
rival the 183 pounds Millar agreed to pay Henry Fielding for his first novel *Joseph
Andrews* (1742), nor the six hundred pounds for the later *Tom Jones* (1749).
Dodsley's fifty-guinea payment to Fielding's sister Sarah for *The Cry* (1754) was
more in line with what he was willing to risk for fiction. Three years earlier, he had
paid the same to Francis Coventry for *The History of Pompey the Little*, and as late as
1759, he and Strahan extended themselves to pay Johnson a hundred pounds for
Rasselas. After the smashing success of *Tristram Shandy* in 1760, Dodsley – no doubt
with some embarrassment – did advise his brother to pay Sterne 250 pounds for the
copyright to the first two books, but he might have had them of Sterne for fifty
pounds a few months earlier.

However, it must be remembered that Dodsley was primarily a publisher of
poetry and the Classics; his forte was not fiction. A fair comparison of his dealings
with authors is more appropriately based on the sums he laid out for works in his
specialty. For instance, one would have to take into account that he paid 210
guineas for Young's *Night Thoughts*, 200 pounds for Warton's edition of Virgil; 250
guineas for Hampton's translation of Polybius; and 600 pounds for Melmoth's
translation of Cicero's letters. Although of a different genre, *The World*, over three
years, earned its editor Edward Moore 858 pounds.

Nothing would better complement this profile of Dodsley's bookselling business

---

[56] Had Young sold Dodsley the copyright for the *Night Thoughts* as they appeared individually, perhaps
      they too would have afforded similar testimony. But Young elected to hold back the copyright until
      1743 when he sold the first five *Nights* for £160: he sold the sixth *Night* for £50 in 1745. By that time, of
      course, the poem had passed through several editions, increasing the author's bargaining power.
[57] p. 34.   [58] Boswell, *Life*, I, 288.

than an account of the cash flow at Tully's Head, one that would show both gross and net receipts during his 24-year career. Unfortunately, such an accounting is impossible. The primary data – Dodsley's ledgers and bank account, together with those of his principal printer, John Hughs – have not survived.[59] Indeed some hard evidence does exist. Copyright purchase agreements and author receipts (Appendix B) afford extensive information regarding seventy-eight works issued from Tully's Head. The printing ledgers of both William Bowyer and William Strahan reveal important details of press runs and costs for many of Dodsley's titles. But even these valuable resources prove too fragmentary for recreating the total picture. In the case of the former, seventy-eight purchases can hardly represent Dodsley's total cash outlay for manuscripts among the several hundred works carrying his name in the imprint. The Bowyer and Strahan ledgers reflect printing details for no more than thirty-nine works, and frequently in an incomplete state, for these two printers were more often than not printing parts of editions farmed out to them by John Hughs.

The unreliable character of eighteenth-century imprints has also worked against such a reckoning. Some general notion of Dodsley's potential income – at least for those works originating solely from Tully's Head – might have been conjectured had eighteenth-century imprints more precisely revealed copyright ownership. But the imprints "Printed for R. Dodsley" or "Printed for R. and J. Dodsley" are of no help in distinguishing those works whose copyrights the Dodsleys purchased (entitling them to full profits, after expenses) from those for which they served merely as the author's publishing agent (and thereby earned only the middleman's usual markup). Had it been otherwise, a reasonable estimate of Dodsley's potential income might have been conjectured by calculating the manuscript and production costs for surviving copies of his publications on the basis of Dodsley's customary payments to authors, together with contemporary price scales for paper, printing,[60] binding, advertising,[61] and, where applicable, drawings and engravings.[62] Under the circumstances, it is impossible to determine whether author or bookseller bore the cost of production and publication for the hundreds of

---

59 Research in Barclays Bank, Gosling's Branch, 19 Fleet Street, London, has turned up an account for James Dodsley but not for Robert. The account, opened on 20 June 1760 (after Robert had retired), shows numerous credits from various London booksellers over the first six years. However it records no payments to individuals, only occasional large withdrawals by James himself. It seems either that James made these withdrawals to pay his creditors in cash, or that he had an account in another bank for that purpose. But research in other surviving eighteenth-century bank records has discovered nothing.

60 See Patricia Hernlund, "William Strahan's Ledgers, II: Charges for Papers, 1738–1785." *SB*, 22 (1969), pp. 179–95; and "William Strahan's Ledgers: Standard Charges for Printing, 1738–1785." *SB*, 20 (1967), pp. 89–111. Hernlund's figures are corroborated by paper costs (18s. per ream) for the production of John Gilbert Cooper's *Life of Socrates* (1749), as cited by Dodsley in a letter to the author on 19 December 1749 (q.v.).

61 Dodsley's bill to John Gilbert Cooper (see previous note) offers a sample of charges (£3.15.0.) for a work's advertisement in three London newspapers (*General Advertiser, London Evening Post,* and *Whitehall Evening Post*) for the period of a week, a typical advertising promotion.

62 Charges for drawings and engravings would be the most difficult to calculate because of varying sizes and degrees of complexity and because of the many hands involved, both professional and amateur.

works for which no publishing agreement or receipt is extant. Consequently the proper attribution of profits and losses among the parties is thwarted.

Yet, whatever value such an exercise might have contributed would have been undermined by still another unknown. Although press runs for many of Dodsley's publications are available and those for the rest might have been reasonably conjectured, few statistics survive to show how many copies of these works were actually sold. As a result, a most important factor in determining real profits and losses would continue to elude our grasp.

Consequently only fragmentary insights to the financial operation of Tully's Head are available. In sum, publishing agreements, receipts, and other notices show that, for sixty-two copyright purchases Dodsley made during twenty-two years (1738–59), together with the purchase of shares in three periodicals and wages accorded three editors of his own periodicals, he laid out a total of £6,498.18.0. For the copyrights alone, he paid £5,183.14.0.[63] A majority of these payments – i.e., a total of £3,129.0.6 – were made in the mid-1750s when Dodsley's business had reached its height. The year 1752 shows expenditure of £400.16.0 to five authors; 1753, £788.10.6 to twelve authors; 1754, £316.6.0 to three authors; 1755, £1,048.16.0 to nine authors; and 1756, £644.12.0 to four authors.

It is regrettable that so little evidence for documenting Dodsley's finances survives. One kind of evidence, the bookseller's accounts to his authors, would have proved eminently useful for such a projection. But, except for that to Cooper (mentioned above) none have been preserved with his correspondence.

Before taking leave of Tully's Head to consider Dodsley's relation with the trade, something should be said of the workers behind the scene, though it is necessarily little. We have already seen that Robert's brother James seems to have joined the firm at least by 1742. He probably assisted Robert as the senior (and perhaps only) apprentice during the early 1740s. When, in 1753, his name begins to appear with Robert's on the firm's imprints, he had more than served his time. In short, it appears that James was at work at Tully's Head for all but the first half dozen years its doors were open.

Only three other apprentices at Tully's Head can be documented, but a fourth is likely. Both John Hinxman (d. 1762) and John Walter (d. 1803) advertised themselves as former Dodsley apprentices when they came to open their own shops, Hinxman taking over John Hildyard's business at York in 1757 and Walter setting up at Homer's Head in Charing Cross in 1759.[64] If both served the typical seven-year apprenticeship, Hinxman would have been the earlier to arrive at Tully's Head; that is, sometime in 1750. Their presence at Dodsley's shop as early as 1753 is

---

[63] To average the cost per copyright (*c*. £83) is tempting but meaningless, for this group includes many of his major purchases and only a handful of the hundreds of pamphlet-sized publications he turned out during these years.

[64] Hinxman, *London Chronicle*, 8–10 September 1757; Walter, *London Chronicle*, 23–25 October 1759. Walter became a close friend of James Dodsley, who appointed the former an executor of his will and left him £1,000. The "Easy and Free, polite and elegant" Walter was memorialized in Henry Dell's *The Booksellers. A Poem* (1766), lines 73–4. (See Terry Belanger, "A Directory of the London Book Trade, 1766." *Publishing History*, 1 (1977), 7–48.)

attested to by the appearance of their signatures on two separate documents originating in that year. Hinxman witnessed the bookseller's agreement with Edward Moore for conducting *The World*, and Walter signed, on behalf of the Dodsleys, a receipt for books purchased by Gilbert West. (See Appendix B.) They were most likely the senior and junior apprentices to whom Dodsley referred in his letter to William Melmoth on 16 December 1756.

Evidence for a third apprentice actually stems from a time after Robert's retirement from Tully's Head, although the apprentice might well have begun his time when Dodsley was still master of the shop. In 1761, an L. Lewis signed a receipt, acknowledging on the Dodsleys' behalf, a payment for books sold to the Earl Grenville-Temple. Perhaps Lewis was a relation of the J. and J. Lewis who printed Nathaniel Weekes's *Barbados. A Poem* for Dodsley in 1754.

Straus proposes a fourth apprentice, offering as evidence the candidate's witnessing of two Dodsley publishing agreements. With James Dodsley's, William Randall's signature first appears in 1750 on the elder Dodsley's agreement with Joseph Warton for a translation of Virgil. Next, together with Hinxman, Randall witnessed the bookseller's agreement with Edward Moore for the conduct of *The World* in 1753. Probably the multiple occasions and the context of each constitutes sufficient evidence for agreeing with Straus. But witnessing a document, of itself, does not necessarily designate an apprentice, as is clear from Richard Berenger's witnessing the Dodsleys' agreement to purchase *Tristram Shandy* from Laurence Sterne in 1760. On the other hand, it must be admitted that the role is suggestive. And, in that case, we might now also consider as possible apprentices a William MacCarthy who witnessed Dodsley's agreement in 1743 with Henry Baker for the purchase of *The Natural History of the Polype*; and a W. H. Wharton who witnessed the bookseller's agreement in 1748 with John Campbell to write a geographical compendium.

3. Dodsley and the trade

Without specific testimony, it is difficult to discern the degree of prejudice exerted against the "outsider" Dodsley by the major trade booksellers during his early years at Tully's Head. We have already seen his frustration in attempting to establish the weekly *Public Register* in 1741, but this failure is primarily attributable to the influence exerted by a single competitor among his colleagues. Normally one's acceptance by the trade's "inner circle" was confirmed by invitation to trade sales, those "semi-public" gatherings of major booksellers at which the stock and copyrights of retired, deceased, or bankrupt members were auctioned. Despite the insistence of participating dealers that these were public auctions, in practice only the certain few who received catalogues had formal notice of the occasions and were truly welcome. Even here, however, the evidence is not conclusive regarding Dodsley's early status. Because catalogues marked with purchasers' names represent the only record of participation in these auctions, surviving evidence does not reflect the sum total of any one bookseller's attendance. None the less, Dodsley can be regarded as at least an occasional attender, for he did make purchases at six different sales between 1737 and 1752. (See Appendix B, section 3.) But whether his attendance must be judged exceptional or the result of invitation cannot be known.

It is equally difficult to speculate on the amount of cooperation a newcomer like Dodsley might expect from the trade in the matter of joint publication. Doubtless it was null among the major dealers, especially in cases of their jealously guarded "bread and butter" reprints. Only sons of tradesmen or otherwise properly "connected" persons stood a chance with these monopolies. A beginner armed only with industry and meager resources was better advised to pursue liaisons with tradesmen of the second or third rank and to negotiate for the joint publication of new works, or at least of works whose copyrights were not already tied up by the monopolies.

So did Dodsley proceed during his first half dozen years at Tully's Head. But his success must be judged modest, at best. Through 1740, we find his name linked with those of other booksellers on only seven occasions. Except for two instances, most of his collaborators in these publications were lesser lights at the time.[65] The appearance of his name with the firm of John and Paul Knapton in two imprints is doubtless explained by the fact that both works belonged to Dodsley's patron Pope. In two other instances, Dodsley himself had probably been the primary undertaker, for his name occurs first in these imprints.

But success breeds success. Although enjoying but a trickle of joint undertakings during these years, Dodsley was making a name for himself with works issued under his own imprint. By 1739, he had published no fewer than forty works on his own, the year 1738 alone showing seventeen. Combined with his recent stage credits, the appearance of his name on Pope's *Works*, Johnson's *London*, Glover's tremendously popular *Leonidas*, and editions of Fénelon's *Télémaque* and Tasso's *Jerusalem*, had begun to attract attention to the newcomer in Pall Mall. As early as 1738, publishers of three other works thought it worthwhile to include Dodsley's name in their imprints as "seller."[66]

The year 1741 brought five joint undertakings, a number that, during Dodsley's first fifteen years in business, was exceeded only in 1746. Significantly, in the latter year, his name is first linked with three major London houses. Although only a small piece, William Best's *The Royal Soldier* occasioned the imprint: "Printed for A. Millar; J. and J. Rivington; and R. Dodesley [sic]." Dodsley took an important stride in 1746 when publishing Volume II of Jonathan Swift's *Miscellanies* with Charles Hitch, Charles Davis, and Mary Cooper. The work would serve not only as a maiden undertaking with Hitch but also as an entrée to a lucrative share in the ongoing, multi-volume edition of the *Miscellanies* and, in turn, to share in Bathurst's twelve-volume edition of Swift's *Works*. The latter would appear as "Printed for C.

---

[65] James Brindley, Henry Chapelle, John Clarke, Lawton Gilliver, Joseph Hazard, Richard Hett, John Jollyffe, Charles Marsh, Francis Noble, Oliver Payne, and W. Sare.

[66] [Anonymous], *What is Man?*, printed for J. Buckland; Robert Smith, *A Compleat System of Optics*, printed for the author at Cambridge, and sold there by C. Crownfield and, in London, by S. Austen and R. Dodsley; Henry Pemberton, *Observations on Poetry*, printed by H. Woodfall, and sold by J. Brotherton, J. Nourse, and R. Dodsley.

Bathurst, C. Davis, C. Hitch and L. Hawes, J. Hodges, R. and J. Dodsley and W. Bowyer. 1754–1755." (For background, see Thomas Sheridan's note of mid-August 1744.)

In other words, by the mid-1740s Dodsley had established his ground in the trade. In 1745 alone, the 27 publications issued solely under the Tully's Head imprint would amount to a career high. In the whole of the decade, he would be solely responsible for 142 new publications. Except for the two opening years and 1745, the average number of publications for all years of the decade ranged in the mid-teens.

Yet, in light of the substantial increase in the number of his own publications, it is notable that his collaborations with other booksellers does not initially keep pace. Taking, for instance, the early years of growth, 1738 to 1749, and dividing them into two equal periods, we find that the total number of his own works had increased from 60 for the first period (1738–43) to 102 for the second (1744–9); in other words, an increase in productivity of approximately 70 per cent. Figured in the same manner, his number of collaborations with other booksellers during the first period – fourteen – increases to a mere eighteen in the second; a rise of 29 per cent.

Why Dodsley did not more fully participate in the webbing effect that an expanding reputation in the trade inevitably produced prompts some speculation. However no simple answer is forthcoming. Surely his impact on the market and on the trade by the late 1740s would have melted the trade resistance he had met with from established booksellers when first entering the business a dozen years earlier. Besides, his joint imprints during the period find his name linked with no fewer than 53 London printers and booksellers, including such major names as Charles Bathurst, William Bowyer, Charles Hitch, Andrew Millar, Samuel Richardson, and the Knaptons, Rivingtons, and Tonsons. Perhaps Tully's Head had become so self-supporting in the 1740s that Dodsley's hands were quite full with his own productions, so that he really had no time to extend his collaborative efforts proportionately. Or possibly his particular business goals did not call for an elaborate scheme of joint undertakings. Perhaps Dodsley was still attempting to establish his identity in the trade and therefore preferred a certain degree of independence so that his public image should not be blurred. Or, finally, it is quite possible that the typical character of his publications did not require collaboration.

Some support for the last two interpretations surfaces in an examination of those titles from the 1740s carrying solely Dodsley's name as publisher. Dealing principally in *belles lettres*, of course Dodsley did not need assistance to finance the many short poetic productions that constituted the bulk of his output. And indeed 56 per cent of his publications during these years averaged 48 pages or less. Another 16 per cent did not exceed 96 pages. In other words, 72 per cent of his trade might have been reasonably carried on without the financial assistance afforded by joint undertaking.

Sizes of the remaining 28 per cent, on the other hand, suggest an extraordinary independence on Dodsley's part, for their production involved considerable financial risk. Among these thirty-nine works – all of which run to more than one hundred pages – eleven span three to six hundred pages, and five others are multi-volume editions. For instance, Dodsley ventured handsome sums on such as his twelve-volume *Collection of Old Plays* (1744) and his three-volume *Collection of Poems by Several Hands* (1748). Of course such confirmed sellers as Duguet's *Institution of a Prince* (1740), Boccaccio's *Decameron* (1741), Henry Baker's *The Microscope Made Easy* (1742), Pliny's *Letters* (1748), and Pindar's *Odes* (1749) afforded reasonable security, but these represented but a handful of his longer publications. Moreover, even such works as these were customarily shared in the trade. The evidence suggests, then, that Dodsley was steering a singular course in the 1740s, one guided by a consciousness of his own needs and interests and directed toward a niche at the head of the trade.

The early 1750s tell a different story, however. A decided shift occurs in the degree of Dodsley's collaboration with other booksellers. Until his brother's name joins the Dodsley imprint in May 1753, the proportion of his joint undertakings leaps ahead. In fact, during this three and a half year period, 35 per cent of his imprints are shared. With James, however, once more the house plan reverses itself, For the rest of the 1750s, joint undertakings with other booksellers fall off to 23 per cent of the total Dodsley output.

His vintage years, then, show a bit more balance. To some extent, perhaps this should be expected, for, by the mid-1750s, Dodsley's business and reputation had reached their zenith. He no longer needed to be the aggressive solicitor of manuscripts; authors and booksellers sought him out, as his correspondence reveals. Except for a curious dip in productivity during 1752 (eight of his own imprints and four collaborations), his output during his last decade at Tully's Head was remarkable. His own imprints totaled 176; or, roughly, one every three weeks. His joint undertakings for the same period amounted to 77. Taken together, the figures mean that Dodsley's name was appearing on a new imprint every two and a half weeks. And, of course, it must be remembered that we are dealing with only first editions and with publications that have been identified. If all were able to be taken into account – later editions, untraced works, and works surreptitiously published under another publisher's name – the statistics would be even more impressive. In fact, the total would most likely approach five hundred.

For his 110 joint undertakings, Dodsley shared the imprint as publisher with 69 other bookselling and publishing firms. As much as imprints can tell us, no bookseller seems to have been a "regular" publishing partner. His most frequent collaborator was Andrew Millar, the publisher of Henry Fielding and James Thomson. Millar's name is linked with Dodsley's in twenty-one imprints; six of these publications find only the two booksellers' names. Immediately behind Millar, with eighteen, are the trade publishers Thomas and Mary Cooper, about whom more will be said presently. The next, the firm of John Whiston and Benjamin White, lags considerably behind, sharing only eight imprints with Dodsley. Five imprints each were shared with Charles Davis, and Thomas Osborne, Sr., and with the firms of John and James Rivington and Charles Hitch and Lacey Hawes. On his own, John Rivington appeared in two additional imprints, and his brother James, when in business with James Fletcher, Jr., is found in another three. Four imprints each were shared with Charles Bathurst, John Clarke, John and Paul Knapton, and William Owen; John Knapton by himself is found in another two. On three occasions each, Dodsley's name is joined with James Brindley, Lawton Gilliver, George Hawkins, James Hodges, John Jollyffe, and John Nourse. The Longman house is also represented three times, once simply as Thomas Longman and twice as the more familiar T. and T. Longman. The names of 49 other firms are found with Dodsley's on one or two occasions.[67]

Of all the firms linked with Dodsley's in imprints, the most frequently occurring name belongs not to a bookseller, strictly speaking, but to a trade publisher.[68] In 1742, the publisher Thomas Cooper, of The Globe, Paternoster Row, joined Dodsley to issue both the second and third "Nights" of Edward Young's *Night Thoughts*. Upon Cooper's death the following year, his wife Mary succeeded to the business and continued the relationship with Dodsley. Over the next seventeen years, her name appeared as publisher with Dodsley's in another sixteen imprints. In addition, four other imprints list her as the publisher and Dodsley as merely the seller. Had this been all, the relationship between the Coopers and the Dodsleys might be dismissed as simply another interesting occasional collaboration. But a closer look at the evidence shows some special connection between the two firms.

During the six years prior to his death, Thomas Cooper's name shows up as the solitary "seller" in twenty of Dodsley's own imprints. But Cooper would be outdone by his wife. From 1743 through 1759, Mary Cooper is listed as the seller in no fewer than 167 of Dodsley's imprints. Together, then, the Coopers were specifically named as Dodsley's associates – although only as sellers – in 187 cases; or, in more than fifty per cent of Dodsley's solo publications. And, of course, if the works for which the Coopers joined Dodsley as publisher are also taken into account, their trade association can be seen to have extended to more than two hundred works, perhaps a unique relationship in the mid-century.

But neither the origin nor the terms of this relationship are known. Although initially tempting, Straus's suggestion (p. 270) that Dodsley had served an apprenticeship at the Cooper house seems highly unlikely. Had Dodsley done so, he would have had to break his indenture in order to open Tully's Head in 1735, for we know he was still serving as a footman in 1732. Moreover, had Dodsley served an

67 Stephen Austin, Robert Baldwin, John Barrett (Oxford), Joseph Bentham (Cambridge), B. Bourne and Cook, William Bowyer, John Brotherton, Daniel Browne, Richard Cave and David Henry, Richard Clements (Oxford), H. Cooke, M. Cook, W. Cook, Charles Corbett, H. Shute Cox, Stanley Crowder, Lockyer Davis, Somerset Draper, T. Durham and D. Wilson, James Fletcher, Sr. (Oxford), James Fletcher, Jr., [Ralph?] Griffith, C. Henderson, [Elizabeth?] James, J. and S. Johnson, William Johnston, W. Lewis, Charles Marsh, John Millan, A. Morley, Francis Noble, John Payne, Oliver Payne, W. Reeves, C. Reymer, J. Richardson, William Russel, J. Ryall, William Sandby, W. Sare, William Shropshire, John Shuckburgh, J. Swan, Paul Vaillant, John Ward, James Waugh, [Robert] Whitworth [of Manchester], George Woodfall, and John Woodyer and W. Thurlbourne (Cambridge).

68 For the distinction between booksellers and trade publishers, see Michael Treadwell, "London Trade Publishers 1675–1750." *Library*, 6th ser., IV (1982), pp. 99–134.

apprenticeship, he might have been freed as a journeyman and become a member of the Stationers' Company. Such a capacity would have proven a distinct advantage when he came to set up in the trade. But his name does not appear in the Stationers' Register. Furthermore, had Dodsley been a freeman of the City, his brother James could also have become a freeman upon the completion of his apprenticeship with Robert. But, as we know, James gained his membership in the Stationers' in 1754 by "redemption," meaning that he had been recommended by an eminent person and had paid a fee.

Whatever the arrangement between Dodsley and the Coopers, certainly Dodsley stood to gain by its terms. Michael Treadwell has pointed out that Thomas Cooper, after succeeding to the business of Thomas Warner in 1733, "was rapidly to become the most important of all the later generation of London trade publishers."[69] Trade publishers, as Treadwell illustrates, seldom purchased copyrights themselves, but by reason of their marketing network provided a valuable distribution service for authors, printers, or booksellers who preferred to retain their copyrights and frequently chose not to put their names to their works. Also, Treadwell shows, the bulk of the work in which trade publishers dealt consisted of pamphlets, small inexpensive works that would require a large sale to turn a profit.

Such services would certainly have fitted Dodsley's requirements. From the beginning, he needed a marketing network for the distribution of his publications, and the Coopers' provided an extensive one. Also, located in the City, the Coopers afforded the Westminster bookseller a useful link with the central location of the trade. But most importantly, the majority of Dodsley's publications fit the nature of the trade publisher's business. As one who made his name largely by the publication of individual poems, Dodsley regularly turned out pamphlet-sized works; in fact, over his 24-year career, 54 per cent of his publications ran to 48 pages or less. Another 16 per cent ranged in the 50 to 96 page category.

Finally, as reflected in his correspondence, the bookseller had reason to conceal his connection with a work on at least three occasions (and one suspects many more). In such instances, it proved convenient to issue a work under Mary Cooper's imprint. Such was the case with John Gilbert Cooper's *Cursory Remarks* in 1751, with Joseph Warton's *Essay on the Writings and Genius of Mr. Pope* five years later, and with Edmund Burke's *A Vindication of Natural Society* in 1757. And one is tempted to think the same for William Whitehead's poem *Honour* (1747), especially since the rest of Whitehead's poetry during the 1740s and 1750s was issued from Tully's Head.

Something of Dodsley and Cooper's familiarity is reflected in the much-noted concluding issue of *The World* in 1756.[70] Pretending to be an account of the editor's fatal accident and deathbed confession, the paper carried Mrs Cooper's name, not Edward Moore's usual "Adam FitzAdam" pseudonym. Although the piece was perhaps written by Moore himself, the choice of Cooper's name for this final number of Dodsley's popular weekly illustrates the working relationship between the two tradesmen on still another level.

[69] Ibid., p. 111.   [70] No. 209, 30 December 1756.

One other occasion is worth noting, although its meaning for the Dodsley–Cooper relationship eludes certain interpretation. When Dodsley first issued his *Oeconomy of Human Life* (1750), a work that saw many editions and translations, it appeared anonymously under Mary Cooper's imprint. When, shortly after its publication, a spurious Volume II appeared on the market, an extended exchange ensued in the newspapers. The projector of the sequel insisted on the authenticity of his work, and his antagonist (Dodsley, presumably) rejected the follow-up with some convincing arguments. Curiously, Cooper had published the sequel, as she had Dodsley's original.

Cooper's decision to publish the sequel admits of at least three possible explanations. As an enterprising publisher, she might simply have concurred with the wishes of the sequel's copyright owner and put her name to it. (She did collaborate with booksellers other than Dodsley.) Or she might have been the true projector and sole publisher of the work, for she did hold many copyrights. In either case, the publisher might simply have stood her ground as an independent and neutral business person and told Dodsley as much. On the other hand, Cooper's conflict of interests might have been only apparent. It is difficult to believe she would have assumed an impertinent air with Dodsley, given the nature of her continuing relationship with the bookseller. (Dodsley would include Cooper's name as seller in the imprint to the many editions of the authentic *Oeconomy* through the next year.) In short, it seems not unreasonable to suggest that Dodsley himself had sanctioned the publication of the sequel, thereby indirectly creating the "paper" conflict by which his own work stood to attract greater attention. If true, the ruse certainly worked, and another dimension is added to our sense of cooperation between the bookseller and publisher.

The testimony of imprints shows that provincial booksellers seldom undertook joint publications with their London counterparts, especially in cases of London printings. Dodsley's publications are no exception. Although, as his correspondence shows, he had developed a considerable business with country booksellers by the mid-1750s, only a handful of them ever shared an imprint with him as co-publisher. As might be expected, Cambridge, and particularly Oxford, do offer such examples. In 1751, *Ode for Music* by Thomas Warton was "Printed for R[ichard] Clements and J[ohn] Barrett [Oxford]; W[illiam] Thurlbourne in Cambridge; and R. Dodsley, London." Barrett's name is also found with those of Dodsley, Mary Cooper, and J. Swan on a London printing of Cornelius Arnold's *Commerce. A Poem* (1751). Perhaps because of the connection with his London-based son (currently in business with James Rivington), James Fletcher of Oxford was listed as an undertaker with the Dodsleys on a pamphlet of 1759. C. Layton of Eton is also listed with the Dodsleys on another pamphlet of the same year. It is not clear whether or not W. Wood of Lincoln shared the copyright with Dodsley, but he did print a sermon for Tully's Head in 1746. Beyond these, Dodsley's imprints show no other provincial collaborators.

However, Dodsley frequently turns up as "seller" for works produced in the country. For each of the Bath booksellers Thomas Boddely and James Leake, Dodsley served as London agent on two occasions. In the same capacity, he handled single works published by William Wood of Lincoln, R. Whitworth of

Manchester, I. Thompson and Co. of Newcastle-upon-Tyne, and John Newbery (when still at Reading). Four booksellers from Oxford listed Dodsley as seller on eight occasions. They include Richard Clements, James Fletcher, James Hetcher, and William Jackson. Other works "Printed at the [Sheldon] theatre" also list Dodsley. The booksellers of Cambridge, however, seemed particularly glad of Dodsley's service. While John Woodyer and T. and J. Merrill listed Tully's Head on but a few occasions and William Thurlbourne did the same on five, Joseph Bentham, the printer to the University, used Dodsley no fewer than thirteen times, particularly for the works of William Mason and Christopher Smart.

One procedure in Dodsley's business marks an interesting transition in English booktrade history. By the mid-eighteenth century, copyright protection against pirating publishers (in England, at least) seems to have been at least as effectively maintained by the close collaboration of major booksellers as it was by the official procedure of registering rights at Stationers' Hall. While the Stationers' Company had enjoyed exclusive powers in earlier centuries, by Dodsley's time its prerogatives and sanctions – at least in the practical order – had considerably waned. What had at one time amounted to the law of the trade had now, for the major dealers anyway, pretty much diminished to ritual. But whatever the practice of the upper echelon of the trade, it is difficult to deny that a broad vestigial respect for the age-old authority lingered to haunt potential violators. At its minimal value, registering a work at the Hall could prove useful when later attempting to exact one's rights in a court of law.

Dodsley's employment of the Stationers' services affords some example of this transition. Unfortunately his correspondence contains only one allusion to registering a work at Stationers' Hall, and it reflects an author's concern, not Dodsley's. Writing on 3 March 1756, William Mason, apprehensive that his *Odes* might be pirated by the magazines, asked whether Dodsley thought registration advisable. Although I can find no record that Dodsley indeed entered the *Odes* at the Hall, newspaper advertisements of the work noted that it had been so registered. Whatever the reality, both Mason's inquiry and the newspaper announcement suggest that the Stationers' name continued to enjoy some dissuasive authority, however mitigated.

More to the point, Dodsley's own practice perhaps more aptly reflects the Stationers' declining importance. Examination of the Company's records shows that the bookseller registered works at the Hall on thirty-four occasions. Of these trips to Amen Corner, at least ten were probably at the urging of the works' authors, for Dodsley did not own these copyrights at the time of registration. Thirteen other instances, however, do suggest Dodsley's personal interest in securing the Stationers' protection, for they include six of his own writings or compilations and seven copyrights he had recently purchased. But the obvious question remains – if registration at the Stationers' afforded precious copyright protection, why did Dodsley register so few of the hundreds of works he published, especially of his own copyrights?

The question becomes further complicated when one considers Dodsley's inconsistent pattern of registration. Why, for instance, did he choose to register particular works, and not others? Why did he enter Melmoth's translation of Pliny's *Letters* (1746) and not the same translator's edition of Cicero's *Letters* (1753)? – the rights to both of which Dodsley had purchased before publication. Or, even more puzzling, why did he occasionally register only parts of serials or only sequels to original works, as in the cases of his fortnightly *Museum* (1746)[71] and Volume II of "Sir Thomas Fitzoborne's" (William Melmoth's) *Letters on Several Subjects* (1749). The explanations usually offered for a bookseller's failure to register a work – the prohibitive expense of surrendering nine copies, or the ephemeral nature of a work – do not adequately address these and many other instances.

However a closer look at Dodsley's registration practice offers a likely explanation, for it does reveal an emerging pattern. When viewed chronologically, it becomes clear that the majority of works he entered at Stationers' Hall were publications of the early part of his career. The last registration of a solely Dodsley-owned copyright occurred in 1753, almost six years before his retirement. In that year, the Stationers' record shows that he deposited nine copies each for his own *Public Virtue* and for Edward Young's *The Brothers*. The next year, apparently upon request of copy-holding authors, he entered MacNamara Morgan's and William Whitehead's tragedies *Philoclea* and *Creusa*. Nothing at all appears in the register for Dodsley's last five years at Tully's Head except Johnson's *Rasselas* in 1759, a copyright he shared with William Johnston. The only reasonable conclusion seems to be that, by the mid-1750s, Dodsley had felt his own stature in the trade afforded adequate protection of his copyrights and that the extra trouble and expense of registration was no longer justified. Such an interpretation appears to respond to the facts, for some of Dodsley's most valuable publications – certainly copyrights he would be anxious to protect – came in the mid-1750s. And yet none is registered at the Stationers'.

Surviving evidence shows that Dodsley used the services of at least thirteen printers during his career. But because printers' names seldom occurred in imprints, only a fragment of his relationship with that integral component of the trade can be known. For instance, only a single work apiece can be identified with the following nine printers: Daniel Browne, Edward Cave (Johnson's *London*), J. Crichley, J. and J. Lewis, C. Reymer, Samuel Richardson (1750 edition of Young's *Complaint*), Charles Say, William Wood (of Lincoln), and J. Wright. Moreover, in imprints reflecting joint undertakings, a direct link with Tully's Head eludes certain determination; one of the other booksellers might have provided the liaison with the printer. This is true in the case of Say and Wright. In both instances, at least three booksellers are concerned, and Dodsley is the last listed in the imprint. Knapton or Gilliver, who had both previously used Wright's services, might have employed him for this edition of Pope's *Letters*. Furthermore, in the case of Thomas Gray's *Odes* and Joseph Spence's *A Parallel in the Manner of Plutarch*, both printed at

---

[71] Only Nos. 10–19 of the *Museum* were registered, on 8 December 1746.

the Strawberry Hill Press, one can hardly say that Dodsley had employed Horace Walpole's printer.

Substantial evidence for Dodsley's employment of printers survives for only three firms. As mentioned above, the ledgers of both William Bowyer and William Strahan attest to the many works their presses turned out for Dodsley. But even here the lines of communication blur, for frequently their services were in the form of shared printing; that is, they printed parts of works that had been farmed out to them by Dodsley's principal printer, John Hughs.

From Hughs's shop, near Great Turnstile, Lincoln's Inn Fields, John Nichols claimed "almost the whole of the valuable and numerous publications of the Dodsleys were produced."[72] Regrettably, Nichols's testimony represents the only existing evidence for such a sweeping statement. In fact, Hughs's name as printer appears in only fourteen of Dodsley's imprints and is mentioned in Dodsley's correspondence on only two occasions. Something of a chronological schema supports Nichols's claim, however. The forementioned imprints carry dates that almost embrace Dodsley's career. The first work was printed in 1738, and the last in 1757. Also significant is that Hughes is known to have printed some of Dodsley's major undertakings, works like Tasso's *Jerusalem*, Pitt's translation of the *Aeneid*, Hampton's translation of Polybius, and most particularly all six volumes of the bookseller's *Collection of Poems by Several Hands*. Unfortunately Hughs's ledgers and papers are missing, and only an intensive study of the peculiarities of his printed product will allow certain identification of other works he turned out for Dodsley.

Two printers deserve separate consideration because of their special relationship with Dodsley. Although a major figure in the history of English printing, Birmingham's John Baskerville had taken an interest in printing only a few years before his first letter to Dodsley in October 1752. As his correspondence with the bookseller reveals, much of the ensuing decade was spent experimenting with types and paper-making. During this period, Dodsley acted as his London agent, selling and distributing his ornamented paper, while encouraging him to complete his Great Primer. After much delay, Dodsley advertised Baskerville's first production, an edition of Virgil, in early 1757. The bookseller avoided the risk of publishing the edition (he subscribed for twenty copies), but he certainly played the role of Baskerville's advocate in the metropolis. The next year found Baskerville printing John Hucknell's poem *Avon*, which was also advertised as for sale at Tully's Head. Despite their close working relationship over a decade, the year 1761 marks perhaps the only occasion on which Dodsley "employed" Baskerville as printer. In that year, the bookseller's three-volume *Select Fables of Esop* was printed at Easy Hill. Dodsley's correspondence of late 1761 and early 1762, when Baskerville's edition of Horace was in progress, more aptly describes the usual mode of their relationship. At the time, Baskerville was churning out the classic in Birmingham, and Dodsley, paving the way in London, was looking after the engravings, obtaining Bute's permission to use his coat of arms, boosting the work among his friends, and securing the necessary advertising.

---

[72] *Literary Anecdotes of the Eighteenth Century* (1812), V. 35.

At present, only a sketch of Dodsley's relationship with the Dublin printer-bookseller George Faulkner has emerged, but, like the tip of the iceberg, it suggests a reality of greater magnitude. Through the 1750s, Faulkner's invasion of London booksellers' copyrights caused sharp resentment within the English trade and led to at least two public repudiations. Chief among the offended parties, Dodsley's friend Samuel Richardson launched a bitter attack on "Irish pirates" and on Faulkner in particular when printing *An Address to the Public* in 1754.[73] Richardson enjoyed further recrimination three years later when Faulkner's proposed membership in the Society for the Encouragement of Arts, Manufactures, and Commerce (the early Royal Society of Arts) was blackballed, the first such rejection in the Society's three-year history. Significantly, the Society's membership roster had currently listed several major London booksellers, including Richardson himself.[74]

Despite the London trade's feuds with Faulkner, his trade and personal relationship with Dodsley appears to have continued amicable throughout the 1750s. On 28 October 1757, for instance – only eight months after the Royal Society of Arts affair – Dodsley is writing to his "friend" to thank him for the gift of a corkscrew, apparently a gesture acknowledging Dodsley's hospitality during Faulkner's visit to London the previous spring. In that same letter, Dodsley reveals his intention to share with Faulkner some of his own publications. He says that he has sent Faulkner a copy of his own *Melpomene* (published anonymously the previous month in London), to which the latter might add the author's name if he cares to publish the work in Dublin. Also, surprisingly, Dodsley promises to deliver to Faulkner's nephew in London some sheets of the fourth (revised) and fifth volumes of his *Collection of Poems by Several Hands*, volumes that will not be published in London until the following March.

Evidence of the two booksellers' collaboration stems from as early as 1749. In April of that year, almost simultaneously from both their shops, appeared Henry Brooke's *The Songs in Jack the Gyant Queller*. Two years later, on 28 May, Faulkner advertised for sale in the *Dublin Journal* a forthcoming edition of Melmoth's translation of Pliny's *Letters*, another edition of which Dodsley himself would be issuing the following month.[75] Dodsley owned the copyright to both of these works, and consequently had these been instances of infringement and not collaboration, most likely he would not have agreed to further cooperation with Faulkner less than two years later. On 13 March 1753, Robert Lowth is writing to Dodsley, reminding him that he had promised to send some copies of Louis Devisme's *Brief Account of the Vaudois* (to be published two days later) to Dublin for sale in Faulkner's shop. Just eight months later, Benjamin Victor, when proposing to Dodsley the

---

[73] For support of Richardson's side of the dispute, see T. C. Duncan Eaves and Ben D. Kimpel, *Samuel Richardson. A Biography* (Oxford: Clarendon Press, 1971), pp. 377–83. Catherine Coogan Ward and Robert E. Ward portray Faulkner as victimized by the "prejudice of the London printing establishment against non-English competitors." See "Literary Piracy in the Eighteenth Century Book Trade: The Cases of George Faulkner and Alexander Donaldson," *Factotum*, 17 (1983), pp. 25–35.

[74] Dodsley was also a member at the time, but he absented himself from the meeting at which Faulkner was rejected. For more on the matter, see the editor's "More on George Faulkner and the London Book Trade," *Factotum*, 19 (1984), pp. 8–11. [75] Dodsley had issued the first edition in 1746.

publication of his *Widow of the Wood*, writes to ask that Dodsley inform him of when he intends "to send the first Sheet to the Press – that I might do the same here with my friend George Faulkner." Such a proposal would have incensed Dodsley had he been at odds with Faulkner.

In short, while many London booksellers and their friends (including Dodsley's friend Samuel Johnson) rallied around Richardson and his protest against Irish infringements on copyright, Dodsley himself seems to have carried on a happy trade relationship with the prime object of their antagonism, George Faulkner.[76]

To illustrate his publications, Dodsley employed the major artists and engravers working in the trade. A full listing of their names and of their contributions would require an examination of surviving copies of several hundred publications, a project for another time. For the present, the mention of a few dozen personalities and some of the works they illustrated must suffice. Many of these are found in Hans Hammelmann and T. S. R. Boase's *Book Illustrators in Eighteenth-Century England*;[77] others are derived from allusions in the Dodsley correspondence or from related research.

Artists, or designers ("del."), who provided Dodsley with drawings, included Nicholas Blakey (fl. 1749–53), Daniel Bond (1721–1803), Charles Brooking (1723–59), John Baptiste Chatelaine (1710–71), Francis Hayman (?1708–76), William Hogarth (1697–1764), William Kent (1685–1748), Arthur Pond (1705–58), John Vanderbank (1694–1739), and Samuel Wale (?1721–86). Among his engravers are numbered: Charles Grignion (1721–1810), John Green (fl. 1758), Thomas Major (1720–99), Charles Mosley (fl. 1745–70), Simon François Ravenet (?1721–74), William Ryland (1738–83), Isaac Taylor (1730–1807), George Vertue (1684–1756), and Gerard Van der Gucht (1697–1776). Another four, talented artists as well, sometimes supplied both drawings and engravings. These were Louis Philippe Boitard (d. *c.* 1760), Gravelot (Hubert François Burguignon) (1669–1773), Gérard Jean-Baptiste Scotin (b. 1698), and Anthony Walker (1726–65).

Present evidence shows Boitard, Grignion, Hayman, Wale, and Walker to have been Dodsley's most frequent illustrators. Boitard was responsible for the portrait of Joseph Spence (engraved by George Vertue) that accompanied the author's *Polymetis* (1747), as well as for many engravings of ancient works of art in the volume. Among other things, Boitard also produced the plates for Richard O. Cambridge's *Scribleriad* and the frontispiece for the 1758 version of Dodsley's popular *Gentleman's* and *Ladies'* memorandum books.

Hayman and Grignion cooperated in many of Dodsley's publications, Hayman providing the drawings and Grignion the engravings. Among them were vignettes for Mark Akenside's *Epistle to Curio* (1744) and William Mason's *Musaeus* (1747) and frontispieces for the *Preceptor* (1748) and the new edition of Edward Young's *Complaint* that Dodsley published with Millar in 1756. Hayman also drew the title

---

[76] Dodsley's publishing cooperation with Faulkner needs further investigation, and perhaps the book advertisements in the *Dublin Journal* would be a good place to begin.

[77] New Haven and London: Yale University Press, 1975. For the following attributions, I am much indebted to these compilers.

page vignette for Dodsley's fortnightly *Museum* (1746–7) and the frontispiece for the third edition, corrected, of Dodsley's tragedy *Cleone*. The former was engraved by Ravenet, and the latter by Ryland.

Grignion also collaborated with the designer Wale. Together they produced the frontispiece to J. G. Cooper's *Letters Concerning Taste* (1755), Baskerville's edition of Horace's *Works* (also a title vignette and a cut of Lord Bute's arms), Dodsley's six-volume *London and Its Environs* (1761), and his three-volume *Select Fables of Esop* (1761), as well as a title page vignette, three headpieces, and three tailpieces for the last. In the 1750s, Walker supplied various engravings for three of Jonas Hanway's works on British trade and mariners, including engravings after Hayman, Blakey, and Wale, four portraits and four headpieces for the four-volume *An Historical Account of the British Trade over the Caspian Sea* (1753). He also did a title vignette and tailpiece for John Duncombe's *Poems*.

Illustrations for a few other Dodsley publications are worth noting. Probably William Shenstone's Birmingham friend Daniel Bond was responsible for the frontispiece, title vignette, five large headpieces, and two tailpieces that Dodsley included in his tribute to the poet, *The Works in Verse and Prose of William Shenstone, Esq.*, Volume I (1764), although only the last mentioned are signed. Grignion's name is also on the tailpieces. Bond and Grignion also collaborated on the title vignette at the head of Shenstone's verses that opened Volume V of Dodsley's *Collection of Poems by Several Hands* (1758), as evident from the Dodsley–Shenstone correspondence in 1758. A version of this illustration (a view of Virgil's Grove at Shenstone's Leasowes) Dodsley used the following year as a tailpiece to the third, corrected, edition of his tragedy *Cleone*.

William Hogarth joined with the engraver Ravenet to provide a frontispiece to Volume I and a plate in Volume II of the Dodsleys' second edition of Sterne's *Tristram Shandy*. Finally, an unusual publication for Dodsley (jointly undertaken with J. and P. Knapton) was advertised in the *London Evening Post* on 5–7 November 1751: "In January next will be ready to be delivered to the Subscribers Six Plates . . . being the first Series of a Set of Prints, entitled English History Delineated . . . Hayman and Blakey, the Artists; and the Engravers, Ravenet, Grignion, and Scotin."

One of Dodsley's ongoing trade interests concerned the quality and supply of English-made paper for printing. If Patricia Hernlund is correct in suggesting that the eighteenth-century bookseller supplied the paper for all jobs contracted with his printer, then Dodsley's interest in the subject is quite understandable.[78] As a businessman, he was naturally anxious to keep his expenses down, but as a leader in the British trade, he was equally desirous of maintaining a quality at least comparable to the Continental paper upon which England was very much dependent at the time.

Through the 1750s, then, Dodsley spent a good deal of energy endorsing indigenous efforts to produce paper of a quality competitive with imports. His

---

[78] "William Strahan's Ledgers, II: Charges for Papers, 1738–1785." *SB*, 22 (1969), pp. 179–95.

support of Baskerville's attempts in this direction has already been mentioned. But a fuller sense of his commitment to the concern emerges from a review of his activities in the newly formed (1754) Society for the Encouragement of Arts, Manufactures, and Commerce. Founded for the purpose of offering premiums to English citizens whose inventiveness could supply practical advances in those areas suggested in the organization's title, the Society early on showed a strong concern for the production of paper. And Dodsley, as one of the Society's early members and its official "Printer and Stationer," proved a leader in this pursuit. In February 1756, the Society's Minutes record Dodsley's heading a committee (which included William Hogarth) authorized to draw up an advertisement soliciting submissions of paper accommodated to the production of fine prints. The aim was refined in committee, as Dodsley reported to the membership on 11 February, to focus on the production of a paper comparable to the French for printing from copper plates. The same month finds him on a similar committee (now joined by Samuel Richardson), whose purpose was to consider the best methods of improving several kinds of British paper. On 31 January of the following year, Dodsley was appointed to a committee for judging submissions of paper produced from silk, an advisory body on which Richardson and Jacob Tonson also served. In April of 1759, both Dodsley and his brother James appear on a committee to judge two parcels of paper made from silk. Perhaps this is the same committee on which the Dodsleys served to judge three pieces of drugget and two reams of marbled paper, a committee mentioned in the Minutes for 13 February 1760.[79]

It is impossible to judge the practical effects of this committee work in terms of its overall impact upon the production and quality of native English paper. But the evidence does afford another dimension in our portrait of Dodsley who, while enjoying personal success and prominence, actively promoted the good of his trade and country.

Son of an obscure schoolmaster, apprentice to a stocking weaver, footman to Quality, poet-protégé of Pope, London playwright, and, as distinguished English bookseller, a preserver of his country's literary legacy – Dodsley confirmed the new mobility in English society and at the same time set a new literate model for the trade. The lavish praise of his friend Richard Graves justly embarrassed him, but Graves's verses, beneath their exaggeration, capture something of Dodsley's powerful influence in the mid-eighteenth-century world of letters:

> Where Tully's Bust, the Honour'd Name
> Point out the Venal Page
> There Dodsley consecrates to Fame
> The Classicks of his Age.

> In vain the Poets, from their Mine
> Extract the shining Mass;
> Till Dodsley's Mint has stamped the Coin,
> And bade the Sterling Pass.[80]

---

[79] For more on Dodsley's contribution to the Society, see note 50.
[80] The full text first appeared on 20 December 1756 in *Aris's Birmingham Gazette*, where it had been inserted by William Shenstone.

B. BIBLIOGRAPHICAL MATTERS

1. The letters and their sources

The present collection numbers 393 pieces of correspondence, two of which are printed with their draft versions. 167 (including the drafts) are written by Dodsley, 220 are addressed to him, two are exchanged between his correspondents, and another two show James Dodsley as author or recipient. Included also are two public letters. Using a Dodsley publication, Sir Charles Hanbury Williams satirizes Lord Wilmington in a piece intended for the newspaper. The second is Dodsley's letter on French servants, first printed in the *London Chronicle*.

Of course the number falls far short of what must have been Dodsley's correspondence over a 24-year career at one of the most respected and busiest bookseller's shops in mid-eighteenth-century London. Such a supposition is easily supported when one multiplies the typical correspondence arising from a work's publication by the number of works turned out at Tully's Head from 1735 to early 1759. As many instances in this correspondence show, the publishing relationship between Dodsley and an author – the offer of a manuscript, its revision, the negotiation of content, format, and payment, the proofing, the work's appearance and reception, as well as the consideration of subsequent editions and their improvement – normally prompted at least three letters from both parties, and frequently more. If only those works published by Dodsley himself are taken into account (357), one can project a correspondence of well over a thousand pieces, even if discounting those works negotiated in person at Tully's Head. And these figures do not take into account his private correspondence.

The uneven spread of Dodsley's surviving correspondence also supports that projection. The first ten years at Tully's Head, during which he negotiated the publication of well over a hundred first editions of living English authors, are represented by only seventeen letters, and four of these years show not a single letter. Although the volume of correspondence increases in the later 1740s, only three letters reflect his activities in 1750, and five in 1751. Perhaps only the years 1757 and 1758, when his publishing affairs are preserved in 121 letters, approach the true complement of his correspondence.

Furthermore, although meager testimony, evidence is available to show the one-time existence of another 128 letters. Appendix D lists 68 untraced letters explicitly referred to in the present correspondence, and another 60 are documented from autograph dealer catalogues or other printed sources. Perhaps this listing will afford assistance in bringing to light additional Dodsley material.

It is the abiding hope of every editor of early manuscripts that his or her particular dragnet will bring to the surface choice morsels missed by predecessors' casts. Although this project has enjoyed its share of eurekas, a lingering regret remains: the search has failed to turn up new correspondence of major literary and trade figures whom Dodsley either published or collaborated with in the publishing business. Perhaps some explanation (and some solace!) is to be found in Samuel Johnson's response to Mrs Desmoulins: "You may tell him [David Garrick] that

Dr. Hawkesworth and I never exchanged any letters worth publication; our notes were commonly to tell when we should be at home, and I believe were seldom kept on either side."[81] As a favored meeting place for his friends and business associates, Dodsley's shop in Pall Mall no doubt often precluded the need for writing. And the present correspondence offers adequate testimony for such an understanding, which included some out-of-towners.

But missing correspondence finds still another explanation – and perhaps the most significant – in an inconceivably witless action of James Dodsley, just three weeks after Robert's death. As Dodsley's letters of 1763 and 1764 show, he, Richard Graves, and John Hodgetts, as William Shenstone's executors, had been at great pains to settle the poet's estate. In fact, the topic dominated their correspondence for a year and a half. Shortly after Dodsley's death – namely, on 12 October 1764 – Hodgetts wrote to James Dodsley, requesting the return of letters he and his niece had written to Robert regarding the settlement.[82] James's reply is exasperating: "In ye Course of looking over my late Brother's Papers I burnt a great number, among which were ye Letters you mention, as they appeared to me to contain nothing material."[83] Carrying on the business until 1797, James might have earned an enviable reputation among booksellers, but he certainly deserves no thanks from the historian of literature or of the booktrade for this deed. One wonders at such an inexplicable action during an age when custom dictated that an author's letter remained his property, to be returned, upon request, at the recipient's death. Whatever else was lost in James's little bonfire remains a subject for speculation, and much regret.

No matter what the explanation, still an editor frets to offer an edition of correspondence where so much is known missing. In the case of the present collection, it can only be said that, over more than fifteen years, the search has been as diligent and as thorough as can be reasonably expected. Either by personal visit or by letter, every college and university library in the United Kingdom known to hold a manuscript collection has been canvassed. The search has extended to all county and major city record offices throughout England and to many of their counterparts in Scotland, Wales, and Ireland. Similarly, libraries of institutions and societies in these countries holding eighteenth-century manuscript materials have been consulted, with a particular focus on Royal societies. Likewise, a search has been conducted of likely repositories in the United States, including libraries of universities and antiquarian societies, as well as the country's older public libraries. Letters of inquiry have been sent to all known private collectors of eighteenth-century materials and to librarians of those large hereditary British collections that house papers originating from the century. In addition, the Reports of the Historical Manuscript Commission have been reviewed, as have all known printed collections of eighteenth-century correspondence published after 1730. Auction house and bookseller catalogues from the late eighteenth century on have been rummaged in the pursuit, especially for items once known to have existed. For the

[81] *Letters of Samuel Johnson*, ed. R. W. Chapman, II, 229–30.
[82] Bodleian MS. Eng. Misc. c. 75, f. 115.   [83] Bodleian MS. Eng. Misc. c. 75, f. 99.

same purpose, advertisements and notices have been periodically placed in journals, newspapers, bulletins, and newsletters consulted by scholars and collectors. Although no editor can hope to lure the last letter from private collectors' caches nor to turn out every country cupboard, the present body of correspondence is printed with the belief that all reasonable efforts have been exerted in its compilation. Some refuge perhaps can be taken in Ralph Straus's boast in the Preface to his biography of Dodsley: "Altogether nearly two hundred letters to and from him [Dodsley] have passed through my hands." The present edition prints twice that number.

In toto, the collection presents Dodsley's exchange with eighty-seven different authors. Nearly half of Dodsley's own letters are addressed to his friend William Shenstone. Although in their respective editions of Shenstone's letters (1939) Marjorie Williams and Duncan Mallam printed the poet's six extant letters to Dodsley and used some of the latter's in their notes, and although Straus used many of Dodsley's to Shenstone, the bulk of Dodsley's side of the correspondence (approximately sixty letters) are printed here in their full text for the first time. That so few of Shenstone's letters to the bookseller have survived is regrettable. Shenstone himself had carefully preserved most of Dodsley's letters, grouping them together as "Letters from my worthy Friend Mʳ Dodsley,"[84] but what happened to his own letters remains a mystery. Given his great respect for the poet, surely Dodsley would have had high regard for their literary value, and saved them. Again, one is tempted to point the finger at James Dodsley.

The next most frequently addressed in the collection are represented by considerably fewer of Dodsley's letters. Ten are written to his cousin Elizabeth Cartwright and six to Joseph Warton. Beyond these, Dodsley's letters are scattered among forty-three different recipients, none addressed with more than four.

Letters written *to* Dodsley originate from a broader range of correspondents. By far the largest number (29) are written by John Gilbert Cooper of Derby, a prolific writer by any standard. Richard Graves ranks second on the list (21), followed by Robert Lowth (17), John Scott Hylton (12), John Brown of Carlisle (11), and William Melmoth (9). Of the other 56 writers, only a few penned as many as six letters, and most are responsible for fewer than three.

The chronological distribution of the letters, considered earlier, offers a mixed blessing. Since Dodsley's most notable contribution to literary history remains his editing and publishing of the six-volume *Collection of Poems by Several Hands* (1748– 58), it is fortunate that 28 per cent of the entire collection arises out of the nineteen months immediately preceding the publication of the last two volumes, on 18 March 1758. Such a concentration allows a fairly comprehensive picture of the process of collecting, editing, and printing of those volumes. The following twenty months claim another 15 per cent of the total, meaning that the other 28 years represented in the collection are spanned by only 57 per cent of the total number of letters. Again, such a concentration during the years 1756–9 – years when Dodsley's reputation was at its zenith – emerges as highly desirable. But it does

---

[84] BL. Add. MS. 28,959.

imply many lean years, as indeed there are, especially during the early part of his career. In fact, the years 1739 through 1742 offer but a single letter, despite the fact that Dodsley negotiated for at least 69 publications during the period, including a few volumes of Pope's works and also Paul Whitehead's *Manners*, a poem that earned the bookseller the censure of the House of Lords and a week in Butcher Row.

Sources of the texts are many. But it is a pleasure to report that 87 per cent of them (341) have been transcribed from author holographs or, more properly, from photocopies of them; only 52 letters depend for their texts upon pre-published sources. The holograph sources include the libraries of 25 separate institutions and societies both in the United Kingdom and the United States, as well as six private collections. (See Acknowledgements for a full listing.) As might be expected, the British Library offered by far the largest number (112), followed by the Bodleian Library, Oxford (51). Other major collections in England are found in Birmingham Public Libraries (34) and the Somerset County Record Office (21). Contributions from eight other British sources ranged in single-digit numbers.

The numbers of holographs and their distribution in the United States proved quite surprising. Harvard University holds the largest share, with twenty-four. The University of Texas at Austin follows, with twenty-one. The James M. Osborn Collection at Yale figures as the next largest source, with thirteen letters. Forty-four other letters are spread through fifteen libraries across the country, from Boston to Berkeley. (See Acknowledgments for a complete listing.) In all, the libraries of institutions and societies hold 319 of the holographs, and those of private collectors, twenty-six.

Although such judgments are always precarious, as close as this editor can determine, only 145 of the total 393 letters have been printed *in toto* at the time of writing. The remaining 248 letters, I believe, are printed here in full for the first time.

In most cases, the transcriptions of texts were prepared from photocopies provided by the libraries represented. A handful were transcribed from the originals when the manuscript's condition prohibited duplication. However many pieces required a return to the original, especially when damaged or obscured texts did not show well in photoduplications. In these instances, the editor either consulted the originals himself or relied upon the assistance of cooperative keepers, archivists, or collectors. In a few cases, scholars currently at work on editions, biographies, and bibliographies of related subjects provided considerable help. Such debts are acknowledged in the notes.

2. Texts

The opinion as well as the practice of modern editors of early correspondence varies on the subject of manuscript transcription. Some prefer diplomatic texts; others, normalized texts. The former render exact transcriptions of the original, with all the author's peculiarities of spelling and puntuation, his abbreviations and superscripts, his capitalization and cross-outs, together with the rest of his age's quaint orthographic practices. The latter, while remaining faithful to the text, accommodate it to modern orthographic standards. Advocates of diplomatic texts traditionally have wished to preserve the character as well as the content of their manuscripts, whereas those preferring normalized texts have regarded the facility of modern readers an overriding value. Editors convinced of one approach or the other from the very start are indeed blessed . . . and few. Some have attempted to offer the best of both worlds by a delicate balancing act that too often suffers the fate of Huncamunca's unsettled acquaintance astride two stools, for the result is neither this nor that. In all cases, the decision to render the text in a particular manner usually pivots upon the individual editor's degree of concern for the much defined and much maligned "accidentals": it is assumed that everyone attempts to preserve the integrity of the author's meaning, traditionally understood to be conveyed in his "substantives."

Indeed it is difficult to dispute the fact that some editions of correspondence are more appropriately rendered in normalized texts. To afford modern readers the utmost ease and unimpeded pleasure, for instance, probably an extensive collection of letters penned by a delightful stylist ought to be relieved of the clutter found in the original manuscripts. To a large degree, such is the case with the monumental W. S. Lewis edition of Horace Walpole's correspondence. The visibly attractive pages of this modern normalized edition make the going extremely negotiable, for the reader's patience is not taxed with the peculiar stylistic mannerisms of the author's age. If one tires of Walpole, it is clearly the fault of Walpole or of his correspondents, not of the edition.

But one wonders about the wisdom of the universal application of the normalizing principle. Are the ease and pleasure of the modern reader the only values to be considered by the contemporary editor? Is it somewhat myopic to translate the orthographic peculiarities of one age into those of another and then to consider such a rendering a definitive edition, one that will adequately serve the needs of future scholars?

Some interesting speculations on the subject are prompted by David Foxon's "Pope and the Early Eighteenth-Century Book-Trade."[85] At some length, Foxon traces the effects of the fashion of dropping capital letters in the printed texts of certain eighteenth-century poets who closely supervised the proofing of their works. He finds that such major figures as Pope, Gay, and Thomson had considerable influence on the gradual discontinuance of the capital letter for common nouns (a practice that would largely disappear by the nineteenth century) when they consciously chose to print certain of their works with common nouns regularly reduced to small initial letters. Although in many cases the poets reverted to capitals for subsequent publication, it is evident that capitals (or the lack of them) in these situations cannot be considered as deriving solely from compositorial mannerisms; they were used or avoided with the explicit intention of the authors themselves. It seems a certain rhetorical value was associated with capitals, a value which, from various statements, can be extended to the use of italics and punctuation. For instance, Foxon notes that Benjamin Franklin, as late

---

[85] Draft of the Lyell Lectures of 1975, on deposit in the British Library, pp. 174ff.

as 6 October 1773, when writing to his brother William regarding a prank piece ("An Edict by the King of Prussia") he had submitted to the *Public Advertiser*, complained that: "It is printed in the *Chronicle*, where you will see it, but stripped of all the capitaling and italicing that intimate the allusions and mark the emphasis of written discourse, to bring them as near as possible to those spoken: printing such a piece all in one even small character, seems to me like repeating one of Whitefield's sermons in the monotony of a schoolboy."[86] And one remembers, of course, that Franklin himself was a printer.

An observation similar to Foxon's, but concerned with eighteenth-century fiction, was voiced about the same time by Martin Battestin in "Fielding's Novels and the Wesleyan Edition: Some Principles and Problems."[87] Battestin later reiterated this attitude most succinctly: "I have tried to demonstrate elsewhere – by showing that the full sense of certain passages in Fielding's novels ultimately resides in his use of capitals, italics, type-sizes, etc. – that accuracy in this matter of rendering even the accidentals of a text is not at all the merely precious or pedantic consideration it is sometimes thought to be."[88]

But to return to Foxon, he found that in the case of at least one poet, the fashion of dropping the capital corresponds chronologically with that poet's gradual discontinuation of the capital in his private correspondence. Such is the case when James Thomson's manuscript letters are compared with his printed texts over the same years. Consequently it seems difficult to understand the capitals in the texts of his poems as anything less than intentional, even though it counters the long-standing rhetorical value that Franklin had attached to the capital.

In response to his discovery, Foxon suggests that if we are to establish accurate definitive texts of eighteenth-century poets, we must pay some attention to those details that hardly appear to have been accidental intrusions on the author's texts by printing-house styles or compositor idiosyncrasies.

If Foxon is correct in saying that we can learn something from an author's private correspondence to help determine authorial intention in his poetry, then it would seem worthwhile to have accurate renderings of that former resource; in fact, editions of correspondence would take on still another value beyond their present worth if the texts of these editions were to reflect author preferences on matters which have been long relegated to the category of "accidentals." And it might be added that the use of such texts in conjunction with contemporary editions of an author's literary works could also facilitate the efforts of eighteenth-century booktrade historians to isolate and identify what indeed was the style of this or that printing house; that is, once a sufficient number of comparisons become available.

Admittedly the mere presence of such stylistics does not always reflect conscious authorial intention. Indeed many eighteenth-century writers seem to have ignored a consistency of style that would permit meaningful inferences, or, happy just to get their works in print (especially if sent from a distance) to have freely subjected their offerings to the style of the London printing house. Some, as will be seen in a few of

---

[86] *The Papers of Benjamin Franklin*, VI, ed. A. H. Smith, p. 145.
[87] *Editing Eighteenth-Century Novels*, ed. G. E. Bentley, Jr. (1975), pp. 9–30.
[88] In *Studies in Bibliography*, 34 (1981), p. 2.

John Gilbert Cooper's letters printed here, showed no interest in even proofing their works when given the opportunity. But as is evident from what has been said above, the failure of "accidentals" to reflect authorial intention cannot be automatically assumed in every case.

What then appears as a valid consideration for editors of modern editions of eighteenth-century poetry and fiction perhaps is equally valid advice for the editors of the necessary adjuncts to those texts – collections of eighteenth-century correspondence, especially correspondence with booksellers and publishers. What might appear preciously technical at the moment might well emerge as standard scholarly procedure for the future. Indeed bibliographical study has made great strides in recent years largely because of a more concentrated study of details formerly ignored. One need only compare the current sense of the term "bibliography" with its use thirty years ago when it designated what is regarded today as a simple "checklist." Or we can reach back a few more years to such a biography as Ralph Straus's *Robert Dodsley* (published in 1910) and be astounded that contemporary practice excused authors from citing the sources of their manuscript material.

The foregoing should have already suggested the manner in which Dodsley's correspondence is presented in this edition. Disposed to the rationale of Foxon and Battestin and to its potential values for future scholarship, the editor has consciously chosen to present a text that follows the original manuscript as faithfully as possible. This manner of presentation should pose few, if any, problems for its most frequent reader, the eighteenth-century specialist. Since the collection's main contribution is informational and not stylistic, absolute ease in its reading seems not a crucial matter. By no means is this meant to imply that the letters are barren of engaging prose. The reader will delight in many passages and sometimes in entire letters, especially those exchanged with Dodsley's closer and wittier acquaintances.

3. Dates

Those letters left undated by their authors have been assigned dates on the basis of both internal and external evidence. Special help in dating many letters arises from the nature of Dodsley's business. Because his correspondence regularly reflects the doings of the literary/publishing world, letters both to and from him carry allusions to works in progress, about to be published, or recently published. Since it is fairly easy (though tedious) work to establish the dates of such publications from contemporary newspaper advertisements, one can at least approximate the dates of most undated letters, if not pin-point them exactly. Such an advantage is not so regularly present in the correspondence of literary men.

In this regard, it should be said that some caution has been exercised in the use of newspaper advertisements. Anyone who has worked with them recognizes the obvious trap: "This day is published." Experience shows that the statement cannot be taken in an absolutely restrictive sense, meaning "this day is the first day of publication." Some works were advertised for a week at a time, sometimes even for weeks, with this same introduction. In other cases, publishers, to promote a second sale of the same edition of a work, re-inserted the exact same advertisement months after the edition had originally appeared. Consequently it is necessary to understand the bookseller's "published" in the broader sense of "promulgated"; namely, the apprising of the public that this volume is "available at this time," not that it is necessarily the first day that the work has become available. Such a broad interpretation, however, does not negate the value of a "This day" advertisement when it is indeed the *first* day that such an announcement occurs. Obviously the volume had not been available to the public (published) before that date. Consequently in all uses of advertisements for dating letters in this edition, only the first appearance of such advertisements has been employed.

In still other cases, as will be seen in Dodsley's correspondence with Christopher Smart and John Baskerville, works advertised as "This day is published" sometimes were delayed beyond the specified date, much to the embarrassment of the publisher. In fact, Smart not only resorted to another publisher after ordering Dodsley to insert one such advertisement but actually allowed some time to pass before publishing the work at all. The timeliness of advertisements was also jeopardized when a work was to be printed outside London – at Oxford, Birmingham, or York, for instance – and then shipped to Dodsley for its London debut. In his letter to John Baskerville on 7 April 1757, RD complains bitterly that the Birmingham printer's tardiness in supplying copies of his edition of Virgil has caused him much embarrassment because he had advertised the work as to appear the previous month.

Nor can it be assumed that an advertised publication date precluded the circulation of finished copies prior to the announced date of publication. Dodsley's letters to Shenstone's circle show him shipping volumes of his *Collection of Poems by Several Hands* several days before an advertisement appeared for the work. In the case of Thomas Percy's Chinese novel, *Hau Kiou Choaan*, an extraordinary gap occurs. Dodsley's letter of 25 June 1761 tells Shenstone he has sent a copy unbound, but adds that the work will not be published until the beginning of the winter.

Further caution must be exercised regarding the frequent discrepancy in dates on which advertisements for a particular work appear in different newspapers. Of course daily papers such as the *Daily Advertiser* and the *Public Advertiser* regularly afford an advantage over papers like the *London Evening Post*, the *St. James's Evening Post*, and the *Whitehall Evening Post*, whose thrice-weekly appearance necessarily meant that, on some occasions, their advertisements would lag a day or two behind the dailies. (The latter appeared for sale on the last of the three days spanned in the date on the masthead.) On the other hand, occasionally only the thrice-weeklies carry the advertisement for a particular work. Since the *London Evening Post* enjoyed a greater circulation in the provinces than any other paper, one can understand its advantages for informing prospective outlying purchasers, especially when a work would be of particular appeal to that market. The columns of this thrice-weekly had particular attraction for Dodsley since he was one of its shareholders. Undoubtedly some of the discrepancies in appearance of ads in different papers can be explained by the fact that advertising space for new books was limited in the dailies, thereby frequently causing the delayed appearance of ads in particular papers or forcing advertisers to make second choices.

Probably the most convincing evidence for determining a specific publication date emerges when a work begins to be heralded some time before its publication with such progressive advertisements as "Next month will be published," "Next week will be published," "Tomorrow will be published," and finally "This day is published." Furthermore, when the same "This day" advertisement appears in several newspapers on the same day, one can believe that tight-fisted eighteenth-century publishers are not wasting their money on meaningless gestures.

Finally, published reviews and book lists in the monthlies are other sources of evidence, although they cannot offer the precision sometimes required. What they do confirm is that a work has indeed been published. In addition, occasional help is derived from reviews and letters to the editor that regularly appeared in the dailies and thrice-weeklies, although obviously they account for a limited number of works.

One last note remains to be made in regard to the dating of publications specifically issued by Dodsley and used in the present annotation. Ralph Straus, at the conclusion of his biography of Dodsley, provides a 63-page listing of Dodsley's publications, complete with dates of appearance largely derived from newspaper advertisements. Although the listing has saved this editor considerable plodding, this edition does not rely upon Straus's assigned dates. In all cases, Straus's dates have been verified or altered by recourse to the original newspaper advertisements. The exercise has shown Straus's dates to be fairly reliable. Only his exclusive use of the *Public Advertiser*, *General Advertiser*, and *Daily Advertiser* is regretted, for occasionally he misses an earlier publication date as found, for instance, in the *London Evening Post* or the *London Chronicle*. In many cases, he assigns a date without indicating the source of the evidence. Because, in several instances, these dates were not able to be corroborated by evidence either from the newspapers or from Dodsley's correspondence – especially when they came earlier than the newspaper advertisements – the earliest possible dates found in newspapers have been employed.

4. Annotation

Protesting against what has been regarded as the pedantry and discursiveness of the past, modern editors of literary materials, with some notable exceptions, have tended to observe a much tighter economy in their annotation. Unfortunately, in some cases, the tendency has produced editions so lean that the scholar whose interest reaches beyond the primary text frequently goes away unsatisfied, sometimes even frustrated. One wonders if the voice raised against past excesses, and supported by budget-minded publishers, has not now resulted in an academic ambition "which o'erleaps itself and falls on the other."

The annotation of this edition attempts to strike a middle course. It observes the general principle: where it has been possible, all questions of an informational nature arising directly out of the text are answered with a degree of thoroughness that should satisfy the curiosity they prompt. The notes attempt to account for all allusions to persons, places, works, agreements, events, and so on, providing pertinent biographical, bibliographical, and descriptive detail where applicable and reasonably expected. Where such is lacking in the following pages, the reader has sounded the outer limits of either the editor's competence or his patience.

Beyond the matter of simple information, the annotation attempts to provide the letters with additional intelligence and coherence in several ways. Where only the nub of a large issue surfaces in a letter, its fuller significance for Dodsley or for his correspondent is elaborated. Where background information is required for the reader's understanding of an allusion, or where a relevant matter goes unmentioned by a letter writer, it is supplied. Where a reasonable conjecture material to the concern at hand seems valuable, it is offered for the reader's consideration. Also, related subjects are cross-referenced so that the reader can pursue a single topic through its various mentions in the text.

Because it constitutes a major concern in Dodsley's correspondence, the mode of reference used for individual poems in his *Collection of Poems by Several Hands* bears special explanation. In this century three different scholars have produced indexes to the *Collection*. In a series of articles published in *Notes & Queries*, beginning in 1907, William Prideaux Courtney provided the first assemblage of all known authors and their poems, based on a 1766 edition in his possession. In 1910, he subsumed all his findings, together with brief biographies of the lesser-known poets, under one cover, entitling it *Dodsley's Collection of Poetry: Its Contents and Contributors*. In 1933, R.W. Chapman extended the work in "Dodsley's Collection of Poems by Several Hands,"[89] adding an alphabetical listing of authors with their works, complete with references. Finally, in 1966, Donald D. Eddy, in "Dodsley's *Collection of Poems by Several Hands* (Six Volumes), 1758 Index of Authors,"[90] offered a revised listing, pointing out that his predecessor Chapman had unfortunately chosen a "mixed set" of volumes, reducing the utility of his references. By "mixed set," Eddy meant that since Dodsley regularly revised the volumes (dropping some poems while adding others), Chapman's choice of the first editions of all six volumes – I–III (1748), IV (1755), V and VI (1758) – prevented him from offering accurate references to the final selection by which probably Dodsley had wished to be remembered: namely, the editions of all volumes issued in 1758. (Volumes I–III, for instance, had reached the fifth edition by 1758.)

Eddy had put his finger on a critical matter that would have to be taken into account by any editor of Dodsley's works or, for that matter, by any scholar referring to poetry in Dodsley's *Collection*. Nonetheless, deciding which edition to use in the annotation of Dodsley's correspondence proved a relatively easy matter when the relationship of the correspondence to the production of the *Collection* was considered. Despite Donald Eddy's wise and accurate appraisal, it seemed necessary to pursue Chapman's path and to refer in all instances to the first editions. To use the 1758 editions of all volumes, as Eddy suggests, would necessarily

---

[89] *Oxford Bibliographical Society: Proceedings and Papers* (III, iii).
[90] *PBSA*, LX (1966), 9–30.

introduce complicated citations and ultimately confuse the reader. Because Dodsley's correspondence was carried on while the initial editions of all volumes were "in progress" and because his letters rarely allude to revised editions of earlier volumes, it has seemed advisable to refer in all cases to those first editions that Dodsley and his correspondents cite in their letters, often by page numbers. Otherwise the present annotation would become unintelligible when attempting to deal with points in the text where Dodsley writes of filling or canceling this sheet or that, or squeezing in someone's poem or dropping another he had originally intended to print. Besides, such statements would have little or no point of reference to editions which Dodsley had yet even to contemplate. A few illustrations should clarify the point. Poems submitted by Thomas Warton, Richard Jago, and William Shenstone for the first edition of Volume IV (1755), and mentioned in their correspondence prior to the publication of that edition, have a different pagination when they come to be reprinted in the second edition of Volume IV in 1758. To provide some form of double allusion in the notes for such instances, simply for the purpose of referring to the 1758 edition of all volumes, seems quite unjustified, even though Dodsley would probably have preferred to be remembered by that later edition.

LETTERS

A. LETTERS, 1733–1764

From Alexander Pope[1]

Feb. 5. 1732/33

Sir,

I was very willing to read your piece, and to freely tell you, I like it, as far as my particular judgment goes. Whether it has action enough to please on the stage, I doubt: but the morality and satire ought to be relished by the reader.[2] I will do more than you ask me; I will recommend it to Mr. Rich. If he can join it to any play, with suitable representations, to make it an entertainment, I believe he will give you a benefit night;[3] and I sincerely wish it may be turned any way to your advantage, or that I could shew you my friendship in any instance.

I am, &c.,

A. Pope.

Source: Dodsley inserted the text of this letter within his own letter, "An Epistle to a Friend in the Country," which was prefixed to a 1736 edition of *The Toy-shop* (Huntington Library copy). See p. 68.

[1] RD might have first met Pope when serving as a footman to the poet's friend Charles Dartiquenave (1664–1737); that is, sometime before 1728 when RD left to become the servant of Hon. Jane Lowther at Whitehall, another patron of literature. Before the date of this letter, RD had already published six of his own poems, implying some encouragement from on high; and Pope's willingness in this letter "to read your piece" and, further, to recommend it to John Rich for performance at Covent Garden, suggests an earlier familiarity with RD's poetry. Certainly *The Toy-shop* marks the solidifying of their relationship. The next year, RD's *The Modern Reasoners* would be issued by Pope's own current bookseller, Lawton Gilliver, and, the following year, Pope's intercession would bring *The Toy-shop* to the stage. With the proceeds of that production, together with a £100 contribution from Pope, RD began the bookselling business that would bring him fame and fortune, forever obliging him to his distinguished patron. For the next nine years, not only would Pope be recommending the new bookseller, but many first editions of his own works would be issued from the sign of Tully's Head in Pall Mall.

David Foxon, in "Pope & the Early Eighteenth-Century Book-Trade" (an unpublished manuscript of the Lyell Lectures lodged in the British Library), pp. 113ff., suggests that Pope had set up RD in business to ensure a tighter control over the subsequent publication of his poetry; that is, parting with established bargain-driving publishers such as Lintot and Tonson, Pope could secure publication of his pieces with an eager protégé without relinquishing the copyright, the same as he had done with RD's predecessor, Gilliver. With the lapse of the copyright for works published earlier with Lintot and Tonson, Foxon suggests that possibly Pope was hoping, within a short time, to have almost complete control of his works that he might issue a grand edition and realize a larger profit. Evidence to support this position is found in both Pope's letters to the printer William Bowyer and in Bowyer's ledger entries for the printing of *The New Dunciad as it was found in the Year 1741* in 1742 (Reginald Harvey Griffith, *Alexander Pope: A Bibliography. Pope's Own Writings* (London: Holland Press, 1962), p. 549), *The Dunciad: Book the Fourth*, 2nd edition (Griffith, p. 556), and *Dunciad in Four Books* in 1743 (Griffith, p. 578). According to Keith Maslen ("Printing for the Author: From the Bowyer Printing Ledgers, 1710–1775," *Library*, 5th ser., 27 (1972), 305–6), the works are entered in the ledger under Pope's

65

name as customer, meaning that Pope was dealing directly with the printer, not through a bookseller. Given that situation, however, one would expect the imprint to read: "London, Printed, and sold by . . ." or "London, Printed for the Author, and sold by . . .," standard formulas for such an arrangement. In fact, the imprints read: "London: Printed for R. Dodsley, and sold by T. Cooper," the standard formula for showing the bookseller acting as the author's agent or owning the copyright. As Maslen notes, "One can only speculate about the relationship of Pope and Dodsley." Whatever Pope's intentions, one can imagine the bookseller who owed so much to the poet concurring with his wishes, especially since it involved a deviation of such minor significance from the standard trade practice.

2 Plotless, *The Toy-shop* consisted of a series of moralistic, satirical dialogues between a master of a toyshop and his customers.

3 When Rich finally produced *The Toy-shop* at Covent Garden on 3 February 1735, the afterpiece was such a success that seven editions of the play were called for in that year alone.

To Alexander Pope

May 8.th [1734][1]

S.r

I beg you will be so good as to look over the Lines to Lady Mar: Harley, & tell me whether you think I should be excus'd in presenting them to her Ladiship. If you think they would be favourably receiv'd, I should be glad (pardon my Freedome) that You would please to make any Alterations You think proper.[2] As to the other, I believe it will be my last Essay of the kind: if it is not too much trouble to You to read it over, I should be very glad of your Opinion of it.[3] Your bearing with my Impertinence is an Instance of Goodness which I shall ever gratefully acknowledge.

I am
S.r
Your most Obed.t Hum.ble Serv.t
R Dodsley

Address: To Alexander Pope Esq.r

To the R.t Hon.ble the Lady Margaret Harley on Her Marriage with his Grace the Duke of Portland.

Fame now has sounded far and wide,
That Beauteous *Harley*, the fair Bride
Of generous *Portland* is to shine;
And Heaven approves y.e grand Design.
All Joy attend the happy Pair!
O Muse thy choicest Song prepare
To aid y.e Mirth of that great Day,
And something new and pretty say.
Something! – but What? – I can't proceed.
"A pretty Compliment indeed!
"Is Harley's Daughter to be wed,

"And can no handsome thing be said?
A sharp and just Reproof I own;
But tell me: what is to be done?
She shines above our highest Praise,
Yet shares ye justest humblest Lays:
And that's so very odd you know,
A Poet knows not what to do.
I cou'd, 'tis true, on this Occasion,
Mount up to Heaven, as 'tis ye Fashion;
Make Goddesses to Her submit,
Venus in Beauty, *Pallas* Wit:
A Thousand pretty Things run o'er,
Each said a thousand times before:
With all their Graces fill my Strains,
And then – be laugh'd at for my Pains.
No, no, such com̃on Place forbear,
There's no Occasion for it here.
Here Truth, in plain and modest Words,
The finest Character affords:
And just to paint Her as she is,
Will be ye fairest loveliest Piece.
But I forbear – I dare not try –
Yet give me leave to prophecy.
If Beauty without Affectation,
A Temper void of Heat or Passion;
Averse to Censure, free from Pride,
The Faults of others glad to hide.
If Modesty with Sweetness join'd,
Not over fond, yet ever kind:
A lively Wit, a Judgment clear,
A Soul good natur'd and sincere:
A Breast with tenderest Passions warm,
And every modest Art to charm:
If these are Blessings in a Wife,
Portland is blest, is blest for Life!

MS: Longleat Portland Papers, Longleat House, Warminster, Wiltshire, Vol. XII, ff. 209v–11.

---

[1] The month and day on the manuscript seems to be RD's, but the year appended by a later hand. (RD customarily dated his letters without the year.) However the ascribed year is accurate in light of the upcoming marriage of Lady Margaret Harley (1714–85) to William Bentinck, 2nd Duke of Portland, on 11 July 1734.

[2] Perhaps Pope passed on both RD's letter and unaltered verses to the Duke or directly to the espoused Lady Margaret, for both items are preserved among the Longleat Portland Papers. The verses seem never to have been published, however.

[3] Possibly RD's *Beauty, or the Art of Charming*, addressed to Frances Seymour, Countess of Hertford, and

issued the following 6 January by Pope's bookseller Lawton Gilliver. This poem was RD's "last" in a series of pieces (*A Muse in Livery*, 1732; *Modern Reasoners*, 1734) addressed to noble ladies during a period when he was obviously seeking patronage.

An Epistle to a Friend in the Country
[to Mr Wright of Mansfield]¹

[1735–6]²

The opinion which you say has prevailed with some, that this piece is not my own, but from a better hand, gives me too much honour to contradict, did it not shew their want of judgment who entertain it.³ I should be very glad if I could persuade myself there were just grounds in the merit of the thing to countenance such an opinion; but since it has been so favourably received, that I am now to print an eighth edition of it, I find I have pride enough to vindicate to myself any credit I may receive from it . . .

You may remember, long before I had the honour of being known to Mr. Pope, the regard I had for him; and it was a great mortification to me, that I used to think myself too inconsiderable ever to merit his notice or esteem. However, some time after, I wrote the *Toy-shop*, hoping there was something in it which might recommend me to him in a moral capacity, at least, tho' not in a poetical one, I sent it to him, and desir'd his opinion of it; expressing some doubt that, tho' I design'd it for the stage, yet unless its novelty would recommend it, I was afraid it would not bear a publick representation, and therefore had not offered it to the actors . . . [At this juncture, RD includes Pope's letter of 5 February 1732/33, q.v.]

Mr. Pope, was as good as his word; he recommended it to Mr. Rich; by his interest it was brought upon the stage; and by the indulgence of the town, it was very favourably received . . .⁴

This is the history of the *Toy-shop*; and I shall always think myself happy in having wrote it, since it first procured me the favour and acquaintance of Mr. Pope . . .

Source: Prefixed as "An Epistle to a Friend in the Country" to a 1736 edition of RD's *The Toy-shop*, pp. iii–iv (Huntington Library).

¹ Straus (p. 31) justly believes Mr Wright of Mansfield to be the addressee. RD's hometown friend (and relative? – see RD's letters of 1757 to Wright's daughter, Nelly) had subscribed to RD's earlier *Muse in Livery* (1732), which included two poems, "To my friend Mr. Wright, upon his commending something I wrote" and "The Footman. An Epistle to My Friend Mr. Wright."

² An eighth edition of *The Toy-shop* has eluded detection, but since a seventh had been printed in 1735 (Library of Congress copy) and the present letter was prefixed to an unnumbered edition of 1736 (Huntington Library copy), the letter must be a product of the interim.

³ Even as late as 1750, RD's style would not be recognized by a public who attributed his *Oeconomy of Human Life* to Lord Chesterfield.

⁴ Although *The London Stage* lists the earliest performance as 6 October 1736, *The Toy-shop* was first produced on 3 February 1735 and the first edition published the following day (*LEP*).

From Alexander Pope

20 August [1737][1]

Pray deliver to Mrs. Pendarves, or bearer, the book of letters, in quarto, or large folio, as she pleases.[2]

A. Pope

Address: To Mr. Dodsley, Bookseller in Pall Mall
Date: August 20

Source: The Autobiography and Correspondence of Mary Granville, ed. Lady Llanover (London, 1861) p. 618.[3]

[1] The year is most likely 1737 by reason of the mention of the "book of letters, in quarto, or large folio." The Stationers' Register shows that RD had entered the *Letters of Mr. Alexander Pope and Several of his Friends* on 17 May of that year, a volume printed by J. Wright and published by Knapton, Gilliver, Brindley, and RD. Furthermore, an advertisement on 19 May advised that "*The First Part of the Works of Mr. Pope in Prose: Consisting of an authentick Edition of his Letters*, in Quarto, large Folio and small Folio" was ready for subscribers (*LEP*, 17–19 May). (The advertisement, incidentally, also noted that none of the quarto would be sold, "the whole number being subscribed for"; and also that the large folio would be sold at a guinea, the small for a half guinea.) Straus's date for the publication, 25 June 1737, is obviously too late.
[2] Mary Pendarves, later Delaney, daughter of Bernard Granville.
[3] On the same page in the *Autobiography*, the Duchess of Portland writes, in a letter to Mrs Ann Granville, that Lady Peterborough (Anastasia Robinson, d. 1755) had given her this letter by Pope. Lord Peterborough had been a friend of Pope, and had also printed some verses in the 17 January 1741 number of RD's *Public Register*. Yet the letter seems not to have survived among the Portland papers.

To [Thomas Hooke?][1]

[1738][2]

Sir,

I sent by the last carrier ye Italian Homer which you desired,[3] together with the Manuscript of Tasso. I am sorry I cannot be concern'd in that Work, but the very late publication of a New Translation of ye same Author, wch hath not been ill receiv'd, seems to me to render ye success of another, even tho' it sh^d be better, at best very uncertain.[4] It is like bringing goods to market when it is over & every one hath supplied himself with what he wanted. I wish you success if you do publish, nevertheless, and am

Sir

Yr most h^ble Servt

for tho' ye commodity sh^d be better, yet as it is of ye same kind, rather than buy again, people will most probably remain satisfied with what they have got.

MS: Harvard Theatre Collection, Harvard College Library.

[1] Thomas Hooke (1693–1772) is a possible recipient of this letter since he is known to have been working on a translation of Torquato Tasso at a time when RD had begun enjoying the success of a "very late

publication of a New Translation of ye same author"; namely, Henry Brooke's translation of 1738, *Tasso's Jerusalem, an Epic Poem.* If the addressee is Hooke, it is obviously not Book I of his translation, published by George Hawkins on 31 January 1738 *(DA)*, that RD is rejecting, for Book I of Brooke's translation had been issued but three days earlier *(DA)*. Hooke could hardly, upon RD's rejection, have succeeded in negotiating, printing, and advertising the work with Hawkins in a few days. Perhaps, since the publication of Hooke's translation ended with Book I, either the bookseller Hawkins decided not to compete with Brooke's translation or negotiations with his translator broke down, causing Hooke to approach RD with a proposal for the additional volumes. If such is the case, probably this letter dates from sometime after 22 August, the day on which the third, and last, book of Brooke's translation appeared *(DA)*. (Book II was advertised on 5 April, *DA*)   ² See note 1.
³ Perhaps A. M. Salvini's translation published in Florence in 1723, which seems to have been the most recent Italian Homer available in England.
⁴ Brooke's translation did not enjoy a second edition, but a later translation by John Hoole (printed for the author and with a dedication to the Queen written by Samuel Johnson) was sold from Tully's Head in 1763 and passed through five editions with the Dodsley imprint.

From Charles Balguy[1]

Peterboro June 14 [1741][2]

I hope you'll be no loser by Boccace; if you can but dispose of the first, I am persuaded it may be greatly improved in a second impression.[3] I have your interest so much at heart in the thing, that I shall spare no pains for that purpose, whenever you think fit to call upon me.

Source: Thomas Thorpe sale catalogue (1833), item 45.

¹ Charles Balguy (1708–67), MD, St John's College, Cambridge, 1750. Balguy practised medicine in Peterborough, where he was also secretary to the literary club. Besides the subject of this letter, he published essays on medicine, although none seems to have originated from Tully's Head.
² The letter appears to have been written shortly after RD's publication of Balguy's translation *The Decameron, or Ten Days' Entertainment of Boccace,* an event of 27 April 1741 *(DA)*.
³ Although later reprinted several times, Balguy's translation did not enjoy a second edition from Tully's Head, despite RD's attempt to puff the work in the initial advertisement: "It is now upwards of an hundred Years since a Translation of these excellent Novels was attempted in English, the Language of which is so obsolete and uncouth, that it is almost unintelligible, and does great Injustice to this ingenious and witty Author." (The notice overlooks a "new" translation published in London by John Nicholson in 1702 and 1712.) As Straus reports, the work was further promoted a few days later in the *General Advertiser:* "As some People have objected to this Author [Boccaccio], on Account of the Levity and Wantonness of his Genius, this is to assure the Publick that such care has been taken in this Translation to render the Expressions delicate and decent, that even the Ladies need not be afraid of reading or having these ingenious Novels."

From John Brown[1]

Carlisle [*c.* 25] Sept: – 1743

S.^r

I wish you had told me directly whether you are willing to purchase the Copy of the Poem I sent You, upon any Terms, or not.[2] If you are, I desire you will let me know what you can give: If you are not, pray inform me particularly upon what Terms you will print, and sell it, upon The Author's Account. I beg you will be as particular as you can in your Answer, because I suppose the proper Time for publishing draws on. Your last Letter has almost miscarry'd for want of a necessary word in the Direction which you will see in my first Letter to You.[3] I am S.ͬ

Your humble Servant –

J: Brown

Address: [?] London
Postmark: Carlisle, 25 [SE]

MS: Bodleian Ms. Toynbee d. 19, ff. 3–4.

[1] John Brown (1715–66), son of the vicar of Wigton, served as a minor canon and lecturer at nearby Carlisle until being appointed chaplain to the bishop of that city in 1747. While rector of Great Horkesley, Essex (1756–61), he gained national recognition for his *Estimate of the Manners and Principles of the Times* (1757). (See RD's letter to Brown in early April 1758 for their altercation regarding the notorious *Estimate*.) Before Brown aligned himself with RD's later antagonist, William Warburton, he had published several of his works from Tully's Head, as evidenced by his letters in this collection. Curiously enough, RD was instrumental in introducing Brown to Warburton (see Warburton's letter of 6 or 7 April 1746), the controversial cleric whom Brown ludicrously portrayed in the first volume of the *Estimate* as a colossus who "bestrides the world." Apparently depressed when he was unable to accept the Empress Catherine's invitation to come to St Petersburg as an advisor for the advancement of culture in Russia, Brown ended his life by slitting his throat.
[2] Most likely Brown's poem *Honour*, which RD would publish on 20 December (*GA*). Although a second edition was not called for, RD reprinted the piece in eleven London editions of his *Collection*. See Brown's subsequent letters for more on *Honour*. For some of the bibliographical details on Brown's work, and for many to follow, I am indebted to Donald Eddy's *A Bibliography of John Brown* (New York: Bibliographical Society of America, 1971).   [3] Not traced.

From John Brown

Carlisle. Oct: 8.ᵗʰ 1743.

S.ͬ

The Terms upon which you propose to print the Poem are reasonable enough:[1] But I did not think the Expence of Print Paper Advertising &c: would have risen quite so high. Perhaps you think of printing it in Folio; but I would have it rather in Quarto; for as ⟨I think⟩ it will hardly exceed twenty-Pages, a Folio of these Dimensions makes in my Eye an awkward disproportioned Figure. I suppose the Expence of printing it in Quarto must be rather less than in Folio. I should chuse to have it done pretty much in the Manner of D.ͬ Young's late Pieces.[2] As to the Time of publishing it, I shall leave that to You, as you must know which is the properest better than I.[3] If such a thing is practicable, ⟨I wou⟩ (as I am told it is) I would have a printed copy sent down by way of Proof, as I cannot expect that You in the hurry of Business should revise it with that Care, as an Author does his own Productions. Whenever you do this, pray divide the Copy into two Packets directed to me, and put them under Covers directed to the Right Rev.ᵈ The Lord Bishop of Carlisle at Rose Castle near Carlisle Cumberland.[4] I thank you for your

Compliments, which I am afraid are higher than the thing deserves. I should think my self much obliged to you, if you could procure me any Emendations or various Readings from any person who has Abilities in this Way: I see you are M.ʳ Pope's Bookseller; but am afraid this is too great a Favour to be expected from Him. I desire the following Alterations may be made;
   In the title Page for "the Lord Viscount Lonsdale" read
"The right honourable the Lord Viscount Lonsdale".
Line 1.ˢᵗ for "See, the whole world" &c:
   read "Yes: All, my Lord, usurp fair Honour's Name",
Line 230.ᵗʰ for "Still sway'd by what is *decent* just & true"
   read "Still sway'd by what is fit and just and true".[5]
These are all I can at present recollect. I am
S.ʳ Your humble Servant
J: Brown
Address: To M.ʳ Robt.ᵗ Dodsley / at Tully's Head, Pall-Mall / London
Postmark: Carlisle 12 OC

MS: Bodleian Ms. Toynbee d. 19, ff. 5–6.

[1] It seems from Brown's letter of 18 February 1745 that RD did not purchase the work outright but rather printed it at the author's expense.
[2] RD acceded to Brown's request. He published *Honour* as he had the first four "Nights" of Young's *Night Thoughts* (16 June), in quarto.   [3] See Brown's letter of September 1743, note 2.
[4] George Fleming (1667–1747), LLD, Bishop of Carlisle (1735–47), had ordained Brown in 1735.
[5] The 1743 edition shows that RD made the changes exactly as Brown had requested. What Brown lists as line 230 is actually line 234.

From John Brown
Carlisle Dec: 24.ᵗʰ 1743.
S.ʳ

   A Day or two after you receive this there will be thirty five Copies of my little Poem called for all stitched in Marble; two of them on fine Paper:[1] Likewise one Copy of your Poem, w.ᶜʰ I desire may be covered the same Way.[2] The remaining Copy on fine Paper I desire you will direct and get convey'd "To the Rev.ᵈ D.ʳ Bolton Dean of Carlisle at Reading Berkshire, Carriage Paid.[3] There must be five more cover'd with Marble Paper and sent as Presents from the Bishop of Carlisle as follows.[4]
   To M.ʳˢ Fleming at M.ʳ Robinson's Watchmaker in the broad Way near Queen's Square Westminster, one.
   To M.ʳˢ Wilkinson at the Rev.ᵈ M.ʳ Wilkinson's in the Savoy, two.
   To M.ʳ Rook at the Roll's Chapel, two.[5]
These five you will place to my Account, unless some other Person should pay you

for them. Pray let me hear what Progress it is like to make as soon as you can judge of it. I am

Sr Your humble Servant

J: Brown

Address: To Mr Robt Dodsley at Tully's-Head / in Pall-Mall / London
Postmark: 28 DE

MS: Bodleian Ms. Toynbee d. 19, ff. 9–10.

¹ *Honour*, published by RD four days earlier.   ² Probably RD's *Pain and Patience*.
³ Robert Bolton, Dean of Carlisle, 1735–65.
⁴ See Brown's letter to RD on 8 October 1743, note 4.
⁵ Mrs Fleming, possibly a relative of George Fleming, Bishop of Carlisle; William Rook, clerk of the Chapel of the Rolls.

From Roger Comberbach¹

Chester   20th Feb: 1744.

S^r

I reced the last Sheet and half, which is perfectly right both in the Latin and English.²

I marked the Erratas in the ⟨f⟩ two first Sheets which I returned to You, but can now remember only two of them. The first is at the latter End of the Dedication, the word like is left out, it should be improve like the Virtues ⟨it⟩ which produce them. It is a much more just thought that Virtue should improve Blessings than that Blessings should improve Virtue; for Virtue is always improving and never reaches its full Growth in this Life.³

The next mistake is in the first page of the Translation. ⟨I should⟩ Instead of have given at present ⟨?⟩ it should have been have ⟨bee⟩ given a sig[nal?] Encouragement to all present, (or all here) ([?] you like better) to hope the best things for [?] *whole* Republick. The word whole is left o[ut] in the Impression. The Latin is de omni republica.

Please to correct with a Pen that which you send to Mr York Whom you may direct to in Red Lion Square⁴

I am S^r

Your most humble Servant

Rog^r Comberbach

There is one mistake in w^t you sent me in the 73 page in the 9th Line other instead of others.

Please to send me down a few of the Impressions, together with Lord Raymonds Report, which if you will let me know the charge of, I will write to a Friend to pay you for them.⁵

Address: To / Mr Dodsley / Bookseller in / Pall Mall / London
Postmark: [27?] FE Chester

MS: Osborn Collection, Beinecke Library, Yale.

¹ Roger Comberbach (d. 1757), LLB, Protonotory of the Palatinate of Chester (1734), and son of Roger Comberbach, former Recorder of Chester. Comberbach published his father's *Report of Several Cases argued and adjudged in the Court of King's Bench . . . Collected by Roger Comberbach* (London: T. and T. Longman, [1755?]) and, besides the present work, his own *A Dispute; consisting of a preface in favour of blank verse* (London, [1755?]). The last was reprinted by Garland Press in 1971. See George H. Marshall, *Collections for a Genealogical Account for the Family of Comber* (London, 1866).
² Comberbach's translation, with the Latin on the facing pages, of *The Oration of Marcus Tullius Cicero, for Marcus Marcellus, address'd to Julius Caesar, Dictator, and the Roman Senate . . . To which is Prefix'd Cicero's Preface to his first Book of Invention . . . Being a Dissertation on the Rise, Progress, and Decay of Eloquence,* RD would publish on 15 March 1745 (DA). The BL copy has sixteen blank pages following the text.
³ That RD made none of the corrections here requested by Comberbach suggests that the sheets had already been printed off and this letter was too late. Secondly, Comberbach had dated his letter Old Style: it was more probably written in 1745.
⁴ The work was dedicated to Simon Yorke Esq. (d. 1767) whose life and early friendship Comberbach says inspired the work. As the author delights in pointing out in the Dedication, Simon's branch of the famous Yorke family had chosen to live in rural contentment while the other pursued its fortunes in government. Simon Yorke and the father of Philip Yorke, 1st Earl Hardwicke, were brothers, being descended from a merchant family of Kent. Whereas Simon retired to the estate at Erthig, Denby, which he had inherited in 1738, his brother's son, Philip, pursued law, was raised to Lord Chief Justice of King's Bench in 1733, and to Lord High Chancellor in 1737 (Collins, *Peerage of England,* IV, 486–9).
⁵ Sir Robert Raymond (1673–1733), 1st Baron Raymond, Lord Chief Justice (1725–33). Raymond's *Report of Cases Argued and Adjudged in the Courts of King's Bench and Common Pleas, in the Reigns of the Late King William, Queen Anne, King George and his present Majesty* (2 vols. London, 1743) became a standard work of legal reference, being reprinted many times throughout the century.

From Christopher Pitt¹

Pimpern [*ante* 1 March 1744]²

Dear Mr Dodsley.–

I rec'd the 2 sets of the new Edition of Virgil, and very much admire the Letter and Paper, and so do my Friends. I have read over the first Book which is very correct. But some Gentlemen who were here yesterday, pointed out to Me 2 leaves wch they lept upon in the third Book wch are wretchedly mangled by the Workmen of the Press, and must be cancel'd, for the Decipherer Himself, could not make either sense or Nonsense of them. I hope I shall not be shock'd with any more of them. see Verse 668 – 676 – 689 – 734 – 736 – 749 – 848 – therefore I beg you to delay the publication for a little while, and I'll write to You again by the next Post.³ when I hope, I shall have gone thro the Whole. My Service to Mrs Dodsley. I am, Sir, Your's.

Ch. Pitt.

I suppose these faults crept in during your Absence from the Town. Compare these lines that I mark'd out in the 3^d Book with the Quarto Edition – the 848th Line need not be cancel'd, tho there is a fault in it.

MS: Harvard Theatre Collection, Harvard College Library.

[1] Christopher Pitt 1699–1748 was born of an affluent family of Blandford, Dorset. His father, a physician, was kinsman to George Pitt, Baron Rivers, who, in 1722, presented Christopher to the rectory of Pimperne, where the clergyman spent his life as a recluse. RD published Pitt's translation of the *Aeneid* in 1740 and its second edition (the present subject) in 1744, although it is dated 1743. Pitt was great uncle to Robert Lowth, another RD correspondent and author.

[2] The date is estimated from Pitt's mentioning a "new Edition" of his translation of Virgil's *Aeneid*. Besides the original, the only other edition published by Dodsley, a 12mo, was first advertised on 1 March 1744 (*LEP*). Furthermore, the printing errors that Pitt notes are found in this edition. Since it seems the edition, although printed, has yet to be advertised, probably the date of this letter does not predate the publication by much.

[3] Although four of the lines Pitt mentions simply involve instances of failure to capitalize, indeed the printer John Hughs "wretchedly mangled" the others. "'Tis Ours to wander still from fate to Fate" (668) becomes "'Tis ours to stwander ill from fate to fate"; and "Then, as her Temple rais'd our Shouts, we paid" (736) reads "urthen, oas her temple rais'd shouts, we paid." In the only copy of this edition I have been able to examine (BL: 1473.b.21), these errors stand, and no list of errata appears, although the condition of the two volumes does not preclude its original existence. No further correspondence on the subject is extant, but perhaps the errors resulted in the late publication of the edition, for it is dated "1743."

From Christopher Pitt

April the 6th [1744?][1] – Pimpern

Dear Sir,

I beg you to send in my Name to Mr Philip Barton of New College in Oxford a Sett of the Aeneid in the small Quarto, ⟨stitch'd in Blue.⟩ bound,[2] and to ask Mr John Pitt of Arlington-Street, for those Papers I lent Him, and send 'em by the Coach.[3] I hope Mrs Dodsley, Mr Spence & are all in good Health. (I speak this for Your Sake) that I believe it would not be amiss for You to call in *Person* on Mr Pitt.[4] I am often ask'd when Mr Spence's Book will appear. I think You have enter'd the Names of all the Subscribers in these Parts, who wait with a kind of Impatience to peruse the Work.[5] Yours in All Friendship and Affection.

C. Pitt.

MS: National Library of Scotland, MS 967, f. 235.

[1] The year is conjectured from internal evidence. During 1744, Pitt seemed to be exchanging works with the two Philip Bartons (uncle and nephew) of New College, Oxford. (See his letters of this year to RD.) Furthermore, in the letter dated "*post* 30 May," he asks RD not to convert the remaining copies of his *Aeneid* to waste, but to send copies to Lord Chesterfield, Colley Cibber, Dr Chapman, and to the Archbishop. It sounds as if he was making virtue of necessity in 1744, and in light of his (expected?) gift of Barton's nephew's Plutarch (letter to RD between 1 June and 9 August), he is reciprocating

through RD. In addition, in the letter dated "*post* 30 May," he asks RD to send him twenty copies of the small quarto and thirty of the large: with such stock of the *Aeneid* on hand, he would hardly be needing RD to send copies on his behalf after mid-1744. (See "Joseph Warton," "Mary Whitmarsh," and "Elizabeth Goldwyre" in Appendix B for RD's purchase of both the copyright to Pitt's *Aeneid* and 500 remaining copies.)

2   See Pitt's letter written between 1 June and 9 August 1744, note 1.

3   Perhaps Pitt's kinsman John Pitt (1706–87), Tory MP for the family seat at Wareham (1734–44) and Commissioner of Woods and Plantations (1744–6) (*Court and City Register*), 1746). In the 1782 edition of Pitt's *Works* (Edinburgh), appear three poems in tribute to John Pitt (pp. 76–8, 89–92, 92–4). In the second poem he speaks of Pitt as having built a home on a cliff overlooking the sea: John Pitt's home was on the coast, near Wareham, Dorchester.

4   The significance of a personal call on "Mr. Pitt" by RD is not known.

5   The allusion to the publication of Joseph Spence's *Polymetis* should have been some help in dating this letter, but since Spence delayed so long in publishing the work, the allusion could be attributed to any one of at least six years. I have not found a newspaper advertisement documenting its initial proposal, but in the *DA* of 11 January 1743, Spence acquainted the public that since he had enlisted 500 subscribers, he would put the work to press. However the work did not appear until more than four years later; namely on 5 February 1747 (*GA*). Pitt, as well as George Pitt, had subscribed for two copies.

From Christopher Pitt

[*post* 30 May] 1744 Pimpern[1]

Dr Mr Dodsley,

I am just returned from the Bath in tolerable good health. I enquir'd for Mrs. Dodsley of Mr. Dalton & hope she has receiv'd some benefit from the Waters.[2] I cannot but condole with the Public & with you in Particular on the loss of *Mr. Pope* of whom I may say in Mr Dryden's words:

"Now he is gone the

World is of a piece".

I had some Conversation at Bath with Mr Cibber & lik'd him the better for speaking with great Candor & Honour of the deceas'd. He very much prest me to let him transcribe some Things rec'd to Lord Chesterfield, with whom it seems he is very intimate.[3] I desire you to give him in my Name a stitch'd set of Vergil in the small Quarto, & to present Lord Chesterfield with a stitch'd Set through his hands, (in my name) of the large Quarto. I also beg you not to convert those that are left as yet, into waste paper, but I will either send for some of them from time to time, stitch'd in the cheapest manner, & oblige some Persons with them who cannot well afford to purchase either Edition.[4] I beg you therefore to send me down Twenty Sets of the small Quarto & thirty of the large, cheaply stitch'd. When I was at Bath I told the Warden of All Souls' College in Oxford,[5] I would present one of the large Sets to the Bodleian Library, & he desir'd you would direct it to him, & he would deliver in the book. My Service to Mr. Spence, Dr. Young & Mrs Dodsley, if in Town.[6]

I am, dear Sir, yr

Affec. Chr. Pitt

I wish you would contrive to present Dr. Chapman at Lambeth with a Small Set in Quarto bound, & thro' his Hands one large Set in Quarto bound to the Archbishop in my name, but let this be a Secret.[7]

Address: To Mr Dodsley / Bookseller in Pall / Mall London
Postmark: Blandford

Source: Handwritten in margin of Ralph Straus's personal copy of *Robert Dodsley* (by Straus himself), pp. 82–3, now in McMaster University Library. Straus gives no source.

[1] The day and month are derived from Pitt's mentioning the recent death of Alexander Pope, which had occurred on 30 May 1744.
[2] Both RD and his wife frequented Bath, he particularly in later years when suffering from the gout. Pitt probably refers to the Rev. John Dalton (1709–63), whose many works RD published between 1736 and 1754. Dalton's "friendship" with Lady Luxborough, said Horace Walpole, resulted in her estrangement from her husband and her "exile" to Barrells (1736), the Baron's estate near Shenstone's Leasowes (*Horace Walpole's Correspondence with Mary and Agnes Berry and Barbara Cecilia Seton*, ed. W. S. Lewis and A. Dayle Wallace (New Haven: Yale University Press, 1944), I, 64–6).
[3] Obviously Colley Cibber (1671–1757), who, the next year, dedicated to Chesterfield his version of Shakespeare's tragedy of King John, *Papal tyranny in the Reign of King John* (*GA*, 27 February 1745), after it had run nine nights at Covent Garden. But probably Cibber professed more intimacy with Chesterfield than he actually enjoyed, for Richard Barker, in *Mr. Cibber of Drury Lane* (New York: Columbia University Press, 1939), p. 249, says the playwright's remuneration was "neither so prompt nor so liberal." RD had published Cibber's *Apology* in 1740. (See Appendix B.)
[4] RD had published Pitt's *Aeneid* in small and large quarto on 14 April 1740 (*GA*), advertised as selling at £1 for two volumes, a few copies on "superfine" paper at £1.12.6. The later edition, in two pocket-size volumes of 12mo, had been advertised in the 28 February–1 March 1744 number of the *London Evening Post*. (See end of note 1 to Pitt's previous letter of 6 April (Whitmarsh and Goldwyre).)
[5] Stephen Nibblett, warden of All Souls, 1726–66.
[6] George Bubb Dodington, Baron Melcombe (1691–1772), wit and patron of literature, entertained his Winchester and Oxford friends Joseph Spence and Edward Young at his Eastbury estate. Another Winchester and Oxford man, Pitt, now Rector of the neighboring Pimperne, dedicated at least three epistles to Spence and one to Young, "Epistle to Dr. Edward Young at Eastbury." See Pitt's *Works* (1782).
[7] John Chapman, DD, chaplain and executor to John Potter, Archbishop of Canterbury (1737–47).

From Christopher Pitt

Blandford: Dorset: – [1 June–9 August 1744?][1]

Dear Sir.

I have just receiv'd Your Obliging Letter,[2] and am very well pleas'd that You and Mr Spence approv'd of the Epigram, wch I am Sensible is far unworthy of the Person's Character on whom it is written. I desire You to send Dr Philip Barton one of the 2^d Edition of Vida,[3] wch I promis'd Him, and He told me *He* intended to return to Me thro *Your* Hands, a Performance of his Nephews on Plutarch. I heartily wish Mr Dobson All Success in his *Scheme*, and believe it deserves All Possible Encouragement; I beg You to enter My Name in the ⟨List⟩ List, And if I can do him any further Service He may command it.[4] I am, with Service to Mrs Dodsley &c.

Your's Affec:

Chr: Pitt

MS: Edinburgh University Library. La.II. 647/313.

[1] The date assigned is suggested by internal evidence. Pitt's previous letter to RD (q.v.) briefly eulogizes Pope, who had just died on 30 May. Since Pitt had some personal as well as professional acquaintance with Pope, it appears not unlikely that the "Epigram, which I am sensible is far unworthy of the Person's Character on whom it is written" had Pope as its subject, thereby urging a date for the letter following closely upon Pope's death. On the other hand, Countess Hartford in her 9 August letter to RD (q.v.) thanks the bookseller for the "Verses upon the Death of M^r. Pope" as well as for the "Epigram upon Old Sarah." Such an epigram did appear in the *Gentleman's Magazine* of December 1744. Should this have been Pitt's "Epigram," then a 1744 date for the letter is still appropriate. (Unfortunately no suitable epigram appears among the 1782 collected edition of Pitt's *Works*.) Secondly the Barton work on Plutarch was most likely, Πλυταρχου Δημοσθενης Και Κικερων *Plutarchi Demosthenis et Ciceronis vitae parallelae, nunc primum semperatim editae,* which had appeared in late 1743, though carrying a 1744 Oxford imprint. Some doubt exists regarding the attribution of this latter work. The British Library Catalogue lists it as the work of Dr Philip Barton (the intended recipient of Pitt's *Vida*), not of his nephew, also a Philip Barton, New College, Oxford (BA 1741; MA 1745). From the context, obviously Pitt refers to a *published* work on Plutarch, and no such work has been attributed to the nephew. Pitt died in 1748, and consequently one is inclined to accept the Plutarch just mentioned as the work to which he refers. The doubt he introduces regarding its authorship poses an interesting question but seems not to argue against the date assigned to this letter.

[2] Not traced.

[3] *De arte Poetica* (1527) by Marcus Hieronymus Vida, Bishop of Alba. Pitt had published a translation of Vida's work, *Vida's Art of Poetry,* in 1726 and RD had published a second edition in 1742.

[4] Probably William Dobson's proposal to publish a Latin translation of Milton's *Paradise Lost*. Dobson, also of New College, Oxford, had been offered £1,000 by William Benson (1682–1754), a generous patron of literature, to produce such a translation, as Benson had earlier encouraged Pitt's translation of the *Aeneid* (Spence, *Anecdotes,* ed. James M. Osborn (Oxford University Press, 1966), I, 137–8). One wonders about the connection of Dobson's "*Scheme*" with the major edition of Milton's epic currently being prepared by Thomas Newton. When an announcement of the publication of Newton's edition appeared in the *London Evening Post* of 2–5 December 1749, the next issue of that newspaper carried Dobson's promise to his subscribers that his translation would appear on the following 1 February. The first volume of Dobson's work, containing Books I–VI, did appear in 1750, but the second volume was not published until 1753.

From Christopher Pitt

Pimpern July 4th [1744?][1]

Dear Mr Dodsley. –

I am afraid You never sent Mrs Walker's Verses on My Virgil to the Magazines as You promis'd Me; Be so good as to write Me a Line or two about it, For I am all most asham'd to see the Lady, till They appear, because She has been at the Trouble of transcribing them two or three times.[1] I hope Mrs Dodsley by this Time has found some Benefit by the Bath.[2] As to My Self they Tell Me I look very well, and indeed find My Self better than I have been for some Years Past. I writ to You not long since but I have rec'd no Answer, wch makes Me fear the Letter Miscarried.³ I am

dear Sir Your's Affect

Ch. Pitt

MS: Harvard Theatre Collection, Harvard College Library.

¹ "Mrs Walker's Verses on My Virgil" are most likely "Verses to Mr. Pitt on his translation of Virgil's Aeneid. By a Lady," which appeared in the *Gentleman's Magazine* of this month, Vol. XIV, p. 386. The lady's verses were probably in response to the 12mo edition of Pitt's Virgil that RD had published in March.   ² See Pitt's letter of 30 May 1744.   ³ An untraced letter.

From Frances Seymour, Countess Hertford¹

Percy Lodge Aug: 9th [1744]²

Mr Dodsley

I was very much obliged to y^u (thô I have not told y^u so sooner) for the verses upon the Death of Mr Pope & without any Compliment think y^r own were much the best amongst them, the ⟨Epitaph⟩ Epigram upon Old Sarah is a very good one.³ I see there is another Complaint come out, which I should be glad to have & my Lord would ⟨be⟩ have the other numbers of Travels & the History of England but does not care for the Naval History.⁴ I directed a Letter to Mr Thomson some time agoe to be left at y^r House I should be glad to know that he has received it.⁵ Is Mr Dalton Dead or Alive? or where is he if above Ground.⁶

I am

Y^r sincere Friend

FHertford

MS: The ALS is laid in before the frontispiece in the British Library copy of *Correspondence Between Frances, Countess of Hertford, (Afterwards Duchess of Somerset) and Henrietta Louisa, Countess of Pomfret, Between the Years 1738 and 1741* (London: Richard Phillips, 1805), I.

¹ Frances Seymour, Countess Hertford (later Duchess of Somerset) (1699–1754), had been an early patron of RD, as well as a friend of Lady Luxborough and William Shenstone, later RD's most frequent correspondent. RD had addressed a poem to her in his *Muse in Livery* (1732), a volume to which she subscribed for four copies. It was also to Countess Hertford that RD dedicated his *Beauty, or the Art of Charming* (1735) and Shenstone, his *Rural Elegance* (1758, RD's *Collection*, V, 1–13). Apparently, from the nature of her request here, RD also functioned as bookseller for both the Countess and her husband, Algernon Seymour, Lord Hertford.
² Except for one detail, internal evidence urges a 1744 dating of this letter. The epigram "Old Sarah" that RD had sent might be the same that appeared in the *GM* of December, 1744, Vol 14, p. 668:

Old Sarah's temper and estate
Made many a Patriot vote and prate
Who, now Old Sarah is no more
Do just as Patriots did before.

However this epigram postdates the death of "Old Sarah," the Duchess of Marlborough, an event of 18 October 1744, which would mean either the epigram anticipated the Duchess's death or the present letter is of 1745. But it does not seem that RD would be sending the Countess a piece from the most popular magazine of the century, nine months after its publication. Besides, she responds here as if RD had sent the epigram among a batch of poems on Pope's death (30 May 1744), his own to be published in his *Trifles* of 7 April 1745. Furthermore, the Countess's mentioning another *Night Thought*'s appearance neatly fits her 9 August dating if she is referring to Edward Young's seventh "Night," which had appeared in July 1744.

³ See note 2, and Christopher Pitt's letter to RD [1 June–9 August 1744?], note 1. RD's "On the Death of Mr. Pope" would appear in his collection *Trifles* (1745).

⁴ Probably the Countess refers to *New General Collection of Voyages and Travels*, published by Thomas Astley in weekly installments from February 1743 to November 1746; *General History of England* (1744) by William Guthrie; and John Campbell's *Lives of the Admirals* (1743).

⁵ Most likely the poet James Thomson (1700–48), who had dedicated his *Spring* (1728) to the Countess and had corresponded with her.

⁶ Surely the fashionable clergyman John Dalton (1709–63), a friend of the Countess and Lady Luxborough. See Christopher Pitt's letter to RD, [*post* 30 May] 1744, note 2.

From Thomas Sheridan¹

Monday Morning [15 or 22 August 1744?]²

Mr Reily's Hampton Wick³

Dear Sir

I should be glad to see you any Day this Week that you are at Leisure, I shall have every thing in Readiness for you. pray let me know by the Return of the Post when I may expect you. My Complements to Mrs. Dodsley. I am with great Truth

Your most obedᵗ Sevᵗ

Thomas Sheridan

MS: Set in an extra-illustrated copy of George William Fulcher, *Life of Thomas Gainsborough* (London, 1856), V, 31ᵥ, Pierpont Morgan Library.

¹ Thomas Sheridan (1719–88) of Dublin, actor, lecturer, and author, son of Thomas Sheridan (1687–1738) and father of Richard Brinsley Sheridan the playwright. The Dodsleys published Thomas Sheridan's *British Education* (1756), *A Dissertation . . . on the English Tongue* (1762), and *A Course of Lectures on Elocution* (1762). Although merely circumstantial, some evidence suggests that his purchase of Swift manuscripts from Sheridan afforded RD the opportunity of being included in the lucrative proprietorship, first, of the ongoing multi-volume edition of Jonathan Swift's *Miscellanies*, a series Charles Bathurst began to redo and expand in 1742; and later of Bathurst's 12-volume Swift's *Works* (see Teerink, pp. 65, 80). Shortly after his father died in 1738, Sheridan had purchased from the executors for £50 the elder Sheridan's manuscripts, which included some sermons, poems, letters, etc. of Swift's. (Although the original has been destroyed, see a transcript of William Hale's Exchequer bill, filed in 1740, among Henry C. Torney's papers, Public Record Office of Ireland, M4855, p. 47.) On 19 March 1744, Sheridan came to London to make his name on the stage, returning to Dublin sometime after mid-December. (See Esther K. Sheldon, *Thomas Sheridan of Smock Alley* (Princeton, 1967), pp. 51–56.) During his visit, he sold at least the Swift manuscripts from his father's collection to RD, as is clear from a £50 receipt issued to RD (see Appendix B), and from RD's publication of new Swift material immediately afterwards. It would seem reasonable to expect that Sheridan would have first approached Bathurst. Perhaps the latter thought Sheridan's price too high, or perhaps the offer was tied in with the publication of Sheridan's father's works (see below). Whatever the case, one can imagine that RD leapt at the opportunity of gaining rights to Swift's works that would give the opportunity of becoming involved with Bathurst's *Miscellanies*. On 31 October 1744, RD claimed

"whole" rights to Swift's *Three Sermons. I. On Mutual Subjection. II. On Conscience. III. On the Trinity* when registering the work at the Stationers' Hall; he advertised it on 2 November (*DA*). Apparently working in agreement with Bathurst, RD published Volume X of the *Miscellanies* on 9 May 1745 (*DA*) under his own imprint. On 31 October 1745 (*LEP*, 29–31 October), he issued Swift's *Directions to Servants*, a piece that would become part of Volume XI of the *Miscellanies* that he would publish with Charles Hitch, Charles Davis, and Mary Cooper on 11 April 1746 (*DA*). The Bowyer Papers (Ledger B, pp. 434–5; Paperstock Ledger, p. 886) show William Bowyer's printing of an edition of *Directions* on 31 November 1748 for Hitch, Davis, and RD, which had been run off from standing type of *Miscellanies*, Volume XI. With this hold on the rights to Swift, RD negotiated himself a share in the forthcoming twelve-volume *The Works of Jonathan Swift*, published together with Bathurst, Davis, Hitch, L. Hawes, Hodges, and Bowyer during 1754–5.

It is just possible that Swift's *Brotherly Love. A Sermon*, published by RD in 1754, had also been acquired from Sheridan. Finally, the one-volume edition of the elder Sheridan's works, advertised (*GA*, 18 January 1745) as to be published by RD and calling for subscribers, never materialized.
2 The context of the note suggests that Sheridan is offering RD something for publication, and, given his "Complements to Mrs. Dodsley," it must have been written before December 1754 when RD's wife died. But the first work of Sheridan's own pen that R&JD will issue, *British Education*, is dated 1756. In addition, Sheridan's promise to have "every thing in Readiness for you" implies that more is involved than a single manuscript (something that would normally be delivered to a bookseller's shop). Although the link is tenuous, the occasion of RD's purchase of the Swift material offers a probable context for this note. Since Sheridan's receipt acknowledging RD's payment for Swift's pieces is dated 23 August 1744, a Tuesday, it is estimated that RD had responded immediately to Sheridan's invitation of the previous day, meaning this note was written on 22 August; or at the outside, the previous Monday, 15 August. For some of the foregoing, I am indebted to James Woolley of Lafayette College; see his "Thomas Sheridan and Swift," *Studies in Eighteenth-century Culture*, 9 (1979), 100, 112.
3 Mr Reily is unidentified; Hampton Wick is in Middlesex.

To Solomon Mendes[1]

[8th November 1744][2]

Dear Sir,
You stand in my books debtor to

	£	s.	d.
The Amorous Widdow	0	0	6
Reflections on Government	0	1	6
Joseph de Costa (dear)	0	10	0
Pinto (cheap)	0	12	0
Cards, and my wife's trumpery	0	4	4

I expect some of the Roman History bound this evening, and will send it you to-morrow morning.[3] My wife and I are going this evening to the solemn foolery of a christening. 'Tis very wisely done, to tye us down so early to believe, what otherwise, perhaps, might never enter into our heads. I think it would be a good way of promoting the sciences, to have godfathers and godmothers at our birth, to promise and vow for this, that he shall be a poet; for that, that he shall be a mathematician: at least, there is as much sense in one as the other.[4]
I am,
Dear Sir,
Your most affectionate,
Humble Servant,
R. Dodsley

Source: The British Magazine and Review; or Universal Miscellany (November, 1782), 334–5.

1 Almost nothing is known of Mendes, who has sometimes been confused with Moses Mendes (G. B. Hill, *Johnson's Lives of the Poets* (Oxford: Clarendon Press, 1905), II, p. 415, n. 1). Cecil Roth reprinted six letters to Mendes from various mid-century figures (including James Thomson, Richard Savage, and John Armstrong) in *Anglo-Jewish Letters*, letters he discovered in the *British Magazine* (see Source above). In a headnote, Roth suggested that the recipient was the same Solomon Mendes who died on 7 January 1762 in Red Lion Street, Holborn. See also Arthur Sherbo "Solomon Mendes, A Friend of the Poets," *Philological Quarterly*, 36 (1957), 508–11.

2 Although Roth claims to have taken this letter from the *British Magazine*, the text of the letter as found in the British Library copy of that periodical carries no date. Nonetheless I have followed his dating, even though he indicates no other source. His assignment of the year 1744, however, does fit the publication of a *Roman History* mentioned in the letter.

3 Thomas Betterton, *The Amorous Widow: or The Wanton Wife* (London, 1706); anon., *Some Reflections upon the Administration of Government* (published by RD, 1739); Joseph de Costa, *Tractado de Cortesia, y politica, que se husa en toda la Europa . . . Todo recopilado, y sacado de diversos authores espanoles, y francises* (Amsterdam, 1726); Ferdinand Mendez Pinto, *The Voyages and Adventures of Ferdinand Mendez Pinto, during his Travels, during the Space of One and Twenty Years in the Kingdoms of Ethiopia, China, Tartaria, Cochin-China, Calaminham, Siam, Pegu, Japan, and a great part of the East Indies.* Translated out of the Portuguese into English by Henry Cogan (London, 1663). The "Roman History" has three candidates, all published in 1744: *The Roman History by Titus Livius* (6 vols. London: J. Clarke); *A New and Accurate Translation of the Roman History of T. Livy* (6 vols. London: W. Payne and J. Rowlands); Charles Rollin, *Roman History* (9 vols. London: J. Knapton).

4 Is this comment for the benefit of RD's Jewish correspondent, or does it represent the publisher's true sentiment, though made whimsically? If the latter, it emerges as RD's sole jibe at the Anglican Church in this collection.

From John Wesley[1]

Windmill Hill, Decr 12th 1744.

S^r

I receiv'd an Anonymous Letter to day, which informs me you are displeas'd at my printing Extracts of the Night-thoughts in "a Collection of Moral and Sacred Poems."[2]

I am not conscious of having done any Wrong herein, either to you or to any other Person. If you apprehended I had, I sh^d have look'd upon it as a favour, had you given me any intimation thereof, at any time after my publishing ye Proposals for that Collection, & I w^d immediately have stay'd my hand.[3]

All I can do now is this. I am ready to refer ye matter to any Number of Arbitrators. And whatever Damage they judge you to have sustain'd, I will willingly make good.[4] I am

S^r

y^r

humble serv^t

John Wesley

Address: To / Mr Dodsley / Bookseller / in / Pall Mall

MS: World Methodist Council Museum, Lake Junaluska, North Carolina.

1 John Wesley (1703–91), founder of Methodism. According to Frank Baker, editor of *The Works of John Wesley*, vol. 26 (Oxford: Clarendon Press, 1982), p. 119, only the signature is in Wesley's hand; the rest is in that of his secretary at the Foundery, Thomas Butts.

2 Not only had the first five "Nights" of Edward Young's *Night Thoughts* (which RD had been publishing in various editions since 1742) appeared in Volume I of Wesley's *A Collection of Moral and Sacred Poems* (3 vols., Bristol, 1744), but in Volume II were also printed at least twenty-four poems by Mrs Elizabeth Rowe (1674–1737) that RD had published, along with Richard Hett, in 1739 in Volume I of a collection entitled *The Miscellaneous Works in Prose and Verse of Mrs Elizabeth Rowe*. RD had entered various editions of *Night Thoughts* at the Stationers' Company from 1742 through 1744. Although no extant document shows RD's right in Rowe's works, Wesley acknowledges the pieces he printed as RD's property in his note of 8 February (q.v.).

3 As noted by Frank Baker (*The Works of John Wesley*, Vol. 26, p. 119), Wesley's *Proposals* had, in fact, made no mention of the specific works to be included in the *Collection*.

4 For the damage settlement, see Wesley's note of 8 February.

From John Wesley[1]

Feb: 8.th 1744/45

Having inadvertently printed, in a Collection of Poems,[2] publishd by me, in 3 Vols. 12°, some Peices, which are the Property of Mr Robert Dodsley, Bookseller, Viz! 5 of the Night Thoughts, and some Peices of Mrs Rowe; for which I have this Day made him Satisfaction, by giving him two Notes, one for 20£ payable in 6 Days, and another for 30£ payable in 9 Months.[3] I hereby give him my Word and promise that I will never again print the same, in that or any other Manner.[4]

John Wesley

MS: The Methodist Archives and Research Centre, John Rylands University of Manchester.

1 For particulars of the case, see Wesley's letter of 12 December. The manuscript is in the hand of neither RD nor Wesley, but the signature is Wesley's. The version of this note printed in *The Letters of the Rev. John Wesley*, ed. John Telford (London, 1931), II, 27–8, does not correspond exactly with the manuscript text. 2 *A Collection of Moral and Sacred Poems* (Bristol, 1744).

3 These payments might at first seem exceptionally large until one realizes that on 24 November 1743 RD paid Edward Young 160 guineas for only the first five *Night Thoughts*. (See RD's publishing agreements and receipts in Appendix B.)

4 In 1770, six years after RD died, Wesley printed an abridged edition of the nine *Night Thoughts*, leaving out the third "Night."

From John Brown

Carlisle Feb: 18.th 1744/5

Mr Dodsley

Along with this I have sent You An Essay on Satire in two small Parcels. As to the Terms of printing – I am sorry to find, in these upon which my other little Poem was printed, that the Interests of the Author and Bookseller are so weakly connected.[1] Upon this Account I do not chuse to have this Essay printed upon that Agreement:

If you think, upon perusing this Copy, that you can purchase it with Convenience to yourself, I desire you will let me know as soon as possible, upon what Terms you 〈wou〉 are willing to purchase it. If not, pray acquaint me with your Resolution, and I shall either desire Mr Dixon to take the Copy, or shall call for it my self.[2] I intended to have been in Town some time Ago, but have been prevented by a very violent Storm of Snow: As soon as the Roads are passable without Difficulty, I hope I shall have the Pleasure of seeing you in Town. In the mean time I am

Sr Your most humble Servt

J: Brown

P.S. I believe I shall add some 30 or 40 lines to the Essay.

MS: Bodleian Ms. Toynbee d. 19, f. 11.

[1] See Brown's agreement in his letter of 8 October 1743.
[2] Rev. Mr Dixon at Dr Brookbank's, Stepney. See Brown's letter of 17 October 1745. Apparently an amicable agreement was worked out, for RD published the essay on 24 April 1745 (*DA*). It was highly praised in William Warburton's letter to RD on 6 or 7 April 1746 (q.v.), although it did not seem to sell well at first. For its later history, see letter of 17 October 1745, note 5.

From John Brown

Carlisle   March 14.th [1745][1]

S.^r

   As I was in Haste when 〈You〉 I wrote last to You, having but about an hour or two to save the Post, I forgot some small Matters I intended to have put in my Letter. I desire you will send me about thirty or forty Copies of the Poem on Honour, along with those of the Essay on Satire. The Frontispiece I told you of being a little uncertain, both as to it's coming in Time, and as to it's being sufficiently finished, I would not have you wait for it: if it does not come, insert this in it's Place.[2]

> – Quemvis media erue turba:
> Aut ob Avaritiam, aut misera Ambitione laborat,
> Hic nuptarum insanit amoribus, hic puerorum:
> Hunc capit argenti splendor: stupet Albius aere.
> Hic mutat Merces surgente a Sole, ad eum, quo
> Vespertina tepet regio: quin per mala praeceps
> Fertur uti pulvis collectus turbine; ne quid
> Summa deperdat metuens, aut ampliet ut rem.
> Omnes hi metuunt versus –[3]

Pray make the two following Corrections wch I forgot.
   L:444. instead of
   "Each tuneful Muse &c": read
   "For thee the graces left th' idalian Grove";

L. last but two in the Conclusion, for
"Cens*o*r" read "Cens*e*r".[4] I am

S.ͬ Yours &:

J:Brown

Address: To / M.ͬ Rob! Dodsley at Tully's Head / in Pall-Mall / London
Postmark: Carlisle March 18

MS: Simon Gratz Collection, British Literary Misc., Case 11 Box 5, Historical Society of Pennsylvania.

[1] The date must fall between the publication of Brown's poem "Honour" on 20 December 1743 (Brown asks for copies of the work) and the appearance of Brown's *Essay on Satire*, which, because of the corrections enclosed herewith, must be close to its 24 April 1745 publication date. The letter is not likely to be 1744, because the *Essay on Satire* is not mentioned in Brown's letters to RD until 18 February 1745.

[2] Apparently the frontispiece arrived in time, for in the first edition appeared a frontispiece showing the heaven-sent figure of Satire hovering among the attentive visages of Beauty, Justice, and Poetry and having just cast out from their midst two serpent-like monsters. It was accompanied by a double couplet extolling Satire as the "sacred Weapon, left for Truth's Defense." RD did not use the passage from Horace that Brown quotes.

[3] Horace, *Satires*, I, 4, 11. 25–33. "Choose anyone from amid a crowd: he is suffering either from avarice or some wretched ambition. One is mad with love for somebody's wife, another for boys. Here is one whose fancy the sheen of silver catches; Albius dotes on bronzes; another trades his wares from the rising sun to regions warmed by his evening rays; nay, through perils he rushes headlong, like dust gathered up by a whirlwind, fearful lest he lose aught of his total, or fail to add to his wealth. All of these dread verses."

[4] RD made the changes in the *Essay on Satire* as Brown requested. Line 444, however, is line 462 in the printed text; "Censer" instead of "Censor" appears in l. 512.

To Thomas Warton, the younger[1]

Mar: 16.ᵗʰ [1745][2]

S.ͬ

I intended to have sent you one of the Eclogues last Post but forgot, for which I beg pardon. I hope it is correctly printed, and to your mind.

I am
S.ͬ
Your most hum.ᵇˡᵉ Serv.ᵗ

R. Dodsley

[Endorsement, in contemporary hand but probably not Warton's:] These were the *German Eclogues*
Address: To / M.ͬ Warton at / Trinity College / Oxford
Postmark: MR
Frank: Free Radnor[3]

MS: BL. Add. MS. 42,560, f. 6.

1   Thomas Warton the younger (1728–90) published his early works with RD, notably his *Observations on the Faerie Queen of Spenser* (1754), which established his reputation as a learned critic and won him the warm regard of Samuel Johnson. Tully's Head was one of his resorts when in London; RD's letter to Berenger on 10 January 1758 mentions him among a "round dozen" of notables at a party where Berenger's health went round. RD was open to the "new" poetry and criticism of both Thomas and Joseph Warton despite their preference for wild and exuberant nature in contrast with the refined neoclassical concerns and style of Pope, his patron, and despite their according Pope a lower ranking among the great English poets. Undoubtedly William Warburton's (Pope's literary executor) annoyance with RD for sponsoring the Warton school led to his remark charging the bookseller with having little regard for the memory of a man to whom he owed so much. (See Warburton's letter of 26 December 1755.) Although the Wartons' poetry would not last, Joseph's *Essay on the Writings and Genius of Pope* (I, 1756; II, 1782) and Thomas's *History of English Poetry* (3 vols., 1774–81), both published by the Dodsleys, proved significant documents in charting changing tastes in eighteenth-century poetry.

2   The year is determined from the allusion within the letter to the recent printing of Warton's *Five Pastoral Eclogues*, published by RD the day before, 15 March 1745 (*DA*). Clarissa Rinaker, in *Thomas Warton: a Biographical and Critical Study* (Urbana: University of Illinois Press, 1916), p. 25n, claims that the *Eclogues* was probably not Warton's, since he had never acknowledged the work and since his sister assured Bishop Richard Mant that he had positively disclaimed it. Consequently the eclogues were excluded from Mant's *Poetical Works of Thomas Warton with . . . Memoirs* (London, 1806); in fact, Mant makes no mention of them. However, a letter by Joseph Warton, *c.* 1790, found in the Swann Collection recently donated to Trinity College, Oxford, makes the attribution: "The pleasures of melancholy was not Mr Warton's first work, but what was Very Extraordinary indeed & what he never would own – German Eclogues." See A. J. Sambrook, "Thomas Warton's German Eclogues," *Review of English Studies*, n. s., 20 (1969), 61–2; Joan Pittock, "Lives and Letters: New Wartoniana," *Durham University Journal*, 70 (1978), 195.

3   For Radnor, see RD's letter to Nelly Wright on 24 February 1757, note 4.

To George Selwyn[1]

Sep 12 [1745][2]

Sr.

I sent up to Mr Parson's in Golden Square he is not in Town, but at Turvin Heath in Buckinghamshire, & they don't know when he will be in town.[3]

I am

Sr

Your most humble Servt

R. Dodsley

Address: To / George Selwyn Esqr / at Oxford
Postmark: 12 SE

Endorsement: Dodsley Septr 12. 1745.

MS: Osborn Collection, Beinecke Library, Yale.

1   This note represents the only piece of correspondence that has turned up between RD and George Selwyn (1719–91), the wit and politician. Having matriculated at Hart Hall, Oxford in 1739, Selwyn was rusticated the year prior to this letter for having made some insult to religion. It appears that no work of Selwyn's was issued from Tully's Head, though he purchased books from the Dodsleys. See

Appendix B.
² The year is taken from a contemporary endorsement on the letter, though not in RD's hand.
³ Probably John Parsons, the only Parsons living at Golden Square in 1745 according to the Watch Book for St James Parish (Westminster Public Library).

From John Brown

Oct. 5ᵗʰ, 1745

. . . The inclosed Paper, will inform you of my Design, and give You a Specimen of the Manner in which I intend to pursue it. If you chuse to engage in an Affair of this nature, please to let me Know your Resolution by the first Opportunity. As to the Method in which these Essays may be published, I have not come to any Determination about it. I should like to have one Essay printed every week in a single Sheet, but that I believe would subject them to the Stamp Duty, which must greatly increase the Expence of Printing them. The other Method which I think may be more feasible will be to throw four Essays together once a Month, which will make up at least a sixpenny Pamphlet. If you approve of this Method, I shall be ready to furnish you with four every month, of which You shall have the Liberty to print one Edition of what Number you please, for five Guineas each Month: This I am certain is a very moderate Share of the Profit that must arise from them if they meet with any tolerable Success, and if there is not a probability of this I think they had much better remain unpublished . . .¹

Source: Straus, p. 85.

¹ From Brown's letter of 17 October it is clear that RD rejected the grand scheme, and from his further letter of 15 February 1746 it seems no other publisher was interested. However, some of the essays seem to have made their way into RD's fortnightly *The Museum: or, Literary and Historical Register*, begun the following March. (See Brown's letter of 15 February 1746.) Straus (pp. 85–6) believes the essays to have been the *Museum*'s Historical Memoirs, but it is clear that John Campbell (1708–75) wrote all of these except four that formed the *Museum*'s "A Succinct History of the Rebellion," which was later published under one cover as *A Complete and Authentick History of the Rise, Progress, and Extinction of the Late Rebellion* (1747). The latter had been accepted as Henry Fielding's work by Wilbur Cross (*History of Henry Fielding* (New Haven: Yale University Press, 1918), II, 55) until Ifan Kyrle Fletcher produced some weighty negative evidence in "Fielding, Dodsley, Marchant and Ray. Some Fugitive Histories of the '45," *Notes & Queries,* CLXXXIX (1945), 90–2, 117–20, 138–41, and reopened the case concerning the authorship of the *Museum* essays. As two current RD authors from the north, both John Gilbert Cooper and John Brown emerge as strong candidates. In his 18 December letter to RD, Cooper even regrets that he did not send RD an account of the rebels' movements in Derbyshire, which the bookseller might have had before the *Gazette* printed its account. Regarding Brown's authorship, Donald Eddy (*A Bibliography of John Brown* (New York: Bibliographical Society of America, 1971), p. 19) says the "answer is probably no." But certain bits of evidence seem not to exclude Brown, even to suggest him. First of all, the rebels had taken Edinburgh and Prestonpans in September, and they were next anticipated to move towards Carlisle, Brown's city. In fact, they reached Carlisle just four weeks after this letter was written. It is significant that Brown admits that the character of his essays would "subject them to the Stamp Duty," a tax which was imposed only on *news.* Certainly there could not have been any more important news for Carlisle at the time, or for England, than the progress of the Pretender's invasion. Furthermore, that the essays were rejected by

RD in October does not preclude their use later on, in March of the following year, when RD began the *Museum*. In fact in his 15 February letter to RD, Brown says that he had been "entirely prevented from proceeding in my late Design by the Progress of the Rebels," but that he is now ready "to throw in my Mite to your Treasury [the *Museum*]." One might conjecture, then, that what had been "news" articles in October could be published in a literary periodical of the following March as "history" and escape the stamp duty. That Brown suggests in that letter that RD might care to reclaim two of the essays which he had sent last October (presumably part of his "late Design") links him even closer with the *Museum* authorship.

From John Brown

Carlisle Oct: 17.th 1745.

S.[r]

I received yours.[1] If my Proposal was out of the Way, it was really what I knew not, as I could only judge by what had already passed between us.[2] I should be glad to oblige you in the Manner you mention, were it consistent with the Plan which I have formed to myself on this Occasion. I know not whether the Title I have fixed on may ⟨pro⟩ promote the Sale of the Essays or not, but it is the most expressive of the Design, and therefore I am determined to retain it. I wish your Correspondent all imaginable Success, and doubt not but he will prove both a good and a useful *Subject*: I dare say he is very well able to carry on his Design without my Assistance, and therefore it is needless for me to interfere, where it is not necessary.[3] I sent you two more Essays by the Post immediately before I received Yours; and the Favour I have to desire of you at present is to seal the four Essays carefully, and send them by the first Opportunity to The Rev.[d] M.[r] Dixon at D.[r] Brookbank's in Stepney.[4]

I am really very sorry to hear of the Success of my other Essay. I am apt to think it was too late in the Season; tho' I think You might have published it three Weeks sooner at least: But perhaps I speak with the Partiality of ⟨the⟩ an Author.[5] I wish I may ever have an Opportunity of reimbursing You, if I have, I shall not omit it. In the mean time I am

S.[r] Your most humble Servant

John Brown

Address: To M.[r] Rob.[t] Dodsley at Tully's Head / in Pall-Mall / London
Postmark: 21 OC

MS: Bodleian Ms. Toynbee d. 19, ff. 12–13.

[1] Not traced.
[2] What RD proposed is not clear. It was probably not the *Museum*, for it had not yet been formulated, and when the *Museum* proposal was made to Brown, he gladly obliged.
[3] Possibly a proposal to cooperate with Brown originating from John Gilbert Cooper of Locko, Derby. In December of this year Cooper begins an extensive correspondence with RD and contributes heavily to RD's new fortnightly *Museum*. (See note 1 in Cooper's letter of 18 December 1745.)
[4] For Brown's change of heart see his letter of 15 February 1746.
[5] Brown's estimate here regarding the reason for the initial weak reception of his *Essay on Satire* (24 April 1745) was probably correct, for the work would ultimately become his most frequently reprinted poem. RD included the essay in the first four London editions of his *Collection* (1748–55), and it also appeared in the 1751 Dublin edition of the *Collection*. The second edition, corrected and enlarged, fared much better. First appearing under separate cover in 1749, this was the version RD included in

the fifth through seventh editions of his *Collection*, and it was also used in a slightly expanded form by Warburton for his edition of Pope's works in 1751. The latter, an immensely popular collection, passed through twelve London editions in Brown's lifetime.

From Glocester Ridley[1]

Poplar Dec: 2. 1745.

S.[r]

I return you the Proof-sheets, & wish you Success in the Undertaking: I should be glad, if you think it may be afforded, to be supplied with 30 copies, which (notwithstanding that I conceal my name) I find I shall be obliged to give away.[2] Towards the beginning of next Week, I believe, there will be three Sermons of mine published by M[r] Clark under the Exchange:[3] I shall be glad if they may be of use in ⟨?⟩ encouraging the Sale of the other. I had ⟨before⟩ last week received a Letter from you, mentioning a Proposal which I shall be very willing to assist by subscribing for the Museum; but I am sure, I am very unfit, any other way to be an auxiliary.[4] I did not trouble you with an answer before, foreseeing I should soon have this opportunity of sending it. I am

Sir,

Your very humble Servant

Glocester Ridley.

MS: Harvard Theatre Collection, Harvard College Library.

[1] Glocester Ridley (1702–74), BCL (1729), DD (1767), New College, Oxford, resided principally at Poplar, east London, where he was chaplain to the East India Company. Ridley was a friend of Christopher Pitt, Robert Lowth, and especially Joseph Spence – all of Winchester and New College, as well as of RD's circle of authors. Lowth wrote Ridley's epitaph and Spence made him his executor.
[2] *Jovi Eleutherio: or, an Offering to Liberty*, Ridley's panegyric on the "British" virtue, RD would publish twelve days later *(DA)* and, in 1748, include in his *Collection* (III, 39–52).
[3] Ridley's *Constitution in Church and State. Three Sermons preached on the occasion of the present Rebellion* at *St. Anne's Limehouse and the Chapel at Poplar in September and October 1745* would be published on 10 December by John Clark, under the Royal-Exchange, Cornhill *(LEP)*.
[4] Despite Ridley's modest protest of being "unfit" to be an "auxiliary" to RD's upcoming fortnightly *The Museum: or, Literary and Historical Register* (1746–7), he would be coaxed into contributing at least three poems: "An Invitation to the Country" (I, 135–6); a translation of John Gay's Fable XVI, entitled "Spinula & Acus" (II, 396–9); and "Psyche or the Great Metamorphoses" (III, 80–97).

From John Gilbert Cooper[1]

Locko Dec: the 18th 1745

S[r]

The visit which the Rebels made us in Derbyshire, I dare say, has fill'd the news papers this fortnight, & as 'tis natural to be sollicitous about what passes at such a time, especially for one in your publick station, I should have sent you a particular account long before the Gasette could have publish'd it, had I not been prevented by the continual apprehensions we have been under, on account of our near situation [to] Derby.[2] on Thursday night the 5th instant, a detach'd Party came to my Father's, & took most of his Coach horses & all his saddle horses, except one, which they left at my request, I alledg'd 'twas the only one my Father could ride on account of his age & indispositions. in other respects they behav'd very civilly. – I suppose by this time you can give me some account of the Power of Harmony, which I desire you would do in the sincerest manner, for tho' an Author, I can bear to hear the truth. how does it Succeed in Sale, & reputation? if there is any likelihood of its' passing the press a second time, correct the following errata, which escap'd me when I revis'd the press.[3] Page the 19th line the 8th for *Medicial* read *Medicinal*. Page the 19th line the 20th after *Peace*; obliterate the Semicolon & place it in the next line after the word *Seats*; Page the 48th line the 2^d after the Word *Torments* make a semicolon instead of a full stop. If there is any news stirring, let me hear it. I am, S^r

Your most humble Servant
John Gilbert = Cooper /Jun.

P.S. Direct for J:G:C:Junior at Locko near Derby.

Address: To Mr Dodsley / at Tully's head / in Pall Mall / London
Postmark: Derby, 20DE

MS: Bodleian Ms. Eng. Misc. d. 174, ff. 1–3.

[1] John Gilbert Cooper (1723–69), poet and miscellaneous writer, published most, if not all, of his works from Tully's Head and was one of RD's most frequent correspondents (thirty-three letters in this collection). Of an ancient Nottingham family, Cooper was born at Thurgarton Priory, the family seat, which he unsuccessfully tried to sell through RD in 1752 after his wife's death. (See the advertisement he sent RD in his letter of 19 January of that year.) His first publication by RD, *The Power of Harmony* (1745), as well as the many essays and poems RD included in the fortnightly *Museum: or, Literary and Historical Register* during 1746 and 1747, show Cooper an avid disciple of Shaftesbury. The *Life of Socrates* (1749) and *Cursory Remarks on Mr. Warburton's New Edition of Mr. Pope's Works* (which RD farmed out to Mary Cooper in 1751) embroiled Cooper in an ongoing dispute with William Warburton, an annoyance that probably had much to do with Warburton's falling out with RD and his refusal to grant the latter a share in his edition of Pope. (See their exchange of letters on 26 December 1755 and 6 January 1756.)

[2] The Pretender's forces entered Derby on 4 December, and accounts began appearing in the *Gazetteer* on 8 December.

[3] Since RD's response is missing, the success of Cooper's *Power of Harmony*, which RD had published on 12 November, escapes specific determination. However, it does not seem to have enjoyed a second edition except as it appeared in Cooper's *Poems on Several Subjects* (1764), where only occasional dictional alterations occur.

From John Brown

Carlisle. Feb: 15th 1745/6

S^r

I have been banished from Carlisle ever since the Rebels took Possession of it till last Night:[1] this is the Reason why I have been so late in receiving and answering Yours. I shall be very ready to throw in my Mite to your Treasury, according to what I have:[2] But I fancy you will not expect very much from me when I assure you I never wrote so many Verses in my whole Life as those I have published, these excepted. I was entirely prevented from proceeding in my late Design by the Progress of the Rebels, who broke off all our Communication with London for several Weeks. If you think the Essays w.ch You sent to M.r Dixon will be of any Use to you in any other shape than what they are now in, they are entirely at your Service:[3] If you will inform me of this, I shall desire him to send them to you. I have been looking among some old Papers, but can find nothing which I think can be for your Purpose Except it be a Translation of two latin Poems from the Musae Anglicanae, one on Scating the other M.r Addison's Puppet show, which were two or three Morning's Amusement last Winter: Strada's Nightingale & the Battle of the Pygmies & Cranes not compleated.[4] If any of these will answer Your design, I shall transcribe them & send them when you please. I shall very probably be sending you some small Matters of Amusement now & then. I shall desire to have your Museum regularly transmitted to me, which you will add to my Account. As our Booksellers here have no very certain Correspondence with London, I should be very glad to have them by the Post in Franks, but whether this be a Proposal which you can conveniently agree to, is what I know not. I ⟨?⟩ wish you success in your Undertaking & am,

S.r Your most humble Serv.t

J: Brown

Address: To M.r Robert Dodsley at / Tully's Head Pall Mall / London
Postmark: Carlisle 19FE

MS: Bodleian Ms. Toynbee d. 19, f. 14.

[1] The Pretender's army took Carlisle on 15 November 1745.
[2] RD's fortnightly *Museum*, to begin on 29 March 1746, carried original essays and poetry, together with historical memoirs and book reviews.
[3] Apparently failure of Brown's grand scheme elsewhere (see letter to RD 5 October 1745) and the attraction of regular publication with other distinguished authors in the *Museum*, softened Brown's hard-line attitude regarding the publication of his essays.
[4] *Musae Anglicanae; sive Poemata quaedam melioris notae, seu hactenus inedita, seu sparsim edita.* The most recent edition would have been that edited by Vincent Bourne and published in two volumes by J. and R. Tonson and J. Watts in 1741. "Skating" was a translation of Phillip Frowde's "Curcus Glacialis"; and Addison's poem, "Machinae Gesticulantis," Brown translated as the "Puppet Show." The "Battle of the Pygmies and Cranes" was also from the Latin of Addison; namely, "Praelium inter Pygmous et Grues commissum," also from *Musae Anglicanae*. The "Nightingale" was the sixth prolusion of Famiano Strada, published in Strada's *Prolusiones Academiae* at Oxford the previous year. The first Brown translation would be published in RD's *Museum* on 24 April, and the second on 5 July. The last two translations seem not to have been completed to Brown's satisfaction; at least they were never published. (See Donald Eddy, *A Bibliography of John Brown* (New York: Bibliographical Society of America, 1971) p. 200.)

From John Brown

Wigton (8 Miles from Carlisle) March 5.th [1746][1]

S.r

I left Carlisle unexpectedly the Day after I wrote to You, & did not receive Yours till last Post:[2] I have enclosed a few Verses which had their Birth here last Week by mere accident: They are at your Service for your Museum, or any other purpose you may think them proper for. You have made an Improvement in your Title Page: I designed to have objected to your *Magazine*.³ Upon Recollection I believe none of the Essays I mentioned will be for your Purpose, except the third, & perhaps the first Page or so of the second, which may be added to the other: but I have no foul Copies, having been reduced to the Necessity of burning these with several other things of a paralel Nature, when Carlisle surrendered to the Rebels.⁴ I shall return thither in two or three Days & will then send you the Translations that are finished.⁵ Upon Consideration I find the Proposal I made in my last was somewhat unreasonable, & must therefore revoke it, especially as I imagine the whole Pamphlet cannot be enclosed in one Frank.⁶ You may put ⟨one or two of the first that are printed⟩ the first and second Nᵒˢ ⟨when⟩ as soon as published, under Covers directed to yᵉ Bishop of Carlisle at Rose Castle. When you have Leisure, I wish you wou'd favour me with an Answer to a few Questions which follow. Pray by what means came these Verses of Mʳ Pope to Light, on the D. of M.? And who had them in keeping? –⁷ What other things do you know or hear of, that Mʳ Pope has left behind him? particularly whether ever he made any Progress in, or ever finished the Design he mentions in one of his Letters to D. Swift, *on Knowledge?*⁸ I am told he had begun something in the Epic Kind, but don't believe it till I have better Authority.⁹ Pray who is the Author of that little Ode to Lord Lonsdale?¹⁰ – And of the Hymn lately published to Liberty, which I have not seen?¹¹ – What & whose is this last new Tragedy of H. the 7ᵗʰ?¹² – I have several other Questions which I want to have resolved but I am afraid I shall tire you. I am Sʳ

Your most humble Servant

J: Brown

MS: Bodleian Ms. Toynbee d. 19, f. 17.

¹ The year is based on Brown's acknowledging the unreasonable proposal – posting the *Museum* in franks – he had made in his fully dated letter on 15 February 1746.   ² Not traced.
³ The early proposed designs for the *Museum* seem no longer extant.
⁴ The *Museum* essays entitled "A Succinct History of the Rebellion"? See Brown's letter to RD on 5 October 1745, note 1.   ⁵ See Brown's letter of 15th February, note 4.
⁶ In his letter of 15 February 1746, Brown had asked RD to send the *Museum* each month in franks.
⁷ "Verses upon the late D[uche]ss of M[arlborough]," published by Mary Cooper the previous month. The verses also appeared in the *GM* of February, p. 104, specified as "From Mr. Pope's characters of women, edited privately." The suppressed lines on "Atosa" (the Duchess) first appeared in Warburton's 1751 edition of Pope's *Works.* Unfortunately no RD response to Brown is extant; otherwise key testimony on the piece's transmission might have been available. For a fuller consideration of the "Verses," see the Elwin Courthope edition of Pope's *Works*, III, 76–94; Norman Ault and John Butt, *Alexander Pope. Minor Poems* (London: Methuen, 1954), p. 59; and F. W. Bateson, *Alexander Pope. Epistles to Several Persons* (London: Methuen, 1951), III, ii, 59–62, 159–70.
⁸ Brown is probably referring to a project mentioned by Pope in a letter to Swift dated 25 March 1736 (*Correspondence of Alexander Pope,* ed. George Sherburn (Oxford: Clarendon Press, 1956) IV, 5). This work, in four epistles, is to take in the "Extent and Limits of Human Reasons and Science," as well as the "Use of *Learning,* of the *Science* of the *World,* and of *Wit.*"
⁹ The eight-line remnant may be seen as "Fragment of Brutus, an Epic" in Ault and Butt, *Alexander Pope. Minor Poems,* pp. 404–5. Pope had mentioned his plan of writing an epic on civic and

ecclesiastical government, using the Trojan Brutus as hero, to Joseph Spence (*Anecdotes*, ed. James Osborn, I, 153), but he never pursued it. Shortly after Pope's death, William Warburton, as Pope's executor, had sent the plan to Brown, with the hope that the latter would complete the work. Writing to Richard Hurd on 30 January 1750, Warburton confided, "Poor Mr. Pope had a little before his death planned out an epic poem . . . The subject was 'Brute.' I gave this plan to Mr. Brown." (*Letters from a late Eminent Prelate to One of his Friends*. (London, [1808]) p. 27). Supposedly Brown began work on the "Brute" but without success. Upon his death in 1766 the manuscript seems to have reverted to Warburton, who apparently passed it to Owen Ruffhead, with other materials, when requesting that author to write Pope's biography, for Ruffhead claimed to have Pope's opening lines for the "Brute" when writing *The Life of Alexander Pope, Esq.* (1769) pp. 410–23. The plan is now in The British Library (Egerton MS. 1950).

¹⁰ *An Ode to the Right Honourable Lord Viscount Lonsdale* (Henry Lowther) by Robert Nugent, a poem published by RD on 5 July 1745 (*GA*). It was reprinted in 1748 in RD's *Collection*, II, 205–8. In 1743, Brown himself had dedicated his poem *Honour* to Lonsdale. (See Brown's letter of 8 October 1743.)

¹¹ Probably *A Hymn to Liberty* by Thomas Cooke of Braintree, published by R. Francklin on 13 February 1746 (*GA*).

¹² Francis A. Congreve, in *Authentic Memoirs of the Late Mr. Charles Macklin, Comedian* (London, 1798) pp, 25–6, claims Macklin wrote this piece in haste to serve the government's cause during the Scottish Rebellion. But the tragedy, advertised as for the benefit of the author and published anonymously by Francklin, Dodsley, and Cooper (*GA*, 13 February 1746), lasted but three nights on the stage.

From John Gilbert Cooper

Locko March the 12ᵗʰ 1745/6

Dear Sʳ

I am glad to see, by an Advertisement in the Sᵗ James's evening Post, that you have encouragement to begin your Museum this Season;¹ I shᵈ take it as a favour if you would let me know who are your coadjutors, in what manner it is to be open'd, & how continued; in regard to which You may depend upon my Secresy if you enjoin it, & any little assistance I can give you, is at your Service.² if it is small enough, send me the first number down in a frank. – how has the *Power* of *Harmony* sold since you wrote to me?³ That your present undertaking may become the greatest channel of conveying the Thoughts of the good & learned thro', for the service of the publick, & for the promotion of your own interest, is the Sincere wish of

Your humble Service

John Gilbert = Cooper Junʳ.

Direct to me as before at Locko near Derby.

MS: Bodleian Ms. Eng. Misc. d. 174, f. 5.

¹ Appearing in the 6–8 March number, the advertisement indicated that *The Museum: or, Literary and Historical Register* would begin on the following 29th, which it did. Thirty-nine fortnightly numbers would appear before the periodical was discontinued eighteen months later with the 12 September 1747 number.

² Whether or not RD shared this information with Cooper is not known; no response survives. He might have told Cooper that Mark Akenside was to be editor (see Appendix B), and John Campbell the

writer of the Historical Memoirs. He could have cited only his own name as undertaker, though modern commentators have obscured the point. The DNB, for one, states that although RD was the projector, he had only a quarter share in the paper, the remaining parts belonging to Thomas Longman, Thomas Shewell, Charles Hitch, and James and John Rivington. However, while the entry in the Stationers' Company Register for 8 December 1746 does indicate that three of four shares were distributed among Longman and Shewell (Shewell was currently associated with Longman), Hitch, and the Rivingtons, the record does specify that the shares pertained only to *Museum* numbers 10 through 19; that is, the numbers issued from 2 August through 6 December 1746. Although the Stationers' Register cannot always be relied upon to show a work's total ownership, when the registration occurs *post factum*, as it does in this case (nineteen numbers already published) and with such specification (listing the individual numbers in which parties share), the ownership, at least to date, seems beyond question. In short, it appears that only RD held rights to numbers 1–9 and that the partners had not been admitted until number 10. Unfortunately, no further entries pertinent to the *Museum* occur in the Stationers' Register, precluding a judgment on the ownership of the twenty numbers yet to be published.

During its lifetime, the *Museum* carried original pieces by Joseph Spence, Christopher Smart, William Collins, the three Wartons, David Garrick, and Samuel Johnson, among others. But Cooper himself would become the periodical's most prolific contributor, supplying at least twenty essays and three poems. (See my articles: "The *Museum* – the Super-Excellent Magazine," *Studies in English Literature*, 13 (1973), 503–15; and "*Museum* Attributions in John Cooper's Unpublished Letters," *Studies in Bibliography*, 27 (1974), 232–5.)   [3] See Cooper's letter of 18 December 1745, note 3.

From William Warburton

[6 or 7 April 1746][1]

Mr Dodsley

I saw, by accident, on ye road a poem called an *essay on Satire occasioned by the death of Mr Pope* & was surprised to see so excellent a piece of poetry & what was still more uncommon so much good reasoning. I find it has been published some time. If it be not a Secret I should be glad to know the Author[2] – If I have leasure I shall give some acc^t of it for the litterary news of your Museum. It will be a better ornam^t to it than y^e dull book of travels in y^e 2^d N$\underline{o}$.

I am your very humble Servant

W. Warburton

Address: To / Mr R. Dodsley / Bookseller at Tully's Head / in Pall Mall / London
Postmark: 7 AP Bath

MS: Osborn Collection, Beinecke Library, Yale.

[1] The year seems clear from Warburton's reference to an account of a "dull book of travels" in RD's second number of the *Museum*, which appeared on 12 April 1746. That number carried reviews of two travel books, though it is not evident which Warburton chose to call dull: Fr. Charlevoix, SJ, *A General History and Description of New France* (pp. 63–6) or Richard Pocock, *A Description of the East* (pp. 66–75; continued in *Museum*, No. 3, pp. 101–9). (The latter work, printed for the author by William Bowyer, listed RD among nine others as a seller.) The exact day on which the letter was written poses some difficulty, however. In his *Literary Anecdotes* (1812–16, V, 587), John Nichols dates the letter 12 April, a specification repeated by Donald Eddy, who reprints the Nichols version of the letter in his *Bibliography of John Brown* (1971, p. 9). Yet the holograph of the letter in the Osborn Collection carries

no date at all, except a postmark of 7 April. Since the second number of the *Museum*, to which Warburton refers, did not appear until 12 April, Nichols's and Eddy's dates would seem to make more sense. However the postmark seems difficult to refute. One can only imagine that Warburton had some advance copy or notice of *Museum* No. 2.

2 The author was John Brown of Carlisle, and the poem, *An Essay on Satire*, had been published by RD the previous April. When RD informed Warburton of the author, Warburton wrote Brown a laudatory letter, promising to print the essay in his future edition of Pope's works (Bodleian Ms Eng. Misc. C390, f. 398; reprinted in *Huntington Library Quarterly*, 17 (1953), p. 22). Warburton kept his word and placed Brown's essay at the head of Volume III of his 1751 edition of Pope's *Works*. (It is ironical that RD was responsible for introducing two of his future antagonists.)

From John Gilbert Cooper

Locko April the 7th 1746

S^r

I have sent enclos'd a small essay, or rather fable on Education, if you approve of it, it's at your Service to insert in the Museum.[1] – I desire you would send me one every time they come out, directed for the Hon^{le} John Stanhope Esqr Member of Parl^t. at Mr Ald.^{n} Frances's Derby, by which means I shall receive it without any post charge;[2] at the end of the year you shall receive the money from

Your humble Servant

John Gilbert = Cooper/$^{Jun^r}$

P.S. in the first Idle hour you have, let me hear from you, & give some account how the World of Letters goes on, [since?] I'm in a place that has no communication with it. [If?] the enclos'd or any other paper I send proves acceptable, [sign] it *Philaretes*.[3]

Address: To [M^r] Dodsley Bookseller / at Tully's head / in Pall Mall / London
Postmark: Derby
Frank: [?]orth

MS: Bodleian Ms. Eng. Misc. d. 174, f. 9.

1 The *Museum*, I, 4 (10 May 1746), 128–30, carried Cooper's "Greek" fable, "On Education."
2 John Stanhope (1705–48), brother of Philip Dormer Stanhope, MP for Nottingham (1727) and Derby (1736), and Lord of the Admiralty for the last ten months of his life. This is one of many indications among RD's correspondence of the regular abuse of the franking system. At this time Members of Parliament were able to send and receive letters free of postal charges, as long as 1) the packets were under two ounces; 2) the Member was actually residing in the place to which it was addressed, and 3) the letter carried the Member's name and address in his own hand on the cover. None of these conditions was closely followed in the mid-eighteenth century. Although not part of the franking system strictly speaking, the privilege allowed to Clerks of the Inland and Foreign Offices of franking newspapers to their correspondents had been in practice from the beginning of the postal service. See George Brumel, *A Short Account of the Franking System in the Post Office, 1652–1840* (Bournemouth: Bournemouth Guardian, 1936).
3 Cooper was quite insistent on the use of this pseudonym for his *Museum* pieces and expressed irritation in his later letters to RD whenever the editor, Mark Akenside, failed to use it.

From John Gilbert Cooper

Locko April the 23[d] 1746.

S[r]

I have sent enclos'd a Paper upon Similitude of Manners in Friendship, wrote in the same manner as the last I sent you upon *Education*.[1] – Your Museum is highly commended on this Side the World. news of this Sort can never be disagreeable to an Author. I am

Yours &c &c

John Gilbert = Cooper/Jun[r]

If you sh[d] See that wandering Knight Collins, pray tell him, that I have not wrote to him because I did not know where to direct my letters, but should think myself honour'd in receiving that Knowledge from his own pen.[2]

MS: Bodleian Ms. Eng. Misc. d. 174, f. 11.

[1] Both essays were published in the same issue of the *Museum*, I, 4 (10 May 1746): "On Friendship," pp. 121–3; "On Education," pp. 128–30. For Cooper's contributions to RD's fortnightly *Museum*, see his letter on 11 February 1747, especially the article cited in note 1.
[2] William Collins (1721–59), another of RD's circle of poets, had been living in London during this period. It is not clear where Cooper first made Collins's acquaintance, but, curiously enough, one of the two known extant Collins letters is addressed to Cooper on 10 November of the next year (BL. Add. 41,178, f. 35). The letter is printed in *The Works of William Collins*, ed. Richard Wendorf and Charles Ryskamp (Oxford: Clarendon Press, 1979), pp. 87–8. Collins is thanking Cooper for the essay he had submitted for their projected Clarendon Review, which was never published. RD had published Collins's *Epistle Addrest to Sir Thomas Hanmer* in 1744, included his "Ode, to a Lady" in the *Museum* (1746), and reprinted Collins's poetry in the *Collection*, both in 1748 (Vol. I 2nd ed.) and in 1755 (Vol. IV). See also Richard Wendorf, "Robert Dodsley as Editor," *SB*, 31 (1978), 235–48.

From John Gilbert Cooper

Locko May the 28th 1746

S[r]

I have sent enclos'd three pieces which will entirely fill the poetical part of one Museum if they meet with approbation from your Directors; as they depend upon one another I would not have 'em Separate, for the first & second are a contrast to each other, as the third is deriv'd from both.[1] – I've been highly entertain'd with an Advertisement in your last. – pray let me know, if 'tis proper, who was the Author of it, & of the Supplement too to *Education*.[2] I am S

yours most Sincerely

J. G. Cooper/Jun[r]

MS: Bodleian Ms. Eng. Misc. d. 174, f. 13.

[1] Cooper is most likely referring to his philosophical piece, "The Estimate of Life. In Three Parts." Although its publication was slightly delayed, the poem did fill the entire poetical part of the *Museum*, I, 10 (2 August 1746), 372–9.

[2] Consisting of merely a title page and table of contents for a "proposed" volume on the topic, "Advertisement for *The History of Good Breeding*," *Museum*, I, 5 (24 May 1746), 169–72, was a playful satire by Horace Walpole, with special thrusts at European political and religious fashions. The author of "Of the Knowledge of the World," subtitled "a Supplement to Education" (see Cooper to RD 7 April 1746, note 1), remains unidentified.

From Samuel Johnson[1]

[June 1746?][2]

Sir

I received yesterday the agreement fairly engrossed which I have examined and find exact, I therefore wrote this morning to Mr Knapton, and find that he is gone from home and that his return is not expected till after mid-summer. I conclude therefore that the writings were sent to me, that I might put an end to the treaty with the rest in his absence, I have therefore given the Bearer a note to be carried if You approve it to Mr Longman who is named the second in the articles, to which You may if you please add your concurrence, or send me word what steps I shall take. I think it is by no means necessary that all the partners should sign on the same day, nor can it be done in this affair because Mr Knapton does not return before the time at which the contract commences. His Brother directed me to apply to the Partners.[3]

I am sir &c

Sam: Johnson

The Bonds I have not seen the Attorney should be directed to send them. I know not who he is.[4]

Address: To Mr Dodsley

MS: Hyde Collection, Somerville, New Jersey.

[1] RD published the first major work of Samuel Johnson (1709–84), *London. A Poem. In Imitation of the Third Satire of Juvenal* in 1738, for which he paid the author ten guineas (Boswell, *Life*, I, 124). Eight years later, together with Andrew Millar, Charles Hitch, the two Longmans, and John and Paul Knapton, RD signed an agreement with Johnson on 18 June 1746 for the production of *A Dictionary of the English Language*, for which, Boswell reports (*Life*, I, 183), Johnson was to be paid £1,575 in installments. Which of the undertakers played the principal role of negotiator and mediator with Johnson over the nine years it took to complete the work is difficult to say, but at least four of them seemed to take a hand at the job over that period. J. A. Cochrane, on p. 24 of *Dr. Johnson's Printer. The Life of William Strahan* (Cambridge, Mass.: Harvard University Press, 1964), says: "Although Millar acted on behalf of the other partners, it is clear that Strahan was employed as their intermediary with Johnson." But the earliest evidence that Cochrane offers for Strahan's role dates from 1750. In the present letter, apparently Johnson's first recourse after having received the contract from the group was Knapton. Finding Knapton not at home, he writes to RD. Johnson's next note to RD on 26 December of this same year no doubt also concerns the *Dictionary*, for here the author is sending RD a receipt for money advanced. But here the evidence ends for RD's role.

RD purchased two more works from Johnson during 1748 and 1749. On 25 November 1748, Johnson sold him the copyright of *The Vanity of Human Wishes* for fifteen guineas, a work published the following January (see Appendix B). On 16 February 1749, RD entered his own name in the Stationers' Company Register as owner of the whole right to Johnson's *Irene. A Tragedy*, which he published on the same day. The actual purchase of the copyright for £100, however, was not until seven months later. Finally, although Johnson's *The Prince of Abissinia* was entered in the Stationers' Register on 19 April 1759 as owned in equal shares by RD and William Johnston, and although only their names appear on the imprint, Boswell notes (*Life*, I, 341) that Strahan had also been a partner in the purchase. Three extant receipts issued to Strahan by Johnson for £25, though after publication of *Rasselas*, seem to bear out Boswell's contention (see Appendix B).

² The text suggests that this letter concerns the signing of the agreement for Johnson's projected *Dictionary of the English Language*. Since Sir John Hawkins, who, when writing *The Life of Samuel Johnson* (1787), said he had the contract "now in my hand" (p. 344), and dated it as 18 June 1746, it can be reasonably assumed that this letter was written about the same time. Boswell also records the same date for the signing (*Life*, I, 183).

³ John Knapton, a partner with his brother Paul, took over the business after his brother's death and later had a share in the publication of Johnson's *Shakespeare* (see Boswell, Life, I, 545).

⁴ Nor, it seems, do any modern Johnson scholars.

From Jacob Calton¹

                                                            Marton June 15. 1746.
Sir,

I don't know whether the Writer will get (or deserves) any Honour or no, by the Notes on Milton's Muse; but the Printer hath been extremely negligent; for the Copy, I think, was correct.² Pray find some vacant Place in the next Number for the following Errata.

Errata in the last Number

P. 211. l. 13. After βοληματων d, the letter of Reference is wanting.

l. 15. For ᾱς ἁς

l. 16. After γην e instead of d. And at the bottom of the Page for ad Aurel read Ad Autol.

l. 20. After *Proverbs* f is wanting.

P. 212 _____ The little Note on *Spenser* should have been in the preceding Page, &g, the letter referring to it, inserted after *Original* 1. 38³

I should be glad to know from you, when you favour me next with a Letter, what Character Mʳ Upton's late miscellaneous Book on Shakespear bears in Town.⁴ He hath been dabling a little with Milton, & designs, I perceive, to proceed further; but the *Corrections* he hath given us do not seem to promise much.⁵ I am every Day almost doing something in Order to fulfill what *I* have promised, when ill Health (which hath no Regard to Promises) does not break in upon my Speculations;⁶ & am

                                    Sir,
                        Your real humble Servant
                                                            J Calton

Address: To Mʳ Robert Dodsley / at Tully's Head in Pall Mall / Sᵗ James's / London
Postmark: 16 IV

MS: Ms Robin Myers, FSA, of London.

1   Jacob Calton, BA, Jesus College, Cambridge (1724–5); ordained deacon (1727) and priest (1729);
    Rector of Kelsey St Nicholas, Lincolnshire, 1729.
2   Calton refers to a brief explication, "Milton's Muse," he had supplied for an issue of RD's fortnightly
    Museum: or, Literary and Historical Register (I, 6 (7 June 1746), 210–12) that had appeared less than two
    weeks earlier. Signed merely "J. C.," its authorship is here identified for the first time.
3   All the errata concern misplaced or omitted footnote letters; the only material error is the substitution
    of "Aurel" for "Autol."
4   John Upton's *Critical Observations on Shakespeare* had been published by George Hawkins on 1 May of
    this year (*LEP*, 29 April–1 May). As one of the learned emendators of Shakespeare's text in the
    century, Upton earned frequent mention in Samuel Johnson's own commentary on Shakespeare,
    although not regularly with favor. Johnson regarded Upton as one who was "skilled in languages and
    acquainted with books, but who seems to have had no great vigor of genius or nicety of taste." See
    Johnson's *Preface to Shakespeare*, ed. Arthur Sherbo (New Haven: Yale University Press, 1968), Yale
    Edition of Johnson, VII, 100–1.
5   Upton's *Critical Observations on Shakespeare* offered some observations on Milton. Thomas Newton, in
    the Preface to his much reprinted edition of *Paradise Lost* (1749), would acknowledge a debt to Upton,
    among other contemporary commentators. Upton did not produce a separate work on Milton.
6   Probably Calton refers to the subject of his short notice at the end of "Milton's Muse": "The Public
    may expect from the Author of these two notes, in a very little Time, a pretty large Specimen of a larger
    Design upon the *Paradise Lost*. He once intended a new Edition, in which the Pointing would have
    been particularly his Care; but he is not displeased to hear that the Work is in better Hands." Probably
    Calton refers to Newton's edition (above), proposals for which would appear on 13 December of this
    year (*GA*). If Calton completed his work, it seems not to have been published.

From John Gilbert Cooper

Derby July the 7th 1746

S^r

You may be sure it gave me pleasure to hear my last little performance was
approv'd of,[1] & who ever asks ⟨you either⟩ about this or any other paper I either
have already, or shall send, you may tell who the Author is. be pleas'd to make the
Printer (for he often forgets) to mark every piece of prose, which I write, *Philaretes* in
the same corner I do; the reason why I Subjoin'd *Musophilus* to the last was because
it Corresponded to the subject. – all your Readers in this country very much admire
your serious Cervantes like exhortation to learn to whistle.[3] – I am return'd again to
my Books after some interval, & will comply with your request as well as I am able,
but had much rather you would write in concert with me in the humorous papers,
that is, make any addition, altaration, amendment &c as you think proper, for I
know nobody's taste I can more rely upon than yours. I sent by last Saturday's Post
an essay on the polite Arts, & a Hymn to Health.[3] – you shall hear from me very
soon. I am, S^r

your most humble Servant

J: G: Cooper/Junr.

MS: Bodleian Ms. Eng. Misc. d. 174, f. 15.

1   "A Project for Raising an Hospital for Decayed Authors" in a letter to the *Museum*, I, 8 (5 July 1746),
    287–91, by "Musophilus."
2   A humorous indictment of misdirected vocations, "A Serious Exhortation to Learn to Whistle" by
    "Democritus" appeared in the *Museum*, I, 6 (7 June 1746), 213–15.

³ A moralistic attack upon the loss of an appreciation for art, "On the Polite Arts" was immediately published in *Museum*, I, 9 (19 July 1746), 321–4. "A Hymn to Health," however, did not appear in the *Museum* until I, 12 (30 August 1746), 460–2.

From John Gilbert Cooper

S^r   Derby July the 26th 1746

I could not answer yours sooner because no Post after the receipt of it came out before this day.¹ I would have the *whole* Poem you mention entitled *the Bioapotimatist*, & the three pieces separately call'd as you see 'em, with the mark of *Philaretes* at the bottom of the last.² I sent you one of the Fables by last Monday's Post, & ⟨another⟩ the other is inclos'd in this with a Turkish Letter.³ If any body thinks it worth while to enquire after the author of any of my compositions you may satisfy their curiosity. if you don't choose to mark any of the poetical pieces at the end you may say ⟨that⟩ at the top of the above mention'd Poem, The following is wrote by the *Gentleman, our correspondent*, (or any thing of that sort with whatever epithet you think proper to bestow upon me) who signs himself Philaretes. you never mention'd whether you receiv'd the Paper *on the Folly of Noblemen paying their debts*, which in my opinion was better than *my project*.⁴ I am, S^r,

your humble Servant

John Gilbert = Cooper/Junr.

P.S. If you think the Title Bioapotimatist not so proper, you make call it; *the Estimate of Life.*

MS: Bodleian Ms. Eng. Misc. d. 174, f. 17.

¹ RD's letter not traced.
² "The Estimate of Life. In Three Parts" was published without Cooper's suggested title. See Cooper to Dodsley, 28 May 1746, note 1.
³ "On Contentment. A Fable," an oriental story and moral very much suggestive of Johnson's *Rasselas*, appeared in the *Museum*, I, 12 (30 August 1746), 450–3; the "other" fable, "On Conjugal Love. A Moral Story," in *Museum*, I 13 (13 September 1746), 490–2. The "Turkish Letter" is "An Epistle from Muli Azareth at London, to the Mufti at Constantinople," published in the same issue of the *Museum* as "On Contentment," pp. 453–5.
⁴ Possibly RD felt this satire on the exploitation of tradesmen by the nobility and gentry a bit sensitive, for he delayed its publication until *Museum*, II, 23 (31 January 1747), 305–8.

From Christopher Smart¹

Sir.   Pemb. Hall Camb^r. ye 6th of August 1746.

I sent you this morning, by the coach, an hundred copies of my affair, which, I suppose, will be as many as you will be able to dispose of.² I wou'd have it advertised but for three days, & only in one paper each day.³ The price of 'em is two shillings a piece. I beg the favor the advertisement may be carefully copied from the title page, because there were too unlucky mistakes in the latin parts of the former three advertisements.[4] If you find they go off tolerably let me know.[5] – I am yours &c C. Smart.[6]

Address: To / Mr Dodsley / at Tully's Head / in Pall Mall / London.
Postmark: Cambridge

MS: Osborn Collection, Beinecke Library, Yale.

[1] Christopher Smart (1722–71), while at Cambridge, seemed to seek out RD as his London bookseller, this Latin version of Pope's *Ode*, coupled with his own, being apparently his first approach. However, coming to London in mid-1749 and soon after introduced to John Newbery by Dr Burney, he turned to Newbery as his bookseller. Professor Betty Rizzo has suggested to me that perhaps RD, hearing that Smart's creditors had had him arrested in November of 1747, had cut off the poet's credit sometime in January 1748. (See Smart's letter on 9 February 1748, complaining of a failure to receive an order of books.) If so, Smart was probably looking for a more venturesome literary midwife when he came to London. Whatever the case, Smart published his *Poems on Several Occasions* from Newbery's shop in 1752, and during the period 1751–3, he conducted *The Midwife, or Old Woman's Magazine* for Newbery. Yet relations with RD seem not to have been entirely strained, for RD's name was listed as a "seller" in the imprints to three of Smart's poems during 1750–3.

[2] "*Carmen cl. Alexandri Pope in S. Caeciliam Latine Redditum.* Editio altera. To which is added *Ode for Musick on St. Cecilia's Day,* by Christopher Smart, Fellow of Pembroke Hall in the University of Cambridge. Cambridge, printed by J[oseph] Bentham, Printer to the University, and sold by R. Dodsley, London, 1746." Bentham had printed the first edition of Smart's translation of Pope's *Ode* in 1743. Claiming to be dissatisfied with Pope's unity of design, which he believed limited the wildness and emotive character of the pindaric, Smart coupled his own rendering with Pope's for the London edition.

[3] The advertisements appeared almost as Smart had instructed: *GEP,* 14–16 August (Saturday); *DA,* 18 August (Monday); *GA,* 19 and 21 August (Tuesday and Thursday).

[4] The "too" [two] unlucky mistakes" – "*Latina Redditam*" for "*Latine Redditum*" – had appeared in pre-publication advertisements in the *DA* on 25 July; the *GA* on 26 July; and the *GEP* of 24–6 July. (Although the *GEP* had correctly printed "*Redditum,*" it referred to Smart as "Fellow og Pembroke-Hall.") For some reason, the mistakes were not corrected in the advertisements mentioned in note 3. However they did stand corrected in the *GEP* of 13–16 September and in the *LEP* of 2–4 September. Smart had cause to be disturbed.

[5] No evidence suggests RD's success with the hundred copies, but it seems a further edition was not called for.

[6] On the inside rear cover of this second edition of *Carmen cl. Alexandri Pope,* appeared the announcement: "There is preparing for the Press, by the same hand, a Latin Version of *Pope's Essay on Criticism,* and of the *L'Allegro* and *Il Penseroso* of *Milton.*" Smart's translation of Pope's *Essay* (*De Arte Critica*) and of *L'Allegro* would eventually appear, on pages 179–93 and 33–9, respectively, in his *Poems on Several Occasions.* London: Printed for the Author, by W. Strahan; and sold by J. Newbery, 1752. (See Betty W. Rizzo and Robert Mahony, *Christopher Smart. An Annotated Bibliography 1743–1983* (New York and London: Garland, 1984).)

From William Whitehead[1]

Bristolwells Aug: 21st 1746.

S^r

At present I am not only idle, but Busy about other things & therefore have not finished the Shield. When I have I will send it; But I hope you have no want of it.[2]

I write now on my L'd Jersey's account, who desires you would send him Foster's account of Ld Kilmarnock [as] soon as it is published, & any thing else that relates to him or Ld Balmerino that is worth sending. They will come in Letters I suppose & must be directed to my Lord at the Hot well, Bristol.[3]

Will Smart's ode come in a Frank? if it will, I should be obliged to you if you would direct to me & enclose it to my Lord.[4] The Pamphlet which is called Considerations on the Treason Bill with some additions I should be glad to have too, perhaps by dividing it it might be brought to a proper compass.[5]

I have my Museums regularly, but Mr Wright complains he has had none since the 5th number.[6]

Your most humble servant

W: Whitehead

Address: To Mr Dodsley / at Tully's Head / Pall Mall
Postmark: 23 AV
Frank: Free / Jersey[7]

MS: The Lewis Walpole Library, Farmington, Conn.

[1] William Whitehead (1715–85) published all his early works from Tully's Head, beginning with *On the Danger of Writing Verse* (1741) through *A Charge to the Poets* (1762), fourteen works in all, with some second editions. Doubtless his correspondence with RD was much more extensive than the three letters printed here would suggest. The calibre of his poetry generally does RD no credit, but his style (in the manner of Pope) apparently proved quite saleable, especially after he had become Poet Laureate in December 1757. His more than a quarter of a century of birthday odes drew much unfriendly comment from contemporaries, Samuel Johnson calling them "grand nonsense." Several of RD's copyright purchases from Whitehead are preserved (see Appendix B).

[2] Apparently Whitehead had planned to print a separate edition of his "dissertation on the Shield of Aeneas," an essay printed earlier in the year as a three-part installment in RD's fortnightly *Museum* (I, 2) (12 April 1746), 53–5; I, 3 (26 April 1746), 89–92; I, 5 (24 May 1746), 172–8), but it did not materialize. RD did include the essay in the edition of Virgil's *Works* (1753) translated by Christopher Pitt and Joseph Warton.

[3] William Villiers (1721–69), 3rd Earl of Jersey. From 1745, Whitehead served as tutor to Villiers' 7-year-old son, Viscount Villiers, later 4th Earl of Jersey, taking the young George on a tour of Germany and Italy during 1754–6. James Foster's *An Account of the Behaviour of the late Earl of Kilmarnock, after his sentence and on the day of his execution* (1746), a provocative work that gave rise to a number of rejoinders. William Boyd, 4th Earl of Kilmarnock (1704–46), was executed after the Battle of Culloden for his role in the '45. Arthur Elphenstone, 6th Baron Balmerino (1688–1746), was similarly executed. The trials of both men prompted numerous works from the press on their lives and careers.

[4] Most likely *Carmen Cl. Alexandri Pope in S. Caeciliam Latine Redditum. Editio Altera. To which is added Ode for Musick on St. Cecilia's Day* by Christopher Smart, which RD had advertised as for sale at Tully's Head on 16 August. See Smart's letter to RD on 6 August 1746.

[5] The pamphlet was probably the anonymous *Some Considerations on the Law of Forfeiture for High Treason*, published by J. Roberts in a second edition the previous month.

[6] Rev. Thomas Wright (*c.* 1717–88), Rector of Birchin, Yorkshire, and Whitehead's college friend (Robert Anderson, *Works of the British Poets* (Edinburgh, 1792–5) II, 896). A few lines (ii, 192) of Whitehead's "On Friendship" were addressed to Wright (DNB).   [7] See note 3.

From John Brown

Carlisle Oct: 27.th 1746.

S.^r

I send you a few Lines in the adjoyning Page which, if you think them worth their Room, you may insert in your Museum: they were a Morning's Exercise done at fourteen years old; I think it would be best to insert them as such but as to this take your own Way.[1] As the rambling Season is now over with me for a while, I may possibly send you some small matters now & then.

I have some thoughts of printing two Sermons, which I preached in the Cathedral during the rebel Assizes here. The Subject is the mutual Connection between religious Truth & civil Freedom, between Tyranny Superstition, Irreligion, & Licentiousness.[2] They are but short Discourses, & may together be decently extended to about forty Pages, tho' they may be included I think in thirty. My only Motive of printing them, is to do a little Justice to my Character as a Clergyman, as I know it hath been objected to me, that I should publish Verses, rather than things belonging to my own Profession.[3] As I am very sensible that Sermons above all other things are a mere Drug, I cannot propose ⟨to⟩ printing these in any other Method than at my own Expence: Tho' if you think the Copy when you see it can be of any Use to you, it is very much at your Service: But as I do not think there is any probability of this, the principal thing I want to be informed of is the Expence that will attend printing 2, 3, 4, or 5, hundred Copies. They are not both larger than many single Sermons that appear; but as I hate to multiply words without Reason, I cannot think of enlarging them much. I would desire therefore to know what will be the Expence of printing them as a twelvepenny Pamphlet in Quarto: 2.dly what will be the Expence of doing it in a smaller Number of Pages as a sixpenny Pamphlet in the same Size: 3.dly what will be the Expence of including them both in one sixpenny Octavo. I would not ⟨by⟩ by any means have them on bad Paper, wch disgraces every thing; a very large margin I should chuse. Please to answer these several particulars as soon as may be; & I shall be preparing a portable Copy in the mean time.[4]

If there is any thing extraordinary likely to appear this Winter in the literary way, I should be glad to hear of it. I am a very lazy Writer, & you are the only Intelligencer I have in town. I am

Sr Your most humble Servt

J: Brown

MS: Bodleian Ms. Toynbee d. 19, f. 16.

[1] The "adjoyning Page" is missing from the Bodleian manuscript, and so the youthful poem is unidentified. Donald Eddy (*Bibliography of John Brown* (New York: Bibliographical Society of America, 1971) p. 17) rightly notes that "Several of the poems in the *Museum* might have been written by a fourteen-year-old boy, but none are so identified." Furthermore, RD might not have even used Brown's verses for the *Museum*.

[2] See Brown's next letter, on 8 November, where the negotiations for the publication of his sermons continues.

[3] Even Brown's friend William Warburton, disappointed with Brown's playwriting, later regretted

that the clergyman's "*love of poetry*, or his *love of money*, should have made him overlook the duty of a Clergyman in these times, and the dignity of a Clergyman in all times, to make connexions with Players" (*Letters from a Late Eminent Prelate*, ed. Richard Hurd, 2nd ed., (Kidderminster, 1809), p. 182).

⁴ Although RD's response to this letter is missing, the substance of his offer and Brown's haggling over the proposal are the principal concern of Brown's next letter, q. v.

From John Brown

Carlisle Nov: 8ᵗʰ [1746]¹

Sʳ

I received yours, but have not yet had Time to transcribe the Sermons.² I would indeed chuse to have them printed as a 12 penny Pamphlet; but I think 7 Pounds is very high for 250 Copies: I am told by a Gentleman pretty well versed in these affairs, that 4 or 500 Copies may be had, with a good Letter & Paper (especially where there is but little Work in a Page) for one Guinea p[er] Sheet: which in this Case, reckoning 40 Pages, would amount to five Guineas, for 4 or 500: there is a very material Difference between this Calculation and yours. You will excuse the Freedom of a Conjecture: I imagine you are accustomed to a greater Profit in printing Poetical Affairs, than those Booksellers have who only deal in plain Prose: If so, I think you must either come down to the Profit of a Sermon Printer, or else I must beg the favour of you to direct me to such a one for this time: But as to any certainty in these particulars, I refer myself entirely to your answer. In short all I want is to have the Sermons handsomely done, & to avoid Expence as far as may be consistent with this.³

There are two little things I should have a Curiosity to see. The one is a Copy of Verses entitled the *Fireside*, wᶜʰ I have heard are well done. The other is a History of yᵉ 12 Hours Administration of Lᵈ Cᵗˢ.⁴ If these (especially the first) could come within the Compass of a Frank, I should be obliged to you for sending them along with your answer, wᶜʰ will be very agreeable to Sʳ

Your most humble Servt

J. Brown

I propose to be in London in January: & if you think that would be as proper a time for publishing these Sermons, I should be almost induced to let them rest till that time.⁵

I have lately met with a french Treatise on Education as it regards the *Understanding*, by Mʳ Morelly: he promises ⟨in it⟩ at the Conclusion, another Essay on the *Passions*: pray have you ever heard of this last?⁶

MS: Bodleian Ms. Toynbee d. 19, f. 7.

¹ The year is clearly 1746, for Brown here continues the negotiation with RD regarding the printing of two sermons, a subject begun in his letter dated 27 October 1746. Furthermore, these sermons would be published on 8 January 1747. See note 3.   ² RD's letter not traced.
³ Apparently RD had chosen not to purchase the copyright for the two sermons Brown had proposed in

his last, and simply submitted an estimate for printing should Brown decide to stand the expense himself. Lacking RD's response to Brown's first letter, it is impossible to pass judgment on the reasonableness of his estimate, £7 for printing. For one thing, Brown's reiteration of RD's estimate does not indicate whether the figure includes the cost of paper, which Patricia Hernlund finds in the Strahan ledgers ("William Strahan's Ledgers, II: Charges for Papers, 1738–1785," *SB*, XXII, 186) "was as great as the cost of setting, correcting, and printing the job." Although the bookseller normally supplied the paper when he owned the copyright, the author would be responsible for this cost when printing for himself. Furthermore, Brown had indicated he wanted good paper and wide margins, two factors that would have raised the cost. The estimate provided by Brown's acquaintance is not far-fetched in that it is somewhat in line with standard charges for printing, at least as reflected in Hernlund's earlier article, "William Strahan's Ledgers: Standard Charges for Printing, 1738–1785," *SB*, XX (1967), 89–111. But the unstated size (it was eventually printed as a twelve-penny pamphlet, running forty-eight pages in 4°), in addition to the "extras" required by Brown, the cost of paper, and RD's commission for handling the job may account for the bookseller's larger figure. Whatever the situation, the two quickly came to an agreement, for *The Mutual Connexion between Religious Truth and Civil Freedom; between Superstition, Tyranny, Irreligion, and Licentiousness: considered in Two Sermons* was published on 8 January of the new year (*DA*), "Printed for R. Dodsley; and sold by M. Cooper." It was later reprinted in Brown's *Sermons on Various Subjects* (1764), pp. 67–118.

4 "The Fire-Side: A Pastoral Soliloquy, On the E[arl] of G[ranville, Lord Carteret] taking the Seals" by Dr Nathaniel Cotton had been published on 2 November 1746 (*DA*). It was reprinted in *The Foundling Hospital for Wit*, No. 4 (1747), pp. 17–18, and in RD's *Collection*, IV (1755), 258–61. The second piece was probably the "Surprising History of a late long Administration" by "Titus Livius, jun.," a satire on the 48-hour administration of Lord Granville, which was printed in *The Foundling Hospital for Wit*, No. 3 (1746), pp. 58–61.

5 RD concurred with Brown's suggestion. See note 3.

6 Morelly seems something of a mystery in the history of eighteenth-century French authorship. None of the details of his life is known, not even his first name. Some of his works are in the Bibliothèque Nationale, Paris. The two works Brown probably has in mind are: *Essai sur l'esprit humain, ou Principes naturels de l'éducation* (Paris: C.J.B. Delespine, 1743) and *Essai sur la coeur humain, ou Principes naturels de l'education* (Paris: C.J.B. Delespine, 1745).

From John Gilbert Cooper

Derby   November yᵉ 15ᵗʰ 1746

Sʳ

having some extraordinary business upon my hands, I have only time this post to acquaint you that whenever the Directors of the Museum would Subscribe ⟨any⟩ a name allusive to the subject of any of my papers, that the mark of *Philaretes* may be plac'd in the opposite corner besides. for instance if they should sign that Paper I sent you upon Lying *Pseudophilus*, as that upon the Beggar was *Philoptochus*, I desire you would still remind the Printers not to reject the other mark.[1] I have almost finish'd two Papers, one Serious, & the other humorous, which you shall have as soon as I can procure Franks,[2] I am in the mean time

your most humble Servant

John Gilbert = Cooper/Junʳ.

Address: To Mʳ Dodsley Bookseller / at Tully's head / Pall Mall / London

Postmark: Derby 17 NO

MS: Bodleian Ms. Eng. Misc. d. 174, 00. 19–[21]

¹ "A Persuasive To erect an Academy for Lying" was later published in the *Museum*, II, 20 (20 December 1746), 216–20, and signed merely "Philaretes." The periodical's editor, Mark Akenside, probably appended "Philoptochus" to "An Account of the Kingdom of Beggars," *Museum*, II, 16 (25 October 1746), 81–4, because Cooper had a second essay in this issue entitled "The Vision of Heaven," pp. 88–91. To have signed both of them "Philaretes" might have suggested an undue influence from one pen in a periodical that tried to create the image of itself as a "sampler" of the learned and fashionable world.   ² See Cooper's letter to RD on 18 February 1747.

From Samuel Johnson

Dec.ʳ 26. 1746

Sir

That You may not have the trouble of sending to me again I have desired Mr Stockton who writes for me to wait on You with a receipt,¹ or I will come myself if it be desired. I am

Sir

Your most &c

Sam: Johnson.

Address: To Mr Dodsley

MS: Pierpont Morgan Library, MA204 V86.

¹ Probably Johnson is sending a receipt for one of the many advances made by the group of booksellers undertaking his *Dictionary of the English Language*. See Johnson's letter of June, 1746. I have not been able to discover anything of Stockton, nor do the Johnson specialists I have consulted seem to know anything about him.

From William Melmoth¹

Ealing Dec.ʳ 26.ᵗʰ 1746.

Sir,

I left the first vol. of Pliny with you, to have the title-page & preface inserted;² I beg you wᵈ send it down to me by the coach, together with the 2ᵈ vol. wᶜʰ is at Dʳ Coxe's.³ Pray send me at yᵉ same time Dʳ Newton's proposals for his Milton.⁴ I am your

very humble serv.ᵗ

Wᵐ. Melmoth.

Address: To / Mʳ Dodsley, / in Pall-mall, / London
Postmark: Peny Post Payd [?]

MS: BL. Add. MS. 35,338, f. 2.

¹ William Melmoth the younger (1710–99), who had abandoned law for writing, published his major works through RD: *Letters on Several Subjects* by "Sir Thomas Fitzoborne" (1747; six editions by 1763); *The Letters of Pliny the Consul* (1746); Cicero's *Letters to Several of his Friends*, (3 vols. 1753). He also

assisted in the writing and correcting of RD's edition of *Select Fables* (1761) and in editing Shenstone's *Works* (1764). He corresponded frequently with RD and sided with him against Garrick in the *Cleone* dispute of 1758. For the last forty years of his life, Melmoth resided in Bath, where, in the Abbey church, appears a Latin inscription in his honor written by his nephew the Rev. John Skynner. Melmoth had adopted and educated Skynner's daughter Sophia (R. E. Peach, *Historic Houses in Bath and Their Associations* (London, 1883–4), II, 52). Perhaps this is the same Rev. John Skynner whose *Sermon Preached at the Funeral of Baptist Earl of Gainsborough* was published by RD in 1751 and enjoyed most unusual success, passing through seven editions in less than three and a half years.

² RD had registered Melmoth's translation *The Letters of Pliny the Consul* at the Stationers' Office on 8 December 1746 and published it three days later (*GA*), although it carries a 1747 imprint. A second, third, and "new" edition appeared in 1747, 1748, and 1757, its success earning its author the name "Pliny Melmoth." RD had purchased the copyright from Melmoth for £50 on 12 February 1746. (See Appendix B.)

³ Dr William Coxe, Melmoth's good friend and a physician to the King's household, lived in Dover Street, London. His son William (1747–1828) continued the friendship with Melmoth after his father's death, addressing him in *Sketches of the Natural Civil and Political State of Switzerland in a Series of Letters to William Melmoth, Esq.* (1779) and *Travels in Switzerland and in the Country of the Grissons in a Series of Letters to William Melmoth, Esq.* (1789).

⁴ Although Thomas Newton (1704–82), Rector of St Marylebone and later Bishop of Bristol, published his proposals for an edition of *Paradise Lost* on 13 December 1746 (*GA*), the work did not appear until 1749, when it was published by J. and R. Tonson and S. Draper, and with prints by Francis Hayman.

From William Melmoth

Thursday.
[26 December 1746 or
2 January 1747]¹

Sir,

I forgot to tell you that I w^d have the Pliny wch I left at your shop, bound up in boards for my self, & sent to me as soon as possible.

When those wch I gave directions about are bound, I beg you w^d send them as follows:

To Mr Skynner at St John's college Cambridge; two setts, one of wch to be bound in Morocco, & to be sent with Mr Thurlborn's parcel.

To Mr Skynner an Attorney in the Poultry, near cheapside.

To Mr Hill, at Grocer's Hall in the Poultry.

To Mr Overton, in Charter house Square.

To Dr Coxe in Dover Street.²

I am sir
your most humble serv^t
Wm Melmoth.

Address: To / Mr Dodsley / in Pall-mall, / London.

MS: BL. Add. MS. 35,338, f. 4.

¹ See Melmoth to RD 26 December 1746 on the same subject. The "I forgot," the further specification regarding the volume's binding, together with the letter's immediate tone, suggest that it might have

been written on the same day as the 26 December letter, also a Thursday. If not, it was probably
written on the following Thursday, 2 January.

2 John Skynner, Melmoth's nephew, earned his BA at St John's in 1746, MA in 1748, and was ordained
in 1752. The Mr Skynner of the Poultry might be the father of the former, for the *Alumni Cantabrigienses*
lists his father as a lawyer, though of Middlesex. Perhaps this is the John Skinner, Esq., designated as
of Poultry when proposed as a member of the Society for the Encouragement of Arts, Manufactures,
and Commerce on 11 February 1761 (see the Society's Minutes). Another Skinner, William (d. 1752),
is mentioned by Edmund Carter (*History of the University of Cambridge*) as a Fellow and Public Orator at
St John's, Cambridge, but Melmoth's nephew seems the more likely recipient of his gift. Probably
Robert Hill (1699–1777), the "learned tailor," who was introduced to the literary world in 1747.
Versed in Latin, Greek, and Hebrew, Hill was the subject of Joseph Spence's *A Parallel in the Manner of
Plutarch between Robert Hill the learned Tailor and Magliabecchi* (1757). Perhaps Hill lived with a relative,
Richard Hill, Poultry, as found in the *List of Liverymen* (1734). "Mr. Overton" is possibly the Henry
Overton, printseller, listed as "without Newgate," precisely the location of Charterhouse Square
(*Kent's Directory for the Year 1759*, p. 85). For Dr Coxe, see Melmoth's previous letter, 26 December.

To Thomas Warton, the younger

Jan 29 [1747][1]

Sir

I rec^d the favour of your letter and shall be very glad to see your Poem on the
Pleasures of Melancholy. As to the Terms, I believe I shall rather chuse to print as I
did your Brothers for so very few Poems sell, that it is very hazardous purchasing
almost any thing.[2]

I am
Dr Sir
Your Most hum^ble Servt
R. Dodsley

MS: BL. Add. MS. 42,560, f. 13.

1 The year "1747" appears on the holograph, but not in Warton's hand. Yet the designation seems
accurate, for RD published Warton's *Pleasures of Melancholy* on 8 April 1747 (*GA*).
2 Probably RD is telling Warton that if he publishes *Pleasures*, it would be printed at the author's
expense, most likely the same arrangement he had worked with Warton's brother Joseph when
publishing his *Odes* during the past year.

From Lucy Pitt[1]

Pimpern Feb ye 9th 1746/7

Sir

My Brother Pitt has bin lately very Ill: so that he cant write without being
troublesom to him:[2] so he desires me, to return you thanks for the Elegant Present of
your Book: which you Miscall Trifles:[3] my Brother desires you to Send him M^r
Spences Books for himself: and those Gentlemen who Subscribed through his

Hands: and he will immeadiatly remitt the last payment:[4] he would have two of the
Sets hansomly Bound for himself: and a friend: in case you Should have lost the list
of Names he gave you: they are as follow
  two Sets for my Brother: one of them a present from the Author: one a peice: for M^r
Dennett Mr Walker Mr Froome Mr Ridout and Mr Bryant:
the Bishop of Bristol desire^d my Brother to write to you: to let you know that he
would Subscribe: so he desires you will wait on him with the Books and his Service
and Duty: my Brother desires you would let him know, how the account Stands
between him and you: having, he beleives, had some Books of you: since he saw you:
my Brother desires to joyn with me in Service to yourself and Lady and to Mr
Spence: which Concluds

from Sir Your Humble Servant

Lucy Pitt

Address: To / Mr Dodsley: Bookseller / at Tullys Head: in Pallmall / London
Postmark: Blandford

MS: Harvard Theatre Collection, Harvard College Library.

[1] Lucy Pitt, Christopher Pitt's sister, is perhaps the Lucy Baskett from whom RD would purchase the
copyright of Pitt's translation of Virgil's *Aeneid*, along with 500 remaining copies, in 1751. (See
Appendix B.) [2] Pitt would die the following year.
[3] RD had published a collection of his own things almost two years earlier under the title *Trifles* (1745).
[4] Joseph Spence's *Polymetis* had just been advertised four days earlier *(GA)*. As is clear from earlier
letters, Pitt had been a subscriber.

From John Gilbert Cooper

Derby Feby the 11th 1746/7

Dear S^r
  As there are papers of mine in the M[useum] to fill a handsome Volume in
Octavo, I am desirous [to have 'em] collected together, & publish'd (if you approve
of the e[ssays)] themselves as soon as possible under this title: ⌈⟨?⟩ [?] Essays, upon
several Subjects, humorous & moral, be[ing] select papers originally publish'd in
the Museum under [the name] of *Philaretes.*⌋[1] in the advertisement I would have
['em so] specify'd. as you have perhaps forgot some which [you have] publish'd the
following list will direct you to 'em[.] N° 4. on Friendship. on Education. N° 7. The
P[lebian Poli]ticians. N° 8. a Project for raising an Hospital for dec[ayed Authors]
N° 9. on the Polite Arts. N° 11. on the Predominant [Passion in] Women. N° 12. on
Contentment, a letter to the [Keeper of] the Museum, containing another from
Muli Azaret[h at London] to the Mufti at Constantinople. ⟨on Conjugal Love⟩
[N° 13 on] Conjugal Love. Vol 2 N° 15. on Good & Beauty. [N° 16. an] account of
the Kingdom of Beggars. The Vision of Heaven. N° 17. on the [death of] Socrates in
a letter to the Keeper of the Museum. [N° 19 on Self Love. N° 20. a persuasive to
erect an Academ[y for Lying.] N° 22. on true and false Religion. N° 23 on the foll[y

of Noblemen and Gentlemen's paying their debts. ?] the same order as I have done,
but mix ['em] as you think proper, or alterna[te the] humorous & moral. if you can
spare time I desire to hear from you by the ret[urn] of the post when you send me
my next Museum. if you don't approve of an Octavo with a pretty large print, I
shall submit to your better judgment. – abou[t] two months ago I sent you some
franks of Mʳ Warren's,[2] & a Poem, entitled Epistle from Theagenes to Sylvia; let me
know if you receiv'd 'em.[3] – I hav[e] been lately very ill & low spirited, & have had
a great deal of family business upon my hands, otherwise you should have heard
oftener from me. – if you thin[k] of publishing these trifles, be pleas'd to alter the
following errata. in the Mot[to] to the essay on Good & Beauty read *oiei* for *aei*. in
the Motto to Conjugal Lo[ve] read ψυχη for ψυ̱κη. in the essay on the folly of
Noblemen &c. line the 3 re[ad] *have* for *has*. & some few more such as these which
will occur, but of no great signification. I am, Sʳ,

Your Sincere Friend

& humble Servant

John Gilbert = Cooper/Junʳ

I would not have any of the Poetry publish'd.[4]

Address: To / Mʳ Dodsley Bookseller / at Tully's head / in Pall Mall / London
Postmark: Derby [13?]FE

MS: Bodleian Ms. Eng. Misc. d. 174, ff. 23–5.

[1] I have not found any evidence that the volume here proposed by Cooper was ever published.
However, the list he provides of his past contributions to the *Museum* is valuable for helping to
determine not only his own canon but his role in the production of the *Museum* especially during its first
year of existence. See my article "Museum Attributions in John Cooper's Unpublished Letters," *SB,*
27 (1974), 232–5.   [2] Borlase Warren, MP for Nottingham (1713–15, 1727–47).
[3] This poem appeared in the *Museum*, III, 31 (23 May 1747), 159–67.
[4] Besides "Theagenes to Sylvia" mentioned above, at least two other poems by Cooper appeared in the
Museum. See Cooper to RD 28 May and 7 July 1746.

From John Gilbert Cooper

Derby Feb:yᵉ 18ᵗʰ 1746/7

Dear Sʳ

According to your desire I have sent enclos'd two Papers, the one, a Serious Essay
on Solitude, the other, a humorous Advertisement.[1] – I am glad to see the Museum
kept up with so much spirit in all Parts but the Poetical, which I think often very
indifferent; I wish it could be conveniently dropt or at least curtail'd in the
beginning of the next Volume. Whatever assistance I can be of, you may always
depend on if I have health & leisure. I am very much afraid I shan't have the
pleasure of seeing you this Spring, which I greatly long for, tho' sometimes the

Flatterer Hope revives me. Remember me to those friends that do me the honour to enquire after me. I am, Dear S^r,

your Sincere Friend

& humble Servant

John Gilbert = Cooper/Junr.

Address: To Mr Dodsley Bookseller / at Tully's Head / in Pall Mall / London
Postmark: 20FE [Derby]
Frank: B. Warren[2]

MS: Bodleian Ms. Eng. Misc. d. 174, ff. 27–9.

[1] Mentioned earlier as still unfinished (Cooper's letter of 15 November 1746), "On Solitude and Society" and "An Advertisement" were published in the *Museum*, II, 25 (28 February 1747), 385–8 and III, 27 (28 March 1747), 10–11.   [2] See Cooper's 11 February letter, note 2.

From Lucy Pitt

Pimpern Feb ye 18th 1746/7

Sir

My Brother desires me once more to trouble you, with a letter about Mr Spences book: I wrote to you by the last post,[1] to desire there might be three Sets bound: and sent to my Brother: ⟨?⟩ with the others: for the set I wrote about Monday: was for Mr Dennett:[2] Mr Dennett Junr: came from London last night: and Says he had the books of you since he was here: so this is only to desire you: to send down, two Setts bound: as was first ordered:[3] and to Strike Mr Dennetts name out of my Bro^{-s} list: he hopes you will excuse this trouble he gives you: and accept of his Service: which Concluds from

Sir your Humble Servant

Lucy Pitt

Address: To / Mr Dodsley, Bookseller / at Tullys Head /in Pallmall / London
Postmark: 20 FE Blandford

MS: Harvard Theatre Collection, Harvard College Library.

[1] Lucy Pitt's letter in the last post – that is, Monday, 16 February – is not traced.
[2] See Lucy Pitt's letter of 9 February.   [3] Apparently, as in her letter of 16 February.

From William Mason[1]

May 31, 1747

. . . I fancy by this time, you can give me a full account of the fate of my *Monody*, and I wish much that you wou'd do so, for you know I told you how great a stress I shou'd lay upon your report because I believ'd it wou'd be a sincere one[2] . . . I cou'd wish also, to know whether Tonson or any other bookseller has a property in the 3rd vol. of Milton. I have often thought it a great pitty that many of the Beautiful Peices it contains shou'd be so little read as they certainly are, I fancy this has arisen from the bad thing they are tack'd to. I want vastly to have a seperate edition of the Tragedy, Mask, Lycidas & Lallegro, &c., but, if you think that it would sell at present I wou'd willingly give you my assistance either for a preface or Notes or any thing that shou'd be thought necessary, & this merely for the sake of the incomparable Poet for whom I am not content with having considerd, & praised as the Author of *Paradise Lost* alone . . .[3]

Source: Straus, pp. 114–15.

[1] The Rev. William Mason (1724–97), poet and scholar, close friend and executor of Thomas Gray, and correspondent of Horace Walpole, published his principal works through Tully's Head: *Musaeus* (1747), *Isis* (1749), *Four Odes* (1756), *Caractacus* (1759, with J. Knapton) all of which passed through at least two editions during RD's lifetime. RD included six of Mason's poems in Volumes III and IV of his *Collection of Poems by Several Hands* (1748, 1755).

[2] Mason's *Musaeus: a Monody to the Memory of Mr. Pope, in Imitation of Milton's Lycidas* was published anonymously by RD on 16 April 1747 (*GA*). Although RD's response is missing, it must have been favorable, for *Musaeus* reached a third edition within a year.

[3] Towards the end of Milton's life, three major editions of his works appeared: *Paradise Lost* (1667), *Paradise Regain'd. A Poem. In 14 Books. To which is added Samson Agonistes* (1671), and *Poems, Etc. upon Several Occasions* (1673). Until the end of the century and into the next, this tripartite division was observed by publishers, particularly by Jacob Tonson, whose family controlled the copyright until the third quarter of the eighteenth century. In this case, then, Mason is thinking of *Poems*, the least edited and reprinted of the three during the first half of the eighteenth century, but containing such "Beautiful Peices" as *Lycidas, Comus, L'Allegro*, etc. For more on the subject see Mason's next letter to RD, [*post* 31 May]; and John Draper, "Queen Anne's Act: A Note on English Copyright," *MLN*, 36 (1921), 146–54 and *William Mason: A Study in Eighteenth Century Culture* (New York: New York University Press, 1924) pp. 28–9.

From Christopher Smart

[*post* 30 May 1747][1]

I beg the favour youd send me by the Maidstone-stage Littleton's Persian letters, & Bruyere's characters in English – & if you possibly can get me Dalton's alteration of Comus you will do me great service,[2] because I am writing a Masque myself[3] – I am affraid you gave me wrong directions to Will Whitehead for I have received no answer to a letter about business[4] –

                                                Yrs. &c

                                                                    C. Smart

P.S. send another Copy of Musaeus[5] & another Prospect of Eton

MS: Hyde Collection, Somerville, New Jersey.

[1] The date is approximated from the postscript where Smart asks for a copy of Thomas Gray's *An Ode on a Distant Prospect of Eton College*, which RD had published on 30 May 1747 (*GA*). In his review (*RES*, XIX (1968), 213–15) of Arthur Sherbo's *Christopher Smart, Scholar of the University* (Lansing: Michigan State University Press, 1967), Cecil Price wrongly suggests this letter to be the same as the one advertised in the Sotheby Catalogue for 4 July 1892, lot 532, there designated as "7 Aug. N.Y., Maidstone" The ALS in the Hyde Collection shows no date nor place of origin.

[2] George Lyttelton, *Letters from a Persian in England* (1735); Jean de La Bruyère, *Caractères* (1688); John Dalton's adaptation of Milton, *Comus, a Masque*, which had been published by RD in 1738 and had passed through seven editions in six years.

[3] Smart's masque was published in 1752 as *The Judgment of Midas*.

[4] William Whitehead, another Cambridge poet and laureate. See Smart's letter to RD on 12 January 1748.

[5] William Mason, *Musaeus: a Monody to the Memory of Mr. Pope, in Imitation of Milton's Lycidas*, published by RD on 16 April 1747 (*GA*).

From William Mason

[post 31 May; *ante* 16 August 1747][1]

. . . I shall not proceed in the Edition I mentioned to you till I see you in London & have your advice more fully about it, for I dont sufficiently understand your Properties &c. nor how you bargain in these cases . . .

Source: Straus, p. 115.

[1] The inclusive dates are determined from this letter's link with Mason's previous letter to RD (31 May 1747) and from the complete absence of the concerns mentioned in his next to RD (16 August 1747, q.v.). His reference to the "Edition I mentioned to you" is doubtless an allusion to his proposal for an edition of the third volume of Milton which he had made to the bookseller in his letter of 31 May. Possibly Mason had discussed the proposal with RD on a visit to London in June or July as he said he had intended, for by the time of his 16 August letter, the matter seems to have been dropped, and he is questioning RD about other publications.

From William Mason

Hull, Aug. 16, [17]47

Sir,

I am told by the booksellers here that the Poem is sold off & that a second Edition is expected; I think if there had been any truth in the report I shou'd have heard from you concerning it, however, I write to you at present to desire that if you shou'd have any such intentions at any time, you wou'd please to give me notice beforehand for there is an Alteration or two that I cou'd wish to make in it.[1] I am come to a resolution of publishing the other Imitations wch will make I believe an eighteen penny pamphlet, but I have not given them the last revisal yet, let me know whether the beginning or latter end of the Winter will be the best time[2] . . . You forgot in your last to let me know what I stood indebted to you & I don't remember exactly how many copies I orderd; please to let me know in your answer to this, wch I beg to have soon because I am going a journey into Derbyshire.

Sir,

Your very humble Ser:

W. Mason

My Compliments to Mr Whithead.[3]

Source: Straus, pp. 334–5.

[1] The second and third editions of *Musaeus* do not seem to have been advertised as was the first. Nor is there an indication of edition in the copies dated 1747 and 1748 which I have inspected at the BL, the Bodleian, and the Huntington. Consequently it is difficult to say whether RD had already printed a second edition by the time of Mason's letter. Collations of two 1747 copies in the Bodleian show them identical except for the last line on p. 20. In the one is found "sad day," and in the other "sadday." If such a minor discrepancy justifies calling the one a second edition, then it would seem to be the copy showing "sad day," for it is this reading that is to be found in an equally identical copy in the BL marked 1748. On the basis of this evidence and from Mason's information, Philip Gaskell's opinion (*The First Editions of William Mason*, Cambridge Bibliographical Society Monographs, No. 1, p. 1) seems justified; namely, that a second edition did appear at the end of 1747. Curiously enough, the text used by RD to reprint the poem in his *Collection* on 12 January of the next year is the same as that of the copy I am suggesting is the first edition; that is, the version with "sadday." In any event, it seems Mason never took the opportunity to make the changes he mentions.

[2] *Musaeus* was written in "Imitation of Lycidas." I cannot find any later poems specifically indicated as imitations, either of Milton or other poets, among Mason's works. Nor does Gaskell list any.

[3] Most likely William Whitehead, another Cambridge graduate and member of RD's circle.

From Lucy Pitt

Blandford Oct. ye 8th 1747

Sir

When I saw you in London: you desire^d me to inform you by a Letter how the account Stood: that my Brother had of you: when he was last: in London: my Brother and I: have carefully look'^t over his papers and cant find the least account of any thing with you: so if ever he had any: he has lost it: but he desires his Service to you: and says he is quite easie about it: knowing that Mr Dodsley is a Man of Honour: and desires that you will Satisfy yourself for what he is in your Debt: and then let him know how the Account Stands: and he Shall be very well pleased: let it be how it will: he is pretty well this Summer: and wishes that Mr Spence, and you, had not only talk^d of coming to See him: but had come this last Summer: for he dont love to expect so great a pleasure: and wait so long for it: as next Summer: I told him that was the time you talk^t off: but he says the sooner: the better.[1]: he desires to joyn with me in Service: to M^r and Mrs Spence, Mrs Dodsly, and yourself: from Sir

your obliged Humble Servant

Lucy Pitt.

MS: Harvard Theatre Collection, Harvard College Library.

1 Although only forty-eight years old, Pitt rightly anticipated the worst: he died little more than six
   months later, on 15 April 1748.

To William Shenstone[1]

Oct.[r] 8 [1747][2]

Sir

When I receiv'd your agreeable piece of Ridicule I was sick in bed, or you would
have heard from me sooner.[3] I suppose you know by this time that y[e] Museum is
dropt,[4] but I think your Essay* too good to be lost, if therefore you have no
objection I will endeavour to get it inserted in some other of y[e] Public Papers.

I am
Sir
Your most hum[ble] Serv[t]

R Dodsley

Address: To / William Shenstone Esq [r] / at the Leasows near / Birmingham /
Warwickshire

Postmark: 8 OC

*[Shenstone's Endorsement:] My good Friend M[r] Jago's prose essay on electricity,
an exquisite piece of Humour, & never yet printed.[5]

May 12, 1759

W. S.

MS: BL. Add. MS. 28,959, ff. 3–4.

1 William Shenstone (1714–63) was, except perhaps for Joseph Spence, RD's most intimate friend
   during the last decade of their lives and certainly his most prolific correspondent. During this period,
   Shenstone, playing the role of the Maecenas of the Midlands, kept RD regularly supplied with the
   writings of his friends from the Birmingham area. It was through Shenstone's intercession that RD was
   introduced to and carried on a correspondence with John Scott Hylton, Richard Jago, John Pixell,
   but particularly with Richard Graves. As early as 1741, RD had published Shenstone's *The Judgment
   of Hercules*, and a year later the poet's most remembered *The School-Mistress*. But by far their most
   intimate publishing relationship occurred during the years 1754–8 when RD was painfully extracting
   revisions of Shenstone's poetry for the last three volumes of *A Collection of Poems by Several Hands*. From
   the mid-1750s until the year before Shenstone's death, RD was almost an annual visitor at the
   Leasowes, Shenstone's *ferme ornée* whose rural delights attracted a regular round of fashionable
   pleasure-seekers. Several of these summer visits were spent poring over works RD had in the press,
   including his own *Collection of Poems*, *Select Fables*, and *Cleone*. Their relationship is attested by an
   extensive correspondence, the largest in this collection. To that part of it preserved by Shenstone, the
   Birmingham poet had ascribed: "Letters from my worthy Friend M[r] Robert Dodsley . . . whose
   Simplicity, Benevolence, Humanity, and Politeness I have had repeated and particular experience"
   (BL Add. MS. 28,959, f. 2). Likewise, the degree of their friendship is evident in Shenstone's
   appointing RD as one of his three executors, a recognition to which RD responded by editing and
   publishing from Tully's Head an edition of Shenstone's works, the year after the poet's death.
2 The year is determined from RD's mentioning the recent discontinuation of the *Museum*, the last
   number of which had appeared on 12 September 1747.
3 An essay on electricity written by Shenstone's friend Richard Jago. Shenstone regularly submitted
   packets of material to RD without specifying which, if any, were his own. (See also RD to Shenstone

on 27 August 1754.) Twelve years later, Shenstone would be asking RD whatever had become of the essay. See RD's response on 20 January 1759.   ⁴ See note 2.
⁵ See RD's letter of 20 January 1759, note 22.

From Edward Young¹

Wellwyn [Hertfordshire]

Oct. 16 [1747]²

Sʳ

I am Sorry Illness prevented your calling on me. I have been near Death my self, but I bless God am better. – If you will give a hundred Guineas you shall have the Whole Copy.³ If you will not I beg You to call on Mʳ Hawkins, & He will direct as to ye small Edition. I am Sʳ

Yr Humble Servᵗ

EYoung.

Address: To Mr Dodsley at / Tullys Head in Pall Mall / London
Postmark: Wellin 17 / OC

MS: University of Colorado Libraries, MS 52a.

¹ Edward Young (1683–1765) had already had a long career as poet and playwright before turning to RD as his bookseller in 1742. RD would then publish the first six in the series of Young's *The Complaint: or, Night Thoughts on Life, Death, and Immortality* (1742–4), registering the "whole rights" for the second through sixth "Nights" at the Stationers' Company as they came out; *The Brothers. A Tragedy* (1753), registered on 16 March; *The Centaur Not Fabulous* (1755), together with Andrew Millar; *A Sea-Piece* (1755); *An Argument Drawn from the Circumstances of Christ's Death, for the Truth of His Religion* (1758); and *Conjectures on Original Composition* (1759), with Millar. For RD's purchase of copyrights to Young's works, see Appendix B.   ² For the assigned year, see note 3.
³ Henry Pettit, the editor of Young's correspondence (Oxford: Clarendon Press, 1971) and of the poet's bibliography, believes the proposal pertains to the collected edition of Young's "Nights," VII–IX, to be published 6 February 1748 (*LEP*) by Mary Cooper and printed by Samuel Richardson. RD had already expended 210 guineas on the first six "Nights" (see Appendix B), and whether for that reason or because he sensed interest in Young's series had begun to wane over the past five years, he apparently refused the offer, for Young did not sell the rights until 1749, and then to Andrew Millar. (See Pettit, *A Bibliography of Young's "Night Thoughts,"* University of Colorado Studies (Boulder: University of Colorado Press, 1954) p. 37). Nine days after the date of this letter, RD did, however, publish the seventh edition of "Nights" I–VI (*GA*), and in 1751, together with Millar, the first complete edition of *The Complaint* ("Nights" I–IX). Apparently the publisher of the individual "Nights" VII–IX, George Hawkins, had not obtained the copyright from Young. Pettit also notes, in determining the year of the letter, that Young's opening statement corresponds with the fact that Young was seriously ill during the autumn of 1747.

To William Shenstone

Octʳ 17ᵗʰ [1747]¹

Sir

I sent you a letter some Posts ago to acquaint you that I had dropt yᵉ Museum but that I would endeavour to get your Satire inserted in some other Paper.² Since that I have rec^d another from You by which you seem not have rec^d mine.³ I have made ye Alterations you directed in your last, & shall wait for your farther instructions.⁴

I am

Sir

Your most hum^ble Serv!

R Dodsley

Address: To William Shenstone Esqr / at the Leasows near / Birmingham
Postmark: 17 OC

MS. BL. Add. MS. 28,959, ff. 5–6.

¹ See RD letter of 8 October [1747], particularly note 2.   ² Ibid., note 3.
³ It is difficult to determine whether RD means another poem or another letter from Shenstone. He published no individual poem of Shenstone's in the late 1740s and only his earlier *The School-Mistress* (1737–42) would be reprinted in the first edition of RD's *Collection* (I, 211–22) in January of the next year. Nor have I traced another RD letter preceding this one, except that of 8 October.
⁴ The alterations were probably intended for Jago's satire, for *The School-Mistress* was printed in the first edition of RD's *Collection* as unchanged from the 1742 edition. However, extensive changes were made for the version found in the second edition of the *Collection*.

From John Gilbert Cooper

Leicester Nov! the 14th 1747

Dear S!

According to my promise I have sent you enclos'd a Fable on the Power of Habit, which I hope will prove acceptable.¹ You know I have not patience to correct, therefore submit that necessary part of the work, to those who have more abilities & inclinations to do it. I should be glad if you who would shew it to Mr Spence, for whose judgment I have as high an esteem, as I have an ambition to be his acquaintance.² My compliments to all Friends. let me hear from you, when you have a leisure hour. I am, D^r S^r,

Your sincere Friend

& humble Servant

John Gilbert: Cooper / Jn!

Remember me to Mrs Dodsley & tell her I hope she'll forgive me writing that essay *on the predominant Passion of Women*, for the sake of another *on Conjugal Love*, & my speedy performance of this trifle.³ When you write enclose that Ode of [Framplon's?] to Handel.⁴ When you publish my estimate of life in your Miscell[anies] prefix those verses I sent you.⁵

MS: Bodleian, MS. Eng. Letters *c.* 198, f. 71.

¹ Perhaps Cooper had RD's *Museum* in mind for this piece but had not been aware that the fortnightly had been discontinued two months earlier. (No correspondence between the two survives for that period.) The fable does not seem to have been published on its own.

2 Joseph Spence (1699–1768), close friend of both Alexander Pope and RD, author of the *Anecdotes*, and, with Cooper, a frequent contributor to the *Museum*.

3 In the essay "On the Predominent Passion in Women" (*Museum*, I, 11 (16 August 1746), 406–9), Cooper advised that women are best mastered by exploiting their main passion: their own beauty. In his moral "On Conjugal Love" (*Museum*, I, 13 (13 September 1746), 490–2), he shows the value of "true" love by portraying a couple who, after a long separation, die in one another's arms upon their reunion.   4 RD published the anonymous *Ode to Handel* on 2 May 1745 (*DA*).

5 Previously published in the *Museum* (I, 10 (2 August 1746), 372–9), "The Estimate of Life" was reprinted in RD's *Collection of Poems by Several Hands* (1748), III, 86–98. Besides using the three-line motto from Shakespeare's *Measure for Measure* (". . . Reason thus with Life; / If I do lose thee, I do lose a Thing, / That none but Fools would weep." III, i. 6–8) that had accompanied the original printing, Cooper had RD prefix the following lines from Plato's *Theaetetus* in the original Greek: "Evils [Theodorus] can never be done away with, for the good must always have its contrary; nor have they any place in the divine world; but they must needs haunt this region of our moral nature. That is why we should make all speed to take flight from this world to the other; and that means becoming like the divine so far as we can, and that again is to become righteous with the help of wisdom" (176 A–B, translated by Francis M. Cornford, *Plato's Theory of Knowledge* (London: Kegan Paul, Trench, Trubner, 1935)).

From Christopher Smart

Pemb. Hall Cambridge
7th of Janry 1747–8[1]

Sir,

I beg the favour you'll advertise my Proposals six or seven times in the papers you think best and make the following addition viz.: There will no more copies be printed, than what are subscribed for, and if there shou'd ever be occasion for a second impression, nothing will be abated from the original price.[2]

Y[rs] etc.

C. Smart

Please to advertize immediately on the receipt of this.

Address: Mr. Dodsley / at Tully's Head / Pall Mall / London

Source: This text is a conflation of two printed sources: a clipping from an unidentified autograph dealer's catalogue that Straus had tipped into his personal interleaved copy of *Robert Dodsley* (p. 333); and secondly, a text printed in the *Times Literary Supplement* (27 May 1926, p. 355) by Edmund Gosse, who claimed the holograph had recently come into his possession. Since the first erroneously prints "Pembroke Hill 1747" and lacks the postscript and address, these elements are taken from the *TLS* version. The autograph dealer text has been followed in one place in the body of the letter where *TLS* prints the nonsensical "There will be more copies be printed. . . ." Unfortunately the holograph does not seem to be among the Gosse papers now in the Turnbull Library, Wellington, New Zealand. The *TLS* text is reprinted by E. G. Ainsworth and Charles E. Noyes in "Christopher Smart: A Biographical and Critical Study," *University of Missouri Studies*, 18 (1943), 33; and, in altered form, by Arthur Sherbo, *Christopher Smart, Scholar of the University* (Lancing: Michigan State University Press, 1967), p. 51.

1 Robert Mahony has called my attention to the sale of what is probably the same letter at Sotheby's on 12 April 1922. However the Sotheby catalogue of that date prints the letter as of "2 January."

Nonetheless, the "7 January" date has been followed because it represents identical testimony from two independent sources. (See "Source.")

RD advertised Smart's proposals for *A Collection of Original Poems* beginning in the *GEP* and the *LEP* on 7–9 January and in the *GA* and *DA* on 9 January, for a total of at least twelve appearances through 16 January. Apparently Smart's letter of 12 January (q.v.), directing RD to discontinue the advertisements, had come too late to forestall the last few appearances. Professor Mary Stewart has pointed out to me that two additional advertisements appeared a month later – in the *DA* on 15 and 26 February – suggesting perhaps that Smart had once more changed his mind about the subscription. But Smart's vacillating had even an earlier history. As Stewart has also discovered, the proposals had first been advertised (with slight alterations) in the *GEP* of 12–14 and 14–17 November 1747. Smart's balking and his financial straits (see his letter on 6 August 1746, note 1) apparently led to the cessation of negotiations with the bookseller, for the collection would ultimately be published by John Newbery in 1752, entitled *Poems on Several Occasions*.

From Christopher Smart

Pemb. Hall Camb^r
y^e 12 of Janry
1747–8[1]

Sir.
On the receipt of this please to defer advertizing till further directions[2] _____
I shall be obliged to you to send the following books to me by the first opportunity.
Observations on the life of Cicero
Lumbard on persecutions
Evelyn's Chalcography
& all Whitehead's (William) Poems. 5 I think they are _____.[3]

Y^{rs}
C. Smart:

Address: To Mr R. Dodsley at / Tully's Head / Pall Mall / London.
Postmark: 13 IA

MS: Poetry / Rare Books Collection, University Libraries, State University of New York at Buffalo.

[1] See Smart's letter of 7 January 1748.   [2] Ibid., note 2.
[3] George Lyttelton, *Observation on the Life of Cicero* (1733; 1741); Daniel Lombard, *Succinct History of Ancient and Modern Persecutions* (1747); John Evelyn, *Sculptura; or the History and Art of Chalcography and Engraving in Copper* (1662; 1755). At this time William Whitehead had printed at least six poems (all published by RD): *The Danger of Writing Verse* (1741), *An Essay on Ridicule* (1743), *Ann Boleyn to Henry the Eighth. An Epistle* (1743), *On Nobility; an Epistle to the Earl of ****** Ashburnham* (1744), *Atys and Adrastus: A tale, in the Manner of Dryden's Fables* (1744), and *Honour* (1747).

From John Gilbert Cooper

Leicester Feb: ye 8th 1747/8

Dear S^r
I sent about a fortnight ago the Pamphlet I wrote to you about in a small Parcel directed to you under the fictitious name of Mr *Andrew Watkins*, to be left at M^r

Garle's warehouse (a tradesman of Leicester) in blue boar court Fryday Street London, which is kept by his servant Joshua Sharpe. as I have never heard from you since, I'm afraid you have not receiv'd it. be so kind to let me hear from you by the return of the Post. whilst the last Sheet is printing off send me those that are finish'd in a frank, that my Friend the Author may correct, if there sh^d be any mistakes.[1] I am, Dear S^r

yours most Sincerely

J G C

Address: To [Mr Dodsley] Bookseller / [at Tully]'s head / [in Pall] Mall / [Lon]don

MS: Bodleian MS. Eng. Mis. d. 174, f. 31.

[1] The reason for the circuitous route, as well as the identity of the piece, has not been discovered. The previous letter from Cooper to RD printed here, 14 November 1747, makes no mention of such a pamphlet. Nor does any earlier or subsequent letter allude to the subject. Cooper's next series of letters begins ten months later and is totally concerned with this publication of his *Life of Socrates* (1749). Possibly the work in question was one of the many pieces RD published anonymously during 1748–9 (see Straus's bibliography), for none of the authors published by RD at this time seems, in any special way, a friend of Cooper's. Mr Garle is probably Richard Garle, a prominent hosier in Leicester in the mid-eighteenth century.

From Christopher Smart[1]

Pemb. Hall Camb^r ye 9th Feb^{ry}
1747–8–

S^r

I sent to you about a month ago for some books, & shou'd be glad to know whether you have forgot, or not received the letter –[2] My service to Mason when you see him, & tell him if he stays much longer in Town, I shall expect to hear from him –[3]

yrs.

C. Smart

MS: Hyde Collection, Somerville, New Jersey.

[1] Although the holograph is unaddressed, I agee with Sherbo (*Christopher Smart*, pp. 52–3) that the letter is most likely to RD and written as a follow-up on Smart's 12 January 1747–8 letter to the bookseller (q.v.).
[2] For the volumes Smart requested, see his letter to RD on 12 January 1747/48. Because this represents Smart's last known letter to RD, Professor Betty Rizzo suggests that RD, now aware that the poet's creditors had begun to close in on him, decided to cut off his credit and hence did not send the books Smart had requested.
[3] Like Whitehead and Smart, William Mason (q.v.), another Cambridge poet and Smart's friend, had turned to RD as his first London bookseller.

From David Fordyce[1]

Aberdeen 11th Feb^{ry} 1747/8

Dear Sir

I am glad to hear that you have got all the Copy safe. I am surprised at Mr Duncan's Tardiness. I thought ⟨it⟩ his Part had been finished before I left London. He has by this delay lost the Opportunity of its being taught by me & a Bro^{yr} Professor in the neighbouring College this winter.[2]

I should like it much that Mr Spence corrected my MS before it went to the Press f he could be prevailed on to undertake that troublesome but obliging piece of work.[3] I should submit implicitly to his Corrections. – But you know best whether you can use so much freedom with him. I'm convinced the work would be much the better for being retouched by so correct & elegant a Pen. As the Sheets are cast off I shall be glad to have them sent me by post. Has Dr Asd. or M^r C__y yet seen & corrected them?[4] Please to send me thro' my Bro^{yr's} Canal the former's late Ode.[5] I imagine my Bro^{yr} will be the most careful of any you can employ in correcting the Press. I am

Dr Sr Yours faithfully

D. Fordyce

The Books you sent for my Assistance in writing the Compend[ium] will be return'd by the first Ship.

In the MS I use the word *Classis* whereas I believe I should have used *Class*. Let it therefore be corrected in the printed Copy. Please to forward the inclosed.[6]

Address: To | Mr Dodsley | Bookseller at Tully's Head | Pall Mall | London
Postmark: 19 FE
Frank: free W. Grant[7]

MS: Simon Gratz Collection, British Literary Misc., Case 11 Box 6, Historical Society of Pennsylvania.

[1] David Fordyce (1711–51) perhaps had first employed RD to issue anonymously his *Dialogues concerning Education* (1745–8). However, most of Fordyce's works emanating from Tully's Head occurred posthumously, the author having drowned in a storm off the coast of Holland in 1751. These included three editions each of *Theodorus, or Dialogue on the Art of Preaching* (1752–4) and the *Elements of Moral Philosophy* (1754–8), a separate printing of the piece that is the subject of this letter. At this time, Fordyce was a professor of moral philosophy at Marischal College, Aberdeen.

[2] The copy consisted of William Duncan's *Elements of Logic* and Fordyce's *Elements of Moral Philosophy*, which comprised Pts. VII and IX of RD's very successful instruction for youth, *The Preceptor* of 1748. Duncan's work was republished by RD under its own cover and with the same title on 16 June (*GA*), and it passed through at least eight editions in the eighteenth century. Fordyce's, however, had to wait until 20 April 1754 (*PA*) for the same treatment. (It had been registered at the Stationers' Office on 10 April.) Duncan was Fordyce's colleague at Marischal.

[3] Joseph Spence regularly advised RD on manuscripts.

[4] In the 1740s Mark Akenside served as one of RD's advisors and correctors of manuscripts; "Mr. C__ y" is unidentified.

[5] Of his several brothers, probably Fordyce refers to William, a practicing London physician in 1750, who seems to have inherited the rights to David's works, or at least negotiated their posthumous

publication. William assigned the copyrights of David's *Dialogue on the Art of Preaching* to RD for £26.5.0. in 1752 and his brother James's *An Essay on the Action Proper for the Pulpit* for five guineas in 1753. (See Appendix B.) The latter work, 86 pages in octavo, had been printed by William Strahan for £3.17.0. (Strahan Papers, BL Add. MS. 48,800). Akenside's *Ode to the Right Honourable the Earl of Huntington* had just been published by RD on 19 January (GA). ⁶ Unidentified.
⁷ The frank of William Grant (1701–64), grandson of the Rev. Alexander Fordyce of Ayton, Berwickshire, currently MP for Elgin, Scotland, and later Lord Prestongrange (1754). Fordyce had dedicated his *Dialogues concerning Education* to Grant.

From James Massey¹

Salford, Manchester, 10 March 1748

It is about fifteen years ago² that, following the profession of a painter in Norfolk, I had the honour, through the favour of Mrs. Hammond,³ to be employed by the present Earl of Orford, at Houghton.⁴ At this Time it was that I first took an account of the collection happily reposited there, which by 2 or 3 journeys that I have since taken, I have at length brought into the condition you find it . . .⁵

Source: J. Waller sale catalogue, 1859, No. 2 (Dawson Turner Collection).

¹ The person of Massey, as well as his "account" of the Walpole collection at Houghton, has eluded detection. Neither he nor his work is mentioned in any of the volumes of the Yale edition of the Walpole correspondence. (For assistance with this letter, I am indebted to John C. Riely, editor of Vols. 40 and 41 of the Yale Walpole and to Mrs Catherine Jestin, Librarian of The Lewis Walpole Library.)
² That is, *c.* 1733 when Horace Walpole was a schoolboy at Eton.
³ Susan Walpole (1687–1763), youngest sister of Sir Robert Walpole, had married Anthony Hamond in 1707 (Yale edition, *Horace Walpole's Correspondence*, ed. W. S. Lewis and J. W. Reed, Jr., Vol. 36, p. 336). ⁴ Robert Walpole (1701–51), 2nd Earl of Orford, Sir Robert Walpole's eldest son.
⁵ It is tempting to imagine some influence of Massey's account of the paintings at Houghton on Horace Walpole's own catalogue, published in 1747 as *Aedes Walpolianae, or a Description of the Collection of Pictures at Houghton Hall in Norfolk* . . . But there is not a clue to any such relationship. Massey seems to have begun his account a few years before the 18-year-old Walpole had begun his in 1736, but had brought it to "the condition you find it" only in recent years. Perhaps RD, who would publish a second edition of the *Aedes* in 1752, had been been interested in using Massey's text for some of the corrections and additions to be introduced to that edition.

To William Shenstone

Mar 24 [1748]¹

Sir

I am much oblig'd to You for so kindly offering me an improv'd Copy of the School Mistress, which I shall be glad of as soon as you please, but I could wish you would not spread the Notion of a new Edition, as that might in some measure retard the Progress of This.² If I should think of another Volume (which is not likely) I will not fail to let you know.³ In the mean time if you have a single Poem or so that you have a mind should accompany the Schoolmistress, I shall be glad to give it a place in yᵉ 2ᵈ Edition, if it is not too long.⁴

I am

Sir

Your most humᵇˡᵉ Servᵗ

R Dodsley

MS: BL. Add. MS. 28,959, f. 7.

¹ The year is determined from the context of the letter which clearly indicates a time between the publication of the first edition of the first three volumes of RD's *Collection* on 14 January 1748 (*GA*) and the second edition the following December.

² Although the text of *The School-Mistress* printed in the first edition of RD's *Collection* was identical to that first printed by RD in 1742 (*DP*), the "improv'd Copy," which Shenstone here offers the publisher became the text of that printed in the second edition of the *Collection* appearing the following December. The alterations are quite extensive and generally favorable. Two original stanzas were dropped, while nine new ones were added, and many words and phrases were altered. In addition, Shenstone had RD drop from the title "Written at *College*, 1736," and also substituted a motto from Virgil in place of the earlier Horatian motto.

³ A fourth volume was not added to the *Collection* until 1755.

⁴ Nothing more of Shenstone's was added to the second edition.

From Henrietta St John Knight, Lady Luxborough¹

[post 3 May] 1748²

You need not make excuses for writing to me again about your Bill, as I am to blame in not having sent you ye money sooner . . .³ I deferred a little 'till I saw Mr Outing⁴ who I heard was in ye Country but not here; however he is now here . . . and Mr Outing will not fail to pay you ye remainder of my bill in ye next month . . . I shall be glad you'd send by Roe (ye carrier) (if 'tis too big for a frank) an Essay upon Delicacy which Lord Hartford mentions to me . . .⁵

Source: A clipping from an unidentified bookseller's catalogue pasted on page 335 of Straus's personally annotated copy of *Robert Dodsley*, now in the McMaster University Library.

¹ Henrietta St John Knight, Lady Luxborough (d. 1756), was half-sister of Henry St John, Viscount Bolingbroke. According to Horace Walpole, she was "exiled" to her husband's estate at Barrells in 1736 when her improper conduct with the Rev. John Dalton (one of RD's authors) became unbearable for her husband Robert Knight. (See *Horace Walpole's Correspondence with Mary and Agnes Berry and Barbara Cecelia Seton*, ed. W. S. Lewis and A. Dayle Wallace, I, 64–6.) In 1746, Robert Knight was created Baron Luxborough in the Irish peerage. At Barrells, Lady Luxborough became a close friend and regular correspondent of her neighbor, William Shenstone.

² The letter must have been written sometime after 3 May, for it was on that day that RD published Nathaniel Lancaster's *The Plan of an Essay upon Delicacy* (*LEP*), mentioned within.

³ RD's letter not traced.

⁴ Williams (*Letters of William Shenstone*, p. 35) identifies "Outing" as Captain Outing, secretary and factotum to Lady Luxborough.   ⁵ See note 2.

To William Shenstone

May 17 [1748][1]

Sir

I have put the Poems to Press for a 2^d Edition & shall be oblig'd to You for a corrected Copy.[2] As to an additional Volume which I had some thoughts of, I find it will be *impossible* to furnish enough that will be good.[3] However if you have a small Piece or two I will try to insert them.[4]

I am

Sir

Your most hum.^ble Servt

R Dodsley

MS: BL. Add. MS. 28,959, ff. 8–9.

[1] For the determination of the year, see note 1 of RD's letter to Shenstone on 24 March 1748.
[2] Ibid., note 2.   [3] Ibid., note 3.   [4] Ibid., note 4.

From Matthew Pilkington[1]

Stanton, near Nottingham
Oct: 1. 1748.

Sir/

I have, ready for the Press, a few sheets which will be entitle'd *A Review of the History, & Order of the Circumstances of the Resurrection of Jesus Christ, being an Appendix to the Evangelical History & Harmony.* I should be willing to have them pass thro' your Hands, if we can agree upon that Point, & therefore defere to know what you will think proper to give, either for the Copy, or what p. 1000. for what you shall vend. I doubt not of their favourable Acceptance, having had the approbation of several of my learned Acquaintance. They will make a Pamphlet of 12^d or 18^d according to the Letter. But I imagine that as I call it an Appendix &c, it should be printed in the Same Size with the Evangelical History. –[2]

I am s^r

Your humble Servant

Matt. Pilkington

Address: To / Mr Dodsley, Bookseller / in Pall-Mall / London
Postmark: 1 OC Nottingham

MS: Harvard Theatre Collection, Harvard College Library.

[1] Matthew Pilkington (1705–65), LLB, Jesus College, Cambridge (1728), and prebend of Ruiton at Lichfield Cathedral (25 January 1748). He is to be distinguished from the lexicographer, and from the husband of Laetitia Pilkington, contemporaries with the same name.
[2] Pilkington's folio *The Evangelical History and Harmony* had been printed for the author and sold in London in 1747. RD seems not to have taken up the present offer, nor can I find that the work was published.

To Joseph Spence[1]

Pall Mall

Oct.ʳ 22ᵈ 1748

Dear Sir

While you are planting the Groves, directing the Walks, and forming yᵉ Bowers that are in all probability to afford You a Retreat for the whole of your future Life; you seem like a man arriv'd at the end of his Labours, and just beginning to enjoy the fruits of them.[2] If I did not love you, I should certainly envy; but as it is, I heartily rejoice; and only wish I was with you to partake of the Pleasure, which I am sensible you must at present enjoy. But here am I, ty'd down to yᵉ World, immerst in Business, with very little Prospect of ever being able to disengage my self. 'Tis true, my Business is of such a Nature, and so agreeable to yᵉ Turn of my Mind, that I have often very great Pleasure in yᵉ Pursuit of it. I don't know but I may sometimes be as much entertain'd in planning a Book, as you are in laying the Plan of a Garden. Yet I don't know how it is, I cannot help languishing after that Leisure which perhaps if it was in my Possession I should not be able to enjoy. I am afraid the Man who would truely relish and enjoy Retirement, must be previously furnish'd with a large & various Stock of Ideas, which he must be capable of turning over in his own Mind, of comparing, varying, and contemplating upon with Pleasure; he must so throughly have seen the World as to cure him of being over fond of it; and he must have so much good Sense & Virtue in his own Breast, as to prevent him from being disgusted ⟨or uneasy⟩ with his own Reflections, or uneasy in his own Company. I am sorry to feel my self not so well qualify'd for this sacred Leisure as I could wish, in any one respect; but glad I have a Friend from whose Example I cannot but hope I shall be able to improve.[3]

[Page of text missing here]

Pray when do you think of coming to Town[4]

[More of the text and signature missing]

MS: Interleaved opposite page 426 in the Henry E. Huntington Library copy of Joseph Spence, *Supplemental Anecdotes*, ed. Samuel W. Singer (London, 1820), RB 131213, v. 4.

[1] Joseph Spence (1699–1768), author of the *Anecdotes*, one of RD's closest friends and his traveling companion in later years. This letter shows the intimacy shared by the two protégés of Pope as early as 1748. After RD's retirement, he regularly travelled north with Spence to visit Shenstone at the Leasowes; to confer or read proof at Baskerville's; or simply to holiday, stopping off at his cousins' in Duffield and Mansfield before proceeding to Spence's Finculo Abbey residence in Durham.

Spence's first literary contributions to Tully's Head appear to have been the eight essays, two translations, and two poems he supplied for RD's fortnightly *Museum* (1746–7). In 1744, RD purchased the copyright for Spence's *Essay on Mr. Pope's Odyssey* (1726) but did not issue another edition until 1747 (see Appendix B). As already noted in David Fordyce's letter, Spence regularly assisted RD in assessing and correcting manuscripts that passed through Tully's Head. The wide-ranging work of Classical scholarship that established Spence's reputation among contemporaries, *Polymetis: or an Enquiry concerning the Agreement between the Works of the Roman Poets and the Remains of the Ancient Artists*, had been published by RD on 5 February 1747 (*GA*). Spence did not sell RD the copyright, however, until 1755 (see Appendix B).

[2] Spence had retired to his house at Byfleet, Surrey, and was busy renovating the grounds that would soon rival Shenstone's Leasowes as a show place for friends and travelers. This allusion to Spence's

redesigning Byfleet in a letter of October, 1748, creates a minor chronological problem in light of Samuel W. Singer's remarks in his edition of Spence's *Anecdotes* (1820). In his Preface (p. 29), Singer says that although Spence was dissatisfied with the possibilities of his "lizard garden" at his cottage in Berchanger, Essex, Lord Lincoln did not present his former tutor with the estate at Byfleet until 1749. Obviously some slight adjustment must now be made in that date.

3 RD's comment is somewhat prophetic of a future landscaping project. See RD's letter to Spence on 19 June 1751, note 2.

4 Except for two lines at the top ("I have a Friend . . . able to improve"), an entire page of the manuscript appears to have been destroyed. At the top of the next page, begins the line "Pray when do you . . .," and then the manuscript breaks off again. In the right top corner of this latter page, appears Spence's endorsement: "Dodesley, Oct: 24."

From John Gilbert Cooper

Leicester Dec.ʳ the 5ᵗʰ 1748

Dear Sʳ

I have now finish'd the Life of Socrates, & have already transcrib'd three parts in four ready for the press, which would have been entirely done by the latter end of Septʳ. had not my marriage writings &c hinder'd me two or three months.[1] If you think that it may be printed off & be fit for publication the latter end of March next, if I ⟨send⟩ put it into the press the first week in January, I will send it the last week in this month to you, ⟨?⟩ with proper directions about the Printing, plates &c. The Text notes Preface & all, in the Same letter as Lᵈ Shaftesbury's work, will take about 280 pages.[2] I desire you would give me your opinion by the return of the post, whether it can be done in the time I mention viz: in ten or eleven weeks, for I would not have it publish'd later than March on account of yᵉ Sale, if it can't I will defer it to another year.[3] the number of the plates will amount only to five, which surely may be engrav'd in two months, but if you think that not long enough I can send you the designs of them next week, which the Engraver may begin upon immediately.[4] My comptˢ. to all Friends. I am, Sʳ,

your most humble Servant

& Sincere Friend

John Gilbert-Cooper/Junʳ.

MS: Bodleian Ms. Eng. Misc. d. 174, f. 35.

1 Cooper's *The Life of Socrates, collected from the Memorabilia of Xenophon, and the Dialogues of Plato . . .* would be published by RD on 14 November of the next year (GA). The "marriage writings" are the formal estate settlement connected with Cooper's recent marriage. He had been obliged to leave Trinity College, Cambridge (which he had entered in 1743), on the occasion of his marriage.

2 Perhaps Cooper refers to the most recent edition of Anthony Ashley Cooper's *Characteristics*, which had been published just four years earlier in 12ᵐᵒ and reduced letter. But apparently RD would recommend otherwise, for *Socrates* would appear in 8° and in a larger letter. Also, it would run only 179 pages.

3 Cooper's letter of the next 16 January shows him deferring to the bookseller's advice to delay the publication until "next October." In his letter of 23 September 1749, however, Cooper is stipulating "[I] would not have it [before] the second week in November at the soonest." RD complied.

4 For the designer and engraver, see Cooper's letter of 15 February 1749, note 1.

From John Gilbert Cooper

Leicester Jany. the 16th 1748/9

Dear S^r

I will defer according to your advice the publication of the life of Socrates till next October, that during the Summer Season there may be time enough to print it accurately, but should be glad to know if you would not have my designs sent you that the copper Plates may be engrav'd.[1] – I desire you would immediately upon the receipt of this send me down by the return of the Post Mr Sewards pamphlet concerning the ⟨?⟩ agreement of Pagan & Popish Idolatry, the exact title I've forgot, but 'twas Printed for Tonson & Draper about the time of the last Rebellion where you may have it.[2] pray don't omit sending it by the return of the post in Frank, which will oblige

Your very humble Servt.

John Gilbert Cooper ^Jun^r.

Send me by the Next Nottingham Stage Coach two Copies of the Power of Harmony.[3]

MS: Bodleian Ms. Eng. Misc. d. 174, f. 37.

[1] I have not traced the letter containing RD's advice. For the progress of *Socrates'* publication, see Cooper's letters of 5 December 1748, 15 February 1749, and 23 September 1749.
[2] Thomas Seward, *The Conformity between Popery and Paganism illustrated . . . Being a sequel to two treatises upon this subject; the one . . . by H. Mower is his exposition of the Apocalypse and the other by . . . Dr. Middleton in his letter from Rome.* (London, 1746).
[3] Cooper's poem, published by RD on 12 November 1745 (*GA*).

From John Gilbert Cooper

Leicester Feb: ye 15th 1748/9

Dear S^r

I have finish'd my designs & according to your advice have sent 'em enclos'd for to be ⟨finished⟩ engrav'd as expeditiously as they can with accuracy, but desire you would let 'em be done by the best Hand, & Send me a specimen of the First or the design delineated, before it is engrav'd, that I may examine it.[1] I propose to have the whole publish'd by next Michaelmas term therefore leave it entirely to you to send for my papers & put the work into the press when it will be most proper or convenient to you.[2] If you want any farther instructions in regard to the plates let me have a line from you, & you shall have an answer by the return of the Post. I am, S^r,

your most humble Servt.

John Gilbert = Cooper.

let me hear when you receive this. comp^ts &c &c.

MS: Bodleian Ms. Eng. Misc. d. 174, f. 41.

[1] See Cooper's letter of 16 January 1749, note 1. L. P. Boitard engraved the frontispiece and the fiv illustrations opening each of the five books.

[2] In the event, Cooper delayed the work's publication beyond 29 September. See his letter of 2 September 1749.

From John Barr[1]

Owmby   April 19.th – [17]4

S^r

Having receiv'd no answer to either of my Letters, nor seeing any account of th publication of my Book in the general Evening post (which I take to be the mos comprehensive paper), I write this to know whether the Letters or the printe copies have come to hand or not.[2] It will not be amiss to repete the Substance c what I before wrote. I desir'd Six might be bound in the most elegant manner; tw for your Neighbour Mr Whickcot in Pall-Mall; one for Lord Scarbrõ in Grosveno Street or Square; one for Lord Chancellor in great Ormond Street; one for ou Bishop in great Marlbrõ Street; & one for Sr Stephen Hales in Hannover Street. I the Dean of Winchester (Dr Cheney) or one for him should call upon you for Book, I desire one may be deliver'd.[3] I suppose they were sent up a Fortnight ago What could be the reason for its not being publish'd before? In my last Letter desir'd an Error in printing which I had discover'd in the Dedication might b rectify'd with the Pen, as I find 'tis practicable, & the alteration not discernible The whole 100 wil not cost Mr Dodsley half a day correcting. The Error is in th first page of the dedication after *accounts*, where I would have a full Stop (.) insteac of a comma (,). Be pleased therefore to make after *accounts* a full Stop in room of comma, or . for ,[4] – Be pleased to let me know by the return of the post whether th parcel is receiv'd, and the Book advertis'd. It should not be sold at less than fou Shillings in Sheets.[5] I am, s^r, your

faithful, humble Servt

J. Bar

Postmark: 21 AP Gainsborough

MS: Bodleian, MS. Montagu d. 11, f. 53.

[1] John Barr (*c.* 1709–78), BA, Sidney College, Cambridge, 1731; ordained, 1734; prebendary of Welto Beckhall, Lincoln, 1755–78. Besides *A Summary of Natural Religion*, the subject of this letter, RD ha also published Barr's *Reflections upon Church Government as a Religious Society* in 1745 and *Sermon Preache on the Ninth of October* in 1746. For the attribution of *Reflections*, see Appendix D.

[2] Barr's *Summary of Natural Religion* was published by RD two weeks later, on 2 May (*GA*). Barr's letter have not been traced.

[3] Probably the Whickcot listed (without a first name) in the Rate Watch and Poll Book for 174 (Westminster Public Library, D506) as owning property valued at £45 on the north side of Pall Mal (perhaps the Thomas Whickcot who later subscribed to the first edition of Laurence Sterne's *Sermons o Mr. Yorick*, published by R and JD in 1761); Thomas Lumley-Saunderson, Earl of Scarboroug

(1691?–1752); Philip Yorke (1690–1764), Lord Chancellor (1737–56), 1st Earl Hardwicke (1754); Dr John Thomas (1691–1766), Bishop of Lincoln (Barr's bishop); Stephen Hales (1677–1761); Thomas Cheyney (*c.* 1694–1760), Dean of Winchester, as of the previous year.

Having been unable to locate a copy of Barr's work, I cannot say whether or not RD complied with this unusual request.

RD sold the work at five shillings. Besides the *General Advertiser* (note 2), the *London Evening Post* carried the advertisement on 6 May.

From William Melmoth

Ealing June 1ˢᵗ 1749.

Sir,

I forgot wⁿ I was in Town last to discharge my debts with you: but as nine guineas was left for me some time ago at your shop, I beg you wᵈ pay yourself, & send me yʳ bill with a receit to it. You will remember to allow me for half a dozen Pliny's wᶜʰ I am entitled to, & have not received,[1] & likewise that I returned Middleton on miracles with the preliminary discourse, for one without that discourse.[2] Pray send me also the two volumes of Univer. Hist. wᶜʰ you had to bind.[3]

Your humble Servᵗ

Wᵐ Melmoth.

Address: To / Mʳ Dodsley, / In Pall mall, / London.
Postmark: Peny Post Payd [?]

MS: BL. Add. MS. 35,338, f. 6.

Copies of Melmoth's translation of the *Letters of Pliny* (1746), which had reached a third edition the previous March.

The "preliminary discourse," entitled *Introductory Discourse*, was published separately by the author, Conyers Middleton, in March 1747 because he had anticipated much controversy when his *Free Inquiry into the Miraculous Powers Which are supposed to have subsisted in the Christian Church, from the Earliest through several successive Centuries* (1749) appeared. As he says in the Preface to the latter work, he "began to think it a duty . . . not to alarm the public at once with an argument so strange and so little understood." Probably Melmoth had already purchased the *Introductory Discourse* and preferred to avoid the extra expense of a second copy.

Through the latter part of April, the evening papers (for instance, *WEP* 8–29 April) had been advertising the completion of the twenty-volume *The Universal History.* Gentlemen were desired "to compleat their Setts as soon as possible, there being but few of some of the Volumes left."

From John Gilbert Cooper

Leicester Septʳ the 23ᵈ 1749

Dear Sʳ

As I have a good deal of business at present upon my hands, & not being very fond of the drudgery of Index making, I leave that part to any Person you think proper to employ, therefore you may put an Index at the end, or prefix a Table of Contents to the whole, or at the beginning of [the] Book just as you find it necessary, of which [you] are a much better judge than myself, or [if you] have a mind you may publish it as it is, wh[en] the Parliament meets, but I would not have it [before]the second week in November at the soonest.[1] I am D[ear Sir]

Your Most obedient humble Ser[v^t]

J G Cooper/Junr

about a fortnight hence send a copy to D^r. Akinside with my compliments &c. let it be neatly bound.

Address: To Mr Dodsley Bookseller / at Tully's head / in Pall Mall / London
Postmark: 25 [SE]
Frank: free / G Wrighte[2]

MS: Bodleian Ms. Eng. Misc. d. 174, f. 45.

[1] Cooper's concern is his forthcoming *Life of Socrates*, which RD would publish on 14 November (*GA*) just as Cooper submitted it; that is, without an index or table of contents.
[2] George Wrighte (*c.* 1706–66), Tory MP for Leicester (1727–66).

To John Gilbert Cooper

Decr 2^d [1749][1]

Dear Sir
   I am afraid you will think me long in giving you any Account of Socrates. I waited in expectation of hearing from Dr Akinside, I saw him Yesterday, & by some Accident or other he had never receiv'd ye Book, so I gave him another.[2] I hear nothing but good of it, and it sells very well. People seem⟨s⟩ in general to expect from the Title that it should have been a larger Work.[3] If I hear any thing particular I will not fail to let you know. I am glad you like the printing of it & am

Sir

Your most obliged

humble Servt

R Dodsley

MS: Letter Book of John Gilbert Cooper, f. 9, Nottinghamshire Record Office, M9659.

[1] The year is determined from the publication of Cooper's *Life of Socrates* on 14 November 1749, almost three weeks earlier.
[2] As the successful author of the influential *Pleasures of Imagination* (1744) – three editions in its first year – Akenside's literary advice was regularly sought by RD's authors. In this case, however, Cooper was probably attempting to ally himself with Akenside against William Warburton, for his *Life* had little to do with poetry. In 1744, Warburton had attacked the *Pleasures* in his *Remarks on Several Occasional Reflections*, to which Akenside's friend, Jeremiah Dyson, had responded with *An Epistle to the Rev. Mr. Warburton. Occasioned by his Treatment of the Author of The Pleasures of the Imagination* (published by RD). As Cooper's next letter of 9 December 1749 shows, he expected his slighting remarks about

Warburton in the *Life of Socrates* would bring a response in kind. He was not disappointed: see his next series of letters, beginning 25 February 1750.

³ The full title did seem rather grandiose for the 179 pages in octavo: *The Life of Socrates, collected from the Memorabilia of Xenophon, and The Dialogues of Plato, and Illustrated farther by Aristotle, Diodorus Siculus, Cicero, Proclus, Apuleius, Maximus Tyrius, Boethius, Diogenes Laertius, Aulus Gellius, and others.* It sold for 3s. 6d.

From John Gilbert Cooper

Leicester Decr the 9th 1749

Dear S^r

Be so good to give me an answer in your next by the return of the Post to the following questions.

what number of my Books did you print?

how many of 'em are dispos'd of?[1]

have you heard any thing either from, or said about, Warburton?[2]

Send me down in two Separate covers (for I'm afraid one will weigh above two ounces) the last *Monthly Review*,[3] directed, for Wrightson Mundy Esqr Memb^r of Parl^t at John Gilbert Cooper's in Leicester, which expedient will save me the expence of carriage, & you two Franks.[4] The reason for my desiring this piece is, I observe in the advertisement that the Life of Socrates is taken notice of in it. I am, D^r S^r,

your most hum^le Servt

J G C:

MS: Bodleian Ms. Eng. Misc. d. 174, f. 47.

[1] The answers to these questions RD provided in his letters of 9 and 19 December. He had printed 500 copies and had sold all he had kept for his shop, although the wholesalers still had some in stock.

[2] Here Cooper anticipated the lengthy quarrel that his contempt of Warburton in the *Life of Socrates* would instigate between himself and the clergyman. This heated exchange, which was also to be one of the chief causes of the rift between Warburton and RD, unfolds in the subsequent letters between the three.

[3] The *Monthly Review* for November (pp. 74–9) believed that "This young author has undeniably, by this performance, given the world a fair promise of a rising genius," but questioned Cooper's judgment, youthful fire, and contempt of such other able writers as Voltaire and *Warburton*. See also Cooper's letter of 23 December 1749, and note 4.

[4] Here Cooper is skirting the regulation which prevented MPs from receiving, free of charge, packages weighing more than two ounces.

To John Gilbert Cooper

Decr 9 1749

Dear Sir

I Yesterday receiv'd a Letter from Dr Akinside, & as you seem particularly to desire his Opinion I will give it you in his own Words.[1] "Pray make my

Compliments to Mr Cooper & thank him in my Name for his Present.² I think hi
Design extreamly good; his Book in general just in point of Sentiment; well adorn'c
with Learning, & that pertinent: only the Style seems too much rais'd, & too full o
Compound Words."

I have the Pleasure to tell you that the Sale has been so brisk that I have none left
but am pushing on the Printer with great Expedition that I may not balk th
Demand, & you will see a new Edition advertis'd I hope in ten days time.³ I an

Dr Sir

Your most obed^t

R. Dodsle

MS: Bodleian Ms. Eng. Misc. d. 174, f. 103.

¹ Not traced.   ² Cooper's *Life of Socrates*.
³ The second edition was not published until the first week of the new year (*GA*, 4 January 1750). RL
  had reminded Cooper that the holiday season was generally considered a bad time to publish. Se
  RD's letter to Cooper on 19 December.

To John Gilbert Cooper

Decr 19 [1749]

Dear Sir

I heartily beg your Pardon for not giving you an Account of ye Expences &
Profits of this First Edition of ye Life of Socrates, which I should never have don
had not You reminded me of our Conditions which had totally slipt my Memory ti
you recall'd it, but which I am very ready to comply with whenever you please t
send your Orders. I printed 500, but there are but small Profits arising from thi
Edition, occasion'd by ye Expence of ye Cutts & the high Price of ye Paper. Th
Profits will be considerably higher in the second Edition as ye Cutts are paid for, &
as I was oblig'd to make use of a cheaper paper (tho' a very good one) none of th
former sort being in the Market. It is not yet proper to advertise the 2^d Edition a
the first, tho' all out of my hands, is not yet out of ye hands of the Wholesale men
who would complain if a 2^d Ed was advertis'd before they had sold the First. But 1
dare say they are very near gone, & ye 2^d Ed will be ready this Week. However a
the Town will be empty I should think it better to defer advertising till after y'
Holidays, but will be directed by You.² The Words *Second Edition* are in ye Titl
Page, & the Errata in the First are corrected in This. But two of ye Errata you las
sent were too late to be corrected, a new Errata will therefore be made for them. 1
have heard nothing of Mr Warburton,³ nor any Criticisms worth mentioning
except what I think I mention'd before viz that several people when they came t
ask for it expected a larger Work.⁴ I send you enclos'd that part of the Monthl
review that contains ye Account of Socrates which I suppose is all you want.⁵ Th
Account is on the other side, & whatever Books You please to order I wil
punctually send.

I am
Dear Sir
Your most obliged hum^{ble} Servt
R Dodsley

You will observe that y^e Acc^t of Socrates is not concluded in this Number.

Account of Socrates

	£	s	d
500 printed all sold at 2ˢ p Book	50 =	0 =	0
Paper 11 Reams & 5 Quire at 18ˢ p Ream	10 =	2 =	6
Printing 11 Sheets & 1/4 at 18ˢ p Sheet	10 =	2 =	6
Engraving 6 Plates & making y^e Drawings	12 =	12 =	0
Working off d° at y^e Rolling Press	1 =	10 =	0
Advertisements	3 =	15 =	0
	38 =	2 =	0
Whole Profit	11 =	18 =	0

MS: Letter Book of John Gilbert Cooper, ff. 11–12, Nottinghamshire Record Office, M9659.

The letter obviously falls between the appearance of the first and second editions of the *Life of Socrates*, 14 November 1749 and 4 January 1750, mentioned in the text.
Cooper deferred to RD's advice (see his letter of 23 December), and the second edition was not published until 4 January.
But he would. See Warburton's letter to RD, 28 September 1751.
See RD's letter to Cooper on 2 December [1749].
November 1749, pp. 74–9, which Cooper had asked for on 9 December.

From John Gilbert Cooper

Leicester Decr. the 23^d 1749
Dear S^r.

Send me down as soon as you can get 'em, the Amsterdam Edition of Diodorus Siculus in two Vols in Folio, of 1745. & Gale's edition of Herodotus.[1] – I must confess that I expected you had dispos'd of double the number of books you mention,[2] by the repeated & complimentary accounts I have receiv'd from my acquaintance in London of the Success of my performance, however to put a Stop to any difference betwixt us in regard to the second Edition, if you will allow me 18 pounds in Classical or other Books, ⟨4⟩ the whole Copy is your own to do what you please with; ⟨can the Page⟩ I mean 18£ including the Clear profits of the first edition, which you know by your own account is 4 already. – if you agree to this I shall from time to time send for such Books as will come to the money, if more I will pay you the ballance. – as to what you mention about the advertisement I leave it entirely to you.[3] let me have one Copy of the second Edition neatly bound, together with the *Review* for the Month of December, (wherein I find an account of Socrates is to be continued) by the Nottingham Stage Coach, which sets out on Monday Jany. the 1st, but if the Review sh^d not be publish'd till that day, then send both on Tuesday the 2^d by the Leicester Carrier.[4] I am, dear S^r,

Your most humble Servt.

J. C. Cooper/Junr.

P.S.[5]

Address: To Mr Dodsley Bookseller / at Tully's head / in Pall Mall [London]
Postmark: 25DE

MS: Bodleian Ms. Eng. Misc. d. 174, f. 53.

[1] Διοδωρον του Σικελιωτου Βιβλιοτηκης ἱστορικης τα σωζομενα, *Diodore Siculi Bibliothecae historicae libri qui supersunt, interprete Laurentio Rhodomano. Ad fidem MSS recensuit Petrus Wesselingius, atque Henr. Stephani, Laur. Rhodomani, Fulvii Ursini, Henr. Valesii, Jacobi Palerii et suas adnotationes, cum indicibus locupletissimis, adjecit.* As evident from the full title of *Life of Socrates*, Cooper had used Diodorus Siculus in the composition of the work and was probably needing it once more for revisions in the second edition. Thomas Gale (1635?–1702), Regius Professor of Greek at Cambridge, had published his translation of Herodotus's *History* in 1679.   [2] See RD's letter of 19 December.   [3] Ibid.
[4] This second account of the *Life of Socrates* in the *Monthly Review* (December, 1749, pp. 94–104), although longer and manifesting the same attitude as the first (see Cooper, 9 December, note 3), is largely a summary of the work's highlights.
[5] The holograph is broken off at this point – the postscript is missing.

To John Gilbert Cooper

Decr 26 [1749][1]

Dear Sir

I am extreamly sorry that you seem not quite satisfy'd about the Number printed of the Life of Socrates.[2] It gives me a pain that I have not been us'd to feel. I wish I could give you any stronger Satisfaction than assuring You that I scorn to impose upon any man, much less upon You whom I have reason to think my Friend. But to put an end to all this, I agree to your Proposal & will send you down the Books order'd by the first opportunity,[3] I will send you one of ye 2^d Edition as soon as I can get one bound & also one to Mr Franklin.[4] I will send the Review when out.[5] I rec'd a Letter from one Mr Bolton Sympson a Clergyman who says you are mistaken in saying that Plato & Xenophon avoid mentioning each other in their Writings, for that in Book 3 Chap 6 Sect 1 of ye Memorabilia Plato is expressly mention'd.[6]

I am
D^r S^r
Your most obed^t &c

R Dodsley

MS: Letter Book of John Gilbert Cooper, f. 14, Nottinghamshire Record Office, M9659.

1 The year is determined on the basis of the appearance of Cooper's *Life of Socrates*, the subject of the letter.
2 See Cooper's letter of 23 December.   3 Ibid.
4 Possibly Thomas Franklin (1721–84), a contemporary of Cooper's at Cambridge and subsequently (1750) a Professor of Greek at Cambridge, a person who would have been interested in a work on Socrates.
5 *Monthly Review* for December, containing the continuation of the previous month's review of the *Life of Socrates*.
6 No doubt the Rev. Bolton Simpson, whose edition of Ξενοφωντος 'Απομνημονευπατων βιβλα Δ. Xenophontis Memorabilium Socratis Dictorum Libri IV (Oxford: Fletcher, 1741) had gone into a second edition the same year. Simpson was correct.

To Thomas Birch[1]

Feb. 24. 1750.

Sir

Please to let ye Bearer have the Vol. of Harleian Miscellany[2] which you have, and if you have not done with it, you shall have another in 2 or 3 Days, from,

Sir,

Your h^ble Servt

R. Dodsley

Address: To / The Revd Mr Birch

MS: BL. Add. MS. 4,305, f. 220.

1 The Rev. Thomas Birch (1705–66), DD, FRS, FSA, was Rector of St Margaret Pattens, London, at the time.
2 "*The Harleian Miscellany: or, a Collection of Scarce, Curious, and Entertaining Pamphlets and Tracts, as well in Manuscript as in Print, Found in the late Earl of Oxford's Library. Interspersed with Historical, Political, and Critical Notes.* London: Printed for T. Osborne in Gray's Inn, MDCCXLIV–VI." Possibly Birch had been using the *Miscellany* in preparing *The Works of Sir Walter Raleigh, Political, Commercial, and Philosophical*, a work to be published by RD the following December.

From John Gilbert Cooper

Leicester [25 or 26 February 1750][1]

Dear S^r

I receiv'd your Bill & the Pamphlet, the balance of the former I will send to town the first opportunity.[2] – pray send me down, as soon as ever it comes out, Mr Warburton's Book about the Miracle which defeated poor Julian's irreligious attempt to rebuild the Temple of Jerusalem; I see 'tis advertis'd to be publish'd the beginning of March, therefore perhaps, Knapton could let you have one immediately in Sheets, which if he can, be so good to send it by the very first Nottingham Stage Coach or Leicester Waggon only ⟨stitched⟩ Sew'd together.[3] – at the same time send me one of your Memorandum Books.[4] – pray don't fail of

sending to Knapton the moment you receive this, for if you can procure me One of
these death doing Books to Infidelity directly it will oblige,[5] Dear S[r]
Your most Obed! Hum^{le} Serv!

J.G. Cooper Jun!

M[r] Jackson, who is going to publish his long expected Book
[a]bout Chronology, desir'd me to acquaint you the next
[ti]me I wrote, that he proposes to have Subscriptions for his
[B]ook taken in at your Shop among others, & desir'd to know
[wh]ether he might put in your Name.[6] I should be
[gla]d to have your answer, but suppose 'tis a thing
[in] course. – I have not a frank, therefore place this
[besid]e other letters You receive from me unfrank'd
[to my] account. I see my Book has not yet been
[adver]tis'd again.[7] let me know how your Subscription for y[e] Prints goes on[8]

Address: To M[r] Dodsley / Bookseller / at Tully's Head / in Pall Mall / London
Postmark: 26FE

MS: Bodleian Ms. Eng. Misc. d. 174, ff. 101–2.

[1] The year is determined from Cooper's mention of an advertisement announcing the appearance in early March of William Warburton's *Julian*, a work that was issued on 7 April 1750; the day is approximated from the postmark.

[2] RD's letter is not traced and consequently Cooper's account and the identity of the pamphlet alluded to remain a mystery.

[3] *Julian, or A Discourse Concerning the Earthquake and Fiery Eruption, which defeated that Emperor's attempt to rebuild the Temple of Jerusalem* was not published until 7 April (*GA*) by J. and P. Knapton.

[4] RD had begun publishing his popular memorandum books for both ladies and gentlemen in 1748.

[5] For the ensuing quarrel, see Warburton's letter of 28 September 1751 and Cooper's of 26 August 1751.

[6] Two years later, John Jackson (1686–1763), Master of Wigston's Hospital in Leicester and conservative theologian, published his *Chronological Antiquities; or the Antiquities and Chronology of the most ancient Kingdoms from the Creation of the World for the Space of Five Thousand Years* (3 vols. London: for the author and J. Noon, 1752), but apparently RD had not agreed to put his name to it in light of the quarrel later to erupt between Cooper and Warburton. See Cooper's letter of 26 August 1751.

[7] A second edition of Cooper's *Life of Socrates* had appeared from Tully's Head on 4 January (*GA*). A third edition was advertised in the *General Advertiser* of 1 November.

[8] In the *London Evening Post* for 1–3 February 1750, appeared the advertisement: "Proposals for Engraving by Subscription, English History Delineated, in a Series of Fifty Prints, representing the most memorable Actions and Events, from the Landing of Julius Caesar to the Revolution." Subscriptions were to be taken by J. and P. Knapton and RD. The appearance of the series was considerably delayed, however. An advertisement in the same paper for 5–7 November 1751 promised that the first six prints would appear the following January. But even this prediction proved inaccurate, for another notice in the 22–25 February *London Evening Post* now promised them on 3 March. Finally in the 7–10 March issue appeared, under the familiar "This Day is published," the long delayed "The Ancient History of England. Delineated in Six Prints. Including the Period from the Landing of Julius Caesar to the Conquest." The prints had been designed by Hayman and Blakey and engraved by Grignion, Ravenet, Scotin, and Vivares. They were being sold by J. and P. Knapton and RD. Possibly the taxing experience of producing these six prints, however, discouraged the Knaptons and RD from continuing the project, which had originally been planned to reach fifty

prints in all, for it seems no others were ever advertised. Amongst Hayman's materials in the BL Print and Drawing Room, while there are some versions of three prints in the first series, no others are found to illustrate later events in English history.

From John Gilbert Cooper

Leicester October the 22^d 1750

Dear S^r

I am very sorry you are necessitated to put a list of any Errata at all to a Third Edition, which might have been prevented if you had let me known that the Publick had been so favorable to my Performance as to require this fresh demand.[1] 'tis true I was six weeks this year at my own house in Nottinghamshire[2] fitting it up & buying furniture against I go there, but I cannot conceive how that could raise a report that I had left this place which I never propos'd to do till next Spring, neither am I altogether so obscure but that a letter directed to me here would have been sent safe to any place I remov'[d] to; however if the success of the sale should so far exceed my expectations, as to occasion a fourth edition (which you may be enabled to judge of by the latter end of next Month) let me know in time that I may send you a small Appendix, if you think it worth having.[3] – the Subject I am now upon you shall be acquainted with before any body else, but at present 'tis known to no one but myself, & considering I'm a *modern* Author that's a great deal to say too.[4] my little Library is not yet compleat [&] till it is so I shall write for Books,[5] for considering the little encouragement ⟨knowledge⟩ Learning meets with, I don't think it justice to my Family to purchase the Tools, and afterwards shall think any Character too dearly bought that is to be paid for at the expence of my ease; therefore you see I have very good reasons to work in the literary Shop just to such a time & no longer, but whilst I do so, you may rely upon having the refusal of my Wares. – when do you begin to publish your historical prints?[6] I would go through with 'em as I have already Subscrib'd, therefore constantly send 'em as they come out, & place the usual expence to my account. – let me have by the return of the Post the Midwife's Magazine if any such Pamphlet is really publish'd,[7] & when The Gout, Business, & your Customers of Quality will afford you leisure I should be glad to have a short answer to the above particulars, in the mean time I am, with sincere wishes that you may live free at present from the first of those three, & hereafter from the two latter, Dear S^r,

Your most humble Servt
& Sincere Friend

J G Cooper/Junr.

My comp^{ts}. to Mrs Dodsley, & if she is not ⟨frightened⟩ utterly averse to being four & twenty hours out of the sweet Smoke of St Jame's, I should be very glad to have the pleasure of her & your company for a week or a fortnight the next Time you come into Nottinghamshire at Thurgarton in that County, for I shall be quite Settled there, (please God my wife & I live!) next Summer.[8]

MS: Bodleian Ms. Eng. Misc. d. 174, ff. 55–9.

[1] The third edition of the *Life of Socrates*, published on 1 November 1750 (*GA*). There seems to have been a break in the Cooper–RD correspondence during 1750. The last letter (traced) from Cooper was written on 25 or 26 February.   [2] Thurgarton. See below.

[3] A fourth edition seems never to have been called for.

[4] Probably his *Letters Concerning Taste* (1754), for the motivation for his next published work, *Cursory Remarks on Mr. Warburton's New Edition of Mr. Pope's Works* (December 1751) was not incited until late summer of 1751. See Cooper's letter on 26 August of that year.

[5] See Cooper to RD, 23 December 1749.

[6] See Cooper's letter to RD on 25 or 26 February of this year, note 8.

[7] *The Midwife, or Old Woman's Magazine* (1750–3), published by John Newbery and edited by Christopher Smart (q.v.).

[8] From Cooper's letter to RD of 26 August 1751, it seems RD did not make the trip the next summer.

To Joseph Spence

[(Dodsley, June 19.) 1751][1]

Dear Sir

I sent you last week by Thatcher's Barge all your Parcels, in which were included two Epping Cheeses which M.rs Dodsley desires M.rs Spence will be so good as to accept. I hope you have before now rec.d all the *cargoe safe*. exc.t y.e Gr H. I have this day sent the *Pope's Works* (which came from M.r *Warburton*) down to Hungerford, to go by the same Conveyance. I am afraid my design *on the Banks of the Thames* will not proceed to Execution, the Landlord and I not having yet agreed.[2] As the idle time of the Year is now come on, I have begun it with the most idle of all Productions, a Love Song: I intend it for M.r Tyer's, to be sung at Vaux-hall.[3] Pray tell me whether 'tis good for ought or not. I wrote it, alas! not from any present feelings or sensations, but by recalling past Ideas to my Mind; and therefore it may possibly want that passionate Tenderness requisite to the Subject: however I think it so much too young for me at present that I shall not let M.r Tyers or any body else know that it is mine.

Mutual Love
a Song.

Whene'er I meet my Caelia's Eyes,
Sweet Raptures in my Bosom rise,
    My Feet forget to move;
She too declines her lovely head,
Soft Blushes o'er her Cheeks are spread,
    Sure this is Mutual Love!

My beating Heart is wrapt in Bliss,
Whene'er I steal a tender Kiss,

Beneath the silent Grove:
She strives to frown, & puts me by,
Yet Anger dwells not in her Eye;
  Sure this is Mutual Love!

And once, O once! the dearest Maid,
As on her Breast my Head was laid,
  Some secret Impulse drove;
Me, me her gentle Arms carest,
And to her Bosom closely prest,
  Sure this was Mutual Love!

And now, transported with her Charms,
A soft Desire my Bosom warms
  Forbidden Joys to prove:
Trembling for fear she should comply,
She from my Arms prepares to fly,
  Though warmed with mutual Love.

O stay! I cry'd – Let Hymen's Bands
This moment tye our willing Hands,
  And all thy Fears remove:
She blush'd Consent with modest Grace,
And sweetly in her glowing Face,
  I read her mutual Love.[4]

Endorsement: Song: by Mr Dodsley.[5]

MS: Interleaved opposite page 427 in the Henry E. Huntington Library copy of Joseph Spence, *Supplemental Anecdotes,* ed. Samuel W. Singer (London, 1820), RB 131213, v. 4.

[1] Most likely the year is 1751, for Warburton's edition of Pope's *Works,* mentioned within as having been sent to Spence as a gift from Warburton, had been published this very day. Besides, RD's enclosure, "Mutual Love," was printed in the *General Advertiser* on 29 July 1751 as "A New Song, sung at Vauxhall by Mr. Lowe." "Dodsley, June 19." is Spence's endorsement.

[2] A drawing by Spence found in the Osborn Collection, Yale, identifies RD's "design on the Banks of the Thames"; it is entitled "Designs for Mr. Dodsley's Gardens at Richmond." However nothing in the Richmond Record Office suggests that RD ever did purchase the property.

[3] Jonathan Tyers (d. 1767), proprietor of Vauxhall Gardens, responded favorably to RD's piece. See note 1.

[4] Although it is impossible to determine whether or not Spence did recommend any alterations in the song, the piece, printed "as sung" in the *General Advertiser,* does show some slight change, primarily in its last three lines. Line 19 becomes "Transported with her blooming Charms," and the last lines read: "She blushed Consent; her Fears suppress'd; / And now we live, supremely bless'd, / A Life of Mutual Love."

[5] This endorsement does not seem to be in Spence's hand.

From John Gilbert Cooper

Thurgarton August the 26th 1751.

Dear S[r]

I rec'd about three days ago a letter from an unknown hand, which was directed & frank'd by you,[1] containing several handsome & undeserv'd compliments on my Life of Socrates, & informing me too at the same time of a thing which I did not know before, that Mr Warburton had made a trifling & insolent reply to some of my notes in his new commentary on Mr Pope's Essay on Criticism[2] P: 151. [?]the same Person exhorts me to make a reply. I should take it therefore as a favor if you would send me down that Volume of the nine which contains his commentary,[3] (for you must know 'tis a wipe inserted only in this very last copy of the whole Works & not in the detach'd piece publish'd a year ago) & I will consider what is to be [don]e. pray send it by the very first Nottingham Coach [di]rected to be left for me at Mr Chappel's linnen [dr]aper in that Town. you may rely upon it that I [w]ill neither blot or abuse the Book, but I promise y[ou if any unforseen accident should happen I will [t]ake the whole Sett. if you know who the Author of [t]his anonymous letter is be so good to favor me with [t]he knowledge of his name, by the return of the Post, [d]irecting your letters always to me at Thurgarton [n]ear *Newark* in Nott[s]. if you should have a hurry [o]f business & can't favor me with an answer yourself [to] this, pray let your Brother give me a Single line.[4]

>   I am, Sr,
>   Your Sincere Friend
>   & humble Servt.

John Gilbert Cooper

[I] expected to see you this Summer with Mrs. Dodsley in Nottinghamshire

MS: Bodleian Ms. Eng. Misc, d. 174, f. 61.

[1] The letter franked by RD has not been traced. Warburton, commenting on verse 92 of Pope's *Essay on Criticism* in Volume I of his edition, *Works of Alexander Pope, Esq* (London: J. and P. Knapton, J. and R. Tonson and S. Draper, and C. Bathurst, 1751), of the previous June, soundly attacked Cooper by calling his *Life of Socrates* (1749) "a late ridiculous and now forgotten thing," an example of ignorance joined with vanity, giving "birth to every iniquity of impudent abuse and slander." RD must have complied with Cooper's request and sent the volume of Pope's *Works*, for a month later Warburton, in a letter to RD (28 September), includes a letter he has received from Cooper and possibly acknowledging the need for some apology to the author of *Socrates*.

The "unknown hand" might have been that of the Rev. John Jackson, the Master of Wigston's Hospital in Leicester and an acquaintance of Cooper's (see Cooper's letter of 25 or 26 February 1750). Although Jackson was a frequent antagonist of Warburton's, his earlier attack on the editor of Shakespeare had indeed been thought to be Cooper's. This is clear from the *Memoirs of the Life and Writings of the late Reverend Mr. John Jackson* (London: T. Field, 1764), when the editor, Dr Sutton, says on page 184: "In 1748, a Piece came out against Mr. Warburton, wherein that Gentleman is sufficiently satyrized, and that in a curious Manner. This Pamphlet for some Time was supposed to be, and accordingly passed with several for the Performance of the Author of the Life of Socrates [Cooper] ... [but] Mr. Jackson authorized me to insert it in the List of his Works. The Title runs thus, A Treatise on the Improvements made in the Art of Criticism, Collected out of the Writings of a celebrated Hypercritic. By Philocriticus Cantabrigiensis. London, for M. Cooper, in Paternoster

Row, 1748. (48 pp).'' Jackson's satire was in response to Warburton's edition of Shakespeare, published the previous year. Warburton's rejoinder to the *Treatise* then prompted Jackson to write *A Defense of a late Pamphlet, called, a Treatise on the Improvement made in the Art of Criticism* (London: J. Noon, 1749). For elaboration on the *Treatise*, see Warburton's letter of 28 September 1751.

[2] "*An Essay on Criticism.* By Alexander Pope, Esq.; with Notes by Mr. Warburton. London: H. Lintot and sold by W. Owen, 1750" (*LEP* 20–3 January 1750).

[3] As seems clear from Warburton's letter to RD a month later, the bookseller supplied Cooper with the requested volume of Pope's *Works.*

[4] James Dodsley (1724–97), Robert's brother and assistant at Tully's Head, whose name would begin to appear in the Dodsley imprint in the mid-1750s.

From William Warburton

Prior Park Sep! 28 1751

M\u1d63 Dodsley

I just now received the inclosed letter from M\u1d63 John Gilbert-Cooper jun!\u02b3[1]

I desire he may have the letter he demands.[2] I am ashamed I was obliged to take notice to you of a thing so much below me as such scurrilous trash. but it concerned the reputation of another honest man.[3] You ⟨will⟩ will readily imagine, that amongst the Dunces who have taken it into their head to be angry, I have a great deal of this miserable ware. But it injuring no body but my selfe, and I very insensible, no body is troubled with it.

M\u1d63 Cooper's sentiments of nameless libellers are very commendable. But it would be well if he would consider, whether putting his name to a Libell would excuse his honesty, tho' it might, his honour. I say his honour, for he must certainly have some very peculiar rules of civil commerce, to tell me to my face, or, which is the same thing, under his hand, that *I have used him very ill.* For how stands the fact! He writes a Book, and finds it proper to confute the sentiments of a preceeding Writer: which certainly he had a right to do. But as this writer was an utter stranger to him, had never any concerns with him, never mentioned his name or his writings in public or in conversation but with honour, had he a right to use this Author with a scurrility worse than billingsgate; to return to it; to repeat it, and to carry it thro' his whole book? Yet this he has certainly done.[4] And what revenge has the Writer taken? no other than the ⟨slight⟩ casual mention of the Author of the life of Socrates, (without the mention of his name) with a slight joke: which he ought to have taken as a friendly admonition of his folly. Instead of this, he tells me *I have used him very ill.* Is it credible he should venture to say this? Or is there a new system of morality come out for the Wits & Poet's of the time! You are in the midst of them, and can tell. I believe you practice the old; and while you do, I shall always be ready to shew my selfe

Your faithful
humble Servant

W. Warburton

MS: Letter Book of John Gilbert Cooper, f. 15, Nottinghamshire Record Office, M9659.

[1] Most unfortunately, not traced. Cooper quotes from this letter in his *Cursory Remarks*. (See Cooper's next letter, of 13 November.)

[2] Possibly a *momentary* apology from Warburton for his attack on Cooper (see Cooper's letter of 26 August, note 1), for the offensive remark was not removed in the 1753 edition of Pope's *Works*.

[3] Probably Warburton did not want his attack to reflect on Pope.

[4] Although Cooper had treated Warburton with some youthful arrogance in his *Life of Socrates* (1749) when speaking of Warburton's *Divine Legation of Moses* (1737–41) (in note 13 on p. 54, Cooper claims Warburton had been led astray by Aelian, a "Scrap-retailing Historian" and promises more of the "renowned Mr. Warburton, whose great Sagacity I shall consider in the following notes"), here Warburton more likely has in mind the acerbic attack *Treatise on the Improvements Made in The Art of Criticism, Collected out of the Writings of a celebrated Hypercritic* (1748), a work currently thought to have been Cooper's but one actually penned by John Jackson, Cooper's friend. Jackson's vicious lampoon of Warburton ran: "As soon as you are able to read *Latin* and *Greek* (and if you understand *English* too, it is so much the better) and have a mind to shew away as a *modern improv'd Critic* . . . whatever Subject you take to improve . . . give it a plausible Title and singular too, as *Divine Legation*, Etc., though any other Title would suit as well, since you intend least of all to be confin'd to treat of your Subject, but chiefly to shew your critical Learning on every other subject" (pp. 2–3). And further, "This demonstrative Argument of our great Critic is called in the modern improved Art of Criticism *Argumentum Asininum*; and is very much used by our Critics: Not that he is literally an *Ass*, but only puts on the *Appearance* of one. It is a beautiful *Prosopopoeia*, and the symbol or Mark by which he is easily known when he goes abroad *incog.* and cares not, for good Reason, to shew his Face, which he has been very cautious of doing, ever since Mr. *Jackson* found him out." The reference to Jackson in the third person, throughout the *Treatise*, no doubt had caused readers – and indeed Warburton himself – to think that Jackson's friend and collaborator, Cooper, had been its author. In his letter to Hurd on 5 July 1752, Warburton, now much offended with Jackson, claimed that "all his account of the mysteries [in that author's *Chronological Antiquities*, 1752] should be one entire theft from me" (*Letters from a late Eminent Prelate*, p. 86).

From John Gilbert Cooper

Thurgarton Nov.ʳ the 13.ᵗʰ 1751.

Dear Sʳ.

Having lost the dearest friend I ever had in the World, my poor Wife, my affliction will only permit me to say in answer to your last, that I must leave the correction of the Press & the publication altogether to you,[1] when it is finish'd be pleas'd to direct, what I order'd before, down to me at Wᵐ. Wrighte's Esqʳ at Leicester.[2] I am, Dear Sʳ

Your ever well Wisher,
& now almost distracted
J G Cooper Junʳ.

MS: Bodleian Ms. Eng. Misc. d. 174, f. 63.

[1] No doubt Cooper's pamphlet response to Warburton's insult: *Cursory Remarks on Mr. "Warburton's" New Edition of Mr. "Pope's" Works Occasioned By That Modern Commentator's injurious Treatment, in one of his Notes upon the "Essay on Criticism", of The Author of the "Life of Socrates." In a letter to a friend,* published by M. Cooper on 5 December 1751 (*LEP*). See also Cooper to RD, 23 November 1751.

[2] William Wrighte, Recorder of Leicester (1729–62) and uncle of George Wrighte, Tory MP for Leicester (1727–66). The latter occasionally franked Cooper's letters.

From John Gilbert Cooper

Leicester Novr the 23^d 1751

Dear S.^r

As you some time ago wrote me word that my Pamphlet would be finish'd as last Saturday the 16th. I fully expected a copy by the Post this day ⟨but⟩ & was not a little disappointed ⟨to? it⟩ in not receiving it, & finding no advertisement about it in the publick Prints. I have particular reasons for having it publish'd the moment you receive this or not at all, which are too long to be at present explain'd in a letter. therefore be so good to comply with my desire in this point.[1] my comp^{ts} to Mrs Dodsley. I pray God preserve you both long from the affliction I now labour under! I am, Dear S^r,

your most Sincere Well Wisher
J G Cooper Junr.

I must insist upon your name being to the Pamphlet as Publisher, for sure what I may write you may publish.[2] pray send is done & an answer by Monday's Post.

MS: Bodleian Ms. Eng. Misc, d. 174, f. 67.

[1] RD letter to Cooper not traced. See Cooper to RD 13 November 1751, note 1. Cooper's *Cursory Remarks* is signed at its conclusion "Oct 30, 1751." It finally appeared on 5 December (*LEP*).
[2] No doubt wanting to avoid a total alienation of Warburton, RD had Mary Cooper publish the pamphlet, leaving his own name off the title page. RD's answer to Cooper has not been traced.

From John Gilbert Cooper

Leicester Jany the 19. [1752]

Dear S.^r

The Death of my poor dea[r] Wife having drove me from the family Seat in Nottinghamshir[e] which I newly fitted up & furnish[ed] last year, I ⟨have advertis'd⟩ shall advertise it to be let in the London Evening Papers n[ext] week. therefore should take it as a favour if you would permit me to refer the enquirers to you for fart[her] Particulars than what can be insert[ed] in an advertisement; which fart[her] particulars I have herein enclos'd [for] you to show any Body who comes [to] you about the Business.[1] I receiv'd [Ju]lia but no Bill as I desir'd in my [last], therefore desire you would let me [know] the first leisure hour you have [wh]at I am indebted to you & I will [send] you an order for the money.[2] What [succ]ess has my Pamphlet had? what [of]Warburton?[3] my comp^{ts} to M^{rs} [Do]dsley. I am, Dear S^r

your most humble Servt
& well wisher
J. G. Cooper Junr

MS: Bodleian Ms. Eng. Misc. d. 174, f. 87.

[1] A "To be sold" advertisement appeared in the *LEP* of 21–3 January 1752, offering "The Priory of Thurgarton at Thurgarton, Notts., two miles from Southwell, ten miles from Mansfield, five miles from Newark, eight miles from Nottingham, and one mile from the River Trent." RD was listed as one of six persons (two in London) for further inquiry. However, it seems Cooper did not indeed sell Thurgarton at this time, for later letters (7 October 1754, 14 October 1754) are addressed from the Priory.

[2] Warburton's *Julian; or A Discourse Concerning the Earthquake and Fiery Eruption which defeated that Emperor's Attempt to rebuild the Temple at Jerusalem*, which had been published on 10 April 1750 (*GA*), and which Cooper had requested of RD in his letter of 25 or 26 February 1750. Cooper's "last" has not been traced.

[3] Warburton seems to have ignored Cooper's *Cursory Remarks*. It is not even mentioned in his correspondence collected by Richard Hurd (*Letters of a Late Eminent Prelate to One of his Friends*, 1808). The *MR* treatment (5 December 1751, pp. 466–75) is lengthy, but uncritical, and the work seems not to have enjoyed a second edition.

From John Baskerville[1]

Birmingham 2d Oct. 1752

Dear Sr

To remove in some Measure Yr Impatience, I have sent You an Impression of the punches of the two lines Great primer, which have been begun & finish'd in 9 Days only, & contain all the Letters Roman necessary in the Titles & half Titles. I can't forbear saying they please Me, As I can make nothing more Correct, nor shall You see anything of mine much less so. You'll observe they strike the Eye much more sensibly than the smaller Characters tho Equally perfect, till the press shows them to more Advantage.[2] The press is creeping slowly towards perfection; I flatter my self with being able to print nearly as good a Colour & smooth a Stroke as the inclos'd; I should esteem it a favour if You'd send me the Initial Letters of all the Cantos, lest they should not be included in the said 14, & three or four pages of any part of the poem, from whence to form a Bill for the Casting a suitable Number of each Letter; The R. wants a few slight Touches & the Y half an hours Correction.[3]

This Day We have resolutely set about 15 of the same Siz'd Italick Capitals, which will not be at all inferior to the Roman, & I doubt not to compleat them in a fortnight. You Need therefore be in no pain about our being ready by the time appointed.[4] Our best Respects to Mrs Dodsley & our friend Mr Beckett concludes me[5]

Yr Most Obedt Servt

John Baskerville

Verte

pray put it in no One's power to let Mr Caslon see them[6]

Endorsement: Oct 2 1752

MS: Typographic Manuscript Collection, Rare Book and Manuscript Library, Columbia University.

[1] John Baskerville (1706–75), the famous Birmingham printer and typefounder, used RD as his London agent for his various experiments in types, paper-making, and printing, as subsequent letters and

other references will show. Their relationship was to be assisted by RD's most frequent correspondent, William Shenstone, Baskerville's neighbor in Birmingham. A visit to Shenstone in the late 1750s usually included a call on Baskerville.

2 As W. Turner Berry and A. F. Johnson observe in *Catalogues of Specimens of Printing Types by English and Scottish Printers and Founders 1665–1830* (1935; repr., with Introduction by James Mosley. New York: Garland, 1983), pp. 28–9, "The Baskerville types mark the beginning in this country [England], of the transition from the old-face to the modern-face." Baskerville, once a writing master himself, paid attention to that trade, as well as to contemporary French experiments in design. In this, he left behind the old-style as found in the most popular type of contemporary England, that of William Caslon. For descriptions of Baskerville's specimens, see Philip Gaskell, *John Baskerville, a Bibliography* (Cambridge, 1959; repr., with corrections and additions, 1973).

3 Baskerville's biographers offer no identification of this work, nor does Straus in *Robert Dodsley*, except to guess it to be some experimental poem. F. E. Pardoe, in *John Baskerville of Birmingham, Letter-Founder and Printer* (London: Frederick Muller, 1975), pp. 30–1, admits speculation on the matter is idle. Fifteen months after this letter, Baskerville will be writing to RD: "I have put the last hand to my Great Primer . . . I shall have Virgil out of the press by the latter end of Jany." One is tempted to believe the allusions in this letter of 1752 are early references to work on Baskerville's edition of the Latin poet, which ultimately would not appear until 1757. But, as Pardoe notes, Virgil's works could hardly be considered a "poem," nor did that edition have engravings; what's more, Virgil's works are not written in cantos. The only poem in cantos that we know RD was preparing at this time, and would publish the next year, was his own *Agriculture*, the first part of the intended tripartite *Public Virtue*. But the typography of the published version of *Agriculture* is not Baskerville's. Consequently the allusion continues a mystery. 4 Christmas – see Baskerville to RD, 19 October 1752.

5 Most likely John Becket, a writing master of New Street, Birmingham. He appears listed, as such, in *Sketchley's & Adams's Tradesman's True Guide . . . to Birmingham* (1770). Furthermore, a "Mr. Becket, Writing Master, Birmingham" appears in the list of subscribers printed in the front of Baskerville's edition of Virgil (1757).

6 Baskerville had just cause for worrying that his work would be leaked to Caslon, for curious family relationships linked Baskerville with Caslon. His apprentice since 1748, Amos Green (1734–1807), was a relative of Caslon's. Green, a neighbour of John Scott Hylton in Halesowen, was also a friend of Shenstone's. In addition, Shenstone's uncle, Edward Cookes, had been Caslon's Master. Finally, Caslon himself originated from Worcester. See Johnson Ball, *William Caslon 1693–1766. The ancestry, life and connections of England's foremost letter-engraver and Typefounder* (Kineton, Warwick: Roundwood Press, 1973), pp. 399 ff.

From John Baskerville

Birmingham 19 Oct. 1752

Dear S^r

As I proposed in my last[1] I have sent You Impressions from a Candle of 20: two Lines Great primer Italick, which were begun & finish'd in 10 Days only; We[2] are now about Figures which are in a Good forwardness, & changing a few of those Letters we concluded finish'd, My next Care will be to strike the punches into Copper & justify them with all the Care & Skill I am Master of; You may depend on my being ready by Y^r time (Christmas) but if more time could be allow'd I should make use of it all in Correcting & justifying;[3] As so much depends on Appearing perfect on first Starting; I have with great pains justified the plate for the Platten & Stone on which it falls, So they are as perfect planes as it will ever be in my Power to procure, for instance, if You Rest one End of Y^r plate on the Stone, & let the other fall the height of an Inch; It falls soft as if You dropt it on feathers or several Folds of

Silk, & when You raise it, You manifestly feel it Suck (if you'll excuse so unphilosophical a Term;) Wet the two, & either would Support the other with (I believe) 500 lbs. added to it, if held perpendicularly; To as perfect a plane will I endeavor to bring the faces of the Types, if I have time;[4] Nor do I despair of better Ink[5] & printing (the Character must speak for itself) than has hitherto been seen

I must beg Leave to remark on the plate sent me, that I fear the performer is capable of doing nothing much better, As he's greatly deficient in Design Drawing & Execution with the Needle, the Composition of the Ornament if it will bear that Name is mean, or if You will, means Nothing;[6] To speak in my own Way the D. is as bad a one as can well be made, If You are determined to have the Initials grav'd, I would refer You to Pine's Horace where the Execution is neat, tho' the proportion is bad;[7] The Letter is Suppos'd rais'd, consequently the side next the light is express'd by a very faint Line, its opposite very strong, like the light & Shadow in a picture; If You'll accept my Judgm^t & Skill is at Y^r Service, Give Me the Initials & Size, or if You please I'll give the Size 4 5 or 6 Lines great Primer & the Letters as Correct as I can draw them in black Lead, the Armament as You & the Graver can agree. Thus Dear Sr You see I readily accept the Terms You are so kind to offer me of treating You freely as my Friend; pray consider the above inter nos only, & give me a Line as soon as You have Leisure As You are [in] the Land of Franks; half a Doz would do me a particular pleasure, As a good many things not worth a Groat might be communicated by

> Y^r Most obed^t hble Servt
>
> J Baskerville

Hast had almost made me forget Complim^ts of the Family &c.

Endorsement: Baskerville Octr 19 1752

MS: Typographic Manuscript Collection, Rare Book and Manuscript Library, Columbia University.

[1] 2 October 1752, q. v.

[2] "We": Baskerville's punch cutter was John Handy (see Johnson Ball, *William Caslon*, p. 401).

[3] Baskerville overestimated his progress. As late as his letter to RD on 16 January 1754, he would announce: "I have put the last hand to my Great Primer."

[4] In the 1750s Baskerville would become much respected for the sharp impression he was able to achieve, primarily through the careful construction of his press. The justifying of the platen and the press stone was essential for a full and even impression because the former pressed the tympans holding the printing paper to the press stone, creating the impression. The sharpness of the impression was also accomplished by the use of hard packing in the tympans.

[5] Philip Gaskell notes that despite Baskerville's efforts to find a good ink, he failed, for the quality of eighteenth-century printing and its materials suffered from competition that drove tradesmen to cut expenses: since there was little call for quality ink, there was no motivation to produce it. (See *A New Introduction to Bibliography*. (New York and Oxford: Oxford University Press, 1972), p. 126.)

[6] RD's engraver for this job is not known.

[7] "*Quinti Horatii Flacci Opera*. Londini: Aeneis Tabulis Incidit Joannes Pine, MDCCXXXIII–VII." Pine's two-volume edition was heavily illustrated.

From Robert Lowth[1]

Winchester
Jan. 16. 1753.

S.r

Instead of informing you that my Book is ready for you, as you might by this time reasonably expect, I can only tell you of the delays & disappointments I have met with.[2] Last Month my Affairs were entirely at a stand for three weeks: My Composer was crippled with the Rhumatism, my Corrector taken ill of the Small pox, & my principal agent forced to fly from it. They are hard at work now, & promise me to finish with all possible expedition: every thing is printed off, but the Outworks, Contents, Index &c.; & I believe I may depend upon being ready to publish early next Month. I find my Expenses will rise higher than I imagined; & they tell me at Oxford that I cannot afford to sell under 12.s unbound; I suppose you will allow me 10.s[3] I will order them to be sent according to your directions.[4]

I have lately receiv'd from Italy, An Account of the Protestants in the Valleys of Piedmont: 'tis drawn up in the form of a Letter by a Friend of mine at my request, as I knew he had peculiar opportunitys & advantages in informing himself: and he gives me leave to publish it.[5] The Subject is interesting & curious: & my Friend's Acc.t will I think give satisfaction. It consists of 12 pages rather larger than this Paper, written very close in a very small hand; & I suppose will at least make a sixpenny Pamphlet.[6] As he is still in the Country & has spoken his mind freely, he does not choose to put his Name to it: but it need be no secret that I am the Publisher. Let me know what you think of this design, & perhaps I may send it to you soon.

I saw 'tother day in a Letter from M.r Garrick, that M.r Spence acknowledges himself to be the Author of y.e *Gamester*, a Dramatic piece now in rehearsal at Drury Lane. Pray explain this to me if you can.[7]

I left in your hands my receipt for D.r Newton's Milton: pray send it to me hither, together with the New Volume, neatly bound.[8]

Believe me, Dear S.r
Your most faithful
Humble Serv.t

Rob.t Lowth.

MS: BL. Add. MS. 35,339, ff. 1–2.

[1] Robert Lowth (1710–87), grammarian, author, Professor of Poetry at Oxford (1741–50), and Bishop of London (1777). Since he published most of his work at Tully's Head during the 1750s and 1760s, Lowth became a regular correspondent of RD's. It was to their friend, and Lowth's fellow prebend at Durham, Joseph Spence, that RD confided that Lowth had suggested the idea for RD's successful *Select Fables of Esop and other Fabulists* (1761).

[2] *De Sacra Poesi Hebraiorum* was published in London by RD and Andrew Millar and at Oxford by Richard Clements on 3 March 1753 (*LEP*), but printed in Winchester, perhaps by William Prior. See Lowth's letter to RD of late February 1753.

[3] It sold for twelve shillings, sewn.   [4] See Lowth's letter to RD of [late February] 1753.

[5] *A Brief Account of the Vaudois, His Sardinian Majesty's Protestant Subjects in Piedmont*, by Louis Devisme (1729–76), was published by RD two months later on 5 March (*LEP*). See Lowth's next letters to RD.

[6] It did.

[7] *The Gamester*, first performed at Drury Lane on 7 February 1753, was the work of Edward Moore (1712–57), the editor of RD's fashionable weekly, *The World* (1753–6). Arthur Murphy, in *The Life of David Garrick* (London, 1801), I, 232, tells us that because Moore's adaptation of Le Sage's *Gil Blas* had lasted only nine nights at Drury Lane two years earlier, the anxious playwright, in order to forestall another failure, managed to get his intimate friend Joseph Spence to whisper it about town that the play was his. See also Lowth's letter of late February.

[8] Thomas Newton (1704–82), to become Bishop of Bristol in 1761, had published an edition of Milton's *Paradise Lost* in 1749. No doubt Lowth's request for "the New Volume" refers to Newton's edition of *Paradise Regained: A Poem, in Four Books. To which is added Samson Agonistes; and Poems upon several Occasions*, to be published by the Tonsons and others the next day, 17 January (*PA*).

From Thomas Gray[1]

Camb:^ge Feb: 12. [1753][2]

Sr

I am not at all satisfied with the Title. to have it conceived, that I publish a Collection of *Poems* (half a dozen little Matters, four of wch too have already been printed again and again) thus pompously adorned would make me appear very justly ridiculous. I desire it may be understood (wch is the truth) that the Verses are only subordinate, & explanatory to the Drawings, & suffer'd by me to come out thus only for that reason. therefore if you yourself prefix'd this Title, I desire it may be alter'd; or if M^r W: order'd it so, that you would tell him, why I wish it were changed in the manner I mention'd to you at first, or to that purpose: for the more I consider it, the less I can bear it, as it now stands.[3] I even think, there is an uncommon sort of Simplicity, that looks like affectation, in putting our plain Christian & Surnames with a M^r before them; but this (if it signifies any thing) I easily give up;[4] the other I can not. you need not apprehend, that this Change in the Title will be any prejudice to the Sale of the book. a showy title-page may serve to sell a Pamphlet of a shilling or two; but this is not of a price for chance-customers, whose eye is caught in passing by a window; & could never sell but from the notion the Town may entertain of the Merit of the Drawings, wch they will be instructed in by some, that understand such things.[5]

I thank you for the Offer you make me, but I shall be contented with three Copies, two of wch you will send me, & keep the third, till I acquaint you where to send it. if you will let me know the exact day they will come out a little time beforehand, I will give you a direction. you will remember to send two copies to Dr Thomas Wharton, M:D: at Durham.[6] perhaps you may have burnt my Letter, so I will again put down the Title

Designs by M^r R: Bentley
for six Poems of
M^r T: Gray.

I am, S^r,   Your Humble Servt

TG:

Address: To / Mr Dodsley

Source: Correspondence of Thomas Gray, eds. Paget Toynbee and Leonard Whibley (Oxford: Clarendon Press, 1935), I, p. 371.

1 Thomas Gray (1716–71), poet and Professor of History and Modern Languages at Cambridge (1768). Although RD was the sole publisher of all of Gray's major poems from 1747 through 1759, including eleven editions of *An Elegy Written in a Country Church Yard*, this letter is the sole surviving example of their correspondence. It seems Gray preferred to conduct business with RD through their friend Horace Walpole. Judging from the tone of this letter and from comments in various letters to Walpole, Gray had little regard for either RD's learning or literary ability. See, for example, his letter of July 1752, No. 169 in *The Correspondence of Thomas Gray*, eds. Paget Toynbee and Leonard Whibley (Oxford: Clarendon Press, 1935).

2 The year is determined from the letter's subject; namely, the forthcoming *Designs by Mr. Bentley for Six Poems by Mr. Gray*, published by RD on 29 March 1753 (*PA*).

3 Lacking his letter to Gray, one can only guess at the title RD proposed. It might well have been the title that appeared in the advertisements for the work, curiously enough, more than a month after this letter from Gray: "Poems by Mr. Gray; with Designs by Mr. Bentley." Nonetheless the actual title page of the work followed the direction Gray gives above. "M.ʳ W" is most likely Horace Walpole. It was to Walpole that Gray had written exactly two years earlier (11 February 1751), urging him to press RD to publish Walpole's copy of the *Elegy Written in a Country Church Yard* within a week's time in order to preempt a version the *Magazine of Magazines* had planned to publish.

4 RD obliged Gray on this matter as well.

5 The drawings were executed by Richard Bentley the younger. See his letter to RD on 20 November 1758. According to Herbert W. Starr, *A Bibliography of Thomas Gray, 1917–1951, with Material supplementary to C. S. Northrup's Bibliography* (Philadelphia: University of Pennsylvania Press for Temple University Publications, 1953), other editions did not appear until 1765, 1766, 1775, and 1789.

6 Thomas Wharton (1715?–94), Pembroke College, Cambridge, MA, 1741; MD, 1752; practiced in London for a few years before moving to Old Park, Durham, his family's estate.

From Robert Lowth

Winchester Feb 24. 1753.

S.ʳ

I am glad M.ʳ Millar agrees to the terms, w.ᶜʰ I thought I had quite settled with you before.[1] I have nothing to add on that head, but that I am willing that you should charge to me the expence of Stitching, for such as you may sell stitch'd, & any thing else that is reasonable or customary.[2] Advertising [I] must entirely committ to your Judgement: [don]'t spare expence to hurt the cause. [I] expect you will advertise now immediatly; [I hope] you will publish as soon as possibly [you can]; for the Season is far advanc'd.[3]

Believe me, Dear S.ʳ

Your most faithful humble Serv.ᵗ

R. Lowth

Address: To M.ʳ Dodsley / in Pall Mall / London

Postmark: 26 FE Winchester

MS: BL. Add. MS. 35,339, ff. 3–4.

1 See Lowth's letter of 16 January where he reports the progress on the printing of his *De Sacra Poesi Hebraiorum* in Winchester, a work he was about to send up to London to be published by RD. Perhaps

Andrew Millar had been a partner from the beginning, but no mention had been made of him in that earlier letter. Strangely enough, as Lowth's next letter indicates, RD will receive his copies from Millar.   ² See Lowth's previous letter, note 3.
³ The work was advertised as published on 3 March (*LEP*, 1–3 March).

From Robert Lowth

[Winches]ter [late February] 1753.¹

S.ʳ

I have receiv'd Newton's Milton, & Setts of M.ʳ Warton's Virgil;² but no [le]tter, or any intimation for whom these [O]ther are design'd.

I believe my Book will be sent to you [&] M.ʳ Millar the beginning of the week: [I] have order'd 200 to you, & 100 to him.³ [I] have forgot whether you did not order [20]o: if this should be a mistake, you [can] easily rectify it by writing to M.ʳ [Clem]ents at Oxford.⁴ I inclose a List [of Per]sons to be Presented, with all necessary [directi]ons about it.⁵ You must order the [Book?] Binder not to *beat* the Title, Inscrip[tion] & 6 last Sheets: the rest will bear [?] well. I leave the business of Advertising to You: R. Clements is the Bookseller concern'd at Oxford.

I send you likewise the Account of [the] Vaudois.⁶ As to the manner of Printin[g] all I can say is, that I would have [it] done very neatly, & as correctly as possi[ble.] The Author, I suppose, will want some Copys for his Friends; I have not ye[t] directions about it; but shall order im[me]diatly a Dozen to a Relation of hi[s.]⁷ I suppose you will allow us as many [as] he will want. I send you his Manu[script] in w.ᶜʰ by his desire I have corre[cted] all inaccuracys of Expression that o[ccur] to me. You will observe that [the line] drawn sometimes at the bottom of [the page] is, not for *Italicks*, but to separa[te the re]ferences from the text. In pa[ge is] a Reference in my hand, w.ᶜʰ I have added [for] the Readers' satisfaction, and have mark'd for *Ita[lic]ks*, as it is an addition. In the same [pa]ge I have taken the liberty of striking [ou]t a Line, w.ᶜʰ seems to me inconsistent, [or] false, or at least obscure: you may, [if] you please, insert in its place the follow[ing] words: "who had as little compassion & [gen]erosity, as zeal for the Protestant cause," – [bu]t it will do very well without any supple[m]ent.⁸ Pray let me know what you pro[p]ose to do in this business, & how my [?] is like to go on & when we are to [pub]lish.⁹ I had pretty well made out [Sp]ence's secret before you told it me, [how] does the plot succeed?¹⁰

[B]elieve me, Dear S.ʳ

Your most faithful
Humble Serv.ᵗ

R. Lowth.

MS: BL. Add. MS. 35,339, ff. 5–6.

¹ The month is fairly certain from Lowth's mentioning in the text that RD will receive two hundred copies of *De Sacra Poesi Hebraiorum* within the week, a work RD advertised for sale, as of 3 March 1753 (*LEP*, 1–3 March); and Lowth's mentioning having received "Setts of M.ʳ Warton's Virgil," a work RD issued on 25 January 1753 (*PA*).

² See Lowth's letter of 16 January 1753, note 8. *The Works of Virgil, in Latin and English*, edited by Joseph
  Warton and published by RD, actually comprised Christopher Pitt's translation of the *Aeneid* (RD,
  1740) and Warton's translation of the *Eclogues* and *Georgics*, as well as essays by Edward Holdsworth,
  Joseph Spence, William Warburton, William Whitehead, and Francis Atterbury.
³ *De Sacra Poesi Hebraiorum*. See Lowth's previous letter, note 1.   ⁴ See below in text.
⁵ Lowth's list seems lost.
⁶ By Louis Devisme. See Lowth's letters of 16 January, and 15 March 1753.
⁷ Apparently Mr Hayward of Throgmorton St., London, to whom RD is later directed to send twelve
  copies. (See Lowth's letter of 15 March 1753. A Mr Thomas Hayward is listed at this address in *A
  Complete Guide to all Persons who have any Trade or Concern with the City of London, and Parts Adjacent*, 6th edn.
  (London: T. & T. Longman *et al.*, 1755) and as a hosier in *Kent's Directory for the Year 1759* (London:
  Henry Kent, 1759), p. 56.
⁸ Lacking the original manuscript, we cannot say whether or not, or how, RD made the change. But he
  did not include the clause suggested above by Lowth.   ⁹ See note 1.
¹⁰ See Lowth's letter to RD on 16 January, note 7.

From Robert Lowth

Winchester Mar. 7. 1753.

Dear Sʳ

  I have just had a letter from Italy from my Friend the Author of the Accᵗ of yᵉ
Vaudois, wᶜʰ I want to answer immediatly, but don't care to write till I can send
him some News of the Pamphlet.¹ If 'tis ready, pray send it me: if not, let me know
when it will be publish'd, & something particular of the form & manner in wᶜʰ 'tis
printed.²

  Pray send by the first opportunity one of my Books (*sew'd*) to the Revᵈ Mʳ Ridley
at Rumford Essex:³ I forgot him in my List. Are all yᵉ Presents deliver'd?

Believe me, Dear Sʳ

Your most Affect. humble Servᵗ

R. Lowth

Address: To Mʳ Dodsley / in Pall Mall / London
Postmark: Winchester [?]

MS: BL. Add. MS. 35,339, ff. 7–8.

¹ Louis Devisme. See Lowth's letter of 16 January 1753.
² The work appeared on 17 March 1753 (*LEP*, 15–17 March) as a 6*d.* pamphlet, running thirty-two
  pages in octavo.
³ *De Sacra Poesi Hebraiorum*, published four days earlier. Like Lowth, Glocester Ridley (1702–74) was an
  alumnus of both Winchester and New College, Oxford.

From Theodore, Baron de Neuhoff, King of Corsica¹

This 8 March [17]53

Sir

ÿou will oblige me Verÿ much to Come to see me The Bearer of this is one Mʳ Taÿlor
Clauss that serves me this 3 ÿear & is plainlÿ Informed of mÿ affaires & procedings

in this place. & to whom I trust all mÿ Commissions. So ÿou could not come the da

here, ÿou maÿ informe the Bearer Clauss of what, I'am to eẍpect from the pub
lished subscription, of w[h]ich, as of the promoter, I'am still unacquainted.² abou
the actions & Charges that are Superseded & the ot[h]er adjusted in paÿing th
half the Bearer will Informe ÿou, and I by our Deliverance shall assure ÿou that i
ani time & place ÿou shall command convinced that I'am ÿr assured & gratefu l
friend³

Th̰ː B̰ⁿ de Newho

Address: To M̰ː Dodsleÿ / At The Tully's head / Pall Mall
[Endorsed by Horace Walpole:] "Letter from King Theodore"⁴

MS: Lewis Walpole Library, Farmington, Connecticut. I am indebted to John C. Riely for calling m
attention to this piece.

¹ Theodore Etienne, Baron de Neuhoff (1694–1756) involved RD in the most remarkable and wryl
pathetic story told in this collection of letters. Theodore, an adventurer from Westphalia, German
had married an Irish girl in the suite of the Queen of Spain and then absconded in 1720; he visite
England and Holland before taking up residence in Florence in the imperial service; then whe
Corsica was in rebellion against France in 1736, he was persuaded by the Corsicans to unite the
forces against France as Theodore I of Corsica. In 1738, he was driven from Corsica by the Frenc
and after two unsuccessful attempts to regain his throne (1738, 1743), he continued to live in exil
Sometime in the 1740s, he came to London, living in Mayfair, where he courted and was courted b
the best of social circles as a rare regal phenomenon. But, living much beyond his means, he was soo
heavily in debt and, in 1749, was arrested by bailiffs and placed in King's Bench Prison. (*The Briti*
Magazine, March 1751, p. 161, claims the Marshalsea Prison, Southwark.) His Majesty initiall
enjoyed celebrity there, entertaining sympathizers and curiosity seekers alike, even investing some i
the "Order of Deliverance" for their gifts and "loyal" attention. But, failing to coax from them a su
adequate to pay his debts, he languished in prison until 24 June 1755, when he was dismissed thanks t
the Act of Insolvency, leaving his kingdom of Corsica to his creditors. He lingered about London fo
another year, broken, poverty-stricken, and abandoned, until he died on 11 December 1756. He wa
buried in St Anne's churchyard, Soho. His story is told in brief by an inscription on a marble ston
marking his grave, supposedly erected by Horace Walpole. As printed in both the *London Chronicle* an
the *London Evening Post*, the inscription read:

> Near this place is interred
> Theodore, King of Corsica,
> Who died in this parish Dec. 11, 1756
> Immediately after leaving
> The King's bench prison,
> By the benefit of the act of insolvency:
> In consequence of which
> He registered his kingdom of Corsica
> For the use of his creditors.
> The grave, great teacher, to a level brings
> Heroes and beggars, galley-slaves and Kings;
> But Theodore this moral learn'd e're dead;
> Fate pour'd its lessons on his living head,
> Bestow'd a kingdom, and deny'd him bread.

(For a scholarly account, see André Le Glay, *Theodore de Neuhoff, roi de Corse* (Paris, 1907). Popula
versions are Valerie Pirie's *His Majesty of Corsica: The True Story of the Adventurous Life of Theodore i*
(London, 1939), and Aylmer Vallance's *The Summer King* (London: Thames & Hudson, 1956

Theodore makes a pathetic appearance, with five other dethroned monarchs, in Voltaire's *Candide*, chap. 26.)
2 Through the instigation of Horace Walpole, RD agreed to print in his new periodical *The World* a subscription appeal for the distressed monarch lying in prison. Accordingly, in the issue of 22 February 1753 appeared "*Date obolum Belisario*" ("Give an Obolum to Belisarius"; Belisarius was the renowned general who, during the reign of Justinian, was imprisoned for conspiring against the Emperor; an "obolum" was a Greek coin worth approximately 1½*d*.). However, so cruelly playful was the petition in suggesting that Garrick give a benefit performance of *King Lear* for the dethroned monarch and in portraying RD as the "high-treasurer and grand-librarian of the Island of Corsica for life" who would receive all subscriptions in Pall Mall that the town responded with more laughs than donations. Consequently RD found it necessary to print a clarifying statement under his own name in the next number of *The World* (1 March), assuring potential contributors that the appeal had not been facetious. Impatiently awaiting the result of the subscription, Theodore sent RD the present letter, inquiring as to how much he might expect from his sympathizers.
3 Theodore's tone changed, however, when RD reported a mere £50 had been collected. According to Horace Walpole, the monarch was so chagrined that he sent his man back to RD, threatening a law suit for using his name in vain! (*Horace Walpole's Correspondence with Horace Mann*, ed. W. S. Lewis, Vol. 20, p. 374.)
4 At one time, Walpole had considered writing a life of Theodore, and RD had probably passed this letter on to him for that purpose. (*Correspondence of Horace Walpole with Thomas Gray*, ed. W. S. Lewis, Vol. 13, p. 28, note 186.)

From Robert Lowth

Winchester March 13. 1753.

Dear Sʳ

I think the Pamphlet is very well printed:[1] I see no material Error in it, except the word *Seal* instead of *Seat*, at wᶜʰ I hesitated my self: 'tis towards the end; I can't tell you the Page, for I have it not just now by me.[2] – I believe I may assure you that the Irish Bishops in the List are all in Ireland, & I suppose at Dublin:[3] You said you would send some Copys thither to Fawkner;[4] you may send these at the same time, sow'd in Marble Paper. Are the Two in Morocco ready? I have sent to Mʳ Dobson an order upon you for a Book, (*sow'd* will do), not knowing how to direct you to him.[5] Remember me to Mʳ Spe[nce.]

Address: To Mʳ Dodsley / in Pall Mall / London
Postmark: 14 MR

MS: BL. Add. MS. 35,339, ff. 9–10.

1 Louis Devisme's *A Brief Account of the Vaudois*, to be published by RD two days later (*LEP*).
2 p. 25. See Lowth's next letter, 15 March.
3 Lowth probably refers to the Irish bishops he wanted presented with gifts of *De Sacra*. He had enclosed a list in his letter of late February and had asked RD in his letter on 7 March whether or not the bookseller had delivered all presents. Apparently RD had difficulty locating all the bishops.
4 George Faulkner (1699?–1775), Dublin bookseller. For his publishing relationship with RD, see RD's letter to him on 28 October and the editor's note in *The Library*, 5th ser. 32 (1977), 52–5.
5 Perhaps the William Dobson (also of New College, Oxford) mentioned in Christopher Pitt's letter to RD 1 June–9 August 1744, note 4.

From Robert Lowth

[Winc]hester [Mar]ch. 15. [1753].[1]

Dear S.[r]

I receiv'd by the last Post another letter from the Author of the *Account*, in w.[ch], he directs me to send some of them to his Friends; w.[ch] as I suppose it is already Publish'd by this time,[2] I must beg you to do immediatly, as follows: To M.[r] Hayward in Throgmorton Street 12,[3] more One Copy to

The Arch B.[p] of Canterbury	The Duke of Bolton
B.[ps] of Bristol	L.[d] George Cavendish
Glocester	L.[d] Frederick Cavendish
Durham	L.[d] Grentham
Exeter	L.[d] Pulteney
Salisbury	Augustus Schutz Esq.[r]
S.[t] Asaph	(*in Brook Street*
Rochester	S.[r] W.[m] Yonge Bar.[t4]

These to be sent without any mention of the Author's name: but if any of them make any enquirys after him of you, you may tell them if you please from me, that 'tis M.[r] Devisme Chaplain to L.[d] Rochford at Turin.[5] Send one if you please from me to the B.[p] Norwich.[6] To the same M.[r] Hayward pray send two more of my Books *bound* directed likewise to L.[d] Rochford at Turin as before, & in the same parcell put up Leland's Answer to L.[d] Bolingbroke's Letters, & any other Answers to the same that are in y.[e] ⟨good⟩ best esteem.[7] My friend orders me 12 Copys of the *Account*; I have no demand for them here: but if you will please to give half a dozen to M.[r] Spence [?] judiciously [?][8] perhaps want more Copys yet; he does not know what number you will allow him, but is ready to pay for those y.[t] exceed [it] Pag. 25. for *Seal* read *Seat*.[9]

I am, Dear S.[r]

Your most faithful

humble Serv.[t]

R. Lowth

If M.[r] Hayward should want any more of the pamphlets, pray let him have them, accounted to the Author.[10]

Address: To M.[r] Dodsley / in Pall Mall / London
Postmark: 16 MR

MS: BL. Add. MS. 35,339, ff. 11–12.

[1] The year is determined on the basis of the appearance of Louis Devisme's *A Short Account of the Vaudois* (15 March 1753), the subject of the letter.   [2] See note 1.
[3] Hayward, a relative of Devisme (see Lowth's letter of late February) was apparently responsible for sending copies to Devisme. In that earlier letter, Lowth ordered twelve copies for Devisme's friends to be sent to the author's relative. In addition, Lowth had RD send copies of his own *De Sacra* for Lord Turin to Hayward. See below.
[4] Canterbury, Thomas Herring (1693–1757); Bristol, Thomas Newton (1704–82); Gloucester, James

Johnson (1705–74); Durham, Richard Trevor (1707–71); Exeter, George Lavington (1684–1762); Salisbury, John Gilbert (1693–1761); St Asaph, Robert Drummond (1711–76); Rochester, Joseph Wilcocks (1673–1756); Bolton, Charles Paulet (1685–1754), 3rd Duke; George Cavendish (1727–94); Frederick Cavendish (1729–1803); Grantham, Henry D'Auverquerque (*c.* 1672–1754); William Pulteney (1684–1764), Earl of Bath; Schutz, unidentified; William Yonge (*c.* 1693–1755), 4th Baronet.

5 William Henry Zuylestein (1717–81), 4th Earl of Rochford and Envoy to Sardinia, 1749–55.
6 Thomas Hayter (1702–62).
7 Henry St John, Lord Bolingbroke's *Letters on the Study and Use of History*, edited by David Mallet, had appeared the previous year. John Leland (1691–1766) answered Bolingbroke on 23 January 1753 (*PA*) with *Reflections on the late Lord Bolingbroke's Letters on the Study and Use of History; Especially so far as they relate to Christianity and the Holy Scriptures* (London: Ben Dodd, 1753). Several other attacks and defenses had appeared, including Voltaire's *A Defence of my Lord Bolingbroke's Letters on the Study of History*, which had been published slightly more than a month before Lowth's letter, on 9 February (*PA*).   8 The manuscript is badly broken off at this point.
9 See also Lowth's letter of 13 March. Apparently it was too late to make the change, and the *Account* did not reach a second edition.   10 See note 3.

From Benjamin Victor[1]

Dublin, August, 1753

My dear Dodsley,

My worthy friend Mr. *Tickell* is just arrived here, and at our first interview he gave me the pleasure of hearing him speak very advantageously of you.[2] He tells me, Sir *William Wolseley* has but very lately apprised you of my intention to be indebted to your care for the printing and publishing a work I have just finished; you have I presume, heard of the subject – It has swelled to three hundred pages in manuscript of a *quarto* size, which perhaps will make about the same number in *octavo*.[3]

I would have it printed on my account, as I take it for granted, you (and any London bookseller) would think me stark mad, if they heard the value I set on the copy. I suppose you will fix the price at two shillings unbound, if it will bear six-pence more, so much the better.[4] I would have three thousand printed off in the first impression; I dont doubt you think that number preposterous– but you are to take this into consideration, that all other *new* books have the curiosity of the public to raise, but that difficulty is conquered already, and not only London, but every county in England is full of expectation; as it is the most unparalleled story, *founded on facts*, that ever appeared since the creation.

I shall send the copy by a safe hand to you, and desire *Sir William Wolseley* (as it is written at his request) to apply to you for a sight of it, because it may be necessary for him to get some able friend of his at the *bar* to look it carefully over, that no offence may be given to the forms of *law*; but I desire the copy may be delivered to no one but *Sir William* in person. The paper and type I shall leave to your choice, only remember the affidavits must be in Italic's.[5]

I know you to be an honest man – and in this case, I expect and desire, that you deal with me as a man of business which admits of no compliment. If you have any doubts about the success of the sale, and of its being able to pay the expence of printing and publishing, let me know it and I will give you any security in London;

for my own part, I shall think myself sufficiently obliged to you, for your care and trouble on this occasion; as the correcting the press must fall to your share; that favour will lay me under an infinite obligation, which I shall gratefully acknowledge whenever you think proper to command the service,

Of your friend and servant.

Source: Benjamin Victor, *Original Letters, Dramatic Pieces and Poems.* (3 vols. London: T. Becket, 1776), I, 209–11.

1 Benjamin Victor (d. 1778) ran an Irish linen business in Pall Mall from 1734 to 1746, and thereby was RD's neighbor during the first decade of their respective businesses. In 1746, he had left England to become treasurer and deputy manager at Smock Alley Theatre in Dublin, positions he held until 1759. The work described in note 3 seems to have been the only one of Victor's issued from Tully's Head during RD's years.
2 John Tickell (1729–82) of Glasnevin, son of Thomas Tickell (1686–1740), and a minor Irish poet. In an undated letter, but one placed immediately before another of 1753 in his *Original Letters* (pp. 204–5), Victor apologizes to John for not having written earlier a letter of introduction for him to his "agreeable" contact in London, especially "knowing you to be in a dangerous place for a man of your sprightly enterprising temper, and one of the *Virtuosi*; but Osborne and Dodsley will prove to you most attractive." For John Tickell, see Richard Tickell, *The Tickells and Connected Families* (London: Witherley, 1948), p. 54.
3 Sir William Wolseley, 5th Baronet of Staffordshire (d. 1779). With Wolseley as his intercessor, surprisingly Victor's work told the real-life story of how Wolseley himself, as a widower aged sixty, was deceived into a quick secret marriage with a 28-year-old neighbor, Anne Whitby, a widow who was already pregnant with her lover's child. Although Victor's next letter (12 November) implies RD's initial interest, the delicate nature of the matter probably caused RD to balk at publishing the work; it didn't appear for another year and a half (*PA*, 2 April 1755), and then with only Charles Corbett's name in the imprint. Victor's work was entitled *The Widow of the Wood, Being an authentic Narrative of a Late remarkable Transaction in Staffordshire.*   4 *The Widow* sold for 2s.6d.
5 Approximately 140 pages of this 206-page account consist of affidavits supplied by witnesses at the hearing of the case. In the printed text, only the reading of each testimony is set off by italics.

To William Shenstone

Pall mall Sep^t 29.th [1753]^1

Sir

I had fully intended my self the Pleasure of waiting on You this Summer, but many Avocations prevented me; but I hope next Summer to be a little more at Leisure. I am now thinking of putting my Fourth Volume of Poems to Press, and shall esteem it as a particular Obligation if You will contribute to render it more acceptable to the Public, by favouring me with any thing which You shall think proper to appear in it.^2 I have a copy of your Pastoral Ballad, but I think you told me you had a more correct one.^3 Any time within a month will be soon enough for my purpose, and the larger your Packet ye greater will be the Obligation laid on^4

Sir

Your most oblig'd & obed^t Servt

R. Dodsley

Address: To William Shenstone Esq.ʳ / at the Leasows near / Stratford upon Avon /
Warwickshire
Postmarks: SE 29; OC 3 Noe such place neare Stratford⁵
Frank: R. Dodsley *free*⁶

MS: BL. Add. MS. 28,959, ff. 12–13.

¹ The year is verified in RD's letter to Shenstone on 10 November 1753, where he admits having missent
  his former letter to Stratford. See the postmark on this letter.
² The fourth volume of RD's *Collection of Poems by Several Hands* did not appear, however, until 18 March
  1755. See RD's letters to Shenstone on 12 January and 23 February 1754.
³ For more than a year, RD would continue to hound Shenstone for the "Pastoral Ballad." When RD
  was approaching his deadline for Vol. IV of the *Collection* in late autumn of the next year, Shenstone
  was still frantically making revisions, resorting to Richard Graves and Thomas Percy for assistance.
  Finally, in his letter of 19 November 1754, RD thanked Shenstone for sending the ballad but still
  questioned its conclusion. The story of the evolution of the often revised and supplemented "Pastoral
  Ballad" and an account of the extant versions, complete with texts, is found in Brooks, pp. 239–304.
  Brooks shows that the first version originates from as early as 1740 or 1741; notes A. J. Sambrook's
  discovery of the first printed edition, published in the *London Magazine* of December 1751 (Sambrook,
  RES, n. s. 18, 169–73); and determines that the final version was that which RD was about to print in
  the fourth volume of his *Collection*. This last text, with some slight (mostly accidental) changes was the
  version RD used in his edition of Shenstone's *Works* (1764).
⁴ By the time of publication, a year and a half later, Shenstone had sent at least five packets containing
  poems written by both himself and his friends. (See RD's letters of 10 November 1753, 12 January
  1754, 27 August 1754, and 18 January 1755; and Richard Graves's letter of 26 October 1754.)
⁵ See RD's next letter, on 10 November, and note 3.
⁶ RD's franking this letter, and thirteen others to Shenstone through 28 July 1755, has proved
  inexplicable to the bibliographical and postal experts I have consulted or read. Nothing we know of
  Dodsley qualified him to use the privilege. Yet he would certainly not have openly defied the law for
  nearly two years, given his keen concern for his reputation and business. Taking a cue from Jeremy
  Greenwood (*Newspapers and the Post Office 1635–1834* (London: Postal History Society, 1971), David
  Foxon has suggested to me that perhaps Dodsley had gained the privilege from the Post Office's Clerks
  of the Roads, who officially franked newspapers sent into the provinces. The clerks employed
  numerous agents in London to collect, wrap, and frank these papers. Dodsley, as the publisher of the
  weekly periodical *The World* and as a shareholder in the most influential paper sent into the country,
  the *London Evening Post*, might have been so employed. If so, perhaps he construed the privilege of
  franking as extending to his letters. In support of Foxon's suggestion, it is significant that the letters
  were franked within the period during which *The World* was appearing (January 1753, through
  December 1756). (In his letter of 26 August 1751, John Gilbert Cooper reports to RD that he had
  received a letter three days earlier "frank'd by you." However it is not clear – since RD's letter is
  missing – whether Cooper means RD *personally* franked the letter or that he had it franked by a
  privileged person.)
    Another explanation is found in the possibility that Dodsley had been appointed by a minister
  enjoying the franking privilege to endorse letters on the latter's behalf. George Brumel (*A Short Account
  of the Franking System in the Post Office: 1652–1840* (Bournemouth: Bournemouth Guardian, Ltd, 1936),
  p. 9) notes that, by a postal act of 1764, "Ministers might appoint others to frank their letters, whose
  names were to be notified to the Postmaster-General: those sending letters were to sign their name on
  the outside and themselves write the address." Although the specification of such an arrangement first
  appears in a law enacted eleven years after Dodsley's initial endorsement, it is not unlikely that such
  extensions of the privilege occurred earlier than the date of legal sanction; in short, that the law merely
  codified custom. If such is the case, Dodsley might have gained the privilege through his friend
  George, Lord Lyttelton, Shenstone's neighbor at Hagley and an author of two works Dodsley had

already put through several editions. Significantly, Lyttelton, throughout the period of these letters, was a lord of the Treasury, the board that controlled the operation of the Post Office.

Although one of these explanations might resolve the mystery, a few questions remain. Why did Dodsley discontinue the practice in mid-1755? Why in the midst of this series of frankings is one of Dodsley's letters to Shenstone – 24 January 1755 – franked by "J. Harris"?

To Joseph Warton[1]

Pall Mall, Sept. 29, 175[3][2]

Dear Sir,

That I am an insufferably bad correspondent, all my friends, with too much reason, complain: and I am afraid I sometimes sin this way beyond forgiveness. However, I have in my own mind made great resolutions of amendment: and when one considers how delightful it is to talk to an absent friend, it is amazing how one can possibly be guilty of the crime of neglect. But the practice of every virtue is delightful, and yet the world continues to be a wicked world: so true it is that man is a heap of contradictions. One good thing however attends this neglect of writing to one's friends too punctually, which is, that one sometimes gets almost to the bottom of the first page in making an apology. I was extremely sorry we could not spare time to call on you in our return from Portsmouth; our party was Mr. Giffard and his wife, and I and mine; and when women are in the way (don't let Mrs. Warton see this) a man can never do what he ought.[3] I prodigiously admire your character of Mr. Bedingfield, who you say has actually refin'd his taste to a degree that makes him dissatisfy'd with almost every composition; don't you think then that he is in almost the same situation with Horace's recover'd madman?[4] What are you doing? and what is your Brother doing? I hear he has laid aside all thoughts of Apollonius.[5] I think he is right: but I would not have him lie still. I am just going to put my fourth volume of poems to press, and wish he would send me a corrected copy of his Pleasures of Melancholy, and Triumphs of Isis.[6] And have you nothing to send me? Whitehead's play does not come on this winter, there is no room for it. Glover's Boadicea comes in in November. And Garrick is engag'd for a play of a Mr. Crisp in February.[7] I have never thought of mine since, and probably never shall.[8] Let me first see what will be said to my Agriculture, which is now finish't, and will be published in November.[9] Compliments to Mrs. Warton and your Brother. Sha'nt we see him or you, or both, in town this winter?

                                        I am ever yours,

                                                        R. Dodsley.

Source: John Wooll, *Biographical Memoirs of the late Revd. Joseph Warton, D.D.* (London: T. Cadell and W. Davies, 1806), pp. 224–5.

---

[1] Joseph Warton (1722–1800), like his brother Thomas, published his early works through RD. In fact their relationship seems to have been quite intimate. In his six letters to Warton printed here, RD, on one occasion, apologizes for not visiting Warton when passing through southern England, on another, looks forward to Warton's London visit, and in several instances inquires after Mrs Warton.

Especially telling is the freedom RD feels in proposing false excuses to mollify public resentment should Warton proceed with his suggested plan of abbreviating the second volume of his *Essay on the Writings and Genius of Mr. Pope* (1756).

2 Wooll's dating the letter as "1754" must be wrong. Within, RD says his poem *Agriculture* is to be published in November, and indeed it appeared on 19 November 1753. (The whole rights were registered to R&JD at the Stationers' Co. on 20 November.) Besides, in his letter to Warton of *post* 19 November 1753, RD says that he has just sent *Agriculture* "last night," presumably upon its publication, for he is hoping it will be well received at Oxford.

3 Possibly the Rev. Richard Gifford (1725–1807), whose poem *Contemplation* RD had published the previous April and who figures in later letters.

4 Robert Bedingfield (1720–1768?) of Oxford. (See Courtney, pp. 75–6.) Bedingfield's "Education of Achilles" had appeared in the *Museum*, III, 30 (9 May 1747), 127–31, and had been reprinted in RD's *Collection*, III, 121–7. Warton praised Bedingfield in his *Essay on Pope*, I, 47; II, 35. On 7 June of this year, Warton wrote to his brother Thomas: "Compliments to Bedingfield. I am glad he is emerging into life from Hertford Coll" (Wooll, *Biographical Memoirs*, p. 217).

5 On 21 January 1752, Warton's brother, Thomas, had signed an agreement with RD by which he promised to deliver a translation of the *Argonautics* of Apollonius Rhodius by January of the present year. (See Appendix B.)

6 Apparently RD had difficulty gathering and preparing the material for the fourth volume, for he later decided not to print it "this winter." (See his letter to Shenstone on 12 January 1754.) In fact, it did not appear until 18 March 1755.

Thomas Warton's *Pleasures of Melancholy* had originally been published by RD in 1747; *The Triumph of Isis, a Poem. Occasioned by Isis, an Elegy* [by William Mason] had appeared under the imprint of W. Owen in 1749. Although the former would be printed in RD's *Collection* (IV, 214), the latter would not.

7 William Whitehead's *Creusa, Queen of Athens* was first acted at Drury Lane on 20 April 1754 and published by RD nine days later, the same day on which he registered the "whole rights" to his name at the Stationers' Company. However it seems RD's purchase of the copyright from Whitehead for 100 guineas did not occur until 21 May (see Appendix B). On 8 December 1753 (*PA*), Richard Glover's tragedy was also published by RD, after its first performance at Drury Lane on 1 December. Samuel Crisp's *Virginia. A Tragedy* was printed for R. and J. Tonson and S. Draper on 7 March 1754 (*PA*) after a luke-warm reception at Drury Lane on 25 February 1754. Crisp's name was "Samuel," not "Henry," as reported in *The London Stage*, Pt. IV, Vol. I. The error seems to have been generated by David Baker *et al.* in *Biographia Dramatica* (1812). See Mrs Clement Parsons, *Garrick and His Circle* (London, 1906), p. 194.

8 RD's tragedy *Cleone*, to become a controversial subject when Garrick refused it a performance at Drury Lane. (See the later correspondence between Garrick and RD.)

9 See note 2.

From John Berckenhout[1]

Brunswick Oct.ʳ 28 [17]53

Sir,

If you are in the least acquainted with what pa[sses] in Germany in the learned way, you must have heard of a famous poem which appeard a while ago under the title of the Messiah. The Author's name is Klopstock; who was, when he publish'd his poem, but a poor student; but is now in the enjoyment of a pension given him by the King of Denmark to enable him to finish is Messiah in tranquility. He has hitherto publish'd but five books; we are promis'd three more very shortly, which are actually in the [press] and the rest will follow as fast as possible: for, [? sch] the whole is nearly finish'd.[2]

[What] hitherto appeard hath met with great Success [in] germany, in spite of its being wrote in a kind of verse intirely new to the Germans. This poem seems to me the best sequal to Milton that can be produc'd.[3] I have therefore amus'd myself in translating it into Miltonic verse: vz the two first books; and if these succeed in England shall continue the work. I shou'd be pleas'd if Mr Dodsley wou'd undertake the publication: for as I am absent, it is by no means indifferent to me to whom it is committed. You will therefore oblige me if, in answer, you will send me your proposals; or rather give me your advice in what manner to proceed.[4] I wou'd willingly have it appear in a manner that may do honor to the Author, translator, publisher and printer. If you cou'd answer for their being very good, I cou'd wish to have a plate expressive of the subject before each book; for which I wou'd transmit you my designs. The Germans have ⟨have⟩ of late begun to Study our language, and in most of their Courts and by most of their literati 'tis at least understood Insomuch that ⟨few of⟩ all our poets of note are well known on the continent.[5] Now as this will be the first translation from this language into English, a very considerable sale may be depended on in this part of the world.[6] But I shall be able to tell you more of this after I have spoke with the booksellers who frequent the Lipzick fare; which affords the most considerable sale of book of any place in Europe.

Your hum^b Serv!

J Berckenhout
Officier dans le Regiment
de Tunderfeld.[7]

MS: Bodleian, MS. Montagu, d. 11, f. 163.

---

[1] John Berckenhout (1730?–91) was the son of a Leeds merchant who had migrated from Holland. The *DNB* indicates that the father had sent young Berckenhout to Germany to learn the language in preparation for a career in commerce but that the youth, shortly after, lost interest in business and joined the Prussian army. However, in an anonymous script on the concluding blank pages of a copy of the younger Berckenhout's pseudonymous *Three Original Poems; being the Posthumous Works of Pendavid Bitterzwigg, Esq.* (1750) (copy belonging to the University of Kentucky Libraries, Lexington), the author claims his own father to have been a "very intimate friend" of Berckenhout's father and explains how Berckenhout had been swindled from his inheritance at his father's death and had fled to Germany, not to learn but to escape his distress. Although the *DNB* and contemporary sources spell Berckenhout's name without a "c," his own signature in this and in the letters to follow clearly show his own spelling, and so it is used here. For a fuller consideration of this letter and of Berckenhout's third and last letter to RD, see my note, "What Ever Happened to Berckenhout's Klopstock?" *Revue de Littérature Comparée*, 51 (1977), 73–9. Unfortunately his 10 December 1753 letter had not yet surfaced at the time of the *Revue* note.

[2] Berckenhout had been somewhat optimistic regarding the schedule pursued by Friedrich Gottlieb Klopstock (1724–1803). Although the *Messias* had been appearing in cantos regularly since 1748, the epic would run to four volumes and not be completed for another twenty years.

[3] For a consideration of the German appreciation of Milton, particularly Klopstock's, see J. H. Tisch, "Milton and the German Mind in the Eighteenth Century," *Studies in the Eighteenth Century. Papers Presented at the David Nichol Smith Memorial Seminar. Canberra, 1966*, ed. R. F. Brissenden (Canberra: Australian National University Press, 1968), pp. 205–29.

[4] Apparently RD had encouraged Berckenhout to submit the translation, for in his next letter from Brunswick he acknowledges that RD's response has prompted him to send off to Tully's Head the first

part of his work on Book I. What ever happened to the packet or to the publishing arrangement is not clear. The third and last letter in their correspondence represented here (26 February 1754) shows Berckenhout complaining of never having received RD's acknowledgement of the packet; nor did the Dodsleys publish a translation of Klopstock's *Messias* except the wretched one done by Mary and Joseph Collyer in 1763. For Klopstock's reaction to the Collyers' prose version, see the 26 February letter, note 2.

5 The increasing German interest in the English language and its authors is corroborated by William Whitehead when writing to RD from Leipsig less than two years later. In that letter of 1 April 1755 (q.v.), Whitehead writes: "every body here almost reads English . . . I am greatly pleased to find our Language grow almost universal."

6 Clearly Berckenhout must mean the first translation of the *Messias*.

7 For more about Berckenhout's military connection, see his next letter, note 3.

From Horace Walpole[1]

Strawberry Hill Nov. 4, 1753.

I am sorry you think it any trouble to me to peruse your poem again; I always read it with pleasure.[2] One or two little passages I have taken the liberty to mark and to offer you alterations; page 79 I would read *thrust to thrust*; I believe *push* is scarce a substantive of any authority. Line 449, and line 452, should I think be corrected, as ending with prepositions, disjoined from the cases they govern. I don't know whether you will think my emendations for the better. I beg in no wise that you will adopt any of them out of complaisance; I only suggest them to you at your desire, and am far from insisting on them.[3] I most heartily wish you the success you so well deserve, and am

> Your very humble servant,
>
> Hor. Walpole.

P. S. – I shall beg you to send me a piece I see advertised, called, 'A True Account of Andrew Frey,' &c.[4]

Source: The Letters of Horace Walpole, Earl of Orford, ed. Peter Cunningham (9 vols. London, 1857–9), IX, 485.

1 RD's relationship with the prolific letter-writer Horace Walpole (1717–97) can in no way be measured by the single letter printed here. From as early as 1744, Walpole had always referred to RD as his bookseller (*Horace Walpole's Correspondence with Thomas Mann*, ed. W. S. Lewis, II, 417). In 1746, RD published Walpole's *Epilogue to Tamerlane* and later included it with two other pieces in his *Collection* (II, 327, 305, 321). It was also through Walpole that RD came to publish Thomas Gray's *Ode on a Distant Prospect of Eton College*, *The Progress of Poesy*, and *The Bard*, as well as the Cambridge poet's *Elegy Written in a Country Church Yard*. Walpole also contributed several numbers to RD's periodical *The World* (1753–6), notably No. 8, a subscription for funds to release Theodore, Baron Neuhoff, King of Corsica (see his letter of 8 March 1753) from debtors' prison. Since Walpole's chief works came out after the setting up of his own press at Strawberry Hill in 1758, and largely after RD had retired from Tully's Head, the publisher was deprived of issuing such works of his friend as *A Catalogue of the Royal and Noble Authors of England* (1758), *Anecdotes of Painting in England* (1762), and *The Castle of Otranto* (1764).

2 Most likely Part I of RD's planned three-part poem *Public Virtue*. The first part, *Agriculture*, would appear on 19 November 1753 (*PA*).

³ On page 79, RD changed the line, but used neither the original nor Walpole's suggestion. Possibly this is the line rendered in the printed version as "The rival Rams, opposing front to front" (l. 363). Lines 449 and 452 were changed, thereby avoiding the use of prepositions at the ends of the lines.

⁴ "*A True and Authentic Account of Andrew Frey. Containing the Occasion of his coming among the Herrnhuters or Moravians, his Observations on their Conferences . . . and the Reasons for which he left them . . .* Faithfully translated from the German. London, printed: and sold by J. Robinson, M. Keith, M. Cook, and J. Jolliff (1753)." Walpole might have seen the advertisement for this work in the *Public Advertiser* of 2 November.

To William Shenstone

Pallmall Nov.ʳ 10.ᵗʰ 1753.

Dear Sir

I receiv'd and read with great pleasure your little poetical Packet, for which I think my self very much oblig'd to You, and shall wait with much impatience for your second.¹ However, it will come time enough if it comes with in a month or five Weeks.² I don't know how I came to think your next Town was Stratford, unless it was because I us'd to direct to Lady Luxborough so, and I thought the Leasows and Barrels had been very near each other.³ I like extreamly what you have sent, but if you think proper I will shew them either to Sir George, or M.ʳ W.ᵐ Lyttelton.⁴ Most of those which compose the three first Volumes, were shewn to Sir George before they were inserted. I am much oblig'd to You for your readiness to contribute on this occasion, & shall endeavour all I can that yᵉ Fourth Volume may not disgrace the three former. I am going to publish a Poem on English* Agriculture, & in a Week or ten days will beg your acceptance of one, which I will direct for You to be left with M.ʳ Baskerville at Birmingham, as I don't know how other ways to convey it to You.⁵

I am
Sir
Your most obliged
humble Serv.ᵗ

R Dodsley

* [Shenstone's endorsement:] By Himself, I see.

Address: To W.ᵐ Shenstone Esq.ʳ / to be left at the Post Office / in Birmingham / Warwickshire
Postmark: 10 NO
Frank: R. Dodsley free⁶

[Shenstone's endorsement on cover:] Return these sometime, if you please.

MS: BL. Add. MS. 28,959, ff. 10–11.

¹ These packets, composed of pieces written not only by Shenstone but also by his friends, were submitted for inclusion in the fourth volume of RD's *Collection*.

² Actually the fourth volume would not be published for almost another year and a half, on 18 March 1755.

³ See the previous "missent" letter to Shenstone of 29 September 1753. This mistake on RD's part is curious, for, as early as 1747 and 1748, he had successfully sent letters to Shenstone at the Leasowes. Possibly this incident, in addition to the lack of extant correspondence between the two from 1749 to 1753 indicates that indeed they had had little contact during that period. Leasowes and Barrells were fifteen miles apart.

⁴ George Lyttelton (1709–73), first Baron Lyttelton, a patron of literature and frequenter of Tully's Head, had published several successful works through RD in the late 1740s, but especially popular had been his monody on his beloved late wife (1747). Lyttelton lent RD much help in deciding the contents and in editing Volume IV of his *Collection* (1755). William Henry Lyttelton (1724–1808), brother of George, MP for Bewdley (1748–55). The next year William would become Subcofferer of the Household and then in 1755 Governor of South Carolina, and, five years later, of Jamaica. Ultimately, he would serve as Lord of the Treasury (1777–82). Like George, William, too, seems to have been of occasional literary assistance to RD in the late 1740s and early 1750s.

⁵ The first book of RD's *Public Virtue: A Poem. In Three Books. I. Agriculture. II. Commerce. III. Arts.* appeared nine days later.

⁶ Regarding RD's franking this letter and others to Shenstone through July, 1755, see RD's letter to Shenstone on 29 September of this year, note 6.

From Benjamin Victor

Dublin 12th of Novr 1753

Dear *Sir*

The *One* Letter you favour'd Me with (containing your mortifying objection to the Number I mention'd for the first impression) I answer'd soon after it came to hand – and, on your better Judgment reduced my desire of 3000 to one thousand, for the first impression.¹ I remember I inform'd Sir William Wolseley of the contents of yours when He was in Staffordshire, and his reply was that the County he was in wou'd demand that Number (1000) and that He wou'd lay Mr Dodsley a Wager of an hundred Guineas of it – but from the beginning of Time = Doctors differ'd! You spoke very justly from the general Sale of most Things publish'd, even of some Merit – But *This* you will find when you read it a most singular Case, and calculated for popularity. and I hope you will have that opportunity soon[,] as the Manuscript is before this in London – Sir William, as soon as he arriv'd there was to wait on the Gentleman who carried it thither [?] directed only to deliver that Pacque[t]² who is only to get it look'd carefully over by some of his learned Friends of the Bar, to see that we are secure from the carpings of the litigious, sorry, Rascals of that profession – after that, Sir William is to deliver it to You to be printed on my Account. I meant to have a large Number printed at once – because (if otherwise) and the first impression soon gone, and the public demand known, some Fleet printer might send forth an impression with more expedition than You – their Dexterity, I dare say, You are too well acquainted with.

I must beg of You to be very early in your Notice of the Time you intend to send the first Sheet to the Press – that I may do the same here with my friend George Faulkner³ a Letter is here in 6 or 7 days – I wou'd have an Advertizment go to the

Papers to give early notice of the Publication – I will enclose One in my next Letter[4]
– and, in [the] mean time, rest assur'd of [your friend's   ]
[Conclusion and signature are missing][5]

P.S. Mrs Joins me in our best [wishes] to Mrs Dodsley.

Pray fav^r Me with a Line [as soon] as ever Sir William has been w[ith] You – the
more frequent the mo[re] Friendly. Brevity I will excuse as it is the Soul of Business.

Address: To | Mr Dodsley | Bookseller in Pallmall | London
Postmark: 19 NO Dublin

MS: Osborn Collection, Beinecke Library, Yale.

[1] RD's letter not traced. Victor's proposed publication, *The Widow of the Wood*, is described in his
August letter to RD.   [2] Manuscript damaged at this point.
[3] George Faulkner (1699?–1775) Dublin printer and bookseller. Apparently Faulkner also refused to
put his name to the work because the Irish edition was published as "Dublin Printed and sold by
S[amuel] Powell in Crane Lane" in the same year as the London edition. For RD's connections with
Faulkner, see my note, "Faulkner and Dodsley: a Publishing Link," *The Library*, 5th ser., 32 (1977),
52–5.
[4] As noted earlier, RD chose not to publish Victor's delicate narrative despite the permission of its
subject, Sir William Wolseley himself.   [5] The manuscript is badly damaged at this point.

To Joseph Warton

[*post* 19 November 1753][1]

Dear Sir,

I sent last night, directed to you in a parcel for some of your booksellers, my poem
on Agriculture; which begs your acceptance. But that an illiterate Muse should be
at all regarded in the Capitol of Learning,[2] would be a wild expectation: however as
she is an innocent country girl, and quite a stranger, I hope you will be civil to her,
and excuse her awkwardness and want of breeding. If she is not dash'd at first, and
put quite out of countenance, she may in time improve.[3] So, trusting her to your
candour and politeness,

I remain affectionately
Yours,

R. Dodsley.

Source: John Wooll, *Biographical Memoirs of . . . Joseph Warton* (London, 1806), p. 227.

[1] The date is determined on the basis of the recent appearance on 19 November 1753 (*PA*), of RD's
Agriculture, mentioned within the letter. Wooll dates the letter simply as "Nov."
[2] Oxford.
[3] Much to RD's disappointment, this first book of blank verse was not successful, and he dropped the
whole project. The last two parts were scheduled to deal with Commerce and the Arts.

To William Shenstone

[c. 28 November 1753][1]

Dear Sir

I sent last week in a Parcel to Mr Baskerville at Birmingham the Poem on Agriculture, directed for You; and I wish You may find in it any Entertainment. My friends here give me some hopes that I have not quite fail'd in my Attempt. I am very much oblig'd to You for the last Pacquet, & wait with impatience for ye next.[2] I shall be extreamly glad of your opinion and remarks on my Agriculture.

I am
Sir
Your most obed^t ⟨&c⟩
R Dodsley

Address: To W^m. Shenstone Esqr at / the Leasows, to be left at the / Post Office at Birmingham
Postmark: 28 NO
Frank: R. Dodsley *free*

MS: BL. Add. MS. 28,959, ff. 15–16.

[1] The date is determined from the postmark and from the fact that RD's *Agriculture* (mentioned within the letter) had been published the previous week.
[2] Poems for the fourth volume of RD's *Collection.*

From John Berckenhout

Brunswick ye 10 Dec^r [17]53

Sir

Since I receiv'd your letter[1] I have, with as much expedition as my military duty wou'd allow, corrected and transcrib'd the first book of the Messiah: part of which I send you at present; which shall precede the remainder but one post.[2] I am ⟨apprehensibe⟩ apprehensive that this manner of expedition will cost us money: but, in case we go on, I believe it will not be difficult to compound with the postoffice.

As to publishing this single book I must own I am alittle fearful. The poem becomes so much more interesting in the following books, and discovers a plan so new, so contrary to all expectations, that I think we shou'd have had nothing to fear if we had made our assay with 3 or 4 books. But you know the publick better than I do. I leave this intirely to you. perhaps the expectation of what is to come may support us. If I am able to prevail with my Prince to give me more leisure (which the success of this translation may be a means of procuring me) I may perhaps be able in time to give you a particular account of the present state of learning in Germany;[3] the character of their ancient and modern Authors of note with translations from their works &e^tc at least I ⟨hav⟩ am promis'd great assistance and am in possession of considerable materials. believe me they have had and have some excellent people! I am desir'd by Ebert (who is mentioned in the preface) to ask you the following questions.[4]

viz.

  In what year were the last editions printed of Fenton's, Pitt's and Somervile's
    poems?[5]

  When we may expect the promis'd edition of Swift's works in 12 Vol?[6]

  When will Warburtons life of Pope appear?[7]

  If it be permitted to ask the name of M.ʳ xxx some of whose poems are in your
    collection?[8]

  Lastly if you dont intend to make a farther collection of the like kind?

  By resolving these questions, and by giving us any new in the learned way, of new Authors, Characters, publications &eᵗᶜ You will obliged the above mentioned English Enthusiast no less than

Your Most obed.ᵗ Serv.ᵗ

Berckenhout

I shall be proud to hear from you as soon as possible

MS: Osborn Collection, Beinecke Library, Yale.

[1] RD's letter not traced.
[2] For Berckenhout's proposed translation of Klopstock's *Messias*, see his letter to RD on 28 October.
[3] Karl I, Duke of Braunschweig (1735–80), a patron of learning and the arts, had established in that city in 1749 the Collegium Carolinum, an institute that included a program for training military officers. Probably this program explains Berckenhout's presence in Braunschweig.
[4] Johann Arnold Ebert, with Klopstock a member of the *Bremer Beitrage* circle, was of the faculty at Collegium Carolinum. Having translated *Night Thoughts* two years earlier, Ebert had become an authority on Edward Young.
[5] Probably Elijah Fenton (1683–1730), whose *Poems on Several Occasions* had enjoyed only one edition, in 1717; Christopher Pitt (1699–1748), although best known for his translation of the *Aeneid* (1740), had published his own poems in 1727, though another edition would appear in 1756; the best known verses of William Somerville (1675–1742), *The Chace*, had been printed most recently in 1749, but his *Occasional Poems* (1727) had not been reprinted.
[6] The twelve-volume, octavo edition of Swift's *Works*, with an account of the author's life and notes historical and explanatory by John Hawkesworth, would be issued in May 1755, by C. Bathurst, C. Davis, C. Hitch and L. Hawes, J. Hodges, R. and J. Dodsley, and W. Bowyer.
[7] Warburton would assist Owen Ruffhead in producing the latter's *Life of Alexander Pope* (1769), but he would not write his own biography of Pope.
[8] Probably Berckenhout refers to William Mason's *Musaeus: A Monody to the Memory of Mr. Pope. In Imitation of Milton's Lycidas*, first published by RD in 1747 and then later included in Vol. III of RD's *Collection* (pp. 136–47). This was the only poem in the three volumes of the *Collection* published to date that carried a by-line approximating Berckenhout's designation; that is, it was signed: "By Mr. M____."

To Solomon Mendes

Saturday Morn. Ten
[December, 1753 or early 1754][1]

Dear Sir,

  A kind letter from a friend, when we are under the pressure of misfortune, is like a chearing cordial to a sick stomach: and such I assure you was yours to me. I am extremely obliged to you for your kind offer of any assistance in your power; and your friendly concern for the uneasiness of my wife, is by so much the more agreeable to me, as her happiness is dearer to me than my own. I keep up my spirits as well as I can: but liberty is a blessing of such value, that the loss of it cannot but be sensibly felt by any one who knows how to enjoy it. Here is one thing, however, which might be a comfort to a man of a lively imagination; I have a map of the whole world to range in, hangs up in the room of my confinement. But –

> Around the world with anxious eyes I roam
> For what's the world to him that has no home?

It would be a very agreeable flattery to persuade myself that I have the good wishes of all the worthy part of mankind; however, I am assured in having one of them, in having yours.

My humble service to the ladies; I am glad they are coming to town. I hope they will comfort the widow in her affliction, and kindly remember the poor prisoner

R. Dodsley

Source: The British Magazine and Review; or Universal Miscellany, (December, 1782), 411–12.

¹ The year is only probable. The reference to Mrs Dodsley shows that the letter predates 12 December 1754, the date of her death. Similarly, it is unlikely that the letter be of a date earlier than December 1753, the month which seems to have marked RD's first confinement with the gout. Writing to Shenstone on 12 January 1754, he indicates that he has been laid up for five weeks with the gout.

From John Mason¹

Cheshunt 7 Jan: [1754]²

Sir

As my little Piece upon Elocution had finish'd it's Course, and was going to submit to the common fate of Pamphlets, you do it an honour to prolong it's existence by giving it a place in the second Edition of the *Preceptor*.³

Had I known your Intention beforehand I should have had no Objection at all to it.

I am oblig'd to you for the polite Acknowledgement you have made of the Liberty you have taken;⁴ than which no other Consideration is desir'd by

Sir

yʳ humble Servᵗ

J Mason

Address: To / Mʳ Dodsley Bookseller / in Pall-mall / London
Postmark: PENY POST PAYD. P, TV.

MS: Bodleian, MS. Eng. Letters d. 40, f. 101.

¹ John Mason (1706–63), Presbyterian minister at Cheshunt as of 1746.
² The year is determined from the mention of the recent appearance of the second edition of RD's *Preceptor* published in December 1753.

³ RD used Mason's slim piece as an introduction to Part I of Vol. I of *The Preceptor*, "On Reading, Speaking, and Writing Letters". *An Essay on Elocution, or Pronunciation* had initially been published by Mary Cooper in 1748; the third and last edition (1751) before the essay's publication in the 1754 *Preceptor* found R. Hett, J. Buckland, J. Waugh joining Cooper as publishers.

⁴ Mason must mean that RD had written to him, for no acknowledgement appears in the 1754 *Preceptor*. In fact, though the authors of many parts of *The Preceptor* are known, all the essays are unsigned. (For some other contributors, see David Fordyce's letter of 11 February 1748.)

To William Shenstone

Pallmall Jan 12 [1754]¹

Dear Sir

I have rec^d two more Paquets from You for which I am very much oblig'd to You; but I think there is very little of your own in either of them, so that I am in hopes of another Paquet from you, especially as I have not yet receiv'd the corrected Copy of the Pastoral Ballad you mention'd.² I believe I shall not print the Volume this Winter, as it will be a Season in which scarce any thing will be thought of except Elections.³ I sent a month or six Weeks ago to Mr Baskerville one of my Poem on Agriculture, together with one directed to You which I hope you have receiv'd, though I am afraid you will not be much entertain'd with it. I have been laid up with the Gout these 5 Weeks, or you would have heard from me sooner. Wishing you all the Compliments of the season I remain

Dr Sir

Your most oblig'd & obed! Serv!

R Dodsley

Address: To Wm Shenstone Esqr / at the Leasows near Birmingham
Seal: RD
Postmark: 12 IA
Frank: R. Dodsley *free*⁴ Warwickshire

MS: BL. Add. MS. 28,959, ff. 17–18.

¹ The year is determined on several bases. First of all, RD says that he would "not print the Volume of the *Collection* this winter." It is clear from his letters of late 1753 to Shenstone (q.v.) that he had intended to publish the volume during the 1753–4 season. Since he did publish the volume in March 1755, a change of heart would only have been possible for January 1754. In addition the letter fits the overall context of the series of exchanges between himself and Shenstone leading to the publication of Volume IV. Finally RD says he sent "a month or six Weeks ago to Mr. Baskerville" his poem, *Agriculture*, to be forwarded to Shenstone. This detail is corroborated in the opening line of his letter to Shenstone on c. 28 November 1753.

² Anonymity frequently characterized Shenstone's submissions. Assuming the role of a Midlands Maecenas, he was regularly sending RD the productions of his neighbors and protégés, and not distinguishing them from his own pieces. Apparently Shenstone had mentioned in some earlier letter that he had a revised version of a "Pastoral Ballad," for RD had mentioned the fact in his letter to Shenstone on 29 September 1753 (q.v.).

³ A general election was scheduled for 7 March. Little did RD know, however, just how distracting the political scene would prove. Henry Pelham, First Lord of the Treasury and Chancellor of the Exchequer, would die on the eve of the election, resulting in much political maneuvering and a change in the ministry's leadership.   ⁴ See RD's letter to Shenstone on 29 September 1753, note 6.

From John Baskerville

Jan. 16. 1754.

. . . I have put the last hand to my Great Primer, and have corrected fourteen
letters in the specimen you were so kind to approve, and have made a good progress
in the English, and have formed a new alphabet of Two-line Double Pica and Two
line Small Pica capitals for Titles, not one of which I can mend with a wish, as they
come up to the most perfect idea I have of letters . . .[1] [*He then details his scheme for
obtaining absolutely correct texts of the work he is about to print.*] . . . 'Tis this. Two people
must be concerned; the one must name every letter, capital, point, reference,
accent, etc., that is, in English, must spell every part of every word distinctly, and
note down every difference in a book prepared on purpose. Pray oblige me in
making the experiment with Mr. James Dodsley in four or five lines of any two
editions of an author, and you'll be convinced that it's scarcely possible for the least
difference, even of a point, to escape notice. I would recommend and practise the
same method in an English author, where most people imagine themselves capable
of correcting. Here's another great advantage to me in this humble scheme; at the
same time that a proof sheet is correcting, I shall find out the least imperfection in
any of the Types that has escaped the founder's notice. I have great encomiums on
my Specimen from Scotland . . .[2]

Source: Talbot Baines Reed, *A History of the Old English Letter Foundries* (1887; rev. A. F. Johnson, London:
Faber and Faber, 1952), p. 269.

[1] Unless Reed's dating of this letter is incorrect, Baskerville seems a bit behind schedule. See his letter to
    RD 19 October 1752, where he promises to finish his Great Primer by Christmas.
[2] The "encomiums" were probably responses to the specimens or prospectuses which Baskerville issued
    during 1754 to advertise his upcoming edition of Virgil. See Philip Gaskell, *John Baskerville: A
    Bibliography* (Cambridge, 1959; repr. Chichelsy: Paul Minet, 1973), pp. 3–6.

From Matthew Pilkington

Stanton (near Nottingham)
Jan. 26. 1754.

S.r

I have just now Sent to S.r George Lyttelton, *A Letter to M.r West relating to His
Observations on the Resurrection.* If they approve the Publishing of it, they will put it
into your Hands, & it shall be your Property, upon Such Terms as you Shall think
⟨proper⟩ reasonable.[1] I am S.r

Your humble Servant

M. Pilkington

Address: To / M.r Dodsley, Bookseller / in Pall-Mall / London
Postmark: 28 IA Nottingham

MS: Harvard Theatre Collection, Harvard College Library.

¹ Friends and near contemporaries at Eton and Christ Church, Lyttelton and Gilbert West had both
  published religious tracts from Tully's Head in 1747 that, by 1754, had reached fourth editions:
  Observations on the Conversion and Apostleship of St. Paul and *Observations on the History and Evidence of the
  Resurrection of Jesus Christ*. Apparently Pilkington's proposed Letter to West did not gain "their"
  approval, for I cannot find that it was ever published.

To William Shenstone

[23 February 1754]¹

Dear Sir

It gives me great pleasure that You do not entirely disapprove of my Poem on
Agriculture, and if at your leisure you would be so good as to favour me with any
remarks upon it, I should be extremely oblig'd to You.² I have quite laid aside all
thoughts of publishing a 4ᵗʰ Vol this Winter, and I please my self with the hopes of
waiting on You at the Leasows next Summer.³ A copy of your Pastoral Ballad was
given to me some weeks ago, but it is very nearly yᵉ same with that I had before.⁴
Pray, have you no poetical Descriptions of your own Place? I wanted to have
introduc'd it amongst my Gardens; but as I had not seen it, I durst not venture to
paint from verbal descriptions.⁵

I am Dear Sir
Your oblig'd humᵇˡᵉ Servᵗ
R Dodsley

Address: To William Shenstone Esqʳ / at the Leasows near Birmingham
Postmark: 23 FE
Frank: R. Dodsley *free*

MS: BL. Add. MS. 28,959, ff. 19–20.

¹ The date is determined from the postmark and from RD's previous letter to Shenstone, 12 January
  1754 (q.v.), where RD mentions the dispatch of his poem *Agriculture*, also referred to here.
² Shenstone's approval of *Agriculture* seems indeed a product of his partiality for his friend. When the
  poem proved unsuccessful, RD abandoned the plan for the larger *Public Virtue*. Even the author's
  dedicating *Agriculture* to the Prince of Wales did not sufficiently encourage its acceptance.
³ The fourth volume of his *Collection*, which he was proposing to Shenstone in his letter of 10 November
  1753. RD did manage to visit the Leasowes the next summer. See his letter to Shenstone of 27 August
  1754.   ⁴ See RD's letter to Shenstone of 29 September 1753.
⁵ "Gardens" probably meant the upcoming Volume IV of RD's *Collection*.

From John Berckenhout

Brunswick. 26 Feb: 1754

Dear Sir.

I sent you the translation of Kloptocks Messiah some weeks ago; and have waited
for your answer with uncommon patience.¹ I have endeavour'd to account for your

silence by every imaginable means; but am now intirely at aloss to assign any probable reason for it: except, that both my letters are miscarried. Is this the case, I beg you will ⟨be so⟩ oblige me so far as to let me know it.[2]

At the time I wrote my last letter I was nothing more than Ensign in this service; but on the sight of a letter wrote to me by Klopstock after he had seen some parts of my translation of his poem, his Highness the Duke has been pleas'd to give me a Captains Comis.ⁿ which will give me sufficient leasure to exicute my design as it ought to be.[3] The 2ᵈ Book is ready and at your service ⟨in⟩ wᶜʰ, if you have been in the least satisfy'd with the first, will give you no small satisfaction. I am, in the greates impatience to hear from You,

Your most Obᵗ Servᵗ

Berckenhout.

Address: To / Mʳ R. Dodsley / at Tully's head in Pall Mall / London
Postmark: MR 6
Frank: Amsterdam

MS: Osborn Collection, f.c. 76/1, Beinecke Library, Yale.

[1] See earlier letters from Berckenhout, on 28 October and 10 December 1753.
[2] Possibly his second and third letters to RD had miscarried, but certainly this one did not, for it carries a London postmark and a quite legible address. In this light, it remains a mystery why RD did not take advantage of a Klopstock-sanctioned translation and chose to publish in 1763 the regrettable prose translation by Mary and Joseph Collyer that served to cripple the German poet's early reputation in England and, justly, to anger him. In 1798, when Coleridge visited Klopstock at Hamburg and suggested that he had been thinking of translating a few of the German's odes, Klopstock responded: "I wish you would render into English some select passages of the Messiah, and revenge me of your countrymen!" (*Biographia Literaria*, ed. J. Shawcross (Oxford 1907), II, 171).
[3] See Berckenhout's previous letter, note 3.

To William Shenstone

Pallmall Augˢᵗ 27 [1754][1]

Dear Sir

As I cannot forget the Pleasures I recᵈ at the Leasows, I ought not to neglect to thank you for them. I shall be extremely oblig'd to You if you will favour me with a copy of the Pastoral, and whatever else you think proper, as soon as is convenient; as I am now printing the Volume with as much Expedition as I can, that it may be publish'd the beginning of the Winter. You desir'd I would send you a list of what I had got. It follows.

The Princess Elizabeth, a Ballad.
Ode to a young Lady, on her Expression.
Verses to Wᵐ L____n 1748.
Inscrib'd in a Shady Valley
In a Root house
On a gothic Building.

The Rake
Ballad in the Scottish Taste.
Address to his Elbow Chair. By Mr Somerville
The Cabinet
The Pepper Box.
The Heroines.
The Panacea.
Lucy, or the parting.
Written at a Ferme ornee near B. 1749
Flowers. by A.W. Esq
Horace & Lydia by ye same
Song. by the same.[2]

These are all I have receiv'd, and I wish You would be so kind as to distinguish which are yours, & to favour me with any others that you may think proper for my purpose.

I am

Dear Sir

Your most oblig'd & obed^t Servt

R Dodsley

MS: BL., Add. MS. 28,959, f. 21.

[1] Since Volume IV of RD's *Collection*, alluded to in the text, appeared on 18 March 1755, this letter of August must belong to 1754.

[2] The first six poems in this list were Shenstone's own and appeared in Volume IV of RD's *Collection* between pages 337 and 353. "The Rake" is designated in the *Collection* (p. 325–6) as by a "Lady in New England." The "Ballad in the Scottish Taste," by William Saunders, did not appear in the *Collection* (See RD to Shenstone, 18 January 1755). The five poems after Somerville's are by Richard Graves, and, except for "The Pepper Box" (which appeared in Volume V, 63–6), all are found in Volume IV, 330–6. The next piece, by Lady Luxborough, was printed on pp. 317–18. Of the next three poems – all by Anthony Whistler – only "Flowers" and "Song" made RD's *Collection* (IV, 327–9).

From John Gilbert Cooper

Thurgarton Sepr the 21st 1754

Dear S^r

I have now finish'd my *letter*[s] *concerning Taste*, & have transcrib'd a great part of 'em for the press. they will all make up a volume as large as my *Life of Socrates* printed in the same letter upon the same paper.[1] as I propose to lay out some money in books at Doc^r. Mead's Sale,[2] I shall expect five & twenty Guineas & the Ruins of Palmy[ra] for the copy. if this suits you let me have a line by the return of the Post, & I will sen[d] up what papers are transcribe'd for your examination by the next Stage Coach; whic[h] if approv'd of, you may put into the pre[ss] immediately,[3] & I will send you afterward[s] a design for a little Title Page Frontispi[ece] I don't propose to put my name to the f[irst] edition therefore enjoin you Secresy.[4] – as I know you are so fond of accurasy, I have taken uncommon Pains & have polish'd these trifles as much as I was able. my best comp^ts to Mrs Dodsley. I was extreamly sorry I was [s]o unfortunate not to see you when you was in Nottinghamshire, which was occasion'd [b]y an engagement I was under to go to th[e] Duke of Rutlands[5] the very week you was [at] Mansfield, however I staid at my Bro^r [ ]wett's four days longer than I intended [on] purpose to see you. I am, Dear S^r,

Your sincere Friend &c

J:G:Cooper Junr.

[dire]ct to me at Thurgarton near Nottingham.

MS: Bodleian Ms. Eng. Misc. d. 174, ff. 71–3.

Cooper's *Letters Concerning Taste* was published by RD on 25 November 1754 (*PA*). *Socrates* was printed in octavo and ran 179 pages, but *Letters* consisted of only 143 pages in octavo.

Richard Mead (1673–1754), a physician to both George I and George II, and a patron of literature, had died on 16 February. A catalogue of his library was issued on 22 October 1754 (*PA*), and his books were scheduled to be sold by Samuel Baker, a bookseller of Covent Garden, on 18 November 1754 and 7 April 1755.

Apparently RD balked at Cooper's asking price, for a receipt signed by Cooper (see Appendix B) reveals only a £20 payment; and a letter to RD of 7 October 1754 (q.v.) shows the author asking for Robert Woods' *Ruins of Palmyra* (1753) as his gratuity for a second edition, should it be called for. *Letters* reached a third edition by March of 1757.

Samuel Wale drew and Charles Grignion engraved the frontispiece, which consisted of a dual representation of the Graces within the same scene. In one, the Graces stand draped and holding plates of fruits and flowers at the open door of a building marked Χαριτων; in the other, they join Cupid in the nude, while attending Venus. All the early editions were published anonymously.

John Manners, 3rd Duke of Rutland (1696–1779).

From John Gilbert Cooper

Leicester   October the 7th 1754

Dear S^r

I rec^d the favor of your letter dated October the 1st,[1] and am very ready to comply with your request to print 750 copies of the first Edition, nor do I desire any gratuity at all for the second Edition, except it be the ruins of Palmyra, & that too only provided it runs briskly off;[2] nay more, I will very readily ⟨comply⟩ relinquish any part of what you propose for the first if the sale should not be successful, or the whole, rather than you should be one shilling out of pocket, for I would ⟨rather⟩ sooner give up the harmless Vanity of saying hereafter to my Child, "this shelf of Books was my own acquisition", than have the mortifying reflection that it was at the expence of another Man, especially of one too ⟨for⟩ whom I have some reason to regard.[3] – I shall return again to Thurgarton tomorrow whither I sh^d be glad if you could send this week a sketch of the copper plate in a letter, that I may correct it if there is any thing therein that does not answer my expectations. I have sent my Papers this day by my Sister Gardiner, who will reach my Father's house in

Hertfordshire next Thursday, & will forward 'em to you the day after. they are seal'd up in a brown Paper with my arms upon it. as soon as the first Sheet is printed off, send it down in a Frank, which I will correct & ⟨return⟩ send back by the return of the Post; & so continue to do sheet after sheet till I can come up to Town, which will be the 12th of November. – I was necessitated by the nature of my Subject to take the little *essay on the polite Arts*, which I wrote in the Museum, as you will observe.[4] all your Friends are well at Mansfield & desire to be remember'd to you. Nelly Wright will send your Testament by me.[5] my comp.^{ts} to Mrs Dodsley. I am, S^r,

your Sincere Friend
& humble Servant

J G Cooper Junr

direct to me at Thurgarton. don't let the Print be less than that the Life of Socrates was publish'd in, in short I would have as many Pages as there is in the Manuscript if possible, or at least very near.[6]

MS: Bodleian Ms. Eng. Misc. d. 174, f. 77.

[1] Not traced.
[2] Cooper had relented on his initial request for the printing of his *Letters Concerning Taste*. See his letter to RD of 21 September.
[3] Cooper usually left the profits from the sale of his works in RD's hands so that he might draw on them from time to time for book purchases. See his letters of 23 December 1749 and 22 October 1750.
[4] *Museum*, I, 9 (19 July 1746), 321–4. See Cooper's letter of 11 February 1746/47.
[5] Nelly Wright of Mansfield, RD's hometown, was to be the addressee of three friendly letters from the publisher in 1757 (q.v.).   [6] See Cooper's letter of 21 September 1754, note 1.

From John Gilbert Cooper

Thurgarton   Monday October the 14.th 1754

S.^r

   I hope you receiv'd my Papers safe the latter end of last week[1] which if you did I ⟨hope⟩ expect to receive the first sheet from the Press next Saturday at the farthest, together with the design delineated, for as the Parliament meets the 14th of next Month there is no time to be lost. I am very sorry Mrs Dodsley is oblig'd to go to Bath on account of her health, but if they stay any time there I shall have the pleasure of seeing 'em proposing to be there myself the latter end of next Month.[2] direct to me for the future at Nottingham, or at Thurgarton near Nottingham, & not near Newark, for the former is the Post town I always send to. I am, S^r,

Your most humble Servt

J G Cooper. Junr.

I have enclos'd four franks and will send more when wanted.

MS: Bodleian Ms. Eng. Misc. d. 174, f. 79.

Cooper's copy for *Letters Concerning Taste*. See his letter to RD a week earlier suggesting a plan for an expedient proofing of the work.
For Mrs Dodsley, see RD's letter to Shenstone of 16 December, and note 2.

From David Hume[1]

14 Oct[r] 1754[2]

Sir

I have us'd the Freedom of sending under Cover to you a Letter to M[r] Spence; because I did not know how to direct to that Gentleman. All the Contents of it regard M[r] Blacklocke, and are equally your Concern, as M[r] Spence's & that of every Lover of Ingenuity.[3] I have therefore left the Letter open, that, if you have leisure, you may read it. I esteem myself very much beholden to you for the Pains you have taken upon my Recommendation. I own, that I still regard S[r] George Lyttelton as our Sheet Anchor; and am infinitely desirous to have him better acquainted with M[r] Blacklocke's Care.[4]

Your Criticisms on his Poems might also be of great Service to him.[5]

I am S[ir]
Your most obedient Servant
David Hume

MS: Victoria and Albert Museum, MS. F. 48. E. 23, f. 169.

David Hume (1711–76), Scottish philosopher and historian, and at this time Keeper of the Advocates' Library, Edinburgh, as well as secretary to the Edinburgh Philosophical Society, had already gained a reputation by his *Political Discourses* (1752). Obviously the present letter is not Hume's first contact with RD on behalf of the young blind Scottish poet Thomas Blacklock (1721–91), whom Hume was attempting to introduce to the London literary world through RD and Joseph Spence. Hume himself did not publish anything from Tully's Head.
Samuel Singer's edition of Spence's *Observations, Anecdotes . . .* (London, 1820) dates this letter "Oct 15 – 54."
Both RD and Joseph Spence were initially very supportive of Blacklock, who must have struck them as a curious phenomenon. Spence, always a benefactor of young talent, wrote a complimentary review of Blacklock's accomplishments, which was published by RD in 1754 as *An Account of the Life, Character and Poems of Mr. Blacklock*. This account subsequently prefaced the two editions of Blacklock's *Poems* published by RD in 1756. Nonetheless, despite early support from RD's circle, Blacklock would soon be complaining of unanswered letters and of the bookseller's failure to consult him on new editions of his poetry. Yet he continued to write to RD through the late 1750s, making some rather personal revelations, which seem to have escaped his biographers.

The holograph of Hume's enclosed letter to Spence, dated 15 October 1754, is interleaved between pages 448 and 449 of the Huntington Library's *Supplementary Anecdotes from Mr. Spence's Papers*, IV. It is printed in John H. Burton's *Life and Correspondence of David Hume* (Edinburgh, 1846), I, 388–92, and in Singer's edition of Spence's *Anecdotes*, p. 447.

Whether or not Lyttelton actually appraised Blacklock's verses is not clear, but since he served as one of RD's critics in reviewing the bookseller's harvest of poems for the volumes of the *Collection*, probably he would have been consulted on Blacklock's pieces.

[5] Possibly RD or his friends did have some criticisms, for the publication of Blacklock's poems was delayed for sixteen months. Unfortunately, I have found no further correspondence on the subject except that written after the work had already been published. However, some partial explanation is found in the *LEP* of 15–17 April 1755 where the public is informed that because some have complained of the shortness of time to subscribe, the publication of Blacklock's poems is to be delayed until the meeting of Parliament the next winter.

To [?George, Lord Lyttelton?] [1]

Prior Park near Bath Oct.[r] 16.th 1754

My Lord

I rec[d] the honour of your Lordship's Commands, but as to the news of this Place, I mix so little with the Company, that I hear scarce any thing: except that M[r] French is this day burying his wife:[2] and that M[r] Nash is writing a History of Bath and Tunbridge during his own Time, & publishing Proposals for printing it by Subscription:[3] ⟨⟨If your Lordship gives me orders I will subscribe for one in Your name: it is thought he will have ⟨for his subscribers⟩ most of the Quality in England ⟨his subscribers⟩⟩ I am extreamly oblig'd to your Lordship for ⟨thinking of me⟩ remembering me in regard to M[r] Backwel's House,[4] but ⟨I think I fool myself⟩ ⟨I believe myself humble enough to⟩ I believe I must humble myself and be contented with the little Cottage I have got. I cannot find the Rule of Life in any of y[e] Booksellers Shops here.[5] It is amazing that Lordship should be so anxious about ⟨the Rule of Life⟩ such a Rule, in an Age when most people live without any Rule at all: ⟨But⟩ ⟨and⟩ but this is not the only Instance of Singularity which might be given to your Honour. ⟨But⟩ However ⟨as⟩ I do not intend a Letter of compliment, w[ch] I know would be disagreable to You I ⟨would rather chuse⟩ will rather endeavor to divert and entertain: and I have found for this purpose in an old obsolete Poet, who wrote about 250 Years ago, and is very little known, an account of ye origin of Mankind and their different conditions & estates, which I think extreamly humorous. His stile is too ⟨obsolete⟩ obscure and his narrative too tedious to be transcribed; I will therefore give you as short an account of it as I can in prose; in which I promise you I will not exaggerate the ridiculousness of the ⟨circumstances⟩ Images, nor the coarseness of the Expressions: if they seem in some instances too ludicrous for the subject, You must impute it to the rude simplicity of the times in which the account was written.[6]

When God had created the world, says my Author, he put Adam & Eve together, and bade them encrease and multiply as fast as ⟨ever⟩ they could. And in order to forward the peopling of this ⟨world⟩ their habitation he endow'd Eve with ye capacity or faculty of bearing twins, a boy and a girl at each Birth. When God assists (says the Poet) Man doth not ⟨work⟩ labour in vain. They fell to this sweet work with such eagerness, and follow'd it with such diligence, that in a few years they had a very numerous progeny. It happen'd one day, when Adam was gone a hunting, or to look after his Sheep or his cows, or on some idle errand or other, (for as he had yet no occasion to be jealous of his wife, he was often rambling abroad) that God almighty saw Eve like a good Housewife sitting at y[e] threshold of her door, lousing and cleaning her Children. She comb'd their heads, wash'd their hands, and wip'd their snotty noses with great neatness and assiduity. He was pleas'd with her behavior, and ⟨sent her word he would⟩ drew near in order to pay her a visit. Eve saw him a coming, and blush'd up to her ears; for says she to herself, if he sees all this heap of children begotten in so little a time I'm afraid he will think I have been too wantonly inclin'd. She hurries therefore as fast as she can, & taking ⟨all⟩ such of her children as were heavy and stupid in their minds, or clumsy and awkward in their bodies, she hides one under a bushel, another in the oven, a third under a heep of sheep skins, a 4th behind a pile of turf, and thus quickly dispos'd of all she did not ⟨like⟩ care to show quite out of sight. She then waited the approach of her visitor with some confusion, and made him a very fine curtesy; but he smiling upon her, quickly dispell'd her fears, by telling her he was come to provide for her children according to their deserts. She scuttled away as fast as she could, and bidding them hold up their heads & behave themselves like men, she ⟨presently⟩ immediately introduc'd to his presense those she had prepar'd for it. He receiv'd them all very graciously; and taking the oldest by the hand, he told him he should be an Emperor, & all his children should be Kings and Princes; to ye next he gave a Trunchion & dubb'd him a General; he ⟨made the third⟩ stuck a flag in the cap of a third and made him an Admiral; the fourth rose a Prime Minister; the fifth an Arch Bishop; & the sixth a Lord Chancellor. ⟨Others he made⟩ Some were swell'd into Judges, ⟨Bishops⟩ Sheriffs Lord Mayors and Constables. To others he gave Wands, Keys, ⟨Stars⟩ Garters and Ribbons. Some he made Dukes Earls Lords and Justices of Peace; and others Historians, Orators, Philosophers,[7] and Poets. Eve was prodigiously pleas'd to find her Visitor in so excellent a humour & thinking ⟨now⟩ this was ye time to make ye fortune of all the rest of her children, she immediately produc'd them also. But when ye Lord saw what uncouth figures they were & how stupidly they behav'd, he look'd upon them with a frowning countenance, & told their mother very cooly that they were scarce ⟨fit for⟩ capable of any thing, and that he could do but very little for them. However, to one he gave a Clever & bade him be a Butcher, to another a hammer & made him a Smith: to this he gave a Thimble & set him up for a Taylor, to that ⟨he gave⟩ a Hand saw, & bade him build a House. To the rest he gave ploughs carts ⟨and⟩ barrows hatchets shovels & wheelbarrows, and bad them get out and labour for their bread, for that bodily toil was all they were fit for. However, that if they behav'd well, he would not forget to reward them some time or other according to their Merits.

If this old account of the origin of the different states of Mankind should give ⟨your Lordship⟩ you a moment's Entertainment, I shall be very glad. ⟨I⟩ Perhaps your Lordship and Mr Peele may be inclin'd to suppose it ⟨might be⟩ written to ridicule some lame account that had been given of this matter, by some contemporary Author; but if Mr Wight ⟨& I⟩ will join me,[8] he and I will undertake to maintain the genuineness of this Account, against your Lordship and that Gentleman, whenever you shall be dispos'd to enter into a polemic debate.

I am etc

Prior Park near Bath.
   Octr 18th

I date my Letter you see from M⸢r⸣ Allen's, and I have just been scrawling on one of his Urns the following Couplet.

> Rais'd on her towering steep ⟨Assent, which few have won⟩
>   so rarely won,
> ⟨The⟩ Yon Seat fair *Virtue* gave her *fav'rite Son.*[9]

MS: Bancroft Library, University of California at Berkeley, Commonplace Book of Robert Dodsley, I ff. 1–6.

[1] Some slight evidence, although nothing substantial, suggests Lyttelton as the recipient. Lyttelton was one lord to whom RD could have written in this friendly tone, for the bookseller had known him well before the latter had succeeded to the baronetcy in 1751; in fact, RD had issued several editions of Lyttelton's *Observations on the Conversion and Apostleship of St. Paul* and *A Discourse on Providence* from Tully's Head during the 1740s and 1750s. The religious nature of both of these works and the subject of the latter fit rather appropriately the subject of RD's letter. Furthermore, RD is writing from Prior Park, the estate of Ralph Allen, a particular friend of Lyttelton's. Likewise significant is RD's bothering to mention that he has "just been scrawling" on one of Allen's urns: "Rais'd on her towering steep so rarely won, / Yon Seat fair *Virtue* gave her *fav'rite Son.*" It was to Lyttelton that Henry Fielding had dedicated his *Tom Jones* and in the novel's second chapter praised his two models for Squire Allworthy, Lyttelton and Allen, as the "favourite of both Nature and Fortune." Finally, the draft letter is found together in RD's Commonplace Book with another to an anonymous recipient who also seems to be Lyttelton (see RD's letter of October–December 1754).

[2] Perhaps the Thomas French who is recorded as a subscriber to the General Hospital at Bath in the subscription list to Edward Bayley's *A Sermon preach'd at the Abbey Church at Bath, on Sunday, April 23, 1749*.

[3] The history proposed by Richard "Beau" Nash (1674–1762), previously the "king of Bath," was not published.

[4] Perhaps William Backwell (d. 1770), banker and RD's neighbor in Pall Mall (*Kent's Directory for 1759* p. 9). According to his will, Backwell owned a country home in Clapham.

[5] The anonymous *Rule of Life* would reach a fifth edition the following year.

[6] An example of the "estates genre," the account RD paraphrases is first found in English as rendered by Amyntas, one of the dialoguists in the fourth of Alexander Barclay's *Eglogues* (c. 1514). Barclay himself had paraphrased the fifth eclogue from *Baptistae Mantuani Adulescentia* (1513), the work of the Italian Carmelite Baptista Spagnolo (1448–1516), Shakespeare's "old Mantuan." (I am indebted to Professor Peter Medine for identifying this piece.)

[7] At this line, "Divines, Physicians," is written in the margin.

[8] Perhaps the John Peele of Hampton, Middlesex, whom RD would nominate for membership in the Royal Society of Arts three years later (RSA, Minutes for 19 October 1757). Possibly Robert Whytt (1714–66), first physician to George III in Scotland; RD would publish Whytt's *Physiological Essays* fifteen months later.   [9] See note 1.

James Dodsley to William Shenstone[1]

Pallmall Oct. 22. [1754]

Sir

   I receiv'd yours with the poem inclos'd.[2] My Brother is at present at Bath. I expect him at home in about a fortnight. None of your poems are yet put to press nor will be till my Brother's return, so that what you desire will be done.[3] Whatever you shall think proper to send will be safe in ye hands of

Sir

Your most obed! Serv!

James Dodsley

MS: BL. Add. MS. 28,959, f. 14.

James Dodsley (1724–97), Robert's brother and successor at Tully's Head, seems to have been taken into the partnership in 1754, when his name is first joined with Robert's in an imprint. Whatever the arrangement, however, his is the solitary bookseller name in the imprint for L. Howard's sermon *The Good Government of a Country its great Object*, issued in December 1753.

Shenstone's letter not traced. Perhaps the poem he had enclosed was Lady Luxborough's. See RD's response on 29 October.

For a list of poems RD had already received from Shenstone for Volume IV of the *Collection*, see RD's last letter on 27 August.

From Joseph Spence

Byfleet; Oct: 25, 1754.

Dear S^r,

I am very glad the 3 Polymetis's are arriv'd safe to you; & all the Remainder of the Copy, corrected for the Press, was inclos'd in the same bundle.[1]

I shall be very glad of the two Copies of the Account &c; & wish you w^d send one, (under two Franks,) to M^r. Blacklocks: & when they are publish't, (which I suppose may be at the Meeting of the Parliament,) I have desired Mr Blacklock to send to you, for whatever number he thinks may be of service to him in Scotland: I mean, to give away among his friends & acquaintance.[2] The Sheet of Polymetis I corrected; & sent for you in a Frank, some days ago. I hope you have receiv'd it, by this. I am

Your very
Obd Servt

Jo: Spence.

I am very much oblig'd to Mr Hume for his kind letter; wch I shall answer soon.[3] How do you direct to him?

Address: To / Mr Dodsley; / at Tully's Head, / Pall-Mall: / London
Postmark: 28 OC

MS: Houghton Library, Harvard University, fMS Eng 1336 (16); originally interleaved in Houghton extra-illustrated copy of Spence's *Anecdotes*, ed. Samuel W. Singer (1820). I am indebted to John C. Riely for calling my attention to this letter.

¹ Spence and RD were preparing a second edition of the former's *Polymetis* (1747) that would appear on 4 September 1755 (*DA*).

² Spence's *Account of the Life, Character, and Poems of Mr. Blacklock*, the blind Scottish poet, would be issued from Tully's Head on 13 November.

³ See Hume's letter to RD eleven days earlier, where he says he is enclosing a letter for Spence. The letter concerned is printed in Singer's edition of Spence's *Anecdotes*, pp. 448–53.

From Richard Graves¹

S.ʳ

Claverton near Bath   26 Octob. 1754.

As I have the highest opinion of Mʳ Shenstone's judgment, I should have no reason to doubt that those little pieces of mine, wᶜʰ *he* has thought proper to transmit to you, deserv'd a place in your collection² – If I cou'd be certain that he was entirely unbias'd by his regard for the Author – They are now however in the hands of a gentleman, whose judgment, I am convinc'd, is not inferior, & who is under the strictest Obligations to Sincerity – Please therefore to use your discretion S.ʳ with regard to the insertion or omission of any or all of them – & to fix my name, if you think proper, to "The Cabinet" tho' it is a name so little known out of the University (& by this time almost forgotten there) that, I am sure, it will rather borrow from, than add any lustre to yʳ Miscellany –

The Cabinet, (or Verses on Roman Medals) is a *subject* that will please the Virtuosi – & tho' nobly treated by the greatest of our modern Poets – yet your Epicures (such are men of Taste) love the same Dish cook'd different ways – & I have descended to some *minutenesses* which will please a *true* Medallist – better evan than Pope's – especially as he has mix'd some Satyrical Raillery in his Poem³ –

As to the Fable of the Pepper-box & Salt-Seller – tho' Mʳ Shenstone w[as] so highly pleas'd with it, as to induce me to inscribe it to him – & to tack some Lines to the End for that purpose – yet he now thinks it rather too lu[dicrous?] for yʳ Collection & more proper to be join'd wᵗʰ some Collection of Ta[les?] [?]⁴ to insert it in yʳ Miscellany – his Name & The [moral at] [th]e End – after "And to the Sideboard still confin'd" should by all means be omitted⁵ –

The Panacea, or Verses on [Fi]shing, may help to make a Variety thro' yᵉ uncommoness of yᵉ Subject – And the Do[c]trine I seriously think of importance – as I am convinc'd most of our Maladies owing to Plethoras & what is call'd Living Well –

The Heroines occasion'd by the Publication of Con. Philips's Mʳˢ Pilki[ng]ton's & Lady V-ne's infamous adventures in Per. Pickle⁶ – have been applauded by my Acquaintance – & if you don't think the Subject too particular, I believe they are the best of my Contribution –

The Stanzas on *Parting*, are favorites of Mʳ Shenstone's, – but I'm afraid are rather too Tender for the Publick Ear – otherwise I shou'd be glad to have *them* inserted – For you must know S.ʳ that I left a Fellowship of All-Souls Coll. for a handsome Wife – & shou'd take some pleasure in letting my Friends see that I was not disappointed in my expectation of happiness⁷ – The adding "Written some

years after marriage" – will disinguish them from a common Love-Song – But I
submitt this & every thing that I send you to your Judgment – & am S^r
y^r humb Ser!

Ric: Greaves.

P.S. Mr Shenstone has promis'd to send his Pastoral Ballad by the Way of Bath –
but I am surpris'd at his Delay – If it comes into [my] [h]ands I will forward it to
you the next Post[8] –

MS: Somerset County Record Office, DD/SK, 28/1, 1.

Richard Graves (1715–1804), Rector of Claverton and author of *The Spiritual Quixote*, was introduced
to RD at this time by Shenstone, though RD did not actually meet Graves until two summers later.
Then a regular correspondence was struck up between the two, which would be continued with the
bookseller's brother James long after Robert's death. Graves would contribute at least eight of his own
poems to RD's *Collection*. At Shenstone's death, RD and Graves served as two of the three executors
and collaborated in preparing the collected edition of the poet's work. See Charles J. Hill *The Literary
Career of Richard Graves*, Smith College Studies in Modern Languages, 16, nos. 1–3 (1934–5) and also
Clarence Tracy's forthcoming biography of Graves.
² That is, for the fourth volume of RD's *Collection of Poems by Several Hands* to appear on 18 March 1755.
The poems mentioned by Graves in this letter had been forwarded to RD by Shenstone sometime
earlier. (See RD's letter to Shenstone on 27 August 1754.) Four of the poems appeared in Volume IV
(pp. 330–6). Although, according to Graves's request, the "Pepper-box" was withheld from Volume
IV, it was printed three years later in Volume V (pp. 63–6). Those in the former volume were
designated as written by "Mr. Greaves"; the "Pepper-box," by "Mr. Graves."
³ No doubt Graves is referring to Alexander Pope's "Epistle V. To Mr. Addison. Occasioned by his
Dialogue on Medals."   ⁴ The manuscript is broken off at this point.
⁵ At the end of the fable, Graves had attached a six-line "Moral," at one point invoking Shenstone.
Despite his directions here to drop that portion, RD did print the "Moral" as the conclusion of the
poem in the *Collection*.
⁶ Theresa Constantia Phillips (1709–65), notorious courtesan; Laetitia Pilkington (1712–50),
adventuress whose *Memoirs* had appeared in 1748; Viscountess Frances Anne Vane (1713–88) whose
apology for her life Smollett allowed to interrupt *Peregrine Pickle* (1751) as Chapter 81, "Memoirs of a
Lady of Quality."
⁷ Graves had been elected to a fellowship at All Souls College, Oxford, as early as 1736, after having
taken his degree at Pembroke. But when he was married (to the 15-year-old daughter of a gentleman
farmer), in approximately 1744, he was forced to resign the position.
⁸ Eventually Shenstone would send it himself, the next month. (See RD's letter to him on 19
November.)

To William Shenstone

Pall Mall Octr 29 [1754]¹

Dear Sir

I do not wonder at the perpetual Interruption which You complain of; the
Possessors of such Beauties as you enjoy, must expect to pay some tax for their
Pleasures. And how happy are You, that the very tax it self is frequently an
additional Pleasure!

I am very much oblig'd to You for the trouble you have taken, & will punctually

follow your directions. I shall be glad now to have your Pastoral Ballad & whatever
else You may think proper to send as soon as possible. May I not prefix to Lady
Luxborough's Lines the Words – *Written by a Lady?*² I rec^d Mr Greave's Pieces by
Yesterday's Post.³ I am sorry I was so circumstanc'd that I could not possibly pay
my respects to Sir George Lyttelton.

I am Dear Sir
Your most oblig'd &c

R Dodsley

Address: To Wm Shenstone Esqr / at the Leasows near Birmingham
Postmark: 29 OC
Frank: R. Dodsley *free*

MS: BL. Add. MS. 28,959, ff. 25–6.

¹ The year is determined from a statement within the letter: "I rec^d Mr Greave's Pieces by Yesterday's
  Post." Graves's letter to RD (q.v.) is clearly dated 26 October 1754.
² The Lady agreed. In her letter of 12 December 1754 to Shenstone, she says: "what Mr. Dodsley I find
  does mention to you, viz. in the Title of the two trifles of mine, to say *Wrote by a Lady* – which is I think
  unexceptionable" (*Letters Written by the Late Right Honourable Lady Luxborough to William Shenstone*, ed
  Wm. Hodgetts (London, 1775). In fact, RD printed "By a Lady of Quality." See RD's letter to
  Shenstone on 15 February 1755.   ³ For a list of the pieces, see Graves's letter of 26 October.

To [George, Lord Lyttelton?] ¹

[October–December 1754]²

Dear Sir,

I rec^d yours, and am much oblig'd to You for your friendly concern on my
account.³ It is true I have fought your battles on some occasions, but I had always
Truth and Justice on my side. You have been more generous on this accusation,
and have innocently defended me, against both: for to confess the Truth I have
really hitherto been a Partner in the London Evening Post; having purchas'd a
Share in it many years ago, when it was by no means so obnoxious as it hath been of
late.⁴ I do not wonder indeed, ⟨from you that you should conclude⟩ from your
knowledge of my Principles & ⟨firm⟩ sincere attachment to the Government, that
you should conclude I had no share in that Paper; But tho' I had a Share in it as a
Proprietor, I can assure You with great truth that I had no more concern in the
management or direction of it than you have;⁵ nor do I know to this day who are the
Writers of it. I, as well as many other of the Proprietors have frequently
remonstrated against their Proceedings, but in vain:⁶ and I believe many others as
well as I, thought themselves (thus circumstanc'd) no more accountable for ⟨the⟩
⟨any⟩ the offenses ⟨that might be⟩ given, than a common Proprietor in any of the
Funds can think himself accountable for every Management in the Court of
Directors. However, since I find that my being a ⟨Partner in this⟩ mere Proprietor
in this Paper hath given particular offence, to show the sincerity of my attachment
to ye Government, I ⟨will⟩ ⟨have given⟩ will give up my Property as a Sacrifice of

Atonement; & have accordingly desir'd that my share may be sold at their next Meeting, tho' I am sensible it will not bring one sixth part of what it is worth.[7]

Thus, as I scorn a Lye, & find it extreamly disagreeable to prevaricate, I have never deny'd my being a Proprietor in the London Evening Post; but that I ever wrote a Line in it, is as far from the Truth, as those who accuse me of it are in this case from Candour, ⟨or Honesty⟩ or Honesty. The rev^d Mr Blaco, whom I never injur'd, whose Person I do not so much as know, & whose Name to the best of my knowledge never went out of my lips till on this occasion, injuriously spread a report that I was the author of some scurrilous lines in ye London Evening Post, which I never saw till after they were printed.[8] His next step was in ye Ev A [Evening Advertiser] to tax me with great assurance in printing 15 years ago, a book translated from the French entitled the *Institution of a Prince*, which he threaten'd to animadvert upon but I suppose upon trial found nothing to his purpose.[9] Upon this strange proceeding I called on Mr Bouquet the publisher of that Paper,[10] to know what offence I had given to ye writers of it that could occasion such a paragraph; and on his acknowledging that Mr Blaco had declar'd that he would take all opportunities of *stigmatizing* ye Proprietors of the London Evening Post, I desir'd that he would give my Compliments to Mr Blaco, and to assure him that I had not to my knowledge done or said any thing to offend him, or any of the Partners, and that if he had any thing to say against me, and would either give me leave to wait on him, or call on me & say it to my face, I should probably be able to give him a satisfactory answer: but that if he proceeded to abuse me in the Papers, I should endeavour to defend my self as well as I could. I was foolish enough to imagine that this might have satisfy'd him, but I was given to understand by a paragraph in the next day's Paper, that this Message be *answer'd publickly*.[11] ⟨and⟩ A few days afterwards, on the remonstrances of a friend against this proceeding, I receiv'd from Mr Blaco, the following extraordinary message: "If Mr Dodsley will in the London Evening Post, ⟨publickly⟩ disclaim his having written any thing against me, I shall have nothing farther to say ⟨to⟩ about him."[12] ⟨A modest Request!⟩ Very gracious truely! but I cannot help wondering how I came to be accountable to Mr Blaco for my Actions. Does ⟨Mr Blaco⟩ he think I am afraid of any thing he can say of me, that I should thus humbly deprecate his anger, by a public attestation of my Innocence? If he does, he is strangely mistaken: and if he does not, how can he have y^e *Assurance*, (to use his own expression) to ⟨think⟩ suppose I could submit to so mean a condescention, to one who I think should first justify, if he can, his own conduct towards me.[13]

MS: Bancroft Library, University of California at Berkeley, Commonplace Book of Robert Dodsley, I, ff. 9–12.

[1] Although hard evidence is lacking, George Lyttelton (1709–73), later Lord Lyttelton, seems a likely recipient of this letter. First of all, RD's various references to the Government and his offer to sell his share in the *London Evening Post* as an "Atonement" to the Government imply that he is addressing some government official. Of current ministers, Lyttelton would have been the most likely to write RD a letter of "friendly concern." As a member of "Cobham's Cubs," he had been one of the leaders of the Opposition at Leicester House (with whom RD sympathized) until, when the Prince of Wales

died in 1751, Henry Pelham brought him and other "Cubs" into the Government, causing new allegiances to the administration. In this context, the addressee's (and RD's) "attachment to the Government" fits the situation. Also, the obvious friendship that marks the letter – "I have fough your battles on some occasions" – amply reflects a familiarity bred of a publishing relationship that had seen eight editions of Lyttelton's works issued from Tully's Head over the last seven years. In addition, RD's particular choice of analogy – the management of funds – seems especially apt in light of Lyttelton's current office as a lord of the Treasury. Finally, RD's distressful situation – implicated in a treasonous attack upon the Crown because of his part ownership of a newspaper allegedly supporting Jacobite sympathies at Oxford – is of a kind that would draw forth a letter of "concern" from a Privy Councillor and friend who needed RD's own explanation in order to deal with the problem in the government.   ² For the dating rationale, see the last paragraph of note 13.

³ Letter not traced.

⁴ An Opposition newspaper, the *London Evening Post* was the most influential London newspaper sen into the country; the provincial newspapers depended upon it for their news and views. (See *Th Connoisseur*, 30 September 1756, and G. A. Cranfield, "The London Evening Post and the Jew Bil of 1753," *Historical Journal*, 8 (1965), 16–30.) The earliest evidence of RD's ownership in the *LEP* comes from a receipt for £150 issued to him by Richard Nutt on 5 May 1747 for 1/15 share in the paper. (See Appendix B.) This minimal share supports RD's contention that he had little contro over or even a knowledge of the paper's writers; it seems to have been merely a financial investment

⁵ The *LEP* had launched a most infamous campaign just the previous year against the Jew Bill, an administration attempt to allow the naturalization of Jews. Doubtless RD, with such friends as Mose and Solomon Mendes, cringed at these openly anti-Semitic attacks.

⁶ Of the "many other" proprietors, I have been able to discover only two: John Meres (d. 1761), who seemed to have the major ownership (at least earlier on), and Richard Nutt (1694?–1780), the printer of the paper. Nutt's marriage into the Meres family, and his signature on the receip mentioned in note 4, suggest that he had gained control of the paper at least by 1747. (See Plomer.

⁷ There is no evidence to show that RD did sell his share. He did continue to use the newspaper (perhaps because of its wide provincial circulation) as a medium for his various authors and for the advertisement of his publications. In a less threatening case two years later, disturbed with "scurrility" printed in the *London Chronicle*, he threatened to sell his share in that paper but did not (See his letter to William Strahan on 14 January 1757.)

⁸ The Rev. Richard Blacow, BA (1744), MA (1747), Brasenose College, Oxford, and a warden o streets at Oxford, embroiled himself on two occasions with what his enthusiasm resented as Jacobite and anti-Georgian incidents at the University. In 1747, he had attempted to arrest some drunken students shouting Jacobite sentiments, and when unsupported by the administration, he brought the case to the court of the King's Bench, securing the reprimand of both the accused and the "lax" Vice Chancellor, Dr William King. (This hostility flared up again in a series of pamphlets during the next and present, incident.) In 1754, considered by many at the University as a traitor and self-promoting troublemaker, Blacow was accused by the *LEP* and by *Jackson's Oxford Journal* as the perpetrator o the notorious "Rag-Plot." Dubbed a "plot" by the *LEP* and the *Journal* because it was viewed as an attempt to stir up public sentiment against supposed Jacobite interests at Oxford, this occasion involved the "discovery" at Oxford on 17 July 1754 of some anti-Georgian verses hidden in a discarded bag of rags. For bringing the verses to the attention of the Grand Jury, Blacow was viciously lampooned in the columns of the *LEP* throughout the period of August through November. Claiming that Blacow himself was the author of the treasonous verses, the number for 30 July–1 August printed "Another Letter from Oxford" in which it was reported that the "*Red Cow of Haslemere* shit this dirty treasonable Paper, as she is no Stranger to the meanest and basest of Undertakings." (On 29 June, the London publisher Charles Corbett had printed a satire on Blacow, entitled *The Cow of Hazlemere*. Regrettably, lacking the early issues of the *Evening Advertiser* (Blacow's voice in London) and whatever correspondence Blacow carried on with RD, it is impossible to determine with accuracy just which *LEP* piece Blacow attributed to RD's pen. Perhaps it was "A hint to the Dignified Informer" (12–15 October) that began: "As that dirty reverend Scribler appears strongly inclined to *hang* and *quarter* Authors, Printers, and Publishers . . ."

⁹ Unfortunately the handful of extant *Evening Advertisers* (in the Beinecke Library, Yale) covering the

period 21 November to 14 December do not carry Blacow's allegation. Apparently he was trying to link RD with the Jacobitism reflected in the Rag Plot by calling attention to a translation from the French that RD had published in 1740, Abbé Duguet's *The Institution of a Prince; or, an Introduction to the Science of Politics.* One allegation of connections with the French Court does appear in the extant *Evening Advertiser* for 7 December, but it is difficult to place chronologically in the ongoing dispute with Blacow, or even to tie to RD with certainty. In that number, a certain proprietor of the *LEP* is urged to tell the public about a letter from the French monarch regarding the raising of funds for the French Court.

    "J. Bouquet, at the sign of the White Hart, in Paternoster-row," published the *Evening Advertiser.* The previous year, his name is found in a number of imprints to anti-Jewish pamphlets and, in this year, in *A Defence of the Rector and Fellows of Exeter College,* a piece by Blacow's faction.

    Again, the appropriate number of the *Evening Advertiser* is missing.

    Not traced.

    The resolution of the dispute between Blacow and RD is not known; the evidence ends here. RD would remember the incident well, however: three years later, when disturbed with "scurrility" in the *London Chronicle,* he would write to his partner Strahan (14 January 1757), warning him that their 2-week-old enterprise could be forced out of business, as had the *Evening Advertiser* in 1756 for a similar practice.

    The fate of the *LEP*'s printer, Richard Nutt, is known, however. On 10 July 1755, he was tried and convicted of printing a libel on the Government under the signature "True Blue" (10 September). He was sentenced to stand in the pillory at Charing Cross for an hour, to be imprisoned in King's Bench Prison for two years, pay a £500 fine, and required to provide sureties for his good behavior for five years (Plomer).

    Despite this letter's yield of internal evidence, the absence of relevant issues of the *Evening Advertiser* precludes an exact dating. It could not have been written before 17 July 1754 when the Rag Plot opened, nor after 10 July 1755 when Nutt was sentenced and the case closed. On the basis of specific allusions to the *LEP* and the *EA,* however, together with the fact that the addressee is just now learning of RD's share in the *LEP,* it would seem the letter was written midway in the unraveling of the Rag Plot; that is, somewhere between October and December 1754.

To Joseph Warton

Pall mall Nov.ʳ 8 [1754][1]

Dear Sir

    I am so far from thinking that any thing malignant will appear in your Work, that I do not think there is anything malignant in your Nature. My sole cause of refusal was what I told you in my last.[2] You may be assur'd I will promote the sale of it as much as if I had publish'd it my self. And if Millar should refuse it (which I dare say he will not) I will transact yᵉ Affair for you with Mʳˢ Cooper or any other Publisher, just as I would for my self.[3] I send you enclos'd Voltaire's Poem, wᶜʰ I thought you had long ago, but which your Brother in one of his Letters says you never had.[4] I am

Dear Sir

most affectionately yʳˢ

R. Dodsley

I will [write soon to] Mʳ Millar about it.

MS: BL. Add. MS. 42,560, f. 29.

¹ The year appears certain from the context of the letter, whose subject – the publication of Warton's *Essay on the Writings and Genius of Mr. Pope* – seems in the next stage of progress in RD's letter to Warton, clearly dated 18 January 1755.

² Unfortunately, the letter is not traced. Because RD expected Warton's *Essay* to contain some adverse criticism of his patron, Pope, apparently he was reluctant to put his name to the piece. As is clear from earlier correspondence, he had already begun to alienate Warburton, Pope's literary executor, from whom he was still attempting to buy a share of Warburton's edition of Pope's *Works*. (See the exchange with Warburton of 26 December 1755 and 6 January 1756), and he did not want to publish a work that would totally sever the connection.

³ Apparently Millar also refused. Warton's *Essay* was published in 1756 by RD's frequent collaborator, Mary Cooper. The second edition in 1762 did carry RD's name, however, and the title was inverted to: *An Essay on the Genius and Writings of Mr. Pope*.

⁴ Most likely Voltaire's *Verses to the King of Prussia*, published by RD on 20 May 1753 (*PA*).

To William Shenstone

Nov.ʳ 19.ᵗʰ [1754]¹

Dear Sir

I recᵈ your excellent Pastoral, with which I am extremly pleas'd; but don't you think there is something too particular in the last Part of it? The Advice of Moschus – and Corydon's changing his Disease – in yᵉ 4ᵗʰ & 5ᵗʰ Stanzas.² I should like much to have them all set, to have it the last in the Book; & let yᵉ Music close the Volume. Arne has a very good Taste for Ballads, if you can perswade him to set them; & I should think it would be for his own Advantage, as he might sell them in his own Collections.³ But in this case you must stipulate with him that I shall have leave to engrave his Music in small Plates for my Volume. If you should not chuse to write to Arne, there is one Oswald with whom I am acquainted, who has a very pretty Taste for scotch airs: I think I could prevail with him to set the four parts.⁴ And I think there is a tenderness in yᵉ Scotch Airs that would suit the Words extreamly if happily set. As to the two questions you ask – I have printed above two thirds of the Volume, but am now standing still, being unwilling to proceed farther till I see what extent your pieces will go to, as I should be sorry to be oblig'd to leave any of them out.⁵ And as to Time, if you can let me have what you intend in about a fortnight or three weeks at most, it will do very well. But I should be glad to be determin'd the Music sooner, as it is to be compos'd, engrav'd, and work'd off. I cannot send any part of your Poems to press till I have the whole.

I am
Dear Sir
Your most obedᵗ Servᵗ

R Dodsley

Address: To William Shenstone Esq.ʳ / at the Leasows near Birmingham / Warwickshire
Postmark: 19 NO
Frank: R. Dodsley *free*

MS: BL. Add. MS. 28,959, ff. 29–30.

¹ The year must fall between two clearly dated events: on 29 October 1754, RD mentions in a letter to Shenstone that he has yet to receive the revised version of the poet's "Pastoral Ballad," a piece that he mentions in this letter as now having; the revised version appeared in Volume IV of RD's *Collection* (pp. 354–63) in March 1755.

² Apparently Shenstone acceded to RD's criticism, for, in the *Collection* text, Corydon does not change his disease, and Moschus does not appear at all. For a thorough comparison of extant texts of the "Pastoral Ballad," see Cleanth Brooks, ed., *The Percy Letters*, VII, 239–306.

³ Thomas Arne's music for only Part I of the "Pastoral Ballad" was printed on the last page of Volume IV of the *Collection*. As we know from RD's letter to Shenstone on 28 August 1756, Arne would also compose the music for the other three parts of the "Ballad"; in fact, in that letter, RD encloses Arne's music for those parts. The mystery that Brooks (note 2) has on his hands (p. 247) might well be explained by the existence of this music. Although Shenstone refers (in "Scruples," some queries for Richard Graves accompanying the later Yale text and printed in Brooks, p. 304) to a line in Part III as "so Arne printed it," he might well have meant not "printed" in the sense of "publish," but merely Arne's printing the text to accompany the measure of the music.

⁴ James Oswald (d. 1769), a Scot who had set up a music shop in St Martin's Lane, had written the music for RD's *Colin's Kisses* (1742), Edward Moore's *The Gamester* (1753), and later for RD's *Cleone*.

⁵ Shenstone's 13 poems covered the last 26 pages of Volume IV.

To William Shenstone

Pall mall Nov.ʳ 30.ᵗʰ [1754]¹

Dear Sir

I have been with Mʳ Arne, but I find he will expect six Guineas for setting the other three Parts; & I must treat with Mʳ Walsh for leave to make use of the 1ˢᵗ part, Mʳ Arne having sold the property of his Music to him.² If therefore You have no objection I will try Mʳ Oswald, & when he has set them will send the Music down to You, & if you do not approve of it I will not insert it.³ Your Pastoral is extreamly admir'd by several whom I have shewn it to, but they think it might be still improv'd merely by being shorten'd: but of this You must be the judge to determine. Should not yᵉ Words "written after leaving a public Place" be left out? I mean because they make it too particular.⁴ I will not speak to Mʳ Oswald till I hear from You. I hope yᵉ remainder of what you intend to favour me with will come in a post or two.

I am Dear Sir
Your most obedᵗ Servᵗ
R Dodsley

Address: To William Shenstone Esqʳ / at the Leasows near Birmingham
Postmark: 30 NO
Frank: R. Dodsley *free*

MS: BL. Add. MS. 28,959, ff. 31–2.

¹ The year is determined both from the letter's following up a suggestion proposed in the former RD letter to Shenstone, namely, negotiating with Arne for setting the music to Shenstone's "Pastoral Ballad"; and a letter from Arne to Shenstone (BL Add. MS. 28,959, ff. 27–8), fully dated 30 November 1754, in which the musician says he received Shenstone's letter through RD and recounts largely what RD writes here.

² John Walsh the younger, musical instrument maker and music printer, publisher, and seller, at the Harp and Hautboy, Catherine Street, Strand, during the period 1736–66. Listed in newspaper advertisements as the "King's printer," Walsh inherited the business from his father who had been music printer to William III.

³ Either Shenstone preferred Arne's services from the beginning or Oswald's did not suit, for only Arne's setting for Part I of the "Ballad" was included in Volume IV of the *Collection*. Arne eventually set the music for the other three parts. See RD's letter of 28 August 1756, and Shenstone's letter to Lady Luxborough 29 March 1755 (Williams, p. 438).   ⁴ The phrase was omitted in the printing.

To William Shenstone

Decr 16 [1754]¹

Dear Sir

I have impatiently expected a Letter every Post last Week, but having not yet receiv'd any, begin to fear it must have miscarry'd. You will see perhaps by the Papers that I have sufer'd the Misfortune of losing my Wife,² 'tis on that Account that I have been for some weeks past in so unhappy a Situation as not to be able to attend to Business at all. I hope you rec'd mine relating to Mr Arne and Mr Oswald.³ I should be extreamly glad if ⟨You⟩ what you intend to favour me with might be sent in a post or two, as I should be glad to publish the beginning of January.

I am
Dear Sir
Your most oblig'd & obed^t Servt
R Dodsley

Address: To William Shenstone Esqr / at the Leasows near Birmingham
Postmark: 16 DE
Frank: R. Dodsley *free*

MS: BL. Add. MS. 28,959, ff. 33–4.

¹ The year is determined from the date of the death of RD's wife.
² Catherine Iserloo Dodsley had died on 12 December 1754 (newspaper citation) and was buried in St James's churchyard, Piccadilly. Her age at death is uncertain. The record of the Dodsleys' marriage at St James's Westminster, on 14 February 1732, shows her to have been "aged twenty-one and upwards."   ³ See RD's letters to Shenstone of 19 and 30 November.

To William Shenstone

Pallmall Decr 31st [1754]¹

Dear Sir

I have waited with great Impatience for your concluding Packet, having long since printed every thing but Yours and your friends pieces. I believe I have enough to finish the Volume, only if there be any thing remaining that You would chuse should be in, I should be glad to have it, as I am desirous of having as much of Yours as I can possibly insert.[2] The Music is engrav'd for the Pastoral; the Ballad you mention'd of the Lass of the Vale I have not yet receiv'd.[3] Pray, if You have any thing more to favour me with, let it come by the return of the Post, as I shall otherwise be in danger of losing the best part of the season for Publication.

I am

Dear Sir

Your most obed^t hum^{ble} Servt

R Dodsley

Address: To William Shenstone Esqr / at the Leasows near / Birmingham
Postmark: [31] DE
Frank: R. Dodsley *free*

MS: BL. Add. MS. 28,959, ff. 35–6.

[1] The year is determined from the impending publication of Volume IV of RD's *Collection*, 18 March 1755 *(PA)*.   [2] RD printed thirteen of Shenstone's poems at the end of Volume IV.
[3] Only the music for Part I of the "Ballad" was published at this time. Shenstone did eventually submit "Nancy of the Vale" but not until 1757, and it would finally appear in Volume V of the *Collection* (pp. 16–19) published on 18 March 1758 *(LEP,* 16–18 March).

To William Shenstone

Saturday night. [18 January 1755][1]

Dear Sir

I receiv'd your final Packet, and am much oblig'd to you, for all the trouble you have so kindly taken on this occasion. I have spent this whole day amongst your Papers & those of your friends, & have put them as nearly in the order you desire as I can. I hope to send you prooft sheets of the whole of them before next week is out, which I beg you will correct & send back by the return of the Post.[2] I have impertinently attempted to alter one Stanza of Lady Luxborough's, which pray restore to it's original reading if you like it better.[3] The Ballad in ye scottish Taste I have omitted.[4] And one of the Songs which you would have kept out (ye Lady's Visit) I have put in.[5] But you will order that as you please. Nancy of ye Vale you never sent.

I am Dear Sir

Your most obed^t Servt

R Dodsley

Address: To William Shenstone Esq. / at the Leasows near / Birmingham
Postmark: 18 JA
Frank: R. Dodsley *free*

MS: BL. Add. MS. 28,959, ff. 22–3.

[1] The month and day are determined by the postmark, and the year by the impending publication of Volume IV of RD's *Collection* (18 March 1755), the subject of the letter.

² Shenstone had sent RD the verses of several of his friends, including those of Lady Luxborough, William Somerville, John Scott Hylton, Richard Graves and Richard Jago.

³ It is difficult to judge to which of Lady Luxborough's four poems in Volume IV RD refers, but most likely it is "Written at a Ferme ornee nr. B. 1749," a poem he had singled out for comment in previous letters to Shenstone (27 August 1754, and 29 October 1754), the subject of which is Shenstone's own Leasowes.

⁴ Probably the poem Shenstone had copied into his Miscellany as "In the scotch Manner, by the Revd. Mr. Saunders." See *Shenstone's Miscellany 1759–1763*, ed. Ian A. Gordon (Oxford: Clarendon Press, 1952), p. 39. In his notes to the poem (p. 146), Gordon identifies Saunders as Shenstone's cousin, the same William Sanders of Tardelrigge, who, together with his brother John, was left a £100 bequest in Shenstone's will.

⁵ "Daphne's Visit" (*Collection*, IV, 347–8), one of Shenstone's five songs in the volume.

To Joseph Warton

Pall mall Jan^ry 18th 1755

Dear Sir

I rec^d your Specimen of an Essay on the Genius of Pope. I dare say you will contrive in your Animadversions to allow him all his due praise; and where you differ from him will do it in such a manner as to render it no impropriety in me to be the Publisher of it.¹ I like your specimen of Paper & Print, & think you should work off 750. But this I leave you to determine. An air of Dogmaticalness I know you will in general avoid, yet in ye beginning of ye 2^d paragraph is there not a little the appearance of it? Might it not run thus? – "It is *somewhat* strange, that in the Pastorals of a young Poet there should not *appear* a single *rural image that is new*: yet this I *am afraid* is ye case &c.".² My 4.th Volume will come out the beginning of February.³ I was in hopes of seeing you in Town before now, when will you come? I think you are right in concealing your self as the Author; and you may be assur'd I will not divulge it.⁴ I will write to your brother to night.⁵ I hope Mrs Warton is well. I endeavour to be as well as I can, and therefore will not attempt to say any thing on my loss.⁶

I am ever
Affectionately Yours
R. Dodsley

P S I have drawn a line you see under ye words I would have you change. You will laugh at me perhaps for changing *something* for *somewhat*, but don't you think there is some difference? In ye 3^d Page should not *explode* precede *extirpate*?⁷ Do complaints of immoderate heat totally lose their consistency in a British Shepherd, in ye midst of Suñer?

MS: BL. Add. MS. 42,560, f. 32.

¹ See RD's letter to Warton on 8 November 1754, notes 2 and 3. Obviously, for the moment at least, he had changed his mind and had now decided to publish Warton's *Essay on Pope*.

² RD's request was not heeded. Warton's criticism of Pope on p. 2 of the 1756 edition was a bit stronger: "It is something strange, that in the pastorals of a young poet there should not be found a single rural image that is new: but this I am afraid is the case." See RD's "PS."

³ RD's *Collection*, Volume IV, did not appear until 18 March.

4 Warton did not keep his own secret. See RD's letter to him on 8 April 1756.
5 RD's letter to Thomas Warton (q.v.) is dated two days later.
6 The death of RD's wife, a month earlier.
7 Warton did not yield on this point either, as the 1756 edition shows. If these few instances are indicative of the haggling that went on through the rest of the manuscript stage between the assertive author and the cautious publisher, it is not surprising that RD ultimately refused to put his name to the imprint and engaged Mary Cooper to publish the work.

To Thomas Warton, the younger

Pall mall Jan 20 1755

Dear Sir

I rec^d a specimen of your brother's Essay on the Writings & Character of Pope, which I take for granted he will write in such a manner as that I can have no objection to publish it.¹ I hope for his own sake that he will allow Pope his just Praise. I like the specimen of Paper & Print, & suppose you will get it done as cheap at Oxford as I should here, and as quick, for the Parliament will rise ye very beginning of April.² If it be well written, and the Criticism new and important, I should imagine you might print 750; if otherwise, 500 may be more than enough. I have sent him 2 or 3 remarks on this first half sheet. What I'm most afraid of is that he will be apt to write in too peremptory a manner.

I am

Dear Sir

very affectionately Yours,

R. Dodsley

MS: BL. Add. MS. 42,560, f. 33.

¹ See RD's letter to Joseph Warton on 18 January.
² For several reasons, the publication of Joseph Warton's *Essay on the Writings and Genius of Mr. Pope* would be delayed until April 1756. At this point, Warton had yet to begin the *Essay*. Through the spring of 1755, he would be trying to keep up with the press, churning out the manuscript in sections, which he would immediately send off to his brother at Oxford, where Thomas saw to its printing and proofing. But domestic disruption took its toll on his output. In March, he was playing nursemaid to a family weathering an epidemic of measles (Joan Pittock quotes his account in a letter recently available in the Swann Collection at Trinity College; see "Lives and Letters: New Wartoniana," *DUJ* (1978), 198), and in May a move to another rectory, though not distant, proved a further distraction. Together, these troubles help to explain his failure to meet the April delivery date RD had recommended and perhaps caused a weakening of his resolution. I am indebted to David Fairer, who, using the brothers' correspondence, pieces the story together in "The Writing and Printing of Joseph Warton's *Essay on Pope*," *SB*, 30 (1977), 211–19.

To William Shenstone

[24 January 1755]¹

Dear Sir

I have not time to write 3 words. Whatever little alterations I have made I beg you will pay no regard to but restore ye old reading where you like it. The most material alteration is in a Stanza of Lady L——— I forgot to insert your reading of ye last Stanza of D^o but I think it better.^{2} All I beg is that you will send them me back by the return of the Post. Mr Somerville's are in ye preceding Sheet.^{3}

I am ever

D^r S^r

faithfully Yours

R Dodsley

Address: To William Shenstone Esqr / at the Leasows near Birmingham
Postmark: 24 IA
Frank: Free J: Harris^4 Warwickshire

MS: BL. Add. MS. 28,959, f. 24.

¹ The date is determined from the postmark and from the impending publication of Volume IV of RD's
   Collection in March 1755.   ² Lady Luxborough. See RD's letter to Shenstone of 18 January.
³ Volume IV of the *Collection* carried "An Address to his Elbow-chair, new cloath'd" (pp. 302–3) and
   the song "As o'er Asteria's fields I rove" by William Somerville (1675–1742).
⁴ Possibly the frank of John Harris, currently an MP from Devon, who kept a house in town near RD, in
   Pall Mall.

To William Shenstone

Pall mall Feb^{ry} 15th 1755

Dear Sir

   I am afraid You have thought me long in giving my thanks for all your kindness, and for all the trouble you have taken on my account.^{1} I am in some pain for those different readings which You left so imprudently to my determination: but I have done as well as I could, & have generally thought it the best way to follow where you seem'd to point. The concluding Stanza in Mr Whistler's Poem I wish You may like.^{2} Pray direct me how I must send you the Volume. I hope to be able to send it in about a week. The Three Vols are at present out of print, but I think they will be ready in about a Month, when I purpose to send you a compleat Sett.^{3} Would Lady L——— think it impertinent if I sent her a Sett?^{4} Pray give me your opinion. I purpose also a Sett for Mr Graves, and Mr Hylton, but know not how I can send them. Mr Jago is in Town & has told me how to send his.^{5} I am in a perpetual hurry & scarce know not what I write. I am ever

most faithfully & truely Yours

R Dodsley

[vertically, along left margin:] I send Lady L———'s Letter enclosed; from which I think it plain she had no objection to my saying – *By a Lady of Quality.*^{6}

MS: BL. Add. MS. 28,959, f. 37.

¹ Shenstone's "kindness" and "trouble" were expended on the editing of his friends' verses for Volume
   IV of RD's *Collection.*

² Shenstone's lately deceased friend, Anthony Whistler (1714–54), had two poems in Volume IV: "Flowers" (pp. 327–9) and a song, "While, Strephon, thus you Teize one" (p. 329). There is no evidence to show which one RD adjusted.

³ The fourth edition of Volumes I–III of RD's *Collection* would appear the same day as the first edition of Volume IV, 18 March (*PA*).

⁴ Lady Luxborough. Shenstone thought it a good idea: see his response of 4 March.

⁵ Richard Graves, John Scott Hylton, and Richard Jago, friends of Shenstone and contributors to Volume IV, would become regular correspondents of RD.

⁵ Lady Luxborough's letter was probably the one addressed to Shenstone on 12 December 1754, which the poet, in turn, had probably forwarded to RD to resolve the bookseller's uneasiness regarding his proposed by-line for her poems: "Written by a Lady." See RD's letter to Shenstone of 29 October 1754, note 2.

From William Shenstone

The Leasowes, March 4.ᵗʰ 1755.

Dear Sir,

I return you many thanks for the Compliment you make my Friends & Me in the offer of a sett of miscellanies x I dare say L.ᵈʸ Luxborough will take it well to be included in it.¹ My Expectation of seeing the last volume advertis'd, was the reason I have not made you this acknowledgment before.

The Delay has given me some Pain; not thro' the least Impatience of seeing my Trifles made publick; for I am really fearfull of the ⟨?⟩ appearance, & could wish a longer time to adjust the state of my contributions. But this very Wish makes me reflect upon the time that has elaps'd since I wrote to you; & of which, I trust, I could have avail'd myself to your satisfaction & my own. I suppose that the Impression must now be taken off; if otherwise, & that for any particular Reason you have chosen it should be deferd I should be glad that you would ⟨acquaint⟩ afford me yᵉ earliest Intelligence.²

> I am ever faithfully
> & affectionately yours
> Will: Shenstone

⟨Mʳˢ Rock⟩³
My Lord Dudley will accept my respectfull Compliments & pardon my Freedom in requesting yᵗ he would frank me these few Covers. We are told here yᵗ my L.ᵈ has lately taken a House in Town, which seems to t[?]⁴

MS: BL. Add. MS. 28,959, f. 38.

¹ Material from "x" through the end of the sentence appears between the letter's lines and is inserted before "My" with a caret. For Luxborough, see RD's letter to Shenstone on the previous 15 February.

² It was too late; Volume IV of RD's *Collection* would appear exactly two weeks later.

³ Mrs Rock is unidentified. This note appears beneath Shenstone's signature on f. 38ᵛ but written perpendicular to the body of the letter. Why Shenstone did not complete the concluding sentence is not clear.

[4] Fernando Dudley Lea (d. 1757), 5th Baron Dudley, was the son of William Lea of Hales-Owen Grange whose sister had married into the Shenstone family (Marjorie Williams, *William Shenstone and His Friends.* London: English Association, 1933). As an executor, Shenstone was called in 1758 to testify in the case of Lord Dudley's will. See Hylton's letter to RD on 2 March 1758.

From John Gilbert Cooper

Thurgarton   Wednesday March the [5th 1755][1]

Dear S^r

I have spent the little leisure [I] have had in the country, since I left Town, in comp[osing] the enclos'd Poem, of which I desire your a[?] I would have it put into the Press immediate[ly?] printed in Quarto as Mr Grey's Elegy w[as,] upon a good paper, & it will make a v[ery] ⟨good⟩ tolerable Sixpenny pamphlet.[2] I shall remain [here] till tomorrow sennight, viz Thursday y^e [13th] &, if you can get the first proof sheet on [to] the press, (which may easily be done) by [next] Tuesday, desire you would send it down [in a] frank by that nights post, directed to [me at] Thurgarton, & I will correct it & re[turn it by the next Post but if not then to Leices]ter where I shall receive it on Saturday [morn]ing the 15th, & will return it by that [nigh]t's Post, let me have the remainder sent [the] Post after. I shall stay at Leicester [from] Thursday the 13th to Wesnesday the 19th, [and] then set out with My Babes for London, [hop]e to be in Town, (please God we all [are] true well & no accident happens) on Saturday [the 2]2^d of this month. – I beg, if there is [a pos]sibility of having it, that you would send [the fi]rst proof Sheet by next Tuesday night's Post, [& the] last by Thursday's, for I would have [it pub]lish'd on Thursday the 20th, neither [earlier] nor later. don't advertise it before [it com]es out, & then only in the Public [Advertiser?][3]

insist upon it that only 500 shall be struck [off] in the first impression. my comp^{ts} to you[r] Brother. I am, Dear S^r,

your Sincere & aff^{te} Fri[end]

J G Cooper ^{Jun^r}

my comp^{ts} to Mr Hughs & tell him I must hav[e] the time. tell Welch, my old Composer, [how] that if he fails me I will never make [him] drunk again.[4] adieu. send it, as soon as you have read it, on Friday

MS: Bodleian Ms. Eng. Misc. d. 174, ff. 91–3.

[1] The day is taken from Cooper's statement: "I shall remain [here] till tomorrow sennight, viz Thursday y^e [13th]," a date which, though obscured in the text, is determinable from the configuration of other dates mentioned in the text. The year is perceived by a process of elimination: the only Cooper poem published by RD in March of any year was *The Tomb of Shakespeare. A Poetical Vision*, a work of 1755.   [2] It was published in quarto, price 6*d*.

[3] An entire line is missing from the holograph at this point. RD cooperated with Cooper's rigid schedule, but he did not advertise *The Tomb* until 23 March 1755, and then in both the *Public Advertiser* and the *London Evening Post* on the same day. Probably vanity is the only explanation for Cooper's

wanting the poem published while he was in town, for the piece is hardly topical or controversial. It was reprinted three years later in Volume IV of RD's *Collection*, pp. 325–32.

⁴ John Hughs (1703–71), printer in Great Turnstile, who is thought to have done most of RD's printing. (See Introduction A.) Apparently Welch was one of Hughs's compositors.

From Thomas Lisle¹

Lincolns-Inn-fields
Holborn Row N:7.
[*c*. 18 March 1755]²

S^r,

When I was at Your house this morning I p[aid] for the fourth Volume of Your Miscellanies, which I left to be bound, & at the same time I paid for Dr Young's Centaur, which I intended to have brought with me, but forgot to take it, & left it on the Counter. – The design of this is only to beg the favor of You, when You send the Miscellanies, to send the Centaur with it.

I Am, S^r,
Your very Humble Servt
Tho: Lisle

As You may probably hereafter print another volume of Poems, I have some few things by me, wrote in my Younger days, & [if] You think it worth while to call upon a Man entirely unknown to You, merely for the chance of finding something You may not di[s]like, You shall be very welcome to look after them, &, if You ap[prove,] to make use of them, if not, they may sleep as they have done for these last twenty years.³ –

Address: To / Mr Robert Dodsley / Bookseller in / Pall-Mall
Postmark: [PENNY POST PAYD]

MS: Bodleian, MS. Eng. Letters d. 40, f. 105.

¹ Thomas Lisle (1709–67), DD Magdalen College, Oxford (1743); Public Orator (1745); rector of Wootton on Wight (1736) and (concurrently) of Burghclere, near Newbury (1746). Besides printing poems in RD's *Collection* (see below), Lisle also employed the publisher in late 1756 to issue his father's, Edward Lisle's, *Observations on Husbandry*. Lisle himself became the subject of a ghostly local legend: "Wootton Lodge . . . formerly the Parsonage . . . was reputed to be haunted by the ghost of a former rector, Dr. Thomas Lisle. At midnight this restless priest, in gown and cassock, regularly ascended the old oaken staircase." W. H. Davenport Adams, *The Isle of Wight: Its History, Topography and Antiquities* (London: T. Nelson & Sons, 1888), p. 164. See Courtney, pp. 108–10.

² The date seems proximate to the publication of Volume IV of RD's *Collection* (18 March 1755) but after that of Edward Young's *The Centaur Not Fabulous*, published by RD and Millar on 4 March 1755 (*PA*), to both of which Lisle alludes.

³ RD printed seven of Lisle's poems in Volume VI of his *Collection*, pp. 162–210.

From John Gilbert Cooper

Newport Pagnel Thursday [night March ye 20 1755][1]

Dear S^r

I rec^d the favor of your letter this day at Northampton, & am got to this place with my Children in my way to London. Surely you'll be able to sell the small number you mention in two or three days.[2] therefore intreat you not to baulk the sale but to keep the types still standing (as it is a small thing) that we may strike off a second impression without loss of time, in case there should be a demand, as I make no question but there will be. have courage, advertise well, you shall have all profits, & I will indemnify you by standing to all loss if there should be any. if the Printer has taken down the types & you find there is a quick demand on Friday, I beg you would make him fall to work to compose afresh that night, make him work all Saturday & have a second impression ready for sale early on Monday morning. I shall be with you on Saturday night. do all you can, for you know I doat upon the words *Second Edition* in a News Paper.[3] adieu. yours in haste

Most Sincerely & affe^tely

J G Cooper Junr

MS: Bodleian Ms. Eng. Misc. d. 174, f. 97.

[1] The date follows from Cooper's letter to RD on 5 March 1755 (q.v.), where he apparently speaks of the same work and the same trip to London and also specifies 20 March as a Thursday, the day on which he had wanted the *Tomb of Shakespeare* to be published.
[2] RD would have the work set in three days, publishing it on 23 March.
[3] *The Tomb* does not seem to have made a second edition.

From William Shenstone

The Leasowes, March the 23^d 1755.

Dear Sir

I had the Pleasure of receiving the fourth volume of your miscellanies, which arriv'd as I remember last thursday was se'nnight. I am oblig'd to you for the care you took to forward it, when printed, as well as for all that Trouble I occasion'd you, *before*. Some Improvements may be made in a subsequent Impression; & whenever this is propos'd I dare say you will give me notice.[1] In general, you have done all that I could expect from a Person of Genius and a Friend.

It remains for me to wish that the Book may fully recompense you, I will not only say, for the Pains you have taken, but for the Discernment you have shewn. It contains many excellent pieces, that are entirely new to me: & if others that are no less excellent have been printed before, it cannot reasonably be objected by such as consider your first Design.

Is it impertinent to ask the Names of those Persons who have not inserted them? If so, I drop my enquiry. The Pages, where their lines occurr, are, 73. 114. 119. 170. 200. 202. 227. 228. 233. 250. 253. 265. 267. 305. 307.[2] Should the parliament sit till

June, I have some thoughts of printing my ode upon Rural elegance; together with some such other Pieces as may make a 12 penny pamphlett. – But if my Purpose continues you will hear from me again soon, & I shall send you up a copy, about half-correct, for your Opinion.[3]

I hope M.ʳ Baskerville meets in London with the encouragement he deserves.[4] I long to hear from you upon all accounts, am, your most affectionate
& most obedient Servant
Will. Shenstone

MS: BL. Add. MS. 28,959. f. 39.

[1] A second edition did not appear until 18 March 1758, the day on which Volumes V and VI were published. This first edition of Volume IV and the fourth edition of Volumes I–III, all advertised as for sale five days earlier, represent an example of what Keith Maslen has termed "shared printing" ("Shared Printing and the Bibliographer: New Evidence from the Bowyer Press," *Studies in the Eighteenth Century: Papers presented at the Fourth David Nichol Smith Memorial Seminar, Canberra 1976*, ed. R. F. Brissenden and J. C. Eade (Australian National University Press, 1979), pp. 193–206). Although the name of RD's regular printer John Hughs appears in the imprint to all volumes, William Bowyer's Paper Stock Ledger, p. 953, reveals that he printed 1,500 copies of signatures A–K⁸ of Volume IV, which he delivered to Hughs on 25 March 1755. (Could this have been a second printing? Volume IV had been advertised for sale a week earlier.) Also, the Strahan Papers (BL Add. MS. 48,800) show this printer charging RD £14.6.0. for work on the fourth edition of Volume II, an additional £10.6.0. for a canceled leaf, and £9 for a ream of paper. (I am indebted to Professor Maslen for the allusion to Bowyer's ledger.)

[2] Soame Jenyns (73), Joseph Trapp (114), Robert Lowth (119), Edward Lovibond (170), unknown (200), David Garrick (202), George Bubb Dodington (227), William Blackstone (228), James Grainger (233), unknown (250), Thomas Warton (253), Gilbert West (265), Edward Moore (267), Charles Parrot (305 and 307). RD identifies most of these authors in his 29 March response to Shenstone (q.v.). But it is surprising that in the place of poems written by his friends Lowth and Garrick, RD should write "unknown," unless, of course, he was not free to identify the authors.

[3] The poem did not appear until three years later when RD opened Volume V of his *Collection* (pp. 1–13) with it. Shenstone had expressed the same desire in a letter to John Scott Hylton two days earlier. (See Williams, p. 434.)

[4] During 1754, Baskerville had been issuing specimens for his proposed edition of Virgil. See Baskerville's letter to RD on 16 January 1754, note 2. In his letter to Shenstone on 29 March 1755, RD says "Baskerville's Specimen is much approv'd & he has met with great Encouragement at both the Universities."

To William Shenstone

Pall mall   March 25.ᵗʰ 1755

Dear Sir

It is with pleasure I inform You that your Poems in my 4ᵗʰ Volume are very much approv'd of by several people, particularly by D.ʳ Akinside, who, desir'd that I would give you his Complimᵗˢ and thanks for the pleasure you had given him in reading them.[1] I shall be very glad to hear how you like the rest of the Volume: it is here in general well approved of.[2] I sent you by yᵉ Carrier last week carriage paid, four setts, one of wᶜʰ I beg You will accept for your self, one for Lady Luxborough, one for M.ʳ Greaves, & one for M.ʳ Hylton. I hope the sending them will not give You much trouble, as I am asham'd, and ought to apologize for what I have already given, instead of adding to it. A sett for Mʳ Jago I have sent by his direction to a relation of his in town, who will forward it to him. And if you have any other friends that you would chuse to make presents to, I beg you will without the least scrupple send me your coñands. I am very glad to find that my favorite, the Pastoral Ballad, is universally admir'd.³ I wish I had had the Lass of the Vale, whom you once mention'd; I dare say she is a beautiful and accomplish'd, tho' rural, Girl; and I therefore wonder how you can be so cruel to lock her up from the World. But I will take care to get it insinuated to her that I intend to fit up another Apartment, where I hope she will prevail with you to permit her with some of her companions to pay me a visit.⁴

I am
Dear Sir
Your most oblig'd
& obed.ᵗ Serv.ᵗ

R Dodsley

Address: To William Shenstone Esqʳ / at the Leasowes near Birmingham
Postmark: 25 MR
Frank: R. Dodsley *free*

MS: BL. Add. MS. 28,959, ff. 40–1.

¹ See previous RD – Shenstone correspondence. Mark Akenside the poet and frequent reader for RD's publications.
² But Horace Walpole, for whom RD was both friend and bookseller, told Richard Bentley he thought Volume IV "the worst tome of the four" (*Correspondence of Horace Walpole with John Chute, Richard Bentley, et al*, ed. W. S. Lewis, A. Dayle Wallace, and Robert A. Smith (New Haven: Yale University Press, 1973), p. 214).   ³ See previous RD – Shenstone correspondence.
⁴ "Nancy of the Vale. A Ballad" would appear in the fifth volume of the *Collection* (pp. 16–18), published in 1758.

To William Shenstone

Pall mall   March 29.ᵗʰ 1755

Dear Sir
      Before this reaches your hands I hope You will have rec.ᵈ the four Setts of Poems I mention'd in my last, which I would not have given You the trouble of if I had known how to send them. I am very glad to hear you have an Ode on Rural Elegance as I know nobody so well qualify'd to write on that subject as your self: but if you intend to publish it this spring, it is time you should send it up, as the Parliament will certainly rise in less than a month, perhaps in three weeks.¹ You have certainly a right to know the writers in the 4ᵗʰ Volume. Those you enquire after are – Page 73 Soame Jennings Esq.ʳ 114 Mʳ Trap. 119 unknown, 170 Mʳ Lovibond. 200 Unknown. 202 Unknown. 227 M.ʳ Dodington, 228 Unknown. 233 D.ʳ Grainger. 250 Unknown. 253 M.ʳ T Warton, 265 Mʳ West. 267 M.ʳ Moore. 305

and 307 M! Parrat.[2] Mr Baskerville's Specimen is much approv'd, & he has met with great Encouragement at both the Universities.[3] I long to see your Rural Elegance, & hope you will be able to send it time enough for this Season.

I am Dear Sir

most sincerely Yours

R Dodsley

Address: To Wm Shenstone Esqr / at the Leasowes near / Birmingham
Postmark: 29 MR
Frank: R. Dodsley *free*

MS: BL. Add. MS. 28,959, ff. 42–3.

[1] See Shenstone's letter to RD on 23 March 1755, note 3.   [2] Ibid., note 2.
[3] Baskerville's specimen for his forthcoming edition of Virgil. See Baskerville's letter to RD on 16 January 1754, note 2.

From William Whitehead

1 April 1755

. . . I am much obliged for your account of my play tho' Mr Sanderson in some measure forstalled you. I still find the *Pythia* does not please; tho' she plays the part sensibly, yet every body tells me she seems to have no idea of the fury and vehemence of her character where she is to assume an air of inspiration. You will make my compliments to Mr Garrick & thank him for the revival.[1] I told him if I met with any dancers that were tolerable I would let him know, but I have seen none at all that were worth his having. They talk of some at dresden, but as I was not there during the carnival I shall probably have no opportunity of seeing them. We shall leave this place the 5 or 6 may, & after having been at dresden, Berlin, Brussels, Hanover, Gotha, Ratisbon, Munich, Vienna, & perhaps too the Courts on the Rhine, we are in hopes of reaching Italy in October or November. If I can be of any service to you there you must write to me immediately, if anywhere afterwards Mr Sanderson will give you directions, & I shall be glad to execute anything you desire. I send you enclosed an account of Dr Lowth's book in the *Acta Eruditorum* at Leipsic, which you will be so good as to transmit to him . . . They talk kindly of him, but at the same time they seem to be his enemies, & therefore you must not believe at most above half what they say. I will speak to him myself the first opportunity.[2] English books, tho' every body here almost reads English, take a good while before they make their way hither, they have sea, & a good deal of Country to pass. However, I am greatly pleased to find our Language grow almost universal . . . I am obliged for your intention of sending the miscellanies but have very little expectation of receiving them, the methods of their getting here are so very dilatory & uncertain.[3] You will make my compliments to all my friends you meet with, & if I can be of any service to them where I am they will oblige me by commanding it.

Source: Straus, pp. 111–12.

¹ *Creusa, Queen of Athens, a Tragedy*, one of three new tragedies brought on by Garrick at Drury Lane during the 1753–4 season, was first acted on 20 April 1754 and revived on three separate nights during the spring of 1755: 25 February, 1 March, and 10 April (*London Stage*). (For RD's purchase of the copyright, See Appendix B and Joseph Warton's letter to RD on 29 September 1753, note 7.) Whitehead seems to be hanging the blame on Miss Haughton who had played the part of Pythia in all performances. But the *Monthly Review* account (May 1754, pp. 374–84) had blamed the deficiency on Whitehead, saying that the author had lowered the character of Pythia, the chief priestess of the Delphic Oracle, by making her an "inquisitive busy-body" for the dramatic purpose of eliciting the play's action in a manner different from that of the Ancients and of the French.

Mr Sanderson, a clergyman of private fortune, had lived the earlier part of his life in town as a coffee house companion of Whitehead's, before marrying and returning to Haslemere. Whitehead addressed Sanderson in his "Elegy VI. To another Friend. Written at Rome, 1756." See *Plays and Poems by William Whitehead. To Which Are Prefixed Memoirs of His Life and Writings by W[illiam] Mason* (3 vols. London and York, 1774–88), III, 42–3.

² Robert Lowth's *De Sacra Poesi Hebraiorum*, published by RD and Andrew Millar in March of 1753, was reviewed in *Nova Acta Eruditorum*, XIV (November, 1754), 644–51.

³ The new Volume IV and the revised Volumes I–III of RD's *Collection* that had appeared on 18 March. RD's letter to Whitehead has not been traced.

From Richard Jago¹

Har[bury] [early April 1755]²

Sir,

I cou'd not prevail upon myself [to write you on the] present Subject, did I not persuade myself that [You w^d] readily credit me; when I assure You, that my Enquiry [was in] Reference to the kind Promise You was pleased to ma[ke me] when I was in Town. This I say, not w.th Intention [to] suggest any Mediocrity of Esteem for y.^{r} favour, but to [prevent] any Imputation of my distrusting the Faithfulness of y.^{r} [Word?] or the Punctuality of y.^{r} Execution of so voluntary an Eng[agement.]

After so cautious a Preface the drift of my Inquiry is [neither] more nor less than this, "Whether your new Impression of [the] 3 first Vol: of y.^{r} Miscell: is already compleated, if not wh[ether] any, & what Part of them is printed, or if Nothing of the kind is yet done, how long it will be before You set it. It is not at all Material that You sh^d know the tr[ue] Reason for my asking these Questions, nor am I at Liberty to give [the Belief] at the same Time that I dissavow any Intention of reminding [You] of y.^{r} Promise hereby, I think it not improper to add that [I] accept the performance of it, as I did the Promise itself, many Thanks.³

I had a Letter from Mr Shenstone last wee[k in] which he mentions his Receipt of the 4.th Vol: of y.^{r} Misc. his Satisfaction in it, & his Belief of its being well rec[eiv'd.]

[I do not know this from?] my Situation nor Correspond[ence for I have little?] w.th the Poetical World; but from [his past suc]cess, and known Judgment I sh^d not in [?] the Truth of his Account of the favorable [reception] of Pieces collected by your hand, was I not consc[ious that] such a Declaration might be construed to imply som[e deg]ree of Self-Commendation.

I desire You will favour me w.th an Answer at [your b]est Leisure directed as below, in wch You will oblige Sir,

Your most Obedient humble Servant,

Ric^d. Jago.

To / The Revd Mr Jago / at Harbury, near Southam in / Warwickshire

MS: Humanities Research Center, University of Texas at Austin, Robert Dodsley / Recipient 1 / Bound, f. 107.

[1] Richard Jago (1715–81) was a school fellow and lifelong friend of Shenstone, who first introduced Jago's work to RD with an "Essay upon Electricity" (q.v.). In 1746 he gained a living at Harbury and subsequently at Snitterfield, where he finished his life. Jago's poems found a place in Volumes IV and V of RD's *Collection*, and as a member of Shenstone's circle the author became an occasional correspondent of RD's. For more on Jago, see the biography prefacing his *Poems Moral and Descriptive* (London: J. Dodsley, 1784) and Isle Dusior, *Richard Jago: A Study in Eighteenth-Century Localism* (Philadelphia: University of Pennsylvania Press, 1945).

[2] The date is approximated from Jago's indicating that Shenstone had written to him, saying that he had received the fourth volume of RD's *Collection*, something which RD had sent during the week previous to 25 March. (See RD's letter of that date to Shenstone.)

[3] It is not clear whether RD had promised a place for Jago's verses in the revised Volume III or whether Jago is merely inquiring about the set of the *Collection* which the publisher had promised to send him through his London relation. Whatever the case, none of Jago's poems appear in the revised Volumes I–III.

To William Shenstone

Pall mall   May 3^d 1755

Dear Sir

I rec^d the favour of your last Packet, which gave me great pleasure, and should have been answer'd immediately had I not waited for another which you gave me some hopes to expect by the following Post. I am extreamly flatter'd with the Honour which my Lady Luxborough does me, in so politely accepting the trivial Acknowledgement of her favour.[1] But how can her Ladyship talk of being vain of the Post of Honour, as She calls it, which I have assign'd her in my Assembly of Wits? Does she not know that she is qualify'd by Genius as well as Birth, to keep the best Company and to shine in the brightest? If she is ignorant of this, she is ignorant of what every body else both knows & allows; and affords an eminent proof how difficult it is to know ones self. I am asham'd that I have not sent before now a Copy of the Poems for Lord Grey, which her Ladyship seems to hint might be agreeable.[2] I had forgot it: but will send two by the next Birmingham Coach, as You may perhaps have some other friend to whom a Casket, however mean, which contains some jewels of your own, may be acceptable.

How extreamly am I also oblig'd to Mr Hylton? But for God's sake, how is it that You and your friends contrive, when you have done one a favour, to make one believe you have receiv'd an Obligation? This is an Imposition not to be borne; a treatment which it is very difficult properly to resent. Is it not horribly provoking to be put into a Situation, in which one knows not how to behave, nor what to say? However, I beg You will be so good as to let one of your Servants convey the enclos'd with my best Compliments to Mr Hylton; I believe he is your Neighbour, & I hope it will not give you much trouble.[3]

What is become of your Ode on Rural Elegance? I was in hopes to have seen it before this time: but I suppose it must now for some Months suffer a severe and and causeless Persecution under your hands, for faults which nobody but your self could accuse it of. I am strongly tempted to come *vi et armis*, and rescue it from your Cruelty. But I suppose you will pretend, like other Inquisitors, that You chastise and correct it for the good of its Soul. Well, You are its Creator, and must do what you please; but I daresay it is already, by its Goodness, in a state of Salvation; and, if You would set it at liberty, would immediately enter into a glorious Imortality.

I am

Dear Sir

most truely Yours

R Dodsley

MS: BL. Add. MS. 28,959, ff. 44–5.

¹ RD had sent Lady Luxborough·a set of his *Collection*, Volumes I–IV, through Shenstone, and Shenstone had conveyed her thanks to RD in a letter not now extant. See Shenstone's letters to her on 29 March and 17 April of this year (Williams, pp. 436, 444).

² Harry Grey (1715–68), 4th Earl of Stamford, a friend of Shenstone's and Lady Luxborough's and a neighbor at Enville Hall. Shenstone's Wood-House at the Leasowes was dedicated to Lord Stamford, as was Stamford's chapel at Enville dedicated to Shenstone. Shenstone had played a significant role in designing Enville. See Samuel Lewis, *A Topographical Dictionary of England* (London: S. Lewis & Company, 1840), II, 159.

³ John Scott Hylton (d. 1793) had one poem printed in each of Volumes IV and VI of RD's *Collection*. RD seems to have awarded Shenstone's neighbor, Hylton, an entire set of the *Collection*; consequently, Hylton's apparent praise of RD.

From Charles Bisset[1]

Skelton in Cleveland

9 May 1755

Sir

Having Just finished a Treatise of the Scurvy, a Product of much Experience and Labour, I purpose putting it in your hands, in order to have it published this Summer.[2] This Treatise is particularly calculated for the use of the Navy, the Prevention, and Cure of the Scurvy, on Ship Board, being its Chief Objects. I have read with great attention Dr Lind's late Treatise of the Scurvy, which contains nothing New that is Material:[3] I flatter myself that mine, which exhibits a great deal that is wholly new, and is very minute, concise and methodical, will be well received, especially at this Juncture; since the War which seems impending must necessarily enhance its Value.[4]

The Transition, I own, is uncommon from Fortification to Physic; The first of these Sciences I acquired, in a very little time, in the low countries, after purchasing into the Army, in 1746; to the last I was regularly bred; and served in a medical Character in the West Indies, during the first five Years of the last War. This Treatise being written almost in the manner of Aphorisms, will make only about 150 octavo Pages: Next Year I intend to publish a more considerable Work, which treats of the Periodical Winds, the Natural Constitution of the Weather, and the Diseases incident to newcomers, and Seasoned Europeans, in the West Indies.[5]

In the close of 1745 I resigned my Place of Second Surgeon to the Naval Hospital in Jamaica, in order to come home for recovery of my Health; soon after my arrival at London I applied to the Board of Sick and Wounded, for employment in the same branch of the Service; but without any Success, notwithstanding my long Service in the West Indies, which had almost ruined my Constitution: After this disappointment I threw my Papers, containing the medical observations I had made in the torrid Zone carelessly aside, and have lost some of them; I relinquished Medicine, and purchassed an Ensignry: at the Conclusion of the Peace, I was dismissed, with the rest of our Brigade, as Engineer, and reduced to half Pay as a Lieut.

After Publishing my Book of Fortification, which being the only original Performance of this kind in our language, wherein I have neither borrowed from, nor imitated, any preceding Author;[6] I was in hopes of being re-established as Engineer; but found the Gentlemen of the Board of Ordnance rather less favourable than the former: they took [no] notice of me till after making application; and then promised to [e]mploy me as practitioner Engineer, a Rank that is only possessed by the youngest Novices, and much Inferior to mine in the last war, which I rejected with great Contempt. I then found myself under the necessity of resuming my first Profession of Physic and Surgery, and settled at Skelton in Cleveland, Yorkshire; in a fine Air; more for my Health than Business: Yet, having been fortunate in my Practice, I have gained a good Character, and very extensive Business among the Country People: whereby the only advantages I acquire are Experience and improvement; for the Peasants, having their Farms high rated, and large Families, I make my – Charges so moderate as to be inequivalent to my labour: I have introduced ⟨?⟩ Inoculation among them, and to incourage them to allow their Children the Benefit of it, I inoculate Gratis, or make only a very small charge for my Medicines.

At my first settling here I was regarded by the Gentlemen as a foreigner, and Interloper; who did what lay in their Power to oppose and discourage me; which only occasioned me to redouble my diligence, and having always expressed a great contempt of them we still continue ⟨?⟩ at variance, which is likely to continue, especially as I can neither drink nor Hunt.

I shall send my Treatise of the Scurvy by the York Waggon about the 20th of this month; whereof I shall give you timely advice, that you may know when to expect it:

I am

Your most Obedient Servant

Cha.ˢ Bisset

Address: To / M.ʳ Dodsley Bookseller / in Pall-Mall London
Postmark: 12 MA

MS: Dreer Collection, Physicians & Surgeons ALS, Historical Society of Pennsylvania.

---

[1] Charles Bisset (1717–91) studied medicine at Edinburgh. He provides his own biographical sketch below.

[2] *A Treatise on the Scurvy, with Remarks on the Cure of Scorbutic Ulcers; designed chiefly for the use of the British*

Navy was published by RD on 9 October 1755 (*LEP*, 7–9 October). It had been printed by William
Strahan the previous month for a sum of £7.7.0.

³ Jame Lind, MD, *A Treatise of the Scurvy. In Three Parts.* (London: A. Millar, 1754).

⁴ The account of Bisset's treatise in the *Monthly Review* (14 January, 1756), pp. 14–25, was not so
optimistic. It urged caution in accepting all that Bisset asserted by way of scurvical distinctions,
assessments, and cures, for it believed much of what the author claimed was theoretical and
unsubstantiated by case studies. Especially bothersome was Bisset's contradicting established
authories like Lind, as well as his apparent striving for novelty.

⁵ I have not been able to discover that such a work was ever published.

⁶ *The Theory and Construction of Fortification*, a 238-page volume in quarto, with plates, had been printed
for the author and sold by A. Millar, D. Wilson, and RD in 1751.

To William Shenstone

Pall mall June 27 [1755]

Dear Sir

I wrote to You the beginning of last Month, in which I enclos'd a Letter to M
Hylton; I also sent by the Birmingham Carrier two Setts of the Poems, which I hope
came safe to your hands. The purport of this is only to say that I have some thought
of coming down to Birmingham this Summer, and if I could know when you would
be at home and at leisure, I should be glad to fix the time of my Journey so as that I
might enjoy the pleasure of spending a day or two with You at the Leasows.²

I am
Dear Sir
Your most obed! hum^ble Serv!
R Dodsley

MS: BL. Add. MS. 28,959, f. 46.

¹ The year is certain from RD's reference to having sent Shenstone a letter at the "beginning of last
Month," in which he had enclosed a letter for Hylton and had said that he was sending two sets of his
Collection. That letter (q.v.) is fully dated 3 May 1755.

² See the next letter to Shenstone, 28 July 1755.

To William Shenstone

Pall mall July 28 [1755]

Dear Sir

I purpose in about a week or ten days to set out for Birmingham, and hope to
have the pleasure of spending a few days with You at the Leasowes. If You should
happen to be engag'd with other company at that time, or are to be from home, if
You will favour me with a Line I will defer my Journey a week or a fortnight longer.
If I do not hear from You I will set out the middle of next week.

I am
Dear Sir
very sincerely Yours
R Dodsley

Address: To William Shenstone Esqr / at the Leasowes near / Birmingham
Postmark: 28 IY
Frank: R. Dodsley *free*

MS: BL. Add. MS. 28,959. ff. 47–8.

The year is fairly certain from RD's reference to a northern trip in his last letter (27 June 1755), as well as from the chronology of this particular summer trip to the Leasowes. See his 28 August letter, thanking Shenstone for his hospitality.

From Edward Young

Aug: 10 1755.

S^r

My heart fails me now I have done what I designd. My Additions, wh are large, will only Disgust former Purchasers; and lengthen wt for its general Use is too long allready. I am therefore determind entirely to drop that Design of[1]

S^r

Y^r Humble Sev^t

EYoung

Address: To Mr Dodsley / at Tullys Head / Pall-Mall / London
Postmark: [W]elwyn 11 AV

MS: University of Colorado Libraries, Boulder, Colorado, MS 52.

It is difficult to be sure of the work to which Young refers. Henry Pettit (*Correspondence of Edward Young, 1683–1765* (Oxford: Clarendon Press, 1971), p. 424) believes it to be the new duodecimo edition of Young's *Night Thoughts* that RD and Andrew Millar would issue on 14 October of this year. Pettit bases his belief on a missing letter listed in a Puttick and Simpson sales catalogue (25 January 1853, lot 698) whose entry carried the notation: "A.L.s. 1 page 4to 1755, Returning portion of a manuscript transmitted by Richardson for his perusal, begs the conveyance to Dodsley, of a parcel, it is for another, smaller edition, of his Night Thoughts." Pettit suggests that the "additions" that Young speaks of in the present letter were the contents of the "parcel" alluded to in the missing letter. On the other hand, although the parcel clearly concerned the new edition of *Night Thoughts*, Young's *The Centaur Not Fabulous. In Six Letters to a Friend, on the Life in Vogue* seems a more likely subject of the "additions." The text of the nine *Night Thoughts* had been completed in the 1740s, and although subsequent editions would show changes, it seems unlikely that Young in 1755 would be offering "additions wh are large" and which would "lengthen wt for its general Use is too long allready." Such a worrying expansion more properly characterizes the development of *The Centaur*, a minor part of which Young mentions in a letter of 1751 but which was now sparked by the anti-Christian elements in Bolingbroke's *Works* published in 1754. As is clear from his correspondence with his friend and printer Samuel Richardson through late 1754 and early 1755, Young's indictment of contemporary pleasure-seekers had amounted to only four letters, which he had intended to print individually as 6*d*. pamphlets. Somewhere in the interim, the project escalated into book-size with the addition of a fifth letter. So it appeared in its first two editions on 4 March and 18 April (*PA*). But the third edition of the ever-expanding work would carry a sixth letter when published on 17 November 1755 (*PA*). Dated between the second and third editions, this letter to RD would mark the appropriate moment for Young's misgivings about adding still more material to *The Centaur*, that might "Disgust former Purchasers" of the two early editions just months before.

In his letter to Richardson on 28 July 1754 (Pettit, p. 406), Young had written: "What I propose is after the thing [*Centaur*] is printed, to let some bookseller have it." Nine days later, Richardson wa⸱ inquiring of Young, who was still planning to publish in pamphlet form: "Have you a wish for ⸱ particular publisher? Roberts or Owen, I think, would either of them do it justice. Yet Dodsle⸱ generally deals with Cooper, against whom there can be no objection" (Pettit, p. 409). In th⸱ meantime, Richardson printed the letters and when it was decided to issue them in book form, RD⸱ rather than his pamphlet publisher Mary Cooper, became involved. On 19 February 1755, Youn⸱ assigned the copyright of *The Centaur* to RD for £200, to be paid six months after the date of th⸱ agreement (see Appendix B). After the signing, RD apparently took in Andrew Millar as an equa⸱ partner, for Millar's name appeared on the imprint of the first edition. Furthermore, as Henry Petti⸱ has shown (p. 409*n*), Young's account at Gosling's bank reveals deposits of £100 each from Millar anc RD on 29 August 1755, the month appointed for the copyright payment.

To William Shenstone

Pall mall Aug.st 28.th [1755]⸱

Dear Sir

It is a common saying, that *Home is home, be it ever so homely.* The Morality of th⸱ Maxim I will not dispute; but after having experienc'd so much Ease anc Politeness, after having been so agreeably entertain'd, and in so elegant a Place a⸱ the Leassowes, I cannot help thinking and saying to my self, *Home is but homely a⸱ best.*[2] This small alteration in the Axiom with regard to Tully's Head, I hop⸱ however you will try to disprove next Winter upon the spot: and indeed you⸱ Company here will go as far towards it as possible. As an inducement to which, ir lieu of the shining falls of your translucent Cascades, Pallmall shall roll over it⸱ Pavement a string of gilt Coaches and Chariots, in brilliant succession. In lieu o⸱ your Larks and your Nightingales, our tuneful Savoyards, from their musica⸱ Coffee-mills, shall grind you as much Melody as your heart can desire. Then as t⸱ your Nymphs and your Naiads, your Dryades and your Hamadriades, are the⸱ more fair, more kind, or more comon than those which shine with us in every Street making Night beauteous? Besides, those Ladies of yours in the Winter creep int⸱ their Oaks, or shrink down to the bottom of their Lakes, and you can have n⸱ enjoyment of them: (which by the bye is doubtless the cause of your low spirits a⸱ that time) whereas ours, in the midst of frost and snow, shine bright as the starrs o⸱ Heaven; and are always obligingly ready to entertain you, even in the colde⸱ season, with a very warm reception. And is not this a comfortable Consideration. Much more might be urg'd in favour of this precious Town; but I hope what hatl been said will have sufficient weight, with a well-dispos'd mind, to induce You t⸱ undertake the Journey. If not, I will change the manner of my attack next time, anc bring down upon you such a force of Artillery as shall soon compel you t⸱ capitulate, if not to surrender at Discretion.

In my return to London I call'd at Barrels, and din'd with Lady Luxborough Her Place is very pretty, and She receiv'd me with great Condescension: but Sh⸱ complains of your Laziness in returning her Visit, says You have not been there thi⸱ Twelvemonth, and I think seems a little angry upon that account. I could have tolc Her, by way of softening matters, that You had treated with more neglect a mucl greater Personage than her Ladyship; but as you was not there to answer for your self, I kept silence even from ill words. The Person I mean is no less than the Goddess of Fame; who, I heard you say (indeed you did not name the Lady) had waited at your door five Years in expectation of ⟨some⟩ certain Elegies which you had promis'd her: and methinks I see her at this instant standing on tiptoe on the top of your Cupola, waiting with great impatience to snatch and bear them to Tully's Head, from whence she intends to distribute them to yᵉ admiring World.

I send you enclos'd the Parody on Dryden's Ode, in which there is a deficiency that I hope you will try to fill up. I have sent also Swift's musical Burlesque, and the World.³ I hope it will not be long before you give me an opportunity of sending one of your own. I had this day the pleasure of Mʳ Hylton's company, and of drinking your health. He talks of staying in Town about a fortnight, and I hope to see him often. I am much oblig'd to Mʳˢ Mary, and beg my compliments to her;⁴ but I think you are not at all so, for her wishing you a humdrum Companion who have nothing upon earth to recommend me but the sincerity and truth with which I am

Dear Sir

Your most obliged

and obedient Servant

R. Dodsley

MS: BL. Add. MS. 28,959, ff. 56–7.

¹ The year is determined from internal evidence whose substance and imagery recurs in John Pixell's fully dated letter to RD on 3 December 1755 (q.v.). There Pixell says Shenstone allowed him to read RD's last two letters and then repeats two particular images RD uses in this letter – the goddess of Fame and her position atop Shenstone's cupola – by way of responding to the bookseller's criticism of the poet's indolence. (See also RD's next letter to Shenstone, on 8 November [1755], which carries further the "indolence" imagery reflected by Pixell.)

² As is clear from "Verses by Mr. Dodsley, on his first arrival at the Leasowes, 1754," which appeared at the end of Volume II of Shenstone's *Works* (1764), RD's second visit to the Leasowes occurred in mid-August 1755.

³ No evidence of such a parody has been discovered. Perhaps it remained deficient. Although a "musical burlesque" only in the broadest sense, Swift's piece is probably "Day of Judgment," printed in *Poems of Swift*, ed. Harold Williams (Oxford: Clarendon Press, 1937), II, 576–79. The verses appear under the title "Dooms-day" in *Shenstone's Miscellany 1759–1763*, ed. Ian Gordon (Oxford: Clarendon Press, 1952), pp. 129–30, accompanied by a revealing note by Thomas Percy through whose hands the miscellany had passed after Shenstone's death. To this poem, which Shenstone had copied into his collection of others' verses, Percy had added: "the foregoing verses were communicated to *Mr. Shenstone* by *Mr. Dodsley*, as the Composition of Dean Swift." At the time, the poem had not appeared in print. The "World" was RD's fashionable weekly edited by Edward Moore. Published on Thursdays, it ran for 209 numbers, from 4 January 1753 through 30 December 1756. For the printing history of *The World*, see William B. Todd, "Bibliography and the Editorial Problem in the Eighteenth Century," *SB*, IV (1951), 41–55; and George P. Winship, Jr., "The Printing History of the *World*" in *Studies in the Early English Periodical*, ed. Richmond P. Bond (Chapel Hill: University of North Carolina Press, 1957), pp. 185–95.

⁴ Mrs Mary Cutler, Shenstone's beloved housekeeper, referred to variously in the correspondence, as "Mrs. Mary," "Molly," or "Mrs. Cutler." In his will, Shenstone bequeathed her a £30 annuity, a sum she had much difficulty in collecting because of the protracted settlement of Shenstone's estate. (See RD's correspondence with Richard Graves during 1763 and 1764.)

To [William Shipley][1]
Secretary for the Society for the Encouragement of Arts, Manufactures and
Commerce

Pall mall Oct[r] 1st [1755][2]

Sir

I send you enclos'd M[r] Powel's Letter, and also M[r] Whitworth's.[3] I must own,
tho' I think M[r] Powel's a very sensible Letter, that I cannot see any good reason
why it should be printed by the Society; nay I do not perceive how it can come with
propriety from us, unless it had contain'd some new Proposals relative to y[e] Objects
of our Society; or some hints towards any Improvements in Arts Manufactures or
Comerce, w[ch] it was proper to lay before the Public in hopes of further Information.
But as it contains nothing of this sort, I do not see what end we propose to answer by
printing it. However [I ?] I may be understood to say this with much diffidence [?]
opinion, and with great deference to y[e] Society who may happen to differ me [on
this?] point. I am aware it may be said that leave hath been asked [to] print it, and
therefore there may be some difficulty in coming handsomely off. To this I can say
nothing, but that y[e] Society will doubtless avoid any thing that may look like an
Incivility to M[r] Powel; and if it shall be thought necessary to print it, perhaps the
manner how it should be done, had better be refer'd to y[e] next General Meeting.[4] I
should not have troubled you with this, but that I am not able to attend y[e] Society
to night, being confin'd with y[e] Gout.

I am Sir
Your most humble Serv[t]
R Dodsley

Endorsement: Mr. Dodsley Oct[r] 1. 1755.

Ms: Royal Society of Arts, Guard Book, Vol. III, No. 26.

[1] Considering its date, D. G. C. Allen, Curator-Librarian of the Royal Society of Arts, thinks this letter
to be almost certainly written to William Shipley (1714–1803), even though it is endorsed on the verso
in George Box's hand. (For Box, see RD's letter to him on 21 June 1757.) For Shipley's role in the
Society, see D. G. C. Allen, *William Shipley, Founder of the Royal Society of Arts: a Biography with Documents*
(London: Hutchinson, 1968).
[2] The year is determined from a dated entry in the extant Minutes of the Society, preserved in its
library. On 1 October 1755, RD's letter is recorded as having been read at that evening's meeting.
Furthermore, a copy of Powell's letter itself, sent by Shipley to Charles Whitworth, is dated 7 August
1755 (Royal Society of Arts, Guard Book, Vol. III, No. 20).
[3] Charles Whitworth (*c.* 1721–78) was one of the original members of the Society and the vice-president
at the time of this letter from RD. Charles Powell (1712–96) was also an original member of the
Society and an influential philanthropist from Castle Madoc, near Brecon, South Wales. (*See
Dictionary of Welsh Biography.*)
[4] Powell's letter proposed the formation of separate county societies with the same objectives as the
London society. He recounts the organization and success of an agricultural society set up at
Brecknockshildwing the past spring. Whitworth's response (RSA, Guard Book, Vol. III, No. 23)
agreed that the formation of such societies would have a salutory effect on the London society, but
thought such groups should be branches of the national organization, not separate entities. The
matter prompted considerable debate among Society members. For a fuller account, see Allen,
William Shipley, pp. 61–6.

Why RD was consulted upon the matter is not entirely clear. Although he had become a member of the Society three months earlier, he seems not to have been an officer. Possibly it was because of his experience in the publishing world or the fact that he had been managing all of the Society's printing and stationery needs. In any event, his advice seems not to have been taken, for the Minutes of 15 October show the Society's ordering Shipley to consult directly with Edward Cave regarding the letter's publication in the *Gentleman's Magazine*. Consequently, a later, fuller proposal amended by the Society appeared in the *Gentleman's* of the next month (XXV, 505–6).

●

To William Shenstone

Pall mall Novr 8.th [1755] [1]

Dear Sir

I was in hopes I should have seen you in London by this time, at least have heard from You. I have been confin'd & very ill with ye Gout almost ever since I left the Leassowes. I suppose Mr Hylton is by this time got into your Neighbourhood, & have therefore ventur'd to give You the trouble of sending him the enclos'd, tho' to confess the truth it contains a Conspiracy against a Gentleman, who, I am sorry to hear it, is a very intimate Acquaintance of yours. He calls himself a *Lover* of *Ease*, and under that smooth Title insinuates himself into the most worthy Bosoms. But I beg You to beware of him, he is an Imposter, his true Name is *Indolence*: I know him well; & from the mischievous Consequences of his Disposition, have frequently been forc'd to kick him out of doors. I confess what alarms me at present is, that I am apprehensive he hath a wicked Intention of suppressing your Elegies;[2] for however desirous he may seem of encreasing your Happiness, he does not even pretend to promote Your Fame: nay I am credibly inform'd, that he hath a lurking Design of climbing secretly up to your Cupola (for he will sometimes even *take pains* to do mischief) in order to drive a nail thro' the foot of that Lady I mention'd in my last to be standing there, & fasten her to ye place. Now a man of this rascally Disposition, however pleasing his Conversation may be, should by no means be allow'd to engross to himself a Person qualify'd to entertain all the World. Let him keep company with such as have nothing of Importance to do, & whose Time perhaps would not be so innocently spent in any other Employment, as in sauntering about with him. These are his proper Companions, & God knows there are enow of 'em, he need not fear admittance to many a noble House & elegant Table. But at the Leassowes! – where Learning and the Muses pay their court! that he should there intrude! – for God's sake give my Compliments to Mrs Mary, & if she has the least desire to oblige me, let her watch his approaches, & shut ye door against him, nay ye outer Gate; that you may not even hear the sound of his Voice.[3] Or, what would be still more obliging, and still more effectual, do you steal away your Papers from him (for I know he keeps them as much out of your sight as possible) and fly up to Town with them with ye utmost Expedition. And this indeed is the Plot in which I have Desir'd Mr Hylton to join me, who has already promis'd that if You will come up to Town, he will be ready to accompany You; where in sober & serious Truth I shall be very glad to see You, either with or without your

Elegies, & will flatter my self that in a post or two you will give me room to hope for that Pleasure, if it be but for a month or two, for I have something that I want You to see of my own.[4]

> I am
> Dear Sir
> most affectionately Yours
> R. Dodsley

MS: BL. Add. MS. 28,959, ff. 60–1.

[1] Internal evidence shows this to be the letter that John Pixell claims (see the next letter) that Shenstone allowed him to read before the former posted his own fully dated letter of 3 December 1755 to RD. Pixell's letter repeats RD's phrasings "Lover of Ease," "Indolence," "kick him out of doors," "climbing . . . up to your Cupola," and "drive a nail thro' the foot." Consequently this letter must immediately precede Pixell's.

[2] This is the first of many RD letters dunning Shenstone for his elegies, the publication of which would not occur until after the poet's death.

[3] For "Mrs Mary," see RD's 28 August letter to Shenstone, note 4.

[4] Probably his tragedy *Cleone*, which by early June of the next year he had sent to Richard Berenger for a reading (see Berenger's response on 10 June 1756) and which would claim much of RD's attention over the next three years.

From John Pixell[1]

Edgbaston Dec: ye 3^d 1755

Dear S^r

I was yesterday at Mr Shenstone's where he favour'd me with a perusal of your two last Letters to him,[2] which not only afforded me a very high Entertainment, but discover'd to Me a good Heart sufficiently fraught with that Virtue which will oblige You to forgive the long Silence of our Friend when I represent to You the situation he is in. –

You pleasantly suppose, which at any other Time I shou'd have easily credited, that it is *Indolence*, rather than his love of *Ease* which causes so long a Silence: but I assure You, S^r, he has for several Months been a Stranger to both: No, S^r, his seeming (for it can never be real) Neglect to You, is owing to a quite different Personage from that which You imagine, One too whom it is as difficult *to kick out of Doors*, I mean that rapacious Harpy – *Law*.[3] Now S^r, You must know this same Harpy has broke in at my Door & has hover'd about my Carcase for these fourteen Years therefore *I know her well*; & (excuse the Pun) notwithstanding all the Costs & Damages I have recover'd to eject her, She has by the force of her long Bill kept me in entire Subjection, & for ought I know may pounce me [t]ill there is nothing left for her to devour. This same [Torture?] is now tormenting Mr Shenstone whom She haunts in various Shapes: & it was but last Night I saw her approach him in the shape of a Commissioner. She makes no scruple of snatching from him his peace by day, his Rest by Night; nay, & so far imitates the Harpy which Virgil mentions as to snatch his food from his Trencher, or, which is the same thing, removes his Appetite. You supposed, S^r, that it was Indolence which climb'd up to his Cupola, & drove a Nail in the Foot of his Fame, but, upon Consideration, You will find it was this said Harpy struck a Fang thro' it.

As for his Indolence, he has been as great a Stranger to that, as his Ease, for he has of late frequently & in the Depth of Night pass'd through a Place which I wish You knew, call'd *Drew's hollow-way*. This was the Road to his Lawyer – a Circumstance of itself sufficient to make it dismal to our Friend. I shall say nothing of it but that after You have stumbled about half a Mile down it You are hem'd in by the River Styx which is the Centre of it.

This S^r is the present State of our Mr Shenstone, & as I was in some Measure depriv'd of his Company Yesterday I strol'd into his Walk a little beyond the Beeches where I copied your Verses which now stand thus –

> Sweet Naid! in this crhystal Wave
> Thy beautous Limbs with Freedom lave;
> By friendly Shades encompast, fly
> The rude Approach of vulgar Eye;
> Yet grant the courteous & the kind
> To trace thy Foot-steps unconfin'd;
> And grant the Swain thy Charms to see
> Who form'd there lovely Shades for Thee.
>
> R. Dodsley.[4]

I cannot conclude without gratifying my Vanity of sending You my Verses design'd for my Garden-Seat, which Mr Shenstone has made me alter 3 times since You saw them; & now strenuously objects to the 3^d Couplet as an invidious Compliment upon him, but if I have You on my Side I shall not in the least regard his Objection. –

> Think not in these paths to view
> Dryads green, or Naiads blue,
> Such as grace fair Enfield's Wood,
> Or Hagley's Lawn,[5] or Shenstone's Flood,
> On whose lov'd Banks the Muses play
> And Echo learns her sweetest Lay——
> Long, long may there unrival'd shine
> Nor shall my temperate Breast repine,
> So Musick lend her willing Aid
> To gladden this ignoble Shade:
> So Peace endear this humble Plain,
> And haply Elegance will deign
> To wander here; & smiling see
> Her Sister-Nymph Simplicity.[6]

I conclude with heartily wishing You may prevail upon Mr Shenstone to come to You, for though his Litigation may soon be ended, a Man of his delicate Sensibility cannot help feeling some time afterwards the ill-Usage he has met with in a near Relation——————

I am S^r yours affectionat[ely]

J.P.P. Pixell

MS: Humanities Research Center, University of Texas at Austin, Robert Dodsley / Recipient 1 / Bound, ff. 121–3.

¹ John Pryne Parkes Pixell (1725–84), Rector of Edgbaston from 1750 and Shenstone's neighbor and friend, published a poem in Volume V of RD's *Collection* (see below) and wrote several letters to the publisher (q.v.). See Courtney, pp. 119–21.   ² 28 August and 8 November 1755.
³ Through his mother Anne Penn, Shenstone had gained an inheritance in Harborough, her brother's estate. But in 1754, Thomas Dolman the younger, a grandson of Penn and also an apparent heir to the property, filed a bill in Chancery against Shenstone regarding the settlement. (See Shenstone's letter to Graves on 15 July 1754, Williams, p. 404). Though Shenstone had expected an early accommodation of the affair, it plagued him for the next six years, despite the intervention in 1758 of his friend Lord Stamford. As late as 7 July 1760, he is writing to Graves: "Since I wrote to you, I have been busied in bringing about a conclusion with D[olman]" (Williams, p. 556). RD expressed sympathy for Shenstone's trouble with Dolman in his letter of *post* 18 February *ante* 21 April 1760: "I shall hate the name of D_____ as long as I live: he is crooked in all his Ways; but the Devil will set strait with him one Day or other."
⁴ Along the paths of Shenstone's much-visited Leasowes, the poet had set up "seats," resting places where his guests could stop to consider a view or to read an inscription or just simply to converse. Some of these he dedicated to his friends and regular visitors. RD's "seat" carried these verses.
⁵ Enville Hall, Lord Stamford's residence; and Hagley Park, George, Lord Lyttelton's.
⁶ These verses, in revised form, appeared in RD's *Collection*, V, 83–4.

From William Warburton

Decr 26 1755

Mr Dodsley

let us not be misunderstood. When you came to me in ⟨?⟩ Town, I told you, *whenever I sold my whole property in Pope I would contrive if possible you should have some share*.¹ And I remember very well, as I found you disposed to understand this as a promise to let you have some share whenever I sold *any*, I set you right, & repeated to you again that my meaning was when I *parted with the whole*. For at that time, I had determined with my selfe to employ Mr Millar & Mr Draper in my concerns. I had my reasons on account of my knowledge of them, & affairs I have had with them. They had always done every thing to my satisfaction. And I must have things done my own way. On which account I sold, what I did sell to them, much cheaper than they bought of Mr Knapton.²

You will ask me then how I came to say I would contrive, ⟨some⟩ if possible that you should have some share when I sold the whole? It was partly on your importunity; partly out of regard I have for your Brother here;³ & partly because Mr Pope had a regard for you: tho', as I told you, I thought you had not been very regardfull of the memory of a man to whom you was so much obliged.⁴

But as you Mention Mr Millar in a complaining way, I must tell you, you do him much injury, to think you had any right to any part of that he bought of me or, Mr Knapton. I chose him preferably to another: I chose him because I would have to do with no other but of my own appointment; and had he, (because you had told him of your willingness to be concerned with him in purchasing some share of Pope) let you have any which he purchased, without my knowledge & consent he had broke his word with me & violated his reputation. I am not a person to be bought & sold. Mr Knapton, who is an honest & a virtuous & a gratefull man, would have suffered me to be as much Master of the sale of his part of this property as if it had been my own. And it is with men of that Character only, that I hope I shall ever be concerned.^{5} ⟨?⟩

You will do Mr Millar & me but justice, (a justice which I must expect of you) to communicate the contents of this to him: and that if you have said any thing contrary to these contents (which in every part is exactly true) that you would own your selfe mistaken.^{6}

I am your very humble Servt

W. Warburton

Address: To: Mr Robt Dodsley Bookseller / in Pall Mall

Postmark: penny post paid

MS: Edinburgh University Library, La. II. 153.

---

^{1} In Pope's last years, Warburton had worked closely with the poet, suggesting revisions for his collected works and offering extensive commentary. Having been willed the copyright of all printed works at Pope's death, Warburton prepared his own edition of Pope's *Works* which he published on 18 June 1751 (*LEP*, 15–18 June) as *The Works of Alexander Pope, Esq. In Nine Volumes Complete. With his last Corrections, Additions and Improvements; as they were delivered to the Editor a little before his Death: together with the Commentaries and Notes of Mr. Warburton* (London: Printed for J. & P. Knapton, J. & R. Tonson and S. Draper, and C. Bathurst). RD, as one of Pope's booksellers, had apparently attempted to buy a share in the Warburton edition. See RD's response on 6 January 1756.
^{2} Andrew Millar, bookseller, opposite Catherine Street, Strand; Somerset Draper, bookseller; John Knapton, bookseller with his brother Paul, at the Crown in Ludgate Street.
^{3} Probably RD's brother Isaac, who had been Ralph Allen's gardener in Bath since 1741, and was therefore acquainted with Warburton, a prebendary at nearby Gloucester for the past two years, and the husband of Allen's niece. See next note.
^{4} As is clear from RD's response to this letter (6 January 1756), Warburton had written another letter on the subject (untraced) a day or two later. Perhaps that letter specified the ways in which Warburton had thought RD had not been "very regardfull of the memory" of Pope, but more likely it concerned his reasons for publishing his edition of Pope through the Knaptons, Tonsons, Draper, and Bathurst and for selling some share to Millar, matters which RD takes up in his 6 January response. Perhaps RD was somewhat disappointed that Pope, at his death, had not provided him with a share in the works that he had issued from Tully's Head, a matter that had become compounded by the haughty dealing he had since experienced at the hands of Pope's literary executor. Whatever the cause, from the mid-1740s on, RD had begun to patronize authors whose Romantic leanings had begun to take some exception to the artificialities of Pope's poetry and much liberty with Warburton's reputation. Although it cannot be certainly tied to RD, Thomas Edwards's *A Supplement to Mr. Warburton's edition of Shakespear*, which criticised Pope "the poet" and Warburton "the critic" for their collaboration on Shakespeare and poked fun at Warburton's enhancing his reputation on Pope's shirt-tail, was published by Mary Cooper, RD's well-known collaborator on "delicate" works. Warburton might also have been thinking of William Melmoth's comment on Pope under the pseudonym "Sir Thomas Fitzoborne" in *Letters on Several Subjects* (3rd ed.; Letter XLI, pp. 201–5),

published by RD in 1750. Amidst lavish praise of the poet, Melmoth did admit that Pope "sometimes sacrifices simplicity to false ornament." But probably if Warburton had any one work in mind, it was Thomas Warton's *Observations on the Faerie Queen of Spenser*, wich RD had issued just the previous year. In his Postscript to the work, Warton had launched another attack on Pope's edition of Shakespeare by supporting Lewis Theobald (Pope's first "Dunce") and outrightly accusing Pope of ignorance. Regarding Theobald's *Shakespeare Restored* (1726), Warton urged: "If Shakespeare is worth reading, he is worth explaining; and the researches used for so valuable and elegant a purpose, merit the thanks of genius and candor, not the satire of prejudice and ignorance. That labor . . . deserves a more honourable repository than the Temple of Dulness."

Nonetheless it is difficult not to imagine that the resentment of the thin-skinned Warburton was fired by attacks on his own reputation that he linked with Tully's Head. He had already shown his displeasure with Mark Akenside's *Pleasures of Imagination* to which Akenside's friend and patron Jeremiah Dyson had responded with *An Epistle to Mr. Warburton. Occasioned by his Treatment of the Author of The Pleasures of the Imagination*, both works published by RD in 1744. In John Gilbert Cooper's letters to RD during 1750 and 1751, we have recounted the feud between this RD author and Warburton, and also Warburton's probable attribution to Cooper of John Jackson's insulting *Treatise on the Improvements Made in the Art of Criticism, Collected out of the Writings of a celebrated Hypercritic* (see Cooper's letter of 26 August 1751). That Warburton's attitude toward RD pivoted largely upon personal offense is supported in a letter by his friend Richard Hurd to William Mason on 8 January 1756, a letter that addresses this very exchange between the clergyman and the bookseller. Hurd writes: "With regard to [Warburton's] letters to D[odsley], I can readily believe that they are written with a frankness which to such a man might have been spar'd. But I think that there is great reason in what he says. You know D[odsley]'s brother [Isaac] is Mr. A[llen]'s servant. And on that account, if for no other, Dodsley should have declin'd having any hand in publishing an abuse on a friend of his, and one of the family." (Warburton was husband to Ralph Allen's niece.) See *The Correspondence of Richard Hurd and William Mason*, ed. Leonard Whibley (Cambridge, 1932), pp. 22–3.

5 This passage exhibits the self-righteousness and pomposity for which Warburton was known among his contemporaries. Edward Gibbon writes of him: "The real merit of Warburton was degraded by the pride and presumption with which he pronounced his infallible decrees; in his polemic writings, he lashed his antagonists without mercy or moderation; and his servile flatterers . . . exalting the master-critic far above Aristotle and Longinus, assaulted every modest dissenter who refused to consult the oracle, and to adore the idol." (*Memoirs of The Life of Edward Gibbon . . . by Himself*, ed. G. B. Hill (London: Methuen, 1900), p. 178).

6 For RD's response, see the next letter. RD was not the only publisher to encounter difficulties with Warburton over the publication of Pope's works. Writing to Henry Lintot the previous October (BL, Egerton MS. 1959, ff.27–8), Warburton warns: "I have only two things to say to Mr Lintot that if he thinks he has any claim to any part of the property of the Dunciad he must prosecute it by Law; his claim of the present profits [£89.13.5½ (f. 29)] must be made on Mr Knapton & his trustees and I shall give them a bond of indemnity.

"If he attempts to print the Dunciad or any part of it at any time I shall immediate print the Homer to which I likewise have a dormant claim, with improvements both in the version & additions to the notes, both of which I have ready. W.W."

To William Warburton[1]

[*c.* January 6, 1756]

Sir

I rec^d your two letters, & should have answer'd them sooner but that I was going out of Town. I must confess your strange treatment of me lays me under some difficulty how to behave. To be silent under such severe Imputations, would be injustice to my self; and I am afraid it will ⟨be difficult⟩ not be easy for me to say vhat ⟨I ought⟩ most modest Resentment would dictate, without giving You ⟩ffence, which ⟨I ⟨would willingly avoid⟩ ⟨am anxious to avoid⟩ ⟨am really ₐnxious to avoid⟩ ⟨to [?] avoid⟩ ⟨to wholly avoid⟩⟩ ⟨to⟩ ⟨I am Sensible however hat I am but a Bookseller, I will endeavour not to forget that Modesty and Respect ᵥhich I owe to your superior Character as a Clergyman⟩ not withstanding all you ₐave said, I would willingly avoid; I know I am but a Bookseller, and You a Divine ⟨but when⟩ tho' pounc'd by an Eagle: but even a wren will complain. I ⟨will⟩ must herefore proceed.

MS: Hyde Collection, Somerville, New Jersey.

This fragment draft is largely repeated and expanded in the following letter, which is also a draft from the Hyde Collection. It is printed here for the purpose of permitting an easy collation with its successor, to show RD's train of thought in the process of revision.

To William Warburton

Pall mall Jan.ʳʸ 6.ᵗʰ [1756]¹

Sir

vide the back of yᵉ Paper

⟨I was favour'd with two letters from you, one on Monday, the other on Tuesday ₗast, which I shoul[ld] have answer'd sooner but that I was then going o[ut] of town.⟩ In the first of your letters I am charg'd (tho' without proof and I hope without foundation) with a want of regard to the Memory of Mʳ Pope, in suffering ₗittle scribb[lers] to defame him thro' my press: and this is given as t[he] reason why you did not chuse to treat with me for [a] share in his works.² In the second this charge is d[ropt?] and I am tax'd with ⟨no want of Insensibility⟩ a want of Sensibility, in applyi[ng] to you for favours, after having, seven years ago, prin[ted] a book in which the Author (who put his name to hi[s] work) had treated You ⟨with disrespect⟩ with ill manners.³ I am also charg'd with not resenting properly, a forg'd Letter se[nt] to You in my name: which last, as I was entirely ignora[nt] of it, and You then did me the Justice to acquit me, have now even forgot ₒn what occasion it was writte[n].⁴ As to the first charge, my want of respect to the Memo[ry] of Mʳ Pope; as it is my pride that he was my friend, so it is my consolation ₐnder the misfortune of your censure, that I cannot charge my self with the least forgetfulness of what I owe him. But ⟨You will pardon my remarking by the way, that your respect to his Memory did not hinder You from employing⟩ ⟨did your respect to his Memory not hinder You from employing⟩ ⟨I suppose it was this respect paid to his Memory that led you to employ⟩ suppose [I h]ad been somewhat remiss in this respect had not you employ'd as the Printer of his works, ⟨him⟩ the person who publish'd the most virulent Libel that has yet appear'd against ⟨your Friend, and who is also a Proprietor in the works of your greatest Enemy, And as⟩ him? ⟨I mean a Preface to yᵉ Patriot Ki[ng.]⟩⁵ As to my having printed a book in which you was disrespectfully treated – I would beg leave to ask,

what You would have said to M.ᵣ Knapton had he ⟨objected against printing th⟨
many invectives which You have thrown out against some of your opponents.⟩
refused to print some of your ⟨Works?⟩ Pieces ⟨And had not he, long⟩ Did yo⟨
⟨make it any objection to him⟩ object to him, that he had, before You employ'⟨
him, printed D.ᵣ Sykes's book, professedly written ag.ˢᵗ You? It does not appear tha⟨
you did.⁶ I do not mention these Instances as charging either M.ᵣ Knapton or M⟨
Millar with the least crime, but only to shew, that what You have thought proper t⟨
make an objection against *me*, was not thought so in regard to *them*. ⟨The next⟩
Another charge ⟨against⟩ upon me is, my want of Sensibility in applying to You fo⟨
favours. I must own I was not conscious that I had ever given you any just cause o⟨
Offence: neither can I look upon my ⟨application to You to purchase at an⟨
valuable Consideration, or at any reasonable price,⟩ offer to You of purchasing a⟨
reasonable price, a share of that Property, part of which you had already dispos'd o⟨
to others, as ⟨applying⟩ an application for any singular favour. + ⟨An[d] as t⟨
giving⟩ But I give my self the air you say, of one who had some mer[it] with you⟨,⟩
– I do not believe, on a perusal of my letter, tha[t] You will find me guilty of an⟨
such Presumption:⁷ but I did so ⟨assume⟩ presume, how strangely was I mistaken⟨
for by your uncharitable ⟨slur⟩ sneer on the morals of a Bookseller, a[nd] from th⟨
very hard conclusion of your last Letter, it ⟨seems⟩ appears ⟨if⟩ that You ⟨coulc
scarce⟩ cannot allow me even the merit of comm[on] Honesty; ⟨since you there⟩
⟨and⟩ but treat me as one with whom Yo[u] would by no means chuse to have an⟨
dealings. This las[t] ⟨charge⟩ stroke I must own would have given me some pain⟨
were I no[t] in hopes that the opinions of all who best know me, and of the public i⟨
general, are somewhat different from that which I am so unfortunate as to find i⟨
yours of

Sir

Your very humble Servant

R Dodsle⟨

P.S. + However, grant it was a favour, I never ask'd but once, & never rec.ᵈ ⟨
denial till now; & the[re]fore your reproaches of Importunity, of not bein[g
content with a simple denial, but forcing You [to] tell me all your mind, I thin⟨
might have been sha[meless?]⁸

MS: Hyde Collection, Somerville, New Jersey.

¹ Clearly a response to Warburton's fully dated letter of 26 December 1755, this letter must be date⟨
   1756.   ² See Warburton's letter, note 4.
³ John Gilbert Cooper, *Life of Socrates* (1749). (For the attack upon Warburton, see Warburton's lette⟨
   to RD on 28 September 1751, note 4.)   ⁴ Untraced. Content unknown.
⁵ In 1749, Andrew Millar had published Henry St John, Viscount Bolingbroke's *Letters, on the Spirit ⟨
   Patriotism: on the Idea of a Patriot King: and On the State of Parties, at the Accession of King George the Firs⟨*
   prefixed with an Advertisement by David Mallet. This Advertisement charged Pope, Bolingbroke⟨
   former friend, with a breach of trust in secretly printing 1,500 copies of the above work, whic⟨
   Bolingbroke had given him merely for circulation among a half dozen friends. Bolingbroke ha⟨
   discovered the copies, printed and kept by J. Wright the publisher, and destroyed all but a few⟨
   Warburton made an attempt to excuse Pope's action in a *Letter to the Lord Viscount B——ke. Occasion'⟨*

by his *Treatment of a Deceased Friend* (1749), and he castigated Mallet in *A Letter to the Editor of the Letters . . . Occasioned by the Editor's Advertisement* (1749). Bolingbroke's response to Warburton was *A Familiar Epistle to the most Impudent Man Living* (1749).

John and Paul Knapton, in 1744, had published Arthur Ashley Sykes's attack on Warburton, *An Examination of Mr. Warburton's Account of the Conduct of the Ancient Legislators, of the Double Doctrine of the Old Philosophers, of the Theocracy of the Jews, and of Sir Isaac Newton's Chronology*. Curiously enough (within the context of the present letter), the Knaptons also published one of Warburton's responses the following year, *Remarks on Several Occasional Reflections: In Answer to the Reverend Doctors Stebbing and Sykes*.

Letter not traced.

This failed negotiation and flare of tempers seems to conclude the formerly friendly relationship between Warburton and RD.

From Thomas Blackwell[1]

Marishal College Aberdeen Jan.[y] 15.th 1756.

M.[r] Doddesley

Sir

Your Jaunt to Holland last Season,[2] just before I left London, deprived me of the Pleasure I had proposed to my self, in some agreable Hours passed at your House.

The public Papers will have informed you some time ago, of the intended Publication of the Memoirs of Augustus Vol II.[d] the 2.[d] day of next Month. As my Subscribers are for the most part Members of Parliam.[t] or Gentlemen of your End o' the Town, they will naturally address themselves to You, for their Books: I persuade myself you will find no Inconveniency in Such People's frequenting your Shop; And hope for the same Friendship and Care in delivering out this Volume as experienced in the Delivery & Sale of the former.[3]

I sho.[d] be very glad to be assured, that you are proceeding in your beautifull and instructive Poem *Public Virtue*. Be not discouraged at the moderate Demand for the first Part: A Work, even of true Merit, must have *time* to work it's Way – the high Runs are upon Pieces that flatter some Passion, or if I may use a low term, Scratch an itching Fancy.[4] Yours, which applies to noblest Faculties of Head & Heart must not expect the Applause of the Mob, like . . . – or the Beggars Opera – And yet if it is pursued in the same Strain, and executed with the Same Spirit it set out with, I will, at any risque, insure it's Reputation & Success.

Be So good as make Complim.[ts] for me to M.[r] Ja.[s] Doddesley and to M.[r] And.[r] Millar, when you have an Opportunity, from whom I have this Day a Letter full of Honesty and Friendship – and always am With unfeigned Esteem

M.[r] Doddesley

Yo.[r] most obed.[t] humb.[le] Serv.[t]

T. Blackwell

Address: To | M.[r] Robert Doddesley | Bookseller at Tully's Head | Pall Mall

MS: Edinburgh University Library, LA. II 646/43.

Thomas Blackwell the younger (1701–57), LLD, Professor of Greek and Principal of Marischal College, Aberdeen.

² No particulars concerning RD's "jaunt to Holland" have been discovered.

³ Volume I of *Memoirs of the Court of Augustus*, Blackwell's father's work, had been published posthumously by the son in 1753, appearing from the house of Hamilton, Balfour and Neill in Edinburgh. The imprint for this second volume carried the Dodsleys' names as the London booksellers when it was published on 2 February of this year (*PA*). RD had taken in subscriptions for Volume I, however (*PA*, 25 January 1753).

⁴ For the "moderate" reception of RD's *Agriculture*, see his letters of November 1753.

To William Shenstone

Pall mall Feb!ʸ 9.ᵗʰ 1756

Dear Sir

And must I then give up all hopes of printing your Elegies this Winter? Does the cruel and voracious Monster M! Pixell told me of devour your whole time, and eat up all your thoughts?¹ Would to God you were writing an Elegy on the Death of your Law-suit! That would be, as ⟨Shakespear⟩ some Author has it in the Title page of ⟨some of⟩ his Play⟨s⟩, a lamentable Tragedy mixt full of pleasant Mirth. Upon my word, Sir, if You do not bring me up these mourning Muses, nothing elegant will come from Tully's Head this season, I shall loose the Fame of being the Muse's Midwife, & my hand for want of practice will forget its obstetrick faculties. Consider too, if these Ladies, from that antiquated steril Precept of Horace, should get a trick of going pregnant nine years instead of nine months, who the devil will be able to get a livelihood by being employ'd as their Mid wife?² Besides, Sir, you exchange the Pleasure of begetting nine children, which might easily be done in that time, for yᵉ plague of nursing one little Embrio: and will the Ladies, think you, have any objection to nine times the pleasure which that old fellow Horace would allow them? No, no; I shall have *them* all on my side to a Girl! They are doubtless for a quick Conception, and an easy Delivery; and so am I. In the Name of all the Muses then, and if You value your Reputation as a Man amongst them, I beg you will make no longer delay. If You do, take notice – I will sit down in Vengeance, and write an Elegy on the Barrenness of your Muse, on the decay of your own Abilities, or on some other scandalous Subject, that shall blast your Character as an able Poet for ever. But in hopes you will think seriously on these things, I will at present suspend my Wrath, and subscribe my self.

Dear Sir
sincerely and affectionately Yours
R Dodsley

P.S. I beg my Compliments to M! Hylton and all Friends. I had the pleasure of enquiring after your Health the other day of my Lord Stamford,³ but not the satisfaction of hearing that you intend to Visit to London this Winter: however, after the dreadful Denunciations above, I hope You will tremble and obey.

MS: BL. Add. MS. 28,959, ff. 49–50.

¹ See John Pixell's letter to RD on 3 December 1755.
² RD's conceit on Horace's famous dictum: "nonumque prematur in annum, membranis intus positus"; i.e. "having buried your manuscript, let it remain into the ninth year" (*Ars Poetica*, ll. 388–9).
³ Harry Grey, 4th Earl of Stamford and neighbor of Shenstone's at nearby Enville Hall, would be bringing RD word of Shenstone's bout of serious illness through the spring of 1758. See RD's letter to Shenstone on 3 May 1755, note 2.

From William Mason

Pemb Hall   March 3ᵈ – [1756]¹

Sir

The Odes are in great forwardness & I believe will be ready to publish the week after next. but as Im apprehensive, that the Magazines will pirate them & greatly hurt their sale, I would ask your Opinion whether it would not be proper to enter them at Stationers Hall. If you think so let me know the expence.² I am

in haste

yours &c

W. Mason

one day next week I desire you would insert the following Advertisement in⟨to⟩ one of the Daily & one of the Evning papers.

Next week will be publishd

four Odes. 1 to Memory 2 to Independency. 3. on Melancholly 4. on the fate of Tyranny, taken from the fourteenth Chapter of Isaiah. By Mʳ Mason. Cambridge printed ⟨for⟩ & sold by W Thurlbourne Dodsley &c ⟨price one Shilling⟩³

Address: To Mʳ Dodsley / Pall. Mall.

MS: Poetry / Rare Books Collection, University Libraries, State University of New York at Buffalo.

The publication of Mason's *Odes*, which Mason here expects within two weeks, occurred on 18 March 1756 (*LEP*).
Newspaper advertisements noted that the *Odes* had been registered at Stationers' Hall, but the Company's Register does not list them. The expense of the registration would have amounted to the author's cost of the usual nine copies the Company required.
Including the mention that the *Odes* had been printed by J. Bentham at Cambridge, RD placed the advertisement in the *London Evening Post* (16–18 March) and in the *Public Advertiser* (23 March).

To Thomas Warton, the younger

Pall Mall   Mar 11.ᵗʰ [1756]¹

Dear Sir

I am glad yᵉ book is at last finisht and I think no time should be lost in in sending it up. The best way will be to let Mʳ Fletcher keep full as many as he thinks he can

use; and send the rest of the Impression up to Mrs Cooper. In her Bale you may tye
up a hundred for me. Your Packet I receiv'd & sent it to Mr Campbell, but have not
seen him since.[2] With Compliments to all friends

I am

Dear Sir

sincerely Yours

R. Dodsley

As ye Work is printed on so good a Paper I should think it might make a 5^s book
bound. But that may be determin'd when I see it, or do you consult Mr Fletcher.[3]

MS: BL. Add. MS. 42,560, f. 50.

[1] The year is determined from the reference to Joseph Warton's *Essay on Pope* to be published in London
   on 27 March 1756 (*PA*) with Mary Cooper's imprint and sold at Oxford by James Fletcher. See also
   RD's letter to Joseph Warton on 8 April.
[2] John Campbell, LLD (1708–75). In a letter to Thomas Warton on 15 July 1756, Campbell
   acknowledges having received Warton's *Life of Sir Thomas Pope* from RD, a piece he would include in
   vol. V (1760) of *Biographia Britannica: or, the Lives of the Most eminent Persons.* (See Wooll, *Biographical
   Memoirs*, pp. 241–2; I am indebted to David Fairer for the substance of this note.)
[3] The price was 5s. bound. See RD's letter to Joseph Warton on 8 April.

**To Jacob, Lord Viscount Folkestone,[1] President of the Society for the
Encouragement of Arts, Manufactures and Commerce**

[*c.* 17 March 1756][2]

My Lord

   As an humble Member of the useful Society, over which your Lordship so
worthily presides, I beg leave to be indulg'd in the liberty of addressing to your
consideration some thoughts which I hope may possibly tend towards its
Improvement. It is with great pleasure that one hears from people of all ranks, a
general approbation of its design; that its Objects are adapted to the genius of a
trading People, that its views immediately open on the improvement of our
Commerce, and that its principal aim is directed to the benefit and honour of our
Country. But it has been thought by many that if our basis and foundation were
somewhat more extended, the Building might not only be rais'd higher and made
more beautiful; but become also much more useful and beneficial. – I wou'd
therefore with great deference propose, that we take into our Scheme the
Encouragement of Letters. – I do not mean that we should offer Premiums to
encourage Persons to write on any given Subjects; that might perhaps tend only to
set many Scribblers at work, and give us much trouble to little purpose; but I cou'd
wish that when any Person of real Abilities, true Genius or useful Knowledge, shall
produce to the Public, any extraordinary Work, in Literature and the polite Arts,
any improvement in Mechanics, or any useful Discovery in the Sciences – I could

wish I say, when any thing of this kind happens, that it fell naturally within our Plan to give to such a Person some honorary Reward, or rather mark of Distinction, such as a gold Medal, or whatever else the Society might on the occasion think proper. This would greatly multiply our opportunities of encouraging Merit in the most genteel way, and at no considerable Expence.[3] – Preparatory to this, as we have not yet assum'd a Name, I would humbly propose we should take that of

The British Society;

for the Encouragement of

Letters, Arts, and Manufactures.[4]

I beg your Lordship's pardon for the Liberty I have taken; to which I could only have been embolden'd by Your known Zeal for the service of your Country in the improvement of this Society.

I am

My Lord

With great Respect

Your Lordship's

most Obed! humble Servant

R. Dodsley

Endorsement: 17 March 1756

MS: Royal Society of Arts, Guard Book, Vol. III, No. 62. The manuscript does not seem to be in Dodsley's hand, but it does carry his signature.

[1] Jacob des Bouveries (d. 1761), created Viscount Folkestone in 1747, was the descendant of well-known Turkey merchants in London. Folkestone was elected the first President of the Society for the Encouragement of Arts, Manufactures and Commerce on 5 February 1755 and held the office until his death. (Henry Trueman Wood, *A History of the Royal Society of Arts* (London: John Murray, 1913), pp. 12, 17, 321.)

[2] The date is determined from an endorsement on the verso of the last page of the letter (17 March 1756), the Secretary's usual indication of the date a letter was received. In addition, the Minutes for the Society's meeting on 17 March 1756 record the reading of RD's letter.

[3] RD's proposal failed to induce the Society to include premiums for literature within its program. During the Society's first year (1754–5), the only premiums offered in the category of the "polite arts" were those for drawings by boys and girls under seventeen years of age. Drawing continued to be the Society's major gesture in the direction of the arts until the mid-nineteenth century. Its early concerns, much influenced by such practical minds as Henry Baker (1698–1774), focused largely on the development of manufactures and commerce. In this light it is surprising to find so many literary men among the Society's active members, persons such as David Garrick, John Hawkesworth, Samuel Johnson, and James Boswell.

[4] Although H. T. Wood (p. 17) indicates that the Society at times abbreviated its somewhat cumbersome title by using simply "Society of Arts," it is only in RD's letters to the Society (this and the next, on 14 December 1756) that the membership's apparent dissatisfaction with the Society's title emerges. But RD's proposed title proved unacceptable because it reflected an expansion in the direction of Letters, a change of program the Society had not been prepared to make. Yet, despite this disappointment, RD's enthusiasm for the organization's work did not flag, as his continuing participation on committees suggests. Also, his letters to David Garrick (November 1757) and to Thomas Gataker (4 November 1757) evidence similar concern, for there he is offering the author's third night proceeds to the Society if Garrick will agree to produce his tragedy *Cleone* at Drury Lane.

To Joseph Warton

Pall Mall, April 8, 1756

Dear Sir,

Your Essay is publish'd, the price 5s. bound.[1] I gave Mrs. Cooper directions about advertising, and have sent to her this afternoon, to desire she will look after its being inserted in the evening papers. I have a pleasure in telling you that it is lik'd in general, and particularly by such as you would wish should like it. But you have surely not kept your secret: Johnson mention'd it to Mr. Hitch as yours – Dr. Birch mention'd it to Garrick as yours – And Dr. Akenside mention'd it as yours to me – And many whom I cannot now think on have ask'd for it as yours or your brother's. I have sold many of them in my own shop, and have dispers'd and push'd it as much as I can; and have said more than I could have said if my name had been to it.[2] Hampton's Polybius is very highly spoken of here; and if one may judge from the preface (which is all I can pretend to judge of) deserves all that can be said of it.[3] I hope Winchester agrees with you in all respects, as it will always give me pleasure to hear of your health and happiness. My compliments to Mrs. Warton; and believe me to be, with great sincerity,

Dear Sir,
affectionately yours,

R. Dodsley.

Source: John Wooll, *Biographical Memoirs of Joseph Warton* (London, 1806), pp. 237–8.

[1] *Essay on the Writings and Genius of Mr. Pope*, published on 27 March (*PA*). See RD's letter to Thomas Warton on 11 March.   [2] See RD's letter to Warton on 8 November [1754], note 2.
[3] *The General History of Polybius*, translated by James Hampton and published by RD on 13 March (*PA*).

To William Shenstone

Pall mall April 17 [1756][1]

Dear Sir

I have receiv'd at last your long-expected letter;[2] and as the making so ample an Apology for your Silence must have been as great a punishment to You as it is a pleasure to me, I readily accept it as a full atonement and satisfaction for all past deficiencies. In this discharge of your debts, I cannot help admiring also your great Generosity, in throwing in, by way of interest for want of prompt payment, several Compliments to which I had no claim, nor even a shadow of right. However, I hope to make them not useless to me, tho' unmerited; as I shall endeavour to come up as near as I can to your ideas: and if You have flatter'd me, I shall this way be reveng'd to some purpose. But if I am inclin'd to doubt of *your* Sincerity, What shall I say to that of your friend Mr *Greaves?* He has certainly strain'd the strings of Compliment till they are quite broken: and tho the pleasing notes were play'd to my own heart, as I could not in searching there, find an adequate cause for such delightful sounds, how can I taste their harmony? All I can suppose is, that You must have given him too strong a bias in my favour, and that is the reason he hath wander'd so far from the mark.[3] Yet if the cause of his mistaken opinion arises from your partiality to me, I will enjoy his error as much as if it was a truth. To the Observation, that "the Taste of the present times runs somewhat higher than the Genius", I have one Objection; but to you I cannot name it. However, if you print your Ode on Rural Elegance, I am perswaded the person who made that Observation, will have but little cause to pride himself in the truth of it. I shall be extreamly glad to see it; and the season is now so far advanc'd, that you have certainly not many weeks or even days to lose. I will hope therefore to receive it by the return of the Post. Pray Heaven it be transcrib'd! – if not, there is a Lion in the way that I am afraid you will not easily overcome. But, courage! –

As to your Shrubbery; if instead of the Phanix you talk of, you will now and then admit a little insignificant Wren to chant its single Note there, You will find the meaning of that note to be when interpreted, that he is as sincerely and affectionately yours, as

Dear Sir
Your most obed! Serv!

R Dodsley

P.S. I certainly intend to publish two concluding Volumes to my Miscellany next Winter, if I can get Materials sufficient, and such as are to my mind; in which I hope for your assistance. There will not be a new Edition of the last four perhaps just at that time, but I fancy it will not be for long after.[4] M! Arne has been in Ireland almost ever since I was at the Leasowes, and still continues there.[5] I beg my Compliments to M! Greaves, M! Hylton, and all friends.

MS: BL. Add. MS. 28,959, ff. 51–2.

[1] The dating of this letter hinges on a minor matter. Sometime between October 1754 and August 1756, Richard Graves began to drop the "e" in the spelling of his family name, "Greaves." In his letter to RD of 26 October 1754, he had signed himself "Greaves" but by the time of his 30 September 1756 letter, he signs "Graves." Even earlier than the latter date, however, Graves must have been employing the simpler version, for in Shenstone's letter of 21 March 1755 (Williams, p. 434), the poet is chiding Graves on the change and urging: "yourself and your Relations should spell their Name Greaves to the End of the World." It is also significant that after RD had met Graves personally for the first time in the summer of 1756, the bookseller in all future references to Graves, spelled his name without the "e," whereas in all previous references to him in letters to Shenstone, he had spelled his name "Greaves." Consequently it seems most likely that this letter in which he spells his name "Greaves" must pre-date the summer of 1756. But the letter cannot fit the context of RD's exchange with Shenstone of April 1755; for a "long-expected Letter" would not be justified since Shenstone *had* written to RD in 1755 just three weeks earlier. Nor would the easy, playful intimate manner of this letter fit the progress of the relationship between RD and Shenstone before 1755. As a result, it seems the letter correctly belongs to 1756.   [2] Not traced.

[3] Graves's compliments might have been conveyed in the form of the highly laudatory "On Tully's Head, in Pall Mall, 1756," a poem which appeared in *Aris's Birmingham Gazette* on the following 20 December, signed by the "Rev Mr. G–––s." See Baskerville's letter to RD of that date and RD's acknowledgement to Graves on 30 December.

[4] This is the first mention of RD's intention to add another two volumes to his *Collection*. They would not

appear for nearly two years, however: they were published on 18 March 1758, along with the fifth
edition of Volumes I–III and the second edition of Volume IV. For a detailed consideration of their
printing in late 1757 and early 1758, see William B. Todd, "Concurrent Printing: An Analysis of
Dodsley's *Collection of Poems by Several Hands*," *PBSA*, 46 (1952), 45–57.

5 Apparently Shenstone had inquired as to whether Thomas Arne had set the music for the other three
parts of his "Pastoral Ballad." RD would enclose the completed parts from Arne in his 28 August 1756
letter to Shenstone (q. v.).

From Thomas Blacklock[1]

Dumfries 3ᵈ May 1756.

Dʳ Sir

I was honoured with your favour of the 25.[2] Curst in due time & quite surpris'd to
hear that the 8ᵛᵒ Edition of my poems is already publishd before I imagind the
Impression begun.[3] I am Sincerely gratefull for that alacrity & expedition with
which you have always exerted yourself to my advantage & for that spirit of
Uncommon disinterestedness which has been so Conspicuous in all your conduct
towards me but I cannot forbear reproaching my own Indolence & forgetfullness in
not begging Mʳ Spence to Alter that Paragraph in the quarto Edition which
concerns Mʳ Hewit as his end in coming to me was really the acquisition of
knowledge.[4] There are still such a number of the Edinr. Edition here & in the hands
of evry one that I am afraid it will be unnecessary to send any of this late Impression
to Scotland except perhaps one or two to gratify my own curiosity and that of a few
friends I shall however consult Mʳ Hume with regard to this &, send you his
opinion[5] If any copys are Transmitted to me they cannot be better Convey'd than
to Messʳˢ Hamilton & Balfour[6] but it appears very probable, ⟨th⟩ if the Booksellers
could be engagd, that a great number of copys might be dispers'd in the north of
England particularly in Yorkshire & Cumberland & the Bishoprick of Durham. I
shall take the liberty of showing Mʳ Willson[7] yours who will be very Sensible of the
favour you did him in directing him to [th]e proper hand but at the same time
much mortifyd that he cannot engage immediately with yourself [Pr]ay is Mʳ
Spence at home or has he proceeded on his Journey Northward[8] The news of the
welfare [of] my friends particularly of yours & his Constitute [the] most essential
Ingredients in the happiness of

Dʳ Sir
Your much obligd &
most huˡ Servᵗ

Thoˢ Blacklock

MS: Bodleian, MS Montagu d. 11, f. 115.

1 Thomas Blacklock (1721–91), of poor but educated parents and deprived of his sight from six months,
early on gained the admiration and sympathy of Dr Stephenson, a physician of Edinburgh, who
sponsored his education at the Grammar School of that city for four years. Despite his handicap, he
began writing poetry at a young age and published a volume of poems in 1746. His friend David
Hume used the second edition of this volume (1754) to intercede with RD for a London edition in

1756, which was prefaced by Joseph Spence's rather vague biography of the Scot. The story of his attempted lecturing at Edinburgh, his ordination and trouble with parishioners, and his marriage, Blacklock himself recounts in his letters to RD. Although initially sympathetic to the phenomenon of a blind poet, RD's interest in Blacklock, like the sale of his poetry, seems to have waned in a few years.

² Letter not traced.

³ A second London edition of Blacklock's *Poems*, in small and large quarto, had been published on 26 February, but I can find no copy of an octavo edition, nor an advertisement for such, predating this letter. The Edinburgh edition of 1754 had been in octavo.

⁴ In Joseph Spence's account of Blacklock, which was prefixed to the 1756 edition of the Scot's poems (though published separately by RD on 13 November 1754 (*PA*), Spence referred to Richard Hewitt as "a boy whom he [Blacklock] had taken to lead him." Apparently Blacklock was a bit embarrassed with the statement, for Hewitt had later left Blacklock to become Lord Milton's secretary and had addressed a laudatory poem to his former tutor, "To Mr. Thomas Blacklock," which was prefixed to the 1756 edition of Blacklock's *Poems* (pp. v–vii).

⁵ For Hume, see note 1.

⁶ The Edinburgh publishers of Blacklock's *Poems*.

⁷ Probably Ebenezer Wilson, a bookseller of Dumfries, whose name appears in the 2nd edition of Blacklock's *Poems* (1756) as a subscriber to two copies. The nature of RD's "favour" on Wilson's behalf is not known.

⁸ Spence's summer trips north were regularly to visit Charles Watson-Wentworth (1730–82), 2nd Marquis of Rockingham, at his home in Kirkby, Leicestershire.

From Richard Berenger¹

Monday May 31: [1756]²

Sir

I yesterday morning told Mʳ Garrick what had past between you and me in reference to him; he has nothing more to say in addition to what he said to you himself, or to what I said to you from him – As so much has been said, and such opposite opinions about your Tragedy, I own I have a curiosity to see it & judge for myself, which if you allow me to do, I assure upon my honor I will decide (as to my opinion of it,) with the coolest & most impartial Judgment I am able.³ You must do me the Justice to believe that if I should not approve, it will not be in complaisance or deference to the sentence past on it by my friend; but merely because I speak as I feel; on the other hand, If in my opinion it should have merit, I will carry it back to him, to examine and reconsider. I am Sir, your obedient

Faithfull Servant

R Berenger

MS: Folger Shakespeare Library Y. C. 141 (1).

¹ Richard Berenger (d. 1782), called by Samuel Johnson "the standard of ideal elegance" (Piozzi, *Anecdotes*, in Johnson *Miscellanies*, I, 254), earned his fashionable reputation at great expense and had to be protected from the bailiffs by the generosity of Garrick, for whom he had served as a sometime reader of plays. He contributed three poems to Volume VI of RD's *Collection* (pp. 271–6), one of which, "On the Birth-Day of Shakespeare," had appeared along with three essays in RD's periodical, *The World* (Nos. 79, 156 and 202). He also produced two works on horsemanship, one a translation of Claude Bourgelat's *Elements d'Hippiatrique* (1750–3).

² The year is clear from the subject of the letter, taken up ten days later in Berenger's fully dated letter to
   RD.
³ RD's *Cleone*, which had been rejected by David Garrick for performance at Drury Lane. RD complied
   with Berenger's suggestion by sending him a copy of the play. See the response in Berenger's next
   letter, of 10 June.

From Richard Berenger

June 10: 1756
S't James's Place

Sir.

I was prevented from sending you my sentiments upon your Tragedy, when I sent the Book to you this morning – I have wrote out what remarks I made as I read it, and inclose a Copy of them – They will be found to be perhaps, but trivial, but they are such as occurred to me, and I submit them to better Judgments, – either your own, or the opinion of your friends – If you intend either to act or print the piece, I most heartily wish you all Imaginable Success – but to give you my opinion upon the whole, independent of my cursory observations, which can easily be alter'd, if you think it worth while; I am apt to think, that it wants force, that it is too full of imitations of other plays, & consequently that it is not original & sufficiently striking, to promise you a great deal – I wish for your sake I may be mistaken, for I am with great truth Sir;[1]

your Faithful & obedient Servant,
R Berenger

Observations[2]
On Cleone
A Tragedy.

The action is not one; for Glanville is incited to his villainy, from a passion which he has for Cleone, and from a desire to gain the possessions of her Husband Siffroy; which disunite and divide it [3] –

Perhaps it may be wrong to make Glanville murder the woman he lov'd, her child, and Lodowick indiscriminately[4] – There is a reason for his killing the child, because he was a bar to his hopes of acquiring Siffroys estate; as well as for the murder of Lodowick, who would have discover'd him, if he had liv'd; but why he should instantly resolve on the death of Cleone whom he lov'd passionately; I don't see; and upon the whole, the character appears to me too outrageously savage and bloody; especially as Glanville is not lead on gradually to this mischief, and the Scenes and incidents don't rise one after another to tempᵗ him on, but he takes his resolution precipitately and seemingly too much in cold blood[5] –

The characters and situations of Glanville & Isabella, have too near a resemblance to those of *Zanga* & *Isabella*, in the *Revenge*[6]

Act 2:^d
Scene 1:st

Glanville says – if *we could but once plant our feet on this Siffroys possessions* – I am apt to think, the expression here of *planting our feet*, is faulty; if we are to understand by it a desire to *arrive at or attain any wish* – it generally meaning figuratively & literally, – to *stop short*, to continue *firm* and *immoveable* in any design or pursuit, and not the accomplishment of a design or wish[7] –

Scene 6:

Glanville says, "the *hand of prudence* is to me the *hand* of *providence* – perhaps this may be too bold an expression in the month of an Asassin, and *prudence* is always used in a good sense[8] –

Act the 3:^d

Scene 5:th

Young Beaumont says, "*murder to night hath dipt his hands in Blood.* Is not this tautology? in what can *murder* dip his hands but in Blood? and ⟨?⟩ it can say no more, than that murder has dipt his hands in murder[9] –

Siffroy says – *Let distraction come and from my Brain tear out the seat of memory* – to do this, it must tear his *brain* out of *his brain*, for the *brain* is the *seat* of memory[10] –

Scene of Cleone & her child –

Though there may be many Instances of children being introduced upon the stage, prattling with their artless innocence, who by their helpless condition moving the compassion of the Audience, yet I think it is generally better not to let them talk, for it is so very easy to make them prattle, that though they talk consistently with their age & notions, yet their conversation is always tedious and trite, and almost known before it is utter'd – for it is not difficult to guess what an infant will or indeed can say, before he opens his mouth to speak – I should think it were therefore better that the *child* should say nothing – not to mention, that this Scene squints stronly at that in *Macbeth*, between Lady *Macduff* & her *child*, as the Madness of Cleone does to that of *Ophelia* in *Hamlet*, though the situation is very interesting – but for calling the *Redbreasts* &c: is the old *Ditty* of the *children in the wood*, and indeed too puerile & trite.[11]

Act 4:

Scene the 3:^d

Siffroy says "O Happiness, thou frail fading Flower – Beauty is frequently compar'd to a *Flower*, and with great propriety, because they answer throughout one to the other, being both objects of our senses, & both of uncertain & short duration – but happiness can be ⟨no more⟩ compar'd to a flower in no other sense than as they are both fleeting & perishable, the allusion therefore is just but in part, & upon that account faulty, for it is a mixture of metaphors which should be always avoided[12] –

Act 5:[th]

Glanvilles attempting to stab Isabella, on her discovering herself & him as accomplices of the murder, is too palpable a Copy of Iago's offering to stab his wife Emelia in Othello.[13]

Cleone going to her dead child – Siffroy follows, and says – "O let pale Horror veil her dreadfull face, her look on this sad Scene – Humans & Pity might wish to veil their faces not to see so sad a Scene, which might shock them, but if any thing is to see a Horrid scene, Horror is surely not improper – but even then – the words convey no Image or Idea to me[14]

MS: Folger Shakespeare Library Y. C. 141 (2–3).

[1] Despite the fact that Berenger's accompaning report helped to doom the chances of Garrick's producing RD's *Cleone* at Drury Lane, Berenger seemed to remain a good friend and correspondent of the publisher. In his letter of 26 October 1757 to John Hoadly (q.v.), RD asks that his compliments be conveyed to Berenger, and when writing to Berenger on 10 January 1758 (q.v.), RD says that at a recent gathering of *literati* at Tully's Head, Berenger's health went round. Also it was Berenger who paid RD considerable praise when the publisher of the most fashionable collection of poetry of the age chose to omit his own successful poem *Melpomene* from Volumes V and VI. Entitled "On *Mr. Dodsley's* publishing 2 Vols. of Poems by Several Hands, in which an Ode, call'd The Regions of *Terror* and *Pity*, is not inserted," Berenger's poem in the *London Chronicle* of 22–5 April 1758 explained:
>   You ask why in that garland fair,
>   Where various sweets abound
>   A *certain* flow'r of merit rare
>   Is no where to be found?
>   . . .
>   Then know, the modest swain, my friend,
>   Who cull'd those flow'rs so gay;
>   Meant *others* worth to recommend,
>   And not his *own* display.

Somewhat ironically, RD's *Melpomene* (1757), the poem to which Berenger refers, had been written amidst the frustration of attempting to get *Cleone* accepted by Garrick.

[2] This is the earliest known criticism of RD's tragedy. The ensuing summer, RD would take the play with him to Shenstone's and then to Graves's, each of whom offered suggestions for revision. In September, John Hawkesworth, too, submitted a lengthy criticism (q.v.) and that fall the Duchess of Leeds, as well as Edward Young, read the play, though no criticisms remain from these quarters. In 1757, RD thanks William Melmoth and Mr (James?) Cawthorne for their comments. But, with all the revisions, Garrick rejected it one more time in September of that year. In December, the Earl of Chesterfield read *Cleone* and sent RD a favorable opinion, and early in the new year, Berenger himself

writes to RD, hoping "that wit [may] come out in folio, and you the publisher or author." Except for the many letters exchanged with Shenstone and Graves regarding the writing and revision of the play's epilogue, the foregoing criticisms represent the recorded commentaries on the play before its first production at Rich's Covent Garden on 2 December 1758. Unfortunately, because early versions of RD's manuscript do not survive, it is impossible to judge the immediate impact of Berenger's objections. However, when one considers them in conjunction with the first edition of *Cleone* in 1758, at least their ultimate effect becomes clear. See below.

[3] In the later text, Glanville can hardly be said to love Cleone passionately, as Berenger observes in his next paragraph; his passion seems purely physical and when rejected turns to hatred. However one would wonder what he would have done had Cleone yielded to him, for indeed her son remained a barrier to Siffroy's possessions.   [4] "Lodowick" becomes "Paulet" in the later text.

[5] "Bloody" was the reputation the play earned.

[6] Edward Young, *The Revenge* (1721). See RD's letter to James Cawthorne, 2 April 1757, where he says he has never read the play.   [7] This line was dropped.

[8] Glanville retains this line, although it occurs in Scene vii.

[9] "Beaumont" becomes "Beaufort." The line was dropped.   [10] Retained.

[11] Cleone's child retains a few lines, and the redbreasts are called for. The likeness to Lady Macduff and her child and to Ophelia are very evident.   [12] Retained as the opening line in the scene.

[13] Another similarity that RD did not attempt to veil.

[14] RD honored this objection by changing the line to: "Let sweet Pity veil / The horror of this scene from every eye."

To William Shenstone

Pall mall June 12.th [1756][1]

Dear Sir

I have some thoughts of setting my face towards Birmingham before 'tis long, and as I should be very sorry to make that Expedition when You are engag'd or from home, I beg the favour of a Line. My Compliments wait on Mr Hylton and all friends.

I am

Dear Sir
Your most faithful
and obed.^t^ Servt

R Dodsley

MS: BL. Add. MS, 28,959, f. 53.

[1] By a process of elimination, this letter is not a likely product of any year in the 1750s except 1756. (Shenstone's collection of RD's letters, now BL Add. MS. 28,959, runs only through 1759.) RD had not met John Scott Hylton, complimented within, until his trip to the Leasowes in 1755. In 1757, when RD is writing to Shenstone regarding his summer plans, Hylton is with him in London. In the summer of 1758, RD takes an extensive trip through Scotland with Joseph Spence. Of significance is the letter's chronological relationship to the following letters to Shenstone: one announces his trip and the next sets the date. The year 1759 is a possible claimant, but the holograph's folio number in Shenstone's collection places it among letters of 1756.

To William Shenstone

June 28.th 1756

Dear Sir

I hope, and it is a hope which gives me great pleasure, that I shall be with You about the 14.th or 15.th of July, as I set out for Oxford on the 9th or 10.th where I shall stay two or three days. I long to see the new Edition of your Place, which, from what You say, will I suppose by that time be compleated: but, were it not that I can despair of nothing, from your Taste in *Rural Elegance*, I should think it impossible that you will be able to make any addition⟨s⟩ to its last year's Beauties.[1] Your politeness in saying that I shall contribute any way to your Enjoyment of these Delights, I am afraid I shall prove to be merely a Compliment, as I bring in my hand, according to your request, an unfortunate melancholy creature, whom you will find so perverse in her Disposition, that she will take pleasure in nothing so much as in causing your tears.[2] However, You shall have as little of her Company as you please, and if we find her in the least disagreeable, we'll lock her up, and banish her from our walks. I hope indeed to be much better entertain'd with the tender Conversation of ⟨those⟩ certain Ladies of your acquaintance, to whom I flatter my self I shall once more have the pleasure of being introduc'd. But take care of me, for tho' I am a grave man, and from my age may perhaps be unsuspected, yet I feel such sparks of Passion lurking in my breast, from the remembrance of their beauties, that I shall certainly be tempted to run away with some of them. I beg my Compliments to Mr Hylton, whom I shall be very glad to see; and tho' I think him at present most virtuously inclin'd shall hope so far to inveigle him, as to engage his assistance in all my attempts, whether of Rapes or Robberies.[3]

> I am
> Dear Sir
> most sincerely Yours

R Dodsley

MS: BL. Add. MS. 28,959, ff. 54–5.

[1] For a chronology of Shenstone's improvements to the Leasowes, see John Riely, "Shenstone's Walks: The Genesis of The Leasowes," *Apollo*, September 1979, 202–9.   [2] The rejected tragedy *Cleone*.
[3] "Rapes or Robberies": snaring poems from the ever-revising, tight-fisted Shenstone.

To William Shenstone

Pall mall Aug.st 28.th [1756][1]

Dear Sir

As you know how difficult it is to prevail w.th ones self to sit down to write, I hope You will pardon my long silence, and not believe me at all the less sensible of those pleasures I receiv'd at the Leasowes, for this delay in acknowledging them. Cleone also makes her Compliments, thanks you for the Improvements she receiv'd under

your correction, seems to hold up her head mightily upon some little Commendations which You were pleas'd to flatter her with, and is vain and silly enough, poor
creature, to fancy you might possibly be in earnest. I had the pleasure of meeting
with Mr Graves, am much oblig'd to You for his acquaintance, & was very sorry I
could have no more time with him. However, he very obligingly made the most of
what we had, read over the Piece, & pointed out to me several little Inaccuracies,
which I doubt not will turn to my advantage. I have made many Alterations since I
came home, and some considerable ones. Have You thought of an Epilogue? I
could wish, if You are so kind, that I might be favour'd as soon as is convenient. I
have enclos'd the other three parts of your Pastoral, set by Mr Arne, and he says, as
well set as any thing he has done.[2] He desires his Compliments. I wish I knew in
what You are just now employ'd. Are You busy with your Architects in the Wing of
your House? Or wandering in little Tempe projecting new beauties? Are You
teaching honest Thomas how to bend your Stream in the most natural meanders?[3]
Or are You listening with a deep regard to his more sage directions? I expect to
hear, when he finishes his mortal course, that he is transform'd into a River God,
and hath taken up his station, reclin'd upon an Urn, at the top of Your great
Cascade; or rather perhaps on that beautiful spot where your River breaks out in
the before mention'd Vale. After all, methinks I do not heartily wish to find you
employ'd in any of these ways; but rather (provided the Epilogue be finish'd) in
correcting & marshaling Your Elegies, or in designing Your Ornaments for them.
Not in contriving beauties that may detain you at home, but in projecting such as
may invite You up to Town: where I will flatter my self with a sure and certain hope
that I shall not fail to have the pleasure of seeing You this Winter.

I am Dear Sir
affectionately Yours

R. Dodsley

MS: BL. Add. MS. 28,959, ff. 74–5.

[1] For several reasons, this 28 August letter is certainly of 1756. RD is thanking Shenstone and his friend
Graves for the many suggestions for the revision of *Cleone*, the "melancholy creature" he had
promised, in his letter of 28 June 1756, to bring with him to the Leasowes. Also, he is thanking
Shenstone for introducing him to Richard Graves. On 27 July 1756 Shenstone had writtent to Graves
saying that RD was to make a quick trip to Bath and wanted to meet him. He urged Graves to "be
acquainted with him at first sight; which, I think should ever be a maxim with persons of genius and
humanity" (Williams, p. 455). And in his letter of 3 September (q.v.), Graves acknowledges to RD
that Shenstone "des[ir'd] me to be acquainted at first Sight" and apologizes for the liberties he took
with *Cleone*. Furthermore, RD must have requested an epilogue for *Cleone* from Shenstone during his
visit, for he asks here, apparently for the first time: "Have you thought of an Epilogue?" But, once
again, it is Graves who helps certify the date when, in his letter of 3 September, he begs pardon for
sending an epilogue of his own making directly to RD, thinking Shenstone's dilatory manner and lack
of acquaintance with the form will prevent his writing anything for RD.

[2] The music Thomas Arne had set for the first part of Shenstone's "Pastoral Ballad" had appeared as
the last page of Volume IV of RD's *Collection*. See also RD's letter to Shenstone on 19 November 1754,
note 3.

[3] Thomas Jackson, Shenstone's servant.

From Thomas Lisle

Burlene Sept: 2. 1756

S[r],

I have sent You a pacquet by the Newbury machine, which inns at the Bell-Savage on Ludgate Hill, & will come to London on Friday; But, as You live at so great a distance from that place, I have directed it to M[r] Parkes in Ivy Lane, & have desired him to convey it to You.[1] It contains the Title Page to the Observations on Husbandry, an Advertisement from the Editor, & the Authors Introduction; all which I beg the favor of You to look over, &, if You think proper they should be printed, be so good as to correct what You find amiss in them, & send them to the Press, without giving yourself the trouble of consulting me: I shall willingly stand to your amendments.[2] But, if You judge them not proper to be published, You will be so kind as to let me hear from You. – In regard to the Index, I should chearfully take that charge upon me, but, as M[r] Hughes has printed [the table of] contents, & as every Section is described in the margin, I am apt to think it will be unnecessary to add to any thing farther;[3] but, if You are of another opinion, let me know it, & my assistance shall not be wanting. – I have not yet looked over the whole, so as to note down all the Errata, but shall do it soon, & send them to M[r] Hughes. I return You thanks for your visit here, & Your Letter since,[4] & Am

Most Sincerely Yours

Tho: Lisle

M[rs] Lisle desires her compliments.

Address: To / M[r] Dodsley / at Tully's Head in / Pall-Mall.
Postmark: [PENNY POST PAYD]

MS: Bodleian, MS. Eng. Letters d. 40, f. 107.

[1] Possibly Nicholas Parkes, listed in *The London Directory for the Year 1768* as an upholsterer at 27 Ivey Lane, Newgate Street.
[2] The work of Lisle's father, Edward, *Observations on Husbandry* had become a joint undertaking. It was printed by John Hughs for Charles Hitch and Lacey Hawes, James Rivington and James Fletcher the younger, William Sandby, John Rivington, and R. and J. Dodsley. The first edition, a single volume in quarto, was published on 21 December of this year (*PA*) but carried a 1757 imprint. The second edition, two volumes in octavo, appeared on 6 October of the following year (*LEP*, 4–6 October 1757). Edward Lisle (d. 1722), a gentleman of fortune with twenty children, had lived at Crux Eaton, Hampshire (*CR*, January 1757, 1–20).
[3] John Hughs (1703?–71), printer in Great Turnstile, Lincoln's Inn Fields (1730–71), printed many of RD's publications.
[4] RD letter not traced. Perhaps RD had taken an indirect route to Oxford the previous summer (see his letter to Shenstone on 28 June) by passing through Burghclere, one of Lisle's livings.

From Richard Graves

[*c.* 3 September 1756][1]

Dear S[r]

I am oblig'd to M[r] Shenstone for many o[ppor]tunities of Enjoyment but for none more than what he [has][2] lately furnish'd me with – by favoring me with a

Visit pr[ay.] I am only afraid, that the Credit of my acquaintance with men of his Genius will gain me a Character for Criticism & Learning which, I am conscious, I cannot support –

As he knew our Interview would be very Short, he des[ir'd] me to be acquainted at first Sight – which however I found a superfluous Request with regard to a person of your benevole[nt] ingenuous appearance – The Consequence I believe, was, That I [appeared] to you in the same Dishabille of Conversation – in which Mr Shen[stone] always indulges me – I am sure at least I took the same [freedom] wth your Play – that I do with his works – wch I cannot [expect to know?] without some Confusion – since I find by Mr Warton (whose [Part?] in a 4. day Excursion to the Helicon Camp) what great hands it [has] before pass'd thro'[3] – However S^r you will easily see what a small [value] I lay upon my Hesitations –

As to the Epilogue, I am asham'd that I did not write to h[im] so soon as I ought to have done – But if he has done anything [I] dare say, it is superior to any Hints I could have given him[4] – [All] I could observe upon the Occasion, was. That the Epilogues w^h have be[en] *popular*, were those that were form'd upon a Satyrical Contrast b[etween] the ⟨the⟩ Romantic Behaviour of some of the chief Characters in your Play – [and the] degenerate Behaviour of y^e moderns = at least this trite method was [what?] occurr'd to me – & I hinted to him something of this kind in regard to Cleone['s] conduct. But as I know him very dilatory – & also suspect it is a way of [writing?] which he has not been us'd to – I have scribbled a few *flippant* [Lines to] this same purpose – wch may serve as a plan for some better hand to impr[ove upon.][5] Tho' I have observ'd that such vulgar Jokes go down better upon such occa[sions than] those things wch require more deep attention –

We shall never come to London without returning y^r Visit in Pal[l mall] Mrs Graves is quite vex'd with me for not ⟨?⟩ bringing her acquainted wth [Cleone.] She has a Turn for affecting Tales – & I think an incomparable Natural Taste I hope to read it to her after it has been upon the Stage – She joins [me] in best Respects –

I am S^r y^r obed hum Ser^t

Ric [Graves]

P.S. The Reason this has not pass'd thro Mr Shenstone's hands is because I would not forestall any thing he may have for the Anvil –

Epilogue to Cleone[6] –

Spoken by –

Well Ladies! so much for the tragick Style –
Behold me now equipp'd to make you smile – "Now, for the epilogue
To make us *smile*! (Methinks I hear you say)
We've laugh'd, behind our Fans – thro' half the Play – "Why child / we've
laughed / alone"
Where did the Poet find this strange Romance!
Cleone sure was never bred in France –
At least, no English Girl, just brought from School –
With such a Dolt would act so like a Fool –
    Captain   One should be good –

The Husband gone three years! Twas vastly good –
But wives, like other folks, are Flesh & Blood
A modern Dame would hardly think it treason
    provok'd – would do it for *that* Reason –
And if accus'd – would give the fool some Reason
Than who so tamely would have slip'd way!
               moral
Like the meek Heroine of this *stupid* play
"Out of my house! This night, forsooth, depart!
⟨modern⟩
A Brittish Wife had said, "With all my heart –
"But think not, haughty Sir! I'll go alone –
"Order your Coach – conduct me safe to Town –
"Give me any Jewels – wardrobe – & my *Maid* –
And pray take Care my Pin-money be paid –
When whims possess the pate of their good-men.
Women must find *protectors* – where they can – &   ) may be omitted
  Well! but the Child! – The tale indeed was sad –
But who, for such a trifle, would run mad!
What could she think – thro' horrid woods to roam!
Who would have brought the little Chit from home!
What has a Mother with her Child to do!
Dear Brats! the Nursery's the place for you –
  Such is the Language of each modish fair –
  But oh! ye Brittish Nymphs, at length, beware!
By Love & Sweetness & the winning arts
  [Of] soft Compliance you must [fix men's hearts]
    [Believe me] Ladies those licentious Lives
May draw vain Danglers but ne're make you wives –
  There was a time when Modesty & Truth
were thought *additions* to the Charms of Youth – "more *lovely* than q
When women hid their necks & veil'd their *faces* –
Nor star'd – nor *rak'd* nor gam'd at publick places * romp'd – q
Domestick Virtues then were all the mode:
A Wife ne'er dream't of Happiness abroad
Obey'd her Spouse – despis'd *coquettish Airs   fantastic
And with the Joys of Wedlock mix'd the Cares–
      Virgins pin'd or dreaded then
No slighted Maids o'er cards, lamented then,
Tho' thin'd by Holy Wars, a Dearth of Men –
No Rake-hell's ridicul'd the married life
      equal to
Nor deem'd a Mistress better than a Wife –

                                R G

Address: To | Mr Dodsley | at his house in Pall-mall | A single sheet London
Postmark 3SE Bath

MS: Somerset County Record Office, DD/SK, 28/1, 77.

The day and month are approximated on the basis of the postmark. The year is quite clear from the context of the letter where Graves is acknowledging his first meeting with RD, an event of the summer of 1756. (See RD's letter to Shenstone on 28 August 1756, note 1.)

The manuscript is badly damaged down the right hand margin, accounting for the many bracketed interpolations.

In his letter to Shenstone on 28 August 1756, RD acknowledged the corrections for *Cleone* suggested by Graves in their brief meeting. Also, in his letter of 28 June 1756 to Shenstone, RD had said that he had planned to visit Oxford for a few days in July before arriving at the Leasowes. Apparently, it was partly for the purpose of gaining Thomas Warton's suggestions for *Cleone*, as well.

Since Graves includes an epilogue for *Cleone* within this letter, it seems RD had mentioned to Graves, as well as to Shenstone, his desire for an epilogue, either during his visit or in a letter on his return to London. (See Graves's letter to RD on 30 September.) As becomes clear in subsequent correspondence, however, RD had hoped Shenstone himself would do the job.

Although the Dodsley–Shenstone correspondence over the next two years would regularly find RD requesting of Shenstone either a new epilogue or corrections for Graves's, ultimately it was Graves's original contribution, with adjustments, that carried the day. (See note 6.)

   RD's attempt to get Shenstone's name on the epilogue rather than Graves's (see RD's letter to Shenstone on 5 October of this year), remains a particularly embarrassing expression of RD's ambition, but in the light of Garrick's continuing refusal of the play, one can have some sympathy for RD's attempt to marshal his strongest resources. See James Gray, "More Blood than Brains: Robert Dodsley and the *Cleone* Affair," *Dalhousie Review*, 54 (1974), 207–27.

Twenty-two of these lines by Graves appeared, only occasionally altered, among the forty-one lines of the Epilogue printed with the first edition of *Cleone*.

From John Hawkesworth[1]

Bromley Kent 14Sep. 1756
Tues[d]:

Dear Sir

   As soon as I had dispatched my last Letter I finished the reading of your Play;[2] what occurred to ⟨?⟩ me is written, as it occurred in the progress of my reading, on the blank page; the substance of which, after reading the whole & *shutting* the Book, I have reduced to the following particulars.[3]

   Glanville designs the death of le Noy and his Child to obtain his Estate[4]

   ⟨?⟩ To effect this Design he contrives to make him jealous of his Wife with Lodowick, supposing that he will murder Lodowick, and suffer death as a murderer by the sentence of the Law, a very indirect and uncertain method at best and the choice of it is yet less probable as Assassins were to be hired who would ask no questions but how they were to be paid.[5]

   Glanville is in love with Cleone le Noy's Wife[6]

   Cleone must either die in consequence of le Noy's jealousy or survive him. in this ⟨?⟩ particular Glanville plots against himself, if Cleone dies he loses her at once, if he lives it is probable in the highest degree that she would learn he was her accuser and knowing this it is morally impossible she should admit him as a Lover.[7]

   But Glanville makes a fresh declaration of his passion at the very time when his main project, the success of which it must endanger, is brought to a Crisis, and must be supposed, at least at that time, to fill his mind with perturbation and solicitude, but this is not all.[8]

He takes the Resolution to ravish her, in her own house, surrounded by her own Servants, without any temptation that had not often occurred before, and against the strongest motive to defer such an Attempt both from hope and fear, fear of the Husband yet alive, and hope for his being soon removed out of the way.[9]

Glanville also seduces Isabella to a criminal intimacy merely that he may use her as an Instrument in the execution of his Design upon le Noy; Yet he proposes at first only to use her as a Witness to prove what he had persuaded her was true, and what indeed she appears to know nothing of but from Glanville himself, so that having no circumstance to attest upon her own knowledge she could as a witness do Glanville ⟨so⟩ no service.

Glanville does not make even this Use of Isabella, nor indeed any other that renders her Character essential to the play.[10]

Glanville having projected the death of le Noy by provoking him to kill Lodowick takes it into his head to kill Lodowick himself, and insinuate that he was living, though his first project succeeds to his utmost wishes, le Noy having assured him he would kill Lodowick with his own hand, and being then coming to do it, and though nothing had supervened that might justify his preventing Lodowick and le Noy from meeting, by so extraordinary and dangerous a measure; for he would have been accused as a Villain, by those who knew he had falsely accused them, if he had not been detected by Lodowick in his address to Cleone.[11]

Glanville also determines to assassinate Cleone without any more adequate ⟨Reason⟩ Motive; for her accusation would have been incurred by his false charge against her, and her accusation, unsupported by collateral Evidence, was all that he had to fear at last.[12]

Thus much for Objections; on the other Side, Supposing the plot to be natural & consistent and Glanvilles conduct [?] well accounted for, the Incidents which it produces are such as must strongly influence the tender passions, particularly those that relate to Cleone and the Child both before and after its death are uncommonly moving.

Mrs. Hawkesworth was so interested that none of these objections occurred to her, except the want of business for Isabella, & paid you the tribute of more tears than, considering her Indisposition, I thought she could afford adieu D[r/sr] I expect Saturday Sev'night with pleasure

I am
Y.[r] Faithfull
humble Serv[t]

J. Hawkesworth

Address: To / M[r] Dodsley

MS: BL. Add. MS. 29,300 A–Y, f. 43.

---

[1] John Hawkesworth (1720–73), whose prolific literary career has only recently begun to be assessed, was, like Richard Berenger, a friend and literary associate of the Dodsleys, as well as a reader and

adviser on plays for Garrick. RD bought a half share in Hawkesworth's periodical *The Adventurer* from John Payne in 1755 (see receipt in Appendix B) and included Hawkesworth's translation "Ode to Death" in Volume V of his *Collection* (1758), pp. 138–43. After Robert's death, Hawkesworth contributed two essays to James Dodsley's weekly *The Spendthrift* (1766), and five reviews to the younger Dodsley's *Annual Register* in 1766. See John Abbott, *John Hawkesworth: Eighteenth-Century Man of Letters* (Madison: University of Wisconsin Press, 1982), as well as Abbott's articles on Hawkesworth in *ECS*, 3 (1970), 339–50, and *SVEC*, 151 (1976), 31–46; also the editor's article in *HLQ*, 42 (1978) 57–72. (Abbott corrects the *DNB*'s date of birth for Hawkesworth.)

² Letter not traced.

³ Without RD's current text, it is impossible to comment on the justness of Hawkesworth's comments. However it is significant that when RD printed the play in December 1758, Hawkesworth's letter to him on the 10th of that month (q.v.) acknowledged that "most if not all the objections I made upon reading the first MS [have been] judiciously removed." And indeed they had, as the following notes show. (All notes assume a comparison with the printed text of 1758.)

⁴ Hawkesworth's reference to the object of Glanville's designs as "le Noy" suggests the existence of a text different from the one criticized in Richard Berenger's letter of 10 June (q.v.), where the character is referred to as "Siffroy," as in the printed version.

⁵ From the beginning, it seems clear that Glanville himself will have Lodowick (later Paulet) murdered.

⁶ In light of a similar criticism in Berenger's letter of 10 June (see note 3 of that letter), it appears Glanville's love of Cleone was made quite plain, whereas in the later version it seems merely physical passion that, when rejected, turns to hatred.

⁷ Major shifts in focus in the revised version eliminate Hawkesworth's objections. There, Glanville is primarily interested in obtaining Siffroy's (le Noy's) property, not his wife Cleone. Secondly, early on, Cleone discovers from Glanville himself that he is her accuser.

⁸ A "fresh declaration" also implies some earlier expression of passion, which does not appear in the later version.

⁹ Glanville's earlier plan to have Cleone murdered removes this objection.

¹⁰ Indeed Isabella plays no essential role in Glanville's plot and is therefore expendable. However as a foil to Glanville (she seems a naive cooperator in his villainy, her heart is touched by the outcome, she confesses her guilt, and testifies against the scoundrel), she does serve to heighten his evil character.

¹¹ In the later version, Lodowick (Paulet) seems scheduled to be murdered at the hands of Glanville's henchman, Ragozin. Consequently the accidental discovery of Lodowick in Cleone's quarters or the need for Lodowick to encounter le Noy returning home from the battlefield loses relevance.

¹² This objection is not totally accommodated in the revised version. Again, lacking true love for Cleone, Glanville might have thought her expendable and more conveniently disposed of with her child, the real barrier to his obtaining le Noy's estate.

From John Scott Hylton[1]

Lapall House 16.ᵗʰ Sep.ʳ 1756

Dear Sir,

How I shall be able to answer your obliging Letter,[2] or at your request to obviate all M.ʳ Shenstone's *ifs* that may retard our journey to London, I cannot foresee; when my Ideas will scarce serve to furnish out the One, or my power be of Force enough to compleat the latter: however I have too much Interest at Heart to refuse my Services where it may possibly be attended with so much pleasure to myself. *Much* I hope; but *More* I fear that I shall not be able to shut M.ʳ Shenstone up with myself in a post Chaize; if I should be so happy, depend upon it that none of the generation of Nimshs shall excell us in driving.

The Reason why I did not write sooner was upon Account of the Books. The 21.ˢᵗ of last Month Lord Dudley receiv'd his set of Poems & M.ʳ Wilmott's also from M.ʳ Male's – All the enquiries that I can make will give me no light concerning mine:[3] M.ʳ Male's people declare they never receiv'd any parcell directed for me; and his Nephew who would be the most likely to know how L.ᵈ Dudley's parcell came, is now out upon a journey, so that I cannot find out the Carrier. – Y.ʳ people probably may remember who they were sent by, so that you may be at no Loss concerning them. If the Parcell should still be at the Inn; I should be glad if you could add to it 2 or 3 Quires of the same paper your letter is wrote upon, & of which I have inclosed a little Bit – otherwise you may send it any time hereafter, directed for me here, to be left at M.ʳ Male's Ironmonger near the New Church Birmingham.

M.ʳ Shenstone receiv'd a Letter from M.ʳ Graves, wherein he speaks of the great pleasure your Visit gave him; I hope your whole Tour was agreable to yourself, and that Cleone has not any reason to repent she left London in Company with M.ʳ Dodsley if wishes could avail, you would easily command the best of mine, or my Pen either, could it serve you as well as M.ʳ Shenstones. alas! I dare not tell you how idle he is – He's order'd me when I wrote to avoid all mention how he was, or had been employ'd. I hope Cleone will not suffer for it – There has been & is continually parties of company at the Leasowes, the attending upon many of them, may in some measure excuse M.ʳ Shenstone's indolence; when Winter approaches I shall open my Intrenchments and endeavour to take him either by *Sap* or *Storm*: However I succeed be assured that I am at all times

D.ʳ Sir
Y.ʳ most Obliged
Hble Servant

John Scott Hylton

Please to make my Compliments to your Brother.

Address: To | M.ʳ Dodsley

MS: Humanities Research Center, University of Texas at Austin, Robert Dodsley / Recipient 1 / Bound, ff. 5–6.

[1] Of the early life of John Scott Hylton (d. 1793), little is known. Courtney (*Dodsley's Collection of Poetry: Its Contents and Contributors* (1910), p. 104) notes that, in a letter of 2 April 1754, Hylton refers to his "shattered fortune" and to a lawsuit. Lady Luxborough, in a letter of 12 December 1753, speaks of his loss of place at Court. Hylton became a neighbor of Shenstone's in March of 1753, when he moved to Lepall House, Halesowen. Although he became a close friend of Shenstone, personally nursing the poet through a long illness in 1758, he had a falling out with his neighbor over a ruse played on him that involved Thomas Percy and which, in a letter to Graves on 22 September 1763 (Stark Library, University of Texas), he attributes to the perfidy of John Hodgetts, Shenstone's cousin. See Hylton's letter of 18 February 1761, note 5, and Brooks, pp. 294–8. Miss Catherine Hutton, writing to Miss Mary Ann Coltman on 7 November 1823, remarked: "I knew John Scott Hylton when I was thirteen years of age. . . . He was a man of taste; but as his flower-edge paper bespeaks, a fribble." (Catherine Hutton Beale, *Catherine Hutton and Her Friends* (Birmingham: Cornish Bros., 1895), p. 177.) In 1784, Hylton edited the poetry of Richard Jago. RD published two of Hylton's poems in his *Collection* (IV, 312; VI, 280).   [2] Letter not traced.

Most likely Pyson Wilmott, parson of Halesowen, Hylton's community. Hylton's set must refer to a *second* set, for in his letter to Shenstone on 25 March of the previous year, RD said he had sent four sets, including one for Hylton. Possibly this first set had never reached Hylton, for when he finally acknowledges having received the books, on 20 January of the next year, he says they have "added greatly to my Amusement" and "have considerably shortened some of the winter Evenings," suggesting he did not previously have a set of his own.

To John Scott Hylton

Sep.^t 28.th [1756]¹

Dear Sir

I am sorry to hear you express so much doubt about your Journey to London: I was in hopes Mr Shenstone had ⟨made⟩ fix'd his resolution so strongly, that he would have set about his preparations for it immediately. I am much surpriz'd that you have not yet receiv'd your books; I sent them at the same time that my Lord Dudley's were sent, but they were directed to you at Lapell Place;² and I dare say You will find them at the Inn at Birmingham. I sent them from ye Bell in Smithfield, by Frimen's Waggon which Inns at Dale End Birmingham. I beg my Comp^{ts} to Mr Shenstone, I hope to write to him in a post or two, but am in such a hurry at present that I cannot half answer Yours.

I am &c

MS: Robert Dodsley Letter Book, Birmingham Public Libraries, f. 2.

The year is evident from Hylton's letter of 20 January of the new year, where he apologizes for having waited three months before acknowledging the receipt of RD's *Collection*, which, at this time, had been lost in transit from London.   ² Hylton's residence.

To Mary Godolphin Osborne, Duchess of Leeds¹

Sep.^t 28.th 1756

Madam

About a fortnight ago Dr Mounsey² acquainted me with the honour your Grace did me in desiring to see my attempt at a Tragedy. I had then ⟨?⟩ no Copy but what was so blotted as to render it scarce legible; and being too well acquainted with its many natural Weaknesses and Imperfections, I was not willing to add to its faults by suffering it to appear before your Grace in so ⟨dis⟩ unadvantageous and disrespectful a Dishabille. I transcrib'd it therefore, and You may now read it with somewhat more ease, but whether with any satisfaction, I am very doubtful. I wish I could flatter my self that it hath merit enough to prevent your Grace from repenting your Curiosity: but ⟨that would be vanity⟩ indeed I lay it before You with real diffidence: should it however be so fortunate as in the least to engage you attention, I shall look upon it as a happy Omen of its future Success.

I am &c

When your Grace hath perus'd it, You will be pleas'd to return it, as I have no othe perfect Copy.

MS: Robert Dodsley Letter Book, Birmingham Public Libraries, f. 1.

[1] Mary Godolphin Osborne (1723–64), second daughter of Francis Godolphin, 2nd Earl of Godolphin had married Thomas Osborne, the Duke of Leeds, in 1740.

[2] Having successfully treated the Duchess's father, Messenger Monsey (1693–1788) had gained th Earl's intercession for the post of physician to Chelsea Hospital. Also by the Earl's favor, he had bee introduced to such Whigs as Sir Robert Walpole and Lord Chesterfield, and became the chief medic officer to the Whigs. An earthy, burly type, who was criticized by some for his familiar manner wit nobility, Monsey willed that, at his death, his body be dissected at the College of Surgeons and th remnants be discarded.

From Richard Graves

Claverton, 30 Sept 175

Dear S[r]

I receiv'd both y[r] kind Letters in due time[1] – The former of which (tho' I forget particular acknowledgment) gave occasion to my own Attempt ⟨of⟩ at a Epilogue[2] – as I was apprehensive of M[r] Shenstone's dilatory temper & as I knew that kind of ludicrous Performance [was] as much beneath the Dignity of a Tragic Writer – as it would be for Rubens or Guido to lacker a Frame – for one of thei Sublimest History-Pieces –

As you only object to the Conclusion of my Epilogue, I am inclin'd to believe tha it has some degree of Merit – but hope however you will be furnish'd with a bette by some of your Friends – & beg that mine may be consider'd, as a mere Nothing

What induc'd me to conclude it, as I have done – was the Consideration of th Effrontery of the present Age – in keeping Mistresses upon Principle – which mad the last Line appear emphatical enough to me – But upon reviewing it – I find it, a you observe, a very abrupt Conclusion[3] – I have been very much engag'd this las week wth Company which our Race on Claverton Down has brought us – or should have answer'd y[rs] sooner. I have now but just sketch'd out 2 or 3 additiona Couplets – w[ch] I must leave you to compleat –

"'Tis yours, ye Fair, to mend a frontless Age[4]
Deaf to the *railing* Pulpit & the Stage –
　　censuring[5]
"In Virtue's Cause, in vain shall Priests engage
　　Tis Y[rs] –

"Till You, ye Fair, resolve to mend the age[6] –
"If Routs & Masquerades are *throng'd* by You
"Grudge not your Lords the Banio & the Stew –
⟨Wives must be blam'd Such Wives⟩
"Yours be the Blame – if husbands go astray –
"Men *will* be Rakes – where women lead the way –

I don't know whether I am not too rude to the Fair Sex – But by all accounts (& even [by] what I see at Bath) the Ladies in high life preserve appearances less in this Age – than they were ever known to do – & deserve some pretty bold Rebukes from the Stage (which they still frequent) – tho' they will not give us an opportunity of shewing them their transgressions f^rm ye Pulpit –

I write this Post to Mr Shenstone from whom I have not heard since I saw you – I am wth Mrs Graves's Compl^ts S^r Y^r

affect. humb Ser^t

Ric: Graves

I hope to get some Franks w^n our Season comes in –

Address: To Mr Dodsley / at his house in Pall Mall / London
Postmark: 4 OC Bath

MS: Somerset County Record Office, DD/SK, 28/1, 2.

Not traced.   ² See Graves's letter to RD of *c.* 3 September 1756.
This conclusion will particularly trouble RD and will be the subject of much revision almost to the time of its presentation at Drury Lane, more than two years later.
Altered to "Tis yours, ye Fair, to bring those days agen," this line became l. 30 in the first edition (1758).
The substantives of this line emerge in l. 35 of the first edition as: "That scorns the Press, the Pulpit, and the Stage."   ⁶ See note 4. The rest of these suggested lines were not used by RD.

To William Shenstone

Pall mall Octr 5.th [1756]¹

Dear Sir

I was in hopes before this time to have seen an Epilogue from You, but as I suppose an old Enemy of mine, whom You still cherish in your bosom, not withstanding all I have said against him, maintains his evil influence over You, to my prejudice, I send for your correction an Epilogue I receiv'd from Mr Graves; which I like very well, only I think it does not close happily: and I could have wish'd for your Name, as it is better known, and would have done me more Honour.² You see my Selfishness; & after this confession, how can I with any grace sollicit You to gratify so mean a Passion in me? But Self love is such a blinder, that I can see no meanness in it: I call it love of Fame, and again confess that I long'd for ye honour of joining your Name to my Piece, as I thought it would contribute to raise my own from Obscurity. I am sensible that I am asking You to bury your Gold in my leaden Coffin, from whence a Resurrection may be very doubtful; but you have other *Good Works* enow to secure your own Immortality, tho' This should be bury'd in eternal Oblivion.

I receiv'd a Letter from Mr Hylton last week, in which I am sorry to find he talks doubtfully about your Journey to London; but I hope he talks from his Ignorance of your Designs, not from his knowledge of them. Dr Akenside desires his compliments to You, and hopes for the pleasure of being acquainted with you this Winter, and longs much to see your Elegies. If you have thought of any Designs for them, I could wish you would send them up, as our Engravers are a very dilatory set of people. And pray bring with You some of your hoarded Treasure to put into my Exchequer of Poetry.[3]

I am ever
Dear Sir
most sincerely Yours

R. Dodsley[*]

Epilogue

Well Ladies. So much for the Tragic stile –
And now the Business is
Behold me now equipt to make you smile –
To make us smile! methinks I hear you say;
We've *laugh'd* behind our fans thro' half the Play.
Where did the Poet find this strange Romance!
Cleone sure was never bred in France.
At least, no English girl just brought from school,
With such a dolt would act so like a fool.
The Captain gone three years! – One should be good –
But wives, like other folks, are flesh and blood.
A modern dame would hardly think it treason;
If thus accused she gave
And if accus'd would give the brute some reason.
Then, who so tamely would have slip'd away
Like the meek Heroine of this moral Play?
"Out of my House! – this night, forsooth, depart!"
A modern Wife had said – "With all my heart –
"But think not, haughty Sir! I'll go alone –
"Order your coach, conduct me safe to Town –
"Give me my Jewels, Wardrobe, and my Maid –
"And *pray* take care my Pin mony be paid."
Well, but the Child! – The Tale indeed was sad –
But who for such a triffle? would run mad!
What could she think – thro' horrid woods to roam!

Who would have brought the little chit from home?
What has a mother with her child to do?
Dear Brats, the Nursery's the place for You!
   Such is the language of each modish fair –
But Oh, ye British Nymphs, at length beware!
By Love, and Sweetness, and the winning Arts
Of soft Affection, you must fix men's hearts:
Believe me, Ladies, those licentious lives
May draw vain danglers – but ne'er make you wives.
There was a time when Modesty and Truth
Were thought additions to the charms of Youth –
When women hid their necks, and veil'd their faces;
Nor star'd, nor rak'd, nor gam'd, at Public Places.
Domestic Virtues then were all the mode,
A Wife ne'er dreamt of Happiness abroad.
Obey'd her Spouse – despis'd fantastic airs;
And with the joys of Wedlock mix'd the cares.
No slighted virgins pin'd, or dreaded then,
Tho' thin'd by Holy Wars, a dearth of Men:
No Rakehells ridicul'd the marry'd life,
Nor deem'd a Mistress equal to a Wife.[5]

MS. BL. Add. MS. 28,959, ff. 58–9.

The year fits the context of the RD–Shenstone correspondence of the last half of 1756, a period much concerned with an epilogue for *Cleone*. RD's 8 October date on the draft version in his Letter Book is initially perplexing. Only the procrastinating letter writer's desire to appear prompt to his correspondent would seem to explain the discrepancy. Realizing that he should have written sooner regarding the epilogue received from Graves and that he had yet to express his regret to Shenstone regarding the failure of the latter's proposed trip to London (whereas he had already done so in a letter to Shenstone's neighbor Hylton a week earlier) RD simply and very humanly backdated this letter. Although the epilogue Graves initially submitted to RD was substantially the one used both on the stage and in print, it was Shenstone's name that was printed with it, though not in the first few editions where it remained anonymous; i.e., "By a Friend." See RD's letter to Shenstone of 16 December 1758. Volumes V and VI of RD's *Collection*, which were in preparation.

Although the RD Letter Book draft copy of this letter does not carry the attached epilogue, it does include some material not found in the BL version. The second paragraph playfully extends RD's plea for assistance with the epilogue: "And will you not lend your little finger to save a friend's whole body from destruction? ⟨but I think⟩ as you are rich, you may afford to be charitable, and let me live on ye crumbs that fall from your Table; I dare say I shall not be the first undeserving beggar you have reliev'd: and so God bless your honor bestow your charity." Secondly the draft version includes a rather significant postscript: "The World closes at Christmas, will you not let us have the credit of *one* Paper from You?" Obviously, RD's weekly journal *The World*, conducted by Edward Moore, ceased publication three months later (on 30 December) not because the world had grown tired of it but because it had been planned that way.

Except for an occasional verbal change, this version represents verbatim the text originally sent to RD, on 3 September. RD has resolved a few of Graves's options.

To Edward Young

Oct! 7.th [1756]

Sir

I have sent You by the Welwyn Carrier my ⟨presumptuous⟩ audacious attempt at writing a Tragedy, ⟨and I⟩ but am afraid, that ⟨next to⟩ ⟨not only to⟩ now my presumption in making such an attempt, ⟨but⟩ my temerity in venturing it under your inspection, will subject me ⟨to some censure in your opinion⟩ to the imputation of much self confidence.[2] As I would not willingly give ⟨just cause⟩ the least shadow of reason for such an accusation, I will confess, that if it had not already receiv'd ye approbation of some very judicious friends (too partial perhaps in this Instance) I ⟨could⟩ durst not have hazarded its appearance ⟨to be try'd⟩ at the Bar of so allow'd and experienc'd a Judge: nor can I yet resign it to its fate without strongly solliciting that ⟨Pity⟩ Tenderness which a first fault ⟨commonly excites,⟩ may ⟨be⟩ hope to find, & that Candor, which the first attempt of an ⟨man⟩ Author unassisted by Learning, may justly claim. I shall be extreamly oblig'd to you for your opinion of it and also for any remarks You will please to favour me with; only as ye Copy is fair & I want to shew it to a friend as soon as you can return it, you will be so good as to put ⟨them⟩ your observations on a seperate Paper.

I am &c

MS: Robert Dodsley Letter Book, Birmingham Public Libraries, ff. 2r–3r.

[1] Since this draft letter appears in a bound letter book in which the individual pieces were entered as they were written – i.e., in chronological order – this letter takes its year from surrounding fully dated letters. This dating principle will be used for other letters to follow, which are found in the same letter book. The reliability of the principle is proven in several cases where the assigned date corroborates that of the "sent" letter, also extant. Furthermore, a response to RD's present request is recorded in Young's 14 October 1756 letter, lot 419 in the Linnecar sale at Puttick and Simpson, 20 March 1850. Although Young's letter has not been traced, its one-time existence at least shows that a finished version of this draft had actually been sent to Young, and in 1756.

[2] The missing Young letter mentioned in note 1 (Linnecar sale) shows that Young agreed to offer comments on RD's *Cleone*, but his comments are not extant.

From David Garrick

Thursday [14 October 1756][1]

Sir

I am told, that You have complain'd of my giving Orders to the Doorkeepers to refuse You admittance into our Theatre –

Since I have been Manager, Every Author, from ye highest to ye lowest, who has wrote for our Stage, has had, & Shall have, the Liberty of the house – It is their Right & not to be taken away at ye Caprice of a Manager; therefore You may Enjoy it freely without being oblig'd to Me;[2] a Circumstance wch will give You no little pleasure, as You have lately boasted wth some warmth that you never *was* oblig'd to Me –

But why would You make y.ʳ Complaints & spread a false report, till You had been convinc'd of yᵉ Truth of y.ʳ Suspicion?

Because an Old Office Keeper at yᵉ Boxes (where you seldom go) was ignorant Enough not to know M.ʳ Dodsley as an Author, M.ʳ Garrick the Manager is immediatly to be tax'd w.ᵗʰ low, impotent Revenge – were You deny'd admittance into yᵉ Pit, y.ʳ usual place⟨,⟩? or Behind the Scenes, w.ᶜʰ indeed is a Matter of Favor? no – had You suspected that particular orders had been given by Me about You, why did you not write to yᵉ Managers to know the Reason of those orders⟨,⟩? had you done this, the Mistake had been clear'd, & You had not been guilty of ⟨?⟩ so much Injustice to Me.

I must desire You to retract the wrong You have done Me in censuring Me too hastily, & I must assure You when any ill usage calls forth my resentments, I take care never to let 'Em carry me into Meañess or Injustice –

I am\
S.ʳ\
Y.ʳˢ

D. Garrick³

MS: BL. Add. MS. 54,224, ff. 236–7.

This letter takes its date from the next, RD's response to Garrick, where the bookseller quotes from Garrick's remarks in the conclusion of this letter. To Garrick's "I take care never to let 'Em carry me into Meañess or Injustice," RD responds "you shall have nothing to fear either from my *Meanness* or *Injustice*," underlining the words to indicate he is quoting Garrick. Since the day of RD's response, 18 October, was a Monday, the "Thursday" with which Garrick simply marked his would most likely have been the previous Thursday; that is, 14 October. For a further elaboration, which corrects the date assigned by Little and Kahrl, *The Letters of David Garrick* (London: Oxford University Press, 1968), I, 318–19, see my note, "The Dating of a Garrick Letter", *PBSA*, 68 (1974), 170–2.

Previously, RD had had four plays – *The Toy-shop* (1735), *The King and Miller of Mansfield* (1737), *Sir John Cockle at Court* (1738), *The Blind Beggar of Bethnal Green* (1741) – and a masque, *The Triumph of Peace* (1749), produced at Drury Lane.

The refusal of free admittance to RD at Drury Lane and the ensuing sharp words exchanged between RD and Garrick over the matter, in this and the next two letters, seem only the acting out of a deeper-seated conflict resulting from Garrick's rejection of RD's *Cleone* for Drury Lane.

To David Garrick

Oct.ʳ 18.ᵗʰ [1756]¹

Sir

When I was refus'd admittance into your Theater, by a Box keeper who declar'd he knew me, but that my Name was not in the list of those who had the freedom of yᵉ House; and when I desir'd M.ʳ Verney who was w.ᵗʰ me to assure him that I was free ⟨of the House,⟩ and M.ʳ Verney refus'd to give him that assurance; what had I to suppose but that You had given orders I should not be admitted?² In this supposition I met two of your friends, to whom I mention'd what had happen'd and my suspicion that you was concern'd in it on purpose that it might come to your ear,

and give You an opportunity of setting me right if I was mistaken. A day or tw
afterwards I mention'd it to another of your friends, for the same purpose, and to n
one else have I open'd my lips about it: and ⟨soon after⟩ when I receiv'd ⟨
message⟩ an assurance from you by ⟨that⟩ this last Gentleman, that you ha
given no orders of that kind; my answer was, that I could easily believe you had no
⟨done it,⟩ and that your denial of it entirely convinc'd me ⟨that⟩ the fault was onl
in yᵉ Door-keepers. Here I thought ⟨had been an end of⟩ an end had been put t
this triffling affair: but it seems this straw was to be catch'd at, in order to give Yo
an opportunity of ⟪pouring out an additional torrent of inveteracy against me. ⟨
will not⟩ But this I pass over, nor shall I return any of ⟨your harsh or indelicat
Expressions in this or your former letter:⟩ ⟨the harsh or indelicate Expressions i
your present or your former letter:⟩⟫ shewing the continuance of your unaccount
able resentment. But I pass over in silence yᵉ harsh and indelicate Expressions i
your present and former Letter.³ I cannot yet bring my self to return them; bu
⟨will⟩ have still endeavour'd to remember tho' you forget, we once were friends
And if ever I should be oblig'd to appeal to the Public on the ⟨usage⟩ treatment
have receiv'd, be assur'd, tho' I may be as you insinuate, the *lowest* Author of th
Stage,⁴ you shall have nothing to fear either from my *Meanness* or *Injustice*; as
⟨hope⟩ trust I shall always preserve my Character ⟨at least⟩ as clear from ⟨those⟩
such imputations, as that of Mʳ Garrick.

I am &c

MS: Robert Dodsley Letter Book, Birmingham Public Libraries, ff. 6–7.

¹ The year is determined on two bases: the Letter Book principle, and Garrick's fully dated letter of 1
  October 1756. By repeating some of RD's language ("what do you mean by my harsh & indelicat
  expressions?") it is obviously a response to this letter.
² Varney was housekeeper at Drury Lane from 1751 to 1761 (Little and Kahrl, I, 284).
³ One of Garrick's letters is not traced.
⁴ In Garrick's previous letter printed here, he had written: "Every author, from yᵉ highest to yᵉ lowest
  who has wrote for our Stage, has had, and Shall have, the Liberty of the house."

From David Garrick

Oct. 18ᵗʰ 1756

but what do you mean by my harsh & indelicate expressions?¹ The Letter, in which
I gave you my opinion of yʳ Tragedy whatever you may think of it was intended by
me as a friendly one; I wrote my honest sincere opinion, as yᵉ matter struck me & i
my expressions were strong they were only strong against what I thought the error
of the play – I acknowledge that I did not gloss over yᵉ business, for I thought it wa
a matter of great concern to us both & that you had been much deceived by you
Friends. I cannot but think that I have behav'd to you with yᵉ greatest sincerity and
integrity, and I must flatter myself that I can judge almost as well as Mʳ Dodsley
can write²

ource: Sotheby sale catalogue, 22 April 1872, Item 36; Ifan Kyrle Fletcher, Catalogue 92 (1946), Item 8, and Catalogue 116 (1955), Item 74.

See RD's previous letter on 18 October.
This last sentence does not appear in the Fletcher catalogues.

From John Ogilvie[1]

Aberdeen Dec[r:] 12.1756.

ir

I take the liberty to trouble You with a few lines though I have not the Honour of your acquaintance & can only excuse myself for such a piece of freedom by the opinion w[ch.] I with the rest of the world have long entertain'd of your candor & ingenuity. – I have been so long accustomed to see every finer performance in Poetry either written or published by M[r:] Dodesly that I have ventured to inclose a specimen of a small Collection of poems which however mean in themselves may yet be screened from the severer censures of criticism under the protection of so celebrated a name. – But that their author may not be suspected of too much presumption he will venture to assure You that his essays have been perused by the best Judges in his own country & have obtained their approbation. – He will not attempt to conceal from You a circumstance You must soon discover – that they are the first productions of early youth. Perhaps your eye will often observe a weed where the mistaken hand meant to have planted a flower. Such a circumstance however will he presumes heighten your benevolence if they are esteemed & moderate your censure if they should be disliked. – At any rate the desire of some people whom I regard & the encouragement I have had from the Publick on former appearances will I hope leave me no room to repent taking this step. I will send You the Collection (which may consist of upwards of an hundred pages) when You have taken the trouble to let me know by a line whether You are pleased with the specimen. – If You think that it will do more than defray it's own charges I shall be satisfyd with a few copys for my friends & any share of the profits that You may think proper to allow me. I depend upon your candor as a Judge & upon your honour as a Gentleman.[2]

I am with true esteem
Sir
Your most obed[t] humble serv[t]
J. Ogilvie

P.S. Will You do me the favour to accept of a little attempt of mine one copy of which I have just now found? – I know You will excuse a multitude of blemishes in it when You are told that it was finished before the author was fully seventeen.[3] A more corrected copy is designed to be inserted in the Collection. But a very few copys of it were sent to England – You may direct – To – To the care of the Rev[d:] M[r:] James Ogilvie att Aberdeen.[4]

MS: Osborn Collection, Beinecke Library, Yale.

¹ John Ogilvie (1733–1813), Presbyterian divine and author, son of James Ogilvie (1695–1776) a
  Aberdeen minister. Ogilvie was one of the Scottish literary clergy who later frequented Londo
  circles. From 1759 until his death, he had a living at Midmar.
² RD does not seem to have accepted the 23-year-old's proposal, for Ogilvie's first poem to be publishe
  in London appeared under the imprint of George Keith in 1758. (See Note 3). The collection he refer
  to here is probably what appeared in 1762 as *Poems on Several Subjects. To which is prefixed, An Essay on th*
  Lyric Poetry of the Ancients' In Two Letters inscribed to the Right Hon. James Lord Deskfoord and published b
  George Keith at the Bible and Crown in Gracechurch St., London. Particularly significant fo
  support of this assumption is Ogilvie's prefixed apology for some youthful poems in the collection, a
  echo of his statement here to RD. The collection gained a favorable acceptance in the *CR* (Octobe
  1762, pp. 294–301). (In 1970 Ogilvie's *Essay on Lyric Poetry* was reprinted, with an introduction b
  Wallace Jackson, by the William Andrews Clark Library at the University of California at Lo
  Angeles as No. 139 in the Augustan Reprint Series. In 1971, Garland Press printed a facsimile of th
  entire 1762 edition.)
³ Apparently, *The Day of Judgment. A Poem. In Two Books.* (Edinburgh: Hamilton, Balfour, and Neill
  1753). A new edition, "corrected and enlarged," was published by Keith in London on 28 Novembe
  1758 (*PA*).   ⁴ See note 1.

To William Shenstone

Pallmall Dec 13.ᵗʰ [1756]

Dear Sir

 I am much oblig'd to the accident, whatever it was, that furnish'd the Mystery o
the Blank Cover, as it has produc'd me, saving the too friendly partiallity of it, a
very agreeable letter.² Nor shall I easily be perswaded that the said blank cover, a
You are pleas'd to call it, was not a very extraordinary Performance; more faultless
and less to be condemn'd than any thing I ever put out of my hands. I cannot take i
kindly therefore, that you should endeavor to depreciate my Talents, by
pretending that yᵉ very Work I least accus'd my self for, has nothing at all in it. I beg
You will answer me seriously. If there was nothing in it, how could you possibly
bring so much Wit & Humour out of it? Should a Highwayman rob You of a
thousand Guineas, count them out before you, and then pretend he found you
pockets quite empty; would you not think him a very audacious Rogue, and
immediately ask him how he came by the mony? I would not be understood to
insinuate here, that You have no Wit and Humour but what you stole out of my
blank Cover; that might be carrying matters too far: Your Poets I have heard, are
in some Language or other emphatically styled *Makers*, and so you may pretend
perhaps that you make Wit and Humour, as God made the World, out of Nothing.
This may be so for ought I know; appearances are indeed against me: but I am a
strict Reasoner, and having learnt it as a Maxim in Philosophy, that Nothing can
give that which it hath not its self, I cannot but conclude that yᵉ aforesaid Cover
was amply replinish'd with Wit and Humour. Now as yᵉ said Wit and Humour was
entirely my own, was all I ever pretended to, and my whole stock, to endeavour to
sink it up[on] me, & pretend there was nothing under this extraordinary Cover, is
very cruel; and in You a mere wanton Cruelty, as it plainly appears You have

nough of your own. "It not enriches You (as Shakspear says) "And makes me poor
ndeed."³ But I have play'd this Battery methinks till my feeble fire begins to fail.
∟et me try from another quarter. I cannot help admiring the ingenuity of your
paradoxical Compliments; they are certainly true Wit, which has been said to
onsist in bringing things together which have *seemingly* no resemblance: but should
∩ arch and judicious Critic happen to change your civil *and yet* into a severe *and
therefore*, what would become of all your Paradoxes and Compliments? I fear they
nust all vanish, like false appearances of old at the touch of Ithuriel's Spear;⁴ and,
o my great mortification, nothing but plain reasoning and naked Truth would
·emain in their stead. But enough of this – Your Letter found me confin'd with the
Gout, & to this I hope You will attribute my idleheadedness in scribbling so much
tuff. I must now be more serious, as I find I am not to expect the favour of seeing
⁄ou in London this Winter. This really gives me great chagrin, as I had promis'd
ny self much pleasure in your company. I hope however you will send up your
∑legies by Mʳ Hylton, as I shall have a convenient opportunity by him of returning
⁄ou the mony for them. As to correcting yᵉ press, the proof sheets may be sent You
lown by the post. Be so good also as to send me the Ode on Rural Elegance, and
vhat other pieces you think of favouring me with for the Miscellany, as I shall put to
press early in the spring, and yours must be the very first things I begin with.⁵ Dʳ
∆kenside also forbears to give me any thing to begin the 6.ᵗʰ Vol till he sees how You
begin the 5.ᵗʰ⁶ You may perceive by this how much depends upon your kindness,
⊥nd upon the speediness of it. As to my Tragedy, Mʳ Garrick has absolutely refus'd
⊥t, and therefore any alterations or improvements I may have made since You saw
⊥t, are I suppose to very little purpose. However, I still continue to file and polish
ᵥow and then, and have made also some small alterations in the conduct. I have
strengthen'd Glanville's Motives to his Villainy, and made him not proceed so far
∩ his attempt upon Cleone. I have alter'd the scene in the 3ᵈ Act which You
)bjected to, where her murder was attempted; and believe I may have added here
& there some touches to the pathetic. I shall be much oblig'd to You for Mʳ
Graves's Epilogue with your Improvements. I have had the pleasure of seeing your
'riend & Neighbour Mʳ Perry two or three times, who intimated to me your
∩tended favour of a Chine and Turkey. He has somewhat to communicate to You
∩ which I shall be very glad if I can be serviceable to him.⁷ I write this whole letter
∩ a hurry in hopes that you may favour me with an answer to the most material
parts of it when you write concerning him. I beg my compliments to Mʳ Hylton, the
ᵥopes of seeing him soon gives me much pleasure. I intend to direct a Hamper with
⊥ Barrel of Oysters and some Porter for the Leasowes against Christmas.

I am ever Dear Sir

Affectionately Yours.

R. Dodsley

[Shenstone's endorsement:] This Letter should be placed previously to one where
Mʳ D. says he has collected 40£ See Lettʳ Jan 11 1757 – This ought perhaps to have
been 1756.⁸

MS: BL. Add. MS. 28,959, ff. 81–2.

¹ Although a later hand has marked the manuscript "1757," several pieces of internal evidence sho
the letter to be certainly of 1756. Fully dated letters of late 1756 and early 1757 verify RD's long attac
of the gout mentioned here. Also, RD mentions Garrick's refusal of *Cleone*, Shenstone's having mac
corrections for the tragedy, and his having asked Shenstone for a corrected version of the epilogu
offered by Graves – all events of 1756. Consequently the letter could not be dated earlier than 175'
Nor can it be dated any later, for here RD is also issuing his first call for Shenstone's intend«
contributions to Volumes V and VI of his *Collection*, whereas, by his letter to Shenstone of 3 Decemb«
1757 (q.v.), he has already sent the poet proofs for Sheets B and D. Finally, a Letter Book draft appea.
for 1756. (RD's 15 December date on that draft is probably explained by the same principle operatir
in his letter to Shenstone on 5 October of this year. See note 1 of that letter.)
² Apparently RD had addressed a cover to Shenstone but had forgotten to include his letter, an«
Shenstone took advantage of the occasion for some whimsical expansion. Neither letter has bee
traced.
³ "But he that filches from me my good name / Robs me of that which not enriches him, / And makes n
poor indeed" (Shakespeare, *Othello*, III, iii, 159–61).   ⁴ *Paradise Lost*, IV, 810.
⁵ Volumes V and VI of RD's *Collection* would ultimately be delayed until March 1758.
⁶ Shenstone's seven poems had ended Volume IV, and apparently RD is attempting to effect son
continuity by having Shenstone's pieces begin Volume V, which they did.
⁷ John Perry (*c.* 1713–80) had entered Pembroke College, Oxford, the year before Shenstone. The tw
became friends and, later, neighbors when Perry was appointed vicar of Clent, Worcestershire (no
in Staffordshire). See Courtney, *Dodsley's Collection* . . ., p. 118. For Perry's "communication," s«
RD's next letter to Shenstone, on 21 December.
⁸ As Shenstone's endorsements on this and RD's next letter suggest, he had been attempting to arrang
this batch of RD's letters (BL. Add. MS. 28,959) in chronological order, probably sometime in 175«
the date of the last letter.

To the Society for the Encouragement of Arts, Manufactures and Commerce

To The Society

Dec.ʳ 14.ᵗʰ [1756]

Gentlemen

As the fixing a Name to our Society has been thought a matter of som
consequence, and seems not yet perhaps to have been happily hit upon, the write
of this begs leave, with great deference to the Society, to propose One to thei
consideration.² He thinks that in chusing a Name three things should ⟨be⟩
principally be regarded, viz: that it be well-sounding, significant, and unaffected
The Name propos'd is indeed a new Word, ⟨but⟩ but it is so easy in it
pronunciation that it would soon be ⟨very⟩ familiar to the ear; and if its meaning i
very obvious, ⟨and⟩ if no harshness impropriety be found in its composition, h«
apprehends its being new should ⟨be⟩ rather be a recommendation ⟨of⟩ than a»
objection to it. He humbly proposes ⟨then⟩ therefore that it be consider'd, whethe»
we may not take the Name of

The Philopatrian Society of London;
for the Encouragement of
Arts, Manufactures and Commerce.

This Name he apprehends ⟨very⟩ most happily includes the very Motive and bon«
of our Association, namely the Love of our Country; and as every man either is o»

)ught to be a Lover of his Country, and as most men wish at least to be thought so, ie is of opinion that so honourable and engaging a Name may induce many to associate with us in these good designs, which he hopes will always continue to give propriety to such an Appellation. He is

Gentlemen

with great respect

a Member & Wellwisher to the Society.

MS: Draft in the Robert Dodsley Letter Book, Birmingham Public Libraries, ff. 11v–13r.

Dated on the Letter Book principle. Also, the Royal Society of Arts Minute Book, under the entry for 15 December 1756, records the reading before the Society of an anonymous letter, dated 14 December 1756, wherein a name was proposed for the Society. The matter was referred for discussion to the next meeting but does not seem to have been taken up.

See RD's letter to the Society on 17 March 1756, note 4.

To William Melmoth

Dec.ͬ 16 [1756][1]

Dear Sir

The perplexing and unaccountable Affair of the five Pounds gives me much disturbance, lest through any neglect of mine you should have been oblig'd to pay the mony twice over. I have again been searching every place where I think it possible I could have put any receit, but can find none. The Letter you have sent me shows that I intended to pay some mony for you the very day I wrote it, whether I did so or not I cannot positively recollect, neither can any of my people remember whether they paid it for me. The older Prentice seemd to recollect that yͤ younger was order'd to pay some mony in Friday street; but yͤ younger does not remember that he ever paid any there.[2] You also recollect your paying me some mony in my back parlour, and asking me for yͤ receit which I could not find;[3] I think I have also some faint remembrance of this circumstance, and if this was the same mony I must certainly have paid it or ought to have done so; but whether it was the same, neither you nor I seem to remember distinctly enough positively to determine. However, it lives upon my mind so uneasily, that I had rather at all events repay you the mony, than bear yͤ thought that I should ⟨any way⟩ by any possibility have occasion'd You unjustly to pay ⟨the⟩ it twice. I have been for this fortnight past and still continue to be confin'd with the Gout, or I should before now have waited upon you, I have the Ladies are well to whom I beg my Compliments & am

Dear Sir

Your &c

MS: Robert Dodsley Letter Book, Birmingham Public Libraries, ff. 14–15.

Dated according to the Letter Book principle.

² Straus (p. 278) suggests that the "younger" apprentice might have been the John Walter who left

Tully's Head in 1759 to open his own business at "Homer's Head in the New Buildings, Charing Cross." (See Walter's advertisement in the *London Chronicle*, 23–5 October 1759.) James Dodsley left Walter £1,000 in his will, indicating a close friendship between the two in the last half of the century. Terry Belanger, in "A Directory of the London Book Trade, 1766," *Publishing History*, I (1977), 7–48, cautions against the error in the *DNB*, which confuses this Walter with the John Walter who founded the *London Times*. The "older" apprentice was most likely John Hinxman (d. 1762), whose name appears as a witness on the contract RD signed with Edward Moore on 23 February 1753 for the conduct of the weekly *World*. (See Appendix B.) Hinxman left Tully's Head in 1757 to open his own shop in York. (See Laurence Sterne's letter on 23 May 1759, note 2.)

³ The nature of the "five-pound" affair has gone undiscovered. The matter is not mentioned again.

From John Baskerville

Birm.ᵐ 20 Decʳ 1756

Dear Sʳ

I have for some past hoped a line from You in relation to the paper Scheme: Whether You have sent, or chose to send any of the thin post to Mʳ Culver, as that is the only Article I lay any Stress upon in his hands; pray do not send it, if You are more inclined to keep it; He shall stay till I can furnish him, which probably may be six Weeks or two months; I have not more than six Ream of that sort, – which If I chose to do it, I could sell tomorrow in Birm.ᵐ at 24/. & if inserting his name makes the least difference in Yʳ Scheme of Advertising, I shall like it quite as well left out.[1] I have sent Samples of the ornamented paper & thin post gilt to several neighbouring towns & have receiv'd Orders freely from them; I told You in my last[2] the prices, but that need not be a Rule to You, perhaps some of Yʳ Customers would like them less if sold too low, all I fear'd was laying an Embargo on them. I propose reducing the price of the octavo from 21 to 18 as it will be more suitable to the Quarto. pray therefore make me Dʳ for that difference in all Yʳ Stock of that Sort.[3] Pray give me Yʳ opinion if it would be wrong to make a present of a quire of each sort, & the thin gilt, to the Princes of Wales, As a Sample of English manufactory;[4] to be had at Mʳ Dodsley's; the Present mine.

I copied with great pleasure from our Birm. Paper a fine Complemᵗ made You, which I shall learn by heart, & of which I give You Joy.[5] I shall have Virgil out of the press by the latter End of Janʸ & hope to produce the Volume as smooth as the best Paper I have sent You. Pray will it not be proper to advertize how near it is finishing, & beg the Gentlemen who intend favouring me with their Names to send them by that time.[6]

When this is done, I can print nothing at home but another Classick, (a Specimen of which will be given with it) which I cannot forbear thinking a grievous hardship, after the infinite pains & great expense I have been at. I have almost a mind to print a pocket Classick in one Size larger than the old Elzivers[7] As the difference will on Comparison be obvious to every Scholer nor should I be very sollicitous whether it paid me or not.

You have not fulfill'd Y^r promise in sending me the printer's Scheme. I am with due Respect to Mr James Dodsley & Comp.^{ts} of the ensuing Season

D^r S^r

Y^r Obed^t Servt

J Baskerville

MS: Beinecke Library, Yale, MS Vault File.

[1] Peter Culver, listed in *Kent's Directory for the Year 1759* (London: Henry Kent, 1759), p. 32, as a jeweler and toyman at the Parrot and Pearl in Fenchurch Street. The advertisement which RD placed in the *Public Advertiser*, on 12 January 1757, was addressed "To the Curious in Writing Paper" and describes the characteristics of this exceeding fine Writing Paper, listing its uses, sizes, and its appeal to ladies, gentlemen, merchants, etc. Although it does not mention Baskerville's name, it concludes: "All the above sorts, particularly the plain thin, for the Use of Merchants, may be had of Mr. Culver, at the Parrot and Pearl in Fenchurch Street."

Perhaps this is the wove paper that, sometime during the past year, James Whatman the elder had made for Baskerville. The Birmingham typefounder used wove paper for the first twenty-eight sheets of his edition of Virgil in 1757. (See Philip Gaskell, *John Baskerville, A Bibliography* (Cambridge, 1959), pp. 19–22.) However the heavy shadows on the paper (caused by the bars of the mould frame) dissuaded purchasers, and Baskerville's "paper Scheme" proved unsuccessful. See RD's letter to Baskerville on the next 10 February. Baskerville continued to experiment with paper, however, Whatman turning out a finer version of wove paper in 1759. But even this refinement took time to catch on. (See Philip Gaskell, *A New Introduction to Bibliography*, pp. 64–6.) Given Whatman's past assistance, it is not clear whether or not the marbled paper for which Baskerville would be awarded a £10 premium by the Society for the Encouragement of Arts, Manufactures, and Commerce in April of 1760 was certainly of Baskerville's own making. (See the Society's Committee Minutes for 2 April 1760.) For RD's concern for paper-making, see the Introduction, pp. 49–50.

[2] Letter not traced.

[3] For RD's negative response to Baskerville's request, see the publisher's letter to him on 10 February 1757.

[4] Augusta (1719–72), widow of Frederick, Prince of Wales, who had died five years earlier.

[5] "On Tully's Head, in Pall-Mall, 1756 by the Rev. Mr. G[rave]s" had been inserted by Shenstone (see Graves's letter to RD on 7 January 1757) in *Aris's Birmingham Gazette* on 20 December 1756, the very day of this letter from Baskerville. The six-stanza praise of RD opens:

> Where Tully's Bust, and Honour'd Name
> Points out the venal Page,
> There Dodsley consecrates to Fame
> The Classicks of his Age.
> In vain the Poets, from their Mine
> Extract the shining Mass;
> Till Dodsley's Mint has stamped the Coin,
> And bade the Sterling pass.

The poem continues in an absurdly laudatory fashion, claiming that if RD had lived in ancient times, he would have been crowned by Caesar and his bust placed next to that of Cicero's at the temple of Apollo. In slightly revised form, the verses appeared as "On Tully's Head in Pall-Mall: To Mr. Dodsley, on his writing *Cleone*, 1756" in Graves's collection *The Festoon: A Collection of Epigrams Ancient and Modern* (1766).

[6] As usual, Baskerville's expected publishing date proves unrealistic. *Publii Virgilii Maronis Bucolica, Georgica, Et Aeneis* will not appear until 5 May of the next year (*PA*). For RD's disappointment and embarrassment with Baskerville's projection, see his letter to the printer on 7 April 1757.

[7] The famous seventeenth-century Elzevier printing family of Antwerp had turned out inexpensive miniature editions of the classics in 24°.

To William Shenstone

Pall mall Decr 21 [1756]¹

Dear Sir

I have just rec^d yours & the Advertisements. I immediately sent one of them with a very little Alteration to the Printer, & hope it will not come too late for the next Paper.² I write in a good deal of pain, and must therefore hasten to conclude, with only telling You that I sent yesterday by ye Birmingham Carrier a Hamper with about 2 Dozen of Porter* and a Barrel of Oysters, which I am inform'd will be in Birmingham on Friday. On account of the Oysters I hope you will contrive to send for it on Friday afternoon or Saturday morning. The Hamper is directed for You carriage paid. I wish you all the Compliments of ye Season and am

> Dear Sir
>> most sincerely & affectionately Yours,
>>> R Dodsley

The Porter may not perhaps come to in ye bottles till it has stood two or three weeks.

* [Shenstone's endorsement:] The Porter came before ye Statue – these L^{rs} are ill placed.³

Address: To / William Shenstone Esqr / at the Leassowes / near / Birmingham
Postmark: 21 DE
Frank: G. free Hunt⁴

MS: BL. Add. MS. 28,959, ff. 85–6.

¹ The year of this letter follows upon the dating of RD's letter to Shenstone on 13 December 1756, wherein he mentions his intention (fulfilled here) of sending the poet a hamper with a barrel of oysters and some porter for the Christmas season. Also the mention of the placing an advertisement for Mr Perry, a piece that appeared in the *Daily Advertiser* on 1 January 1757, corroborates this evidence.
² The advertisement appeared two days later in RD's weekly *The World* (No. 208) and was repeated in the next number. RD placed a duplicate notice in the *Daily Advertiser* on 1 January. A pathetic notice, the advertisement begs for funds to allow a "Clergyman in the Country, who has a numerous family, and but a slender Income" and who "has been near twenty Years afflicted with a severe chronical Disorder" to visit a "distant" mineral spa to seek relief of his malady. Interested subscribers were advised that their contributions would be accepted at RD's shop in Pall Mall. As revealed in RD's next letter to Shenstone, where he reports the result of the subscription, the clergyman was the Rev. John Perry (see RD's letter to Shenstone, 13 December, and note 7). If one can judge from the title of Perry's poem of the next year, "Malvern Spa, 1757," published in RD's *Collection* (V, 84–7), the spa was not exceptionally "distant," lying about fifteen miles southwest of Worcester. For an unfortunate development in this subscription fund, see Perry's letter to RD on 7 March 1757.
³ See RD's letter to Shenstone of 13 December, note 8.
⁴ Probably George Hunt (?1720–98), M.P. for Bodmin, Cornwall, 1753–84.

To Richard Graves

Decr 30th [1756]¹

Dear Sir

There is not a more certain nor a more wholesome Truth, than that every Crime brings its proper punishment upon ye Delinquent. Of this Truth my present distress is not knowing how to apologize for my past silence, renders me a flagrant instance. I will begin however with laying ye fault on Mr Shenstone; and yet I am afraid he has ⟨enough⟩ so much to answer for to you on ye score of his own Indolence, that to impute mine to him may appear quite cruel: ⟨however⟩ but he has promis'd me from time to time some alterations in your Epilogue, and I have ⟨defer'd⟩ delay'd writing that I might ⟨?⟩ confer with you about them; but behold they are not yet ⟨come⟩ arriv'd.[2] This appears but a frivolous excuse methinks now I have made it; how much more honest would it have been to have confess'd my fault at once, and beg'd your pardon? But one crime begets another; my neglect of You had almost betray'd me into an abuse of Mr Shenstone, by way of apology. As to poor Cleone, Mr Garrick's refusal to take her into his House, and give her a legal Settlement in Drury Lane, has thrown her into a state of absolute Vagrancy; and whether she will ever find a settled habitation is very difficult to say. She meets with many Admirers 'tis true, but few friends; all pity, but none help her: ⟨and⟩ 'tis in the little World of the Theater, as in ye Great; none rise but by favour, and Cleone hath not been so happy as to find any in his eyes to whom she made her addresses. Yet this is the chef d'ouvre of that Author whom you have taken it into your head so lavishly to adorn with unmerited Panegyrick.[3] The Master of Tully's Head is extremely oblig'd to you that in his present humbld and mortify'd state, you would vouchsafe to spend a thought upon him; it is a great comfort to a poor author, ⟨that tho⟩ when his wisdom is despis'd & his words not heard in one place to find that in another they are deem'd worthy of praise and honour. But why, dear Sir, in so high and exalted a strain? Rank'd with Tully – crown'd by Cesar – plac'd in the Temple – indeed I am afraid we are much too high here. You have strain'd the Peg of Compliment till there is no harmony in the string. However it is certainly very pretty and I heartily wish it was more just. It must be my endeavour to make it so, by striving to live and write up to your idea of me. Pray when did you hear from Mr Shenstone? I cannot yet learn whether his Elegies will be publish'd this winter or not. Surely he is indolent beyond all bounds. I beg my Compliments to Mrs Graves and am

Dear Sir

&c

MS: Robert Dodsley Letter Book, Birmingham Public Libraries, ff. 16–18.

[1] The year is determined from RD's reference to Richard Graves's "Panegyric" by which the author of *Melpomene* was "Rank'd with Tully – crown'd by Cesar – placed in the Temple." All these honors heaped upon RD allude to Graves's poem printed ten days earlier in *Aris's Birmingham Gazette*. See Baskerville's letter on the 20th of the month, note 5. Also the year 1756 is corroborated by the letter's placement in RD's Letter Book.
[2] For Graves's epilogue, see RD's letters to Shenstone and Graves during the past autumn, especially the letter from Graves of 30 September.   [3] See note 1.

From Richard Graves

Claverton Jan-7-1757–

Dear S^r

   Tho' it is a great pleasure to me to hear from you some times yet I am sorry you should consider y^rself as under any obligation of ceremony – to answer every Letter

which I may have occasion to trouble you with – I know you are generally much
better employd –

As to Mr Shenstone's delay in sending you an improv'd Copy of the Epilogue[1] – I
must take part of the Blame upon myself – I receiv'd his *Alterations* as long since, a.
the 21st of Decemb^r. and to my Shame, I own, have not return'd my hyper-critica
Remarks upon his Criticisms[2] – ⟨?⟩ till this last Post – I don't know how it is – but I
generally find a greater want of leisure upon these festival Occasions – than at any
other time – The truth of the case, I believe, is, That from considering it as a Season
of Indulgence – I sink into down-right *Idleness* – wch I think is distinguish'd from
Laziness – as the latter implies *doing nothing* – and the former *doing nothing* to y^e *purpose*
The being employ'd – but not about our *proper* business – wch at ⟨present⟩ that time
was the finishing our Epilogue – In short, I think you have so much reason to be
disgusted with me and my friend in this affair, That you would serve us right – to
throw yourself into better hands – & deprive us of the Honour of serving even as
Pages in the *Train* of your Cleone –

For I hope S^r you do not look upon us, as such tame Criticks – as to give up our
Opinions of that Lady to a mere Superficial Hero of the Stage – or think that we
cannot distinguish between *Merit* & *Success* – The latter, you know, It is not in the
power of Mortals to ⟨m⟩ *command*, – but, I am sure, you have done more – you have
deservd it – I know enough of the Theatre from Report – to be convinced, tha
Delicacy of Sentiment – Beauty of Diction – Moral Reflections & the other
Perfections of Composition are of little moment when the M-n-g-r is no
Complimented with a shining Character – to display his Personal Merit to the bes
advantage[3] –

Well; but to return to the Business in hand. Mr Shenstone has so well unravell'c
& Connected my Sentiments – and added 3 or 4 Lines towards the end – which so
happily apply those last Lines of mine to ye Subject of the Play[4] – that I begin to look
upon what I only sent to keep a place (like a footman in the Boxes – till its arch-type
should appear –) as not entirely undeserving your Notice – at least I think it is as
much corrected as it is capable of being – I have sent him 4 Lines alluding to the
prophane Employments of our modern Ladies on Sunday Nights. Which I think
might be introduc'd instead of ye present after *"ne're dreamt of Happiness abroad"* –
because tho' he has taken some pains to connect the present Lines – yet I think it y^e
most exceptionable part of the Epilogue – I only want to have him make it worthy
of his Adoption – as I imagine his Name is respectable – & mine cannot appear[5] –

As to my Panegyrick upon the Master of the Tully's Head[6] – I own – it would be a
fulsome Compliment to any modern Author – to pick out one of the celebrated
Ancients – & without any other Reason but a Similitude of their Studies, to form a
comparison between them in favour of the modern – But I must insist upon the
propriety of my taking an occasion from a particular Circumstance – to lament –
That a Person of true Genius & real *Learning* should be forc'd to make a mercenary
Use of the Honour paid to a Brother-Genius –; who, if he had liv'd in happier time
– would probably have receiv'd the same Honour himself – Tully indeed was but an
unsuccessful Poet – yet the circumstance alluded to – will be an excuse for
comparing you to him rather than to Virgil or Horace or any other Writers of the
Augustan Age –

Mr Shenstone has omitted the Name of Augustas to avoid the clashing of ss – but ᴀe has certainly made me sacrifice sense to Sound in this instance – because *Caesar* ᴀlways means *Julius* unless restrain'd by some additional Name or Circumstance. I ᴅid not know of his inserting it in the Birmingham Journal – till he sent me word ᴀimself[7] – I have put him in mind of publishing his Elegies – but he makes no Reply – Mrs Graves joins with me in best Respects & compl^{ts} for ye year 57. I am S^r
y^r affect: humb Sert
Ric: Graves

Address: To / Mr Dodsley / at Tully's head / in Pall Mall / London
Postmark: 10 IA Bath

MS: Somerset County Record Office, DD/SK, 28/1, 5.

Epilogue for RD's *Cleone*. See previous RD–Graves–Shenstone letters.
Shenstone's letter not traced.
An obvious reference to Garrick who remained unmoved in *Cleone*'s case. Later, Thomas Davies would claim in his *Memoirs of the Life of David Garrick* (1808), I, 253, that, lacking a premier role for Garrick, *Cleone* did not interest the manager.
Lacking any letter at this time from Shenstone to RD, it is impossble to determine which were the "3 or 4 Lines towards the end" added by Shenstone, or whether they were used by RD.
It seems RD's "message" must have filtered through to Graves, and, one might expect, much to the publisher's embarrassment. In his letter to Shenstone on 5 October of the previous year, RD, though expressing his pleasure in the epilogue Graves had sent, says quite clearly that he would prefer to have Shenstone's name appear as its author because he is better known.
See Baskerville's letter to RD on 20 December 1756, note 5.
Apparently Shenstone had made some adjustments before sending it to *Aris's Birmingham Gazette*.

To William Shenstone

Pall mall Jany 11.th 1757

ᴅear Sir

What you was pleas'd to call a heterogeneous Present was both very good and ᴠery acceptable, and I thank you for it. I had yesterday a letter from Mr Graves, ᴠho tells me that You have made such alterations in the Epilogue that he now likes ᴛ very well, and hopes you will adopt it for your own, as his Name cannot possibly ᴀppear.[1] He sent it to you he says by the last post, so that I think it very unlikely I � should be above a post or two without seeing it. Not a word of the Elegies! Not a ᴠord of the Ode &c!^{2} For God's sake when comes Mr Hylton to town?[3] I long to see ᴀim that I may have an opportunity of venting my spleen against You. I wish You ᴠas to hear how we shall rail! But what would that signify? You would wrap ᴄourself up in your dear Indolence, and laugh at all our vain emotions. I have ᴠritten by this post to Mr Perry to acquaint him that I have collected near forty ᴅounds in consequence of his Advertisement; I was in hopes it would have arisen to ᴀfty, but am afraid it will fall somewhat short.[4] I am still confin'd with the Gout, ᴀnd have not been able to set my feet to the ground these six weeks; you will therefore excuse the shortness of my letter, but how charitable it would be in You to write me a long one?

I am ever

Dear Sir

most affectionately Yours

R. Dodsley

Address: To William Shenstone, Esqr / at the Leasowes near / Birmingham
Postmark: 11 IA. / RG

MS: BL. Add. MS. 28,959, ff. 62–3.

[1] Cf. Graves's letter of 7 January, and note 5.
[2] RD had been hounding Shenstone for the elegies for more than a year. The "Ode" might be "A Pastoral Ode, To the Honourable Sir Richard Lyttelton," a piece that according to Graves in his letter of 25 April 1763, Shenstone had intended for RD's *Collection* but could not refine to his satisfaction.
[3] Although Hylton had expected to come to London in the spring (see his letter on 20 January), he did not arrive until July.
[4] For Perry's advertisement, see RD's letter on 21 December 1756, note 2.

To William Strahan[1]

Jan. 14 1757

Dear Sir

I was surpriz'd beyond expression, after what I had desir'd you to say to Mr Spens, to see in last night's Paper, a personal Invective of the most infamous & scurrilous kind.[2] I suppose you have not had an opportunity of seeing him. But I beg you will give my Compliments to him & let him know, that as my Name appears to ye Paper I think it is using me extreamly ill to make me answerable for such low scurrility as I not only detest but am asham'd of. If Mr Spens will put his name to ye Paper as its author I shall have the less cause of complaint: but if he will not he ⟨must not expect that⟩ may be asur'd I will never suffer mine to give a sanction to such despicable stuff. How does Mr Spens know but that I am by his means disobliging & of course losing some of my best friends?[3] ⟨But⟩ And why is our Paper immediately to become ye vehicle of private scandal and low detraction? ⟨expressly contrary to our declar'd resolution in ⟨the⟩ our very ⟨first Number?⟩ ⟨Introduction?⟩ entrance on the work.⟩ Does any paper of credit give into this dirty practice? The Daily the Public Advertiser; ye General the Whitehall Evening Posts; are they not all extreamly cautious of admitting personal abuse? And did not the Evening Advertiser destroy its self by ⟨this very practice⟩ these very measures?[4] Besides, as our Plan is universally approv'd of, and as our Paper I can plainly perceive is likely to succeed prodigiously, have not we the strongest motives to avoid giving particular offence? And to suppose that we shall lessen the offence by impartially admitting abuse on both sides, is just as absurd as it would be, to expect, were two men quarreling under my window, & I should throw a stink pot on both their heads, that either of them should look up and thank me for the favour. There is another thing which I must mention, & which I think it equally behoves us to be guarded against, and that is, that we give no just cause of ⟨offence⟩ complaint to yᵉ Trade, either by taking the whole of any periodical Papers, or by giving such large extracts of Pamphlets as may prevent their sale, and consequently instead of serving injure the Proprietors.⁵ As to yᵉ Tests Contests and all such Papers as deal in personal satire, we should certainly have nothing at all to do with them.⁶ And as to pamphlets, it is not only ungenerous but unjust to think of giving such large extracts as may be construed into a Pyracy, and tend to prevent instead of encouraging, the sale. In order to obviate all these objections to our Paper I have drawn up an Advertisement, which I think should be prefixt for some nights successively, and am of opinion that it will conduce to promote the sale of it. However as I am but a single person I desire you will take yᵉ sense of the Partners on all I have said; ⟨& if it shall be thought⟩ only assuring you that if yᵉ paper cannot be carry'd on without giving any of these causes of offence, I ⟨must⟩ shall desire to dispose of my share, being determin'd not to sacrifice my character to other people's indiscretions, nor to any lucrative consideration whatsoever.

I am &c

⟨To the Public.⟩

Advertisement.

As the Public have shewn a general approbation of the Plan & design of this Paper, we take this early opportunity of acknowledging our obligation, and of obviating some objections that have been made. ⟨As⟩ By ⟨some⟩ an indiscretion or inattention naturally ⟨attending⟩ liable to attend the Infancy of every Design, some personal abuse, transcrib'd from other Papers, has been unwarily admitted into this: ⟨and as⟩ some Book sellers ⟨having⟩ also have express'd an apprehension that we intend to make such large Extracts from Pamphlets &c as may tend to prejudice their sale: ⟨of them:⟩ we therefore take this opportunity of assuring the Public in general, and the Trade in particular that for the future the utmost caution shall be ⟨taken⟩ observ'd ⟨that no⟩ in not transcribing any unjustifiable liberties ⟨shall be⟩ taken by other Writers with private or particular Characters; and that no unfair depredations ⟨shall⟩ shall be made on the property of any Bookseller whatsoever: it being our intention to serve, not injure, the cause of Learning; & to promote, not obstruct, the sale of every good and useful work.⁷

MS: Robert Dodsley Letter Book, Birmingham Public Libraries, ff. 18–21.

¹ William Strahan (1715–85), printer in New Street, London, was a partner with RD in the publication of the new thrice-weekly *London Chronicle; or Universal Evening Post*, the subject of the letter. As revealed in his ledgers, Strahan printed many works for RD. Their most significant common undertaking was Samuel Johnson's *Dictionary of the English Language* (1755).

² Spens, the editor, has eluded historians; even his Christian name is not recorded. The matter that disturbed RD in "last night's" number was probably a reprint from the 8 January number of the anti-administration paper *The Test*, which had shown the royal household and the Ministry responding to the quack cures of "Dr. Bombasto." The satire was obviously aimed at William Pitt whose new administration (the previous month) had been forced upon George II, primarily through domestic pressures.

³ This was RD's second conflict in the course of three years with the editorial policies of newspapers in which he had a share. (See his letter to George, Lord Lyttelton in October–December 1754, regarding his encounter with the *London Evening Post*.) A modest manner and a concern for his business reputation made RD a regular enemy of "scurrility" in works appearing under his name. See his next two letters to Strahan (24 January 1757 and 12 December 1758). One of the "best friends" RD felt he was disobliging was doubtless Samuel Johnson, who had written the Introduction to the *Chronicle*' first issue (Boswell, *Life*, I, 317).

⁴ RD well remembers the strident affair initiated by Richard Blacow in the columns of the *Evening Advertiser* in 1754. See his letter to George, Lord Lyttelton, October–December 1754.

⁵ Several lengthy extracts from such as *The Test*, *The Con-Test*, and *Inspector* had appeared in the *Chronicle*. (See note 6.) Likewise, in each number since its inception, the *Chronicle* had printed two long extracts of newly published books and pamphlets, some of them running seven or eight columns and serialized over a few issues. One printed the author's recipes for pills and ointments to cure the bites of "mad animals," obviously the work's market secret. Significantly, three of the pamphlets had been issued by RD's regular publisher and distributor, Mary Cooper – no doubt this caused much protest.

RD's comments here somewhat anticipate the suit he would enter in Rolls Court against Thomas Kinnersley, the publisher of the *Grand Magazine of Magazines*, on 15 June 1761. Kinnersley was charged with infringement of copyright for printing in his periodical large extracts from Johnson's *Rasselas*, a work in which RD and William Johnston had equal shares. Ironically, the case was dismissed, largely because the proprietors themselves had printed similar extracts in RD's *Annual Register* (1759), pp. 477–9, as well as in the *London Chronicle* (19–21 April 1759; 28 April–1 May 1759) the subject of this letter.

⁶ Four of the seven numbers of the *Chronicle* to date had carried reprints from *The Test*, while three of those numbers had also run reprints from *The Con-Test*. All of these pieces viciously attacked a range of vulnerable subjects, from the inactive Duke of Newcastle to certain eccentricities of the royal household.

⁷ RD's proposed advertisement was not printed. For further developments in the case, see his next letter to Strahan, on 24 January.

From John Scott Hylton

Lapall = House near Hales–Owen
Birmingham 20 Jan.ʳʸ 1757

Dear Sir,

I am both sorry and ashamed to think that I have been more than 3 months regardless of your Letter, which I ought to have answered the next post, had it been only to have inform'd you that I receiv'd the Books, which have considerably shortened some of the winter Evenings, and added greatly to my Amusement.¹ – Altho' I am now set down to my Buroe in order to furnish out a Letter which may in some measure compensate for my long silence, I fear my magazine of intelligence will appear rather like the unconnected narratives of an old woman, than like a regular Epistle. – However, I will begin with Mʳ Shenstone, who all the Summer since your departure from hence, has been principally occupied in laying out his Valley of Tempe, and attending the Nymphs and Swains who came to visit it; exclusive of this, he has been obliged to transact a good many (tho' not a many good) Things in regard to the Law = suit he has been for some time engaged in with his perverse Cousin; which to one of his Disposition, wᵈ give infinitely more Pain, than to those of a less delicate Turn of Mind: But I hope an amicable reference, which is now on Foot, will terminate all these disagreable Occurences, and establish his Peace.[2] No wonder that the Muses have been neglected: yet I will not hold him altogether blameless, for he might have devoted some time to them; and I often threaten to inform against him to M.ʳ Dodsley. *That, that*____. I do not know what name bad enough to call it by – *that lazy procrastination*, has infected his whole Habit both of Body and of Mind, and as the Disease is desperate, palliatives will work no good – What a pity it is, that some nay many fine Things which he has wrote must be buried in obscurity? like the alterations he has made in y.ʳ Epilogue, but believe he has not quite finish'd it. – Surely M.ʳ Garrick is the most absolute Monarch that ever govern'd the Stage, and I am almost ready to question his judgement after rejecting your Cleone; but as you have now an opportunity of adding to her Beauty & Merit, I hope she will some time hence shine forth with redoubled Charms. – I see very little of the World here, and learn very little News, and since M.ʳ Shenstone has left off taking in the News, I neither see the World or the News = mongers of it. But not to pun – I have not seen one of y.ʳ papers called the World these three Months or more, and M.ʳ Shenstone as well as myself cannot conceive what goes with them.[3] – As touching my journey to London I will not say (in excuse for my Laziness) there is a Lion in the way – but really it is now become precarious. My Lawyer has not my Business in readiness which I was to transact; and I have got a rogue of a Tenant who is playing the Devil with one of my best Farms, and unless I watch him close up to Lady = Day, I shall be a great sufferer by him: however I hope to be in London this Spring,[4] and want no incentives to enjoy the Pleasure I should have in your Company: I wish I could be of service to you when I come for I greatly pity your Sufferings, and I am sorry to hear of them. The Gout is the *approbium Medicinae*, and past the Art of Me, or My Brethren, to eradicate; but I hope you are at Liberty to walk about, & enjoy Life again. – It will be a mere Compliment, to say, that I have laid out for a Hare this month past, for you, and cannot find one; however if I do, no Friend that I have should be more welcome to it than yourself.

M.ʳ Baskerville & Doc.ʳ Ash have had a great quarrel; the latter aspersed the Character of the former most vilely touching his Wife, w.ᶜʰ M.ʳ Baskerville resented, and wrote a very sensible and smart Letter in vindication of himself, which is shown about privately.[5]

Will your two Vol.ˢ of poems come out, to compleate the Set? this Winter, or not?[6] if it must depend in some measure upon M.ʳ Shenstone's Contributions, give me a Commission, and I will persecute him so, that He shall take up Pen and Ink in mere Despair, & self Defence.

I hope y.ʳ Bro.ʳ is well, please to make my Compliments to him; & if I have tired your Patience by the length of my Letter, I hope you will impute it to the desire I have of testifying by any means that I am ever D.ʳ Sir

Y.ʳ most Obliged & Obd.ᵗ

Hble Servant

John Scott Hylton

MS: Humanities Research Center, University of Texas at Austin, Robert Dodsley / Recipient 1/Bound, ff. 9–11.

¹ See Hylton's letter to RD on 16 September 1756 and RD's response on 28 September.
² See Pixell's letter to RD on 3 December 1755, note 3.
³ RD's fashionable weekly, *The World*, edited by Edward Moore, had just been discontinued. Begun on
  4 January 1753, it had run for 208 numbers through 30 December 1756.
⁴ According to RD's letter to Shenstone on 21 April, Hylton had yet to reach London. However, RD's
  later letter of 13 July speaks of having had dinner with Hylton in London.
⁵ The "aspersion" of Dr John Ash (1723–98), Shenstone's and Baskerville's personal physician, is
  unrecorded. Probably it was some reflection on Mrs Eaves's living in Baskerville's house while her first
  husband was still alive. See Ralph Straus and Robert K. Dent, *John Baskerville: A Memoir* (Cambridge:
  Printed at the University Press for Chatto and Windus, London, 1907), pp. 39–40.
⁶ Volumes V and VI of RD's *Collection* did not appear until March 1758.

To William Strahan

                                                              Pall Mall Janʸ 24 1757
Dear Sir,
    As I find a clamour is rais'd in the Trade, and that clamour is levell'd directly and
particularly at me, I have determin'd to part with my share of the London
Chronicle, which I hereby offer to the Partners, desiring no profit from it, tho' I
think it in a very prosperous way, only a return of the mony advanc'd. If the
partners do not chuse it, I believe I can dispose of it. I beg my compliments to all the
partners, and heartily wish them success.¹ – I am,
                                                              Dear Sir,
                                                              Your most obed Servᵗ
                                                                           R Dodsley

You will be so good as to omit for the future yᵉ Names of R and J Dodsley.

Address: To Mʳ Strahan² / Printer / in / New Street.

Source: Straus, pp. 98–9. Straus claims that a holograph of this letter was in his possession at the time of
the writing of *Robert Dodsley*.

¹ Despite RD's letter of "counsel" to Strahan on 14 January, the *London Chronicle*'s attack on the
  Newcastle Ministry continued, and the apologetic advertisement to readers he had suggested seems to
  have been ignored. Although editor Spens had restrained himself in the 18–20 January number, the
  15–18 January number had carried an attack upon the Minister of Trade and Plantations (George
  Montagu Dunk, 2nd Earl of Halifax), and that of 20–2 January had reprinted an article from *The Test*
  (15 January), calling for reform in an age of decay, obviously aimed at the Ministry. Also, curiously
  enough, at the bottom of the front page of the issue of 18–20 January, had appeared for the first time:
  "Advertisements and Letters to the Authors are taken in by R. and J. Dodsley in Pall Mall." Since this
  comes *after* RD's disgruntled letter of the 14th, it almost seems as if the other partners were attempting
  to coerce RD to sell his share.
² As of the twelfth number, 25–7 January, the Dodsleys' names are no longer carried at the foot of the
  front page. This letter, together with the dropping of the Dodsleys' names from the paper, is usually
  taken to mean that RD did sell his share in the *London Chronicle* at this time. But several pieces of
  evidence over the next four years suggest that he did not. First of all RD did not completely turn his
  back on the paper but continued to contribute to its columns and its revenue. His own letter to the
  editor appears in the paper on 24 December of this year. In April he sends Shenstone an article which

had appeared in "tonight's" *Chronicle*, and he gets Hylton's poem inserted in the number for 14 September 1758. But two other matters seem even more convincing. When his tragedy *Cleone* was successfully produced at Covent Garden and thereby turned the town against Garrick, he writes to Strahan, asking that the letters in "our paper" praising *Cleone* and deriding Garrick be discontinued lest Garrick's friends think that a vengeful RD is responsible. Secondly, in the case of RD vs. Kinnersley, before the Rolls Court on 15 June 1761 (see RD's letter of 14 January, note 5), the case is dismissed largely because two of the plaintiffs had themselves printed large extracts of *Rasselas* in their own periodicals; namely, in The *Annual Register* and in the *London Chronicle*. As mentioned earlier, RD becomes distressed when his *name* is linked with abusive material, but he does not seem particularly distressed about the substance of the material; that is, whenever the enterprise represents a successful investment – all, of course, within the limits of good business sense. Consequently, lacking any contrary evidence, it seems entirely likely that the removal of his name from the paper allowed RD to continue his share in the ownership of the *London Chronicle*.

To William Melmoth

Jan 27 [1757][1]

Dear Sir

I am much oblig'd to you for your excellent Prescriptions to the poor sickly patient I sent You; I fear you could not avoid looking upon it as somewhat like trying hopeless experiments in order to infuse new life into a dead or dying body.[2] It was generous however and humane to try your skill in so desperate a case, and as I believe you have done all that was possible, I shall not call in any further advice or assistance, but ⟨consider⟩ regard it as dead, and bury it privately. I hope however you will consider it as ye offspring of Disease, ⟨and attribute⟩ and attributing to that the weakness and infirmity of its constitution, ⟨and firmly⟩ kindly believe, that if the ⟨father⟩ parent had been in a better shape himself, he would doubtless have been able to produce a more healthy child. But to leave this languid metaphor before it expires under my hands, I ⟨must⟩ must acknowledge that I approve of all your criticisms save one. That circumstance of a tragic Poet's starting, as you humourously express it, at his own Ghosts, I am somewhat inclin'd to defend, ⟨which I⟩ and think it may be done upon the known maxim, that to ⟨move⟩ affect others one must first be really mov'd ones self: ⟨And⟩ The Tragic Writer who is not ⟨moved himself⟩ himself moved to Terror or Pity by his own conceptions or his manner of expressing them, I should fear would stand but a small chance of ⟨moving⟩ affecting his Audience. I have made many alterations in consequence of your criticisms, but believe I shall not venture it with the public. I beg my Compliments to ye Ladies and am

Dear Sir &c

MS; Robert Dodsley Letter Book, Birmingham Public Libraries, ff. 22–3.

[1] The year follows from the RD Letter Book principle.
[2] Melmoth's criticism seems not to have survived. RD is most likely to be referring to the manuscript of his poem, *Melpomene: or The Regions of Terror and Pity*, a work that he was to send to Shenstone three weeks later for correction and which was eventually published anonymously by Mary Cooper on 29 September 1757 (*LC*). The identity of the poem seems clear from RD's reference to "ghosts," a subject of the poem, and to "Terror or Pity," terms in the title and the poem's primary concern.

To John Baskerville

Feb.ry 10 [1757][1]

Dear Sir

I am very sorry we seem a little to have misunderstood each other. I think I have somewhere your direction to charge Mr Culver 24^s p Ream for whatever plain Paper he had of me; and thought, as I had paid You for it, he was to pay me.[2] However, if I am mistaken, let it be as you say, it is a matter of but small consequence & I hope it will sell both with Mr Culver and me, he having had a second parcel. I sent a small sortment of every kind to Mr Leake at Bath.[3] But I beg you will take notice that if you don't stop your hand in the ornamented Paper, you will certainly be at a very great loss, as You are to take all back of that kind you know which I don't dispose of; and to tell you the truth I have not open'd a single Ream of ⟨what you⟩ either parcel you sent me this Winter Quarto or Octavo, & have used but very few dozens of the Messages. So that I think you should not ornament another sheet, till you see how you can dispose of what I have, & let me send it back immediately for that purpose. As to lowering the price, I am very sorry You thought of it so late. You may remember how earnestly I press'd you to set it at first as low as possibly you could, for your own sake, and that nobody might interfere with you. But to sell it now at a lower price than we set out with, I think is hardly fair, I am sure not creditable either for You or me, and what I believe upon reflection you will hardly think proper for either of us to do. Besides, I am far from thinking it would now revive the sale.[4] The account you give me of the Virgil pleases me much, & I hope you will in that have all the success your heart can wish. I beg if you have any objection addition or alteration to make in the following Advertisement, you will let me know by ye return of the post. If I don't hear from You I will immediately advertise. Pray let me know at ye same time ⟨what I must⟩ about sending back ⟨of⟩ the ornamented Paper.

To the Public.

John Baskerville of Birmingham thinks proper to give notice that ⟨he has⟩ having now ⟨very nearly⟩ finish'd his Edition of Virgil in one volume Quarto it will be publish'd the latter end of next month. Price one Guinea in Sheets, ⟨&⟩ He therefore desires ⟨that those⟩ that such Gentlemen ⟨who⟩ as intend to favour him with their Names, will be pleas'd to send them either to himself at Birmingham or to R & J Dodsley in Pall mall, in order that they may be inserted in the List of his Encouragers.[5]

MS: Robert Dodsley Letter Book, Birmingham Public Libraries, ff. 23–5.

[1] The year is derived from the letter's placement in RD's Letter Book. Furthermore, it is clearly a response to Baskerville's letter of 20 December.

[2] See Baskerville's letter of the previous 20 December, particularly note 1.

[3] James Leake the elder, bookseller at Bath (1724?–64). See RD's next letter to Baskerville on 7 April, where he says Leake has sold all his supply of Baskerville's paper and has requested more.

[4] Nonetheless RD did lower the price. See his letter on the following 7 April.

⁵ RD would place a similarly worded advertisement for Baskerville's Virgil on 23 February (*PA*), something he would regret. See his next letter to Baskerville on 7 April.

To William Shenstone

Pallmall Feb!ʸ 17.ᵗʰ [1757]¹

Dear Sir

You must think me a most absurd fellow, that at the very time I am waiting with great impatience for some of your Pieces to begin the 5.ᵗʰ Volume of my Miscellany, I should think of troubling You with a triffle of my own.² But I shall be glad if You will just favour me with a few moments to read over the enclos'd, and should you happen to think it capable of being made fit for the Public, I should be very glad it might receive your corrections. I know I ought not to trouble You on this account, but as I intend in case it be publish'd to lie quite conceal'd, I do not chuse to shew it to any one here. I send another copy of it by to night's post to M! Graves. I have sate in a chair near three months & cannot yet set either foot to the ground.³ I flatter my self with hopes that you are preparing to enable me to put my 5.ᵗʰ Volume to press, which I shall be glad to do as early in the spring as possible. I send you enclos'd a small collection of Poems just publish'd by M! Whitehead.⁴ I was to have had two Odes by M! Gray, but they are not yet sent me.⁵ I was to have had too a collection of Elegies, but ah!⁶ − I am ever

Dear Sir
affectionately Yours
R. Dodsley

MS: BL. Add. MS. 28,959, f. 64.

¹ For several reasons, this letter is certainly of 1757. The "triffle" RD mentions as enclosed for Shenstone's "corrections" is undoubtedly his ode, *Melpomene*, a work which appeared (anonymously, as RD herein projects) on 29 September of this year (*LC*). He says, furthermore, that he has also sent another copy by the same night's post to Mr Graves: Graves's fully dated letter of five days later (q.v.) is completely concerned with criticism of *Melpomene*. Secondly, RD is asking Shenstone, here, in rather unhurried fashion, to enable him to put his "5th Volume" of the *Collection* to press "as early in the spring as possible." But by this time in 1758, both Volumes V and VI had already gone to press. Consequently, the letter could not be any later than 1757. Finally, although RD had published many individual poems by William Whitehead in the past, the first *collection* of Whitehead's poems he had issued was *Elegies: With an Ode to the Tiber*, a publication of 4 February 1757 (*PA*). His mentioning within, then, that he is sending Shenstone a "small collection of Poems just publish'd by M! Whitehead" clearly identifies the letter as a product of 1757.
² *Melpomene: or The Regions of Terror and Pity*, according to the advertisement in the *LC* of 27–9 September 1757, was printed for Mary Cooper. However, the Huntington Library copy of 1757 carries no author's or publisher's name on the imprint. The poem was printed *in toto* in the *LC* of 29 October–1 November 1757 with one variant. In stanza 24, "assenting" becomes "creative."
³ RD's attacks of gout now became more frequent. He had reported his first attack to Shenstone in late 1750.　　⁴ See note 1.

From Richard Graves

Claverton, 22, Feb. – 1757

Dear S^r

I have read y^r Melpomene with great pleasure – & am sure it will require but little *Correction* to make it *fit* for ye publick – How far it is qualified to please the gross Taste of that fickle Lady – you are a better Judge than I can be – who have had but a very slender acquaintance wth her.[1]

I take the first vacant moments to answer yours; Because I think there is little Room for any *Verbal* Criticism (which is the height of my Aim) – & therefore I will refer to your own Revisal, what occurs to me (on the first Perusal) to be capable of Improvement in a higher Sphere[2] –

In the Region of Terror I would have you consider whether another Source of that Passion is not to be sought after in Superstition – or that ⟨natural⟩ Propensity which, I think, is natural to us, to be afraid of Ghosts & Apparitions = especially as you profess to follow Shakespear to his hidden Recesses – who has certainly made a fine Use of it – I know it is y^e Fashion of this enlighten'd age utterly to reject every notion of this kind – But, if something of it is not natural to us, how can we account for y^e Prevalence of those apprehensions, thro' all ye ages of ye world – The greek word for Superstition – Deisi-Daimony – signifies ⟨y^e⟩ properly y^e *fear* of *Ghosts* or Demons – either good or bad – And the Appearance of Brutus's Genius – which (according to true History) appear'd with circumstances of Terror – and another Story in Pliny's Epist. – quite ⟨upon ⟩ in ye modern Taste of Apparitions – proves these Fears to be natural ⟨&⟩ at least not ye Invention of ye Monkish Ages, as is commonly said[3] – For my part, I have still so much of ye Nursery about me – That I never see Hamlet's ⟨G⟩ or Banquo's Ghosts but my Blood runs Chill – & fills me wth a surprising Terror – But I only hint this – & would have you try to introduce a *Ghost* after ye Image of *murder* – Stanza 9 – "But whence that murmering Noise! The Earth opens – & a horrid Spectre rises – & beckoning stalks amid visionary Tombs & Charnels to where his mangled Corpse is deposited without ye Rites of Sepulture – &c – in ye usual Style – & ye Effects of raising the Hair, like Quills on ye fretful Porcupine – but you are acquainted with Shakespear's Language & will find no difficulty in executing such a Stanza – if perhaps you have not already rejected it as improper[4] — — St. 7 Stran – inverted – Encircled – [9] –[5]

As to ye Language it is very elegant – & I can see nothing that *needs* correction. except ye Rhymes – in one or two Stanzas – which return too near together – There is *rise* & *his* – St. 3 – *eyes* & *dies* St. 5 – *Eyes* & *Tyes* St. 7 – *arise* Blasphe*mies* – St. 9 – & *arise Sighs* St. 10 – *rise eyes* St. 11 – *Sighs Eyes* St. 13 – one alteration however in Stanza

10 – I think will be enough as all the rest are at a sufficient Space – between these[6] – The three Epithets – St. 3 – express ye thing vastly well – But Milton having used The *Vast Profound*, as a substantive – makes it sound ambiguous – qv[7] – St. 5 – 'Powers of Manhood" – sounds to me as relative only to ye male Sex in opposition to ye female – qv. whether *Powers* of *Nature* would do[8] – St. 7. – *disowns* all Human Types – hardly strong enough –?[9] – ⟨feels not the⟩ St. 9. – *Despair* us'd as a Person L.1. & as a *Passion* L.7. – "A Reprobate to Heaven the Caitiff *dies*" "with Execrations, Groans & horrid Blasphemies"[10] – q – St. 10 – I cannot assist you – but think the two last Rhymes should be alter'd – *appear* – & *Fear* – q – To melt y^r feeling heart – ⟨petrified⟩ with Fear ⟨callous groan⟩[11] St-11-12-13-14 – & – all very beautiful & y^r Instances finely chosen & Picturesque – St-14 – "What is so sweet as Friendship" – How *sweet y^r* Charms of Friendship?" qv[12] – St. 20 – "And art thow kill'd in raising the Passions? 24 – whether this is not the very thing – which he desires to be instructed in? – If so however it will be easily alter'd – But I believe you are right. He desires to be instructed in Shakespear's art of *pleasing* – She bids him study Nature & ye wit of raising ye Passions.[13]

You see S^r I take the freedom of – deliberating & proposing my most unreasonable Samples in your Company – I depend upon Mr Shenstone's Decision – who is generally infallible in his Criticisms[14] – But sometimes lays too great stress upon Trifles – Mrs Graves & myself are at present under ye greatest anxiety – on acct of our Children – whom we have banish'd from our care – to be inoculated – She joins in best respects with S^r y^r affect – humb Ser^t

Ric: Graves

MS: Somerset County Record Office, DD/SK, 28/1, 6.

[1] See RD's letter to Shenstone on 17 February. The "fickle Lady" is Fame.

[2] The following criticisms Graves offered for RD's *Melpomene*, to be published in September of this year. Without Graves's working copy, it is difficult to determine the value of the alterations or, in some instances, their placement since the piece will be the subject of further changes. Furthermore, the reader, without *Melpomene* in hand, will make little sense of the alterations considered in the following notes. They are offered merely to afford a further example of the collaborative revising carried on within RD's circle.

[3] Probably Graves refers to the goddess Diana's appearance to Brutus in a vision, whereby the grandson of Ascanius was directed to seek out the land of Albion for his people. In the Brutus legend, the event is recounted, for instance, in Geoffrey of Monmouth's *Historia Regum Britanniae*, Bk. I, Chpt. XI. The episode in Pliny's epistle is no doubt that recounting the eruption of Mount Vesuvius that destroyed Pompei and killed Pliny's uncle. In Letter 20 of Book VI, Pliny relates: "The people followed us in the utmost consternation, and (as to a mind distracted with terror, every suggestion seems more prudent than its own) pressed in great crowds about us in our way out. . . Among these there were some who augmented the real terrors by imaginary ones." RD would have been familiar with the allusion, having published *The Letters of Pliny the Consul*, translated by William Melmoth, the source of this quotation, in 1747. (See Appendix B, under Melmoth.)

[4] RD concurred with Graves's recommendation of a ghost, introducing it in a new eleventh stanza.

[5] Indecipherable without Graves's text.

[6] "Rise" and "his" were eliminated; "eyes" and "dies" are retained as the rhymes of the concluding couplet, but in Stanza VI "tyes" and "arise Blasphemies" were cut; "Sighs" is coupled with "eyes" instead of with "arise" as the concluding couplet of Stanza IX; "rise" and "eyes" are retained as the

rhymes of the next to last couplet in Stanza XIV, as are "sighs" and "eyes" in Stanza XVI
Generally, RD recognizes Graves's criticism and responded to it by dropping some of the repetitiou
sounds and by introducing additional material that spaced the rimes somewhat.
7   Graves's recall of Milton is slightly askew. In *Paradise Lost*, Bk. VII, the son of God enters the "vas
profundity obscure" to create the world (l. 229). Graves has confused this phrase with Milton'
"Darkness profound" (l. 233).
8   RD retained "Powers of Manhood."
9   This phrase was dropped, but because of the change in stanza numbering, it is difficult to say wha
replaced it.   10   "Despair" was dropped altogether.
11 The order of lines in Stanza 10 must have been changed. "Appear" and "fear" constitute the firs
rhyme in the alternating-rhyme stanzaic pattern, and are later in the third person singular.
12 Ultimately the opening line in Stanza XVII became: "How strong the bands of Friendship?"
13 At first, Graves seems to miss the rhetorical value of Melpomene's question, but then realizes it
import in the midst of his comment.
14 See RD's letter to Shenstone on 21 April for further alterations.

To Miss Nelly Wright[1]

Feb.ry 24th [1757]

Dear Madam

You judged ⟨very rightly⟩ (as indeed you always do) very rightly, when yo
imagin'd that ye flavour of the Hare would be improv'd to my taste by its coming
from Your fair hands: I will not therefore thank your *father* for it, ⟨but I am⟩ being
much more oblig'd to him that he has thus given me an opportunity of thanking
You. I hope it will not be long however before I see him in Town, & am glad to hea
his confinement has been owing to a sprain only, as I had heard before it was th
gout, and very sincerely sympathiz'd with him, having not been able myself to set
foot to the ground these three months ⟨past⟩. Your friend M.r Cooper is just come ir
upon me & thinks himself very happy in having an opportunity of sending you hi
Compliments.[3] I beg You will make mine to every friend in Mansfield who may
happen to enquire after me: I cannot help feeling a kind partiallity in favour of th
place, but fear I am growing too infirm ⟨ever⟩ to entertain the hope of ever seeing i
again, which to confess the truth is a reflection by no means agreeable to me. I hav
no news to send you except that it is now generally believ'd Admiral Bing will suffe
on monday next, all ye ⟨attempts⟩ sollicitations of his friends to procure a pardor
having prov'd in vain. I am sorry to hear ⟨your⟩ Mrs Wright was so ill when yo
wrote, I beg my compliments to her, and hope this will find her better. My goo
Lord Radnor I am afraid will scarce get over this winter, in whom you will lose a
Admirer, who often us'd to enquire after your health; and I a friend for whom I ha
a very great regard.[4] Thus our friends drop from us one after another, leaving us a
last alone, joyless, comfortless, unconnected; but thereby kindly disposing us t
rejoice in the hope of following them. But methinks I hear You cry out, Good Lord
how grave the man is? One might have heard a sermon in ones own parish church
'Tis very true, as you say, & I don't know how it has happen'd; but believe I am lo
spirited, which I never us'd to be you know, and so for fear I should preach yo
quite asleep, I will put an end to my letter & my moralizing together.

I am &c

MS: Robert Dodsley Letter Book, Birmingham Public Libraries, ff. 26–7.

Nelly Wright of Mansfield, Notts., seems to have been the daughter of a boyhood companion of RD's. Although there are several Wright families listed for Mansfield in the period, Nelly's father was probably the William who subscribed for two copies of RD's *Muse in Livery* (1732), in which appeared two poems addressed to "Mr. Wright." Straus (pp. 293–4) claims that Miss Wright seems to have helped RD's sister Alice Dyer to nurse him when he was beset with attacks of gout. It is John Gilbert Cooper who supplies Miss Wright's first name. Writing to RD on 7 October 1754, he says all RD's friends at Mansfield are well and that "Nelly Wright will send your Testament by me."

The year is assigned on two bases; from the Letter Book principle and from RD's mentioning within the letter that all attempts to forestall Admiral John Byng's execution have been in vain. Byng, who had been sentenced to death by court-martial on 27 January 1757 for his neglect of duty in the battle for Minorca the previous year, was executed at Portsmouth on 14 March 1757. The letter cannot have been written after 1757, for Lord Radnor, whom RD says "will scarce get over this winter," died in 1757.   3 John Gilbert Cooper. See note 1.

John Robartes, 4th Earl of Radnor (1686?–1757), did, in fact, die on 15 July 1757. See RD's letter of 30 August 1757 to Miss Wright. How Miss Wright had made Radnor's acquaintance is not clear. Straus (p. 294) suggests she had visited his residence in Twickenham.

From John Perry[1]

Clent   March 7th 1757

My Dear Friend

Your benevolence, so laudably exerted in my behalf, has produced an uncommon Spirit of Malevolence in some of my Neighbors; who have been at the pains, to write to London to a Correspondent in Pall Mall, who pretends to have the enclos'd account from Mr Dodsley; several Copies of wch are industriously spread abroad. The malicious intent of it is to suggest that I impos'd upon you, by representing my Living to be but poor £20 p^r An^m.[2] I have the utmost abhorrence of lying & prevarication, & if I can find out the Author of this Villainous attempt upon my Character, will not let him escape wth impunity. In the mean while if you would favour me wth a letter to satisfy a Particular friend or two, that I never did represent my Living of that Value, I shall take it kind.[3] By Mr Shenstone's advice, I have neither acknowledg'd or deny'd, that I was ye Person whose case was describ'd in the World, but only said, "it was a good natur'd Action in Mr Dodsley, let it be for whom it would.[4] I think you may wth truth & justice say that the Person who wrote the Advertisement & sent it to you & recommended the Clergyman's Case to ye Public was a Gentleman of Fortune & too much honour to impose upon you or any man.[5] But I ask pardon for dictating to a much abler Pen, & am

Wth ye utmost Sinerity & Gratitude
Y^r Most Obliged Servt

J. Perry

P.S. I have wrote to Mr Caesar & for the sake of my Girl shall endeavour to come up wth her to London about ye middle of April that I might get her a proper place.

MS: Harvard Theatre Collection, Harvard College Library.

¹ For a biographical note on Perry, see RD's letter to Shenstone on 21 December 1756, where also is found an account of the benefit that prompted this "Villainous attempt" on Perry's character.

² Perry's maligner is not known nor is RD's role in representing Perry's income as only twenty pounds per annum, for the "enclos'd account" is missing. Perhaps RD had innocently speculated on the sum, and someone who knew better took offense. At any rate, Perry and RD apparently sorted out the misunderstanding, for on the next 11 April the bookseller is thanking Shenstone for sending Perry's poem "Malvern Spa, 1757," which he would include in his *Collection* (V, 84–87).

³ RD's response is missing.

⁴ Two days after receiving the advertisement for Perry's cause from Shenstone, RD printed it at the conclusion of No. 208 of his weekly *The World* (23 December 1756) and repeated the notice the following week. It was identical to that which would appear in the *Daily Advertiser* on 1 January (see RD's letter to Shenstone on 21 December, note 2), but its second printing carried the heading: "To those who are pleased with finding an opportunity to do good." Giving Perry such exposure to the "right" kind of audience in the limited space available in *The World*, RD could hardly be suspected of malevolence, especially since Perry's appeal had been sponsored by RD's dear friend Shenstone.

⁵ Most likely Shenstone himself.

To William Shenstone

Pallmall   March 11ᵗʰ 1757

Dear Sir

I cannot help feeling awkwardly to my self in sitting down to write this Letter, being sensible that any modest man who had ask'd a friend's opinion of his piece, and receiv'd no answer, ought to take that silence not only as the civilest, but the tenderest kind of Disapprobation.¹ To confess the truth, from any body but You I should certainly have so construed it; but, not to mention the partiallity of your friendship which I flatter my self with, I know I have such a chance of its being in You mere Indolence, that, notwithstanding the imperfections of the Poem, & the probability that your silence proceeds from the polite motives hinted at above, I will just venture once more to put you in mind of it. After this, it would be quite tearing & impertinent to say a word of your long-expected Elegies – Epilogue – Poems for the Miscellany – or any such things. I will therefore pass them over at present in silence – tho' I could be very glad to read the Elegies in print, to see the Epilogue as you have now corrected it, & to put yᵉ 5ᵗʰ & 6ᵗʰ Volumes of the Miscellany to press as soon as You please, that I might have yᵉ Summer before me to print them in the best manner.² Is not Mʳ Hylton coming to Town? May I not expect a packet by him? Or, why cannot You accompany him? Methinks I could start up on my feet with great alacrity, to see You come in; which is more than I have been able to do these four months; having been so long confin'd by the Gout, which still continues its tyranny over me, and chains me down to my chair. In this wretched situation, for Charity's sake have some pity upon me; send from your Pharmacopoeia of Wit some cordial drops to cheer my spirits, et eris mihi magnus Apollo.³

I am
Dear Sir
very truely & affectionately Yours
R. Dodsley

Address: To William Shenstone Esqr / at the Leasowes / near / Birmingham
Postmark: 12 MA.
Frank Ed: ffree Walpole

MS: BL. Add. MS. 28,959, ff, 65–6.

See RD's letter to Shenstone of 17 February, with which he had submitted his ode *Melpomene* for Shenstone's suggestions.

Apparently RD had now decided not to attempt to publish Volumes V and VI of his *Collection* this spring, as he had formerly planned.

All the subjects RD mentions in his letter have appeared in earlier letters, where the reader will find them annotated.

To [James?] Cawthorn[1]

April 2^d [1757][2]

Dr Sir

My friend Mr Hitch has been so kind as to shew me your ⟨Letter to him containing some⟩ candid and judicious remarks on my Tragedy of Cleone. It plainly appears from your letter that you have not thought it unworthy of being read with attention, and your general approbation of it, after such a perusal, gives me a very sensible pleasure. To dwell on ye particular circumstances you have ⟨commended⟩ approv'd, ⟨would⟩ might perhaps too plainly indicate the ⟨too easy acquiescence of an Author⟩ great complacence I feel in what so agreably flatters ⟨his⟩ my own vanity; I ⟨will⟩ shall therefore pass them over in silence; only give me leave to observe, that the encreasing gradation of Sifroy's distress, tho' a point I labour'd with particular care, hath ⟨not⟩ been taken notice of ⟨by⟩ only by one person besides your self.[3] But I am really more oblig'd to You for your criticisms than your commendations, & hope when you come to town I shall have an opportunity of spending a few hours with you that I may reap the benefit of your minutest objection: at present I will confine my self to the two most considerable.

⟨You think⟩ Your first is that the stile is not sufficiently rais'd for the dignity of Tragedy. I must own I am so great an enemy to ⟨pompousness of Expression⟩ that tumidity of style so often made use of in Tragedy, that I may probably have err'd on the other side. However, if I have, it is an error of my judgment; as I think a domestic distress like this, should be as far remov'd from all pomp of expression as elegance will permit. Ribbons and starrs, diamonds and embroidery are only fit for Kings ⟨and⟩ or heroes ⟨and⟩ or the highest Nobility; and in a Tragedy where ⟨these are the personages⟩ such personages as these sustain the dialogue, their ⟨diction⟩ sentiments may ⟨indeed share⟩ with propriety be cloath'd in a more ⟨adorn'd & elevated⟩ superb and ornamented Stile: but in the humbler dress of private life, such decorations would surely be somewhat misplac'd.[4] As to ye versification, I have not ⟨so much study'd⟩ endeavour'd at a smooth & flowing harmony of numbers (which I ⟨have⟩ always look'd upon in Rowe[5] as a fault) ⟨as⟩ but at such a natural ease and simplicity of ⟨Expression⟩ language, as might flow without harshness or inelegance from the lips of the Speaker. In this endeavour I doubtless may have fail'd in many places, and when we meet shall be very glad to have them pointed out by so good a Judge.

⟨As to⟩ Your objection against the appearance of old Beaumont in the last ⟨scene⟩ Act I have some hopes ⟨that⟩ upon ⟨a reconsideration you⟩ your reconsidering it may possibly ⟨change your opinion⟩ be remov'd.⁶ To ⟨divide the distress⟩ multiply the objects of Pity, as you well observe, ⟨could certainly⟩ may sometimes divide & weaken ⟨it⟩ the passion: but I meant ⟨the⟩ in this instance to make the grief of the father an accumulation of distress on the head of yᵉ husband; ⟨and have accordingly⟩ having drawn ⟨him⟩ the old man so much of a Philosopher as to bear his misfortunes with great firmness; and it is the observation of a very ingenious french writer, that it is not they who bear their ⟨misfortunes⟩ griefs the most steadily, but they who feel them with the ⟨most⟩ tenderest sensibility, that affect yᵉ Passions of an audience with the greatest force.⁷ Now as the action of the piece is *the Rashness of Sifroy, and its punishment*, & as all these calamities, viz the grief of the ⟨old man⟩ father, yᵉ murder of the child, and yᵉ distraction and death of Cleone, take their rise from that same fatal Rashness. They must certainly contribute, ⟨not only⟩ as to aggravate the ⟨distress of the Husband, and⟩ Husband's distress, so in consequence greatly to encrease the pity and concern of an audience in his behalf. But a thorough discussion of this point would probably stretch beyond the bounds of a letter, I will therefore defer it till I have the pleasure of seeing You. As to Glanville and Isabella being an Imitation of Zanga & his Mistress in yᵉ Revenge I never read that Play in my life, nor ever saw it acted but once, so could not possibly copy any thing from thence: but I suppose there is some resemblance as yᵉ observation has been made before:⁸ I will therefore certainly read it the first opportunity, and if possible remove the objection.

I am &c

MS: Robert Dodsley Letter Book, Birmingham Public Libraries, ff. 30–33.

¹ Although Straus (p. 245) considers this letter to be addressed to Cawthorn, a bookseller, RD is more likely to be addressing James Cawthorn (1719–61), the clergyman and poet. Hitch, whom RD mentions as the friend who passed on Cawthorn's criticism of *Cleone*, must be Charles Hitch the bookseller – an occasional collaborator with RD and apparently Cawthorn's bookseller. In 1745, Hitch had published the latter's *Sermon preached before the Worshipful Burgesses of Westminster at St. Margaret's Church on Thursday April 18 1745*, the advertisement for which (*LEP*, 23–5 May) carried the additional note: "Speedily will be published" Cawthorn's *Essay upon Education*.
² The year is assigned on the Letter Book principle.
³ See Richard Berenger's letter of 10 June 1756.
⁴ As both the characters and language of his plays show – middle-class folk void of "pompousness of Expression" – RD played a significant role in domesticating drama on the mid-eighteenth-century London stage.
⁵ Nicholas Rowe (1674–1718), poet and dramatist, who consciously imitated Shakespeare in his many tragedies.
⁶ RD retained old Beaumont ("Beaufort" in the printed version) in the last act.
⁷ In this regard, RD's plays show him to be squarely in the eighteenth-century middle-class sentimental tradition.   ⁸ See Berenger's letter of 10 June 1756, and note 6.

To John Baskerville

April 7.th [1757]¹

Dear Sir

I am very sorry I advertis'd yᵉ Virgil to be publish'd last Month, as You have not enabled me to keep my word with the Public; but I hope it will not be delay'd any longer, as every day You lose now the season is so far advanc'd is certainly a great loss to You. I hope I shall have yᵉ pleasure of seeing You and it together. However, if the delay is occasion'd by your making corrections, I think that a point of so much consequence that no consideration should induce You to publish till it is quite correct. As to the ornamented Paper I will lower the Price ⟨if⟩ since you think it proper, but am still of opinion that it will not sell at our end of the town, tho' for what reason I cannot immagine. I sent a sortment of it to Bath which is sold, & Mʳ Leake has sent for a small parcel more; I will send it him at the reduc'd price, & will advertise ⟨his⟩ it to be sold by him also.² I shall be glad of twenty Reams of Post made from your own molds as soon as you can.

I like exceedingly your specimen of a Com̃on Prayer, & hope you are endeavouring to get leave to print one. There is an error in the Exhortation, ⟨of⟩ *shall* for *should*.³ Your small letter is extreamly beautiful, I wish I could advise what to print with it. What think you of some popular French book? Giblas, Moliere, or Telemaque? In the Specimen from Melmoth,⁴ I think you have us'd too many Capitals, which is generally thought to spoil the beauty of printing: but they should never be us'd to adjective verbs or adverbs. My best Compliments attend your whole family, and in hopes of seeing you soon I remain

Dear Sir &c

MS: Robert Dodsley Letter Book, Birmingham Public Libraries, ff. 34–5.

¹ RD had advertised Baskerville's *Publii Virgilii Maronis Bucolica, Georgica, Et Aeneis* on 23 February (*PA*), as he mentions in the letter. The work was ultimately advertised as ready for subscribers on 5 May 1757 (*LC*). Consequently the letter is clearly of 1757, as its placement in RD's Letter Book also indicates.

² Here RD accedes to Baskerville's suggestion (letter of 20 December 1756) regarding the sale of the latter's ornamented paper at a lower price, something RD had advised against in his letter of 10 February. Perhaps the sale in Bath offered some hope.

³ F. E. Pardoe, on p. 46 of *John Baskerville of Birmingham: Letter-Founder and Printer* (London: Frederick Muller, 1975), says no specimen for Baskerville's edition of the *Common Prayer Book* seems to have survived. Nor indeed was Philip Gaskell able to provide one for his *John Baskerville: A Bibliography* (1959). Without the text, it is impossible to decide the justness of RD's minor adjustment, suggesting that "shall" be replaced with "should." Baskerville did "get leave" to print the *Common Prayer Book* a year and a half later, on 1 December 1758, when he was appointed Printer to the University of Cambridge. Pardoe (p. 53) prints the agreement with Cambridge, whereby Baskerville was given permission to print the Prayer Book in octavo, as well as the Bible in folio.

⁴ In this specimen of his type for 1757, Baskerville had used Melmoth's edition of Cicero's *Letters to Several of his Friends*, first published by RD in 1753. Baskerville had also used Melmoth's Cicero in 1754 for a specimen of his proposed edition of Virgil. See Gaskell's *Bibliography*, where both are described (pp. 3–6).

To William Shenstone

Pallmall April 11th [1757]¹

Dear Sir

After the pains you have so kindly & so effectually taken with my Ode, I can never with any face accuse you again of Indolence. I have adopted, as You will see, most of your Alterations; and as I had made several others since You saw it, I was desirous of letting You see it again as soon as possible, that it may receive the benefit of another revisal, which You have so generously promis'd to bestow upon it. I must own I could wish it might appear soon, if it can be made tollerable: but am afraid of being too troublesome to You. I write in such a hurry that I shall not ⟨say⟩ remember half of what I have to say. I thank You and M.ʳ Graves however most heartily for yᵉ Epilogue. It has no fault but too much length, which is easily mended. Must I put your name to it, or Mʳ Graves's?² I thank You also for Mʳ Perry's Poem, and for what I hope is but the beginnings of your own.³ All the doubtful readings in the enclos'd I beg You will determine. If I should think of another Stanza I will send it to You. I wish this may be either sense or english, but I cannot read it at present being quite press'd for time.

                                        I am ever
                                        Dear Sir
                        Your most oblig'd & affec. Serv.ᵗ
                                                    R. Dodsley

MS: BL. Add. MS. 28,959, f. 68.

¹ For several reasons, this letter can be considered a product of 1757. The "Ode" RD refers to is almost certainly his *Melpomene*, a poem he had first sent Shenstone on 17 February 1757 (see letter) and which he would publish on 29 September of this year (*LC*): the "Ode" that RD resubmits to Shenstone in his fully dated letter of 21 April 1757 is also *Melpomene*. Secondly, Perry's poem for which RD is thanking Shenstone, "Malvern Spa, 1757. Inscribed to Dr. Wall," will have already been printed by RD in volume V of his *Collection* by this time the following year. Finally this letter was entered in the Letter Book between others whose dates are certainly determinable.
² Since the Epilogue to *Cleone*, on which Shenstone has worked changes, has not been extensively altered from Graves's original submission, obviously RD is attempting to justify putting the better known name to the piece in order to enhance the tragedy's appeal.
³ For Perry's poem, see note 1.

To William Shenstone

Pallmall Ap. 21.ˢᵗ 1757

Dear M.ʳ Shenstone

I have already so much obligation to You for the pains you have taken with my Ode, & for your improvements in it, that I am asham'd to give You any farther trouble, being apprehensive your Goodnature may be quite weary'd out with my Impertinence.¹ But ⟨have⟩ having made some small alterations since I sent you the last copy, I cannot forbear submitting them to your consideration.

Stanza 1st
Tumultuous tides of various Passion rise
   Inspire his kindling mind
   With Sentiments refin'd;[2]
2^d
  – whence human sorrows charm
Bid Terror shake us, or Compassion warm;
   As different strains controul,
   And freeze, or fire the soul:
While, set to sympathy, the heart's true tone,
Shall) Feel⟨s for⟩ another's woe, or modulate⟨s⟩ its own.[3]
6th
And sees, or seems to see, black fiends from hell,[4]
7th
A wretch with jealous brow, and[5]
8th

O dire effect! his changing &c. I hope you have alter'd y^e last lines of this stanza. I
cannot please my self.[6]
9th
His haggard looks impress &c.[7]
10
And hark! ah, mercy! whence that doleful sound?
   My bristling hair starts up! unusual groans
Strike my chill'd heart! While $^{Lo!}$ from unhallow'd ground,
   A pale ghost rising, points to where the bones
     Of its unhonour'd corse,
     Murder'd without remorse,[8]
11
And all the powers of Reason feel controul.[9]
Is that expression allowable?
12
A dawning twilight[10]
16
What more engaging to a generous mind
   Than female trust in love? Yet lost, forlorn,
No pity yon fair mourner hopes to find,
   Expos'd by him she lov'd to want and scorn.
   Left by the man she lov'd[11] –
I had thought of a new stanza to be introduc'd here, but I don't like it. I will
transcribe it however, as you may possibly strike out something from it, or supply its
place with somewhat better.

In helpless age, from regal state cast down,
   That poor old man, with hand extended, see.
He sway'd a sceptre once, & wore a crown,
   Now craves the passing alms of Charity:

From filial rage and strife
To screen his closing life,
He quits his throne; a father's wrongs he feels;
And in the lap of Want his patient head conceals.[12]
I think this image wrong, as it is difficult to imagine a King should become a Beggar. I once thought of making it suit Belisarius; but that would be historical, and all the rest is visionary. In short, I submit the whole Ode to your Judgment; and shall be very glad, if you think it at all fit for the public, that I may receive your last corrections as soon as is convenient, as I would willingly publish it before the Town grows empty, which will now be very soon.[13]

Mʳ Spence meditates a visit to my Lord Wentworth in Leicestershire in about two months, when he intends to perswade my Lord to come with him to see the Leasowes, having a great desire to be acquainted with You.[14] I need say nothing on this occasion. Two persons of tempers so congenial, as they must certainly like each other, will easily become acquainted. I beg my Compᵗˢ to Mʳ Hylton, whom I was in hopes to have seen in Pall mall long before now.[15] I suppose You are not content with hating London your self, but will perswade all your neighbours to hate it. I wish however You would come see it, if it was but even for a week.

I am ever
Dear Sir
affectionately & sincerely
Your oblig'd humble Servᵗ
R. Dodsley

MS: BL. Add. MS. 28,959, ff. 69–70.

¹ *Melpomene: or The Regions of Terror and Pity*, to be published in September. Without Shenstone's response, it is impossible to determine whether he advised against some of these changes or whether they would be abandoned during the summer when RD was making still further alterations before printing the ode. The apparent lack of correspondence between stanza numbers in the text and those in the notes is explained by the introduction of additional stanzas before the printed version appeared. The following notes will show merely what was used in that printing. Generally the ode was improved by the changes and additions, but, clearly, changes yet to be made considerably strengthened the poem.

² Only the first line is reflected in the final copy: "The swelling tides of mighty Passion rise."

³ An additional line appears between lines 1 and 2, and the fourth line was not used. The final couplet became: "Adjust its passions, harmonize its tone, / To feel for others' woe, or nobly bear its own."

⁴ Line 7 in Stanza VII reads: "And sees, or fancies, all the fiends below."

⁵ Ultimately used (Stanza VIII).

⁶ The opening and concluding lines of Stanza IX became: "The storm proceeds – his changeful visage trace: / . . . And not a tear bedews those vacant eyes – / But songs and shouts succeed, and laughter-mingled sighs."

⁷ The final version of the third line of Stanza X reads: "His look malignant chills with boding fears."

⁸ The idea of introducing a ghost had been proposed by Graves (see his letter of 22 February). RD used some of Graves's phrasing both here and in the printed text (Stanza XI), although every line here was somewhat altered.

⁹ Line 4 in Stanza XIII reads: "And Reason calls her boasted powers in vain."

¹⁰ The opening of line 3 in Stanza XIV.

¹¹ Although the sense was maintained, this Stanza was changed considerably.

¹² Except for lines 1, 2, and 4, this remained intact as Stanza XIX. Line 3 became line 4, and the first four lines read: "Ah! who to pomp or grandeur will aspire? / Kings are not rais'd above misfortune's frown; / That form, so graceful even in mean attire, / Sway'd once a Sceptre, once sustained a crown."

¹³ Further proposed alterations sent to Shenstone throughout the summer delayed the ode's appearance until the autumn.

¹⁴ Charles Watson-Wentworth (1730–82), 2nd Marquis of Rockingham, resided at Kirkby, Leicestershire. Wentworth is not mentioned in Shenstone's extant letters, and so it is difficult to tell whether or not their meeting took place.

¹⁵ Hylton did not reach London until late June or early July. In his letter to Shenstone on 13 July, RD says that Mr and Mrs Baskerville, Miss Eaves, and Mr Hylton dined with him the previous day.

To John Smith, 11th Earl of Clanricarde¹

April 25ᵗʰ [1757]²

My Lord

As the Memoirs & Letters of the ⟨Earl⟩ Marquiss of Clanricarde are now quite finisht, I must beg your Lordship's directions with regard to the presents, particularly what must be done with that intended for his Majesty.³ I was in hopes your Lordship would have come to Town on ⟨that⟩ this occasion; and the more so, as I am in some concern about the sale of ⟨it⟩ yᵉ work, being apprehensive, as it proves imperfect, that the public may not be so ready to purchase, as I expected.⁴ In which case, as I was entirely ignorant of this imperfection, I hope your Lordship will not let me be a sufferer. I shall send one neatly bound to your Lordship by yᵉ next Carrier; & that for his Majesty is ready to be deliver'd, as soon as I receive directions. I am

My Lord &c

MS: Robert Dodsley Letter Book, Birmingham Public Libraries, f. 39.

¹ John Smith, 11th Earl of Clanricarde (1720–82).

² The year is determined from RD's mentioning the readiness of Clanricarde's edition of his ancestor's memoirs and letters, which RD would publish on 21 May 1757 (*LEP*) and also from the letter's position in RD's Letter Book.

³ "*The Memoirs and Letters of Ulick, Marquis of Clanricarde and Earl of St. Albans; Lord Lieutenant of Ireland, and Commander in Chief of the Forces of King Charles the First in that Kingdom during the Rebellion, Governor of the County and Town of Galway, Lord Lieutenant of the County of Kent, and Privy Counsellor in England and Ireland . . . now first published by the present Earl of Clanricarde,* London. Printed by J. Hughs for Robert and James Dodsley." In his notes to the William Bowyer ledgers (p. 840), which Keith Maslen kindly shared with me, Professor Maslen indicates that, sometime before July 1757, Bowyer had printed 220 copies of 16½ sheets of this folio volume; Hughs had printed 116 sheets. Ulick de Burgh, 5th Earl and Marquis of Clanricarde (1604–57), who, for many years, had been a loyal general to Charles I, especially in the Irish campaign, capitulated to Parliament in 1652. No response to this letter has been located.

⁴ Possibly the "imperfection" was that mentioned in the *Monthly Review* of the following September (pp. 218–20), where the reviewer regrets that the editor of the *Memoirs* had not accounted for a publication of 1722: *Memoirs of the Rt. Hon. the Marquis of Clanricarde . . . Published from his Lordship's original Manuscripts*. Though this earlier publication was slighter and covered a single transaction, the reviewer thought it should have been the basis for the present work. Furthermore the present work, he claims, removed some of the Earl's imputations against the Catholics of Ireland in order to enhance the memory of his character.

To William Shenstone

Pallmall   April 26 [1757]

Dear Sir

I am afraid You will think this Ode has turn'd my head; but forgive me this onc‹ & I will sin no more. I just beg leave to submit to You an alteration or two, tha have occur'd to me since I wrote last, and I have done.

Stanza 8

And not a tear bedews his vacant eyes;
But songs, and bursts of rage, in mingled fragments rise,

16

No succour yon fair mourner &c.

19

Aw'd into reverence, my rapt soul attends –
    The Power, with eyes complacent, saw my fear;
And, as with grace ineffable she bends,
    These accents vibrate on my listening ear.
        "Aspiring son of Art,
        Say, does thy feeling heart
Glow with these wonders to thy fancy shewn?
Then shall th' impassion'd Muse make all her charms thy own.

20

The lares of Affectation &c.

21

Then seize the daring pen &c.[2]

I beg You will pay no regard to these or my former alterations, should they happen to interfere with any which you may have made. I shall be very glad to see your least hints, as I am sensible you alter nothing without a reason.[3] But I thought I was to have heard from you within a week. Ah Mr Shenstone! – What a rascal I am! I had like to have forgot my promise never to accuse You of Indolence again.

I am
    Dear Sir
    Most sincerely & affectionately Yours
                    R. Dodsley

MS: BL. Add. MS. 28,959, f. 71.

[1] RD's concern for his ode *Melpomene*, a publication of the following September, clearly identifies this letter as a product of 1757. See RD's letter to Shenstone on 11 April 1757, note 1.

[2] Since the manuscript revealing the current state of the text of *Melpomene* is missing, it is impossible to judge the advisability of RD's recommended changes, or even exactly which words or phrases he is recommending be changed. But, in reference to the changes herein suggested, the first printed edition the following September shows that: at least two more stanzas were added in the interim, for what RD refers to as "Stanza 8" above becomes the ninth stanza and "19" becomes 21; in "Stanza 8," "his" becomes "those," and the second line is not used at all; the line for "16" is not used at all; in "19," "Know" replaces "Say" at line 6, "does" is dropped, and the last line is abandoned; in "20," "lares" "lares" becomes "lures"; the line for "21" is not used. See also the textual changes recommended in RD's letter of 21 April.

Shenstone's response has not been traced, if in fact he did respond, though the opening of RD's letter to him of 13 July seems to imply that he might not have.

To William Shenstone

[30 April 1757][1]

Dear Sir

An Essay on the Chinese manner of laying out Garden Ground in to night's Chronicle has pleas'd me so much that I cannot forbear sending it to You, as I think it cannot fail to afford you a peculiar pleasure. I am miserably relaps'd & totally unable to walk across the room. I write in pain & so stop short.

Ever faithfully Yours

R. Dodsley

MS: BL. Add. MS. 28,959, f. 67.

The date is taken from RD's mentioning "An Essay on the Chinese manner of laying out Garden Ground in to night's [London] Chronicle." In the *LC* of 28–30 April 1757 appeared a long review of Sir William Chambers's *Designs of Chinese Buildings, Furniture, Dresses, Machines, and Utensils. Engraved by the best Hands, from the Originals drawn in China by Mr. Chambers. To which is prefixed a Description of their Temples, Houses, Gardens, etc.* Chambers's work had been published "for the author" on 28 March (*PA*). In the imprint, the "Mess. Dodsley" are listed among the sellers.

To Miss Nelly Wright

May 3ᵈ [1757][1]

Dear Miss

I hope your good father got well home, & did not encrease his cold that night at Drury Lane, where we parted. For my own part I waited there, tell him, above half an hour before I could meet with a chair, so that getting a cold which again reduc'd me to my flannels, I am now practicing Philosophy upon crutches: & you cannot conceive what a complacency & respect I grow to have for my self, on the contemplation of my own virtues of Patience & Resignation. I heartily thank you for your kind invitation to Mansfield: yᵉ single consideration of being so charmingly nurs'd, would be a strong temptation let me tell you. But God bless your Charity, & send you better employment with a man than to wrap his legs in flannel. He must be an impudent fellow that could think of subjecting You to such a task! You, who have had no benefits from the Creature! Let those who have known what he is good for, take care of him when he is good for nothing. But it is of a piece with the rest of your ⟨Goodness⟩ Character; your virtues are not of yᵉ selfish kind, but pure & disinterested; & I wish I could flatter my self with the hopes of being able to get down, that I might give you an opportunity of exercising them in my behalf.

MS: Robert Dodsley Letter Book, Birmingham Public Libraries, f. 40.

[1] The year is determined from the letter's entry in RD's bound Letter Book, where it appears betwee other letters to Miss Wright that can be certainly dated; namely, between that of 24 February [175; and that of 30 August [1757]. For Miss Wright's father, see the former letter to her.

From John Dyer[1]

12 May 175

. . . You should have had my thanks before for your very handsome publication of the *Fleece*, had I not flattered myself with a journey to town, and with seeing you but very ill health still confines me, and I almost despair of the journey[2] . . . I hop these remarks will be agreeable to you. If you are inclined to make use of them, of any others, which I may send you, be pleased to acquaint me. I have no frank, an am your debtor for postage.

Source: Straus, p. 110.

[1] John Dyer (1700?–57), poet and landscape painter. RD had published Dyer's *The Fleece. A Poem.* *Four Books* on 7 February 1757 (*PA*). Earlier, the bookseller had reissued the poet's *Grongar Hill* (172€ and *The Ruins of Rome* (1740) in Volume I of his *Collection* (1748). A posthumous edition of Dyer's *Poem* also appeared from Tully's Head on 5 November 1761 (*PA*). See Ralph M. Williams *Poet, Painter, ar Parson: The Life of John Dyer* (New York: Bookman Associates, 1956).
[2] Originally from Wales, Dyer currently had a living in Coningsby, Lincs., which had been presented him by Sir John Heathcote. Here he died at the end of the present year.

To David Garrick

June 17 [1757]

Sir

Having made very numerous, & some considerable alterations in my Play sinc You saw it; & ⟨being also inform'd⟩ having been inform'd that You are nc unwilling to give it ⟨another⟩ second reading in company with some of ou common friends, I take the Liberty of ⟪desiring to know whether you would nc rather chuse to give it ⟨another⟩ ⟨such a⟩ another reading first alone. I have tw reasons for this proposal; ⟨first that⟩ one is that I am not without hopes that⟩ letting you know that I am very ready to submit it to such a perusal. But as I flatte my self you ⟨might⟩ may possibly find most of your former objections now remov' ⟪by the Alterations I have since made; ⟨that⟩ the other, that I should be ⟨very sorry to engage any of my friends in so disagreeable an office as that of defending m weaknesses: and I am very far from the vanity of thinking it so perfect as tha nothing can be objected against it. However, I by no means decline submitting it t such a perusal; I only mean that I would willingly avoid any altercation about i

xcept what might be adjusted between our selves. For though it has had the
pprobation of many of ye best Judges, & that to a degree much beyond my
xpectations, yet I do not feel my self so partial in its favour, nor so tenacious of its
ιilings, as not to be very willing to remove or correct whatever may yet be found
bjectionable in it.》 would it not be more agreeable to You to give it another
eading first alone? If it would, I will send it to You whenever you find your self at
·isure.²

1S: Robert Dodsley Letter Book, Birmingham Public Libraries, ff. 40v–42r.

Besides being derived from the RD Letter Book principle, the assigned year fits the chronology of
events recorded in four additional pieces of correspondence during the last half of 1757. On 15
September, Garrick would inform RD that despite the changes in *Cleone*, he believes it still "defective"
and "too bloody." Five days after Garrick's letter, RD wrote to Shenstone to say that Garrick had
rejected the tragedy for the final time. A further letter to Garrick, sometime in November, responds to
the theatre manager's rejection, as does a letter to Thomas Gataker on 4 November.
Apparently Garrick acceded to RD's request, as evident from the exchange of letters recounted in
note 1.

·o George Box,¹ Secretary of the Society for the Encouragement of ᴧrts, Manufactures and Commerce

[*c.* 21 June 1757]²

ir
Sometime ago chance threw me into Company with a Gentleman who is a
ubscriber to y^r Society. He enumerated the many advantages that accrue to the
νhole by the virtuous and worthy encouragem! and Industry of a part of the Nation.
.e pointed out the Benefits that had already evinced the *necessity*, and utility of such
n Undertaking; and the Premiums – Honourable and Pecuniary, which were
llotted such as excell in any Art or Science propos'd by the Society; and concluded
νith Informing the Company that any Hint or Design which might, (tho in the
mallest degree) [?] promote the Utility of y^r Plan, or render its good effects more
xtensive, would be rec'd by *you*, considered with Candor & Impartiality, & if
·racticable and agreeable to the Laws of the Society and its Interests, be put into
xecution.
This was the Motive which urged me to be thus troublesome and to offer my Mite
ɔ improve & promote so laudable a Plan, but alas! I fear my Scheme will meet with
ᴧany objections against its [?] practicability! yet I am induced to hope, that the
ood effec[ts] which must necessarily result from its being put into execution, will
utweigh any difficulties! not to keep you longer in suspense, It [?] is to promote the
ᴋnowledge of our *own* Language ⟨by⟩ in its several Branches of Reading,
·peaking, & writing it, with Elegance & propriety: & could this great design be
·rought about under y^r Influence I flatter myself I could (tho indeed I need not)
·rove, that it will redound as much to the Hon! of the Society, as any of their

present or former Labours; & as advantageous to the Nation as any Essay that ha
been made towards its Improvem! since its first Establishment. I confess S.r som
difficulties lie in the way, and it is possible (tho I must say I think not very probable
under the Auspices of y.r Society it may fail, but should that be the Case, it will, i
must be allow'd by all ⟨the⟩ incorrupti Judices to be a noble attempt, worthy
Englishmen! – This is the worst that can happen but if we permit ourselves to enjoy
the prospect of its succeeding, what happy and glorious effects may we not expec
from it! what Immortal Honour will your Society derive from it? What advantage.
would accrue to every art, science, and profession, from a Taste for Eloquence? [?] i
we look back into History, we shall find that many Nations before they were clear'd
from the Rusticity of their Barbarous Origin by the force of Eloquence, were
strangers to the Polite Arts; that as Eloquence grew powerful the Arts flourished
their dominions were extended and their glory & the fear of them was known thro
the world; we shall also find that when that divine Art began to decline, the rest fel
into their primitive Obscurity. but I wander from my Point. I intended a Hint, and
am run into a History. it is time for me to Conclude and put an end to y.r trouble and
mine. However, should what I have so incoherently thrown together appear o
Consequence enough to be enquir'd into, my Assistance, and the few abilitie
heaven has been pleas'd to Entrust me with, shall be at the Society's Service; and in
my next I shall Endeavour to be more Correct, (for indeed I despair of success) and
full but sh.d it happen to be (as many are) considered as a chimerical Scheme. I hope
S.r the Intention with which I wrote will plead my Excuse.

I am S.r

Y.rs & the Society's

most Obed.t Serv.t

& well wisher

Honestu

P.S. a line acknowledging the Receipt of this directed for B. Z. at M.r Lindsay
Orange Merchant on Ludgate Hill, will be esteem'd a favour.

Address: To Mr. Box / These
Endorsement: Rcvd June 21 1757. No Answer[3]

MS: Royal Society of Arts, Guard Book, Vol. III, No. 63.

[1] Box had become Secretary to the Society on 2 March 1757. Although this letter is signed with merely the
pseudonym "Honestus," the hand is clearly Dodsley's. Besides, not only is the proposal in line with an
earlier request to include Letters within the Society's scope (see Dodsley's letter to Lord Folkestone, *c.* 1
March 1756), but the use of similar expressions ("render its good effects more extensive" and "Wel
wisher") as found in the letter to Folkestone and in the 14 December 1756 letter to the Society, betray
Dodsley as the author.

[2] Although undated, the letter is endorsed as having been received on this date.

[3] Just what Dodsley expected to accomplish with this bit of levity is not clear. The Society's Minutes do
not indicate that this letter was ever read at one of its meetings, as other Dodsley letters had been. In
fact, the endorsement "No Answer" suggests that the piece, though entered in the Guard Book
effected little more than office amusement.

From Thomas Blacklock

Dumfries June 27. *1757.*

Dear Sir

The year has now almost, if not fully evolv'd, since I had the Pleasure of hearing from you. My last[1] enclos'd a small Treatise on Universal Grammar,[2] & let me confess it, I was vain enough to hope you wou'd send me your Oppinion of it; not that I esteem'd it so highly, as to imagine your Oppinion would be to it's Advantage, for long Study & repeated Experience has made it plain to me, how great, & how numerous the Difficulties are, which a Scotch Man has to encounter, before he can write with that facility & Chastness which occur naturally to an Englishman; And which are necessary to give him that Elegant Satisfaction so justly expected from every one that pretends to instruct, or entertain the Publick. I am sensible that the strictest Attention & Care are too little to guard us against harsh Periods, & exotick Idioms which are rendred familiar to us from our Infancy by the Difference of our manners, Conversation & Accent, besides it is no easy matter, for one who converses More with Books than Men, to disengage him-self from that Scholastick turn, which is the natural Consequence of Study. – I fear your Answer has been delay'd, till you could give some Account of the Octavo Edition of my Poems.[3] But tho' the Success of that should prove as bad as an Author jealous of his Reputation can imagine it, the Misfortune will still be greater if aggravated by the Silence of a friend. If it continues not to sell in London, perhaps some copies may be dispos'd of here, whatever is it's fate, I only wait for your Orders to reimburse you. I remmember you once inform'd me, that Sir George Littleton had mentioned me to the Duke of Argyle,[4] his grace might now now interpo[se] very seasonably & successfully for me, as I have some Thoughts of attempting a Course of Lectures upon Eloquence, History & Poetry, in Edinburgh at the opening of the Winter Session. For without any regard to the present fluctuating State of Politicks, a hint from Sir George would engage the Duke in my favour, who could easily determine Lord Milton to exert him-self for me.[5] Supported by such a powerfull Intrest, I might not only hope, to succeed in a precarious Subscription of Lectures from year to year, but even for an Establishmen[t] in the Colledge. There are few Sciences proffest there, except such as more immediately depend upon sight, which with some preperation I wou'd not undertake to teach. Men of such extensive Influence as Sir George Littleton & the Duke of Argyle might accomplish this Scheme, however easy it may seem with a word of power.[6] And by a Single fiat qualifie me to deserve & obtain from Society that Reputation & Competency which are still wanting to me, give me leave only to add; That as Friendship is an enjoyment which no Difference of external Circumstances can palliate, so your continued Correspondence will always contribute much to the Honour & Happiness of your most humble

Serv! Thomas Blacklock –

Address: To / Mr. Robert Dodsley Bookseller / in Pall mall / *London*

MS: Osborn Collection, Beinecke Library, Yale.

[1] Neither RD's nor Blacklock's letter has been traced.
[2] This "Universal Grammar" might have been the work Blacklock had published the previous year in Edinburgh, entitled *An Essay of Universal Etymology; or, the Analysis of a Sentence* and through which he was attempting to expand his London reputation, as he had the previous year by republishing his Edinburgh *Poems* (1756) in London. RD did respond a few weeks later (16 July), but in an evasive manner and ultimately did not publish Blacklock's grammar.
[3] RD had advertised the octavo edition, the third, on 25 May 1756 (*PA*). Unfortunately RD's response in this matter would also prove disappointing for Blacklock. See his letter on the 16th of the next month.
[4] Archibald Campbell, 3rd Duke of Argyll (1682–1761), the Chancellor of Aberdeen University.
[5] Andrew Fletcher, Lord Milton (1692–1766), Lord Justice Clerk, acted as the Duke's confidential agent in Scotland during this period, when Scottish affairs had been entrusted to the hands of the latter.
[6] It seems from his letter of 19 March of the next year, Blacklock was still marshalling his resources to bid for this position. However, as he recounts to RD in his letter of 4 March 1759, he decided not to enter the lists when he discovered that the leading candidate was a person of "great genius, a correct taste & a liberal education," a youth named Adam Ferguson! Whether Lyttelton ever interceded for Blacklock is never mentioned in the correspondence. RD responded (16 July) by informing the poet that Lyttelton was now "much out of power," and, at the moment, out of town.

To William Shenstone

Pallmall July 13.th [1757][1]

Dear Mr Shenstone

It is so long since I wrote to you, or heard from you, that I am really at a loss what to say, & seem as if I was going to begin a new correspondence. However, I do recollect that I made a promise never to accuse you of indolence again, but I did not think you would have taken so ungenerous an advantage of that hasty promise as to grow ten times more indolent than ever upon it. But to scold at this distance I find has no effect, I shall therefore come down and give it you face to face, till I make every echo in the Leasowes ring again: & till then I will suppress my wrath. I had a letter from Lord Lyttelton a day or two ago,[2] desiring me to acquaint Lord Wentworth & Mr Spence, that he was going into Wales for about three weeks, & hoping they would contrive not to come into Worcestershire till his return. I should be very glad to be at the Leasowes at the same time Mr Spence is there, but am afraid he will not be soon enough for me. I fancy M.^r and Mrs Baskerville will set out in about ten days or a fortnight, & they have perswaded me to accompany them.[3] I have this day sent M.^r by Timmon's Waggon, which will be in Birmingham on Saturday about two o'clock, a large deal case directed to You carriage paid, and order'd to be left at the Inn till sent for. If You will be so good as to send your cart for it, and two horses, for it is somewhat above eight hundred weight, you will find on opening it, a Gentleman who is very desirous of spending the rest of his days as a tenant in your shades. He is a leaden companion indeed, but very inoffensive by word or deed, has an easy agreeable air, and seems always inclin'd, heavy as he is, to enliven the company and place where he is admitted. He calls himself the piping Fawn. If You can make him acceptable to You I shall be very glad; and thus much I will venture to say in his behalf, his parts have been commended, & I know he will be happy, at least contented, in whatever situation you may think proper to place him.[4] I have made many alterations in my Ode, & will bring it down with me in hopes it may receive many more. What have you got for my fifth Volume? I hope a large packet: if not, pray give my Compliments to M[rs] Cutler,[5] and tell her I trust (if she has any regard for your fame and honour) that I shall so far corrupt her honesty as to induce her to join with me in robbing your Bureau of every scrap of Poetry in it. But I hope I shall have no occasion to proceed to these extremities: the Rural Elegance I dare say is before now alter'd to your mind, & if You can send it me by the return of post, I will put it to press before I set out, and order a proof of it to be sent after me.

I am

Dear Sir

most affectionately Yours

R. Dodsley

turn over.

P.S. M[r] and M[rs] Baskerville Miss Eaves[6] & M[r] Hylton din'd with me yesterday: I wish you had been with us, but that is a happiness which I must never hope to enjoy in Pallmall. They have unkindly determin'd to set out this day sennight; any line therefore in answer to this must be sent so as to be here on Tuesday next, & I don't know whether that is possible or not. M[r] Hylton obstinately set forwards this morning, for which I hope he will be roasted all the way home. I have upon second thoughts enclos'd the Ode that You may have time to give it due correction before I come.

MS: BL. Add. MS. 28,959, ff. 72–3.

[1] For several reasons, this letter is clearly of 1757. Spence's anticipated trip north to Lord Wentworth's, mentioned within, was announced in RD's fully dated letter of 21 April 1757: "M[r] Spence meditates a visit to my Lord Wentworth. . . in about two months." Secondly, RD says he would be bringing his ode with him to Leasowes for Shenstone's alterations. Obviously this is *Melpomene*, an ode mentioned in several letters to Shenstone since 17 February 1757 and published on the following 29 September. Finally a draft version of this letter in the RD Letter Book corroborates a 1757 dating.
[2] Letter not traced.   [3] See RD's "P.S."
[4] Shenstone would use his gift of the piping fawn to grace "Dodsley's Bower" on the south-eastern border of the Leasowes.
[5] Shenstone's housekeeper.
[6] Miss Sarah Eaves, Mrs Baskerville's daughter by her former marriage.

To Thomas Blacklock

July 16 [1757][1]

Dear Sir

Very often hath my conscience reproached me with my indolence, my neglect, (I am really asham'd to give it so hard a name as it deserves) in not writing to You ⟨in⟩ for so long an interval: and your kindness in studying excuses for me doubles my confusion. But I have really had a most dreadful year of it with the Gout; I was for five months nail'd down to my chair incapable of setting a foot to the ground; and am now after eight months confinement not able to walk 100 Yards. But this I must acknowledge is no sufficient apology, and I therefore throw my self entirely on your good nature. I thank you very kindly for the pleasure your short but very comprehensive grammar gave me: but ⟨am⟩ tho' I like it exceedingly I am really so far from being a competent judge of it, having never had a grammatical education, that it would be impertinent in me to pretend to give any ⟨other⟩ opinion of it. ⟨than that I lik'd it my self⟩ I will venture however to say that tho' very concise it is to me quite clear: and I believe when explain'd by a good master, will contribute to give boys a better idea of ⟨Lang⟩ yᵉ nature of Language than they commonly gain at school. And I really and sincerely think that you have as little occasion to apologize for the purity of your language (I will not say as any scotchman but) as any Englishman I know. I heartily wish I could give you as good an account of the sale of your poems as they deserve, but to say the truth they sell but very slowly; & I will send any number you please to Scotland whenever you ⟨please to ⟩ direct me to whom I must send them. As to settling the account I beg you will not be in haste about it, I should be very sorry to send you an account without a ballance in your favour. Lord Lyttelton is not at present in London; I may possibly see him at his house in the Country in about a ⟨month⟩ fortnight when I will speak to him; but as he is at present quite out of place, I believe he is much out of power. However, if he can do you any service only by writing to the Duke of Argyle, I should hope he will not be averse to it: and if you will let me know particularly what it is you would have his Lordship ask of the Duke, I will certainly mention it to him; for I beg you will believe, however lazy my hand may be, my heart is very sincerely and affectionately Yours.[2]

MS: Robert Dodsley Letter Book, Birmingham Public Libraries, ff. 46–8.

[1] Three matters mentioned within the letter – the grammar submitted to RD by Blacklock, the bookseller's account of the sale of Blacklock's *Poems* in the octavo edition, and Lord Lyttelton's possible intercession for the position Blacklock seeks at Edinburgh – mark this letter as a response to Blacklock's fully dated letter of 27 June 1757. A 1757 dating is corroborated by the letter's position in RD's Letter Book.

[2] Specifications for all the foregoing matters can be found in Blacklock's letter of 27 June or in the accompanying notes.

To Nicholas Herbert[1]

July 20 [1757][2]

Sir

   I just now receiv'd yᵉ honour of your Letter:[3] I am setting out to morrow morning for Worcestershire, but my brother will take care to get your Volume of Acts, & send ⟨them⟩ it as directed.[4] He will also send the two Odes of Mʳ Gray. I sincerely lament the unhappy accident which befel my good friend's ⟨friend's⟩ fingers, as it will ⟨prevent his Biographer⟩ so far lessen his Character, that his Biographer cannot say *all* his actions left a *sweet* savor behind them. What pity it is that a perfect Character should thus be destroy'd ⟨&⟩ – that a clergyman so well respected, so generally thought to be ⟨pure & holy⟩ ⟨undefiled before God and ye World⟩ spotless & untainted with Corruption, should thus be found guilty of gross Uncleanness? But I hope he will take particular care to wipe this stain from his flesh, & present himself pure and undefiled before God & the World. Repentance may do much: if he sincerely repents, & forsakes his left-handed unrighteous ways, he shall save his fingers clean. I doubt not but you will take care to give him proper admonition on ye occasion: and for the sake of a friend's Character I will keep this ⟨unhappy⟩ unfortunate *slip* a profound secret.

I am &c

MS: Robert Dodsley Letter Book, Birmingham Public Libraries, ff. 48v–50.

¹ The Hon. Nicholas Herbert (1706–75), of Glenham, Suffolk, MP for Wilton (1757–75) and treasurer to Princess Amelia (1757–60). RD had published two of Herbert's poems in his fortnightly *Museum* (II, 26 (14 March 1747), 426–8; III, 28 (11 April 1747), 51–3) and reprinted them in Volume III of his *Collection* (1748), pp. 313–19. Another poem was to follow in Volume VI (1758), p. 162.
² For several reasons, this letter appears to be a product of 1757. RD says he is setting out "to morrow morning for Worcestershire," the very day he had announced such a trip in his letter of 13 July to Shenstone. He tells Herbert that his brother James will send him the "two Odes of Mr Gray," probably because they had not yet been published, but would be in 16 days; that is, on 6 August 1757. Also, as a draft copy in RD's Letter Book, the letter can be dated as 1757.
³ Had Herbert's letter been preserved, the identity of the erring clergyman in the following might have been established.
⁴ The volume of Acts of Parliament regularly produced by the King's printer.

From Robert Lowth

Sedgefield near Dur[ham]
Aug. 9. 1757.

Dear S^r

I have been obliged to publish a Serm[on]¹ preach'd at ye meeting on occasion of the Pub[lic] Infirmary at Newcastle.² It is printed the[re] & I have taken the liberty of putting You[rs] & Mr Millar's name in the Title-page I have order'd 150 to be sent to You, of wch be so good as to send a part to Mr Millar with my humble Service & request that he would be so kind as to assist in ye sale. 'Tis publish'd for the Benefit of the Infirmary, & if it produces any gain, it will so far do some good.

I must further beg the favour of you [to] send a few Presents of them for me, [?] wch I will give you a List inclos'd³ [?] The Life of William of Wykeham is fin[is]h'd; & ready for the Press.⁴ I beg you [to] confer with Mr Millar about the Pub[li]cation of it, & give me your joint advice [up]on ye matter. As far as I can guess, it [wi]ll make a pretty large Octavo, without [sw]elling it in the printing; tho' I would have [it] printed well & decently. It will not be [a] Book for Common Readers; it will not have [mu]ch either in the matter or the manner [th]at will be entertaining to the generality: [it] is chiefly calculated for those that have [so]me relation to the Subject of it, & may [m]erit the attention of a few others that [see?] something more curious than ordinary in [?] Antiquities & History. So that it [will] not safely admit of a large Impression. [The Title] is to be "The Life of W^m of W^m["] [?] are all the circumstances I can think of [to] direct you in forming a Judgement upon [it.] And when I have told you, that I wo[uld] not part with the property of ye Copy & shall want a number (about 60 or [?)] for Presents, you may easily determine [?] upon your Proposals, & I shall as easily agree to them. – If you choose to print now, ⟨to be⟩ ready to publish early [in] ye winter, I can send it as soon as you please. I have nothing to add but a P[re-]face, giving an account of my Materials for wch the Book itself need not wait.

Believe me, Dear S^r

Your most obedient
humble Servt
Robt Low[th]

P.S.　The Sermons for Oxford [?]

MS. BL. Add. MS. 35,339, ff. 13–14.

¹ The text is broken off down the right side of the recto, and down the left, on the verso.
² "*A Sermon preached at St. Nicholas Church in Newcastle, before the Governors of the Infirmary for the Counties of Durham, Newcastle, and Northumberland, on Thursday June 23, 1757, being Their Anniversary Meeting.* Printed by I. Thompson at Newcastle, and sold by W. Charnley; J. Richardson in Durham; R. and J. Dodsley in Pallmall; and A. Millar in the Strand." The London publication occurred on 4 September 1757 (*PA*).
³ The list, which begins in Lowth's "P.S." is missing, possibly torn off for RD's convenience.
⁴ *The Life of William of Wykeham, Bishop of Winchester. Collected from Records, Registers, Manuscripts, and other authentic Evidences* would be published by Andrew Millar and R. and J. Dodsley the following 27 May (*PA*). The cost of printing the first and second editions, both octavo, is found in the Strahan Papers (BL. Add. MS. 48,800). For the 432-page first edition, with plates, Strahan's ledger for May 1758 shows £26.2.0; under April 1759, the cost of the 446-page second edition is listed as £25.14.0. Numerous corrections and additions to the first edition apparently necessitated a good deal of resetting. Lowth, like several of RD's New College authors, was a product of Winchester.

To Miss Nelly Wright

Augst 30th [1757]¹

Dear Miss

　　When your ⟨letter⟩ kind Invitation came to ⟨Town⟩ Pall mall I was set out for Birmingham, where I have been for five weeks. My brother sent your Letter to me thither, and I should have answer'd it sooner, but that I fully intended to have stolen a week from my business there, and slipt away in a Postchaise to Mansfield. But this I found it impossible to accomplish; tho' it was very much in my wishes. However, if I should be so happy as to escape the Gout this Winter, I may probably

)e bold enough to make an attempt at seeing Mansfield next Suɱer. ⟨But at⟩ At ɔresent I am very lame, & tho' I have been so long from home, I am not yet able to ᴡalk but with great difficulty. I am much afraid, if I should have another attack ᴛhis winter, that the use of my legs will be quite taken from me. Poor Lord Radnor is ᶃone. He dy'd a day or two after his birth day, having rounded seventy years. He ᴇft me a hundred pounds, which I would very gladly have stay'd for some years ᴏnger. I beg my compliments to all friends, and am

&c

MS: Robert Dodsley Letter Book, Birmingham Public Libraries, f. 51.

The letter is dated from RD's reporting to Miss Wright the recent death of John Robartes, 4th Earl of Radnor, who had died on 15 July 1757. Also RD's saying that he had been, as of 30 August, five weeks in Birmingham fits in chronologically with his trip to the Leasowes in 1757. He left London on 21 July (letter to Herbert on 20 July), and probably arrived on the 24th or 25th. Finally the letters entry in RD's Letter Book shows it to be a product of 1757, coming as it does before RD's letter to Graves which can certainly be dated as 24 October 1757.

From Robert Lowth

[September 1757][1]

Wᵐ. of Wykeham sets out this day from Dur[h]am to wait of you. He travels slowly, ⌐&] will not arrive in Town till this day fortnight. If he does not come to your hands ᶊoon after that, be so good as to enquire after him, at the Newcastle Carrier's at the ᴡhite Horse in Cripplegate.

I have no objection to your Proposals; & if upon looking over & examining it you ᶊhall think proper to alter your design in any particular, I shall as readily agree to ᴀny alterations you shall propose.[2] Tho' you'll find, as I told you, that it will not be a ᴃook of amusement for common Readers, yet the number of persons that bear some ᴇelation to Wᵐ. & his Colleges, [to] satisfy whose Curiosity it is chiefly design'd, i[s] ⌐pretty?] considerable. This is a circumstance yᵗ [shᵈ] [enter?] into the account: the ᴄhief hopes [? you] advise [dwelling?] upon it to enlarge your [sale I?] leave yᵗ ᴇntirely to your judgement. I am [very?] much for your being of the cautious side, ⌐& wᵈ] rather have you under than above the mar[k.][3]

I must beg of you to get a careful & in[tel-]igent Corrector. There will be no ɔarticula[r] difficulties in the Book itself; the References [&] Notes will require the ᴄhief care: the Appendix, tho' better written, will be more troublesom[e] especially ᶇ the old French in one part, & in abbreviations of the Latin.[4] You might send me ɔy the Post any particular sheets where there are the chief difficulties: if you do, ᴇemember to send [yᵉ] Ms. too, for I have no Copy. You'll think it proper to print ᴛhe Appendix on a different & smaller Letter; & I suppose, put it to press together ᴡith the Book.[5] In the beginning of the Appendix you'll find two loose Papers; one ⌐a] Contents; the other a genealogical Table. [The] [la]tter is to go at the end of ᴀppenˣ & [?][6] [? I have] made inquiries about [yᵉ] [d]rawing of Wᵐ.s Monument ᶇ Winchester Cathe[dr]al for a Frontispiece; & have some hopes of [h]aving it tolerably done by one now in that neighbourhood. But if you should chance to know [o]f any Artist going that way, that could do it well, pray send him to the Dean of Winchester.[7]

I should be glad to see your first sheet by way of specimen; perhaps you won't care to stay for my opinion upon it: however, send it me to satisfy my curiosity.

But before you send the Book to the press, I must beg the favour of you to take the trouble of rea: :ding it over carefilly yourself: & not only to alter any mistakes in writing, spelling, &c. but to give me your observations, & objections to any passages; & mark all improprieties of expression, obscurity, &c. for all wch I shall be much obliged to you.

Mr Spence is return'd to Byfleet:[8] he has seen [pa]rt of it; but if you can catch him, make him [look] it over again.

[The Pre]face is done; & you shall have it [?] [?] & communicate this to him.

I forgot to desire you to send a Sermon [to y^e] D. of Newcastle. Send one now: his Grace w[ill not?] think of its being too late, if he thinks about [?] I find they are over weight for the Post; so [?] those out of Town wait till you have an oppo[rtu-]nity: & pray add to the List, Lord Wentworth.[9]

This has put me in mind to look over my form[er] List of Presents; & I find I cannot reduce it [to] under Fourscore for Wykeham.

What you saw in the Papers is true. I shall be very glad of your Company at The Chaplain['s] Table; but don't yet know when I am to be in Waiting.[10]

My Wife presents her humble service; & You will believe me to be,

Dear S^r

Your most Affectionate

humble Servt

R. Lowth

P.S. / W^m of Wm Section 1. pag. 1. [be]fore ye word *[inquisitive]* insert, *[idly.]*[11]

MS: BL. Add. MS. 35,339, ff. 18–19.

---

[1] Two matters mentioned within the letter urge this dating. Lowth's *Sermon preached at St. Nicholas Church*, which he is asking RD to send to the Duke of Newcastle, had appeared on 4 September 1757 (*PA*). In order for the Duke of Newcastle to believe that his gift copy of Lowth's *Sermon* was not sent "too late" – on the basis that it was sent by coach and not by post because of its weight – it would have to arrive in Newcastle sometime within a few weeks of its 4 September publication date. This, of course, would date Lowth's request for such a delivery even earlier. Secondly, Lowth's appointment as a Chaplain in Ordinary to George II, alluded to at the end of the letter, had been announced in *Lloyd's Evening Post* on 26 August 1757, where RD might have read the news. Allowing a few weeks for their exchange of correspondence on the subject would suggest an early September 1757 dating.

[2] RD's letter is not traced.

[3] Since Lowth did not want to sell the copyright, he was financing the publication himself and was therefore understandably cautious of an overrun. A second edition was called for a year after the first, however, followed by a supplement to the second edition.

[4] The 48-page appendix is almost entirely in Latin; some French names appear.

[5] The appendix was printed in smaller letters.

[6] The genealogical table was placed at the very end of the volume, in fold-out form.

[7] Isaac Taylor (1730–1807) drew the monument of William of Wykeham at Winchester and F. Patton did the engraving. Whether or not it was Taylor whom Lowth had in mind at this point is not clear. See Lowth's letter to RD on 3 November and Thomas Cheyney's letter to RD on 6 February 1758.

[8] One of Joseph Spence's residences.

[9] Lowth's *A Sermon preached at St. Nicholas's Church in Newcastle*. Sir Thomas Pelham Holles (1693–1768), Duke of Newcastle, and Charles Watson-Wentworth (1730–82), 2nd Marquis of Rockingham.

[10] Curiously, Lowth's name does not appear among the names of Chaplains in Ordinary as listed in *Court and City Register* or *Court and City Kalendar* for either 1757 or 1758.

[11] RD complied.

From David Garrick[1]

Sep.^{br} 15.th 1757.

Sir.

I have kept the Tragedy a Week longer than I should have done, that I might thoroughly consider it at different Readings, & be the better Enabled to give my Opinion of it – where ye particular Alterations have been made I cannot positively point out, but I really think, that ye Play is the better for them – Yet notwithstanding these Amendments, and ye other Passages of Merit, it is still my Opinion that y.^r foundation of ye Whole is defective, & that ye Schemes that are form'd & the Circumstances that arise in ye Course of ye Fable are too bloody, shocking & improbable – If you please to remember these were partly my Objections to the Plan before You had written a Line of y^r Tragedy – If you will do me the Justice to believe that this Judgment of mine is sincere & unprejudic'd, I will very readily agree that it may be Erroneous; & I hope that it will prove so, whenever Your Master, & Mine, the Public, shall determine the Question.[2]

I am
S.^r
Your most
hum^{le} Servt
D: Garrick.

MS: laid in copy of Richard Brinsley Knowles, *Life of Sheridan Knowles* (London, 1872), II, 94. Harvard Theatre Collection, Harvard College Library.

[1] Although the letter carries no address, it most probably was directed to RD and concerns Garrick's final refusal of *Cleone*. The theater manager's complaint that the tragedy's "Circumstances . . . are too bloody" echoes the contemporary impression of the tragedy. Furthermore the additional reading of a revised tragedy fits the history of RD's application to Garrick on behalf of *Cleone*. Three months earlier, on 17 June, RD wrote to Garrick (q.v.), petitioning another reading of the play, in which he claimed he had "made very numerous, & some considerable alterations . . . since You saw it." It is unlikely that Garrick would have refused it another reading. In fact, five days after the date of this Garrick letter, RD told Shenstone that the theater manager had refused *Cleone* for the final time.

[2] See RD's next letter to Garrick, in November 1757, where the author has decided to print *Cleone* "with some faint hope. . . of a more favourable reception from the Public than You thought proper to afford it."

To William Shenstone

Pall mall Sep.! 20.th [1757]

Dear Sir

I have delay'd thanking you for all the Civilities, the Kindness, and the pleasures I receiv'd at y.e Leasowes, that I might send you at the same time a proof of your Poems and of your Grove; and that I might give you the time for filing and polishing which you desir'd.[2] I think the Design is executed very neatly, & hope you will like it; M.r Giles went to Grignion & gave him some useful directions.[3] I have interleav'd the Proofs, that you may insert any alterations you think proper. You will see I have omitted the Evergreen, and Candour, which You seem'd most afraid of, & intend to insert them without a name.[4] I beg my Compliments to M.r Hylton: pray what becomes of his meditated Pastoral?[5] I enquir'd about a Green Shagreen Pocket-book, but as I am told it will come to two guineas exclusive of the Clasp, I defer'd buying it, till I have your farther orders: in the mean time have sent You the Morrocco one mended. When you shall have corrected the four Sheets I have sent, which I hope will be in about a month or six weeks at most, you may send them up in the four franks I have enclos'd for that purpose: I hope by that time to have finish'd both the volumes. The Printer says he shall be able to keep the press standing of these four sheets, till you can send them back, which is a great convenience to me, as it permits me to go on with the rest. As You have so much time, I have sent no proof to M.r Graves, because I thought you might possibly make some corrections, & would rather chuse to send your own proofs to him. I have shew'd D.r Akenside your Elegy; he is prodigiously struck with it, & hopes you will some time or other before 'tis long, let the public enjoy the pleasure of the whole Collection.[6] I have sent you one of my Ode, & one for M.r Hylton: I have also sent by the Penny post one to L.d Lyttelton's House in Town, whether they will send it to him, in the Country I know not; but if they should, and You should happen to see him, pray don't say whose it is, as I would by no means be known.[7] M.r Garrick has finally rejected Cleone; so instead of dying of Grief, she may now go hang her self in Despair.[8] Or rather truely, ought not the Authur to be hang'd, for wasting so much time to so little purpose? But he is penitent, and will do so no more. I beg my Compliments to Molly, and thank her for all her care of me: and pray let her give my love to the Cows for their delicious suppers.

I am
Dear Sir
Your mostd affectionate & oblig'd
humble Servant
R. Dodsley

MS: BL. Add. MS. 28,959, ff. 76–7.

[1] The year of the letter is certain for several reasons. First of all, RD is sending proofs of Shenstone's poems which were to appear in Volumes V and VI of RD's *Collection* the following March; the prospective poems for the *Collection* had not reached this stage by September of 1756. Secondly, the ode

which RD is sending to Shenstone and Hylton is his own *Melpomene*, which would be advertised as published the next week (*LC*, 27–9 September 1757). Finally, RD says Garrick has *finally* rejected *Cleone*, a disappointment he likewise admits to Moses Mendes in a letter that can certainly be dated 26 October 1757. More significantly, Garrick's rejection was conveyed in his letter on 15 September, five days earlier.

2 An engraving of Virgil's Grove at the Leasowes would be printed at the head of Shenstone's "Rural Elegance," the poem which opened Volume V of the *Collection*. The same scene, but now with a variant design by Daniel Bond and engraved by Charles Grignion, would appear at the end of that edition of *Melpomene*, which was appended to the 1759 edition of *Cleone* (3rd, corrected). Virgil's Grove, Shenstone's first major improvement to his farm, became universally acknowledged as his masterpiece of landscaping. The engraving by James Mason (1710–*c*. 1780) after the painting by Thomas Smith (d. 1767) is now at the Lewis Walpole Library, Farmington, Conn. See John C. Riely, "Shenstone's Walks: The Genesis of the Leasowes," *Apollo* (September 1979), 202–9. Virgil's Grove is frequently referred to in the RD–Shenstone correspondence of 1757–8.

3 Probably Joseph Giles, the engraver, Shenstone's neighbour and friend. See Williams, p. 430n. John Scott Hylton never seems to have liked Giles. See his letter to RD on 21 February 1759. Charles Grignion (1721–1810) executed many engravings for RD's publications.

4 "The Evergreen" and "Candour" appeared anonymously and apart from Shenstone's designated poems, in Volume VI of the *Collection*, pp. 211–13.

5 In subsequent correspondence, it will be clear that Hylton was attempting to finish an Indian eclogue in time for RD's *Collection*, but he failed to make the deadline. See his letter to RD on 24–5 February 1758.

6 Probably Shenstone's elegy "Jessy," which he eventually withdrew from among his poems to be published in RD's *Collection*. See the later correspondence, especially the publisher's letter to the poet on 16 January 1758.   7 *Melpomene*. See note 1.

8 See Garrick's letter of 15 September. Thomas Percy, who seems never to have got on well with RD, improves upon Garrick when noting in the margin of Shenstone's letter to Richard Graves on 25 November 1758: "Garrick had rejected it [*Cleone*] in a billet to this effect – 'I will have nothing to do with your d——n'd, bloody, and improbable Tragedy'." (Brooks, VII, 227) One wonders if Percy resented Shenstone's relationship with RD in the late 1750s; certainly he was angered when he felt that RD's influence on James Dodsley had considerably delayed the publication of his *Reliques of Ancient English Poetry* (finally published in 1765). (However, see Shenstone's letter of 20 November 1762, and note 6.)

From Richard Graves

Claverton 10 Octob. 1757 –

Dear S^r

I ought sooner to have acknowledg'd the Receipt of your Poem – which I have perus'd again & again with fresh pleasure: And, to speak like a Critick, will venture to pronounce it an excellent Composition! It is finely imagined & (now at least) vastly correct – I suppose Mr Shenstone put you upon re-considering & methodizing it – and altering several particulars – which neither my self nor, I am sure, any common reader would have suspected Capable of any improvement – This Ode must necessarily do you Credit with every Reader of Taste & Delicacy – I only wish you had prefix'd your Name to engage the *Curiosity* of those, who may not have Judgment enough at first Sight to fathom its Beauties – or may over-look it amidst the daily Productions of the Press[1] –

I hope this Performance is only ⟨preparat ?⟩ prepatory to ye printing – if not ye acting of y^r Tragedy[2] – I am (with Mrs Graves's Respects)

S^r y^r oblig'd humb Ser^t

Ric: Graves.

I have waited a Post or two for a Frank – but was unwilling to defer my Acknowledgements any longer –

Address: To / Mr Dodsley / at his house in Pall-Mall   London
Postmark: 13 OC Bath

MS: Somerset County Record Office, DD/SK, 28/1, 7.

[1] *Melpomene* was published anonymously from Mary Cooper's shop.
[2] *Cleone*, recently rejected by Garrick for the last time. At this time in the following year RD would be considering printing the play.

From Robert Lowth

Sedgefield Octr 17. 1757.

Dear S^r

What can be become of our friend Mr Spence? When a man of his punctuality does not keep to his time, one is always in pain about him. He said he was to be in town the first week of this month; & therefore I had troubled him with a small Commission wch otherwise I sh^d have mention'd to you in my last.[1] I am now afraid of deferring ye matter any longer lest I should interrupt your proceedings. It was to send me back again one page of my W^m of W^m in wch I wanted to make some alteration, as I had forgot to do it before I sent it to you & cannot recollect it sufficiently to do it otherwise. In the Sixth Section towards the middle [yo]u will find a Paragraph beginning with these words, *The Original Drawings* – Be so good as to cut out the next leaf after that, & send it to me; I will return it to you in a Post or two aft[er.]

I want to know about what time you will want the Preface & Dedication; because with regard to the latter I must make some preparations, wch I would not do till all is near ready.

Once more I be[g y]ou w^d get a Corrector for all the Latin part, or our Book will certainly be disgraced.

Believe me, Dear S^r

Your most Affectionate

R. Lowth

MS: BL. Add. MS, 35,339, f. 15.

[1] Writing in September, Lowth had asked RD to have the manuscript of *William of Wykeham* read by Joseph Spence, who, he expected, would soon be in town.

From John Hoadly[1]

St. Maries, Oct.r 18. 1757.

Sir

First, with Regard to my own Things: I know of no Property either Mr. Russell ye Printer, or his Brother, (as I was told ye Gentleman was who applied to me for the Copy,) has in ye Translation of ye Muscipula. I only permitted him to print it, as Mr. H. had spoken of it handsomely in a Letter, & approv'd of it more than of any other Translation.[2] Tho' I think I collected *Six* upon that Occasion, before I sat down to work upon it. Whether You will preface it with any Thing to that Effect, you are to judge. I think, it wd. not be amiss.

The verses under Mr. Hs. Prints have been much admir'd by ye best Judges; but being put under ye Plates in detach'd Pieces, were never thoroughly understood as ⟨a⟩ one compleat Poem. The References to ye Plates may be plac'd either at ye bottom of ye Page, or on ye Sides. At ye end of them I have given You a List of ye Refs in ye Order in which I wd have them plac'd; & number'd Them accordingly. They are plac'd in that Order, & will be easily understood, at one View.[3]

Mr. Berenger has been with me this last Week, & has tempted me, against my Opinion, to send You a few most excellent Copies of Mr. Straight; particularly one to me, when I was a Youngster at ye Temple, design'd for the Study of ye Law; & another upon ye Change of my Resolution to That of ye Gospel. Both These are as good in their Kind as can be writt, & I wd have You *begin* my Pieces with Them, as they are number'd; tho' I may expose myself alittle by my Letter to Him on the Delay of his Promise.[4]

The Bird of Passage is better as a Poem than as a Ballad, & I desire it may be inserted, & in that shape.[5]

The Epil. & Prol. that follow have been so often copied out & lik'd, that I was easily persuaded to add them to the Number. – The Epitaph you may do as you will with.[6]

I send You also ye best of a greater Number of Epigrams from Martial, address'd to Mr. Harris of Salisbury. Whether you print 'em all, or whatever Number of them, let 'em begin & end with those to Mr. Harris. I wou'd beg that no Names be printed at length; only initial Letters.[7] –

You mention'd to me Mr. Taylor's Copy of Verses on *The Dropsical Man*; but as ye Joke is old, & too tediously told, I chose to omit that, & have sent You some much better, particularly ye two first, full of Wit & true Humour. The Rest are excellent in their way, particularly N.os 22, 23, 24, 25 – which I wonder you cou'd put a Negative upon.[8]

If you can possibly make Room for ye whole Collection, as they stand, I shd be glad; as ye Authors were my particular Friends, & I shou'd be well supported on each side. – The Others, which You return'd into my Hands, are either not so worthy of Publication, or improper so soon after my poor Brother's Death: else You shd be wellcome to Them.[9]

You may add *Mr. H.'s Fragment of Chaucer* after Mr. Taylor's Pieces.[10] – And I hope ye whole will answer to You both in Reputation and Profit.

If hereafter you may think of another Volume, I may supply You with some

Curiosities; as, a few of Ld Hervey – English Pieces of Tony Alsop, quite unknown – of George Stubbs – &c, &c^{11} –

I am, Sir,

Your very humble Servan^t

J. Hoadly

MS: BL. Add. MS. 30,262 A-W, ff. 70–1.

1 John Hoadly (1711–76), LLD, son of Bishop Benjamin Hoadly, was, at the time of this letter, Rector of St Maries, Southampton. He corresponded frequently with RD during 1757 and early 1758; that is, during the period when Volumes V and VI of RD's *Collection* were being composed. In these volumes, Hoadly placed thirteen poems (V, 248–51, 258–88; VI, 229, 294–5). Both R. W. Chapman and Donald Eddy attribute "To Chloe. Written on my Birth-Day" (III, 2nd edn., 270 and reprinted in VI, 229), in the first printing, to Hoadly's father, Benjamin Hoadly. But John Hoadly's letter to RD on 8 March 1758 identifies the piece as his own.
2 Probably William Russell (1726–75), listed by Plomer as a bookseller at Horace's Head by Temple Bar, 1751–5. "KAMBROMYOMOXIA: or the Mouse-Trap," Hoadly has translated from Edward Holdsworth's *Muscipula, sive-Cambro-muo-machia* (Londini, 1709), a piece later reprinted in *Musae Anglicanae*, II (1741), 106–14. Apparently Russell had no share in "The Mouse-Trap," for Hoadly's verses were printed in RD's *Collection*, V, 258–68. "Mr H." is Hoadly's good friend William Hogarth.
3 Although RD had said he planned to omit Hoadly's verses that had accompanied Hogarth's prints in *Rake's Progress* (1735), he did include them in his *Collection* (V, 269–74) as a single poem, with references to the individual prints and their titles.
4 Rev. John Straight (1688?–1736), an intimate of Benjamin Hoadly's sons, was rewarded by the Bishop with a prebend at Warminster, Salisbury Cathedral, in 1732 (Courtney, pp. 133–4). In an advertisement in the *LEP* on 22–5 January 1743, Straight is referred to as the late vicar of Finden, Sussex, and sometime Fellow of Magdalen College, Oxford. RD carried out Hoadly's instruction by printing Straight's "To Mr J. H[oadly] at the Temple, occasioned by a Translation of an Epistle of Horace" in the *Collection* (V, 244–8), following it with Hoadly's response, "To the Rev. Mr. J. S." (pp. 248–51), which, in turn, was succeeded by Straight's "Answer to the Foregoing, 1731" (pp. 251–3).
5 "The Bird of Passage" appeared together with Hoadly's other poems in Volume V, 258–78.
6 The "Epilogue to Shakespear's first Part of King Henry IV" and the "Prologue to Comus" appeared in Volume V, 281–5. What happened to "Epitaph" is not clear, unless it is the piece printed as "Verses said to be fixed on the Gate of the Louvre at Paris 1751" (V, 279).
7 James Harris (1709–80), author of *Hermes* (1751), father of the first Earl of Malmesbury, and friend of George IV when Prince of Wales (*Victoria County History. Wiltshire* (London: Oxford University Press, for the Institute of Historical Research, 1953–), VI, 78, 142). His *Works* were edited by his son, the Earl, in 1801. RD printed the epigrams in the *Collection* (V, 285–8), but used Harris's full name, not merely his initials as Hoadly had requested.
8 RD printed nine of William Taylor's poems in V, 288–95 and, despite Hoadly's advice, "The Dropsical Man" in VI, 125.
9 Hoadly's brother Benjamin (1706–57), a physician to George II, had died on 10 August.
10 James Harris's piece was printed in V, 296, and, as requested, after Taylor's "Fragment."
11 John Hervey, Baron Hervey of Ickworth (1696–1743); Anthony Alsop (d. 1726); George Stubbs (1681–1742), friend and neighbor of Bubb Doddington in Dorset. For Hervey, see RD's response on 26 October 1757, note 4. Poems by Alsop would cover eleven pages in VI, 239–49, but Stubbs would not be represented in the *Collection*.

To Richard Graves

Octr 24th [1757]^1

Dear Sir

Your approbation of my Ode gives me great pleasure: I have ye satisfaction to find that it is here also pretty generally approv'd. I am sensible however it owes much of its correctness to Yours and M.ʳ Shenstone's judicious criticisms, of w.ᶜʰ You will easily perceive the effects. The hint of a Ghost was your own; I hope you are not shock'd with yᵉ manner of its appearance.[2] As yᵉ Piece comes out with no name to it, I expect but a very small sale; and to have prefix'd mine would have done it but little service. Your mention of Cleone is very kind, as she is a poor neglected creature whom nobody regards insomuch that she sometimes splenatickly talks of shutting herself up in the cloyster of a Beaureau and avoiding all commerce with mankind. Whether her merits were sufficient to have qualify'd her for shining in yᵉ public eye, I am by no means a proper judge; but ⟨whatever may be her deficiencies,⟩ if, in yᵉ state of obscurity to which she is condemn'd she still preserves a few such judges as You to think of her with kindness and to regret her fate; I hope whatever may be her other deficiencies she will always have Modesty enough to think her self highly honour'd. – But to quit my own ⟨paltry⟩ concerns, let me now, my dear Sir, come to Yours. I have heard a whisper that you are preparing ⟨a Work⟩ an Entertainment for the public.[3] I am much in the dark indeed as to what it is, & if it be not too great a secret, pray indulge me! ⟨but⟩ I dare say it will be a feast and an elegant one; and I long methinks for a taste, or a glimpse of your bill of fare: ⟨If it be not too great a secret, pray indulge me; and⟩ if you are not provided with a Clerk of the Kitchen, I hope I shall have the honour of serving it up to the Public.

I am &c

MS: Robert Dodsley Letter Book, Birmingham Public Libraries, ff. 51v–53r.

¹ The year is fairly easily established from RD's reference to the recent acceptance of his ode both by Graves and by the London literary world; *Melpomene* had been issued by Mary Cooper on 29 September 1757. Secondly, the fair copy of this letter, which RD had sent to Graves, dated 25 October, is acknowledged by Graves as a product of the "25.ᵗʰ of Octob. last" in his next letter to RD on 3 February 1758. Finally, the letter is another draft entered chronologically in RD's Letter Book.
² See Graves's letter to RD on 22 February 1757. RD introduced a ghost in Stanza XI, though "spectres" also appear in Stanza IV and "phantoms" in Stanzas VIII and XIII.
³ This allusion might be the earliest known reference to Graves's *The Spiritual Quixote* (to be published in 1772 by James Dodsley), drafts of which, by reason of internal evidence, can be dated as early as 1757. For considerations of the matter see Charles J. Hill, *The Literary Career of Richard Graves, the Author of The Spiritual Quixote*. Smith College Studies in Modern Languages. Volume XVI. Nos. 1–3 (October, 1934–April 1935), pp. 17 ff; and Clarence Tracy, ed. *The Spiritual Quixote or The Summer's Ramble of Mister Geoffrey Wildgoose. A Comic Romance*. (Oxford: Clarendon Press, 1967), XV, pp. 491–2.

From Richard Jago

Oct.ʳ 25.ᵗʰ 1757.

Sir,

I had the Pleasure of spending the greater Part of the last Week at the Leasows w.ᵗʰ M.ʳ Shenstone who inform'd me of y.ʳ Intention to oblige the public w.ᵗʰ a Continuation of y.ʳ Miscellaneous Collection this Winter, and that he had given You some Trifles of mine w.ᵗʰ a View to their being inserted in one of the succeding Volumes.[1]

I am sensible, Sir how advantageous M.ʳ Shenstone's Recommendation is, and that it is no inconsiderable Compliment to be admitted to a Place in a Collection under so judicious a Compiler: At the same Time Sir, You must permit me to claim such an Interest in my own, as to give my Consent both to the Dress, and the Manner of its Insertion; for w.ᶜʰ Purpose I must desire the Favour of You to send me Proof Sheets, if You have thought proper to print any thing belonging to me, as soon as conveniently You can, w.ᵗʰ an Account of the Time of Publication, & of y.ʳ Intention of reprinting, or not reprinting your former Volumes.²

I shall always be extremely glad of the favour of Yours, and M.ʳ Shenstone's Corrections, yet so as to acquiesce thro' Conviction, rather than implicit Obedience, to w.ᶜʰ Principle You will neither of You have Occasion to object, because it is most rational & I dare say will not be less operative.

I have Reason to believe that y.ʳ approaching Publication will be a Succesful one, as indeed there is the greatest Probability that all in w.ᶜʰ You engage will be, to w.ᶜʰ I am sensible how little I can contribute any further than w.ᵗʰ my good Wishes, who am Sir

Your most Obedient
Humble Servant

Ric. Jago

Please to direct to me at Harbury near Southam in Warwickshire

MS: Humanities Research Center, University of Texas at Austin, Robert Dodsley / Recipient 1/Bound, ff. 65–7.

¹ Six of Jago's poems appeared in Volume V of RD's *Collection* (pp. 70–83).
² Jago is one of Shenstone's few versifying friends who sought to maintain his own artistic integrity by refusing to give his patron and RD *carte blanche* authority over the text of his poems. See his subsequent correspondence with RD on this issue.

To John Hoadly

Oct.ᵗ 26 [1757]¹

⟨Dear⟩ Sir

I rec.ᵈ your excellent Packet of Poetry, for which I am much oblig'd to You & return You my thanks. I will print y.ᵉ the whole of ⟨them⟩ it in the order which you have directed, only omitting one or two of Martial's Epigrams, & y.ᵉ Verses on M.ʳ Hogarth's ⟨Prints⟩ Rake's progress, which I think will be improper, on account of their having been at the bottom of his Prints, and as they will not perfectly be understood by any reader who has not the Prints before him to show the particulars to which the lines refer & this is the opinion of others as well as my own.² M.ʳ Taylor's Dropsical man is already printed.³ Any thing of Lord Hervy's I should be very glad of; a Dialogue of his between Atticus & Eugenio I have.⁴ And if you have any ⟨other⟩ pieces that are perfectly good, either by him or others, I would strive to

nake room for them, as I shall certainly close the Miscellany with these Two
Volumes. To extend it farther would make both the collection & the price too large.
I am ⟨very⟩ much oblig'd to Mʳ Berenger for prevailing with you to send me Mʳ
Straight's Pieces. If he is still with you I beg my compliments. You talk'd of
correcting the Mouse-trap; if you have any alterations I beg You ⟨would⟩ will be so
good as to favour me with them by yᵉ first opportunity, as I have already sent them
o yᵉ Printer.

I am &c

MS: Robert Dodsley Letter Book, Birmingham Public Libraries, ff. 54–55.

On the basis of the verses mentioned within – designed for the next two volumes of RD's *Collection*
(March 1758) – this letter is clearly a response to Hoadly's fully dated letter of 18 October 1757 (q.v.
for subjects mentioned in this letter). Furthermore, as a draft letter in RD's Letter Book, it appears
within the series which are certainly of 1757.
Apparently RD changed his mind, for "Verses under The Prints of Mr. Hogarth's Rake's Progress,
1735" appeared in Volume V, 269–74.
Although Hoadly thought William Taylor's "The Dropsical Man" "old" and "tediously told," it
appeared in Volume VI, 125.
Apparently Hoadly did not send any other pieces of Hervey's, for only one poem of his appeared, "A
Satire in the Manner of Persius, in a Dialogue between Atticus and Eugenio" (V, 147–55).

To Moses Mendes[1]

Octʳ 26 [1757][2]

Dear Sir
    I am much oblig'd to you for yᵉ favour of your elegant Epistle. I assure You it has
given me great pleasure, not only from its Liveliness and Wit, with which
⟨however⟩ it is very richly fraught, but as I ⟨receive⟩ look upon it as a testimony of
your regard and friendship.[3] I have neither time nor abilities to answer it in the
same strain and therefore shall very wisely & prudently decline the attempt,
desiring You will be pleas'd to accept of my acknowledgments in humble but very
honest Prose. ⟨But⟩ It happens oddly enough that saving my belly I am just in the
same situation with regard to Mʳ Garrick, in which you describe the scribblers of
the age. The Tyrant, Sir, has refus'd my Tragedy! I leave you therefore to judge
with what grace I can join with you in laughing at those who rail at him. ⟨on a
similar account⟩ Ought I not rather to join with yᵉ railers? But why should I
trouble You with an affair, of which I take it for granted you are entirely ignorant?
When you come to Town 'tis probable You may hear more of it. I desir'd Mʳ
Tucker to send You an Ode on Terror and Pity; if it should afford you half an hour's
entertainment it will give me pleasure.[4] I am glad to hear you are this Winter
⟨coming⟩ to be my neighbour in Pall mall. ⟨I hope⟩ When you come to Town,
which I suppose will not be long first, I hope I shall have the pleasure of seeing You
more frequently than I have done.

I am &c

MS: Robert Dodsley Letter Book, Birmingham Public Libraries, ff. 56–7.

1 Moses Mendes (d. 1758), poet and dramatist, had acquired a considerable fortune while carrying on his father's business in stocks, which, in turn, enabled him to acquire a substantial estate, St Andrew at Old Buckenham, Norfolk. He had also obtained an MA at Oxford in 1750. In 1755, Mendes had placed two poems in Volume IV of RD's *Collection* (121–55, 300–1).
2 The year is easily established from RD's reference to both *Cleone* and to *Melpomene*. From the context *Melpomene*, published on 29 September 1757, has already appeared, but *Cleone* (December 1758) had yet to be produced. Since Mendes died in February 1758, the letter must be of 1757.
3 Mendes's epistle is not identified.
4 Tucker is most likely the individual addressed in Mendes's "To Mr. S. Tucker," an epistle that appeared later in *A Collection of the Most esteemed pieces of Poetry that have appeared for several Years. With Variety of Originals, by the Late Moses Mendez, Esq; and other Contributors to Dodsley's Collection*. (London Richardson and Urquhart, 1767). As addressed in the poem, Tucker seems to be a businessman "Health to my friend, and to his partner, peace." Since RD says he is having Tucker send him a copy of *Melpomene*, it would seem his business was bookselling, but I cannot find him listed as such anywhere. Possibly this is the Samuel Tucker whose name appears in the list of subscribers prefixed to Spence's *Polymetis* (1747).

To George Faulkner[1]

Oct.ʳ 28.ᵗʰ [1757]

Dear Sir

I am oblig'd to You for making me acquainted with your Nephew Mʳ Smith, have yet had the pleasure of seeing him only once;[3] he tells me You have favour'd me with a present of a Corkscrew; ⟨for which I thank You,⟩ but alas! I have ver near drank up my liquor; or rather, I have quitted the bottle for the pail, and am become a toper in Milk.[4] However, I shall always be very glad to draw a cork for a friend, and therefore I thank you for your present. I transmitted to You an Ode on Terror & Pity which I hope you rec.ᵈ I have not put my Name to it here, but if you think it worth reprinting, you may prefix or omit it just as You please.[5] I shall deliver to your Nephew ⟨some⟩ before Christmas some sheets of my 4ᵗʰ & 5ᵗ Volumes of Miscellanies.[6] I have this day sent to Mʳ Hitch according to your order the remainder of Sir Thomas Prendergast's Numbers (viz: all from N.º 40) of th Body of ⟨Husbandry⟩ Architecture, which I hope you will receive by your firs order from M.ʳ Hitch.[7] I am charg'd here by D.ʳ Shebear with having said in a Letter to you, that he was committed to Newgate for some of his writings. I do no remember that I ever open'd my lips to you about him; ⟨or⟩ and so I told him. but i I had, I dare say you have both more ⟨friend⟩ prudence & more friendship for m than to shew any letter of mine that might do me a prejudice. ⟨with any ⟨one⟩ ⟨body⟩.⟩ I beg You will let me know by a line the first post whether he or any on has the least foundation from You for asserting this.[8]

I am Sir &c

MS: Robert Dodsley Letter Book, Birmingham Public Libraries, ff. 57v–59r.

¹ George Faulkner (1699?–1775), printer and bookseller, of Essex Street, Dublin, has never been adequately linked with RD. But this letter (not mentioned in Robert E. Ward's *Prince of Dublin Printers: the Letters of George Faulkner* (Lexington: University of Kentucky Press, 1972)) helps to call attention to a personal and publishing relationship between RD and Faulkner that lasted for at least ten years. RD twice alludes to his friendship with Faulkner, once thanking him for the gift of a corkscrew, most likely a gesture of appreciation for RD's company during Faulkner's visit to London six months earlier. RD's promise to deliver "sheets of my 4th [second edition] and 5th Volumes of Miscellanies" through Faulkner's nephew clearly expresses the London publisher's cooperation with Faulkner for Dublin editions of his *Collection of Poems by Several Hands*, volumes slated for London publication the following March. In addition, he mentions having sent a copy of his own *Melpomene* ("Ode on Terror & Pity"), published anonymously through Mary Cooper the previous month, and allows Faulkner the decision of whether or not to add the author's name to the Dublin printing. Other matters strengthen the overall portrait suggested in this letter. The son of Faulkner's former master in the trade, William Bowyer the London printer, handled a lot of RD's printing and shared a number of copyrights with RD, among them an edition of Swift (1755), Faulkner's prize publication; Tully's Head is listed in Faulkner's *Dublin Journal* (27 February–3 March 1759) as the only London house taking in subscriptions for *Miscellanies in Prose and Verse* by Samuel Derrick, Faulkner's friend; Faulkner and RD simultaneously published editions of Frances Sheridan's *Memoirs of Miss Sidney Bidulph* (1761).

² The year is determined from the letter's appearance among other letters of 1757 in RD's chronologically arranged Letter Book.

³ Ward (*Prince of Dublin Printers*, p. 75) noted that columns of Faulkner's *Dublin Journal* from 1759 to 1762 show an "S. Smith at Mr. Faulkner's in Essex street." Plomer (*Dictionary of Printers . . . 1726–1775*) lists a Samuel Smith, Bookseller, of Essex Street, from 1758 to 1767. It is not clear whether one or both of these are the same nephew RD met. Plomer also notes, however, that the nephew who took over Faulkner's business in 1776 was Thomas Todd.

⁴ Regularly troubled with the gout, RD seems to be making another attempt at abstinence.

⁵ See note 1.

⁶ Ibid.

⁷ Apparently Faulkner had ordered through RD for Sir Thomas Prendergast (d. 1760), the Irish Postmaster-General, copies of the installment issues of Isaac Ware's *Complete Body of Architecture*, which had finally been published under a single cover the previous year. RD's sending Prendergast's numbers to Charles Hitch, bookseller of Paternoster Row, to accommodate Faulkner, suggests a further working relationship with that bookseller.

RD's pique must arise from his alleged role as *messenger* of information, not as the discoverer of scandal, for the notorious John Shebbeare (1709–88) had already been imprisoned twice (in 1754 and 1755) for his attacks on the Government in his novel *The Marriage Act* and in his sixth in a series of *Letters on the English Nation*.

To Richard Jago

Oct.ʳ 29.ᵗʰ [1757]¹

Sir

I rec^d the favours of yours, in which ⟨it gives⟩ I think I can perceive, & it gives me much concern, that you are not altogether pleas'd with Mr Shenstone's having given me some of your pieces without ⟨your knowledge⟩ first consulting You about them. I acknowledge ye reasonableness of what You urge, & believe it was mere indolence in him that he did not write to You, for I know he intended it. ⟨But⟩ And it gives me ⟨the more pain⟩ ⟨great⟩ the more uneasiness, as I have entirely

⟨printed⟩ work'd off the sheets in which they are inserted. However, I hope Yo
will find them printed correctly, & quite to your mind: or if there should be an
material alterations which You would have made, I will insert them in ⟨the⟩ ⟨an
the Errata at the end of the Volume.² I beg you will believe that nothing was farthe
from my thoughts than yᵉ intention of disobliging a Gentleman of your character
& from whom I had before receiv'd such agreeable favours: & be assur'd that in th
next Edition which I will not print without acquainting You, I shall be very read
to make whatever alterations you may think proper.

I am &c

MS: Robert Dodsley Letter Book, Birmingham Public Libraries, ff. 61v–62r.

¹ The year is certain from the fact that this letter is an obvious response to Jago's fully dated letter to R
on 25 October 1757 in which he gently complains of Shenstone's having submitted his poems to R
for the *Collection* without his sanction or without giving him an opportunity to correct them.
² Jago responded graciously with only two corrections. See his letter of 3 November 1757.

To William Shenstone¹

Pall mall Oct.ʳ 29ᵗʰ 175

Dear Sir

I was in hopes by this time to have had *some* if not *all* of the sheets return'd which
sent for your correction, & which keep a great quantity of the Printer's Lette
lock'd up, much to his inconvenience & disadvantage. As I have now very nea
finish'd both the Volumes, I beg You will be so good as to let me have them with a
possible expedition.² I have this day receiv'd a Letter from Mʳ Jago which gives m
great uneasiness, as I have printed off all his pieces, & he seems desirous to have ha
the proof sheets, that he might have corrected them himself. I shall be very sorr
that by your willingness to oblige me, you should disoblige him. And yet, as they ar
quite printed off it is now impossible he should correct them, unless I cancel the tw
sheets in which they are contain'd; to do which would cost me ten or twelve pounds
I will send him to night the pages which contain his Poems, & tell him, if he find
any material errors, that I will insert them in a list of Errata at yᵉ end of the Volume
I should be extreamly sorry to disoblige any of your friends on this occasion.³ I ha
a letter from Mʳ Giles a post or two ago, in which he told me you desir'd two or thre
proofs of your Grove, which I have here enclos'd.⁴ Where is Mʳ Hylton's India
Eclogue? Is he gone thither to learn their manners? If not, pray give m
Compliments to him, & bid him make haste or he will come too late.⁵ I believe
shall go with Mʳ Spence into the north next Sum̃er, & we intend to call on You for
day or two in our way. I imagine yᵉ *Rural Elegance* will give you most trouble i
correcting: if therefore you can dispatch any of the other sheets first, it will be ver
agreeable to the Printer as it will set *some* of his Letter at liberty. I am

Dear Sir
ever affectionately Yours
R. Dodsle

MS: BL. Add. MS. 28,959, f. 78.

*   A draft copy of this letter is found in RD's Letter Book, ff. 60–1, dated 28 October.
²   This letter is merely the first of RD's many distressful requests to Shenstone to complete work on his portion of the next two volumes of the *Collection*, a matter that would dominate their correspondence for the next three months.
³   See RD's letter to Jago on this same day and Jago's letters of 3 and 21 November.
⁴   See RD's letter to Shenstone on 20 September, notes 2 and 3.
⁵   Hylton did "come too late." See his letter to RD of 24 February 1758.

To Elizabeth Montagu¹

[late 1757?]²

. . . My Vanity is extreamly gratify'd in your approbation, and I am very sensible how much its being countenanced by a Person of Your acknowledg'd Taste, must tend to give a favourable impression of its Merit to others, and I beg You will do me the further favour of accepting the Piece to which You have done so much Honour . . .

Source: Straus, p. 217.

¹   Mrs Elizabeth Montagu (1720–1800), despite her central role in London's fashionable and literary circles, is represented in RD's correspondence by this single fragment of a letter, which, according to Straus, was RD's response to her letter of praise for his recently published *Melpomene*. Only one other occasion of her contact with the bookseller is recorded. In his letter to Graves on 20 November 1762 (Williams, p. 638), Shenstone mentions the visitors that he and RD had entertained at the Leasowes during the past season, and among them is Elizabeth Montagu. Straus's identification of the letter's subject, *Melpomene*, indicates that he had seen either the full text of the letter or Mrs Montagu's holograph, but neither has been discovered; nor is the letter printed in any of the collections of her correspondence.
²   If Straus's determination of the letter's subject is correct, then the letter must post-date 29 September 1757, the day *Melpomene* was published (*LC*).

From Richard Jago

Harbury Nov 3ᵈ 1757

Sir,

Tho' I cannot retract the Right wᶜʰ I claim'd of being advised wᵗʰ concerning the Insertion of some Pieces of mine in yͬ Miscellany, & must regret your Neglect of it in some trivial respects of no Consequence to any body but myself, yet as You inform me that the sheets in wᶜʰ they are contain'd are work'd off, I will give You no more trouble than to insert the annex'd Alterations amongst the Errata at the End of the Volume.

In the Swallows Part ii:

Page 75. Line 11. instead of Forget read Forgot.
Page 76. Line 18. for dark read dank.¹

Whatever Concern I have shewn about this Publication, please Sir, do understand it as respecting the Manner, more than the Substance of what has been done in it: for I cannot be insensible of the Advantage of having any thing of mine pass thro' y.ʳ hands of w.ᶜʰ I see a Fresh Proof in a restored M.S. more than sufficient to attone for The Theft committed on the Cover. I am Sir,

Y.ʳ most humble Servant

Ric Jago.

Address: To / M.ʳ Dodsley Bookseller / in Pall-Mall / London
Postmark: 9 NO   Southam

MS: Humanities Research Center, University of Texas at Austin, Robert Dodsley / Recipient 1 /Bound, ff. 69–71.

¹ See Jago's letter to RD on 25 October and RD's response on 29 October. RD kept his word and included the errata Jago requests at the end of Volume V, the volume in which his poems had appeared.

From Robert Lowth

Sedgefield
Nov.ʳ 3.ᵈ 1757.

Dear S.ʳ

I return your proof-sheet, as so[on as I go?]¹ from hence. I shall be able to do it one[?day or ot-]her, when I get to Durham. In the mea[n time?] observe that what you send me by your [Tuesday?] nights' Post will probably be still a post long[er] in getting back again; for I have no regular m[e-]thod of getting my Letters from Durham y.ᵗ come by that Post. Send me no more Copy: I can do well enough without it, if you will but compose the pages & other *figures* in the references, & see that they are right. I believe there is a Copper Plate of W.ᵐ'ˢ Crosier, w.ᶜʰ is preserv'd at New Coll., engraving at Oxford by Green:² You may perhaps hear something about it from M.ʳ Thos. Warton. When you receive the Monument from Taylor, pray send it on to me.³ If I don't like it, I beleive I shall employ Green to go & take it at Winchester, & engrave it.

Observe, that I spell *Bulle* always with an *e* [at] the end, as being more regular & agreable to t[he ge?]niology, & also to distinguish it from that [other?] word of the same so[und w.ᶜ]ʰ has been [the source of so many?] puns upon this. You will tell [?me that prac]tice & customs are against me, & [?make an app]eal to Johnson's Dictionary, &c. Re-[gardless,?] I think I am right, & believe I could [give?] authorities: but if you contest y.ᵉ matter, [I sub]mit.⁴

[I] am sorry you have let into y.ᵉ secret of [M]elpomene.⁵ I had intended to have made some [in]quiries of you about it. I should have desir'd you to inform me who was the Author; for that I had read it several times, & could not guess at him, not knowing any one that was capable of writing it. I observe that y.ᵉ prevailing fashion of Odes at present is to be drest out in abundance of fine imagery & fine words, which do not permit the reader to come at the sense that may be at the bottom, but at the expence of the Tenth reading & hard study into the bargain: here I found a Noble Plan invented, dispos'd, & excecuted, [w]ith great spirit, sublimity, & force of imagination; [at] ye same time clear & perspicuous throughout, [?] connexions, descriptions, & ye whole expres-[sions] wch excells in an unaffected simplicity [and warm]th: – thi[s & more] I should have said to you; but since I find I a[m informed of the?] Author, I have nothing further now to [say; however?] there is one word in it to wch I have an [objection?] & the greater, because it is the *last* [?] Be pleas'd to consider, whether to *fly* [*away?*] & to *fly*, or to go swiftly away, are not two [distinct?] words; whether *flew*, the past time of ye fo[rmer?] expresses more than *was upon the wing*, with [out] any intimation of *to* or *from*, coming or *going*; [&] whether to express what you mean, you should n[ot] have said, *fled*, or *flew away*.⁶ I mention this, because I am willing to suppose y^t ye Public have taste enough to call for a new Edition of Melpomene soon; when, if you approve of my remark, you may easily alter it: and I expect that you repay me my Criticism in kind & with interest. I should have thought that this Prologue might have easily introduced Cleone: but perhaps it may be an objection against Melpomene in the Ode too, that she deals too muc[h] in the strong, the simple, & the intelligible. If [such] is the case I enter my Protest ag^t ye public [?senti-]:ment, & heartily thank you for the unus[ual plea]sure it has given me.

[I have finished?] the leaves wch I wanted to [revise and will?] return y^m by the next Packet. [Warton?] may perhaps send you from Oxford [? a drawin]g of W^m's Arms for ye Pedigree: if [not, I?] shall send you a small print of y^m to [use?] for direction, as soon as I hear from him.

Believe me ever,

Dear S^r
Your most Affectionate
humble Servt

R. Lowth.

MS: BL. Add. MS. 35,339, ff. 16–17.

¹ The manuscript has deteriorated down the right margin. The letter is principally concerned with the preparation of Lowth's *The Life of William Wykeham* to appear the following May.

² John Green (fl. 1758) ultimately drew and engraved the cut of William of Wykeham's crosier that appears facing p. 286 in Lowth's *Life*.

³ See Lowth's letter to RD of early September 1757, note 7.

⁴ Johnson used the traditional spelling, "bull."

⁵ *Melpomene* had been published anonymously and from Mary Cooper's shop, not from RD's own. Initially RD had let only Shenstone and Graves in on his secret.

⁶ Within the context, Lowth's criticism seems apt. The last stanza of *Melpomene* ran:

While awe-struck thus I stood,
The Bowers, the lawn, the wood,
The *Form Celestial*, fading on my view,
Dissolv'd in liquid air, and all the vision flew.

Nonetheless, RD seems either to have disagreed with or to have forgotten Lowth's suggestion when he reprinted *Melpomene* in December 1758, appending it to his new, successful tragedy, *Cleone*, for in that edition the text remains "flew."

To Thomas Gataker[1]

Novr 4.th [1757][2]

Dear Sir

Your kind offer to mediate a reconciliation between Mr Garrick and me I look upon as proceeding from ⟨your friendship, and am⟩ ⟨a⟩ your mutual regard ⟨for⟩ to us both, and for my part, I am much oblig'd to You for it. I have no objection to a renewal of that friendship which subsisted for so many years between us; on the contrary You know I have regreted the loss of it, both on his own account, and on account of many ⟨agreeable⟩ friends with whom we are both connected. But however desirous I might be of renewing ⟨& living⟩ a friendship with so agreeable a man as Mr Garrick, I cannot meanly seek it, as he well knows I was not the first who sought ye quarrel, and as I cannot help thinking my self ye injur'd person. I will explain what I mean by this last, as he will probably say he has done me no injury, having a right to act or refuse whatever he may think proper. No doubt he has such a right, and I only mean that I suffer a *consequential* injury, as the public will be very apt to ⟨judge that⟩ imagine a Play refus'd, is a Play unworthy to be acted. Now I had some reason to hope that ye Tragedy in question was not of this kind, having shewn it to ⟨many⟩ several of the very best judges ⟨which⟩ amongst ye circle of my acquaintance persons of acknowledg'd taste & abilities, from whom I receiv'd such testimonies in its favour ⟨(many of which you have seen)⟩ wch you shall see whenever you please as gave me fair ground ⟨to hope⟩, if not ⟨for its⟩ to expect its success, at least to ⟨hope⟩ flatter my self that it would have been thought ⟨not unworthy⟩ worthy of a trial, especially as I look'd upon Mr Garrick as my particular friend. I will not at present repeat the manner in which all these hopes were frustrated, because I am willing to bury in oblivion every disagreable circumstance that has past between us. You tell me ⟨he⟩ Mr Garrick is in the same disposition; it will give me great pleasure to find ⟨that he is⟩ him so far in earnest, as to accept of the following Proposal. If Mr Garrick will act the Tragedy of Cleone, in the manner I intended it to be cast, any time betwixt ⟨the present⟩ now and ye latter end of Feb.^{ry} either this year or the next, I will agree to give up all ⟨my⟩ rights to any profits that may arise from ye author's nights in case of its success: that is, the profits of the 3.^d Night shall be appropriated to ye use of the Society for the Encouragement of Arts, Manufactures & Commerce;[3] of the 6.th night, to the Foundling Hospital, and of ye 9.th night to whatsoever ⟨purpose⟩ public use Mr Garrick shall think proper.

I am &c

MS: Robert Dodsley Letter Book, Birmingham Public Libraries, ff. 63–65.

[1] Dr Thomas Gataker (d. 1768), surgeon at Charing Cross Hospital, was the author of several medical works published by the Dodsleys in the 1750s and 1760s. Gataker also contributed an essay on vocations to RD's periodical *The World* (No. 184, 8 July 1756, pp. 143–8). The physician and his wife appear to have been particular friends of RD's as this letter and other RD letters (to Berenger, 10 January 1758; to Shenstone, 22 August 1758 and 20 November 1762) suggest. Edmund Burke's letter of *c.* 6 September 1759 informed RD: "You cannot meet anybody who is more your friend than Mrs. Gataker."

² This letter seems surely a product of 1757, a time when RD openly referred to Garrick as a "tyrant."
  (See his letter to Lowth, *post* 4 November 1757.) It cannot be of 1758 because, by October of that year,
  Cleone, the subject of this letter, is already in rehearsal at Rich's Covent Garden. Although its sense
  could fit 1756 (see RD's heated exchange with Garrick in October), its entry in draft form in RD's
  Letter Book follows that of his letter to Jago on 29 October, a piece that can easily be dated as 1757.
³ See RD's letter to Garrick November 1757, note 4.

To Robert Lowth

[*post* 4 November; *ante* 3 December 1757][1]

Dear Sir

I did not apprehend any danger in corresponding with You; but I am afraid I shall grow so proud & ⟨vain⟩ conceited on your opinion of my Ode, that my friends will not be able to bear my vanity: and you will have the sin to answer for of having made me a bad man, by endeavouring to perswade me that I am (in this instance at least) a good Poet. To confess the truth, ⟨I made my addresses to the Lady Melpomene with some assiduity,⟩ I have long been ⟨her⟩ an admirer of the fair Melpomene, of late had made my addresses to her with some assiduity, and ⟨may?⟩ flatter'd by my friends, that ⟨by the means⟩ thro' the intrest of one Cleone a retainer of hers, I had made some impression on her heart, I thought my self in a fair way of gaining her good graces. But the King of her Country,[2] being inform'd by the said Cleone of my ⟨audacious⟩ design on his favorite ⟨Daughter⟩ Melpomene forbad my entrance into his Dominions on pain of Damnation, deem'd my humble suit audacious and presuming, and dismiss'd ⟨the ward?⟩ poor Cleone from his presence with visible marks of ⟨disgrace⟩ unkindness and disgrace. Piqued at this repulse, I publish'd my Ode on Terror and Pity, to shew yᵉ World my pretensions, and to let the Tyrant see, ⟨how familiar I had been with his Daughter⟩ tho' he scorn'd my offers, that the Lady had not disdain'd to admit me into ⟨her most⟩ some of her secret Misteries. But as I must endeavour to suppress my Passion, the best way is to talk of it as little as possible, so with Compliments to Mʳˢ Lowth I conclude my self, Dʳ Sir

MS: Robert Dodsley Letter Book, Birmingham Public Libraries, ff. 65v–67r.

[1] RD's acknowledgement of Lowth's praise for *Melpomene* (published 29 September 1757) identifies this
  letter as a response to Lowth's letter of 3 November 1757. The letter's placement in RD's Letter Book
  shows it to have been entered after RD's 4 November letter to Thomas Gataker, but before his 3
  December letter to Shenstone, which has its date corroborated in the "sent" version among the BL
  manuscripts.   [2] Garrick.

From John Pixell

Edgbaston Nov: yᵉ 7ᵗʰ 1757

Dear Sʳ

If I am not too late in my Application, I beg You to correct the following Verses, so as allow them a Place in your Collection. They were written but a few days ago, just as You see them, by Miss White – the young Lady who lives in my house, & was first set a scribling by Mr Shenstone.[1] You must know She has lately found out an Echo in my Garden near the Screen on which my Verses are inscribed, which You know Complain of Mr Shenstone, that Echo wants his sweetest Lay. If these Verses are inserted immediately after mine, they will serve to explain that little Obscurity of Expression, & at the same time You will by this means have the Pleasure of greatly obliging[2]

your truly affectionate Friend

J P P Pixell –

P.S. I am just this moment return'd from Mr Shenstone who is put into a violent Hurry by your last letter.[3] –

Address: To | Mr Dodsley at | Tully's head | in | Pall-Mall | London
Postmark: 9 NO Birmingham

Verses occasion'd by an Echo found in
the above-mention'd Garden.
written by a Young Lady.
Art thou the Nymph in Shenstone's Dale
That dost with plantive note bewail,
That he forsakes the Aonian Maids
To court inconstant Rills and Shades?
Mourn not, sweet Nymph; Alas! in vain
Do They still smile, & Thou complain;
Yet whilst he woo'd the gentle Train
With softest Song, & sweetest Strain,
Along the Lawn, or through the Wood,
Or by the Margin of the flood,
The list'ning herd around him stray'd
With Wanton Frisks the Lambkins play'd;
In speechless Joy the Faunus stood
And ev'ry Dryad of the Wood[4]
And ev'ry Naiad ceas'd to lave
Her azure Limbs amid the Wave:
The Graces danc'd, the Rosy Band
Of Smiles & Loves went hand in hand,
And purple Pleasure strow'd the Way
With sweetest Flow'rs; & ev'ry Ray
Of each fond Muse, with Rapture fir'd
To glowing thoughts his breast inspir'd.
The hills rejoic'd, the Vallies rung
All Nature smil'd, while Shenstone sung
His tuneful Lay – But now no more –
Ah! why dostd *thou* repeat – no more?

Ev'n *now* he hies to deck the Grove,
And ev'ry Scene the Muses love;
He soon again will own their Sway,
And Thou shalt catch the tender Lay;
And with harmonious Number fill
Each rocky Cave, & vocal Hill.[5]

I fear M[r] Hylton will be too late with his Indian Eclogue –

MS: Humanities Research Center, University of Texas at Austin, Robert Dodsley / Recipient 1/Bound, ff. 125–7.

[1] Pixell's plea on behalf of Miss White's abysmal verses (see below) strikes a humorous note. The "Miss White – the young Lady who lives in my house" became Pixell's second wife in 1759. She was the daughter of the former rector of Edgbaston. (See Courtney, pp. 119–21, and Ian Gordon, ed. *Shenstone's Miscellany* (Oxford: Clarendon Press, 1952) p. 139).
[2] Apparently RD politely excused himself, "sacrificing" the value of placing Miss White's verses immediately after Pixell's "Transcrib'd from the Rev. Mr. Pixell's Parsonage Garden near Birmingham 1753" in Volume V of his *Collection* (p. 83).
[3] See RD's letter of 29 October.
[4] Here Pixell adds the note, "A Statue in the farm at the Leasowes."
[5] Although Ian Gordon says (p. 139) that none of Miss White's poems seem to have been published, the enclosed verses, in a much altered state, were included in RD's edition of Shenstone's *Works* (1764), II, 378–9. Perhaps Shenstone's affinity for Miss White's poems – he copied six of them into his Miscellany – supplied the motivation.

From Richard Jago

Nov[r] 21st 1757.
Harbury near Southam, Warwickshire

Sir,

I cannot suffer so feeling a Mind as Yours to remain a Moment in Perplexity upon my Account, and therefore I sit down to releive it from that distress, into w[ch] my last has brought You contrary to my Intentions w[ch] were only to allude to a Fact of so late a date as the last Summer, and which I thought the Circumstances mention'd by me wou'd have been sufficient to recall to y[r] Memory. The whole Affair is neither more, nor less than this, that M[r] Shenstone, amongst other things, put into y[r] hands at the Leasows a Pastoral, on w[ch] I have the Pleasure to see You have bestow'd some Corrections, of w[ch] I purpose to avail myself and to account for its being in greater outward Deshabille than when it was sent to him, he thought proper to tell me that it was owing to some desire You had shewn of taking it along wth my other Pieces for y[r] Miscellany; but that upon his recollecting that I had not settled the Reading, nor the Manner of its appearance, he had withdrawn it, & laid it by for my determination.[1]

And now my hand is in Sir, I will tell You another Secret relating to this Subject, w[ch] is that if M[r] Dodsley can contrive, without damage to himself, to make this

same Pastoral Writing convey a few Guineas into my Pocket, I may possibly make
Use of them before the rising of the Parliament to consult further wth him about its
Publication. I am very sensible of the Slenderness of its Merit, but I am fully as
sensible that my hoarding Money has in so small a Compass that it is highly
expedient by some lawful Means or other to meditate an Addition to it before I set
forward on such an Expedition. How honest, or practicable an Expedient this may
be for the above purpose must be referr'd to y.^r Consideration by Sir,

> Your most Obedient Humble Servant
>
> Ric. Jago.

_MS:_ Humanities Research Center, University of Texas at Austin, Robert Dodsley / Recipient 1/Bound,
ff. 73–5.

¹ It is not clear whether this "pastoral" is indeed one of the Jago poems published by RD in Volume V of
the _Collection_ or whether it represents still another not represented in the miscellany. In any event, it
does not seem that RD ever published a poem of Jago's in pamphlet form, as the author proposes
below.

To David Garrick¹

[November 1757]

Sir

I have at last, tho' with some reluctance, determin'd to publish the following
Scenes, w.^ch ⟨I will not venture⟩ it may be presumption to call a Tragedy, as You
have not thought them worthy of being represented as such at the Theater in Drury
Lane. It is now ⟨upwards of⟩ between two & three Years since you first favour'd
me with a perusal of this Piece, which I then told You I should not have ventur'd to
offer to ye public had I not been encourag'd to it by the favourable opinions of
several of the best Judges amongst my Acquaintance. I forbear to mention Names,
for tho' the list would do me ⟨infinite⟩ Honour, ⟨but⟩ it might carry an air of ⟨?⟩
ostentation & vanity which I should chuse to conceal. I will ingenuously confess
however, I ⟨kept⟩ have kept ⟨it⟩ ye Piece by me thus long, in expectation ⟨?⟩ that
from the concurrence of these opinions, with those of several others of your own
friends, very eminent in the republic of Letters, you might possibly ⟨be⟩ have been
induc'd to honour it with the indulgence of a Trial. But no ⟨such intention
appearing⟩ intimation of change ⟨of⟩ in your sentiments appearing, I have now
relinquish'd ⟨that⟩ the vain hope of seeing it on the Stage, (ye only point of view in
which a Dramatic Performance can be seen to an advantage) and must content my
self with setting it before the public in ye dim light of a printed Pamphlet. How
much of ⟨the⟩ its Terror & Passion ⟨will⟩ ⟨may⟩ will be lost in this imperfect view,
may be easily ⟨imagin'd⟩ conceiv'd; for ⟨that⟩ it is not ⟨quite destitute of passion
the view of every one⟩ who ⟨has⟩ reads it, ⟨[?] But let me not be betray'd into any
thing that may look like a defense of my own Performance⟩ that ⟨can⟩ will be able
to supply his Imagination the striking Graces of Action, & expressive Feelings, with
which I have sometimes flatter'd my self, You & Mrs Cibber ⟨would⟩ might have
animated some of the Scenes.

Let me not be betray'd into saying any thing ⟨that⟩ which may look like self-
pprobation: ⟨it is extreamly disagreeable to me to speak at all on this Subject; and
othing but the mortification of being obliged to publish a reject'd Play ⟨Piece⟩
Play⟩ could have induc'd me so far to differ with a person of your judgement as
ill to suppose to say ⟨that either⟩ but if I have not been more flatter'd than it can
e ⟨supposed⟩ well imagin'd a person of my small consequence would be, the Piece
may yet have⟩ ⟨is certainly⟩ not quite ⟨is probably⟩ destitute of some degree of
heatrical Merit.⟩ I am sensible the Play has many defects, ⟨which⟩ ⟨but⟩ & I will
nly apologize for them by ⟨saying I⟩ confessing that I could make it no better; ⟨&
hat⟩ I ⟨never⟩ had not the vanity to think of producing a perfect Tragedy, as I
ever remember to have seen that way so. but if I have not been more flatter'd than
: can well be imagin'd a person of my small consequence would be, it might
robably have pass'd with pardon, if not with applause. I will not venture to say
ore in its behalf; I am afraid this is full as much as it deserves: besides, it is now
efore the Public, ⟨and who⟩ and must ⟨speak for itself, they⟩ tell its own story as
ell as it can; they will not be bias'd in its favour by any thing I could say, ⟨?⟩ were I
ver so much dispos'd to defend it, which however I am by no means inclin'd to
ttempt.

After all, tis very possible I may be more oblig'd to You for refusing it, tho' it
night somewhat chagrin me at first, than to any of those Friends ⟨I have⟩ whose
entiments (perhaps too partial in its favour) might have betray'd me into dangers,
rom which I am now Sir happily preferr'd by your more kind severity. For tho' I
ave endeavour'd and at yᵉ expense of some time and pains, ⟨to give to the Public
Tragedy⟩ in yᵉ production of this piece, to form a Fable on one single striking
ʿimportant⟩ Action tho' I have attempted to ⟨draw⟩ draw ⟨and⟩ and enforce
rom ⟨every part of⟩ this Fable an important Moral, have labour'd that ye conduct
of the ⟨Whole⟩ Piece should be easy and unembarrass'd, & the Passions strong and
arious; tho' I have aim'd at nature and simplicity in the Language, at propriety in
he Sentiments, and that the circumstances and incidents should be interesting and
ffecting, yet I am very sensible how probable it is I may have fail'd of success in the
xecution of ⟨all or any⟩ some or all of these things: only give me leave once more to
bserve that if I have so entirely fail'd as You seem to think ⟨I have⟩ I have ⟨some⟩
everal persons of the best and most ⟨allow'd Judges⟩ acknowledg'd taste and
udgment have either been mistaken themselves, or have unaccountably concurr'd
n flattering and deceiving me. But whatever may be the case, for I will seek no
arther into your reasons for rejecting it, I assure you all animosity and resentment
ave long subsided in my breast; I now submit it to yours and to ye Public
ʿconsideration⟩ view with perfect tranquility and resignation, & if you should ever
o far change your opinion as to think it worthy of a trial on your Stage, I hereby
ive up all claim to any profits which might possibly arise ⟨to the author from⟩
rom the author's nights in case of its success, and if such faint shadow of advantage
s worth acceptance, transfer & assign them, ⟨as far as I have power to do so⟩ to the
se of the Society for yᵉ Encouragement of Arts, Manufactures & Commerce.

I am &c

MS: The Bancroft Library, University of California at Berkeley, ff. [13?]–17.

¹ Though it bears no address or signature, this holograph letter is a draft of RD's letter to David Garric
that follows. It is printed here because it carries approximately thirteen more lines than the fair cop
showing RD's numerous turns of mind as he came to grips with a difficult topic. For the annotatio
see the fair copy, presented next.

To David Garrick

[November 1757]

Sir

I have at last, altho' with some reluctance, determin'd to print the Tragedy c
Cleone. I am sensible of the prejudice that will lie against it from your refusal; an
that it will have your popularity to struggle with, as well as its own defects: but
resign it to its fate; with some faint hope, however, of a more favourable receptio
from the Public than You thought proper to afford it.

It is now almost three years ago, since I offer'd this Piece to your perusal
declareing that I should not have ventur'd to risk the opinion of the Public, bu
thro' the encouragement I had receiv'd from the best Judges amongst m
⟨acquaintances⟩ Friends; of whose sincerity in giving me their sentiments, I coul
have no doubt; & several of whose Names I then mention'd to You. I forbear t
repeat them here; for tho' the list would do me honour, it might carry an air c
ostentation which I would chuse to avoid. However, 'twas the concurrence of thes
opinions with those of several of your own friends, Gentlemen of abilities an
acknowledg'd eminence in the Republic of Letters, that gave me hopes You migh
at length have honour'd it with the indulgence of a trial. But as no intimation ha
yet appear'd of any change in your sentiments, I relinquish all expectation of eve
seeing it upon the Stage, (where *alone* a dramatic performance can be seen to an
advantage) and am content to set it before the public in the dim light of a printe
pamphlet. How much of its force and passion must be lost in this imperfect view
may be readily enough conceiv'd by a person of the least degree of candor
doubtless, there are not *many* readers, who can supply to their imagination, thos
striking graces and expressive feelings, with which, I flatter myself, it might hav
been animated by *yourself* and M.ʳˢ *Cibber*.²

Let me not be betray'd into the appearance of self applause. I am sensible yᵉ Pla
has defects, and will only apologize for them by a confession that I could render i
no better. I had not the vanity of hoping to produce a perfect piece, no
remembering ever to have *seen* one. But if I have not been more flatter'd than it ca
well be imagin'd a person of so small importance would be, it is not totally withou
merit, and might have succeeded, had you thought fit, to the extent of my moderat
ambition. However, it is now before the public, and must speak for itself.³ After all
it is very possible I may be more oblig'd to You, than to those friends whose mor
favourable sentiments might have betray'd me into danger. For tho' I hav
endeavour'd to form a Fable upon one single striking Action; have attempted from
this fable to deduce an important Moral; have striven to render the Conduct of it
easy & unembarrass'd; the Passions, lively and various; the Incidents an

ircumstances, interesting and affecting: tho' I have study'd truth and propriety in
e Sentiments; & have aim'd at Nature and Simplicity in ye Language; yet 'tis
robable I may have been deficient in some, or all of these particulars. Give me
:ave only to repeat, that if I have been entirely unsuccessful, many persons of the
10st acknowledg'd Taste, have either been mistaken *themselves*, or have unaccount-
bly concurr'd in flattering & deceiving *me*. An Apology of some significance for the
uthor, if not for the Play.

But I will seek no farther into your reasons for rejecting it, as all resentment on
hat account has long subsided in my bosom. To yours, and to the public perusal I
ubmit it, with the utmost tranquility, & most perfect resignation. And should You
ver so far change your Sentiments as to think it worthy of a trial, I here relinquish
ll profits that can possibly arise from its success on the Stage, and (might so faint a
1adow of advantage be deem'd worthy of acceptance) could wish to transfer them
) the SOCIETY for the ENCOURAGEMENT of ARTS, MANUFACTURES, and COMMERCE.[4]

[unsigned][5]

1S: Harvard Theatre Collection, Harvard College Library.

The year is fairly certain and the month approximated. Within, RD says that it has been almost three
years since he first proposed *Cleone* to Garrick. The first hint of that offer – in this collection – occurs in
Richard Berenger's letter of 31 May 1756 (q. v.). There Berenger offers to read RD's tragedy and to
intercede with Garrick (who had already rejected it) if he thinks it stageworthy. He indicates that
Garrick, at the moment, "has nothing more to say [about *Cleone*] in addition to what he said to you
himself, or to what I said to you from him." Apparently some time had elapsed since Garrick's
rejection. Given the reading time for a new play, one might reasonably expect that Garrick had
received the work at least a month or two earlier. But then when Berenger adds "As so much has been
said and such opposite opinions about your Tragedy," it seems as if the play had been read by several
people, perhaps by a few of Garrick's readers. That would mean that several months had passed since
RD had first submitted the play, perhaps at the beginning of the year, or even the end of the previous
year, 1755; that is, "almost three years" before the proposed date of this letter.

Additional evidence for a November 1757 dating is found in the similar proposals in both this letter
and RD's letter to Thomas Gataker on 4 November 1757 (q. v.). In response to Gataker, who was
attempting to patch up the quarrel between RD and the theatre manager over the final rejection of
Cleone, RD likewise proposes that if Garrick would act the tragedy at Drury Lane, RD would donate
the profits of his author nights to the Society for the Encouragement of Arts, Manufactures, and
Commerce. Such a singular proposal had never been hinted at in all of RD's previous correspondence
regarding *Cleone*. Finally, in all Garrick's earlier rejections of the play, RD begrudgingly acquiesced
and simply went about making further revisions. This is the first time that he has considered printing
the play, suggesting a certain finality to his negotiations with Garrick, the situation in later 1757. On
the other hand, by 19 December 1757, it is clear from RD's letter to Lord Chesterfield on that date that
he has given up the idea of printing the play in favor of offering it to John Rich for performance at
Covent Garden.

Susannah Cibber (1714–66), estranged wife of Theophilus Cibber. A celebrated actress since the mid-
1740s, she had joined Garrick's company at Drury Lane in 1753. RD had published her comedy *The
Oracle* in 1752, having paid £31.10.0 for the copyright. (See Appendix B.)

RD is speaking rhetorically; the tragedy was not printed until 7 December 1758 (*LEP*); that is, until
after it was acted at Covent Garden.

RD had been elected a member of the Society on 2 July 1755 and, on 6 April 1757, had been
unanimously elected "Printer and Stationer" to the Society. He remained a dues-paying member
until his death in 1764. See my article, "Robert Dodsley: The First Printer and Stationer to the
Society," *Journal of the Royal Society of Arts* (July, August, 1983), 480–3; 563–6.

⁵ A signed, "sent" copy of this letter has not turned up. If RD had delayed in sending one, perhaps in the meantime he had learned of Mrs Bellamy's and Mr Barry's joining John Rich's company at Covent Garden (see his letter to the Earl of Chesterfield on 19 December), causing him to seek the tragedy' performance at Rich's theatre rather than its printing. If such was the case, the motivation for actuall sending this letter would have disappeared.

To William Shenstone

Pall mall Decr 3^d [1757]

Dear Sir

I have receiv'd both Sheet B and D, but by the alterations you have made, ther will want about three pages to fill up Sheet C, wch I hope you will take care t supply from your hidden stores. I fill'd up Sheet D with your verses on Riddles, & with Mr Whistler's two small pieces, which I put in between Mr Graves's & yours. I think ye Speech of Nancy of the Vale had better be mark'd as it is, than printed i Italics.³ I cannot like – *Paradise's* – Nor do I think there is the least occasion for Note to explain the other reading.⁴ I have not been able to find a better word tha *mouldering* in The Ode to Health but I will keep the sheet unwork'd for a week, tha you may have time to find a better, but I think it will be difficult.⁵ What think you o the word *blame* instead of *tax*, in the Winter's Visit?⁶ Surely You have mucl improv'd ye Ode after Sickness. Suppose the 3^d Line of it should be

And wander'd forth alone;⁷

I have taken care to indent the Lines in this Ode as You directed, and the whole of i comes into this sheet, so that there will want at least three pages to fill up Sheet C.⁸ am extreamly sorry to hear you are not well, & on that account am really bot afraid and asham'd to press you about the other two Sheets; if therefore you can le me have them any time before Christmas, it will do very well. I am just upon th point of concluding both the Volumes, and if any farther touches are to be given t the plate, pray let me have your directions.⁹ I beg my compliments to Mr Hylton & to Molly, and am

Dear Sir

most affectionately yours

R. Dodsle

MS: BL. Add. MS. 28,959. ff. 79–80.

¹ From the clearly stated forwardness of Volumes V and VI of RD's *Collection*, which would appear i March 1758, this letter must be of December 1757. A draft copy of this letter in RD's Letter Boo corroborates this dating.
² "Upon Riddles" (V, 57–8); Anthony Whistler's two pieces (V, 60–1); Graves's poems began on p. 6 of Volume V.   ³ Italics were not used, merely quotation marks.
⁴ RD was probably referring to the use of "paradise's" in the second stanza of "Ode to Indolence" (V 19–20), the poem that followed "Nancy of the Vale" in the *Collection*. In this instance, Shenstone di not yield.
⁵ See RD's letter to the poet on 18–[20?] December, note 3. "Mouldering" was eventually used in th text.   ⁶ "Blame" was used.

⁷ RD's suggestion was accepted, although Shenstone had penned in on the otherwise blank f. 80ʳ, "Forth I rang'd alone."

⁸ Shenstone cooperated, supplying at least three additional poems to fill sheet C of Volume V: "Ode. Written 1739" (pp. 34–5), "Song I" of "Love Songs" (p. 38), and "Compliment in 1743." RD did not use the last. See his letter of 18–[20?] December.

⁹ The plate for the cut of Shenstone's famed Virgil's Grove at the Leasowes, which was used at the head of Shenstone's "Rural Elegance," the opening poem in Volume V. RD also used the same scene, but a different engraving, to conclude that printing of *Melpomene* which was appended to the 1759 edition of *Cleone*.

To John Hoadly

Dec 5 [1757]¹

Sir

You will doubtles wonder why I have been so long silent after receiving yᵉ favour of your ten Volumes of Poetry. The reason was, that I was desirous of reading them all over, that I might give you but one trouble, & I have been so interrupted with business of other kinds that I could not accomplish that point sooner. I find I have already many pieces, which have been sent me from different quarters, that are in your volumes, but I heartily wish I had had them sooner, as there are many which I might have inserted ⟨which I⟩ but now have not room for. However I have mark'd several which I send You in a paper enclos'd, & if there are any of them which you would not have me insert, you will favour me with a line to point out which they are. I have mark'd yᵉ *Indolent*, I wonder you omitted it, however as it cannot come with your others I will not insert it unless you permit.² You expected Mʳ Berenger to call on You at Winchester; if he is with you I beg my compliments. And now, tho' I have been so long in answering yours, I am so unreasonable as to beg you will favour me with an answer as soon as possible, as I am desirous of finishing yᵉ Volumes before Christmas.

MS: Robert Dodsley Letter Book, Birmingham Public Libraries, ff. 70–1.

¹ The letter is obviously a follow-up to RD's letter to Hoadly on 26 October and a response to Hoadly's untraced reply. In the former, RD thanked Hoadly for the packet of poetry he had sent for Volumes V and VI of the *Collection* and asked for more. Furthermore, in light of the implied progress of these volumes, the letter can fit only 1757. Finally, the year 1757 is corroborated by the letter's placement in RD's Letter Book.

² "The Indolent" appeared in Volume VI, 294–5.

From John Scott Hylton

Lapall = House, Hales = Owen near Birmingham
6ᵗʰ Decʳ 1757.

Dear Mʳ Dodsley,

I am ashamed, and almost afraid to take up the pen to write to you, considering of how little importance my letter is likely to prove, and how much less my pretentions are to expect any further Indulgence from you, in point of time I mean, wherein I may be able to finish my Eclogue.[1] I have wrote about 60 lines, which will be the better half of my production, but M.ʳ Shenstone tells me I shall now be too late, and I have small encouragement to proceed, for he is too much embarras'd with his own peices to attend to mine; add to this I have now a great deal of Tenants business upon my Hands and other unforeseen and unavoidable Avocations, that exclude Poetry, and every other Amusement. – What can I do, how long will it be before you print off, will it be 3 weeks? If the day of Grace be not past, I will repent me of my Idleness and double my endeavours to complete my peice as well as I am able. – I have been often with M.ʳ Shenstone, and he is now busy in correcting the remainder of the Sheets, he has not been either in good Health or good Spirits to attend to any Thing, and it has caused him no small degree of uneasiness that the attention requisite to his own Affairs should prove prejudicial to the execution of yours.[2] – I have a Box of papers and Writings that my Attorney will send down to me by the Coach next Monday, and should be obliged to you if you would send the following Books for me in two parcels to M.ʳ Edw.ᵈ Inge Attorney at Law in great Brook Street near Hanover Square.[3] – West on the Resurrection, [& L.ᵈ Ly]ttelton's Letter annexed to it, and the Preceptor.[4] – any time this [week.] I am much obliged to you for your Ode, which you were so kind as to send me, & think it an exceeding good one: M.ʳ Shenstone w.ᵈ have your Name affixed to it; and I do not see why it should not.[5] – I wish I could come to Town, I would but can not, then should I know all that I have to hope or fear, and if there is no prospect of my compleating my Eclogue time enough, I hope you will forgive me for so vain an Attempt to shine in an Undertaking superior to my Genius.

I am Dear Sir

Y.ʳ most obliged & obedient,

Hble Servant,

John Scott Hylton

P.S. I beg my compliments to your Bro.ʳ who I hope is well. Lord Dudley's death has put an end to all Franks, with me.[6]

Address: To / M.ʳ Dodsley / in / Pall = Mall / London
Postmark: 8 DE Birmingham

MS: Humanities Research Center, University of Texas at Austin, Robert Dodsley / Recipient 1 /Bound, ff. 13–16.

[1] Hylton did not complete his "Indian Eclogue." See his letter to RD on 24 February 1758.

[2] Shenstone's health continued to deteriorate to the point where Hylton, acting as his nurse through early 1758, withheld incoming letters so as not to tire him.

[3] See Hylton's letter to RD on 9 February 1758.

[4] Gilbert West, *Observations on the History and Evidence of the Resurrection of Jesus Christ*, published by RD in 1746; George, Lord Lyttelton, *Observations on the Conversion and Apostleship of St. Paul*, in a *Letter to G. West, Esq.*, also published by RD in 1747. RD had edited and published *The Preceptor: Containing a General Course of Education* in 1748 and had issued a second edition of the two-volume work in 1753.

⁵ RD had published *Melpomene* anonymously.
⁶ Fernando Lea Dudley, 5th Baron Dudley, had died on 21 October.

To William Shenstone

Pall mall Dec.ʳ 18.ᵗʰ[–20? 1757]¹

Dear Sir

   I am extreamly sorry your corrections of Mʳ Whistler's Song came too late: that sheet was work'd off a week before.² And I have this morning put to press Sheet B, taking it for granted you will not easily find a Word that will suit a decay'd Cell and a sickly Carkass better than *mouldering*.³ I am now in daily expectation of Sheet C; in which You will be so good as to send as much new Copy as will fill three pages and a half, as half the first page of C is taken into B, & three of the latter pages carry'd into D. If any more touches are to be given to the plate, pray send me yᵉ improvements as soon as possible.⁴ The whole of the two volumes is now sent to press and will be finish'd next week; so that I only wait for your two remaining sheets. I beg however you will not so hurry your self in your corrections as not to give time to satisfy your self in them; as I am sensible how disagreeable ⟨that⟩ it will be to You either to hurry too much, or correct too little; and it really gives me additional pain, as you complain of ill health and low spirits. I wish you would come and keep your Christmas in Town, surely it would do you good; I am certain at least it would do me good. Thus far I had written on Saturday but was call'd away & did not finish my letter; & yesterday I receiv'd your packet. I observe you have sent me some pieces to fill up Sheet C, but not the sheet it self, but I suppose that will come by the next post. As to your various Readings, however flattering to my vanity your Partiallity may be, I feel my self unequal to the task of deciding where You are doubtful. I think in general you have fixt the best readings, but if I must expose my self, suppose the first three lines of yᵉ Ode in 1739 were to stand thus –

aid

'Twas not by beauty's charms alone,

That Love's imperial Power was known,

Or hearts were captive made:⁵

betray'd seems there not quite yᵉ proper word; besides you have it in the next Stanza.
Stanza 3ᵈ L 1. for, the lightings – suppose quick Lightening? Ibid. L 5

Till lips & eyes at once conspire.⁶

Stanza 4.ᵗʰ I think *love-sick* best – there are too many nn's in yᵉ line the other way.⁷
Stanza 5 on Every charming lip and eye – I like.
Stanza 7 *their* Deity, I should prefer.⁸
In the Compliment in 1743, I think your first readings are best, except perhaps at the conclusion, where I think the Roses blend better on the *cheek* than on the *face*.⁹
In the Song, methinks I would prefer in
Stanza 1 While faltering accents spoke my fear –
Stanza 2 *fruits*, instead of *crops*, as they are destroy'd by *vernal* cold; and the blossoms are more liable to be hurt by that than yᵉ early corn.

Standa 3ᵈ   How chang'd by Fortune's fickle wind,
                 The friends I lov'd became unkind;¹⁰
I prefer this reading much before the other. But in all these cases I beg you will
determine by the return of yᵉ post when I hope you will send Sheet C. I am sorry I
have printed off Lysander to Cloe & the Answer in the middle of yᵉ Vol without any
name.¹¹ You will perceive my hurry & excuse what I have written. I am most truely
yours

                                                            R. Dodsley

MS: BL. Add. MS. 28,959, ff. 83–4.

¹ The letter is certainly of 1757, for Shenstone responds to the items mentioned here in his fully dated
  letter of 21 December 1757. RD wrote approximately the first third of the letter, stopped, and then
  did not take it up again until probably two days later. (Otherwise, when resuming, he probably
  would have said "yesterday" rather than "Thus far I had written on Saturday.") But the letter must
  have been posted no later than the 20th for Shenstone to respond on the 21st.
² Whistler's "Song" (V, 61).
³ And so "mouldering" appeared in the fifteenth stanza of Shenstone's "Ode to Health, 1758" (V, 21–
  4), despite his mild objection. See Shenstone's letter to RD on 21 December.
⁴ See RD's letter to Shenstone on 3 December, notes 8 and 9.
⁵ The text used in the *Collection* for an "Ode, Written 1739" (V, 34–5) included the first line suggested
  by RD, but not the last two.   ⁶ These readings were not accepted by Shenstone.
⁷ Shenstone concurred in this instance.   ⁸ These last two preferences were printed.
⁹ Ultimately this poem was not used in the *Collection*.
¹⁰ For the song "I Told my nymph" (V, 38), RD followed his own readings for the first and third
  stanzas. However, though Shenstone accepted his advice on the second stanza (see Shenstone's letter
  21 December), RD did not print "fruits" instead of "crops."
¹¹ "Lysander to Chloe" was separated from Shenstone's other pieces and printed anonymously in
  Volume VI, 213–14, as was "Answer," VI, 212.

To Philip Dormer Stanhope, 4th Earl of Chesterfield ¹

                                                    Decʳ 19.ᵗʰ [1757]²
My Lord
     The Consequences of Good-nature are too frequently troublesome. Relieve a
beggar at your ⟨door⟩ gate, and you are sure to find him there again. Your
Lordship's ⟨favourable⟩ favourable opinion of Cleone, has encouraged me to
sollicit a boon in her ⟨favour⟩ behalf, which if it be not improper for your Lordship
to grant, will certainly be of great service to me.³ As Mʳ Rich has at last engag'd Mʳ
Barry and Miss Bellamy at his house, I have determin'd to offer my Tragedy to him;
but am advis'd to strengthen my application with a line from some great person
whose opinion would have weight & consequence with him. Your Lordship's
favourable ⟨interposition⟩ sentiments signify'd by a Line for me to take ⟨with me⟩
to Mʳ Rich, ⟨as ⟨I am⟩ being but very little acquainted with him,⟩ as it would do
me great honour, I am convinc'd would also give me so much credit with Him, that
he would at least be favourably dispos'd towards receiving it. ⟨I hope your
Lordship continues to receive benefit from the use of yᵉ Waters;⁴⟩ I would not have

presum'd to trouble your Lordship with a letter on this occasion, intending to have waited for your return to Town, but am advis'd to be as expeditious as may be in my application, as 'tis expected some thing else will be offer'd him.[5]

I am &c

MS: Robert Dodsley Letter Book, Birmingham Public Libraries, ff. 72–3.

[1] RD's acquaintance with Chesterfield (1694–1773) reaches back to his first days at Tully's Head, if not earlier. In fact, Straus (p. 7) suggests that RD's father might have been school teacher to some of the Stanhope family back in Mansfield. (RD does supply a report to Chesterfield on the latter's godson at Mansfield in 1758. See his letter to Arthur Stanhope on 19 September of that year.) Perhaps RD had come to know Chesterfield through either Pope or Lyttelton, when the three notables were associated with the Opposition at Leicester House. The Earl's patronage of RD is certified by 1739, when, as Straus recounts (p. 51), Chesterfield and Lyttelton offered bail when the bookseller had been confined to prison for issuing Paul Whitehead's *Manners*. Chesterfield contributed poetry to RD's short-lived *Publick Register* in 1741, no fewer than twenty-four pieces to RD's *World* (1753–6), and early on was thought to have been the author of RD's *The Oeconomy of Human Life* (1750). His two papers in *The World* praising Johnson's *Dictionary* prompted Johnson's famous letter to the Earl in 1755. The present letter, and two later ones, show Chesterfield's intercession on behalf of RD's *Cleone*.

[2] For several reasons, the year of this letter must be 1757. Prior to late 1757, RD is known to have applied only to Garrick for a performance at Drury Lane; there is no previous hint that he would offer it to John Rich for Covent Garden. Secondly, it was for the theatrical season of 1757–8 that Rich had first engaged Spranger Barry (1719–77) and George Anne Bellamy (1731?–88) for the Covent Garden company. Finally, this draft letter is entered in RD's Letter Book between a letter to John Hoadly which can be confidently dated 5 December 1757 and a second fully dated letter to Chesterfield of 5 January 1758, which is clearly a follow-up to his response to this letter on 22 December 1757.

[3] Chesterfield's earlier expression of favor for *Cleone* is untraced.

[4] That RD addressed the letter to Chesterfield in Bath is confirmed in his patron's reply three days later.

[5] In fact, Rich was entirely booked for the current season and was unable to accommodate RD until the next.

From William Shenstone

Tuesday Dec.[r] 21. 1757.

Dear Sir,

I receiv'd your Letter this morning to my no small Confusion – Yet blame I *no* alone can One beside *myself*; or rather that Incapacity I feel for *Criticism*, which ⟨makes me wish, in any sort, desire to delay ⟨y.[e] progress of⟩ your publication. When I sent my last Packet, I purpos'd by y.[e] next post to explain the uses for which it was intended[1] – I have *not* done so – have not been *able* to do so – & *now* am *surpris'd* to find y.[t] another Sheet is gone to the Press – for According to y.[e] Construction I put upon y.[r] last Letter, I thought it might be not altogether too *late*, if I *regulated* y.[e] whole by *X.[tmas]* I hope y.[e] *Elegy* is not yet begun in Sheet B.; & even ⟨then⟩ thus, if it were not inconvenient to stop y.[e] press a little, I would rather it were Too many of my Pieces are entirely t[?] done, y.[n] otherwise[2] – I think to write again, & have reserv'd my *only* Frank, for tomorrow – Mean time I give you my Thoughts in regard to y.ᵉ Compositions *your Letter mentions*. In y.ᵉ Ode to Health, I could propose no better word y.ⁿ *falling* instead of *mouldering*; & if you happen to prefer y.ᵉ *Latter*, I will by no means disagree with you.³

In regard to the Song "I told my nymph" I desire y.ᵗ you would follow *all* y.ᵉ readings you propose⁴ / The same, as to "y.ᵉ Compliment 1743.⁵ / As to y.ᵉ Ode 1739, I am neither wholly satisfyd with y.ʳ reading or my *own*. However; does not *Aid* in y.ᵉ first Line *run* better y.ⁿ Charms? Love's *imperial pow'r was known* is flat, & Love *here* is a *Person*, tho a *Passion* in y.ᵉ 5.ᵗʰ Line⁶ / But I leave you to *penetrate* my reasons, why I propose y.ᵉ following alterations, for y.ʳ *Choice*.

I	II
'Twas not by Beauty's aid alone	'Twas not thro Beauty's aid alone
fancy'd	
That love usurped his airy throne⁷	That Love's insidious pow'r was known
fancy'd	
His magic powr displayd	Or ever breast, betrayd
His tyrant sceptre swayd	
improve	
⟨A mutual kindness must conspire	A mutual kindness &c:
languid of love	
To fan y.ᵉ sparks of young desire	
flames soft	
Which &c.⟩	

I think y.ᵉ *second* preferable; as "*insidious*" suits better with "*betrayd*" in y.ᵉ *next* Line, & not ill with "was known" in *this*. The "*betray'd*" us'd in y.ᵉ next stanza may be exchangd for *reveal'd*, or some word of equal Import – I don't know *why* I prefer "Lips at once & Eyes" &c: so very probably you are in y.ᵉ right – *Quick* Lightnings doesn't *run* so well as "*the* Lightnings &c: but is is perhaps preferable on *another* score – As to the rest, please to follow your own readings in regard to this Ode – The Plate will require but very trifling alterations, if any; & may be sent at a Minutes warning.⁸

I have but a mean Opinion of two or three amongst y.ᵉ songs; & was thinking, (with this last ode Lysander & some few other Pieces in my manuscript) y.ᵗ I could have supply'd their Place to advantage. Do you remember y.ᵉ Verses on y.ᵉ Kid? – but I will write again to-morrow, & speak more Explicitly on the Occasion⁹ –

Do you think M.ʳ H. Walpole wou'd oblige me w.ᵗʰ a Copy of y.ᵉ Travels he has lately printed? (Hentznerus, I think is y.ᵉ Name –) I do not mean any otherwise then thro' *your* Mediation.¹⁰

You judge rightly of me in thinking how much it pains me to print precipitately – My *gratitude* suffers equally in subjecting you to Inconvenience. I am therefore truly under much anxiety – but w.ᵗʰ abundance of good-will, Dear M.ʳ Dodsley

Y.ʳˢ very affectionately

W. Shenstone

Pray write.

Address: To: M.ʳ Dodsley / at Tully's head, in / Pall-mall London¹¹

MS: BL. Add. MS. 28,959, ff. 87–8.

¹ See RD's letter to Shenstone on 18 December.
² "Jessy," the "Elegy" mentioned here, was subsequently withdrawn by Shenstone. See RD's letter to Shenstone on 16 January 1758.
³ See RD's letter to Shenstone on 18 December 1757, and note 3.   ⁴ Ibid., note 10.
⁵ Not used in *Collection.*   ⁶ See RD's letter to Shenstone on 18 December, note 5.
⁷ Only these two lines became part of the printed text of "Ode, written 1739." (V, 34–5).
⁸ The plate of Shenstone's grove to head "Rural Elegance," which opened Volume V.
⁹ "The Dying Kid" was eventually used in Volume V, 36–7. See RD's letters to Shenstone on 27 December 1757 and 16 January 1758.
¹⁰ The original work by the German Paul Hentzner had been translated by Richard Bentley and printed by Horace Walpole at Strawberry Hill in 1757 as *A Journey into England in the Year 1598.* It was subsequently reprinted in Volume II of RD's *Fugitive Pieces* in 1761, 1762, 1765 and 1771. See RD's letter to Shenstone on 5 January 1758, note 2.
¹¹ Shenstone had scribbled the following along the right edge of the cover: "a Sheet a-piece of those work'd off / The [?] to Sheet C."

From Philip Dormer Stanhope, 4th Earl of Chesterfield

Bath. Decem: yᵉ 22ᵈ 1757

Mʳ Dodsley.

I am glad to hear that Cleone is going to make her appearance upon the Stage, being persuaded that both you and Mʳ Rich will find your accounts in it. I can by no means agree to the Criticism of it's being, what they call, too deep a Tragedy. The old Tragedys, which our Classical Superstition makes us all adore, seldom turned upon a Love-tale, but were calculated to excite horror and terror. And most of our English Tragedies, present, and not without success, upon our stage heaps of mangled carcases, bloody Daggers, and bleeding wounds. In yours, If I remember right, no person is murthered upon the Stage, and the Child previously murthered, only seen at a distance. Your Villain is not greater than Iago, and many others whom I could mention, I am sure not a greater, than many in Nature. I hope you have taken care to bring the Audience to be better acquainted with the Character and motives of Isabella in the first Scene in which she appears; for as I red it, I thought you had not sufficiently explained her. You should also instruct the Actors, not to mouth out the Y, in the Name of Siffroy, as if they were crying Oysters, but to lay on the accent upon the O, and soften the final y. Thus I have given my opinion of your Play very sincerely, which, you may show Mʳ Rich and Mʳ Barry if you please, though I see no reason, why it should have any weight with those Gentleman who are certainly from their acquaintance with the Stages, and with the Town, the best Judges of what will, and what will not *do.*¹ When your Play shall be acted, I heartily wish you a good run and a ninth night, for I am very truly

Your friend and servant.

Chesterfield

Address: To Mr Dodesley at his House / in Pall Mall / London
Postmark: 24 DE
Frank Free / Chesterfield

MS: Houghton Library, Harvard University, f. MS. Eng. 42.50.

¹ In appreciation of Chesterfield's support for *Cleone* (requested in his letter of 19 December), RD
dedicated to the Earl the printed version of his tragedy, published a little less than a year later, on 7
December 1758.

To William Shenstone

Pall mall Decr 27th [1757]¹

Dear Sir

I am really in pain for You, and in shame for my self: I have plung'd You in
difficulties, from which I know not how to extricate You without doing violence
both to my self and You by these tearing Letters. The only hope which comforts me
is, that You are in the last stage of your drudgery, and one good effort will deliver
You from it. I am afraid You must for some months past have consider'd your own
habitation as a kind of Purgatory & have suffer'd accordingly: you have try'd your
self as it were by fire, but I doubt not you will come out pure & perfect, &
immortality will be your reward. For my part, I have not the least fear for any of y^e
Songs, but if you can supply the place of any of them with what you like better, I
have no objection: the dying Kid, if I remember right, was extreamly pretty, & I
should be extreamly glad to see it. The last Sheet of ye 5th Volume is compos'd, but
cannot be work'd off, because I cannot fix the Index till I have got Sheet C from
You. The 6th Volume is quite finish'd. I certainly did not express my meaning
rightly, if you understood that all the four sheets were to continue unwrought till
Christmas, I meant only that A and C might wait till then, B and D I thought were
finish'd to your mind. You should leave nothing to be penetrated by so blunt a Wit
as mine, which I assure you is amazingly dull: however, what think you of adopting
from your own readings the following?

'Twas not by Beauty's aid alone,
That Love usurpt his airy throne,
    His boasted power display'd;
'Tis kindness that secures his aim,
'Tis hope that feeds the kindling flame
    Which Beauty first convey'd.

Then in what is now the 3^d Stanza, but wch I think with you had better be ye 2^d,
suppose

In Clara's eyes the lightenings view;
Her lips with all the rose's hue
Have all its sweets combin'd; &c²

I enclose Sheet D which except ye error of one word, *iroin* for *iron*, I hope is pretty correct.[3] On Monday next I will send you by the Birmingham Carrier, Hentznerus,[4] & to my good friend Mrs Mary a small Canister of Tea. With Christmas compliments to all friends, I subscribe in great hurry,

Dear Sir

Yours most affectionately

R. Dodsley

MS: BL. Add. MS. 28,959, ff. 89–90.

[1] The year is certain, as the letter concerns the last stages of the preparation of Volumes V and VI of RD's *Collection*, to be published the following March. Also RD's mentioning his eagerness to see Shenstone's "The Dying Kid" clearly responds to the latter's offer of the poem in his letter of the previous Tuesday. Finally, the draft copy of this letter is found in RD's Letter Book.

[2] See Shenstone's letter to RD on 21 December. The above reading was used for "Ode, written 1739." (V, 34–5).

[3] This error occurred in the first verse of Shenstone's "Upon Riddles" (V, 57). The poem was printed without correction.

[4] See RD's letters to Shenstone on 21 December 1757 and 5 January 1758.

To Thomas Percy[1]

[December 1757–10 March 1758][2]

Sir

    The two Poems you favour'd me with are printed off, & it is therefore too late to make any alteration in the Name.[3] I have not any of the proof sheets by me at present & cannot now take them out of the Impression without spoiling a sett.

I am

Sir

Your most obed^t Servt

R. Dodsley

A Song[4]

Paraphras'd from the Spanish of Cervantes

Mariners soi d'amor

Gen su pielago &c,

Thro' Loves profound & stormy Main
  An hapless Mariner I sail
· Nor hopes my weary Bark to gain
  Or welcome Port or friendly Gale

Led by a star my Course I steer
  Ah! too remotely shine it's Rays
A star more bright & lovely ne'er   A lovlier Star did ne'er appear
  Bless'd Pilot's fond amiring gaze
  drew   To Pilots &c

Regardless wheresoe'er it leads
With crowded sail I follow on
My Soul, nor Rocks nor Quicksands heeds   My Skiff
Attentive to it's Rays alone

Yet oft the Clouds of cruel Slight
Reserve & Coldness interpose
And hide them from my longing sight
At random then my Vessel goes

O lovely Star: with fav'ring gleams
Direct me to the wish'd-for Coast
But ah! shouldst thou withdraw thy beams
I sink forever wreck'd & lost.
         Or
O lovely clear & brilliant Flame
For whose dear Sake I'm gladly lost
The Moment thou withdrawst thy beam   sh^d thou thy fav'ring beam
I sink &c

Address: To / the Revd Mr Percy

MS: Houghton Library, Harvard University, b MS Eng 893 (251).

1. Thomas Percy (1729–1811), later Bishop of Dromore, was in his late twenties when he became a protégé of Shenstone, who seems to have introduced him to RD. Shenstone advised him on his writings and then channeled them to RD, who provided further suggestions. But, despite an early rapport with RD, Percy soon preferred to deal with James Dodsley, who would take over the business in early 1759. In fact, writing to Shenstone on 27 November 1760 (Cleanth Brooks, ed. *The Correspondence of Thomas Percy and William Shenstone* (New Haven: Yale University Press, 1977), pp. 79–80), he complains that negotiations with James for the publication of the "Old Ballads" had broken down because RD who never "had much opinion of the work has I suppose persuaded him to desist: for the other has receded from his own offers." JD, he says, has "shown too much of the bookseller in this affair," whereas "in our former engagement he acted with great honour and civility." He then recalls Baskerville's distinction between the two brothers: "as a Tradesman Mr James Dodsley is the more generous man to deal with," to which Percy adds "Unless Mr Robert Dodsley influences him." But Percy had allowed his personal disappointment to blind him to the true causes of RD's uneasiness with the work – literary objections shared (apparently unbeknownst to Percy) by his advisor, Shenstone. (See Shenstone's letter to RD on 20 November 1762.) Nonetheless, JD purchased the copyright to the ballads for 100 guineas on 22 May 1761 (see Appendix B) and, shortly after RD's death, published them as Percy's *Reliques of Ancient English Poetry* (3 vols. 1765). Issued from Tully's Head during RD's lifetime were Percy's *Hau Kiou Choaan* (1761), a Chinese novel; *Miscellaneous Pieces Relating to the Chinese* (1762; assigned as "Chinese Proverbs"); *The Matrons* (actually 1772, but copyright purchased by JD in 1761); *Five Pieces of Runic Poetry* (1763); and *The Song of Solomon* (1764), a translation. See copyright agreements for all except *The Matrons* and *The Song of Solomon* in Appendix B.

2. The date is approximated from various pieces of evidence. The "two Poems" mentioned here were given the "final Perusal" by Percy and RD on 24 November 1757 (see Percy's letter to Shenstone of that date; Brooks p. 1); that is, the poems were not beyond proof stage in late November. On 18 December, RD wrote to Shenstone that volumes V and VI of the *Collection* were "now sent to press and

will be finish'd next week." This letter, then, must post-date Percy's of 24 November and probably RD's of 18 December. In "Concurrent Printing: An Analysis of Dodsley's *Collection of Poems by Several Hands*" (*PBSA*, XLVI, 45–57), William B. Todd estimates the printing of Signature P of Volume VI (the signature within which Percy's poems fell) to have been carried on during the week of 12 December. As quoted above, RD did not expect the printing to be completed until sometime around Christmas, meaning that he is writing this letter sometime after that point. On the other hand, we know that RD had some, if not all, the volumes bound by 10 March. (See his letter to Shenstone on 15 March, note 2.) Since the gathering, collating, and binding of the estimated 3,000 copies of Volumes V and VI (Todd, p. 53), as well as the same for the new editions of Volumes I to IV, would have taken some time, and since RD says nothing to Percy about the sheets' being at the binders, probably he is writing sometime before the end of February.

3 "A Song" and "Cynthia, an Elegaic Poem" appeared in RD's *Collection*, VI, 233–4; 234–9. Perhaps Percy was wanting to give a more endearing title to "A Song," since it was addressed to his future wife ("O Nancy, wilt thou go with me . . ."). From both the Percy letter to Shenstone alluded to in note 2 and from Shenstone's response on 4 January (Brooks, pp. 4–5), it is clear that both RD and Shenstone had been responsible for alterations in the two pieces.

4 A very liberal rendering of a song from the opening of Chap. 43, Bk. 4, Pt. 2 of Cervantes' *Don Quixote*. A curious problem arises from the fact that the poem, in Percy's hand, appears on the verso of RD's note. Either RD, in returning the poem Percy had perhaps left with him when in London in November, merely turned the sheet over, jotted the note, and posted it; or Percy, at some later date, used the blank verso of RD's note to write out the poem. The latter is more likely since Shenstone, to whom Percy first broached new pieces before presenting them to RD, is first informed of a Spanish piece in Percy's letter of 9 August 1759 (Brooks, pp. 31–2).

Five contemporary manuscript versions of "The Mariner of Love" survive: 1. the verso of RD's letter; 2. one Shenstone copied into his Miscellany sometime between 1759 and 1763 (Ian Gordon, *Shenstone's Miscellany* (Oxford, 1952), pp. 52–3); 3. a text in Percy's hand (Harvard b MS. Eng 893 (249), with the Spanish on the facing page; 4. BL Add. MS. 32,237, f. 195, also the original Spanish and Percy's translation on facing pages; 5. Bodleian MS. Percy c. 7, a fair copy in Percy's hand printed in David Nichol Smith, *Ancient Songs Chiefly on Moorish Subjects* (Oxford, 1932), the work that Percy had partially printed in 1775 but dropped when apparently it seemed out of taste with his ecclesiastical ambitions. It is very difficult to assign a chronological order to the production of these texts, but the Bodleian fair copy that Smith used is no doubt the latest. The "RD text," because of the total abandonment of lines from Stanza 5 (that also fail to appear in other versions), is probably the earliest. The similarity of the British Library text in stanza 3, line 3, to the RD text places it next in line. For assistance with these texts, I am indebted to Professors Cleanth Brooks and Ian Gordon.

From Richard Berenger

Lymington, Hants
Jan: 1: 1758

My good Friend[1]

Being well appriz'd that you have many mouths to fill, many maws to cram, and that your Wits and Authors are voracious Animals; being here in the Land of *Hog*, I send you a Morsel wherewith to regale some of the *Master Spirits*, some of the Fellows who adorn your *back* parlour, and who can furnish Salt and sauce to whatever dish you set before them – By the Southampton Coach I have sent a parcel of Swine flesh, it will be in Town on Tuesday Night. Oblige me by accepting it, and may it prove as good and agreable as I wish it, and every thing else that is or may be yours.[2] I past a long long while ago thre days with Mr Warton at Winchester – He is a most valuable and excellent Creature I am happy & proud to be of his acquaintance I have sent two Letters to Him, but can't get a word in answer to either – can you give me any Intelligence of Him – I wrote some time since to Mr Gataker, I hope he and his are well, but in writing to Him, I sing to the Death – I have never heard from Him – Make my cordial compliments, and tell him I love and respect Him.[3] The Laurel has at last been properly bestow'd, and Parnassus should make bonefires and rejoicings[4] – I am here intrench'd in Books, [?] rather not many books but what is better, and not so usual, much reading, & this is the only business, the only amusement I have – Plautus and I are grown pretty Intimate. He is a dry, pleasant, tedious, sensible old fellow – I am now got to Warton's Virgil, vastly delighted with Him, he contributes hugely towards making the tedious *hours more* s[we]et, *more* sweet I should not say,[?] he makes them absolutely sweet and short – *with Him conversing I forget all Time*[5] – Adieu my dear Sir, that Wit ⟨may⟩ come out in Folio, and you the Publisher or Author, that the Gout may dread to approach you, and that all manner of Good may attend you this New Year, and each Suceeding one, and that they may roll on one after the other, in Health and Tranquillity, till your friends stop that course, is the Hearty wish of your Hearty friend, and obedient Servant.

R Berenger

Address: To / Mr Robert Dodsley / Bookseller / Pall-Mall / London
Postmark: 2 IA

MS. Bodleian, MS. Eng. Letters *c.* 75, ff. 35–6.

[1] Berenger's addressing RD as "My good friend" suggests, as does RD's reply, that their friendship had survived the occasion in 1756 when, functioning as Garrick's consultant, Berenger had given a lengthy adverse criticism of RD's tragedy *Cleone*. See also Berenger's letter of 10 June 1756, note 1, regarding their friendship.

[2] Although four days earlier RD had told Shenstone that Volume VI of the *Collection* was "quite finish'd," the "Morsel" which Berenger is sending by the Southampton Coach might well have been his playful "To Mr. Grenville on his intended Resignation," which RD printed in that volume of the *Collection* ((pp. 271–2). On the other hand, when acknowledging the receipt of the piece on 10 January, RD makes no mention of including it. George Grenville (1712–70), MP for Buckingham (1740–70), had resigned as treasurer of the Navy in 1756 upon the impending dismissal of William Pitt and of his brother Richard, Earl Temple, but regained the position in 1757 under the Newcastle–Pitt Ministry.

[3] Why Joseph Warton and Thomas Gataker did not answer Berenger's letters is not clear. No resentment seems involved, for when RD responds nine days later, he mentions that, the day after receiving Berenger's letter, when Warton and Gataker were in his company for dinner, "your health went round, and much regret was exprest that You was not with us."

[4] William Whitehead (1715–85) had recently been appointed Poet Laureate.

[5] Joseph Warton's translation of Virgil's *Eclogues* and *Georgics*, had appeared, along with Christopher Pitt's translation of the *Aeneid*, as *The Works of Virgil, in Latin and English*, published by RD in 1753.

[From Thomas Blacklock][1]

[early January 1758][2]

D^r S^r

You will perhaps be at a loss to account for a silence so long, from one so fond of your correspondance – believe me, when I recollect ye number & variety of events, whose conspiring influence could cause an interruption so considerable I am at a loss to account for it to any other but myself. Permit me only to say in general, that nothing of less importance than the pursuit of a Settlement for life, could have suspended an intercourse so agreeable & usefull. I had propos'd a great many plans to my friends & prepar'd myself for ye accomplishment of some; but in each there were unhappy circumstances against me, sufficient to render them impracticable, or at least unsuccessfull.[3] A State like this will be better imagin'd than describ'd. The anxiety & uneasiness with which it is attended deprives ye mind of that gay serenity which is necessary to qualify it either for entertaining itself or others. No moments therefor can be more unfit than these, for writing to ones friends. I am at last a Candidate for orders in our Church & have performed the most arduous part of my probation not without success – a probation it may justly be call'd from ye length of its duration, the extent of its subject, & the severity of its rules. Students of Divinity from the time they assume that character, are under perpetual censure and tuition, either at ye College or with ye Ministers of ye District where they live, & are obliged periodically to produce written approbations of their conduct, from ye College to ye Presbytry, & from ye Presbytry to ye College. The tryal itself continues for a year – it begins with a Strict examination, extending almost to ev'ry branch of science. It demands a solemn & particular assent ⟨to⟩ to ye most rigorous Calvinistical principles It ends in different exercises of Eloquence & Composition. But it is now over with me in effect, & leaves me more at ease than I have been for some time, because it gives me a prospect, tho' a faint one, of rising above necessity & of becoming in some measure usefull to ye World.[4] Yet I did not without sensible regret exchange the green retreats of ye muses, the flowry regions of fancy, the early haunts of rational & elegant delight, for ye barren Deserts of School Divinity, the Rugged paths of Controversy & ye dull employment of hunting Heresys. ⟨Yet⟩ But these were indispensible preliminarys to ye imployment I had chosen, & ye Horror of living in vain, inspird me w^t sufficient courage to confront & overcome every dificulty; A more agreeable task now remains that of endeavouring to improve ye heart and understanding of my fellow Creatures – an attempt wch must always be in some degree its own reward. I have still ⟨some⟩ a few Tractical pieces by me, which some remains of unmortified vanity strongly importune me to transmit to you – particularly now that I hear you are going to publish two voll^s more of your Collection[5] – The inclosed is written by the earliest & most intimate of my friends.[6] I have reviewed it w^t as much care & impartiality as I could – it is now submitted to your criticism, not without expectation that it may obtain a place in your Miscellany, if it comes not too late. Should this be ye case you may send it to ye Author of ye London or Gentlemans Magazine[7] – I will send you the Poems mentiond above so soon as they can be transcrib'd – It is perhaps unecessary to enquire into ye success of my last Edition, there is too much reason to presume it still uniform.[8] You'l oblige me however by sending a few dozens of it Directed for me, to ye care of Messrs Hamelton & Balfour[9] – Mr G.G[10] & I have each of us your first four voll^s., so when

continued on ye cover

MS: Harvard Theatre Collection, Harvard College Library.

¹ Although the final lines of this letter (supposedly written on the cover) and the signature are missing, Thomas Blacklock is undoubtedly its author. The writer resides in Edinburgh ("Directed for me, to yᵉ care of Messʳˢ Hamelton and Balfour"), has been studying for the Presbyterian ministry, has published a few editions of his poetry with RD, and writes a long personally revealing letter – all features of other Blacklock letters to RD at this time. In addition, the author refers to "Mʳ G. G." (probably "the earliest & most intimate of my friends" of a few lines above); that is, Gilbert Gordon, who had written an account of Blacklock prefixed to the second Edinburgh edition of the poet's works (1754). In the *London Magazine* of January 1758 (pp. 45–7), appeared Gordon's poem "To a young Lady . . ." that corroborates Blacklock's sentiment:"Nor must I here forget to recommend, / Blacklock – my fav'rite – intimate and friend. / We from our earliest youth to each were known. / Alike our pleasures, our associates one."

² In the light of its contents, this is probably the letter that Blacklock says he sent "two months agoe" when writing to RD on 19 March 1758. There he mentions having enclosed a manuscript poem written by a friend that he wishes RD to publish, and he also reminds the bookseller to send copies of his octavo edition "mentioned in my former [letter]."

³ For one such plan, see Blacklock's letter on the previous 27 June.

⁴ A little more than two years later (4 February 1760), Blacklock would be writing RD in despair of his ministry, claiming that the people rejected him because of his blindness, and his clerical colleagues refused him support.

⁵ Volumes 5 and 6 of RD's *Collection* would appear two months later.   ⁶ See note 1.

⁷ As is clear from RD's letters to Shenstone at this time, where he pleads for the final proofs for Volume VI of the *Collection*, Blacklock had submitted his friend's poem too late for it to be included in the miscellany. If this is indeed "G. G.'s" poem that had appeared in the *London Magazine* for this month, RD had complied with Blacklock's request to secure its insertion in that periodical. It is strange, however, that Blacklock, writing on 19 March, had yet to notice its placement there.

⁸ In his letter to Blacklock on the previous 16 July, RD had regretted to inform the poet that the octavo edition of his poems was selling "very slowly."

⁹ Hamilton and Balfour, Blacklock's bookseller in Edinburgh.   ¹⁰ See note 1.

To William Shenstone

Pall mall Janʳʸ 5ᵗʰ 1758

Dear Sir

I begin now to wait with great impatience for Sheet A and C, as much time will be taken up (the Impression being 6 Vols) in gathering and making them fit for the binder, and in binding a pretty large number before I must venture to publish.¹ You will therefore be so good as to send them me with all convenient dispatch, as I am desirous of giving them as much of this season to spread in as possible. I was disappointed last Monday of Mʳ Walpole's book, there being none to be had; I therefore did not send the Tea; but will endeavour to procure one by some means or other & send them together. Mʳ Walpole made me a present of one, which I have lent to a Gentleman in the Country; if I can get no other I will send You that as soon I can get it.² I am ever

most sincerely & affectionately Yours
R. Dodsley

MS: BL. Add. MS. 28,959, f. 91.

¹ Besides Volumes V and VI, RD was also putting out the fourth edition of Volumes I–III, and the second edition of Volume IV.

² See RD's letters to Shenstone on 21 December 1757, note 10, and on 16 January 1758. Still extant in the Lewis Walpole Library, a copy of Walpole's printing of Hentzner's *Journey into England* shows an inscription that traces a history of ownership most pertinent to this letter. On the inside fly-leaf, in the hand and with the initials of Shenstone's friend John Scott Hylton, appears the following: "This Volume was given by Mʳ Walpole to the late Mʳ Robert Dodsley, who presented it to Mʳ Shenstone, from whom I had it." Obviously RD succeeded in retrieving his gift copy of Hentzner from the country and sent it to Shenstone.

To Philip Dormer Stanhope, 4th Earl of Chesterfield

Jan 5 1758

My Lord
 I have delay'd my acknowledgments of yᵉ Honour your Lordship did me in giving your Opinion of Cleone, till I could ⟨give⟩ obtain a definitive answer from Mʳ Rich, wᶜʰ I have not been able to ⟨obtain⟩ do till yesterday.¹ He tells me his Engagements will not permit him to perform it this season, but promises ⟨me⟩ it shall be done if I think proper the beginning of the next. ⟨season.⟩ To this I have acquiesc'd, provided Mʳ Barry & Miss Bellamy continue with him; but if they leave him I can by no means think of venturing it at his house.² I am extreamly oblig'd to your Lordship for your favourable interposition, and hope you will pardon my ⟨presuming⟩ having presum'd to request it.

I am with real Gratitude & great respect,
My Lord, &c

MS: Robert Dodsley Letter Book, Birmingham Public Libraries, f. 76.

¹ See Chesterfield's letter to RD on 22 December 1757.
² As RD had hoped, George Anne Bellamy (1731?–88) did play Cleone (and with great success), but Spranger Barry (1719–77) did not appear.

To [?]

[5–6 January 1758]¹

Sir
 I do not wonder that Mʳ – should justify what he has done; but let me ask both him & you whether either of You would have inserted such an account of a work written or printed by your selves

MS: Robert Dodsley Letter Book, Birmingham Public Libraries, f. 77.

¹ As a fragment, without addressee or date, this piece is very different from the usual fulsome drafts RD entered into his Letter Book. Although by the Letter Book dating principle, it is assigned a 5–6 January 1758 date, its subject seems more in line with RD's bitter complaints to William Strahan in January 1757 regarding the scurrilous material appearing in their newly founded *London Chronicle*. Such might be the case since these few lines appear in the closing pages of the Letter Book, where RD might have turned, earlier on, to try a thought before abandoning the idea.

To John Rich

Jan 6.th [1758][1]

Sir

I have so many reasons to wish my Play may be brought on this season rather than the next; and am so prest by many people of Consequence who are desirous of seeing it, from the favourable character that has been given of it by persons of the most acknowledg'd taste & judgment, that I cannot avoid once more desiring it as a favour, ⟨that⟩ if you are not so circumstanc'd as to render it quite impossible, that you would comply w.th my request in bringing it on now. I would by no means interfere with ye interests of any other person, nor hinder ye performance of any Play which you may be getting up, but would be satisfy'd with y^e ⟨alternate⟩ performance of mine ⟨three times⟩ along with any other play or plays that you may be engag'd for. I have reason to think that many people whom you would wish to oblige will be pleas'd ⟨with⟩ at your compliance with this request, & ⟨hope it⟩ will endeavour that it may turn out to your own advantage as well as mine. I ⟨will wait on⟩ could wish You to think of it two or three days before you return me an answer.[2]

I am &

MS: Robert Dodsley Letter Book, Birmingham Public Libraries, ff. 78–9.

[1] The year quite fits the sequence of letters negotiating for *Cleone*'s performance, and is determined by the Letter Book principle.
[2] Apparently Rich could not oblige, though his written response has not been discovered.

To Richard Berenger

Jan 10.th 1758

Dear Sir

I receiv'd your agreeable Letter and Present, which were both very acceptable, and demand my ⟨warmest⟩ best acknowledgments and thanks.[1] You judg'd extreamly well, or rather were inspir'd with a prophetic spirit, when you imagin'd the society of Wits and choice spirits ⟨would⟩ might be very numerous at Tully's head; for the day after I heard from You, I had no less than a round dozen of them din'd with me, ⟨when your health went round and much regret was exprest that You was not with us.⟩ The two Mr Wartons, Mr Spence Mr Burke Mr Cooper Mr Langton Mr Gataker Mr Beddingfield, and Mr Garrick were of the party, when your health went round, & much regret was ⟨not with us.⟩ exprest that You was not with us.[2] But no Happiness on earth is perfect; ours was not so, for want of ⟨Your enlivening Company.⟩ You. But I hope it will not be long before you visit again ye purlieus of St James.

> Haste thee, haste, & bring with thee
> Jest and youthful jollity –
> Sport that wrinkled Care derides,
> And Laughter holding both his sides.[3]

For what should you do in the Country? You, who are made for Society – the Soul of social mirth. You who can delight a circle of polish'd friends, what should you do amongst Clowns & Rustics Besides, it is not now the Season

    1 ⟨And⟩ When the mower whets his scythe
    2 ⟨When⟩ And the milkmaid singeth blithe,
       Nor can you now tell amorous tales
       Under the hawthorns in the dales.

Come to Town therefore, if not for our sakes at least for your own. The Piazzas of Covant Garden afford in January ⟨afford⟩ a better shelter than any Grove in Christendom; and what are now your mossy banks and purling streams, in the Country, to a sparkling bowl & a downy bed at the Hummums? Your Naiads, your dryads & your Hamadryads are enough to starve a man to death; but with yᵉ Nymphs of Drury you may be as warm as your heart can wish – and warmer too. And will not those comfortable considerations invite You to Town?

Joe Warton tells me he wrote to You by the last Post; & I should have written sooner but that I have been in one perpetual hurry for this last fortnight, feasting & rioting noon & night at home and abroad, as if I had set the Gout at defiance, or had totally forgotten the last seven months confinement. But ⟨they go out of town to morrow morning, and tho' robb'd of much glee & social pleasure,⟩ I ⟨shall⟩ must return to my milk and my sober senses ⟨with great satisfaction.⟩ and bid adieu to yᵉ jovial cups of mirth & social pleasure, at the bottom of which, Prudence, ⟨pulling⟩ twitching me by yᵉ sleeve, points to Crutches and cloath shoes. I am much oblig'd to You for your concluding kind wishes, and in return, may all your own, in whatever relates to your self, be crown'd with success! & may your own heart ⟨always⟩ still dance to that mirth which your ⟨vivacity for⟩ good humour ⟨always⟩ always gives to others!

                I am &c

MS: Robert Dodsley Letter Book, Birmingham Public Libraries, ff. 80–3.

For some of the subjects mentioned here, see Berenger's letter on 1 January.
Ibid. Garrick's presence at Tully's Head suggests that RD and the theatre manager had temporarily patched up their differences.
Here and in the following couplets, RD tailors Milton's *L'Allegro* to his purposes.

To William Shenstone

                Pall mall Jan. 16.ᵗʰ 1758

Dear Sir

    I had expected every day for some time to have receiv'd the two remaining Sheets from You, when behold another Letter came without a Proof! Ah, dear Mʳ Shenstone! consider what a sad situation I am in – big with *twins*, at my *full time*, and no hopes of your assistance to *deliver* me!¹ Was ever *man* in such a situation before? You will tell me, perhaps, You are only sollicitous that those features of my offspring which may resemble You, should not come into the world imperfect or blemish'd: I feel your plea, my dear Sir, and allow it a kind one; but for Heaven's sake let the finishing touches be no longer delay'd! I dare be answerable for it, those features which You are so diffident about, will be allow'd by every one else, most strikingly beautiful. Besides, why should you alone insist upon that *absolute perfection*, to which no human production did ever yet arrive?

I have for this month past told every body that I had finish'd, that I only waited for two sheets from You, and that I should certainly publish in January. This is already impossible, and if the sending your sheets should be any farther defer'd, will scarce be done in February. And as the four first Volumes are now quite out of print, not a book to be had, and as the proper season for publication will be far advanc'd before I can possibly get them ready, a longer delay would be very detrimental to me. I beg You will believe that it hurts me extreamly to *press You* so earnestly, and that I would by no means do it were not the necessity of Publication on many accounts equally *pressing on me*.

Thus far I had written, & was just going to close my letter, when your cruel prohibition of Jessy arriv'd[2] – God grant me patience! – But you cannot be in earnest! – What, rob me of the most beautiful piece in ye Collection! What I have boasted of to every body, shewn to several, and what all have admir'd. Dr Akenside says it is the most charming Elegy in any Language. I beg, my dear Sir, You will not think of depriving me of so valuable a treasure. I thank you for the dying Kid, the Simile, the ceremonial, and for all your corrections.[3] I am quite asham'd of the repeated trouble I give you, but hope another Post or two will end it. Pray thank Mr Hylton for his Tale which I think is a very pretty one and am sorry it came so late.[4] But O poor Jessy! let me not think of losing her if you love me! And I am really

very affectionately Yours

R. Dodsley

Hentznerus & the Canister of Tea were sent this sennight: I hope you have before now receiv'd them.[5]

MS: BL. Add. MS. 28,959, f. 92–3.

[1] "Big with twins" – Volumes V and VI of the *Collection* from which Shenstone was withholding Sheet A and C.

[2] Despite RD's urging, Shenstone excluded "Jessy" from the *Collection*. RD would continue to prod him for his elegy but it had to await the posthumous edition of the poet's *Works* (1764), where it was printed simply as "Elegy XXVI" (I, 97–101).

[3] All three pieces appeared in the *Collection* (V, 36–7, 45–6, 46–7), supplying the place in Sheet C from which Shenstone had apparently withdrawn some "Songs." (See Shenstone and RD's exchange on 2 and 27 December 1757.)

[4] Apparently RD later found room for Hylton's tale in Volume VI of the *Collection*: see RD's letter to Hylton on 20 February. On p. 280, appeared "'True Resignation' by Mr. H___." Obviously Hylton had sent this little satirical piece to RD when he had been unable to finish more than sixty lines of his proposed "Indian Eclogue," the subject of occasional reference in RD's correspondence with Hylton, Shenstone, and Pixell, of late 1757.

[5] See Shenstone's letter of 21 December 1757 and note 10.

To [Thomas?] Thackray[1]

Jan 16 [1758][2]

Dear Sir

I receiv'd the favour of your letter & was very sorry to hear of Mr Stephenson's death, and of the bad circumstances in which he dy'd.[3] However, as I suppose no dishonesty will appear in his conduct with regard to his Office, I do not apprehend any harm will come to me as his Surety. If You think otherwise, and that there will be any danger ⟨of that⟩, I beg you will let me know. But as I have not yet heard any thing from the Board and think it would be very hard if they should expect me to make good any deficiencies, perhaps 'tis best to say nothing about it.[4] I do not know where Mr Hargreaves lives, nor how to enquire after him; if You think it proper that I should enquire after him, you will be so good as to let me know where he lives.[5] With my kindest wishes for your health and happiness I remain Dear Sir
&c

not sent.[6]

MS: Robert Dodsley Letter Book, Birmingham Public Libraries, ff. 85v–86r.

Perhaps the Thomas Thackray who subscribed for six copies of RD's *A Muse in Livery*, one of the latter's first published works while still a footman in Whitehall and fresh from the country. Probably Thackray had been an acquaintance of RD's in his youth, for two other matters place him in Duffield, Derby, a town but twenty miles from RD's birthplace, Mansfield, and where RD had cousins. In letters of 1761 and 1763 to his cousin Elizabeth Cartwright of Duffield, RD asks that his compliments be given to a Mr Thackray. Secondly, the subject of this letter, the recently deceased Mr Stephenson, is probably Hugh Stephenson of Duffield. (See note 3.)
The year follows from its placement in RD's Letter Book.
Probably Hugh Stephenson of Duffield, a supervisor of excise in Derby, whose will would be probated on 22 July 1758 (PRO). (Unfortunately Thackray is not mentioned in the will.) The "bad circumstances in which he dy'd," as clear from RD's next letter to Thackray on 18 February, refers to some indebtedness at his death.
RD's letter on 18 February suggests that Thackray had played the intermediary with RD in procuring the surety for Stephenson. RD was held responsible for £50 on Stephenson's account by the Board of Excise.   [5] Hargreaves' identity is unknown.
"not sent" is in RD's hand. See RD's letter to Thackray on 18 February.

To William Shenstone

Pall mall Jan^{ry} 21st [1758][1]

Dear Sir

I have just receiv'd a letter from You which I perceive was written before You received my last.[2] I find you have enabled me to fill Sheet C without the help of Jessy, but I hope what I said in my last, will induce You to revoke her doom. I could add to those reasons many others. I really look upon it as the most striking Poem in the whole Collection. I think it will do You more credit than any other of your

Pieces. It will certainly do no disservice to ye Collection of Elegies, but may be
inserted amongst them, whenever they appear and will in the meantime mos
strongly recommend them to ye Curiosity of the Public.[3] Besides, so many o
the best Judges have seen it, so many more have heard of it, and in short such ar
expectation has been rais'd about it, that to be disappointed of it will be very
mortifying, and may do mischief. Many more reasons might urg'd for her presen
appearance, all to whom I have mention'd it cry out against you for the thought o
suppressing it: so pray by the next post give us the satisfaction of hearing that she i
to appear. I have a thousand things to say, but am seiz'd with the Gout hand and
foot & write in great pain. I can put Mr Hylton's Tale into a leaf which I have been
oblig'd to cancel.[4] The Sentiment I had printed before with ye Evergreen &
another without your Name. Pray send the Rural Elegance, & let me finish, for I
shall now be in great trouble & anxiety which accompany'd with pain is too much.
The Season is wasting, and I have between 6 and 7 hundred pound bury'd in the
Paper & print of this Edition, which I want to pay and cannot till I publish. I fear i
is impossible You should read or understand what I have writ.

I am ever
most affectionately Yours
R. Dodsley

MS: BL. Add. MS. 28,959, f. 94.

[1] From the context, the letter quite evidently fits RD's exchange of correspondence with Shenstone in
     January 1758, when the publisher was trying to finish the last two volumes of his *Collection*. RD's regret
     regarding the "doom" of "Jessy" is obviously a follow-up on his 16 January letter where he mention
     just hearing of Shenstone's decision against printing "Jessy" in the *Collection*.
[2] Not traced.   [3] See RD's letter to Shenstone on 16 January, note 2.   [4] Ibid., note 4.
[5] The "Sentiment" was withdrawn from the *Collection*. "The Evergreen" appeared in Volume VI, 211
     12. It is impossible to identify the unnamed poem to which RD refers, for there were four other poem
     by Shenstone grouped with "The Evergreen." "Rural Elegance," of course, opened Volume V.

To William Shenstone

Pall mall Feb^ry 2^d [1758]

Dear Mr Shenstone

I do most heartily congratulate You on having got thro' the disagreeabl
business of correction. But for god's sake do not make me blush with talking of m
Patience, when I am holding up my hands in admiration of *yours*! If You hav
forgiven me all my tiezing impertinence, what a fund of Good Nature you mus
have! A Wife could not have been a greater plague to You than I have been for som
time past. I am extreamly sorry for your ill health, & fear I have contributed t
make it worse: but bear with me this once, & forgive me, pray do! I have look'd ove
the Ode as carefully as I could, & according to your directions have transpos'd th
Stanzas, & indented the Lines, but I could not send it to press without troublin
You with it once more, lest there should be any thing which You might wish t

alter; tho' I must confess I see nothing amiss, nothing but what is excellent.² In the 3ᵈ Stanza I have put the word *sport* instead of *joy* which was us'd in yᵉ 2ᵈ In yᵉ 5.ᵗʰ Stanza I lik'd – 'Ariconium pours her gems profuse better than – flowering plant profuse – so left the two lines as they were. But You will determine. In the 8ᵗʰ I put in the word *Ev'n*, I thought there were too many *the*'s.³ I have no doubt about your Philosophy in the 17ᵗʰ Stanza; if it is not Physically true, it is at least Poetically so, and that is sufficient; but I think it is both. The Transpositions afterwards I think mend the connexion; & perhaps it is safest to let the Compliment stand. Poor Jessy! – But I will not, I dare not tieze you any more about her. She would certainly do You honour – her Loss will be greatly lamented – but your will be done! – Only be so good as by the return of yᵉ Post to send back this Sheet, with your final determination in regard to that *sweet girl*! It is past my time of day to ravish, otherwise I should certainly be tempted to take her from you by force.⁴ I am ever

Dear Sir

Affectionately Yours

R. Dodsley

In the 16.ᵗʰ Stanza of the Elegy, what think You of

> Hope not delight in *us*, methinks they say

instead of

> Hope not to find delight in *us*, they say⁵ –

MS: BL. Add. MS. 28,959, f. 95–6.

¹ Again, RD's concern within this letter for finishing Volumes V and VI of the *Collection* identifies it as belonging to February 1758.
² Shenstone's "Rural Elegance. An Ode to the late Duchess of Somerset," the opening poem in Volume V. If the editor, John Hodgetts, has properly dated a letter from Lady Luxborough to Shenstone as a product of 12 December 1753 (*Letters Written by the Late Honourable Lady Luxborough to William Shenstone, Esq.* (London, 1775), p. 361), then it would seem that Shenstone had been contemplating printing "Rural Elegance" over four years earlier; that is, more than a year before it becomes a subject of the poet's correspondence with RD. In that letter, Lady Luxborough had enclosed a letter from the Duchess of Somerset in which the latter expressed appreciation of Shenstone's dedicating "Rural Elegance" to her, but asked that her name not be printed. As Lady Luxborough explained, "every body will know she is the Heroine of the piece."
³ Shenstone must have agreed with RD's suggestions (that is, if he responded), for all are found in the version of "Rural Elegance" printed in the *Collection*.
⁴ Regarding "Jessy," see RD's letters to Shenstone of 16 and 21 January.
⁵ Either Shenstone disagreed or RD simply forgot his own suggestion six years later when he was putting out the edition of Shenstone's *Works*.

From Richard Graves

Claverton, 3. Feb. 1758

Dear Sʳ

I am oblig'd to you for a kind Letter of the 25.ᵗʰ of Octob. last¹ – which perhaps I ought to have acknowledg'd before this time – But when I consider the importance

of *your* engagements – & your connections with all the great Genii of the Age,
cannot but look upon *my* Correspondence, as beneath your Consideration – Aft
almost half-a-years Silence however I am favour'd with a Letter from M
Shenstone – who laments (as, I, &, I believe, you, have reason to do) his dilato
temper – yet hopes at least that I correspond with his friend Dodsley – Who, I
informs me, is endeavouring to rescue more of my Rhymes from utter Oblivion

Now, as the mere admission amongst your eminent Hands has, I find, rais'd m
to some degree of Consequence with many People[2] – I should be sorry to forfeit
again, by exposing any more of my Levities – as I expect to be pardon'd for once
by insinuations – that those Trifles crept into Print – thro' the partiality of m
Friends – But should think myself inexcusable to be repeating those Follies at n
Age – & amidst the Avocations of a serious Profession – by Mr Shenstone's accou
however, matters are advanc'd too far for my Remonstrances – & I know I am sa
in the Hands of a Person of your Judgment & Character. But should be glad
know, in one Line, what particular Piece or Pieces of mine, you have honour'd w
y^r approbation – I ⟨?⟩ dare say, that wch I gave you upon my *own place* is not one –
it appears excessively insipid to me = after four years – and it would be ridiculous
⟨to⟩ even to have made *such* a place y^e subject of any Meditation – However I ha
made one or two alterations in ⟨that⟩ those Stanzas – which to me, appear of
much Importance as the Thing itself[3] –

The most material Article of my last Letter to Mr Shenstone – was a Request
him to publish his Elegies – upon which head, I think I us'd some forcib
arguments – But he vouchsafes me no answer – as, I believe, he is at a Loss – Wh
Answer to make – Tho' perhaps a Person that is capable of writing with so muc
Delicacy – may see many nice Objections – wch are invisible to my gross
Perception –

Mr Shenstone agrees with me, that you ought to have affix'd your Name to
Melpomene – not only for the Sale of it – but, as I am certain, your Name wou
have been a proper Introduction of it to the Notice of all People of Taste[4] –

You greatly surprise me, by what you hint about my being engag'd in a
Entertainment for ye Public[k] as I communicated something of such a Scheme
Mr Shenstone under ye Seal of inviolable Secrecy[5] – and could have forgiven hi
for whispering it to any one, rather than to you – As I should be sorry to have yc
think, that I would publish any thing which I should be asham'd to submit to
Inspection – Something of that kind however I must now own, that I have bestow
(at different times) perhaps two months Labour upon. But ⟨the⟩ a number
disagreeable domestick Concerns – have put, I believe, a final Period to m
Labours – You will not ⟨be⟩ suspect that there was any thing immoral in m
undertaking – for I intended the Reverse – But the Species of writing was of the ⟨?
lowest kind – & my many Interruptions – would have prevented my executing
wth any degree of Perfection – It was begun in a Pique – & continued from t
amusement I found in it – & if I had ever publish'd it, I own it would have been w
a View – of getting about as much money – as w^d have purchas'd 2 or 3 Folio's of
ornamental kind – wch out of regard to my family, I could not prudently do – But

ave at present no prospect of Leisure to compleat it – ⟨&⟩ before the Date of its
opularity will probably be expir'd – I am S^r

y^r oblig^d hum^b Ser^t

Ric: Graves

ddress: To / Mr Dodsley / at Tully's head in / Pall-Mall   London
ostmark: 6 FE [Bath]

S: Somerset County Record Office, DD/SK, 28/1, 8.

q.v.
Probably Graves alludes to the four poems he had placed in Volume IV (330–5) of RD's *Collection* in
1755.
Graves is probably referring to his "Written near Bath, 1755," a "meditation" on his own living
quarters, which RD included in his *Collection* (V, 67–9).
Melpomene: or The Regions of Terror and Pity, published the previous September.
Clarence Tracy (biography of Graves, in preparation) believes this to be almost certainly a reference
to the beginning of Graves's *The Spiritual Quixote* (1773).

rom John Scott Hylton

The Leasowes
4 Feb.^ry – 1758.

ear Sir,
   As it is now near Eight o'Clock, I shall not have time to write you any long Letter,
ut I am desired by Mr Shenstone who has really been extremely ill, ever since he
as wrote to you, to acquaint you that he purposes if he have a tolerable Day
morrow to return your proof Sheet. He could not possibly do so to night, upon
count of the time at which he receiv'd it. Upon just casting an Eye over it, he
inks the transpositions of Stanzas will occasion the first Line of the 23^d Stanza to
e (as it now stands) not altogether intelligeable.[1] But he hopes when he returns the
heet to fix all necessary alterations. The kind Letter you was so obliging to favour
e with, I will answer soon.[2] Mr Shenstone joins with me in the Compliments with
hich I am

Dear Sir
Y^r most Obliged & Obed^t
Hble Servant

John Scott Hylton

ddress: To / Mr Dodsley / in Pall=mall / London
ostmark: 6 FE

S: Humanities Research Center, University of Texas at Austin, Robert Dodsley / Recipient 1 /Bound,
17.

Reference to Shenstone's "Rural Elegance," which he was still tuning up for RD's *Collection.* It was in
Sheet C, which RD had returned on 2 February.   [2] Not traced.

From Thomas Cheyney[1]

Wintõn. Feb. 6. 175[8]

Sir.

I here enclose ye Print taken out of Gales' Book, as also a Drawing of W^m [
Wickham's Tomb & Effigies by a less Scale.[2] Y^e Operator, Mr Isaac Taylor,
needfull, may be heard of at Alderman Baker's.[3] He has I think perform'd tolerabl[
well – after comparing it wth ye Original, I note only two Imperfections – ye Hand[
lifted up, seem to me rather too large in proportion – And of 7. Compartments o[
ye Tomb, each containing an Escutcheon wth Arms, 3 are distinguish'd by a Mitr[
ye Middle One & two Alternate. On ye Tomb, ye Middle one is a double-Arm[
encircled w.^th°ye Garter, ye 2 Alternate being double also, but with! ye Garter. M[
Taylor in his drawing distinguishes ye two Alternate wth a Mitre, but exhibits onl[
single Arms (in) ye 3 Roses. This mistake, I presume, if worth while, may easily b[
rectify'd by ye Engraver.

This you'l please to cõmunicate in due time to Dr Lowth, who, I fear, has bee[
too much engaged by his Wife's Illness to make any great Dispatch of his Work[

You may phaps be a little surpriz'd by a lett^r under my hand after reading in y[
Genl Ev'ning-Post of Feby 2^d, that I was dead [&c]

If you have any Knowledge of Mr Say,[5] or an easy Access to his Office, I shall b[
oblig'd if you'l ask him upon what Information & Autority he made so free wth m[
& gave so circumstantial an ac ⁓ ct of my death. I think a Man in his calling migh[
easily eno' have discern'd som'what ludicrous in ye Paragraph, intended to affror[
me, & impose upon him, unless he professes to make his Paper a vehicle for an[
Buffoonery y^t shall be laid before him.[6]

I ask pardon for this trouble, but you see my Provocation to it, tho' I don't la[
any great Stress on such an Idle Attempt.

I am, Sir,

Y^r Faithful & Humble Servt

Tho: Cheyne[

P.S. Ab^t a week before ye date of my Paragraph, anoth^r fiction of ye like nature wa[
inserted in ye same Paper, of ye death of Captn Imber, an officer residing here – An[
this, tis said, how truly I know not, prov'd a real Injury to him, wth respect to
Promotion in ye army then depending.[7] This sh^d be a Hint to Mr Say to recollec[
who his Wintõn Correspond^ts are, & w^t regard for ye future he ought to pay to thei[
Intelligences.

MS: Bodleian Library, MS. Eng. Letters d. 40, ff. 108–9.

[1] Thomas Cheyney (1694–1760), in the Wykehamite tradition, was educated at Winchester and Ne[
College, Oxford. He became Dean of Lincoln in 1744 and, four years later, returned as Dean t[
Winchester, where he died. (See G. H. Blore, *Thomas Cheyney, Wykehamist, Dean of Wincheste[
(Winchester: The Wykeham Press, 1950).)

[2] In a letter to Thomas Warton at Oxford on 20 October 1757 (John Wooll, *Biographical Memoirs [
. . . Joseph Warton* (1806), p. 249), Lowth asks Warton to engage John Green (fl. 1758) to make[
drawing of the unique version of William of Wykeham's arms found in the New College seal,

drawing he plans to send to RD as a headpiece for the genealogical table at the rear of *William of Wykeham*. Lowth had also told RD to expect the drawing from Oxford, when writing on 3 November 1757 (q.v.). In the latter letter, Lowth had likewise told RD that if the engraving of William's tomb by Isaac Taylor (1730–1807) proves unsatisfactory, he would send Green to Winchester to redo it. Except for the adjustments noted here by Cheyney, which the engraver F. Patton carried out, all worked out satisfactorily. Green's "arms" headed the genealogical table, his crosier appeared as the plate facing p. 286, and Taylor's tomb graced the frontispiece. Apparently the print Cheyney enclosed from Samuel Gale's *History and Antiquities of the Cathedral Church of Winchester* (1715) was intended as a visual representation of the corrections he was suggesting.

3 Probably William Baker (1705–70) of Winchester Street, London, an alderman of the City since 1739.

4 Lowth's distraction is evident in his next letter, six days later. Without asking to see Taylor's drawing, for which Cheyney here suggests changes, Lowth tells RD he can send it directly to the engraver.

5 Edward Say, in Avemary Lane, was the printer and publisher of the *General Evening Post*.

6 It is ironic that Cheyney should complain to RD about the misinformed obituary. He obviously had not seen the *London Chronicle* – in which RD had a major share – which printed on the same day as did the *General Evening Post* the following notice: "Sunday died, of a mortification, at Winchester, Dr. Cheyney, Dean of that cathedral. In November last he was on a visit at the Vicar of Blandford's; and as he was hurrying on one of his boots, the spur, which had been unfortunately left in it, run into one of his toes, which gave him excessive pain, and occasioned his death." Unfortunately no extant copy of the *General Evening Post* for 2 February has been located in order that the text for that notice might be verified. RD quickly attempted to undo the blunder in the 7–9 February *London Chronicle*: "The Rev. Dr. Cheyne, Dean of Winchester, is not dead, as was mentioned in the papers on Friday." The subject of death haunted Cheyney from the age of 30, when he drew up his first will. As an unmarried Winchester recluse, he continually revised his will (ultimately worth £28,000), making significant changes. This eccentricity apparently became known among his local acquaintance, and perhaps prompted the prank mentioned here.

7 Again, no extant copy of the *General Evening Post* has been located, and consequently Captain Imber's "obituary" cannot be verified. Perhaps he was the officer noted in the *London Chronicle* of the previous week (31 January–2 February): "A few days ago died of consumption at Shrewsbury, where he was recruiting, Captain Evers."

From John Scott Hylton

The Leasowes. Sunday Night 8 o'clock.
9th [–13] Feb.^{ry} – 1758.^{1}

Dear Mr Dodsley,

I have the pleasure to inform you that we think Mr Shenstone out of Danger; Dr Ash who has just left him, hearing me say that I would Write to you this post, desired I would present his Compliments to you & assure you of the same^2 His recovery gives us all good Spirits; tho' he is yet too weak and low to bear the Light, or the Visits and Messages of his Friends, who send from all Quarters to know how he does. I exclude every thing from him that may cause the least disturbance, & by so doing, and giving him the Bark, we shall be able to prevent a relapse, which might be dangerous, if not fatal.

I have not been six Hours from hence, since I last wrote to you for he will not permit me to leave him; indeed I could not, it would have been cruel in me if I had! When he is able to bear it, I will communicate the tender concern you feel for his sufferings to him. – His discourse since his being confined to this Bed, has been only what related to his Affairs, and that I have endeavoured to let be, no more than

what was needful; and I dare say you do not doubt my cure of him, as the pleasure
& Happiness I enjoy in this part of the world is connected with his Friendship and
Affection to me! – I am glad you have not taken Jessy into the Collection: He
probably means to amend it, and if he never had been able so to do; it, and other
Things would not have been supress'd.[3] – When you write I beg the Favour of
about half a doz.^{n} prints of the Grove, to colour for 2 or 3 Ladies, one of which I
mean to send to y.^{r} Coz.^{n} at Duffield.[4] – I am sorry I have no Frank, to enclose my
Letter. I thought to have sent this away to the post this Evening, but must defer it
now till tomorrow, tho' I am sorry to think what you must suffer every time the
post = man goes by your Door without calling at it. – Mr Inge my Attorney in Brook
Street has not sent the Books I ordered from you to be sent thither, but as he is over
Power'd with Business, and I am an idle Fellow, it is my own fault that I do not send
to him. – I mean however to write to him in a week or two, and will desire you to
send for them if I do not receive them soon after.[5] – Pray do inform me whether D^{r}
Smollet's History of England be worth purchasing, the cuts 167 in Number if well
engraved must be worth the Money[6] – The Natural History of the County of Kerry
excites also my Curiosity[7] – you know my Taste for Curiosities – All this however
does not exhibit any Taste in me for poetry, indeed I dare not presume to like or
dislike any thing of that kind before I know M^{r} Sh——e's Opinion, and tho' he is so
very delicate, I would scorn to be his Echo, because it precludes all Taste of one's
own, did I not know him to be as just, and generous, as he is correct and delicate.
God preserve his valuable Life, 'till we have had a larger share of the Happiness he
confers upon all around him! – if I do not hear from you in a week, I will write again.
When will your two Vol.^{s} come out? – I am Dear Sir

Y^{r} most Obliged

Hum^{b} Servant

John Scott Hylton

Monday Morning 9 o'clock

I am this moment come from him, he has had rather a bad Night, occasioned partly
by the weather, which was very stormy 'till after Twelve. I have dress'd his Blisters,
and the fatigue of that has thrown him into a dose, which I hope may refresh him. –
His Head was clearer this Morning, & his Ideas less confused than they have been
hitherto. – I will write sooner than a week, should he happen to be worse, which I
do not however Apprehend.

Address: To M^{r} R: Dodsley / in Pall = Mall / London
Postmark: 15 FE Birmingham

MS: Humanities Research Center, University of Texas at Austin, Robert Dodsley / Recipient 1 /Bound
ff. 25–28.

[1] Begun on Thursday 9 February, the letter was not completed until the 13th, as evident from th
"Monday" postscript. It took Hylton almost a week to write and mail this letter, as the postmark of th
15th shows.

Dr John Ash (1723–98) of the General Hospital, Birmingham, Shenstone's physician.
See RD's letters to Shenstone of the previous month.
An engraving of Virgil's Grove at the Leasowes, which RD was preparing for use with Volumes V and
VI of his *Collection*, and which he would also use for *Cleone* (1758) and *Melpomene* (1759 edition). See
RD's letter to Shenstone on 22 August 1758 for identification of his "Coz." at Duffield."
Edward Inge, attorney in Great Brook St, near Hanover Square.
A Complete History of England deduced from the Descent of Julius Caesar, to the Treaty of Aix la Chapelle, 1748 by
Tobias Smollett (4 vols. London, 1757–8). For RD's response, see his letter to Hylton on 20 February,
and for Hylton's order, see his letter of 24–5 February.
Hylton is probably referring to Charles Smith's *The Antient and Present State of the County of Kerry, being a
Natural, Civil, Ecclesiastical, Historical, and Topographical Description thereof* (Dublin, 1756).

From John Hoadly

Bath, Feb.ʸ 11. 1758.

Sir,

I beg y.ᵉ Favour of You, immediately on y.ᵉ Receipt of This, to send y.ᵉ Enclos'd to
Mr. Boyce of the Chapel:Royal,[1] (whose Place of Residence I know not,) and He will
send You a Parcel of Musical Papers, in a Box or Bundle; which I shall be much
oblig'd to You if You will send, y.ᵉ very first Opportunity, by one of the Bath-
Machines or Coaches, directed to me at Mr. Skrine's in Galloway's Buildings,
Bath. Together with These be pleas'd to send all my Volumes of P[oetry] as
carefully pack'd as possible; for they [?] begin to be as crazy outwardly, as [?] some
of them, with their Authors, are inwardly. How well You complied with my former
request, of sending me y.ᵉ Proof Sheets of Those Poems of M.ʳ Taylors & others, for
which I was particularly concern'd, that I might correct the Stopping, &c!² – I
have not hear'd a Syllable from y.ᵉ bold Berenger these 3 Months, but I hear, with
Wonder, that He is still at Lymington. I am,
　　　　　　Sir,
　　　　　Yours Sincerely
　　　　　　　J Hoadly –

I have forgot whether y.ᵉ *Epigrams* were call'd Translations – or Imitations – or only
Epigrams from Martial. Let 'em not be call'd *Translations* by any means.[3]

Address: To M.ʳ Dodsley, / Bookseller, at Tully's Head, / in Pall Mall, / London
Postmark: [13?] FE Bath
Frank: Free Henley[4]

MS: Bodleian, MS. Eng. Letters d. 40, f. 110.

William Boyce (1710–79), organist at the Chapel Royal in 1758.
See former RD-Hoadly correspondence for authors and titles of poems Hoadly had submitted for
RD's *Collection*.
Hoadly's poems were printed in the *Collection* as "Epigrams from Martial" (V, 285–8).
Probably Robert Henley (1708?–72), 1st Earl Northington; MP for Bath (1747–57); Speaker of the
House of Lords (1757–60).

From Robert Lowth

Sedgefield   Feb. 12. 175

Dear S.

'Tis so long since I have had from you any proof Sheet, that I think it high time
enquire whether you have sent any that have not come to my hands. The last that
had & return'd, came towards the end of Section 7.ᵗʰ. I forget the number of it. –
find the Dean of Winchester has sent you a Drawing of W.ᵐ's Monument for th
Title-page. He says 'tis well done; & he is best judge, as he could compare it w.ᵗʰ y
Monument itself. If you are in any haste therefore you may put it into th
Engraver's hands, without sending it to me.[1]

Dear S. Your's most aff.ˡʸ

R. Lowt

MS: BL. Add. MS. 35,339, f. 20.

[1]   The letter concerns the preparation of Lowth's *William of Wykeham*, to appear in May. For the Dean
Winchester's submission, see Thomas Cheyney's letter to RD of 6 February. Lowth does not seem t
least disturbed about the engraver's deviations from his model.

From John Scott Hylton

The Leasowes   16 Fe:ᵇ 175

Dear Sir,

The Bearer of this, M. Winwood of Birmingham, is a Gentleman who
acquainted in M. Baskerville's Family, also with our Friend M. Shenstone, and is
Friend of mine.[1] He Breakfasted here a few Days ago, and inform'd me he was goin
to London, when I desired him to wait upon you with this, and to give you wha
Account he could of M. Shenstone's Illness; who is now, thank God! much bette
than when I wrote last, he is quite free from his Fever if we can but keep him so, fc
he will not think himself that it is possible he should live, therefore (by the D.
order) I shall apply the Eighth blister to him this Evening – These are severities, bι
I hope wholsome ones.

Lord Stamford went for London yesterday, and sent a servant to inquire how M
Shenstone did – I told the servant, if at anytime he should pass by your shop i
Town, he might hear how M. Shenstone did, as his Lordship might be desirous (
knowing.[2] – If you can send a print or two of the Grove M. Winwood will put the
in his pocket Book for me.[3] – I will write again soon, and am in great Haste, which
hope you will excuse D. Sir

Y. Most Obed. Serv.

John Scott Hylto

Address: To / M. R: Dodsley / at Tully's Head / in / Pall = mall / London.

MS: Humanities Research Center, University of Texas at Austin, Robert Dodsley / Recipient 1/Boun
f. 21.

No doubt the Daniel Winwood to whom Hylton asks RD to send an order of books, in his letter of 18 February 1761. He indicates Winwood's address as New Hall Walk, Birmingham. The same address is listed in Sketchley and Adams's *Tradesman's True Guide and Universal Directory* (Birmingham, 1770) for a Daniel Winwood, toymaker.

Harry Grey (1715–68), 4th Earl of Stamford, of Enville Hall. For his relationship with Shenstone, see RD's letter to the poet on 3 May 1755, note 2.   ³ See Hylton's letter of 9 February, note 4.

To [Thomas?] Thackray

Feb.ry 18 [1758]¹

Dear Sir

I am not yet come to any certainty what share of Mr Stephenson's debt will be allotted me to pay, but believe it will be as you say about 50£. It goes extreamly against my heart to lessen your small income; & on ye other side it is very hard that I should lose 50£ by a person with whom I was but very little acquainted.² I have thought of two expedients. One is, that you give me now 50£ & let me pay you four P Cent for it during your life, which I suppose is as much as you make of it. The other is, that you give me a bond for the whole Sum that ⟨I⟩ may be allotted me to pay, to be paid by your Heirs Execturors, &c after your death, to me or my Executors. If you chuse either of these ways I shall be very well satisfy'd: or if you chuse neither of them, I leave it to your self to do whatever you shall think reasonable.³ And be assur'd whatever You determine upon, I shall always preserve that esteem and affection for you, which I owe to your friendship, & with which I have ever been,

Dear Sir
Your sincere & cordial friend.

MS: Robert Dodsley Letter Book, Birmingham Public Libraries, ff. 87–8.

The year is assigned by the RD Letter Book principle.
See RD's first letter to Thackray on 16 January, and especially notes 3 and 4.
Thackray's response to this unusual offer is not known, but apparently the matter was settled amicably, for in later letters to his cousin Elizabeth Cartwright RD sends Thackray his compliments.

To [John Scott Hylton]¹

Pall mall Feb.ry 20.th [1758]²

Dear Sir

I am extreamly oblig'd to you for the comfort your last letter gave me; and ⟨I⟩ hope as I have not heard from You since, our dear friend Mr Shenstone continues to recover. But do let me hear from you I beg: And tell him that to see his Name sign'd by himself only to those three words – *I am better* – would give me infinite pleasure. I should have written sooner, but could not get the enclos'd prints till now. I have seen some of the Cutts of Dr Smollet's History, & think as you say that

⟨the cutt⟩ they alone will be worth the mony.[3] The History of the County of Kerry I have not seen nor heard any character of.[4] ⟨Your little Tale⟩ I have found an opportunity of squeezing your little Tale into the last Volume; and shall publish now in about ten days or a fortnight.[5] Lord Lyttelton who is just gone from me, i very sorry to hear M.[r] Shenstone has been so ill, and desires his Compliments. With my most cordial wishes for the safe and speedy recovery of my Friend, I remain

Dear Sir

MS: Robert Dodsley Letter Book, Birmingham Public Libraries, ff. 89–90.

[1] Unquestionably the addressee is Hylton, for his letters to RD designate him as the one providing daily care for Shenstone during the latter's illness. Also RD herein responds to the requests in Hylton's letter of 9 February.
[2] RD's responses to matters mentioned in Hylton's letter on 9 February 1758, requires this letter to be assigned the same year.
[3] For the second corrected edition of his *Complete History of England* to appear in weekly numbers Smollett advertised engravings by Strange, Grignion, Ravenet, Miller, Houbraken, and Picquet among others.   [4] See Hylton's letter to RD on 9 February, note 7.
[5] See RD's letter to Shenstone on 16 January, note 4.

From John Scott Hylton

The Leasowes 24[-5] Feb: 175[8]

Dear Sir,

I wrote you a Letter this day week, which I sent by a gentleman of my Acquaintance whose Name is Winwood, & who set out for London in the Birmingham Stage last Monday, and also desired him to wait upon you with i himself. since then I wrote a Letter to him with some little Account how M. Shenstone was which I desired him to inform you of the first oppertunity. - Yesterday Evening I had the favour of yours with the prints, for which I return you many Thanks. The certainty of M.[r] Shenstone's recovery need not be doubted; he has occasion for very few Medicines now, & with the use of good restorative diet and the fresh Air by riding out a little way in a post = Chaize, (which I hope to get him into in a few Days.) now and then, as he can bear it will soon set him up again He had had some very good Days, & on Thursday was so well as to see Company, & sit in the Library – to day he has been rather low = spirited, but is not near so bad a he thinks himself to be. – I do all I can to raise him, and nothing that can do him good is omitted, indeed he wants nothing but to pursue the Rules laid down for him, and I would engage my Life, as D.[r] Ash would his, if he did not get well in a Month, to forfeit both. – He said, (for I shew'd him your Letter) that he would write a postscript to This, if he was able. Do not be uneasy if he should not, for it will be want of Spirits and not want of inclination if he should do otherwise – Lord Stamford hears once or twice a week how M.[r] Shenstone amends, by M.[r] Saunders his Lordship's Apothecary, whom he orderd to write to him for that purpose, who sends hither for Intelligence.[2]

25.th Feb: 1758.

Mr Shenstone I heard slept well last Night, which I am glad of, as it gives me an Assurance of his having a good Day in Consequence of it. I am glad to hear that our two Vol.^s will so speedily come out, and must confess it will be with some degree of impatience that I shall expect to see them after they are publish'd. I think you have done my little tale and me more honour than we deserve, and really hope you have not mark'd it out to be mine; for tho' written upon a Fact, in this part of the world, yet it is so very a trifle that I would not lay any great stress upon it.[3] Had my Indian Eclogue been finish'd, or fit to publish it would have given me great pleasure; but I have laid it aside for want of Mr Shenstone's pen to enable me to correct it's faults.

   The second Edition of Smollet's His: of England will be so long in coming out in d.^d Numbers that it will tire any one's patience to take it in that way; if you could procure me the whole at once, I should be very glad to have it (in Sheets) as soon as you can.[4] The reason why I chuse it in Sheets, is, because I mean to have the Cuts bound by themselves, or not as I shall like best. I will conclude my Letter now as Mr Shenstone will add a postscript, the sight of which will be a great pleasure to you, as it will be as much satisfaction to me to send it – I am Dear Sir,

                  Y.^r most Obliged Hum.^{le} Servant

                              John Scott Hylton

Shenstone's Note:] It was ever my Inclination to contribute to my dear dear friend Mr Dodsley's satisfaction; I may venture to say that I feel myself, to -day, as did likewise on thursday last, somewhat better than I have been. – Very willingly would I launch out into a greater Length of Letter, but as I cannot write to +

Hylton's postscript:]
   Dr Sir;
   Mr Shenstone was so fatigued at the place where I have made the Cross that I was obliged to take it from him – he will be better soon, and when able, will write to you, but I must trouble him no more till he is more composed – on Monday I hope he will take an Airing. He has been 4 or 5 Hours before he could attempt to write what he has written. – Adieu!

                     JSH

Address: To / Mr Dodsley / Pall = mall / London

Postmark: 27 FE

MS: Humanities Research Center, University of Texas at Austin, Robert Dodsley / Recipient 1 / Bound, f. 29–32.

The Winwood mentioned within as the bearer of Hylton's letter of the previous week is also specified in that previous, fully dated letter as the conveyor.

Probably the "Mr. Sanders" Shenstone mentions in his letter to Lady Luxborough on 11 September 1748 (Williams, p. 168) as "an Apothecary of Stourbridge, eminent in his *Way*."

See RD's letter to Shenstone on 16 January, note 4.

4 The fourth and last volume of the first edition of Smollett's *Complete History* had been available since the beginning of the year, whereas the projected 110 numbers of the weekly edition would not be completed until 1760.

From Robert Lowth

Sedgefield Feb. 24. 1758.

Dear S!

The sheet preceding these wch I return, y! is, the Sheet G, I have not seen: I hope you have taken care to correct it well. When you have finish'd the *Life*, I wish you w.^d send it all to me by the Newcastle Coach, directed to me at ye College Durham, that I may look it over, in order to make an *Errata* of any material mistakes that may remain.[1] The Appendix I suppose you will print on a less Letter: I think that will be more proper, & besides the Volume is big enough. Remember to send me with ye proof sheets of it, the Copy of N.ºs 5,6,7,8,12,13,14,15: I shall otherwise have no Copy to correct by. When shall you want the Preface, &c? – My Wife, tho' better than she has been, yet still continues very ill. – Believe me, Dear S!

Your's most Affectionately

R. Lowth

MS: BL. Add. MS. 35,339, f. 21.

[1] Lowth's *Life of William Wykeham*, which appeared in May.

To Joseph Warton

Pall mall Feby 27.th [1758][1]

Dear Sir

I verily think that if you leave off your agreeable Excursions and occasional Criticisms you will rob your work in a great deg[ree of] that variety which render'd it so ent[ertaining;] you will make it seem not all of a pie[ce and] lead your readers to think that the best [part] of Pope's Works are huddled together in haste, if not slubber'd over and neglected.[2] If you are afraid of any severe or ill-natur'd [remark] in the College, might not that be obvi[ated by] letting the second volume come out by your Brother?[3] Or might you not say in a prefatory Advertisement, that tho' you had collected your materials long ago, your present avocations which you thought it your duty not to neglect, had prevented your putting them together sooner?[4] I really think that another volume is as little as can possibly be employ'd to make the Work at all uniform; but it is certainly of more importance not to risk the censure of neglecting your present Business. Would not an Advertis[ment] prefix'd, professing, from your own want of [time t]hat you had given up all your materials [to you]r brother, obviate all blame, & save [the wo]rk? To confess the truth, I am

.fraid such a hasty jump to the end of the work will look like being in too much haste
o [be ri]d of it, and may prejudice the reader [against] it, as You have led him to
xpect rather more than a volume than less.

I am ever

dear Sir

Affectionately Yours

R. Dodsley

f Vernon's poems come to Fletcher push them[5]

Address: To the Revd Mr Warton / at the College / Winchester / Hants
Postmark: 28FE

MS: BL. Add. MS. 42,561, ff. 227–8.

The year assigned is based on RD's postscript, where he is urging Warton to encourage the sale of William Vernon's *Poems on Several Occasions* when it comes to the Oxford bookseller James Fletcher. Issued by W. Reeves in Fleet St, *Poems* appeared sometime in October 1758, for in that month it was listed in the *Monthly Review* (though not advertised in the usual places). Joan Pittock, in "Joseph Warton and His Second Volume of the *Essay on Pope*," *RES*, n.s. 18 (1967), 272, has suggested a 1760–1 dating for the letter, but RD seems to be giving a pre-publication "push" for the work. The assigned date shows that Warton had some of Volume II of his *Essay on Pope* ready for the press in 1758, supporting his statement in the Advertisement to the volume (which eventually appeared in 1782) that the first two hundred pages had been in print for more than twenty years. Such a claim is convincingly argued in David Fairer's bibliographical study of the volume in *Studies in Bibliography*, 30 (1977), esp. pp. 211–12.
This statement also supports the assigned date, for RD is obviously not referring to Volume I, published in 1756. In that volume, Warton had considered primarily Pope's early works, but Pope's "best" – *Essay on Man*, moral essays, *Dunciad*, etc. – were to be taken up in the second volume. Although RD did not live to see Volume II, its content does justify some of the fears he expresses here. Despite its dealing with Pope's longer, more mature work, the second volume is no heftier than the first; the *Dunciad*, for instance, earns only fourteen pages of commentary.
Thomas Warton, at the time Professor of Poetry at Oxford, had worked closely with his brother in preparing the first volume of the *Essay*. See RD's letter to Thomas on 20 January 1755, note 2, and David Fairer (above, note 1).
Warton had become Second Master at Winchester College in 1755, increasing the demands on his time.
Born at Wolverhampton of poor parents, William Vernon gained a rudimentary education before being bound to a buckle maker, an apprenticeship he left to enlist as a private in the Buffs. Various pieces of evidence, chiefly in his *Poems on Several Occasions*, show that, in 1757, he was in camp on the Isle of Wight, that he visited Winchester and the Wartons, and that they encouraged him to print his poems by subscription. One of the poems in the collection is dated "From the camp, on the Isle of Wight, September 4, 1757." Another poem published in the *Gentleman's Magazine* (August 1759) is entitled "Written in a copy of Dr. Young's Night Thoughts at Winton College, December, 1757." When *Poems* was published in 1758, its lengthy subscription list included both Joseph and Thomas Warton, as well as a surprising number of students of "Winchester College." Finally, its Advertisement acknowledged "The many obligations I am under to a very valuable friend of mine at Winchester (The Rev. Mr_____)" – most likely a reference to Joseph Warton. (I am grateful to Mr Harold Forster of Woodstock, Oxford, for helping to bring these details together. RD's interest in Vernon's success is not clear.

From John Scott Hylton

Thursday 2^{d}[–4] March. 1758

Dear Sir,

I am glad my Letter reach'd your Hands, as I was fearful of your impatience when I heard that Mr Winwood did not set out for London till 3 or 4 days after I had wrote the Letter he brought to you from me.[1] I am convinced you feel a grea deal for the Sufferings of your friend, who tho' mending apace I hope; is yet too weak and low to bear the intelligence of your affectionate good wishes for hi Recovery – He ask'd me if I had heard from you, & what you said to his imperfec postscript, to my letter. – I told him you were greatly concerned for him, & beg'c that he would ask me no further, which he did not – He suffer'd greatly about a week since, upon my telling him that I had had a Letter from Mr Jago, and was no composed of some Hours after, altho' he knew nothing of the Contents of it. – He sometimes mentioned you, and two or 3 more of his best Friends. – I hope you wil be so kind to let Lord Stamford know how he does when you have an oppertunity from the following Acc.^{t}[2] – last Sunday he had a tolerable good Day, and or Monday Dr Ash & Dr Roebuck perswaded him to go out in a post = Chaize which he did for an Hour, and bore it Very well,[3] on Tuesday he was low again (the Day being windy & somewhat rainy) and by no means c.^{d} I perswade him to go out for a $\frac{1}{4}$ of an Hour – on Wednesday not much better, but he went out for ab.^{t} $\frac{1}{2}$ an Hour, or Thursday he would have had a tolerable good Day – but he being unfortunately a Witness to Lord Dudley's Will, which had Caveat lodg'd ag.st it, and a Commissior at present held to enquire into the sam[?] caused them to apply for hi Examination, which Dr Ash and my self mentioned to him in the best manner we were able, he said he would do what he could to give his Evidence, and the paper were left in my Hands to take his Depositions, but his Head was too confused to beax it, or to do justice to the parties.[4]

The 3rd March 1758

Thank Gods! we have postponed the Comission to the 3^{d} of April. and by that time Mr Shenstone will be as well and as capable as ever to go thro' a fatigue of that kinc – 'tis a fine Day and I have sent Tom[5] for The Chaize and he must ride out anc mend of course; I will not let him be low = spirited again – Do (I know you will) rejoyce with me! – Alack Tom is come back without a Chaize from Dr Ash's – ! – I will send him away if I can, to borrow Mr Kendall's directly. – Dr Roebuck told M Shenstone that he should be in London this week, and should see you, therefore, nc doubt but you have had a particular Account of Mr Shenstone's illness from hin before this time. – Mr Piercy was here last Night, and saw Mr Shenstone for about 5 or 6 minutes, I wish we could have enjoy'd his Company, for he inform'd me that he had his M:S: collection of Old = Ballads in his portmanteau[6] – But it c.^{d} not be. I an to write to Mr Piercy in 3 week's time, and send him word how Mr Shenstone is by that time for he will not be return'd to Lord Sussex's before then.[7]

I have sent for Mr Saunders to come & bear M.^{r} S: company to day or to-morrow as he was desirous of seeing him, and who will also (probably) write some account o his Visit, and how he found Mr Shenstone, to Lord Stamford.[8] – Oh! how shall I rejoyce to see you here again, & I am sure M.^{r} S: will, & think himself much obligec to you, if you introduce M.ʳ Spence to his Aquaintance as you gave us to hope for.⁹ I will be sure to make M.ʳ Spence's Compliments to him in the manner you mention; and to avoid repetitions of this kind in my Future Letters to you, I will take care to inform him of every Thing by Degrees, that will add to his pleasure, and the restablishment of his Health, as I find he can bear it – I would go thro' any thing upon Earth to serve him, for his own sake, for your sake, and for the sake of many more, who as Men of Taste and Literature must ever esteem him. – And surely my own interest in his preservation will be no small Consideration with me. For he is my best and only Friend in this Country – my only conversible Companion, & Director, and without him I would quit Lapall; For the Leasowes would be worse than a Desert to me! – I will not now suppose it possible to loose him!

I am greatly oblig'd to you for your kind intention of sending me your 5.ᵗʰ and 6.ᵗʰ Volˢ¹⁰ by next Monday's Carrier (Friman I suppose) and will let you know in my next Letter whether I can venture to shew them to M.ʳ Shenstone when they come, or not. – I am wanted – therefore will finish this if possible after Dinner.

5 o'Clock. Friday Afternoon.

No post = Chaize to be had! – I am afraid to go up up stairs but must; and my only Consolation, is, that to morrow may be a fine a Day as this has proved.

4.ᵗʰ March – 8 o'Clock Saturday Morn.

M.ʳ Shenstone was in very good Spirits last Night, read to us in D.ʳ Young's Satires, and made us laugh Very heartily, eat his Supper, went to Bed ab.ᵗ Ten, took his Medicines, slept well, and has rung the Bell, to have a Fire lighted in the Library that he may get up. – The day promises fine, and I will not let him sit still at Home, if post Chaize can be had. I am ever Dear Sir

y.ʳ most Obliged & Affec.ᵗ

John Scott Hylton

P.S. Pray do you know who that Scotch man is in the London Magazine for January last? He signs G.G.[,] is (as his Verses intimate) the Friend & Acquaintance of Blacklock, and makes mention of M.ʳ *Shenstone* among others – M.ʳ Graves mention'd it in a Letter to *him* which I opened.¹¹

I have found a Frank in M.ʳ Shenstone's pocket Book, which I stole for you – I wish I could procure some and then I should write with greater Satisfaction to you, than to make you pay postage for my incorrect scrawl so often as I have done.

MS: Humanities Research Center, University of Texas at Austin, Robert Dodsley/Recipient 1/Bound, f. 33–6.

¹ See Hylton's letter to RD on 16 February, note 1.   ² Ibid., note 2.

³ John Roebuck (1718–94), Birmingham inventor and chemist, supported Shenstone's literary career, as he did Baskerville's printing projects. For Dr Ash, see previous Hylton letters in 1758.

⁴ For Lord Dudley, see Shenstone's letter to RD on 4 March, 1755, note 4. Dudley had died on the previous 21 October. Shenstone was an executor of his will.

⁵ Thomas Jackson, Shenstone's servant.

6　Thomas Percy (1729–1811), poet and editor of the *Reliques*. See RD's letter to Percy, December 1757
7　Henry Yelverton (1728–99), 3rd Earl of Sussex, had presented Percy to a second living at Easton Maundit. Percy had taken up residence in the vicarage adjacent to Sussex's groves in 1756.
8　See Hylton's letter on 24 February, note 2.
9　The meeting occurred the following June.
10　Of RD's *Collection*.
11　Robert Anderson, *A Complete Edition of the Poets of Great Britain* (1794), XI, 1151, identifies Gilbert Gordon (d. 1789), intimate friend of Blacklock and Collector of Excises in Dumfries, as the author of "On the Cultivation of Taste" (which had been printed in Alexander Donaldson, *A Collection of Original Poems by the Rev. Mr. Blacklock and Other Scotch Gentleman* (1760), pp. 27–39). The same poem had appeared in the January 1758, *London Magazine* (pp. 45–7), entitled "To a young Lady in Scotland, who desired the author would favour her with a Sight of what Manuscript Poems he had in his Possession." It is addressed: "My dear Miss G———n." The poet tells the lady not to limit herself to manuscripts but to study the best poets past and present. On Shenstone and Blacklock, he writes

> The soft distress of Shenstone's rural lay
>
> . . .
>
> Nor must I forget to recommend,
> Blacklock – my fav'rite – intimate and friend.
> We from our earliest youth to each were known
> Alike our pleasures, our associates one.

Anderson also identifies Gordon as the one who provided the introductory biographical account for the second Edinburgh edition (1754) of Blacklock's poems. See also Blacklock's letter to RD on 19 March, note 2.

From Robert Lowth

Sedgefield March. 5. 1758

Dear S.ʳ

I think M.ʳ Green has done the Crosier extremely well.[1] I inclose directions for finishing the Plate. 'Tis plainly too large for our Page, especially in the width: & it may be [le]ssen'd without any damage to it. You'll be so good as to give him the proper dimensions.

The Engraver would have perform'd better in the Genealogical Table, if he had not so scrupulously follow'd the Copy as to the Manner of it, w.ᶜʰ was never meant as a Rule for him.[2] Pray see that he makes the Corrections & Alterations given there. And let me have another Proof of Both before they are work'd off.

The Dean of Winchester tells me, you will see M.ʳ Taylor.[3] I had desir'd him to satisfy him for his 2 Drawings. [He?] says, that you will not only have an earlier opportunity, but will know better how to do it. I beg therefore that you will undertake it.

Believe me, Dear S.ʳ

Your's most Affectionately

R. Lowth

MS: BL. Add. MS. 35,339, f. 22.

1　For Green, see Cheyney's letter of 6 February, note 2.
2　From the context of the correspondence, it seems that neither Green, who engraved the crosier, nor

Taylor, who did the two engravings of William of Wykeham's tomb and monument, was responsible for producing the fold-out genealogical table at the rear of the volume. But the latter is unsigned, and no other engraver is mentioned in the correspondence.
3 See Thomas Cheyney's letter of 6 February, notes 1 and 3.

From John Hoadly

Bath, Mar: 8. 1758

Sir,

I am much surpriz'd to see You advertize, to publish this Month; for except what Pieces you have had corrected by ye Authors themselves, (which I think I can plainly trace,) ye Volumes are miserably printed.[1] I have run over them both, with out great Attention indeed & have mark'd a good many Faults, which occur'd – & hope they will not come too late, (by ye next Machine,) to be of Service to You.[2] I was surpriz'd to see a Poem of mine, (to Chloe, written on my Birth Day) printed again, when it is in one of the former Volumes. I have cross'd it out, & you must put some other Piece in it's Place, for such Heedlessness will never be overlook'd.[3] I *have* some notion that T. Warton's Poem upon Ale was printed before in another [?] yet I may be mistaken.[4] Why cou'd You [not] have bro't all mine together, & all Mr Tay[lor's,] some of which you have printed, that You formerly resolv'd not to take?[5] The Titles you have added to his are some of 'em very wrong and absurd. If it is not too late, I beg they may be alter'd. Dr Ibbot's Fit of the Spleen is made mortal Nonsense.[6] For my sake, let ye Pieces taken from my Volumes be corrected; or People will think I don't understand common Grammar.[7]

I hope, Dear Sir, that ye Work will alltogether turn out both to your Honour and Advantage. I desire no other Return for my Share of it, than that You will reserve a compleat Sett for me, & send another by the Winchester-Coach, directed to ye Revd Mr Taylor at Crawl[ey] to be left at Mr Newbolt's in Win[chester] with a Note from You, acknowledging ⟨you⟩ the Favour of his Permission (given to me) to print so many of his Father's Pieces.[8] – and that You will believe me to be,
Sir,
Your's sincerely
J. Hoadly.–

I sh^d say more but Writing gives me great Pain, having ye Gout in my Elbow and both Feet – tho' I have [?] up near a Month.

Address: To / Mr Dodsley, / Bookseller, in Pall Mall, / near St James's. / London.
Postmark: MR B[ath]

MS: Bodleian, MS. Eng. Letters d. 40, ff. 111–12.

1 An advertisement, announcing that Volumes V and VI of RD's *Collection* would be published "In a few Days," had appeared in the *London Evening Post* of 4–7 March.
2 Unfortunately Hoadly's next communication, indicating "Faults" he had discovered in the new volumes of the *Collection*, is missing; but see notes 3–6.

3 Hoadly's letter came too late for RD to remove the poem "To Chloe. Written on my Birth-Day, 1734'
   (VI, 229). It had also appeared in the second edition of Volume III (1748). A significant error on
   RD's part, the same poem, with a slightly altered title, appeared in two volumes of the *Collection*
   published in 1758, the fifth edition of Volume III and the first edition of Volume VI.

4 Hoadly was in error. Thomas Warton's "A Panegyric on Ale" appeared only in Volume VI, 258–62.

5 Hoadly's poems appeared on pp. 248 and 258–88 of Volume V; William Taylor's on pages 288–95 of
   Volume V and on page 125 of Volume VI. For the poems which RD had earlier suggested he would
   not use, see his letters to Hoadly on 26 October and 5 December 1757.

6 Hoadly justifiably resented at least two stupid errors in Ibbot's piece (V, 202), which, though not able
   to be changed in the first edition, were corrected in later editions. In line 3, "teeming" certainly made
   more sense that "seeming," as did "Fears" for "tears" in line 14. Later editions also showed the
   alteration of line 31, "But that of falling water, friend to thought," to "But that of Water, even friend to
   thought," a dubious gain.

7 The loss of Hoadly's manuscript volumes precludes the possibility of checking the discrepancies.

8 Henry Taylor (1711–85), son of William Taylor (see note 5), and a friend of Hoadly. He had received
   preferment through Hoadly's father, Benjamin, Bishop of Winchester, and at this time he had a living
   at Crawley, Hampshire.

From Thomas Lisle

Lincolns-Inn-fields.
Saturday evening.
[13 March, 1758?][1]

Dear S[r],

On the Receipt of your collection of Poe[ms] this evening, I ran over those which
are placed u[nder] my name, & return You my thanks for the care Yo[u] have
taken of the Press;[2] there is one line howeve[r] I could wish had been alter'd, & that
is the ninth, as it now stands, in my Letter from Smyrna, Vol. 6 Page 167 – *Besides,*
my –
The whole passage, in my manuscript, was as follow[s]

> Say first (but one thing I premise,
> I'll not be chid for telling lies;
> X Greece is a damn'd notorious nation,
> X And Bards are Lyars by profession;
> Besides, my Granum us'd to say,
> I always had a knack that way.

The two lines mark'd thus X are omitted in the print[ed] Copy, & I think,
deservedly, but then the following wor[ds] besides should have been alter'd
[beginning with ?] reason mentioned before. In the Book [you] sent me I have
altered it with my pen, & it now [re]ads thus, –

> I'll not be chid for telling lies;
> *My good old* Granum us'd to say,
> I always had a knack that way;

[Co]u'd it not be altered in the same manner in all the Copies not yet disposed of? if
it could, I should [b]e better satisfied with it.[3]
One thing more I have to mention, & that is the [R]ant to Venus, of which You
promised me no part [s]hould be printed, except the Anacreontic at the [e]nd; but

somehow, I find, it slipped your memory, &, since the real date is put to it, it is of no [g]reat signification.⁴ I wish You success in the [s]ale, & am,

Sʳ,

Your very faithful

Humble Servᵗ

Tho: Lisle.

Address: To / Mʳ Robert Dodsley / Bookseller in / Pall-Mall.
Postmark: Peny Post Payd

MS: Bodleian, MS. Eng. Letters d. 40, ff. 103–4.

¹ The month and year are certain; the day approximated. Within the letter, Lisle thanks RD for a set of the *Collection*, the last two volumes of which were published on 18 March (*LEP*). If RD had sent Lisle his set on the same day that he had sent sets to so many other contributors – namely, on the 13th (see RD's letter to Shenstone on 15 March) – then Lisle would probably have received it at Lincoln's Inn that very day, making this letter, acknowledging its receipt "this evening," a product of the 13th.
² Lisle's poems covered pp. 162–210 in Volume VI.
³ It is hardly likely that RD would have agreed to such a request. That he did not is suggested by the fact that later editions carried the text of the first 1758 edition.
⁴ "To Venus. A Rant, 1732" (VI, 164–5). The 49-year-old Reverend Doctor was probably a bit embarrassed by the youthful effusion at the poem's opening.

To William Shenstone

Pall mall Mar. 15.ᵗʰ [1758]¹

Dear Ṃʳ Shenstone

I have long'd to write to You almost as much as to hear from You: I venture at last, & hope this will find you so much recover'd, that You may favour me with a line to confirm me in that hope: but I beg, if it still continues to be uneasy to You to write, that you will by no means attempt it. I sent by Frimen's Waggon on Monday,² Carriage paid, a compleat Sett of the Poems, & two or three 5.ᵗʰ and 6.ᵗʰ which beg your acceptance, and which I suppose you will want to give to those who had the former four from You. I have my self sent the two last to Mʳ Graves, Mʳ Jago, and Ṃʳ Giles: I have also sent a compleat sett to Mʳ Bond and Mʳ Pixel.³ I hope You will be able to look into them, and that they will afford you some amusement. I shall be very glad to hear your opinion of them as soon as it shall become not disagreeable to You to take a pen into your hand. Ḍʳ Akenside presents his Compliments, & desires your acceptance of the enclos'd which will be published in a day or two.⁴ He, and many others very much regret yᵉ loss of your Elegy in the Collections.⁵ I will not tire you with a long letter – God bless you, and restore you to perfect health! I know not any thing that will give me so much pleasure as to hear it, being ever most sincerely and affectionately Yours

S. Dodsley

P.S. I intended to have written to Mʳ Hylton to night but find I have not time. I beg my compliments, & that he will accept of the two Volumes which are inclos'd in your parcel: & if You are not yet well enough to let me hear *from* You, I hope he will continue his indulgence in letting me hear *of* You.

MS: BL. Add. MS. 28,959, f. 97

¹ The year is clear within where RD indicates that he is sending the recently published Volumes V and VI of the *Collection* to Shenstone.
² That is, 13 March. The volumes must have been delivered to Tully's Head, then, by Saturday 10 March.
³ Richard Graves, Richard Jago, Joseph Giles, Daniel Bond, and John Pixell of Edgbaston, all friends of Shenstone. All except Bond had poems in the new volumes of the *Collection*. Bond (1721–1803), a local Birmingham artist, was responsible for the drawing of Virgil's Grove engraved by Grignion, which illustrated the opening poem of Volume V, Shenstone's "Rural Elegance."
⁴ Mark Akenside's "Ode to the Country Gentlemen of England," published by RD on 16 March (*PA*)
⁵ "Jessy." See RD's correspondence with Shenstone of the previous December and January.

From Thomas Blacklock

Dumfries 19 Mar 1758

Dʳ Sʳ

I wrote you about two months agoe inclosing a M:S Poem, & about a week after, sent you another letter upon the same subject; to neither of which I have receiv'd any return¹ – As my friend has been enquiring from time to time at me, whether any return has been made to those letters I could wish to hear from you as soon as possible – If you have not leisure to give the poem that critical examination you could wish it may be put into any other hand you think proper² – It woud likewise be extremely obliging to send me yᵉ copys of yᵉ octavo Edition of my Poems mentioned in my former, for there are a great many of them Commissiond here;³ & besides it will soon become necessary for me vigorously to sollicit all my old friends, & exert myself by every method possible in accquiring new ones of importance so that a quantity of these poems by me might facilitate my introduction to some people of superior Rank – You will know my meaning by connecting this with what I wrote formerly.⁴

By a letter lately receivd from Mʳ Spence I am allowd to entertain some hopes of seeing you here with him – it is a prospect on which I wou'd ruminate with inexpressible pleasure, if it cou'd obtain your sanction – perhaps you are a man of less courage than he, & dare not trust the effects of presbyterian Air & Presbyterian eloquence – for he bravely tells me that he hopes you will both hear me preach without being converted – You may perhaps escape the Aerial contagion, but I solemnly advise you to beware of the other – You are unacquainted with the forse of Scots eloquence – you neither know the sweetness nor variety of our Recitativo – you are not familiar to the real Thunder of our Rhetorick which according to Hudibras or Sam: Calvin is

On Pulpit Drum eclesiastick
To beat with fist instead of a stick⁵

Remember S^r tho' my hand is weak my spirit is willing, let your ears therefor be prepar'd against these batteries when you resolve to hear[6]

your most obedient Servt

Thos Blacklock

Address: To – / Mr Robert Dodsley – / at Tully's head Pall-mall / London
Postmark: 2 [?] MR Dumfries

MS: Osborn Collection, Beinecke Library, Yale.

[1] Neither letter traced.
[2] Could this be the poem by Gilbert Gordon, signed "G.G.," in the *London Magazine* for January, which praised Blacklock as poet ("Blacklock – my fav'rite – intimate and friend"), and which Hylton wrote to inquire about (see his letter to RD on 2–4 March, note 11) because it had also mentioned Shenstone's poetry favorably? Perhaps Blacklock had missed its appearance in the *LM*, although it is probably unlikely that RD would not have written to take credit for getting it inserted.
[3] The third edition of Blacklock's *Poems*, published by RD in 1756.
[4] For the significance of this statement, see Blacklock's letter of March 1759, where he explains his abortive attempt to lecture at Edinburgh University.
[5] Hudibras, Pt. I, Canto I, ll. 11–12.
[6] RD visited Blacklock on his trip through Scotland the following August.

To William Shenstone

Pall mall Mar. 30th [1758][1]

Dear Sir

As I have heard nothing either from You or of You this long while, I cannot help flattering my self that you are on the mending hand; & this prodigious fine weather gives me an additional pleasure, as I think it must be much in your favour. I Yesterday receiv'd a Letter from Mr Graves acquainting me that he & Mrs Graves intend to be in London in the Whitsun Week. I have wrote to him by this post to desire he will take up his abode with me whilst in Town, my house will then be empty.[2] And Oh, if You could but contrive to give him the meeting how happy I should be! Would not Mr Hylton come with You? I dare say he would. And I have room for You all. Can You withstand such an opportunity of seeing Mr Graves? I hope not! And I dare say the Journey would do You great good. Think of all these things, my friend, and make me happy by a visit.

I am ever
most affectionately Yours

R. Dodsley

MS: BL. Add. MS. 28,959, f. 98.

[1] Shenstone's "mending" determines the year. Hylton's and Graves's next letters, fully dated 22 April 1758 and 25 April 1758 respectively, both acknowledge RD's invitation to London, given here.
[2] Neither Graves's letter nor RD's has been traced.

To [John Brown][1]

[2–6 April 1758][2]

Sir

I did not see S^r C W till this morning when I deliver'd him only the short Message You desir'd viz: "That if he persisted in his design of inserting any personalities in his intended Answer to your book it might be attended with Consequences disagreeable to both parties." In answer to this Sr Cha dictated to me the following Words which he desir'd me to send to You.

Sir Cha W little thought ⟨that⟩ after what he had sent at Mr Ranby's request to Dr T.[3] which he supposes D^r B saw, that he would endeavour to intimidate M^r D from printing what he writes.[4] He is above entering into Personalities with D^r B, & shall concern himself only with his Book, unless his own Impertinence sh^d make it necessary.

In regard to ye rest of what pass'd between You and me on Saturday night, & your Letter on Sunday, I thought it not proper, for your sake as well as my own, that Sir Cha should know it from me. But for the sake of Truth, I thought it not amiss that one friend of Sir C's & one of your own sh^d be made acquainted with the whole.[5] If it goes any farther I suppose it will be your own fault. As to what regards my self, my Disposition is not to offend,[6] but not to be frighted: I shall certainly print what I may judge proper; and think, if you please to reflect on what pass'd between us, that a caution agst personalitites may at least be as proper for your self as for

Sir etc[7]

MS: Harvard Theatre Collection, Harvard College Library.

[1] Although unaddressed, the letter is certainly written to John Brown (1715–66), for its content concerns Sir Charles Hanbury Williams's proposed book-length response to the first volume of Brown's *Estimate of the Manners and Principles of the Times*, printed the previous year. The evidence is found in a letter of Sir Charles's (see note 4) and in Horace Walpole's colorful account of the heated exchange, when writing to George Montagu on 4 May 1758:

> The History promised you of Dr Brown is this. Sir Charles Williams, had written an answer to his first silly volume of the Estimate, chiefly before he came over [from St Petersburg], but finished while he was confined at Kensington. Brown had lately lodged at the same house, not mad now, though he has been so formerly. The landlady told Sir Charles, and offered to make affidavit that Dr Brown was the most profane curser and swearer that ever came to the house . . . Well – in a great apprehension of Sir Charles divulging the story of his swearing, Brown went to Dodsley in a most scurrilous and hectoring manner, threatening Dodsley if he should publish anything personal against him; abusing Sir Charles for a coward and a most abandoned man, and bidding Dodsley tell the latter that he had a cousin in the army who would call Sir Charles to account, for any reflections upon him, Brown. Stay; this Christian message from a divine, who, by the way has a chapter in his book against duelling, is not all: Dodsley refused to carry any such message, unless in writing. The Doctor enough in his senses to know the consequences of this, refused; and at last a short verbal message, more decently worded, was agreed on. To this Sir Charles made Dodsley write down this answer: "that he could not but be surprised at Brown's message, after that he, Sir Charles, had at Ranby's desire sent Brown a written assurance that he intended to say nothing personal of him – nay, nor should yet, unless Brown's impertinence made it necessary." This proper reply Dodsley sent: Brown wrote back, that he should send an answer to Sir Charles himself; but bid Dodsley take notice, that printing the works of a supposed lunatic might be imputed to the printer himself, and

which he, the said Doctor, should *chastise*. Dodsley, after notifying this new and unprovoked insolence, to me, Fox, and Garrick, the one, friend of Sir Charles, the other of Brown, returned a very proper, decent, yet firm answer, with assurances of repaying chastisement of any sort. Is it credible? this audacious man sent only a card back, saying, "Footman's language I never return, J. Brown." . . . On the same card he tells Dodsley that he cannot now accept, but returns his present of the last two volumes of his Collection of Poems, and assures him they are not spoiled by the reading. (W. S. Lewis, *Horace Walpole's Correspondence*, 9 (New Haven: Yale University Press, 1941 pp. 219–21).

2 The subject matter and the chronology of events require the letter to have been written between the occasion of Sir Charles Hanbury Williams's letter of 28 March 1758 (mentioned by RD and printed in note 4) and the publication of the second volume of Brown's *Estimate* on 10 April 1758 (*DA*). Had this second volume already appeared, it would certainly have caused the modification of the content of RD's letter. More particularly, RD's mentioning of Brown's failure to grasp the intent of Williams's letter to "Dr. T.," a product of Wednesday 28 March, together with his reference to a meeting with Brown on Saturday and to Brown's letter of Sunday – that is, 31 March and 1 April – would necessarily place RD's letter in the first week of April.

3 "Dr. T." is perhaps Robert Taylor, who, as a physician to George II and with an enviable practice in London, would be a likely person to be tending Williams, recently returned from St Petersburg where he had been in the King's service. Probably John Ranby (1703–1773), sergeant-surgeon to George II.

4 Probably what Sir Charles "had sent at Mr Ranby's request to Dr T." was the following unpublished letter found in the Bodleian Library (MS Toynbee, d. 19, ff. 18–19):

My Good Friend .

Kensington 28. March 1758

As you contributed very much to make me well, I will do all I can to make you Laugh, you gave me Spirits and you shall reap the Benefit of 'em.

I yesterday went with Mr Ranby to take the air, and during our Drive who should come to wait upon me but John Brown D. D. he seemed extremely eager to see me, and the people of the House say he looked as if he was frighted out of his Wits, but finding I was not at home, he inquired earnestly when I should return, my good Landlady told him, that I had ordered my Dinner at half an Hour after three, upon which he said he would call again between 4. and 5. but upon Recollection said he would call between 6. & 7. we expected him here but he never came,

But this Morning our Friend Ranby came in Laughing, and said he came with an humble Petition to me from Dr Brown the Contents of which was, that he beggd very hard that I would not mention his Addiction to Cursing and Swearing, in the Answer which I Intend his Book.

As I find you are acquainted with Dr Brown I desired you would read him what follows from me, It is his Book I mean to answer, and not to asperse him and I think myself in Hon^r obliged to do it from some passages which he will find in the Dedication and which are not at all relative to him.

He certainly is a Man of too Warm an Imagination as appears by his Work In which he is particularly Defective in Two Things Want of Knowledge and ⟨Caprice⟩ Practice in the persons, and Things, which he writes about, and which are quite out of his Sphere; and Judgment, what Would he think of a person in my Situation who have been constantly for above these Twenty Years in State Affairs, If I should write a Book ⟨about Divine affairs⟩ in Theological Writings in ⟨Christian⟩ public Business and abuse a great many Divines and Fathers I never read. This Warmth of Imagination may betray him into that Vice which he is afraid I should mention but as I found my Morality in this World and my Hopes of Salvation in the next upon the Truths and Lights of the Gospel I am thereby taught as to ⟨my⟩ the Wordly part not to return Injuries, I freely forgive the Doctor as far as I am concerned in the Book he may depend upon it I will not touch upon any thing that may hurt his moral Character andsofar from mentioning the Vice which I have heard from more than one pson/ and which if mentioned would do him Irretrievable Mischief I only advise him to amend it.

I have another Story which has been Confirmed to me by two persons one of ⟨which⟩ whom is a Friend of yours and perhaps you may know it yourself that Doctor Brown who is very severe upon such Clergymen as Dont do their Dutys and appear in all public places, Except their pulpits, has instead of attending his own Parish and warning and Exciting his parishioners to Do that Duty, and perform those Devotions which our Church has enjoyn'd so particularly for this Season he has been employing himself even during Passion week in Correcting a second Volume for publication and instead of a Weeks Preparation for the Holy Sacrament he has employed that week in preparing his Works for the Press, he sees the Moat in his Neighbors Eye but overlooks the Beam in his own, but of this also you may assure him that I shall not say one Word in my Book.

If I might give him, to show him that I do not wish him ill, what I think rather a Friendly peice of Advice I would do it by Counselling him not to publish his second Volume.

I am / My Dear Doctor / Your m! hble Serv!

CH

⁵ Henry Fox (1705–74), 1st Baron Holland (1763); and David Garrick, who had produced and acted in Brown's *Barbarossa, a Tragedy* (1754). See Walpole's letter in note. 1.

⁶ For better or for worse, Sir Charles's response to Brown did not make it into print.

⁷ This was RD's penultimate letter to Brown; according to Walpole, the firmness of the next (untraced) brought forth Brown's peevish: "Footman's language I never return."

From John Scott Hylton

Lapall House 22ᵈ April 1758

Dear Sir,

I have neglected writing to you for a long time, and that upon the Supposition that M! Shenstone's Health being in a manner re = established, my Correspondence would not be of so much Consequence as it had been. – I do now, and ought sooner to have return'd you my best thanks for your kind present of y! 4 and 5ᵗʰ Vol⁵ of the poems,¹ which are more than my *little squib* of an Epigram could merit by way of return. I think there are many good things in the Collection, and I was in great Hopes of seeing One very good thing there to have render'd the whole more pleasing to your Friends; what I mean is your Melpomene.² Perhaps you may publish it with other peices of your own seperate, some time hence: This is a point to be wish'd for, and I hope not to be despair'd off. – M! Shenstone is to all appearance as well as ever, he rides, and walks out almost every Day, but he is still weak and low = spirited at times. a journey to London, Bath &c would do him much service; I wish he would accept your kind invitation to meet M! and M!ˢ Graves at your House in May, and I would very gladly do myself the pleasure to accompany him to such agreable Company – I am in haste, & hope you will excuse me with an assurance that I am ever dear Sir

Y! most Obliged and Obed! Servant

John Scott Hylton

Address: To / M! Dodsley / in / Pall = mall / London

MS: Humanities Research Center, University of Texas at Austin, Robert Dodsley / Recipient 1 / Bound, ff. 37–40.

¹ Hylton's specifying Volumes IV and V must have been a slip on his part. Surely he meant V and VI, which had just been published, and which he had through Shenstone. See RD's letter to Shenstone on 15 March. ² See Berenger's letter to RD on 10 June 1756, note 1.

From Richard Graves

Claverton, 25 April 1758

Dear S.ʳ

The great Civility of your Offer deserv'd my earliest acknowledgment – But when I consider yᵉ particular nature of that offer, I am quite asham'd to have kept you so long in suspense – about my accepting of it – as it may have been highly inconvenient to you on many accounts[1] – You will imagine, that I have been deliberating upon it – or waiting for Mʳ Shenstone's Resolution – But alas! yᵉ chief Motive for our taking a London Journey is entirely inconsistent with the agreeable Scene you have so kindly deck'd out for us – You must know then S.ʳ that I shall be ⟨?⟩ on this occasion a Sort of Bear-leader to a Young Gent – whom I have had for 5 Years under my Care – and who is so destitute of friends amongst his own family – ⟨whence⟩ capable of taking care of him, that his Father has requested me to take him with me into Berkshire – & when we are there, to *shew* him London Town for a few days – So that, tho' we will contrive to be somewhere within Distance of you we cannot make a mere Convenience of your house – as we should be forc'd to do – if we accepted yʳ kind Offer[2] –

I have not heard yet from Mʳ Shenstone but am in hopes his Physicians will force him from his beloved Retreat – as a Change of Air must necessarily be of great service to him –.

I hope your Person is more at liberty than it was last summer – but perhaps the Publick will be the better for yʳ confinement – as I am sure yʳ mind is always free – For my part – tho' I long to be more at Leisure – for Meditation & Recollection – Yet I find my present Connections engage me in a Life of absolute Dissipation – and I never have a moment to myself –

Mʳˢ Graves joins in best Respects wᵗʰ

s.ʳ yʳ oblig'd humb Serᵗ

Ric. Graves

Address: To | Mʳ Dodsley | in Pall-mall | London
Postmark: 28 AP

MS: Somerset County Record Office, DD/SK, 28/1, 9.

[1] See RD's letter to Shenstone on 30 March 1758.
[2] Mr and Mrs Graves did visit London, but curiously – after this effusion – did not visit RD. (See RD's complaint to Shenstone in his letter of 23 May.) Even stranger, Graves did not explain his "rudeness" to RD until seven months after the visit; namely, in his letter of 20 December 1758 (q.v.).

To William Shenstone

Pall mall May 23ᵈ 1758

And so You think, dear Sir, that your having been ill last Winter, is to serve You as an excuse for not writing to your friends this Summer. But do not flatter your self that we will be put off in this manner, and bear it tamely. For my part, I declare I think it neither reasonable nor honest; and, in short, am so provok'd, that I verily believe I shall come and tell You so to your face. I am very much inclin'd to place to your account also my Disappointment in not seeing M.ͬ and M.ͬˢ Graves these Holidays: I have expected them all last week, but they never came.[1] Why would not You make their Journey sure, and my Happiness compleat, by promising to meet them here? They would then have certainly come. But you are the most – O how I could abuse You! But I will suppress my cholar at present, to show what a Philosopher I am, and how much my Passions are under Command.

M.ͬ Spence and I intend to set out for Scotland on the 23ᵈ of next Month.[2] We shall stay two or three days at his Living in Bucks, & then in our way Northward, we propose if You are at home to spend a day or two at the Leasowes. M.ͬ Spence desires his Compliments, and, as much of the pleasure of our Tour depends on seeing You, I beg if it be possible for You to take a pen into your hand, that You will favour me with a line, to let us know whether You will about that time be disengag'd. I beg my Compliments to M.ͬ Hylton, and am ever

Dear Sir

most truely & affectionately Yours
R. Dodsley

MS: BL. Add. MS. 28,959, f. 99.

[1] Actually Graves and his wife had already visited London. See Graves's letter of 25 April, note 2.
[2] Joseph Spence and RD would begin their trip a week earlier. See RD's next letter to Shenstone, of 13 June.

To Sir Charles Hanbury Williams[1]

May 23ᵈ 1758

Sir

By Yesterday's Monmouth Carrier I sent You two Bourn's Justice & the 4ᵗʰ Volume of the Biographia: Also the Numbers of Smollet's History of England, as far as they are come out. I will send next Monday Ainsworth's Dictionary, & if any thing should come out worth sending I will not fail to enclose it.[2]

I am
Sir
Your most obed.ͭ Serv.ͭ

R Dodsley

On D.ͬ Brown's Declaration, that, in his Business of exposing the People of England, he will not be content with a smaller District than that of his Majesty's Dominions.[3]

The Devil and Doctor take their Tour,
Their business much the same;
One seeking whom he may devour,
The other, whom defame.

Both prowl for Culprits – Brown, beware!
Satan's a subtil elf:
Twou'd make you swear, if you *cou'd* swear,
To be pick'd up your self.

Endorsement on overleaf: May 23, 1758 Dodsley

MS: The Lewis Walpole Library, Farmington, Conn.

[1] Just the year prior to this letter, Williams had returned frustrated from St Petersburg where, as ambassador, he had succeeded in working a triple alliance, only to have British policy reverse itself and to see his victory go unacknowledged and unrewarded. Probably these circumstances caused the emotional breakdown that led to his suicide in late 1759.

[2] Samuel Bourn, *The Scripture Account of a Future State Considered,* 1754 (although RD refers to the work as "Bourn's Justice," justice was the subject of the work, not part of its title); *Biographia Britannica; or the Lives of the most Eminent Persons who have flourished in Great Britain and Ireland from the earliest ages down to the present time* (6 vols. London: W. Innys 1747–66) (Volume IV had just appeared on 6 May); Tobias Smollett's *Complete History of England deduced from the Descent of Julius Caesar, to the Treaty of Aix la Chapelle, 1748* (4 vols. 1757–8), was currently being re-issued in a corrected, second edition in installments and at this point had reached No. XIII (*LEP*, 20–3 May); Robert Ainsworth, *Thesaurus Linguae Latinae Compendiarius: or a Compendious Dictionary of the Latin Tongue* (2 vols. 1736).

[3] John Brown's highly controversial *Estimate of the Manners and Principles of the Times,* first published in 1757, had been expanded into a second volume, appearing on 12 April of this year (*PA*). For Williams's clash with Brown regarding the former's proposed review of Volume 2, see RD's letter to Brown in early April of this year.

From Robert Lowth

Durham June 9. 1758.

[D]ear S^r

[I] have rec^d your packet. I must [beg] of You to send two more of W^m [of W^k]^m to Winchester directed to Dr Eden, [&] one to Mr Prince at Oxford, for [p]resents.[1] To me also two more: & [w]ith them be pleas'd to send, Four Essays upon the English Language, by Professor Ward; An Introduction to Languages &c, by Mr Bailey; Tragoediarum Graecarum Delectus by Dr Burton, wth De Graec. Litt. Institutione Dissertatio, by the same, bound together: Voltaire's Histoire Universelle, the best Edition in French. All bound & Letter'd. The first Volume of Duncombe's Horace, wch Mr Duncombe says he order'd for me, as a Present; & pra[y en]ter my name as a Subscriber for [the] same.[2] Pray send me likewise [a] Specimen of different sorts of your best Letter writing Paper. An[d] add likewise to the Books above order'd, Theatre des Grecs, par [le] Pere Brumoy, the very best Edition (in 8vo or 12[^{mo})] handsomely bound.[3]

I wish you a good Journey into the North; pray let me know your Route, & when you are to be at Edinburgh[4] I have never a Frank.

Believe me, Dear S^r

Your's most affectionately

R. Lowth.

Address: To M.ͬ Dodsley / Bookseller in Pall Mall / London.
Postmark: 12 IV Durham

MS: BL. Add. MS. 35,339, ff. 23–4.

[1] Lowth's gifts of *Life of William of Wykeham*, just published on 27 May, were to his son-in-law, Robert
Eden, DD (1701–59), prebend at Winchester, and probably to Daniel Prince, bookseller at Oxford,
who is listed in *Alumni Oxoniensis* as "privilegiatur" in 1750 and described by David Foxon ("Pope and
the Early Eighteenth-Century Book-Trade," Lyell Lectures, Oxford University, 1977 (unpublished
Ms.), p. 124) as "overseer of the Learned side of the Oxford University Press from 16 February 1758."

[2] John Ward, *Four Essays Upon the English Language* (1758); Anselm Bayly, *An Introduction to Languages
Literary and Philosophical; especially to the English, Latin, Greek, and Hebrew* (1758); Πενταλογια, *Sive
Tragoediarum Graecarum Delectus* edita Joannis Burton (1758); *De Literarum Graecarum Institutione
Dissertatio*, also by Burton; Voltaire's *Abrégé de l'Histoire universelle, depuis Charlemagne jusques à
Charlequint* (1753), which had appeared in English as *The General History and State of Europe, from the
Time of Charlemain to Charles V* (1754–7). *Works of Horace in English Verse. By Several Hands*, collected and
published by John Duncombe. Volume I (1757). Volume II, to which Lowth is here subscribing,
appeared in 1759.

[3] Pere Brumoy, *Théâtre des Grecs* (1730). In 1760, RD, along with several other booksellers, would
publish Charlotte Lennox's translation *The Greek Theatre of Father Brumoy*, in 3 volumes.

[4] Most probably RD visited Lowth when he reached Durham. See his romantic description of Durham
in his letter to Shenstone on 22 August 1758.

To William Shenstone

Pall mall June 13.ᵗʰ [1758][1]

My dear Friend

For how many months in vain have I hastily cast my eye over the superscriptions
of my Letters, when the Post came in, to spy out your hand? You have at last made
me very happy in receiving a Letter from You which gives me a tollerable account
of your health.[2] But if I was pleas'd merely with the receit of it, I was delighted with
its length & its Contents. I see you are well by the spirit of your Lines, as one knows a
Bird is in health by the shining of its plumes: and if I may judge by my own feelings
on the sight of your Letter, I can easily believe a heart like yours will feel some
additional pleasure on the visit of a friend: but you will die in no man's debt on this
account, as the pleasure which You give your friends will always leave the ballance
sufficiently in your favour. I will not answer the whole of your Letter now, as I hope
to have the pleasure in a few days of doing it vive voce, Mͬ Spence and I purposing
to set out on our tour on Friday next. This being a week sooner than we intended,
we shall probably be with You about the 21.ˢᵗ or 22.ᵈ[3] I beg my Compliments to Mͬ
Hylton; I am much his Debtor for the accounts he was so good as to give me from
time to time of your health; in which if he sometimes made you better than you
really was, it was a kind deceit, and I am the more oblig'd to him. Mͬ Spence is just
come in, and desires his Compliments.

I am ever
Dear Sir
Affectionately Yours
R. Dodsley

MS: BL. Add. MS 28,959, f. 100.

¹ The year is derived from the mention of RD's impending trip north with Joseph Spence, which coincides exactly with the trip announced by RD in his letter to Shenstone on 23 May 1758. Also, the allusion to Hylton's accounts of Shenstone's illness must refer to the former's letters of February 1758.
² Not traced.   ³ See RD's letter to Shenstone on 23 May.

To William Shenstone

Pall mall Aug.ˢᵗ 22.ᵈ [1758]¹

Dear Sir

I did not finish my long Tour till Saturday last, & this is yᵉ first Letter I sit down to write. I left M.ʳ Spence in good health at Durham, where he comes into Residence as this day, & will consequently be there for three weeks longer at least.² But I suppose you have heard from him before now, & how much he admires your Elegies, &c I have sent them to go by tomorrow's Coach, which will be in Birmingham on Thursday night, where I hope You will receive them safe, & that you will lose no time in putting them to press.³ The other two Volumes I will send if you desire it, but had rather keep them till You come to Town, which I hope I may now most certainly depend upon. I will not forget the Pidgeons as soon as I have an opportunity of enquiring about them.⁴ I beg you will send me (and by the return of the Post if you possibly can) yᵉ Letter I left in your hands, with your corrections.⁵ You will also let me have as soon as you have opportunity, a Description of yᵉ Leasowes, for yᵉ use I mention'd to You.⁶ I call'd at Duffield in my return, & thank you for pointing out to me so agreeable a relation.⁷ She is indeed a fine Girl, & desires her Compliments to You & M.ʳ Hylton; and pray be so good as to give him mine. I hope I am secure of seeing You next Winter, as I know M.ʳ Spence will very strongly insist on your returning his visit at Byfleet. He is not without hopes of seeing you also at Durham; and indeed you would be pleas'd with it, as it is one of the most romantic places I ever saw. It is situated on four or five Hills, & the river Weare encompasses almost yᵉ whole of it. On the North of yᵉ Cathedral is an old Castle which is the Bishop's Palace, where yᵉ present Bishop, Dʳ Trevor, has made very considerable Improvements.⁸ On the South is a large Court call'd the College, round which are the Dean's & Prebends' Houses, which are handsome & convenient. From the upper end of this Court, a short passage leads directly to what they call the Water-Walks, a Scene more delightful than can well be conceiv'd. It consists of a sweet Walk on a large sweep or bend of the River, arch'd over with wild hanging Woods & intermingled Rocks, on a steep ascent that goes up almost perpendicular from it. There are Seats here and there on the bank of the River, & some interspersed in the retir'd parts of the woody ascent, affording various and delightful prospects. The whole City is surrounded with hills, not high, but pleasing; & on the other side is Pella Wood, which is a scene of the same kind with yᵉ former, only bolder, wilder, & both more rural & more retir'd. But amongst all these enchanting Prospects, let me not forget, what is as much so as any of them, the

Retirement of our friend at his Abby of Finculo, about four miles from Durham.[9] It consists of the Ruins of an old Abby, enough of which is remaining to render it a fine venerable Object. It is situate in a romantic valley, by the side of ye River, which here tumbles along amongst rough Stones & pieces of rock; & on the opposite side is a steep craggy ascent intermingled & overhung with Woods, in a very picturesque manner. Hither we brought a cold Collation, drank your health, & heartily wish'd for your Company.[10] I must conclude abruptly, for I shall not have time to finish several other letters which must go by this night's Post.

I am ever

Affectionately Yours

R. Dodsley

P.S. Pray don't neglect to return me ye Letter. It may be of Consequence. Has Mrs Gataker yet call'd on You? If she should, she will well deserve your particular regard.[11]

Address: To / William Shenstone Esqr / at the Leasowes / near / Birmingham
Postmark: 22 AU
Frank: Free E. Rudge[12]

MS: BL. Add. MS. 28,959, ff. 101–2, 108.

¹ Once the year of RD's letter to Shenstone on 19 September 1758 is established (q.v.), it becomes clear that this letter too is a product of 1758, for several matters mentioned in that letter are follow-ups on points found in this. First of all, the "long Tour" alluded to here is doubtless RD's trip to Scotland with Spence, which he had announed in his letters of May and June of 1758 and about which, in the September letter, he apologizes to Shenstone: "I wish we had known You had ye least inclination to have seen Scotland." RD's request for "ye Letter I left in your hands" (probably the dedicatory letter to Chesterfield prefacing *Cleone*) is explained in the later letter. Also, his request for a description of Leasowes is elaborated in his later letter, as is his promise not to forget the "Pidgeons." Finally, regarding the elaborate description of Durham which concludes this letter, RD says in the later piece: "Durham is certainly all and more than I have describ'd."
² Spence had been appointed a prebendary at Durham.
³ The publication of Shenstone's elegies would be considerably protracted; in fact, they would appear posthumously in RD's edition of Shenstone's *Works* (1764).
⁴ See RD's letter to Shenstone on 19 September.
⁵ Ibid, note 4.
⁶ Ibid, note 5.
⁷ Probably Elizabeth Cartwright, whom Hylton, in his letter of 9 February 1758, calls RD's "Coz^n." See RD's later correspondence with Miss Cartwright.
⁸ Richard Trevor, Bishop of Durham (1752–71).
⁹ Spence's residence in Durham.
¹⁰ A certain auspiciousness surrounds RD's enthusiasm for Durham in this elaborate description: six years later, on his next visit, he would be buried there! In September of 1764, whils visiting Spence, the close friend of his later years, he would die in the "romantic valley, by the side of ye River." Spence's epitaph for his friend can still be read on the large, flat brown stone that marks his grave in Durham Cathedral burial ground.
¹¹ Probably Mrs Thomas Gataker (d. 1797), wife of the London surgeon, several of whose works RD

had published in the late 1750s. The last two sentences, together with the address, postmark and frank, appear on folio 108.

[12] Probably Edward Rudge (1703–63), MP for Evesham, Worcester (1741–54: 1756–61).

From Thomas Blacklock

Dumfries 23 Aug. 1758

Dear Sir

By this time I hope You are got home, & have recovered the fatigue of so long a journey.[1] Tis my misfortune, & that of a great many others to be less capable of expressing friendship when they ought to do it, than at any other time. When we form ideas of Mankind per advance it frequently happens that the Picture is superiour to the original. I was extreamly disappointed, but nothing cou'd be more agreeable than the disappointment. For whatever advantageous impressions Mr Dodsley's former Conduct had made upon my mind, his appearance only served every moment to heighten & improve them. The Young Gentleman who will probably give You this is one of the most universal accomplishments I ever met with. Every human creature is almost mark'd & predestin'd by nature for some particular science or pursuit; but when You converse with Mr Shand, You will be at a loss for what part he is intended, so much does he excell in all. From his easy genteel behaviour in company One wou'd imagine he had been always in the world. From the profoundity & extent of his learning, it wou'd be hard to perswade one that he had ever been out of the closet. He is passionately fond to obtain the acquaintance of People of reputation & learning in England, & as I know none more proper to recommend him than Mr Dodsley, I cannot forbear wishing that You would exert Yourself in introducing him to company. Believe me, every Man of taste will think his acquaintance an acquisition when he is known.[2] – Pray let me hear from You at your first leisure. I shou'd be sorry to be forgot just when You have seen me. At the same time I shall not wish to be longer, nor more warmly remembered than You are always, by

> Your sincere friend, &
> most humble Servant
>
> Thomas Blacklock

P.S. Perhaps this may be delivered You by Mr Chapman whom You saw when the Magistrates of this place were with You. He is Master of the Grammar School here.[3] I am not sanguine in my opinions of Mankind, but if I am at all a judge of the human Character, there is no Sphere in life which Mr Chapman wou'd not dignify, as far as Virtue & integrity of life can adorn it.

MS: Osborn Collection, Beinecke Library, Yale.

RD's trip to Scotland, begun in late June and ended the previous week.

[2] The illustrious Mr Shand seems to have escaped Blacklock's biographers.
[3] George Chapman (1723–1806), master of the grammar school in Dumfries (1751–74), and afterwards
     a printer at Edinburgh.

From Sir James Stonhouse[1]

Northampton Aug: 24. 1758.

Sir

The Essay on Monopolies is written by a Person of excellent Sense, whom you
well know – but He chuses *at present* to conceal his Name.[2]

If you'll please to print ye Pamphlet (at Six Pence) with all possible Expedition
He will indemnify you from any Loss, which may accrue from the Deficiency of it's
Sale.[3]

If you have any *particular Reasons* for not printing it, you'll then please to send the
Manuscript, as soon as you receive this, to Mr Cluer Dicey's in Bow Church Yard,[4]
directed for

Your humble Serv

James Stonhouse

P.S. Please to write on ye Outside
"Dr Stonhouse desires this may be sent with ye Packet on Saturday Morning." –
Every Saturday Morning at Six a Packet with ye News Papers comes from M^r
Diceys by a special Messenger to Northampton. Probably you'll receive this Letter
Fryday afternoon ab^t five.

MS: Harvard Theatre Collection, Harvard College Library.

[1] Sir James Stonhouse, MD (1716–95), eleventh baronet (1792), the clergyman characterized by
     Hannah More as the "Shepherd of Salisbury Plains." In 1761, the Dodsleys sold from Tully's Head
     Stonhouse's *Universal Restitution a Scripture Doctrine*, but seem not to have been the publishers of any of
     his works.
[2] George Tymms's *Essay on Monopolies, or Reflections on the Frauds practiced by Dealers in Corn* would be
     advertised as published on 18 September 1758 (*PA*). The author acknowledged the work in a letter to
     RD, written probably in late August or early September (q.v.).
[3] The pamphlet sold at 6*d*. In the letter mentioned in note 2, Tymms assumes all responsibility for RD'
     possible loss on the sale.
[4] Cluer Dicey, a printer and publisher at the Maiden-head in Bow Church Yard, London, had also
     inherited his father's print shop in Northampton, where Stonhouse had a medical practice from 1743
     to 1763.

From George Tymms[1]

[*post* 24 August; *ante* 9 September 1758][2]

I flatter my Self that you know me enough to believ[e it] is not without great
reluctance ⟨that⟩ I commence Author at this time of Life . . . At the request of my

'riend Doctor Stonhouse of Northampton, I left in his hands a few Observations I ₁ad made upon the Monopolies of Corn and Flour, and his partiality for the Writer ₁as so far misled his better Judgment, as to make him insist upon their being put ₁nto form and printed.[3] This I have at last consented to, but I assure you very ₁nwillingly; and upon the express condition that my name shall not be put to it.[4] I ₁eave intirely to your discretion, whether it may be proper for this little Pamphlet to ₁ome out (if out it must come) under the Title of an Essay upon Monopolies: or ₁eflexions &c. *in a letter to a Friend. –* If so, be pleased to let it be subscribed ₁ublicola. – I was asked for a Motto, but have not been able to hit upon one that ₁leased me; and should be much obliged to you or any Friend of yours for a better.[5] N.B.: I give you an absolute power not only over the Title page, but every other ₁age and Sentence of it; and beg of you at least to correct any blunder wch. you may ₁bserve, that your Friend may be as little exposed as possible.*]* – If you can ₁onvince the good Doctor[6] that we had better *keep the piece ten years,* you will oblige ₁ne much: as I hope before that time, there may cease to be a reason for any ₁iscourse upon the Subject, which would have been better relish'd Six months ₁go.[7] – I now know that I ought, and most readily will, be accountable to you for y^e ₁aper wasted, and other Expences of printing, what I am very sensible no body ₁vould buy, if they cou'd see more of it than the Title.

I am Dr Sir,

Most faithfully and Sincerely

Yours

Geo. Tymms

n ye M.S. pag. 1. I find the word *Turtles* omitted; viz it should stand – *let these ₁ngrossers of Turtles*[8] [?] conclusion. – *Whenever a* [?] *the Proof:.* &c. The note here ₁eferred to (if it be proper [?] come in better in another place; viz. under Page . . . ₁vhere ye Par. [?] that the Grain sells for nothing; and immediately after thes words . . *We know by him when the times are likely to be good*:[9] &c. But I must own, that were it ₁ot for my deference to a superior Judgment, I should have struck out that Note ₁nd the reference to Yarrenton's Book:[10] wch I was apprehensive wou'd give y^e ₁Vriter of this Pamphlet too much ye appearance of a Schemist, or what the French ₁all a *Visionaire.*

₁S: Harvard Theatre Collection, Harvard College Library.

₁ George Tymms (1699–1781), son of a saddlemaker of Doncaster, Yorkshire; LLB, Sidney College, Cambridge (1753); Vicar of Raunds, Northampton (1731–55), and at this time Rector of both Harpole (1740–59) and Cottesbrook (1755–81).
₁ The letter is an obvious follow-up to James Stonhouse's letter to RD on 24 August 1758 (q.v.), but it must predate Tymms's next letter on 9 September, for the printing of his *Essay on Monopolies, or Reflections upon the Frauds and Abuses practiced by Wholesale Dealers in Corn and Flour* is then in a more advanced state.   3 See note 2.
₁ The *Essay* was published anonymously on 18 September.
₁ "In a letter to a *Friend*" was not used, nor was the subscript "Publicola." (Latin: "people's friend." Valerius Publicola was the first consul of the Roman republic.) The title page carried two mottoes

taken from Cicero's letters to Publius Cornelius Dolabella, Consul, and to T. Pomponius Atticus. Perhaps RD himself chose the mottoes, for he would have had a copy of Cicero's letters at hand having published Melmoth's translation five years earlier.   6 James Stonhouse, see above.

7 Although standard in the modern market, the manipulation of commodity supplies for purposes of increased profit had only begun to take hold in the English agricultural world during the eighteenth century. Bad harvests played into the hands of stock-piling and engrossing millers and middlemen to the detriment of both farmers and the poor. Bounties and the remission of duties on exports exacerbated conditions during lean years. The years 1756 and 1757 produced bad crops, and the subsequent short supply of grain caused a starving and angry populace to riot and to destroy the property of their enemies. Tymms's pamphlet, like so many others of its kind during the period, took aim at all the guilty parties, focusing on the hoarding farmer and the brace of middlemen, at the center of which stood the greedy miller. But the harvest of 1758 proved a good one, relieving the pressure for reform. What then "would have been better relish'd Six months ago" – in the spring – was now "out of fashion." None the less, Stonhouse's extract of Tymms's pamphlet, as printed in the *Northampton Mercury* on 18 September (see Tymms's letter on 9 September, note 3), claimed that the *Essay* would "be put into the Hands of every Member of both Houses of Parliament" with the hope that the problem would be taken up at the next session. Whether the copies were actually delivered is not known, but Parliament seemed sufficiently anxious that the new session brought at least a renewal of the Corn Laws of the previous year. (See Donald Grover Barnes, *A History of the English Corn Laws from 1660–1846* (1930; rept. New York: Augustus M. Kelly, 1961), passim.)

8 The right top corner of the manuscript is broken off. On p. 5 of the printed text of *Monopolies*, "Turtles" is included in the line that begins: "Let there be Ingrossers of *Turtles, Ortalons, French Claret . . .*"

9 The line, on p. 16, runs: "Mr. A buys now, and we can tell by him when the times are likely to be good."

10 The footnote to the line referred to in note 9 alludes to Andrew Yarranton's *England's Improvement by Sea and Land* (1677–81). Tymms wonders "Whether a Scheme proposed by Mr. Yaranton in his ingenious Book . . . p. 209 . . . may not be worthy the Attention of the Legislature." Noting that "this valuable Book is out of print," Tymms recalls the proposal's intention to establish public granaries where the farmer might store his grain when the price is low. The grain could then be used as a tradable commodity at any time and also afford landlords security against the farmer's rent.

To Sir Charles Hanbury Williams

Pall mall Augst 31st [1758]^1

Sir

I have this day been up at your House in Brook Street, but as there are not yet any shelves put up, I cannot at all judge of the size or quantity that will be wanted. However, when you come to Town, and let me see a List of what Books will be wanted, I dare say we shall not disagree about the Terms, as it will always be a pleasure to me to obey your Commands, being

Sir
Your most oblig'd
and obed! Servant

R Dodsley

Endorsement on overleaf: Augst 31.58 / Mr Dodsley

MS: The Lewis Walpole Library, Farmington, Conn.

1 The year is taken from the endorsement, which seems to be in Williams's hand.

From William Whitehead

Middleton Park, Sept. 2, 1758.

Dear S.!

Inclosed I return you the receipt, & am much obliged for the trouble you have had about it. I should have let it go on 'till the half year, had not they told me that they always chose to pay it quarterly. The deductions bring it down somewhere about nineteen pounds.[1] I have no accounts with me in the Country, or I would tell you the exact sum, but Mr Adams will settle it all with you. I will send you the Ode in Honour of the King's Birthday][2] in about a fortnight or less.[3] Have you anything literary in prospect for this winter? The playhouses, I presume, are near opening. Are we to expect any novelties either in plays or actors? I had the pleasure of seeing your friend Mr Melmoth at Bristol this summer, but had much less opportunity of being in company with him than I could have wished.[4] I have some thoughts of being in Town about the 1st of November whether I stay the birthday or not, & can then hear a rehearsal, if it should be necessary.

I am, dear Sr.,

Your most obedient
Humble Servant,
W. Whitehead.

Source: Straus, p. 113.

Unidentified.   [2] Brackets appear in Straus text.
In the *London Evening Post* of 9–11 November appeared, printed in full but without the music: " 'Ode for his Majesty's Birth-Day, Nov. 10, 1758.' Written by William Whitehead, Esq; Poet Laureate; And set by Dr. Boyce, Master of the King's Band of Musick. The Vocal Parts by Mess. Beard, Savage, Wass, Cowper, Barrow, and the rest of the Gentlemen and Children of the Royal Chapel: The Instrumental by his Majesty's Band, Etc."   [4] William Melmoth, the younger (1710–99).

From George Tymms

Harleston Sep.!br 9.th 1758.

Dear Sir!

Doctor S.[1] is so impatient about y.e trifling Pamphlet w.ch probably may be printed before this reaches You, that he will not be satisfied without my troubling you again to desire it may be published and advertized as expeditiously as possible. For my own part I can't see why we should be compelled to print *before Term ends*, as our Hunger is happily satisfied, & 'tis but *one Friend* who requests it.[2] – But to be serious, he wants to have a Number of y.m down, and offers to bear y.e expense of y.e publication, w.ch I can by no means admit of. It is ⟨by⟩ not ⟨means⟩ reasonable that any body else should pay for my follies, nor will I suffer that, where I can prevent it. The honest Gentleman is likely to have some of his own to pay for. – He sent me y.e inclosed this morning, w.ch he intends for y.e Northampton Mercury.[3] He is welcome to extract, parcel out, or comment as he pleases, provided he makes no

use of my name: but surely he is too hasty, and should at least let y.ᵉ Pamphlet b·
published before he quotes & refer's to it in print.

I am D.ʳ Sir,

Your most obedient humble
Serv.ᵗ

Geo. Tymm·

If you have not already seen our Friend M.ʳ Jackson, since my last, I beg you will sa·
nothing to him about it.⁴

MS: Harvard Theatre Collection, Harvard College Library.

¹ James Stonhouse of Northampton. (See his letter on 24 August.) Tymms's *Essay on Monopolies* woul·
  not be advertised until 18 September.
² Michaelmas term, 29 September. The "one Friend" is Stonhouse. Regarding the satisfaction of "ou·
  Hunger," see Tymms's letter of late August, note 7.
³ Although the "inclosed" is missing, two days later a 106-line single-column extract of Tymms's *Essa·*
  appeared in the *Northampton Mercury*, but without the mention of the author's name; an additiona·
  extract was printed in the same paper one week later, on 18 September, the day of the pamphlet·
  publication in London.
⁴ Most likely John Jackson (1686–1763), theological writer, Master of Wigston's Hospital, Leiceste·
  (1729), author of *Chronological Antiquities* (1752), and also friend of another RD author, John Gilber·
  Cooper of Leicester. Tymms and Jackson were both born in Doncaster, Yorkshire, where the latt·
  probably became acquainted with Tymms, or at least with his family by reason of the elder Tymms'·
  trade as saddle maker. Jackson had married the daughter of the collector of excise at Doncaster·

From John Scott Hylton

Lapall = House 14.ᵗʰ Sep.ᵗ 1758

Dear Sir,

I heard some time since by M.ʳ Shenstone that you were return'd from Scotland·
and hope you had as much pleasure in your Expedition as you expected, of which]
have heard no Acc.ᵗ more than that D.ʳ Roebuck inform'd me that you and M·
Spence were at Edenburgh when he was at Glascow, which was a little unfortunate·
as his Company and Information might have been of service to you in your Tour. –·
I have been at Worcester Musick meeting, and was extremely delighted with ever·
Thing during my stay in that City, from whence I return'd last Saturday;¹ I me·
with several of my Acquaintance at the Oratorios, amongst whom was our Friend·
M.ʳ Shenstone, who staid two Days, and seem'd very well pleas'd with the whole –·
Lady Coventry shone as brilliant as ever, & M.ʳ Beard & Frasi were the same swee·
Singers as they were when I heard them four years ago.² – M.ʳ Wilmot of Worcester·
desir'd me when I wrote to you to enquire the prizes, of the two following Books·
whether they can be procured, and what Character they bear. you may find them·
in the list of Foreign Books at the End of the Gent.ᵐ'ˢ Magazine for December 1757·
Collection Academique composer, des Memoires, Actes, et Journeaux des plu·
celebres Academies, et Societies Literaries, concernant l'Historie Naturelle &c·
Dijon The 6.ᵗʰ Vol: what is the price of it, and also of the former Volumnes? Th·

ther Book is, Monnoies en Argent qui composent une des differentes parties du
Cabinet des sa Majeste l'Empereur, depuis le plus grandes pieces jusq au Florin
nclusivement – Folio Vienna. Containing all the Silver Coins of the European
rinces &c from 1460 to this time. engraved by M. Winkler.[4]

I have not either Time or Materials to make this Letter much longer, but shall
just add that I think M.ʳ Shenstone & you have done me more honor than I have the
ight to claim, by the Insertion of my Verses upon his place, in the London
Chronicle; indeed I was not privy to it, and they are so much improved that I have
scarce Vanity enough to think them my own Offspring.[5]

Do be so kind to let me hear from you soon, & believe me ever most
Affectionately,

D.ʳ Sir

Y.ʳ Most Obliged Hble Servant

John Scott Hylton

D.ʳ Grainger, and M.ʳ Tho.ˢ Warton have been both of them at The Leasowes.

MS: Humanities Research Center, University of Texas at Austin, Robert Dodsley / Recipient 1 /
Bound, ff. 41–2.

In the *London Evening Post* for 5–8 August 1758, had appeared the following advertisement:
The meeting of the Three Choirs of Gloucester, Hereford, and Worcester will be held at Worcester
upon the 30th of this Month, and the two following Days . . . Care has been taken to engage the best
performers from London and other places; amongst whom are Signiora Frasi, Messrs Beard, Wass,
Pinto, Miller, Thompson, Adcock, Vincent, Etc."

Richard Lyttelton } Stewards
Tho. Birch Savage

Maria, Countess of Coventry (1733–60); John Beard (1716?–91), actor and vocalist; Giula Frasi, a
popular Italian voice of opera and the stage in the third quarter of the eighteenth century.
Probably Pynson Wilmott, Parson of Halesowen, Hylton's residence.
Jean Berryat, *Collection Académique, composée, des Mémoires, Actes, ou Journaux des plus célèbres Académies et
Sociétés Littéraires étrangères, des Extraits des Meilleurs Ouvrages Périodiques, des traités particuliers, et des Pièces
fugitives les plus rares . . . traduits en Français, et mis en ordre par une Société de Gens de Lettres* (13 vols. Paris,
1755–79). Although Berryat had died in 1754, the work was completed according to his plan.
Valentin Jameray Duval, *Monnaies en or et en argent qui composent une des parties du Cabinet de S. M.
L'Empereur* (2 vols. Folio. Vienna, 1759–69). The engravings for the latter were done by Jean
Christophe Winkler (1701–70). I could not discover the prices of these volumes on the English market;
they seem not to have been advertised.
Hylton's "Verses, written at the Gardens of William Shenstone, Esq., near Birmingham, 1756"
appeared in the *London Chronicle* for 24–6 August 1758. It was reprinted in the *Public Advertiser* on 30
August, and RD saw to its third appearance in the *London Magazine* for September, (p. 440). See RD's
letter to Shenstone on 19 September.

From George Tymms

[*ante* 18 September 1758][1]

I was favour'd with yours & y.ᵉ Pamphlet inclo\sed.[2] I am greatly obliged to You for
not printing more than 250, which are at least 200 more than there can be a chance
to sell. Good D.ʳ S. do's not consider y.ᵗ y.ᵉ Season is over and y.ᵉ Subject *out of fashion*,[3]
but I wou'd oblige him at a greater expence than that of this impression, w.ᶜʰ I beg

you will let me know, and I will discharge it immediately. I am determined not t father y.ᵉ untimely Brat for many reasons:⁴ nor is y.ᵉ world in danger of being furthe troubled with my Works: but certain it is that had I y.ᵉ Pen of Voltaire, my Mss would all travel into Pall Mall.

The words *In a letter to a Friend,* in y.ᵉ Title Page, & y.ᵉ Subscription *Publicola* do no well agree with *an Essay*: much less are they consistent with y.ᵉ Assurance given to y Reader, page 21, that I am no Physician, or with y.ᵉ words pag: 28. *The justice &c must be submitted to y.ᵉ Public, for whose benefit they were invented.* – I heartily wish it ma not be too late to have them expunged, for I would much rather have M Anonymous roasted, than poor *Publicola.*⁵

All y.ᵉ Errata I can observe are as follow.

Page 18. line 6. for *makes* read *make.* page 21. 1. 22.ᵈ for *easily* read *easy,* page 26, lin 16, for *groud* read *ground.*⁶

Pardon my hast, and be assured that I am

D.ʳ Sir

Most faithfully & sincerely Yours

Geo. Tymm,

Page 14. line 1.ˢᵗ, *important Man* had better be, *important Person,* as the words *friendl, Man* occur at the bottom of the same Page.⁷

If you see our Friend M.ʳ Jackson, I beg his acceptance of my respects. He may b intrusted with y.ᵉ Secret, but I am sure will be surprised y.ᵗ such a Subject cou'c enter into my head: and concern'd that I shou'd be weak enough to consent to y. publication.⁸

The Northampton Carrier M.ʳ Cooke sets on Thursday Mornings from y George Inn [Sm]ithfield.

Obliged and most obedient humble
Servant.

Geo. Tym[ms]

MS: Harvard Theatre Collection, Harvard College Library.

¹ The letter's content suggests a date prior to the publication of the author's *Essay on Monopolies.* Sinc the pamphlet did not reach a second edition, the title-page revisions Tymms hopes do not come "to late," as well as the errata he notes, must have been designed for the first edition that RD advertised o 18 September 1758.   ² See note 1.
³ James Stonhouse. Regarding the subject's being "out of fashion," see Tymms's letter of *post* 24 August note 7.   ⁴ I.e. Tymms would have the work published anonymously.
⁵ See Tymms's letter of *post* 24 August, note 5.
⁶ Except for that on p. 21, RD made the adjustments. That on p. 26 occurred in line 17, not 16.
⁷ RD printed "important Man."   ⁸ For Jackson, see Tymms's letter of 9 September, note 4.

To William Shenstone

Pall mall Sepᵗ 19.ᵗʰ [1758]

Dear Sir

I am very glad to hear that you got as far from home as Worcester; I hope it was by way of inuring your self to travel, in order to enable you by degrees to reach

London. I shall probably see M.ʳ Beard & Mʳ Havard before 'tis long, & will deliver
your Compliments.² I do not wonder You was pleas'd at Worcester Music-
meeting,³ as I am inform'd there was much more eagerness amongst yᵉ Ladies to see
You, than to hear the Music. My reason for sending for the Letter, (which is much
improv'd by your Corrections) was in order to have printed the Play; but my Lord
Chesterfield has disswaded me from it: and thinks it will still at some time or other
be acted.⁴ A description of the Leasowes suitable to our book cannot be very long;
however, we are not in haste for it, as yᵉ Work goes on but very slowly.⁵ M.ʳ Hylton's
Poem is extreamly pretty, and I intend to get it inserted in the London Magazine.⁶ I
wish we had known You had yᵉ least inclination to have seen Scotland; we should
certainly have try'd to push it forward into a resolution; and indeed it would have
much enliven'd those dreary hills. Durham is certainly all and more than I have
describ'd; and M.ʳ Spence I know would be extreamly glad to see you there for a
month or two; but I hope You will first pay him a visit in this Neighbourhood.⁷ I
have not yet had an opportunity of seeing M.ʳ Henly, to know whether he still
intends to part with his Pidgeons: he has been in the West almost ever since I came
home.⁸ As to Franks, you could not have ask'd at a worse time, as I have no body in
Town to apply to: however I have enclos'd three, & will send You more as soon as I
have an opportunity of getting any. But pray never shorten your Letters to me on
that account, nor lessen their numbers: do you think I should be sorry to pay double
Postage? I heartily congratulate You on your friend Lord Stamford's great
acquisition of Fortune.⁹ Not a word about the Elegies? I hope you have put them
into M.ʳ Baskerville's hands; or if not, that You will bring them to Town with You.¹⁰

I am ever
Dear Sir
most sincerely Yours

R. Dodsley

MS: BL. Add. MS. 28,959, ff. 103–4.

¹ The year is evident from RD's response to matters mentioned in Hylton's fully dated letter of 14
September 1758. In addition, RD's trip to Scotland through Durham alluded to within, occurred in
1758.
² Apparently another untraced letter from Shenstone to RD conveyed Shenstone's compliments to
John Beard (1716?–91), actor and vocalist, and William Havard (1710?–78), actor and dramatist.
Both had been scheduled to appear at the Worcester Music Meeting. See Hylton's letter of 14
September, note 1. Hylton had praised Beard's performance in that letter.
³ See Hylton's letter to RD on 14 September.
⁴ The "letter" (mentioned in RD's last letter to Shenstone) is most likely the dedicatory letter to Lord
Chesterfield that RD would print at the front of his first edition of *Cleone* in December. As letters
exchanged with Lord Chesterfield at the end of 1757 and the spring of 1758 show, the latter had been
the patron and advisor to RD on the matter of *Cleone*. In fact, it was apparently Chesterfield who
saved RD from the rash plan of printing the play as mentioned here. Writing to Graves on 25
November 1758, Shenstone says: "I suppose he acts by Lord Chesterfield's opinion: for I know, when
he was going to print it (since he came home) with a *proper* dedication to Mr. Garrick, my Lord then
prevented him, telling him, it *would* be acted one day or other" (Williams, p. 495).
⁵ The description was probably intended for the edition of Shenstone's elegies, which never
materialized except as printed in RD's edition of the poet's *Works* (1764)
⁶ See Hylton's letter to RD on 14 September, note 5.

[7] See RD's letter to Shenstone on 22 August.

[8] Ibid. In his letter to Shenstone on 14 October, RD spells the name of his pigeon-fancier friend as "Hindley." This might be the same individual whom RD proposed as a candidate for membership at the 1 December 1756 meeting of the Society for the Encouragement of Arts, Manufactures, and Commerce (RSA): Frederick Atherton Hindley, Esq., of Bury Street, St. James's. (Minute Books of the Royal Society of Arts.)

[9] In his letter to John Scott Hylton on 8 August, Shenstone wrote: "My L⁴ Warrington, it seems dy'd about a week ago, an event of yᵉ utmost importance to L⁴ Stamford" (Williams, p. 448). Indeed it was. At his father-in-law's death, Stamford inherited Warrington's estates in Cheshire and Lancashire.

[10] Regarding Shenstone's publishing of his elegies at Birmingham, see Graves's letter to RD on 2 March 1759.

To Arthur Charles Stanhope[1]

Pallmall Sep^t 19th [1758]

Sir

Tho' it has given me pain to be so long without making acknowledgements for the many Civilities receiv'd from You whilst at Mansfield, yet I was very unwilling to do it till I could let you know that I had seen my Lord Chesterfield, which I had the Honour to do on Sunday morning last at Blackheath. I was extreamly sorry to find Him much out of order, occasion'd by a sickness, & giddiness in his head which had attack'd him with some violence the day before: And You will be the more particularly concern'd, as it prevented his Lordship from putting in execution a design he had laid, of setting out that very morning, in order to have paid you a visit at Mansfield. He came as far as London in his way on Saturday, but was forc'd to turn back again to Blackheath. He enquir'd very kindly, and very particularly after your Son; of his health, complexion, countenance, & temper concerning all which particulars, it really requir'd nothing more than a strict adherence to truth, to give him a very pleasing Account. He enquir'd also about your House: whether it was large and good. I told him it was not very large; but that it was much the best house in the Town, and very pleasantly situated. I should think it not impossible that his Lordship might still pay You a visit this Autumn tho' he seems to be afraid that this attack will render it imprudent for him to venture. I beg my Compliments to Mrs Stanhope, and am

Sir

Your most obliged
and obed^t Servant

R Dodsley

MS: Spencer Library, University of Kansas, MS P297.

[1] Arthur Charles Stanhope (1716–70) of Mansfield was the cousin of Philip Dormer Stanhope (1694–1773), 4th Earl of Chesterfield. This letter represents one of a series in the negotiations in which the Earl selected A. C. Stanhope's son Philip to be educated as his successor. Apparently RD's friendship with Chesterfield, as well as his own Mansfield origins, explains his involvement. For the full story, see Frank C. Nelick, "Lord Chesterfield's Adoption of Philip Stanhope," *PQ*, 38 (1959), 370–8.

² The year is determined from Stanhope's fully dated letter of 25 September 1758 to the Earl, also in the Spencer Library. Here Stanhope writes: "M�r Dodsley is very obliging in his description of our Boy." Although he does not mention the city expressly in his letters of the previous month, RD most likely passed through his hometown, Mansfield, on his long trip north with Spence during July and August. At that time, he could have conveniently visited Stanhope and gained an impression of the latter's three-year-old son.

To William Shenstone

Pall mall Oct.ʳ 10.ᵗʰ [1758]¹

Dear Sir

I wrote to M.ʳ Hylton yesterday, which I enclose, and put off writing to you till to day, when I meditated a very long letter: But behold I am seized by the Gout in my right elbow, & fear I shall scarce be able to write, or to think, or to hold the pen for ten minutes. But I will try to give you some short hints of what I intended to say; in which if I am either dull, or imperfect, or should stop short in the middle, you will charitably lay the fault on my elbow not my head; and heartily join with me in cursing the Gout, not rail at my Stupidity. The first part of my letter was to have consisted of a Panegyric on your Punctuality, for which you know I am furnisht with ample materials. In the next place I should have told you, that I have some thoughts of bringing on my Play at Covent Garden: but this some of my friends tell me will be only changing the risk of its Damnation by the Town, into yᵉ certainty of its murder by the Actors.² What a damn'd thing it is to have written a Play!

Were I to curse the man whom most I hate,
On Managers & Actors let him wait.

I might next have proceeded to let you into a secret, which is, that I am at present now writing from Esop and others, an hundred select Fables in prose, for the use of schools; we having no book of that kind fit to put into the hands of youth, from the wretched manner in which they are written.³ Tell me what you think of this attempt. I am forced to lay down the pen – I have resumed it, but feel I cannot write long. I will look over your letter, and set down hints as they occur from it.⁴ M.ʳ Hylton's verses were inserted in yᵉ London Magazine before I recᵈ your last.⁵ Bring yᵉ Description of the Leasowes with you, when you come to visit Mʳ Spence at Wheel barrow-Place. You have got the exact Idea of Finculo, how the Devil did you come by it?⁶ And your picture of Tom Warton is as like as two Peas.⁷ I have not half answer'd your Letter, but cannot possibly write any longer. If this fit goes off I will write again very soon.

I am
Dear Sir
Affectionately Yours
R. Dodsley

MS: BL. Add. MS. 28,959, f. 105.

¹ The year is certain from various bits of internal evidence. Nowhere in RD's correspondence before 1758 is there a hint that he had been thinking of producing an edition of Aesop's fables. But by this

time in 1759 he is beyond the point of letting Shenstone in on a "secret"; in fact, in January he is saying
that he is trying to select the best from all the fabulists. Secondly, Hylton's verses had been inserted i
the *London Magazine* of September 1758. Finally, RD's saying that Shenstone had "got the exact Ide
of Finculo" is clearly a follow-up on his letter to Shenstone of 22 August 1758, wherein he described i
detail Spence's residence at the Abbey of Finculo.

² Reference to RD's intent to produce his tragedy, *Cleone*, at Covent Garden, an event of the following
December.
³ *Select Fables of Esop and Other Fabulists*, eventually published in 1761, contained 159 fables, fifty-two o
which were originals by RD and friends.
⁴ Shenstone's letter has not been traced.
⁵ See John Scott Hylton's letter to RD on 14 September, note 5. Perhaps Shenstone had som
alterations for Hylton's poem.   ⁶ See note 1.
⁷ Unfortunately Shenstone's description of "Tom Warton" appears in an untraced letter.

To William Shenstone

Pall mall Oct.ʳ 14 [1758]

Dear M.ʳ Shenstone!

   The Gout in my elbow is somewhat abated, and I will try to answer the
remainder of your Letter, beginning where I left off.² I have spoken to D.ʳ Akenside
he desires his Compliments, but will not hear of printing the Ode you mention, &
says he has told the Doctor his reasons.³ You have not mention'd your Elegies, bu
promise that in your next *perhaps* you *may*. Very cautiously exprest, and mean
exactly *perhaps* you *may not*. But after what you tell me of your several Avocations, I
do not wonder that you seem *doubtfull* whether you shall be able to do any thing else
However, I expect to see you this winter, & after what has past, which I will take no
notice of even to your self, I think it probable the Elegies may travel with you i
Manuscript up to London. Since I wrote last, I have absolutely fixt with M.ʳ Rich
for the acting of my Play: it is going immediately into Rehearsal, & must be acted
the latter end of next Month.⁴ And now perhaps you may think me very whimsica
should I intimate that upon looking again at the Epilogue, I am not quite satisfy'd
with it; & very unreasonable if I should desire you would try your hand about a new
one. But the truth is, I should be proud of the Honour of your Name, & glad that yᵉ
Entertainment might at least have yᵉ advantage of *ending* with spirit.⁵ My friend M.ʳ
Hindley⁶ is so far from parting with his Pidgeons, that he has built them a new
house: but he has promis'd me some young ones in the spring, which he says may be
likely to settle more kindly with you than old ones. In the mean time however, I
have sent you by Mʳ Allen's Birmingham Waggon of this day, carriage paid, *five*
pair of old ones. viz: 1 pair Fan tails, 1 Turbots, 1 Barbs, 1 Capuchins, 1 Cropers. I
have sent them in a large Cage, sent a peck of Tares along with 'em, gave the
Waggoner great charge of them, & hope they will come safe. The Waggon should
come into Birmingham on Thursday night; but he says he shall have some repair to
make in it on Thursday, so it may be Friday morning before he gets in. You will
probably find them, like some other London Beauties, a little dirty and draggle-

ail'd, but they will spruce themselves up at the Leasows: where, if they do not settle
ʳery kindly, I shall think them birds of no *Taste*, whatever may be their *Beauty*.

I am

Dear Sir

Affectionately Yours

R. Dodsley

MS: BL. Add. MS. 28, 959, f. 106.

The year determined from RD's mentioning that he has "absolutely fixt with Mʳ Rich" for the acting
of *Cleone* the "latter end of next Month." Although delayed a week, the play was produced on 2
December 1758. Also RD's promise of pursuing the matter of the pigeons with Mr Hindley is a follow-
up on his letter of 19 September 1758.

See RD's previous letter to Shenstone, four days earlier.

Regrettably the identity of the ode and of the "Doctor" is obscured with Shenstone's missing letter.

Regarding the production of *Cleone*, see RD's correspondence over the next three months.

In his next letter, RD would change his mind regarding a new epilogue for *Cleone*.

See RD's letter to Shenstone on 19 September, note 8.

From George Tymms

Huntingdon Octʳ 14.ᵗʰ 1758

Dear Sir!

I am utterly ashamed not to have made an earlier acknowledgment of your last
Favour, with yᵉ Pamphlet inclosed very accurately printed, and in every respect
much better than it deserved.[1] It gives me great concern to find that one Fact in it,
wᶜʰ I thought I had from unquestionable authority, is mistated.[2] A Man who
presumes to publish, should take nothing upon trust, for if his veracity can be
impeach'd in any one particuar, he justly forfiets all claim to credit. – I have but one
satisfaction; that amongst my own Acquaintance there are but two Persons who
know, and not one other whom I have reason to think do's in yᵉ least *suspect* me to be
yᵉ Scribbler of that weak, tho' well meant performance.[3] The publication of it
indeed was contrary to my own opinion and remonstrances: but I must now desire
you to send me down 50 of them, for yᵉ use of that Gentleman's Summer house, who
will have them by him, and to whom I shall recommend yᵉ most proper application
of them.[4] All yᵉ rest of yᵉ Impression I will be accountable to you for hereafter.

I beg you will at yᵉ same time send me your Collection of Poems wᶜʰ Mʳ Hughs
printed. Brown's Estimate, yᵉ 2 Volˢ. – Dalrymple's Feudal Tenures & a French
Book sold by Vaillant – yᵉ title of wᶜʰ if I forget not, is L'Ami de l'homme. – *wᵗʰ a
Bill*.[5] I beg they may all be bound in Calf & letter'd. I have been rambling ten days,
out return home next Week. I now write with 6 females chattering in yᵉ room, &
must hasten to yᵉ assurance that I most sincerely am

Dear Mʳ Dodsley's

Address: To | Mʳ Robᵗ Dodsley | Bookseller | in Pall Mall | London
Postmark: 16 OC [Huntingdon?]

MS: Harvard Theatre Collection, Harvard College Library.

¹ Most likely RD had sent Tymms a copy of the *Essay on Monopolies* shortly after its publication on 18 September. See Tymms's letters of the previous month on the subject.
² Tymms does not specify the "one Fact" here or in his other letters to RD.
³ James Stonhouse (see his letter on 24 August) and RD.   ⁴ Stonhouse.
⁵ RD's *Collection* printed by John Hughs, the last two volumes of which had appeared the previous March; John Brown, *Estimate of the Manners and Principles of the Times,* (2 vols. 1757, 1758); Sir John Dalrymple, *Essay towards a General History of Feudal Property in Great Britain* (1757); Victor de Ruguetti Mirabeau, *L'Ami des hommes, ou Traité de la population* (Avignon, 1756–60), four parts of which had been published at this time, touching on population, commerce, and agriculture.

To William Shenstone

Pall mall Oct.ʳ 24.ᵗʰ [1758]¹

Dear Sir

Since my last hasty Letter I have changed my opinion. I now think you cannot send me a more spirited Epilogue.² My only objections against it were, that it was too long, and so hard upon the Women, that I was afraid of affronting the Boxes. I have endeavoured to shorten it, as you will see by the enclosed: with what success I know not; be so good as to consider it.³ If you can soften the Conclusion, or change the last four lines into a Compliment to the Ladies, I think the whole will do extreamly well. I would not by any means lose the Satire of it, as it is strong, spirited, and just: but a sugar-plumb at the close, may sweeten it on yᵉ palate, & prevent it from rising upon their stomachs.⁴ The Play is in rehearsal, & is intended to appear on the 18ᵗʰ of next month: if you can let me have yᵉ Epilogue about a week or ten days before that time, it will do very well.

I am ever
Dear Sir
Affectionately Yours
R. Dodsley

MS: BL. Add. MS. 28,959, F. 107.

¹ The year is certain from the mention within that RD's *Cleone* is about to be produced.
² See RD's letter of 14 October for his balking at the use of the frequently revised epilogue to *Cleone.*
³ This manuscript version of the epilogue is unaccounted for.
⁴ Without interim texts, it is impossible to say how much the conclusion of the epilogue had changed since the original version, or even since alterations had been introduced in the late summer of 1756. Undoubtedly, however, the final version concludes on a much more positive – even patriotic – note.

To William Shenstone

Pall Mall Novʳ 4.ᵗʰ [1758]¹

Dear Mᵣ Shenstone

I have not time to write more than a very few words. There was no probability of my Play being ever receiv'd by Mᵣ Garrick. I had therefore no alternative, but either to suppress it, print it unacted, or try it at Covent Garden. What will be the event I know not, but my friends give me hopes, and yᵉ Performers like it, & seem inclin'd to take pains with it. Mʳˢ Bellamy is my Cleone, & I hope she will do it very well.² I beg you will send me the Epilogue in a post or two. I will only put the Epilogue – *Written by a Friend* – if you desire it so.³ But Success I suppose may remove your objection. Rehearsals are yet but very imperfect, but I think the performance will be much better than I expected. I will not fail to enquire, as opportunities offer, about a Place for Maurice.⁴ I suppose he wants a Footman's place, and that he is not marry'd. The Vindication of Natural Society is written by that Mʳ Burke who wrote on the Sublime and Beautiful.⁵

I am ever
Dear Sir
most affectionately Yours
R. Dodsley

Mʳ Rich & the Actors still propose to bring on the Play this day fortnight, but for my part I think it cannot be till yᵉ week following.⁶ However you will be so good as to let me have the Epilogue as soon as possible.

MS: BL. Add. MS. 28,959, f. 109.

See RD's previous letter to Shenstone.
George Ann Bellamy (1731?–88), formerly a member of Garrick's company at Drury Lane.
And so it was.
Apparently a neighbor, or possibly a tenant, of Shenstone's. In a letter to Jago on 16 June 1754 (Williams, p. 402), Shenstone speaks of "your old acquaintance Maurice, who lives at the corner of my coppice."
RD had published Edmund Burke's *A Vindication of Natural Society: or, a View of the Miseries and Evils Arising to Mankind from Every Species of Artificial Society. In a Letter to Lord . . .* anonymously in 1756, signing it "by a late noble Writer." A second edition, with a new preface, had appeared at the end of 1757. RD had purchased the copyright from Burke on 10 May for the slight sum of £6.6.0 (See Appendix B.)   ⁶ See RD's letter to Shenstone of 14 October, note 1

From Richard Bentley¹
With a concluding note by Horace Walpole

Strawberry-Hill, Noᵛ 20 1758

Mʳ Dodsley

If we print the Lucan in 4ᵗᵒ, it is to be consider'd that the notes are not compleat, and it will be called an imperfect Edition. to remedy which I think it will be adviseable, to revert to my Fathers design of printing Grotius's notes along with his own,² by which means a number of notes I had discarded, as being only relative to Grotius will find their place again. but to prepare this for the press, I must be at the trouble of transcribing pretty near the whole work, a toil I w'd willingly contrive should pay me a little better.³

No doubt, you are the best judge of how many we are likely to dispose at home, but when I talkd to Mr Franklyn upon our first scheme of printing it in 8vo, he said he had no doubt, but half the Edition might be disposed of in Holland.[4] I shd be glad to know your opinion.

Suppose therefore we were to print 500. at 1⅜ each, the Trade to sell again at 16. I imagine the account wd stand thus.

Paper – – – – – – – – – –   84-0-0

Advert^nts – – – – – – – – –   10-0-0

500 books at 1⅜ each   – – –   300-0-0

Profit to ye Bookseller   – –

If you agree to this proposal, we can begin upon it immediately.[5] I am

Sir

Your Humble Servant,

R Bentley.

Mr Dodsley

I shall be in town on wednesday, & if you will call on me thursday or friday with yr opinion, we will settle this affair.

Yrs etc

Hor Walpole

Address: [by Bentley] To Mr Dodsley / Bookseller in Pall Mall / London
Postmark: 21 NO
Frank: Free Hor. Walpole

MS: Lewis Walpole Library, Farmington, Conn. The manuscript is laid in a copy of Lucan's *Pharsalia*, printed at Walpole's Strawberry Hill Press in 1760. I am indebted to Professor John C. Riely, who supplied me with a copy of the text and reviewed my notes prior to the letter's first printing in *The Yale Edition of Horace Walpole's Correspondence*, Vol. 40, ed. W. S. Lewis and John C. Riely (New Haven: Yale University Press, 1980), 148.

[1] Richard Bentley (1708–82) was the son of the distinguished Richard Bentley (see note 2) and friend and correspondent of Horace Walpole until their relationship ended in 1761. Bentley had executed the designs for six illustrations to Thomas Gray's poems published by RD in 1753 (see Gray's letter to RD on 12 February 1753).

[2] Bentley's father, Richard Bentley (1662–1742), classical scholar and Master of Trinity College, Cambridge, had supplemented the notes to Lucan's *Pharsalia* which had been provided earlier by Huig van Groot (1583–1645), the Dutch jurist and theologian known as Hugo Grotius. The volume did appear in quarto a little over two years later and included Grotius's notes: *M. Annaei Lucani Pharsalia. Cum notis H. Grotii et R. Bentleii, etc.* (Strawberry Hill, 1760). In a letter to William Mason on 30 January 1780, Walpole explains how the name of Richard Cumberland (1732–1811), grandson of Bentley, Sr., came to be printed as editor of the *Pharsalia*. Walpole reveals that Cumberland had actually come into possession of Bentley's manuscript notes and had given them to his uncle, Richard Bentley, "for the latter's benefit." But although Bentley alone selected and revised the notes, he did not wish his name to appear; consequently Cumberland's name was affixed. (See *Journal of the Printing-Office. With Notes by Paget Toynbee* (London: Constable and Houghton Mifflin, 1923), pp. 38–9.)

3 William Cole is quoted in Nichols's *Literary Illustrations*, VIII, 573, as claiming that Bentley had told him that he had "got about £40" for the edition printed at Strawberry Hill.

4 Richard Francklin (d. 1765), was a printer, bookseller, and publisher at Tom's Coffee House, Covent Garden, from 1726 to 1756 (Plomer). It seems, however, that Francklin had taken up residence at Strawberry Hill before 1747, living in a cottage in the enclosure that Walpole called the "Flower Garden." In a letter to Bentley on 17 July 1755, Walpole had mused: "Can there be an odder revolution of things, than that the printer of *The Craftsman* [anti-Robert Walpole periodical] should live in a house of mine?" In a letter of 8 June of the following year, Walpole writes again of Francklin in the same context to John Chute. (Lewis, *Correspondence of Horace Walpole*, Vol. 35, pp. 237, 94.) Walpole's entry in the *Journal of the Printing-Office* (p. 7) for 11 December of this year includes the note: "Began to print Lucan in quarto with Dr Bentley's notes. At first It was intended to print only the notes in octavo without the text."

5 Allen T. Hazen, *A Bibliography of the Strawberry Hill Press* (New Haven: Yale University Press, 1942), pp. 46–8, indicates that Walpole's press turned out 500 copies of the *Pharsalia* during 1758–60. However the following brief account, laid in Horace Walpole's manuscript volume *Journal of the Printing House* (Lewis Walpole Library 49.2506A), suggests otherwise:

350	Lucan received by Mr Dodsley
186	Remain in hand
51	Delivered to Mr Walpole
33	D.^o to Mr Bentley & Mr Cumberland
80	Sold
350	

The volume had been printed at Walpole's Strawberry Hill Press and distributed through RD, who served as publisher and secured advertisements in the papers, the first appearing on 8 January 1761 (*LC*).

From David Garrick

Sunday Morn.^g
[3 December 1758][1]

Dear Sir

I most sincerely congratuate You upon Your Success last Night[2] – I heard with much concern, that some of y.^r Friends, particularly Mr Melmoth were angry with me for playing the *Busy Body* against y.^r Tragedy.[3] this I think is very hard upon Me, for I am certain that Your house was far from receiving any injury from Ours – however if You will call upon Me, & let me know, how I can support y.^r Interest, without absolutely giving up my own, I will do it; for whatever You or y.^r Friends may think I am most sincerely

Y.^r Wellwisher
& hum^{bl} Ser^t

DG.

[Garrick's endorsement:] My first letter to Dodsley.[4]

MS: Victoria & Albert Museum, MS.F. 48. F. 7, ff. 1–2.

1 See note 2.

2 The success of RD's *Cleone* at the Covent Garden theater on the evening of 2 December was one of the sweetest moments in his entire career. As traced in these letters, he had been revising the tragedy again

and again for nearly three years, only to have it continually refused by Garrick for Drury Lane, despite the recommendations of several of their mutual friends. For a thorough consideration of the play's favorable acceptance and of Garrick's attempt to undermine its success by "splitting" the town on the occasion, see Straus, pp. 200–25; James Gray, "'More Blood than Brains': Robert Dodsley and the *Cleone* Affair." *Dalhousie Review*, 54 (1974), 207–27; and the next series of letters.

3 It seems more than coincidence that Garrick scheduled Susanna Centlivre's *The Busy Body* – with himself playing Marplot for the first time – to open the same evening as *Cleone*. And then, when *Cleone*'s production was delayed for a few nights, Garrick likewise delayed *The Busy Body*. (See Straus, p. 228.) William Melmoth had provided the Prologue for *Cleone*.

4 See the following exchange of letters.

To John Stuart, 3rd Earl of Bute[1]

Pall mall Dec.[r] 5.th 1758.

My *Lord*

Your Lordship's known Candour and Benevolence, and Your favourable Disposition to encourage every attempt that may tend towards the improvement of the Stage, encourages me, though I have not the Honour to be known to your Lordship, humbly to apply for Your Assistance in behalf of the new Tragedy of Cleone; which, tho' it has hitherto been favourably receiv'd by the Town, is in danger of sinking, for want of that Countenance and Support, which the Great alone have power to make effectual to Theatrical Productions.[2] If I may presume to hope that it might be favour'd by the Presence of His Royal Highness the Prince of Wales, I should esteem it as the highest honour that could be done it.[3]

Hoping your Lordship will pardon the Presumption of this unsupported Application, I beg leave to subscribe my self, with profound respect,

My Lord,
Your Lordship's
most obedient
and
most humble Servant

R Dodsley

MS: Papers of the 3rd Earl of Bute, Mount Stuart, Rothesay, Isle of Bute, Scotland.

1 John Stuart (1713–92), 3rd Earl of Bute (1737) and, in 1761, George III's Secretary of State. A patron of literature and the arts, Bute gave Samuel Johnson a pension of £300 a year, among his many other benevolent intercessions. Dodsley would apply to him again in 1762, this time to secure his permission that John Baskerville's *Horace* might be dedicated to him. (See Shenstone's letter to RD on 11 February 1762.)

2 In the light of the town's support for *Cleone*'s first two performances, Dodsley's fear for the tragedy's "sinking" is probably exaggeration to gain the Earl's sympathies. On the other hand, he had already suffered the damaging review printed anonymously by Sir John Hill. (See Hawkesworth's letter on 10 December, note 3.)

3 Bute's dominant influence at the Court of the Prince of Wales had been well known; in fact, his relationship with the Princess had raised eyebrows. And indeed he did honor RD's request. Writing to Shenstone four days later, RD boasts: "At present I can only tell You Cleone has been acted this Night for the 7th. time, & has been receiv'd with great and unanimous applause. Last night y[e] Prince of Wales Prince Edward, Princess Augusta & three more of the Royal Family were there."

To David Garrick

Dec.ʳ 5.ᵗʰ [1758][1]

Sir

I thank you for your Compliments on the success of Cleone, and could have wish'd You had thought proper to have put it in my power to have thank'd you for contributing towards it: but I think it is not now in your own to redress the injury you have done me. You know full well that *profit* was but my second motive for bringing this piece on the Stage, and you have taken effectual care to nip its *Reputation* in the bud, by preventing yᵉ Town, as far as lay in your power, from attending to it.[2] As to my proposing any means in which you can now be of service to me, I hope you do not think that, after what has past, I can possibly bring my self to ask a favour of you. In short, if your behaviour to me has been right, I see no cause you have to be concern'd about it; if wrong, why was it so? I am certain I gave you no provocation for it.[3] I therefore leave it on your self to pursue what measure you may think most consistent with your own reputation; as to mine, you have certainly in this instance done all you could to lessen it. However, I beg you will believe it is with some regret I feel I cannot at present subscribe my self, with that cordiality I have always wish'd to be,

Sir
Your friend and Servant
R Dodsley

[Garrick's endorsement:] Dodsley's ⟨Answer. Letter⟩ Answer

MS: Victoria and Albert Museum, MS. F. 48. F. 7 ff. 3–4.

The content, RD's response to Garrick's letter of 3 December 1758, determines the year.

RD refers to Garrick's playing *The Busy Body* on the opening night of *Cleone* to distract theatergoers. George Anne Bellamy, RD's Cleone, admitted in her autobiography that Garrick had indeed damned the play publicly. When, shortly before its performance, RD had asked the actress to be more forceful in her opening performance, Bellamy peevishly assured him that "Mr Garrick had anticipated the damnation of it [*Cleone*], publicly, the preceding evening, at the Bedford Coffee-house, where he had declared, that it could not pass muster, as it was the very *worst* piece ever exhibited." (George Anne Bellamy, *An Apology for the Life of George Anne Bellamy. Written by Herself.* (4 vols. London, 1785), III, 109.) For RD's rejection of the profit motive, see his letters to Garrick and to Thomas Gataker in November of 1757.

James Gray, in "'More Blood than Brains'," poses some interesting, but still unanswered, questions regarding not only Garrick's motivation in the affair, but also that of Johnson: "Why was Garrick so resolutely opposed to putting on *Cleone* at Drury Lane? Why was Johnson so determined the play should be a success? Was he still, nine years after the disappointment of his own *Irene*, smarting under the treatment Garrick had given his tragedy? Did he sink his recent and much publicized differences with Lord Chesterfield in order to throw his full support behind RD at the rehearsals? Was there, in effect, a pro-RD conspiracy at work against David Garrick? Did the merits of *Cleone* justify all the elaborate teamwork?" Thomas Davies, sometime actor in Garrick's company, might have been correct in *Memoirs of the Life of David Garrick, Esq.*, ed. Stephen Jones (2 vols. London, 1808), I, 253, when saying that Garrick's probable role in *Cleone* as Siffroy would have been overshadowed by Mrs Cibber's Cleone and therefore the play was not in his interest. On the other hand, Garrick had, at least earlier on, submitted the play for a reading to his and RD's friend Richard Berenger and received a decidedly negative evaluation. (See the criticism in Berenger's letter to RD on 10 June 1756). Of all the extant contemporary criticisms of *Cleone*, Berenger's probably most approximates that of a modern reader when he complains that it is "too full of imitations of other plays, & consequently that it is not original & sufficiently striking." Of course, RD revised it several more times, but the lack of originality is not usually overcome by revision, something which Garrick, too, realized.

From David Garrick[1]

[Wednesday 6 December 1758][2]

Master Robert Dodsley.[3]

When I first read Your peevish Answer to my well meant proposal to You, I was much disturb'd at it[4] – but when I consider'd, that some minds cannot bear the smallest portion of Success, I most Sincerely pity'd You; and when I found in ye same letter, that You were graciously pleas'd to dismiss Me from y^r Acquaintance; I could not but confess so apparent an Obligation, & am wth due Acknowledgm^{ts}

Master Robert Dodsley
y^r most oblig'd
D.G

[Garrick's Endorsement:] My Answer to Master Robt Dodsley.

MS: Victoria and Albert Museum, MS. F. 48. F. 7, ff. 5–6.

[1] Three autograph copies of this letter exist. David Little and George Kahrl (*Letters of David Garrick*, I 296–7) print the text found in the Harvard Theatre Collection, saying that it "appears to be the letter sent Dodsley" and that the Forster text (Victoria and Albert Museum, see *Source*) "may be the first draft." A third copy – identical to the Harvard text but not mentioned by Little and Kahrl – is found in the Folger Shakespeare Library (laid in an extra-illustrated copy of Percy Fitzgerald, *The Life of David Garrick* (London: Tinsley Brothers, 1868), III, 379. Perhaps Little and Kahrl rejected the Forster copy as the sent letter because of the endorsement on the reverse that suggested it to be the copy Garrick kept. On the other hand, in both the Harvard and Folger texts, a "that" which is crossed out in one place and reinserted in another finds its proper place in the completely fair Forster text. Another subtle difference between the Forster text and the other two also suggests the poignancy of the later thought. Where the latter two read "but when I consider'd, that few Minds can bear as they ought, the smallest portion of Success," the Forster text takes more pointed aim at RD: "but when I consider'd, that some Minds cannot bear the smallest portion of Success." If one understands the Forster text as the final version, and if one accepts the meaning Little and Kahrl attach to the endorsement, it would seem necessary to conclude that Garrick suppressed his anger and did not send this letter to RD at all, unless perhaps a fourth copy once existed. That a fourth, sent copy once existed seems entirely possible in light of Garrick's first letter in this exchange (3 December), whose fair copy is also found in the Forster Collection, and with the endorsement: "My first letter to Dodsley." We know RD answered this letter (on 5 December). Consequently, either later copies of the Forster manuscripts once existed (the letters sent) or the Forster copies were the sent letters, which, after RD's death, fell back into Garrick's hands, at which time he endorsed them accordingly.

[2] This heated note is clearly an immediate response to RD's letter of 5 December. There RD's saying he cannot sign himself "with that cordiality I have always wish'd to be, Sir, Your friend and Servant" is here construed by Garrick as the playwright's "dismissing" the theater manager from his company. This internal evidence for the assigned date is corroborated by both the Harvard and Folger copies of the latter (see above), which carry the date "Wednesday" in Garrick's hand; that is, 6 December.

[3] Garrick peevishly reminds the successful playwright of his "trade" origins with the address "Master." Doubtless he was angered at RD's aligning many of their mutual friends behind *Cleone*. The opening night applause of Samuel Johnson, for instance, must have been difficult to abide.

[3] Garrick's "proposal" was made in his letter of 3 December (q.v.).

To William Shenstone

I have no Frank.

Pall mall Decr 9 [1758]^1
almost 11 at Night.

Dear Mr Shenstone

I have not time to say three words, and therefore beg You will not look on this as a letter, but expect a long one from me in a three or four days. At present I can only tell You Cleone has been acted this Night for the 7th time, & has been receiv'd with great and unanimous applause. Last night ye Prince of Wales Prince Edward, Princess Augusta & three more of the Royal Family were there.^{2} Mrs Bellamy has got vast reputation in ye Character of Cleone & in your Epilogue. My great hurry must excuse all present omissions. I have not been able to think of any thing this month past: I wish you had been here. When your things are ready I will send You & Mr Hylton a book & Mrs Mary.^{3}

I am

R. Dodsley

Address: To William Shenstone Esqr / at the Leasowes near Birmingham
Postmark: 9 DE

MS: BL. Add. MS. 28,959, ff. 110–11.

^{1} Since RD mentions within that Cleone "has been acted this Night for the 7th time," the letter is clearly of 1758. ^{2} See RD's letter to the Earl of Bute, on 5 December.
^{3} That is, a printed copy of *Cleone*, with Shenstone's Epilogue.

From John Hawkesworth

Sundaynight 10 Decr 1758

Dear Sir

Many thanks for your agreeable Present of Cleone which I have again read and think most if not all the objections I made upon reading the first MS judiciously removed;^{1} sure the Effect upon the audience in the 4th & 5th Act must have been very great: I see a Letter in Lloyd's on the Subject which I think friendly but injudicious; to regret so very much that Mr Pope did not form a Tragedy on the story, and to expatiate so copiously on the powers *he* would have exerted & the Beauties *he* wou'd have display'd is tacitly to take more from your Cleone than any express commendation cou'd give.^{2} I have read also an Account of the Tragedy printed for Cooper which by the pert self sufficient prattle it contains I think must be Hill's.^{3} I shou'd before now have given you my hand & paid the tribute of my Eyes to Cleone if Mrs Hawkesworth had not caught so bad a Cold ⟨as confined her⟩ as to be confined to the house, she joins with me in the kindest Wishes & hopes to wait on you very soon I am D^r S^r

Affectionately Yours

Jn Hawkesworth

[?]

MS: Henry E. Huntington Library, HM 12238.

¹ See Hawkesworth's criticisms in his letter of 14 September 1756.
² The review in the *Lloyd's Evening Post and British Chronicle* of 4–6 December praises both RD and Bellamy, but, as Hawkesworth says, undermines the playwright's success by regretting that Pope had not written the play. In his Preface to the printed edition of *Cleone*, RD himself called attention to the fact that Pope had encouraged him to expand an original three-act text into five acts, after admitting that he had burned his own attempt at a play on the subject.
³ In his letter to Shenstone on 20 January 1759, RD identifies the author of *An Account of the New Tragedy of Cleone*, published three days after opening night, as Sir John Hill. RD saw the work as an attempt to prejudice the town against *Cleone*, for which Hill did not "miss his reward," Garrick bringing on for him two days later "the Farce call'd *The Rout*, which was damn'd the second Night." Straus (p. 235) recalls Garrick's regret for connecting himself with Hill, which resulted in the manager's stinging verse:

> For physic and farces, his equal there scarce is,
> His farce is a physic, his physic a farce is.

It is curious that Mary Cooper, one of RD's regular collaborators in the trade, was listed as one of the two sellers of Hill's work.

To William Strahan

Pall mall Decr 12.th [1758]¹

Dear Sir

As Mr Garrick has not treated me with all the civility I could have wish'd, in the affair of my Play, I am apprehensive the Letters in our Paper, censuring his conduct, may be thought by several to come from me, which is an imputation I would chuse to avoid.² I should be sorry to be the occasion of any injury to his Character as a Man, tho' he refus'd to favour mine as a Writer. Besides, Mr Garrick has doubtless many friends, who I should think will all be disgusted with a Paper that should persist in endeavouring to cast an Odium upon him. Perhaps, therefore, in prudence it might be better to forbear all personal reflections: for my own part, I do not feel at present the least disposition to Revenge, but on the contrary could wish his behaviour might be forgotten.

I am

Dear Sir

affectionately yours

R. Dodsley

Address: To Mr Strahan / Printer in New Street / Shoe Lane.
Postmark: Penny Post Paid / W.F.U.

MS: Letter #56 in a bound manuscript volume of 39 letters from David Garrick to George Colman, the elder. Berg Collection, New York Public Library.

¹ The subject of the letter, RD's conflict with Garrick regarding *Cleone*, surely marks it as having been written in 1758. The reviews of *Cleone* in the *London Chronicle, or Universal Evening Post*, mentioned within, had appeared in the issues beginning 5 December 1758.
² Along with Strahan, RD had been a proprietor of the *London Chronicle*. In the number for 5–7 December, only the Prologue and Epilogue to *Cleone* had been printed, without commentary. But the

number for 7–9 December noted how *Cleone* was gaining strength, effecting a "revolt against fashion" for this "long neglected theatre [Covent Garden]." More to the point, it reported that the "Malevolent *Vade mecum*, which a well known scribbler [Hill] recommends to all who intend to see this play . . . hath totally missed its aim." The attack was then focused on Garrick: "It may, indeed, gratify the Manager, for whose use it was principally written: But it will never justify his refusal of a piece, which, had it been acted at Drury Lane, would . . . have compensated for all the bawdy that has been there exhibited." Then the number for 9–12 December continues a consideration of Marplot, Garrick's role, as acted at Drury Lane, and notes the increasing crowds for *Cleone*.

To William Shenstone

Pall mall Decr 16 [1758]^1

Dear Mr Shenstone

I did not think it ever could happen that I should have occasion to make an Apology for not writing to You, as I am never better pleas'd than when so employ'd. Yet so it is, and I am afraid You will think me inexcuseable: but when You consider the perpetual hurry I have been in for this month past, I know You will forgive me. I have such a chaos of things in my head to say to You, that I feel it will be impossible to reduce them to any order. I must therefore throw them out as they rise, and that with all the rapidity I can, as I am still very much press'd for want of time. This is the 12.th Night of the Play, & it has been receiv'd with great Indulgence. It has stem'd the Tide of Fashion, which runs very strong against that House;^{2} and has supported its self against the strength and popularity of Mr Garrick, which have been remarkably exerted against it.^{3} On its first night he acted the part of *Marplot* in the Busy body, a Character he had never appear'd in before; and this he continued to run against it the 2^d 4th 5th & 7th Nights which at first had the effect he intended, of making the Town, who he knew would follow him, appear to neglect Cleone; and thus he hop'd to have justify'd his former conduct in refusing it. It happen'd, however, that after ye 3^d or 4th Night, it rose in reputation, the audiences encreas'd, and tho' they have not been crowded, they have been better than have usually appear'd at that House, and sufficient to induce the Manager to carry it on for his own advantage. The Epilogue was receiv'd with great applause, and I wish, for my own credit, your Letter had come time enough for me to have prefixt your Name to it ye first Edition. However, that Edition, which was 2000, was sold off the first day; and I have printed 2000 more with your Name.^{4} But what will you say to me for the alteration I have audaciously ventur'd to make in the close? What apology can I offer for adulterating your spirited Wine with my flat Cydar? I will make none but the Truth, which is, that I was afraid of offending the Ladies, and desirous of palliating matters with them at taking leave.^{5} The whole Town have been unanimous in blaming Mr Garrick for his behaviour in this affair, and it has occasion'd a fresh quarrel between him and me, the particulars of which are too long for a letter, but I will acquaint You with them when I see you, which, as you have got a Chaise & Horses, I hope I shall do soon after Christmas. Mr Spence will be in Town in February, & will not be happy if he does not see you. I am glad to hear of your application to the correction of your Works: how many days did it last?

Do you like the Title of Shenstoniana?[6] Is it not now too trite? At first when I read your Dream I was amaz'd, and thought some God had been whispering to You in your slumbers; but I soon began to suspect, that your Inspiration was not, as usual, from Apollo, but the Post Office: & was not long ere I discover'd that a certain Wren had flown that way, & sung the song of Triumph in your ear.[7] I hope you have before now rec^d a book for your Self, Mr Hylton & Mrs Cutler. I sent them to Mr Giles, & desir'd him to forward them directly.[8] The Books you bespoke are all in hand, but Mr Montagu is very slow; however, as it is on so good an occasion, I shall not fail to hasten him all I can.[9] I am ever

Dear Sir

Affectionately Yours

R. Dodsley

MS: BL. Add. MS. 28,959, ff. 112–13.

[1] The contents – an extended consideration of the events surrounding the production of *Cleone* – require a dating of 1758. Specifically, RD mentions that "this is the 12th Night of the Play," which corroborates the letter's 16 December date. (No performances on Sunday.)

[2] Covent Garden had long been in the "shadow" of Drury Lane.

[3] See RD's exchange of correspondence with Garrick of the previous two weeks.

[4] This amazing sale of *Cleone*, at 1s. 6d., in a single day, clearly shows the play to have been the theatrical event of the season.

[5] Lacking the copy of the Epilogue Shenstone had returned to RD, one cannot determine precisely the change made at the end. The London author's fear of offending the ladies in his audience will continue to mark his exchange with the 44-year-old country bachelor through the latter's revisions for the third edition to be published in April 1759. For more on RD's last-minute changes in the Epilogue, see his letter of next 20 January.

[6] Despite this early attempt to publish his *Works*, Shenstone would have to rely upon his faithful friend RD to produce a posthumous edition in 1764.

[7] A curious allusion. Possibly Shenstone had written RD, claiming to have seen success for *Cleone* in a dream, when all the time he had been informed of the play's acceptance by a friend visiting London at the time. RD might be identifying the informer by punning on the name of Shenstone's neighbor at Wroxall Abbey, Christopher Wren.

[8] No doubt copies of *Cleone*, which RD had promised in his letter of 9 December. For Giles, see letter to Shenstone of 20 September 1757, note 3.

[9] For Montagu, see RD's letter to Shenstone on 20 January 1759, note 12.

From Richard Graves

Claverton, 20 Dec. 1758

Dear S^r

I receiv'd y^r tragedy of Cleone – which I shall deposit in my Archives with double pleasure – both as a valuable performance, & as a testimony to my descendants, that I was acquainted with so worthy an Author – And what can be more glorious for You, than to have entertain'd the whole nation in its most rational Amusement – without flattering the bad taste of the multitude or any vicious passion of the great world – ?

I drew tears from Mrs Graves even by *my* reading of your play; so can easily conceive the Effect of it, in Mrs Bellamy's Action – which I find attested by the publick Chronicles of the transactions of the town. – I have no idea of any thing more mortifying to a certain M--g-r[1] than to see his rival Theatre crowded by the very performance, which (I'm certain) *he* refus'd thro envy to the Author –

I hope Sr Mr Shenstone thought my Affairs of importance enough – to explain to you at ye Leasowes – our unaccountable Behavior – when we [w]e were last in London[2] – We took Lodgings for a [w]eek – but staid in town only two days – (on acc^t of Mrs Graves's illness) one of which was spent in waiting on my late Patron – the other on a gentleman, who is so kind as to act as my Banker – & on whom I depended for money to carry me down again – If we take ye same Journey next Whitsuntide – Mrs Graves has determin'd to make our first Visit to our worthy friend in Pall-mall –

I am S^r
Y^r affect. hum^b Ser^t

Ric. Graves

P.S. I have had the Small-pox this Autumn – after escaping it 40 years – which is one reason – why I did not sooner take some notice of our rudeness when in Town –

MS: Somerset County Record Office, DD/SK, 28/1,10.

[1] An obvious allusion to David Garrick.
[2] One wonders why Graves himself had not written to explain his failure to meet RD when in London eight months earlier. (See his last letter on 25 April.) His smallpox in autumn (see postscript) seems a weak excuse. Could there have developed some coolness regarding RD's desire to have Shenstone's name on the Epilogue to *Cleone*, for which Graves himself had actually written the original text? Also, in Graves's letter to RD on the previous February, he mentions that "After almost half-a-years Silence" he had received a letter from Shenstone, as if communication between the triumvirate had broken down.

From Richard Jago[1]

[1758?]

S^r,

I receiv'd y^rs of the 15th, and am satisfied I cannot expect any Share of Profit from so small a number as you mention, unless it shou'd run to another Edition & in that Case I know You wou'd do by me as well as You cou'd afford – I am much surpris'd at y^r not remembering to hear M^r S___ tell me He wou'd print my Book in y^e Winter, as He was obliged to speak so very loud & repeated it several times; it was not an absolute Promise, but (if He cou'd afford it) that was the term. Several Circumstances concurr to make me doubt whether You were really the Person introduc't to me last April in M^r S___'s Dressing-room under the name of Mr Dodsley. I must have entirely forgot [y]^r Features since I had the pleasure of seeing you [at] our House about a dozen years ago, wch was the [on]ly time I think – Be so good to set me right in that particular it will clear up some things wth regard to the aforesaid Gentleman's Conduct wch now I don't know w! to make on – besides saving me the trouble of repeating some things that pass't there – this Book of Verses lay then upon the Table & was open'd & show'd to You but you did not take the smallest Notice of it; only as Mr S. mention'd the *Complaint of Deafness* wch He said He had show'd you before, You (or y! Representative) expres't a high approbation of it.

I am sorry my Friend the transcriber put those lines of Dr Cobden's² in the Front, they were sent me above 30 years ago upon sight of some humorous pieces, trifles most of wch I have thought proper to suppress, & it wou'd look too vain in me to publish them now – If that Gentleman is living perhaps He may have forgot them, at least wou'd not like they shou'd be printed, He only Knew me by the Name of *Long*.

But, I think it wou'd be the best way to let the Dream come out by it Self first, or with only that One, of the Author's Complaint of Deafness, at the end of it. – as it wou'd both increase the Expence of printing to put more in, & also make it too large for a Pamphlet wch I suppose you design it for now. The Letters are out of my Hand at present but I have got a Friend to transcribe some of them wch being intermixt with affairs of a private Nature must be wrote over again – & – the Persons they were wrote to will not part with the originals.

You oblige me very much, S^r, in promising to speak to Mr S. it cannot be long before You will have an Opportunity of seeing him – & it will be better for you to sound him first, if he seems averse to do it it will save me the Mortification of a Refusal, but need take no notice of my questioning the Identity of the Person.

It was a very young Clergyman that advis'd me not to publish it least it shou'd give Encouragem! to the Method [ists] but have had Testimonies from much older & perhaps wiser Heads that no such thing need be apprehended. I know no more of their Principles than you, nor don't see how any body can know unless they wou'd publish some articles of their *Credenda* in wch they were all agreed.

The allegoricall way of writing is common enough & Dreams & Visions are often look't upon as the best way of conveying Ideas of Religion & Virtue, but if people will be so mad to take such things in a Literal Sense who can help it?

Sir, I have given You a great deal of trouble already, or else I cou'd say more on the Subject – when you favour me with an Answer please to send Y^r Letter by the Gen^{rl}. Post – I am wth Respect S^r

Y^r Hum^{ble} Serv!

R. J.

we are out of the Reach of the penny Post
Y^{rs} was put by that into ye general

— — — — —

P.S. I am determin'd not to send the Letters till I see how the Dream takes – besides as the Correspondence is going on there will be more of them.

An imperfect Copy of the Complaint of Deafness was publisht last Winter in the Grand Magazine also the Apology for Tea – but never any of the others that I know of Mr Ireland sends his Compliments.³ wou'd be very glad to see you at the Menagerie⁴

Address: To | M^r R Dodsley

MS: Humanities Research Center, University of Texas at Austin, Robert Dodsley | Recipient 1 | ff. 109–[16].

¹ This letter totally defies comprehension. Certain facts are clear: 1) Despite its apparent non-sequiturs, the letter is written as a single continuous piece on the recto and verso of two legal-size sheets; 2) the letter is written in Jago's hand, and therefore the signature "R. J." is presumably Jago's; 3) on the verso of the second sheet appears: "To | M^r R Dodsley," but without an address (not posted?); 4) from the author's mentioning within that the verses "Complaint of Deafness" and "Apology for Tea" had been published "last Winter in the Grand Magazine," we can conclude that the letter is most likely a product of 1758, for these two poems had been printed in the *Grand Magazine of Magazines* in February and April 1758, respectively (pp. 93–4; 96).

Beyond this, the letter proves inscrutable. The most perplexing statement occurs when Jago writes: "Several Circumstances concurr to make me doubt whether You were really the Person introduc't to me last April in M^r S——'s Dressing-room under the name of Mr Dodsley: I must have entirely forgot [y]^r Features since I had the pleasure of seeing you [at] our House about a dozen years ago, wch was the only time I think." Although Jago had written to RD on four occasions in 1757, of course it is entirely possible that he might be unacquainted with Dodsley's features, or perhaps had forgotten them in the dozen years since their meeting. However this is not the case. Only three years earlier – that is, in April, 1755 – Jago wrote to remind RD of the "kind Promise You was pleased to ma[ke me]" when I was in Town." Is it possible that Jago would remember Dodsley's visit of a dozen years ago and forget his meeting with the bookseller just three years earlier? One is tempted to think that Jago is proposing a publication to James Dodsley at some later date, but Robert is clearly the addressee, and Jago's reference to the verses in the *Grand Magazine* specifies a time when RD was still at the helm of Tully's Head.

Furthermore, all efforts to identify the work he is proposing, in whole or in part, have proved futile. None of Jago's pieces in his major collection during life, *Poems Moral and Descriptive* (published by James Dodsley in 1784), bear any relation to the present descriptions. Nor do any collections of Jago's poems (as in Chalmers's *Works of the English Poets*) contain verses that can be related to the subjects he mentions in the letter.

Finally, it is not clear whether or not Jago is suggesting that he wrote the "Complaint of Deafness," but it is printed in the *Grand Magazine of Magazines* as "By a Lady." The phrasing and signature of the letter do not suggest that he is proposing a work on behalf of anybody but himself. Given the obstacles to publication he seems to be facing, perhaps the work was never printed.

² Perhaps Edward Cobden (1685–1764), divine and poet. RD had been one of several booksellers listed in the imprint to Cobden's *Poems on Several Occasions* (1748).

³ Probably Samuel Ireland (d. 1800), a painter from Spitalfields. Marjorie Williams (*Letters of William Shenstone*, p. 540) quotes from RD's letter to John Scott Hylton in January 1760 (untraced): "Mr. Ireland ye Painter, here also."

⁴ The dens at the Tower of London featured wild beasts from many lands that regularly attracted painters and sketchers.

To William Shenstone

Pallmall Jany 20th 1759.

Dear Sir

You have indeed wrote (rode) round me, till You have almost turn'd my head giddy. I have no hopes of *coming up* with You, you have *left me out of sight, beat me hollow*, nor can I *save my distance* even with *whip and spur. Three heats*,[1] without giving one time to *breathe*, is enough to break ones heart. But methinks I hear you cry out, that I am in danger of *running on the wrong side of the Post*; I will therefore *check my steed*, which may easily be done as he can hardly *make a gallop*, and endeavour to put him into the plain & safer road of comõn Sense, and a dog *trot*. But I know not what to write, nor where to begin: or if I should begin, it appears to me that I shall never be able to come to an end of all I have to say. First, You rejoice with me on the success of Cleone. I heartily thank you for your obliging Congratulations, & pray let this suffice at present, as I am almost sick of the Subject. You ask me who is the Author of the Remarks on it? D.ʳ Hill, the precipitate D.ʳ Hill; who came to see it acted on Saturday night, wrote his Criticism on Sunday, printed it on Monday, and with great Good-nature publish'd it on Tuesday morning, the third day of its being acted, & two days before the Play its self was printed: such was the industry exerted in predjudicing the Town against it.[2] But he did not miss his reward; M.ʳ Garrick brought on for him, some days afterward, the Farce call'd the Rout, which was damn'd the second Night.[3]

You next proceed to tell me that M.ʳ Graves pass'd four or five days with You at the Leasowes –

"O charming Noons, and Nights divine!"

what would I have given to have spent them with you! I might have enjoy'd, tho' I could not have improv'd them. Your Elegies I doubt not are now perfect – You will not dare to shew them to any one else – his judgment is decisive, I know 'tis in their favour, nor can you longer continue your injustice in hiding them from the World. I intend a tour into Wales next Summer, & purpose to stay some days with him at Bath. Why won't you trust me with his Plan? I am very secret, and very honest for a Bookseller.[4]

As to Fables, I am indeed trying to select some of the best, from all the Fabulists, & to new write them in plain simple prose, for yᵉ use of schools.[5] It is a task which I was first perswaded to undertake by Dʳ Lowth, when I had yᵉ pleasure to seeing him last Sumẽr at Durham.[6] I wrote between thirty and forty soon after I came home, & happening to shew them to Mʳ Melmoth, his partiality approv'd them so well, that he was pleas'd to join me in the work, & whilst I have been busy'd in my Play, has written between thirty & forty more.[7] I shall be very glad to hear your reasons for entertaining but a mean opinion of Fables; & that you would favour me with what rules you think should be observ'd in writing them.[8] Indeed we have no collection of Fables in prose, that are fit to be read; and as they are amongst the first things that are put into yᵉ hands of young people, were they judiciously chosen, well told, in a Style concise & clear, & at yᵉ same time correct and elegant; were Sentiments proper to their natures and circumstances given to yᵉ persons of the Fable, & were the Maxims they teach so plainly couch'd in the Narration, as to need no detach'd explanatory Moral at the end, I think it might possible be a useful and acceptable Work, and not altogether unentertaining.[9] But pray send me your thoughts on it more at large.

And now I come to your exclamation ag.ˢᵗ Second Editions, with Additions & Alterations. I shall dispatch this point in a very few words. Would you have an

Author, after he has once publish'd, ty'd up from correcting his errors, or improving his Work? Second thoughts you know are said to be the best, & therefore second Editions corrected, are no bad things – I speak as a Bookseller.[10]

I have prevail'd with Tonson to give me a Sett of the octavo Cutts for Milton (ye Quarto would no[t] do) which I have sent to Montagu.[11] Roubiquer is dead or dying, & Montagu I believe is near fourscore.[12] Michael Drayton's Works were printed a few years ago in one Vol Folio, & in three Vols octavo.[13] The price of ye Folio 25^s the octavo 18^s. There was an Edition of ye Earl of Surry['s] Poems printed by Curl in one Vol. royal octavo, but I believe it is out of print.[14] As to my own trash, I will send the[m] You as they are; but they are so small that they will not bind single, & of such different sizes that they will not bear to be bound together. Besides, I am asham'd of some of them already, & should be much more so to see them pompously bound in Russia leather. Think of the impropriety of dressing up a beggar in Lace & Embroidery, & I will trust your good Taste to get the better of your partiality, and your good Nature, to save me from blushing at my own absurd finery. I should be sorry to have it said of my *Triffles*.[15]

"*That their fond Author was so good to gild 'em.*"

or to hear any one cry out – *how much more cost than worship!* If I should live however to print a more careful Edition of my things, I may endeavour, as far as I am able, to remove the objection.

And have You really taken up your Winter Quarters in your Study? I am glad You had ye Grace to tell me in so oblique a manner, that I am to entertain no hopes of seeing you here. Pray dispatch one of those Pidgeons to let me know what you are about. Do not think I will be satisfy'd with this disappointment, unless I hear by and bye that you have executed some great and important Work. Nothing else can excuse You. I wish you had *indeed* been made Poet Laureat: this might perhaps have forc'd you up to Town: tho' I fancy you would rather, in that case, have wish'd that his Majesty would have been graciously pleas'd to have come down to hear your Ode at the Leasowes.

I think I have now run thro' your first letter, & answer'd it pretty punctually. I come now to your second.[16] The World, with the Names of the Authors, as far as I know them, I will send, together with ye Epistles philosophical & moral, but I cannot learn the name of the Author.[17] That Mr Burke who writes so ingeniously, is an Irish Gentleman, bred to the Law, but having ye grace not to follow it, will soon I should think make a very great figure in the literary World.[18] He, with many others, to whom I had given hopes of seeing You in Town, would have been glad of your Acquaintance: but O shame to London! has it nothing that deserves your notice? You say you are in a vein for *correction*; for my part I think you well deserve to be *corrected*: however, I will send you the two manuscript Volumes, & hope you will make good use of them. Mr Percy's information in relation to Dr Grainger is true. I have heard his Tibullus well spoken of, & believe it sells.[19]

I am very sorry you are not satisfy'd about the Epilogue: but it was partly your own fault, as you confess, in sending it so late that I had no time to consult with you about it. Besides, I was afraid some parts of the Irony on the Play, should be taken in earnest, & that might have been dangerous. Then that phrase in the last Line occurs twice before; & I am doubtful, so were some others to whom I shew'd it, whether it be allowable or not – Was never age &c – In regard to that Line.

Why child, we've *laugh'd aloud* thro' half yᵉ Play, the case was so very much the reverse, that it would not have been proper to have been spoken even in jest – For Men as well as Women *wept aloud*.[20] However, your Letter comes very opportunely, for I am just going to print a new edition, and have not *now* the least objection to printing yᵉ Epilogue exactly as you shall write it: so pray send a copy of it as soon as you please, & if you have any corrections to make in the Play, be so good as to send them to me, I shall esteem it as a great favour, being now determin'd to put the last hand to it.[21]

And now, dear Sir, have patience for a few more words, in answer to your last Letter, and You shall be releast. I well remember the humorous Essay on Electricity. I sent it to Mʳ Moore, who being now dead, I know not what is become of it. But I will enquire of his Widdow, & recover it if I can.[22] I have just been to ⟨have⟩ wait⟨ed⟩ on Lady Northumberland for the Vista, but she was not at home: I spoke however to my Lord, & he promis'd me that he will remind her Ladiship of it, and that it shall be sent to me if found.[23] And thus I have written a Letter longer than all your three; so that your boast of riding round me must fall to yᵉ ground. And tho' you may not allow that I carry weight for inches, I hope you will at least confess that I have behav'd very handsomely.

> I am ever
> Dear Sir
> Affectionately Yours
> R. Dodsley

MS: BL. Add. MS. 28,959, f. 114–17.

[1] In this letter, RD responds, one by one, to three letters he had received from Shenstone, none of which has been traced.

[2] See Hawkesworth's letter to RD on 10 December 1758, note 3. Apparently Sir John Hill (1716?–75) had attended the Saturday opening of *Cleone* and launched his attack on the following Tuesday in *An Account of the New Tragedy of Cleone*. This piece stirred up a storm, further ingratiating *Cleone* with the town. Although the *Critical Review* had some adverse criticism of RD's play (December 1758, pp. 463–75), it vehemently attacked Hill when reviewing *A Letter to the Hon. Author of the New Farce called the Rout*, claiming the author of *The Rout* to be "beneath all ridicule."

[3] Hill's *Rout* was produced at Drury Lane on 20 and 21 December and then discontinued. Despite its failure, Hill published it on 26 December (*PA*) and had the courage to attach to the advertisement: "There is nothing personal in this Piece. The Run is interrupted only by the Illness of one of the Performers." Hill's sham was exposed by a review in the *Gentleman's Magazine* of the next month (p. 37).

[4] Possibly a reference to Graves's early work on *The Spiritual Quixote*, which he had been trying to keep a secret. For even earlier hints of the work, see RD's letter to Graves on 24 October 1757 and Graves's to RD on 3 February 1758.

[5] RD's correspondence over the next two years would make frequent reference to his forthcoming edition *Select Fables of Esop and Other Fabulists*, which appeared in February 1761 from Baskerville's press.

[6] Although Robert Lowth might have persuaded RD to undertake the work, probably the idea had originated with RD, for he was no stranger to fables. As Jeanne K. Welcher and Richard Dircks point out (*An Essay on Fable. Robert Dodsley*. Augustan Reprint Society, No. 112 (William Andrews Clark

Library, University of California, Los Angeles, 1965), p. i), RD had printed many fables in such works as his *Museum* (1746–7), *The World* (1753–6), Joseph Spence's *Moralities* (1753), and Edward Moore's *Poems, Fables, and Plays* (1756). In fact, he had issued his own edition of Aesop's *Fables* in 1753.

7 Melmoth not only contributed fables (though unidentified) to RD's collection but did a critical reading of the collection for RD in November of this year. See his letter to RD on the 20th of that month.

8 Ultimately RD wrote his own essay on the rules for writing fables, that prefaces *Select Fables*, though borrowing much from the Frenchman Antoine Houdart de la Motte's *Discours sur la Fable* (translated for him by Shenstone), and relying much on Shenstone's corrections and recommendations. See RD's letter to Shenstone on 24 June 1760. Shenstone's "mean opinion of Fables" seems to have sustained itself, for he did not respond to RD's repeated efforts to secure a half dozen fables from him. Thomas Percy claims that Shenstone contributed No. 41 "The Waterfall" and No. 41 "The King-fisher and the Sparrow" to the volume of original fables (Bodleian MS Percy, B. 2, f. 24, printed in Brooks, *The Correspondence of Thomas Percy and William Shenstone*, p. 236). But since RD was himself the author of this second fable (see his letter of 27 March 1759), one wonders about Percy's reliability. In a letter to Graves on 1 March, 1761, Shenstone himself says, "I can hardly claim a single fable as my own" (Williams, p. 572).

9 All of these topics RD will take up in his Essay on Fable in the first edition of *Select Fables*.

10 Probably RD is arguing against Shenstone's reluctance to provide a revised edition of the Epilogue to *Cleone*, for the third edition of the play to be published on 26 April (*LC*).

11 On 25 January 1759 (*LC*), J. and R. Tonson would re-issue, in octavo and printed by Baskerville, Milton's *Paradise Lost . . . from the Text of Thomas Newton, D. D.*, a work they had published the previous year in quarto, with cuts by Francis Hayman.

12 Most likely the "Richard Montagu, Bookbinder in Great Wild Street" (St Giles) who announced in the *Daily Advertiser* on 4 July 1760 that he had invented and now offered for sale a "beautiful Marble Paper to fit all Sizes of Books without piec'ng." Ellic Howe (*A List of London Bookbinders 1648–1815* (London: Bibliographical Society, 1950)) lists a Richard Montague (fl. 1743–58) as located in St Giles in the Fields. (Plomer lists a Richard Montague of Wild St. as a "book and pamphlet-seller.") Since linked with Montagu in the same sentence, "Roubiquer" is probably another bookbinder, John Roubiquet, also found in Howe and praised in the *Address to the Booksellers of London and Westminster* (1781): "It cannot be disputed, that Bookbinding has arrived at a Degree of Perfection in the Course of the last sixteen Years, unknown to any former Period, both in the useful as the ornamental Part . . . We have seen, during that time, a Roubiquet, a Johnson, a Roger Payne, and a Baumgarten" (quoted by Howe, p. xxvi). Apparently RD used Montagu's bookbinding services.

13 *The Works of Michael Drayton, Esq.*, in one volume folio, had been printed by John Hughs in 1748 and sold by RD, J. Jollyffe, and W. Reeve. W. Reeve had issued the three-volume octavo set himself in 1753.

14 *The Praise of Geraldine, a Florentine Lady. Being the celebrated love poems of the Right Honourable Henry Howard, Earl of Surrey* (London: Henry Curl [Edmund Curll?], 1728.

15 By "my own trash," RD probably refers to his own publications that had indeed appeared in "different sizes." Much of what he had written up to 1745, he had issued that year under one cover entitled *Trifles*. No other collection was issued during his lifetime.

16 Not traced.

17 *The World*, the weekly edited for RD by Edward Moore during the years 1753–6. If RD ever did write to Shenstone to reveal the authors of *The World*, his letter, regrettably, has not turned up. William Kenrick wrote *Epistles Philosophical and Moral* (London: T. Wilcox, 1759).

18 One of RD's sagest judgments as critic and bookseller was to publish the first works of Edmund Burke.

19 RD probably refers to the manuscript of the new fables, apparently for Shenstone's correction. James Grainger's *Poetical Translations of the Elegies of Tibullus, and of the Poems of Sulpicia, with the Original Text, and Notes Critical and Explanatory* (2 vols. London: A. Millar), though dated 1759, had actually appeared on 12 December 1758 (*PA*).

20 The Epilogue calls for Mrs Bellamy (Cleone) to offer some initial comic relief by which to drive home the point of her closing moral prescription. She begins by assuming the expected sentiment of the modish ladies of the audience, who would naturally find something comical in the blind fidelity of a

wife whose husband chose to be off to the wars for three years. After depicting the independent attitude assumed by a modern wife in such a situation, the argument switches to a bygone time when wives, steeped in virtue, never dreamed of happiness outside of the domestic scene. The obvious injunction follows: "Tis yours, ye Fair, to bring those days agen." Apparently Shenstone's line – "Why child we've *laughed aloud* thro' half the play" – was not only blatantly at odds with the audience's true reaction, but, prior to the performance, was thought by RD too weighted in favor of the modish lady's sentiment and therefore destructive of the intended irony. Consequently he changed the verse to induce a more docile, receptive frame of mind in the females of the audience: "To make us smile? – methinks I hear you say – / Why, who can help it, at so strange a Play?" Lacking Shenstone's last revision of the Epilogue, one cannot say more than RD does about the phrase "Was never age etc."

21 For RD's use of the criticisms of Shenstone and of others, see his letter on 20 February 1759, note 4.
22 More than eleven years earlier, Shenstone had sent Richard Jago's essay on electricity for inclusion in RD's fortnightly *Museum*. (See RD's letters to Shenstone on 8 and 17 October 1747.) Because the *Museum* had already been discontinued, RD wrote that he would try to get the essay inserted in another London periodical, though he seems to have been unsuccessful. He had even given it to Edward Moore six years later for *The World*, but neither did Moore use it. Just two weeks before this letter, on 6 January, Shenstone had written to Jago, asking the author for a copy of the essay and saying that he had been thinking of publishing a "small Miscellany from neighbor Baskerville's press" (Williams, p. 503).
23 Probably Shenstone's "The Vista." But this piece had to await the posthumous edition of Shenstone's *Works* (1764), where it appeared as "The Ruin'd Abbey; or the Effects of Superstition" (I, 308–21). Elizabeth Seymour, Lady Northumberland (1716–76), wife of Hugh Percy, 2nd Earl of Northumberland and later 1st Duke of Northumberland of the third creation (1766).

To William Shenstone

Pall mall Feb 8 [1759][1]

My dear M.ʳ Shenstone

I am in too much hurry to write you a letter, tho' I have ten thousand things to say. And first I thank You for every thing relating to Cleone, but cannot at present descend to particulars. I have sent all the books you bespoke. I could get no other copy of La Motte but that I sent.[2] There is a better Edition of Sir John Davis printed in Scotland, which I believe I can get if you are dissatisfy'd with this.[3] But my people brought it in, & I did not see it till 'twas packing up. D.ʳ Grainger's Present to You was sent to me, but as you had bespoke one bound in Russia, I sent that, & kept his, which was bound common, & shall only charge you yᵉ difference.[4] As to the Epilogue – I like what you have last sent very well – If I should object to any thing besides the blotted Lines it would be – the *mad folks & murder'd babes*, which hardly looks like Irony. That Couplet –

Else know I wield a Pen &c

will be thought to point particularly at Lady Vane, which I would chuse to avoid.[5] And is not the image of a husband reading a Sermon to his wife somewhat strange in an Epilogue? Is not the word *Matron* improper for a Lady of intrigue?[6] But truce with Objections, I have no more to make. I had a Letter from Mʳ Pixel in which he says M.ʳ *Garrick has sent some varnish'd reasons into that neighbourhood for his strange conduct.*[7] Pray what are those reasons & to whom sent? The pompous Edition of 'ontaine's Fables is in 4 Vols Folio (three of which are publish'd) price 12 Guineas inbound.[8] O you literary Triffler! are not you asham'd to spend your time on the outside of books? It goes against my conscience to send you the Letters you desire: hall I not by this means be deem'd an Accomplice with you in defrauding the World of your better Labours?

I thank you again & again for all your hints concerning Cleone. I should be glad o have a frontispiece &c but will it not look like a partial fondness for ones own offspring? You will send me however the drawing & the Epilogue.[9] The best Edition of Warburton's Pope is the large Octavo: if you have the Duodecimo I think ye maller of the two is the prettiest.[10] Like the true Lion I find you chuse to turn your backside on the false Knight.[11] Where Victory would be disgrace, contempt is better than Courage. I wish you may understand what I have written but I am in too much haste to read it or to add more than that I am Yours

R. Dodsley

MS: BL. Add. MS. 28,959, ff. 118–19.

[1] From internal evidence, the letter requires the year 1759. Much of the concern of the letter has to do with RD's preparation of a new edition of *Cleone* (3rd) with Shenstone's revised Epilogue, a volume that would appear on 26 April 1759. Also "Dr Grainger's Present to You" is undoubtedly James Grainger's *Poetical Translations of the Elegies of Tibullus, and of the Poems of Sulpicia*, which had been published just two months earlier, on 12 December (*PA*).

[2] See RD's letter to Shenstone on 20 January 1759, note 8. Apparently Shenstone was dissatisfied with this edition of de la Motte, which might have been the translation printed in 1721 by Robert Samber, for, in his letter to Graves on 9 February 1760, he says he has purchased a quarto edition in French (Williams, p. 548). There he speaks of a prose translation he regards as "beneath contempt."

[3] Perhaps Sir John Davies (1569–1626), poet, lawyer, and Attorney-General for Ireland, but the only work by Davies with a Scottish imprint in the British Library or in the National Library of Scotland is *The Original, Nature, and Immortality of the Soul* (Glasgow: R. and A. Foulis, 1749).

[4] See note 1. No doubt the work had come from Andrew Millar, its publisher.

[5] RD gave in to Shenstone, for both of these lines were retained in the third edition of *Cleone*. Frances Ann, Viscountess Vane, nicknamed "Lady Fanny," had managed to get the memoirs of her indiscretions inserted as Chapter 81 in Tobias Smollett's *Peregrine Pickle* (1751).

[6] These last two objections were sustained; neither a preaching husband nor a "Matron" appeared.

[7] Regrettably, this letter and Garrick's "varnish'd reasons" have not been discovered.

[8] Jean de La Fontaine (1621–95). A "Grand Folio Edition just published at Paris" of Fontaine's *Fables choisies mises en vers* (1668), with 276 prints by J. B. Oudry, had recently been advertised as on sale at R. and J. Dodsley's (*LEP*, 25–7 January 1759).

[9] It is not clear, without Shenstone's letter, just whose drawing he is proposing, but it seems to have been of Mrs Bellamy as Cleone. (See RD's next letter to Shenstone.) However the frontispiece to the third edition, Cleone's death scene from Act V, was designed by Francis Hayman (?1708–76) and executed by William Ryland (1738–83).

[10] The large octavo, Warburton's first edition, had fuller notes than the small.

[11] Seemingly a reference to Shenstone's young friend Edward Knight, a wealthy and learned resident of Wolverley, Worcester. But Shenstone's letters of this period show only cordial relations with Knight. Perhaps RD's "Knight" is a metaphorical allusion to Shenstone's friend, the engraver, Joseph Giles. The evidence is sparse (Shenstone's brief letters to Matthew Boulton of Snow Hill, Birmingham, in Williams, p. 491), but it seems that Shenstone, in August 1758, had amused himself with some verses at the expense of his friend John Baskerville, copies of which he had secretly shared with Boulton and Joseph Giles. Apparently Giles had shown them to Baskerville, putting Shenstone in an embarrassing way with his friend and causing the poet to urge Boulton either to return his copy or burn it. Nothing

remains of his exchange with Giles on the matter. Significantly, Hylton, writing to RD on the 21st o
this month, says: "I never liked him [Giles] in my Life, I know him to be a sycophant, & a peice c
mischief he intended me with M! Shenstone has render'd him detestable to me!"

To William Shenstone

Pall mall Feb.ᶠʸ 20.ᵗʰ [1759]

Dear M! Shenstone!

How much am I oblig'd to you for your kind attention to my affairs? I like you
idea for the Title page extreamly; a Gentleman of my acquaintance, from the stag
Box one night with his pencil made a little sketch of M!ˢ Bellamy in the very attitud
you mention, and he tells me if he can finish it to his mind, he will also etch it for m
for that purpose;² Hayman is desiging a frontispiece from the dying Scene, & I hop
in a post or two to receive the new Edition of your Grove together with th
Epilogue, & then let any Lady say if they dare that the Play is not a *fine* one.³ I an
oblig'd to You for your Criticisms on it, & shall avail my self of them; I will conside
also every thing that has been said against it in the Reviews & Magazines, &
endeavour by this means to make my Enemies do me the Office of Friends.⁴ M
Deane has done me the favour to drink a dish of Tea with me this afternoon; he set
out for the Country on Monday next, and desire his Compliments to You.⁵ I sen
you by Trimen's Waggon yesterday two setts of Letters, Burke's new Edition of y
Sublime, with two Quires of blue Paper, & I enclose with this D! Grainger's Lette
to Smollet.⁶ I will not put Cleone to press till I hear from you again, as I am willing
to do all I can towards rendering her less unworthy of that indulgence with whicl
the Public overlook'd her Imperfections.

The last Edition of Sir William Temple is four Vols in Octavo Price 24.ˢ There is ⁚
fine Edition of Montaigne in French 3 Volumes Quarto, Price 30.ˢ and in English ⁚
Vols Octavo, Price 15.ˢ⁷ You must perceive in what a hurry I write, & will therefor
pardon all imperfections. I hope I shall in a little time contrive to be somewha
more at leisure.

I am ever
Dear Sir
Affectionately Yours
R. Dodsle

MS: BL. Add. MS. 28,959, f. 120.

¹ RD's mentioning revisions that would become part of his third edition of *Cleone* to appear in Apr
1759, require that the year be 1759.
² The ornament for the title page would be neither of Cleone nor the sketch offered by RD'
acquaintance (George Steevens), but rather a scene of a vulture killing a lamb, as he suggests in hi
letter to Shenstone on 19 March. (See Steevens's letter of 9 April.)
³ For the frontispiece, see RD's last letter to Shenstone, note 9. For the "Grove," see RD's letter t
Shenstone on 20 September 1757, note 2.
⁴ Despite Thomas Percy's peevish attempt to portray RD as obstinate on literary matters (Brooks, pِ

235–8), the author of *Cleone* listened carefully to his critics and made considered changes in the play accordingly. Even prior to the first printing of *Cleone*, he had sought the advice of several friends, especially that of Shenstone and Graves and, as already seen, accommodated the many crucial objections expressed in Richard Berenger's letter on 10 June 1756 and in John Hawkesworth's on 14 September of the same year. The third, corrected, edition would see still further alterations (on fifty-nine of the eighty printed pages) and, as RD says, he made "my Enemies do me the Office of Friends." The new text shows no major additons or excisions: no actions, motivations, or characters are introduced nor deleted, although some refinement of character motivation occurs. Merely twenty-seven lines were added, and two dropped (other than those for which substitutions were included). Additions and substitutions serve to clarify the nature of some individual characters and their relationships with others; to effect more intelligent linking of one or two scenes; to create a better sense of verisimilitude (the *Critical Review*'s complaint, December 1758, pp. 463–75) by effecting greater correspondence between characters' motivation and their utterances; and particularly to better realize the emotional potential of some scenes.

Most of the alterations are aimed at verbal refinement. For help on this count, RD would be much indebted to Shenstone, whose many handwritten corrections survive in the latter's own copy of the first edition, now in the Bodleian Library. This copy carries corrections both for the text and Advertisement of *Cleone*, as well as for the Epilogue. (In addition, attached to the rear fly-leaf of the Bodleian volume is a 5″ × 6″ sheet of queries and criticisms that is endorsed on the reverse side: "By Mr. [Robert] Bedingfield.") In response to the likes of *Lloyd's Evening Post* (4–6 December 1758), RD attempted to achieve more power and "beauties" in his poetry by heightening his imagery; by elevating his imagery at times from the simply perceived to poetic abstraction ("to quench / A loose desire, and gain a moment's pleasure" becomes "to quench / A loose desire, a lawless passion's rage," I, iv, 14–15); by smoothing his rhythms, sometimes simply by inversion; by substituting the more precise, more logical word; by occasionally opting for the classical nuance in preference to the Christian ("Guardian Powers" for "Gracious Heaven," III, iv, 4). Most obvious is the elimination of the flatulent "O" that had opened so many lines and had made the verse loose or naively over-charged. By these means, RD likewise responded to the complaint of the *Critical Review* that had regretted the language was so "humble." Finally, this verbal tinkering also gained RD a degree of naturalness of language. In all, the third edition of *Cleone* is quite evidently a more polished text because of the assistance of both friends and enemies. Nonetheless both its poetry and characters continued to languish in the shade of their more accomplished models. RD did not rise to the power of Pope, and visions of Lady Macduff and her child, Ophelia, Othello, Macbeth, even of Falstaff, dance in our heads.

5 Probably Anthony Deane, Jr. (1729–?), an ironmonger who frequented Shenstone's circle and is often mentioned in the poet's correspondence. Johnson Ball (*William Caslon*, pp. 59, 176) indicates that Deane lived at Hagley, but his name appears in the subscription list of Baskerville's *Bible* (1763) with the designation: "of Whittington, Staffs." Ball notes, however, that Deane spent much of his time either in London or in Bath. (See also RD's letter to Shenstone on 30 December 1760).

6 These unidentified letters, RD had promised to send when he wrote on 8 February. The books were: the second edition of Edmund Burke's *A Philosophical Enquiry into the Origin of our Ideas of the Sublime and Beautiful*, which had been published from Tully's Head the previous month; *A Letter to Tobias Smollett, M. D., occasioned by his Criticism upon a late Translation of Tibullus* (*PA*, 30 January 1759), a response to Smollett's attack (*Critical Review*, December, 1759, pp. 475–82) on James Grainger's *Poetical Translation of the Elegies of Tibullus*. Smollett had belittled Grainger's work as a "huge farrago of learned lumber, jumbled together for very little purpose" and in a "great part borrowed from Brochfus," that there was "very little either to inform, interest, or amuse the reader." Grainger had anticipated Smollett's treatment in a letter to Thomas Percy in February where, complaining of the printer's slowness in providing proof sheets, he consoles himself: "but while I am not in the hands of the public I consider myself as so long reprieved from the cruel fangs of those savage beasts the Critical Reviewers" (Nichols, *Illustrations of Literature*, VII, 249).

7 *The Works of Sir William Temple Bar^t* (4 vols. London: J. Clarke *et al.* (sixteen other publishers), 1757); perhaps RD refers to J. Tonson and J. Watts's three-volume edition *Les essais de Michel seigneur de Montaigne* (1724), for no other contemporary London edition in French seems to have been available.

From John Scott Hylton

Lapall Hous
21 Feb.^ry 1759

Dear Sir,

I am so very much your Debtor, that I can scarce think I am able to compound with you if that might set me clear in your Account. – Indeed, I do not know how to exculpate myself for not writing to you long ago; and to offer up my congratulations upon your Success of Cleone, would be paying a Compliment because the rest of the World have paid it. However I was not without my Hopes and Fears for you before Cleone ma[de] her Appearance; and I can only truly say that the reputation & Fame you have thereby aquired gave me the Sincerest pleasure.

I return you many Thanks for the present you made me of your Play, which, however I did not receive till a Fortnight after it came to Giles's Hands; & hope nothing of mine may ever come into his Hands again. I never liked him in my Life, I know him to be a sycophant, & a peice of mischeif he intended me with Mr Shenstone has render'd him detestable to me![1]

But enough of this – Mr Shenstone has sent to have an improv'd drawing of the Grove, I think he said, to decorate y.^r intended Edition of Cleone[2] – which when it comes out I w['d] desire to be set down for one or two. I dare say it will sell. –

Mr Shenstone has put me (by his own Example) upon adding a few more Books to my Collection – can you be so good to send me the following, in a Box, directed for me here, or to Mr Aris's?[3]

Borlace's Nat: Hist.^y of Cornwall, in Sheets, let the Cuts be a good Impression.
The Elabratory laid open, Oct.^yo a new Book last year, bound & letter'd.
Edward's Canons of Criticism & the last Edition, bound, gilt, & letter'd.
A set of Dr Newton's Cuts (if to be purchas'd) for my Baskerville's Milton.
Dr Grainger's Tibullus, bound, gilt, and letter'd.
Mrs Lenox's Female Quixote 2 Vol.^s – bound & letter'd.

I want also to know the price, size, & reputation of Oudenhorp's Seutonius.[4] The person who takes this to Birmingham, is in such haste, that I must conclude, but will write a more orderly Letter next time, if you will accept this from

Dear Sir
Y.^r most Obliged & Obed.^t Servant
John Scott Hylton

Poor Thomas at the Leasews, was releas'd from all his Pain & Sufferings last Tuesday Morn.^g he was sensible 'till ab[t] an Hour before he died.[5] – Mr Shenstone had long expected it, and therefore bore it better than he otherwise would have done.

Address: To | M.^r R: Dodsley | in Pall=mall | London
Postmark: 24 FE [Birmingham?]

MS: Humanities Research Center, University of Texas at Austin, Robert Dodsley | Recipient 1/ Bound, 45–8.

¹ Probably the Joseph Giles who produced Shenstone's seal, assisted Grignion in engraving the print of Shenstone's grove, and published some poems in RD's *Collection*. See Shenstone's letter to Lady Luxborough on 17 April 1755 (Williams, p. 444) and RD's letters to Shenstone on 20 September 1757 and 15 March 1758. The nature of Giles's alleged "peice of mischeif" is not known, but it seems Shenstone had mentioned the affair to RD. See RD's letter of 8 February to Shenstone. See also Pixell's letter to RD on 20 April in which the author says RD once offered Giles the opportunity of opening a pamphlet shop in London.

² So it did, designed by Daniel Bond, Shenstone's friend in Birmingham, and engraved by Charles Grignion in London. See Shenstone's letter to RD on 31 March.

³ Probably Thomas Aris, a printer in High Street, Birmingham, 1741–61 (Plomer).

⁴ William Borlace, *The Natural History of Cornwall*, published by RD on 8 February (*LC*); Robert Dossie, *The Elaboratory laid open, or the Secrets of Modern Chemistry and Pharmacy Revealed* (1758); Thomas Edwards, *The Canons of Criticism* (1758); for Newton's cuts, see RD's letter to Shenstone of 20 January, note 11; for Grainger's Tibullus, see RD's letter to Shenstone of the previous day, note 6; Charlotte Lennox, *The Female Quixote; or the Adventures of Arabella* (1752); Franciscus Van Oudendorp, *Caius Suetonius Tranquillus ex recensione F. Oudendorpii, qui variantes lectiones, suasque animadversiones adjecit, intermixtis, J. G. Graevii & J. Granovii, nec non ineditis C. A. Dukeri annotationibus* (Lugduni Batavorum, 1751).

⁵ Thomas Jackson, Shenstone's servant.

From Thomas Blacklock

Dumfries 4th March 1759.

Dear Sir

Before I proceed either to apologize for my former Silence, or to give you the reasons why I break it at present, give me leave to congratulate you on your New Character of a Dramatic Poet. None since the days of Otway & Shakspear have so well deserved it, & I wish w.^t all my Soul, the Nations for whom you write may have a full & just sense of your Merit.¹ I heard of Cleone in Edinburgh, but for reasons to be afterwards mentioned, was obliged to deny myself the pleasure of reading it, till my return to Dumfries. Even then it's distress proved too high for me, & I had Scarce spirits enough to bear me home from a friend's house, who read it to me. Still however I was master of sufficient deliberation, to admire it's propriety & variety of Stile, It's beautifull & interesting plan, it's tender & natural incidents, the justness & consistency of it's Characters, & in short a whole piece in which the two irresistible charms of spirit & regularity, so rarely united in British productions, reflected mutual lustre, each upon the other. You'll wonder at my premature return from Edinburgh, & why I did not read Cleone whilst there. Forgive me therefore if I enter into a detail of these, since thus I shall be most naturaly lead to the design of the present Epistle. And that my account may be less imperfect, I must beg leave to recapitulate the views of My conduct, as well as the incidents of my life.² The generous subscription promoted by you & Mr Spence, gave me the first distant prospect of independency, still however there appeared something wanting to make that easy & agreeable.³

I found (or imagined) myself possessed of talent, which if exerted might contribute both to my own & the advantage of others arround me. With these ideas, I commenced a severe course of Study, to prepare a course of Lectures on

Criticism, or if you please on the Belle Lettres wch I intended to deliver to the Students in Edin.^h[4] I had known others, less qualified for this task, successfull in it. But when I consulted my friends there,[5] I found that a set of Gentlemen, who superintended the progress of learning here under the name of the Select Society, were prepossessed in favour of one Mr Adam Fergusson; a youth who added, to all the advantages he could derive from a great genius, a correct taste & a liberal education, all those improvements which are acquired by travelling & which a just & comprehensive knowledge of Mankind can bestow.[6] Sensible of the importance of this Society, & check'd by my sincere friendship for Mr Fergusson, I resolved never to enter the lists, though perhaps I might have lost no honour by the competition. Whilst I revolved, uncertain whey^r to sit down contented w^t my present acquisitions, or make oy^r efforts to increase my fortune & my reputation, I was soon determined by the arrival of a family amongst us, who had for sometime lived in the country, but now being deprived of both their fay^r & mother, & as they were all females, finding themselves less qualified for agriculture & oy^r Such rural employments, they returned to this place where they were born, & where a considerable number of good relations, the amiable Character of their Parents, & their own Merit, entituled them to esteem. As their habitation was contiguous to mine, I thank'd my Stars for the opportunity to pass some hours of relaxation, so agreeably as in their Company. My heart was likewise still warm w^t gratitude for a favour I had received from their fay^r, whose recommendation, had in no small degree influenced Dr Stevenson, to become my Benefactor.[7] How easy is the transition from gratitude or any tender passion to anoy^r which I need not Name! One of these Ladies, whom nature had eminently distinguished w^t all these perfections which constitute the happiness of conjugal life, was soon distinguished by me. This may appear imprudent & even absurd, but when you reflect, how strictly God & nature has allied the susceptible w^t the amiable, when you reflect what are the feelings of an ingenious heart, & how strongly virtue is enamoured of her own image where ever found, if you cannot excuse, you will at least pity me. Hitherto I had formed no views, but those of friendship & an agreeable Intercourse; If I felt wishes that tended further, they were treated as ridiculous & chimerical, till fortune should give a more favourable turn to my affairs. I flattered my self however, that an innocent & honourable intimacy, w^t one of my Character, infirmity & Circumstances, might pass uncensured, but I was miserably mistaken, for ill natured observation, soon made it necessary eiy^r to explain my views, or decline my pursuit. Which alternative was the most natural? When you have determined this, it will apologize for me. The issue of this eclaircissment, was at least not desperate. Fired therefore w^t oy^r views & oy^r Motives that had hitherto inspired me, I listned to the importunities of some of my best friends, in Edin^h, & resolved to enter into orders. This event, & the course of the tryal are not quite unknown to you. It ended on the 23^d of Novr last, to the Satisfaction of a Number who had formerly declared ag^t me.[8] Thus superior to all my difficulties, & almost secure, not only of friends but popularity, I set out for Edin^h But the transition from warmth, repose & Study, to cold weather, & the fatigues of a very inconvenient journey, hurt my constitution, to a degree, which it never before had felt, &

rendered all my sanguine hopes, perhaps for ever, abortive. What I could humbly wish therefore, is to know whey^r you are reimbursed the expenses of my Octavo edition, because w^t out being too decisive, in my sentiments concerning my present state, it is at least possible, that I may soon be gathered to my fathers.[9] And if this should happen, whilst accounts remain unadjusted between us, you'll find it less easy to reclaim from my relations, what Ballance may be found in your favour, than during my own life.[10] Shall I presume to beg you will present my kindest compliments to Mr Spence? This letter will furnish him w^t the means of relating the Catastrophe of my Romance, if it should finish at this Period, and if the Publick are kind enough to my memory, to wish for a Posthumous edition.[11] I have only to add that

I am

Dr Sir

Your sincere friend & hu^{le} Ser^t

Thos Blacklock.

MS: Osborn Collection, Beinecke Library, Yale.

[1] A reference to the success of RD's *Cleone* at Covent Garden the previous December.

[2] Some of the details in the following account have eluded all of Blacklock's biographers, even Henry Mackenzie, who had the cooperation of Blacklock's widow in writing the biography that prefaced the 1793 edition of Blacklock's *Poems*. The accounts offered by Mackenzie, Robert Anderson (*Works of the British Poets, with Prefaces Biographical and Critical* (1795), and Robert Chambers (*Biographical Dictionary of Eminent Scotsmen*, rev. T. Thomson (1868)), for instance, fail to mention the fact that his wife's father, the Dumfries surgeon Joseph Johnston, had been the intercessor with the Edinburgh physician who had funded Blacklock's early education at Edinburgh, Dr Stephenson; and that Blacklock had actually courted his wife four years prior to their marriage. All accounts give the impression that a sudden marriage was contracted when the poet succeeded in gaining ordination for the presbytery of Kirkcudbright in 1762. Anderson even adds that the "connexion [with Joseph Johnston] . . . formed the great solace and blessing of his future life," as if Johnston had not already played a major role in Blacklock's life.

[3] The subscription for the London edition of Blacklock's *Poems* (1756), promoted by RD and Joseph Spence, had carried the "life" of the poet that Spence had published separately in 1754.

[4] This plan occurred to Blacklock in late 1757 or early 1758.

[5] The "friends" included David Hume (himself an unsuccessful candidate for the Chair of Ethics at Edinburgh in 1745), who, although principally responsible for the London edition of Blacklock's *Poems* (see Hume's letter of 14 October 1754), saw little chance of Blacklock's getting on at Edinburgh.

[6] Adam Ferguson (1723–1816), Hume's successor as librarian at the Advocates' Library in 1757 and Professor of Philosophy at Edinburgh as of this year.

[7] Blacklock here proceeds to consider his early courtship, in late 1757 or early 1758, of his future wife Sarah Johnston and clearly identifies her father as the intercessor with Dr. Stephenson, his benefactor.

[8] Blacklock's account is a bit garbled, but "It" probably refers to his present pursuit of the relationship with Sarah Johnston, not his resolve "to enter orders." In a letter of the same day (q. v.), Richard Jameson tells RD that Blacklock went to Edinburgh about the end of November (to enter orders?), but stayed little more than two months. Those who had "declared ag^t me" probably refers to those who were antagonistic to his courting Miss Johnston.

[9] If Blacklock's intimate friend Richard Jameson is to be believed (see his letter of this day), the poet's fear of impending death was largely imaginary. In fact, Blacklock lived for another thirty-two years.

[10] If the sale of Blacklock's poems had not improved since RD's last report on 16 July 1757, perhaps RD had not been reimbursed for his printing and advertising expenses, but an account of the octavo's sale does not survive.

[11] Spence did not update his biography of Blacklock, nor did RD publish another edition of his poems. It seems the poet's warm verses "To the Rev. Mr. Spence. Written at Dumfries in the year 1759" had little effect at Byfleet.

From Richard Jameson[1]

Dumfries March 4. 1759

Dear Mr Dodsley,

Some Weeks ago, I used the Freedom to write a few Lines to you with a young Gentleman, Mr Welch, who was very desirous to be acquainted with you. I'm afraid I was to blame in recommending him to you in the Manner I did; for I have not the Happiness of a *very intimate* Acquaintance with you, and I was entirely unacquainted with him: but if I have committed a Fault, ⟨I hope⟩ you are good, and will, I hope, forgive me. – Hang all Apologies. They are ugly, awkward things at best; and I'll have no more to do with them, happen what will.

Poor Mr Blacklock is not well.[2] I am in great Uneasiness about him. He went to Edinburgh about the End of November, and continued there for above two Months, during which Time he did not enjoy one hour's Health; and was obliged to return at last to his native Air, in a very sickly Condition. I think him rather better since he came home, but he is of a different Opinion himself; for he firmly believes that his present Illness is to carry him out of this World very soon. I hope, however, he'll for once be disappointed; for I really think almost one half of his Illness is imaginary. Had he studied Poetry as much as he has done Divinity of late, he would have had every whit as good a Mind, and I'm sure he would have had a much better Body than he has at present.

Mr. Story, a Gentleman who supp'd with you one Evening in Mr Graham's at Dumfries, has promised to deliver you this. His Stay in Town will be some two or three Weeks; and I hope I shall have the Pleasure of hearing of your Welfare when he returns. He is a worthy Man, and one of my best Friends; and will be very glad to oblige either Mr Dodsley or me.[3] – I owe dear Mr Spence a Letter, but I have not time to write him at present: My best Wishes and Services to him if you happen to see him.

I ever am, Dr Sir, your most sincere Friend and
humble Servt

Rich. Jameson

Address: To——— | Mr Robert Dodsley Bookseller | at Tully's Head Pall Mall | London.

MS: Osborn Collection, Beinecke Library, Yale.

[1] The Rev. Richard Jameson, formerly a minister of the Episcopal Church at Dumfries, later of the English congregation at Dantzie, was at this time residing principally at Newcastle upon Tyne.

² Henry Mackenzie's "Account of the Life and Writings of Dr. Blacklock," written at the request of Blacklock's widow, describes Jameson as Blacklock's most intimate friend for the seven years following the poet's obtaining a license to preach at Dumfries. That relationship seems confirmed in Blacklock's addressing a poem to Jameson in which occurs the line "For thee my spirits shall more languid flow" (*Poems*, 2nd ed. (1756), pp. 181–5). The "Account" prefaced the edition of Blacklock's *Works* published in 1793. For Blacklock's own description of his illness, see his letter to RD on the same day.

³ Probably this is the John Story listed among the subscribers in the second edition of Blacklock's *Poems* (1756) as a "Writer, in Dumfries."

To William Shenstone

Pall mall Mar. 15.ᵗʰ [1759]¹

Dear Sir

I write this not to answer any of your Letters, but merely to tell you that I sent by last Monday's Waggon in a parcel directed to Mʳ Hylton, Blackstone's Analysis, Collection of Farces, & a Skin of green Morocco Leather.² You will wonder why I am in so much hurry that I cannot write you a Letter; the reason is I am settling my affairs, and leaving off the business to my brother, so that if you write a Letter that will not reach me till after Lady-day, you will be so good as to direct it to me at the Chinese Porter in Cockspur Street near Charing Cross.³ I hope the Swans came safe; they will change their colour next moulting time, & I am told will be very fine ones.⁴ I send you enclos'd a proof of the Epilogue; if you have any Corrections to make, You will send them by the return of the post. The drawing of the Grove is very beautiful, vastly improv'd, & I hope to send you a proof of it by the next Post:⁵ The Halcyon is the prittiest thing I ever saw. I hope Grignion will do justice to them both.⁶ I have not yet got any ornament for the Title page from the Gentleman I mention'd. But perhaps it is better without, as it might have been thought over-adorn'd.⁷ Hayman has made I think a very good Drawing for the Frontispiece, it is the Scene of Cleone's Death. I expect Mʳ Spence in Town in about a Week, I wish You and he might meet at my new Habitation.

I am ever

Dear Sir

Affectionately Yours

R. Dodsley

Address: To William Shenstone Esqʳ

MS: BL. Add. MS. 28,959, f. 121.

¹ RD's mentioning within that he is in the midst of "leaving off the business to my brother" dates the letter as 1759, for it was in April of that year that he retired from Tully's Head – at least formally.

² Apparently Shenstone had written RD a few times since RD's letter to the Leasowes on 20 February, but none of these have been traced. William Blackstone's *An Analysis of the Laws of England*, first published in 1756, reached a fourth edition in 1759. The farces might have been some of the twenty-seven farces advertised in the *London Daily Post and General Advertiser* of 9 March as published by J. Watts and B. Dodd.

³ Apparently RD took up temporary residence at the Chinese Porter before moving into his sister and brother-in-law's house in Bruton Street, several streets north-west of Tully's Head. See his letter to Shenstone on 3 April.

⁴ More adornment for the Leasowes, which Shenstone had probably requested in one of his missing letters.

⁵ Preparations for the third, revised edition of *Cleone*, for which see the previous correspondence of RD and Shenstone.

⁶ Probably a reference to a drawing to be engraved by Grignion for RD's fable "The Halcyon and the Sparrow" which appeared in RD's *Select Collection of the Fables of Esop and Other Fabulists* in 1761. RD would send Shenstone the text of the fable in his 27 March letter.

⁷ See George Steevens's letter to RD on 9 April. Possibly RD's suggestion that the title page might look "over-adorned" had his "gentleman acquaintance" succeeded in providing the drawing reveals a mild case of "sour grapes," for, in fact, the title page did carry an adornment, the one mentioned in RD's letter. Hayman's drawing of Cleone's death scene was used as the frontispiece.

To William Shenstone

Pall mall Mar.ᶜʰ 19.ᵗʰ [1759]¹

Dear M.ʳ Shenstone!

You must excuse another hasty letter; the unsettled state I am in will not permit me to think at all, and my departure from Tully's Head is defer'd for a fortnight longer. I have not yet got the ornament for the Title Page, and I begin to question whether I shall have it at all or not.² I think Hayman has done the dying Scene for a Frontispiece very well. What think you of somewhat emblematical for the Title Page? Would it not be better than telling the story thrice over, in the Frontispiece & in the Title too? Would a vulture killing a Lamb, be understood to allude to yᵉ Murderer killing the Child? Or would it not at least be expressive of Terror & Pity, especially if assisted by an apt Motto?³ But I believe if You would think for me, You could find something better. I expect a proof of the Grove to night, if it comes I will enclose it; if not, you may expect it in a post or two. If the Swans will not be civil and contented where they are, I think they are Geese, and ought to be treated accordingly, that is, if they will not stay in the water, run a spit thro' them, and fix 'em at the fire.⁴ I forget every thing. I subscrib'd for You to M.ʳ Johnson, and should have sent you the enclos'd Receit a month ago.⁵ The present Translation of Montaigne is Cotton's, only it is said to have been revis'd. There is no Edinburgh Virgil but a very small bad one in 18ᵐᵒ Neither is there any Edition of Hutcheson's Morality in Octavo. The Works of celebrated Authors are binding for You.⁶ I hear Cleone was to be acted by yᵉ Company at York as last Saturday, & that all the Boxes were taken a week before.⁷ Pray don't forget the Fable of the two Swans, and I wish you would write it in prose, that I might have the advantage of inserting it in my Collection.⁸ I have not yet had your thoughts on that Subject. Pray think on a Device for my Title Page. No proof of the Grove is come, but a message which tells me I shall have both that and the Halcyon on Saturday. I like the Epilogue now very much, & can think of no alteration in it, unless you leave out the Couplet of yᵉ Husband reading his Wife a sermon; and the middle line of the last Triplet.⁹ An answer in a post or two will come time enough.

I am

most affectionately Yours

R. Dodsley

MS: BL. Add. MS. 28,959, ff. 123–4.

RD's mentioning his surrendering of the business at Tully's Head to his brother in a fortnight requires this letter to be of 1759.
For *Cleone,* third edition; see his previous letter to Shenstone, note 7.
¹ Both Francis Hayman's drawing for the frontispiece of *Cleone* and the cut of the vulture and the lamb would become realities for the third edition of the play in the next month.
For both the grove and the geese, see RD's previous letter to Shenstone.
² Shenstone's subscription to Samuel Johnson's *The Plays of William Shakespeare.* A little more than a year earlier, Shenstone had written to Thomas Percy: "Do you hear that Mʳ Johnson's Shakespeare will be publish'd this Winter? I have a Prejudice (if *Prejudice* it may be call'd) in favour of all he undertakes; and wish the world may recompence him for a Degree of Industry very seldom connected with so much real Genius" (4 January 1758; Brooks, VII, 6).
³ *Essays of Michael Seigneur de Montaigne . . . with marginal notes . . . and an Account of the Author's Life,* trans. Charles Cotton (3 vols. London: T. Basset, 1685); a seventh edition, with "amendments and improvements," would be advertised on 23 November 1759 (*PA*). Perhaps either RD or Shenstone confused Virgil with Horace. Two weeks later, RD would write that he was sending the "*Glascow* not *Edinburgh* Horace." (See his letter of 3 April.) Francis Hutcheson, *A System of Moral Philosophy* (2 vols. Glasgow: Foulis; London: A. Millar and Longman) was available only in quarto. *The Works of Celebrated Authors of whose Writings there are but small remains* (2 vols. London: J. and R. Tonson and S. Draper, 1750).
⁴ Unfortunately no copy of a York newspaper for the date seems to have survived, that the performance's dates and actors might be known.
⁵ Shenstone's fable, if he ever did write it, does not appear in the *Select Fables.* RD has obviously entrapped Shenstone with the gift of the swans mentioned earlier.
⁶ The drawing for the title page of *Cleone,* the print of Virgil's Grove, the Halcyon, the epilogue for *Cleone* are all subjects of the last few letters to Shenstone. Both the couplet and triplet's middle line were omitted in the printed version.

From Richard Graves

Claverton 27 March 17[59]¹

Dear Sʳ

Tho' you have probably several Correspondents at Bath – who have inform'd you of the reception your Cleone met with, in that epitome of the polite world – yet I think myself hardly excusable in my absolute silence upon the Subject – I am tired with pleading the continual embarassments, which my threefold Character of Rector- Curate- & Pedagogue involve me in – but have really been entirely engross'd this fortnight – by an *accident* which has happen'd to one of my Pupils & by the apprehension of a *misfortune* to myself – in the death of an Irish Baronet – by which I am in danger of losing near 50£² – and now having be[en] thus impertinent – to convince you of the reality of my Plea – I will give you my account of what You have ⟨be⟩ heard in a better manner already – as we are pleased to hear the successes of our army – related – even by the Pen of an ignorant subaltern – even a private Soldier –

I need not tell you that it was represented to a *crowded* audience – & I think the principal parts were well perform'd – I never saw Miss Bellamy – but even ⟨from⟩ in Miss Ibbot's Person – Cleone appear'd very amiable in her distress – but as I had heard Sifroy complain'd of – as (*comparatively* with Cleone) but a tame Character – I was surpris'd to see how spirited he appear'd upon the stage – tho' Mʳ Keasbury has

nothing very pathetick in his voice or m[an]ner – Glanville rais'd Hull above hi
usual self – who, tho' he *speaks* well, is generally but an *insipid Actor* – Paulet &
Beaufort jun.^r made the worst appearance – as being perform'd, the former by a
good *Comedian* – the latter by a good *Harlequin* – but both equally bad *Tragedians*³ –

I fixed myself (with I. Wiltshire) in the Centre of the Pitt⁴ – in the midst of young
Milliners & Abigails – where [I] had the pleasure of observing the Effect of your
Genius upon undisguis'd humanity – Neither indeed was there a young or
handsome face in the Boxes but what [was] conceal'd with an hankerchief – Shew'd
that the fa[ir] Lady either *was* deeply affected – or was conscious that she *ought* to be
so – I had the satisfaction [?] of silencing (with a single Hiss) one or two young
fellows who – either to shew their Stoical ⟨sensibility⟩ Command over their
Passions – or their absolute Contempt of the rest of the audience – were clamorously
rallying M^{rs} Br___ias & two or three more very pretty women upon their amiable
Sensiblity⁵ –

I heard but one Criticism – & that was of an elderly Lady (who had read the
play) & was offended at Isabell's remaining so long upon the Stage in Sc. 2 Act. II
to hear the horrid conversation between Glanville & Ragozin – & said she might as
well have been dismiss'd at the End of the first Scene – I don't know what force
there is in this – but dare say *you* do – & that there is a good Reason for ye present
Conduct –

If you have heard f^{m.} Mr Shenstone lately – you will be surpris'd to hear, that I
took such a journey at Xmass – I was there but 3. days – However I was prevail'd on
to contribute my mite towards polishing the Elegies – tho' I found they had pass'd
Mr Spence's Censure – as I was bold enough to offer some Strictures upon y
Tragedy – ere tho' (I afterwards heard) it had been criticis'd by ye greatest Genii of
the Age – But I am an insignificant mortal – & venture boldly – because I have no
character to lose –

I found Mr Shenstone somewhat dispos'd to have them consign'd to the super-
excellent Type, that has made Virgil & Milton more beautiful. – But I told him It
would give him the Air of a *local* Author – & that for my part, I should not have so
high an opinion of any Production, that did not make its first Appearance in the
Metropolis⁶ – And I believe there are many people that have the same prejudice –
It puts one in mind of one Doughty's *country* Sermon – preach'd in a *country* Church –
& published at ye request of a *Country* Congregation – In short, I hope you will get
them into *Your* clutches early in the next winter –

You give us hopes of seeing you here this Summer – which gives me great
pleasure – as I shall not be able to stir from home the Whitsun-holidays – All the
world (except M^r Ga k) now admire you as an Author – but no one has a greater
personal Regard than S^r

Y^r affect. humb sev^t
Ric. Graves

Mrs Graves desires her best Respects –
[Endorsement in Graves's hand:] Mr Dodsley

MS: Somerset County Record Office, DD/SK, 28/1, 75.

Unfortunately, resources are unavailable to determine the exact dates of *Cleone*'s run in Bath. However, when writing to Shenstone on 3 April 1759, RD mentions having received a letter from Graves recounting the performance at Bath, and the play could not have opened at Bath before its London debut in December 1758. Moreover, Graves's reference to Garrick's continuing resentment of RD's success with the play identifies the letter as a product of early 1759.

Graves conducted a boys' school in a building provided by Ralph Allen at Prior Park. The anticipated loss of £50 perhaps arises from the withdrawal of a student by reason of his father's death.

George Anne Bellamy was RD's Cleone in the play's London debut. Sarah Ibbott (d. 1825) spent most of her acting career at Bath. William Keasbury (1726–97), actor, singer, manager, playwright and novelist, had begun a long association with the Orchard Street Theatre, Bath, in the 1756–7 season. Alfred Barbeau (*Life and Letters at Bath in the Eighteenth Century* (London: William Heineman, 1904), p. 76) notes that Keasbury, with Dimond, became manager of the Bath theater in 1785. Thomas Hull (1728–1808) began his stage career at Smock Alley Theatre, Dublin, in the 1753–4 season, came to the Bath theater in 1759 but left over a dispute regarding the managership, and then joined the Covent Garden company where he enjoyed a long career. Lacking a contemporary account of the performance at Bath, it is impossible to identify the actors who played the roles of Paulet and Beaufort, Jr. Most of the foregoing information is taken from Philip Highfill, Jr., Kalman Burnim, and Edward Langhans, *A Biographical Dictionary of Actors, Actresses, Musicians, Dancers, Managers, and Other Stage Personnel in London, 1660–1800* (Carbondale: Southern Illinois University Press, 1973), Vol. 2.

William Wiltshire (d. 1762) kept one of the two chief rooms for public assemblies in Bath. The room was named after him from 1737 until 1771 when it was closed for construction of the new Upper Rooms. (David Gadd, *Georgian Summer. Bath in the Eighteenth Century* (Bradford-on-Avon, 1977) pp. 65–7.) *The Bath and Bristol Guide* for 1755 (rept. Bath: Kingsmead Bookshop, 1969) charted certain distances in Bath "From the Front Door of Mr Wiltshire's."

"Mrs Br—ias" is unidentified.

Shenstone had planned to have his elegies printed at Baskerville's press in Birmingham, the origin of editions of Virgil (1757) and Milton (1758) in "super-excellent Type." RD had supported the idea when writing to Shenstone on the previous 19 September: "I hope you have put them into Mr Baskerville's hands." The elegies would not be printed until RD included them in his edition of Shenstone's *Works* (1764).

To William Shenstone

Pallmall Mar: 27.th [1759]¹

Dear Mr Shenstone

When shall I be able to write you a Letter? Not now I am sure. I will endeavour to get you a Sett of the Quarto Cutts for Milton, which perhaps may suit Mr Baskerville's next Edition. How you came not to have ye Cutts for the 2.^d Vol: I cannot imagine.² The leaving Tully's Head makes me melancholy as well as You; but it is a Sacrifice to brotherly Love. I have not thought of my Fables for three months past till yesterday, when I wrote the following.

The Halcyon & the Sparrow.

As a Halcyon was sitting beneath ye shade of a retir'd Grove, on the bank of a River, she was startled with the fluttering visit of a Sparrow from the neighbouring Town. After the first Compliments were over – How is it possible, said ye Sparrow, that a bird so finely adorn'd, can think of spending all her days in this obscure Retreat? Those beauties, that shining plumage, were sure not given you to be hid, but to attract the wonder of every eye. You should endeavour to know the World, in order that your self may be known and admir'd. You are very complaisant, said the Halcyon, to conclude that the consequence of my being known must be that of being admir'd. But I have been told, it does not always follow that ever Beauty is admir'd, or Excellence belov'd: and I have learnt besides, not to place my happiness in the opinion of others, but in my own feelings. I am a Halcyon, & these peaceful Shades are my delight; why therefore should I seek the bustle of a World, which suits not with my temper? Tittle tattle may be agreeable to a Sparrow, but I love Silence & Contemplation. Let every one study his own Genius, and cultivate that Taste and Talent, which Nature has given him.[3]

This may serve as a Specimen of what I intend: and pray tell me how you like it. But instead of giving me your thoughts on the Subject, you ask me what I think the precise distinction betwixt a Fable and a Tale. This is not fair dealing. However, I will give you my opinion, in order that it may be corrected. I think a Tale may be
                    one or more events
defin'd – A Series of Events, related – without regard to any Moral: whereas a Fable is one single Event, contriv'd on purpose to illustrate and enforce some useful Moral Truth or to enforce some moral Duty or Prudential Maxim. And now pray give me your opinion! and I could wish you would favour me with half a dozen or half a score Fables by way of Specimen. I expect Mᵣ Spence in Town to morrow, how long he may stay I cannot tell. I wish my neighbourhood would be as liberal in confering Posts on You, as your own has been.[4] I was in hopes of having another Letter from you before now, correcting the conclusion of your Epilogue, & giving me your opinion on the Vulture & Lamb. I am this moment enabled to send you proofs of the two Plates; I think they are extreamly well done, however I will wait a post or two to see whether you propose any alteration.[5] You must perceive what a hurry I write in, & will therefore excuse all imperfections.

I am
Dear Sir
Affectionately Yours

R. Dodsley

MS: BL. Add. MS. 28,959, ff. 125–6.

[1] RD's allusion to his "melancholy" at leaving Tully's Head requires that this letter be of 1759, the year he left the business to his brother. That evidence is corroborated by the reference to the drawing of the vulture and the lamb, a matter introduced in his last letter to Shenstone on 19 March 1759. Furthermore RD's mentioning of his attempt to obtain for Shenstone the quarto cuts for Milton is echoed in Shenstone's fully dated letter four days later.

[2] Shenstone must have changed his mind regarding the particular cuts he wanted, possibly because he had changed his mind regarding the edition he would purchase. In his letter two months earlier (20 January), RD had told Shenstone that he had managed to get him the octavo cuts from Tonson. Both quarto and octavo editions of Milton's *Paradise Lost* and *Paradise Regained* had been printed by Baskerville in 1758 (Philip Gaskell, *John Baskerville: A Bibliography*, 1959). On the other hand, as RD might be implying, Shenstone had wanted to purchase a quarto edition as well.

[3] This fable was printed in *Select Fables* (III, 201–3) as "The King-fisher and the Sparrow." Although a somewhat expanded text, the printed version retains essentially the same fable and continuity; only the sentiments are enlarged and diction altered in several places.

[4] An obscure allusion. Perhaps by local "Posts" conferred on Shenstone, RD meant the role he played as literary critic of Birmingham, serving as Maecenas to new poetic talent that sought him out, the

latest of which seems to have been Thomas Percy. Regarding the honor RD's neighborhood might have conferred on Shenstone, see RD's letter of 30 December 1760, note 6.

See RD's letter to Shenstone on 19 March, note. 3

From William Shenstone

March 31, 1759.

Dear Mr. Dodsley,

I am afraid you think me negligent; know then that I sat down last *Thursday*, to write you a long Letter, about seven o'Clock at Night, when I discovered that the Post went out at that very Hour I sat down to write. I had immediate Recourse to such Consolation as the Case admitted; and supposed a Letter received on *Monday* Morning, might do near as well as one on *Saturday* Night, considering that *Sunday* intervened; which must be a leisure Day, *even* for *Printers*. But in good Earnest now, do you think me lazy? Or have not you, under your present *Dissipation*, an *heavier* Complaint against my *Diligence*? You and I shall hardly agree about the *Means* of *estimating* Letters; you, conscious of your own Genius, are desirous to value them by their *Weight*; while I, conscious of my late *Industry*, would fix their Value by the Number of *Words*. What Pretensions, pray, can you suggest, for so very *perverse* a Manner of Reckoning? Is not *Industry* a *moral Virtue*? And are not many written Words a *Proof* of Industry? But though your *Ingenuity* be even a Miracle, you will hardly prove it to be a *moral Virtue*, unless, indeed, in the *Way you manage it*; and *so, all* your Faculties are moral virtues: however, we less *artful*, or less *heroick* Personages, must magnify the Virtues that we *have*; of these, Industry is one, though perhaps *this* had been scarce *allowed* me, till within these three or four Months past. I say, that we, who are the *Animae nil magnae Laudis egentes*; we, the *Animae viles, inhumata nfletaque turba*: In other Words, the *Numerus*, and the "*nati Fruges consumere;*" if we would appear considerable, pray what Method can we take?[1] I know, indeed, but two; the one of disparaging your Abilities, which is not quite so feasible; the other, of taking all occasion to magnify our own good Qualities. If then, Industry be a Virtue, I am possessed of it very remarkably: Not a Moment of my Time passes, but I am employed, either in overseeing Labourers; reading Robinson's *History of Scotland*;[2] writing in my Paper Books, ('tis not material *what*, but writing;) perplexing the *Birmingham* Artists with Sketches for Improvements in their Manufactures, which they *will* not understand; and lastly, and finally, feeding my Poultry, my Ducks, my Pigeons, and my Swans; which last give me as much Pleasure, as what I had before gave me Vexation. No inconsiderable Panegyric, I'll assure you! And surely this is not only *Industry*, but an *Industry* of a *better Kind* than what employs the *Animae viles* of a Drawing-room. And now this *last Instance* of my great Industry puts me in Mind of asking you a Question:

Pray now, you that are a Mythologist, what an absurd Man you are, not to jump at an Invitation to come directly to the *Leasowes*? Here am I, (like your Friend ÆEsop, before Ogilby's *Fables*; or like Adam, in our old *Bibles*) sitting once or twice a Day with every created Animal before me. Is not this the only residence for a

Person that is writing Fables? 'Tis true, this very Person may contemplate better in a *Crowd*, than *another* in the Depth of Solitude: *you* may far surpass *me*, who thus *converse* with *Birds*: while he describes a Sparrow from *Pall-Mall*, or a King-fisher from *Charing-Cross*: but *Imagination* is a prodigious *Heightener*; and unless he paints them from Life, may he not *attribute* to a *King-fisher* much finer Feathers than he in Truth possesses?[3] Pray take the Opinion of Mr. Spence – How I blush, while I recollect that Name! And yet, were it not for my *own* Omissions, it must revive *only* my most *favourite* Ideas. Surely 'tis written in the Book of Fate, that I shall discharge my Debt within a Post or two; for Fate evidently enough interferes, or I could never have been so long silent. I am almost ashamed to desire my humble Respects to him, and yet it is impossible for me to suppress my Feelings.

I must now proceed to Business. Past six o'Clock once more; but the Post now goes out at ten. If you *can* procure me the quarto Cuts for Milton, it will be a very desirable Favour.[4]

Mr. Bond has made some Alteration in your *Grove*, which I thought very pretty on its *Arrival*; yet, perhaps, he may be right enough, if Mr. Grignion can comprehend his Meaning.[5] The Trees he means *on the wrong Side the Water*, are some of those opposite to the Letter *S*, which I have put upon the Back: but I am fearful of *spoiling*; and must beg Mr. Grignion would re-compare the Print with Mr. Bond's original Drawing, then retouch his Plate, and let me have a few more Proof-Sheets of both the Prints. Give me one or two Lines by *Return* of Post, if possible.

No Books ready? I want Mallet's Works, bound in *Russia* Leather, and lettered on Green.[6] Pray excuse this last vile Page. I have wasted my Time, and now am utterly at a Fault for it.

W. Shenstone.

Source: Thomas Hull, *Select Letters* (London, 1778), II, 253–8.

[1] "Souls desiring little praise . . . inferior souls, an unburied and unwept multitude: . . . the crowd . . . born to eat the fruit of the ground." From Virgil, *Aeneid*, XI, 372.
[2] William Robertson's *History of Scotland* had just appeared on 20 January. (See the editor's "Unpublished Garrick Letters to Robertson and Millar," *YES*, 5 (1975), 130.)
[3] Four days earlier, RD had sent Shenstone the text of his fable "The King-fisher and the Sparrow."
[4] See RD's last letter to Shenstone, note 2.
[5] Daniel Bond. See Hylton's letter to RD on 21 February, note 2.
[6] A new edition of *The Works of David Mallet*, in three volumes, had just been issued by Andrew Millar and Paul Vaillant on 28 February (*PA*).

To William Shenstone

Pall mall April 3^d [1759][1]

Dear Sir

You may gather from my haste in answering You, the haste in which I expect your Answer. I have not a book to sell, nor have had for this fortnight past, therefore shall take it for granted that I may proceed, if I have not an answer by the very first return of the Post. Mr Grignion has done all he can in both the Plates, & thinks they are extreamly well, and exact according to the Drawings. He will let me have some green proofs in two or three days.² I have got you the six Cutts for the 2ᵈ Volume of Milton, but there are no Quarto Cutts to be had. The reason why yours were printed on a small Paper was, that Mʳ Tonson had not then determin'd to print any of them for sale.³ Your volumes of the Authors of whose Works there are but small remains, were sent by last Thursday's Coach. Mallet's Works, & the *Glascow* not *Edinburgh* Horace I will send You by the first opportunity.⁴ I remove to my new Habitation this day sennight, & shall hope after that to be able to write You a Letter.⁵ I had a Letter from Mʳ Graves last post, he tells me they are acting Cleone at Bath with applause. They have also acted it at York & some other Places.⁶

I am ever & ever

Yours

R. Dodsley⁷

MS: BL. Add. MS. 28,959, f. 127.

¹ The letter's year is certified by a fully dated Shenstone letter to John Scott Hylton on 6 April 1759 (see my article "Four New Shenstone Letters," *PLL,* 11 (1975), 264–78) in which Shenstone says that he had just received a short note from RD indicating that *Cleone* was "acting with applause, both at Bath and York," which, of course, is the conclusion of this letter. In addition, other matters mentioned in the letter respond to letters of the previous weeks.

² The subject of these three sentences is the publication of the third, revised edition of *Cleone,* to occur on 26 April (*LC*). Apparently RD had sold off the first two editions, another indication of the play's popularity. The first two editions alone (see RD's letter to Shenstone on 16 December 1758) had numbered 4,000 copies. ³ See RD's letter to Shenstone on 27 March, note 2.

⁴ See RD's letter to Shenstone on 19 March, note 6; also Shenstone's 31 March letter to RD, note 6. Some slip of the pen must have occurred in RD's 19 March letter, where he writes of sending a Virgil printed at Edinburgh among the books Shenstone requested. In the present letter, he says he is sending a "*Glascow* not an *Edinburgh* Horace." The Glasgow edition of Horace's *Works* was probably the third octavo edition published by R. and A. Foulis in 1756.

⁵ Painted during June and early July 1760, Sir Joshua Reynolds's portrait of RD shows the publisher holding a letter addressed to him at Bruton Street. His "new Habitation" as of "this day sennight," then, was most likely that of his sister, Alice, and her husband, Francis Dyer, on Bruton Street. Although RD's name had regularly appeared in the Westminster Rate, Watch, and Poll Books while he lived in Pall Mall, his name does not appear in 1759; nor does it appear for Bruton Street. However, Francis Dyer's name is listed for Dover Street (enters Bruton Street) at a £20. rent for 1759. As the Reynolds portrait suggests, and as the addresses of subsequent letters, as well as their authors' compliments to the Dyers, confirm, RD lived at the Dyer residence from 1760 until the time of his death in September 1764. In this connection, it is probably not inconsequential that RD named Francis Dyer one of his two executors. (His brother Alvory served as the other.)

⁶ See Graves's 27 March letter and RD's letter to Shenstone on 19 March.

⁷ After RD's signature appear approximately 2⅓ lines heavily crossed out and blotted. Whether they were RD's postscript or Shenstone's endorsement is impossible to tell.

From [George Steevens]¹

Burstead Ap: 9.ᵗʰ [1759]²

Mʳ Dodsley

I have delay'd thus long writing to you that I [might] have further opportunity of repeating my endeavours [to] finish the design I intended for the frontispiece of Cleone but have been unsuccessful in the execution, th[ough] indefatigable I assure you in the attempt; and am on[ly] sorry I ever mentioned it to you least you should thi[nk] I promised what I had no intent to perform; but [as] I could not please myself in it (and you know the par[ty?] of painters to themselves is very great) I am sure I cou[ld] never expect to please others, or produce an ornament [any] way worthy of your tragedy: But had I succeeded even [to] the utmost of my own expectations in it, I should hav[e] look'd on it as a trifling embellishment which could have added nothing to a piece which without either flattery or compliment has too many beauties of its own to stand in need of any foreign aid or support. I shall soon be in town myself and will wait on you, an[d] settle accounts with your Brother; but am at present confin'd with a sore throat & a cold: in the meantime[e] I wish you may live to enjoy at ease the fame you have so justly deserved, and continue to have a better opinio[n] of me than to think that wish an unsincere one which comes from the heart of

Your obliged

Humble Serv!

Address: To | Mr Robert Dodsley | at Tulley's Head | in Pall-mall | London
Postmark: PENNY POST PAID

MS: Folger Shakespeare Library, C. b. 11 (2).

¹ Although the signature is broken from the bottom of the holograph, the letter was almost certainly written by George Steevens (1736–1800), later editor of Shakespeare. The hand is identical to that of Steevens's letter to RD in January 1762. Secondly, the letter is written from Burstead, Steevens's home in Essex. Finally, it is probably not coincidental that this letter is catalogued in the Folger Shakespeare Library, together with the other Steevens letter to RD.
² The year is evident from RD's three previous allusions in 1759 to a gentleman friend who had promised a drawing for the title page of *Cleone*'s third edition. See his letters to Shenstone during February and March.

From John Pixell

Edgbaston   April ye 20th [1759]¹

Dear S^r

When I was lately in London I was so unfortunate, as not to find You at home, notwithstanding my repeated Endeavours. I wanted to settle my Account with You for the favour of inserting my Advertisement in the Chronicle. I have printed my Songs, & sent them to Mr Walsh, where You will please to send for the two Collections You subscrib'd for.² I am acquainted with a Person in Birm. who tells me, that as You once made a Proposal to Mr Giles to keep a Pamphlet = Shop, he wou'd gladly accept of the same Offer. He is a married Man in Business, but as he will have leisure-time upon his hands, he thinks he can executing such an undertaking punctually.³

If you approve of it, You will please to send me Word. *Success to your Fables.* –

I am your obliged humble Ser^t

J P P Pixell

Mr Shenstone has been doing every thing this Winter but correcting his Poems. –
Address: To / M^r R Dodsley / at Tully's head / in / Pall = Mall / London
Postmark: 23 AP Birmingham

MS: Humanities Research Center, University of Texas at Austin, Robert Dodsley / Recipient 1/
Bound, ff. 133–5.

¹ The year is certain by reason of the letter's subject; namely, the publication of Pixell's *Collection of Songs, with their Recitatives and Symphonies for the German Flute, Violins, Etc., with a thorough Bass for the Harpsicord. Set to Musick by M^r. Pixell* in April 1759.
² Apparently RD had placed the advertisement calling for subscribers to the *Collection of Songs* in the *London Chronicle* of 23–6 September 1758, where Tully's Head is the only London shop to which subscribers might send their names. However it seems Pixell changed his mind regarding the publishing venue, for the imprint shows that the *Collection of Songs* was printed at Baskerville's "for the Author and sold by Mess. Walsh and Johnson." Perhaps significantly, this is the last of Pixell's letters to RD until 1764.
³ Perhaps Joseph Giles, the engraver and poet, mentioned in RD's former correspondence with Shenstone. The identity of Pixell's candidate for the pamphlet shop is not known; the subject does not come up again in this correspondence.

From Laurence Sterne¹

York. May 23. 1759

Sir

   With this you will rec^{ye} the Life & Opinions of Tristram Shandy, wch I choose to offer to You first – and put into your hands without any kind of Distrust both from your general good Character, & the very handsome Recommendation of Mr Hinksman.² The Plan, as you ⟨may⟩ will percieve, is a most extensive one, – taking in, not only, the Weak part of the Sciences, in wch the true point of Ridicule lies – but every Thing⟨,⟩ else, which I find Laugh-at-able in my way⟨,s⟩ –

   If this 1st Volume has a run (wch such Criticks as this Latitude affords) say it can't fail of) We may both find our Account in it. – The Book will sell; – What other Merit it has, does not become me either to think or say, – by all Acc^{ts} You are a much better Judge – the World however will fix the Value for us both. –

   If You publish it now – a 2^d Volume will be ready by Christmas, or Nov^r – the Reason for some such Interval, You will better see in reading the Book.³ – I think it will make a Volume in Oct^{vo} of about the Size of the Essay upon ingenious Tormenting, by Millar – that is, allowing the same Type & Margin.⁴ –

   Be so good as to let me have the favor of a Letter when You rec^{ye} the Mans. – wth What You think it worth, to You. – tho' I believe the shortest Step is to tell You what I think tis worth myself – wch I hope is 50 pounds.⁵ –

> I am Sir
> with great Esteem
> for Y^r Character
> Y^r most Obed^t & hum^b Servt
>
> Laurence Sterne

PS Please to direct for me Prebendary of York, – to be left at M! Hinksman's York
Some of our best Judges here w.^{d} have had me, to have sent into the world – $\langle$w.$^{th}\rangle$
cum Notis Variorum – $\langle$but I$\rangle$ there is great Room for it – but I thought it better to
send it naked into the world[6] – if You purchase the MS. We shall confer of this
hereafter –
Address: To | Mr Robt Dodsley

MS: Robert H. Taylor Collection on deposit at Princetown University Library.

[1] The brief two-and-a-half-year relationship of the Dodsleys and Laurence Sterne (1713–68) pivoted
solely upon the publication of the Yorkshire's clergyman's *Life and Opinions of Tristram Shandy,
Gentleman*, Volumes I-IV, and the two-volume *Sermons of Mr. Yorick*. For reasons discussed below,
Sterne employed the booksellers Thomas Becket and Peter Dehondt for the last five volumes of
Tristram. This letter represents Sterne's first approach to the Dodsleys. A consideration of the
bibliographical problems associated with the publication of *Tristram* is pieced out among the notes to
this and to Sterne's other letter, in early October.

[2] John Hinxman (d. 1762), a former apprentice of RD's in Pall Mall, had moved to York sometime in
1757 and took over the bookselling business of the late John Hildyard (d. 1757) at the Sign of the Bible
in Stonegate. (See his advertisement in the *London Chronicle*, 8–10 September 1757). A later
advertisement in the *London Evening Post* on 21–3 January 1759 announced a sale catalogue listing
15,000 volumes (formerly Hildyard's) as available at Dodsley's shop in Pall Mall. In 1761, he moved
to London and took over the business of Mary Cooper, a publisher who frequently collaborated with
RD (Plomer).

[3] As is clear from Sterne's next letter in early October, the first volume would undergo considerable
revising and supplementing during the summer and would not be ready for the press until autumn.

[4] Lewis P. Curtis (*Letters of Laurence Sterne* (Oxford: Clarendon Press, 1935), p. 75) identifies Sterne's
"intended" model as Jane Collier's *Essay on the Art of Ingeniously Tormenting*, published by Andrew
Millar in 1753. Although *Tristram* and the *Essay* were both printed in octavo, the latter had 234 pages
compared with the 179 pages in *Tristram*, Vol. I.

[5] By refusing to pay Sterne's price, the normally shrewd RD missed his opportunity with *Tristram* – that
is, financially: the copyright his brother might have had for £50 in June 1759 would cost him fivefold
the following March (see Appendix B). Yet there is little reason to think that RD refused to purchase
the copyright in June because he was completely ignorant of the novel's merits or of its market value.
In fact, RD must have expressed substantial interest in the madcap manuscript when responding to
Sterne at the time (letter unfortunately missing), for the author's second letter in October indicates
that not only had Sterne troubled himself to revise the work according to RD's recommendations but
now he also offered RD the "whole Profits of the Sale" at Tully's Head if the bookseller would agree to
patronize the work as if he had purchased the copyright. Furthermore, according to Sterne's friend
John Croft, RD had actually offered the author £20 for the first volume (*Whitefoord Papers*, ed. W. A.
S. Hewins (Oxford: Clarendon Press, 1898), p. 227), not a slight sum for a first work of an unknown
author. (Three years earlier, RD had paid the newcomer Edmund Burke £6.6.0 for his *Vindication of
Natural Society*.) RD would also have to stand the costs of printing, paper, binding, and advertising.
Besides, Sterne was asking RD to risk his money on a "plotless" piece that violated all the rules that
had come to be associated with fiction, as well as to offend the morals of the graver sort who looked for
instruction, not bawdy, in fiction. (For a further consideration of the offer, see Sterne's October letter,
note 4.)

Evidence is lacking to show whether or not Sterne, after failing to get his price from the Dodsleys,
had attempted to peddle his "crack-brain" prodigy elsewhere. But, as John Croft relates, certainly his
friends at York were less encouraging than RD, for they believed this "laughable book" had no chance
with the booksellers, "nor wou'd they offer any price for it" (*Whitefoord Papers*, p. 226).

Contemporary publishing practices also help to explain RD's role in the *Tristram* saga.
Unfortunately the long-standing debate on whether the first two volumes were printed in York or in
London, although an intriguing bibliographical problem, has actually distracted from the main issue,
Tristram's publication. Confusing the separate functions of printing and publishing, past commenta-

tors have seemed to think determining the work's printer amounted to identifying its publisher. Although Kenneth Monkman's thorough bibliographical study of the first two volumes of *Tristram* (*The Library*, 25 (1970), 17–38) has surely convinced this editor that the first edition of these volumes was printed in York at the press of Ann Ward, it is surprising that the same careful bibliographer seems to make publication hinge on printing. He concludes: "Dodsley seemingly had nothing to do with publishing the first edition, beyond, presumably, selling on commission those copies Sterne sent up to him in London" (p. 16).

But publishing is not printing, and the Dodsleys were not printers but booksellers (publishers). Printers, sometimes outside London, produced the books the Dodsleys published. Several works authored by Dodsley's correspondents, for which he has always been regarded as the publisher, were printed outside London, and the impressions sent up to the metropolis where RD *published* them. Joseph Warton's first volume of an *Essay on the Writings and Genius of Mr. Pope* (1756), seen through the press at Oxford by his brother Thomas, is a case in point.

Likewise, there is no reason to believe that because a bookseller did not purchase a copyright in advance of publication he was not its publisher. Many of the author–publisher negotiations recorded in this edition show RD publishing works he had not bought. Appendix B lists several copyright assignments (Edward Young's *Night Thoughts*, for one) that postdate RD's publication of the work's first edition. It must be understood, then, that even if RD did not agree to purchase a work outright, his sponsorship – publishing – of the piece was valuable to an author (as clearly Sterne realized). Not only had he established a reputation for quality publication in *belles lettres* but the literary and social circles in which he moved and sold his books afforded the right kind of audience for an aspiring author. More often than not, unknown authors, especially if their manuscripts were judged questionable sellers, would not succeed in convincing RD to purchase their works in advance of publication, except at a low rate. In such cases, often authors, rather than looking elsewhere, would choose to stand the expense of printing and advertising themselves just to have RD's imprint. Such, it seems, was Sterne's understanding, and his interest.

It should also be mentioned that sometimes RD was the full-fledged publisher of a work even though his name did not appear in the imprint. If, for one reason or another, he felt uneasy about putting his name to a work, he would regularly engage the publisher Mary Cooper to issue it with her imprint. Joseph Warton's *Essay on the Writings and Genius of Mr. Pope* (1756) for a while was so threatened, and John Gilbert Cooper's *Cursory Remarks on Mr. Warburton's New Edition of Mr. Pope's Works* (1751) was published in this manner. (See their correspondence.) In effect, merely because the Dodsley name did not appear in the imprint did not mean that the work had not originated from Tully's Head, that RD was not the publisher, or even that RD did not own the copyright, as was the case with Cooper's *Cursory Remarks*.

In the light of the above, it is interesting that the first known advertisement for *Tristram* – normally advertising was the publisher's responsibility – occurred not in a York newspaper but in the *London Chronicle*, a tri-weekly owned in part by RD. The 18–20 December number announced that *Tristram* would appear "In a few Days" as "printed for and sold by John Hinxman (Successor to the late Mr. Hildyard) Bookseller in Stonegate: J. Dodsley in Pallmall and M. Cooper in Pater-noster-row." Although copies for December 1759 are not extant, the first advertisement in the only York newspaper, the *York Courant*, appeared on 12 February, more than a month after the work had been offered for sale in London. Although J. Dodsley's name does not appear in the imprint, it is conceivable that Hinxman, given his former association with the Dodsleys, was acting as the "front man," as sometimes did Mary Cooper. It might be significant that, two years later, Hinxman took over Mary Cooper's business.

⁶ Apparently RD agreed with Sterne's advisors, for, in his next letter to the bookseller, Sterne reports that "Notes are added where wanted."

From William Melmoth

Ealing, July 28th 1759.

Dear Sir,

I finished my peregrinations the day before you began yours: for the day after my arrival at this place I called at your lodgings, & was informed you set out that very morning for M.ʳ Shenton's.¹ I have often thought you in many respects a man to be envied: but in your present situation you are in possession of a happiness too great for mortals; enjoying in one of the hottest seasons that ever was known in England, the shade & ⟨?⟩ coolness of the finest groves, perhaps, in the world, rendered still more enchanting by the conversation of one of the best poets as well as one of the worthiest men of the age. A certain monarch of old broke off all connection & alliances with a brother king in greece, for no other reason but because ⟨?⟩ the latter experienced an uncommon share of felicity: if his example deserved to be followed, you are the man of all others whose friendship I w.ᵈ renounce.² But the truth is, you cannot have more happiness than I wish you, nor more, I am persuaded, than you deserve: & therefore I will e'e.ʳ be contented to hold on my amity with you till I have a better reason for parting with it; which I am very sure I ⟨?⟩ shall never be furnish'd with.

With respect to my own travels, I have little to say worth relating. Finding my health not equal to so long ⟨at⟩ a journey as to scarborough, & the weather at the same time proving extremely cold & wet, I turned out of the high road at Newark & crossed the country to Nottingham. As I found the air of that place agree with me, & [when?] met with an old friend, who lives like a true Arcadian in a little rural cottage at a short distance from the town, I continued there 'till my return hither. I saw every thing in the neighborhood ⟨wort⟩worth looking at: but what pleased me most, was Lord Byron's abbey upon the forest; w.ᶜʰ without doubt you have visited.³

If I am not mistaken, you talked of passing through Ludlow in your way to Wales. If you hold in that resolution, I will trouble you with a commission. I beg the favor of you to inquire if there is any boarding house in that town pleasantly situated, in w.ᶜʰ two or three persons may be well & genteely accomodated. If any thing of this kind is to be had there, be so good as to inform yourself of the terms; as likewise whether y.ᵉ air of the place is dry, or moist; ⟨?⟩ what kind of society it supplies; & whether the roads about it are tolerably good for a four wheeled carriage. Adieu, dear sir, I am, with the ladies comp.ᵗˢ to you,

Your faithful
& affectionate humble Serv.ᵗ
W.ᵐ Melmoth.

Address: To | M.ʳ Dodsley, | At W.ᵐ Shenstone's Esq.ʳ | at the Leassows near Birmingham, | Warwickshire.
Postmark: 28 IY.

MS: BL. Add. MS. 35,338, f. 8.

¹ Melmouth addresses RD at Shenstone's Leasowes, where the now retired bookseller would spend all of August and a good part of September before a stay in Bath.
² Melmoth expresses envy of RD's new state: with a reputation and fortune, he is free to travel and to enjoy his friends, especially Shenstone. Playfully, Melmoth compares their relationship to that of Amasis and Polycrates in Herodotus's *History* (III, 40). Amasis, King of Egypt, distressed with the continual good fortune of Polycrates, tyrant of Samos, recommended that the latter rid himself of something precious. Polycrates threw a treasured jewel into the sea, only to have it served up to him days later in the belly of a fish. Terrified with this uncanny stroke, Amasis deserted Polycrates. (For the discovery of this allusion, I am indebted to Mr J. Lavery, a reader in the British Library.)

³ Newstead Abbey, Lindby, Nottinghamshire, home of the Byrons, and at the moment in the hands of William, 5th Baron Byron of Rochdale (1722–98). Lord Byron, the poet, sold the Abbey in 1818, supposedly to pay his debts. (See *Thoroton's History of Nottinghamshire*, ed. John Thorosby (London, 1797), II, 280 ff.).

From Edmund Burke¹

[*c*. 6 September 1759]²

Dear Sir,

I admit that I am greatly to blame for having so long denied myself the pleasure of corresponding with you. The agreeable places you have been in, and the very agreeable people you have been with, could not have failed through your hands of paying me abundantly for any trouble I should have had in sending you now and then a little false news of the Town, or a few lines of nonsense of my own. It is but an indifferent compliment to myself to say that I find trouble in writing to a friend I value and esteem as much as I do you. But the fact is so; and I have observed it in general of those who are very fond of scribbling other things that they are of all people the least to be depended on for writing Letters. God forbid that any of my friends should judge of my regard for them by the punctuality of my correspondence. This is, I am sensible a bad habit, but along with other bad ones it grows upon me every day. Now Sir, I am to tell you a piece of news which will make you ample amends for all those which I have omitted to send you. If it were not for this I do not know how I should be able to meet your indignation. Know then that Mrs Gataker is at the point of setting out for Bath where you will see her about the End of next week.³ I congratulate you on this meeting; though, upon my word we suffer not a little by what you gain. You are a lucky man and meet friends wherever you go. You cannot meet anybody who is more your friend than Mrs Gataker is, or whose friendship does you more honour. I claim some of the merit and satisfaction of this meeting by being the first to tell you of it. Other news I have none. The Town, and I suppose the Country too, rings of Lord George Sackville; he meets some friends, and a good many Enemies; but Grubstreet I think is unanimous against him, and Grubstreet is no despicable Enemy in affairs of this Nature. However there does not seem to be the same Violence nor the same artifice against him that was used against Byng. Besides a party in his favour seems to be forming much earlier: The Duke of Richmond, and the aid de Camps Fitzroy and Legonier I am told lean against him.⁴ When Politicks are so dead in the middle of Summer which is their Season what can you expect of the Literary world? The Literary campain does not, you know, open until the other is closed. If you have had the happiness of Mr Shenstones company on your Ramble, and that he is now at Bath pray present my best complements to him. I am much obliged to him for the partial Sentiments he is pleased to entertain of me.⁵ I know that I am indebted to you for this. If he should at any time come to Town, I should desire you to go a Stop further to introduce me to his acquaintance. I do not know whether you have met a Mr Frampton at Bath. He is a Clerg[yman] and a very particular friend of Mine.⁶ He has a little living somewhere near Lansdown, though I am afraid he does not come to it at this time of the year. If you see him be so good to remind him of me; and be acquainted with him; for he is a very worthy man and very clever. I saw your brother two or three days ago, He is very well. Mrs Burke desires her compliments to you very particularly. So does my Brother. Mr Wm Burke is very much yours. He is not yet set off for his part of the world.[7] Believe me

dear Mr Dodsley

yours very Sincerely

Edm Burke.

Address: To | Mr Robert Dodsly at | Mr Leakes Bookseller in | Bath

Postmark: 6 SE B.

Source: The Correspondence of Edmund Burke, ed. Thomas Copeland (Cambridge University Press, 1958), I, 127–8.

---

[1] Edmund Burke (1729–97) had entered the Middle Temple in 1750, but when his interest wandered from law to letters and he gave up legal studies in 1755, his father discontinued his allowance. It is not certain how or when Burke first met RD (Straus, p. 354, suggests Arthur Murphy introduced them in 1752), but undoubtedly he was financially pressed when, on 10 May 1756, he signed over to the bookseller his rights to *A Vindication of Natural Society* (1756) for the paltry sum of £6.6.0. On the following 5 January another receipt shows RD purchasing Burke's (or more likely his kinsman William Burke's? see Appendix B) *Account of the European Settlements in America* (1757), but now for £50. Burke had tasted success, for the very next month – even before *An Account* was published – he signed over to RD the rights to his *Philosophical Enquiry into the Origin of Our Ideas of the Sublime and Beautiful* (1757) on 16 February for 20 guineas; and nine days later signed an agreement with RD to produce a *History of England from the Time of Julius Caesar to the End of the Reign of Queen Anne*, for which he was to be paid £300 in installments, and the manuscript to be delivered by Christmas Day of the next year. When Burke's progress on this ambitious work flagged, one can imagine RD's recommending that the young writer take his history in smaller doses and then engaging him to conduct the *Annual Register*, to begin in 1758. It seems clear from the sudden outpouring of major works within two years of leaving the Middle Temple, that Burke had long abandoned law before his father knew of it. (For agreements and receipts to all the foregoing works, see Appendix B.)

[2] The day and month are estimated from the postmark; the year is certain from the mention within of the current trial of 1st Viscount Sackville, an event of 1759.

[3] Most likely Mrs Anne Gataker (née Hill), wife of Thomas Gataker, Surgeon Extraordinary to George II. Mrs Gataker is spoken of in exceptional terms also in RD's letter on 22 August 1758 and in Shenstone's on 20 November 1762. Also, in his letter to Thomas Percy on 1 October 1760, Shenstone writes: "I am also made to expect a very clever woman, one Mrs. Gataker, with a party of ingenious Persons from London, in a fortnight's time" (Brooks, VII, 75).

[4] George Sackville Germain (1716–85), 1st Viscount Sackville, was currently being tried for his failure to obey Prince Ferdinand's command to lead the British cavalry in pursuit of the French at Minden. Sackville's inaction could not help but be compared with that of Admiral Byng, who had been executed two and a half years earlier; in fact, one pamphlet *A Parallel, between the case of Admiral Byng and Lord George Sackville*, openly pursued the likeness. Though not suffering the same fate as Byng, Sackville was dismissed from the King's service by a court martial. Burke's estimation of the case's notoriety and his account of Grub Street's position on the issue were quite accurate. The *London Magazine*'s monthly catalogue of publications for this month, for instance, showed fifteen of a total of thirty-nine works to be concerned with the case. The magazine itself did not hesitate to show its colors when dismissing all the defenses of Sackville as inept. *A Vindication of Lord George Sackville*, it called a "confused jargon and jumble"; *His Lordship's Apology*, it termed a "sham"; and *A Reasonable Antidote against the Poison of Popular Censure* was "idle, contradictory and absurd."

Charles Lennox (1735–1806), 3rd Duke of Richmond, a Colonel with Prince Ferdinand's forces at the Battle of Minden; Colonel Charles Fitzroy (1737–97), later 1st Baron Southampton, and Colonel Edward Ligonier (d. 1782), later Earl Ligonier, had both been aides-de-camp to Ferdinand.

5 Though his letter is missing, Shenstone's admiration for Burke is easily inferred from RD's letter of response on 20 January of this year: "That Mr Burke who writes so ingeniously, is an Irish Gentleman." Shenstone had written to Richard Graves, on 20 February of this year: "Of all books whatever, read Burke 'Of the Sublime and Beautiful'" (Williams, p. 525). RD had sent Shenstone a copy of the second edition. See RD's letter of 20 February.
6 The Rev. Matthew Frampton (b. *c.* 1719), Rector of Langridge, near Bath (1750–69). (See Thomas Copeland, *The Correspondence of Edmund Burke*, I (Cambridge University Press, 1958), p. 128, note 5.
7 William Burke (1729–98) of Beaconsfield, Buckinghamshire, and Edmund Burke referred to one another as "cousins," but it is not certain that they were even related (Namier and Brooke). However their relationship was close, as denoted by William's signing the articles of agreement and receipt for Edmund's *Vindication of Natural Society*. (See Appendix B). "His part of the world" probably refers to Guadeloupe, West Indies, to which William would soon depart to assume his duties as Secretary and Registrar (1759–63).

From Laurence Sterne

[*c.* 5 October 1759][1]

Sir

What You wrote to me in June last[2] in answer to my demand of 50£ for the Life & Opinions of Tristram Shandy – "That it was too much to risk on a single Vol. – which, if it happen'd not to sell, w^d be hard upon your Brother – I think a most reasonable Objection in him against giving me the Price I thought my Work deserved.[3] – You need not be told by me, How much Authors are inclined to over-rate their Productions – for my own part I hope I am an exception, – for if I could find out by any Arcanum, the precise Value of Mine – I declare, Mr Dodsley should have it 20 p Cent below its Value.[4]

I propose therefore to print a lean Edition in 2 small Vols, of the Size of Rasselas, & on the same paper and Type,[5] – at my own Expence merely to feel the Pulse of the World[6] – & that I may know what Price to set upon the Remaining Volumes, from the reception of these – If my Book sells & has the run our Criticks expect, I purpose to free myself of all future troubles of this kind, & bargain with You, if possible for the rest as they come out which will be every six Months.[7] – If my Book fails of Success, the Loss falls where it ought to do.

the same Motives which inclined me first to offer You this Trifle[8] – incline me to give you the ⟨usual⟩ whole Profits of the Sale (except what Mr Kinksman[9] sells here wch will be a great many[10]) – & to have them sold only at y^r Shop, upon the usual Terms in these Cases. The Book shall be printed here, & the Impression sent up to You; for as I live at York & shall correct every Proof myself, it shall go perfect into the World – & be printed in so creditable a way as to Paper Type etc – as to do no Dishonour to You, who I know never chuse to print a Book meanly. will you patronise my Book upon these Terms – & be as kind a friend to it as if you had bought the Copy?[11] –

Be so good as to favour me with a Line by the return, & believe me

Sir Y^r Obliged &

most humble Servt

Laurence Sterne

P.S. All Locality is taken out of the Book – the Satyr general, – Notes are added where wanted – & the whole made more saleable – about a hundred & 50 pages added[12] – & to conclude a Strong Interest form'd & forming on its behalf which I hope will soon take off, the few I shall print on this Coup d' Essai. –

I had desired Mr Kinksman to write the purport of this to You, by this Post, – but least he should omit it – or not sufficiently explain my Intention – I thought best to trouble You wth a Letter myself.[13] –

direct for me

Prebendary of York.

Address: To / Mr R. Dodsley / Bookseller in / Pall Mall / London

Postmark: 5 OC York

MS: Dreer Collection, English Prose Writers, ALS, Historical Society of Pennsylvania.

---

¹ The day and month are based on the 5 October postmark, and the year determined from the fact that the letter must fall between Sterne's fully dated letter of 23 May 1759 and the publication of the first volumes of *Tristram Shandy* on 1 January 1760 (*LC*). Although not having seen the original, and relying upon Thomas Frognall Dibdin's printing in *Reminiscences of a Literary Life* (London, 1836), Pt. i, 207–8, Lewis Perry Curtis in *The Letters of Laurence Sterne* (Oxford: Clarendon Press, 1935), pp. 80–1 correctly assigns an October 1759 date.

² Most regrettably, not traced.

³ Although officially retired from Tully's Head, RD continued to advise his brother on the purchase of copyrights.

⁴ Some confusion occurs regarding the amount of RD's offer. "20 p Cent below its [Sterne's] Value" would mean £40 for the first volume submitted in May. In choosing this particular figure, Sterne could be reflecting RD's offer in the June letter to which he refers. Both Wilbur Cross (*The Life and Times of Laurence Sterne* (New Haven: Yale University Press, 1929), p. 193) and Ralph Straus (*Robert Dodsley*, p. 263) claim that RD offered £40 for the work, although subsequent to this second letter from Sterne; that is, after the author had revised it and added 150 pages. But neither Cross nor Straus specifies whether the £40 was the proposed price for both volumes. Furthermore, omitting a specific reference, both give Sterne's friend John Croft as their source for the information. However, Croft's sole mention of RD's offer (*Whitefoord Papers*, pp. 226–7) stipulates £20 and implies that the offer was made before Sterne wrote the present letter, meaning that it applied to only the first volume. Perhaps Cross and Sterne were extrapolating Croft's figure to include a second volume.

⁵ On 19 April of this year (*LC*), RD and William Johnston had issued Samuel Johnson's *Rasselas* in two volumes, small octavo, priced at 5s. The first two volumes of *Tristram* would appear in octavo, as did the subsequent ones, in Caslon pica (the "new Letter" in the advertisement perhaps meant a new fount), priced at 5s. (Vols. V–VIII, 4s.; Vol. IX, 2s.), but, in part, on a "superfine Writing Paper." For details, see Kenneth Monkman, "The Bibliography of Early Editions of *Tristram Shandy*," *Library*, 25 (1970), 14–22.

⁶ After RD refused to meet Sterne's price, a Mr Lee, according to Croft (*Whitefoord Papers*, p. 227), loaned Sterne £100 to print the work. Lee has been identified as William Phillips Lee by John H. Harvey in "A Lost Link with Laurence Sterne," *Yorkshire Archaeological Journal*, XLII (1966), 103–7. Monkman (p. 22) questions the sum Lee provided, observing that £100 was far in excess of the amount required to publish the first volumes of *Tristram*.

⁷ Sterne would "free myself of all future trouble of this kind" when he came to London the following March and signed a preliminary agreement, selling the copyright of the first two volumes to James Dodsley for £250 and, likewise, Volumes III and IV for £380. On 19 May, it appears a second agreement was signed, either raising Dodsley's payment for the first two volumes or according a rather large sum for the two-volume *Sermons of Mr. Yorick*, to be published three days later. Isaac Reed's "Memoranda from Mr. Dodsley's Papers" (Reed says he received the Dodsleys' papers from

James's executors) shows the following entries: "19 May 1760 Laurence Sterne for £450 assigns to Ja^s Dodsley his property in the 2 Vols of Tristram Shandy and the two Vols of Yoricks Sermons. The same day Mr Dodsley agrees wth Sterne for the purchase of the 3rd & 4th Volumes of Tristram Shandy for the sum of £380. to be paid six Months after publication." (See Appendix B.)

Except for the last, which appeared on 29 January 1767, the first editions of the nine volumes of *Tristram* came out two at a time on the following dates: 1 January 1760, 29 January 1761, 22 December 1761, and 23 January 1765 (*LC*). Although he did not publish them exactly as planned, Sterne was able to keep his production schedule, at least for the first six volumes. Only Vols. I–IV would be purchased and published by Dodsley, however; the rest would be issued by Thomas Becket and Peter Abraham Dehondt, interestingly, at Tully's Head in the Strand. A former apprentice to Andrew Millar, Becket had set up shop two weeks after the first edition of *Tristram* had been published and took Dehondt into partnership later that year.

Not a shred of hard evidence remains to explain why Sterne switched booksellers with Volumes V and VI, although various conjectures have been offered. (See Wilbur Cross, p. 284; Melvyn and Joan New, eds. *The Life and Opinions of Tristram Shandy, Gentleman* (2 vols. Gainsville: University Presses of Florida, 1978), II, 826; Monkman, pp. 25–6.) Of course, a disagreement with the Dodsleys or an unacceptable offer for the next volume would naturally stand as prime candidates. However Sterne's resorting to two newcomers in the trade and retaining the copyright while dealing directly with the printer is reminiscent of Alexander Pope's maneuver with the trade in the late 1720s and 1730s when he treated such newly established booksellers as Lawton Gilliver rather like distributors. (See David Foxon, unpublished draft of the Lyell Lectures (1977), pp. 113ff.) Such an arrangement, Pope had once said, should clear two-thirds of the profits for the author (Joseph Spence, *Anecdotes*, ed. James M. Osborn (Oxford, 1966), I, 85). Perhaps Sterne now wanted more of the immediate profits, as Monkman suggests, and saw the retention of the copyright as a hedge against the future. In this light, Monkman (pp. 27–8), after calling attention to an entry in William Strahan's ledger that shows Sterne did indeed pay for 4,000 copies of Volumes V and VI, estimates that Sterne, after the sale, would have had more than £600.

On the other hand, perhaps the Dodsleys had sensed that the town's passion for *Tristram* had peaked and thought laying out additional large sums for the work was risky. Indeed, although a second edition of Volumes III and IV (the latter, a concealed edition) was called for on 21 May 1761 (*LC*), apparently there was not another in Sterne's lifetime. Significantly, the price of the new volumes was reduced from 5s. to 4s., and more than a year after their appearance, the publisher Becket noted that almost a quarter of the 4,000 volumes remained unsold (Curtis, *Letters*, p. 192). A second edition was not required until 1767. But more importantly, the last two volumes published by the Dodsleys had been subject to the kind of criticism that would have made the cautious RD cringe. If Dr Thomas Newton's comments in a letter of 26 February 1761 are at all representative, perhaps the Dodsleys were not anxious for more of *Tristram*, even though additional profits were to be had. Newton claimed: "The last two volumes of Tristram Shandy have had quite contrary success to the two former. It is almost as much the fashion to run these down, as it was to cry up the others . . . All the Bishops and Clergy cry out shame upon him. All the graver part of the world are highly offended; all the light and trifling are not pleased" (L. P. Curtis, "New Light on Sterne," *MLN*, LXXVI, 501).

8   In his letter of 23 May, Sterne had claimed that RD's "general opinion of the Character, & the very handsome Recommendation of M^r. Hinksman" had moved into the offer.

9   How curious that Sterne should misspell his own bookseller's name. Curtis (*Letters*, p. 81) adjusted the spelling to "Hinksman," rejecting Dibdin's transcription (his source) as an "obvious blunder."

10 In a letter that Sterne coaxed Catherine Fourmantel to write David Garrick on 1 January 1760, for the purpose of currying support for *Tristram* from that fashionable quarter, the visiting London singer tells Garrick that Hinxman had sold 200 copies in the first few days of its sale. (See Curtis, pp. 85–6.) Given the motive of the letter, the figure might be a bit inflated.

11 For some observations on the Dodsleys' role in the publication of *Tristram*, see Sterne's letter on 23 May, note 5.

12 Lacking RD's letter in June, we can only infer that Sterne's purpose in mentioning these matters specifically – "Locality" removed and notes added – was to point out to the publisher that he had indeed observed the recommendations made in that June letter. For a consideration of some of the

likely differences between the manuscript Sterne had submitted to RD in May and the one he is here preparing to print, see Melvyn and Joan New's Introduction to the Florida Edition of *Tristram*, II, 817–20.   [13] If Hinxman did in fact write to RD, his letter has not survived.

To William Shenstone[1]

Oct. 12, 1759.

Dear Sir,

What Apology can I make for not writing to you now for more than a Month, after receiving so much Pleasure and so many Civilities? However, as you too well know how easy it is for such Things to happen, I will make none, but leave you to *forgive us our Trespasses, as we forgive them that trespass against us.* And this would lead me to expostulate with you for not coming to Bath:[2] but I forbear, having many Things to be pardoned in myself, as well as many to deliver to you, and therefore so much for Apology.

I have seen *Persfield*, Mr. Morris's Seat; and Mr. Spence was just come from seeing it, when he arrived at *Bath*: he is much struck with it, and has attempted somewhat towards a Description of it. I shall have a Copy of his Papers soon, and will transmit it to you.[3] The Place is certainly of the great and sublime Kind; most of the near Views are seen below you from the Top of high Precipices, consisting of steep Rocks, hanging Woods, the Rivers *Severn* and *Wye*, which last winds about the Feet of the Rocks below you, in a very romantic Manner, almost surrounding a very pretty Farm, where Cattle and Sheep are feeding in the Meadows, at such a Depth below your Eye, that they seem very much diminished. The Rocks are bold and numerous, half covered with Woods, and rise almost perpendicular from the Edge of the Water to a surprising Height, forming, from the great Cliff a Kind of double Amphitheatre. A Gun fired from the Top of this Cliff, creates, by the Reverberation of the Report amongst other rocks, a loud Clap of Thunder, two or three Times repeated, before it dies away: but even this Echo, conformably to the Pride and Grandeur of the Rest of the Place, will not deign to answer a smaller Voice than that of a Musket; with a Culverin, I suppose, it would hold a noble Dialogue. The Town of *Chepstow*, and its ruined Castle, appear in the near View at somewhat more than the Distance of *Hales Owen* from your Grove;[4] and the romantic Windings of the *Wye* are seen all the Way to them, except now and then that its Stream is hid among the Rocks; and all the Way below them, till it is swallowed up by the *Severn*, at about two miles distance, where that River is also near two Miles over, and from whence it extends, enlarging in Breadth, quite down to *King-Road*, below *Bristol*. I can conceive nothing finer than these Views would be, were the Waters of the Rivers as clear as that of the *Thames*: but, alas! they are so muddy, that they will scarce return the Images of the Rocks, Trees, and other Objects, that rise upon their Banks. The distance Views are very extensive, and lets the Eye into Parts of fourteen different Counties. The Extent of the Walks is near four Miles, which in about five Hours Time I made shift to accomplish. I went from *Bath* with a polite Party of Gentlemen and Ladies, and our three Days Excursion was altogether exceeding agreeable.

Dr. L[owth] has favoured me with six new Fables, which are very clever and ingenious. Poor Mr. M[elmoth] has been so ill, that he has done but one. I have written one myself, since I came Home; the *Butterfly, Snail, and Bee*: and one Mr. G[raves] gave me, the *Tube-Rose and Sun Flower*: the two last I send you enclosed.[5] So that if you will favour me with half a Dozen, I shall have got my Number. I will, therefore, set about writing the Preface and the *Essay on Fable*; and shall be glad to publish this Winter, that I may get them off my Hands, and out of my Head, before I am quite sick of them.[6] Mr. G[raves] was so kind as to read them all over, and gave me several Corrections, and an Imitation of the squeaking Pig from Phaedrus.[7] Mr. M[elmoth] is now employing himself the same way;[8] and when he has done with them, Dr. L[owth] will go over them again; so that I shall hope they may be pretty correct. I shall throw out several of the weakest of my own new ones, and shall endeavour to supply their Places with better.

As you seemed to like the *Madeira*, I shall send by Trimen's Waggon, next *Monday*, Carriage paid, four dozen Pints of the same, which beg your Acceptance. Believe me to be ever,

dear Sir,

sincerely and affectionately yours,

R. Dodsley

P.S. Mr. Spence's Drawing, which I took to be the *Arcadia*, was only a Drawing that he directed to be made at *Rome* for a Lady's Monument in a Garden.[9]

I am this Instant favoured with a more particular Description of the Scenes and Views[10] I have attempted to describe, and for your better understanding the Situation of them, have copied them. First you enter the serpentine Walks, (which are near four Miles and a Half in length) from *Chepstow*, and the

I.	View, the Town.
II.	The Sea and the Rocks.
III.	The two Passages over the *Severn*, from *England* to *Wales*, where the Passage-Boats are continually passing and re-passing.

IV.	Three Avenues from which are seen	*Chepstow*,
V.		The Church,
VI.		Castle and Rocks.

VII.	A confined View of the Rocks and Channel.
VIII.	A Balcony, from whence are beautiful Views of the River Wye, and its Windings, the Rocks, Woods, &c. &c. beyond Description.
IX.	A Seat; the View, the Woods continued.
X.	A *Chinese* Bridge; a pretty confined Prospect.
XI.	A large Oak, with Ivy, and two Seats under it.
XII.	A beautiful Green by the Wood.
XIII.	A Seat under two Oaks.
XIV.	A delightful Shrubbery.
XV.	A Cave of Stone and Pebbles, with an extensive Prospect.
XVI.	The Top of the Mount, with the Prospect of seven Counties, the Sea, the Rocks, *Berkley* Castle,[11] the Shipping, &c. &c.

XVII.   A Mew for Pheasants, with Shrubberies of the finest foreign Shrubs.

XVIII.   A fine Beech Tree, exceedingly large.

XIX.   A Druid's Throne and Temple *in a Parterre*.

XX.   The Cave where we dined; the opening before it in Form of a Semi-
             circle, which the Prospect from thence resembles, from whence are
             seen the Rocks, the Wood, the River, with fine Lawns.

XXI.   A *Chinese* Semi-circle; the View, the River, Rocks and Lawns, *Berkley*
             Castle, and a very extensive Prospect of *Bristol*, &c. &c.

XXII.   A Cave, with Iron Rails before it; the View, looking down a Precipice,
             the most beautiful Woods imaginable.

XXIII.   An octagon Temple, surrounded with *Chinese* Rails, from whence is a
             most extensive Prospect of many Counties, with *Kings-Road*, the
             Shipping, &c. &c.

Source: Thomas Hull, *Select Letters* (London, 1778), II, 264–70.

[1] The italics in this and in subsequent RD letters taken from Hull are most likely that editor's doing, for
     they do not reflect RD's style.
[2] In his letter to Thomas Percy on 3 October (Brooks, p. 40), Shenstone relates that RD had stayed at
     the Leasowes for six weeks before proceeding to Bath "where he is now, I believe, with Spence and
     [William] Whitehead, and in full expectation of seeing me."
[3] Persefield, near Chepstow, in Monmouthshire was the seat of Valentin Morris (d. 1789). Spence's
     description of Persefield is now among his gardening papers in the Osborn Collection, Beinecke
     Library, Yale.
[4] Approximately a half mile. Halesowen, seven miles from Birmingham, and Shenstone's birthplace,
     was now also the residence of his neighbor, John Scott Hylton.
[5] RD's "Butterfly, Snail, and Bee" (*Select Fables*, III, 151–2) mentions the Leasowes as a favorite
     visiting place of travelling butterflies. Neither the text of this nor that of Graves's "The Tuberose and
     the Sun Flower" (*Select Fables*, III, 153–4) were preserved with RD's letter.
[6] *Select Fables of Esop, and Other Fabulists* would be delayed another year and a half.
[7] Graves's version of Phaedrus's "Scurra et Rusticus" (Bk. V, Fable IV) appeared in RD's *Select Fables*
     (I, 47–9), as "The Mimic and the Countryman." Phaedrus's Latin verse translations of Aesop's fables
     were available in many editions through the first half of the eighteenth century.
[8] See Melmoth's letter on 20 November.   [9] Unidentified.
[10] RD's source for the following account of Persefield is not traced, but it is certainly not that of Spence
     that RD mentions above.
[11] Berkley Castle, the baronial fortress where King Edward II was murdered.

From Richard Graves

                                                      Clav[er]ton – 15 Oct. 1759
Dear S^r

If you have open'd a general Subscription for Aid, amongst your learned friends,
I dare say your Collection of Fables is by this time completely fill'd – To let you see,
however, that I sometimes think of you – & remember you more than a common
"guest that tarrieth but a day" I have ventur'd to send you one more of my own
Composition – which you may either admit ⟨or⟩ reject or model – as you please – It

⟨has⟩ is liable to the same Objection with my other of being too verbose &, I was afraid, it might coincide with ⟨some⟩ one or two subjects wch you have already mythologiz'd – wch made me endeavour to prefix ye moral – wch I think is different from any of yours –

The Mag-pie & the / old / Raven –

He whose affections are dissipated by too general an *acquaintance*, is (usually)
endearments
unqualified for the warmth of *friendship* –

There was a certain Mag-pie, more busy & more loquacious, than any of
= kind = species –

the = *chattering tribe*. His tongue was in perpetual motion – & he himself continually
And he
upon the wing – fluttering from place to place – But seldom appear'd twice together in the same company –

Sometimes you might see him with a flock of pidgeons – plundering a field of ⟨?⟩ new-sewn Corn – [Then perch'd upon a cherry-tree with [a] par[ce]l of Tom-tits].[1] The next moment, he was engag'd with a flight of Crows – & feasting upon a delicious carkase –

[In the Evening perhaps he was hopping about & dancing the Lay – wth a party of popin-jays – The next morning, he was to be found in company with two or three solemn owls – talking politicks – & abusing the ministry –] government.

He one day took it into his [gallant] head, to visit a venerable Raven – who liv'd retir'd among the branches of a spreading oak – at the foot of a solitary mountain – "I admire this romantick situation (says ye prating [bird] & am charm'd with the wildness of the prospect – & the murmuring of that waterfall – [which [invites one to repose] &] diffuses a calmness of soul, superior to all the violent gratifications of publick life – what an agreeable retreat do you enjoy here! [sequesterd from the bustle & impertinence of the world] & wrapt up in the contemplation of the beauties of nature –] I shall certainly quit the gaieties of the Town – & for the sake of your Company, my good *friend*, spend the remainder of my days in this neighbourhood –

Well! S^r says the Raven; I shall always be glad to see you at my homely Retreat – But you and I should certainly be the most unsuitable Companions imaginable – Your whole ambition seems to be, to shine in conversation – &, by your popularity & complaisance, to recommend yourself to the *world* – whereas my greatest
consists in ease & privacy
happiness is in retirement & the conversation of a few select friends – I prefer a good heart to a voluble tongue – And tho' I am oblig'd to you for your polite professions – yet your benevolence seems divided amongst such a numerous acquaintance – that a very small share of it can be reserv'd for those – whom you
absurdly call
honor with the title of your *Friends*[2] –

I have just rec^d a Letter from Mr Shenstone – who repeats to me his opinion of your *polishing* & *abridging* – "He *wishes* you to chuse uncommon Subjects – &

inculcate refin'd Morals" – and to keep a medium between the naked Simplicity of Phaedrus – & the superfluous ornament of Fontaine³ –

One friend Mʳ Scot ask'd me "Whether I thought Fables were "*quite the Thing*" at this time of day – " I told him that *Fables* were certainly inferior to a Tragedy – if he meant that you were writing below yrself – But however, that you were probably doing as much real Service to the publick – And that a *new* Collection were certainly wanting – By the way, however, it were not amiss to let the world know in a preface. That you had been set upon this work – by people concern'd in the Education of Youth – as well as by a perso[n] of the first Rank in polite Literature (as I think you mention'd Dʳ Lowth as yᵉ first Suggester of it –⁴

Re-consider Mʳ Shenstone's litteral translation of the Wolf & yᵉ Lamb – & (as Rollin has pay'd that Encomium upon it.) whether you ought to alter it from *Father* to *Brother* – tho' I really think it more *probable*⁵ – I believe I had more to say to you – But yᵉ Servant waits & I am unwilling to lose a Post – Mʳˢ Graves joins in more than Compliments wᵗʰ

Sʳ yʳ affect:

Ric: Graves.

Address: To / Mʳ Robᵗ Dodsley / to be left at Mʳ Dodsley's at / Tully's head in Pall-Mall / London
Postmark: 17 OC Bath

MS: Somerset County Records Office, DD/SK, 28/1, 11.

¹ Slanted brackets represent Graves's square brackets in the manuscript.
² Graves's "The Magpye and the Raven" was printed in the *Select Fables* (III, 154–6) immediately following his "Tuberose and the Sun Flower." The text Graves includes here was thoroughly but not substantially revised before printing, most of the changes coming in simple word choice and, not surprisingly, in a tightening of the syntax. The paragraph Graves encloses in brackets (third) was deleted.
³ See Williams, p. 523. For Graves's own fable borrowed from Phaedrus, see RD's letter to Shenstone on 12 October, note 7. For La Fontaine, see RD's letter to Shenstone on 8 February of this year, note 8.
⁴ RD told Shenstone on 20 January that Robert Lowth had been the person who prompted the undertaking.
⁵ Some confusion occurs here. Though Graves speaks of Shenstone's literal translation of "The Wolf and the Lamb" (*Select Fables*, I, 14–15), in Shenstone's letter to Graves eleven days later, Shenstone says, "The Fable which I literally translated from Phaedrus was 'The Wolf and the Crane' [*Select Fables*, I, 22] in order to give Dodsley an idea on what Rollin laid stress in Fables" (Williams, p. 527). At first, it would seem Graves had simply mistaken which fable Shenstone had taken from Phaedrus. This sense seems corroborated in the statements of both: Shenstone says Rollin "laid stress" on this kind of fable, and Graves that "Rollin has pay'd that Encomium upon it." And when what seems to have been their common source is considered – Charles Rollin, *The Method of Teaching and Studying Belles Lettres. Translated from the French* (4 vols. London: Hitch and Hawes, 1759) – it seems that "The Wolf and the Crane" is the piece, for it is the only fable Rollin considers individually (I, 165–7). The case is clouded, however, with Graves's next statement: "Whether you ought to alter it from *Father* to *Brother*." Of the two fables, only "The Wolf and the Lamb" carries the word "father." The point is significant only for determining which of the fables Shenstone did indeed translate. But, for this, it seems best to rely on Shenstone's own, later statement.

From Philip Parsons[1]

Oakham Octr 29. 1759

Sir

I have finish'd a Poem on the *Nativity* from the Original of the Italian Poet Sannazaro (entitled *de Partu Virginis*) which I am inclined to publish.[2] The Poem is in three Books and is now under the Examination of an ingenious Friend. I chuse to treat with You about the Publication, because You will see by the enclosed Letter of Yours that You are not an absolute Stranger to my Poetry, tho' You are to my Person.[3] If You be willing to publish it (I mean if it shall appear to deserve publishing) be so good to let me know, and the Manuscript shall be with You in about 3 Weeks time.[4]

I am S^r
Your Obedt Servant
P. Parsons.

Direct to me at Oakham in Rutland

MS: Beinecke Library, Yale.

Philip Parsons (1729–1812), clergyman and Master of Oakham School, Rutland, contributed the first nine papers to Richard O. Cambridge's *The Student* (1751) and later the major portion of No. 169 (25 March 1756) to RD's periodical *The World.* The hexameter *De Partu Virginis* (1756) of Jacopo Sannazaro (1456–1530) had appeared in an Italian edition in 1740, but the BL shows no eighteenth-century English translation. Some of his Latin poems had been included by Pope in *Selecta Poemata* (1748). [3] RD's "enclosed letter" not traced. I can find no evidence that such a poem was ever published.

From William Melmoth

Novr 20.th 1759.

Dear Sir,

I hoped to have returned these M.S.S. to you in person, but being prevented, I must in this manner desire you to make my acknowledgements to Dr Lowth for ye pleasure & advantage I have received from his fables & grammar.[1] His observations on the structure of our language, wch he has ranged under the article of *sentences*, are ⟨?⟩ particularly judicious & useful. I was pleased to find several instances of gross inaccuracies produced from Swift: a writer w^m I have always looked upon as enjoying a reputation much higher than he deserves, in many respects.[2] I am persuaded, if he had flourished in these times, w^n his character c^d receive little, or no advantage from party, that he w^d not have been held in much esteem as a prose writer. In poetry I acknowledge his excellence.

I fear my notions of fable-writing are not what they ought to be, since they do not perfectly co-incide with ⟨those⟩ wch seem to be Dr Lowth's. To me it appears, that fables calculated principally for ye instruction of youth, sh^d turn upon the obvious qualities of common & familiar objects. In this view, the fables of the [?] & y.^{e}

Crocodile; the Diamond & the Loadstone; the Toad & the Ephemoron; tho extremely ingenious & well imagined, are too much raised above common observation to be addressed to the general purpose of this species of composition. Simplicity seems essential to this sort of writing in all its parts; it its subject as well as in its language. The Ostrich & the Pelican is therefore, according to my ideas, a perfect fable; or at least, it wants nothing to render it so but to be a little more concise. For altho' the Ostrich & the Pelican are foreign birds, & consequently not familiar to ye eye, yet they are extremely common by representation; & there is scarcely a boy in England a dozen years old, who has not heard of the two qualities under wch they are respectfully characterised in ye present fable. – But these observations I only whisper in your ear, where I trust you will let them die: for I am persuaded you are too much my friend to ⟨?⟩ mention them to Dr Lowth, w^m I w^d wish to have a better opinion of me than to believe I w^d oppose his judgement by mine.[4] Adieu, Dear Sir,

Y^{rs} sincerely

Wm Melmoth

Address: To / Mr Dodsley.

MS: BL. Add. MS. 35,338, f. 10.

[1] Melmoth refers to Lowth's contributions for RD's *Select Fables* and to an early manuscript of Lowth' *Short Introduction to English Grammar*, the latter to be jointly published by R & JD and Andrew Millar ir 1762. See Lowth's letter on 19 June 1760 for his response to Melmoth.

[2] Heavily footnoted, Lowth's *Grammar* cites, passim, errors and inconsistencies in writers of the last hundred years, but particularly in those of the Milton and Pope–Swift–Bolingbroke circles. It i curious that Melmoth focuses on Swift because Lowth does not.

[3] If RD agreed with Melmoth's criticism of Lowth's subjects, he did not let on in that section of his Essay on Fable prefixed to the edition where he takes up the "Persons" and "Characters" proper to fables Nor did he hesitate to print Lowth's in *Select Fables* (I, 49–50 now entitled "The Dog and the Crocodile"; III, 156–7, 170–2), together with the next that Melmoth mentions, "The Ostrich and the Pelican" (III, 136–7).

[4] RD did acquaint Lowth with Melmoth's remarks on the *Grammar*, something which Lowth gratefull acknowledges in his letter to RD on 19 June 1760, but it seems he made no mention of the comments on the fables.

From John Hawkesworth

[mid-November 1759]

Dear Sir

I cannot help thinking my self unreasonably treated by B. about Oroonoko, for i it is ⟨worth while to give me but⟩ not worth while to give me more than £20 fo that, upon what calculation can it be worth while to give £100 for a new play? no the difference of Six-pence in the price for the disproportion is by no means equal and as to the Sale there is the greatest reason to suppose that will not be less than a new play as it will be performed with the whole Strength of Drury Lane Theatre. think I should ma[ke] a better Bargain if they would give me leave to print it my sel for £20 – this however I dare say they will not do if I was to make the offer;[2] and as you seem to think it is best I should comply with their proposal of £20 and ten pounds, I will comply, with whatever indignation at a Tyranny from which I cannot now set my self free. many thanks ⟨by⟩ dear Sir for the trouble you have been at on my Behalf.[3] I shall come to Town to morrow & hope to return on Monday by the Stage. – the business I come to Town to transact engages me to morrow night. I should be glad if our meeting with Mʳ Gally could take place so as to permit my return on Monday, if not let it be Monday Evening and I will defer my return till Tuesday.[4]

> I am
>
> ever & truely Yʳ Affectionate
>
> humble Servᵗ[5]

[?]

Address: To / Mʳ Robᵗ Dodsley / at a Grocers overagainst the End of Suffolk Street / Charing Cross / London

Postmark: NO 1[?] Bromley

MS: Henry E. Huntington Library, HM 12235.

[1] A partially obscured postmark – "NO 1[?]" – gives the month and the approximate week of this letter. Allusions to two specific events identify the year. Here Hawkesworth seems to say the cast for the Drury Lane performance of his adaptation of Thomas Southerne's *Oroonoko* (1695) is set; its debut will in fact occur on 1 December 1759, Garrick playing the lead. Secondly, his troublesome negotiation with the play's publisher, Charles Bathurst, and his compliance with RD's advice obviously predate the play's printing, an event of 4 December 1759. A third event supports such a dating, but not absolutely. Hawkesworth's requesting RD to set up a meeting with Alexander Galley within the next few days probably concerned their signing a contract with James Dodsley for the writing of *A Compendium of the Geography, Natural History, and Antiquities of England*, a meeting that was delayed until 6 December 1759. (See Appendix B.) Finally, Hawkesworth's addressing RD at Charing Cross marks a time after the bookseller's retirement in early 1759 but before his moving in with his sister in Bruton Street by mid-1760.

[2] Perhaps Bathurst had a monopoly on the printing of Southerne's play, the last edition of which had appeared fifteen years earlier.

[3] Apparently RD had interceded with Bathurst on Hawkesworth's behalf.

[4] See note 1.   [5] The signature is missing, the manuscript having broken away.

To William Shenstone

December 1[-4], 1759.

Dear Mr. Shenstone,

I suppose you have some Time ago received from my Brother the Things you ordered. I desired him to send them, as also the Poems for Mr. Woodhouse, to whom I beg my Compliments, and am sorry he had them not sooner, but I had really forgot them.[1] I have been such a Rambler since I came to Town, that I have not had Time to attend to any Thing. I have not written a single Fable since that I sent you, and yet am so unreasonable, as to wonder you have not sent me your half

Dozen, I am writing an Essay on Fable, and thinking of a Preface, both of which I shall desire you to take the Trouble of reading and correcting, as soon as I have done them; however, I believe I shall take your Advice, and not think of printing this Winter. I was glad to hear you had some Hopes of finishing your Affairs with Mr. D—, and hope they are compleated to your Satisfaction.[2] I have been favoured with a Letter from Mr. Wren, which I answer by this Post.[3] You said, my Lord Lyttelton was to be at the Admiral's till after Christmas, but I saw him pass by in his Chariot a few Days ago. You have given me Hopes of seeing a Survey of your Farm;[4] I beg you will not delay what will give me so much Pleasure: would to God you would bring it yourself, with all your verbal Descriptions, Mottoes, &c, and let them be engraved and printed. I wish I could hear that you was writing somewhat. What think you of an Elegy on the Death of General Wolfe?[5] You know, I suppose that he was to have been married to a Sister of –, before he went on his last Expedition, but that she desired it might be deferred till his Return. I think the Scene might be laid in her Chamber, on the rejoicing Night for the taking of *Quebec*; her Friends may be supposed to have concealed his Death from her, and her Anxiety for his Welfare, in the Midst of the Rejoicings, might have a fine Effect: when suddenly his Ghost should appear, inform her of his Fate, and endeavour to comfort her in her Affliction. Here is Room for Description, Reflection, and the true Pathetic. Such a Story as this in your Hands could not fail to be fine: I wish you to try, and that right soon.

I have searched all the Shops in *London* for a *Pan* proper for the Subject we talked of, but in vain. What think you of the enclosed Sketch? I think it might be mended. Is not the left Hand raised too high?[6]

I had written thus far on *Saturday* Afternoon, when your Letters and Plans arrived by the Penny-Post, which determined me to stay till *Tuesday* before I finished my Letter. You have now embarrassed me; I have so many Things to reply to, that I know not where to begin: I must take them as they lie.

Did I ever tell you of Mr. P—'s *Chinese* Novel? If I did, I have quite forgot it, and will therefore never own it.[7] I shall be very glad to see Mr. H—'s Picture: my Compliments to him, and tell him, I suspect he intends it as a reconciling Present to Miss S—.[8] I wish Mr. Alcock would finish my two Drawings for the Fables; as to my Face, it is a Subject not worth considering;[9] however, I will make you an impudent Proposal: if you will exchange Faces with me when you come up to Town, we will both sit to the same Painter.[10] Notwithstanding you have taken Pains to forfeit all Claim to Favour from Mr. Spence, I am very well satisfied, the Letter you promise will effectually cancel all your Offences: I shall go down to him in about a Month, (you see I give you Time enough) enclose it to me, and I will carry it to him, with one of your small Plans, to which I will put References;[11] at the same Time, I will endeavour to get the *Scotch* Paper on Gardening.[12] As to my Sketch of the *Leasowes*, I have not yet had Time to think of it; but as soon as I have finished my Essay, especially if you make it unnecessary for me to write any more Fables, by sending me your half Dozen, I will certainly sit down to it; you see I am willing to make good Bargains.[13] The Duchess of Somerset's Letters I have safe, and will send them to you.[14] I am glad Mr. Graves is going on; and doubt not but the Work will turn to his

Advantage.[15] I shall certainly not print the Fables this Winter; and as to the Essay, I hope to have gone through it in about a Fortnight. I have read Dr. Hawksworth's *Adventurer* on the Subject, in which I exactly agree with you; and I have read a bad Translation of La Motte's Essay: I know nothing else on the Subject worth reading.[16] When I send you my Essay, I beg you will give it any Improvement which you may think it wants, either in correcting Imperfections, or in supplying Deficiencies. I have got six more new Fables from Dr. L––.[17]

Do not think that I will tamely hear my Friend's *Custard* abused; I shall certainly find a Time to vindicate his Honour, and to make your proud Foreigner own the superior Merit of *English* Custard.

And now for your Plans: I am much obliged to you for sending them; and if I might have my Wish, I would engrave the small coloured one, with Figures of Reference. This should be the Frontispiece to a Pamphlet, which should contain a Description of the Places and Things referred to, somewhat more at large than they are in this Drawing; together with all your Mottos, Verses, Compliments &c. as also a verbal Description of the rising and falling of the Ground; the Objects, Prospects, &c. all the Way round. In the Middle of the Title-Page, I would put the last Plate of Virgil's *Grove*; as a Head-piece at the Beginning of the Pamphlet, I would have a Print of your House; and at the End, which should be contrived to be almost a whole Page, I think the chief Cascade might be placed. The Plate should be worked off in Green; the road through the Path round the House, and the Water, should be afterwards coloured by Hand.[18] Think of these Things; and may Heaven give you Resolution to put them in practice!

I am, dear Sir,

most affectionately yours,

R. Dodsley.

P.S. Get a Drawing, by Bond, of the great Cascade, and of your House, of a proper Size, and I will be at all other Expence;[19] and if you have any Delicacy about being the Editor of this yourself, I will write a short Preface, and sign my Name to it, in which I will say, that I teized you into it, which is no more than Truth.[20] Dec. 3.[21]

Source: Thomas Hull, *Select Letters* (London, 1778), II, 271–7.

[1] James Woodhouse (1735–1820), the "shoemaker poet" of Rowley, near the Leasowes. Woodhouse's own collection, *Poems on Sundry Occasions*, would be published by James Dodsley in 1764 and earn the poet much attention in London. Woodhouse was the recipient of Samuel Johnson's dictum: "Give nights and days, Sir, to the study of Addison, if you mean . . . to be a good writer" (Mrs Piozzi, *Anecdotes of Dr. Johnson* in *Johnsonian Miscellanies*, ed. G. B. Hill (2 vols. 1897; repr. New York, 1966), I, 223). Johnson was later contemptuous of Woodhouse's reputation: "He may make an excellent shoemaker, but can never make a good poet" (Boswell, *Life*, II, 127).

[2] For the lawsuit brought against Shenstone by his cousin Thomas Dolman the younger, regarding the settlement of the estate of their grandfather, William Penn of Harborough Hall, Hagley, Worcestershire, to which they both had claims, see Shenstone's letters of 1754 and 1760, in Williams. Since his parents had died in his youth, Shenstone had spent a portion of his early years under the roof of his uncle, the Rev. Thomas Dolman, father of his litigious cousin.

[3] Christopher Wren (1711–71) of Wroxall Abbey, grandson of the famous architect and friend of Shenstone. Neither Wren's letter nor RD's response has been traced.

[4] John Riely (see note 11) identifies this survey as that executed by William Lowe. On this plan was based, Riely says, the engraving that accompanied RD's Description of the Leasowes in his edition of Shenstone's *Works* (1764). Shenstone had mentioned this survey in a letter to Percy on 3 October 1759 (Brooks, p. 39).

[5] Apparently Shenstone thought very little of it; he would not be coaxed into writing an elegy on James Wolfe, who had recently lost his life while commanding the English army in their victory over the French at Quebec. When writing to Thomas Hull on 7 January, 1761, Shenstone recommended that Hull try his hand at such an elegy (Hull, I, 279; Williams, p. 567).

[6] Pan was not used as the frontispiece for *Select Fables*. Instead, the frontispiece shows a barebreasted female seated on the porch of a temple, holding a palm branch in her left hand and a sun-like disc in her right (symbol of Truth?). A figure that probably represents Aesop is lifting her veil, revealing her to three youths in Western dress. Samuel Wale provided the drawing, and Charles Grignion engraved it. (See Hans Hammelmann and T. S. R. Boase, *Book Illustration in Eighteenth-Century England* (New Haven: Yale University Press, 1975), pp. 92–3.)

[7] Most likely Thomas Percy's *Hau Kiou Choaan or The Pleasing History: A Translation from the Chinese Language*, to be published by the Dodsleys in 1761. Apparently Percy had been keeping his work a secret. See RD's letter, *post* 18 February 1760, to Shenstone. James Dodsley would pay Percy £50 for the copyright. (See Appendix B.)

[8] Probably John Scott Hylton's picture. "Miss S—" is unidentified.

[9] Edward Alcock's drawings were not forwarded. Among those that Shenstone told Percy in early 1761 he had substituted for RD's cuts in his own copy of *Select Fables* (Williams, pp. 568–9) was one of RD himself, after (Jonathan) Richardson. See John Scott Hylton's letter on 18 February 1761, note 2.

[10] For their exchange of pictures – RD's by Sir Joshua Reynolds and Shenstone's by Alcock – see their subsequent correspondence.

[11] "one of your small Plans, to which I will put References" most likely refers to the "Survey of your Farm" for which, RD says in his next letter to Shenstone, Joseph Spence is much obliged. The original of this "small Plan," a line drawing tracing the walks of the Leasowes, together with a listing of fifty-one references to the features of the Leasowes, written in RD's hand, is preserved in the Henry E. Huntington Library (HM 30312). It had originally been bound in the Library's extra-illustrated copy of Spence's *Anecdotes*. Also formerly bound in this copy was Spence's own unfinished account, "The Round of Mr. Shenstone's Paradise." For alerting me to these materials, I am indebted to John C. Riely, whose "Shenstone's Walks: The Genesis of Leasowes," *Apollo* (September 1979), 202–9, also prints William Lowe's *Plan of the Leasowes* (1759), preserved in the Osborn Collection, Yale. Professor Riely believes that the latter was the original from which the presently mentioned "Survey" was traced.

[12] Possibly an *Essay on Landscape Gardening* by Sir John Dalrymple (fl. 1750), one of the Barons of the Exchequer of Scotland. In his next letter to Shenstone (4 January 1760), RD says he has "not been able to get Dalrymple's Essay on Garden Grounds." The only copy of this work I have been able to locate is an 1823 version edited by Boulton Carney (BL).

[13] RD's "Description of The Leasowes, the Seat of the Late William Shenstone, Esq." appeared in his edition of Shenstone's *Works* (1764; II, 331–71). See note 19.

[14] Shenstone's request for the letters of Frances Seymour, Countess of Hertford and Duchess of Somerset, might suggest he had some interest in printing the letters together with those of Lady Luxborough, since both ladies had been his friends and both had died within the last five years. Ultimately, Lady Luxborough's letters would be issued from Birmingham in 1775 by John Hodgetts, who, as Shenstone's executor, had the letters from the poet's estate.

[15] Probably another allusion to Graves's early work on *The Spiritual Quixote*, to be published by RD's brother in 1773.

[16] John Hawkesworth's "Critical Remarks on fable" appeared in the *Adventurer*, No. 18 (6 January 1753), 103–8. The "bad Translation" was probably that by Robert Samber prefixed to *One Hundred New Court Fables* (1721).

¹⁷ Robert Lowth, whose fables, perhaps, are the "Custard" of the next few lines. In those lines, the "proud Foreigner" is probably La Motte. See RD's letter of 24 June.

¹⁸ For the background and consequence of these "Plans," see note 20.

¹⁹ Whether Shenstone acted on RD's recommendation is unknown, but the Birmingham artist Daniel Bond would later provide drawings of the Leasowes for RD's edition of Shenstone's *Works* (1764).

²⁰ Apparently when visiting the Leasowes in the summer of 1758, RD had suggested that Shenstone print a description of his now famous *ferme ornée*, for after his return to London, he reminds Shenstone in a letter on 22 August to send a description of the Leasowes "for yᵉ use I mention'd to You." The next month (19 September), he tells Shenstone the description cannot be too long and the following month (10 October) reminds him to bring it with him when visiting Spence. About the same time, Shenstone employed Lowe to survey the Leasowes. In the interim, as this letter reflects, he had sent off his "Little Plan of my Farm . . . reduc'd to a small scale" (Brooks, p. 39) and drawings to RD, but apparently without an adequate verbal description. Probably what had delayed Shenstone's efforts with the plan was an opinion he expressed in a letter to RD on 20 November 1762 (q. v.): "I am more and more convinced, that no description of this Place can make any Figure in print, unless some *strictures* upon *gardening* . . . be superadded." But in the same letter, he says that Thomas Percy and Richard Jago, while touring the Leasowes recently, had begun writing the description RD wanted. Although the plan for the pamphet was terminated by Shenstone's death less than three months later, Percy later claimed that the description printed in RD's edition of Shenstone's *Works*, II, 331–71, was essentially that written by Jago, himself, and a few other friends of Shenstone in 1762; that it was not by RD, as had long been believed (Brooks, p. 216). That Shenstone had been attempting to resolve his own objection is clear from his own notes that would accompany the Description in his *Works*: "Unconnected Thoughts on Gardening."

²¹ Since the present text depends upon Hull's printed version, it is difficult to be certain whether "Dec. 3" was added by RD or assigned by Hull. If the letter was begun on Saturday and completed on Tuesday – see third paragraph – the correct date would be 4 December.

To William Shenstone

Jan. 4, 1760.

Health, Happiness, and all the Compliments of the Season, to dear Mr. Shenstone! I have enquired of all the Spilsbury's in Town, but I cannot find that my little Drawings are yet sent up. This, if Mr. Alcock be still with you, I wish you would be so good as to tell him, with my Compliments.¹ When am I to expect an Answer to my last long Letter? And when am I to have your half dozen Fables? I have sent my Preface, and my Essay on Fable, to Mr. Graves, by this Night's Post, with a Desire, that he will transmit them to you in a Post or two.² When you get them, I shall be very glad if you will look them carefully and critically over: they are both very short; and there are blank Pages on one Side, for whatever Alterations or Remarks you shall favour me with. I beg you will be so good as to let me have them back, with your Fables, as soon as possible. I shall not publish this Winter: but I want to have all my Materials together, that I may begin to think of disposing them in the Order they are to stand.

I have Compliments to you from Mr. Spence, and he is much obliged to you for the Survey of your Farm. He has never been able to get Dalrymple's *Essay on Garden Grounds*.³ I enclose a few Lines on the *Leasowès*. If you should think them not totally unworthy of the Subject, I should be glad if you would please to bestow such Correction upon them as you may think will tend to their good. I have other

Matters to communicate to you, and to advise with you about; but you have so much upon your Hands already, from my last Letter and this, that I will not discourage you from sitting down to write to me, by adding at present any Thing further to your Trouble.

I am, dear Sir,

affectionately yours,

R. Dodsley.

Source: Thomas Hull, *Select Letters* (London, 1778), II, 277–9.

[1] RD soon abandoned hopes of getting Alcock's drawing for *Select Fables* and had others executed. See his next letter to Shenstone.   [2] Neither letter, nor enclosures, traced.
[3] See RD's previous letter to Shenstone, notes 11 and 12.

From Thomas Blacklock

Dumfries 4th Feb[ry]. 1760.

Dear Sir

To what shall I impute this long pause of our intercourse? The vanity of my own heart, and my consciousness of your goodness, prevent my drawing any inferences, much to my own disadvantage. Yet I should have considered a Gentleman in your situation, an inhabitant of the Metropolis of England, which now appears to me the Metropolis of the world, as always capable of being more agreeably amused than by any thing I could send, if your advice had not been necessary to me, which I can now ask with more freedom as you are disengaged from business. Without further preamble, the affair is this. – My uneasiness tho' not entirely gone, is yet so much abated, that there is no probability of it's being immediatly decisive. In vain have I suffered the toil and difficulty of passing tryals in this Church, there is no probability that She will receive me into her bosom. The common people, on account of my blindness, are prejudiced against me, & the popular Clergy, who alone have it in their power to remove such a prejudice, are, for reasons best known to themselves, far from being sanguine in their attachment to me – Though the common dictates of humanity, the circumstances in which I am involved, my moral Character & my learning which they have tried – ought to have inspired them with different sentiments.[1] These disadvantages have induced me to undertake the most desperate of all employments, that of publishing Sermons. I beg to know therefore, how far you think such a scheme practicable, whether it can be done by subscription, whey[r] any Bookseller will take the Copy, or whey[r] I may prudently run the risk myself. The subjects are ey[r] entirely new, or treated in a different manner from any oy[r] I have seen. I was intended that they should be both curious & useful. The purity & Idiom of the English Language, has been as carefully as possible observed.[2] I beg pardon for this trouble which I can assure you would not have been given, had I not been informed, that you were not longer concerned in trade. Your answer can not be less favourable than I expect, when therefore it proves convenient for you to write, your sentiments on this subject will greatly oblidge

Your most hu^{le} Ser^t

Thos Blacklock

P.S. Please send, directed as before a dozen or two of the poems Octavo edition as soon as convenient with an Acct of the number transmitted.[3]

T.B.

MS: BL. Add. MS. 21,508, ff. 44–5.

---

[1] Blacklock had been presented to the ministry of Kirkcudbright upon the application to the Crown by Lord Selkirk. But his blindness was objected to by the parishioners, and consequently, after a few years of legal dispute, Blacklock would resign the post, receiving a small annuity from the parish and returning to Edinburgh, where he took in pupil-borders.

[2] I can find no record, either in bibliographies or in periodicals, that his proposed collection of sermons was ever published.

[3] The third edition of Blacklock's *Poems* had been published in 1756 by RD.

To William Shenstone

[post 18 February; ante 21 April 1760][1]

Dear Sir,

I am sorry I hurried my Essay out of your Hands, before you had done with it; but if I think of publishing my Fables next *October* or *November*, it is high Time I should put both to Press now, that the Printer may have good Weather to print in, and that the Work may have time to dry, after it is finished, before the Books are bound. But as it happens, I cannot begin till the latter End of this Month, as the Printer is not at Leisure; however, I have put my Plates in Hand, and they are going on as fast as possible. I never received Mr. Alcock's Drawings; so I have got two others executed, of somewhat a different Design.[2] I will not put the Essay in Hand till the last, which may, perhaps, be about *July*, as I shall be very desirous of its having the Advantage of your Corrections. But am I not to hope for a new Fable or two from you? You see how I dwindle in my Expectations: but pray don't let me be *quite* disappointed. I propose, if possible, to finish the Printing of my Fables before I set out on my northern Expedition. Mr. M––, and his Lady, will be at *Nottingham* about the latter End of *August*; they have wished I would meet them there, and in their Return to Town, bring them round by the *Leasowes*.[3] Mr. Burke has also a strong Inclination to meet us there; so that possibly we may be happy enough to spend a Day with you; another must be spent at Lord Lyttelton's, (as they are both acquainted with him) and a third at *Birmingham*.[4] I shall hate the Name of D–– as long as I live: he is crooked in all his Ways; but the Devil will set strait with him one Day or other.[5] I have not seen a Page of Mr. Percy's Novel, and therefore cannot at all explain it to you; but I suppose he makes no Secret of it. I wish Mr. Graves would finish his.[6] – And will you really consent to an Exchange of Pictures? Upon my

Word, you make but a sorry Bargain for yourself: however, to give you as little Reason as may be to regret your Compliance, I will sit to one of our best Artists; and to supply the Want of Merit in the Original, will endeavour to give as much as I can to the Copy. If you have any Thing to suggest on this Subject, (as you seem to hint) you will be so good as to let me have a Line, because, as soon as I am able to get abroad, which I hope will be in a few Days, I intend to consult with Reynolds about it.[7] Ay, I forgot to tell you, that I have been confined this Month with the Gout; every Man has his D—n;[8] *that* is mine. I am glad your Likeness is a strong one; and I think the Attitude, you are drawn in, is a good one: pray, is that the Picture you intend for me? The Writer of *Tristram Shandy* is a Mr. Sterne, one of the Prebendaries of *York*. As to Mr. Baskerville's *Bible*, he will easily be dissuaded from the marginal Ornaments; but the Title-Page is a Favourite, and for my Part, I have not much Objection to it.[9] Mr. Webb's Book, on *Painting and Painters*, is reckoned ingenious, and if you like the Subject, will be worth your Perusal. *Antient and Modern Rome*, I also think a good Poem.[10] My Compliments to Mr. Hylton, and all Friends.

I am ever,
Dear Sir,
most faithfully yours,
R. Dodsley.

Source: Thomas Hull, *Select Letters* (London, 1778), II, 103–6.

[1] Hull does not date this letter, and Straus's assigned date (p. 288), May 1760, is a bit too late. From internal and external evidence, the date can only be approximated as within a certain two-month period. It must post-date 18 February 1760 because Daniel Webb's *Inquiry into the Beauties of Painting and into the Merits of the most Celebrated Painters, Ancient and Modern* – mentioned within as "reckoned ingenious" – was published by R&JD on that day (*PA*). On the other hand, the letter must be dated as prior to 21 April, 1760, for at 10.00 a.m. on that day RD had his first appointment to sit for his portrait at Sir Joshua Reynolds's studio, something about which, according to this letter, he had yet to consult Reynolds. He says he hopes to see Reynolds "in a few Days," for at the moment he is still confined with the gout. Since, with Reynolds's busy schedule, it is not likely that RD sat for him at the first consultation, it is conceivable that at least a week or two intervened, and consequently this letter might be dated earlier than 21 April. (See Reynolds's Sitter Book for 1760, Royal Academy of Arts, REY/1.)

[2] See RD's two previous letters to Shenstone in which he awaits Alcock's drawings for *Select Fables*. The "two others" might be those by Samuel Wale, which, engraved by Charles Grignion, were used for *Select Fables*.

[3] William Melmoth. See Melmoth's letter of 9 October, where he apologizes for not keeping the rendezvous.

[4] Edmund Burke and George, Lord Lyttelton.

[5] Probably Thomas Dolman, Shenstone's cousin. The settlement of their claims to the family estate at Harborough had been unfavorable to the poet. See RD's letter to Shenstone of 1 December 1759, note 2.

[6] See RD's letter to Shenstone of 1 December 1759, notes 7 and 15.

[7] See note 1.

[8] See note 5.

[9] Baskerville's edition of the Bible would appear in 1763. Though without illustration, the title page of Volume I shows an intermixture of varying sizes and types of characters, featuring "Holy Bible" in

scroll. The title page of Volume II, however, the New Testament, is extremely plain by contrast. As RD indicates, Baskerville was "dissuaded from the marginal Ornaments."

George Keate's *Ancient and Modern Rome. A Poem Written at Rome in the Year 1755* had been published by R&JD on 5 February (*PA*).

To William Shenstone

June 17. [1760][1]

Dear Mr. Shenstone,

I was yesterday searching for Figures for your two Niches – I have found three Pair, the Figures good, that will do as to Size, *viz.* the Antinous I mentioned, and the Apollo with his Arm over his Head; a Flora and a Ceres; and a Homer and Virgil. The Antinous and Apollo are two Feet high, Flora and Ceres twenty-three Inches, and Homer and Virgil twenty-one. These last are each of them leaning upon a Pedestal; on one of which, in *Basso Relievo*, is *Troy* in Flames; on the other, Romulus and Remus sucking a Wolf. These are both pretty Figures; and don't you think them better Ornaments for a Library, and more suitable Companions for Sappho, than either of the others?[2] A Line by the Return of the Post, will just give me Time to get which of them you choose finished, and sent to you, before I set off for *Nottingham*, for I find I must go thither before I come to the *Leasowes*; but I shall stay only a few Days. I had a Letter from my Friend Mr. M––, by the last Post, who is at *Nottingham*, and I find him wavering in his Resolutions, about coming by the *Leasowes*.[3] I am glad you like my Design for the Picture: and how agreeably you have contrived to flatter me about it! But say what you will, I shall have a Picture of Mr. Shenstone; you will have one only of Dodsley; and a Shenstone by Alcock, will certainly be more valuable than a Dodsley even by Reynolds.[4] I read to him that Part of your Letter which related to him; he desires his Compliments, and would be glad, if you came to Town, that you sate to him. I hope I shall be able to send the Picture to you, before I set out on my Journey; but it is not yet finished.

I am,

affectionately yours,

R. Dodsley.

Source: Thomas Hull, *Select Letters* (London, 1778) II, 107–8.

By reason of the reference within to the near completion of RD's portrait by Reynolds, the letter must be of 1760. RD would last sit for Reynolds at 9.30 a.m. on Friday, 4 July, 1760. (Reynolds's Sitter Book, Royal Society).

As has become clear through the correspondence, RD was regularly supplying Shenstone with ornaments for the Leasowes.

Melmoth's letter is not traced, but see his next letter to RD on 3 July.

When Shenstone had received RD's portrait by Reynolds, he confessed to Percy: "I am ashamed to mention the Price." A month earlier he had specified to James Prattinton, a merchant of Bewdley: "the Head of Mr. Dodsley, by Reynolds . . . cost him at least 10 Guineas" (Williams, pp. 559, 655).

From Robert Lowth

Sedgefield June 19. 176(

Dear S!

I am very sorry to hear by our good Friend M! Spence, that you have been s cruelly handled by the Gout this Spring. I hope it will prove all for your Good, & that it has left you in good spirits, with a stock of health that may last you a grea while, before it shall think proper to discipline you again.

I ought to have thank'd you long ago for the Papers you sent me from M Melmoth, & to have desired you to present my Comp!ˢ & Thanks to him for bein so kind as to communicate them.[1] The remarks are all very proper, & many of ther have been of use to me in my design; ot[hers are?] above the rank of Grammatica [use.] If M! Melmoth desires to have his papers back again, I will take care t return them to you. I am very sorry to find you speak of him, as in a bad state c health.

I am glad to hear the Fables are in such forwardness. As to the form & th decorations I do not presume to say any thing; well knowing that you are the bes Judge of what will please the public.

We have lost our good Friend D! Chapman, than whom no man had bette pretensions to long life.[2] Our Society is a Memento Mori. The six uppermos Houses in our College all in a line [have] been vacant by Death withi[n] [the]s three years.

I hope your Brother is quite gott well of his fever in w꜀ʰ I left Him. Pray put hin in mind that I forgot to call for my Moreton's Table of Ancient Alphabets, w꜀ʰ I lef with him to be put upon Cloth: he may give [i]t to my Brother when he meets wit‍ [hi]m.[3]

My Wife is, I thank God, perfectly well, & desires her Comp!ˢ to You. Believe me ever,

Dear S!
Your most affectionate
humble serv!

R. Lowth

Address: To M! Dodsley.

MS: BL Add. MS. 35,339, ff. 25–6.

[1] See Melmoth's letter to RD on 20 November 1759.
[2] Thomas Chapman (1717–60), a fellow prebendary with Lowth at Durham.
[3] *Edwardi Bernardi, S.T.D. et astronomicae apud Oxoniensis professoris Saviliani, orbis eruditae literatura charactere Samartico deducta, nunc restaurata, et supplementis quibusdam egregis aucta Carolo Morton, M.D. Reg e ant. Soc. Lond. S. e col med. Etc.* William Lowth (1707–95), Lowth's brother, was a prebend o Winchester from 1759 until his death.

To William Shenstone

June 24. [1760]*

Dear Mr. Shenstone,

How much am I obliged to you for the Pains you have taken in translating La Motte's Discourse on Fable! and though I fancy you will find, upon comparing the

wo, that I have made a good Deal of Use of it, I shall be very glad to have more of it
nterwoven, if you shall think I have not sufficiently extracted the Essence of it. I
nust own, my Pride (or call it my Folly, if you please) would rather choose to prefix
omewhat of my own on that Subject, than servilely adopt the Thoughts of a
?renchman, though I acknowledge them to be very ingenious. Besides, I have had
he Hardiness to differ with him in some Respects, which makes it still more
mproper to take his whole Discourse. Proceed, therefore, if you please, in
·orrecting my Essay; and interweave with it as much more of La Motte as you may
hink proper.² If you defer this till I come down, which I wish you would not, pray
n the mean Time think of half a Dozen new Fables, that we may not have too much
o embarrass us when together. My Face is quite finished, and I believe very like.³ I
ancy I shall send it, together with the Figures, on *Monday* Se'ennight;⁴ but I shall
1ot be able to set out myself till *Monday* Fortnight, and staying a Week or ten days at
Vottingham and *Mansfield*, will detain me from the *Leasowes* till the latter End of next
Vlonth. If the picture should be turned yellowish, by being packed up, Mr.
₹eynolds advises, that it be set in the Sun for two Hours, which will quite recover
t.⁵ Why did you leave the Choice of your two Figures to me? How could you put me
ınder such a Difficulty? If I have done wrong, you will suffer for it; and say what
·ou will, I have not sufficient Firmness of Taste to direct me right; besides, I do not
:xactly remember the Niches: it is therefore your Fault to trust me; and if I have
:rred, your Duty to forgive me. I have ordered the Homer and Virgil to be bronzed:
hey are very pretty Figures; and if you have, as you say, no other Objection to
hem, but the Want of two or three Inches more of Height, I hope some Means may
›e found to obviate so small a Deficiency. I should not, however, have ventured to
end them, but that you seemed, at last, to acquiesce in their being sent. I think,
1owever, I have been somewhat happy in my Urns; and I am not without Hopes,
hat you will approve the whole Cargo. The Folio Virgil will come in the same
²ackage.⁶ I feel myself very happy in the thoughts of seeing you soon, and will
1asten the Day as much as is in my Power. I hope Mr. Baskerville will be quite
·eady for me; I shall send him the Paper in a Fortnight.⁷ I am

faithfully yours,

R. Dodsley.

Source: Thomas Hull, *Select Letters* (London, 1778), II, 109–11.

The reference within to the near completion of Sir Joshua Reynolds's portrait of RD supports Hull's
assignment of the year 1760 to the letter, for RD's last appointments in Reynolds's Sitter Book
occurred on 3 and 4 July 1760. The mention of final preparations for the printing of *Select Fables* by
Baskerville also argues for the 1760 date.

The English translation of Antoine Houdart de la Motte's essay on fable, provided for Dodsley by
Shenstone, was produced from *Fables nouvelles dediqueés au roy par M. de la Motte . . . avec un discours sur la
fable*, a quarto Paris edition of 1719 that Shenstone himself had purchased for the occasion, according
to Welcher and Dircks (*An Essay on Fable. Robert Dodsley*, Augustan Reprint, No. 112). From this, and
from Joseph Addison's *Spectator* essays (Nos. 183 and 512), RD borrowed freely, drawing his outline
and many notions from La Motte, but observing Addison's directives regarding economy of style.

Specifically, RD was indebted to La Motte in Section I for the instruction that a fable's moral
truth ought not be too obvious but should be conveyed beneath the "shadow of allegory"; on the other
hand, it ought not be trivial, dubious, or dark. Although RD agreed that a fable must first please if it is

to convince, he chose to place his maxim at the head of the fable as a guide, whereas La Motte appended his to the end. In Section II, "On the Action and Incidents," RD stresses La Motte' directive that a fable must be clear, one complete action, and natural to life. In Section III, he echoe one of the advantages that La Motte sees in the use of animals: it enlarges one's store of characters that is, if the animals' actions suitably reflect their natures and respective properties. In the las section, "Language," RD concurs with the Frenchman's call for a familiar style as more effective fo insinuating the moral. Only natural language will beget the appearance of nature. Finally, RI embraces La Motte's belief that occasional strokes of humor and incidental reflections add furthe value to the fable's rhetorical and resulting moral effectiveness. But RD's Essay was not wholly dependent on the Frenchman. His original contributions to the understanding of fable writing included such matter as the relationship between the fable as a genre in itself and epic and dramati fables; the nature and role of the moral within each; the value for instruction of the lower and simple forms of fable (as he would offer in *Select Fables*, particularly in Vol. III); the utility and prope. implementation of animals in fables; and the rhetorical need for brevity and for the familiar bu elegant style. A brief but useful introduction to RD's *Essay* is found in Welcher and Dircks's editio (above), where the editors acknowledge that RD presented "For the first time in English, a comprehensive and original study of the genre."   ³ Reynolds's portrait of RD.

⁴ See RD's last letter, where he mentions selecting statues for Shenstone's library. "On Monday Se'ennight" would mean that RD would be sending the figures and his portrait on 7 July, just thre days after his last appointment with Reynolds. On 20 July, Shenstone told James Prattinton that he had received RD's portrait "yesterday" (Williams, p. 655).

⁵ Passed through several hands over the years, RD's portrait by Reynolds now hangs in the Dulwich Ar Gallery, a donation of H. Yates Thompson, whom Straus indicates (frontispiece) as having been the owner at the time of the publication of *Robert Dodsley* in 1910. A full provenance is available a Dulwich. I am indebted to Dr Hazel Simpson for calling my attention to its location.

⁶ In his letter to Graves two weeks later (Williams, p. 556), Shenstone, proudly recounting the items he is to receive from RD, includes mention of "Ogilby's Virgil," almost certainly the "Folio Virgil" RI mentions here. The first folio edition of Ogilby's elegantly printed Virgil appeared in 1654.

⁷ Probably a reference to the paper RD would supply to Baskerville for the printing of *Select Fables*. RI did come to the Leasowes, as promised, and stayed for more than two months to correct the edition while Baskerville printed off the sheets, something which Shenstone tells Percy in a letter of 11 Augus (Williams, p. 559). In another letter, on 1 October, Shenstone informs Percy that "Dodsley is gone te spurr *Baskerville*; returns on Friday to spurr *me*" (Williams, p. 563).

From William Melmoth

Nottingham, July 3ᵈ 1760

Dear Sir,

    In the hope that you continue your intentions of visiting us about the time you named,¹ I will trouble you with a commission or two, wᶜʰ I beg the favor of you tc let yʳ servant execute. I inclose a note for some tea, wᶜʰ you will be so good as orde him to carry to Mʳ Twining's in Devereax Court, but not to pay for it; as also to get two bottles of cephalic snuff from a Pamphlet shop the lower end of Pall-mall ove against the house yᵗ was once the King's arms Tavern. I shall be obliged to you i you will give these small parcels a place in yʳ Portmanteau. I have one request more to make: it is, that you wᵈ desire yʳ Brother to insert the inclosed in the daily advertiser.²

    We defer our expedition to Matlock 'til the Assizes, wᶜʰ begins here yᵉ 24.ᵗʰ of this month; at wᶜʰ time we shall be obliged to quit our Lodgings, as they are always appropriated to the Judges. We shᵈ promise ourselves more satisfaction from this excursion, if we had a prospect of y.ʳ accompanying us: but I fear we must not expect that pleasure.³ I wish you a great deal in your journey hither, & the continuance of this mild weather to render it the more agreable. Adieu, dear sir, & be assured that I am

most faithfully yours,

W.ᵐ Melmoth.

The Ladies expect you [?] especially M.ʳˢ M. who begs to show you [?] window. I s.ʰᵈ be very glad of a few Franks, if you c.ᵈ easily procure them for me.⁴

MS: BL. Add MS. 35,338, f. 12.

¹ Despite the mention of their projected visit to Nottingham in a number of letters during the summer of 1760, Melmoth and RD never did meet. See the former's final letter on the subject written on 9 October.

² Through July 1760, the *Daily Advertiser* carries no notice obviously linked with Melmoth, nor one by RD that might be regarded as placed on Melmoth's behalf. Perhaps he had intended an advertisement for the sale of his house in Ealing, which he would leave shortly to take up residence in Shrewsbury.

³ As his correspondence during the summer of 1760 reveals, RD would spend a good part of August and all of September in the Birmingham area, revising and correcting his fables with Shenstone, as well as chivvying Baskerville's press. He would follow this with a visit to Bath.

⁴ This last sentence appears on the verso of the holograph.

From William Melmoth

Nottingham, Aug. 29.ᵗʰ 1760.

Dear Sir,

In y.ᵉ letter you favored me with about a fortnight ago,¹ you mentioned your intention of sending the candlesticks the following week; but the waggon having since that time twice returned hither without bringing them, I imagine you find a difficulty in procuring them. If that sh.ᵈ by y.ᵉ case, I beg you w.ᵈ not give yourself any farther trouble about them: but if you have employed any workman to make them, & sh.ᵈ not have sent them away before this reaches your hands, pray keep them 'till I call upon you & receive them in person, w.ᶜʰ I hope will now be in 3 weeks at farthest.² I proposed indeed y.ᵗ it sh.ᵈ have been sooner, as I had determined to leave this place the 12.ᵗʰ of next month; but finding by the papers that if I held my resolution I sh.ᵈ fall in with your concert at Birmingham,³ I postpone my journey a week longer in order to avoid the crowd w.ᶜʰ this music meeting will probably bring to your principal Inn. I shall be glad to know what sign that Inn bears, & shall thank you for informing me at the same time w.ᶜʰ are the best Inns to lie & dine at in the road between Nottingham & Birmingham, & also if there is any thing in the way worth a traveller's observation. The rest when we meet: in y.ᵉ mean while accept the Ladies best compliments, with the assurance of my being Dear Sir,

most sincerely y.ʳˢ

W.ᵐ Melmoth.

Address: To / M.ͬ Dodsley, / at M.ͬ Baskerville's / in Birmingham, /
Warwickshire.
Postmark: Nottingham

MS: BL. Add MS.35,338, ff. 13–14.

¹ RD's letter not traced.
² That is, at the Leasowes where RD would be staying through early October.
³ The Birmingham Music Festival in 1760 was held on 16–18 September. (I am indebted to Dr S. W.
  McVeigh of Goldsmith's College, University of London, for discovering this date.) Melmoth's next
  letter, on 9 October (q.v.), shows that he did not make the trip to Birmingham at all.

From William Melmoth

Nottingham, Oc.ͬ 9.ᵗʰ
1760.

Dear Sir,
    Your letter of y.ͤ 4.ᵗʰ is just now come to my hands; & I cannot suffer y.ͤ Post to
return without taking my thanks to you along with it.¹ I imagined you w.ᵈ wonder
what was become of me; & therefore ⟨you⟩ wrote an account to you of the
reasons w.ᶜʰ had prevented me from joining you at Birmingham, as I hoped &
intended to have done long ago. This Letter I directed to y.ͬ lodgings in London,
supposing you by that time in possession of y.ͬ winter-quarters.² To the reasons you
will find in that letter w.ᶜʰ occasioned me the disappointment of not seeing you,
another has since arisen, w.ᶜʰ I fear will detain me in this place till I return to
Ealing:³ Peter is confined to his Bed by a Fever, & I do not expect he will be in a
condition to drive me again sooner than the end of this month. This being the case, I
have now no chance of saluting you till we both return to the south; where I hope it
will not be long before we are both of us once more well settled. In the mean while
do me the favor to assure M.ͬ Shenstone, that I am extremely sensible of the honor
he does me by his obliging invitation. I much wish it were in my power to take the
benefit of his compliment: but y.ͤ season is now too far advanced.⁴ If you see L.ᵈ
Lyttleton before you leave the country, pray assure him of my best respects. Adieu,
dear sir, & believe me to be most sincerely
                                Y.ͬˢ
                                                        W.ᵐ Melmoth.

The Ladies present their best compliments to you.
Address: To / M.ͬ Dodsley, / at M.ͬ Baskerville's in / Birmingham /
Warwickshire.
Postmark: Nottingham

MS: BL. Add. MS. 35,338, ff. 15–16.

¹ RD's letter not traced.   ² Melmoth's letter not traced.

³ Melmoth's residence, west of central London.
⁴ Shenstone had looked forward to Melmoth's visit. Writing to Percy on 1 October, he complained, "Mʳ Melmoth is not yet come, but is expected every Day" (Williams, p. 563).

To William Shenstone

Dec. 30, [1760]¹

Dear Mr. Shenstone,

I am very sorry you have been so much indisposed since I left you. Bleeding, Vomiting, Purging, the Doctor, and the Disease, are too many Enemies for a Man to struggle with at once; and I heartily wish you Joy of your Victory against such apparent Odds. I am sure, I have very little Reason to suppose, you make Sickness a Plea for Laziness, since you have taken infinitely more Pains on my Account, than you seem disposed to take on your own. Pray think of this, and learn to love yourself as well as you do your Friends; pay as much Regard to your own Fame as you do to theirs, and the World will be obliged to you.

I received a Letter from Mr. Eaves; he tells me, the Fables are finished, and that they will come up to Town this Week.² I shall be very glad of it; for I find even then, that I shall not be able to publish before *February* You tell me the Portrait is *only* delayed till you can see Alcock.³ – Can it be delayed to a more uncertain Time? You do not imagine how many Friends are longing to see it; and here the Winter is passing away, and I am losing the Pleasure of obliging *your* Friends as well as my *own*. I hope I shall see Mr. H–– when he comes to Town.⁴ I expect Mr. D–– soon after New-Year's Day – Would to God you would come with him!⁵ Now is *your* Time to make Interest for Preferment, as Merit seems, at present, the best Recommendation to Favour. Come, and give the Ministry an Opportunity of doing themselves Credit.⁶ With the Compliments of the Season, and my best Wishes in all Seasons, I conclude, and am,

Dear Sir,

ever affectionately yours,

R. Dodsley,

Source: Thomas Hull, *Select Letters* (London, 1778), II, 100–1.

¹ The mention within of the completion of RD's *Select Fables* (1761) and his statement that he will not be able to publish them until February requires this letter to be dated 1760; the *Fables* were published on 23 February 1761 (*PA*).
² Since *Select Fables* was being delivered from Baskerville's in Birmingham, where the volume was printed, "Mr Eaves" would probably be John Eaves, the son of Baskerville's wife by a former marriage, who, adopted by Baskerville, seems to have been his intended successor in the business (Johnson Ball, *William Caslon 1693–1766* (Kineton: Roundwood Press, 1973), p. 400).
³ Shenstone's portrait by Edward Alcock was the subject of former letters.
⁴ Most likely Shenstone's now estranged neighbor, John Scott Hylton. See Hylton's letter on 18 February 1761, note 5.
⁵ Probably Anthony Deane. See RD's letter to Shenstone on 20 February 1759.
⁶ As will become clear later (see Shenstone's letter of 20 November 1762), RD was now laying the groundwork to secure Shenstone a government pension. Such was the probable reason for his errands to Sir Harry Erskine (friend of Lord Bute, Secretary of State) and to Lord Stamford (Shenstone's neighbor and patron) mentioned in his letter to Shenstone on the next 12 February. The time was

ripe, as Boswell, introducing the subject of Samuel Johnson's pension, observed: "The accession of George the Third to the throne of these kingdoms [1760], opened a new and brighter prospect to men of literary merit, who had been honoured with no mark of royal favour in the preceding reign. His present Majesty's education in this country, as well as his taste and beneficence, prompted him to be the patron of science and the arts" (*Life*, I, 372).

From Robert Lowth

Durham Jan. 9. [1761]¹

Dear S.ʳ

I am very glad to hear that your Fables are pretty near re[ady] to make their appearance:² My [little man] is impatient for them; he presents his Comp.ᵗˢ, & desires you to make haste. Be pleas'd, as soon as they are ready, to send one very ha[nd]somely bound, with a Note in *my Name* To the Honᵇˡᵉ Master Legge; to M.ʳ Legge's House at the Treasury:³ & one neatly bound, in my Name likewise, To M.ʳˢ Galand at the Boarding School at Newington Butts: and also to send to me here Six neatly bound.

I shall be in Town probably about the latter end of March: I shall [brin]g up the Grammar with me, a [goo]d deal improved.⁴ I am not re-[sol]ved, whether to print a few Copies [to] give about to friends & critics, to [ge]t their remarks; or to publish an [Ed]ition of a small number, with yᵉ [sa]me design, & to feel the pulse [of] the public. However, in the mean time I should be obliged to you, if you could get or borrow for me, S.ʳ *Thomas Smith, Of the correct writing of English*: printed in 1568; of what size, I know not; but suppose 'tis a small Treatise.⁵ Your Friend M.ʳ Walpole may perhaps be able to give you some information about it. If you should happen to meet with it, keep it till I come; unless you could send it with the Fables.

M.ʳ Spence desires his Service to you: he has something material to say [to] you, but has forgot what. My [Wife] is much at your service; & I t[hank] God, has been perfectly well ever [since] I saw you.

Believe me ever,

Dear S.ʳ
Your most Affectionate
Humble Serv.ᵗ
R. Lowth.

MS: BL. Add. MS. 35,339, ff. 31–2.

¹ Lowth's allusion to the imminent publication of RD's *Select Fables*, an event of 23 February 1761, urges a dating of 1761,

² In his letter to Shenstone a little more than a week earlier, RD announced that Baskerville had completed the printing of *Select Fables* and that his shipment was due in London the first week in January, although the work was not to be published until February.

³ Henry Bilson Legge (1708–64) was currently the Chancellor of the Exchequer.

⁴ Lowth's *Short Introduction to English Grammar*, to be published by Andrew Millar and the Dodsleys in 1762, and for which JD would pay Lowth £50 for a moiety on 18 April 1763, four days after issuing the second edition. (See Appendix B.) The improvements were perhaps in part due to William Melmoth's suggestions. See Melmoth's letter to RD on 20 November 1759 and Lowth's on 19 June 1760.

⁵ *De recta et emendata Linguae Anglicae Scriptione, Dialogus* (1568) by Sir Thomas Smith (1513–77).

To William Shenstone

Feb. 12. [1761][1]

Dear Mr. Shenstone,

Hoping by this Time you are in a fair Way of Recovery, I venture to write to you. Indeed, I was extremely alarmed by the Account Dr. Ash gave me of you in his first Letter, and also by a Line from Miss H—: but by a second Letter from the Doctor, and by a Note afterwards from Mr. Baskerville, I received some Hopes of your Recovery, tho' not enough to encourage me to write to yourself, for fear of the worst.[2] I have been extremely uneasy indeed, and still continue so. Pray let Molly, or somebody, give me a Line, to satisfy me how you are.[3] Don't offer to write yourself, if it be the least uneasy to you: I will be satisfied with hearing from any Hand that you are better, and when you are able to write yourself, I shall be happy. Lord S— is come to Town, and in a Day or two I purpose to wait on him. I have not yet seen Sir H. E—: I think I had better see Lord S— first.[4] God preserve you, and send you a speedy Recovery.

I am ever most affectionately yours.

R. Dodsley.

Source: Thomas Hull, *Select Letters* (London, 1778), II, 102–3.

[1] The allusion to Shenstone's serious illness would seem to make this letter a follow-up to RD's letter to Shenstone on 30 December 1760. Except for a time in early 1758, these months were the only ones during which the poet had been gravely ill. Also, the subject alluded to in note 4 was business of 1761.

[2] None of these letters traced. For Dr John Ash, see Hylton's letters of 1757 and 1758. Probably Miss Catherine Hutton, daughter of William Hutton, the antiquary, bookseller of Birmingham, and author of the *History of Birmingham* (1782). As a fellow bookseller, RD had probably met the noted Hutton and his family through Shenstone. Also, the Huttons were related to Miss Elizabeth Cartwright, who visited the family when returning from her visit to her cousin RD in London during the spring of 1763. Miss Hutton's relations with the Cartwright family are recounted by her cousin Catherine Hutton Beale in *Catherine Hutton and Her Friends* (Birmingham: Cornish Bros., 1895). Writing to Miss Mary Ann Coltman, daughter of Elizabeth Cartwright Coltman, on 7 November 1823, Miss Hutton says: "I thank thee for the manuscripts thou hast sent me; those of Spence, Dodsley, and Hall are very valuable autographs" (Beale, p. 177).

[3] Mary Cutler, Shenstone's housekeeper.

[4] "Lord S—" is most likely Harry Grey, Lord Stamford, Shenstone's friend and patron at nearby Enville Hall. "Sir H. E—" could be Sir Harry Erskine (d. 1765), friend of Lord Bute, a patron of literature and Secretary of State in 1761. See RD's letter of 30 December 1760, note 6.

From John Scott Hylton

Lapall = House. 18[–20] –Feb.[ry] –1761
Hales = Owen near Birmingham

Dear Sir,

On Friday the 13.th Instant, I receiv'd the favour of your Fables, for which I return you my most grateful thanks: they are indeed but a trivial acknowledgement, for your kind Present, yet however small, I could by no means delay the Offering. – To give my Opinion of the Book, would be only ecchoing its merited Fame, & adding a Drop to the Ocean; yet must beg you to accept it however in two or three Lines. The Life of Esop & the Essay on Fable, will be read, I think, with applause, and afford satisfaction to your learned readers; as well as the Fables themselves convey, Improvement to youth.[1] The Head and Tail Peices are very elegant: some few may think the Prints of each Fable too *petite*, yet they may be pleasing to more than *petite* Folks.[2]

I can trace you in many places – M.ʳ Shenstone here & there; yet I should be glad to know (if allowable) each Writer.[3] – Ah! how could I think a Ventle = Trap could be wrought into a Fable?[4] I am sufficiently punished for my Vanity & stand reproved. I fancy it would have been quite unintelligible to all, except *Connoisseurs* & the *Gents of Virtu.*

I meant to have been in London about this time, & to have had the pleasure of seeing you. That I have not so done, is in great measure oweing to my not having compleated my purchase with my Bro.ʳ but that is the Lawyer's fault, & not either his or mine. however I have more chances for my seeing Town this Spring, than I have against it. I wish I could have so agreeable a companion in my journey as M.ʳ Shenstone might have proved, had not Things turned out, *as they are!*[5]

I beg my Compliments to your Bro.ʳ whose Bills I should be glad to have, which I will discharge when I come to Town: in the mean while should be much obliged to him, if he will send in a Box, directed for me to be left at M.ʳ Dan: Winwood's in New = Hall = Walk Birmingham,[6] the Books underneath

London & its Environs – 6 Vol: Bound in Calf & gilt Backs.

Blacklock's poems &c price 2ˢ/6.ᵈ

Allan Ramsay's Poems. the last Edition.

M.ʳ W.ᵐ Hamilton's poetical Works, w.ᶜʰ I see advertised, if you can recommend it.

Also

Millar's Gardener's Kalender, the last Edition

A catalogue of all the Books mentioned in the Monthly Reviews. price 1ˢ/6.ᵈ[7] I hope to have the favour of a few Lines from you soon, and am with the greatest regard

> Dear Sir,
> Your most Obliged
> & Obedient Hum.ᵇ Servant
> John Scott Hylton

20.ᵗʰ Feb.ʳʸ I forgot your Address, therefore am obliged to send this to y.ʳ Brother's – I hope he will send the Books Soon.

MS: Humanities Research Center, University of Texas at Austin, Robert Dodsley / Recipient 1/ Bound, ff. 49–51.

[1] Although RD composed the Essay on Fable prefacing the body of fables, Thomas Percy observes in his notes on *Select Fables* (Bodleian Library, MS Percy, B. 2, f. 24; printed in Brooks, *The Percy Letters*, VII, 236–7) that the Life of Aesop, given to RD by Joseph Spence, had been translated from the French of Claude-Gaspar Bachet de Meziriac (1581–1638), with notes added by Spence.

² Shenstone, for one, had complained about the smallish size of the cuts, when writing to Richard Graves on 1 March (Williams, p. 572). In a letter to Percy in early 1761 (Brooks, 86–8), Shenstone says he had even procured a copy of the fables from Baskerville before the cuts were inserted and that through the help of the painter Edward Alcock he has supplied his own illustrations, which he lists for Percy. (Shenstone's copy is now in the Birmingham Public Library.) Perhaps two of them were the illustrations RD complained of not receiving from Alcock the previous spring (letter to Shenstone between February and April 1760), which necessitated, when RD was anxious to get to press, the employment of Samuel Wale to do the head and tail pieces.

   Indeed one wonders why RD chose to illustrate the first edition of a major production, on fine paper from Baskerville's press, so ineffectually. The edition is divided into three books, containing fifty-four, fifty-three, and fifty-two fables, respectively. Ganged twelve to a plate at the head of each group of twelve fables, the one-inch illustrations of the individual fables demand not only a keen eye but also some page-shuffling to relate them to the fables they illustrate. (For Shenstone's own illustrations, see RD's letter to him on 25 June 1761, note 8.)

³ Unfortunately, no complete list of the fables' authors has survived. In his letter to Percy in early 1761 (Williams, p. 569), Shenstone says he can procure the names, but, if he did, his account is lost. Percy, however, in his notes to the *Select Fables* (Brooks, 234–8) did record the origin of some, although an error in one case renders his attributions suspect. In Volume II, he finds La Motte the source of nos. 2, 3, 6, 9, 10, 15, 16, 19, 39, 42, and 45–53. That Richard Graves authored "The Tuberose and the Sun Flower" and "The Magpye and the Raven" has been shown earlier. Percy claims that Joseph Spence provided "Many of the Ancient and some few of the Modern (but few or none of the Original Fables)." For Shenstone's contribution, see RD's letter on 20 January 1759, note 8. As is clear from the foregoing correspondence, Percy is accurate in attributing many of the Original Fables to Robert Lowth, but *which* is not known. Doubtless some were also contributed by William Melmoth, as RD himself mentioned in former letters. Percy also gives one fable to RD's brother James and claims one for himself, "The Toad and the Gold-fish" (III, 216–17). The rest, he says, were written by RD.

⁴ Apparently RD had rejected Hylton's proposed fable on a "ventraltrap" (archaic form of "vemtletrap," meaning a spiral-shaped sea shell).

⁵ Hylton had for several years found support and admiration from Shenstone for his avocation, the collecting of antiquities, old coins, and natural curiosities. In the summer of 1759, however, Shenstone, with the (innocent?) help of Percy, had some fun with Hylton's proclivity in what has been called "The Tobacco-stopper Plot." Percy supplied Hylton, through Shenstone, with a tobacco-stopper that he had purchased from Moody, a toymaker of Birmingham, and that was pretended to have been made from the wood of a tree planted by Shakespeare, and Shenstone accompanied it with a forged letter from Moody. Shenstone has Moody say that a "Mr. Fitzdottrel, Cabinet-Maker," the source of the tobacco-stopper, had given a deposition before the mayor of Stratford regarding the authenticity of the tree and was now offering the whole tree for sale to Moody, if Hylton would be interested in joining the purchase. Hylton took the bait, but Shenstone intercepted his response to Moody. Since Hylton had expressed interest in only a part of the tree in order to make a bass-relief cup, "Moody" (Shenstone) writes that he will send just a branch and that he has already had such a cup made for Hylton (which Shenstone had). The ruse carried on with the gathering of other bogus antiquities and curiosities until a visit to Birmingham the following year revealed to Hylton that he had been duped. What Shenstone later tossed off as simple good-natured raillery angered Hylton, and a falling-out ensued from which the two neighbors never fully recovered. (See the unravelling of the story in Brooks seriatim, but particularly pp. 28–9, 194–9.) Two weeks after the present letter, Shenstone recounts to Percy a futile effort to resume a relationship with Hylton (Brooks, p. 91).

⁶ Daniel Winwood, a Birmingham toymaker.

⁷ *London and Its Environs,* a six-volume encyclopedia, taking in all aspects of the topography and society for twenty miles around London, and published by the Dodsleys the previous December; *Original Poems by the Rev. Mr. Blacklock and other Scottish Gentlemen* (1760); Ramsay's *Poems* had appeared the previous November; RD had been one of the publishers on 21 January (*PA*) of William Hamilton's *Poems on Several Occasions*; Philip Miller, *The Gardiner's Kalendar, directing what works are necessary to be done every month, in the garden and in the conservatory* (1732; 12th edn., 1760); *A Complete Catalogue of all the Books and Pamphlets published in Great Britain and Ireland, from the Year 1749, inclusive; with their Prices, and References to their Characters in the Monthly Review*, which had appeared the first week of the month.

To William Shenstone

[March or April 1761][1]

Dear Mr. Shenstone,

I am very glad, that with the Return of Spring, your Strength and Spirits begin also to revive. May they proceed and encrease with the Season, and communicate such Health and Vigour to your vernal Shoots, as will encourage and enable them to bud, blossom and bear; for 'tis Pity, that Fruit of so exquisite a Flavour should be lost to the Taste of Mankind! But your Generosity and Benevolence lead you to cultivate and improve the barren Soil and sorry Shrubs of your Friends, to the Neglect of your own rich Fields and more excellent Plantations. You will see in the *Critical Review* a Character of my Fables sufficient to make me excessively proud, were I not inwardly checked by considering how much they owe to your Correction: but I ought to be proud of that, and I am so.[2] They do not, however, yet appear to be much taken Notice of; but it is early Days, and my Friends encourage me to hope, that when they are known, they will not be neglected.[3] I am much pleased with the further Honour you have done them, in getting new Head and Tail Pieces executed, and shall be very impatient till I see your List of the Subjects.[4]

As to your Picture, you may be sure I long to receive it, as it will at once adorn my Room, and do Honour to myself; and I think farther, that as it will, probably not be much mended by Alteration, the best Way will be to send it up without Delay: but this, however, I leave intirely to your Determination.

I have applied to Mr. Rich, in Behalf of Mr. Heron; but he has no Vacancy in his House, nor Room to employ him: as to Mr. Garrick, I am not on such Terms, at present, as to ask a Favour of him.[5] I have spoken also to two or three Printers about Mr. W––,[6] but I have not yet been able to hear of any Thing for him – but I will not give it up: I shall be glad to know what Pay he will expect.

Mr. Jennyns's Book will be published in about a Fortnight – When Mr. Percy's will be ready is uncertain.[7] All your Letters are very acceptable to me, as they assure me of your Friendship; therefore, pray write to me as often as you can, though you should have nothing more to say, than to give me that Assurance.

I am, dear Sir,

ever affectionately yours,

R. Dodsley.

Source: Thomas Hull, *Select Letters* (London, 1778), I, 300–2.

[1] RD's thanking Shenstone for his editing of the *Select Fables* (now published), his mentioning of the "Return of Spring," his alluding to the *Critical Review*'s praise of the *Fables* (reviewed in the February *Critical Review* published on 2 March 1761), and his forecasting the publication of Soame Jenyns's book, *Miscellaneous Pieces in Two Volumes* (*PA*, 10 May 1761), taken together, argue for a March or April dating of the letter, and not a 5 January date as assigned by Hull.

[2] The reviewer had written: "[Dodsley's] unaffected ease, natural elegance, and propriety of character, cannot we think, be surpassed. Mr. Dodsley has not only given the best rules for writing apologues, but he has exhibited the most perfect examples of these rules, and is himself the pattern of that beautiful simplicity which he recommends. We must confess we never perused any thing in this kind with so much satisfaction . . . In a word, we may venture to recommend Mr. Dodsley as the best prose-writer of apologues of this or any other country."

[3] In a letter to Percy in April (Williams, p. 576), Shenstone says, "Dodsley has sold 2000 of his Fables, & begins to talk of second & third editions." He repeats the same figure in a letter to Graves on 2 May (Williams, p. 578) but adds that RD "complained that he should *lose* thirty pounds by my neighbor Baskerville's impression; and that he should not be more than ten pounds gainer, upon the *whole*." (As might be expected, the "common," or school, edition had proved a sounder economic venture than Baskerville's edition on fine paper.) Although Shenstone acknowledges having encouraged RD to print one more edition (with new illustrations) at Baskerville's "for the polite world," he urges RD not to become discouraged about the work's future return: "I told him it was enough, in books of *this sort*, if the first edition paved the way for their future establishment in schools. And surely so it is: for a book of this kind, once established, becomes an absolute estate for many years." And so it would become, although RD would not live to fully appreciate the merit of Shenstone's judgment.

[4] See RD's letter to Shenstone of 25 June, note 8.

[5] In the two allusions to Heron in Shenstone's letters (Williams, pp. 540, 554), Shenstone refers to him as "Poor Heron." On 8 March 1760, he writes to Hylton: "Poor Heron's Letters, particularly his account of the *thriving* trade he carries on, are as humorous as may be. He seems to have wit, and a ready application of ye promiscuous matters he has perused – I would advise him not to waste his talent upon epistles, but to write a Novel; or detach'd Characters; or little essays, or somew^t, by wch he may get money and recommend himself to Friends" (p. 554). Only Shenstone's connection with Thomas Blacklock and the writing of plays would suggest that this is the same Robert Heron, who, in his youth, served as a guide to the blind poet and as an assistant to Hugh Blair. This Heron produced plays, pamphlets, travels, biographies, and translations. He wrote *The Comforts of Life* while imprisoned in Newgate, where he died in 1807. No further mention of him occurs in RD's correspondence.

[6] Unidentified.

[7] For Jenyns, see note 1. Thomas Percy's *Hau Kiou Choaan* would not appear until 14 November (*PA*).

To Elizabeth Cartwright[1]

May 1st [1761][2]

Dear *Cousin*

The receit of your agreeable Letter reproaches me with a want of Politeness in not accompanying my triffling Present with a line or two to desire your acceptance of it.[3] However, if it has afforded You any pleasure, I hope you will forgive me. I cannot possitively determine about the time that I shall be in Derbyshire, but it certainly will not be before July: however, you so elegantly describe the Beauties of your Village, that I shall certainly endeavour to see them before they begin to fade. As to my Entertainment, since You remember the Fable, You know the Country Mouse was happier than her friend the Courtier: as all Creatures, both Mice and Men, will be, the more simply they fare.[4] For my own particular, (and I will quote You a better Poet for it than you quoted to me)

I have (with Pope) the Virtue & the Art,
To live on little, with a cheerful heart. –
Nor am I one among those curious Men,
Who chuse a Pheasant still before a Hen. –
When the tired Glutton labours thro' a Treat,
He finds no relish in the sweetest meat;
He calls for something bitter, something sour,
And the rich feast concludes extreamly poor.[5]

But You have Farms, and Dairies, and Gardens: how many Dainties do these afford? Have you not new-milk-whey? Curds and Cream? Eggs and Bacon? nay Bacon & Fowls upon occasion? Have you not Pease and Beans, and Spinage and Brocoli? The Plenty of a Farm, and the Delicacies of a Garden. By your own Confession, You enjoy in Flowers the sweetest Perfumes of Nature: and do not your Groves afford You a band of *M*usic whenever You dine? And whenever you repose are You not attended with the profoundest Silence? Is not this the truest Elegance, the highest Pomp? And, after all, You pretend to apologize for your Entertainment. I will come and prove to You that you live in the greatest Luxury.

I desire my Compliments to M.ʳ Giffard; and tho' he has taken himself out of the way of a Bishoprick, I hope he is not removed out of the reach of Happiness; and that is a better thing.[6] He perhaps may dispute this point with me: if he does, pray tell him

_____He prefers, I doubt,

the Rogue with Venison, to a Saint without.[7]

If you should chance to see my good Friends Mʳ Thackray and M.ʳ Bradshaw, I could wish to be kindly remembered to them.[8] My best Respects attend upon my Cousins both known and unknown: and, tho' last not least in love, I beg You will accept of the same your self from,

> Dear Madam,
> Your affectionate Cousin
>
> R Dodsley

MS: Leicester Record Office, 15D57/2.

[1] Elizabeth Cartwright (1737–1811), the "Lilly of Duffield," was the only daughter of Samuel Cartwright (d. 1792) of Duffield, Derbyshire. In 1766, she married John Coltman of St Nicholas Street, Leicester, a noted Midlands hosier during the latter half of the eighteenth century. RD seems not to have known of his "cousin" until she was called to his attention by Shenstone. (See RD's letter to Shenstone on 22 August 1758.) From their first meeting in Duffield during the summer of 1758, she seems to have ignited a spark in the aging RD and prompted a regular "Dutch uncle" correspondence through the early 1760s until his death. Through RD she probably met Joseph Spence, several of whose letters are preserved among the family papers. RD chaperoned her about London during the spring of 1763. (See his letters of that period.) A talented young lady, she executed paper landscapes, one of which RD saw fit to present to the Queen. Regrettably, only one of her letters to RD is extant, but that letter shows an especially personable and clever style.

[2] Although the year is obscured on the manuscript, Catherine Hutton Beale, who had either access to or ownership of the manuscript when preparing her *Catherine Hutton and Her Friends* (Birmingham: Cornish Bros., 1895) prints the letter (pp. 13–14) with a 1761 dating. Straus does likewise (p. 246). Internal evidence argues the same. RD says he will be going to Derby in July, something he also tells Shenstone in a letter of 25 June 1761. Also RD makes a veiled reference to a present he recently sent Miss Cartwright, which, because he goes on to allude to a particular fable, most likely was a copy of his *Select Fables*, recently published.   [3] Letter not traced. For RD's "triffling Present," see note 2.

[4] "The Court and Country-Mouse" (RD's *Select Fables*, I, 38–39) tells the story of a country mouse who accepts an invitation from a city mouse to visit the Court. When they arrive, they happen upon the remnants of a sumptuous meal, but are soon routed, in turn, by a dog, a cat, and servants. The moral: even poverty with peace is preferable to the greatest affluence amidst anxiety.

[5] RD's adaptation from Pope's *Second Satire of the Second Book of Horace*, ll. 1–2, 17–18, 31–34; the last two couplets are verbatim from Pope.

6 The Rev. Richard Gifford (1725–1807), Vicar of Duffield from 1759 until his death. In 1753, RD had published Gifford's *Contemplation. A Poem* and in that year reports to Joseph Warton that Gifford accompanied him and his wife on a trip. Perhaps RD's comment regarding the Vicar's taking himself "out of the way of a Bishoprick" refers to Gifford's settling down in the village of Duffield. For an account of Gifford, see John Nichols, *Illustrations of Literature* (1828), V, 182–97.

7 RD's borrowing from Pope's *Moral Essays*, I, 78–80.

8 See RD's letters to Thackray. Perhaps Joseph Bradshaw of Duffield (d. *c.* 1770). Miss Joan Sinar, Archivist of Derbyshire, tells me that Bradshaw was a warden of the parish of St Alkmund, Duffield, and that his signature, allowing the payment of accounts during the period 1737–48, is occasionally found in the parish Wardens' Book. Mrs Jane Hampartumian, Assistant Archivist, Lichfield Joint Record Office, adds that Bradshaw's will was probated in 1770.

To William Shenstone

June 25. [1761][1]

Dear Sir,

Your Picture really affords me many pleasing Reflections, and I have ordered the Frame to be full gilt, whilst I am out of town, that it may not give you any unpleasing ones.[2] I am going to *Derby* and *Nottingham* for three Weeks or a Month: I can't stay longer, as I must attend to the Press, having put my Fables in Hand for a new Edition.[3] I have last *Monday* sent you Percy's Novel; I sent it unbound, as we had not Time to bind it: it will not be published till the Beginning of next Winter.[4] I have sent you the *Fables*, bound in *Morocco*,[5] and the common Edition in Boards, for your future Corrections: but I would not have you begin till you see the next Edition, as I hope you will find it altered somewhat for the better; I will send you one of them as soon as it is printed.[6] You will find, likewise, in the Parcel, Soame Jennyns's Works, and a Pamphlet or two;[7] also the Fables, with your Drawings in them, many of which I like extremely; that at the Head of the second I approve the least: but those that are placed in the Life, I think should be transferred to the Head and Tail-Pieces of the Fables – but there will be Time enough to talk of this hereafter.[8] As to Italics, I believe I shall steer a middle Course; and make Use only of a few.[9] I send you a List of some Statues, about the same Size with that Pair you have;

DEMOSTHENES	LOCKE	CHAUCER	SHAKESPEARE
and	and	and	and
CICERO,	NEWTON,	SPENCER,	MILTON.

When you have fixed upon which Pair you will have, you will let me know whether you will have them white or bronzed, and what Kind of a Bronze.

I really don't know how to appease Mr. W——. I told him, I was very sorry I had pretended to meddle with his Ode, and begged his Pardon. He is still unappeased, writes me another angry Letter, and desires me to give him my Reasons for every Alteration; this it is impossible for me to do, as I have forgot how it originally was; and I really think it of very little Consequence, as no Name appears to it.[10]

Mr. Stuart is just now with me, and desires his Compliments. He thinks of seeing your Place the latter End of this Summer, and believes the Attorney-General, Mr.

Pratt, will be with him.[11] I have just been struck with the bad News, that Mr. ——
has lost his Wife.[12] You will perceive I write in a Hurry; Mr. Stuart sits by me.

I am

ever affectionately yours

R. Dodsley.

Source: Thomas Hull, *Select Letters* (London, 1778), II, 112–14.

[1] Percy's Chinese novel, *Hau Kiou Choaan*, has already been printed for Tully's Head, RD says, and will be published at the beginning of the winter. It was published on 14 November 1761 (*PA*). Also RD's first edition of his *Select Fables of Esop* had appeared in February 1761 and the second edition, for schools ("common Edition"), on 21 April (*PA*). Falling between the appearance of these editions of the *Fables* and that of Percy's novel, the letter must be of 1761.

[2] Shenstone's portrait by Alcock, the subject of past letters, now hangs in the National Portrait Gallery.

[3] That is, the third edition of the *Fables*. But his plans seem to have been delayed, for it would not appear until 17 March 1762 (*PA*). Perhaps the appearance of another edition of the late Samuel Richardson's *Aesop's Fables* on 25 October (*PA*) influenced his decision.

[4] See note 1.

[5] Perhaps this was a first edition of the *Fables* that had been binding for Shenstone. Shenstone's personal copy of the *Fables*, first edition printed by Baskerville and bound in morocco, sold at Sotheby's on 2 October 1978, lot 229.

[6] The "common Edition," a London printing on 21 April and intended for instruction in schools; the "next Edition" refers to the third edition. (See note 1.)

[7] See RD's last letter to Shenstone, note 1.

[8] Writing to both Percy (Brooks, pp. 86–8) and Graves (Williams, p. 572), Shenstone confesses that, disliking the illustrations RD had chosen for *Select Fables*, he had obtained a copy of the work from Baskerville before the cuts were inserted and had "my painter" (Edward Alcock) "supply the vacancies." At some length, Shenstone goes on to describe the individual drawings, probably those that RD alludes to above. However despite the bookseller's apparent liking for some of Shenstone's illustrations, none of them found a place in subsequent editions, including that by Baskerville in 1764. RD simply had the plates for the frontispiece and for the individual fables recut. But they were hardly improved, at least in terms of Shenstone's criticism. On the other hand, many of the emendations to the Index found in Shenstone's own copy of the first edition (in his own hand) were incorporated in the cheap school editions of 1762 and in Baskerville's of 1764. The 1762 editions also carried a new Preface and Life of Esop. The former indicated: "The Life of Esop prefixed to the former editions of these Fables having been thought not so full and satisfactory as it might have been, a learned and ingenious Friend has been so kind as to consult the ancient Writers who have made any mention of Esop."

Shenstone's illustrations in his personal copy either substitute for or supplement RD's originals. (For a description of RD's, see John Scott Hylton's letter on 18 February 1761, note 2.) He replaced the frontispiece and the title-page vignette with his own; added further illustration at the head and tail of the Preface, at the head of each chapter of the life of Esop, and at each of the sections of the essay on fable; omitted RD's minuscule, ganged illustrations for the individual fables, substituting his own at the head and tail of each of the three books of fables. Throughout the books, appear various abstract designs of curling lines, some simply pencilled in. Perhaps most importantly, Shenstone's illustrations differ from RD's in terms of their function. Whereas RD's attempt to illustrate each fable literally and narratively, Shenstone's – typically portraying scenes of youth admiring figures of wisdom – focus upon the instructive value of fables, thereby more properly addressing RD's stated intention and audience for the work.

Shenstone's copy of the *Fables* containing Alcock's wash drawings was purchased at Sotheby's on 23 July 1956 for the University of Birmingham Library (where it is now in the Baskerville Collection, 44A). Because it came to light late in my research, and because it was too fragile for photocopying, I have not been able to inspect the set personally. The foregoing comments are derived from pages of three British university theses kindly supplied by the following authors to whom I am much indebted: Francis Burns (Newman College, Birmingham), "William Shenstone: A Biographical and Critical Study" (University of Sheffield, 1970); Sylvia I. Martin (Director, Burchell & Martin Ltd., Birmingham), "Illustrations in Baskerville's Printed Books" (University of Birmingham, 1977); Robert A. McKee (Department of Librarianship, Birmingham Polytechnic), "A Commentary on the Life and Works of William Shenstone" (University of Birmingham, 1976). See also Philip Gaskell, *John Baskerville, A Bibliography* (Cambridge University Press, 1959), Item 14.

9 Shenstone's own manuscripts show him to have been an inveterate underliner (italicizer), and as a reader and corrector of RD's modern fables, he himself might have been occasionally responsible for their use. Curiously, when writing to Graves on 2 May (Williams, p. 569), he aligns himself with Burke, Lowth, Melmoth, and Spence. who, he says, had tried to discourage RD from using italics at all.

10 Perhaps Christopher Wren (1711–71), grandson of the architect and friend and neighbor of Shenstone. "An English Sapphic," by Wren, had appeared anonymously in the *London Magazine* (1761, p. 214). This was a variant (RD's alteration?) of the text Shenstone had copied into his Miscellany about this time (Ian Gorden, ed. *Shenstone's Miscellany 1758–1763*, pp. 110, 158).

11 Most likely James "Athenian" Stuart (1713–88), painter and architect, and together with RD a member of the Society for the Encouragement of Arts, Manufactures and Commerce; Charles Pratt (1714–94), Attorney-General since 1757.

12 Perhaps refers to the death of William Melmoth's wife, which had been announced in the *Public Advertiser* this very day.

To [Elizabeth Cartwright] [1]

Sep. 27.th [1761] [2]

Dear Madam

I am afraid You will think me a very slow Correspondent; and, to confess the truth, I think my self so. However, I beg You will not imagine my Silence proceeds either from want of Respect or Affection. But if you should ask me from what it proceeds, I must own I should be at a loss what to say, unless You will admit of the honest but unpolite excuse of Laziness. I have put into a neat gilt Frame your very excellent Favour; I look upon it as one of the chief Ornaments of my Room, & I assure You it is highly admired by the best Judges, even by some Ladies who have seen extream fine things of that kind in the Nunneries abroad.

Our glorious Coronation is now over; I wish You had been here to have seen it: as to my self, I durst not venture: but by all accounts it was the most superb and magnificent Sight that ever was exhibited in Europe. The amazing number of Spectators, and the Joy that appeared in every Countenance; the Richness of the Cloaths, the elegant Patterns of the Silks, & their vast variety; the Profusion of Jewels, the Beauty of the Ladies, set off by all that Art & Elegance, assisted by Wealth, could furnish; displayed a Scene so grand and so enchanting, that some of the Spectators have declared they could scarce forbear imagining themselves transported to Fairy-Land.

If You are still at my Cousin Sanders's,[3] I beg you will give my Compliments to her, and to y.e Family, & many thanks for all Civilities there:[4] if You are so little of a Rake as to be got home again, pray let me be most kindly remembered to all friends at Duffield: & also to dear M.r Thackray whenever You or your Papa may chance to see him.[5] My Sister desires her Respects to You & to my Cousins, and I am with great truth & sincerity

Dear Cousin

Your most faithful & obed[t] Serv[t]

R Dodsley

MS: Royal Archives, Windsor Castle, RA Add 2/40. Printed by the gracious permission of Her Majesty the Queen.

[1] Undoubtedly to Elizabeth Cartwright, RD's only known female correspondent at Duffield. (See ten other letters to her in the early 1760s.) In his letter to her on 15 December 1763, RD acknowledges the receipt of her "exceeding pretty Landskip for M[r] Spence," and that by the latter's order "have got it fram'd in the same manner that mine is," a reasonably clear reference to "one of the chief Ornaments of my Room" mentioned here. Furthermore RD had visited Duffield a few months earlier; consequently his wish to be remembered to friends there, his mentioning her papa and the local Mr Thackray (alluded to in other letters to Miss Cartwright) help to secure the identification.
[2] The year is certain because RD includes an account of the recent "glorious Coronation" of George III, an event of 22 September 1761.   [3] An unidentified cousin.   [4] See note 1.
[5] See RD's letter to Thackray on 16 January 1758.

From Richard Graves

Claverton, 10 Jan. 1762

Dear S[r]

M[r] Shenstone desires me to make any remarks that occur upon these designs – & transmit them to you – I have never turn'd my thoughts this way – But 'tis obvious to remark. That the first will be most interesting to those who have a fondness for Horace himself – & the latter to those who are pleas'd with M[r] Baskerville's elegant manner of adorning [ye] Classicks – I am alittle dubious about the propriety of representing a real Poet with an allegorical harp – It might lead a modern Gentleman into a mistaken notion – that the Roman Poets sang their Ballads about the Streets to their Instruments.[1] –

M[r] Shenstone asks my permission to insert that popular Epigram upon our young monarch in the London Mag – at the same time that he informs me it is too late to refuse my Assent[2] – If I thought such a trifle could contribute the least degree of Credit to a work in which I find You have some small share – I should be very well pleas'd with my friends communication of them – I take it for granted no initial Letters – or the least hint will be given of the Authors –

M[r] Shenstone us'd to be pleas'd with these Lines upon proclaiming war ag[st] France in the Year 44 – They are now applicable to the war with Spain.[3] I was struck with the insignificance of a little market town in Glostershire but to make the humor generally relish'd, it. sh[d] be Brentford or some place near the metropolis

War proclaim'd at Bren'ford –

a Climax

Written in y[e] year 1744 –

> Brittain at length her wrath declares
> And now to meet her Foe prepares
> Bellona mounts her Iron car
> Grac'd with ye implements of war –
> *Augusta* sounds the dread alarm   London
> And all our Ports their Gallies arm.
> Bristol & York have Heralds sent
> Denouncing George's fell intent
> Nay – Brentford now proclaims defiance
> Let Bourbon tremble at th' alliance⁴ –

I am (in a hurry as usual) S^r

Y^r affect. humb. ser^t

Ric. Graves

MS: Somerset County Record Office, DD/SK, 28/1, 12.

¹ The subject of this paragraph is the publication of Baskerville's edition of Horace (1762). For Shenstone's role in the production of the edition, see the appropriate letters in Williams for 1762 and 1763, and particularly Shenstone's next letter to RD, which is more fully annotated in my article "Four New Shenstone Letters," *PLL* 11 (1975), 264–78. This Graves letter, with the accompanying designs, doubtless is the one Shenstone anxiously anticipated when writing to John Livie, the editor of Baskerville's Horace, on 14 January 1762: "Dodsley says, in his Letter of to-day, that he has not received the Designs from *Bath* – but he certainly *has* before ye date of this." (RD's letter has not been traced, but for the text of Shenstone's to Livie, see *PLL* article, above.)

² Graves's "The Patriot King: or George the Third" would appear on p. 44 of the *London Magazine* for January 1762.

³ Despite having signed a peace treaty with France and Spain the previous August, England had once again declared war on France eight days before this letter was written.

⁴ This piece too would appear on p. 44 of the *London Magazine* for January 1762, thereby explaining Graves's use of the plural "Authors" in the close of the letter's second paragraph. In the *London Magazine*, the title is simplified to "War declared at Brentford. A Climax," line 6 is missing, and a few verbal changes occur.

From George Steevens

[Hunt]ingdon Jan [1762?]¹

Mr Dodsley.

You may perhaps think that I am very negligent [of] my friends for not having written to you before to [en]quire after your health and to apologise for having impos'd [upon] you in the account I gave of the poem you are now p[rep]aring to publish; but our march being so very sudden, [I] had not leisure to settle my own affairs which have emp[loy'd a] great part of my time since I have been here, and wha[t] with our necessary duty and marching backwards & forwards to make room for other regiments I have scarce had an hour to myself.

This poem is the work of a man who is of all others dearest to me in the world; he was afraid of declaring himself to be the author at once for fear of [its] being disapproved, tho I always told him that he had no reason to doubt of its success; and if my judgment should be found deceitful, he would be sure to find himself treated with candour and tenderness even tho it should be rejected.

Your very genteel behaviour to him I find from what he writes has made him your own for ever; and the great opinion I have of Mr Dodsley independent of his literary merit will tempt me the first leisure I [have] [?] his hands being fully resolved to be guided by ⟨your⟩ his judgme[nt;] if he shall approve it I ask no other praise, if he rejects it I assure him it shall never appear as a candidate for publication any where else.

I durst say you will not only find ⟨in⟩ Mr Keate a genteel scholar; but as you know him more intimately, a valuable friend with every amiable and good quality that either gives us pleasure or satisfaction; and I assure you it is no small joy to me to think I have been the means of introducing him to you: I confess I am under many obligations to you but shall never be able to make you a more valuable return than I have already done in ⟨making⟩ bringing you acquainted with a man whom I have so great an opinion of.[2]

As soon as we are sent back into Essex (which I suppose will hardly be before there is a peace) I shall persuade him to revise several other things he has by him which I durst say will meet with your approbation; but unfortunately for me I have been prevented either by illness or one accident or another from being so much in his company as I could have wish'd, and he pays that partial regard to me never to undertake a thing of that kind without my knowledge; which deference shewn to me I know not how to acknowlege unless it be by appearing sollicitous, as, I shall always really be, for the sucess of every thing he attempts, and occasiond my [?] him to appear [before] you without visible concern, it was necessary that [you] should not think the performance was his own.

I beg the favour of you not to mention to him that I have said he has several other things by [him] because he might think that a breach of friendship wh[en] I only would have to be the means of making the wor[ld] as well as you more acquainted with him.

As soon as the poem is publishd I beg the favour that you will desire your Brother to send me [some] copies of it to Huntingdon, directed to Geo: Steevens of the first battalion of the Essex Militia at the headquart[ers] at Huntingdon.

I am deeply indebted to your brother and ough[t] to be ashamed of myself to own it, but whenever he chuse[s] to be paid (tho I shall be in London in a short time mysel[f)] he need only to send me his bill with a line & it shall be paid immediately.

I am Sir with the compliments of the season and the sincerest wishes for your health and happiness.

Your most obliged
humble Servt
Geo: Steevens.

Let a quire of Mr Baskervilles paper be sent with the books.

I would not have Mr Keate know that I have sent for those copies of his poem because he will insist on paying for them

MS: Folger Shakespeare Library C. b. 11(1).

The letter is most likely of 1762, for the Dodsleys' first publication of a George Keate poem – the subject of the letter – occurred on 23 February 1762 (*PA*), when *An Epistle from Lady Jane Gray to Lord Guildford Dudley* was issued from Tully's Head. The 23 February date also fits in nicely with Steevens's speaking of Keate's verses as "the poem you are now p[rep]aring to publish." Apparently the earlier publication by the Dodsleys of Keate's *A Short Account of the Ancient History, Present Government, and Laws of the Republic of Geneva* (*PA*, 11 March, 1761) did not involve a meeting with the author.

² Keate's poem *The Alps* would be published by James Dodsley in April 1763 and his *The Ruins of Netley Abbey*, in February 1764. In fact, Keate relied on Tully's Head for further publications, selling James Dodsley the copyright to his *Works* (2 vols.) for 150 guineas in 1781. (See Appendix E.)

From William Shenstone

[Feb: 11.th 1762][1]

Dear Mr Dodsley,

I have spoken to Mr Livie upon the Subject of his dedication; & he agrees with Me that there *can* be no properer person to procure the Leave we want y.^{n} Mr Dalton.[2] Suppress therefore, if you please, my Letter to Mr Lackey; and engage Mr Dalton, as soon as ever you can, to do his best offices in this affair.[3] They wait only for the Plates; & for my Lord's answer, before they can order his Arms to be engraved. I *blundered* in regard to Livie's University; a blunder so much the more unlucky, as they have *no* Masters of Arts at Edingburgh – He was of Aberdeen – As to the rest, you will give Mr Dalton any proper information my Letter affords you. Livie does *not* expect a Present; He will be perfectly satisfied, if the work entitle him to any degree of Lord Bute's esteem: And this Mr Dalton m[ay] *say*, should his Lordship give him an opportunity. Perhaps it need not be mentioned that Livie is a *Scotchman*; unless my Lord should make particular Enquiry – *Betwixt Friends*, I believe, that, having no establishment, he means hereafter to ask some little matter, by means of a scotch Lady who is my Lord's relation.

The smaller drawing you enclosed is really a perfect beauty, & must be executed at all events. When I return it, which I mean to do on saturday, I shall give the graver one or two directions.[4]

I wish I could think as highly of the Frontispiece. In truth, it does not please me; & what to do, I cannot tell. The designer does not seem to enter into the spirit of ye Story; A single pillar of ye temple had been sufficient. and the circumstance of the Shield hung upon ye Pillar with ye motto, being wholly omitted, throws the whole *Stress* upon the merit of the *two Figures in the Foreground* – I am sorry to say, these do not answer. Maecenas appears with no dignity, & Horace's attitude I can't explain. If the Floor had been raised one step where the Patron sits; & his Person, tall; or his Chair embellished a little &c And if Horace were shorter, (as his Stature was) his attitude, no way violent – & his head, down-cast; it would perhaps have removed some of my Objections – But if there were no possibility of hanging a Shield &c on a *Piece* of a temple, & so making ye back ground *important* (as the designer surely might have done) yet there evidently were means of rendering it more *beautifull*, than it appears here. Hayman certainly should have been y.ᵉ Man! But more of this when I write on saturday.⁵

When shall I see Baptista Porta? as also ⟨?⟩ "the *Frontispiece*" only to the ornaments &c of temples and churches?⁶ The verses in the Lond. Magazine are tolerably well printed, tho my punctuation is not observed⁷ – Y.ʳ Brother was to send me also the annual Registers; all except that for the year 1759.⁸ I believe Woodhouse has or *will* desire Y.ʳ Brother to supply him with the few magazines he distributes here⁹ – This Letter is written amid much hurry & confusion of Brain, when I can really express nothing, to my mind; much less the esteem & affection with which I am, dear Sir,

Y.ʳ most obed.ᵗ

W Shenstone

MS: Houghton Library, Harvard, ALS File.

¹ Without the holograph, and therefore dependent upon Thomas Hull's text (*Select Letters*, 1778), both Duncan Mallam and Marjorie Williams date this letter as 1761. Although the "Feb: 11ᵗʰ 1762" date on the holograph seems clearly not in Shenstone's hand, internal evidence bears it out. Shenstone's familiarity with John Livie, the corrector of Baskerville's *Horace*, is here too advanced to date the letter 1761. Secondly, the Shenstone–RD circle's correspondence of February 1761 was totally concerned with RD's publication of his *Select Fables*, and Baskerville's *Horace* is never mentioned, whereas the reverse is the case in 1762. Although the "Feb: 11ᵗʰ" cannot be certified exactly, internal evidence requires that the letter be a product of the period between 14 January and 3 March, the first date representing Shenstone's letter to Livie (see below) and the second a letter to Thomas Percy (Williams, p. 619). In the first Shenstone indicates that RD had yet to engage Samuel Wale as the designer, but here he is commenting on designs that RD has already sent him. In his 3 March letter, Shenstone tells Percy that Lord Bute accepts the dedication, whereas at this point RD has yet to secure that permission. For a fuller consideration of the dating of this letter (together with the text of the letter to Livie alluded to above), see my "Four New Shenstone Letters," *Papers in Language & Literature*, 11 (1975), 264–78.

² John Livie, classicist and tutor to the family of the noted Birmingham physician and chemist John Roebuck, was Baskerville's editor/corrector for the printer's edition of *Horace*. Richard Dalton (1715?–91), librarian to George III and Keeper of the Royal Pictures (through the favor of Lord Bute, the Secretary of State) was the appropriate person to secure Lord Bute's acceptance of the dedication of Baskerville's *Horace*. Living at St James's Palace, Dalton had regular access to the Secretary of State.

³ "Lackey" is probably Shenstone's phonetic spelling of the name of Stephen Martin Leake (1702–73), who, as Garter King-of-Arms, had initially been thought by Shenstone to be the proper person for interceding with Bute and for acquiring his coat of arms. It was Leake's job to administer all matters concerned with the granting of arms.

⁴ Probably the drawing that appeared on the title page, the only other illustration besides the frontispiece that was printed in the first edition. It shows Athene – patroness of the arts and protectress of children – seated with a British shield resting against her right thigh and a long spear against her left shoulder, while her right arm draws a youth toward an open volume of Horace's works atop a pedestal, to which she is pointing with her left hand.

⁵ Despite Shenstone's objections and his attempt to offer a substitute (see his letter to Livie on 24 February in my *PLL* article), Samuel Wale's drawing for the frontispiece was printed without alteration.

⁶ Giambattista Porta (*c.* 1538–1615), Italian physicist. R&JD had published on 25 April 1761 *The Ornaments of Churches considered* by William Hole.

⁷ Five poems in the *London Magazine* for January 1762 had probably received Shenstone's correction, though none were actually his: "To William Shenstone, Esq., The Production of a half hour's Leisure. August 30, 1761" by "Cotswouldia"; "The Patriot King: or, George the Third" and "War declared

at Brentford, A Climax" by Richard Graves; "To Miss Loggin; from Miss Whately" and "To Mr. S. upon his desiring her to paint his character" by Miss Whately.

⁸ The Dodsleys began publishing the *Annual Register* in 1759, with Edmund Burke as the editor/ compiler. For the contract with Burke and his receipts for payment, see Appendix B.

⁹ James Woodhouse. See RD's letter to Shenstone on 1 December 1759, note 1. Apparently the shoemaker-poet also distributed periodicals.

From Robert Lowth

Durham Mar. 5. 1762.

Dear Sᵣ

I am very glad to find the Public has so good an Appetite for Grammer: but hope, that what we have already treated them with, will stay their stomachs for some time. For I shall certainly wait for the opinions of the Critics; & when I have leisure, will endeavour to give it all the improvements I can. So that possibly by about this time two years we may be able to give them another Edition.¹

I desired you in my last, about 3 weeks ago, to enquire at Mᵣ Best's the Hanover Secretary for a Pacquet left with him by Professor Michaelis of Gottingen for me.² It is not come by the Carrier of this week; & you mention nothing of it in your Letter; perhaps Your Brother might enquire for it. However, if it is not already sent, it will be too late now; for I think of setting out for London about the end of this Month. – I have heard from Mᵣ Spence, since he has been in Nottinghamshire. – I have the pleasure of informing you, that my Wife has just now brought a little Boy into the world.

Dear Sᵣ

Yours most Affᶦʸ

R. Lowth.

Address: To Mᵣ Robᵗ Dodsley / at Tully's Head / Pall Mall.

MS: BL. Add. MS. 35,339, ff. 27–8.

¹ Together with Andrew Millar, the Dodsleys had published Lowth's *Short Introduction to English Grammar* on 8 February (*PA*) and apparently had already been pressing the author for a second edition. Although Lowth here suggests a two-year wait, probably he succumbed to the favorable reviews which had already begun to appear, for a second edition was published in April 1763. The *Monthly Review* would print a very favorable account in its July issue (pp. 37–41) and the *Critical Review* gave a laudatory but tempered review the previous month (pp. 510–4).

² William Best (d. 1785). Johann David Michaelis (1717–91) contributed to the annotation of the second edition of Lowth's *De Sacra Poesi Hebraiorum* (1763). The package Lowth was seeking through RD might have been the notes for the revision of this work, which had first been printed in 1753.

From William Melmoth

Bath, Mar: 13ᵗʰ 1762.

Dear Sir,

I cannot send a frank to your Brother without slipping in a line or two to yourself, tho' I have nothing more material to trouble you with than to express my concern for the account you gave me of your own health, & to say that mine is tollerabl well. I am persuaded if you c^d contrive to spend some part of your winters at Bath you w^d pass the rest of the year with more freedom from y^r unwelcome visitor:[1] regret therefore, for your sake as well as my own, that any affairs sh^d occasion you t drive the thoughts of a journey hither so far off as ⟨till⟩ to Autumn. Before that tim (if a Peace sh^d take place; of wch it seems, there is some faint glimmering) I ma perhaps be induced to make a tour ⟨of⟩ to ye Southern part of France: a scene wch have long wished to view, & wch health no less than curiosity w^d tempt me to visi the first favorable opportunity.[2]

Dr Lowth was so very obliging as to favour me with a present of his grammar.[3] I is clear, succinct, & elegant; & will contribute more towards recovering ou language from its vague, uncertain State, than any performance of the same kin that ever was published. As I know not where the very ingenious author is to b found, I must request you to forward the inclosed acknowledgement to him.

Farewell, dear Sir, I am most affectionately yours
Wm Melmoth

Address: To | Mr Dodsley Senr

MS: BL. Add MS. 35,338, ff. 17–18.

[1] The gout.
[2] Although England had signed a peace treaty with France and Spain at Paris on 15 August 176 rivalry for supremacy of the seas and for control of the colonies caused England to declare war agai on 2 January 1762. Although this war was of short duration, a preliminary treaty was not signed unt 3 November, and then not confirmed until the Treaty of Paris on 10 February 1763. It is not likel then, that Melmoth toured southern France in the autumn of 1762. At least he had not as of earl September, for RD's letter to Shenstone on 18 September reports having seen him in Bath at that time
[3] No doubt Lowth's gift to Melmoth for having given, a few years earlier, a critical reading to th former's *Short Introduction to English Grammar* that had just been published by Andrew Millar and R on 8 February (*PA*). See Melmoth's letter on 20 November 1759, as well as Lowth's on 19 June 1760

To Elizabeth Cartwright

The Leasowes, July 26, 176

Dear Madam, –

I did not receive your kind accusatory letter till a few days ago, at the Leasowe where I have been for about a month past[1] . . . Mr. Shenstone desires hi compliments to you; he is preparing to publish his works by subscription, in on volume, quarto, at a guinea, and I fancy he will have a large number o subscribers.[2] Pray give my compliments to Mr. Gifford, and tell him we have los Mrs. Brooke and Miss Moore; they are in Lincolnshire, and are preparing to go t Quebec.[3]

Your affecting story of the poor miller and is wife has raised my curiosity so muc as to make me wish you would give me a relation of the whole, with all i circumstances. You wish me to send you some people of taste to reside in you village, that you might learn politeness; upon my word you want them not, and we have as much reason to envy Duffield its Miss Cartwright, as you have to envy London its Miss Carter;[4] and, believe me, the manners of our women of fashion in general would by no means improve your natural politeness. Be contented, therefore, with what you have, and do not wish to exchange a natural politeness for studied refinement, nor truth and simplicity for art and affectation.

R. Dodsley

Source: Catherine Hutton and Her Friends, ed. Catherine Hutton Beale (Birmingham: Cornish Brothers, 1895), p. 15.

[1] Letter not traced.
[2] On the previous 14 September, Shenstone had conveyed essentially the same information about his prospective edition in a letter to Richard Graves (Williams, pp. 585–9). The collection never materialized, however; Shenstone died less than seven months after this July letter.
[3] For Gifford, see RD's letter to Miss Cartwright on 1 May 1761, note 6. Mrs Frances Brooke, née Moore (1724–89), who had conducted the weekly called *The Old Maid* (1755) would publish through the Dodsleys the next June the very popular *The History of Lady Julia Mandeville.* Her husband, the Rev. John Brooke, DD, was chaplain to the garrison at Quebec. Sarah Moore, her sister, accompanied her on this trip to Quebec and kept a record of the passage. (See Frances Brooke, *The History of Lady Julia Mandeville,* ed. E. Phillip Poole (London: Eric Partridge, 1930), p. 16.
[4] Elizabeth Carter (1717–1806) poet and miscellaneous writer, whose translation of Epictetus RD had published in 1758.

From Joseph Baretti[1]

Milan Sept.ʳ 13.ᵗʰ 1762.

Dear Sir

A Friend of mine wants to know whether it was probable or not to sell in London ⟨of⟩ a few Copies of a Latin Poem,[2] of which the Bearer will deliver you one with this. I cannot avoid begging of you the favour of showing this work to some of the Learned that visit your Shop, and in case you were willing to have some, the Proprietor would be glad to have a return partly in Books and partly in money. I suppose that delivered in London they would not cost above a Crown each copy.

Whether you incline to listen to this proposal or not, I am glad of having found this opportunity to tell Mʳ Dodsley that I am with all respect and affection

His Most obedient and most humble ser.ᵗ

Joseph Baretti

My hearty Compliments to our good Friend Johnson.[3]

MS: Folger Shakespeare Library. Tipped in at p. 434, Vol. 8, of Copy 4 of an extra-ill. Percy Fitzgerald, *The Life of David Garrick* (1868).

[1] Giuseppe Marc'Antonio Baretti (1719–89) had come to England from his native Italy in 1751. Probably through Charlotte Lennox, to whom he taught Italian, he had met Samuel Johnson in 1753.

Johnson immediately took to Baretti's learning and vitality, introducing him to his literary circle, among whom would have been RD. In 1753, RD published Baretti's *Dissertation upon the Italian Poetry, in which are interspersed some remarks on Mr. Voltaire's Essay on the Epic Poets*. Baretti seems to have spread his business among a number of London booksellers during his stay, but on 2 February 1759 (*PA*) appeared an advertisement of proposals for printing by subscription *La Poesi de Giuseppe Baretti*, subscriptions to be taken in by RD, Paul Vallaint, and the author at his residence in Poland Street. The collection did not materialize.

Baretti left London for Milan in 1760, shortly after printing his *Dictionary of the English and Italian Languages* (2 vols). This letter stems from a period in 1762, when, forbidden by his former patron, Count Firmian, to print his four volumes of travels, because of certain passages offensive to the Portuguese Court, he was about to leave Milan for Venice.

2 An unidentified poem (Italian imprint?), not mentioned again in RD's correspondence.

3 Signing himself "Your most affectionate friend," Samuel Johnson wrote long letters to Baretti after the latter had left England for Milan. Always encouraging him to return and sending the greetings of all his English friends, Johnson wrote on 10 June 1761: "all that you embraced at your departure, will caress you at your return." (See R. W. Chapman, I, 132–5; 138–40; 145–7.)

To William Shenstone

Sept. 18, [1762][1]

Dear Mr. Shenstone,

After I parted from you at *Broomsgrove*, I arrived very safe and speedily at *Worcester*, as I hope you did at the *Leasowes*. I found Dr. D—— in the same infirm State of Health, in which he has lingered for some Years past; but by keeping up his Spirits and his Appetite, by great Temperance, and by taking an Airing regularly twice a Day in his Chaise, for six or eight Miles at a Time, he has so nicely trimmed his feeble Lamp of Life, that he has prevented it from going out, and may possibly preserve it burning some few Years longer.[2] I employed Mrs. D—— to get me a Pot of Lampreys, which I sent, Carriage paid, to be left for you at Mr. Hodgett's:[3] I hope you received them safe, and that they proved good.

On the *Monday* following, I went from *Worcester*, in the *Birmingham* Stage, to *Bristol*, and the next Morning in a Post-Chaise to *Bath*. I found a Letter at Leake's,[4] which had lain for me eight or ten Days, and the Morning after my Arrival received another, both earnestly pressing my Return; I set out again, therefore, in two or three Days for *London*, where, without the least Fatigue, on *Tuesday* last I arrived. If I can be of any Service to the Widow,[5] I shall be very glad; but I am afraid the Father is inclined to take every Advantage which the Law will allow him.

At *Bath*, I saw Mr. Melmoth, who arrived there with his Lady the Day before I set out. He laments very much his Misfortune in missing you at the *Leasowes*; but hopes he shall have the Pleasure of seeing you some Time or other at Bath, where for the future (except two or three Months in the Winter, which he will dedicate to his Friends in *London*) he intends to reside.[6] I spent a Day with Mr. W——, who is meditating an Essay on *Simplicity*, of which he shewed me an imperfect Plan, and some few Sketches of the Work; he considers it in Sentiments, Language, Actions, and Works of Art, and I fancy will make a good Performance of it.[7] I spent also a

Day with Mr. Graves. Mr. Allen has built him a good additional Room, and a handsome School.[8] He is very earnest in his Wishes, that you would pursue your Subscription without farther Delay, and desires that I will press you to it without Intermission; I told him, I had said all I could, and hoped you would proceed. You are in the Meridian of your Fame, he says, and should not let your Sun decline one Moment, before you put your Work in Agitation.[9]

> I am, dear Sir, with great Truth,
> affectionately yours,
> R. Dodsley.

Source: Thomas Hull, *Select Letters* (London, 1778) II, 314–16.

[1] Hull dates this letter as 1761, but it must be of 1762, for a number of subjects presented here find their response in Shenstone's fully dated holograph letter of 20 November 1762. Among them are Shenstone's acknowledgement of RD's gift of lampreys, his prodding RD regarding the latter's hasty departure from Bath to aid a London widow, and his pleasure at the news of Daniel Webb's planned essay on "Simplicity."

[2] Most likely the Rev. John Dalton, DD (1709–63), a canon of Worcester. RD had published a number of Dalton's works from 1736 through the 1750s, including his masque, *Comus* (1738). RD would report Dalton's death to Elizabeth Cartwright in his letter of 3 August 1763. For Dalton's earlier reputation and his link with Shenstone, see Christopher Pitt's letter to RD, of *post* 30 May 1744, note 2.

[3] John Hodgetts of Hagley, Shenstone's cousin.

[4] James Leake, bookseller at Bath.

[5] Jane Morgan Hinxman, widow of RD's former apprentice, John Hinxman, and sister to the late publisher, Mary Cooper. See Shenstone's letter of 20 November, note 2.

[6] William Melmoth had moved to Bath in 1761 and lived at No. 12 Bladud Buildings (R. E. Peach, *Historic Houses in Bath*, II, 52).

[7] Daniel Webb (see Shenstone's letter on 20 November), who lived in the Bath area and whose *Remarks on the Beauties of Poetry* had been issued from Tully's Head the previous March. Regarding Webb's more notable work, *An Enquiry into the Beauties of Painting*, Shenstone had told Richard Graves on 7 July 1760: "I bought Webb instantly" (Williams, p. 556). On the *Beauties of Poetry*, he commented to Percy on 16 May 1762: "On the whole you must needs read it; but I think you will not esteem it equal, to his Treatise upon Painting" (Williams, p. 624). Needless to say, Shenstone would be interested in Webb's next work.

[8] After Ralph Allen (1694–1764) of Prior Park had purchased the adjoining Claverton Manor in 1758, he assisted Richard Graves, the parson of Claverton, by providing quarters for the conduct of a school, where Graves instructed as many as forty students per year for the next thirty years. See Charles J. Hill, *The Literary Career of Richard Graves* (Northampton, Mass., 1934–5) and Clarence Tracy's forthcoming biography.

[9] For the past year, both RD and Graves had been pressing Shenstone to publish an edition of his works by subscription. Although the initial suggestion is unaccounted for, Shenstone writes to Graves on 14 September 1761: "There is nothing can be more rational than what you say about the expediency of *losing no time*, if I mean to collect and publish what I have written" (Williams, pp. 586–7). The next month (although Brooks, on p. 119, thinks it early December), he writes to Percy: "I have just mentioned it in a letter to Mr Graves & to Mr Dodsley, *only* – I should like to collect my trifles in some such manner, y^t a Friend may buy them together, at a Bookseller's" (Williams, p. 603). (In the latter, Shenstone continues with interesting insights on contemporary opinion on the use of subscription.) By 26 July 1762, RD was able to write to Miss Cartwright that Shenstone "is preparing to publish his works by subscription, in one volume, quarto, at a guinea." Nothing came of the plan, however; Shenstone died the following February.

From William Shenstone[1]

The Leasowes, Nov.ʳ 20, 1762.

My dearest Friend,

It is a very *surprising* and a *cruel* thing, that you will not suppose me to have been *out of Order*, after such a Neglect of writing as can hardly be *excused* on any *other* Score. I cannot indeed lay claim to what the doctors call an *acute disease*: but *dizziness of Head* & *Depression of Spirits* are at best no *trivial* Maladies, & great *discouragements* to writing. There is a lethargick state of *Mind* that deserves your Pity, not your Anger; tho' it may require the Hellebore of sharp reproof. Why then did you not apply this pungent Remedy, before the disease was gone so far? – But seriously, I pass too much of yᵗ sort of time, wherein I am neither *well* nor *ill*; and being unable to express myself at large, am averse to do so by Halves. From the strange Laconicism of your Letter, I am really in doubt whether you are not angry at me; & yet had rather this were owing to Anger that *may* subside, than to any perservering *Fondness* you may have for such unusual Brevity. Should the Latter become hatitual, I shall see the Letters of a Genius dwindle to "per first will advise the Needful." God forbid such a transformation!

Your *former* Letter, to my great confusion, was dated Sept.ʳ 18.ᵗʰ Let me speak first to some few Parts of it – The Lampreys arrived safe, & were as good as I ever tasted; but every time I tasted them, I wanted *you*; and you are mistaken, if you imagine, I can half relish such Cates, *alone*. However I return you thanks.

You gave me no account how far the Bath-waters &c. were judged expedient for you. A *charitable* action called you up to town; & you, in the benevolence of your Heart, presume, that this *accounts for* the neglect of every advantage that concern'd *yourself*. Pray Let me know whether the Bath was proper for you, at the same time that you inform me whether you were able to serve M.ʳˢ H{inxman}.[2] I shall be sorry for *you*, as well as *Her*, if you should miss the Gratification you would derive from the success of such an Endeavour.

Were I rich I would erect a Temple to *Simplicity* and *Grace*: or, as the Latter word would be *equivocal*, to Simplicity & *Elegance*. I am glad to hear that M.ʳ Webb has undertaken to deify the *Former*; as he will produce better *grounds* for such a *Consecration* than was ever done by Pagans or by Papists, on any *such* occasion.[3] By the way, I take that Goddess to be a remarkable Friend to Ease & Indolence – There is another well-deserving personage; *Delicacy*; whose Cause has been strangely deserted by either M.ʳ Melmoth, or D.ʳ Lancaster.[4]

Will it make better for me, or Worse, to say I've not yet written to M.ʳ Graves? but I will positively write, within this week, if it cost me a dose of Salts to clear my brain. As to wᵗ he says about my printing immediately, he *may* be *right*, and I am *sure* he is *friendly*; but more of this in a little time.[5]

{What you say of Percy's ballads is perfectly just & sensible – I have preached so long to the same purpose, that I am quite weary & will preach no more. I am willing to *hope* that this collection will *still* have merit to engage the Publick: but am less sanguine than I should have been, had he shortened his notes, admitted more improvements, and rejected all such ballads as had no Plea but their *Antiquity*.[6] Thus far in answer to your former Letter.}

Since y.ᵉ receipt of ⟨that,⟩ your last Letter M.ʳ Percy & his wife came & spent good part of a week here; and *He* also would needs write a description of the Leasowes. During the Latter part of his circuit My friend Jago & I accompanied Him; & what was produced on that occasion, you will go near to know in a Little time.⁷ Mean while I am more and more convinced that no description of this Place can make any Figure in print, unless some *strictures* upon *gardening*, & *other* embellishments be superadded.⁸

M.ʳ Jago has been with me twice; having written a Poem in blank verse, which he leaves here for my revisal. Tis a descriptive Poem, called Edge-hill; and admits an account of y.ᵉ battle fought there, together with many legendary tales & episodes.⁹

About a week ago, I paid a visit of ⟨?⟩ two or three Days, which I had long promised, to Lord Foley.¹⁰ His table, for a constancy, is y.ᵉ most magnificent of any I ever saw. Eighteen or twenty elegant dishes; a continual succession of Company: his behavior perfectly hospitable; & his conversation really entertaining. I most readily own myself to have been under a mistake with regard to his *companionable* Character. My reception was as agreeable, as it could possibly be. As to the rest, he has a most admirable house, & furniture; but without any room or utensil that would stand the test of *modern* Criticism. The views around him wild, & great; & the Park capable of being rendered *fine*[,] *twice* as striking as it is at present, if he would fall some ⟨?⟩ Oaks under y.ᵉ value of a crown, & some hawthorns under y.ᵉ value of a half-penny. But 'tis possible, at his time of Life &c, nothing of this Sort will be undertaken. The two things at present remarkable are *his Lodge* & *his Chapel*. The Portico of y.ᵉ former, ⟨?⟩ (designed by Fleetcroft¹¹) affords three different & striking Prospects. The Chapel is so very superb & elegant, that M.ʳˢ Gataker has nothing to do but send you & me *thither*, to say our Prayers in it.¹² In reality, it is perfect Luxury: as I truly thought it, last sunday Se'nnight. *His Pew*, is a *room* with an handsome Fire-place. The Ceiling Coved, painted in compartments, & y.ᵉ remainder enriched with gilt stucco-ornaments; the walls enriched in y.ᵉ same manner; the best painted windows I ever saw: the Monumᵗ to his Father, Mother & Brothers, cost, he said, £2,000. The middle Ayle rendered comfortable by iron stoves in y.ᵉ shape of Urns. The organ perfectly neat, & good in proportion to it's size: And to this Chapel you are led thro a Gallery of paintings seventy feet Long – what would you more? you'll say, a good sermon – I really think his Parson is able to preach one.

And now I come, lastly, to speak of y.ʳ Letter I received on Monday.¹³ What an uncommon Man you are! to take so *much* thought for *those*, who never took any for themselves! {And so, you flew immediately to M.ʳˢ Cholmondely, so soon as ever she arrived in town¹⁴ – I really am at a Loss what I can say to that Lady: Were she *only* generous, ⟨?⟩ or *only* witty, or *only* the politest woman breathing, I might attempt, however awkwardly, to express my thanks on this occasion; but as you have convinced me she is *all* these, & *more* than these *together*, I despair, and grow too much in *earnest* to offer my acknowledgements with any kind of Grace. Be so good however as to assure her, if any good can possibly befall so *helpless* a Person as I really am, how proud I shall be to stand indebted for it to one I esteem so much as M.ʳˢ Cholm'ley. My L.ᵈ Bute will *certainly* take no farther notice, till some of my noble Friends revive the Subject. I purpose to wait on four or five before they go up to town; *any* of which I am very sure will be ready to give me a good word, if my L^d should speak to them upon the Subject: But if *they* are all silent, *he* will be so too. I shall begin this series of visits, so soon as ever the Frost is gone; and when I have been at my Ld Stamfords, will explain my sentiments a Little farther.[15] Mean time accept my most lively thanks; & rather *contrive for* me, than *leave me* to think, in my own behalf. I can *make* my own Fortune answer all necessary purposes; at the same time a degree more affluence would be very desireable for the Latter part of Life; & if it can be obtained reputably, & without too too great an Encroachment on my way of Life that is become habitual, there is no Person Living to whom I would more gladly owe it y^n to yourself & Mrs Cholmley.}[16] I have enquired after Mr Wedderburn, and it seems he is a very clever & a very rising Lawyer; to whom I am the more obliged for mentioning me, as I fear I have not the Honour of being the least known to him.[17] Pray write to me as soon as possible, & I will make you amends (if *writing* make amends) for the scandalous *omissions* of which I have been guilty – I have somewhat to tell you of L^d L____'s usual *great kindness* when y^e L^ds D{artmouth} & W{illowby} were last at Hagley – But I have not time, & must conclude – my dearest worthiest Friend![18]

> y^r ever obliged

> > Will Shenstone

MS: The Honourable Michael Shenstone, Canadian Ambassador to Austria, Vienna, Austria.[19]

[1] Shenstone acknowledges this letter to be a response to three earlier RD letters: one dated 18 September; a second, whose date is not mentioned; and one "received on Monday," that is, 15 November. Only the first has been traced and appears in this collection.

[2] Text enclosed within this form of parentheses throughout the letter designates material that Thomas Hull had struck through in the holograph when editing Shenstone's letters to be included in his *Select Letters* (1778).

John Hinxman, RD's former apprentice, had taken over the bookselling business of John Hildyard at York in 1757 and then had returned to London in 1761 where he came into possession of the publishing business of the recently deceased Mary Cooper, through marriage to her sister, Jane Morgan. (See Michael Treadwell, "London Trade Publishers, 1675–1750," *Library*, 6th ser. IV, 111, note 26.) Hinxman's death on 9 July 1762 (*York Courant*, 20 July 1762) – a few months before the first RD letter to which Shenstone alludes – had no doubt prompted RD's "*charitable* action," his coming "up to town." But perhaps more than a lady's distress urged his hasty departure from Bath. Since Hinxman had succeeded Cooper, RD's frequent publishing collaborator, his finances and copyrights were likely of concern to RD. In fact, Shenstone's language ("the Gratification you would derive from the success of such an Endeavour") suggests that RD was anxious to play a role in the settlement of Hinxman's affairs, perhaps even to purchase the business.

[3] See RD's letter on 18 September, note 7.

[4] Nathaniel Lancaster's *Plan of an Essay on Delicacy*, issued more than thirteen years earlier from Tully's Head, had just been reprinted by RD on 2 November (*PA*) in his *Fugitive Pieces* (I, 277–352). Probably Shenstone had been expecting more of "Delicacy" from Lancaster, given the long interim. Melmoth, too, is charged as a deserter of "Delicacy" most likely because, as RD had reported in his 18 September letter, Melmoth had removed himself from London society to live in Bath.

[5] Shenstone wrote to Graves the same day, apologizing for his delinquency and taking up the matter of the proposed edition of his works to be sold by subscription. See Williams, pp. 636–41.

[6] Appearing here in print for the first time, Shenstone's objections to Percy's proposed edition of

ancient ballads counteracts Percy's complaints against the Dodsleys (especially against Robert) in late 1760 for reneging on their initial offer for the ballads. At that time, he bitterly decried Robert's influence on the new master of Tully's Head; influence which, he assumed, had caused the breakdown in negotiations. (See RD's letter to Percy in late 1757, note 1.) As seems clear from this passage, he little knew that the person who had encouraged the work and to whom he had issued his complaints – Shenstone – had serious objections to the work, as well. Perhaps Shenstone had been a bit two-faced in dealing with his young protégé. In any event, these specific literary criticisms of Percy's work relieve RD of the long unanswered charge of acting "too much of the bookseller in this affair."

7 See RD's letter to Shenstone on 1 December 1759, note 20.
8 Although Shenstone would never complete such a piece, he had certainly gathered the materials for it. Pages 125 to 147 of Volume II of his posthumously published *Works* comprised a section of practical observations on effective gardening, entitled "Unconnected Thoughts on Gardening."
9 *Edge-Hill; or, the Rural Prospect delineated and moralized* would be published by James Dodsley in 1767. Shenstone's encouragement of the author is found in letters to Jago of the period, to one of which (Williams, pp. 644–5) Percy appended the following note: "Shenstone always thought it wanted much more finishing to render it worthy of the Public . . . It is but a dull poem" (Brooks, p. 232).
10 Thomas Foley (1703–66), 2nd Baron Foley, resided at Witley Court, Kidderminster, Worcester, approximately 19 miles south-west of Birmingham.
11 Henry Flitcroft (1697–1769), first gained recognition in 1720 as the assistant and draftsman to Lord Burlington. From 1726 until his death, he was employed by the Office of the Works, becoming Comptroller in 1758. He was responsible for the design of many buildings, including the seat of the Duke of Bedford, Woburn Abbey.
12 See Edmund Burke's letter, *c.* 6 September 1759, note 3.
13 Untraced. Obviously that letter, as does the rest of the present one, concerned RD's attempt to rally support among influential friends for the purpose of securing Shenstone a government pension. Although RD had urged the poet to undertake the cause as early as December 1760 (see his letter of 30 December of that year), only now, it seems, was Shenstone moved to take action (see below). Between them, they enjoyed influential resources for mounting a case with John Stuart, 3rd Lord Bute, currently First Lord of the Treasury and a patron of literature. As Graves recalled in *Recollections of some Particulars in the Life of the late William Shenstone* (1788, pp. 165–6), the fine relations Shenstone had cultivated with Scottish literary figures might have been turned to his favor in the application to their countryman, Lord Bute. RD himself had succeeded with two earlier requests of Bute, when applying on behalf of Baskerville's *Horace* and his own tragedy *Cleone*; and his powerful London acquaintances were numerous. Actually, according to Graves (*Recollections*), Shenstone had thought a patent had already been drawn up. Thomas Percy is even more specific. On page 399 of Volume III of his own copy of Shenstone's *Works* (Bodleian Library), his marginal note claims that the poet "was to have had a Pension from the Crown, of £300: p^r ann____," the same amount accorded Samuel Johnson the previous summer. But Shenstone died within three months of the date of this letter and before the pension could be awarded.
14 Most likely Mary Cholmondely (*c.* 1730–1811), wife of the Hon. Robert Cholmondeley and younger sister of Peg Woffington, the actress. Much admired in London society, her wit and beauty had endeared her to Samuel Johnson, for whose edition of Shakespeare she had actively solicited subscriptions. (See Boswell's *Life*, especially I, 318.)
15 Bute would most likely have known Shenstone's poetry and have been familiar with his role in the publication of Baskerville's *Horace* (see Shenstone's letter to RD on 11 February of this year.) Besides Lord Stamford (see Shenstone's letter to Richard Jago on the next January 11; Williams, pp. 650–1), another of the "noble friends" to be approached was John Ward (1704–74), Baron Ward of Birmingham (see Shenstone's letter to Percy on the next 16 January; Williams, p. 651).
16 The entire passage within brackets was omitted in Hull's edition and consequently absent from both Williams and Mallam.
17 Alexander Wedderburn (1733–1805), later Baron Loughborough, was currently MP for Ayr burghs and a favorite of Lord Bute. Wedderburn's favor was significant: the previous summer he had been the intermediary in securing Johnson's pension through Lord Bute.

[18] George, Lord Lyttelton, Shenstone's neighbor at Hagley; William Legge (1731–1801), 2nd Earl of Dartmouth; and John Peyto Verney (1738–1816), 14th Baron Willoughby de Broke, Richard Jago's patron. In a letter to Graves on this same day (Williams, p. 638), Shenstone ticks off a long list of recent visitors at the Leasowes (as if copying from a guest book), and near the end of the list, immediately following Lyttelton's name, appear those of Dartmouth and Willoughby.

[19] For assistance in locating this holograph, I am indebted to Francis Burns of Newman College, Birmingham.

To Elizabeth Cartwright

[January 1763][1]

Dear Madam,

You pretend to be proud of my correspondence, but how can that be possible when I am, as you see, so wretched a correspondent? I am afraid you are a little flatterer, and only say this to make me proud of myself; for sure if either of us have cause to be proud, it is I, to have so fine a young lady not disdain now and then to favour with a letter so old a fellow. I thank you for your history of the honest miller; it gave me much pleasure in the reading, yet there was one part of your epistle which gave me more[2] – it is that which contains an intimation of your design of coming up to town. Pray who are you coming with? I hope with somebody that will not have room for you when in London, as I have now a spare apartment, that will be very much at your service; and it will give both me and my sister, who desires her compliments, a real pleasure if you will favour us with your company while you stay in London.[3] I shall be impatient to know when you come, so pray inform me. You will always be welcome; but I should think the best time for yourself would be about the middle of March, as the town will then be full, the Play-houses open, and probably Ranelagh and Vauxhall too, before you need to return. And the weather also, it may be hoped, will be so good as to permit us to take a voyage up the river to Richmond, or down to Greenwich, and will with more pleasure allow us to see the town, than in the darkness and dirt of winter. Pray favour me with a line soon, to confirm my happiness in the certainty that you will come, and when. I beg my compliments to all my cousins; also to Mr Gifford, Mr Bradshaw, and Mrs Mytton.[4]

I am, my dear cousin,

Affectionately yours,

R Dodsley

Source: Catherine Hutton and Her Friends, ed. Catherine Hutton Beale (Birmingham: Cornish Brothers, 1895), 16–17.

[1] C. H. Beale gives merely the date "December 1762" for this letter, implying that the manuscript (if she saw it) lacked a date. Probably it did, for RD never dated his letters simply with the month and year. Actually the month is more likely January 1763, if Miss Cartwright is not guilty of being too free with chronology in another letter she writes on 20 January 1763 to Mrs Fieldhouse (Beale, pp. 8–11). There she says of her projected trip to London: "Mr Dodsley wrote me ye other day, says it must be in March, or ye beginning of April," a clear reference to RD's recommendation in this letter.

[2] Letter not traced.

³ Miss Cartwright did come to town, with friends from Sutton-in-Ashfield, Miss Unwin and her mother. There is no indication that they lodged with RD and his sister. Either Mr Unwin or his son had introduced Miss Cartwright to her future husband, John Coltman, at Matlock in 1757. See Beale, pp. 10, 43, 66.
⁴ For Mr Gifford, see RD's letter to Miss Cartwright on 1 May 1761, note 6. Mrs Mytton was an elderly acquaintance whom Miss Cartwright, in a letter to Mrs Fieldhouse the same month, says visits her house twice a week (Beale, p. 11). For Bradshaw, mentioned in a few other letters to Miss Cartwright, see RD's letters on 1 May 1761, note 8.

To Samuel Cartwright¹

April 12ᵗʰ 1763

Dear *Sir*

This comes to thank you for the favor you have done us, and the pleasures you have given us, in letting us have Miss Cartwright in London.² We have only this further to ask that you will suffer us to enjoy this Happiness as long as you can possibly spare her. I will promise you to do all in my power to entertain her, and to make her absence from you as supportable as her affection to you will permit. She is in very good health, extreamly agreeble to us, and I hope very happy in herself. I hope both my Cousins are well, to whom I beg my Compliments in which Miss joins me with sincere duty and affection. Pray be so good as to let somebody convey the enclosed to Mʳ G____ & Miss R____ and to give my compliments when you see them to Mʳ Bradshaw & Mʳˢ Mytton³

I am Dear Cousin
Affectionately Y'ʳˢ

R Dodsley

Source: Leicestershire Record Office, 15D57/448. This transcription, supposedly from the original, by Samuel Coltman (1772–1857), grandson of the recipient, is found in his three MS volumes of reminiscences, written *c.* 1850 and entitled "Time's Stepping Stones."

¹ Samuel Cartwright (1701–92), father of Elizabeth Cartwright, RD's young correspondent. According to C. H. Beale (*Catherine Hutton and Her Friends*, pp. 67–8), Cartwright was a staunch "republican" and "dictator of his village" (Duffield). Samuel Coltman, Elizabeth's son, who preserved family reminiscences in "Time's Stepping Stones," was named after his grandfather, who had come to live with the Coltmans in Leicester after his wife died, arriving the day of his grandson's birth (Beale, p. 66). ² For Miss Cartwright's visit to London, see RD's January letter to her. ³ Probably Mr Gifford, mentioned in other letters to Miss Cartwright, and Miss Roten, Miss Cartwright's neighbor and friend. For Bradshaw see RD's letter to Elizabeth Cartwright of 1 May 1761, note 8. For Mrs Mytton, see RD's letter to Miss Cartwright in January, note 4.

From Richard Graves

Claverton; 25 April 1763

Dear Sʳ

Tho' I thought it most adviseable, on many accounts, not to accept your kind offer of a share in the MSS – Yet I hope you do not intend to deprive me of the

pleasure which I propos'd to myself, of giving you all the Assistance in my power –
to correct & prepare them for the press[1] – The situation in which I left the affair,
when I came from London, was, I think, that you should consult Mr Melmoth, D^r
Lowth or any third person, of whom you could ask such a favour; ⟨?⟩ – and when
they had decided the merit of the several pieces you were to allot me such a Task as
you thought proper – And this scheme I hope you will pursue.[2]

Instead of my coming to Town however at Whitsuntide, as I propos'd, I am
afraid you must have the trouble of conveying me a volume or two, by any friend,
that you can trust – or in default of such an opportunity – in a Packet by Wiltshire's
Waggon, directed for me at Mr Indenick's in the Grove[3] – For tho' I fully intended
(& sincerely wish) to give Mrs Graves her annual Dose – of Relaxation &
Amusement – yet we are so unfortunately circumstanc'd this year, that we should
refuse two new Scholars, & run the hazards of losing two more of great
consequence, if we could not engage for one of us at least to be at home the whole
ensuing holidays – whilst their parents are absent upon a Summer's Expedition –

However I am determin'd myself to take a journey to the Leasowes – as you, &
probably others may, judge it a proper Compliment to our late friend's memory:
Tho' I am convinc'd that by exhibiting my insignificant person, & by betraying my
inexperience in business, & law affairs, I shall forfeit that high opinion (&
consequently loose my influence as an Executor) which the people in that country
may ⟨of⟩ have conceiv'd of me, from poor Mr Shenstone's partiality in my
favour[4] –

I have been looking over some of our friend's Letters, but cannot meet with any
directions relating to any of his pieces except those that are already publishd – The
ode to Sr R. Lyttleton was intended for your miscellany – but, I suppose, M^r Sh. –
could not alter it to his mind – I have sent two Letters in which he lays great Stress
upon omitting or al[te]ring the Stanza relative to the (stet) Dear Lyttle^n [w]hich, if
it should be in your Copy – you will correct accordingly[5] – I shou[ld like my]
Letters return'd – or carefully preserv'd – as they make part of our Series of
Correspondence.[6]

I wish you could contrive to make this in y^r way from the North: There is a Coach
all the Summer now advertis'd from Birmingham to Bath – I always want to talk to
you about our valuable friend – & when I see you waste half the time upon
indifferent Subjects – This Loss has set the vanity of all my amusements – (which
were of the solitary kind) in the strongest light – & tends greatly to veer my
Affections from the world – to which the pleasures of the Imagination have always
attach'd *me* more strongly than any others –

I have but just now finish'd my business attending the taking possession of my
new preferment: wch terminates rather more agreeably than I expected, as it will
bring me in a *clear* 40 £ a-year & I have put about 10 Guineas in my pocket after
near 70 £ expence – & a hundred pound worth of trouble & fatigue[7] –

I beg my best respects to Mrs Dyer & family[8] – & – am with Mrs Graves's Compl^{ts}

S^r y^r affect. humble

Ric Graves

MS: Somerset County Record Offices, DD/SK, 28/1, 14.

[1] Much of the following letter concerns Graves's and RD's roles as literary executors of William Shenstone, who had died on 11 February of this year. Like the subsequent letters between RD and Graves, this one involves preparations for the printing of Shenstone's *Works*, the first two volumes of which will appear only a few months before RD's own death in September 1764.

[2] Much effort would be expended by RD and his friends examining Shenstone's literary remains and deciding what would be printed and what suppressed in the forthcoming edition of his *Works*.

[3] Indenick is unidentified, but the "Grove" was the "Orange Grove," one of Graves's haunts in Bath. There, at Mrs Henderson's boarding house, Graves and Shenstone had first met. (G. W. Peach, *Historic Houses in Bath*, I, 98).

[4] In his letter to RD on 21 May, Graves says that he has plans to set out for the Leasowes about 6 June. Apparently he did, for his letter to RD on 20 June recounts early complications frustrating the claims of various parties involved in the settlement.

[5] RD's "miscellany" was his *Collection of Poems by Several Hands*; Sir Richard Lyttelton (1718–70), brother of George, Lord Lyttelton; "A Pastoral Ode, To the Honourable Sir Richard Lyttelton" would be printed in the *Works*, I, 174–81, but it is unclear which correction Graves stresses.

[6] Presumably Shenstone's letters.

[7] A year before his death, Ralph Allen had procured for Graves the vicarage of Kilmersdon, near Radstock. (Peach, I, 92).   [8] RD's sister.

From Richard Graves[1]

Thursday night 8 o'clock
[*post* 25 April; *ante* 21 May 1763][2]

Mr Graves's Complt^s to Mr Dodsley –

He having met with fresh difficulties – by the Bishop's being gone out of town, – has had but little time to attend to the MSS. However has read over the *Vista* (very improperly so call'd) which with short notes, referring to ye several Kings reigns & a few connections would pass very well. The Story of the *Spanish Lady* or "*Love & Honour*" is an excellent thing, to my taste – & the *progress of Delicacy* – very pretty – *The Snuff-box* quite a juvenile & servile Imitation of Pope's Rape of the Lock – & by no means to be printed[3] –

Mr Graves is for placing these good things at the Head of each Volume – & the less perfect in their train – Suppose V. 1. The Elegies – the progress of Taste – Odes – Songs &c – & all that ⟨w^{ch}⟩ relate to Mr Shenstone's State of mind – Vol. II – The School-mistress – ⟨Oe⟩ Oeconomist[4] – Ludicrous Subject – Epigrams &c – Vista or Effects of Superstition (as I would call it) – Love & Honour – &c – Verses to Dr Radcliff to be suppress'd The fatal Exotic, but middling[5] – Vol. III – Rural Elegance or [?], Pastoral Ballad⟨s⟩ (unless this at the end of the first Vol) – & ⟨all⟩ some that have been printed already – Vol. IV – Prose works[6] –

Mr Graves has only sketch'd this out for hints to M [?][7] take any Manuscript with him – because he hopes M$^{[r]}$ Milmoth or some third person will give their Opinion about printing or suppressing –

Mr Graves has had so much trouble about this paltry preferment, that the prospect of *gain* would hardly engage him in any more anxiety[8] – However he will be happy if it is in his power to give Mr Dodsley any Assistance –

"Rural Elegence" – is not sufficiently expressive of the Subject of that Poem – ⟨The superiority⟩[9]

MS: Somerset County Record Office, DD/SK, 28/1, 76.

¹ Graves's writing in the third person to his friend Dodsley gives this letter an unusually impersonal air almost as if it had been written by an assistant. Nonetheless, the holograph is in Graves's own hand One can only imagine that, given the cross-outs, the letter is a draft, and this was Graves's manner with such things.

² The inclusive dates are those of Graves's former and subsequent extant letters to RD. The former reminds RD of their agreement to have William Melmoth or Robert Lowth help select the Shenstone pieces to be printed in RD's edition of the poet's *Works*, and the latter shows that arrangement a *fair accompli*. In this letter, however, although Graves himself has made more progress with the manuscripts, he is still hoping that "Mʳ Milmoth or some third person will give their Opinion about printing or supressing."

³ In the *Works*, "The Vista" was entitled "The Ruin'd Abbey; or The Effects of Superstition" (I, 308–21); it was accompanied by footnotes. "Love and Honour" was also printed (I, 321–32), and "progress of Delicasy" appeared as "The Progress of Taste; or the Fate of Delicacy" (I, 264–84). Graves's opinion of "The Snuff-box" seemed supported by RD and his advisors, for it was not printed. Curiously enough, however, many years later when writing his *Recollections of Some Particulars in the Life of the late William Shenstone, Esq.* (1788), Graves admitted that the piece "has some merit" and might have been an "agreeable present to the many admirers of Mr. Shenstone" (p. 90).

⁴ "Oeconomy, a Rhapsody, addressed to Young Poets" (*Works*, I, 285–307).

⁵ Both "Verses to Dʳ Radcliff" and "The fatal Exotic" were suppressed. John Radcliffe (d. 1775) had been Master of Pembroke College while Shenstone was at Oxford.

⁶ Apparently agreement on the number of volumes for Shenstone's *Works* had yet to be reached; when published, the set would number three volumes: poems, prose, and letters.

⁷ Because "hints to M" concludes one page of the holograph letter, and because the next page, beginning with "[?] take," does not follow the sense of the former, possibly an entire page of the manuscript is missing at this point.   ⁸ See Graves's previous letter (25 April), note 7.

⁹ Apparently more of the text is missing at this point.

From Richard Graves

Bath, 21 May – 1763

Dear Sʳ

Having a few minutes leisure upon my hands (af[ter] hurry of dismissing above 20 boys with the proper instructions for the holidays) I am willing to say something more (tho' I hardly know what) about our friend's [MSS]

As I find your most judicious friends have pronounc'd what we thought the most *perfect* of them very incorrect, I [am] certain they would condemn several other pieces to eterna[l] oblivion – In which case, I should think it very hard up[on] you, to be oblig'd to ⟨give⟩ venture so large a sum upon the remainder, for fear of their falling into mercenary hands. Now I don't know that the will gives the Executors any particular directions about the *Papers* – & therefore I suppose we are oblig'd to dispose of them, as well as the other goods & chattels – to the best advantage – But still in such a manner as a *majority* of us shall judge most respectful to the memory of our friend – I should think therefore after *you* & *I* have rejected what our friends shall determine not equal to the Reputation which Mʳ Shenstone has already establish'd in the world – we might venture to trust Mʳ H. with the liberty of getting even 200, £ for them else-where¹ –

This however I only mention for your consideration – as yo[u ar]e infinitely more capable to judge of this affair than [I] am –

So far however I think it certain, that any *two* of th[e] Trustees must have a power of determining – what shall [be] publish'd & what suppress'd – Tho' I dare say M^r H––g––s would think of offering to Sale, what we think proper to reject –

I think of setting out about Monday the 6.th of June – & – continuing 2 or 3 days at the Leasowes – but will write to Mr Clarke to meet me there – as I know I can do nothing by myself^2 –

I beg my Respects to M^r & Mrs Dyer & y^r niece & am

Dear S^r y^r affect humb Ser^t

Ric Graves

I am sorry to make you pay postage for this Scroll – but my Franks are gone. – I din'd wth Mr Web. last Saturday – who I suppose will soon appear in publick again^3 –

Address: To Mr Dodsley / at Mr Dyer's in Bruton Street / Berkley Square / London

Postmark: 23 MA Bath

MS: Somerset County Record Offices, DD/SK, 28/1, 15.

---

^{1} Without the correspondence between RD and his advisors (either William Melmoth or Robert Lowth or both; see Graves's letter on 25 April), it is impossible to say what was recommended to be printed and what to be suppressed. Perhaps their advice was not wholly observed, for RD's edition of Shenstone's *Works* largely reflects the choices and rejections found in Graves's former letter. Also, although some unpublished Shenstone poetry has turned up in this century, it has been slight in both quantity and quality. (See Alice Hazeltine, *A Study of William Shenstone and His Critics. With Fifteen of his Unpublished Poems and Five of his Unpublished Latin Inscriptions* (Menasha, Wisc.: George Banta, 1918).) "Mr. H." is undoubtedly John Hodgetts, Shenstone's cousin and the third of the three executors. Noting the early nineteenth-century bookseller William Hodgetts, Williams suggest (p. 631n) that the business might have originated in the eighteenth century and that John Hodgetts might have been connected with it. The suggestion would seem to support Graves's statement. Besides, John Hodgetts would see through the press Lady Luxborough's *Letters . . . to William Shenstone* (1775), as well as a posthumous edition of Richard Jago's *Poems Moral and Descriptive* (1784). However, neither Plomer or Maxted list a Birmingham tradesman named Hodgetts in the eighteenth century.
^{2} Richard Clark (1739–1831), later sheriff and mayor of London, was probably the attorney recommended to Shenstone's executors by Lord Stamford. (See Graves's next letter, of 20 June).
^{3} Mr Daniel Webb, whose *Fingal Reclaimed* would be published this year.

From Richard Graves

Claverton, 20 June 1763

Dear S^r

As I have taken it upon me, to give you an account of the Situation affairs are in at the Leasowes, I am afraid, you begin to be very impatient on that head – But the continual embarassment of my own Affairs has prevented me from writing to You before this time.

From the interfering interests of the several parties concern'd, I found them violently exasperated against each other. As our friend Mr Hds however is in the most invidious situation, I found all the rest united against him – and accusing him of protracting the Sale of the Estates, appropriated to the payment of Debts & Legacies, with some interested views, which they could not well explain[1] – But upon an interview with M[r] Clark (the Attorney recommended by Lord Stamford) I am pretty well convinc'd that things cannot be transacted in a hurr[y][2] great difficulties – For the Will is so ambiguously express'd – as to leave room for various Litigations –

The most important Question is, I find, this: As the first Clause of the Will charges the Whole Estate with the payment of the Debts & Legacies – whether, the mortgages upon John Shenstone's & M[rs] Cutler's Estates, are to be consider'd as *Debts* – to be paid out of the whole Mass – or whether the two particular estates devis'd to them are liable to the Incumbrances – The latter, at first sight, appears most plausible – But one or two experienc'd persons, that I have mention'd it to, are clearly of the former – M[r] Clarke however ⟨will⟩ has thrown the whole Will into proper Questions to be laid before Council – at once – as soon as they have got in all the Debts –

M[r] Hodgetts seems very desirous of keeping the Leasowes – which may *incline* him to protract affairs & (as they tell me) M[r] Clark is his old [?][3] in some of the parties concern'd – but a farther reason for M[r] Clark's deferring, is, to see whether the heirs at Law (who have lately made pretensions to the Leasowes Farm, as having been entail'd) will pursue the Affair[4] – in which Case we must have an Opinion upon the whole together –

Mr. Hodgets desir'd me to let you know, that he could have £400. for the MSS – But had rather you should have them at 300, certain ⟨wh⟩ which (with a few Copies for friends) he strenuously insists upon[5] – Especially (as he says) things are likely to turn out much less to his advantage than he expected –

M[r] Clark, when he has had the Opinion of some Counsell, will transmitt a Copy of it to you & myself – He seems a very honest & very sensible man –

M[rs] Graves desires her best Compl[ts] may be join'd wth those of S[r]

y[r] affect. humb Ser[t]

Ric Graves

Address: To | M[r] Dodsley at M[rs] Dyer's in | Bruton Street, Berkley Square | London
Postmark: 22 IV Bath

MS: Somerset County Record Offices, DD/SK, 28/1, 16.

[1] The rest of the letters from Graves, through 1764, are concerned with the on-going attempt by the three executors to resolve the complexities of Shenstone's will (dated 5 February 1763 and proved on 10 May). The affair was complicated, as Graves says here, because the estates out of which some of the annuities were to be paid had been mortgaged, and the negotiations became exacerbated because the various parties to the will, motivated by resentment and greed, fell into factions.

   Since Shenstone had no children and probably because his heirs-at-law, first cousins Mary Shenstone and Elizabeth Audley, had little to do with him during his lifetime, the poet left his treasured Leasowes, "together with the priory House and other Lands in Haywood lately Exchanged with Lord Lyttelton," to his second cousin John Hodgetts. Thereafter it was to pass to Shenstone's cousin Edward Cookes of Edinburgh, but all with the recommendation that if the Leasowes afforded more value to the cousins if sold, then it should be offered for sale to some of Shenstone's "Chief friends prefering the Honble John Grey Youngest Son of Lord Stamford." Ivy Farm at Quinton and a house in Birmingham were left to John Shenstone, a cousin. Mary Cutler, Shenstone's housekeeper, received £150 and a yearly rent charge of £30 to be paid from the Churchill estate, as well as an additional £12 yearly for the care of Mrs Arnold, Shenstone's aged servant. Another cousin, Mary Southall, received an annuity of £10, and other cousins, John and William Saunders, were bequeathed £100 each. Others, including the executors, were left various sums for mourning.

The bequests were straightforward enough, but when it was discovered that Ivy Farm and other lands at Quinton, the Cross Keys Inn in New Street, Birmingham, and the houses in Halesowen were still mortgaged to Edward Foye, who wanted £600 owed him as well as interest due, the executors feared that there would not be enough in reserve if all the annuities were paid outright. And Hodgetts, wanting to retain the Leasowes, was not anxious to sell it for the pleasure of the other claimants.

Finally, in 1764, Hodgetts arranged with Edward Cookes (next to inherit the Leasowes) to sell the property and to divide the proceeds. In November, negotiations were begun with Joseph Turnpenny, buttonmaker, who purchased the estate for £5,350 and took possession on the following 25 March. But the sale did not resolve the difficulties for Shenstone's executors. RD's participation, of course, was ended by his death in September 1764. But Mary Cutler, who had begun a seemingly endless series of proceedings in Chancery against Hodgetts and Graves and others, merely added Turnpenny's name to her list of bills. (For Cutler's actions, see Graves's letter on 30 March 1764, note 3. Here, as there, I am indebted to Dr Francis Burns of Newman College, Birmingham, for many details.)

² The manuscript has deteriorated at this point, and a whole line is missing.
³ Manuscript deteriorated. Several words are missing.
⁴ Shenstone's first cousins, Mary Shenstone and Elizabeth Audley.
⁵ RD purchased the manuscripts for £300. The evidence was given by Richard Graves in "Cutler vs. Graves," 1765, Chancery Proceedings (P.R.O. c.12. 1892.22). Thomas Percy, however, thought they were sold for £250 (Percy to Dalrymple, Lord Hailes, 16 June 1763, *Correspondence of Thomas Percy*, IV, 39). (Quoted from Burns, p. 321, note 2).

To Elizabeth Cartwright

Aug: 3^d 1763

It was not till two or three days ago that I recollected the Letter you intrusted me with for Miss Unwin: I immediately enclosed it, and wrote to her confessing my fault.[1] I hope no ill consequences have arisen from my carelessness, or rather let me call it my unhappy want of memory, for surely I would not be guilty of carelessness or any thing blamable towards my dear Miss Cartwright. Have you yet forgiven me my not calling at Duffield? How unhappy I am to be pleading for pardon where I would willingly do any thing that might oblige. Mr Dalton has got your paper Landskip in order to show to the Queen.[2] I wish he may have an opportunity before her Majesty lies in, as I should be very glad to be any way instrumental in doing you honor, being with great truth

Dear Madam
Your most obed^t Servant
R Dodsley

Dr Dalton I suppose you see by the Papers, is dead[3]

Source: Transcription by Samuel Coltman (1772–1857), son of Elizabeth Cartwright Coltman, found in the manuscript volumes "Time's Stepping Stones" (*c.* 1850), Leicestershire Record Office, 15D57/448.

¹ Miss Unwin, with whom Miss Cartwright had traveled to London during the past spring. The routeing of the letter is puzzling. Certainly Miss Cartwright would not send a letter to London to be delivered to a friend who lived only twenty miles from her. But RD says explicitly he had not called at Duffield during his recent trip north (where he might have otherwise been entrusted with the letter). Perhaps Miss Unwin was once more in London, or had never left since her spring visit.
² See RD's letters of 10 November, note 2, and 15 December for the result of his application to the Queen on Miss Cartwright's behalf, and for Richard Dalton's role in the affair.
³ For the Rev. John Dalton, see RD's next letter to Miss Cartwright, on 25 August, and note 1.

To Elizabeth Cartwright

Aug 25ᵗʰ 1763.

Dear Madam

I am very much alarm'd for fear you are ill, for surely nothing else could cause you to keep silence so long, you cannot bear malice with such a continuance on account of my not calling at Duffield in my return, I will not think you capable of it. Whatever it be, I beg you will favor me a line that I may be freed from this disagreeable suspense. I have not seen Mʳ Spence since my return; I fancy he is still in Wiltshire. I suppose you saw in the Papers that we have lost Dʳ Dalton, which surely by Mʳˢ Dalton must be regarded as a deliverance: but she is so good a creature that I am afraid she will be afflicted.¹

I am not very well and purpose in about a fortnight to go to Bath, in order to try the Waters for about six weeks. I hope I shall hear from you before I go. My best respects to all my Cousins – to Mʳ & Mʳˢ G––d & to all Friends.²

I am, Dear Madam
Affectionately Yours
R Dodsley.

Source: "Time's Stepping Stones" (*c.* 1850), Leicestershire Record Office, 15D57/448.

¹ Mrs Dalton's "deliverance" might be explained by her husband's libertine social reputation. See Christopher Pitt's letter to RD, *post* 30 May 1744, note 2.
² Probably the Rev. and Mrs Richard Gifford, mentioned in earlier letters to Miss Cartwright.

To Elizabeth Cartwright

Novʳ 10ᵗʰ 1763.¹

Dear Madam

I did not return from Bath till last Saturday night, and I think I am return'd without receiving any benefit from the Waters, tho' I both drank and bath'd. Mʳ Spence is at Byfleet, and I purpose to pay him a visit in a few days, when I will carry him your Letter, and your extreamly pretty Landskip, both which I am sure he will receive with great pleasure. I endeavor'd to see Mʳ Dalton yesterday, but he was not at home; so I know not whether the Queen has seen your handiwork or not; if not, she has miss'd an Entertainment, which even a Queen might regret.² My brother

Dyer promises himself the pleasure of seeing you next Summer, a pleasure which I shall envy him.[3] Pray give my Compliments to M.ʳ Giffard, I am sorry for his Misfortune, and wish him success in his future endeavours to repair it.[4] To M.ʳ Thackray & M.ʳ Bradshaw I beg my Compliments when you see them.[5] My Brother and Sister Dyer present their Compliments and thank you for your intended hare, as much as if it had taken its course this way; and as you lik'd it, were better pleas'd that you ate it, than if they had eaten it themselves. M.ʳˢ Brooke embark'd for Quebec before I set out for Bath.[6] You promis'd my Sister to write to me as soon as you heard of my return: I therefore give you this early notice that I may claim your promise. I also desire two pair of shoes as soon as possible. With my best respects to all my Cousins, I remain,

Dear Madam
most affectionately Yours

R Dodsley

MS: Leicestershire Record Office, 15D57/3.

[1] In his next letter to Miss Cartwright, RD refers to this letter as having been written on 8 November.

[2] See RD's letters of 3 August and 15 December. Mr Richard Dalton was George III's librarian, a contact in royal quarters used by RD on other occasions. See RD's letter from Shenstone on 11 February 1762, note 2.   [3] Francis Dyer, RD's brother-in-law.

[4] For Gifford, see RD's letter to Miss Cartwright on 1 May 1761, note 6. The clergyman's "Misfortune" has not been discovered.

[5] See RD's letters to Thackray in January and February of 1758. For Bradshaw, see RD's letter on 1 May 1761, note 8.

[6] For Mrs Brooke, see RD's letter to Elizabeth Cartwright, 26 July 1762, note 3.

From [Elizabeth Cartwright][1]

Clifton Nov. 24th [17]63[2]

After returning thanks to my good F.ᵈ M.ʳ Dodsley for his two very obliging little, little Letters, I cannot help telling him how griev'd I am to find him only a Man of Words – the Chocolate ready, the Balm Tea prepar'd, my Cap (if not better) put on much tighter than usual; all this done two mornings together, yet no M.ʳ Dodsley appeared – Oh, but he was truely mortify'd that he cou'd not! yes my good speech making F.ᵈ so I do suppose; and am most cruelly concern'd for you. For my part as I put not my trust in Man, nor the Children of ⟨Eve⟩ Man, knowing them all to be deceitful upon the wieghts, yea lighter than Vanity itself, – I set down in a musty Philosophical mood enough, and moraliz'd over the Chocolate that you shou'd have partook of – the result of w.ᶜʰ was, that all is vanity – for a Philosopher must not talk of vexation of spirits, you know.

Seriously speaking, and without flourish, I shou'd have [been] extremely glad to have seen you, and (tho' not cruelly), was not a little disappointed that I had not that pleasure. after all perhaps 'tis well for you that you did not come, for ⟨?⟩ most probably you w^d have been question'd almost to death, which I suppose you in your wisdom forsaw, and like a ⟨wise⟩ prudent man avoided. Well Sir, (tho' a disappointed Woman) I assure you I have no malice, for I shall be very glad to hear that you got safe to London, and that you are well and happy; if the former, I make no doubt of the latter, for you seem to have a disposition form'd to be so; may it continue to the last with you – can you tell me where there is such another to be purchas'd at an easy rate? after concluding you well & happy; I desire to know what you are about; busy with Mr Shenstone still, or are you minding your own affairs?[3] – A propos, I take it mortally ill that you did not send me the Monody – no, nor say one word about it.[4] indeed, tho' you are a Man of words, it is but of few, for I think there is about nine in both your Epistles, and if you don't give me nineteen in the next, don't expect to be thank'd for it. I protest against your saying you want subject – for that I know to be – that is – I know it not to be so – Why what a thousand things you might have told me, and without going from home too – now you must have your Ten thousands to be sure, to tell one. Pray is there any such things as Plays now in Town? and do you ever go to them? When does Mrs Sheridan's Comedy make its appearance and when – in short, I expect much intelligence of this nature from you.[5] tell it not in Gath, but I have not read Lady Julia yet[6] – but I protest to you Sir that it has not been my fault; the Horrid Book-Man at the Hotwells (who by the way is the least Homo I ever saw) promis'd that he w^d get it me, – but alas! I know too well how promises are kept sometimes.[7] Well I am sure I don't belong to the promise breaking tribe, for tho' what I said did not amount to half a promise, rather than come under that Denomination, you see how I expose myself (and that not with a scanty hand) to your censure and laughter; the first I know will be gentle, and the latter I ⟨?⟩ should be the most unreasonable creature in the World if I did not indulge you in very heartily – but you are to know I allways was much less afraid of real Judges than smatterers – they make great allowances for Human infirmities – and female frailties in particular – Comforted with these reflexions, and relying on your good nature I scrawl on; wch of all the Scrawl you may have seen, I am sure you must think the oddest and I expect that you w^d be honest enough to own it. if you correspond with me Sir, you must expect more incoherence, incorrectness, and more Ins, aye and outs too, than ever you met with before – but I have still another comfort, and that is, that I don't think you will be able to decipher above half on't –

As to myself I have nothing to tell you (how *ever curious you shou'd happen to be*) only that my Motto is Semper Eadem, as the Irishman construed it – I suppose I need not tell you how that was.[8] I think this place most delightfuly situated, which I suppose you are no stranger to, but am sorry to add that I am not ⟨for long?⟩ fix'd for long here I am almost certain. I shou'd be extremely glad if time and chance w^d bring my good Neighbors and me together anywhere, that we might talk over old Stories, but whatever I may be of other People's, I am sure I am none of Fortune's Favorites; so don't expect it, so must be content with offering you my best wishes. I flatter myself with hearing from you very soon, and that you will tell me a little how the World goes – for alas! I am in the country.

MS: Folger Shakespeare Library, C. b. 11 (3).

¹ Most probably the writer is Elizabeth Cartwright, RD's cousin. She complains that although she had prepared for RD's visit, he had disappointed her. Furthermore, she informs him that his two "little, little Letters" of apology had hardly redeemed him. Indeed the size and content of RD's letters on the previous 3 and 25 August reflect that assessment precisely. On 3 August, he asks: "Have you yet forgiven me my not calling at Duffield?" Apparently Miss Cartwright did not respond, for on the 25th RD worries: "you cannot bear malice with such a continuance on account of my not calling at Duffield in my return." Actually RD had sent another letter on 10 November, but apparently it had not reached her. (See his letter of 15 December.) Perhaps the present letter was not even posted, for it is not signed, and RD would have acknowledged it in his letter three weeks later.

² Clifton was a suburb south of Nottingham, about fifteen miles from Miss Cartwright's home. The occasion of her stay is not known. Clifton Hall, a sightseer's attraction, had been the residence of Sir Robert Clifton, who had died the previous December.

³ Graves's and RD's troubles with Shenstone's unsettled estate are the major concern of their correspondence until RD's death.

⁴ Unidentified.

⁵ Probably a reference to Frances Sheridan's *The Dupe*, a comedy that had been hissed from the stage on opening night, the 10th of the month.

⁶ The fashionable *History of Lady Julia Mandeville* published by RD the previous 20 June (*PA*), reaching a second edition on 15 September and a third on 21 December.

⁷ On the basis of the slim evidence, it is impossible to identify the "Book-Man." Of the four hot-well spas in England, Matlock would have been the closest to Miss Cartwright's home in Duffield (*c.* fifteen miles), but no bookseller is listed for Matlock in D. F. McKenzie, *Stationers' Company Apprentices 1701–1800* (Oxford: Oxford Bibliographical Society, 1978) nor in Ian Maxted, *The British Book Trades, 1710–1777* (Exeter: by the author, 1983).

⁸ Reference unidentified. *Semper eadem* was the motto of Elizabeth I.

To Elizabeth Cartwright

Dec.ʳ 15.ᵗʰ [1763]¹

Dear Madam

I think it appears by your Letter to my brother Dyer that you have not receiv'd mine of the 8.ᵗʰ of Nov.ʳ in which I acquainted You with my return from Bath. I rec.ᵈ no benefit from the Waters, and since my return I have been worse than ever. I also told you that I had not seen Mʳ Dalton, but I have seen him since, and the Queen has seen your Performance, and admir'd it much. I have now got it back. I am sorry for Mʳ Gifford's Misfortune, and wish him better luck another time. I receiv'd your exceeding pretty Landskip for Mʳ Spence, and by his order have got it fram'd in the same manner that mine is. He is at present with my Lord Lincoln in Nottinghamshire, and will write to you as soon as he comes home: in the mean time he sends you his Compliments and thanks. We drank your health yesterday at the eating of your hare which was a very good one. I hope I shall have two pair of Shoes very soon, for these grow extreamly thin, tho' I now scarce ever walk at all, and am afraid my future Journies will al be confin'd to a Chair or a Coach.² But we must submit to these things, they are annex'd to humanity, & serve a very good purpose in weaning us from the World. For my part, I am quite ready to be wean'd, having long thought this earthly bubby but a very insipid sort of diet. I long methinks to be quaffing Immortality, in which 'tis said there is no worriness, nor want of appetite. But I shall grow grave, and forget that I am writing to a young Lady in the prime of her youth and beauty, and who of consequence has no wishes to die about her. May she therefore live long and happy as her heart can desire! So prays sincerely her affectionate Cousin

R Dodsley

MS: Leicestershire Record Office, 15D57/4.

¹ The year is certain from the similarity of contents of this letter to RD's fully dated letter to Miss Cartwright on 10 November, which he here recalls as his last letter to her on 8 November.
² For all subjects in the foregoing, see RD's letters of August and November to Miss Cartwright.

From Richard Graves

[c. 6 January 1764]¹

Sir

I am oblig'd to you for the happy word, "diffusive" in yʳ Criticism on my verses² – I sent them to Mʳˢ A [?] as spoke by our young gentlemen on their dismission for the holidays – & bespoke her interest at yᵉ same time to get our Road mended – in consequence of which Mʳ A – sent his men yᵉ very next week³ –

I alter'd yᵉ two Lines on a tender point

"But see the men of *Virtuous parents* born,"
"Whose *useful Life* exalted acts adorn –

Has Mʳ Clark yet laid the Will before Mʳ Blackstone?⁴ –

I am destitute of Franks – & good news –

Address: To | Mʳ Dodsley | at Mʳ Dyer's in Bruton Street | near Berkeley Square | London
Postmark: 6 IA Bath

MS: Somerset County Record Office, DD/SK, 28/1, 79.

¹ The day and month are approximated from the postmark. The year must be 1764 because Graves asks if Shenstone's will has been laid before William Blackstone, an application that could not have been made in a January of any other year than 1764: Shenstone had died in February 1763, and RD would be dead in January 1765. Besides, in his letter on 30 March 1764, Graves mentions that Blackstone's opinion had arrived.
² Graves's verses were published the next year as "Mr. Allen, or the Great Plebeian" in his anonymous *The Festoon*; the collection later appeared in Dublin as *The Christmas Treat* (1767). For the identification of this piece, I am indebted to Professor Clarence Tracy.
³ Graves seems quite pleased with flattering his landlord, Ralph Allen, into mending his road. (See note 2.)
⁴ See note 1. Sir William Blackstone (1723–80), the first Professor of English Law at Oxford (1758–66), had been at Pembroke College with Shenstone and, as subsequent letters show, advised the executors regarding the settlement of the poet's estate. For Clark, see Graves's letter of 21 May 1763, note 2.

To Elizabeth Cartwright

Feb.ʳʸ 2ᵈ [1764]¹

Dear Madam

Tho' I have sometimes reprov'd You for your delay in writing to me, yet I think in my Conscience you never deserv'd reproof half so much as I do at present on that very account. I cannot, nor will not try to make any apology on this head, but rather chuse to throw my self entirely on your mercy: so pray forgive me! and I will never do so again. Not but I have been very ill since I came from Bath, and am very listless & unwilling to set about any thing. But this is not intended as an apology, since it ought to be, and really is, a pleasure and a relief to me to write to so dear friend as Miss Cartwright. I am much oblig'd to You for your Turkey which was exceeding good; and for your pot of Honey which I dare say is excellent. My Sister gives her best Compliments and desires you will be so good as to send her your Receit for making Mead.[2] She is much oblig'd to You for your kind offer of sending her some Cowslips, but those she thinks she can get better and fresher from Covent Garden Market than you can possibly send them from Duffield. My Shoes fit me exactly as they should do, and I shall be glad to know to whom I must pay the money for them. I could send it by my brother Dyer, who intends You a visit in the Summer, but That I think is too long to trust. I expect Mr Spence in about a week, who will then take your Landskip into his own care, being unwilling to trust any body else with the conveyance of so valuable a charge. I am, with Compliments to all friends,

Dear Madam,
Affectionately Yours,

R Dodsley

MS: Leicestershire Record Office, 15D57/5.

[1] The year is certain from internal evidence. The shoes that "fit me exactly," RD had requested of Miss Cartwright in his letters of 10 November and 15 December 1763. In the former letter, RD mentions that his brother-in-law, Francis Dyer, planned a trip to Duffield "next Summer," a subject repeated here. Also in the December letter, RD mentions that he has had Miss Cartwright's "landskip" framed for Joseph Spence, who, in this letter, has yet to return to claim it.
[2] According to C. H. Beale (*Catherine Hutton and Her Friends*, p. 20), Miss Cartwright and her mother made both mead and metheglin, and Mr Cartwright's "banks" were well furnished with bees, Duffield having been long celebrated for its honey.

From John Hoadly

Bath. Feby 15. 1764.

Sir,

I saw lately advertis'd a new Edition of your Miscellany.[1] I beg the Favour of You to take upon yourself the correct printing of what little Pieces of mine there are in it; as they were most shamefully neglected in the last Edition, even to ye leaving out whole Lines; to the utter Confusion of Grammar, Sense, and what some Poets might resent more – even Rhime.[2] – I hope You enjoy your Health, & are freer from Gout than your very

humble Servant

J. Hoadly

MS: Bodleian, MS. Eng. Letters d. 40, f. 113.

¹ This advertisement has eluded detection. It certainly did not appear in any London paper that Dodsley normally used for advertising. In fact, there would not be another edition of Dodsley's *Collection* ("Miscellany") issued during his lifetime. The most recent edition had been advertised for sale on 22 November 1763 (*DA*), less than three months prior to Hoadly's letter, and the next would not appear until 1765.

² In the light of note 1, the 1763 edition would seem to have been the only one to which Hoadly could be referring. But it is unlikely that he would be asking RD to look after the "correct printing" of poems already published. Whatever the case, he certainly had reason to complain of the printer's shameful neglect, as he had also in his letter of 8 March 1758 when the first edition had appeared. A collation of the 1758 and 1763 editions shows seven obvious errors in the former and four in the latter, together with many other discrepancies about which it is impossible to judge without the original manuscript. The 1763 edition had corrected the seven obvious errors of the 1758 edition, but had introduced its own. Hoadly's poems, together with two by John Straight, had occupied the same pages in both editions: V, 244–88; VI, 294–5.

From Richard Graves

Claverton, 30 Mar[ch 1764]¹

Dear Sʳ

Nothing could be more fortunate th[an] the arrival of Mʳ Blackstone's opinio[n] soon enough to prevent your writing, [of] my request to Mʳ Clark² – Tho' I still thin[k] that matters have been protracted mu[ch] longer than was necessary –

I suppose the Sanction of the court [of] Chancery will skreen us from the impo[r]tunities of the creditors – But as I en[join'd] Mrs Cutler to consult you & myself ([or] her friends) about accepting a Sum of mo[ney] for her Annuity – I should be gla[d if] you could find an opportunity of learn[ing] the Value of such a Life, from any pers[on] skill'd in those sorts of Calculations –

I think she told me that Mʳ Hodgetts [of]fered her £300 – which, I believe, is [?] price – And would probably [do?] as well for her – Because with the ad[diti]on of her labour I suppose she could [con]trive to live upon the Interest – & then [such] a Sum of money would be more than [she] would probably ever save out of her [ann]uity – & she seems to have a regard for [her] family, to whom it might be of great [ser]vice – Tho perhaps Mʳ Hodgetts might [fi]ght to give more than that, to get [ri]d of such an Incumbrance³ –

I am glad to find by your advertise[men]t that your publication is in such [for]wardness⁴ – I am quite uneasy at being [pla]ce'd in the front of the complimentary [sup]port – & that not only my name – but [pl]ace of abode should be added – the [we]ak forces should always be rank'd in the middle.⁵

As you talk'd of sending me more than one Copy (which you really ought not) I should be glad to compliment Mʳ Blackstone wᵗʰ one: unless you would like to make it our joint present or even your own – as he had a regard for Mʳ Shenstone – & his approbation may be of consequence at Oxford⁶ – His house is in Carey Street – But as you always Err on yᵉ generous side, I ought not to make this request –

I hope we shall find you in Town at Whitsentide where we intend to pass a fortnight. I am with Mʳˢ Graves –

Good wishes Sʳ yʳ affect humbˡᵉˢᵗ

Ric Graves

P.S. Since I wrote this your Brother has been here, with Mr Allen's Compliments to know whether Mr Shenstone's works are yet pubish'd or not. He has sent 2 or 3 times to Mr Leake – & I find is very impatient – cheifly, y^r Brother says, as he hears there are some sentiments upon Gardening[7] –

MS: Somerset County Record Office, DD/SK, 28/1,63.

[1] The settlement of Shenstone's will had not reached this state by 30 March 1763, and RD, the recipient of the letter, died in September 1764.

[2] For Blackstone, see Graves's letter on 6 January of this year, note 4. His "opinion," presumably written, has not survived. For Clark, see Graves's letter on 21 May 1763, note 2.

[3] To Mary Cutler, his housekeeper, Shenstone had left "one Annuity or Yearly Rent charge of Thirty pounds clear of Taxes and all other Outgoings – to be paid . . . to her Half yearly," and charged to his "Estate in Church hill in the holding of Benjamin Whitaker." Shenstone also directed that Mrs Cutler be paid an additional annuity of "Six pounds half yearly" for the care of his "old servant Mary Arnold." But the executors found that the estates from which Mrs Cutler's annuities were to be drawn had been mortgaged, preventing the easy dispersal of the payments due her. The executor on the scene and inheritor of the Leasowes, John Hodgetts, became the villain in the eyes of the various claimants. John Scott Hylton had written to Graves on 22 September (Humanities Research Center, University of Texas at Austin, Robert Dodsley / Recipient 1/Bound, ff. 53–5) that Mrs Cutler "has been obliged to quit the Priory [at the Leasowes], because Hodgetts will not repair it, & the rain comes into every Room . . . & old Mrs. Arnold is with her." Hylton says that Cutler wants Hodgetts to sell the estates so that she and Mrs Arnold might be relieved of their condition, but that Hodgetts refuses (somewhat understandably!). Hylton also complains that Hodgetts has failed to release to himself and to Thomas Percy their letters to Shenstone, as well as to pay certain bills that Hylton had submitted as one of Shenstone's creditors.

    Among these and other disgruntled parties, Mrs Cutler seems to have been the most aggressive. She wanted the payment of her £150 bond given by Shenstone, as well as £165 for wages due from the beginning of her service to Shenstone; £100 from a bond and £20 from a note (with interest), both dating from 1758; and money owed from the estate of Thomas Jackson, Shenstone's servant who had died in 1759. All amounted to £500, but for some of the debts Mrs Cutler could not produce sufficient evidence. (See below, Francis Burns, pp. 324–5.) Frustrated, she began Chancery proceedings against the executors during April 1764. Of course, the complaint against RD was dropped with his death in September, but Mrs Cutler continued to file numerous bills against Hodgetts and Graves through 1766, bills that either named or required testimony from another score of people associated with Shenstone toward the end of his life.

    Tracing the case's development in the Public Record Office becomes extremely complex and much beyond a concern with RD. I am much indebted to Dr Francis Burns of Newman College, Birmingham, who recently pursued it to the bitter end. He tells me that the crucial judgment occurs in C.33 Index 1808 Michaelmas 1766 f. 61. There the entitlements of the annuitants were recognized, and it was ordered that the properties in Churchill and Romsley and the houses in Halesowen be sold, the proceeds to pay remaining debts, funeral expenses, and legacies. Mrs Cutler agreed to stay all proceedings, but she, Mary Arnold, and Richard and Mary Southall – the annuitants – consented to have a value set on their several annuities by the Master. Because no specific sums are mentioned, perhaps the Master made all parties accountable to him and took responsiblity for settling all claims on the basis of stipulations in Shenstone's will. (I am also indebted to Dr Burns, for supplying me with pages from his University of Sheffield thesis "William Shenstone: A Biographical and Critical Study" (1970).)

[4] RD had advertised on 15 March 1764 (*DA*) that the first two volumes of Shenstone's *Works* would be published "In a few Days." However the volumes did not appear until 6 April (*DA*).

[5] Graves refers to the appearance of his "To William Shenstone, Esq. at the Leasowes" among the "Verses to Mr. Shenstone" that concluded Vol. II of Shenstone's *Works*. His verses were second in line to Lady Luxborough's, but they preceded RD's and James Woodhouse's, as well as those by five others.

6 Blackstone was currently Professor of English Law at Oxford.
7 RD's brother Isaac had served Ralph Allen as gardener for over twenty years (Benjamin Boyce, *The Benevolent Man*, (Cambridge: Harvard University Press, 1967) p. 116). James Leake was Allen's bookseller in Bath. The "sentiments upon Gardening" were printed as "Unconnected Thoughts on Gardening" in Volume II.

From Richard Graves

Claverton, 9. April 1764

Dear S^r

I receiv'd your kind present on Saturday[1] – for which you have mine & Mrs Graves's acknowlegements – I knew *you* would not send them embossed – but I really do not love such very fine Books – perhaps because they disgrace the rest of my Study.

I am surpris'd at your Expedition – ⟨and⟩ but think no deliberation would have been attended with equivalent advantages either to the Sale or to our friends Reputation[2] – I have only had time to dip – but hope there are no inaccuracies of any moment – I met with a few Latin words falsely printed – one or two of them so as to puzzle me – As there will probably be a smaller Edition soon, I will take the first opportunity to send you a catalogue of Errata – with the pages mark'd[3] –

There is one thing of consequence which I should currently desire to have omitted, as such a piece of Buffonery will discredit our friend & may hurt the Sale of ye Book: I mean the first Sentence in the article of Religion: I am certain it was not in the Manuscript that I saw – or if it was, I must certainly have put a Cross upon it – The third Number will displease the Clergy – who are a powerful body in the reading world[4] –

I wonder also at your placing the Essay on Gardening – in a place so little conspicuous – as it is certainly ye most striking of all ye prose – would have conclud'd well, after ye Essay on Taste – & have introduc'd in some measure, your Description of ye Leasowes – Unless you would likewise transpose ye Essay on Taste – & put in next to that on gardening – & let ye Article on Religion conclude ye Prose[5] – But of this you may consider – I must conclude in haste wth Mrs Graves, Comp^{ts}

y^r affect humb ser^t

Ric Graves

Mr Melmoth says he offer'd his Assistence both by Letter & in person – and seems rather displeased that you did not accept of it. I have not seen him since ye work came out[6] –

MS: Somerset County Record Offices, DD/SK, 28/1, 17.

1 Volumes I and II of Shenstone's *Works*, published three days earlier.
2 Graves apparently was worried about a hasty publication of the volumes, for he had also evinced some surprise at their early appearance in his letter of 30 March.

³ Graves did send a sheet of corrections to RD; he inquires about it in his letter to James Dodsley on 1 October, shortly after Robert's death. The sheet has not been traced. Volume III of Shenstone's *Works* would not appear until 1769, and another edition of the first volumes not until 1773.
⁴ The opening sentence in the article "On Religion" read: "If people were to bawl out, 'God for ever! Huzza!' (which is a mark of respect to kings upon any event that is deserving of national gratitude) why were not this equivalent to a regular thanksgiving?" The third section of this article cynically censures hypocrisies in contemporary religious practice.
⁵ Among the thirty articles – some continuous essays, others extended but loosely connected notes on individual topics – arranged under the heading "Essays on Men, Manners, and Things" and comprising the body of Volume II, Shenstone's "Unconnected Thoughts on Gardening" is the twentieth in numerical order and separated from the last article, "On Taste," which immediately precedes RD's "Description of the Leasowes."
⁶ This statement suggests that, contrary to his original intentions, RD did not engage William Melmoth's assistance in preparing his edition of Shenstone's *Works*.

From John Pixell

Edgbaston April yᵉ 16ᵗʰ 1764.

Dear Sʳ

I cannot help troubling You with my Thanks for this fresh Instance of your unmerited kindness in making me the valuable Present of the Writings of Mʳ Shenstone – most of which needed not (though They had it.) the charm of Novelty to recommend them to Me.¹ You have certainly done your utmost to hand them down to Posterity in the most elegant manner, which must be esteem'd as the highest Instance of your friendly Zeal for his Fame & Reputation. –

I am pleas'd that You have given yᵉ Publick the Ground-Plot of the Leasowes, that Posterity may, by having recourse, see what rural Taste was in a state of Innocence before the Fall; for surely whatever Changes Time & Caprice may make, must be so many Deviations from Simplicity.² – but I forget that the only design of this Letter is to tell You how much Sʳ,

I am your obliged humble Servᵗ

J Pixell

MS: Humanitites Research Center, University of Texas at Austin, Robert Dodsley / Recipient 1/ Bound, f. 129.

¹ As a friend of Shenstone, Pixell received the first two volumes of RD's edition of the poet's *Works*.
² See RD's letter to Shenstone on 1 December 1759, notes 11 and 20.

To Elizabeth Cartwright

April 28, 1764¹

Yes, my dear Madam, I am very well content to continue yet awhile in this "dirty Planet," nay, am afraid I shall be very sorry to leave it, when I consider that I shall probably leave behind me some very agreeable Friends. Mʳ Spence talks of setting out about the middle of June, and of staying a week or ten days at his Living on the road, and a day or two at L.ᵈ Wentworth's,[2] but for his servants you need give yourself no trouble, for he will have none with him but John, who may lie at the public House at the Bridge. We shall have no horses but those we hire, and get rid of at every Post. As to Mͬ Spence and I, if it will not be too troublesome we shall chuse to lie at your house, which will want neither hills, nor rivers, nor lawns to make it agreeable: I flatter myself we shall find there somewhat much more agreeable than all these. We shall certainly go by Matlock where I did purpose to stay a few days while Mͬ Spence made his visits to the Duke, but of this we shall better determine when we are upon the spot.[3] My brother Dyer seems yet strongly inclined to see Duffield; and if he does I fancy it will be in July. I had a letter the other day from ⟨?⟩ Quebec, from Mͬˢ Brooke who is very well.[4] A third Edition of Lady Julia is printed, which continues to sell, and is much admir'd. All here join me in Compliments to all your good family.

I am   Dear Madam
Affectionately Your's
R Dodsley[5]

Source: "Time's Stepping Stones" (*c.* 1850), Leicestershire Record Office, 15D57/448.

[1] Although Samuel Coltman's copy of RD's letter shows no date, C. H. Beale (*Catherine Hutton and Her Friends*, p. 20), who apparently had seen the holograph letter, dates this piece as "April 28, 1764."

[2] On his return from his last tour of the Continent in 1742, Spence was presented by his college to the living of Great Horwood, Buckinghamshire. Charles Watson-Wentworth (1730–82), Earl of Malton and 2nd Marquis of Rockingham, had been Lord of the Bedchamber from 1751 until he fell from favor and was dismissed from his offices in 1762. He lived at Kirkby, just north-east of Duffield, Miss Cartwright's home. For more specific details of the itinerary and for a later account of RD's failing health, see the next two letters to Elizabeth Cartwright, from his travelling companion Joseph Spence.

[3] William Cavendish (1720–64), 4th Duke of Devonshire, to whom Spence had earlier served as a travelling tutor. If Spence ever reached the Duke's, it was none too early: Cavendish died four months later at the age of forty-four.

[4] See RD's letter to Miss Cartwright on 26 July 1762, note 3. Coltman's transcription shows an asterisk after "Brooke" referring to the marginal note: "The Author of Lady Julia Mandeville." It is not clear whether the inclusion is RD's or Coltman's.

[5] This is the last of RD's letters in the collection. Indeed its opening was prophetic: RD departed this "'dirty Planet'" while on the trip he is here planning.

From Joseph Spence to Elizabeth Cartwright

June 12, 1764

Dear Miss Cartwright, –

I return you a thousand thanks for your delightful letter, in which you are so good as to treat me with three descriptions instead of one. I have been in a perpetual round of business, and visits, and visitors for a long time, which have kept me in (what I heartily abhor) a continual hurry. Pray forgive me, or rather pity me.

Mr. Dodsley came here the 9th, is better than when I saw him before, and I hope the air and exercise may give a new turn to him.[1] We set out to-morrow morning for my living in Buckinghamshire, not such a paradise as Duffield is; but rich for the farmer and deep (very deep) for the traveller [alluding to the roads], at least in all the winter months, and probably still.[2]

We are to set out from thence on Monday, the 18th, and if it should not be too much for Mr. Dodsley, he going on for Duffield, I turning aside for my old engagement Kirkby, the seat of Lord Wentworth, when I am to rejoin him at your house, and then we may settle the rest of our route. I am exceedingly obliged to Mr. Gifford[3] for his most kind invitation, but if you have two beds to spare without inconvenience, I should on all accounts rather desire to be under the same roof as my friend. My chaise and servant will be very well at an inn, and horses – I have none. I heartily wish you and all the good family health and happiness, and am your most obliged humble servant,

Jos. Spence.

Source: Catherine Hutton Beale, *Catherine Hutton and Her Friends* (Birmingham: Cornish Bros., 1895), pp. 21–2.

[1] For all subjects in this letter, see RD's letter to Miss Cartwright on 28 April, where he gives the same itinerary in anticipation of the trip with Spence. See also Spence's next letter, of 24 July.
[2] Great Horwood, a living Spence had had from his college since 1742. "Alluding to the roads" is apparently Catherine Hutton's addition.
[3] For Gifford, see RD's letter to Miss Cartwright on 1 May 1761.

From John Scott Hylton

Lapall House, Halesowen, near Birmingham
24 June 1764

Dear Sir__,

When you was so kind as to make me a present of Shenstone's Works, you signified your intention of doing the same to Mr. Jago. . .

Source: John Waller sale catalogue (Dawson Turner Collection), 1859, No. 2.

From Joseph Spence to Elizabeth Cartwright

Durham, July 24, 1764

Dear Miss, –

Mr. Dodsley, who is pure well for a man in his condition, joins me in hearty thanks to you and all the good family for all your goodness to us at Duffield; and in all services to all friends there. We came on so leisurely that we did not get hither till the 17th in the evening, and on the road I had prevailed on my very honest cripple of a companion to promise me that he would attempt to walk round my garden here (which is about 500ft.)¹ once every day for the first week, twice for the second, and so on to four times a day, which would have been towards half-a-mile; but all this fine scheme was defeated the very first morning after he arrived here; for, upon making the experiment of one round only, Mr. Dodsley was so excessively fatigued that I have never been able to get him to venture upon a second. I am now endeavouring to make it practicable by preparing three resting places for him; one is a chair placed in a sort of grotto hollowed under the house; another is by a little turning seat on a small knoll that takes in a prospect of the country, and particularly the London road; and the third is a bench with a foot board, quite covered and surrounded with a little grove. Now, if he will take 'Gil Blas,' or any other good book in his hand, he may walk from one of these seats to another, and read as long as he pleases at each, and by this means may very well be in the air an hour or two whenever he pleases. The seat on the knoll is not yet finished, but as soon as it is, and the weather is inviting, I hope for better success in this experiment than we had in the former . . . Mr. Dodsley begs you would return his visit to you at London, and, whenever you so do, I beg you would come together for a good long visit to me at Bifleet. I am already your much obliged and affectionate humble servant,

Jo. Spence

Source: Catherine Hutton Beale, *Catherine Hutton and Her Friends*, pp. 22–3.

¹ As a prebendary of Durham, Spence resided at Finculo, the ruins of an old abbey four miles outside the city. For a description, see RD's letter to Shenstone on 22 August 1758.

From Richard Graves¹

Claverton – 30 Aug 1764

Dear Sʳ

I have heard nothing from Shropshire² these 2. *months* – & therefore know not in what situation Mʳ Shenstone's affairs now are – But a gentleman who has a considerable place in the house of Commons – & knows business, din'd with us this week – and says, "If we trust the affair entirely to our Lawyer tho' never so honest in his way, he will keep ⟨the⟩ it in his hands, till his Bill amounts to half the Estate in Question – He adds then, That we should consult together and form some pla[n] of selling the Estates – &c – and order him to execute it immediatly – And, I think, if all the parties concern'd could be brought to have a proper confidenc[e] in us as Executors –&c, by being persuaded that this is yᵉ only chance they have for their Legacies & Annuiti[es] being paid, acquiesce & wait with patience till [we] had sold the Estates and rais'd the money – it w[ould] soon be dispatch'd without any danger to us³ – th[en] we should not be at the expence of an amica[ble] Suit⁴ – which, I hear, will cost at least 50£ – an[d] may not be determin'd in some years – I have wrote to Mʳ Hodgets, to know how things [lie] & to desire him to bring all the parties concer[n'd] to submit to our Authority – But perhaps so[me] other Schemes may be carrying on, of which I [am igno]rant –

I have sent you the inclos'd verses – which I sketch'd out last Summer – but never had time [to] look them over till last week – They please m[e] better at present, than those already printed in [M^r] Shenstone's works^5 – And I was thinking whether [they] might not be inserted somewhere – tho' by n[ow] to *follow* Mr Cunningham's^6 – which make [?] you have any other Edition to come out – And you may dispose of them as you please –

I hope your Journey has had a good effect upon y^r health – I don't hear how your brother disposes of himself – but I find he has offers enough – in his present way, very advantageous^7 – I am with Mrs Graves's Comp^{lts}

s^r y^r affect. humb ser^t

Ric Graves

I wish you could have appointed a meeting of all parties & gone down – & acted for me by Letter of Attorney.

ToM^r Dodsley.^{8}

'Tis past, my friend, the transient scene is clos'd!
              th' enchanted vision
The fairy Piles, the enchanted visions rais'd
By Damon's magic skill – is lost in air.
    What tho' the Lawns, the pendant woods remain.
Each tinkling stream and rushing cataract
With Lapse incessant ecchoes through ye dale!
Yet, what avails the lifeless landscape *now*?
The charm's dissolv'd; the Genius of the woods
Alas! is fled – For Shenstone is no more –
    As when from fair Lyceum, crown'd with pines,
Or Menales, with leaves autumnal strew'd,
The fabled Pan retires⟨,⟩ the vocal hills
Resound no more – *but* all Arcadia mourns!
    Yet here we fondly dream't of lasting joys:
Here we had hop'd from busy throngs retir'd,
To drink large draughts of friendship's cordial stre[am]
In sweet oblivion wrap'd, by Damon's verse
And social converse, many a summer's day.
    Romantic wish! In vain we mortals trace
Th' imperfect sketch of human bliss. – Whilst yet
Th' enraptur'd Sire his well-plan'd structure views
Majestic rising 'midst his infant groves:
Sees the dark laurel spread *its* glossy shade; *her*
Its languid bloom the purple Lilac yield   *her*
Or pale Laburnum drop *its* golden chain   *her*
Death speeds the fatal shaft, & bids his heir
Transplant the Cypress round his Father's tomb.
    Oh teach me then like you, my friend to raise
To moral truths my groveling muse: For ah [!]

Too long, by wanton Fancy led astray
[Of] Nymphs & groves [?]
Oh: could I learn to sanctify my strains
With Hymns like those by tuneful Meyrick sung![9]
Or rather catch the melancholy sounds
That breath in Grey's or Warton's verse,[10] to paint
The sudden gloom that damps my Soul – But see!
Melpomene herself has sntach'd the Pipe,
With which sad Lyttelton his Lucia mourn'd[11]
And plaintive cries, "My Shenstone'⟨s⟩ is no more"!

                                                                R.G.
                                                        ⟨Aug. 1763.⟩

[P.]S. The moment I had finish'd this Letter – I receiv'd one [fro]m Clark – who gives a sad account of yᵉ State of Affairs – [he] talks of our being serv'd with attachment [&c] from yᵉ Sheriff.[12] [I] have wrote him a very angry Letter – & as he says "no Bill [of] Chancery can be fram'd which will answer our purpose." [I have asked] him why we cannot agree to sell the Estates – & [?] which will make all parties easy – but yᵉ Lawyer [?] in getting Shen[stone's ?]
Address: To Mʳ Dodsley, at Mʳ Dyer's / in Bruton Street near / Berkley-Square / London
Endorsement: a Single Sheet
Postmark: 3 SE Bath

MS: Somerset County Record Office, DD/SK, 28/1, 18.

[1] Unless it was forwarded to him in Durham where he had travelled with Joseph Spence, RD would never have seen this letter, for he died in that city a little more than three weeks later.
[2] Probably meaning from Hodgetts, the third executor.
[3] For the foregoing matters related to the settlement of Shenstone's estate, see Graves's letters since mid-1763, especially those of 20 June 1763 and 30 March 1764.
[4] A friendly action instituted by agreement between the parties in order to secure a judicial decision on a point of law (*OED*).
[5] By "those already printed in [Mʳ] Shenstone's works," Graves meant his own verses at the end of Volume 2, entitled "To William Shenstone, Esq. at the Leasowes."
[6] John Cunningham's "Corydon, A Pastoral. To the Memory of William Shenstone Esq." was the last of the "Verses to Mr. Shenstone" and the last item in Volume II of Shenstone's *Works*.
[7] Most likely a reference to RD's brother Isaac, whose position as gardener at Ralph Allen's Prior Park might have terminated with Allen's death on 29 June of this year.
[8] Although RD would not be able to honor Graves's request, his brother included the verses in the next edition of Shenstone's *Works* (1773). However, they did not replace Graves's earlier verses but were added to the group eulogizing Shenstone; that is, they were inserted immediately after "Verses by Mr. Dodsley, on his first arrival at the Leasowes, 1754." The printed text is faithful to that which Graves presents here, except that a three-line motto from Milton's *Lycidas* is added; "Shenstone," in the first mention, becomes "Damon"; and, curiously, "Mason" is substituted for "Grey."
[9] The verses of James Merrick (1720–69) had been published by RD in his *Collection* (IV–VI) and later collected as *Poems on Sacred Subjects* (1763).
[10] In the context, probably Graves is thinking specifically of Thomas Gray's *Elegy* and Thomas Warton's *Pleasures of Melancholy*, both published by RD.

[11] George, Lord Lyttelton's "To the Memory of a Lady [Lyttelton's first wife, Lucy] lately deceased. A Monody" (1747).

[12] "Attachment" involved the taking of property into the actual or constructive possession of the judicial power (*OED*). This action probably resulted from Mary Cutler's proceedings against the executors. Since it is doubtful that RD ever saw this letter (see note 1), he probably remained ignorant of the new turn of events in the protracted settlement of Shenstone's estate.

From Richard Graves to James Dodsley

Claverton, near Bath
1. Oct. 1764.

S^r

I receiv'd a confirmation of the death of my late valuable friend, your brother; (but no particulars – of that melancholy event) from Mr Dyer.[1] As Mr Dodsley's executors will of course succeed to his Trust in Mr Shenstone's affairs, I should be glad to know, who they are ⟨in⟩ as soon, as those enquiries can decently be made[2] –

I sent my late friend a whole Sheet of particulars – absolutely necessary to be alter'd in any future Edition of Mr Shenstone's works, which, I take it for granted he communicated to you – If not please to let me know, & I would write them over again[3] –

I also sent a Copy of Verses upon Mr Shenstone['s] death about a month since – which if he had thought proper, I desir'd to be inserted next to Mr Dodsley's blank verses – I know not what became of that Letter – as I suppose poor Mr Dodsley was then too ill – to be troubled with things of that kind[4] – I am

Sr Y^r Most obed Ser^t

Ric Graves.

MS: Somerset County Record Office, DD/SK, 28/1, 19.

[1] Francis Dyer, husband of RD's sister Alice.
[2] RD's brother Alvory and his brother-in-law Francis Dyer were his executors. See Appendix A.
[3] Not traced. See Graves's letter of 9 April.
[4] Apparently Graves's letter of 30 August had been saved by James Dodsley, or retrieved from Durham, for it was preserved among the Skrine MSS printed here. For the text of Graves's verses, see that letter.

B. PUBLIC LETTERS

From Sir Charles Hanbury Williams[1]

Grub-Street, February, 1742-3[2]

Fis Anus et tamen[3]

Sir;

– Though, for the generality, the books you usher into the world come forth as correct as possible, for which (as a man of reading) I take this opportunity of thanking you; yet, give me leave to tell you that, in your edition of Dr. Young's Poem, called, "The Complaint, or Night Thoughts," Part II., there is one erratum so gross and apparent, that I am surprised it could escape you.[4] It is in the first of the two following lines, at the bottom of the 28th page.

> A Wilmington[5] goes slower than the Sun,
> And all mankind mistake their time of day.[6]

Now, suppose you should, to use your own phrase, *dele the Sun*, and *lege a snail*; and then the verses would run thus;

> A Wilmington goes slower than a snail,
> And all mankind mistake their time of day.

And, as the last line is plainly intended by the poet, as an excuse for this noble person's having mistaken his time of day, I would also submit it to you, whether that likewise should not receive a small alteration of, *But* instead of *And*; and then the verses will run thus:

> A Wilmington goes slower than a snail
> But all mankind (i.e. all mankind as well as his lordship),
> _____ mistake their time of day.

Which is a genteel excuse for a superannuated person's accepting such an employment as his lordship is now in;[7] seeing that, according to this author, it is no particular failing in his lordship; but that all mankind are subject to the same error of mistaking their time of day.

> A Wilmington goes slower than a snail,
> But all mankind mistake their time of day.

But, to return to the most material error, which is that of the word Sun. I must beg leave to impute it entirely to your negligence, and to be almost certain, that it can be no other than a false print; for do you, Mr. Dodsley, believe, that Dr. Young really thinks it necessary to keep up a character of orthodoxy among his brethren, by pretending to believe literally the old story of Joshua? Does not he yet know, from the concurrent assent of all astronomers, that the sun never stirs out of its place? And how can Lord Wilmington go slower than that which never moves? I really believe he could, if any man in England could; but having so lately made himself *first minister*, it would be hard to put his Lordship so soon upon attaining any more impossibilities. Another reason why I think this Sun must have been a

494

mistake is, that I have myself been preparing a panegyric in honour of this able, active, supreme, sole minister, throughout which I could never connect his Lordship with the Sun, so as to bring them both into the same sentence; and, Good God, how could a man think of his Lordship and the Sun in the same line? 'Tis, I must confess, a vast extent of thought, far beyond my compass. The Sun shines fixed, and immoveable in its own proper sphere. Is his Lordship in his sphere? Is his Lordship immoveable? Is his Lordship bright? Does he shine? Does he dazzle? Does he influence? Does he enlighten? Does he warm? Or can he create? When he retires from mortal eyes for some short time to Chiswick, do men wish to see his face again?[8] Do they wait impatiently his coming out? Don't they rather think it time he should go out? How could his Lordship put any body in mind of the Sun? Nay, the Poet himself owns that his Lordship has mistaken his time of day; and that too is a thing which the sun never does. There is another remarkable instance in which he likewise differs from the Sun. The Sun is less favourable to England, than to almost any other country. Whereas, his Lordship's whole bent and study is, to make glorious and happy this already, totally, undone, nation. For what else, but a heart entirely English, could have persuaded an old infirm decay'd body and understanding, high in nobility, rich in excess, and without issue (for as I before observed he can create nothing), to take upon himself the *sole* government of this hard-ruled people? But for their good, what would he not? Nay, what does he not submit to? He stalks about, a first minister; not like the Sun: for he cannot show us even the shadow of power. Condescends to preside at a board where he has no influence; to sit in a parliament where he has no utterance; and most assiduously attend a council where he has no *opinion*. Look at his employments, and you will wonder at his power. Look at his power, and you will be amazed at his employments. If he must be in the heavens, then it cannot be as a Sun; it must be as a Pheanomenon, and such a one as never appeared in our hemisphere before; an inoffensive great man, an unregarded first minister, so much so, that I verily believe I am the only person who has his greatness enough at heart, ever to mention his name to the world; where, however, in spite of all my endeavours, it may happen to be forgot, unless his Lordship should prudently make an order at the Treasury (and I do not doubt Mr. Sandys will consent to it upon proper application through my Lord Bath),[9] that the following advertisement be published weekly in the London Evening Post:

This is to assure the public, that the Earl of Wilmington, &c. &c. still continues to act and sit at the Treasury-board, and carry on the business there, to the great advantage of these kingdoms, very methodically, and *slower than the sun*; by their Lordships' command.

J. Jeffreys.[10]

And I cannot but think, that it would be right, too, to get this Mr. J. Jeffreys to certify to the public (for people don't believe Mr. Cary),[11] that it was his Lordship, and not the late Mr. Pultney, that made him Secretary to the Treasury.[12] – But whatever is to be done of this kind, if his Lordship should submit so far as to take advice from so mean a hand as mine, I would, for fear of accidents, entreat him to put it immediately into execution; a week's delay may be dangerous; and, I believe, a month's would be fatal. And now, Mr. Dodsley, I must beg pardon for this long digression; but the subject fired me, and you, who are yourself an author, know how much pains it costs us, not to follow started Game, though I fear you won't allow my temptation to have been great, since so little diversion was to be expected from the pursuit of game that goes *slower than the Sun*. But, to return to my subject: – You won't, I hope, now wonder that I so confidently believe, that if you will again look over the MS. from which the Poem was printed, you will find the word *snail*, instead of *sun*. That word suits every way: it fits the place in the verse, and nothing can be more applicable. A snail being the slowest creature in the Creation, except that which the ingenious poet has placed behind it; but, if after looking over the Ms., it should still prove to be *sun*, I beg you will write to the doctor, lest it should have been a fault in the transcribing; but if there again I should be (or rather if the doctor should have been) mistaken, I beg of you in all humility to propose, and in the second edition (which I dare hope this letter will a little conduce to its having) insert my emendation. Insert it, if it be only in regard to common sense; for, really, to say that a man moves slower than a thing that does not move at all, is nonsense.[13] But to say Lord Wilmington is slower than the slowest reptiles, is very intelligible. Thus have I sent you my thoughts upon this trifling subject; but don't imagine it proceeds from any pique of spleen to the Poet or his Hero. Though, as a friend to learning, I own myself a little hurt, that his Lordship ever since he stumbled into his great employment, has cut off those small remains of encouragement, given by his predecessor to us men of letters. The disbanding the regiment of Gazetteers, and introducing Hanover forces in their stead, I will venture to tell, is not at all popular in our neighborhood; and, however despised the writings of my friends may have been, I dare affirm they did as much real service to the cause they were engaged in, as ever the Electoral troops will do.[14] The one contributed a little to support the late administration; the other, I believe, and hope, will destroy the present. Both have been paid extravagantly; but the Gazetteers did something, whereas the Hanoverians, whenever they are wanted against the Emperor, will, I dare say, be found to move as slow as the *snail*, or his *Lordship*, or the *sun*. Before I conclude, I should excuse myself, that this letter makes its first appearance in a public newspaper.[15] But you must consider it is a sort of appeal to the public, as well as to the printer, and author and his Hero.

And now if any thing herein should give offence, which (considering the taste of the age we live in) I think next to impossible, I shall only beg of those who condemn it, that they will do it in Doctor Young's own words; and let me find a little flattery mixed with their censure, when struck with just admiration of the character and talents of his Hero, and astonished at my daring familiarity, with so *great* and so *powerful* a man, they cry out with him

> *Wits* spare not *Heav'n*, O Wilmington, nor *thee*.
> I am, Sir,
> Your very humble servant,
> John Grub.

Source: *The Works of the Right Honourable Sir Charles Hanbury Williams . . . from the Originals in the Possession of his Grandson, the Right Hon. the Earl of Essex, With Notes by Horace Walpole, Earl of Orford*. (3 vols. London: E. Jeffrey, 1822), I, 102–11.

¹ Charles Hanbury (1708–59) had assumed the surname of his godfather, Charles Williams, in 1729 and thereby inherited a fortune. Although a staunch supporter of Robert Walpole, Williams did not lose his offices as MP for Monmouthshire (1735–47) and Paymaster of the Marines (1739–46) when the great minister fell in 1742. From 1747 until 1757, he served as an envoy to various countries on the Continent, the last two years as ambassador to St Petersburg. Frustrated in this last mission, he suffered an emotional breakdown on his way home, a condition that eventually led to his suicide in 1759. Known for his wit and gallantries, Williams was an original member of White's and of the Dilettante Club and authored many clever but vicious lampoons during the early 1740s (many printed in the *Westminster Journal*) that might easily have deprived him of the opportunity to take his own life. His friend Horace Walpole said of him: "He had innumerable enemies, all the women for he had poxed his wife, all the Tories, for he was a steady Whig, all fools, for he was a bitter satirist, and many sensible people, for he was immoderately vain" (W. S. Lewis, ed. *Correspondence*, XXX, 312–13). RD's letters to Williams in 1758 show him serving as the latter's bookseller, but their acquaintance predates this year, as this letter and Williams's contributing No. 37 to RD's periodical *The World* in 1754 show.
    About this same time, Williams attacked Wilmington in another piece, "New Ode to a Great Number of Great Men" (*Works*, I, 139): "See yon old dull impotent Lord."
² The February date appearing at the end of the letter (seemingly from the holograph) inexplicably differs from that assigned by the editor, January, 1742–3. The former is used here as representing Williams's own ascription.
³ "You are old, and yet . . ." is borrowed from Horace, *Odes*, IV, 13:2. Horace's ode is addressed to the aging Lyce, who refuses to recognize that she can no longer stir Cupid's fire but lives on like an old crow, a target of public jeers.
⁴ RD had published *The Complaint . . . Night Second* on 4 December (*DA*), just a few months earlier.
⁵ The target of this satirical letter, Spencer Compton (1674?–1743) Lord Wilmington, after a long undistinguished government career that earned him such epithets as "old woman" and "amiable cipher," had been appointed as a stopgap First Lord of the Treasury in the Pelham administration that followed Walpole's fall in 1742. Williams's biting lampoon on the 69-year-old lord predated the latter's death by only four months.
⁶ Young had dedicated the second "Night" to Wilmington. In these few lines, the poet was attempting to persuade the reader of the quick passing of life and was warning the reader not to be deceived by the example of Wilmington who had lived so long.
⁷ Wilmington (1674?–1743) would have been approximately sixty-nine years old at this point.
⁸ Chiswick was Wilmington's home.
⁹ William Sandys (1695–1770), an untiring opponent of Robert Walpole, had been appointed Chancellor of the Exchequer in 1742 upon Walpole's downfall. Williams caricatured him in *The Motion* (*c.* 1742). William Pulteney (1684–1769), Earl of Bath, had supported Sandys's motion for the recall of Walpole in 1741, and was invited to form a government when Walpole finally resigned in 1742. However, his career was ruined in July of the same year when he deserted the Opposition to accept a peerage. Williams satirized Bath in a number of pieces, particularly "A Dialogue between the Earl and Countess of Bath," "The Country Girl," "Ode to the Earl of Bath," and "The Statesman" (*Works*, I, 174–5; 32–6; 146–9; 150–2).
¹⁰ In the new government succeeding Walpole's administration, John Jeffreys (1706–66) became Joint Secretary to the Treasury. Like Wilmington, he quickly distinguished himself as an ineffective official.
¹¹ Walpole's note: "Walter Cary, friend to Lord Wilmington."
¹² By indicating that Wilmington had been made Secretary to the Treasury by "Lord" and not by "Mr." Pulteney, Williams wryly comments on the political aspirations that characterized Pulteney before he deserted the Opposition for a peerage.
¹³ Needless to say, Young's lines remained intact in subsequent editions.
¹⁴ The emptying of English coffers to hire Hanoverian troops had been a heated issue during Walpole's twenty-year adminstration. In 1743, when Parliament proposed similar action, the controversy was renewed, prompting an extensive pamphlet war, featuring Lord Chesterfield ("Geoffrey Broadbottom") as the principal antagonist.
¹⁵ Although Williams had apparently intended his letter to appear in a contemporary newspaper

(probably the *Westminster Journal*, where so many others had been printed), Horace Walpole, in "Some Anecdotes Relating to Sir Charles Hanbury Williams and His Works" (taken from Williams's MS *Commonplace Book of Verses*), writes: "He [Williams] soon after wrote a dissertation in prose on those two lines of Dr. Young in one of the *Night Thoughts*. [Quote lines.] It was to abuse Lord Wilmington, but was never printed." Williams's *Commonplace Book* was first printed in *Horace Walpole's Correspondence with George Selwyn, Lord Lincoln, Sir Charles Hanbury Williams, Henry Fox, Richard Edgcumbe*, ed. W. S. Lewis and Robert A. Smith (New Haven: Yale University Press, 1961), pp. 311–23; the above quote is from p. 313.

To the *London Chronicle*
[from Robert Dodsley?] [1]

24–7 December 1757

The Observations of your Correspondent (p. 463.) concerning the national Advantages arising from the Employment of foreign Servants are very pertinent and just: But as the Benefits which he has pointed out are merely accidental, without any patriotic Intention in the Persons who retain them as Domesticks, it occasions the Liberty of a few Animadversions on the Subject, which, I apprehend, deserves to be further canvassed and considered before we adopt the Maxims of either Side for true Doctrine. [2]

The whole Number of foreign Servants (except a few Swiss) are of the French Nation: I shall therefore consider the Propriety or Impropriety of receiving this particular Class of People into the Families of the Nobility and Gentry of this Kingdom.

I think the Sentiments of the Gentleman are both harsh and exaggerated, where he asserts, 'An Englishman in Livery is a kind of Monster,' and adds, 'That he is a Person born free with the obvious Badge of Servility.' And also, 'That he who wears another's Habit, tho' for Pay, forfeits his Freedom.' A Livery Suit may indeed be fitly called a Badge of Servility, but then it does not convey Ideas of Slavery. The Necessity of the subordinate Ranks, Conditons, and Offices of Men, sufficiently obviates the Dishonour and Disgrace of Servitude. It rests only to determine whether a Person by wearing a Livery loses his Freedom. Slavery and Freedom are mere relative Terms, and the Import of them only to be gathered when applied to particular Circumstances; as England to its great Honour knoweth not Slavery, nor Loss of Freedom, (but by Covenant and Consent) in the Persons of the most menial and servile of her Subjects, the Position is too absurd to require a further Illustration. The Reduction of the Price of Labour may be better effected, if necessary, by a Naturalization of Foreign Protestants, useful Labourers, and industrious Artificers, than by an Importation of fifty thousand French Servants, professed Papists, whose religious and political Principles have an apt and natural Tendency to the Subversion of our Religion, Laws and Government.

The Qualities of foreign Servants as opposed to English ones, their suppliant and submissive Obedience, certainly deserves the Preference; but not therefore to be envied: And, if I mistake not, it is this Behaviour, joined with a Fondness for French Fashions, which induced our Men of Fortune to retain them in their Service; For what can be a more proper Indication of true Greatness, Independence, and Power, than an English Lord or Gentlemen, many of whom value themselves only on their Title, Rank, and Dignity, contrasted with the abject, servile Flattery and Obedience of a fawning Frenchman. The known Reputation of English Food, Wages and Freedom are powerful Incentives to a poor meagre Frenchman, to visit this Island, especially as he meets with no Difficulty in acquiring a Place, nor needs any other Character than being of that Nation: So that the false Vanity of the English Gentry, and the right Measures which the French Servants pursue for their real Interests, are the true mutual Motives I conceive of each of their Grounds of Action.

Can it be agreeable to sound or good Policy to wish or desire an Increase of Foreign, or rather French Servants, from the accidental and slender Advantages which may accrue to our Country, when our Principles and Conduct are liable to be injured by an Imitation of French Manners, Language and Dress? And altho' the same cannot be produced without our Permission, yet *similis similo gaudet*, the Force of Custom is very great and prevalent, and always begets a Similarity of Manners; else when the general satyrical Expression of our Countrymen being *Frenchified*?

The Interests of the English and French Nations seem incompatible in a State of Peace; can it therefore be consistent with the Rules of Prudence, when we are engaged in a War, in Defence of our natural and just Rights, with a People, cruel, barbarous and tyrannical, to receive its Subjects into our Bosom and caress them as Friends, when they are undoubtedly our avowed Enemies, and are bound by the Ties of Love of their Country, as far as their Abilities and Influence can extend, to communicate whatever may be necessary for their Safety and our Destruction? The Admission therefore of these Servants into the Families of the Great is certainly very impolitick, and the public Vindication of the Practice I shall ever esteem very imprudent.

I am, Sir, yours, &c.

R.D.

Source: London Chronicle; or the Universal Evening Post, 24–7 December 1757, pp. 612–13.

[1] As one of the proprietors of the *London Chronicle* from its inception at the beginning of the year, Dodsley is most likely the "R.D." who submitted this letter. In addition, the sentiments are very much his.

[2] This RD letter is a response to a letter in the *London Chronicle*, which, in turn, had been a response to an earlier piece in the same newspaper. The first article, signed 'B.B.," appeared on 15–18 October 1757 (p. 375). The author recounted a survey which found that 28,000 servants from Catholic countries were currently working in England, and then he supplied a "typical" letter sent home to France by such servant "spies." The second letter (*LC*, 12–15 November 1757, pp. 468–9), objected to the first reader's solution by claiming it shameful that free-born Englishmen be put in servitude, whereas using foreign servants released Englishmen for productive jobs in agriculture and manufacture, and for the army and navy. Actually the subject was not a new one. For instance, the *LEP* for 10–12 April 1744 had carried an advertisement for *French Snakes in British Clover*, a publication which expressed the same worry regarding the great number of French servants in English households, a condition which it thought destructive of the love of "our country" and religion.

APPENDIXES

APPENDIX A
ROBERT DODSLEY'S WILL

In the light of the fact that three of Dodsley's brothers were principal beneficiaries in his will, it is surprising that none of them was either author or recipient of a single letter in this collection; and it is even more surprising that never once are they mentioned in any of Dodsley's own letters. Perhaps he regarded the preservation of family correspondence, especially when exchanged with relatives who shared few of his interests, as of small value for posterity, and therefore simply discarded the letters over time. On the other hand, perhaps James, his fourth brother and successor at Tully's Head, destroyed his family correspondence shortly after Robert's death, as it seems he did so many other letters. Nonetheless, one might have expected at least the occasional allusion to the brothers in those letters that have survived, especially in personal letters written to their mutual acquaintances. When writing to Nelly Wright of Mansfield in 1757, for instance, Dodsley sends his compliments to cousins but omits mention of the immediate family in the Mansfield area. Although Dodsley's letters to Richard Graves are missing, Graves, in his extensive correspondence with the bookseller, only once seems prompted to mention anything of Dodsley's brother Isaac, who lived and worked on Ralph Allen's estate where Graves conducted a school for boys.

Perhaps the omission in early letters finds some explanation in the state of family relations following Robert's leaving (or deserting) his stocking-weaver apprenticeship in Mansfield. Although the circumstances of his departure are obscure, his father apparently took it badly, for when the latter died in 1750, the family property in Mansfield was willed not to Robert, the oldest of the children, but to John, the second son. John Dodsley (c. 1704–77) had apparently earned his father's favor by carrying on the farmer-maltster tradition of earlier Mansfield Dodsleys, first at Bolsover and later at Stoney Houghton. Evidence is lacking to suggest the effect of the father's will on the relationship of the two brothers, but certainly, as Robert's own will proves, they seemed to be on good terms in later years. After retirement Dodsley occasionally visited Mansfield – most notably two weeks after writing the present will – where, it can be assumed, he enjoyed the hospitality of his brother as well as that of other local relatives.

Likewise, it can hardly be imagined that Dodsley's visits to Ralph Allen's Prior Park in Bath during the 1750s did not include visits to his brother Isaac, who served as Allen's gardener from 1741 at least until 1764, the year of his employer's death.[1] Seeking relief from the gout, Dodsley made several trips to Bath in the 1750s and early 1760s, and one of his letters in 1754, addresssed perhaps to George, Lord Lyttelton, was dated from Prior Park, where he had been Allen's guest. Yet Isaac is not mentioned in this correspondence except on two occasions: once by Warburton and once by Graves, but never by Robert.

In the service of Sir George Savile until his death, Alvory Dodsley (1706–65) was probably the least successful of the brothers. Straus does suggest (p. 9) – although without revealing his evidence – that Alvory might have run a Westminster pamphlet shop through the support of his influential brother. If this is true, such a tie could well explain why Alvory is accorded the largest inheritance of any family member other than James and why the bookseller chose him as one of his two executors. A London location and a familiarity with the business would prove valuable assets for one executing a London will and dealing with Dodsley's extensive copyright holdings.

As would have been expected, Dodsley's sister Alice received not only a sizeable bequest but also all of her brother's furniture, linen, china and so on, for the retired bookseller had been living with Alice and her husband, Francis Dyer, in Bruton Street, St James's, during the last four years of his life. Apparently Francis had also earned Dodsley's particular respect during this time, for he was designated as the second of the two executors.

Applying simple arithmetic to the figures in the will shows that James, Robert's youngest brother and his successor at Tully's Head, enjoyed the largest bequest of all, £500. The sum proves a pittance, however, when compared with the value of the many copyrights Dodsley ceded to his brother, not to mention the good will and shop established at Tully's Head. Proceeds from whole or partial rights in the works of such as Henry Baker, Edmund Burke, Samuel Johnson, and Edward Young, as well as in Dodsley's own *Collection of Poems by Several Hands*, *The Preceptor*, and *Select Fables of Esop*, would alone amount to a small fortune. Indeed the value of the legacy James inherited would not become apparent until many years later, when it came time for proving his own will in 1797. He left his relatives not hundreds of pounds but thousands; eight thousand apiece, for instance, to two nephews in Derby.[2]

The Will[3]

This is the last will and testament of me Robert Dodsley, of the Parish of Saint George Hanover Square, being willing and desirous to settle and dispose of such temporal estate as God hath been pleased to intrust me with whilst I have strength and ability so to do. In the first place I desire that all my just debts and funeral expences may be paid and satisfied as soon as conveniently may be after my decease. Item I give and bequeath unto my brother Alvory Dodsley the sum of four hundred pounds. Item I give and bequeath to my brother John Dodsley the sum of two hundred pounds. Item I give and bequeath unto my niece Sarah daughter of my said brother John the sum of one hundred pounds. Item I give and bequeath unto my brother Isaac Dodsley the sum of two hundred pounds. Item I give and bequeath unto my niece Kitty, daughter of my brother Isaac Dodsley, the sum of one hundred pounds. Item I give to my sister Alice Dyer wife of Mr. Francis Dyer the sum of two hundred pounds and all my household furniture, plate, linen, china, and pictures, to and for her own sole and separate use and benefit, and I do direct that the same shall not be subject or liable to the debts controul power or disposition of her present or any future husband. Item I give and bequeath unto my niece Kitty Dyer the sum of three hundred pounds: all which legacys I do direct shall be paid within two years after my decease out of the principal sum of two thousand pounds due to me on Bond from my brother James Dodsley. Item I give and bequeath unto my said brother James Dodsley the remaining sum of the said two thousand pounds (after payment of said legacys) together with all the residue and remainder of my personal estate, ready money, books, copys, shares of copys, and all other my effects whatsoever of which I shall die possessed or intitled unto at the time of my decease. And I do hereby nominate, constitute, and appoint my said brother Alvory Dodsley and my brother-in-law Francis Dyer executors of this my Will, hereby revoking and making void all former and other Wills by me at any time heretofore made, and do declare this only to be my last Will and Testament. In witness whereof I the said Testator Robert Dodsley have hereunto set my hand and seal this seventh day of July one thousand seven hundred and sixty.

R Dodsley [seal]

Signed, sealed, published and declared by the said Testator Robert Dodsley as and for his last Will and Testament in the presence of us who in his presence and in the presence of each other have hereunto set our hands as witness thereto:

Bern^D Young ⎱   Clerks to Messrs Hindley and Eamonson,
W. Martindale ⎰   Bury Street, St. James's.

THIS WILL was proved at London on the third day of October in the year of our Lord one thousand seven hundred and sixty four before the Worshipful George Harris Doctor of Laws and Surrogate of the Right Worshipful George Hay also Doctor of Laws Master Keeper & Commissary of the prorogative Court of Canterbury lawfully constituted by the oaths of Alvory Dodsley the Brother of the said Deceased and Francis Dyer the Executors named in the said Will to whom Adminstration of all and singular the Goods Chattels and Credits of the said Deceased was granted they having been first sworn duly to administer

[1] See Benjamin Boyce, *The Benevolent Man. A Life of Ralph Allen of Bath* (Cambridge, Mass.: Harvard University Press, 1967), p. 116.

[2] For much of the biographical detail regarding RD's brothers, the foregoing relies upon Straus's *Robert Dodsley*, pp. 6–9.

[3] The text of the will has been transcribed from a photocopy supplied by the Principal Probate Registry, Somerset House, Strand, London. It is not in RD's hand, but carries his signature.

APPENDIX B

I. ABSTRACTS OF ROBERT DODSLEY'S PUBLISHING AGREEMENTS, RECEIPTS, AND BILLS

To avoid the repetitive formal language that characterizes the original texts of most of the following documents, only abstracts are printed here. Care has been taken, however, to preserve all detail thought to be of interest to the student of publishing history. In agreements to publish, for instance, are included arrangements regarding not only full payment for a copyright, but also the manner of payment, whether before or after publication, whether by the whole or by the sheet, and the actual payment per sheet, for both first and later impressions. Also retained are such details as the responsibility for providing materials (books, pamphlets, etc.) necessary for composing a work; the acquisition and disposal of plates for a work; reversions of copyright, given certain conditions; forfeitures resulting from the author's failure to deliver a manuscript on the date agreed; the rights of vested parties should one or the other decide to discontinue the contractual agreement; the specification of a model work (size, paper, type, etc.) for the proposed publication; the responsibility for correcting the press; the number of copies to be printed for a given impression. Where pertinent, these details have been woven into the annotation of the body of correspondence.

These abstracts, referring to 125 separate transactions, originate from autographs, citations in printed texts, extracts from original Dodsley papers, and bookseller and auction house catalogues. Sixty-four documents are available in their full texts. In all, the entries reflect fifty-one extant autographs, thirty-four extracts made by Isaac Reed (1742–1807) from the Dodsley's papers (see below), and forty abstracts from printed sources, including twenty-one from Sotheby catalogues and nine from Straus, *Robert Dodsley*. All documents but thirty-three concern RD and authors, booksellers, printers, book purchasers, or their representatives. Ten carry James Dodsley's name linked with RD's; another twenty-two show James's name alone; and one is signed on the Dodsleys' behalf by L. Lewis. These last mentioned are included because, in each case, the agreement is a follow-up on a work originally negotiated or contracted for by RD himself, alone or in conjunction with James.

Curiously enough, fate has preserved a record of publishing agreements that to a large extent covers different periods of RD's career from those represented in his correspondence. Of the one hundred and three parties involved in these documents, only twenty-three are found among his correspondents; although much more than half of the correspondence dates from after 1753, less than forty per cent of the documents originate from that period. The effect on the present work has been both positive and negative. Although the concentration of the correspondence in the 1750s would have profitted from corroborative evidence afforded by the documents, such resources supply for the period where the correspondence is light; namely, during RD's earlier years at Tully's Head. Consequently the agreements can be viewed as truly a supplement to the correspondence, and a most valuable one.

The format of the entries follows in this manner. The first item in each entry, the name in bold print, represents the party with whom RD is engaged in that document. Regularly, articles of agreement with authors, or even receipts from them, were drawn up by the bookseller or an appointed person and merely signed by the author entering the agreement or giving the receipt, but not always. Agreements between booksellers and printers must be treated *ad hoc*.

The next item is a short-title of the work with the year it was first published from Tully's Head which, in most cases, means its first edition. Where RD is publishing his first edition of a previously published work, the year of its original first edition occurs as well.

The third item designates the source of the contractual information. It can be assumed that where institutional or private libraries are listed, the full text of the agreement is on hand. Where an agreement has been taken from a printed source, "full text" occurs in parentheses if indeed that is the case; if otherwise, no designation occurs. Those sources specified "Reed/Chalmers," are Isaac Reed's extracts from the Dodsley papers that had come into his possession in 1797 upon the death of James Dodsley. (See below for a fuller citation.)

In a few cases where the same document has been offered for sale at different times by the same or by different dealers or auctioneers, all the pertinent detail found in the manuscript seems not to have been listed in each entry, for the supply of information varies. In such instances, the abstract represents a conflation of those sources.

Frequently, additional references to the same document are extant. These are placed next in the listing, following "*Also:*". Such references are almost always secondary to the initial source supplied at the heading, in terms of their meaner supply of information or their further remove from the original manuscript. In entries that show distinctly numbered documents, each document is presented in numerical sequence as it pertains to the publication in question. Normally additional documents concern revised agreements, second or later editions, or multiple receipts.

The next item – only occasionally appearing (for example, in Henry Baker, *Employment for the Microscope*) – records such matters as RD's registering a work at the Stationers' Company and pertinent printing information, usually taken from the ledgers of William Bowyer[1] or William Strahan.[2]

At the conclusion of each entry, the imprint (where a copy survives) has been provided to show additional persons known to have been involved in the publication or sale of the work. Occasionally, especially in the case of receipts, only one bookseller's name will appear whereas, in fact, one or more other people owned a share or shares in the copyright. For example, Reed/Chalmers records that JD paid £50 for a moiety of the copy of Robert Lowth's *Short Introduction to English*

Grammar (1762). Presumably the other half was purchased by Andrew Millar whose name appears with R & JD's on the imprint. That half seems not to have been retained by Lowth, for James Dodsley later purchased some of Millar's share. (See entry for Thomas Cadell.) Of course there is no intention to suggest that all names appearing in an imprint are those of shareholders. In many cases, persons such as Mary Cooper were involved merely in the sale of a work. Where a copy has not been seen, other publishing data are supplied instead of an imprint. Finally, an occasional note or query follows the imprint.

Reed/Chalmers. Agreements assigned this origin have been taken from a manuscript entitled: "Memoranda from Mr. Dodsley's Papers, which I received this day, 29th April 1797, from the Extors." The Memoranda are in the hand of Isaac Reed (1742–1807), whose collaboration with RD's brother James is clear from Reed's issuing another edition of RD's *Select Collection of Old Plays* in 1780 and a revised *Collection of Poems by Several Hands* in 1782. This 25-page document later passed into the hands of the biographer Alexander Chalmers (his name appears on the front fly-leaf) and today is lodged in the New College Library, Edinburgh. The pagination is assigned by the editor; the original shows no pagination nor foliation.

Very occasionally (see entries for John Collet; William Melmoth, "Fitzoborne's" *Letters*), Reed/Chalmers is at odds with extant documents regarding dates, but frequently it supplements the information provided by other sources. Most importantly, it contributes more than a quarter of the following entries.

¹ Grolier Club, New York, 19471, 19472, 19474; Bodleian Library, MS. don. b. 4. For references to the Bowyer Ledgers, I am indebted to Professor Keith Maslen, University of Otago, whose study of the subject is forthcoming.   ² BL. Add. MS. 48,800.

Akenside, Mark (1721–70)

The Museum: or, Literary and Historical Register (1746–7)

National Library of Scotland, MS. 582, f. 27.

RD engages A. for six months, beginning 25 March 1746, to prepare and have ready for the press, once a fortnight: one essay whenever necessary for carrying on the *Museum*; also for the same work, an account of the most notable, recently published books in English, Latin, French, or Italian to fill one and a half sheets of small pica; books to be furnished by RD; A. to supervise all and correct press. On his part, RD agrees to pay A. £50 on or before 27 September 1746, and thereafter £100 per year as long as both parties agree to continue the publication. Dated 20 January 1746.

Also: Reed/Chalmers, p. 3, which notes that RD admitted [Thomas] Longman, [Charles] Hitch, and [John] Rivington as partners and engaged John Campbell to undertake the Historical Memoirs in the *Museum; Gentleman's Magazine*, n.s. 39 (1853), p. 158; Straus, pp. 82–3.

Imprint: London: Printed for R. Dodsley in Pall-mall. M.DCC.XLVI and M.DCC.XLVII (collected edition)

Amey, Robert, pamphlet seller in Craig's Court, Charing Cross, and Westminster Hall, Court of Requests (1737–53)
  See: Austen, Stephen

Atkinson, John
  See: Woodward, Thomas

Austen, Stephen (d. 1750), bookseller in Newgate Street (1730–50)

BL. Egerton MS, 738, f.1.

Autograph signed articles of agreement, dated 15 December 1743, by Amey, John Jollyffe, Stephen Austen, John and Henry Pemberton, RD, and John Hughs to print the trial between the Earl of Anglesey and Mr Annesley. Austen to pay $\frac{1}{4}$ for $\frac{1}{4}$ of copy; rest to pay $\frac{1}{8}$ for $\frac{1}{8}$ of copy.

No copy located.

Baker, Henry (1698–1774)

The Microscope Made Easy (1742)

BL. Egerton MS. 738, f. 3.

Autograph signed articles of agreement, dated 3 June 1742, assigning the copy of B.'s *The Microscope Made Easy* to RD for the following payment: 5*s.* (herein receipted); 20 printed copies before publication; one guinea per sheet, half to be paid at publication and remainder two months after; additional guinea per sheet after 1,000 copies sold. To be printed in 8° in same sized letter as Lord Paget's Miscellanies. RD to procure and pay for copper plates. If second impression is needed within two years, RD to pay B. $\frac{1}{2}$ guinea per sheet additional. If no second edition within two years, copy and plates revert to Baker, the latter at one half RD's cost. Witnessed by Dan. Highmore, attorney, and JD.

Also: Straus, p. 324.

Imprint: London. Printed for R. Dodsley, and sold by M. Cooper, and J. Cuff. 1742.

Natural History of the Polype (1743)

BL. Egerton MS. 738, f. 5.

Autograph signed articles of agreement, dated 22 August 1743, assigning copy of B.'s *Natural History of the Polype* to RD for the following payment: 5*s.* (herein receipted): two guineas per sheet + 20 printed copies before publication. To be printed in 8° in the same letter as B.'s *Microscope Made Easy* (1742). For each future edition, RD to pay B. five guineas and six printed copies. Witnessed by William MacCarthy and JD.

Also: Straus, p. 325.

Imprint: London. Printed for R. Dodsley, and sold by M. Cooper and J. Cuff, Optician. 1743.

Employment for the Microscope (1753)

Straus, p. 347 (full text)

Autograph signed receipt whereby Baker acknowledges payment of £88.11.6. by RD, as per agreement, for copy of *Employment for the Microscope*. Dated 26 January 1753.

Also: Reed/Chalmers, p. 8.

"Whole rights" registered to RD at Stationers' Company, 31 January 1753.

Imprint: London. Printed for R. Dodsley: and sold by M. Cooper, and J. Cuff. 1753.

Baskett, Rev. John & Mrs Lucy
    See: Whitmarsh, Mary

Blackwell, Thomas (1701–57)

Memoirs of the Court of Augustus (1753–5)

Sotheby sale cat., 22 March 1855, lot 19 of John Wilks Collection; purchased by Webster.

Assignment of B.'s copy of *Memoirs of the Court of Augustus* to Hitch, Thomas Longman, Millar, RD and John Rivington for £500. Also, B.'s wife's discharge to the booksellers. Three documents, 1753–7.

Imprint: No copy located; *LEP*, 28 February–2 March 1756.

Bowyer, William, the younger (1699–1777), printer in Whitefriars
    See: Griffiths, R

Brooke, Henry (1703?–83)
See: Griffiths, R

Burke, Edmund (1729–97)

A Vindication of Natural Society (1756)

Berg Collection, New York Public Library.

Autograph articles of agreement and receipt for £6.6.0 signed by RD and William Burke, for the first edition of B.'s *Vindication of Natural Society*. 500 copies to be printed. RD agrees to pay an additional six guineas if second edition is printed. Dated 10 May 1756.

Also: Reed/Chalmers, p. 7 (full text); John Waller, Cat. 83, *Autographs and Historical Documents* (1870), item 91.

Imprint: London. Printed for R. and J. Dodsley, 1756.

A Philosophical Enquiry into the Origin of Our Ideas of the Sublime and Beautiful (1757)

Alfred Morrison Collection (HMC Ninth Report, 1883, Pt. II, p. 478).

Autograph signed receipt for twenty guineas from R&JD for the copy of Burke's *A Philosophical Enquiry* . . . Dated 16 February 1757. R&JD agree to pay an additional ten guineas if a third edition is called for.

Also: Reed/Chalmers, p. 7 (full text); Sotheby sale cat., 26 April 1869, lot 114 (purchased by Addington); Sotheby sale cat. (Samuel Addington Collection), 24 April 1876, lot 35.

Imprint: London. Printed for R. and J. Dodsley. 1757.

History of England from the time of Julius Caesar to the End of the Reign of Queen Anne

Reed/Chalmers, pp. 5–6 (full text).

On 25 February 1757, B. agreed to deliver to R&JD a work entitled a *History of England from the time of Julius Caesar to the End of the Reign of Queen Anne*, not less than 80 sheets to be printed in 4°, by 25 December 1758, for which R&JD will pay £300 in installments. Only 1,500 copies to be printed. Option to R&JD to pay £200 more for future rights.

(Work never finished. John Hughs's account to JD on 11 March 1769 says that in 1760 "6 sheets of it were worked off, and 9 sheets composed" (see ALS by Isaac Reed among Boswell papers, Yale. Ref: *Corresp. of E.B.*, ed. Copeland, I, 164).)

Annual Register

1. Reed/Chalmers, pp. 11–12 (full text).

Copy of autograph signed agreement between B. and R&JD, dated 24 April 1758, whereby B. agrees to write, collect, and compile the *Annual Register* for 1758 to be printed in 8° in the manner of Miller's Kalendar 800; to run neither less than 30 nor more than 34 sheets; to be completed, corrected and published by Lady Day, 1759. Both parties to give one another three months' notice if either chooses to discontinue the work or the contract as set forth. R&JD agree to pay B. £100 for the first volume, one moiety on or before next Michaelmas, the other upon publication. R&JD agree to supply all pamphlets and books necessary to carry on the work.

Also: Sotheran and Willis sale cat. (Tennysoniana), n.d., item 24; Straus, pp. 257–8.

2. Sotheby sale cat., 15 June 1882, lot 202.

Autograph signed receipt from B. for £53.15.0. acknowledging RD's payment for B.'s work on *AR* for 1759 (purchased by Thibandeau).

3. Pierpont Morgan Library, R-V Autographs Misc. English (Originally laid in extra-illustrated copy of Herbert Paul, *Queen Anne*, 1906).

Autograph signed receipt, dated 4 June 1762, acknowledging R&JD's payment of £50 to B. for work on the *Annual Register* for 1762.

4. James Crossley, *N&Q*, 1st ser., III, 441 (mention).

Receipt from B., dated 1763, acknowledging payment for work on the *Annual Register*.

Also: perhaps same document listed in Sotheby sale cat., 12 May 1851, lot 93 of John Wilks Collection (purchased by Morgan).

Burke, William (1729–1798)

An Account of the European Settlements in America (1757)

Reed/Chalmers, p. 6.

On 5 January 1757, R&JD paid B. £50 for the copy of *An Account of the European Settlements in America.*

Also: Sotheby sale cat., 22 March 1855, lot 23 of John Wilks Collection (purchased by T & W Boone). (The catalogue lists this document under *Edmund* Burke's name and quotes Noteby Evans, who sold it in 1835, as saying that it "decides the point frequently controverted, whether [Edmund] Burke was the author of the work. Burke himself has omitted it in the collection of his works." Current opinion believes Edmund contributed to and revised the work, but that it is essentially William's); Straus, p. 362 (mention).

Imprint: London. Printed for R. and J. Dodsley. 1757.
   See also: Burke, Edmund, *A Vindication of Natural Society.*

Cadell, Thomas (1742–1802), partner and successor to Andrew Millar

English Grammar (1762)

John Johnson Collection, Bodleian Library.

Autograph signed receipt, dated 13 July 1769, acknowledging JD's payment (by notes of hand) of £315 for seven $\frac{1}{20}$ shares of Robert Lowth's *English Grammar*, large and small (lots 557–62; 564–5); and 18 books in 1,500 of Dodsley's *Collection of Poems by Several Hands*, first three volumes (lot 254). All purchased at sale of Andrew Millar's copyrights on 13 June 1769 at Queen's Arms Tavern.
   See also: Lowth, Robert

Campbell, Archibald (1726?–80)

Alcides

Reed/Chalmers, p. 10 (full text).

Articles of agreement between C. and RD that C. will write an epic in 24 books entitled *Alcides* on the plan and quantity of the eight books now deposited with RD. For latter, RD advances C. £15.15.0. and C. agrees to produce one book every three months. RD to pay 5 gns. each. The total to be 150 gns. RD to print 500 copies. For 2nd edn. C. to receive 50 gns. more; the same for a 3rd. If RD prints 750 of first edn., then 100 gns. more for 2nd and 50 more for 3rd. Dated 16 March 1754.

(No copy located. Probably not completed.)

Campbell, John (1708–75), misc. writer

Museum: or, Literary and Historical Register (1746–7)
Reed/Chalmers. p. 4.

C. undertook the "Historical Memoirs" of RD's *Museum.*

Geography, Natural History and Antiquities of England and Wales
BL. Egerton MS. 738, f. 6.

Autograph signed articles of agreement whereby C. agrees to write *Geography, Natural History and Antiquities of England and Wales* to be printed in one volume, 4°, in same size letter and page as Jarvis's translation of *Don Quixote*, and containing not less than sixty nor more than eighty sheets. RD to pay two guineas per sheet in following manner: one guinea per sheet as work goes forward and remainder three months after publication. C. agrees to finish work in ten months or forfeit £50; RD to publish or forfeit £50. C. to prefix name to work and to correct press. Document shows only C's signature and that of witness, W. H. Wharton. Dated 15 October 1748.

(Work was not completed, perhaps not even agreed to by RD since his signature is missing. See John Hawkesworth and Alexander Galley, who, ten years later, RD engaged for the same work.)

Chapelle, Henry, bookseller & stationer, Grosvenor Street (1741–64)

BL. Egerton MS. 738, f. 8.

C.'s autograph signed receipt for £1.5.6. received from RD for one eighth of printing expenses for one thousand copies of each volume of "Tommy Thumb." Dated 11 January 1749.

Cheselden, William (1688–1752), surgeon and anatomist

Anatomy of the Human Body (1713)

1. BL. Egerton MS. 738, f. 7.

Autograph unsigned proposal, dated 1 May 1748, whereby RD agrees to pay 200 guineas for the copy, plates, and remaining volumes (providing 450 remain) of C.'s *Anatomy of the Human Body*. Also RD to pay 50 guineas for C.'s notes on Le Dran's *Operations in Surgery* to be printed with Thomas Gataker's translation (1749) and the plates to be directed by C. RD to pay 100 guineas upon delivery of plates and books and 100 guineas six months later; an additional 50 guineas for the notes on Le Dran as soon as plates engraved and copy printed.

2. Royal College of Surgeons, London, MSS Box 31 33.

Signed articles of agreement (including receipt), assigning the copyright and copper plates for C.'s *Anatomy* to Charles Hitch and RD for £200. Dated 8 April 1749. Witnessed by James Dodsley.

W. Bowyer printed 1,000 copies between 14 May 1750 and 1754 (Paper Stock Ledger, p. 714).

Imprint (Anatomy): London. Printed for C: Hitch & R: Dodsley. 1750 [i.e. 1756]

(*Anatomy* included forty plates. RD had printed the 6th edition in 1741 according to an advertisement in the *General Advertiser*, 26 March 1741.)

Henri François Le Dran's *Operations in Surgery*, translated by Thomas Gataker (q.v.) and with notes by C., was published by C. Hitch and RD on 5 May 1749 (*GA*).

Cibber, Colley (1671–1757)

Apology for the Life of Colley Cibber (1740)

Sotheby sale cat., 10 May 1875, lot 31 (purchased by Marshall).

Signed receipt, acknowledging RD's payment of £52.10.0. for the copy of C.'s *Apology*. Dated 24 March 1749/50.

Also: Reed/Chalmers, p. 4; Straus, p. 340.

Cibber, Susannah Maria (1714–66), actress

The Oracle. A Comedy in One Act (1752)

Sotheby sale cat., 10 May 1875. lot 32 (purchased by Naylor).

Receipt acknowledging RD's payment of £31.10.0. for the copy of C.'s *Oracle* and £18.18.0. for the expense of paper and printing. Dated 1 April 1752.

Also: Reed/Chalmers, p. 4 (copy only); Straus, p. 344 (full text).

Imprint: London. Printed for R. Dodsley; and sold by M. Cooper; and W. Reeve. 1752.

Clive, Catherine (Kitty) (1711–85), actress

The Rehearsal: or, Bays in Petticoats (1753)

Sotheby sale cat., 10 May 1875, lot 37 (purchased by Harvey).

Receipt for £21, assigning RD copy of C.'s *Rehearsal*. Dated 24 March 1753.

Also: Reed/Chalmers, p. 8; Straus, p. 347 (mention).
Imprint: London. Printed for R. Dodsley. 1753.

Collet, John (1725?–80), painter

Chit-Chat, or Natural Characters (1755)
Straus, p. 355 (full text).
1. RD's receipt for having received C.'s *Chit-Chat*, together with his promise to pay C. 20 gns. on or before its publication. Dated 6 November 1754.
Also: Reed/Chalmers, p. 8.
2. C.'s receipt for RD's note of promise to pay C. 20 gns. for the copy of *Chit-Chat* upon its publication. Dated 6 November 1754.
W. Strahan printing bill, entered February, 1755: £18.10.6.
Imprint: London. Printed for R. and J. Dodsley. 1755.

Cooper, John Gilbert (1723–69), misc. writer

Letters Concerning Taste (1754) [Dated 1755]
Straus, p. 352 (full text).
Autograph signed receipt by C. acknowledging RD's payment of £20 in books for the copy of *Letters Concerning Taste* (n.d.).
Also: Reed/Chalmers, p. 8.
Imprint: London. Printed for R. and J. Dodsley, 1755.

Cotton, Nathaniel, the elder (1705–88)

Visions in Verse (1751)
Reed/Chalmers, p. 13.
On 1 October 1757, RD paid C. £50 for *Visions in Verse* (1751; 5th edition by 1755).
Imprint: London. Printed for R. and J. Dodsley. 1755.

Coventry, Francis (d. 1759?)

The History of Pompey the Little (1751)
Reed/Chalmers, p. 8.
1. RD purchased of C. on 5 January 1751 the copy of *The History of Pompey the Little* for £52.10.0.
2. On 2 November 1751 RD paid C. £30 for the alterations in the 3rd edition.
"Whole rights" registered to RD at Stationers' Company on 12 February 1751.
Imprint: London. Printed for R. and J. Dodsley. 1751.

Curll, Edmund (1675–1747), bookseller

Philomela (1736)
Osborn Collection, Beinecke Library, Yale.
Autograph receipt from Curll, acknowledging payment of £45 by Richard Hett and RD for 300 copies of Elizabeth Singer Rowe's *Philomela* (1736) and for the sole copyright complete in two parts. Dated 5 March 1738/9.

Dilly, Charles (1739–1807), bookseller, 22 Poultry
See: Strahan, William

Dodsley, Robert

Sotheby sale cat. (Lewis Pocock Collection), 10 May 1875, lot 50.

RD's signature to a promissory note. Dated 10 June 1758.

Duncan, William (1717–60)

Commentaries of Caesar (1753)

BL. Egerton MS. 738, f. 9.

Autograph signed articles of agreement, dated October 1744, whereby D. agrees to deliver a translation of *Commentaries of Caesar* to be printed in the same size, type, and letter as Horace's *Satires* printed for J. Oswald, and to have Latin text printed on facing pages. RD agrees to pay D. £1.11.6. per sheet in the manner: 20 gns. upon the delivery of Gallic Wars, 20 gns. upon delivery of the rest, and remainder three months after publication. Not more than 1,000 copies to be printed. If 2nd edition, RD agrees to pay 10s. 6d. per sheet. In consideration of which, D. assigns copy to RD. Witnessed by James Dodsley.

Also: Straus, p. 347, suggests that agreement was voided when other booksellers entered the undertaking.

Imprint: London. Printed for J. and R. Tonson and S. Draper, and R. Dodsley. 1753.

See also: Rivington, John

Lives

Sotheby sale cat., 12 May 1851, lot 914 of John Wilks Collection; purchased by Pickering.

Articles of agreement for D.'s translation of Plutarch's *Lives*. Dated 1753.

Emonson, James (d. 1780), London printer in St James's, Clerkenwell (1754-80)
  See: Strahan, William

English, Thomas

Annual Register for 1766

Pierpont Morgan Library, R-V Autographs Misc. English (originally laid in extra-ill. copy of Herbert Paul, *Queen Anne* (1906).

Autograph signed receipt, dated 6 November 1767, acknowledging payment of £140 from JD for E.'s writing and compiling *Annual Register* for 1766.

Annual Register for 1790

Pierpont Morgan Library, R-V Autographs Misc. English (originally laid in extra-ill. copy of Herbert Paul, *Queen Anne* (1906)).

Autograph signed receipt, dated 30 December 1793, acknowledging payment of 150 gns. from JD for E.'s writing and compiling history of Europe in 8 chapters in *Annual Register* for 1790.

Fielding, Sarah (1710–68)

The Cry (1754)

Houghton Library, Harvard, 51*–178 (35).

Autograph signed receipt, dated 19 November 1753, acknowledging RD's payment of £52.10.0 for half of copy of F.'s *The Cry* (1754), to be printed in 3 volumes, 12°. RD to be accountable to F. for profits from other half.

Also: Reed/Chalmers, p. 8.

Imprint: London. Printed for R. and J. Dodsley. 1754.

Fordyce, David (1711–51)
  See: Fordyce, William

Fordyce, James (1720–96)

An Essay on the Action proper for the Pulpit (1753)

Puttick and Simpson sale cat., 23–4 March 1864, lot 104.

Receipt for 5 guineas assigning RD the copy of F.'s *Essay on the Action proper for the Pulpit* (n.d.).

Imprint: London. Printed for R. and J. Dodsley. 1753.

Fordyce, William (1724–92)

Theodorus; or Dialogue on the Art of Preaching (1752)

Sotheby sale cat., 10 May 1875, lot 54 (purchased by John Waller).

Receipt for £26.5.0 paid by RD for F.'s right in his brother David Fordyce's *Theodorus*. Dated 12 March 1752.

Also: Reed/Chalmers, p. 4 (addenda: £26.5.0. + twenty copies; if more than 1,000 copies sold, £5.5.0 additional); Straus, p. 344.

"Whole rights" registered to RD at Stationers' Company on 10 April 1752.

Imprint: London. Printed for R. Dodsley, 1752.

Galley, Alexander

A Compendium of the Geography Natural History and Antiquities of England

Bodleian Library, MS. Eng. Misc., c. 143, f. 304.

On 6 December 1759, G. signed articles of agreement to write a work entitled *A Compendium of the Geography Natural History and Antiquities of England*, based upon a Plan and Specimen supplied by John Hawkesworth (q. v.), and from materials provided by JD. Galley was to be paid £210 in eight equal quarterly payments. Witnessed by RD, the agreement was also signed by Hawkesworth, an Ann Smith, and JD. (The work was never completed.)

See also: Campbell, John.

Gataker, Thomas (d. 1768), surgeon

Operations in Surgery (1749)

Sotheby sale cat., 10 May 1875, lot 61 (purchased by Dutton).

Receipt for £63, assigning to RD G.'s right in his translation of Le Dran's *Operations in Surgery*. Dated 13 May 1748.

Also: Reed/Chalmers, p. 8; Straus, p. 338 (mention).

W. Bowyer printed 1,500 small, 150 large, 8° (Paper Stock Ledger, p. 711).

Henri François Le Dran's *The Operations in Surgery*, translated by G. and with notes by William Cheselden, was published by C. Hitch and RD on 5 May, 1749 (*GA*).

Goldwyre, Elizabeth

Aeneid (1740)

Reed/Chalmers, p. 8.

On 21 October 1751, RD paid G. £52.10.0 for Christopher Pitt's translation of Virgil's *Aeneid*.

Imprint: London. Printed for R. Dodsley. And sold by Mr. Hitch; Mr. Hinchliffe; Mr. Clements at Oxford; Mr. Crownfield and Thurlebourne at Cambridge; and Mr. Leake at Bath. 1740.

See also: Whitmarsh, Mary.

Gray, Thomas (1716–71)

Odes ("Progress of Poetry" and "The Bard") (1757)

Henry E. Huntingdon Library, laid in copy of Gray's *Odes* (1757), 148587PF.

Autograph signed receipt for 40 guineas, assigning RD copy of G.'s Odes, "Powers of Poetry" ("Progress of Poetry") and "The Bard," and reserving G. the right of one impression in an edition of his works. Dated 29 June 1757.

Also: Reed/Chalmers, p. 13; Straus, p. 164 (full text).

Imprint: At Strawberry-Hill, for R. and J. Dodsley, 1757.

Grenville-Temple, Richard, Earl Temple (1711–79)

Colonial Williamsburg Foundation, Williamsburg, Virginia.

Autograph receipts (3) for T.'s payments to "Messrs Dodsley" for books received:

1. JD's signed receipt on 4 May 1759, acknowledging payment of £19.13.3. for these books received on the following dates: 1756: 2 December, *Genius of Britain* (6d.); 10 December, *Court Register* (2s. 6d.); 1757: 28 July, abridgement of two last *Philosophical Translations* (£2); 19 November, binding Purcell (1s.); 1758: 13 February, *Statutes at Large*, 6 vols. fol. (£14.10.0.); 1 March, half binding Journals, 3 vols. (9s.) and sewing Index to Vol. I of same (1s. 6d.); Swift, *History of the Four Last Years of the Queen* (5s.); 29 April, *Dialogue on the Exchequer*, fine paper (10s.); 1759: 11 January, *Court Register* (2s. 9d.); 21 February, *Militia Arts* (3s.); 26 February, Robertson, *History of Scotland* (£1.1.0); 3 May, half binding Chambers, *Treatise of Civil Architecture* (7s.).

2. Receipt signed by L. Lewis on behalf of R&JD on 1 January 1761, acknowledging payment for books received by T. during 1760: 6 February, *Court Register* (2s. 9d.); 30 May, binding of Lyttelton, *Dialogues of the Dead* (1s. 6d.); 23 October, Martin, *Description of the Western Islands* (4s.).

3. JD's signed receipt on 6 June 1763, acknowledging payment of £22.1.3. for books received by T. during 1763: 27 May, Grey, *Debates of the House of Commons, 1667–1694*, 10 vols. lettered (£3.3.0.); 31 May, *State Trials*, 8 vols. fol. (£18.18.0), with lettering (3d.)

Griffiths, R[alph?] (1720–1803)

Jack the Gyant Queler (1749)

BL. Add. MS. 38,728, f. 108.

Autograph receipt for £1.1.0. signed by G. and dated 8 April 1749, assigning all rights in the copy of Songs in *Jack the Gyant Queller* by Henry Brooke (1703?–1783) to RD and William Bowyer. (Note on MS.: "in Bowyer's Hand.")

W. Bowyer printed 500 copies and delivered them on 11 April 1749 (2nd Ledger Book, p. 486), the same day RD advertised the work (*GA*).

Guthrie, William (1708–70)

An Historical and Critical Account of the Theatres in Europe (1741)

Reed/Chalmers, p. 1

On 29 September 1740 [T] Waller and RD agree to pay William Guthrie £10.16.0 for a translation of Luigi Riccoboni, *An Historical and Critical Account of the Theatres in Europe.*

Imprint: London. Printed for T. Waller; and R. Dodsley. 1741.

Hampton, James (1721–78)

The General History of Polybius (1756)

Boston Public Library.

Autograph signed articles of agreement, whereby H. assigns RD the copy of his translation of *Polybius* for 250 guineas to be paid in the following manner: 50 guineas upon delivery of the first three of five books, and the remaining sum on the date of publication. H. agrees to put the work to press within one month of the present date and to furnish the rest of the text, together with Preface and Index, by the next 29 December. H. also agrees to correct the press. Dated 26 April 1755.

Four autograph receipts from H., appearing on the same document, acknowledge RD's payments according to the following schedule: 14 June 1755, £52.10.0.; 1 October 1755, £52.10.0; 27 December 1755, £31.10.0.; 9 March 1756, £126. (Total: £262.10.0.; i.e. 250 guineas).

Also: Reed/Chalmers, p. 8 (details of agreement only).

Imprint: London. Printed by J. Hughs, for R. and J. Dodsley. 1756.

Hatchett, William

Fortunes Tricks in Forty-Six [1747]

Reed/Chalmers, pp. 1–2

On 20 February 1746, John Jollyffe and RD paid W. Hatchett 8 guineas for a pamphlet called "Fortunes Court of Requests," with a promise of 2 guineas more upon the sale of 750. (Reed/Chalmers note: "NB this, I believe is the drama published under the title of *Fortunes Tricks in Forty-Six.* [*An Allegorical Satire* (1747)]."").

Imprint: London. Printed for M. Cooper. 1747.

Hawkesworth, John (1720–73)

Compendium of the Geography, Natural History, and Antiquities of England and Wales

1. Reed/Chalmers, p. 13.

On 26 April, 1758, R & JD agreed with H. for the writing of a *Compendium of the Geography, Natural History, and Antiquities of England and Wales* to run not less than eighty nor more than a hundred sheets in 4° in the manner of Stanley's *Lives of the Philosophers* and to be printed with H.'s name at the rate of four guineas a sheet. (Not completed.)

Also: Sotheby sale cat., 10 May 1875, lot 73 (purchased by John Waller). (Does not include "Wales" in proposed Title.)

(Apparently this agreement was voided in favor of the next.)

2. Bodleian Library, MS. Eng. Misc., c. 143, f. 304.

On 6 December 1759, H. signed articles of agreement to supply Alexander Galley with a Plan and Specimen for a work to be entitled *A Compendium of the Geography Natural History and Antiquities of England.* Galley was to write the work from materials provided by JD. H. also agreed to superintend and revise the work, for which he would be paid £105 for the first edition and £52.10.0. for the second. Galley, Ann Smith, and JD also signed the agreement. Witnessed by R.D.

(The work was never completed.)

See also: Campbell, John; Galley, Alexander

Hay, William (1695–1755)

Religio Philosophi (1753)

Reed/Chalmers, p. 9.

On 2 June 1753, RD purchased from H. for £100 the copy of *Religio Philosophi.*

Imprint: London. Printed for R. Dodsley. 1753.

Select Epigrams (1755)

Sotheby sale cat., 10 May 1875, lot 74 (purchased by Dutton).

Signed receipt, acknowledging RD's payment of £60 for H.'s translation of Martial, *Select Epigrams.* Dated 21 April 1755.

Also: Reed/Chalmers, p. 9; Straus, p. 354.

Imprint: London. Printed for R. and J. Dodsley. 1755.

Hett, Richard, bookseller in the Poultry (1726–66)

See: Curll, Edmund

Hinxman, John (d. 1762), RD's apprentice and York bookseller
See: Moore, Edward

Hitch, Charles (d. 1764), bookseller, Paternoster Row, London (1733–64)

Museum: or, Literary and Historical Register (1746–7)

Reed/Chalmers, p. 4.

Hitch admitted to partnership in RD's *Museum* (1746–7).

> *See also:* Johnson, Samuel, *Dictionary of the English Language;* Cheselden, William, *Anatomy of the Human Body;* Blackwell, Thomas, *Court of Augustus;* Thomson, William, *Orpheus Caledonius.*

Hughs, John (1703?–71), printer nr. Great Turnstile, Lincoln's Inn Fields (1730–71)
See: Austen, Stephen

Jarvis, Charles (1675?–1739)
See: Jarvis, Penelope

Jarvis, Penelope, wife of Charles Jarvis

Don Quixote (1742)

Straus, p. 323.

On 7 May 1742, P.J. assigns copy of her husband's translation of *Don Quixote* (1742) to RD for £21 and 15 free copies.

Straus (p. 323) also notes the existence of an agreement between RD and the Tonsons for the work's publication, wherein Alexander Pope is mentioned as a referee in case of dispute.

Johnson, Samuel (1709–84)

London (1738)

Boswell's Life, ed. G. B. Hill; rev. L. F. Powell, I, 124.

RD paid J. 10 guineas for *London*.

Imprint: London. Printed for R. Dodsley, 1738.

A Dictionary of the English Language (1755)

Boswell's Life, ed. G. B. Hill; rev. L. F. Powell, I, 183.

On 18 June 1746, J. signed agreement with Andrew Millar, Charles Hitch, the two Thomas Longmans, RD, and John and Paul Knapton to deliver his *Dictionary* for which J. was to be paid £1,575 by installments.

Imprint: London. Printed for W. Strahan, for J. and P. Knapton; T. and T. Longman; C. Hitch and L. Hawes; A. Millar; R. and J. Dodsley. 1755.

The Vanity of Human Wishes (1749)

Hyde Collection, Somerville, New Jersey.

Autograph signed receipt, acknowledging RD's payment of 15 guineas for the copy of J.'s *The Vanity of Human Wishes* (1749) but reserving J. the right to print one edition. Dated 25 November 1748.

Also: Reed/Chalmers, p. 2 (full text); Boswell, *Life*, I, 193 (mention).

Imprint: London. Printed for R. Dodsley, and sold by M. Cooper. 1749.

Irene (1749)

Pierpont Morgan Library, R-V Autographs, Misc. English. (Originally laid in a copy of Johnson's *Irene*, 1749.)

Autograph document signed, dated 8 September 1749, assigning copy of J.'s *Irene* to RD for £100 but reserving to J. the right of one impression.

Also: Reed/Chalmers, p. 4.
"Whole rights" were registered to RD at the Stationers' Company on 16 February 1749.
Imprint: London. Printed for R. Dodsley and sold by M. Cooper.

London Chronicle (1757–)
Boswell, *Life*, I, 317.
J. received one guinea in 1756 from RD for writing the Introduction to the *London Chronicle* (1 January 1757).

Rasselas (1759)
1. Boswell, *Life*, I, 341.
William Strahan, William Johnston, and RD paid J. £100 for the copy of *Rasselas* and £25 additional when it reached a second edition.

2. Berg Collection, New York Public Library.
J.'s signed receipts to Strahan for payment of three installments on Rasselas: £10, 21 May 1759; £6.6.0. 22 June 1759: £8.14.0. (n.d.).
Half right registered to RD at the Stationers' Company on 19 April 1759; the other half to W. Johnston.
Imprint: London. Printed for R. and J. Dodsley; and W. Johnston.

Jollyffe, John, bookseller in Pall Mall (1731–76)
See: Austen, Stephen; Hatchett, William.

Jones, Henry (1721–70), poet and dramatist

The Earl of Essex. A Tragedy (1753)
Reed/Chalmers, p. 8.
On 5 March 1753, RD paid J. £100 for the copy of *The Earl of Essex.*
"Whole rights" registered to RD at Stationers' Company on 28 February 1753.
Imprint: London. Printed for R. Dodsley, 1753.

Knapton, John and Paul, booksellers in Ludgate St., London (1735–70?)
See: Johnson, Samuel, *Dictionary*

Layng, Henry

Circe (1745)
Reed/Chalmers, p. 1.
On 29 April 1746, L., for 10 guineas, assigned RD the copy and plate for his translation of Giovanni Battista Gelli's *Circe.*
Imprint: London. Printed for R. Dodsley, 1745.

London Evening Post (1727–1806)

Reed/Chalmers, p. 4.
On 5 May 1747, RD purchased a 15th share of the *London Evening Post* for £150.
Also: With details as above, a receipt signed by Richard Nutt listed on clipping from unidentified bookseller's catalogue laid in Straus's personal copy of *Dodsley* at p. 333 (now in McMaster University Library).

London Magazine (1732–85)

1. Reed/Chalmers, p. 4.
On 9 December 1748, RD purchased a quarter share of the *London Magazine* for £350.

2. Bodleian Library, John Johnson Collection.

At the King's Head in Ivy Lane on the first Tuesday in December 1764, all partners present, RD's ⅙ share dividend in the *London Magazine* for 1763 was declared to be £283.6.8. Against this sum, James Dodsley's purchase of ⅛ share in the *London Magazine* for £236.5.0. was subtracted, leaving a residue to JD of £47.1.8. Agreement drawn up by John Rivington.

Longman, Thomas (d. 1765), bookseller in Paternoster Row, London (1726–65)

Museum: or, Literary and Historical Register (1746–7)

Reed/Chalmers, p. 4.

L. admitted as partner in publication of RD's *Museum: or, Literary and Historical Register* (1746–7).

    See also: Johnson, Samuel, *Dictionary*; Blackwell, Thomas, *Court of Augustus*.

Lowth, Robert (1710–87), Bishop of London   *

Short Introduction to English Grammar (1762)

Reed/Chalmers, p. 17.

JD paid Robert Lowth £50 for a moiety of the copyright of the *Short Introduction to English Grammar*. *Imprint:* London. Printed by J. Hughs; for A. Millar; and R. and J. Dodsley, 1762.

    See also: Cadell, Thomas.

Melmoth, William, the younger (1710–99)

The Letters of Pliny the Consul (1746)

Reed/Chalmers, p. 2.

On 12 February 1746, RD purchased from M. the copy of M.'s translation of *The Letters of Pliny the Consul* for £50.

Imprint: London. Printed for R. Dodsley, and sold by W. Thurlbourne in Cambridge. 1747.

(Item 266 in J. Waller's sale cat., 1870–3, is puzzling: "Assignment of his [Melmoth's] translation of Pliny's Letters to James Dodsley . . . 3 February 1794."

Letters on Several Subjects, Vol. I (1747)

1. Sotheby sale cat., 10 May 1875, lot 150 (purchased by Dutton); Sotheby sale cat., 15 March 1888, lot 347 (purchased by Bennett).

M.'s signed receipt for 30 guineas received from RD for the copy of "Sir Thomas Fitzoborne's" *Letters on Several Subjects*, Vol. I (1747). Dated 26 December 1747.

Also: Straus, p. 334.

2. Reed/Chalmers, p. 2.

RD paid M. £60 for "Fitzoborne's" *Letters* on 27 December 1747.

W. Bowyer printed 1,000 copies each of the 1st, 2nd, and 3rd editions, which he delivered on 29 Nov. 1747, 2 April 1748, 21 Oct. 1749 (Paper Stock Ledger, pp. 905, 904, 915, 917). *Imprint:* London. Printed for R. Dodsley. 1748.

3. Straus, p. 338 (full text).

M.'s receipt for a note of £100, payable within six months, assigning copy of "Fitzoborne's" *Letters*, Vol. II (1749), together with a translation of Quintilian's *Dialogues Upon Eloquence*. Dated 12 December 1748. *Also:* Reed/Chalmers, p. 2.

"Whole rights" were registered to RD at the Stationers' Company on 10 March 1749. W. Bowyer printed 1,500 copies for the 1st edition and 750 copies for the 4th edition (1753) (Paper Stock Ledger, p. 911).

Imprint: London. Printed for R. Dodsley, 1749.

Letters to Several of His Friends (1753)

1. Bodleian MS. Eng. Misc. c. 107, f. 138.

Autograph (in M.'s hand) signed articles of agreement, dated 29 November 1752, assigning copy of M.'s translation of Cicero's *Letters to Several of His Friends* (1753), for which RD to pay M. £600 in three installments: £100 at this signing, £100 on date of publication, and £400 twelve months after date of publication, on which last date RD to gain all property and rights.

Also: Reed/Chalmers, p. 9; Sotheby sale cat., 12 May 1851, lot 997 of John Wilks Collection; Straus, p. 348 (full text).

2. Reed/Chalmers, p. 9.

On 30 April, 1755, M. received full payment from RD for Cicero's *Letters.*

Also: Straus, p. 348 (mention); Sotheby sale cat., 12 May 1851, lot 997 of John Wilks Collection.

W. Bowyer printed 3,000 copies of Vol. I, delivered on 10 April 1753 (Paper Stock Ledger, p. 944).

Imprint: London. Printed for R. Dodsley. 1753.

Millar, Andrew (1707–68)
   See: Cadell, Thomas; Johnson, Samuel, *Dictionary;* Thomson, William, *Orpheus Caledonius;* Blackwell, Thomas, *Court of Augustus.*

Montagu, Lady Barbara, sister of 2nd Earl of Halifax

Sarah Scott, *Agreeable Ugliness: or, The Triumph of the Graces* (1754)

Reed/Chalmers, p. 13

On 30 November 1753, RD paid M. £7.7.0. for a translation of Pierre Antoine de la Place's *La laideur aimable et les dangers de la beauté* (Londres, et se vend, à Paris, Rollin, 1752).

Imprint: London. Printed for R. and J. Dodsley. 1754.

(Separated from her husband, Scott lived with Lady Barbara.)

Moore, Edward (1712–57)

The World (1753–6)

1. BL Egerton MS. 738, f. 16.

Autograph signed articles, whereby M. agreed to write or cause to be written *The World*, a paper of one and a half sheets in the manner of the *Rambler*. RD agreed to pay M. three guineas for each paper, as long as both parties agree to publish under that title. If either party decides to discontinue his part, the other party will be allowed to continue the paper under the same title, M. with another bookseller, RD with another author. Whenever the paper shall be collected and printed in smaller volumes, each of the parties shall have a moiety of the copy and profits from that publication. Signed in the presence of John Hinxman and William Randall and dated 23 February 1753.

Also: Reed/Chalmers, p. 10 (date: 23 May 1753); Straus, pp. 186–7 (full text).

2. Bodleian Library, John Johnson Collection.

Autograph signed receipt for £400, assigning R&JD M.'s moiety of the copy of *The World* in 209 numbers. Dated 28 December 1756.

Also: Reed/Chalmers, p. 10

Morgan, MacNamara (d. 1762), dramatist

Philoclea, A Tragedy (1754)

Reed/Chalmers, p. 8.

On 6 February 1754, RD paid M. £100 for the copy of *Philoclea.*

"Whole rights" were registered to RD at the Stationers' Company on 31 January 1754.

Imprint: London. Printed for R. and J. Dodsley. And sold by M. Cooper. 1754.

[Nugent, Robert, later Earl (1702–88)]

Copy of receipted bill for purchase of books.

Essex Record Office, D/DU 502/2, p. 129.

RD's signed receipt acknowledging payment for Rollin, *Histoire ancienne* (£2.4.0), S. Fielding, *David Simple* (6s.), and [?], *Lady's Travels into Spain* (3s.). Dated 24 May 1744.

Nutt, Richard (1694?-1780)
See: London Evening Post

Paltock, Robert (1697-1767)

Life of Peter Wilkins, a Cornish Man (1751)
Reed/Chalmers, p. 4.

On 11 January 1749, Jacob Robinson (bookseller in Ludgate St., 1742–58) and RD purchased of P. the copy of his *Life of Peter Wilkins* for £21 and twelve copies.

"Whole rights" were registered at the Stationers' Company to Robinson and RD on 1 December 1750.

Imprint: London. Printed for J. Robinson and R. Dodsley, 1751.

Payne, John (d. 1787)

The Adventurer
Beinecke Library, Yale, MS File.

Autograph signed receipt, dated 11 December 1755, acknowledging payment of £120 by R&JD for purchase of ½ share of copy of *The Adventurer* in four volumes, 12°, and for all future impressions.

Imprint: London. Printed for C. Hitch, and L. Hawes, J. Payne, and R. Baldwin; and R. and J. Dodsley. 1756.

Peele, John, bookseller in Amen Corner, Paternoster Row
See: Woodward, Thomas

Pemberton, Henry, bookseller in Fleet St (1739?-44?)
See: Austen, Stephen

Pemberton, John, Jr., bookseller in Fleet St (1739–44?)
See: Austen, Stephen

Percy, Thomas (1729–1811)

Five Pieces of Runic Poetry (1763)
Sotheby sale cat., 12 May 1851, lot 1031 of John Wilks Collection (purchased by Webb).

P.'s assignment of copyright to JD of *Five Pieces of Runic Poetry* for 10 guineas. Dated 25 March 1763.
Imprint: London. Printed for R. and J. Dodsley. 1763.

Reliques of Ancient English Poetry (1765)
1. Reed/Chalmers, pp. 15–16.

Signed articles of agreement whereby P. assigns JD the copy of his Collection of Ancient English Ballads, proposed to be printed in three volumes, 12mo, for 100 guineas. Should only two volumes be printed, payment to be £70; an additional £35 for a third volume, for which P. hereby engages JD. If any accident prevents P.'s completing the work after he had received any part of the payment, the folio manuscript of ballads shall become JD's property. Dated 22 May 1761.

Also: Sotheby sale cat., 12 May 1851, lot 1031 of John Wilks Collection (purchased by Webb).

2. Sotheby sale cat., 12 May 1851, lot 1031 of John Wilks Collection (purchased by Webb). P.'s assignment of copy of "Collection of Ancient Songs and Ballads" to JD. Dated 1763.

Hau Kiou Choaan or The Pleasing History, 4 vols. (1761)
Sotheby sale cat., 12 May 1851, lot 1031 of John Wilks Collection (purchased by Webb). P.'s assignment of copy of *Hau Kiou Choaan* to JD for £50. Dated 10 June 1761.
Also: Reed/Chalmers, p. 16.
Imprint: London. Printed for R. and J. Dodsley. 1761.

"Chinese Proverbs, Chinese Poetry, and Argument of a Chinese Play" (1761) (Published with *Hau Kiou Choaan*, above)
Reed/Chalmers, p. 16.
P.'s assignment of copy of "Chinese Proverbs . . ." to JD for 10 guineas.
Also: Sotheby sale cat., 12 May 1851, lot 1031 of John Wilks Collection (purchased by Webb). (Mentions only "Chinese Proverbs.")

Philips, Ambrose (1675?–1749)
See: Woodward, Thomas

Pitt, Christopher (1699–1748)
See: Whitmarsh, Mary; Goldwyre, Elizabeth

Pope, Alexander (1688–1744)
See: Jarvis, Penelope

Popple, William (1701–64)
See: Woodward, Thomas

Randall, William
See: Moore, Edward; Warton, Joseph

Riccoboni, Luigi (c. 1675–1753)
See: Guthrie, William

Rivington, James (1724–1803), bookseller in St Paul's Churchyard (1742–56)
See: Smollett, Tobias

Rivington, John (1720–92), bookseller in St Paul's Churchyard (1740–92)

Museum: or, Literary and Historical Register (1746–7)
Reed/Chalmers, p. 4.
R. admitted as a partner in publication of RD's *Museum* (1746–7).

William Duncan, *Commentaries of Caesar* (1753)
Bodleian Library, John Johnson Collection.

Autograph receipt, signed by R. and dated 18 September 1767, acknowledging JD's payment of £1.10.0. for ⅛ share of Wm. Duncan's *Caesar's Commentaries*, 8°, purchased at Queen's Arms Tavern on 18 August 1767 (sale of Mess. Tonsons' copyrights). Promises further assignment on demand by virtue of letter of attorney from Richard Tonson, dated 20 May 1767.

See also: London Magazine (John Johnson Collection); Blackwell, Thomas, *Court of Augustus*.

Robinson, Jacob, bookseller in Ludgate St., London (1742–58)
See: Paltock, Robert

Rowe, Elizabeth Singer (1674–1737)
See: Curll, Edmund

Salmon, Thomas (?1697–1767)

Tradesman's Dictionary
BL Egerton MS. 738, f. 12.

Autograph signed articles of agreement, dated 22 August 1749, whereby S. agrees to deliver by the next summer the *Tradesman's Dictionary* for which RD will pay 1½ guineas per sheet for 20–28 sheets in the following manner: one guinea per sheet as copy prepared and made ready for press: ½ guinea per sheet when the whole work is delivered. If not delivered by next summer, S. forfeits ½ guinea per sheet. S. acknowledges payment of £4.

(No copy published by RD located. Perhaps this became *Tradesman's Director; or, The London and Country Shopkeeper's Useful Companion.* London: Printed for W. Owen. 1756.)

Scott, Sarah (d. 1795), novelist
See: Montagu, Lady Barbara

Selwyn, George (1719–91)

1. John Waller sale cat., 1873, item 114.
JD's autograph signed receipt for S.'s payment of a bill for books. Dated June 1755.
2. Sotheby sale cat. 21 August 1872, lot 116.
JD's autograph signed receipt to S. for payment of a bill for books, etc. Dated 8 March 1756.

Sheridan, Thomas (1719–88)

Jonathan Swift, *Three Sermons* (1744); *The Difficulty of Knowing Oneself* (1745); (?*Directions to Servants*, 1745)
Sotheby sale cat., 12 May 1851, lot 1076 of John Wilks Collection; Sotheby sale cat., 22 March 1855, lot 274 of John Wilks Collection (purchased by John Anderdon); Sotheby sale cat., 10 June 1870, lot 650 (purchased by John Waller); John Waller sale cat., 1870, item 248.
S.'s receipt for £50, acknowledging RD's payment for copy of Jonathan Swift's Sermons, Letters, Poems, etc. Dated 23 August 1744,
(Swift is named only in the Sotheby cat. for 22 March 1855 and in the Waller catalogue.)
Imprint: (Three Sermons) London. Printed for R. Dodsley: and sold by M. Cooper. 1744. (Others not seen.)

Smart, Christopher (1722–71)

Fables of Phaedrus (1765)
John Waller sale cat., 1855, item 142.
Receipt from S. for 10 guineas, acknowledging payment for his translation of Phaedrus. Dated 4 August 1764.
(Probably JD was the recipient; RD had been in Durham since 9 June and would not return.)
Imprint: London. 1765. (Copy not seen.)

Smith, Ann
See: Galley, Alexander

Smollett, Tobias (1721–71)

A Compendium of Authentic and Entertaining Voyages (1756)
Sotheby sale cat. (John Wilks Collection), 12 May 1851, lot 1084 (purchased by Hodgson); Sotheby sale cat. (? John Wilks Collection), 22 March 1855, lot 288; John Waller sales cats. (William Upcott

Collection), 1855, item 144, and 1856, item 143; Puttick and Simpson sale cat., 23–4 March 1864, lot 104; Sotheby sale cat., 21 June 1881, lot 164 (purchased by Thibandeau); Sotheby sale cat., 15 April 1918, lot 1098 (purchased by Sotheran).

Autograph signed articles of agreement between S., RD, James Rivington, and William Strahan, whereby S. agrees to compile, before 1 August 1754, seven volumes in 12° entitled *A Compendium of Authentic and Entertaining Voyages*, for which S. to be paid 1½ guineas per sheet for approximately 100 sheets. Dated 5 May 1753.

Also: Reed/Chalmers, p. 9; Alfred Morrison Collection, HMC Ninth Report (1883), Pt. II, p. 478.

Spence, Joseph (1699–1768)

Essay on Mr. Pope's Odyssey (1726, 1747)

BL Egerton MS. 738, f. 13.

Autograph receipt, dated 1 September 1744 and signed by Sam. Wilmot of Oxford, acknowledging payment of £15.15.0. for copy of S.'s *Essay on Mr. Pope's Odyssey* (1726, 1747).

Also: Straus, p. 328.

Imprint: London. Printed for R. Dodsley. 1747.

Polymetis (1747, 1755)

Sotheby sale cat., 10 May 1875, lot 173 (purchased by Harvey).

S.'s autograph receipt for £200, assigning the entire right in the copy and plates of *Polymetis* (1747). Dated 1 February 1755.

Imprint: London. Printed for R. Dodsley. 1747.

Sterne, Laurence (1713–68)

Tristram Shandy

1. New York Public Library, Berg Collection.

Autograph signed articles of agreement assigning the copy of the first two volumes of *Tristram Shandy* to JD for £250, £50 in hand and remainder in 6 months. Profits of all books already printed to be S.'s Further agreed that the third and fourth volumes to be purchased by JD for £380. Dated 8 March 1760 and witnessed by Richard Berenger.

2. Reed/Chalmers, p. 14.

On 19 May 1760, S. assigned the copy of the first two volumes of *Tristram Shandy* and of two volumes of *The Sermons of Mr. Yorick* (1760) to JD for £450.

Imprint: London. Printed for R. and J. Dodsley. 1760.

3. Reed/Chalmers, p. 14.

On 19 May 1760, S. agreed with JD for the purchase of Volumes 3 and 4 of *Tristram Shandy* for £380 to be paid six months after publication.

Imprint: London. Printed for R. and J. Dodsley. 1761.

Stillingfleet, Benjamin (1702–71), botanist and author

Sotheby sale cat., 10–12 May 1875, lot 175 of Lewis Pocock Collection.

S. agrees with RD to receive ⅔ of profits from sale of the oratorio *Paradise Lost* (performed Covent Garden, 1760). Signed 14 February 1760.

Imprint: London. Printed for R. and J. Dodsley; and sold by Mr. Baker. 1760.

Strahan, William (1715–85), printer in New Street, London (1737–85)

William Cheselden, *Anatomy of the Human Body* (1713, 1741, 1756)

Royal College of Surgeons, London MSS Box 31 33.

Autograph signed receipt, dated 25 November 1778, acknowledging JD's payment of £4.7.0 for $\frac{1}{16}$ share of William Cheseldon's *Anatomy of the Human Body*, purchased at the sale of the estate of William Nicoll on 22 October 1778 at Globe Tavern (Lot 15). Signed: W. Strahan, Jamey Emonson, and Chas. Dilly.

See also: Smollett, Tobias.

Swift, Jonathan (1667–1745)

Three Sermons (1744); *The Difficulty of Knowing Oneself. A Sermon* (1745); (?*Directions to Servants*, 1745)
See: Sheridan, Thomas

Thompson, William (1712?–66?)

On Sickness, A Poem (1745–6)

Straus, p. 328 (full text)

Autograph receipt, signed by John Thomas for T., acknowledging RD's payment of ten guineas as the first payment for the first part of T.'s *On Sickness*. Dated 17 February 1745.

Also: Reed/Chalmers, p. 1.

"Whole rights" registered to RD at the Stationers' Company for Bk. I on 26 February 1745; Bk. II on 24 April 1745; Bk. III on 14 February 1746.

Imprint: London. Printed for R. Dodsley, and sold by M. Cooper. 1745 (Bks. I & II); 1746 (Bk. III).

Thomson, William

Orpheus Caledonius (1725, ?)

BL Egerton MS. 738, f. 11.

Autograph signed receipt, dated 3 March 1753, for £52.10.0., assigning copy and plates of T.'s *Orpheus Caledonius* to RD. (Note indicates Hitch, Millar, & John Rivington equally concerned in copy.)

(No copy published by RD located.)

Tonson, Jacob and Richard (d. 1767; d. 1772)
See: Rivington, John, Duncan's *Commentaries of Caesar*; Jarvis, Penelope

Waller, T[homas?], London publisher at the Mitre and Crown, opp. Fetter Lane, Fleet St
See: Guthrie, William

Warton, Joseph (1722–1800)

The Works of Virgil, in Latin and English . . . The Aeneid translated by . . . Christopher Pitt. The Eclogues and Georgics, with notes . . . by . . . Joseph Warton (1753)

1. BL Egerton MS. 738, f. 14.

Autograph signed articles of agreement, dated 7 March 1749–50, whereby W. agrees to deliver a translation of Virgil's *Eclogues* and *Georgics*, complete with critical and explanatory notes upon these works and the *Aeneid*, together with occasional dissertations, a life of the author, and an index to the whole work, within fifteen months of this date. On his part, RD agrees to pay W. £200; £100 when the work is ready for press (except index), and £100 when corrected from press. RD also agrees to furnish all books necessary for carrying on the work. Signed in the presence of James Dodsley and William Randall.

(In 1751, RD had purchased the copy of Pitt's *Aeneid* and here engaged Warton as editor of the collection. The work included observations by Holdsworth, Spence, *et al.*; dissertations by William Warburton, William Whitehead, late Bishop Francis Atterbury; three essays on poetry by W.)

Also: Straus, p. 346 (complete)

2. Sotheby sale cat., 10 May 1875, lot 186; purchased by Dutton.

Autograph receipt for £221, assigning RD the copy of W.'s translation of Virgil's *Eclogues* and *Georgics*. Dated 15 November 1752.

Also: Reed/Chalmers, p. 8; Straus, p. 346.

Imprint: London. Printed for R. Dodsley. 1753.

Warton, Thomas (1728–90)

Argonautics

1. Eisenhower Library, Johns Hopkins University.

Autograph signed articles of agreement, dated 21 January 1752, whereby W. promises to deliver by January next, a translation of the *Argonautics* of Apollonius Rhodius, for which RD will pay W. £80 in two installments.

2. Bodleian Library Dep. c. 638, f. 45, on deposit by Trinity College, Oxford.

Autograph signed articles of agreement (with slight accidental variations from the above).

Also: Sotheby sale cat., 10 May 1875, lot 51 (purchased by John Waller); Reed/Chalmers, p. 9; Straus, p. 350 (mention).

(Work never published.)

West, [Gilbert?], (1703–56)

Lewis Walpole Library, Miscellaneous Manuscript Collection.

Receipt for W.'s purchase of single copies of John Gilbert Cooper's *Life of Socrates* (1749) and William Hay's *Religio Philosophi* (1753) for seven shillings. Dated 3 November 1753. Signed for R&JD by John Walter.

Whitehead, William (1715–85)

The Danger of Writing Verse (1741)

Reed/Chalmers, p. 1.

RD paid W. £10.10.0. for the copy of *The Danger of Writing Verse.*

Imprint: London. Printed for R. Dodsley; and sold by T. Cooper. 1741.

An Essay on Ridicule (1743)

Reed/Chalmers, p. 1.

RD paid W. £15.15.0. for the copy of *An Essay on Ridicule.*

Imprint: London. Printed for R. Dodsley; and sold by M. Cooper. 1743.

Ann Boleyn to Henry the Eighth. An Epistle (1743)

Straus, p. 324 (full text)

Articles of agreement between W. and RD for publishing *Ann Boleyn to Henry the Eighth.* RD runs all risk of printing, paper, and publishing. After expenses deducted, W. and RD to share equally in profit. Dated 28 April 1743 and signed by Thomas Wright on behalf of W.

Also: Reed/Chalmers, p. 1 (date: 20 April 1743).

Imprint: London. Printed for R. Dodsley; and sold by M. Cooper. 1743.

On Nobility (1744)

Bodleian Library, John Johnson Collection.

W.'s autograph receipt for ten guineas received from RD for the copy of poem *On Nobility* (1744), but reserving right to print poem in any miscellany that W. may print by subscription. Dated 30 April 1744.

Also: Reed/Chalmers, p. 1 (date: 20 April 1744); Sotheby sale cat., 10 May 1875, lot 190 (purchased by Waller); Straus, p. 326.

Imprint: London. Printed for R. Dodsley; and sold by M. Cooper, 1744.

The Roman Father (1750)

Reed/Chalmers, p. 4.

On 17 March 1750 RD paid W. £100 for the copy of *The Roman Father*. "Whole rights" registered to RD at the Stationers' Company on 10 March 1750. *Imprint:* London. Printed for R. Dodsley; and sold by M. Cooper. 1750.

Creusa, Queen of Athens. A Tragedy (1754)

Boston Public Library, Ch. G. 13.66.

Autograph signed receipt for 100 guineas, assigning RD the copy of W.'s *Creusa, Queen of Athens*. Dated 21 May 1754.

Also: Sotheby sale cat., 10 May 1875, lot 190 (purchased by John Waller); Reed/Chalmers, p. 8 (receipt: £100; date: 21 March [May?] 1754); Straus, p. 352.

"Whole rights" registered to RD at the Stationers' Company on 29 April 1754. *Imprint:* London. Printed for R. and J. Dodsley; and sold by M. Cooper. 1754.

Whitmarsh, Mary (with Lucy Baskett, executrix of Christopher Pitt)

Christopher Pitt, trans., *The Aeneid of Virgil* (1740, 8°; 1744, 12°)

BL Egerton MS. 738, ff. 10–11.

1. Autograph signed receipt for £52.10.0., acknowledging RD's payment for the copy of Virgil's *Aeneid* translated by Christopher Pitt. Signed by Mary Whitmarsh and Lucy Baskett. Dated 21 October 1751.

2. Autograph signed receipt for £62.10.0. acknowledging RD's payment for 500 unsold copies of Pitt's translation of Virgil's *Aeneid* (one half of impression). Signed Mary Whitmarsh and Lucy Baskett. Dated 21 October 1751. (8° or 12°?)

3. Order for RD to pay £115 to Rev. John Baskett ten days after sight. Signed by Mary Whitmarsh. At bottom of document: "Accepted Novr 18". Signed by Lucy Baskett and Robert Dodsley.

(In a bracket to the right of W.'s and B.'s signatures on each receipt appears the designation of their executorship, followed by the name Elizabeth Goldwyre, perhaps their representative in the negotiation with RD.)

Imprint: London. Printed for R. Dodsley. And sold by Mr. Hitch; Mr. Hinchcliffe; Mr. Clements at Oxford; Mr. Crownfield and Thurlebourne at Cambridge; and Mr. Leake at Bath. 1740.

Woodfall, William (1746–1803)

William Cheselden, *Anatomy of the Human Body* (1713, 1741, 1756)

Royal College of Surgeons, MSS Box 31 33.

Autograph signed receipt, dated 19 October 1771, acknowledging JD's payment of £6.6.0 for $\frac{1}{16}$ share of copyright of Cheselden's *Anatomy of the Human Body*, with a promise of further assignment on demand. *See also:* Strahan, William

Woodward, Thomas, bookseller against St Dunstan's in Fleet St.

Ambrose Philips, *Humphrey, Duke of Gloucester* (1723), *Briton* (1722); William Popple, *Double Deceit* (1735) (*See also:* Appendix B, section 3, Ward (120).)

Straus, p. 345 (full text)

RD paid £3.3.0. for $\frac{2}{3}$ share in Ambrose Philips' *Humphrey, Duke of Gloucester* (1723) and *Briton* (1722) and one half in William Popple's *Double Deceit* (1735), shares formerly belonging to W. and John Peele but sold at Queen's Head Tavern in Paternoster Row on 12 March 1752. Payment to be used for Alice Grove, W.'s widow, and John Peele. Signed John Atkinson.

(It does not appear that RD ever printed these plays.)

Young, Edward (1683–1765)

Night Thoughts, I-IV

Reed/Chalmers, p. 1; Public Record Office, C33, Part 2 420/244; Case of Andrew Millar and James Dodsley against Alexander Donaldson.

For the first five parts of *Night Thoughts*, RD paid Y. in two installments of 110 guineas and 50 guineas for which consideration Y. sold the copyright to RD on 24 November 1743.

Also: Sotheby sale cat., 12 May 1851, lot 1114 of John Wilks Collection (purchased by Jones); Sotheby sale cat., 22 March 1855, lot 347 of John Wilks Collection (purchased by John Anderdon); Sotheby sale cat., 10 June 1869, lot 1031 of John Dillon Collection (purchased by John Waller); John Waller sale cat., 1870–3, item 426.

Imprint: London. Printed for R. Dodsley; and sold by M. Cooper. 1743.

Night Thoughts, VI

Houghton Library, Harvard, fMS Eng 760.1.

Autograph signed receipt for fifty guineas, dated 26 January 1744/45, assigning RD the copy for the sixth "Night" of Young's *Complaint* (1744).

Also: Sotheby sale cat., 12 May 1851, lot 1114 of John Wilks Collection (purchased by Jones); Sotheby sale cat., 22 March 1855, lot 347 of John Wilks Collection (purchased by John Anderdon); Sotheby sale cat., 10 June 1869, lot 1031 of John Dillon Collection (purchased by John Waller); Winifred Myers sale cat., No. 3, item 453.

Imprint: London. Printed for R. Dodsley. 1744.

The Infidel Reclaimed

John Waller sale catalogues, 1870–1 (unnumbered item); 1870–3, item 425.

Receipt for 50 guineas, acknowledging RD's payment for the copy of "The Infidel Reclaimed," Part I. Dated 26 January 1744/45.

The Brothers. A Tragedy (1753)

Reed/Chalmers, p. 9.

On 7 March 1753, RD purchased from Y. the copy of *The Brothers. A Tragedy* (1753) for £147.

Imprint: London. Printed for R. Dodsley. 1753.

The Centaur Not Fabulous (1755)

1. Hyde Collection. Somerville, New Jersey.

Autograph, signed receipt, dated 19 February 1755, assigning the copy of Y.'s *The Centaur Not Fabulous* (1755) to RD for £200, to be paid six months after the date of this agreement.

Also: Sotheby sale cat., 12 May 1851, lot 1115 of John Wilks Collection (purchased by Webb); Sotheby sale cat., 22 March 1855, lot 348 of John Wilks Collection (purchased by John Anderdon); Sotheby sale cat., 17 May 1879, lot 216 (purchased by Naylor).

2. Reed/Chalmers, p. 9.

On 25 August 1755, R&JD purchased from Y. the copy of *The Centaur Not Fabulous* for £100. (Reed/Chalmers notes the existence of the earlier agreement, above, but fails to mention that, in the interim, Andrew Millar had purchased a moiety of the copy. R&JD's payment of £100 represents only half of that due Young.)

Also: Sotheby sale cat., 27 May 1887, lot 441 (purchased by Foster); Sotheby sale cat., 3 December 1888, lot 229 (purchased by Barker); Sotheby sale cat., 27 November 1890, lot 475 (misprints date: 20 August 1755; purchased by Barker); Sotheby sale cat., 5 May 1900, lot 246 (purchased by Barker).

Imprint: London. Printed for A. Millar; and R. and J. Dodsley, 1755.

2. COPYRIGHTS REGISTERED AT THE STATIONERS' COMPANY

These works are listed separately here because they found no appropriate point of reference in the body of the text or in the foregoing appendices. Unless otherwise specified, it should be assumed that RD registered "whole rights" to his name. The date following the name of the work is the day of registry at the Stationers' Company. (Dates prior to 25 February reflect "Old Style.") This date regularly corresponds to the advertised date of publication, or closely approximates it, and so no additional date of publication is supplied in the entry. In one instance, an imprint is supplied for purposes explained below.

The case of RD's publication of Alexander Pope's works offers a knotty problem. David Foxon has implied that the poet, attempting to establish a new relationship with the booktrade in 1728, abandoned his earlier, established booksellers, Lintot and Tonson, and set up Lawton Gilliver and then RD in business in order that he might retain the copyrights for all future works to himself. Thus, when the fourteen-year copyrights for earlier works ran out, he would be able to publish his own edition of his works and reap fuller profits.[3]

The account found in William Bowyer's ledgers regarding the printing of Volume III, Pts I & II, of Pope's *Works*, which RD published, would seem to lend support to Foxon's suggestion. On p. 391 of Bowyer's 2nd ledger, Pope's name heads the entry as "customer," normally the person paying for the job and, presumably, the one holding the right of copy. RD's name does not appear except in the Paper Stock Ledger (p. 895), which ordinarily lists the person who had supplied the paper and to whom the job was to be delivered. This evidence throws into question the copyright suggested in the imprint on Volume III and, by extension, the "Whole rights" to Volumes V & VI that RD had registered to his name at the Stationers' Company almost seven years earlier. The doubt is strengthened in the case of *Letters of Mr. Alexander Pope, and Several of his Friends* (see below), where RD's registration of "Whole rights" is not verified in the imprint.

Unfortunately no evidence survives to explain Pope's specific arrangement with RD. The larger implication of the matter, of course, is to question once more the reliability of both imprints and the specification of "rights" in the Stationers' Register for the purpose of determining the true holders of copyright.

Akenside, Mark. *The Pleasures of Imagination.* 14 January 1743
    Epistle to Curio. 14 November 1744
    Odes on Several Subjects. 26 March 1745
Cambridge, Richard Owen. *The Scribleriad. A Heroic Poem*
    Bk, 1, 26 January 1750/51
    Bks. 2 & 3. 5 March 1750/51
    Bk. 4. 18 March 1750/51

---

[3] See David Foxon, "Pope and the Early Eighteenth-Century Book-Trade," unpublished, first, uncorrected draft of the Lyell Lectures, 1977, pp. 113ff.; lodged at the British Library, X.902/2958.

Bk. 5. 7 April 1751
Bk. 6. 7 May 1751
Coventry, Francis. *The History of Pompey the Little: Or the Life and Adventures of a Lap Dog.* 12 February 1750/51 (Mary Cooper's name scratched out and RD's inserted. The next work entered, *History of a Woman of Quality*, was registered to Cooper.)
Dodsley, Robert. *The Blind Beggar of Bethnal Green.* 3 April 1741
The King and Miller of Mansfield. 7 February 1736
Fordyce, David. *Theodorus, a Dialogue concerning the Art of Preaching.* 10 April 1752
Miller, Philip. *The Gardiner's Dictionary.* $\frac{1}{32}$ share
Pope, Alexander. *The Second Epistle of the Second Book of Horace, Imitated.* 22 April 1737
Letters of Mr. Alexander Pope, and Several of his Friends. Printed by J. Wright for J. Knapton, L. Gilliver, J. Brindley, and R. Dodsley. 17 May 1737. ("Whole rights" registered to RD.)
The Works of Alexander Pope, Esq. Vols. 5 & 6. 2nd edition, corrected. 31 October 1737

3. DODSLEY'S PURCHASES OF COPYRIGHTS AND STOCK AT BOOKSELLERS' SALES

From available evidence, it does not seem that Dodsley purchased heavily at trade sales. Perhaps the London monopoly was slow to invite him to the sales when he first set up in business, for he was an "outsider," one who had not served an apprenticeship and had no forebears in the business. As early as 2 August 1737, however, he did make a purchase from the stock of John Walthoe, Sr., as a marked catalogue of that date tells us (Ward, No. 56, see below). But then his next documented attendance and first recorded copyright purchase at a sale does not occur until 1743, at the Daniel Midwinter sale.

On the other hand, it is unlikely that the thrifty Dodsley would have been especially anxious to make such purchases in his early years. His cash reserve when opening Tully's Head was decidedly slim, and what he realized from sales seems to have been poured back into the purchase of copyrights directly from authors. In some ways, then, it is not surprising that he does not become seriously involved in buying at trade sales until the mid-1740s, when his business had become well established and his resources more plentiful.

The following listings are taken primarily from two collections of trade sales catalogues compiled by two families of eighteenth-century booksellers: the collection of Aaron and John Ward, now in the John Johnson Collection, Bodleian Library; and that of the Longmans, now in the British Library. Together, they cover (with much overlap) trade sales during the period 1718 to 1768[4].

---

[4] For a discussion of both, see Terry Belanger, unpublished Columbia University dissertation (1970), "Booksellers' Sales of Copyright: Aspects of the London Book Trade, 1718–1768"; and "Booksellers' Trade Sales, 1718–1768," *Library*, 30 (1975), 281–301.

Where discernible, the full title and other particulars have been substituted for the abbreviated version in the cataloge. The number following the collection's name refers to the number assigned, in pen (by the compiler?), to the individual catalogue. The sums marked in the margins of the catalogue with RD's name seem to be evidence of extended credit, for they would hardly be equivalent to total purchase prices.

Ward (56) 2 August 1737. Sale of John Walthoe, Sr., stock.

Lot 69. Rapin's *Works*, 2 vols. 220 of 1,000. 20 sets. £5.15.6.

Ward (100) 4 August 1743. Daniel Midwinter sale.

Lot 91.⅓ share of George Savile, Lord Halifax, *The Lady's New-year's Gift; or Advice to his Daughter* (1st edn., 1716). £1.18.0.
Lot 92.⅓ share of same. £1.12.6.

Ward (111) 13 January 1747.

Lot 17. £1.1.0.
Life of the Black Prince (the Whole).
    [? Anon. *Life and Death of Edward surnamed the Black Prince*, as in the Harleian Miscellany, 1744]
John Kelly, *The Levee. A Farce*. (London. Printed for M. Cooper. 1744) (Two-Thirds).
Sir Creswell Levinz. *Reports of* . . . 1702. 3 Pts in 2 vols. (an Eighth).
    A Collection of Select and Modern Entries . . . *referring to Cases in* . . . *Levinz's Reports*. 1702 (an Eighth).
Laws of Bastardy (an Eighth).
[?Daniel Defoe] *Letter from a Country Whig*. 2 Pts. by the Author of the *Caveat* (the Whole).
Letters of the Antients (a Tenth).

Lot 18. (included in £1.1.0. for Lot 17.)
Niccolo Machiavelli, *Works*. fol. (Mr Ward's share).
François Misson, *Voyage to Italy*. 1688 [1739]. 4 vols. 8°. 147 in 1,000 (stock).
Mechanisms of the Fires made in Chimnies. 4°. 147 in 1,000 (stock).
Memoirs of the Royal House of Savoy. 1707. 147 in 1,000 (stock).
Mercurius Politicus. 8°. (One-sixth).

Lot 19. £2.2.0.
Nathaniel Marshall, *Penitential Discipline of the Primitive Church*. 1714. (Half).
    Defence of our Constitution. 1717. (Half).
    The Royal Patten . . . *Sermon upon the Death of* . . . *Queen Anne*. 1714. (Half).
    Recompence of Virtue . . . *preached at the Funeral of Mr. R. Blundel*. 1718. (Half).
    Letter to a Clergyman about Oaths. (Half).
    Works of St. Cyprian. 1717. (Half).
    New Danger from Popery (Two-Thirds).

Lot 20. (included in £2.2.0 for Lot 19).
William Nelson, *An Abridgement of the Common Law*. 1725, 1726. 3 Vols. fol. (an Eighteenth).
    The Rights of the Clergy. 1712. (Two-Thirds).
    Reports of Cases decreed . . . *in Chancery*. 1725 (a Sixth).

Lot 21. (included in £2.2.0. for Lots 19 & 20).
Sir Isaac Newton, *The Chronology of Ancient Kingdoms*. [? ed. J. Conduitt. 1728] (a Ninth).
De Mundi Systemate Liber. [?J. Tonson. 1728] (a Ninth).
    The Elogium of Isaac Newton (trans. from Le Bovier de Fontenelle). J. Tonson, 1728. (a Ninth).
James Nihell, *New and Extraordinary Observations concerning* . . . *the Pulse*. 1741. (Two-Thirds).
Newborough's Copies (Mr Osborne's share of) consisting of thirty Articles, a List of which will be produced, and the Share declared.

Longman (55) 14 November 1751. Stock and Copies of John Osborn.
Lot LXIV £1.10.0.
Roger de Piles, *The Principles of Painting*. (Half). [English translation published by J. Osborn, 1743.]

Longman (56) 19 November 1751. Stock and Copies of John Osborn.
Second Sale.
Lot LXIV £1.10.0.
Roger de Piles, *The Principles of Painting* (Another Half).

Ward (120) 12 March 1752. Books in Quires and Copies of Thomas Woodward, deceased.
Lot XXXII £3.3.0.
Ambrose Philips, *Humphrey, Duke of Gloucester* (1723) (Two-Thirds).
  Briton, a Tragedy (1722) (Two-Thirds).
William Popple, *Double Deceit* (1735) (Half).
(See also Appendix B, section 1, under Woodward, Thomas.)

Tonson and Watts Sale. 19 December 1753 (MS., Lawrence G. Blackmon, Stamford, Connecticut).
Daniel Browne and John Whiston purchased from Jacob Tonson the younger and [John?] Watts ten sets each of Plutarchi Vitae (5 vols.), Tasso (2 vols.), Racine (2 vols.), Rousseau (2 vols.), and Montaigne (3 vols.), to be the joint and equal property of Browne, Whiston and Benjamin White, Andrew Millar, Samuel Baker, and RD. No purchase price specified. Fifteen guineas were deposited with Whiston & Co. to advertise the volumes, and Whiston to be accountable to the partners every six months.
(The memorandum includes a price scale for the sets, as they were to be offered to gentlemen, booksellers, and the partners. These editions were the "Tonson Classics," in royal quarto.)

The verso of the MS. shows a memorandum dated the same day as the agreement and specifying small sums (deposits?) for the individual sets.

[Stationers' Sale?] 5 April 1759 (Stationers' Company MS)
R&JD one of nine bookselling firms, each purchasing one set of *The History of the Life of Gustavus Adolphus King of Sweden*, quarto, in sheets. JD's signature appears on a note with the others, each for 10s. 4d.

Longman (132) 3 May 1764 Copies of Mrs Hinxman.
Lot 57 £1.11.6.
  Geography of England, done in the manner of Gordon's Geographical Grammar. R. Dodsley, 1744, octavo.
  [James Dodsley purchase?] (One-Eighth).

APPENDIX C

PROVENANCE OF AUTOGRAPH LETTERS AND CITATIONS TO MAJOR
PRINTED VERSIONS

As much as has been discovered regarding the transmission of the autograph letters in the body of the text is printed below. In many cases the pedigree is traceable to the eighteenth century, but in many others there are gaps in the continuity. In some, no record at all has been found to carry the letter's history back beyond the present owner or holder. For obvious reasons, these last are not included in the list.

Although eighteenth-century notables were usually careful to preserve their correspondence for posterity, collectors' interest in the letters of other than history's distinguished figures did not become keen until the second decade of the nineteenth century. It is after this time that such collectors as William Upcott, Dawson Turner, and Sir Thomas Phillipps began to amass their prodigious stores of autographs, a story A. N. L. Munby records in *The Cult of the Autograph Letter*.[1] Consequently, it is from that time that autograph letters begin to become part of the public record, as they were listed in sales catalogues issued by the dealers and auction houses.

Anyone engaged in tracing the provenance of letters dating from the eighteenth century, then, is very much dependent upon these sale catalogues. The most useful ones, of course, are those whose owners attended the sales and troubled themselves to write in purchasers' names next to the items purchased. Regrettably, Englishmen did not systematically preserve their trade catalogues as did their Continental counterparts, and today we are left with incomplete runs, especially in the case of the lesser dealers. As Munby points out, even the British Library lacks consistent runs of some important material.

Nonetheless, surviving catalogues number in the thousands, enough to daunt the most patient researcher who would follow his subject into the early nineteenth century. For Dodsley's correspondence, some limits were set for purposes of efficiency and sanity. Since most nineteenth-century dealers were in tune with their customers' particular collecting interests, they regularly indicated in the titles of their catalogues whether indeed the sale included autograph letters, a custom rather faithfully continued into our own century. Consequently this search began by identifying all nineteenth-century catalogues whose titles indicated that autograph material was included in the sale. For the most part, they were extracted from that giant folio volume that sits to the left of the Supervisor's circle in the Main Reading Room of the British Library. To this list were added all catalogues recording sales of any properties related to Dodsley's correspondents or to other contemporary figures with whom it was thought he might have had a connection.

[1] *The Cult of the Autograph Letter in England* (London: Athlone Press, 1962).

The same approach has been followed for twentieth-century catalogues, through to the present time. When pertinent citations were found in the latter and the dealer remained in business (e.g. Maggs Bros., Sotheby & Co.), the dealer's assistance was solicited in tracing the piece further. Finally, all leads supplied by friends, colleagues, and printed works were pursued.

In all, well over a thousand catalogues were reviewed. Among them were runs of catalogues issued by John Bell, T. & W. Boone, James Coleman, Christie, F. S. Ellis, Robert Evans, Goodspeed, Hodgsons, Thomas Kerslake, Joseph Lilly, Maggs Bros., Payne and Foss, Puttick and Simpson, Bernard Quaritch, Thomas Rodd, John R. Smith, Sotheby & Co., Thomas Thorpe, John Waller, and Willis & Sotheran. Although the time and effort expended on this portion of the project has been considerable, the editor is well aware that the net might have been of a finer mesh.

For ease and efficiency of reference, the following entries are presented according to collections in which the letters are lodged. Collections in the United Kingdom are listed first, followed by those in the United States; and both follow alphabetical order. Those wishing to make use of this information while reading the body of the text need only be armed with the letter's location as cited at the foot of the letter. Should this procdure fail to turn up an entry, the reader can assume that no earlier record has been traced.

The first item following the library entry and its particular collection is a listing of the letter(s) in that collection, cited by the name of RD's correspondent ("to" or "from") and accompanied by the date and foliation or pagination (in parentheses, but without "p" of "f"). Next, under "A," appears the provenance itself. Section "B" records principal printed versions of the letters cited. No attempt has been made to provide a complete listing of all such extant sources. In this section, for economy's sake, references to Straus's *Robert Dodsley* have been abbreviated to "*RD.*" When no Section "B" appears, or when only selections from the forementioned letters occur, it can be assumed that no major printed versions were located.

The provenance is listed in order of transmission, the first citation being the earliest. A citation followed by an "equals" sign (=) means that the holograph was transmitted directly to the party mentioned in the next citation. This method will eliminate much duplication (for instance, as would arise from the need to mention Sir Thomas Phillipps in connection with a sale of his property at Sotheby & Co. when the previous citation refers to his collection). In all citations, the use of brackets indicates transmissions that have not been certified in print.

United Kingdom

Birmingham Public Libraries

Robert Dodsley Letter Book, ff. 1–90.
RD to: (1756): Duchess of Leeds, 28 Sept. (1); John Scott Hylton, 28 Sept. (2); Edward Young, 7 Oct. (3); David Garrick, 18 Oct. (6–7); Society for the Encouragement of Arts, Manufactures, and

Commerce, 14 Dec. (11–13); William Melmoth, 16 Dec. (14–15); Richard Graves, 30 Dec. (16–18); (1757): William Strahan, 14 Jan. (19–21); William Melmoth, 27 Jan. (22–23); John Baskerville, 10 Feb., 7 Apr. (24–27, 34–35); Nelly Wright, 24 Feb., 3 May, 30 Aug. (26–27, 40, 51); James Cawthorn, 2 Apr. (30–33); 11th Earl of Clanricarde, 25 Apr. (39); David Garrick, 17 June (41–42); Thomas Blacklock, 16 July (46–48); Nicholas Herbert, 20 July (48–50); Richard Graves, 24 Oct. (51–53); John Hoadly, 26 Oct., 5 Dec. (54–55, 70–71); Moses Mendes, 26 Oct. (56–57); George Faulkner, 28 Oct. (57–59); Richard Jago, 29 Oct. (61–62); Thomas Gataker, 4 Nov. (63–65); Robert Lowth [4 Nov.–3 Dec.] (65–67); 4th Earl of Chesterfield, 19 Dec., 5 Jan. 1758 (72–73, 76); (1758): Anon., [c. 6 Jan.] (77); John Rich, 6 Jan. (78–79); Richard Berenger, 10 Jan. (80–83); [Thomas?] Thackray, 16 Jan., 18 Feb. (85–86, 87–88); John Scott Hylton, 20 Feb. (89–90).

A. [Joseph Lilly Collection = Sotheby sale cat., 22 April 1872, lot 28, purchased by Waller]; Samuel Timmins Collection = Sotheby sale cat., 20–2 April 1899, lot 225, purchased by Downing; Birmingham Public Libraries acquired in November, 1899.

B. Duchess of Leeds, *RD* (206-7); Young, Henry Pettit, ed. *The Correspondence of* (Oxford, 1971), pp. 437–8; Garrick (1756). *RD* (209–10); Melmoth, *RD* (277–8); Graves (1756), *RD* (211–12); Strahan, *RD* (96–8); Baskerville (10 Feb.), T. B. Reed, *History of the Old English Letter Foundries* (1887), pp. 271–2; Straus and Dent, *John Baskerville* (Cambridge, 1907), pp. 96–7; Leonard Jay, *Letters of* (1932), pp. 12–13; Baskerville (7 Apr.), Reed, p. 272; Straus and Dent, p. 97; Jay, p. 14; Wright (24 Feb., 3 May, 30 Aug.), *RD* (294–95); Cawthorn, *RD* (245–6); Clanricarde, *RD* (362–3); Garrick (17 June), *RD* (218–19); Blacklock, *RD* (359); Graves (24 Oct.), *RD* (219–20); Hoadly (26 Oct.), *RD* (142–3); Jago, *RD* (139–40); Gataker, *RD* (221–2); Lowth, *RD* (214–15); Chesterfield (19 Dec. 1757, 5 Jan. 1758), *RD* (224–5); Rich, *RD* (225); Berenger, *RD* (144–6).

Bodleian Library, Oxford

MS Eng. Letters, c. 198, f. 71.
from John Gilbert Cooper, 14 Nov. 1747.
A. Purchased by the Bodleian from E. Hall, Gravesend, Kent, 1958–61.

MS Eng. Letters, d. 40, ff. 101–14.
from John Mason, 7 Jan. 1754 (101); Thomas Lisle, [c. 18 Mar. 1755] (103–4), 2 Sept. 1756 (105), 13 Mar. 1758 (107); Thomas Cheyney, 6 Feb. 1758 (108–9); John Hoadly, 11 Feb. 1758 (110), 8 Mar. 1758 (111–12), 15 Feb. 1764 (113–14).
A. Elkin Mathews sale cat., No. 56 (1933), item 85; purchased by Bodleian.

MS Eng. Misc. c. 75, ff. 35–6.
from Richard Berenger, 1 Jan. 1758.
A. Charles E. Doble Collection; bequeathed to Bodleian by Doble's widow in 1915.

MS Eng. Misc. d. 174, ff. 3–102.
from John Gilbert Cooper, 18 Dec. 1745 (3);
1746: 12 Mar. (5), 7 Apr. (9), 23 Apr. (11), 28 May (13), 7 July (15), 26 July (17), 15 Nov. (19);
1747: 11 Feb. (24–25), 18 Feb. (28–29);
1748: 8 Feb. (31), 5 Dec. (34–35);
1749: 16 Jan. (37), 15 Feb. (41), 23 Sept. (45), 9 Dec. (47), 12 Dec. (52–54);
1750: [25 or 26 Feb.] (101–2), 22 Oct. (55–58);
1751: 26 Aug. (60–61), 13 Nov. (63), 23 Nov. (67); 19 Jan. [1752] (87–88);
1754: 21 Sept. (71–72), 7 Oct. (76–77), 14 Oct. (79);
1755: [5 Mar.] (91–93), [20 Mar.] (96–97).
from RD, 9 Dec. 1749 (103).
A. Sir Thomas Phillipps Collection (MS 13846) = Sotheby sale cat., 5 June 1899 lot 455; W. A. Lindsay Collection = Sotheby sale cat., 14 Feb. 1927, lot 380; P. J. & A. E. Dobell sale cat., No. 66 (1927), item 58, purchased by Bodleian. RD letter (103–4) purchased by Bodleian from Birrell and Garnett, Cat. 16 (1927), item 228c. Perhaps it had become separated from Cooper's letters after the Lindsay sale.

MS Montagu d. 11, ff. 99, 163–4, 196–7.
from John Barr, 19 Apr. 1749 (99); John Berckenhout, 28 Oct. 1753 (163–64); Thomas Blacklock, 3 May 1756 (196–97).

A. Collection of Walter Wilson (1781–1847), London, bookseller = sold to Captain Montagu Montagu, RN in 1847 = bequeathed by Montagu to Bodleian in 1864.

MS Toynbee d. 19, ff. 3–17.

from John Brown, 1743: [c. 25] Sept. (3–4), 8 Oct. (5–6), 24 Dec. (9–10); 1745: 18 Feb. (11), 17 Oct. (12–13); 1746: 15 Feb. (14), 5 Mar. (17), 27 Oct. (16), 8 Nov. (7).

A. Sir Thomas Phillipps Collection (MS 13852) = Sotheby sale cat., 5 June 1899, lot 453; F. Edwards sale cat., No. 507 (1928), item 8, purchased by Paget Toynbee = bequeathed by Toynbee to Bodleian in 1928.

B. Donald D. Eddy, *A Bibliography of John Brown* (New York: Bibliographical Society of America, 1971): 18 Feb. 1745 (pp. 5–6), 17 Oct. 1745 (pp. 15–16).

The British Library

Correspondence between Frances, Countess of Hertford . . . and Henrietta Louisa, Countess of Pomfret, between the years 1738 and 1741 [ed. W. Bingley] (London, 1805). ALS laid inside front cover of Volume I.

to Frances Seymour, Countess of Hertford, 9 Aug. [1744].

A. Rev. Sundius John Stamp Collection = Puttick and Simpson sale cat., 6 Aug. 1850.

Add. MS. 4,305, f. 5.

to Dr. Thomas Birch, 24 Feb. 1750.

A. Bequeathed by Birch to British Museum in 1766.

Add. MS. 21, 508, f. 44.

from Thomas Blacklock, 4 Feb. 1760.

A. Henry Belward Ray Collection = Sotheby sale cat., 23–6, July 1856, lot 137, purchased by British Museum.

Add. MS. 28,959, ff. 3–11, 15–37, 40–127.

to William Shenstone, 1747: 8 Oct. (3–4); 17 Oct. (5–6); 1748: 24 Mar. (7), 17 May (8–9); 1753: 29 Sept. (12–13), 10 Nov. (10–11), [c. 28 Nov.] (15–16); 1754: 12 Jan. (17–18), [23 Feb.] (19–20), 27 Aug. (21), 29 Oct. (25–26), 19 Nov. (29), 30 Nov. (31–32), 16 Dec. (33–34), 31 Dec. (35–36); 1755: 18 Jan. (22), [24] Jan. (24), 15 Feb. (37), 25 Mar. (40), 29 Mar. (42–43), 3 May (44–45), 27 June (46), 28 July (47–48), 28 Aug. (56–57), 8 Nov. (60–61); 1756: 9 Feb. (49–50), 17 Apr. (51–52), 12 June (53), 28 June (54–55), 28 Aug. (74–75), 5 Oct. (58–59), 13 Dec. (81–82), 21 Dec. (85); 1757: 11 Jan. (62–63), 11 Mar. (65–66), 11 Apr. (68), 21 Apr. (69–70), [30 Apr.] (67), 13 July (72–73), 20 Sept. (76–77), 29 Oct. (78), 3 Dec. (79–80), 18 Dec. (83–84), 21 Dec. (87–88), 27 Dec. (89–90); 1758: 5 Jan. (91), 16 Jan. (92–93), 21 Jan. (94), 2 Feb. (95–96), 30 Mar. (98), 23 May (99), 13 June (100), 22 Aug. (100–2), 19 Sept. (103–4), 10 Oct. (105), 14 Oct. (106), 24 Oct. (107), 4 Nov. (109), 9 Dec. (110–11); 1759: 20 Jan. (114–17), 8 Feb. (118–19), 20 Feb. (120), 15 Mar. (121), 19 Mar. (123–24), 3 Apr. (127). from James Dodsley to Shenstone, 22 October [1754] (14). from Shenstone to RD, 4 and 23 Mar. 1755 (38, 39).

A. Joseph Lilly Collection = Sotheby sale cat., 22 April 1872, lot 79, purchased by G. Manners for British Museum.

B. Except for thirty-two, Straus (*RD*) prints fragments or in many cases the whole texts of the foregoing. Marjorie Williams, *The Letters of William Shenstone* (Oxford, 1939): from Shenstone, 4 and 23 Mar. 1755 (pp. 431, 435). Duncan Mallam, *The Letters of William Shenstone* (Minneapolis, 1939): from Shenstone, 4 and 23 Mar. 1755 (pp. 316–17, 320–1).

Add. MS. 29,300, f. 43.

from John Hawkesworth, 14 September 1756.

A. Lewis Pocock Collection = Sotheby sale cat. 10 May 1875, lot 72, purchased by British Museum.

Add. MS. 30,262, ff. 70–1.
from John Hoadly, 18 Oct. 1757.
A. Puttick and Simpson sale cat., 2–3 June 1878, purchased by British Museum.

Add. MS. 35,338, ff. 2–17.
from William Melmoth, 26 Dec. 1746 (2), [26 Dec. 1746 or 2 Jan, 1747] (4), 6 June 1749 (6), 28 July 1759 (8–9), 20 Nov. 1759 (10–11); 1760: 3 July (12), 29 Aug. (13), 9 Oct. (15–16); 13 Mar 1762 (17).
A. Sir Thomas Phillipps Collection (MS 13844) = Sotheby sale cat., 5–10 June 1899, lot 458, purchased by British Museum.

Add. MS. 35,339, ff. 1–32.
from Robert Lowth, 1753: 16 Jan. (1–2), 24 Feb. (3), [late Feb.] (5–6), 7 Mar. (7–8), 13 Mar. (9–10), 15 Mar. (11–12);
1757: 9 Aug. (13–14), [early Sept.] (18–19), 17 Oct. (15), 3 Nov. (16–17);
1758: 12 Feb. (20), 24 Feb. (21), 5 Mar. (22), 9 June (23);
19 June 1760 (25–26); 9 Jan. 1761 (31–32); 5 Mar. 1762 (27).
A. Sir Thomas Phillipps Collection = Sotheby sale cat., 5–10 June 1899, lot 456, purchased by British Museum.

Add. MS. 42,560, ff. 6, 13, 29, 32, 33, 50.
to Thomas Warton, 16 Mar. [1745] (6), 29 Jan. [1747] (13), 20 Jan. 1755 (33), 11 Mar. [1756] (50).
to Joseph Warton, 8 Nov. [1754] (29), 18 Jan. 1755 (32).
A. James Ingram, President of Trinity College, Oxford, sold copyright to John Murray, publisher, on 4 November 1826; Sir John Murray, publisher, presented to British Museum on 10 October 1931.
B. "P" and "F," respectively, in the following refer to Joan Pittock, "Joseph Warton and His Second Volume of the *Essay on Pope*," *RES*, n.s. 18 (1967), 264–73; and David Fairer, "The Writing and Printing of Joseph Warton's *Essay on Pope*," *SB*, 30 (1977), 211–19. Only two are printed in their entirety. T. Warton: 20 Jan. 1755 (P, 271; F, 213); 11 Mar. 1756 (F, 216). J. Warton: 8 Nov. 1754 (P, 271); 18 Jan. 1755 (P, 270).

Add. MS. 42,561, ff. 227–8.
to Joseph Warton, 27 Feb. [1758].
A. (Same as in 42,560).
B. Pittock, p. 272 (see 42,560).

Add. MS. 54,224, ff. 236–7.
from David Garrick, [14 Oct. 1756].
A. Joseph Lilly Collection = Sotheby sale cat., 22 April 1872, lot 35, purchased by John Waller = John Waller sale cat., 1872, item 120; presented to British Museum by National Portrait Gallery on 9 December 1967.
B. *The Letters of David Garrick*, ed. David M. Little and George M. Kahrl. (London: Oxford University Press, 1963), pp. 318–19.

Bute, 3rd Earl of (Papers) Mount Stuart, Rothsay, Isle of Bute
to John Stuart, 3rd Earl of Bute, 5 Dec. 1758.
A. Since eighteenth century, among Earl of Bute's Papers.

Edinburgh University Library
La.II.153.
from William Warburton, 26 Dec. 1755.
A. Rev. John Lee Collection; Nisbet sale cat., 4 April 1861, item 336; Collection of David Laing (1793–1878), bequeathed to Edinburgh University Library in 1878.

La.II 646/43.
from Thomas Blackwell, 15 Jan. 1756.

A. [Joseph Lilly Collection = Sotheby sale cat., 22 April 1872, lot 27]; Collection of David Laing (1793–1878), bequeathed to Edinburgh University Library in 1878.

La.II 647/313.

from Christopher Pitt, [1 June–9 Aug. 1744?].

A. Collection of David Laing (1793–1878), bequeathed to Edinburgh University Library in 1878.

Leicestershire Record Office

15D57/2–4.

to Elizabeth Cartwright (later Coltman), 1 May [1761] (2), 10 Nov. 1763 (4), 15 Dec. [1763] (4), 2 Feb. [1764] (5).

A. Elizabeth Cartwright Coltman; Mrs C. H. Parkes (née Sarah Clarke), great-granddaughter of Elizabeth Cartwright and John Coltman = 1892, Mrs Jane Hudson (née Clarke) = 1936, Miss J. D. Parkes, Petworth, Sussex, who bequeathed Coltman family papers to Leicestershire Record Office in 1957.

B. Catherine Hutton Beale, *Catherine Hutton and Her Friends* (Birmingham: Cornish Bros., 1895): 1 May [1761], pp 13–14; 15 Dec. [1763], pp. 19–20.

15D57/448 Samuel Coltman, "Time's Stepping Stones" (transcript).

to Elizabeth Cartwright (later Coltman), 3 Aug. 1763, 25 Aug. 1763, 28 Apr. 1764.

to Samuel Cartwright, 12 Apr. 1763.

A. Elizabeth Cartwright (Coltman); Miss Nancy Clarke, of Swithland, granddaughter of Thomas W. Clarke, great grandson of Elizabeth Cartwright and John Coltman = Miss J. D. Parkes, Petworth, Sussex, who bequeathed Coltman family papers to Leicestershire Record Office in 1957.

B. Catherine Hutton Beale, *Catherine Hutton and Her Friends*

to Elizabeth Cartwright, 28 Apr. 1764 (p. 300).

to Samuel Cartwright, 12 Apr. 1763 (pp. 18–19).

Longleat House
Portland Papers, Vol. XIII, f. 209.

to Alexander Pope, 8 May [1734].

A. Among Portland Papers since eighteenth century.

B. *Correspondence of Alexander Pope*, ed. George Sherburn (Oxford, 1956), III, 407.

Methodist Archives and Research Centre, John Rylands University Library of Manchester

from John Wesley, 8 Feb. 1745.

A. Robert Evans sale cat., 22 December 1835, lot 1131, purchased by John Wilks; John Waller sale cat., 1855, lot 175.

B. *Morning Chronicle*, 21 Dec. 1835; Thomas Marriott, "Wesley Papers," *Weslyan Methodist Magazine*, 1848, p. 976; *The Letters of John Wesley*, ed. John Telford (London, 1931), II, 27–8; *The Journal of the Rev. John Wesley*, ed. Nehemiah Curnock (London: Epworth Press, 1938), III, 162; John Wesley, *The Works of*, ed. Frank Baker (Oxford: Clarendon Press, 1982), Vol. 26, p. 119, note 16.

Robin Myers, London

from John Calton, 15 June 1746.

A. Thomas Thorpe sale cat., 1833, item 164; Dawson Turner Collection; John Waller sale cat., 1859, No. 2; Richard Hatchwell, *Malmesbury Miscellany*, 32 (October, 1982), item 17, purchased by Myers.

National Library of Scotland
MS 967, f. 235.

from Christopher Pitt, 6 Apr. [1744?].

A. Contained in volume of autograph letters apparently compiled between 1820 and 1840 by Thomas Thomson, Liverpool; purchased by National Library of Scotland in 1933.

Nottinghamshire Record Office

M9659, Letter Book of John Gilbert Cooper, ff. 9, 11–12, 14–15.

to John Gilbert Cooper, 1749: 2 Dec. (9), 19 Dec. (11–12), 26 Dec. (14).

from William Warburton, 28 Sept. 1751 (15).

A. [John Gilbert Cooper family?]; Everard Charles Gilbert Cooper bequeathed to Nottingham Public Library [Nottingham City Archives Office (formerly part of Nottingham Public Library) amalgamated with Notts. Record Office in 1974] in 1956.

Royal Archives, Windsor Castle

RA Add 2/40.

to Elizabeth Cartwright, 27 Sept. [1761].,

A. Maggs sale cat., autumn, 1921, item 1729; Maggs sale cat. No 451, 1924, item 787; Maggs sale cat., 1942, item 1433, purchased by Royal Archives.

Royal Society of Arts

Guard Books, Vol. III Nos. 26, 62, 63.

to William Shipley, 1 Oct. [1755] (26).

to Jacob, Lord Folkestone, [c. 17 Mar. 1756] (62).

to George Box, [c. 21 June [1757] (63).

A. Preserved in Royal Society of Arts Guard Books since 1757.

Somersetshire Record Office

DD/SK 28/1–79.

from Richard Graves, 26 Oct. 1754 (1);
1756: [c. 3 Sept.] (77), 30 Sept. (2);
1757: 7 Jan. (5), 22 Feb. (6), 10 Oct. (7);
1758: 3 Feb. (8), 25 Apr. (9), 20 Dec. (10);
1759: 27 Mar. (75), 15 Oct. (11); 10 Jan. 1762 (12);
1763: 25 Apr. (14), [25 Apr.–21 May] (76), 21 May (15), 20 June (16);
1764: [c. 6 Jan.] (79), 30 Mar. (63), 9 Apr. (17), 30 Aug. (18).
from Richard Graves to James Dodsley, 1 Oct. 1764 (19).

A. Sir Thomas Phillipps Collection (MS 13851); Miss Dorothea Skrine, Warleigh Manor, Bathford, Somerset, deposited at Somerset County Record Office in 1956.

B. Charles Jarvais Hill, *The Literary Career of Richard Graves*. Vol. XVI, Nos. 1–3. Smith College Studies in Modern Languages. Northampton, Mass., 1934. (Hill used Warleigh MSS. extensively, but none *in toto*.)

Victoria and Albert Museum

Forster Collection, MS. F. 48 F. 7, ff. 1–2, 3–4, 5–6.

from David Garrick, 3 Dec. 1758 (1–2), [6 Dec. 1758] (5–6) to David Garrick, 5 Dec. [1758] (3–4).

A. Collection of John Forster (1812–76) bequeathed to Victoria and Albert Museum in 1876–7.

B. from Garrick, 3 Dec.: *Private Correspondence of David Garrick*, ed. James Boaden (London, 1835), I, 79; *RD*, pp. 228–9; *Letters of David Garrick*, ed. Little and Kahrl (Oxford, 1963), I. 294; [6 Dec.]: Boaden, I, 80; *RD*, p. 230; Little and Kahrl, I, 296–7.

to Garrick: Boaden, I, 79–80; *RD*, pp. 229–30.

MS. F. 48 E. 23. f. 169.

from David Hume, 14 Oct. 1754.

A. Puttick and Simpson sale cat., 3–7 June 1868, item 514; Collection of John Forster (1812–76), bequeathed to Victoria and Albert Museum in 1876–7.

B. *New Letters of David Hume*, ed. Raymond Klibansky and Ernest Mossner (Oxford: Clarendon Press, 1954), p. 37.

United States

University of California, Bancroft Library
Robert Dodsley Commonplace Book
to [George, Lord Lyttelton], 16 Oct. 1754 (ff. 1–6)
to [George, Lord Lyttelton?], [Oct.–Dec., 1754] (ff. 9–12)
A. [? Sotheby sale of Isaac Reed Collection, 2 Nov. 1807]; Sir Thomas Phillipps Collection (MS 20112).

University of Colorado Libraries
MS. 52a.
from Edward Young, 16 Oct [1747]
A. Collection of R. E. Egerton-Warburton, Arley Hall, Chester (3rd Report of the Royal Commission on Historical Manuscripts, 1872); Dobell's Antiquarian Bookstore = 1937, Henry Pettit, University of Colorado.
B. *Correspondence of Edward Young,* ed. Henry Pettit (Oxford: Clarendon Press, 1871), pp. 284–6.
MS 52.
from Edward Young, 10 Aug. 1755.
A. Sotheby sale cat., 18 February 1963, item 443, purchased by University of Colorado Libraries.
B. Pettit, p. 424.

Columbia University, Butler Library
from John Baskerville, 2 Oct. 1752, 19 Oct. 1752.
A. John Anderdon Collection = Evans sale cat., 14 February 1833, lot 331, purchased by Wilson; Joseph Lilly, bookseller = Sotheby sale cat., 22 April 1872, lot 11, purchased by John Waller; [Sotheby sale cat., 22–3 March 1899]; Samuel Timmins Collection = Sotheby sale cat., 20 April 1899, lot 230; Maggs Bros. purchased from Sotheby; (2 Oct.) Ralph Straus, Straus and Dent, *John Baskerville. A Memoir,* 94n.; American Typefounders Company = 1941, purchased by Columbia University.
B. Talbot B. Reed, *History of the Old English Typefoundries* (1887); rev. A. F. Johns (London: Faber, 1952), pp. 270, 272; Straus and Dent, *John Baskerville,* pp. 94–5; *RD,* pp. 271–2.

Folger Shakespeare Library
PN 2598 G3F5 Copy 4. Extra-ill. copy of Arthur Murphy, *Life of Garrick* (1801), VIII, 434.
from Joseph Baretti, 13 Sept. 1762.
A. Collection of Alexander Meynick Broadley (1847–1916) (bookplate in *Life of Garrick* dated 1902); Myers & Company sale cat., No. 236, item 17 = Henry Clay Folger purchased on 6 April 1923.
Y.c. 141 (1–3).
from Richard Berenger, 31 May [1756] (1–2), 10 June 1756 (3).
A. Joseph Lilly, bookseller = Sotheby sale cat., 22 April 1872, lot 13, purchased by Harvey; purchased by H. C. Folger in 1925.
C.b. 11 (1–3).
from Elizabeth Cartwright, 24 Nov. 1763 (3).
from George Steevens, 9 Apr. [1759] (2), January [1762] (1).
A. Sir Thomas Phillipps Collection = Sotheby sale cat., 6 July 1892, lot 544, purchased by Fenwick (?Phillipps' grandson, Sir T. Fitzroy Fenwick); purchased by H. C. Folger in 1925.
PN 2598 G3F5, Copy 3, extra-ill. copy of Percy Fitzgerald, *The Life of David Garrick* (London 1868), III, 379.
from David Garrick [6 Dec. 1758] (See also Harvard University and Victoria and Albert Museum).
B. Boaden, I, 80; Little and Kahrl, I, 296–7.

Harvard University

Houghton Library

Extra-ill. copy of Richard Brinsley Knowles, *Life of Sheridan Knowles* (London, 1872), II, 94.
from David Garrick 15 Sept. 1757.

A. Joseph Lilly, bookseller = Sotheby sale cat., 22 Apr. 1872, lot 37, purchased by Harvey; presented to Harvard by Robert Gould Shaw in 1915.

B. Little and Kahrl, I, 267 (not identified as letter to RD).

f MS Eng. 1336 (16) (originally interleaved in extra-ill. copy of Joseph Spence, *Anecdotes*, 1820).
from Joseph Spence, 25 Oct. 1754.

A. John Dillon Collection = Sotheby sale, 6–10 June 1869; Collection of John Ruskin (1817–1900); Goodspeed's, Boston = 3 November 1977, Harvard.

f MS Eng. 42.50.
from Philip Dormer Stanhope, 4th Earl of Chesterfield, 22 Dec. 1757.

A. John Anderdon Collection = Evans sale cat., 14 Feb. 1833, lot 307, purchased by Glynn; Sir Thomas Phillipps Collection = Sotheby sale cat., 5 July 1892, lot 203, purchased by G. Pearson; Sotheby sale cat., 5 Apr. 1894, lot 397 [mistakenly dated "Dec 7th 1757"]; Maggs sale cat., No. 320 (1914); Library of Harold Murdock bequeathed to Harvard, June 1935.

B. *RD*, pp. 224–5; *The Letters of Philip Dormer Stanhope*, ed. Bonamy Dobree (London, 1932), V, 2273–4.

bMS Eng 893 (251).
to Thomas Percy, [18 Dec. 1757–late Feb. 1758].

A. [Sotheby sale cat., 9 March 1870, lot 169, purchased by Waller]; John Waller sale cat. #83 *Autographs and Historical Documents*, 1870, item 90; Waller, *Interesting Autograph Letters* (London, 1872); Sotheby sale cat., 28 Apr. 1884 = lots 146 and 302 of Percy Papers purchased by Quaritch for Harvard.

ALS File.
from William Shenstone, 11 February 1762.

A. Thomas Thorpe sale cats., 1833, item 3442; 1844, item 2131; Collection of John Davies, Manchester = Puttick and Simpson sale cat., 9–10 Sept. 1851, lot 241; Sotheby sale cat., 27 Nov. 1945, lot 513; Maggs sale cat., 12 July 1946, item 264 = Harvard.

B. Thomas Hull, *Select Letters* (1778), I, 303–6; Williams, pp. 569–71; Mallam, pp. 404–6 (all print as of "1761").

Harvard College Library, Harvard Theatre Collection

Extra-ill. copy of Asia Booth Clarke, *The Elder and Younger Booth* (Boston, 1882).
from David Garrick, [6 Dec. 1758] (See also Folger and Victoria and Albert Museum).

A. Evert Jansen Wendell bequeathed to Harvard in 1918.

B. Boaden, I, 80; *RD*, 230; Little and Kahrl, 296–7.

Henry E. Huntington Library

RB 131213, v. 4. Joseph Spence, *Supplemental Anecdotes* (London, 1820).
to Joseph Spence, 22 Oct. 1748 (interleaved opposite p. 426), [19 June 1751] (interleaved opposite p. 427).

A. Daly Collection = American Art Galleries sale, 19 March 1900.

B. Joseph Spence, *Anecdotes*, ed. Samuel Weller Singer (1820; repr. Carbondale: Southern Illinois University Press, 1964), pp. 251–2, 252–3; *RD*, pp. 117–18, (22 Oct. 1748).

HM 12235, 12238.
from John Hawkesworth, 10 Dec. 1758 (12238), [Nov. 1759] (12235).

A. Sir Thomas Phillipps Collection (MS 13847) = Sotheby sale cat., 5 July 1892, lot 353, purchased by Pearson; Anderson Galleries sale cat., 13–14 February 1918, lot 447, purchased by Henry E. Huntington.

University of Kansas, Spencer Library
MS P297.
to Arthur Charles Stanhope, 19 Sept. [1758].
A. Miss Elizabeth Dransfield (d. 1907), of Doncaster = Col. Ralph Watson Hallows (1885–?).

Lewis Walpole Library
from Theodore, Baron de Neuhoff, King of Corsica, 8 Mar. 1753.
A. Collection of Sir Wathen A. Waller = Sotheby sale cat., 5 Dec. 1921, lot 185; Christie's sale cat., 15 Dec. 1947, lot 27, purchased by Maggs for W. S. Lewis.
from Richard Bentley (with note by Horace Walpole), 20 Nov. 1758, laid in copy of Lucan's *Pharsalia* (printed at Walpole's Strawberry Hill Press, 1760).
A. Purchased from Sir Robert Abdy, Bt., by Maggs for W. S. Lewis in 1938.
B. Allan T. Hazen, *Bibliography of Strawberry Hill Press* (Yale University Press, 1942), p. 48 (partial); *Horace Walpole's Miscellaneous Correspondence*, ed. W. S. Lewis and John C. Riely (Yale University Press, 1980), I, 148–9.
Bound MSS Williams, Vols. 73, 77.
to Sir Charles Hanbury Williams, 23 May 1758 (73), 31 Aug. [1758] (77).
A. Sir Thomas Phillipps Collection (MS 11388) = Sir T. Fitzroy Fenwick; William H. Robinson, bookseller = June 1949, W. S. Lewis.

Mary Hyde Collection
from Samuel Johnson, June, 1746.
A. Sotheby sale cat., 3 Dec. 1900, lot 1036; Montagu David Scott; B. F. Stevens; Robert B. Adam Collection, Buffalo, N. Y.
B. *The Robert B. Adams Library* (New York, 1929), I, 42; *Letters of Samuel Johnson*, ed. R. W. Chapman (Oxford, 1952), I, 29–30.
from Christopher Smart [*post* 30 May 1747], 9 Feb. 1748.
A. Robert B. Adam Collection.
B. Arthur Sherbo, *Christopher Smart, Scholar of the University* (Michigan State University Press, 1967), pp. 52–3.
from William Warburton, 6 Jan. 1756 (with fragment draft of).
A. Robert B. Adam Collection Liii, 196.

State University of New York-Buffalo, Lockwood Memorial Library, Poetry Collection
from Christopher Smart, 12 Jan. 1748.
A. Thomas Thorpe sale cat., 1833, item 914; George Linnecar Collection = Puttick and Simpson sale cat., 20 Mar. 1850, lot 370, purchased by Bird; Christie sale cat., 23 July 1856, lot 572; Myers sale cat. No. 348 (1947), item 383.
B. Sherbo, *Christopher Smart*, p. 53.
from William Mason, 3 Mar. [1756].
A. Maggs sale cat. No. 299 (Nov. 1912).
B. *Correspondence of Thomas Gray*, ed. Paget Toynbee and Leonard Whibley (Oxford, 1935), II, 459.

New York Public Library, Berg Collection
Bound ms. volume of 39 ALS from David Garrick to George Colman, the elder.
to William Strahan, 12 Dec. [1758].
A. Purchased from Myers & Co. on 28 October 1954.

Historical Society of Pennsylvania

Simon Gratz Collection, British Literary Misc., Case 11, Boxes 5, 6.

from John Brown, 14 Mar. [1745] (5).

A. Puttick and Simpson sale cat., 3 June 1878, lot 38; Simon Gratz Collection, formed 1870–1925 = bequeathed to Historical Society during 1912–25.

from David Fordyce, 11 Feb. 1748 (6).

A. Joseph Lilly, bookseller = Sotheby sale cat., 22 Apr. 1872, lot 27 [?purchased by Fawcett]; Simon Gratz Collection (see above) = bequeathed to Historical Society, as above.

Dreer Collection.

Physicians and Surgeons, ALS.

from Charles Bisset, 9 May 1755.

A. [? Joseph Lilly, bookseller = Sotheby sale cat. 22 Apr. 1872, lot 27, purchased by Fawcett]; Ferdinand J. Dreer Collection, formed during 1855–90 = bequeathed to Historical Society in 1890.

English Prose Writers, ALS.

from Laurence Sterne, [c. 5 Oct. 1759].

A. John Anderdon Collection = Evans sale cat., 14 Feb. 1833, lot 313, purchased by Rich; Ferdinand J. Dreer Collection (as above); bequeathed to Historical Society in 1890.

B. Thomas F. Dibden, *Reminiscences of a Literary Life* (1836), Pt. i, 207–8; *Letters of Laurence Sterne*, ed. Lewis P. Curtis (1935; repr. Oxford, 1965), pp. 80–1.

Pierpont Morgan Library

Extra-ill. copy of G. W. Fulcher, *Life of Thomas Gainsborough* (London, 1856), V, 31.

from Thomas Sheridan [15 or 22 Aug. 1744].

A. Sir Thomas Phillipps Collection = Sotheby sale cat., 6 July 1892, lot 525, published by Ridge.

from Samuel Johnson, 26 Dec. 1746 (now removed from Fulcher volume).

A. Sotheby sale cat., 3 Dec. 1900, lot 1038 (ALS alone), purchased by Pearson.

B. *Letters of Samuel Johnson*, ed. R. W. Chapman, I, 30.

Robert H. Taylor Collection, Princeton University Library

from Laurence Sterne, 23 May 1759.

A. Charles Mathews Collection = Sotheby sale cat., 22 Aug. 1835, lot 767; Collection of John Wild (d. 1855); R. N. Carew Hunt (great-grandson of Wild); Taylor purchased from W. H. Robinson & Sons in 1953.

B. *RD*, pp. 261–3; R. N. Carew Hunt, *Unpublished Letters from the Collection of John Wild.* 1st Ser. (London, 1930), pp. 41–3; Curtis, *Letters of Laurence Sterne*, pp. 74–5.

University of Texas at Austin, Humanities Research Center

Robert Dodsley/Recipient 1/Bound, ff. 5–135.

from John Scott Hylton, 16 Sept. [1756] (5–6);

1757: 20 Jan. (9–11), 6 Dec. (13–16);

1758: 4 Feb. (17), 9–13 Feb. (25–28), 16 Feb. (21), 24 Feb. (29–32), 2–4 Mar. (33–36), 22 Apr. (37–40), 14 Sept. (41–42);

21 Feb. 1759 (45–48); 18–20 Feb. 1761 (49–51).

from John Pixell, 3 Dec. 1755 (121–23), 7 Nov. 1757 (125–27), 30 Apr. [1759] (133–35), 16 Apr. 1764 (129).

from Richard Jago, [early April 1755] (107), 25 Oct. 1757 (65–67), 3 Nov. 1757 (69–71), 21 Nov. 1757 (73–75), [1758?] (109–[116]).

A. Sir Thomas Phillipps Collection (MS 13845) = Sotheby sale cat., 28 June 1965, lot 81, purchased by Texas.

Yale University

Beinecke Library, MS Vault File

from John Baskerville, 20 Dec. 1756.

A. [John Anderdon Collection = Evans sale cat., 14 Feb. 1833, lot 331]; Lewis Pocock Collection = Sotheby sale cat., 10 May 1875, lot 7, purchased by Waller; Samuel Timmins Collection = Sotheby sale cat., 20 Apr. 1899, lot 230, purchased by Maggs.

B. Reed, *History of Old English Letter Foundries*, p. 271; Straus and Dent, *John Baskerville*, pp. 96–7.

James M. Osborn Collection

from Roger Comberbach, 20 Feb. 1744.

A. Thomas Thorpe sale cats., 1833, item 209; 1839, item 110; [1840?], item 216; 1842–3, item 94.

to George Selwyn, 12 Sept. 1745.

A. Thomas Thorpe sale cat., 1833, item 3185; Sotheby sale cat., 21 Aug. 1872, lot 103.

from William Warburton, [6 or 7 April 1746].

B. John Nichols, *Literary Anecdotes*, V, 587 (dates as 12 Apr., but no date on ms.); *RD*, p. 84.

from Christopher Smart, 6 Aug. 1746.

B. Sherbo, *Christopher Smart*, p. 50.

from John Berckenhout, 26 Feb. 1754.

A. [Thomas Thorpe sale cat., 1833, item 73].

from John Ogilvie, 12 Dec. 1756.

A. Thomas Thorpe sale cat., 1833, item 761.

World Methodist Council Museum

from John Wesley, 12 Dec. 1744.

A. Collection of Dr Elmer T. Clark.

B. *Works of John Wesley*, ed. Frank Baker, Vol. 26, p. 119.

APPENDIX D
UNTRACED CORRESPONDENCE OF ROBERT DODSLEY

The following list of 139 untraced letters is compiled from allusions found in extant Dodsley correspondence and from printed sources, including autograph bookdealer/auction house sale catalogues. Perhaps a few instances are duplicates, for the information discovered in the sources is not always adequate to make absolute distinctions. Although all letters in the body of this edition taken from printed sources are indeed untraced letters, it was thought that eleven of them, because they survive only in fragmented state, deserve special mention here. These entries are marked with an asterisk. In all entries, material in brackets represents the editor's additions.

The first item in each entry names the author or recipient of the letter listed. Following is the reported or approximated date of the letter(s), sometimes preceded by a number in parentheses, which indicates the number of letters mentioned in the source. The third item is the source itself. When the source happens to be another letter, a hyphenated double name indicates the author and recipient, respectively. Finally, an extract from the letter, when available, appears in parentheses. In this last item, only that information is included which is thought relevant to present concerns. Since they are printed in the body of the text, no extracts are provided for items marked with an asterisk.

from Anonymous
  (2) Early September 1761
  RD-Shenstone, 18 September 1761
to   Alcock, Edward, Birmingham painter
  late 1759
  RD-Shenstone, 4 January 1760
from Ash, John (1723–98), MD, Birmingham
  (2) January–February [1761]
  RD-Shenstone, 12 February [1761]
from Bagnell, Rev. Gibbons
  1750
  Sotheby sale cat. (16–17 December 1763), lot 456
  (seeking anonymous publication of his translation of Hesiod)
from Baillie, James, of Boalhough, Scotland
  15 November 1746
  Edinburgh University Library (missing from collection);
  Thomas Thorpe sale cats. (1833), item 42; (1839), item 69
  ("conjuring Dodsley 'by Pope and Apollo' to apprise him of his determination relative to his poem called 'Deliverance': 'We poets, like indulgent parents, are very fond of our offspring, and like other good Christians, very anxious about our salvation and damnation.'") [If published by RD, no copy traced.]
*from Balguy, Charles (1708–67), MD
  14 June [1741]
  Thomas Thorpe sale cat. (1833), item 45

from Barford, Richard
Chilmark, 24 January 1757
Thomas Thorpe sale cat. (1833), item 50
(Instructions for RD's publication of Barford's poem)
[Unidentified]
from Barnard, Edward (1717–81), of Eton
n.d.
Thomas Thorpe sale cat. (1833), item 52
(Relative to some translation. "My Compliments to the Wartons, when you see or write them.")
from Barr, John (*c.* 1709–78), Rector of Oumby, near Lincoln
(3) (n.d.); 1 January 1744)
Thomas Thorpe sale cat. (1833), item 53
(January, 1744, letter concerns his book entitled *Reflections upon Church Government.* Only known attribution of *Reflections* to Barr.)
from Barton, Philip (uncle or nephew? – both classicists at New College, Oxford, at this time)
New College, Oxford, 12 Febuary 1753
Thomas Thorpe sale cat. (1833), item 675
("sending [Robert] Lowth's book *Poesi* [*De Sacra Poesi Hebraeorum,* 1753]; no time to correct errata")
from Baskerville, John (1706–75), Birmingham printer
January–February [1761]
RD-Shenstone, 12 February [1761]
from Bisset, Charles (1717-91)
n.d. in catalogue
Sotheby's sale cat. (Joseph Lilly Collection) (22 April 1872), lot 27
from Bisset
1756
Thomas Thorpe sale cat. (1883), item 82
(Supposes a particular review will prejudice the sale of his book [*Treatise on Scurvy,* 1755?])
from Blacklock, Thomas (1721–91), Scottish poet
12 September 1754
Sotheby sale cat. (Sir Thomas Phillipps Collection) (4 July 1892), lot 152 (purchased by Pearson)
from Blacklock
Edinburgh, 20 January 1756
Thomas Thorpe sale cat. (1883), item 83
(Relative to the publication, this year, of the 4° edition of his poems under supervision of Joseph Spence)
to Blacklock
25 April 1756
Blacklock-RD, 3 May 1756
from Blacklock
30 May 1756
Puttick and Simpson sale cat. (S. George Christison Collection) (19–21 December 1850), lot 64
[Perhaps same as referred to in Blacklock-RD 27 June 1757]
from Blacklock
31 October 1756
Clipping from sale catalogue laid in Straus's personal copy of *Robert Dodsley,* p. 359
from Blacklock
January 1758
Blacklock-RD, 19 March 1758
from Boyle, John, 5th Earl of Cork (1707–62)
n.d.
Sotheby sale cat. (J. M. Rainbow Collection)/(25 February 1854), lot 142

from Brooke, Frances (1724–89), author
      (2) n.d.
      John Gray Bell sale cat. (1851), items 208, 209
*from Brown, John "Estimate" (1715–66)
      5 October 1745
      Straus, *Robert Dodsley*, p. 85
to   Brown
      5–17 October 1745
      Brown-RD, 17 October 1745
to   Brown
      early 1746
      Brown-RD, 15 February 1746
to   Brown
      end of February 1746
      Brown-RD, 5 March 1746
to   Brown
      early November 1746
      Brown-RD, 8 November 1746
from Burke, Edmund (1729–97), author and statesman
      (4) n.d. in catalogues
      Evans sale cat. (13 February 1833) (purchased by Wilks);
      Sotheby sale cat. (John Wilks Collection) (12 May 1851), lot 93 (2, purchased by Morgan); lots
      98, 889 (purchased by Webb)
from Burke
      Dublin, 9 February 1764
      John Waller sale cat. (1857) (H. Belward Ray Collection), item 214
      (Regarding a work in progress [*Annual Register* for 1763?]
      which "please God I propose to send over next week, executed rather more to my satisfaction
      than I could have flattered myself was practicable, considering what I had to go upon")
from Cheyney, Thomas (*c.* 1694–1760), Dean of Winchester
      n.d. in catalogue
      Thomas Thorpe cat. (1833), item 197
      (Relating to Joseph Spence's *Polymetis*, 1747)
from Comberbach, Roger (d. 1757), of Chester
      (4) Chester, 1744
      Thomas Thorpe sale cats. (1833), item 209; (1839), item 110; [1840?], item 216 ("containing
      corrections for, and observations on, his translation of Cicero's Orations"); (1842–3), item 94
from Comberbach
      1754
      Thomas Rodd sale cats. (1836), item 513; (1838), item 812; (1841), item 1244; (1847), item 1697
from Cooper, John Gilbert (1723–69), miscellaneous writer
      Thurgarton, 7 October 1751
      Puttick and Simpson sale cats. (29 July 1861), item 365; (29 July 1867) (Robert Cole
      Collection), item 251 (about beginning a quarrel with William Warburton)
to   Cooper
      November, 1751
      Cooper-RD, 23 November 1751
to   Cooper
      1 October 1754
      Cooper-RD, 7 October 1754
to   Cooper
      mid-March, 1755
      Cooper-RD, 20 March 1755

from Cooper, Maria Susanna, novelist [to James Dodsley?]
30 October 1762
Thomas Thorpe sale cat. (1833), item 211
(relating to her novel *Letters between Emilia and Harriet,* 1762)
from Cooper, Samuel (1739–1800), of Shottisham, near Norwich [to James Dodsley?]
1762
Thomas Thorpe sale cat. (1833), item 210
("Relative to his essays [?] and Mrs. [Maria Susanna] Cooper's novels published by Dodsley"
[*Letters between Emilia and Harriet,* 1762; other two novels published in 1769 and 1775])
*from Dyer, John (1700?–57), poet
12 May 1757
Straus, *Robert Dodsley,* p. 110
*from Garrick, David (1717–79), actor and theater manager
18 October 1756
Sotheby sale cat. (Joseph Lilly Collection) (22 April 1872), lot 36
from Graves, Richard (1715–1804), poet and novelist
n.d.
John Waller sale cat. (1860), item 87
(letter on military affairs addressed to RD at Bath)
to Graves
(2) August–September, 1756
Graves-RD, 30 September 1756
to Graves
30 March [1758]
RD-Shenstone, 30 March [1758]
from Graves
late March [1758]
RD-Shenstone, 30 March [1758]
to Gray, Thomas (1716–71), poet
November 1752
Gray–Horace Walpole, 17 December 1752 (*Correspondence of Thomas Gray,* ed. Paget Toynbee
and Leonard Whibley (Oxford, 1935), I, p. 365)
from Gray
November 1752
Gray–Horace Walpole, 17 December 1752 (Toynbee and Whibley, I, p. 366)
to Gray
c. 15 December 1752
Gray–Horace Walpole, 17 December 1752 (Toynbee and Whibley, I, p. 366)
from Gray
Stoke, 25 July 1757
Sotheby sale cat. (27 November 1945), lot 464
(Concerning the printing of the Pindaric Odes at Strawberry Hill. He is sending a parcel of
copies as soon as ready and gives list of friends for presentation copies) [*Odes,* 1757]
from Miss H.
January–February [1761]
RD-Shenstone, 12 February [1761]
from Hawkesworth, John (1720–73), author
early September 1756
Hawkesworth-RD, 14 September 1756
from Hawkesworth
3 November 1757
Robert E. Gallagher, dissertation, Northwestern University (1957), p. 207, claimed the
holograph was in possession of Geoffrey Tillotson, but it is not now in the Tillotson Collection.

from Herbert, Nicholas (1706–75), of Glenham, Suffolk; MP, Newport
    c. 20 July [1757]
    RD-Herbert, 20 July [1757]
from Hume, David (1711–76), philosopher and historian
    12 March 1754
    Joseph Spence. *An Account of the Life, Character, and Poems of Mr. Blacklock* (1754), p. 4.
to   Hylton, John Scott (d. 1793), of Halesowen, near Birmingham
    early September [1756]
    Hylton-RD, 16 September [1756]
to   Hylton
    December 1757–4 February 1758
    Hylton-RD, 4 February 1758
to   Hylton
    9 October [1758]
    RD-Shenstone, 10 October [1758]
*from Hylton
    1764
    John Waller sale cat. (Dawson Turner Collection), 1859, No. 2
from Knight, Henrietta St John, Lady Luxborough (d. 1756)
    3 June 1747
    Christie sale catalogue, 19 December 1963, item 230
    (Asks RD to send Mallet's *Hermit* to the Saracen's Head on Snow Hill; states she was
    misinformed when she wrote for the British Compendium of 1741, for she has an older copy; asks
    for any new poem, play or pamphlet; states that what were probably the last plays – the *Suspicious*
    Husband and *Miss in her Teens* – were sent to her by a friend.)
*from Knight, Henrietta St John, Lady Luxborough (d. 1756)
    [*post* May] 1748
    Clipping from unidentified sale catalogue laid in Straus's personal copy of *Robert Dodsley*, p. 335
    (Now in McMaster University)
to   Lowth, Robert (1710–87), Bishop of London
    February 1762
    Lowth-RD, 5 March 1762
from Lowth
    February, 1762
    Lowth-RD, 5 March 1762
from Lyttelton, George, Lord (1709–73)
    early July 1757
    RD-Shenstone, 13 July 1757
*from Mason, William (1724–97), poet
    31 May 1747
    Straus, *Robert Dodsley*, pp. 114–15
*from Mason
    [*post* 31 May, *ante* 16 August 1747]
    Straus, *Robert Dodsley*, p. 115
*from Massey, James
    Salford, Manchester, 10 March 1748
    John Waller sale cat. (1859) (Dawson Turner Collection), No. 2
from Melmoth, William (1710–99), author
    early December 1756
    RD-Melmoth, 16 December [1756]
from Melmoth
    16–17 June [1760]
    RD-Shenstone, 17 June [1760]

to   Melmoth
     mid-August 1760
     Melmoth-RD, 29 August 1760
from Melmoth
     September 1760
     Melmoth-RD, 9 October 1760
to   Melmoth
     4 October 1760
     Melmoth-RD, 9 October 1760
from Mendes, Solomon (d. 1762?)
     23 December 1746
     Thomas Thorpe sale cat. (1883), item 723
to   Mendes
     late 1753
     S. Mendes-RD, December 1753
*from Montagu, Elizabeth (1720–1800), author
     late 1757
     Straus, *Robert Dodsley*, p. 217
to   Parsons, Philip (1729–1812)
     n.d.
     Parsons-RD, 29 October 1759
to   Percy, Thomas (1729–1811), editor of *Reliques*
     11 January 1757
     RD-Shenstone, 11 January 1757
from Pitt, Christopher (1699–1748), poet and translator
     26 March [?]
     Puttick and Simpson sale cat. (4 June 1878), lot 218
from Pitt
     5 May [1744]
     Sotheby sale cat. (Sir Thomas Phillipps Collection), 4 July 1892, lot 479 (purchased by Pearson)
     [Same as June 1744 letter?]
from Pitt
     June [1744?]
     Pitt-RD, 4 July [1744]?
from Pitt, Lucy, sister of Christopher Pitt [later Lucy Baskett?]
     16 February 1747
     L. Pitt-RD, 18 February 1747
from Ridley, Glocester (1702–1774), miscellaneous writer
     20 January 1745
     Sotheby sale cat. (Sir Thomas Phillipps Collection) (6 July 1892), lot 501 (purchased by Barker)
to   Ridley
     late November 1745
     Ridley-RD, 2 December 1745
from Shenstone, William (1714–63), poet
     n.d.
     Sotheby sale cat. (Peter Cunningham Collection) (26 February 1855), lot 130
from Shenstone
     22 April 1754
     Sotheby sale cat. (27 July 1885), lot 886 (purchased by Waller)
     (Respecting death and funeral of his relative Miss Dolman to whose memory he erected an urn in
     "Lover's Walk" at the Leasowes)
from Shenstone
     early April [1756]
     RD-Shenstone, 17 April [1756]

from Shenstone
    early December [1756]
    RD-Shenstone, 13 December [1756]
from Shenstone
    December [1756]
    RD-Shenstone, 21 December [1756]
from Shenstone
    23 November 1757
    Shenstone–John Scott Hylton, 26 November 1757 [abstract in Maggs sale cat., No. 652
    (Christmas, 1937), item 850]
from Shenstone
    18–19 December [1757]
    RD-Shenstone, 18–20 December [1757]
from Shenstone
    14–15 January 1758
    RD-Shenstone, 16 January 1758
from Shenstone
    19–20 January [1758]
    RD-Shenstone, 21 January [1758]
from Shenstone
    June 1758
    RD-Shenstone, 13 June 1758
from Shenstone
    early September 1758
    RD-Shenstone, 19 September 1758
from Shenstone
    September–October [1758]
    RD-Shenstone, 14 October [1758]
from Shenstone
    early October [1758]
    RD-Shenstone, 10 October [1758]
from Shenstone
    (3) December, 1758–January, 1759
    RD-Shenstone, 20 January 1759
from Shenstone
    1759
    Thomas Thorpe sale cat. (1844), item 2130; Sotheby sale cat. (27 July 1885), lot 884 (purchased
    by Barker)
from Shenstone
    early March 1759 (?)
    RD-Shenstone, 15 March 1759
from Shenstone
    late November 1759
    RD-Shenstone, 1 December 1759
to Shenstone
    November 1761
    Shenstone-RD, 20 November 1761
from Smart, Christopher (1722–71), poet
    7 August (?)
    Sotheby sale cat. (Sir Thomas Phillipps Collection) (6 July 1892), lot 532 (purchased by
    Pearson)
from Smart
    30 January 1747
    Puttick and Simpson sale cat. (3 June 1878), lot 267

from Smart
1749
John Gray Bell sale cat. (September 1856), item 630
from Stevenson, John Hall (1718–85)
Skelton Castle, 4 March 1764
Thomas Thorpe sale cats. (1833), item 3598; (1838), item 1869; (1840), item 1595
(Introducing Mr Thompson)
from Stonhouse, Sir James (1716–95), MD, of Northampton
Northampton, 8 May 1746
Sotheby sale cat. (Sir Thomas Phillipps Collection) (6 July 1892), lot 545 (purchased by
Pearson)
from Thackray, (Thomas?)
January [1758]
RD-Thackray, 16 January [1758]
to Unwin, Miss
July–August 1763
RD-Elizabeth Cartwright, 3 August 1763
to Victor, Benjamin (d. 1778), theater manager
August–October 1753
Victor-RD, 12 November 1753
from Victor
August–October, 1753
Victor-RD, 12 November 1753
from W., Mr. [?Christopher Wren, 1711–71; see below]
(2) early [1761]
RD-Shenstone, 25 June [1761]
from Warburton, William (1698–1779), Bishop of Gloucester
24 December 1743
R. E. Egerton Warburton, Orley Hall, Chesterfield, *3rd Report of the Royal Commission on Historical
Manuscripts* (1872)
(Regarding RD's *Select Collection of Old Plays*, 1744)
from Warburton
25 December 1746
Sotheby sale cat. (Sir Thomas Phillipps Collection) (6 July 1892), lot 578 (purchased by Barker)
from Warburton
end of December 1755
RD-Warburton, *c.* 6 January 1756
(Regarding W.'s refusing RD a share in his edition of Pope's *Works*, 1751)
to Warton, Joseph (1722–1800), poet and critic
October–November [1754]
RD-J. Warton, 8 November [1754]
from Warton, Thomas (1728–90), historian of English poetry
[January 1747]
RD-T. Warton, 29 January [1747]
from Warton
[mid-1754]
RD-J. Warton, 8 November [1754]
from Whitehead, William (1715–85), Poet Laureate
n.d.
Puttick and Simpson sale cat. (S. George Christison Collection) (19–21 December 1850), lot 693
from Whitehead
Clare Hall, 6 November 1743
Thomas Thorpe sale cat. (1833), item 1006
(New poems ready for press but declines parting with them for same price as sold previous pieces
to RD; asks his ultimatum as to an advanced sum)

*from Whitehead
    1 April 1755
    Straus, *Robert Dodsley*, pp. 111–12
to   Wren, Christopher (1711–71), grandson of Sir Christopher Wren
    1 December 1759
    RD-Shenstone, 1–3 December 1759
from Wright, Miss Nelly, of Mansfield
    January–February [1757]
    RD–N. Wright, 24 February [1757]
from Wright
    July–August [1757]
    RD–N. Wright, 30 August [1757]
from Young, Edward (1683–1765), poet and dramatist
    Wellwyn, 3 January 1744
    Sotheby sale cat. (John Dillon Collection) (10 June 1869), lot 1031 (purchased by John Waller);
    John Waller sale cat. (1870–3), item 424
    (Regarding the purchase of a portion of *Night Thoughts*)
from Young
    14 October 1756
    Puttick and Simpson sale cat. (Linnecar Collection) (20 March 1850), lot 419

APPENDIX E
CORRESPONDENCE AND DOCUMENTS OF
JAMES DODSLEY

The following listing records both extant holograph texts and printed citations to James Dodsley correspondence and documents that have come to hand in the course of the search for Robert Dodsley material. Although items belonging to James have never been overlooked during the research on Robert, this list does not pretend to be complete. Because James was not the primary subject of the project, some stones were left unturned. For instance, little effort was expended in attempting to trace holographs listed in autograph dealer catalogues where the date and correspondent cited made it clear that the piece had no bearing on Robert's world. The same applies to materials found or listed in other printed sources. However, such citations are listed among the following; in fact, they make up the bulk of the appendix.

None the less, the results of library searches suggest that James's correspondence has fared much worse than Robert's. Proportionately, fewer letters survive, despite his longer career at Tully's Head (38 years as compared with Robert's 24). In fact, this search has discovered only 79 extant pieces. Of these, only three are authored by James; the rest are addressed to him. The same condition characterizes James's surviving purchase agreements and receipts.

In the case of citations found in auction house and autograph dealer catalogues, normally just the earliest citation has been presented. (Some items turn up again and again.) In several instances, details found in later catalogues (author's full name, dates, etc.) have been silently introduced into these earlier citations. Where sparse detail in an earlier source rendered its subject questionable, the later has been used. Generally, where an extant manuscript has come to hand, economy has dictated that secondary, catalogue citations to the same are not listed. Although not included, frequently informative abstracts or quotes accompany entries in these catalogues.

I. EXTANT LETTERS

to [?] 7 January 1791. National Library of Scotland MS582.
from [?] Dublin, 6 December 1790. Bodleian MS. d. 11, f. 125.
from [?] 10 February [n.y.] (one-page fragment). Harvard Theatre Collection.
from Christopher Anstey, 29 May 1774. Bath Reference Library, AL 377.
    from Anstey, 25 January 1776. Henry E. Huntington Library HM 11438.
    from Anstey, 14 June 1780. Bodleian MS Montague d. 11, f. 29.
    from Anstey, [2] February 1781. Beinecke Library, Yale.
    from Anstey, 15 November 1786. Bath Reference Library, AL 378.
    from Anstey, 6 March 1787. Bath Reference Library, AL 1345.
from George Anne Bellamy, "Sunday Even" [1772?]. A. N. L. Munby Collection, Cambridge.
    from Bellamy, "Monday" [1772]. Folger Shakespeare Library, Y. C. 132 (1).
    from Bellamy, "Monday Noon" [1772]. Dreer Collection, Historical Society of Pennsylvania.

from Edmund Burke [*post* 1765]. Osborn Collection, Beinecke Library, Yale.
from Richard Burke, Jr., 7 April [n.y.]. Bodleian MS. Montagu d. 11, f. 175.
from John Gilbert Cooper, 12 July 1762. Bodleian MS. Eng. Misc. d. 174, ff. 84–5.
from Thomas Davies [n.d.]. Osborn Collection, Beinecke Library, Yale.
from William Dodd. 22 November [n.y.]. Boston Public Library.
from Oliver Goldsmith, 10 March 1764. W. M. Elkins Collection. Philadelphia (ref.: Katharine
    Balderston, *The Collected Letters of Oliver Goldsmith* (Cambridge, 1928), p. 73).
from Richard Graves, 13 [i.e. 12] October 1773. Bath Reference Library, AL 287.
from Graves, 13 October 1773. Bath Reference Library, AL 2316.
from Graves, 31 July 1783. Bath Reference Library, AL 2317.
from William Hall, 10 April 1769. Bodleian MS. Eng. Letters d. 40.
from John Hawkesworth, "Wed morn." Henry E. Huntington Library, HM 12234.
from Robert Hill, [n.d.]. Bodleian MS. Eng. Letters d. 40, f. 100.
from William Holmes, Exeter, 15 July 1778. Bodleian MS. Eng. Letters d. 40, f. 121.
from William Holmes, Exeter, 18 July 1778. Bodleian MS. Eng. Letters d. 40, f. 124.
from John Scott Hylton [3 Jan., n.y.]. Humanities Research Center, University of Texas at Austin,
    Robert Dodsley / Recipient 1/Bound, f. 56.
from Richard Jago, 5 August 1765. H.R.C., University of Texas at Austin, ff. 77–9.
from Jago, 25 November 1765. H.R.C., University of Texas at Austin, f. 81.
from Jago, 3 February 1766. H.R.C., University of Texas at Austin, ff. 85–7.
from Jago, 20 April 1767. H.R.C., University of Texas at Austin, f. 89.
from Jago, June 1767. H.R.C., University of Texas at Austin, f. 93.
from Jago, 15 August 1769. H.R.C., University of Texas at Austin, ff. 97–9.
from Jago, 11 November 1769. H.R.C., University of Texas at Austin, f. 107.
from Jago, 26 December 1769. H.R.C., University of Texas at Austin, f. 105.
from Samuel Johnson [*c*. 1765?] Sotheby sale cat. (5 December 1902), lot 213.
from W. King, Oakfield [Ireland], 1785. Bodleian MS. Eng. Letters d. 40, f. 126.
from King, Woodstock, 24 July 1793. Bodleian MS. Eng. Letters d. 40, f. 128.
from King, Woodstock, 2 August 1793. Bodleian MS. Eng. Letters d. 40, f. 130.
from Charlotte Lennox, 10 May 1784. Frederick W. Hilles, Yale (ref.: Mirian Small, *Charlotte Ramsey
    Lennox* (New Haven, 1935), p. 55).
from Robert Lowth, 2 May 1763. BL Add MS. 35,339, ff. 29–30.
from Lowth, 21 March 1764. BL Add. MS. 35,339, ff. 33–4.
from Lowth, 5 May 1764. BL Add. MS. 35,339, f. 35.
from George, Lord Lyttelton, "Monday Morning" [1767–71]. Beinecke Library, Yale.
from [William] Mason, 25 October 1782. Boston Public Library.
from William Melmoth, 12 February 1763. BL Add. MS. 35,338, f. 21.
from Melmoth, "Thursday." BL Add. MS. 35,338, ff. 19–20.
from T. and J. Merrill, Cambridge, 1 November 1776. Harvard Theatre Collection.
from Merrill, Cambridge, [n.d.]. Harvard Theatre Collection.
from Bellamira Mornay, Clapham, 25 July 1755. Harvard Theatre Collection.
from Mornay, Clapham, 9 August 1755. Harvard Theatre Collection.
from Richard Muilman [later Trench Chiswell], King Street, Covent Garden, 15 June 1770. Harvard
    Theatre Collection.
from Nicholas Owen, 22 March 1776. Bodleian MS. Don d. 89, f. 267.
from Philip Parsons, 13 April 1770. Bodleian MS. Don d. 89, f. 291.
from Thomas Percy, [*c*. 1762]. Bodleian MS. Percy C.2, ff. 233–4.
from Edward Popham, 20 November 1777. Harvard Theatre Collection.
from Popham, Lacock, "Xtmas day" 1777. Harvard Theatre Collection.
from Popham, Lacock near Chippenham, 13 September 1778. Harvard Theatre Collection.
from Samuel Jackson Pratt, Crown's Coffeehouse, Charles Street, Covent Garden, "Thursday
    Morning." Harvard Theatre Collection.
from Pratt, Middle Temple, 6 Feb. 17[??]. Harvard Theatre Collection.
to [Isaac] Reed, [n.d.] No. 11 Staples Inn. Folger Shakespeare Library.

from Glocester Ridley, Poplar, 8 June 1768. Harvard Theatre Collection.
from Charles Rutledge, Paris, 24 May 1778. Boston Public Library.
from Eliza Ryves, 11 February 1776. Harvard Theatre Collection.
from Ryves, 15 February 1776. Harvard Theatre Collection.
from Ryves, Woburn, 26 November 1777. Harvard Theatre Collection.
to William Shenstone – Pallmall – 22 October [1754]. BL. Add. MS. 28,959, f. 14. (Printed in this edition.).
from Thomas Sheridan, 4 August [1762?]. National Library of Scotland, MS. 968, f. 14.
from Charlotte Smith, 4 May 1784. Henry E. Huntington Library HM 10800.
from Philip Stanhope, 5th Earl of Chesterfield, [and witnessed? co-signed? by Beaumont Hotham, later Baron Hotham]. Addressed to Mrs Eugenia Stanhope and JD, waiving injunction against publication of 4th Earl of Chesterfield's letters. Dated 29 March 1774. Lilly Library. Indiana University.
from George Stonhouse, Grey fryers, Bristol, 21 December 1769. Harvard Theatre Collection.
from Deane Swift, 24 February [n.y.]. Dreer Collection, Historical Society of Pennsylvania.
from Philip Thicknesse, 20 November 1777. Laid in Vol. I of G. Fulcher, *Life of Gainsborough* (1856), Pierpont Morgan Library.
from G[eorge?] Tierney, Eton, 27 November 1777. Harvard Theatre Collection.
from John Toup, 13 March [1767?]. Bodleian MS. Eng. Misc. C. 75, f. 37.
from Ed[ward] W[alpole?], Luxborough, 21 September 1771. Harvard Theatre Collection.
from Thomas Warton, 23 June 1769. Milton S. Eisenhower Library, Johns Hopkins University.
to Thomas Webster, 30 November 1785. Pierpont Morgan Library, Autographs Miscellaneous.
from William Whitehead, 3 July 1764. Lewis Walpole Collection.
from Whitehead, 18 September 1783. Lewis Walpole Collection.
from Arthur Young, Bradfield Hall, 2 April 1782. Boston Public Library.

2. UNTRACED LETTERS CITED IN AUCTION HOUSE AND AUTOGRAPH DEALER CATALOGUES

from [?] 1771. Sotheby cat., 22 March 1855, lot 125.
from Mark Akenside, 22 November 1768. Sotheby cat., 30 June 1879, lot 6.
from Christopher Anstey, 15 December 1776. Maggs cat., 1950, No. 794, item 20.
from Anstey, 20 December 1777. Thorpe cat., 1833, item 23.
from Anstey, 25 December 1777. Thorpe cat., 1833, item 24.
from Anstey, 3 December 1777. Thorpe cat., 1833, item 25.
from Anstey, 4 January 1778. Thorpe cat., 1833, item 26.
from Anstey, 11 January 1778. Thorpe cat., 1833, item 27.
from Anstey, 22 January 1778. Thorpe cat., 1833, item 28.
from Anstey, 23 January 1778. Thorpe cat., 1833, item 29.
from Anstey, 27 May 1778. Thorpe cat., 1833, item 30.
from Anstey, 30 August 1778. Thorpe cat., 1833, item 31.
from Anstey, 24 January 1787. Thorpe cat., 1833, item 33.
from Anstey, 29 October 1787. Sotheby cat., 27 May 1875, lot 10.
from Anstey, 13 January 1793. Thorpe cat., 1833, item 34.
from Anstey, 27 April 1793. Thorpe cat., 1833, item 35.
to John Balfour, bookseller, [rough draft with n.d.]. Thorpe cat., 1833, item 309 [from RD or JD?].
from Oliver Beckett, 20 December 1791. Thorpe cat., 1833, item 60.
from George Anne Bellamy, [n.d.]. Thorpe cat., 1833, item 65.
from Richard Bentley, Jr., [1761?]. Sotheby cat., 22 January 1828, lot 237.
from Richard Beresford, Theobald's Park [n.d.]. Thorpe cat., 1833, item 72.
from George Monck Berkeley [n.d.]. Thorpe cat., 1833, item 74.
from William Bolts, November 1775. Thorpe cat., 1833, item 89.
from Frances Brooke, 29 August [1769]. Sotheby cat., 31 March 1875, lot 63.

from Edmund Burke [*c.* 1770]. Sotheby cat., 2 July 1962, lot 225.
from Richard Burke, 9 August 1775. Sotheby cat., 3 December 1888, lot 26.
from Thomas Cadell, 24 July 1783. Sotheby cat., 2 June 1980, lot 1220.
from Thomas Cave, Stanford Hall, Leicester, 1767. J. Waller cat., 1859, No. 2 [unnumbered].
from Cave, 30 August 1767. J. Waller cat., 1859, No. 2 [unnumbered].
from Richard Chandler, 21 March 1773. J. Waller cat., 1866–8, item 89.
from Chandler, 23 March 1773. Thorpe cat., 1833, item 183.
from Thomas Chatterton, December 1768. Thorpe cat., 1837–8, item 307. [Includes next item.]
from Chatterton, 15 February 1769. Sotheby cat., 4 July 1892, lot 201 (Phillipps MS).
from Samuel Cooper, 1762. Thorpe cat., 1833, item 210 [to RD or JD?].
from Maria Susanna Cooper, 30 October 1762. Thorpe cat., 1833, item 211 [to RD or JD?].
from George Crabbe, 23 July 1795. Sotheby cat., 17 May 1839, lot 139.
from Herbert Croft, 14 July [n.y.]. Thorpe cat., 1833, item 220.
from Thomas Davies [n.d.]. J. Waller cat., 1859, No. 2. [unnumbered].
from Irwin Eyles (3) [n.d.]. Thorpe cat., 1833, item 604.
from Richard Graves, 26 December 1766. Thorpe cat., 1833, item 610.
from Graves, 13 March, 1769. Thorpe cat., 1833, item 611.
from William Green, 1783. Thorpe cat., 1833, item 308.
from Green, 18 February 1783. J. Waller cat., 1859, No. 2 [unnumbered].
from Thomas Hull [n.d.]. Laid in copy of Hull, *Select Letters* [William Upcott Collection], listed in Joseph Lilly cat., 1846 [unnumbered].
from Charles Jenner, 1771, Sotheby cat., 12 May 1851, lot 410.
from Paul Joddrell [n.d.]. J. Waller cat., 1859, No. 26, item 180.
from George Keate, 8 October 1787. Thorpe cat., 1833, item 626.
from William Keate, 23 May 1790. Thorpe cat., 1833, item 627.
from Bartholomew Kieling, 1767. Thorpe cat., 1833, item 628.
from Kieling, 31 January 1767. J. Waller cat., 1859, No. 2 [unnumbered].
from Thomas King (3) [n.d.]. Thorpe cat., 1833, items 634–6.
from Charles Knowles, Baronet, Admiral, 8 April 1767. Thorpe cat., 1833, item 638.
from Thomas Knowles, Bury, Suffolk, 23 March 1777. Thorpe cat., 1833, item 639.
from James Lind, MD, Warsaw, 10 September 1767. Thorpe cat., 1833, item 659.
from Thomas Lloyd, July, 1782. Thorpe cat., 1833, item 662.
from Robert Lowth, 19 December 1767. Thorpe cat., 1833, item 676.
from W. Lowth, 25 January 1790. Thorpe cat., 1833, item 677.
from M[artin?] Madan, 11 January 1785. Thorpe cat., 1836, item 2401.
from Martin Madan (2) [n.d.]. Thorpe cat., 1833, item 684.
from Spencer Madan, 5 November 1782. Thorpe cat., 1836, item 2402.
from J. Mainwaring (3), 1776 & 1787. Thorpe cat., 1833, item 686.
from Daniel Malthus [n.d.]. Thorpe cat., 1833, item 700.
from Charles Martyn [n.d.]. Thorpe cat., 1833, item 710.
from William Mason, 1 April 1775. Sotheby cat., 26 April 1769, lot 416.
from Matthew Maty, 29 September 1774. Thorpe cat., 1833, item 715.
from T. R. Maunsell, 1774. Thorpe cat., 1833, item 999.
from Henry Meen (2 notes), 1779. Sotheby cat., 12 May 1851, lot 543.
from Meen, 17 November 1779. Thorpe cat., 1838, item 1300.
from Meen, 18 August 1780. Thorpe cat., 1833, item 719.
from Meen, [2] March 1781. Thorpe cat., 1833, item 720.
from W. A. Merrick, 20 October 1784. Thorpe cat., 1833, item 724.
from W. Miller (See Scott.)
from Edward Moses, Newcastle upon Tyne, September 1790. Thorpe cat., 1833, item 729.
from David Murray, 7th Viscount Stormont, 1 March 1774. Thorpe cat., 1833, item 939.
from Jeremiah Whitaker Newman, 1783. Thorpe cat., 1833, item 753.
from Norton Nicholls, 15 July 1775. Thorpe cat., 1833, item 755.
from William Northey, 13 August 1769. Thorpe cat., 1833, item 759.

from William O'Brien, 5th Earl of Inchiquin, 18 January 1789. Thorpe cat., 1833, item 602.
from Nicholas Owen, 4 September 1777. Thorpe cat., 1833, item 766.
from John Pinkerton [n.d.]. Sotheby cat., 31 March 1875, lot 405.
to [John?] Pinkerton, 1792. Puttick and Simpson cat., 3 April 1869, item 185.
from Edward Popham, 1770. John Gray Bell cat., 1864, item 3688.
  from Popham, 29 June 1776. Thorpe cat., 1833, item 823.
  from Popham, 22 December 1776. Thorpe cat., 1836, item 3083.
  from Popham, 22 December 1779. Thorpe cat., 1838, item 1599.
from Thomas Potter [n.d.]. J. Waller cat., 1866–8, item 190.
from Thomas Powell, 1773. Thorpe cat., 1833, item 831.
from Samuel Jackson Pratt, 1792. J. Waller sale cat., 1851 [unnumbered].
from A. Purshouse, 2 August 1782. Thorpe cat., 1833, item 836.
from Edmund Rack, 17 April 1780. Thorpe cat., 1833, item 839.
from John Rayner, 1789. Thorpe cat., 1833, item 846.
from William Renwick, 27 February 1776. Thorpe cat., 1833, item 854.
from William Richardson, 12 June 1770. Thorpe cat., 1833, item 857.
from J. Robertson, 27 April 1785. Thorpe cat., 1833, item 863.
from Robert Robinson, 20 August 1774. Thorpe cat., 1833, item 865.
from T. P. Robinson, [n.d.]. Thorpe cat., 1833, item 864.
from Eliza Ryves, 23 January 1776. Sotheby cat., 4 July 1792, lot 511 (Phillipps MS).
from Scott and W. Miller, [n.d.]. Sotheby cat., 8 August 1864, lot 176.
from Thomas Sheridan, 8 December 1766. J. Waller cat., 1866–8, item 385.
from E. Smithson, Stanwick, 18 August [n.y.]. Thorpe cat., 1836, item 3501.
from George Georgeson Stahlberg, 1772. Thorpe cat., 1833, item 931.
from William Stevens, 1775. Thorpe cat., 1833, item 937.
from George Stonhouse, October 1767. Thorpe cat., 1833, item 938.
from Deane Swift, 1764. Thorpe cat., 1838, item 1901.
from Philip Thicknesse, February 1780. Thorpe cat., 1833, item 949.
from Matthew Tomlinson [n.d.]. Thorpe cat., 1833, item 953.
from Dr [Richard?] Watson, 1776. Southgate & Barrett cat., 25 November 1847, item 264.
from Thomas Wilson, 2 February 1767. Thorpe cat., 1833, item 1039.
from J. Yonde [n.d.]. Thorpe cat., 1833, item 1047.
from Arthur Young, April 1782. Thorpe cat., 1833, item 1048.

3. EXTANT PURCHASE AGREEMENTS AND RECEIPTS

Anstey, Christopher. Signed receipt acknowledging JD's payment of £250 for copyright of *The New Bath Guide*. 31 July 1766. Bath Reference Library, MS. 1017.

Cadell, Thomas. Acknowledgement of sale (13 June 1769) and signed receipt for £315 in notes rendered on 13 July 1769 by JD for purchase of Andrew Millar's eight twentieth shares in the copyright of Lowth's *English Grammar*. Includes £9 for a lot consisting of copies of RD's *Collection of Poems by Several Hands*. John Johnson Collection. Bodleian Library.

Caslon, Catherine. Acknowledgement of purchase (5 June 1783) and signed receipt for 10s. 6d. (5 July 1783) received from JD for one twenty-fourth share in Child's *Plaything*. National Book League. London.

Dilly, Charles. See Strahan, William.

Emonson, Jamey. See Strahan, William.

Johnston, William. See Weld, Isaac.

Leland, Ann. See Weld, Isaac.

Leland, John. See Weld, Isaac.

Melmoth, William. Signed agreement whereby M. promises to deliver a manuscript for a work to be entitled *The Translator of Pliny's Letters defended from the Objections of Jacob Bryant*, and JD, on his part, agrees to pay £100 for the work. Should the work have a 2nd edition or should Pliny's *Letters* have a

9th edition, JD agrees to pay M. an additional £100. In either case, M. is to have the opportunity of revising. Boston Public Library.

Millar, Andrew. See Cadell, Thomas.

Nicholl, William. See Strahan, William.

Peyton, V. J. Signed receipt acknowledging JD's payment of £8.13.3. for P.'s translation of the Art of Painting[?]. 27 December 1762. John Johnson Collection, Bodleian Library.

Reed, Isaac. Autograph receipt acknowledging JD's payment of £20 for R.'s correcting, improving and adding notes to a new edition of Pearch's *Collection of Poems*. R. promises to assign JD all right to the notes. Boston Public Library.

Rivington, John. Acknowledgement of sale (18 August 1767) and signed receipt for £1.10.0. (18 September 1767) received from JD for purchase of one eighth share in Duncan's translation of Caesar's *Commentaries*. John Johnson Collection. Bodleian Library.

Russell, J. Acknowledgement of sale (25 May 1784) and signed receipt for £1.16.0. (25 June 1784) received from JD for purchase of one twelfth share in Child's *Plaything*. National Book League, London.

Stanhope, Eugenia. Signed articles of agreement whereby JD consents to pay S. 1,500 guineas for the copyright of the late Earl of Chesterfield's letters and other pieces. 22 November 1773. Lilly Library, Indiana University.

Stanhope, Eugenia. Running from 1 April 1774 to 4 November 1775, six signed receipts acknowledging JD's installment payment of 1,500 guineas for the copyright to the 4th Earl of Chesterfield's letters. Lilly Library, Indiana University.

Strahan, William, Jamey Emonson, and Charles Dilly. Acknowledgement of sale (22 October 1778) and signed receipt for £4.7.0. (25 November 1778) received from JD for purchase of one sixteenth share in William Cheselden's *Anatomy of the Human Body*. (From estate of William Nicholl.) Royal College of Surgeons, MSS. Box 31 33.

Strahan, William. Acknowledgement of purchase (27 October 1772) and receipt for £2.2.0. in notes (1 December 1772) as payment for one twenty-fourth share in Child's *Plaything*. National Book League, London.

Ware, Catherine and Richard. Acknowledgement of sale (15 December 1767) and signed receipt for £8.5.0. in notes rendered on 16 January 1768 for two twenty-fourth shares in the copyright of Child's *Plaything*. John Johnson Collection, Bodleian Library.

Weld, Isaac, of Dublin. Signed articles of agreement whereby Weld, acting on behalf of Ann Leland, executrix of the late John Leland, assigns to JD and William Johnston the copyright of Leland's sermons [published as *Discourses on Various Subjects* (4 vols., 1768–9)] for the consideration of 400 copies of the work. 9 July 1767. National Book League, London.

Whalley, Eliza. Signed settlement of publishing account for Thomas Whalley's *Edwy and Edilsa*, whereby JD and E. Whalley divide profits of £6.12.0. and 254 unsold copies. 6 May 1783. Laid in Pierpont Morgan Library copy of W. M. Thackeray, *The Four Georges* (1861).

Whalley, Thomas. See Whalley, Eliza.

Whitehead, William. Signed receipt for 100 guineas received from JD for copyright of *The School for Lovers*. 16 February 1762. Unidentified clipping from bookseller's catalogue laid in Straus's copy of *Robert Dodsley*, p. 376.

Woodfall, W. Signed receipt acknowledging JD's payment of £6.6.0. for one sixteenth share of Cheselden's *Anatomy*. 19 October 1771. Royal College of Surgeons, MSS. Box 31 33.

4. PURCHASES RECORDED IN "MEMORANDA FROM MR DODSLEY'S PAPERS"[1]

Anstey, Christopher. On 31 July 1766, JD paid A. £250 for *The New Bath Guide*. (See section 3.)

---

[1] Isaac Reed's manuscript extracts, compiled on 29 April 1797, now in New College Library, Edinburgh.

Ayscough, George Edward. On 4 January 1774, A. agreed to sell JD the manuscripts of George, Lord Lyttelton for £250 in cash, £150 in six months, and £200 on a 2nd edition.

Ayscough. On 18 December 1776, JD paid A. £100 for *Semiramis* (adaptation of Voltaire), with a promise of £50 more if acted fifteen nights the first season.

Barrington, Daines. On 28 May 1764, JD paid B. 15 guineas for Evan Evans's translation, *Some Specimens of the Poetry of the Antient Welsh Bards.*

Berckenhout, John. On 26 September 1776 JD paid B. £200 for Vol. I of *Biographia Literaria.*

Blower, Elizabeth. On 25 September 1781, JD paid B. £31.10.0. for B's novel, *George Bateman.*

Bongout, Robert. On 9 February 1778, JD paid £21 for B.'s *Journey of Dr. Robert Bongout, and his Lady, to Bath.*

Brooke, Frances. On 5 July 1763, JD paid B. 100 guineas for *The History of Lady Julia Mandeville.*

Burke, Edmund. On 26 May 1791, B. received £1,000 from JD, "being the Consideration for the profits arising from the Sale of" *Reflections on the Revolution in France. See also* King, Walker.

Cockin, William, On 21 December 1774, JD paid C. £21 for *The Art of Delivering Written Language.*

Cooper, Mr, of Shottisham, Norfolk. On 10 February 1763, JD paid C. £24.15.0. for a novel, *The School for Wives.*

Cumberland, Richard. On 12 February 1766, JD paid C. £150 for *The Summer's Tale.*

Davies, Thomas. On 3 October 1761, JD paid D. 12 guineas for an account of the Colony of South America [Carolina?] written by Joseph Massie.

Davies. On 20 March 1773, JD paid D. £25 for half of the right in Parnell's *Works* with the "Life" by Oliver Goldsmith.

Davies. On 20 March 1773, JD paid D. £25 for half of the right in Waller's *Works* with the "Life" by Percival Stockdale, together with corrections and improvements by Thomas Percy.

Elliott, Ann. On 15 May 1765, JD paid E. £31.10.0. for *Indiana Danby*, a novel.

English, Thomas. On 28 January 1782, JD paid E. £150 for the "History of Europe" in the *Annual Register* for 1780. *See also* Appendix B.

Evans, Evan. *See* Barrington, Daines.

Fawkes, Francis. *See* Fawkes, Mrs Francis.

Fawkes, Mrs. Francis. On 6 April 1780, JD agreed with F. and Henry Meen to purchase Fawkes' and Meen's translation of *The Argonautics of Apollonius Rhodius* for 150 copies of the same.

Gibbes, Phebe. On 24 February 1789, JD paid G. £20 for *Hartley House Calcutta.*

Goldsmith, Oliver. On 31 March 1763, G. agreed to write a Chronological History of the Lives of Eminent Persons of Great Britain and Ireland in approximately two volumes for which JD would pay three guineas a sheet.

Goldsmith. On 3 August 1764 JD paid G. 30 guineas for compiling the *History of England.*

Goldsmith. On 31 October 1764, JD paid G. 10 guineas for "The Captivity: An Oratorio" [first printed in *Miscellaneous Works*, Vol. 2 (London, 1820?)].

Goldsmith. JD paid G. £5.5.0. for improving the 2nd edition of *An Enquiry into the Present State of Polite Learning. See also* Davies, Thomas.

Graves, Richard. On 17 December 1772, JD paid G. £60 for *The Spiritual Quixote.*

Graves. On 22 March 1774, JD paid G. £25 for *Galateo* (translated from the Italian of Giovanni De La Casa), *The Love of Order*, and *The Progress of Gallantry.*

Graves. On 25 March 1776, JD paid G. 20 guineas for *Euphrosyne.*

Graves. On 2 January 1779, JD paid G. 40 guineas for *Columella*, 2 vols.

Graves. On 8 June 1780, JD paid G. 10 guineas for the 2nd vol. of *Euphrosyne.*

Graves. On 20 June 1780, JD paid G. £40 in full for *The Sorrows of Werter.* [Note: "R.G. received as much afterwards as made it £200."]

Hall, J. S. On 8 August 1761, JD paid H. 6 guineas for a pamphlet, *The Kept Mistress.*

Holdsworth, Edward. *See* Spence, Joseph.

Home, Charles. On 4 July 1791, JD paid H. £100, which, with £50 additional in twelve months, amounted to full payment for *A New Chronological Abridgement of the History of England.*

Hoole, John. On 7 May 1791, JD agreed with H. to purchase the copyright and all unsold copies of *Ariosto* in 5 vols., all the copies of *Orlando Furioso* reduced, and all the copies of *Rinaldo* upon the condition of JD's defraying all the expenses of the publications and paying £250 and 150 copies of

Orlando reduced and *Rinaldo*. Hoole also confirms JD's right to his translation of Tasso's *Jerusalem Delivered* (1763).

Hoole, Samuel. On 28 January 1782, JD paid H. £21 for *Modern Manners*.

Hughes, Anne. On 24 August 1782, JD paid H. £5.5.0. for H.'s *Poems*.

Hull, Thomas. On 18 June 1777, JD agreed to pay H. £100 for *Select Letters between the Duchess of Somerset, Lady Luxborough, William Shenstone et al.*, 2 vols.

[Hutton, James]. On 15 February 1771, JD paid the "authoress" (?) twenty guineas for *The Disguise. A Dramatic Novel*. (See section 5, under "Hutton".)

Irwin, Eyles. On 3 April 1780, JD agreed to purchase I.'s *Series of Adventures in the Course of a Voyage up the Red Sea, Etc.* for 200 copies of the same.

Jenyns, Soame. On 4 June 1776, JD paid J. £250 for *A View of the Internal Evidence of the Christian Religion*.

Jenyns. On 25 May 1782, JD paid J. £50 for *Disquisitions on Several Subjects*.

Johnston, William. *See* Leland.

Jones, Henry. On 13 December 1760, John Taylor and J. received £50 from JD for the *Life and Extraordinary History of the Chevalier John Taylor*.

Keate, George. In May, 1779, JD purchased K.'s *Sketches from Nature in a Journey to Margate*. [Payment not mentioned.]

Keate. On 13 March 1781, JD paid K. 150 guineas for K.'s *Poetical Works*, 2 vols.

Kindersley, Jemima. On 28 July 1781, JD paid K. £25 for *An Essay on the Character, the Manners and Genius of Women*, a translation of Antoine Léonard Thomas's *Essai sur le caractère, les moeurs, et l'esprit des femmes*.

King, Walker. On 25 November 1791, K. accepted from JD on Edmund Burke's behalf £300 as B.'s share of the profits from the sale of *A Letter to a Member of the National Assembly* and *An Appeal from the New to the Old Whigs*.

Knight, Henrietta St John, Lady Luxborough. On 21 July 1775, JD purchased L.'s letters for £73.

Lee, [?John]. On 13 August 1778, JD made partial payment of £10.10.0, and, on 31 October 1778, full payment of £10.10.0. for L.'s *Introduction to the Study of Natural History*. [Note: "It was printed by Mr D but condemned as unfit to be published by him."]

Leland, [John?] On 9 July 1767, JD and William Johnston agreed to purchase L.'s Sermons, giving 400 copies for the copyright and an additional 50 copies for a second edition.

Lennox, Charlotte. On 25 October 1766, JD paid L. 20 guineas for half of the right to the *History of Eliza*.

Lennox. On 10 January 1774 JD paid L. £10 in part and, on 17 February 1774, £25 in full for a translation of *Meditations and Penitential Prayers*, by Madam de la Vallière.

Lowth, Robert. On 18 April 1763, JD paid L. £50 for a moiety of the copy of *A Short Introduction to English Grammar*.

Lyttelton, George, Lord. *See* Millan, John; Ayscough, George.

MacPherson, James. On 14 April 1761, M. sold JD the right of printing *Fragments of Ancient Poetry* for 10 guineas.

Madan, Spencer. On 29 April 1769, JD paid M. £52.12.6. for Alexander Pope's "letters to a Lady"[?].

Marshall, William. On 3 March 1784, JD paid M. 100 guineas for *Planting and Ornamental Gardening*.

Martin, M. On 29 November 1779, JD agreed to purchase M.'s *Philytoron* for £100.

Massie, Joseph. *See* Davies, Thomas.

Meen, Henry. *See* Fawkes, Mrs Francis.

Melmoth, William. On 24 April 1773, JD purchased M.'s *Essays on old Age and Friendship*, a translation from Cato [Cicero!] for 100 guineas.

Melmoth. On 10 November 1777, JD purchased M.'s translation of Lelius for 100 guineas.

Melmoth. On 3 February 1794, JD agreed to pay M. £100 for a work called *The translator of Pliny's letters vindicated from the objections of Jacob Bryant* and £100 more when he should print a second edition of it or the 9th edition of Pliny's *Letters*.

Melmoth. On 23 January 1779, JD paid M. (for the use of William Coxe) £70 for C.'s Letters on Switzerland [?*Sketches of the Natural, Civil and Political State of Switzerland*].

Millan, John. On 20 December 1773, JD purchased of M., for £105, the property of George, Lord Lyttelton's *Persian Letters*, together with any other pieces by L. to which M. had claim.

Minifie, Margaret. On 19 January 1763, JD agreed to give M. 700 sets of *The Histories of Lady Frances S-*, *and Lady Caroline S-*, and to divide the profits equally with her.

Parnell, Thomas. *See* Davies, Thomas.

Percy, Thomas. On 21 May 1761, JD agreed to pay P. 10 guineas for each of the *Song of Solomon* and *Five Pieces of Runic Poetry*; also 10 guineas each for future impressions and for a collected volume.

Percy. On 22 May 1761, P. sold JD, for 100 guineas, his Collection of Ancient English Ballads, proposed to be printed in three volumes 12ᵐᵒ. P. promises that three volumes is all he intends to print of the work. If two volumes only are printed first, P. to receive £70, and £35 for a later third volume. If an accident prevents the work's completion after P. has received any part of the payment, then the folio manuscript becomes JD's property.

Percy. On 23 May 1761, JD paid P. 20 guineas for *Miscellaneous Pieces relating to the Chinese*.

Percy. On 10 June 1761, JD paid P. £50 for the Chinese history [*Hau Kiou Choaan*].

Percy. On 10 June 1761, JD paid P. 10 guineas for the "Chinese Proverbs, Chinese Poetry, and Argument of a Chinese Play" [all added to the edition of *Hau Kiou Choaan*]. *See also* Davies, Thomas.

Pope, Alexander. *See* Madan, Spencer.

Potter, Robert. In 1781, JD agreed to purchase P.'s translation of *The Tragedies of Euripides* for 525 copies of the same.

Powlett, Edmund. On 5 December 1761 JD agreed to become joint partners with P. in *The General Contents of the British Museum* and to pay the author 5 guineas for the work and a like sum for future editions.

Pratt, Samuel Jackson. On 23 December 1772, JD paid P. £20 for some unspecified manuscripts.

Rutherford, John. On 1 March 1781, JD paid R. £50 for *Sentimental Journey through Greece*.

Shilleto, Charles. On 9 November 1779, JD paid S. 3 guineas for *The Sea Fight. An Elegaic Poem from Henry to Laura.*

Smart, Christopher. On 4 August 1764, JD paid S. 10 guineas for *A Poetical Translation of the Fables of Phaedrus.*

Spence, Joseph. On 24 March 1767, S. agreed with JD: (1) to confirm JD's right in *Polymetis*; (2) to assign JD all rights in S.'s printed works upon payment of £100; (3) for £100, to assign JD the copyright of Edward Holdsworth's Observations [*?Remarks and Dissertations on Virgil*] to be printed during the summer, 1767, S. to receive 25 bound copies; (4) for £100, S. assigned JD the copyrights to all unpublished works that S.'s executors would judge proper to be published. [Note: "There are receipts for the first two sums."]

Stanhope, Phillip Dormer, 4th Earl of Chesterfield. On 22 November 1773 JD agreed to purchase C.'s letters for £1,500 in three equal installments. [Reed's Note: "By the Assignmᵗ dated 1st April 1774 he appears to have paid £1575 for them." (*See* Section 3.)]

Sterne, Laurence. *See* Appendix B.

Stewart, John. On 14 June 1771, JD settled with S. for *Critical Observations on London*. [No payment given.]

Stillingfleet, Benjamin. On 14 February 1760, S. agreed that JD would have one third of profits arising from the sale of his oratorio *Paradise Lost*, S. retaining two thirds.

Stockdale, Percival. *See* Davies, Thomas.

Streit, John Angus. On 1 May 1771, JD paid S. £7.11.1. for 140 sets and the copyright of *Memoirs of Count P———*, in 2 vols. 12ᵐᵒ.

Taylor, John. *See* Jones, Henry.

Thomson, Alexander. On 6 March 1767, JD purchased T.'s *Letters on the British Museum* for 10 guineas.

Topham, Edward. On 3 April 1776, JD paid T. £60 for *Letters from Edinburgh*.

Turner, Richard. On 10 December 1778, JD paid T. 10 guineas for *A View of the Earth as far as it was known to the Ancients.*

Vigor, Mrs. On 26 December 1775, JD paid £21 for V.'s letters, and 10 guineas more in February, 1789.

Walpole, Horace. On 23 January 1768, JD purchased W.'s *Historic Doubts on Richard III* for £100.

Walpole. On 25 October 1781, JD paid £20 to Thomas Kirgate (Walpole's printer) for the privilege of one impression of *The Castle of Otranto*. [Note: On 16 March, £20 additional for a 5th edition.]

Warton, Jane. *See* Warton, Joseph.

Warton, Joseph. On 16 January 1782, JD paid W. £200 for the *Essay on the Genius and Writings of Mr. Pope*, together with the remaining copies.

Warton. On 18 January 1782, JD paid W. £50 for two works written by Jane Warton entitled *Letters to two young unmarried Ladies* and *Letters on the Christian Life*.

Weston, William. On 19 June 1762, JD paid W. 40 guineas for the first edition of *New Dialogues of the Dead*.

White, James. On 22 October 1788, JD paid W. £40 for the romance *Earl Strongbow*.

Whitehead, William. On 16 February 1762, JD paid W. 100 guineas for *The School for Lovers*, a comedy. (See section 3.)

Whitehead. On 14 April 1770, JD paid W. £50 for *A Trip to Scotland*.

Wimpey, Joseph. On 19 September 1776, JD purchased of W. the remaining copies of *Rural Improvements*.

Young, Arthur. On 2 March 1770, JD agreed to purchase Y.'s *A Course of Experimental Agriculture* for £500, paid in installments, and twelve sets of the work.

5. CITATIONS TO PURCHASE AGREEMENTS AND RECEIPTS IN AUCTION HOUSE AND AUTOGRAPH DEALER CATALOGUES

Akenside, Mark. A.'s autograph statement, giving JD permission to publish his poems under certain restrictions. 2 November 1768. Sotheby sale cat., 10–12 May 1875, lot 1.

Ayscough, George Edward. Original agreement between A. and JD regarding the purchase of the copyrights and manuscripts of the late Lord George Lyttelton. 4 January 1774. [no price]. Thorpe sale cat., 1838, item 1217.

Ayscough. Receipt acknowledging JD's payment of £200 for the second edition of *The Works of George Lord Lyttelton*, edited by A. 18 December 1775. Thorpe sale cat., 1838, item 1217.

Ayscough. Agreement with JD for the purchase of A.'s tragedy *Semiramis* for £100. 1776. Sotheby sale cat., 12 May 1851, lot 22.

Baldwin, Robert. *See* Johnson, Samuel.

Barrington, Daines. Signed receipt to JD. 1774. Sotheby sale cat., 22 March 1855, lot 18.

Berckenhout, John. Assignment of copyright of *Biographia Literaria*, Vol. I, to JD for £200. 1776. Sotheby sale cat., 12 May 1851, lot 882.

Brooke, Frances. Receipt to JD on 24 November 1770 [no details; for *The Excursion?*]. Sotheby sale cat., 12 June 1876, lot 242.

Buckland, James. *See* Johnson, Samuel.

Burke, Edmund. Assignment of the profits to JD from B.'s *Reflections on the Revolution in France* for £1,000. 26 May 1791. Sotheby sale cat., 12 May 1851, lot 890.

Burke. Receipt signed by Walker King on B.'s behalf, acknowledging JD's payment of £300, the profits arising from the sale of B.'s *Letter to a Member of the National Assembly* and *An Appeal from the New to the Old Whigs* [n.d.]. J. Waller sale cat., 1857, item 215.

Cadell, Thomas, the elder. JD's endorsement on a C. draft. 1783 [no details]. John Gray Bell sale cat., 1863, item 656. *See also* Johnson, Samuel.

Carnan, Thomas. *See* Johnson, Samuel.

Conant, Nathaniel. *See* Johnson, Samuel.

Corbett, C. Signed receipt acknowledging JD's payment of £18.8.0. for the copyright of C.'s first three volumes of *Collection of Poems*. 12 February 1773. Thorpe sale cat. [n.d.; *c.* 1833–6], item 182.

Corbett. Signed receipt acknowledging JD's payment of £4.16.0. for the first impression of 3 vols. of *Collection of Poems*. 12 February 1773. Thorpe sale cat. [n.d.; *c.* 1833–6], item 183.

Cumberland, Richard. Signed receipt acknowledging JD's payment of £150 for the copyright of C.'s *Summer's Tale*, consequent on the ninth performance. 14 February 1766. Thorpe sale cat. [n.d.; *c.* 1833–6], item 206.

Davies, Thomas. Signed receipt acknowledging JD's payment of £92.5.0. for shares of copies and expenses paid by D. 22 June 1773. Sotheby sale cat., 10–12 May 1875, lot 47.

Davies. D.'s signed receipt acknowledging JD's payment of £36 for the copyright of Edward Moore's *Fables for the Female Sex* [n.d.]. Sotheby sale cat., 10–12 May 1875, lot 48.

Davies. D.'s signed receipt acknowledging JD's payment of £31.10.0. for half of the copyright of John
Hoole's translation of Tasso's *Jerusalem Delivered*. January 1766. Sotheby sale cat., 10–12 May
1875, lot 48. *See also* Johnson, Samuel.

Davis, Lockyer. *See* Johnson, Samuel.

Dilly, Charles. *See* Johnson, Samuel; Woodfall, H. S.

English, Thomas. *See* Appendix B.

Evans, Thomas. *See* Johnson, Samuel.

Gardner, Henry. *See* Johnson, Samuel.

Graves, Richard. Autograph receipt acknowledging JD's payment of £25. 28 May 1774. Thorpe sale
cat., 1838, item 859.

Graves. Autograph receipt acknowledging JD's payment of 20 guineas. 25 March 1776. Thorpe sale
cat., 1838, item 860.

Grenville-Temple, Richard, Earl Temple. *See* Appendix B.

Hayes, S. (bookseller). *See* Johnson, Samuel.

Hoole, Samuel. Agreement with H. for *Modern Manners*. 1782. Sotheby sale cat., 12 May 1851, lot 914.
(See section 4.)

Hull, Thomas. Assignment to JD of H.'s *Select Letters between the Duchess of Somerset, Lady Luxborough,
William Shenstone et al*, 2 vols., for £100. 1777. John Gray Bell sale cat., April 1855, item 642.

Hutton, James. Signed receipt for 20 guineas received from JD for copyright of *The Disguise*. 15
February 1771. Sotheby cat., 12 May 1851, lot 967.

Jeffs, W. Agreement with J. for compiling the Index to the first twenty-two volumes of the *Annual
Register*. 1780. Sotheby cat., 12 May 1851, lot 914.

Jenner, Charles. Receipt acknowledging JD's payment of £30 for J.'s *The Placid Man*. 1769. Sotheby sale
cat., 12 May 1851, lot 410.

Jenner. Order to JD for £20. 1773. Sotheby sale cat., 22 March 1855, lot 123.

Jenyns, Soame. Autograph assignment to JD of J.'s *View of the Internal Evidence of the Christian Religion* for
£250. 4 June 1776. J. Waller sale cat., 1870–3, item 210.

Johnson, Samuel. Agreement for printing and publishing the first separate edition of J.'s *Lives of the Poets*.
Grecian Coffee House, 12 March, 1781. In the hand of John Nichols and signed by him, T. Cadell,
JD, T. Longman. C. Dilly, T. Evans, G. Robinson, N. Conant, G. Nichol, and T. Davies. Sotheby
sale cat., 14–16 December 1931, lot 333.

Johnson. Agreement signed by the publishers for the printing of the first complete edition of J.'s *Works*
and the first "Life of Dr. Johnson" (by Sir John Hawkins). Chapter Coffee House, 24 December
1784. Signed by John Rivington & Sons, Jas. Buckland, C. Dilly, T. Longman, L. Davies. T.
Cadell, T. Payne, W. Lowndes. G. and T. Wilkie, R. Baldwin, T. Carnan, J. Murray, S. Hayes, B.
Law, J. Robson, J. Nichols, JD, H. Gardner, and G. Nicol. Sotheby sale cat., 14–16 December
1931, lot 334.

Keate, George. Assignment of copyright of K.'s *Poetical Works* to JD for 150 guineas. 13 March 1781.
Sotheby sale cat., 22 March 1855, lot 128.

Keate. Autograph assignment to JD of K.'s *Sketches from Nature in a Journey to Margate*. May 1779. [no
price] Sotheby sale cat., 27–8 October 1980, lot 831.

King, Walker. *See* Burke, Edmund.

Kirgate, Thomas. Two receipts for £20 each, acknowledging JD's payment for the right of publishing
The Castle of Otranto. [n.d.] Sotheby sale cat., 12 May 1851, lot 435.

Law, B[edwell?]. *See* Johnson, Samuel.

Luekomber, [?] JD agreed with L. for compiling *The Present Peerage*. 1784. Sotheby sale cat., 12 May
1851, lot 914.

London Magazine. *See* Appendix B.

Longman, Thomas. *See* Johnson, Samuel; Woodfall, H. S.

Lowndes, W. *See* Johnson, Samuel.

Lyttelton, George, Lord. *See* Ayscough, George Edward.

Madan, Martin. Assignment of M.'s copyright of *Thelyphthora* to JD for £100. 8 December 1780.
Sotheby sale cat., 12 May 1851, lot 991.

Melmoth, William. Assignment to JD of M.'s translation of *The Letters of Pliny the Consul*. [no price]. 3
February 1794. J. Waller sale cat., 1870–3, item 266.

Murray, John. *See* Johnson, Samuel.

Nichol, George. *See* Johnson, Samuel.

Nichols, John. *See* Johnson, Samuel.

Payne, Thomas. *See* Johnson, Samuel.

Percy, Thomas. Assignment of P.'s Collection of Ancient English Ballads to JD for 100 guineas. 22 May 1761. Sotheby sale cat., 12 May 1851, lot 1031.

Percy. Assignment of P.'s *Hau Kiou Choaan* to JD for £50. 10 June 1761. Sotheby sale cat., 12 May 1851, lot 1031.

Percy. Assignment of P.'s "Chinese Proverbs" to JD for 10 guineas. 10 June 1761. Sotheby sale cat., 12 May 1851, lot 1031.

Percy. Assignment of P.'s *Five Pieces of Runic Poetry* to JD. [No sum mentioned.] 25 March 1763. Sotheby sale cat., 12 May 1851, lot 1031.

Percy. Assignment of P.'s Collection of Ancient Songs and Ballads to JD for 100 guineas. 25 March 1763. Sotheby sale cat., 12 May 1851, lot 1031.

Percy. Agreement for the sale of P.'s *Collection of Antient Poetry* to JD for 100 guineas. 1771[?]. John Gray Bell sale cat., April 1855, item 696.

Percy. JD's agreement to allow P. to print additional volumes to the *Reliques of Ancient Poetry*. 7 March 1775. Sotheby sale cat., 12 May 1851, lot 1031.

Percy. Agreement between P. and JD for the 3rd edition of *Reliques of Ancient English Poetry*. 1775. [Same as previous?] John Gray Bell sale cat., April 1855, item 695.

Pine, John. Signed receipt for £16.5.0. received from JD for P.'s engraving of plates to illustrate Horace's *Works*. 1797. Sotheby sale cat., 12 May 1851, lot 1032.

Potter, Richard. Assignment of copyright to JD of P.'s translation of Euripides' *Tragedies* for 525 copies of same. 1785. Sotheby sale cat., 12 May 1851, lot 1055.

Power, James. Receipt acknowledging JD's payment of 10 guineas. 28 May 1774. Thorpe sale cat., 1838, item 1619.

Pratt, Samuel Jackson. Signed receipt acknowledging JD's payment of £20 for the manuscript of P.'s poems. 23 December 1772. Thorpe sale cat., 1838, item 1623.

Reed, Isaac. Agreement between R. and JD whereby R. consents to edit [Robert Dodsley's] *Select Collection of Old Plays* for the sum of £100. 1779. Sotheby sale cat., 22 March 1855, lot 247. [Six receipts for the same, written at various times, also in this lot.]

Reed. Receipt to JD [no details]. Sotheby sale cat., 12 June 1899, lot 1374.

Rivington, John. *See* Johnson, Samuel; Woodfall, H. S.

Robinson, George. *See* Johnson, Samuel.

Robson, James. *See* Johnson, Samuel.

Rutherford, John. Assignment to JD of the copyright of R.'s *Sentimental Journey through Greece* for £50. 1781. Sotheby sale cat., 22 March 1855, lot 248. (See section 4.)

Selwyn, George. Receipt signed by JD acknowledging S.'s payment of book bill. 12 September 1745. Sotheby sale cat., 21 August 1872, lot 103.

Sheridan, Thomas. Signed receipt for £42 received from JD for copyright of S.'s *Lectures on Elocution*. 1776. Sotheby sale cat., 12 May 1851, lot 1076.

Sheridan. Signed document by which S. acquits JD of liens on certain copyrights for 60 guineas. 5 August 1768. Sotheby sale cat., 10–12 May 1875, lot 171.

Smart, Christopher. Signed receipt for £10, acknowledging payment for S.'s *Poetical Translation of the Fables of Phaedrus*. 1764. Sotheby sale cat., 12 May 1851, lot 1084.

Stillingfleet, Benjamin. S.'s agreement with JD to receive two thirds of profits from the sale of his oratorio, *Paradise Lost*. 14 February 1760. Sotheby sale cat., 10–12 May 1875, lot 175.

Topham, Edward. Agreement between T. and JD for the purchase of Letters from Scotland [*Letters from Edinburgh*] for £60. 3 April 1776. Thorpe sale cat., 1838, item 1950.

Trusler, John (2). Articles of agreement to T.'s writing a work on English etymology [*The Difference between Words . . .*]; also his receipt for £63 for the same. 1766. Sotheby sale cat., 22 March 1855, lot 311.

Walpole, Horace. *See* Kirgate, Thomas.

Warton, Jane. Assignment to JD of the copyright of two works by W. for £50. 1782. Sotheby sale cat., 12 May 1751, lot 1103.

Warton, Joseph. Assignment to JD of the copyright of W.'s *Essay on the Genius and Writings of Mr. Pope* for £200. 16 January 1782. Sotheby sale cat., 12 May 1851, lot 1103.

Wilkie, G. and T. *See* Johnson, Samuel.

Woodfall, Henry Sampson. The balance sheet of the *Public Advertiser* for 1775, signed by the following shareholders: John Rivington, Thomas Longman, Charles Dilly, Woodfall, and JD. J. Waller sale cat., 1859, No. 2 (unnumbered).

INDEX

All materials, from the Introduction through Appendix D, including both letters and notes, are indexed. References are to page numbers. Principal features of entries and their usual order are as follows. Page numbers of principal biographical notes for Dodsley's correspondents appear in bold print. In each entry for Dodsley's correspondents, references to the letters themselves appear under the bold-face subheadings "Letters from" or "Letters to," or both. References to missing letters are also included under these subheadings, but, to distinguish them from references to the letters printed here, they are placed in italics. At the end of each author entry appear references to that author's works cited in the text.

Titled persons are indexed under family names, with cross references from their titles or from the age's more familiar denominations for them. Titles of works cited in the correspondence carry cross references to main author entries. Author pseudonyms are separately listed in quotation marks and cross referenced with proper surnames. In the case of booksellers, publishers, and printers, it can be assumed that, unless otherwise designated, their businesses were located in London. All scholars and critics cited in the notes are indexed.

Abbreviations in the index reflect the same usage employed in the text: "RD" and "JD" are used for references to Robert Dodsley and James Dodsley. (See also "Cue Titles," pp. xxiii–xxv.)

For two reasons, items listed in Appendix E, "Correspondence and Documents of James Dodsley," are not included. The contents of that brief appendix are arranged almost entirely in alphabetical order and consequently are readily accessible to the reader. Unnecessary duplication and a protracted index would be the only result of repeating those entries here. Secondly, since the subject of this edition is Robert Dodsley, it seemed advisable not to mislead users of the index with references to material irrelevant to Robert's concerns.

Abbott, John, 237
Aberdeen, University of, 459
Abrégé de l'histoire universelle (Voltaire, François Marie Arouet de), 361–62
"Account of the Kingdom of Beggars" (Cooper, John Gilbert), 105–6, 109
Account of the Life, Character, and Poems of Mr Blacklock, see Spence, Joseph
Acts of Parliament, 287
"Adam Fitzadam," *see* Moore, Edward
Adams, Mr, 369
Adcock, Mr, vocalist, 371
Addison, Joseph (1672–1719), 433; "Machinae Gesticulantes," 91; "Praelium inter Pygmous . . .," 91; *Spectator* (on fable), 441
"Address to his Elbow-chair" (Somerville, William), 172, 192
Address to the Booksellers of London and Westminster (1781), 395
Adventurer, The (1752–54), 522; *see also* Hawkesworth, John
Adventures of Télémachus, The (Fénelon, Salignac de la Motte), 29, 38
"Advertisement, An" (Cooper, John Gilbert), 110–11

"Advertisement for *The History of Good Breeding*" (Walpole, Horace), 96
Aeneid, see Virgil
Aesop, 434; fables of, 27, 395, 411; *see* RD, *Select Fables of Esop*
Agriculture, see RD, *Public Virtue*
Ainsworth, E. G., 118
Ainsworth, Robert (1660–1743), *Thesaurus Linguae Latinae Compendiarius* (1736), 360–61
Akenside, Mark (1721–70), 8, 14, 95, 121, 130, 197–98, 214, 222, 242, 249, 292, 332, 376; *Epistle to Curio* (1744), 8, 48, 530; *Museum* (1746–7), 8–9, 33, 93, 106, 508; "Ode to the Country Gentlemen of England," 353–54; *Ode to the Rt Honourable the Earl of Huntingdon* (1748), 8; *Odes on Several Subjects* (1745), 8, 530; *Pleasures of Imagination* (1744), 7–8, 29, 130–32, 214, 530
Alcock, Edward, painter, 432, 434–38, 449, 454; portrait of W. Shenstone, 437–39, 445, 453–54; **Letter to,** *546*
Allen, D. G. C., 208
Allen, Ralph (1694–1764), 4, 178, 213–14, 409, 465, 473, 482, 485–86, 492, 503; *see also* Graves, Richard

Allen, Mrs Ralph, 482
Alsop, Anthony (d. 1726), 296
Alumni Cantabrigienses, xxii–xxiii
Alumni Oxonienses, xxii–xxiii
Amasis II, King of Egypt (d. *c.* 525 BC),
     418
Amelia, Princess Sophia Eleanora (1711–86),
     2nd daughter of George II, 287
Amey, Robert, pamphlet seller, 508–9
Analysis of the Laws of England, An (Blackstone,
     Sir William), 405
Ancient and Modern Rome. A Poem (Keate,
     George), 438–39
Anderson, Dorothy, 6
Anderson, Robert (1750–1830), 403
Anglesey, 6th Earl of, *see* Annesley, Richard
Ann Boleyn to Henry the Eighth. An Epistle, see
     Whitehead, William
Annesley, James (1715–60), 509
Annesley, Richard, 6th Earl of Anglesey
     (1694–1761), 509
Annual Register, The, see RD
Anonymous, **Letter to**, 329
Antient and Present State of the County of Kerry
     (Smith, Charles), 340–41, 344
Apollonius Rhodius, *Argonautica*, 158–59, 527
"Apology for Tea," 390–91
Argyle, 3rd Duke of, *see* Campbell, Archibald
Aris, Thomas, Birmingham printer, 400–1; *see*
     Aris's Birmingham Gazette
Aris's Birmingham Gazette (1741–   ), 50, 223,
     253, 255, 257
Arne, Thomas (1710–78), music composer,
     186–88, 223–24, 231
Arnold, Cornelius (1711–57?), *Commerce* (1751),
     43
Arnold, Mary, W. Shenstone's servant,
     inheritance from Shenstone, 477, 485
Ash, John (1723–98), physician, 261–62, 339,
     341, 344, 348, 447; **Letter from**, *546*
Atkinson, John, 508, 528
Atterbury, Francis (1662–1732), Bishop of
     Rochester, 151, 526
Atys and Adrastus. A Tale (Whitehead, William),
     119
Audley, Elizabeth, cousin of W. Shenstone,
     476–77
Augusta, Princess of Wales (1719–72), 12, 21,
     252–53, 382, 385
Austen, Stephen, bookseller, 38, 41, 509
"Author's Complaint of Deafness," By a Lady,
     390–91
Avery, E. L., *see* Van Lennep, W. B.

Backwell, William (d. 1770), banker, 176, 178
Bagnell, Rev. Gibbons, **Letter from**, *546*;
     trans. of Hesiod, 546

Baillie, James, **Letter from**, *546*;
     "Deliverance," 546
Baker, Frank, 83
Baker, Henry (1698–1774), 221, 504, 507;
     Employment for the Microscope (1753), 509;
     Microscope Made Easy (1742), 10, 30–1, 40,
     509; *Natural History of the Polype* (1743), 31,
     37, 509
Baker, Samuel (d. 1778), bookseller, 533
Baker, Sir William (1705–70), London
     alderman, 338–39
Baldwin, Robert (d. 1810), bookseller, 41
Balfour, John (d. 1795), *see* Hamilton &
     Balfour
Balguy, Charles (1708–67), 70; **Letter from**,
     70, *546*; *Decameron . . . of Boccace* (1741), 70
Ball, Johnson, 145, 399, 445
"Ballad, in the scotch-manner" (Saunders,
     William), 189–90
Balmerino, Lord, *see* Elphenstone, Arthur
Barbeau, Alfred, 408
Barclay, Alexander (1475?–1552), *Eglogues*
     (*c.* 1514), 176–78
Barclays Bank, 35
Baretti, Joseph (1719–89), 29, **463–64**; **Letter
     from**, 463–64; *Dictionary of the English and
     Italian Languages* (1760), 464; *Dissertation on
     Italian Poetry* (1753), 464; *La Poesi de . . .*,
     464
Barford, Richard, **Letter from**, *547*
Barker, Richard, 77
Barnard, Edward (1717–81), **Letter from**, *547*
Barnes, Donald Grover, 368
Barr, John (*c.* 1709–78), **128**; **Letter from**,
     128–29, *547*; *Reflections upon Church
     Government* (1745), 128, 547; *Sermon preached
     on the Ninth of October* (1746), 128; *Summary
     of Natural Religion* (1749), 128
Barrels, *see* Knight, Henrietta St John, Lady
     Luxborough
Barrett, John (d. 1753), Oxford bookseller, 41,
     43
Barrow, Mr, musician, 369
Barry, Spranger (1719–77), actor, 314, 318–19,
     321, 329
Barton, Philip, DD, 75, 77; **Letter from?** *547*
Barton, Philip, nephew of Philip Barton, DD,
     Letter from? *547*; *Plutarchii, Demosthenis et
     Ciceronis vitae parallelae* (1744), 77–78
Baskerville, John (1706–75), 16, 46, 50, 58,
     125, **144–45**, 162, 165, 168, 197, 261–62,
     277, 284–85, 324, 342, 349, 373, 394,
     396–97, 408–9, 444, 447; paper-making,
     252–53, 264, 273, 458; **Letters from**,
     144–46, 169, 252–53, *547*; **Letters to**,
     264–65, 273; *Bible*, 273, 399, 438–39; *Book
     of Common Prayer* (1758), 273; *Horace*

Baskerville, John (*cont.*)
(1762), 22, 46, 49, 382, 456–57, 459–60,
469; Milton's *Paradise Lost* and *Paradise
Regained* (1758), 400, 410, 413; RD's *Select
Fables of Esop*, 441–43, 445–46, 449, 451,
454; *Virgil* (1757), 46, 58, 145, 169, 197,
199, 252–53, 264–65, 273
Baskerville, Mrs John, 284–85
Baskett, Rev. John, 509, 528
Baskett, Mrs Lucy, 509, 528
Bath coach, 341
Bath, Earl of, *see* Pulteney, William
Bath, theater of, 407–9, 413
Bathurst, Charles (d. 1786), bookseller, 7,
38–39, 41, 80–1, 213, 430–31
Battestin, Martin, 56–57
Battista, Giovanni, *Circe* (trans., Layng,
Henry), 519
"Battle of the Pygmies and Cranes" (Brown,
John), 91–2
Bayley, Anselm, *Introduction to Languages Literary
and Philosophical* (1758), 361–62
Beale, Catherine Hutton, 238, 447, 452, 470,
483, 488
Beard, John, actor and vocalist, 369–71, 373
Becket, John, Birmingham writing master,
144–45
Becket, Thomas, bookseller, *Tristram Shandy*,
18, 423
Bedford Coffee House, 383
Bedford, 4th Duke of, *see* Russell, John
Bedingfield, Robert (1720?–68?), 158, 330, 399
399
Beggar's Opera, The (Gay, John), 217
Belanger, Terry, 36, 252, 531
"Belisarius," 153
Bell, The, Smithfield inn, 239
Bellamy, George Anne (1731?–88), actress, 12,
314, 318–19, 329, 379, 382, 385–86, 389,
395, 397–98, 407–09
Bell-Savage Inn, Ludgate Hill, 232
Benson, William (1682–1754), 78
Bentham, Joseph (d. 1778), Cambridge printer,
41, 44, 101
Bentinck, William, 2nd Duke of Portland,
66–67
Bentley, Richard the elder (1662–1742),
scholar, 379–80; Lucan's *Pharsalia* (1758),
379–81
Bentley, Richard the younger (1708–82),
Letter from, 379–81; *Designs by Mr
Bentley for Six Poems by Mr Gray* (1753),
148–49
Berckenhout, John (1703–91?), **160; Letters
from**, 159–61, 165–66, 170–71; trans. of
Klopstock's *Messiah*, 160–61, 165–66,
170–71; *Three Original Poems* (1750), 160

Berenger, Richard (d. 1782), 37, 86, 210, **225,**
237, 295, 299, 313, 315, 341, 399, 525;
Letters from, 225–29, 325–26; **Letter
to,** 330–31; "On Mr Dodsley's Publishing
2 Vols. of Poems," 228; "To Mr Grenville
on his intended Resignation," 326
Berkley Castle, 425–26
Bernard, Edward (1638–96), DD, *Orbis eruditae
literatura* ("Table of Ancient Alphabets"),
440; *see also* Morton, Charles
Berry, W. Turner, 145
Berryat, Jean (d. 1754), *Collection Académique,
composée, des memoires, actes, ou journaux des
plus célèbres académies et sociétés littéraires
étrangères* (1755–58), 370–71
Best, William (d. 1785), Hanover Secretary,
461; *The Royal Soldier* (1746), 38
Betterton, Thomas (1635?–1710), *Amorous
Widow* (1706), 81, 82
Bevis, Richard, 6
Bible, *see* Baskerville, John
Bibliography Newsletter, xv
Bibliotheke Historike (Diodorus Siculus), 133
Biographia Britannica (1747–66), 360–61
Birch, Thomas (1705–66), **Letter to,** 135;
Works of Sir Walter Raleigh (1750), 135
"Bird of Passage" (Hoadly, John), 295–96
Birmingham coach, 201, 204, 254, 323, 344,
464
Birmingham Music Concert, 443–44; *see also*
Worcester, music meeting
Birmingham waggon (Mr Allen's), 376
Bisset, Charles (1717–91), **202–3; Letters
from,** 202–4, *547; Theory and Construction of
Fortification* (1751), 202–4; *Treatise on the
Scurvy* (1755), 202–4, 547
Blacklock, Thomas (1731–91), poet, 20, 22,
175–76, 179–80, **224–25,** 225, 349–50, 547
("To Mr Thomas Blacklock"), 404–5,
451; **Letters from,** 224–25, 283–84,
326–28, 354–55, 365–66, 401–4, 436–37,
547; **Letters to,** 285–86, *547; Collection of
Original Poems* (1756), 175, 224–25,
283–84, 286, 327–28, 354–55, 403–4,
436–37, 547; *Essay of Universal Etymology*
("Treatise on Universal Grammar"?)
(1756), 283–84, 286; *Original Poems by . . .
Blacklock and other Scottish Gentlemen* (1760),
448–49; "To the Rev. Mr Spence," 404;
see also Spence, Joseph
Blacklock, Mrs Thomas (née Johnston), 402–3
Blackstone, Sir William (1723–80), 197;
settlement of W. Shenstone's estate, 482,
484–86; *Analysis of the Laws of England*
(1756), 405
Blackwell, Thomas the elder, *Memoirs of the
Court of Augustus* (1756), 217–18, 509

Blackwell, Thomas the younger (1701–57), **Letter from**, 217–18; *Memoirs of the Court of Augustus* (1756), Vol. I, 218, 509, Vol. II, 217–18; 509

Blackwell, Mrs Thomas, 509

Blacow, Rev. Richard, 183–85, 260

Blair, Hugh (1718–1800), 451

Blakey, Nicholas (fl. 1749–53), designer, 48, 49, 136

Blore, G. H., 338

Boadicea (Glover, Richard), 158–59

Board of Excise, 333

Board of Ordnance, 203

Boccaccio, Giovanni (1313–75), 29, 40 (*see also* Balguy, Charles; Nicholson, John)

Boddeley, Thomas, Bath printer and bookseller, 43

Boitard, Philippe (d. c. 1760), artist/engraver, 48, 126, 128

Bolingbroke, 1st Viscount, *see* St John, Henry

Bolton, 3rd Duke of, *see* Paulet, Charles

Bolton, Robert, DD, Dean of Carlisle, 72–73

Bond, Daniel (1721–1803), artist/designer, 48–49, 293, 353–54, 401, 412, 433, 435

book, auction sales, xiv

bookseller, eighteenth-century, xiv

Booth, George, 2nd Earl of Warrington (1675–1758), 373–74

Borlase, William (1695–1772), antiquary, *The Natural History of Cornwall* (1758), 400–1

Boswell, James (1740–95), xiii, 221; *Life of Johnson*, xxiii, 8, 12, 15, 446

Boulton, Matthew, 397

Bouquet, J., bookseller, 183, 185

Bourn, Samuel (1714–96), *The Scripture Account of a Future State Considered* (1754), 360–61

Bourne, B. and Cook, booksellers, 41

des Bouveries, Jacob, Viscount Folkestone (d. 1761), **221**; **Letter to**, 220–21

Bowyer, William the younger (1699–1777), printer, 17, 29, 35, 39, 41, 46, 65, 81, 197, 301, 507–9, 512, 515–16, 520–21, 530

Box, George, Secretary to Society for the Encouragement of Arts, Manufactures, and Commerce, 208; **Letter to**, 281–82

Boyce, Benjamin, 505

Boyce, William, DD (1710–79), musician, 341, 369

Boyd, William, 4th Earl of Kilmarnock (1704–46), 102

Boyle, John, 5th Earl of Cork (1707–62), 14; **Letter from**, 547

Boyle, Richard, 3rd Earl of Burlington (1695–1763), 469

Bradshaw, Joseph (d. 1770?), 452–53, 470–71, 479

Brief Account of the Vaudois, A, see Devisme, Louis

Brindley, James, bookseller, 5, 23, 38, 41

Bristol, Bishop of, *see* Newton, Thomas

British Museum General Catalogue of Printed Books, xiii

Brooke, Frances (née Moore) (1723–89), 462, 479, 488; **Letter from**, *548*; *The History of Lady Julia Mandeville* (1763), 463, 480–81, 488

Brooke, Henry (1703?–83), *Songs in Jack the Giant-Queller* (1749), 30, 47, 510, 516; *Tasso's Jerusalem* (1738), 70

Brooke, John, DD, 463

Brooking, Charles (1723–59), designer, 48

Brooks, Cleanth, 325; *Correspondence of Thomas Percy & William Shenstone*, xxiii, 157, 187

Brotherton, John, bookseller, 38, 41

Brown, John, of Carlisle (1715–66), 53, **71**, 360–61; **Letters from**, 70–73, 83–85, 87–93, 103–5, *548*; **Letters to**, 356–58 (feud with RD), *548*; **Works**, *Barbarosa* (1754), 358; "Battle of the Pygmies and Cranes," 91–92; *Essay on Satire* (1745), 83–85, 88–89, 94–95; *Estimate of the Manners and Principles of the Times* (1757, 1758), 71, 356–58, 360–61, 377–78; *Honour* (1743), 7, 70–73, 83–85, 93; RD's *Museum* (1746–47), 87–88, 90–92, 103; *Mutual Connexion between Religious Truth and Civil Freedom* (1747), 103–4; "Puppet-show," 91–92; "Scating," 91–92; *Sermons on Various Subjects* (1764), 105

Browne, Daniel, printer, 41, 45, 533

Brumel, George, 95, 157

Brumoy, Père (1688–1742), *Théâtre des Grecs* (1730), 361–62; *see also* Lennox, Charlotte

Brutus, legendary founder of England, 266–67

Bryant, Mr, 109

Buckland, James, bookseller, 38

Burguignon, Hubert François (Gravelot), 48

Burke, Edmund (1729–97), xiv, 17, 330, 393, 395, **420**, 437, 455, 504; **Letters from**, 419–21, *548*; **Works**, *Account of European Settlements in America* (1757), 17, 420, 511; *Annual Register* (1758–), 14, 17, 33, 420, 461, 510; proposed *History of England*, 420, 510; *Philosophical Enquiry . . . Ideas of the Sublime and the Beautiful* (1757), 17, 31, 33, 398–99, 420–21; *Vindication of Natural Society* (1756), 17, 30, 32–33, 42, 379, 416, 420, 510

Burke, Mrs Edmund, 420

Burke, William (1729–98), 17, 420–21, 510–11; *Account of the European Settlements in America* (1757), 17, 420, 511

Burlington, 3rd Earl of, *see* Boyle, Richard

Burney, Charles (1726–1814), musician, 18,
    101
Burnim, Kalman, *see* Highfill, P., Burnim, K.,
    and Langhans, E.
Burns, Francis, 455, 470, 477, 485
Burton, John, DD (1696–1771), classicist, *De
    literarum Graecarum institutione dissertatio*
    (1758), 361–62; *Pentalogia, sive
    Tragoediarum Graecarum Delectus* (1758),
    361–62
Busy-Body, The, see Centlivre, Susannah
Bute, 3rd Earl of, *see* Stuart, John
Butler, Samuel (1612–80), *Hudibras* (1663–68),
    354
Butts, Thomas, Methodist secretary, 83
Byfleet, Surrey, *see* Spence, Joseph
Byng, Admiral John (1704–57), 268–69,
    419–20
Byron, George Gordon, 6th Baron
    (1788–1824), poet, 419
Byron, William, 5th Baron of Rochdale
    (1722–98), 418–19

"Cabinet, The" (Graves, Richard), 172, 180
Cadell, Thomas (1742–1802), bookseller,
    Lowth's *English Grammar*, 508, 511
Caesar, Julius, Emperor (102?–44 BC), 27, 136
Caesar, Mr, 269
Caius Suetonius Tranquillus (Oudendorp,
    Franciscus), 400–1
Callimacus (fl. 265 BC), Greek poet, 27
Calton, Jacob, of Kelsey, Lincs., **99; Letter
    from**, 98–99; "Milton's Muse," 98–99
Calvinism, training in, 327; mode of preaching,
    354
Cambridge, Richard Owen (1717–1802), 14;
    Scribleriad (1751), 48, 530–31; *Student*
    (1750–51), 429
Cambridge University Press, xv
Campbell, Archibald, 3rd Duke of Argyle
    (1682–1761), 283–84, 286
Campbell, Archibald (1726?–80), 31, 32, 511
Campbell, John (1708–75), *Biographia Britannica*
    (1760), 220; *Complete and Authentick History
    . . . of the late Rebellion* (1747), 87;
    *Geography, Natural History, and Antiquities of
    England and Wales*, 31–32, 37, 511–12; *Lives
    of the Admirals* (1742–44), 80; RD's *Museum*
    (1746–47), 87, 93–94, 508, 511
"Candor" (Shenstone, William), 292–93
Canons of Criticism (Edwards, Thomas), 213,
    400–1
Canterbury, Archbishop of, *see* Herring,
    Thomas
Capel, William, 3rd Earl of Essex (1697–1743), 6
Caractères (La Bruyère, Jean de), 112–13
Carlisle, Bishop of, *see* Fleming, George

Carlisle, city of, 70, 87, 90, 91
*Carmen Cl. Alexandri Pope in S. Caeciliam Latine
    Redditum* (Smart, Christopher), 100–2
Carter, Edmund, 108
Carter, Elizabeth (1717–1806), classicist and
    poet, 463
Carteret, John, 1st Earl Granville (1690–1763),
    105
Cartwright (later Coltman), Elizabeth
    (1737–1811), 20, 53, 340–41, 343, 363–64,
    447, **452**, 465, 471; **Letter from**, 479–81;
    Letters to, 451–53, 455–56, 462–63,
    470–71, 477–79, 481–83, 487–88
Cartwright, Samuel (1701–92), 452, 455, **483;
    Letter to**, 471
Cary, Walter, 495, 497
Caslon, William (1692–1766), typefounder,
    144–45
Catherine II, Empress of Russia (1729–96), 71
Cave, Edward (1691–1754), printer, 45;
    Gentleman's Magazine (1731–), 9, 15
Cave, Richard, bookseller, 41
Cavendish, Lord Frederick (1729–1803), 154–55
Cavendish, Lord George (1727–94), 154–55
Cavendish, William, 4th Duke of Devonshire
    (1720–64), 488
Cawthorn, James (1719–61), 12, 228; **Letter
    to**, 271–72
Centaur not Fabulous, The, see Young, Edward
Centlivre, Susannah (1667–1723), dramatist,
    The Busy-Body (1709), 12, 381–83, 387
"Ceremonial, The" (Shenstone, William), 332
Cervantes, Saavedra de (1547–1616), 29; *Don
    Quixote*, 323–25
"Cervantes, A Song Paraphrased" (Percy,
    Thomas), 323–25
Chadwyck-Healey, publishers, xv
Chalmers, Alexander (1759–1834), 507–8;
    Works of the English Poets (1812), xiii
Chambers, Robert (1802–71), 403
Chambers, William, *Designs of Chinese Buildings,
    Furniture, Dresses, Machines, and Utensils*
    (1757), 279
Chapelle, Henry, bookseller, 38, 512
Chapman, George, of Dumfries (1723–1806),
    365–66
Chapman, John, DD (1704–84), at Lambeth,
    75, 77
Chapman, R. W., 3–4, 7, 60, 296
Chapman, Thomas, DD (1717–60),
    prebendary of Durham, 440
Chappel, Mr, linen draper of Nottingham, 140
Characteristics of Men, Manners, Opinions, Times
    (1711) (Cooper, Anthony Ashley), 21, 126
Charles Edward, the "Young Pretender"
    (1720–88), 87, 90; *see also* Jacobite
    Rebellion

Charlevoix, Fr, SJ, *General History and Description of New France*, 94

Charlotte, Queen (1744–1818), 452, 477–78

Chatelaine, John Baptiste (1710–71), designer, 48

Chaucer, Geoffrey (1340?–1400), *Canterbury Tales*, 27

Chepstow, town of, 424–25

Cheselden, William (1688–1752), *Anatomy of the Human Body* (1713), 32, 512, 526, 528; notes to Gataker's trans. of Le Dran's *Operations in Surgery*, 515

Chesterfield, 4th Earl of, *see* Stanhope, Philip Dormer

Chesterfield, 5th Earl of, *see* Stanhope, Philip

Cheyney, Thomas (*c.* 1694–1760), Dean of Winchester, 128, 290–91, **338**, 339 (his "death"), 342, 350, 548; **Letters from**, 338–39, *548*

Chinese novel, *see* Percy, Thomas, *Hau Kiou Choaan*

Chinese Porter, inn in Cockspur St, London, 405–6

Cholmondely, Mary (*c.* 1730–1811), 469; intercessor for W. Shenstone's pension, 467–69

Cholmondely, Hon. Robert, 469

Chomley, Nathaniel, 18

Chrichley, J., printer, 45

Chronological Antiquities (Jackson, John), 136, 142

Churchill, Sarah (née Jennings), Duchess of Marlborough (1660–1744), 78–80, 92

Cibber, Colley (1671–1757), actor and theater manager, 6, 75, 77; *Apology* (1740), 32, 512; *Papal Tyranny in the Reign of King John* (1745), 77

Cibber, Susannah Maria (1714–66), actress, 310, 312–13, 383; *The Oracle* (1752), 34, 313, 512

Cibber, Theophilus (1703–58), actor, 313

Cicero, Marcus Tullius (106–43 BC), 27, 256, 368; *Letters, see* Melmoth, William; *see also* Lyttelton, George

Cicero, Observations on the Life of (Lyttelton, Sir George), 119

Clanricarde, 5th Earl of, *see* de Burgh, Ulick

Clanricarde, 11th Earl of, *see* Smith, John

"Clarendon Review," 96

Clark(e), John, bookseller, 38, 41, 89

Clarke, Richard (1739–1831), attorney, settlement of W. Shenstone's estate, 475–76, 482, 484, 492

Clauss, Taylor, 151–52

Claverton Down, race at, 240

Clements, Richard, Oxford bookseller, 41, 43–44, 150

Cleone, see RD

Clifton, Sir Robert (1690–1762), Clifton Hall, Notts., 481

Clinton, Henry Fiennes, 9th Earl of Lincoln (1720–94), 126

Clive, Catherine (1711–85), actress, *The Rehearsal* (1753), 34, 512

Cobden, Edward, DD (1684–1764), 390–91; *Poems on Several Occasions* (1748), 30, 391

"Cobham's Cubs," 183

Cochrane, J. A., 15, 97

Cockayne, George, *Complete Baronetage*, xxii–xxiii; *Complete Peerage*, xxii–xxiii

Cole, William, 381

Coleridge, Samuel Taylor (1772–1834), 171

Collection Académique (Berryat, Jean), 370–71

Collection of Farces, 405–6

Collection of Moral and Sacred Poems (Wesley, John), 82–83

Collection of Original Poems, A, see Blacklock, Thomas

Collection of Poems by Several Hands, see RD

Collections of Songs (Pixell, John), 414–15

Collet, John (1725?–80), painter, 508; *Chit-Chat* (1755), 513

Collier, Jane, *Essay on the Art of Ingeniously Tormenting* (1753), 415–16

Collins, A. S., *Authorship in the Days of Johnson*, 3–4, 33–34

Collins, William (1721–59), poet, 9, 94, 96; *Epistle . . . to Sir Thomas Hamner* (1744), 96

Collyer, Joseph the elder (d. 1776), 161, 171

Collyer, Mary (d. 1763), 161, 171

Coltman, John, Leicester hosier, 452, 471

Coltman, Mary Ann, 447

Comberbach, Roger the elder, Recorder of Chester, *Report of Several Cases . . . in the Court of King's Bench* (1755?), 74

Comberbach, Roger the younger (d. 1757), **74**; **Letters from**, 73–74, *548*; *Dispute . . . in favour of blank verse* (1755?), 74; *Oration of Marcus Tullius Cicero* (1745), 73–74, *548*

Common Prayer, Book of, see Baskerville, John

"Complaint of Deafness," 390–91

Complaint; or Night Thoughts, see Young, Edward

Complete Body of Architecture (Ware, Isaac), 300–1

Complete History of England, A, see Smollett, Tobias

"Compliment in 1743," *see* Shenstone, William

Compton, Spencer, Earl of Wilmington (1673?–1743), 51; Williams's satire on, 494–98

Comus, a Masque (Milton), *see* Dalton, John

Conformity between Popery and Paganism (Seward, Thomas), 127

Congreve, Francis, *Authentic Memoirs of . . . Macklin* (1798), 93

"Conjugal Love, On," *see* Cooper, John Gilbert, *Museum*
"Contentment, On" (Cooper, John Gilbert), 100, 109
Con-Test, The (1756–57), 15, 259–60
Cook, bookseller, *see* Bourne, B.
Cook, M., bookseller, 41
Cook, W., bookseller, 41
Cooke, H., bookseller, 41
Cooke, Mr, Northampton carrier, 372
Cooke, Thomas (1703–56), *Hymn to Liberty* (1746), 93
Cookes, Edward the elder, W. Shenstone's uncle, 145
Cookes, Edward the younger, inheritance of Leasowes from his cousin W. Shenstone, 476–77
Cooper, Anthony Ashley, 3rd Earl of Shaftesbury (1671–1713), 90; *Characteristics of Men, Manners, Opinions, Times* (1711), 21, 126
Cooper, John Gilbert ("Philaretes") (1723–69), 31, 53, 57, 87–88, **90**, 126 (marriage), 157, 268–69, 330, 370; Thurgarton, 143–44; feud with Warburton, 90, 131–32, 135–36, 140–44, 214–16; **Letters from**, 89–90, 93–97, 99–100, 105–6, 109–11, 117–18, 126–31, 133–38, 140–44, 172–75, 196, *548*; **Letters to**, 130–35, *548*; **Works**, essays and poems in RD's *Museum*, 90, ("Account of the Kingdom of Beggars," 105–6, 109; "Advertisement," 105, 110–11; "Conjugal Love," 100, 109–10, 117–18; "Contentment," 100, 109; "Death of Socrates," 109; "Education," 95–96, 109; "Epistle from Muli Azareth at London," 100, 109; "Epistle from Theagenes to Sylvia," 110; "Estimate of Life," 96, 100, 118; "Folly of Noblemen and Gentlemen's Paying their Debts," 109–10; "Friendship," 96, 109; "Good and Beauty," 109–10; "Hymn to Health," 99–100; "Persuasive to Erect an Academy for Lying," 105–6, 109; "Plebian Politicians," 109; "Polite Arts," 99–100, 109, 174; "Predominant Passion in Women," 109, 117–18; "Project for Raising an Hospital for Decayed Authors" (by "Musophilus"), 99–100, 109; "Self-Love," 109; "Solitude and Society," 105, 110–11; "True and False Religion," 109; "Vision of Heaven," 106, 109); *Cursory Remarks on Mr Warburton's New Edition of Mr Pope's Works* (1751), 24, 42, 90, 138, 142–44, 417; *Letters concerning Taste* (1754), 49, 138, 172–75, 513; *Life of Socrates* (1749), 30, 35, 90, 120, 126–38, 140–41,

172–74, 215–16; *Poems on Several Subjects* (1764), 90; "Power of Habit," 117; *Power of Harmony* (1745), 90, 93, 127; *Tomb of Shakespeare* (1755), 194–96
Cooper, Mrs John Gilbert, 90, 142–43
Cooper, Maria Susanna, **Letter from**, *549*; *Letters between Emilia and Harriet* (1762), 549
Cooper, Mary (d. 1761), publisher, 10–11, 13, 24, 38, 40–43, 81, 90, 185–86, 206, 220, 222, 260, 385–86, 416–17, 468 (her death), 508, 531; *World*, 42
Cooper, Samuel, **Letter from**, *549*
Cooper, Thomas, publisher, 40–42
Corbett, Charles (d. 1752), bookseller, 41, 156, 184
Cork, 5th Earl of, *see* Boyle, John
Corn Laws, 366–68
Cornwall, *see* Borlase, William
Corsica, king of, *see* Neuhoff, Baron de
"Corydon, a Pastoral" (Cunningham, John), 491–92
"Cotswouldia," *see* Thomas, Mrs Elizabeth
Cotton, Charles (1630–87), poet, trans., *Essays of Michael Seigneur de Montaigne* (1759), 406–7
Cotton, Nathaniel (1705–88), physician, "The Fire-side," 104–5; *Visions in Verse* (1751), 29, 32, 513
Courtney, William P., *Dodsley's Collection of Poetry*, xxiii, 60, 238, 309
Covent Garden Theatre, 5, 12, 18, 65, 307, 313–14, 319, 375, 379, 381–82, 387–89, 409; *see also* Rich, John
Coventry, Francis (d. 1759?), *History of Pompey the Little*, 33–34, 513, 531
Coventry, Maria, Countess of (1733–60), 370–71
Cowper, Mr, musician, 369
Cox, H. Shute, bookseller, 41
Coxe, William (d. 1760), physician, 106–8
Coxe, William (1747–1828), 107
Cranfield, G. A., 15, 184
Crébillon, Prosper Jolyot de (1674–1762), 29
Creusa, Queen of Athens, *see* Whitehead, William
Crisp, Samuel (d. 1783), *Virginia* (1754), 158–59
Critical Review (1756–), xxiii, 16, 394, 399, 450 (RD's *Select Fables*)
Croft, John (1732–1820), 18, 416, 422
Cross, Wilbur, 87, 422–23
Crowder, Stanley (d. 1798), bookseller, 41
Crownfield, Cornelius, Cambridge bookseller, 38
Culver, Peter, jeweller and toymaker, 252–53, 264
Cumberland, Richard (1732–1811), 380

Cunningham, John (1729–73), "Corydon, a Pastoral. To the Memory of William Shenstone," 491–92
Curl, Henry, printer, 393, 395
Curll, Edmund (1675–1747) [393? 395?]; Rowe's *Philomela* (1736), 513
Cursory Remarks on Mr Warburton's New Edition of Mr Pope's Works, see Cooper, John Gilbert
"Cursus Glacialis" (Frowde, Philip), 91–92
Curtis, Lewis P., 416, 422–23
Cutler, Mrs Mary ("Molly"), W. Shenstone's housekeeper, 207, 209, 285, 293, 314, 323, 385, 388, 447; pursuit of annuity from Shenstone's estate, 476–77, 484–85, 493

Daily Advertiser (1730–   ), xxiii, 58–59, 258, 442–43
Daily Post (1719–46), xxiii
Dale End (inn?), Birmingham, 239
Dalrymple, Sir David, Lord Hailes (1726–92), 14
Dalrymple, John, 4th Baronet of Cranstoun, *Essay on Landscape Gardening*, 432, 434–35; *Essay Towards a General History of Feudal Property in Great Britain* (1757), 377–78
Dalton, John, DD (1709–63), 7, 76–77, 80, 123, 464–65, 477–78; *Comus, a Masque* (1738), 29, 112, 465
Dalton, Mrs John, 464, 478
Dalton, Richard (1715?–91), George III's librarian, 459–60, 477–78, 481
Danger of Writing Verse, The, see Whitehead, William
"Daphne's Visit" (Shenstone, William), 189
Dartiquenave, Charles, 4, 65
Dartmouth, 2nd Earl of, see Legge, William
D'Auverquerque, Henry, Earl of Grantham (c. 1672–1754), 154–55
Davies, David W., xv
Davies, Sir John (1569–1626), 396–97; *Original, Nature, and Immortality of the Soul* (1749), 397
Davies, Thomas (1712?–85), bookseller, *Life of Garrick* (1780), 383
Davis, Charles (d. 1755), bookseller, 38–40, 81
Davis, Lockyer (d. 1791), bookseller, 41
Day of Judgment (Swift, Jonathan), 207
Day of Judgment (Ogilvie, John), 248
Deane, Anthony the younger (1729–?), ironmonger, 398–99, 445
"Death of Socrates" (Cooper, John Gilbert), 109
de Burgh, Ulick, 5th Earl of Clanricarde (1604–57), *Memoirs and Letters of* (1757), 277
de Costa, Joseph, *Tractado de Cortesia* (1726), 81–82

Defoe, Daniel (1661?–1731), 5
De Hondt, Peter, bookseller, *Tristram Shandy*, 18, 416, 423
De literarum Graecarum institutione dissertatio (Burton, John), 361–62
Dell, Henry (fl. 1766), *The Bookseller* (1766), 36
Denmark, King of, see Frederick V
Dennett, Mr, 109, 111
Dent, Robert K., see Straus & Dent
De partu Virginis (Sonnazaro, Jacopo), 429
Derbyshire, county of, 89, 90
Derrick, Samuel (1724–69), *Miscellanies in Prose and Verse*, 301
De sacra poesi Hebraeorum, see Lowth, Robert
Description of the Leasowes, see RD
Designs by Mr Bentley for Six Poems by Mr Gray (Bentley, Richard the younger), 148–49
Designs of Chinese Buildings . . . (Chambers, William), 279
Desmoulins, Mrs (b. 1716), 51
Devisme, Louis (1720–76), *A Brief Account of the Vaudois* (1753), 47, 147, 150–51, 153–55
Devonshire, 4th Duke of, see Cavendish, William
"Dialogue between Atticus and Eugenio" (Hervey, John), 298–99
"Diamond and the Loadstone, The" (Lowth, Robert), 230
Dibden, Thomas Frognall, 422–23
Dicey, Cluer, printer and publisher, 366
Dictionary of National Biography, xxii–xxiii, 10
Dictionary of the English Language, A, see Johnson, Samuel
Dilettante Club, 497
Dilly, Charles (1739–1807), bookseller, 513, 526
Dimond, Mr, theater manager, 409
Diodorus Siculus (fl. 44 BC), *Bibliotheke Historike* (1745), 133
Dircks, Richard, see Welcher, J. and Dircks, R.
"Dissertation on the Shield of Aeneas" (Whitehead, William), 101–2
Divine Legation of Moses, The (Warburton, William), 142
Dixon, Rev., 84, 88, 91
Dobson, William, 153; *Paradisus Amissus . . . Latine redditum* (1750), 77–78
Dodd, Anne, bookseller, 3
Dodd, Benjamin, bookseller, 3
Dodd, William (1729–77), 3
Doddridge, Philip (1702–51), 3
Dodington, George Bubb, Baron Melcombe (1691–1762), 3, 77, 196–97, 296; "On Sir Robert Walpole's Birth-day," 196–99
Dodsley, Alice, RD's sister, see Dyer, Alice
Dodsley, Alvory (1706–65), RD's brother, 4; RD's executor, 413, 493, 505; RD's last will, 503–5

Dodsley, Isaac (d. 1781?), RD's brother, gardener, 4, 212–14, 485–86, 491–92; RD's last will, 503–4

Dodsley, James (1724–97), RD's brother, bookseller, xiv, 3–4, 10–11, 14, 16, 18, 24, 35–37, 40, 42, 50–53, 140–41, 169, 179, 181, 194, 217, 238, 251, 253, 261, 286–88, 293, 316, 324, 391, 414, 416–17, 420–22, 431, 434, 440, 442, 446, 448, 449 (RD's *Select Fables*), 458–61, 469, 487, 492, 503–5 (RD's last will), 506–8; Corresondence and Documents (Appendix E), 555–67; *Annual Register* (1758–ˑ), 237; *Spendthrift* (1766), 237; Letter to William Shenstone, 178–79

Dodsley, John (1704?–?), RD's brother, 4; RD's last will, 503–4

Dodsley, Kitty, RD's niece, 504 (RD's last will)

Dodsley, Lucy (1704?–?), RD's sister, 4

Dodsley, Robert the elder (1681–1750), 4, 503

Dodsley, Robert (1703–64), apprentices, 251–52; apprenticeship, 4, 503; birth and early life, 4; Richard Blacow, dispute with, 183–85; business, 22–50; businessman, 20–21; copyrights, xiv, 35, 506–33 (Appendix B); death, burial, and epitaph, 20, 52, 364; designers and engravers, 48–49; book distribution, 42; drama, xiii–xiv (see *Cleone*); editing, xiv; editing Shenstone's mss., 471–75; RD's executors, 413, 493; finances, 34–36; franking, 157–58; on French servants, 498–99; gout, 166–67, 209, 249, 251, 254, 257, 261, 265, 270, 279, 286, 300–1, 326, 334, 375, 376, 438, 440, 462, 481, 483; imprints, 23–24; imprisoned, 6; last days, 488–90; "Letter Book," xxi, xxiv; paper-making, 49–50; patriot, 22; poetry, xiii–xiv; politics, 21, 27; Pope's bookseller, 72; portraits of: by Joshua Reynolds, 432, 434, 437–38, 441–42, by Jonathan Richardson, 434; press runs, 29–30; printers, 45–48; provincial booksellers, 43–44; publishing agreements, xiv, 30–34, 506–33 (Appendix B); purchase of Shenstone's mss., 474–77; religion, 21, 27; retirement, 405–6, 409–10, 413; Richmond, proposed purchase at, 138–39 (see Spence, Joseph); science, 27; W. Shenstone's executor, 471–75, 482, 484–86, 490, 492–93; Society for the Encouragement of Arts, Manufactures, and Commerce (RSA), *see under heading*; Stationers' Company, *see under heading*; trade relations, 37–49; trade sales, 37–38, 531–33; Tully's Head, 5, 22–23, 52; last will, xiv, 503–5 (Appendix A); *Letter to London Chronicle*, 498–99

Works and Publications: *Agriculture* (1753, Pt. I of *Public Virtue*), 11, 45, 145, 158–59, 161–65, 168, 170, 217–18; *Annual Register*, 14–15, 260, 460–61; *Beauty: or the Art of Charming*, 5, 67, 79; *Blind Beggar of Bethnal Green* (1741), 6, 245, 531; "The Butterfly, Snail, and Bee," 425–26; *Cleone*, 11–13, 15, 18–19, 21–22, 49, 115, 158–59, 187, 210, 221, 225–31, 233–45, 249–50, 255–57, 261, 263, 270–72, 280–81, 291–94, 297, 299–300, 305–7, 310–15, 318–19, 321–22, 326, 329–30, 341, 373, 375–79, 381–89, 392–401, 405–7, 406 (at York), 407–9 (at Bath), 412–14, 469 (for the Epilogue, *see also* Graves, Richard, and Shenstone, William); *Colin's Kisses*, 187; *Collection of Poems by Several Hands*, xiv, xxii, 7, 10, 13–14, 19–20, 30, 40, 46–47, 49, 53, 58, 60–61, 71, 88–89, 96, 112, 114–15, 117–18, 123–24, 156–59, 161–63, 165–66, 168, 170–72, 180–81, 186–93, 196–202, 204, 223–25, 231, 237–39, 243, 249–50, 258, 260–61, 265, 270–71, 274, 280, 285, 287, 292–93, 295–304, 307–10, 314–28, 331–35, 337, 340–41, 345, 349–54, 357–58, 401, 431, 472, 483–84, 504, 508, 511; "Common-place Book," 12; *Description of the Leasowes* (1764), 432, 434–35, 486–87; *English History Delineated* (1752), 49, 136–37; *Epistle to Mr Pope* (1734), 5; *Fugitive Pieces*, II (1761), 321, 468; *King and Miller of Mansfield* (1737), 6, 245, 531; "King-fisher and the Sparrow" ("Halcyon and the Sparrow"), 405–7, 409–10, 412; *London and its Environs* (1761), 49, 448–49; *London Chronicle* (1757–ˑ), 184, 258–60; *London Evening Post*, 157, 182–85; *Melpomene* (1757), 13, 19, 228, 263, 265–68, 270–71, 274–78, 285, 292–94, 296–97, 299–301, 303–5, 307, 315–17, 336–37, 341, 358; Memorandum Books, 135–36; *Miseries of Poverty*, 4; *Modern Reasoners* (1734), 5, 65, 68; *Muse in Livery* (1732), 5, 68, 79, 269, 333; *Museum: or, Literary and Historical Register* (1746–47), 9–10, 14, 45, 48–49, 87–103, 105–6, 109–11, 115–18, 174, 287, 395–96; "Mutual Love," 138–39; "Ode on the Death of Pope," 80; *Oeconomy of Human Life* (1750), 10–11, 42, 68, 319; *Pain and Patience*, 73; *Preceptor* (1748), 8, 21, 48, 121, 167–68, 316, 504; *Public Register* (1741), 9, 37, 69, 319; *Rex et Pontifex* (1745), 6; *Select Collection of Old Plays* (1744), xiv, 6–7, 29, 40, 508, 553; *Select Fables of Esop* (1761), 15–16, 19, 46, 49, 107, 115, 147, 375–76, 392, 394–95,

405–6, 409–12, 414, 425–38, 440–42,
445–55, 460, 504; *Servitude* (1729), 5; *Sir
John Cockle at Court* (1738), 6, 245; *Toyshop*,
5–6, 21–22, 65–66, 68, 245; *Trifles* (1745),
80, 108–9, 395; *Triumph of Peace* (1749),
245; "Verses by Mr Dodsley, at his first
arrival at the Leasowes, 1754," 492–93;
Wish, 11; *Works in Verse and Prose of
William Shenstone* (1764; see Shenstone,
William); *World*, 10, 14, 42, 153, 157, 161,
207, 225, 243, 261–62, 269–70, 306, 319,
393, 395–96, 521 (*see also* Moore, Edward)
Dodsley, Mrs Catherine (née Iserloo)
 (d. 1754), RD's wife, 11, 13, 74–76, 78,
 80–81, 109, 114, 117, 137–38, 140,
 143–44, 164, 167, 173–75, 188, 191
Dodsley, Sarah, RD's niece, 504 (RD's last will)
"Dodsley's Collection" (Yale), xiv
Dodwell, Henry (d. 1784), 3
Dodwell, William (1709–85), 3
"Dog and the Crocodile, The" (Lowth,
 Robert), 429–30
Dolman, Thomas the elder, 433
Dolman, Thomas the younger, 212, 260–61,
 432–33, 437–38
Dossie, Robert, *Elaboratory laid open* (1758),
 400–1
Douglas, Dunbar Hamilton, 4th Earl of
 Selkirk, 437
Draper, John, 112
Draper, Somerset, London bookseller, 41,
 212–13
Drayton, Michael (1563–1631), *Works* (1748),
 29, 393, 395
"Dropsical Man, The," *see* Taylor, William
Drummond, Robert Hay, Bishop of Asaph,
 154–55
Drury Lane Theatre, xiii, 5–6, 12, 18, 244–46,
 310, 394, 430–31
Dryden, John (1631–1700), 76, 207
Dublin Journal (1728–   ), 47
Duck, Stephen (1705–56), poet, 4, 7
Dudley, Baron, *see* Lea, Fernando Dudley
Dudley, Lord Guilford, *see* Keate, George
Duguet, Abbé, *Institution of a Prince* (1740), 40,
 183, 185
Dulwich Art Gallery, 442
Duncan, William (1717–60), professor,
 Marischal college, *Caesar's Commentaries*
 (1753), 30, 32, 514, 523; *Elements of Logic*
 (1748), 121; Plutarch's *Lives*, 514
Duncombe, John (1729–86), *Poems* (1756), 49;
 Works of Horace in English Verse (1757–59),
 361–62
Duncombe, William (1690–1769), 7, 22
Dunk, George Montagu, 2nd Earl of Halifax
 (1716–71), 262

Durham, Bishop of, *see* Trevor, Richard
Durham, city of, 20, 362–64, 373
Durham, college of, 440
Durham, T., and D. Wilson, booksellers, 41
Dusior, Isle, 201
Duval, Valentin Jameray, *Monnaies en or et en
 argent qui composent une des parties du cabinet
 de S. M. L'Empereur* (1759–69), 371
Dyer, Alice, RD's sister, 4, 269, 406, 413, 456,
 470, 472, 475, 479, 483; RD's last will, 504
Dyer, Francis, husband of Alice, 4, 475, 479,
 481–83, 488, 492–93; RD's executor, 413,
 493; RD's last will, 504–5
Dyer, John (1700?–58), **Letters from**, 280,
 549; *The Fleece* (1757), 280; *Grongar Hill*
 (1726, 1748), 280; *Poems* (1761), 280; *Ruins
 of Rome* (1740, 1748), 280
Dyer, Kitty, RD's niece, 504 (RD's last will)
"Dying Kid, The" (Shenstone, William),
 320–23, 332
Dyson, Jeremiah (1722–76), *Epistle to the Rev.
 Mr Warburton* (1744), 130

Eamonson, Mr, 505
Eaves, John, stepson of John Baskerville, 445
Eaves, Sarah, 277, 285
Eaves, T. C. Duncan, and Ben D. Kimpel, 47
Ebert, Johann Arnold, 166
Eddy, Donald, 7, 60–61, 71, 87, 91, 94–95,
 103, 296
Eden, Robert, DD (1701–59), prebendary of
 Winchester, 361–62
Edge-hill (Jago, Richard), 467, 469
Edinburgh, University of, 283, 402–3, 459
"Education, On" (Cooper, John Gilbert),
 95–96, 109
Edward Augustus, Prince of Wales (1739–67),
 12, 22, 170, 382, 385
Edwards, Thomas (1699–1757), *Canons of
 Criticism (Supplement to Mr Warburton's Edition
 of Shakespeare*) (1758), 213, 400–1
Eighteenth-Century Short-Title Catalogue, xv, 23
Elaboratory laid open, The (Dossie, Robert),
 400–1
Elegies (Whitehead, William), 265
Elements of Logic (Duncan, William), 121
Elements of Moral Philosophy (Fordyce, David),
 121
Elphenstone, Arthur, 6th Baron Balmerino
 (1688–1746), 102
Elzevier editions, xv, 252–53
Emonson, James (d. 1780), printer, 514, 526
English, language, 160–61, 199, 281–82
English History Delineated (RD), 49, 136–37
English, Thomas, *Annual Register*, 514
Epictetus (*c.* AD 50–*c.* 138), stoic philosopher,
 27

"Epilogue to Shakespeare's first Part of King Henry IV" (Hoadly, John), 295–96
"Epistle from Lady Jane Grey to Lord Guilford Dudley" (Keate, George), 457–58
"Epistle from Muli Azareth at London to the Mufti at Constantinople" (Cooper, John Gilbert), 100, 109
Epistles Philosophic and Moral (Kenrick, William), 393, 395
Erasmus, Desiderius (1466?–1536), 29
Erskine, Henry, 5th Baron of Alva and Cambuskenneth (d. 1765), 445, 447
Essai sur la coeur humain (Morelly), 104–5
Essai sur l'esprit humain (Morelly), 104–5
Essay on Criticism (Pope, Alexander), 140–41
"Essay on Electricity," *see* Jago, Richard
Essay on Landscape Gardening (Dalrymple, John), 432, 434–35
Essay on Ridicule (Whitehead, William), 119, 527
Essay on Satire, see Brown, John
Essay on the Writings and Genius of Mr Pope, see Warton, Joseph
Essay on Universal Etymology (Blacklock, Thomas), 283–84, 286
Essays of Michael Seigneur de Montaigne, see Montaigne, Michel Eyquem
Essex, militia of, 458
Essex, 3rd Earl of, *see* Capel, William
"Estimate of Life," *see* Cooper, John Gilbert, *Museum*
Estimate of the Manners and Principles of the Times, An, see Brown, John
Evans, Noteby, 511
Evelyn, John (1620–1706), *Sculptura; or the History and Art of Chalcography and Engraving in Copper* (1662, 1755), 119
Evening Advertiser (1754–58), 183–85, 258, 260
"Evergreen, The" (Shenstone, William), 292–93, 334
Evers, Captain, 339
Exeter, Bishop of, *see* Lavington, George

Fables, see RD, *Select Fables of Esop*
Fables nouvelles . . ., see La Motte, Antoine
Fairer, David, 191, 220, 347
Fasti Ecclesiae Anglicanae, xxiii
Fasti Ecclesiae Scoticanae, xxiii
"Fatal Exotic, The" (Shenstone, William), 473–74
"Father Francis's Prayer" (West, Gilbert), 197–98
Faulkner, George (1699?–1775), Dublin bookseller, 47–48, 153, 163–64, **301**; **Letter to**, 300–1; *Dublin Journal* (1728–   ), 47, 301; Swift's *Works*, 301
Fawkener, Sir Everard (1684–1758), 16–17

Female Quixote (Lennox, Charlotte), 400–1
Fénelon, Salignac de la Motte (1651–1715), *Adventures of Télémachus* (1699), 29, 38
Fenton, Elijah (1683–1730), 166
Ferdinand, Duke of Brunswick (1721–92), 420
Ferguson, Adam (1723–1816), professor at Edinburgh, 284, 402–3
Fielding, Henry (1707–54), 14, 34, 87; *Tom Jones* (1749), 178
Fielding, Sarah (1710–68), novelist, *The Cry* (1754), 31, 34, 514
Finculo Abbey, *see* Spence, Joseph
"Fire-side, The" (Cotton, Nathaniel), 104–5
Firman's Waggon, *see* Frimen's Waggon
Firmian, Count, Plenipotentiary at Milan, 464
"Fit of the Spleen, A" (Ibbot, Benjamin), 351–52
Fitzroy, Charles, 1st Baron Southampton (1737–97), 419–20
Five Pastoral Eclogues (Warton, Thomas), 7, 85–86
Fleece, The (Dyer, John), 280
Fleming, Mrs, 72–73
Fleming, George (1667–1747), Bishop of Carlisle, 71–73, 92
Fletcher, Andrew, Lord Milton (1692–1766), 225, 283–84
Fletcher, Ifan Kyrle, 87
Fletcher, James the elder (1710–95), 41, 43–44, 219–20, 347
Fletcher, James the younger (d. 1798), Oxford bookseller, 41, 43
Flitcroft, Henry (1697–1769), 467, 469
"Flowers" (Whistler, Anthony), 172, 192–93
Foley, Thomas, 2nd Baron Foley (1733–66), 467, 469; his Witley Court, 469
Folkestone, Viscount, *see* des Bouveries, Jacob
Fontaine, *see* La Fontaine, Jean de
Fordyce, Rev. Alexander (d. 1789), of Ayton, 122
Fordyce, David (1711–51), **121**, 125; **Letter from**, 121–22; *Dialogues concerning Education* (1745–48), 121; *Elements of Moral Philosophy* (1754–58), 121; *Theodorus, or Dialogue on the Art of Preaching* (1752–54), 121–22, 514–15, 531
Fordyce, James (1720–96), *Essay on the Action Proper for the Pulpit* (1753), 122, 515
Fordyce, Sir William (1724–92), physician, 121–22, 515
Forster, Harold, 347
'45, The, *see* Jacobite Rebellion
Foster, James, *Account of . . . the late Earl of Kilmarnock* (1746), 102
Foundling Hospital, 306
Four Essays upon the English Language (Ward, John), 361–62

Fourmantel, Catherine, singer, 423
Fox, Henry, 1st Baron Holland (1705–74),
  357–58
Foxon, David, 55–57, 65, 157, 362, 423, 530
Foye, Edward, W. Shenstone's creditor, 477
"Fragment of Chaucer, A" (Harris, James),
  295–96
Frampton, Rev. Matthew (*c.* 1719–?), 419, 421
France, war with, 456–57, 462; *see also* French
  servants
Frances, Mr, alderman of Derby, 95
Francklin, Richard (d. 1765), bookseller,
  380–81
franking, system of, 95, 157–58, 373
Franklin, Benjamin (1706–90), 55
Franklin, Thomas (1721–84), 134–135
Frasi, Giula, Italian vocalist, 370–71
Frederick, Prince of Wales (1707–51), 6, 21,
  183–84
Frederick V, King of Denmark (1723–66), 159
Frederick William II, King of Prussia
  (1744–97), 186
Free Inquiry into the Miraculous Powers . . .
  Christian Church (Middleton, Conyers), 129
French, (Thomas?), 176, 178
French servants, 51, 498–99
"Friendship, On" (Cooper, John Gilbert), 96,
  109
Frimen's Waggon, 19, 239, 349, 353, 398, 425
Froome, Mr, 109
Frowde, Philip (d. 1738), "Cursus Glacialis,"
  91–92; *see also* Brown, John, "Scating"

Gadd, David, 409
Galand, Mrs, schoolmistress, 446
Gale, Samuel (1682–1754), *History and*
  Antiquities of the Cathedral Church of
  Winchester (1715), 338–39
Gale, Thomas (1635–1702), trans. of
  Herodotus's *History* (1679), 133–34
Gallagher, Robert E., 549
Galley, Alexander, proposed *Compendium of the*
  Geography, Natural History, and Antiquities of
  England, 431, 512, 515, 517
Gamester, The, see Moore, Edward
Gardener's Kalendar, see Miller, Philip
gardening, *see*: Dalrymple, John; Dodsley,
  Isaac; Miller, Philip; Shenstone, William
Gardiner, Mrs, 173
Garle, Richard, 120
Garrick, David (1717–79), 6, 51, 94, 147, 153,
  158, 197, 199–200, 221–22, 237, 330–31,
  357–58, 423, 431, 450; rejection of RD's
  Cleone and their falling out, 12–13, 15, 18,
  22, 107, 225–26, 228, 249–50, 255–57,
  261, 263, 280–81, 291–93, 299, 306–7,
  310–14, 319, 326, 331, 373, 378–79,

381–84, 386–87, 389, 392, 396–97, 408–9,
  450; **Letters from**, 244–47, 291, 381–82,
  384, *549;* **Letters to**, 245–46, 280–81,
  310–14, 383–84; *Miss in Her Teens* (1747),
  550
Gaskell, Philip, 114, 145–46, 169, 253, 273,
  455
Gataker, Thomas (d. 1768), surgeon, 221, 281,
  306, 313, 326, 330, 364–65; **Letter to**,
  306–7; trans. of LeDran's *Operations in*
  Surgery, 512, 515; essay in *World,* 306
Gataker, Mrs Thomas (née Anne Hill), 306,
  364, 419–20, 467
Gay, John (1685–1732), 55; *The Beggar's Opera*
  (1728), 217
Gelli, Giovanni Battista, 29
General Advertiser (1734–52), xxiii, 35, 59, 258
General Evening Post (1733–), xxiii, 338–39
General History of England, A (Guthrie, William),
  79–80
General History of Polybius, see Hampton, James
Gentleman's Magazine (1731–), xxii, xxiv,
  9–10, 15, 327
George I (1660–1727), 173
George II (1683–1760), 8, 173, 259, 277,
  290–91, 296
George III (1738–1820), 446, 456–57;
  coronation of, 455–56; *see* Whitehead,
  William
George IV (1762–1830), 296
George Inn, Smithfield, 372
Germain, George Sackville, 1st Viscount
  Sackville (1716–85), 419–20
Germany, English language in, 160–61, 199;
  learning in, 165
Gibbon, Edward (1737–94), *Memoirs* (1827,
  1830), 214 (on Warburton)
Gifford, Rev. Richard (1725–1807), 158–59,
  452–53, 462–63, 470–71, 478–79, 481, 489;
  Contemplation (1753), 453
Gifford, Mrs Richard, 478
Gilbert, John (1693–1761), Bishop of Salisbury,
  154–55
Gilbert, John, father of John Gilbert Cooper,
  173
Gil Blas (Lesage, Alain-Renée), 490
Giles, Joseph, Birmingham artist, 292–93, 302,
  353–54, 388, 397–401, 414–15
Gilliver, Lawton, bookseller, 5, 38, 41, 45, 65,
  68, 423, 530
Gloucester, Bishop of, *see* Johnson, James
Glover, Richard (1712–85), *Boadicea* (1753),
  158–59; *Leonidas* (1737), 5, 38
Godolphin, Francis, 2nd Earl of Godolphin
  (1678–1766), 240
Goldwyre, Elizabeth, C. Pitt's trans. of Virgil's
  Aeneid, 76, 515, 528

"Good and Beauty, On" (Cooper, John Gilbert), 109–10

Gordon, Gilbert (d. 1789), 349–50; "To a young Lady . . .," 327–28, 350, 354–55

Gordon, Ian, 190, 309, 325

Gosling's bank, 206

Gosse, Edmund, 118

Gough, Lady, 3

Gough, Sir Henry, 3

Graham, Mr, 404

Grainger, James (1721?–1766), physician, 197, 371; *Letter to Tobias Smollett* (1759), 398–99; *Poetical Translation of the Elegies of Tibullus* (1759), 393, 395–400; "Solitude, an Ode," 196–99

Grand Magazine of Magazines, The (1750), 260, 390–91

Grant, William, Lord Prestongrange (1701?–64), 121–22

Grantham, Earl of, *see* D'Auverquerque, Henry

Granville, 1st Earl of, *see* Carteret, John

Granville, Ann, 69

Granville, Bernard, 69

Granville, Mary, 69

Gravelot (Hubert François Borguignon) (1669–1773), artist/engraver, 48

Graves (Greaves), Richard (1715–1804), 16, 19, 50, 52–53, 115, 157, **181**, 182, 187, 190, 192–93, 198, 222–23, 228–29, 231, 238–39, 257, 265, 274, 276, 292, 314, 349, 353–55, 358, 360, 392, 399, 413, 435, 464–66, 468, 469 (on Shenstone's pension), 503; editing of Shenstone's *Works*, 471–75, 486–87, 491–93; his living at Kilmersdon, 473; first meets W. Shenstone, 473; W. Shenstone's executor, 471–75, 482, 484–86, 490, 492–93; **Letters from**, 180–81, 232–35, 240–41, 255–57, 266–68, 293–94, 335–37, 359, 388–89, 407–9, 426–28, 456–57, 471–77, 484–87, 490–93, *549*; **Letters to**, 254–55, 296–97, *549*; Letter to James Dodsley, 493; **Works**: "Cabinet," 172, 180; Epilogue to RD's *Cleone*, 233–35, 240–43, 249–50, 255; *Festoon* (1766), 253, 482; "Heroines, or Modern Memoirs," 172, 180; "Lucy, or the Parting," 172; "Magpye and the Raven," 426–28, 449; "Mimic and the Countryman" [Phaedrus], 425–26; "Mr Allen, or the Great Plebeian," 482; "On Tully's Head . . . 1756," 222–23, 253, 255, 257–58; "Panacea: or the Grand Restorative," 172, 180; "The Parting," 180; "Patriot King; or George the Third," 456–57, 460; "Pepper-box," 172, 180–81; *Recollections of . . . Shenstone* (1788), 469; *Spiritual Quixote* (1772), 181, 297, 336–37,

392, 394, 432–34, 437; "To Mr Dodsley," 491–93; "To William Shenstone," 485; "Tuberose and the Sun Flower," 425–26, 449; "War proclaim'd at Brentford," 456–57, 460–61; "Written near Bath, 1755," 336–37

Graves, Mrs Richard, 233, 241, 255, 257, 267, 294, 359–60, 389, 408, 428, 472, 476, 484, 486, 491

Gray, James, 235, 382–83

Gray, Thomas (1716–71), xiv, 13–14, 112, **149**, 380, 549; **Letters from**, 148–49, *549*; **Letter to**, *549*; **Works**: *Elegy Written in a Country Church Yard* (1751), 29, 149, 161, 492; *Ode on a Distant Prospect of Eton College* (1747), 7, 112–113, 161; *Odes* ("Bard" and "Progress of Poetry," 1757), 31, 33, 45, 148–49, 161, 265–66, 286–87, 515–16, 549

Greek Theatre of Father Brumoy, The (Brumoy, Père), 361–62

Green, Amos (1734–1807), engraver, 145

Green, John (fl. 1758), engraver, 48, 304–5, 338–39, 350–51

Greenwood, Jeremy, 157

Grenville, George (1712–70), MP, 326; *see also* Berenger, Richard.

Grenville-Temple, Richard, Earl Temple (1711–79), 37, 326, 516

Grey, Harry, 4th Earl of Stamford (1715–68), 201–2, 211–12, 218–19, 342–43, 348, 373–74, 445, 447, 468–69, 475–76

Grey, Lady Jane (1537–54), *see* Keate, George

Grey, Hon. John, son of Harry Grey, 4th Earl of Stamford, 477

Griffith, Reginald Harvey, 65

Griffiths, Ralph (d. 1803), bookseller, 41(?), 516

Grignion, Charles (1717–1810), engraver, 48–49, 136, 173, 292–93, 344, 354, 401, 405–6, 412, 434, 438

Grotius, Hugo (Huig van Groot) (1583–1645), 379–81

Grove, Alice, 528

Guthrie, William (1708–70), *General History of England* (1744–51), 79–80; trans. of Riccoboni, *Historical and Critical Account of the Theatres in Europe* (1741), 516

"Halcyon and the Sparrow," *see* RD, "King-fisher and the Sparrow"

Hales, Stephen, DD (1677–1761), 128–29

Halifax, 2nd Earl of, *see* Dunk, George Montagu

Hall (? Sir James, 4th Baronet, 1761–1832), 447

Hamilton, Gavin, *see* Hamilton & Balfour

Hamilton, William (1704–54), *Poems on Several Occasions* (1761), 448–49

Hamilton & Balfour, Edinburgh booksellers, 224–25, 327–28
Hammelmann, Hans, and T. S. R. Boase, 48
Hammond, Anthony, 122
Hammond, Susan Walpole (1687–1763), 122
Hampartumian, Jane, 453
Hampton, James (1721–78), *General History of Polybius* (1756), 34, 46, 222, 516–17
Handel, George Frederick (1685–1759), *see* "Ode to Handel"
Handy, John, 146
Hanway, Jonas (1712–86), 49; *Historical Account of the British Trade over the Caspian Sea*, 49
Hardwicke, 1st Earl of, *see* Yorke, Philip
Hargreaves, Mr, 333
Harleian Collection of Old Plays, 6
Harleian Miscellany (1744–46), 135
Harley, Lady Margaret Cavendish, 66–67
Harris, George, DL, 505
Harris, James (1709–80), "Fragment of Chaucer," 295–96
Harris, John (*c.* 1690–1767), MP, Devon, 158, 192
Harris, Michael, 9
Harvey, John H., 422
Hatchett, William, *Fortunes Court of Requests* (1746), 30, 517
Haughton, Miss, actress, 200
Hau Kiou Choaan, *see* Percy, Thomas
Havard, William (1710?–78), actor, 373
Hawes, Lacey, bookseller, 39, 40, 81
Hawkesworth, John (1720–73), 14, 52, 221, 228, **236–37**, 549; **Letters from**, 235–37, 385–86, 399, 430–31, *549*; **Works**: *Adventurer* (1752–54), 237, 433–34 (on fables); "Ode to Death," 237; proposed *Compendium of the Geography, Natural History, and Antiquities of England*, 512, 515, 517; adaptation of Southerne's *Oroonoko* (1759), 430–31; Swift's *Works* (1755), 166
Hawkesworth, Mrs John, 236
Hawkins, George (d. 1780), bookseller, 41, 70, 116
Hawkins, Sir John (1719–89), 98
Hay, George, DL, 505
Hay, William (1695–1755), *Religio Philosophi* (1753), 517; *Select Epigrams* (of Martial), 517
Hayman, Francis (1708?–76), artist, 48–49, 107, 136–37, 398, 405–7, 460
Hayter, Thomas (1702–62), Bishop of Norwich, 154–55
Hayward, Thomas, tradesman, 150–51, 154
Hazard, Joseph, bookseller, 38
Hazeltine, Alice, 475 (previously unpublished W. Shenstone poems)
Hazen, Allen T., 381

Heathcote, Sir John (1689–1759), 280
Henderson, Mrs, proprietor of Bath boarding house, 473
Henderson, C., bookseller, 41
Henley, Robert (1708–72), 341
Henry, David (1710–92), bookseller, 41
Henry VII; or The Popish Imposter (Macklin, Charles), 92–93
Hentzner, Paul, *Journey into England in the year 1598* (1757), 320–21, 323, 328–29
Herbert, Nicholas (1706–75), 10, **287**; **Letter from**, *550*; **Letter to**, 286–87
Hernlund, Patricia, 35, 49 105
Herodotus (484?–425? BC), 27; *History*, 418; *see also* Gale, Thomas
"Heroines, or Modern Memoirs, The" (Graves, Richard), 172, 180
Heron, Robert, 450–51
Herring, Thomas, Archbishop of Canterbury (1747–57), 154
Hertford, Lord, *see* Seymour-Conway, Francis
Hervey, John, Baron of Ickworth (1696–1743), 9, 296; "Atticus and Eugenio," 298–99
Hetcher, James, Oxford bookseller, 44
Hett, Richard, bookseller, 38, 83, 513, 517
Hewitt, Richard, 224–25; "To Mr Thomas Blacklock," 225
Highfill, Philip, Jr, *see* Highfill, P., Burnim, K., and Langhans, E.
Highfill, P., Burnim, K., and Langhans, E., *Biographical Dictionary of Actors, Actresses . . .* (1963), 409
Highmore, Daniel, attorney, 509
Hildyard, John (d. 1757), York bookseller, 36, 416, 468
Hill, Charles J., 181, 297, 465
Hill, Sir John (1716?–75), 382, 385–87; *Account of . . . Cleone* (1758), 385–86, 392–94; *History of a Woman of Quality* (1751), 531; *The Rout* (1758), 386, 392–94
Hill, Richard, 108
Hill, Robert (1699–1777), 107, 108; *see also* Spence, Joseph, *Parallel in the Manner of Plutarch*
Hindley, Frederick Atherton, 373–74, 376–77, 505
Hinxman, Jane (née Morgan), wife of John Hinxman, 464–66, 468
Hinxman, John (d. 1760), RD apprentice and bookseller, 17, 36–37, 251–52, 415–17, 421–24, 468, 518, 521; death of, 464–65, 468
History and Antiquities of the Cathedral Church of Winchester (Gale, Samuel), 338–39
History of Lady Julia Mandeville, The, *see* Brooke, Frances
History of Scotland (Robertson, William), 411–12

Hitch, Charles (d. 1764), bookseller, 38–40, 94, 97, 222, 271–72, 300–1, 508–9, 512, 515, 518, 526

Hoadly, Benjamin the elder (1676–1761), Bishop of Winchester, 296, 352

Hoadly, Benjamin the younger (1706–57), physician, 295–96; *Suspicious Husband* (1747), 550

Hoadly, John (1711–76), **296** ; **Letters from**, 295–96, 341, 350–51, 483–84; **Letters to**, 298–99, 315; **Works**: "Bird of Passage," 295–96; epigrams from Martial, 295–96, 298–99, 341; "Epilogue to Shakespeare's first Part of King Henry IV," 295–96; "Epitaph," 295–96; "The Indolent," 315; "Mouse-trap," 295–96, 298–99; "Prologue to Comus," 295–96; "To Chloe," 296, 351–52; "To the Rev. Mr J. S.," 296; "Verses . . . Gate of the Louvre," 296; "Verses under the Prints of Mr Hogarth's *Rake's Progress*, 1735," 295–96, 298–99

Hodges, Sir James, bookseller, 39, 41, 81

Hodgetts, John, of Hagley, 238, 464–65; editor of Jago's *Poems*, 475; editor of Lady Luxborough's *Letters*, 335, 434, 475; Shenstone's executor, 52, 434, 474–75, 484–85, 490; designs on W. Shenstone's Leasowes, 476–77

Hodgetts, William, 19th century bookseller, 475

Hogan, Charles B., *see* Van Lennep, W. B.

Hogarth, William (1697–1764), artist, 48, 50, 295–96; *Rake's Progress* (1735), 295–96, 298–99

Holdsworth, Edward (1684–1746), 151, 526; *Muscipula, sive Cambro-muo-machia* (1709), 295–96

Hole, William, *Ornaments of Churches considered* (1761), 460

Holland, RD's trip to, 217

Holland, 1st Baron, *see* Fox, Henry

Homer, 69

Honour, *see* Brown, John

Honour (Whitehead, William), 42, 119

Hooke, Thomas (1693–1772), **69**; **Letter to**, 69

Hoole, John (1727–1803), *Jerusalem Delivered* (1763), 70

Horace (Quintus Horatius Flaccus) (65–8 BC), 27, 49, 84–85, 123, 218–19, 256, 407, 413, 514; *Odes*, 497; *Quinti Horatii Flacci Opera . . . incidit Joannes Pine* (1733–37), 146; *see also* Duncombe, John, and Baskerville, John

"Horace and Lydia" (Whistler, Anthony), 172

Houbraken, Mr, engraver, 344

Howard, Henry, Earl of Surrey (1517?–47), *Poems* (1728), 393, 395

Howe, Ellic, 395

Howe, Sir Richard, 4

Hucknell, John (1729–71), poet, *Avon* (1758), 46

Hudibras (Butler, Samuel), 354

Hughs, John (1703–71), printer, 35, 46, 75, 194–95, 197, 232, 377, 509–10, 518

Hull, Thomas (1728–1808), actor, manager, writer, 408–9, 434; *Select Letters . . . William Shenstone* (1778), 468

Hume, David (1711–76), 20, **175**, 179–80, 224–25, 403, 550; **Letters from**, 175–76, *550*

Hunt, George (1720?–98), MP, 254

Hurd, Richard (1720–1808), Bishop of Worcester, 93, 214

Hutcheson, Francis (1694–1746), *System of Moral Philosophy* (1755), 406–7

Hutton, Catherine, 238, 447, 489

Hutton, William, Birmingham bookseller, 447

Hylton, John Scott (d. 1793), 17, 19, 53, 115, 145, 190, 192–93, 197–98, 201, 204, 207, 209, 218, 223, 229–30, **238**, 242, 249, 257–58, 263, 270, 276–77, 285, 292–93, 302–3, 309, 314, 329, 353–55, 360, 362–64, 375, 385, 388, 398, 405, 426, 432, 434, 438, 445, 550; claims against W. Shenstone's estate, 485; "Tobacco-stopper Plot," 449; **Letters from**, 237–39, 260–62, 315–17, 337, 339–41, 358, 370–71, 400–1, 447–49, *550*; **Letters to**, 239, 343–46, 348–50, *550*; **Works**: "Indian Eclogue," 292–93, 302–3, 309, 316, 345; "True Resignation," 332, 334, 344–45, 358; "Verses, written at the Gardens of William Shenstone, Esq.," 371, 373, 375–76

"Hymn to Health" (Cooper, John Gilbert), 99–100

Hymn to Liberty (Cooke, Thomas), 93

Ibbot, Benjamin (1680–1725), "Fit of the Spleen," 351–52

Ibbott, Sarah (d. 1825), actress, 407, 409

Imber, Captain, 338–39

"In a Root House" (Shenstone, William), 171–72

"In a Shady Valley" (Shenstone, William), 171–72

Indenick, Mr, 472

"Indian Eclogue," *see* Hylton, John Scott

"Indolent, The" (Hoadly, John), 315

Inge, Edward, attorney, 316, 340–41

Inoculation (smallpox), 203, 267

Inquiry into the Beauties of Painting (Webb, Daniel), 438, 465

Inspector, The, 260

Institution of a Prince, see Duguet, Abbé
Introduction to Languages, An (Bayley, Anselm), 361–62
Ireland, Samuel (d. 1800), 391
"Irregular Ode after Sickness" (Shenstone, William), 314

Jackson, John (1686–1763), 140–41, 370, 372; *Chronological Antiquities* (1752), 136, 142; *Treatise on the Improvements made in the Art of Criticism . . . by a celebrated Hypercritic* [William Warburton] (1748), 140–42, 214; *Defense of* (former), 141
Jackson, Thomas (d. 1759), Shenstone's servant, 231, 348–49, 400–1, 485
Jackson, Wallace, 248
Jackson, William (d. 1795), Oxford printer, 44
Jackson's Oxford Journal (1753–), 184
Jacobite Rebellion, 87–90, 92–93, 102; *see also* Charles Edward, the "Young Pretender"
Jacobitism, 183–85
Jago, Richard (1715–81), 19, 61, 115, 190, 192–93, 198, **201**, 238, 302, 348; **Letters from**, 200–1, 297–98, 303–4, 309–10, 353–54, 389–91; **Letter to**, 301–2; **Works**: description of Shenstone's Leasowes, 435, 467; *Edge-hill* (1767), 467, 469; "Essay on Electricity," 115–16, 201, 394, 396; *Poems Moral and Descriptive* (1784), 201, 391; "Swallows," 303
Jamaica, 203
James, (Elizabeth?), bookseller, 41
Jameson, Richard, 403, **404–5**; **Letter from**, 404–5
Jarvis, Charles (1675?–1739), trans. *Don Quixote*, 511, 518; *see* Jarvis, Penelope
Jarvis, Penelope, wife of Charles Jarvis, assignment of *Don Quixote*, 518
Jeffreys, John (1706–66), MP, 495, 497
Jennyns, Soame (1704–87), 9, 14, 197; *Miscellaneous Pieces* (1761), 450, 453
Jersey, Lord, *see* Villiers, William
"Jessy," *see* Shenstone, William
Jestin, Catherine, 122
Jew Bill, 184
"John Grub," *see* Williams, Sir Charles Hanbury
Johnson, A. F., 145
Johnson, J. and S., booksellers, 41
Johnson, James, Bishop of Gloucester (d. 1759), 154–55
Johnson, Samuel (1709–84), xiv, 9, 12, 18, 27, 34, 48 (RD, "Doddy" his patron), 51, 70, 86, 94, **97**, 99, 102, 221–22, 225, 382–84, 433, 463–64 (friend of Baretti), 504; pension, 446, 469; **Letters from**, 97, 106;

Works: *A Dictionary of the English Language* (1755), 14, 18–19, 97–98, 106, 259, 304–5, 319, 518; *Irene* (1749), 18, 33, 98, 383, 518; *London* (1738), 5, 18, 29, 31, 34, 38, 97, 518; *London Chronicle*, 15, 260, 519; *Plays of William Shakespeare* (1765), 406–7, 469; *Rambler* (1750–52), 521; *Rasselas, Prince of Abissinia* (1759), 18, 34, 45, 98, 260, 422; *Vanity of Human Wishes* (1749), 18, 31, 33, 97–98, 518; "Vision of Theodore," 8
Johnston, Joseph, Dumfries surgeon, 402–3
Johnston, Sarah (Blacklock, Mrs Thomas), 402–3
Johnston, William, bookseller, 41, 45, 98, 260, 519
Jollyffe, John, bookseller, 38, 41, 509, 517, 519
Jones, Henry (1721–70), *Earl of Essex* (1753), 34, 519
Jonson, Ben (1573?–1637), *Eastward Ho*, 29
Journal of Newspaper and Periodical History, xv
Journey into England in the year 1598, see Hentzner, Paul
Julian (Warburton, William), 135–36, 143–44
Juvenal (Decius Junius Juvenalis) (1st–2nd cent. AD), 27

Kahrl, George M., *see* Kahrl, G. and Anderson, D.; *also* Little, D. and Kahrl, G.
Kahrl, G. and Anderson, D., *Garrick Collection of Old English Plays*, 6
Karl I, Duke of Braunschweig (1735–80), 165–66, 171
Keasbury, William (1726–97), actor, 407, 409
Keate, George (1729–97), friend of George Steevens, 457–59; *Alps* (1763), 459; *Ancient and Modern Rome. A Poem* (1760), 438–39; *Epistle from Lady Jane Grey to Lord Guilford Dudley* (1762), 457–58; *Ruins of Netley Abbey* (1764), 459; *Short Account of . . . Geneva* (1761), 459; *Works* (1781), 459
Kendall, Mr, 348
Kenrick, William (1725?–79), *Epistles Philosophic and Moral* (1759), 393, 395
Kent, William, designer, 48
Kerry, natural history of, *see* Smith, Charles
Kilmarnock, 4th Earl of, *see* Boyd, William
Kimpel, Ben D., *see* Eaves, T. C. Duncan
King, William (1685–1763), DCL, 184
"King-fisher and the Sparrow, The," *see* RD
Kinnersley, Thomas, publisher of *Grand Magazine of Magazines* (1750), 260, 263
Klopstock, Friedrich Gottlieb (1724–1803), German poet, *The Messiah*, 159–61, 165–66, 170–71
Knapton, James, bookseller, 23, 39, 45

Knapton, John (d. 1770), bookseller, 5, 38–39, 41, 49, 97–98, 135–36, 212–14, 216–17, 518–19

Knapton, Paul, bookseller, 38, 41, 49, 97–98, 216–17, 518–19 .

Knight, Edward, 397

Knight, Henrietta St John, Lady Luxborough (d. 1756), 19, 77, 80, **123**, 162, 179, 182, 192–93, 197, 201–2, 238, 335, 485; **Letters from**, 123, *550*; "Written at a *Ferme Ornee* near Birmingham," 172, 189–90, 192; *Letters* (1775), 434

Knight, Robert, Baron Luxborough (1702–72), 77, 123

Kolb, Gwin J., 18

La Bruyère, Jean de (1645–96), *Caractères* (1688), 112–13

"Lady's Visit" (Shenstone, William, "Daphne's Visit"), 189

La Fontaine, Jean de (1621–95), *Fables choises misis in vers* (1668), 396–97, 428

la Motte, Antoine Houdart de (1672–1731), *Fables nouvelles . . . avec un discours sur la fable* (1719), 16, 395–97, 433, 435, 440–42, 449

Lancaster, Nathaniel (1701–75), *Plan of an Essay upon Delicacy* (1748), 123, 466, 468

Langbaine, Gerard, *Lives and Characters of the English Dramatic Poets*, 6

Langhans, Edward, *see* Highfill, P., Burnim, K., and Langhans, E.

Langton, Bennet (1737–1801), 12, 330

La Place, Pierre Antoine, *La laideur aimable* (trans. Scott, Sarah), 521, 524

Lavery, J., Mr, 418

Lavington, George, (1684–1762), Bishop of Exeter, 154–55

Layng, Henry, trans. of Battista's *Circe* (1745), 519

Layton, C., Eton bookseller, 43

Lea, Fernando Dudley, 5th Baron Dudley (d. 1757), 193–94, 238–39, 316–17, 348

Leake, James the elder (d. 1764), Bath bookseller, 43, 264, 273, 420, 464–65, 485–86

Leake, Stephen Martin (1702–73), 459–60

Le Dran, Henri François, *Operations in Surgery*, 512, 515

Lee, William Phillips, 422

Legge, Henry Bilson (1708–64), Chancellor of Exchequer, 446

Legge, William, 2nd Earl of Dartmouth (1731–1801), 468, 470

Le Glay, Andre, 152

Leicester carrier, 134–35

Leicester House, 21, 183, 319

Leipzig, 160–61

Leland, John (1691–1766), *Reflections on the late Lord Bolingbroke's Letters* (1753), 154–55

LeNeve, John, *Fasti Ecclesiae Anglicanae*, xxiii

Lennox, Charles, 3rd Duke of Richmond and Lennox (1735–1806), 419–20

Lennox, Charlotte (1720–1804), 463; *Female Quixote* (1752), 400–1; *Greek Theatre of Father Brumoy* (1760), 362

Lesage, Alain-Renée (1668–1747), *Gil Blas* (1715), 490

Letter to Tobias Smollett (Grainger, James), 398–99

Letters concerning Taste, *see* Cooper, John Gilbert

Letters from a Persian in England (Lyttelton, Sir George), 112–13

"Letters from Smyrna" (Lisle, Thomas), 352–53

Letters of Mr Alexander Pope, *see* Pope, Alexander

Letters of Pliny the Consul, The, *see* Melmoth, William

Letters on the Study and Use of History (Bolingbroke), *see* Leland, John

Lewis, J. and J., printers, 37, 45

Lewis, L., RD's apprentice, 37, 516

Lewis, W(illiam?), bookseller, 41

Lewis, Wilmarth Sheldon, xiv, Horace Walpole's *Correspondence*, 55

Life and Opinions of Tristram Shandy, The, *see* Sterne, Laurence

Life of Socrates, *see* Cooper, John Gilbert

Ligonier, Edward, 2nd Viscount Ligonier (d. 1782), 419–20

Lincoln, Bishop of, *see* Thomas, John

Lincoln, 9th Earl of, *see* Clinton, Henry Fiennes

Lincoln's Inn Fields Theatre, 5

Lind, James, MD, *Treatise of the Scurvy* (1754), 202, 204

Lintot, Bernard (1675–1736), bookseller, 23, 65, 530

Lintot, Henry (1709–58), bookseller, 214

Lisle, Edward, *Observations on Husbandry* (1756), 195, 232

Lisle, Thomas (1709–67), **195**; **Letters from**, 195, 232, 352–53; "Letters from Smyrna," 352–53; "To Venus. A Rant, 1732," 352–53; *see also* Lisle, Edward

Lisle, Mrs Thomas, 232

Little, David M., *see* Little, D. and Kahrl, G.

Little, D. and Kahrl, G., *Letters of David Garrick*, 245, 384

Lives of the Admirals (Campbell, John), 80

Livie, John, classicist, Baskerville's *Horace*, 459–60

Lloyd's Evening Post (1757–), 385–86, 399

Lombard, Daniel, *Succinct History of Ancient and Modern Persecutions* (1747), 119

London, Bishop of, *see* Sherlock, Thomas
London Chronicle, or Universal Evening Post
(1757–1823), xxiv, 15, 51, 56, 59, 184,
258–60, 279, 329, 339, 371, 386–87, 414–
15; **RD's letter to**, 498–99; *see also* RD
London and Its Environs (RD), 44, 448–49
London Evening Post (1727–   ), xxiv, 15, 35,
58–59, 182–85, 260, 499, 519
London Gazette, The (1666–   ), 87, 89
London Magazine, The (1732–   ), xxiv, 15,
327–28, 349, 373, 375–76, 420, 460–61,
519–20
London Stage, 1660–1800, The, see Van Lennep,
W. B.
Longman, Thomas (1699–1765), bookseller,
41, 94, 97, 508–9, 518, 520; sales
catalogues, 531–33
Longman, Thomas II (d. 1797), bookseller, 41,
518; sales catalogues, 531–33
Lonsdale, Lord, *see* Lowther, Henry
Lords, House of, 5, 54
Loughborough, 1st Baron, *see* Wedderburne,
Alexander
"Love and Honour" (Shenstone, William),
473–74
"Love Songs" (Shenstone, William), 315
Lovibond, Edward (1724–75), 197; "Tears of
Old May-Day," 197
Lowe, William, artist, survey of Shenstone's
Leasowes, 434–35
Lowth, Robert (1710–87), 9, 13, 16, 47, 53, 75,
89, **147**, 197, 550; editing Shenstone's
Works, 472, 474–75; RD's *Select Fables of
Esop*, 392, 394, 425, 428–30, 433, 435,
440, 449, 455; **Letters from**, 147–51,
153–55, 287–91, 294, 304–5, 342, 346,
350–51, 361–62, 440, 446, 461, *550*;
Letters to, 307, *550*; **Works**: *De sacra
poesi Hebraeorum* (1753), 147, 149–51,
153–54, 199–200, 461, 547; "The
Diamond and the Loadstone," 430; "Dog
and the Crocodile," 429–30; "Ostrich and
the Pelican," 429; *Sermon preached at St
Nicholas Church* (1757), 287–88, 290–91;
Short Introduction to English Grammar (1762),
429–30, 440, 446, 461–62, 507–8, 520;
"Toad and the Ephemeron," 430; *William
of Wykeham* (1758), 287–91, 294, 304–5,
338–39, 342, 346, 350–51, 361–62
Lowth, Mrs Robert, 290, 307, 338, 346, 440,
446, 461
Lowth, William (1707–95), 440
Lowther, Henry, 3rd Viscount Lonsdale
(d. 1751), 72, 93 ("Ode to")
Lowther, Hon. Jane, 4, 65
Lucanus, Marcus Annaeus (Lucan) (AD
39–65), 27; *Pharsalia*, 379–81; *see also*

Bentley, Richard, the elder and the
younger
"Lucy, or the Parting" (Graves, Richard), 172
Lumley-Saunderson, Thomas, 3rd Earl of
Scarborough (1691?–1752), 128
Luxborough, Lady, *see* Knight, Henrietta St
John
Lycidas (Milton, John), 112, 492
"Lysander to Cloe" (Shenstone, William), 318,
320
Lyttelton, Sir George (1709–73), 7, 9, 15,
21–22, 157–58, 162–**63**, 175, 182, 211–12,
260, 283–84, 286, 292, 319, 344, 432, 437,
444, 468, 470, 550; **Letter from**, *550*;
Letters to, 176–78, 182–85; **Works**:
Discourse on Providence (1747), 178;
*Observations on the Conversion and Apostleship
of St Paul* (1747), 29, 170, 178, 316;
Observations on the Life of Cicero (1741), 119;
Letters from a Persian in England (1735),
112–13; *To the memory of A Lady: A Monody*
(1747), 163
Lyttelton, Sir Richard (1718–70), KB, 371;
Shenstone's "To the Hon . . .," 472–73
Lyttelton, William Henry (1724–1808), 162–63

MacCarthy, William, 37, 509
"Machinae Gesticulantes" (Addison, Joseph),
91
McKee, Robert A., 455
McKenzie, Donald F., 15
MacKenzie, Henry, biography of Thomas
Blacklock, 403, 405
Macklin, Charles (1697?–1797), actor and
manager, *Henry VII; or The Popish Imposter*
(1746), 92–93
McVeigh, S. W., 444
Magazine of Magazines (1750–51), 149
"Magpye and the Raven, The" (Graves,
Richard), 426–28, 449
Mahony, Robert, 101, 118
Maidstone, 113
Maidstone stagecoach, 112
Major, Thomas (1720–99), 48
Male, James, ironmonger, 238
Mallam, Duncan, *Letters of William Shenstone*,
xxiv, 53, 460
Mallet, David (1705–65), poet, editor of
Bolingbroke's *Letters on the Spirit of
Patriotism . . .* (1749), 215–17; *Amyntor and
Theodora, or the Hermit* (1747), 550; *Works*
(1759), 412–13
"Malvern Spa, 1757" (Perry, John), 270, 274
Mandeville, Lady Julia, *see History of Lady Julia
Mandeville*
Manners, John, 3rd Duke of Rutland
(1696–1779), 173

Mansfield, city of, 4
Mant, Richard (1776–1848), Bishop of Down,
    86
Mantuan, *see* Spagnola, Baptista
Marlborough, Duchess of, *see* Churchill, Sarah
"Marplot" (in Suzannah Centlivre's *The Busy-
    Body*), 12, 381–83, 387
Marsh, Charles, bookseller, 38, 41
Marshall, George H., 74
Martial (Marcus Valerius Martialis, *c.* AD
    40–102), 27; epigrams of, *see* Hoadly,
    John, and Hay, William
Martin, Sylvia I., 455
Martindale, W., 505
Maslen, Keith, 65–66, 197, 508
Mason, James (1710–*c.* 1780), engraver, 293
Mason, John (1706–63), **Letter from**, 167–68;
    Essay on Elocution (1748), 167–68
Mason, William (1724–97), 13, 44, **112**, 120,
    492; **Letters from**, 111–14, 219, *550*;
    Caractacus (1759), 29, 112; *Isis* (1749), 112;
    Musaeus (1747), 7, 48, 111–14, 166; *Odes*
    ["To Memory," "On Melancholy," "On
    the Fate of Tyranny," "To
    Independency"] (1756), 44, 112, 219
Massey, James, painter, **Letters from**, 122,
    550
Massinger, Philip (1583–1640), *New Way to Pay
    Old Debts*, 29
Maurice, 379
Mead, Richard (1673–1754), MD, 172–73
Medine, Peter, 178
Melmoth, William (1710–99), 16, 37, 53,
    106–7, 228, 369, 381–82, 437–40, 446,
    464–66, 468; death of wife, 454–55; editing
    Shenstone's *Works*, 472–75, 486–87; RD's
    Select Fables, 392, 395, 425, 449, 455;
    Letters from, 106–8, 129, 417–19,
    429–30, 442–45, 461–62, *550–51*; **Letters
    to**, 251–52, 263, *551*; **Works**: *Letters of . . .
    Cicero to Several of his Friends* (1753), 30–32,
    34, 45, 106, 273, 368, 521; *Letters of Pliny
    the Consul* (1747), 40, 45, 47, 106–7, 129,
    266–67, 520; *Letters on Several Subjects* ("Sir
    Thomas Fitzoborne") (1747–49), 29–30,
    45, 106, 213–14, 508, 520; trans. of
    Quintilian's *Dialogues upon Eloquence*,
    520
Melmoth, Mrs William, 437, 443, 454–55 (her
    death)
Melpomene, see RD
Memoirs and Letters of Ulick de Burgh (Smith,
    John), 30, 277
Memoirs of the Court of Augustus (Blackwell,
    Thomas), 217–18, 509
Menagerie, 391
Mendes, Moses (d. 1758), 184, 293, 300;

Letter to, 299–300; *Collection . . . of Poetry*
    (1767), 300
Mendes, Solomon (d. 1762?), **82**, 184; **Letter
    from**, *551*; **Letters to**, 81–82, 166–67, *551*
Meres, John (d. 1761), printer, 184
Merrick, James (1720–69), poet, 492; *Poems on
    Sacred Subjects* (1763), 492
Merrill, Thomas and J., Cambridge
    booksellers, 44
Messiah, The, see Klopstock, Friedrich Gottlieb
Methodism, 390
Meziriac, Claude-Gaspar Bachet de
    (1581–1638), life of Aesop, 448
Michaelis, Johann David (1717–91), Professor
    at Göttingen, 461
Microscope Made Easy, The, see Baker, Henry
Middleton, Conyers (1683–1750), *Free Inquiry
    into the Miraculous Powers . . . in the Christian
    Church* (1749), 129
Midwife, or the Old Woman's Magazine
    ([1750]–53), 137–38
Midwinter, Daniel the younger (d. 1757),
    bookseller, 531
Millan, John (d. 1784), bookseller, 41
Millar, Andrew (1707–68), bookseller, 9, 34,
    38–40, 48, 97, 116, 149–50, 185–86, 206,
    212–13, 215–17, 287–88, 397, 415, 423,
    508–9, 511, 518, 521, 526, 529, 533
Miller, Mr, engraver, 344
Miller, Mr, vocalist, 371
Miller, Philip (1691–1771), *Gardener's Kalendar*
    (1732, 1760), 448–49, 510, 531
Milton, John (1608–74), 112, 160, 408, 430;
    Comus, 112; *L'Allegro*, 112, 330–31; *Lycidas*,
    112, 492; *Paradise Lost*, 5, 112, 267–68,
    393, 395, 409–10, 412–13; *Paradise Regained*
    (1758), 410 (*see also* Calton, Jacob;
    Dobson, William; Newton, Thomas)
Milton, Lord, *see* Fletcher, Andrew
"Milton's Muse" (Calton, Jacob), 98–99
"Mimic and the Countryman, The" (Graves,
    Richard), 425–26
Minden, Battle of, 419–20
Mirabeau, Victor de Ruguetti, *L'Ami dès
    hommes* (1756–60), 377–78
*Miscellaneous Works in Prose and Verse of Mrs
    Elizabeth Rowe*, 83
Modern Reasoners, The, see RD
Monkman, Kenneth, 417, 422–23
Monmouth carrier, 360
Monnaies en or et en argent qui composent . . .
    (Duval, Valentin Jameray), 271
Monsey, Messenger (1693–1788), physician,
    239–40
Montagu, Lady Barbara, 521
Montagu, Elizabeth (1720–1800), **303**; **Letter
    from**, *550*; **Letter to**, 303

Montagu, Richard, bookbinder, 388, 393, 395
Montaigne, Michel Eyquem (1533–92), *Essays of* (1759), 398–99; *see also* Cotton, Charles
Monthly Review (1749–), xxiv, 16, 131–35, 144, 200, 204, 277, 448–49, 461
Moody, Mr, Birmingham toymaker, 449
Moore, Edward (1712–57), 197; *Fables for the Female Sex* (1744), 15; *Gamester* (1753), 147–48, 150, 187; *Gil Blas* (1751), 148; *Poems, Fables, and Plays* (1756), 395; *World* (1753–56) by "Adam Fitzadam," 14, 33–34, 37, 42, 147, 243, 252, 394, 396, 521
Moore, Mrs Edward, 394
Moore, Sarah, 462–63
Mordaunt, Charles, 3rd Earl of Peterborough (1658–1735), 69
More, Hannah (1745–1833), 366
Morelly, Mons., *Essai sur la coeur humain* (1745), 104–5; *Essai sur l'esprit humain* (1743), 104–5
Morgan, McNamara (d. 1762), *Philoclea* (1754), 34, 45, 521
Morley, A., bookseller, 41
Morris, Valentine (d. 1789), 424–26
Morton, Charles (1716–99), MD, *Orbis eruditae literatura . . . supplementis* (1759), 440
Mosley, Charles (fl. 1745–70), 48
Mosley, James, 145
"Mouse-trap, The" (Hoadly, John), 295–96, 298–99
Munby, A. N. L., 534
Mundy, Wrightson (1712?–62), MP, 131
Murphy, Arthur (1727–1805), 420; *Life of David Garrick* (1801), 148
Musae Anglicanae, 91, 296 (*see also* Addison, Joseph; Brown, John; Frowde, Philip; Holdsworth, Edward)
Musaeus: a Monody to the Memory of Mr Pope, see Mason, William
Muscipila, sive Cambro-muo-machia (Holdsworth, Edward), 295–96
Museum: or, Literary and Historical Register, see RD
Musgrave, Sir William, *Obituary Prior to 1800*, xxii, xxiv
"Musophilus" (pseud. of John Gilbert Cooper), 99–100, 109
Mutual Connexion between Religious Truth and Civil Freedom (Brown, John), 103–4
"Mutual Love" (RD), 138–39
Mytton, Mrs, 470–71

Namier, Sir Lewis, and John Brook, *History of Parliament*, xxii, xxiv
"Nancy of the Vale," *see* Shenstone, William
Nash, Richard "Beau" (1674–1762), history of Bath, 176, 178

National Union Catalogue, xiii
Natural History of Cornwall, The (Borlase, William), 400–1
Nelick, Frank C., 374
Neuhoff, Baron de, King Theodore of Corsica (1725?–56), **152–53**, 161; **Letter from,** 151–53
New College, Oxford, 304, 338
New General Collection of Voyages and Travels (1743–46), 80
New General History of England (1744), 80
New, Melvin and Joan, 423–24
Newbery, John (1713–67), bookseller, 44, 101, 119, 138
Newbolt, Mr, 351
Newbury carrier, 232
Newcastle carrier, 289, 346
Newcastle-upon-Tyne, 1st Duke of, *see* Pelham-Holles, Thomas
Newgate Prison, 300
Newstead Abbey, Notts., 418–19
Newton, Thomas, Bishop of Bristol (1704–82), 99, 109, 154, 423; *Paradise Lost . . . with Notes of Various Authors* (1749), 78, 99, 106–7, 147–48, 393, 395, 400, 409–10, 412–13; *Paradise Regained* (1753), 147–48, 150
Nibblett, Stephen (1726–66), 77
Nichols, John, 46; *Literary Anecdotes* (1812–16), 94–95
Nicholson, John, *Il Decamerone* (1702, 1712), 70
Nicoll, William, bookseller, 526
Night Thoughts, see Young, Edward
"Nightingale" (Strada, Famiano), 91
Nobility, On, see Whitehead, William
Noble, Francis (d. 1792), bookseller, 38, 41
Northampton carrier (Mr Cooke), 372
Northampton Mercury (1720–), 368–70
Northumberland, 1st Duke of, *see* Percy, Hugh Smithson
Northumberland, Lady, *see* Seymour, Elizabeth
Norton, Thomas (1582–1634) and Thomas Sackville (1536–1608), *Gorboduc*, 29
Norwich, Bishop of, *see* Hayter, Thomas
Nottingham stagecoach, 134–35
Nourse, John, bookseller, 38, 41
Nova Acta Eruditorum (Leipzig), 199–200
Nugent, Robert, Earl Nugent (1702–88), 522; *Ode to the Right Honourable Lord Viscount Lonsdale* (1745), 93
Nutt, Richard (d. 1780), printer, 184–85, 519, 522

Observations on Husbandry (Lisle, Edward), 195, 232
Observations on the Antiquities . . . Cornwall (Borlase, William), 400–1

Observations on the History and Evidence of the Resurrection, see West, Gilbert
Ode on a Distant Prospect of Eton College, see Gray, Thomas
"Ode on Rural Elegance," *see* Shenstone, William
"Ode to a Young Lady" (Shenstone, William), 171
"Ode to the Country Gentlemen of England" (Akenside, Mark), 353–54
"Ode to Handel" (1745), 117–18
"Ode to Health," *see* Shenstone, William
"Ode to Night" (Parrott, Charles), 197
Ode to the Rt. Honourable Lord Viscount Lonsdale (Nugent, Robert), 93
Ode to the Rt. Honourable the Earl of Huntingdon (Akenside, Mark), 8
"Ode. Written 1739," *see* Shenstone, William
Odes, see Mason, William
"Oeconomy, A Rhapsody" (Shenstone, William), 473–74
"Of the Knowledge of the World" (anon.), 96
Ogilby, John (1600–76), *Aesop's Fables* (1651), 411; *Virgil* (1654), 441–42
Ogilvie, Rev. James (1695–1776), 247–48
Ogilvie, John (1733–1813), **248**; **Letter from**, 247–48; *Day of Judgment* (1753), 248; *Essay on Lyric Poetry*, 248; *Poems on Several Subjects* (1762), 247–48
"On a small Building in the Gothick Taste" (Shenstone, William), 171–72
"On Melancholy," *see* Mason, William
"On Religion" (Shenstone, William), 486–87
"On Sir Robert Walpole's Birth-day" (Dodington, George Bubb), 196–99
"On Solitude and Society" (Cooper, John Gilbert), 105, 110–11
"On Taste" (Shenstone, William), 486–87
"On the Discovery of an Echo at Edgbaston" (White, Miss), 307–9
"On the Fate of Tyranny," *see* Mason, William
"On the Folly of Noblemen and Gentlemen's Paying their Debts" (Cooper, John Gilbert), 109–10
"On the Polite Arts," *see* Cooper, John Gilbert, *Museum*
"On True and False Religion" (Cooper, John Gilbert), 109
"On Tully's Head . . . 1756," *see* Graves, Richard
Orbis eruditae literatura, see Bernard, Edward; *also,* Morton, Charles
Orchard Street Theatre, Bath, 407–9
Ornaments of Churches considered, The (Hole, William), 460
Osborn, John, bookseller, 532–33

Osborne, Mary Godolphin, Duchess of Leeds (1723–64), 228, **240**; **Letter to**, 239–40
Osborne, Thomas (d. 1767), bookseller, 40
"Ostrich and the Pelican, The" (Lowth, Robert), 429
Oswald, James (d. 1769), musician, 186–88
Otway, Thomas (1652–85), dramatist, 401
Oudendorp, Franciscus Van, *Caius Suetonius Tranquillus* (1751), 400–1
Oudry, J. B., illustrator, 397
Outing, Captain, 123
Overton, Henry, print seller, 107–8
Owen, William (d. 1793), bookseller, 41

Paget, Thomas Catesby, Baron Paget (1689–1742), 509
"Pain and Patience" (RD), 73
Paltock, Robert, *Life of Peter Wilkins* (1751), 31, 522
"Panacea: or the Grand Restorative" (Graves, Richard), 172, 180
"Panegyric on Ale, A" (Warton, Thomas), 351–52
pantomime, 6
Paradise Lost . . . with Notes of Various Authors, see Newton, Thomas
Paradisus Amissus . . . Latine redditum (Dobson, William), 77–78
Pardoe, F. E., 145, 273
Parkes, Nicholas, 232
Parrott, Charles, 197 ("Ode to Night")
Parsons, Mrs Clement, 159
Parsons, (John?), 86–87
Parsons, Philip (1729–1812), schoolmaster, **429**; **Letter from**, 429; **Letter to**, *551; World* (No. 169), 429
"Parting, The" (Graves, Richard), 180
"Pastoral Ballad," *see* Shenstone, William
"Pastoral Ode, to . . . Richard Lyttelton" (Shenstone, William), 257–58, 472–73
"Patriot King; or George the Third, The" (Graves, Richard), 456–57, 460
Patton, F., engraver, 291, 339
Paul, Sir James Balfour, *Scots Peerage*, xxiv
Paulet, Charles, 3rd Duke of Bolton (1685–1754), 154–55
Payne, John (d. 1787), bookseller, 41, 237, 522 (*Adventurer*)
Payne, Oliver, bookseller, 38, 41
Peele [John?], 177–78
Peele, John, bookseller, 522, 528
Pelham, Henry (1695?–1754), statesman, 168, 184
Pelham-Holles, Thomas, 1st Duke of Newcastle-upon-Tyne (1693–1768), 260, 262, 290–91, 326, 497
Pemberton, Henry, bookseller, 38, 509, 522

Pemberton, John, bookseller, 509, 522
Pendarves, Mary Delany (née Granville) (1700–88), 69
Penn, Anne, mother of W. Shenstone, 212
Pentalogia, sive Tragoediarum Graecarum Delectus (Burton, John), 361–62
"Pepper-box, The" (Graves, Richard), 172, 180–81
Percy, Hugh Smithson, 1st Duke (3rd creation) of Northumberland (1715–86), 394
Percy, Thomas (1729–1811), 3, 8, 14, 16, 19, 157, 207, 238, 293, **324**, 348, 350, 393, 395, 398–99, 411, 439, 467, 477, 485; on Jago's *Edgehill*, 469; prank on John Scott Hylton, 449; Shenstone's pension, 469; **Letters to**, 323–25, *551*; **Works**: "Cervantes, A Song Paraphrased from . . .," 323–25; "Cynthia," 323, 325; description of Shenstone's Leasowes, 435, 467; *Hau Kiou Choaan* (1761), 58, 324, 432, 434, 437, 450–51, 453–54, 523; *Matrons* (1772), 324; *Miscellaneous Pieces Relating to the Chinese* (1762), 324; *Reliques of Ancient English Poetry* (1765), 3, 293, 324, 348, 466, 468–69, 522; *Five Pieces of Runic Poetry* (1763), 324, 522; *Song of Solomon* (1764), 324; "Toad and the Gold-fish," 449
Percy, Mrs Thomas, 467
Perry, John (*c.* 1730–80), 249–50, 254, 257–58; **Letter from**, 269–70; "Malvern Spa, 1757," 270, 274
Persefield, Monmouthshire, 424–26
Persius (Aulus Persius Flaccus) (AD 34–62), 27
"Persuasive to Erect an Academy for Lying" (Cooper, John Gilbert), 105–6, 109
Peterborough, Countess of, *see* Robinson, Anastasia
Peterborough, 3rd Earl of, *see* Mordaunt, Charles
Pettit, Henry, 116, 205–6
Phaedrus (1st century AD), 428 (*see also* Graves, Richard; Shenstone, William)
Pharsalia, see Lucanus, Marcus
"Philaretes" (pseud. for John Gilbert Cooper's pieces in RD's *Museum*)
Philips, Ambrose (1675?–1749), *Briton* (1722), 523, 528; *Humphrey, Duke of Gloucester* (1723), 523, 528
Phillipps, Sir Thomas (1792–1872), antiquary, 534
Phillips, Theresia Constantia (1709–65), courtesan, 180–81
Philosophical Enquiry into the Origin of our Ideas of the Sublime and the Beautiful, see Burke, Edmund
Picquet, Mr, engraver, 344
Pilkington, Laetitia (1712–50), 124, 180–81

Pilkington, Matthew (1705–65), **124; Letters from**, 124, 169–70; *Evangelical History and Harmony* (1747), 124; *Letter to Mr West relating to his Observations on the Resurrection*, 169–70
Pindar (518?–438 BC), 27, 30, 40; *see also* West, Gilbert
Pine, John (1690–1756), engraver; *see* Horace
Pinto, Mr, vocalist, 371
Pinto, Ferdinand Mendez, *Voyages and Adventures of* (1663), 81–82
Pirie, Valerie, 152
Pitt, Christopher (1699–1748), **75**, 89, 108, 111, 114–15, 166; **Letters from**, 74–80, *551*; *Aeneid* (1740), 30, 32, 46, 74–79, 326, 515, 523, 526, 528; *Vida's Art of Poetry* (1726, 1742), 77–78; *Works*, 76
Pitt, George, 1st Baron Rivers (1722?–1803), 75
Pitt, John (1706–87), MP, 75–76
Pitt, Lucy, **Letters from**, 108–9, 111, 114–15, *551*
Pitt, William, 1st Earl of Chatham (1708–78), 259, 326
Pittock, Joan, 86, 191, 347
Pixell, John Prynne Parkes (1725–84), 19, 115, 207, **212**, 218–19, 353–54, 401; **Letters from**, 210–12, 307–9, 414–15, 487; *Collection of Songs, with their Recitatives and Symphonies . . .* (1759), 414–15; "Transcrib'd from the Rev. Mr Pixell's Parsonage Garden," 308–9
Pixell, Mrs (née White), 309, 396–97; "On the Discovery of an Echo at Edgbaston," 307–9
Plan of an Essay on Delicacy, see Lancaster, Nathaniel
Plato (*c.* 427–347 BC), 27, 118, 134
Plautus (*c.* 250–184 BC), 326
Pleasures of Melancholy, see Warton, Thomas
"Plebian Politicians, The" (Cooper, John Gilbert), 109
Pliny, the younger (Caius Plinius Caecilius) (AD 62?–113), 27; *see* Melmoth, William
Plomer, H. R. et al., *Dictionary of the Printers and Booksellers*, xxii, xxiv
Plutarchii, Demosthenis et Ciceronis vitae parallelae, see Barton, Philip
Pococke, Richard (1704–65), *Description of the East*, 94
Poems on Several Occasions (Hamilton, William), 448–49
Poems on Several Occasions (Smart, Christopher), 101, 118–19
Poems on Several Occasions (Vernon, William), 347
Poems on Several Subjects (Cooper, John Gilbert), 90

Poetical Translation of the Elegies of Tibullus
(Grainger, James), 393, 395–400
Polybius (203?–*c.* 120 BC), 27; *see* Hampton,
James
Polycrates, King of Samos (d. *c.* 522 BC), 418
*Polymetis: or an Inquiry concerning the Agreement
between the Works of the Roman Poets, and the
Remains of the Antient Artists, see* Spence,
Joseph
Pond, Arthur (1705–58), designer, 48
Pope, Alexander (1688–1744), xiv, 5, 7, 11, 14,
19, 21–23, 38, 50, 54–55, **65–66**, 68, 72,
76–80, 86, 90, 92, 101–2, 118, 125,
212–17, 319, 385–86, 423, 430, 451–53,
518, 523; **Letters from**, 65, 69; **Letter
to**, 66–68; **Works**: *Dunciad*, 65, 214;
"Epistle V. To Mr Addison . . . on
Medals," 180–81; proposed epistle on
reason and knowledge, 92; *Essay on
Criticism*, 140–41; "Fragment of Brutus,"
92–93; *Homer*, 214; Horace, *Epistles*, II, II,
531; *Letters of Mr Alexander Pope* (1737), 5,
45, 69, 530–31; *Rape of the Lock*, 473;
"Verses upon the late D[uchess] of
M[arlborough]" (1746), 92; *Works*, 531,
(II), 5, (III), 30; *Works* (ed. Warburton,
q.v.), 92, 138, 139, 212–17; *Works of
Shakespeare* (1725), 214; *see also* Warton,
Joseph
Popple, William (1701–64), *Double Deceit*
(1735), 523, 528
Porta, Giambattista (*c.* 1538–1615), 460
Post Office, clerks of, 157; *see also* franking,
system of
Potter, John (1674?–1747), Archbishop of
Canterbury, 75, 77
Powell, Charles (1712–96), 208–9
"Power of Habit" (Cooper, John Gilbert), 117
Power of Harmony, The, see Cooper, John Gilbert
"Praelium inter Pygmous et Gues commissum"
(Addison, Joseph), 91
Pratt, Sir Charles (1714–94), Attorney
General, 453–55
Prattinton, James, merchant, 439, 442
*Preceptor: Containing a General Course of Education,
see* RD
"Predominant Passion in Women, The"
(Cooper, John Gilbert), 109, 117–18
Prendergast, Thomas (*c.* 1700–60), 2nd
Baronet Prendergast, 300–1
Presbyterian, preaching, 354; clerical study,
327
Price, Cecil, 113
Prince, Daniel (d. 1796), Oxford bookseller,
361–62
"Princess Elizabeth: A Ballad" (Shenstone,
William), 171–72

"Progress of Taste; or the Fate of Delicacy"
(Shenstone, William), 473–74
"Project for Raising an Hospital for Decayed
Authors" (Cooper, John Gilbert), 99–100,
109
"Prologue to *Comus*" (Hoadly, John), 295–96
Public Advertiser (1752–94), xxiv, 56, 58–59,
258
Public Virtue, see RD
Publicola, Valerius, 1st Roman consul, 367,
372
*Publii Virgilii Maronis Bucolica, Georgica, et Aeneis,
see* Virgil
publisher, eighteenth-century, xiv
Publishing History, xv
Pulteney, William, Earl of Bath (1684–1764),
14, 154–55, 495, 497
"Puppet-show, The" (Brown, John), 91–92

Quebec, battle of, 432, 434
Quebec, city of, 462–63
Quinti Horatii Flacci Opera, see Horace
Quintilian, Marcus Fabius (AD *c.* 35–*c.* 95),
William Melmoth's trans. of *Institutio
oratoria*, 520

Radcliffe, John (d. 1775), Master of Pembroke
College, 473–74
Radnor, 4th Earl of, *see* Robartes, John
"Rag Plot" (1754), 184–85
"Rake, The," 172
Rake's Progress (Hogarth, William), 295–96,
298–99
Ralegh, Sir Walter (1552?–1618), *Works*, 29
Ramsay, Allan (1686–1758), *Poems*, 448–49
Ranby, John (1703–1773), sergeant-surgeon to
George II, 356–57
Randall, Dale, 8
Randall, William (RD apprentice?), 37, 521,
523, 526
Ranelagh, 470
Ransom, Harry, 33
Rasselas, Prince of Abissinia, see Johnson, Samuel
Ravenet, Simon François (1721?–74),
engraver, 48–49, 136, 344
Raymond, Robert, 1st Baron Raymond
(1673–1733), *Reports of Cases Argued and
Adjudged in the Courts of King's Bench and
Common Pleas* (1743), 73–74
Reed, Isaac (1742–1807), 422–23, 506–8
Reeve, W., bookseller, 41, 395
Reily, Mr, 80
*Reflections on the late Lord Bolingbroke's Letters on
the Study and Use of History* (Leland, John),
154–55
Reliques of Ancient English Poetry, see Percy,
Thomas

Reports of Cases Argued and Adjudged in the Courts of King's Bench and Common Pleas (Raymond, Robert), 73–74

Revenge, The, see Young, Edward

Reymer, C., printer, 41, 45

Reynolds, Sir Joshua (1723–92), portrait of RD, 432, 434, 437–39, 441–42

Riccoboni, J. (*c.* 1675–1753), 29; trans. by William Guthrie, *Historical and Critical Account of the Theatres in Europe* (1741), 516, 523

Rich, John (1682–1760), theatre manager, 5, 12, 65–66, 68, 229, 313–14, 318–19, 321, 329, 376, 379, 387, 450; **Letter to,** 330; Covent Garden theatre, 307, 376

Richardson, J., bookseller, 41

Richardson, Jonathan the younger (1694–1771), portrait painter, portrait of RD, 434

Richardson, Samuel (1689–1761), printer and novelist, 39, 45, 47, 50, 205–6; *Aesop's Fables* (1740), 454

Richmond, 3rd Duke of, *see* Lennox, Charles

Ridley, Glocester (1702–74), **89,** 151; **Letters from,** 89, *551*; **Letter to,** *551*; *Constitution in Church and State* (1745), 89; Gay's "Fable XVI" (trans.), 89; "Invitation to the Country," 89; *Jovi Eleutherio* (1745), 89; "Psyche," 89; "Spinula & Acus," 89

Ridout, Mr, 109

Riely, John C., 122, 179, 230, 293, 380, 434

Rinaker, Clarissa, 86

Rivington, James (1724–1803), bookseller, 31, 38–41, 43, 94, 523, 525

Rivington, John (1720–92), bookseller, 38–41, 94, 508–9, 520, 523, 526

Rizzo, Betty, 101, 120

Robartes, John, 4th Earl of Radnor (1686?–1757), 85–86, 268–69, 289

Robertson, William (1721–93), *History of Scotland* (1759), 411–12

Robinson, Mr, watchmaker, 72

Robinson, Anastasia, Countess of Peterborough (d. 1755), 69

Robinson, Jacob, bookseller, 522–23

Rochdale, 5th Baron of, *see* Byron, William

Rochester, Bishop of, *see* Wilcocks, Joseph

Rock, Mrs, 193

Rockford, 4th Earl of, *see* Zuylestein, William Henry

Rockingham, 2nd Marquis of, *see* Watson-Wentworth, Charles

Roe, the carrier, 123

Roebuck, John (1718–94), MD, 348–49, 370, 460

Rollin, Charles (1661–1741), French historian, 428

Roman History (1744), 81–82

Rook, William, clerk of the Chapel of the Rolls, 72–73

Roten, Miss, 471

Roth, Cecil, 82

Roubiquet, John, bookbinder, 393, 395

Rout, The (Hill, Sir John), 386, 392–94

Rowe, Elizabeth (née Singer) (1674–1737), *Miscellaneous Works* (1739), 83; *Philomela* (1736), 513, 524

Rowe, Nicholas (1674–1718), 13, 271–72

Royal Society of Arts, *see* Society for the Encouragement of Arts, Manufactures, and Commerce

Rudge, Edward (1703–63), MP, 364–65

Ruffhead, Owen (1723–69), 93, 166

"Ruin'd Abbey; or the Effects of Superstition," *see* Shenstone, William

Ruins of Paymyra (Wood, Robert), 172–73

Rule of Life, The (1742), 176, 178

Russell, John, 4th Duke of Bedford (1710–1771), 469

Russell, William (1726–75), bookseller, 41, 295–96

Russell, William (d. 1793), printer, 295–96

Russia, Empress of, *see* Catherine II

Rutgers University, 8

Rutland, 3rd Duke of, *see* Manners, John

Ryall, J., bookseller, 41

Ryland, William (1738–83), engraver, 48–49, 397

Ryskamp, Charles, 96

Sackville, 1st Viscount, *see* Germain, George

St Asaph, Bishop of, *see* Drummond, Robert Hay

St James area, London, 23

St James Evening Post (1715–60?), 58

St John, Henry, 1st Viscount Bolingbroke (1678–1751), 123, 215–17, 430; *Familiar Epistle to the most Impudent Man Living* (1749), 217; *Letters, on the Spirit of Patriotism: on the Idea of a Patriot King . . .* (1749), 216; *Letters on the Study and Use of History* (1752), 154–55, 205; *see also* Leland, John

Salisbury, Bishop of, *see* Sherlock, Thomas, and Gilbert, John

Sallust (Caius Sallustius Crispus) (86–*c.* 34 BC), 27

Salmon, Thomas (1697?–1767), *Tradesman's Dictionary*, 32, 524

Samber, Robert, *One Hundred New Court Fables* (1721), 397, 434

Sambrook, A. J., 86, 157

Sandby, William (d. 1799), bookseller, 41

Sanders, Mrs, RD's cousin, 455

Sanders, Charles, apothecary, 344–45, 348
Sanderson, Mr, 199–200
Sandys, William (1695–1770), Chancellor of Exchequer, 495, 497
Sannazaro, Jacopo (1456–1530), Italian poet, *De Partu Virginis*, 429
Sare, W., bookseller, 38, 41
Saunders, Mr, *see* Sanders, Charles
Saunders, John, inheritance from his cousin W. Shenstone, 477
Saunders, William, inheritance from his cousin W. Shenstone, 477
Saunders, William, "Ballad, in the scotch-manner," 189–90
Savage, Thomas Birch, musician, 369, 371
Savile, George, 7th Baronet (1678–1743), 503
Say, Charles (d. 1775), printer, 45
Say, Edward, printer of *General Evening Post*, 338–39
Scarborough, 3rd Earl of, *see* Lumley-Saunderson, Thomas
"Scating" (Brown, John), 91–92
Schoolmistress, The, see Shenstone, William
Schutz, Augustus, 154
Scot, Mr, 428
Scotin, Gérard Jean-Baptiste (b. 1698), artist/engraver, 48–49, 136
Scotland, language of, 283
Scott, Sarah, trans. of La Place, *Agreeable Ugliness* (1754), 521, 524
Scouten, Arthur H., *see* Van Lennep, W. B.
Scripture Account of a Future State Considered, The (Bourn, Samuel), 360–61
Sculptura; or the History and Art of Chalcography and Engraving (Evelyn, John), 119
Sedgwick, Romney, *History of Parliament*, xxii, xxiv
Select Fables of Esop, see RD
"Self-Love" (Cooper, John Gilbert), 109
Selkirk, 4th Earl of, *see* Douglas, Dunbar Hamilton
Selwyn, George Augustus (1719–91), **86**, 524; **Letter to,** 86–87
"Sentiment, The" (Shenstone, William), 334
Sentimental comedy, 6
"Serious Exhortation to Learn to Whistle, A" (anon.), 99
Sermon preached at St Nicholas Church in Newcastle (Lowth, Robert), 287–88, 290–91
servants, 498–99 (English); 498–99 (French)
Seven Years War, 462
Severn, River, 123
Seward, Thomas, *Conformity between Popery and Paganism illustrated* (1746), 127
Seymour, Algernon, Earl of Hertford and 7th Duke of Somerset (1684–1750), 79, 123

Seymour, Elizabeth, Lady Northumberland (1716–76), 394, 396
Seymour, Frances, Countess of Hertford and Duchess of Somerset (1716–76), 67, 78, **79**, 80, 335, 432, 434; **Letter from,** 79
Seymour-Conway, Francis, 1st Marquis of Hertford (1719–94), 123
Shaftesbury, 3rd Earl of, *see* Cooper, Anthony Ashley
Shakespeare, William (1564–1616), 12, 118, 266–67, 399, 401, 449; *Hamlet*, 227, 229, 266; *Macbeth*, 227, 229, 266; *Othello*, 228, 249–50, 321 (*see also* Hoadly, John; Upton, John)
Shand, Mr, 365–66
Sharpe, Joshua, 120
Shebbeare, John (1709–88), 300–1; *Letters on the English Nation* (1755), 301; *Marriage Act* (1754), 301
Sheldon, Esther K., 80
Shenstone, John W., inheritance from his cousin W. Shenstone, 476–77
Shenstone, Mary, W. Shenstone's first cousin, 476–77
Shenstone, William (1714–63), 3, 8, 10, 12–14, 16–17, 19, 52–53, 61, **115**, 123, 125, 145, 180–81, 200–1, 210–12, 228–229, 232–33, 235, 237–41, 255–57, 260–63, 267, 269–70, 281, 291, 293, 297–98, 301–3, 308–9, 316, 324, 336–37, 339–40, 342–45, 348–50, 358–59, 370–71, 389, 400–1, 408, 415, 418–19, 421, 427–28, 444–45, 452, 456; Baskerville's *Horace*, 456–57, 459–60; death of, 463; executors, 52, 434; Leasowes, 19, 49, 77, 79, 170, 206, 211–12, 230, 285, 292–93, 302–3, 315, 340–41, 354, 363, 373, 375–77, 398, 400–1, 405–7, 412, 426, 432–35, 476–77, 477 (sale of), 486–87 (RD's "Description of"); proposed pension, 445, 447, 467–70; on Percy's *Reliques*, 466, 468–69; portrait by Alcock, 432, 438, 445, 450, 453–54; prank on John Scott Hylton, 448–49; RD's *Select Fables of Esop*, 395 (trans. of La Motte's *Discours sur la Fable*), 432–33, 437, 440–42 (La Motte), 443, 448, 450–51, 454–55; settlement of last will and estate, 475–77, 480, 484–86, 490, 492–93; **Letters from,** 193–94, 196–97, 231, 319–21, 411–12, 459–61, 466–70, 55 1–52; **Letters to,** 115–17, 122–24, 156–58, 162–63, 165, 168, 170–72, 181–82, 186–93, 197–99, 201–2, 204–7, 209–10, 218–19, 222–24, 229–31, 241–43, 248–50, 257–58, 265–66, 270–71, 274–79, 284–85, 292–93, 302–3, 314–15, 317–18, 322–23, 331–35, 353–55, 359–60, 362–65, 372–79, 385, 387–88, 391–99, 405–7,

409–13, 424–26, 431–42, 445–47, 450–51, 453–55, 464–65, *552*; Letter from James Dodsley, 178–79; **Works**: "Answer," 318; "Candor," 292–93; "The Ceremonial," 332; "Compliment in 1743," 315, 317–18, 320–21; "Daphne's Visit" ("Lady's Visit"), 189; "Dying Kid," 320–23, 332; elegies, 207, 209–10, 218, 231, 242, 249, 255, 257–58, 265–66, 270, 334, 336, 363–64, 373–74, 392, 408, 473; Epilogue for RD's *Cleone*, 231, 241, 249, 256–57, 261, 270, 274, 393–99, 405–7, 410; "The Evergreen," 292–93, 334; "Fatal Exotic," 473–74; "I Told My Nymph," 317–18, 320; "In a Root house," 171–72; "In a Shady Valley," 171–72; "Irregular Ode after Sickness," 314; "Jessy," 292–93, 319, 321, 332–35, 340, 353–54; *Judgment of Hercules* (1741), 7, 115; "Love and Honour," 473–74; "Love Songs," 315; "Lysander to Cloe," 318, 320; *Miscellany* (ed. I. Gordon), 309, 455; "Nancy of the Vale," 189, 198, 314; "Ode to a Young Lady," 171; "Ode to Health," 314, 317–18, 320; "Ode to Indolence," 314; "Ode. Written 1739," 315, 317–18, 320, 322–23; "Oeconomy, A Rhapsody," 473–74; "On a small Building in the Gothick Taste," 171–72; "On Religion," 486–87; "On Taste," 486–87; "Pastoral Ballad," 156–57, 168, 170–71, 181–82, 186–89, 198, 224, 231, 473; "Pastoral Ode to . . . Richard Lyttelton," 257–58, 472–73; "Princess Elizabeth: A Ballad," 171–72; "Progress of Taste" ("Progress of Delicacy"), 473–74; "Ruin'd Abbey" ("The Vista"), 394, 396, 473–74; "Rural Elegance," 79, 197–99, 201, 223, 230, 249, 285, 293, 302, 315, 320–21, 334–35, 337, 354, 473; *Schoolmistress* (1742), 115, 117, 122–23, 473; "Sentiment, The," 334; "Simile," 332; "Snuff-box," 473–74; "Unconnected Thoughts on Gardening," 468, 486–87; "Upon a Visit to the Same in Winter, 1748," 314; "Upon Riddles," 314, 322–23; "Verses to a Writer of Riddles," 314; "Verses to Dr Radcliffe," 473–74; "Verses . . . 1748 to William Lyttelton," 171–72; "The Vista" (*see* "Ruin'd Abbey"); "Wolf and the Crane" (Phaedrus) [? "Wolf and the Lamb" (Phaedrus)], 428; *Works* (1764), 19, 49, 107, 157, 309, 335, 364, 373, 434–35, 462–63, 465, 468, 471–75, 484–87, 491–93
Sherbo, Arthur, 82, 113, 118, 120
Sheridan, Frances (1724–66), *The Dupe* (1763),

480–81; *Memoirs of Miss Sidney Bidulph* (1761), 301
Sheridan, Thomas the elder (1687–1738), 80–81
Sheridan, Thomas the younger (1719–88), actor, lecturer, 7, **80–81**, 524; **Letter from**, 80–81; *British Education* (1756), 80–81; *Course of Lectures on Elocution* (1762), 80; *Dissertation . . . on the English Tongue* (1762), 80
Sherlock, Thomas (1678–1761), Bishop of Salisbury and London, 5
Shewell, Thomas, bookseller, 94
Shipley, William (1714–1803), **Letter to**, 208–9
Short Introduction to English Grammar, see Lowth, Robert
Shropshire, William, bookseller, 41
Shuckburgh, John (d. 1761), bookseller, 41
"Simile" (Shenstone, William), 332
Simpson, Rev. Bolton, 134; *Xenophontis Memorabilium Socratis Dictorum* (1741), 135
Simpson, Dr Hazel, 442
Sinar, Joan, 453
Singer, Samuel W., Spence's *Anecdotes* (1820), 126
"Sir Harry Beaumont," *see* Spence, Joseph
Skinner, William (d. 1752), 108
Skrine, William, 341
Skynner, John, attorney, 107–8
Skynner, Rev. John (1724?–1805), 107; *Sermon preached at the Funeral of Baptist Earl of Gainsborough* (1751), 107–8
Skynner, Sophia, 107
Smart, Christopher (1722–71), 44, 58, 94, **101**, 138; **Letters from**, 100–1, 112–13, 118–19, 119, 120, *552–53*; *Carmen Cl. Alexandri Pope in S. Caeciliam Latine Redditum* (1746), 100–2; *Judgment of Midas* (1752), 113; *Midwife* (1750–51), 101; trans. of Phaedrus, 524; *Poems on Several Occasions* (1752), 101, 118–19
Smith, Ann, 515, 517, 524
Smith, Charles, *Antient and Present State of the County of Kerry* (1756), 340–41, 344
Smith, David Nichol, 325
Smith, John, 11th Earl of Clanricarde (1720–82), **Letter to**, 277; *Memoirs and Letters of Ulick de Burgh* (1757), 30, 277
Smith, Robert, bookseller, 38
Smith, Samuel, 300–1
Smith, Sir Thomas (1513–77), *De recta et emendata linguae Anglicanae Scriptione* (1568), 446
Smith, Thomas (d. 1767), painter, 293
Smock Alley Theatre, 156, 409

Smollett, Tobias (1721–71), xiv; *Compendium of Authentic and Entertaining Voyages* (1756), 31, 524–25; *Complete History of England* (1757–58), 340–41, 343–46, 360–61; *Peregrine Pickle* (1751), 180–81, 397; *see also* Grainger, James
"Snuff-box, The" (Shenstone, William), 473–74
Society for the Encouragement of Arts, Manufactures, and Commerce (Royal Society of Arts), 22, 47, 108, 220–21, 253, 306, 311, 313; **Letters to**, 208–9, 220–21, 250–51, 281–82
"Solitude, an Ode" (Grainger, James), 196–99
Some Considerations on the Law of Forfeiture for High Treason (2nd ed. 1746), 102
Some Reflections on . . . Government (1739), 81–82
Somerset, Duchess of, *see* Seymour, Frances
Somerville, William (1675–1742), 190, 192; "Address to his Elbow-chair," 172, 192; *Chase* (1735, 1749), 166; *Occasional Poems* (1727), 166; "Song," 192
"Song" (Somerville, William), 192
"Song," *see* Whistler, Anthony
Sonnazaro, Jacopo, *De partu Virginis* (1526), 176–78
Southall, Mary, inheritance from her cousin 429 W. Shenstone, 477, 485
Southall, Richard, inheritance from W. Shenstone's estate, 485
Southampton coach, 325
Southerne, Thomas (1660–1746), *Oroonoko* (1695), 430–31
Spagnola, Baptista ("Mantuan") (1448–1516), 176–78
Spain, war with, 456–57
Spectator (1711–12), 14, 441
Spence, Joseph ("Sir Harry Beaumont") (1699–1768), 7, 9, 16, 19–20, 76, 77, 89, 93–94, 114, 117–18, **125**, 147–48, 150–51, 154, 175, 224–25, 229, 276, 284–85, 290–91, 294, 302, 330, 349, 354, 360, 362–64, 370, 373, 375, 401, 403–5, 408, 410, 412, 424–26, 432, 435, 440, 446–47, 452, 456, 461, 478, 481, 483, 487–88, 492, 526, 550; living at Byfleet, 125–26; design for RD's garden at Richmond, 139; Finculo, 20, 125, 364, 375–76, 490; RD's *Select Fables of Esop*, 448–49, 455; **Letter from**, 179–80; **Letters to**, 125–26, 138–39; Letters to Elizabeth Cartwright, 488–90; **Works**: *Account of the Life, Character, and Poems of Mr Blacklock* (1754), 20, 175, 224–25, 404; *Anecdotes*, 125; *Essay on Mr. Pope's Odyssey* (1726), 125, 525; *Moralities* (1753), 395; *Museum*, 19, 125; *Parallel in the Manner of Plutarch* (1758), 45, 108; *Polymetis* (1747), 19–20, 32, 48,

75–76, 108–9, 111, 125, 179–80, 525, 548; "Round of Mr Shenstone's Paradise [Leasowes]," 434; *see also* Blacklock, Thomas
Spence, Mrs Joseph, 114, 138
Spens, Mr, editor of *London Chronicle*, 258–59, 262
Spilsbury (engraver?), 435
Spiritual Quixote, The, see Graves, Richard
Stamp tax, newspaper, 9, 87–88
Stanhope, Arthur Charles (1716–70), **374**; **Letter to**, 374–75
Stanhope, Mrs Arthur Charles, 374
Stanhope, John (1705–48), MP, 95
Stanhope, Philip Dormer, 4th Earl of Chesterfield (1694–1772), 10, 12, 14, 21, 68, 75–77, 228, 240, 313, **319**, 363–64, 373–75, 383, 497; **Letter from**, 321–22; **Letters to**, 318–19, 329; poems in *Public Register*, 319; pieces in *The World*, 319
Stanhope, Philip, 5th Earl of Chesterfield (1755–1815), 3, 319, 374–75
Stanley, Thomas, *History of Philosophy* (1655–62), 517
Starr, Herbert W., 149
Stationers' Company, xiv–xv, xxiv, 10, 42, 44–45, 81, 83, 94, 98, 107, 116, 159, 219, 507, 509, 513, 515, 519–22, 526, 528, 530–31, 533
Steevens, George (1736–1800), 398, 405–6; **Letters from**, 413–14, 457–59
Stephenson, Hugh (d. 1758), 333, 343
Sterne, Laurence (1713–68), xiv, 13, 17–18; **Letters from**, 415–17, 421–24; *Life and Opinions of Tristram Shandy* (1760–67), 17–18, 34, 37, 49, 415–17, 421–24, 438, 525; *Sermons of Mr Yorick* (1760), 18, 128, 416, 422–23, 525
Stevenson, Dr, 402–3
Stevenson, John Hall (1718–85), **Letter from**, *553*
Stewart, Mary, 119
Stillingfleet, Benjamin (1702–71), *Paradise Lost* (oratorio, 1760), 525
Stockton, Mr, 106
Stone, George W., *see* Van Lennep, W. H.
Stonhouse, Sir James (1716–95), **366**, 367, 369–72, 377–78; **Letters from**, 366, *553*; *Universal Restitution* (1761), 366
Story, John, 404–5
Strada, Famiano (1572–1649), *Prolusiones Academiae* ("Nightingale"), 91
Strahan, William (1715–85), printer, 29, 31, 34–35, 46, 97–98, 197, **259**, 288, 329, 423, 507–8, 513, 519, 525–26; **Letters to**, 258–60, 262–63, 386–87; *London Chronicle* (1757–), 15, 258–60, 262–63, 386–87

Straight, Rev. John (1688?–1736), 295–96, 298–99, 484; "To Mr J. H[oadly] at the Temple," 295–96; "Answer to the Foregoing, 1731," 295–96
Strange, Sir Robert (1721–92), engraver, 344
Straus, Ralph, xiii–xxiv, 4, 10–11, 15, 23, 37, 41, 53, 57, 59, 87, 118, 251–52, 262, 269, 272, 303, 319, 382, 386, 420, 422, 442, 452, 504–6, 514, 518; *see also* Straus & Dent
Straus & Dent (Robert K.), *John Baskerville, Strawberry Hill Press, see* Walpole, Horace 262
Stuart, James "Athenian" (1713–88), 453–55
Stuart, John, 3rd Earl of Bute (1713–92), 22, 46, 48, **382**, 445, 447, 459–60, 467–69 (Shenstone's pension); **Letter to**, 382
Stubbs, George (1681–1742), 296
Succinct History of Ancient and Modern Persecutions (Lombard, Daniel), 119
Suetonius, *see* Oudendorp, Franciscus
Summary of Natural Religion (Barr, John), 128
Surprising History of a late long Administration by "Titus Livius, jun." (1746), 105
Surrey, Earl of, *see* Howard, Henry
Sussex, 3rd Earl of, *see* Yelverton, Henry
Swan, J., bookseller, 41, 43
Swift, Jonathan (1667–1745), xiv, 92, 207, 429–30, 526; *Day of Judgment*, 207; *Brotherly Love* (1754), 81; *Difficulty of Knowing Oneself* (1745), 524; *Directions to Servants* (1745), 81, 524; *Miscellanies*, 38, 80–81; *Three Sermons* (1744), 81, 524; *Works*, 7, 80–81, 166
Sykes, Arthur Ashley (1684–1756), DD, *Examination of Mr Warburton's Account of the Conduct of the Ancient Legislators* (1744), 216–17; *System of Moral Philosophy, see* Hutcheson, Francis

Tacitus, Cornelius (AD *c.* 55–*c.* 117), 27
Tasso, Torquato (1544–95), 29; *Jerusalem* (1738), 38, 46, 69–70
Taylor, Henry (1711–85), 351–52
Taylor, Isaac (1730–1807), engraver, 48, 291, 304, 338–39, 350–51
Taylor, Robert (1710–1762), physician to George II, 356–57
Taylor, William, 351–52; "Dropsical Man," 295–96, 298–99, 341
"Tears of Old May-Day, The" (Lovibond, Edward), 197
Tedder, Henry Richard, 10
Temple, Sir William (1628–99), *Works* (1757), 398–99
Test, The (1756–57), 15, 259–60, 262
Thackray, Thomas, **333**, 452, 455, 479; **Letter from** ? *553*; **Letters to**, 333, 343

Thatcher's Barge, 138
"Theagenes to Sylvia" (Cooper, John Gilbert), 110
Théatre des Grecs (Brumoy, Père), 361–62
Theobald, Lewis (1688–1744), *Shakespeare Restored* (1726), 214
Theophrastus (*c.* 372–*c.* 287 BC), 27
Theory and Construction of Fortification, The (Bisset, Charles), 202–4
Thesaurus Linguae Latinae Compendiarius (Ainsworth, Robert), 360–61
Thomas, Mrs Elizabeth ("Cotswouldia"), "To William Shenstone, Esq," 460
Thomas, John (1691–1766), Bishop of Lincoln, 128–29
Thomas, John, 526
Thompson, Mr, 553
Thompson, Mr, vocalist, 371
Thompson, H. Yates, 442
Thompson, Isaac (d. 1776), Newcastle-upon-Tyne bookseller, 44
Thompson, William (1712?–1766?), *On Sickness* (1745–46), 526
Thomson, James (1700–48), poet, 55–56, 80
Thomson, William, *Orpheus Caledonius* (1725, ?), 526
Thorpe, Thomas, autograph dealer, 6
Thurlbourne, William, Cambridge bookseller, 43–44; *see also* Woodyer, John
Tibullus, Albius (*c.* 54–19 BC), *see* Grainger, James
Tickell, John (1729–82), 155
Tickle, Richard, 156
Tickle, Thomas (1686–1740), 156
Timmen's Waggon, 284
Tisch, J. H., 160
"Titus Livius, jun.," *see Surprising History* . . .
"To ******" (Whistler, Anthony), 314
"To Chloe" (Hoadly, John), 296, 351–52
"To Independency," *see* Mason, William
"To Memory," *see* Mason, William
"To Miss Loggin; from Miss Whately" (Whately, Mary), 461
"To Mr Dodsley" (Graves, Richard), 491–93
"To Mr Shenstone" (Whately, Mary), 461
"To Venus. A Rant, 1732" (Lisle, Thomas), 352–53
"To William Shenstone, Esq" (Thomas, Mrs Elizabeth), 460
"Toad and the Ephemeron, The" (Lowth, Robert), 430
Todd, Thomas, bookseller, nephew of George Faulkner, 301
Todd, William B., 207, 224, 325
Tomb of Shakespeare, The (Cooper, John Gilbert), 194–96
"Tommy Thumb," 512

Tonson, Jacob the elder (1656?–1736), bookseller, 23, 65, 530
Tonson, Jacob the younger (d. 1767), bookseller, 39, 50, 112, 213, 393, 395, 413, 518, 523, 526, 533
Tonson, Richard (d. 1772), bookseller, 523, 526
Tower of London, 391
Toyshop, The, see RD
Tracy, Clarence, 181, 297, 337, 465, 482
Tragoediarum Grecarum Delectus (Burton, John), 361–62
"Transcrib'd from the Rev. Mr Pixell's Parsonage Garden" (Pixell, John), 308–9
Trapp, Joseph (1679–1747), 197
Treadwell, Michael, 41–42, 468
Treatise of the Scurvy (Lind, James), 202, 204
Treatise on the Scurvy (Bisset, Charles), 202–4, 547
"Treatise on Universal Grammar" (Blacklock, Thomas), 283–84, 286
Treaty of Paris (1763), 462
Trevor, Richard (1707–71), Bishop of Durham, 154–55, 363–64
Trimen's Waggon, *see* Frimen's Waggon
Tristram Shandy, see Sterne, Laurence
Triumph of Isis, The (Warton, Thomas), 158–59
True and Authentic Account of Andrew Frey, A (trans., 1753), 161–62
"True Resignation," *see* Hylton, John Scott
"Tuberose and the Sun Flower, The" (Graves, Richard), 425–26, 449
Tucker (Samuel?), 299–300
Tully's Head, see RD
Turner, Dawson (1775–1858), antiquary, 534
Turnpenny, Joseph, buttonmaker, purchase of Shenstone's Leasowes, 477
Twining, Thomas, tea merchant, 442
Tyers, Jonathan (d. 1767), 138–39
Tymms, George (1699–1781), 366, **367**; **Letters from**, 366–72, 377–8; *Essay on Monopolies* (1758), 366–72, 377–78
Tyson, Jeremiah, *Epistle to Mr Warburton* (1744), 214

"Unconnected Thoughts on Gardening" (Shenstone, William), 468, 486–87
Universal History, from the earliest Account of Time to the Present (1736, 1765), 129
Unwin, Miss, 471, 477–78; **Letter to**, 553
Unwin, Mr, 471
Upcott, William (1779–1845), autograph collector, 534
"Upon a Visit to the Same in Winter, 1748" (Shenstone, William), 314
"Upon Riddles" (Shenstone, William), 314, 322–23

Upton, John (1707–60), *Critical Observations on Shakespeare* (1746), 98–99

Vaillant, Paul (d. 1802), bookseller, 41
Vallance, Aylmer, 152
Vanderbank, John (1694–1739), designer, 48
Van der Gucht, Gerard (1697–1776), engraver, 48
Vane, Frances Anne (née Hawes), Viscountess Vane (1713–88), 180–81, 396–97
Van Lennep, W. B., Avery, E. L., Scouten, A. H., Stone, G. W., and Hogan, C. B., *The London Stage, 1660–1800*, xxiv
Varney, Mr, 245–46
Vaux Hall Gardens, 138–39
Verney, John Peyto, 14th Baron Willoughby de Broke (1738–1816), 468, 470; Richard Jago's patron, 470
Vernon, William (1735–?), *Poems on Several Occasions* (1758), 347; "Written in a copy of Dr Young's Night Thoughts," 347
"Verses to a Writer of Riddles" (Shenstone, William), 314
"Verses to Dr Radcliffe" (Shenstone, William), 473–74
Verses to the King of Prussia (Voltaire, François Marie Arouet), 185–86
"Verses under the Prints of Mr Hogarth's *Rake's Progress*, 1735" (Hoadly, John), 295–96, 298–99
"Verses upon the late D[uchess] of M[arlborough]" (Pope, Alexander), 92
"Verses, written at the Gardens of William Shenstone, Esq.," *see* Hylton, John Scott
"Verses written . . . 1748 to William Lyttelton" (Shenstone, William), 171–72
Vertue, George (1684–1756), engraver, 48
Victor, Benjamin (d. 1778), 6, **156**; **Letters from**, 155–56, 163–64, 553; **Letter to**, 553; *Widow of the Wood, The* (1755), 47–48, 155–56, 163–64
Victor, Mrs Benjamin, 164
Victoria History of the Counties of England, xxii, xxv
Vida, Marcus Heronymus (c. 1490–1566), 29; *De Poetica* (*see* Pitt, Christopher)
Villiers, George Bussy, 4th Earl of Jersey (1735–1805), 102
Villiers, William, 3rd Earl of Jersey (d. 1769), 102
Vincent, Mr, vocalist, 371
Vindication of Natural Society, A, see Burke, Edmund
Virgil (Publius Virgilius Maro) (70–19 BC), 27, 123, 145, 256, 408, 413; *Aeneid*, 411–12 (*see also* Pitt, Christopher); *Publii Virgilii Maronis Bucolica, Georgica, et Aeneis*

(Baskerville, 1757), 252–53; *Works of . . . in Latin and English* (J. Warton, 1753), 150–51 (*see* Baskerville, John; Ogilby, John; Warton, Joseph)
Virginia. A Tragedy (Crisp, Samuel), 158–59
"Vision of Heaven, The" (Cooper, John Gilbert), 106, 109
"Vista," *see* Shenstone, William, "Ruin'd Abbey, The"
Vivares, engraver, 136
Voltaire, François Marie Arouet de (1694–1778), 29, 131, 372; *Candide* (1759), 153; *Defence of my Lord Bolingbroke's Letters* (1753), 155; *Le siècle de Louis XIV* (1751), 16–17; *Abrégé de l'histoire universelle* (1754–57), 361–62; *Verses to the King of Prussia*, 185–86

Wale, Samuel (1721?–1786), painter/designer, 48–49, 173, 434, 438, 449, 460
Wales, Prince of, *see* Frederick; *also* Edward Augustus, Duke of York
Wales, Princess of, *see* Augusta, Princess
Walker, Mrs, 78–79
Walker, Anthony (1726–65), artist/engraver, 48
Waller, T., bookseller, 516, 526
Walpole, Horace, 4th Earl of Orford, (1717–97), 9, 14, 77, 112, 122–23, 148–49, 152–53, **161**, 198, 271, 320, 328–29, 356–58, 380–81, 446, 497–98; RD his bookseller, 161; Thomas Gray, 161; Strawberry Hill Press, 46, 381; **Letter from**, 161–62; **Works**: "Advertisement for *The History of Good Breeding*," 96; *Aedes Walpolianae* (1747), 122; *Anecdotes of Painting in England* (1762), 161; *Castle of Otranto* (1764), 161; *Catalogue of the Royal and Noble Authors of England* (1758), 161; *Epilogue to Tamerlane* (1746), 161; *World*, 161
Walpole, Robert, 1st Earl of Orford (1676–1745), 122, 240, 381, 497
Walpole, Robert, 2nd Earl of Orford (1701–51), 122
Walpole, Susan, *see* Hammond, Susan Walpole
Walsh, John the younger, music printer, 187–88, 414–15
Walter, John (d. 1803), RD apprentice and bookseller, 36–37, 251–52
Walter, John (1776–1847), proprietor of *London Times*, 252
Walthoe, John the elder, bookseller, 531
"War Proclaim'd at Brentford – a Climax" (Graves, Richard), 456–57, 460–61
Warburton, William (1698–1779), Bishop of Gloucester, 71, 84, 86, 90, 93, 103–4,
130–33, 143, 151, 503, 526; feud with J. G. Cooper, 90, 131–32, 135–36, 140–44, 548 (*see also* Jackson, John); **Letters from**, 94–95, 141–42, 212–14, *553*; **Letter to**, 214–17; **Works**: *The Divine Legation of Moses* (1737), 142; *Julian*, 135–36, 143–44; *Letter to the Editor [Mallet] of the [Bolingbroke's] Letters, on the Spirit of Patriotism* (1749), 217; *Letter to the Lord Viscount B[olingbroke]* (1749), 216–17; *Remarks on Several Occasional Reflections* (1745), 217; Pope's *Works* (*see also* Pope, Alexander), 11, 89, 90, 95, 138–39, 140–42, 166, 186, 212–17, 397, 553
Ward, Aaron, bookseller, sales catalogues, 531–33
Ward, Ann (d. 1789), York printer, 417
Ward, Catherine C., and Robert E., 47
Ward, John, 6th Baron Ward of Birmingham (1704–74), 469
Ward, John, bookseller, 41; sales catalogues, 531–33
Ward, John, *Four Essays upon the English Language* (1758), 361–62
Ward, Robert E., 301; *see also* Ward, Catherine C.
Ware, Isaac (d. 1766), *Complete Body of Architecture* (1756), 300–1
Warner, Thomas, publisher, 42
Warren, Borlase (1677–1747), MP, 110–11
Warrington, 2nd Earl of, *see* Booth, George
Warton, Joseph (1722–1800), 9, 14, 19, 53, 76, 86, 94, **158–59**, 325–26, 330–31, 338; **Letters to**, 158–59, 164, 185–86, 190–91, 222, 346–47, *553*; **Works**: *Enthusiast* (1744), 7; *Essay on the Writings and Genius of Mr Pope* (1756, 1782), 11, 24, 42, 86, 159, 185–86, 190–91, 219–20, 222, 346–47, 417; *Odes on Several Occasions* (1746), 108; *Works of . . . Virgil* (1753), 34, 37, 150–51, 326, 526–27
Warton, Mrs Joseph, 158, 190, 222
Warton, Thomas the elder (1688–1745), 94, 346–47
Warton, Thomas the younger (1728–90), 9, 14, 61, **86**, 94, 158, 185, 190–91, 197, 233, 235, 304–5, 330, 371, 375–76; **Letters from**, *553*; **Letters to**, 85–86, 108, 191, 219–20; **Works**: Apollonius, *Argonautics*, 158, 527; *Five Pastoral Eclogues* (1745), 7, 85–86; *History of English Poetry* (1774–81), 86; *Life of Sir Thomas Pope* (1760), 220; *Observations on the Fairie Queen* (1754), 86, 214 (on Pope); *Ode for Music* (1751), 43; "Panegyric on Ale," 351–52; *Pleasures of Melancholy* (1747), 108, 158–59, 492; *Triumph of Isis* (1749), 158–59

Wass, Mr, vocalist, 369, 371

Watson-Wentworth, Charles, 2nd Marquis of Rockingham (1730–82), 225, 276–77, 284–85, 290–91, 488–89

Waugh, James, bookseller, 41

Webb, Daniel (1719?–98), 464–66, 475; *Fingal Reclaimed* (1763), 475; *Inquiry into the Beauties of Painting* (1760), 438, 465; *Remarks on the Beauties of Poetry* (1762), 465

Wedderburne, Alexander, 1st Baron Loughborough (1733–1805), 468–69

Weekes, Nathaniel, *Barbados* (1754), 37

Welch, Mr, 404

Welch, Mr, compositor, 194–95

Welcher, Jeanne, *see* Welcher, J. and Dircks, R.

Welcher, J. and Dircks, R., 16, 394–95, 441–42

Welwyn carrier, 244

Wendorf, Richard, 96

Wesley, John (1703–91), **Letters from**, 82–83; *Collection of Moral and Sacred Poems* (1744), 82–83; *Letters* (1931), 83

West, Gilbert (1703–56), 7, 37, 169–70, 197, 527; "Father Francis's Prayer," 197–98; *Observations on the History and Evidence of the Resurrection* (1746), 29, 170, 316; *Odes of Pindar* (1749), 30, 40

West Indies, 202–3

Westminster Journal (1741–43), 497–98

Wharton, Thomas (1715?–94), MD, 148–49

Wharton, W. H., 37, 511

Whately, Mary (later Darwell), "To Miss Loggin; from Miss Whately," 461; "To Mr Shenstone," 461

Whatman, James, papermaker, 253

Whickcot (Thomas?), 128

Whistler, Anthony (1714–54), 19, 314; "Flowers," 172, 192–93; "Horace and Lydia," 172; "Song" ("While, Strephon . . ."), 172, 192–93; "Song" ("Let Wisdom boast . . ."), 317–18; "To ******," 314

Whiston, John (1711–80), and Benjamin White (d. 1794), booksellers, 40, 533

Whitaker, Benjamin, tenant of W. Shenstone, 485

Whitby, Anne, 156

White, Miss, *see* Pixell, Mrs

White, Benjamin, *see* Whiston, John

White Horse Inn, Cripplegate, 289

Whitefield, George (1714–70), 56

Whitehall, 5, 23

Whitehall Evening Post (1746–), xxv, 35, 58, 258

Whitehead, Paul (1710–74), *Manners* (1739), 5–6, 54, 319; *State Dunces* (1733), 34

Whitehead, William (1715–85), 9, 14, **102**, 112–14, 119–20, 151, 161, 326, 426, 526;

Letters from, 101–2, 199–200, 369, *553–54*; **Works**: *Ann Boleyn to Henry the Eighth. An Epistle* (1743), 31, 119, 527; *Atys and Adrastus* (1744), 119; *Charge to the Poets* (1762), 102; *Creusa, Queen of Athens* (1754), 34, 45, 158–59, 199–200, 528; *Danger of Writing Verse* (1741), 7, 102, 119, 527; "Dissertation on the Shield of Aeneas," 101–2; *Elegies* (1757), 265; "Elegy VI . . . written at Rome, 1756," 200; *Essay on Ridicule* (1743), 119, 527; "Friendship," 102; *Honour* (1747), 42, 119; *Nobility* (1744), 33, 119, 527; "Ode for his Majesty's Birth-Day," 369; *Roman Father* (1750), 34, 528

White's Chocolate House, 497

Whitmarsh, Mary, 76, 528

Whitworth, Charles (*c.* 1721–78), 203

Whitworth (Robert?), (Manchester?), bookseller, 41, 43

Whytt, Robert (1714–66), physician, 177–78; *Physiological Essays* (1756), 178

Widow of the Wood, The, see Victor, Benjamin

Wight, Mr, *see* Whytt, Robert

Wilcocks, Joseph (1673–1756), Bishop of Rochester, 154–55

Wilkinson, Mrs, 72

Wilkinson, Rev, 72

William of Wykeham, Life of, see Lowth, Robert

Williams, Sir Charles Hanbury (1708–59), 14, 50, 356–58, 496 ("John Grub"), **497**; satire on Sir Spencer Compton, Lord Wilmington, 494–98; **Letter from** (public), 494–98; **Letters to**, 360–61, 368; "New Ode to a Great Number of Men," 497; parody of Young's *Night Thoughts*, 494–98; *The Motion* (1742), 497; *World* (No. 37), 497

Williams, Marjorie, *Letters of William Shenstone* (1939), xxv, 3, 53, 123, 460

Williams, Ralph M., 280

Willoughby de Broke, 14th Baron of, *see* Verney, John Peyto

Wilmington, Earl of, *see* Compton, Spencer

Wilmot, Pynson, 238–39, 370–71

Wilmot, Samuel, 525

Wilson, D., bookseller, *see* Durham, T.

Wilson, Ebenezer, Dumfries bookseller, 224–25

Wiltshire, William (d. 1762), 408–9

Winchester, cathedral of, 289

Winchester coach, 351

Winchester, Dean of, *see* Cheyney, Thomas

Winkler, Jean Christophe (1701–70), engraver, 371

Winship, George P., Jr., 207

Winwood, Daniel, Birmingham toymaker, 342–45, 348, 448–49

"Wolf and the Crane, The" (Phaedrus) (Shenstone, William), 428
"Wolf and the Lamb" (Phaedrus) (Shenstone, William), 428
Wolfe, James (1727–59), general, elegy on, 432, 434
Wolseley, William, 5th Baronet of Staffordshire (d. 1779), 155–56, 163–64; *see also Widow of the Wood*
Wood, Henry Trueman, 221
Wood, Robert (1717?–71), *Ruins of Palmyra* (1752), 172–73
Wood, William (d. 1804), Lincoln bookseller and printer, 43, 45
Woodfall, George, bookseller, 41
Woodfall, Henry (1739–1805), bookseller, 38
Woodfall, William, bookseller, 528
Woodhouse, James (1735–1820), poet, 431, 433, 460–61, 485
Woodward, Thomas, bookseller, 528, 533
Woodyer, John, and W. Thurlbourne, Cambridge booksellers, 41, 44
Woolley, James, 81
Wootton Lodge, 195
Worcester, music meeting at, 370–73; *see also* Birmingham Music Concert
Works of Celebrated Authors (1750), 406–7
Works of Sir William Temple, 398–99
Works of Virgil, in Latin and English, 150–51
World, The (1753–56), *see* RD; *also* Moore, Edward
Wren, Christopher (1711–71), grandson of architect, 388, 432, 434, 453, 455; **Letter to**, *554*
Wright, J., printer, 45
Wright, Nelly, 68, 174, **269**, 503; **Letter from**, *554;* **Letters to**, 268–69, 279–80, 288–89
Wright, Rev. Thomas, 102, 527
Wright, William, **68**, 268, 279; **Letter to**, 68
Wright, Mrs William, 268
Wrighte, George (*c.* 1706–66), MP, 130, 142
Wrighte, William (d. 1762), recorder of

Leicester, 142
"Written at a *Ferme Ornee* near Birmingham," *see* Knight, Henrietta
Wye, River, 424–25
Wykeham, William of, *see* Lowth, Robert

Xenophon (*c.* 435–354 BC), 134; *see* Simpson, Rev. Bolton

Yarranton, Andrew, *England's Improvements by Sea and Land* (1677–81), 367–68
Yelverton, Henry, 3rd Earl of Sussex (1728–99), 348, 350
Yonge, William, 4th Baronet Yonge (*c.* 1693–1755), 22, 154–55
York, city of, 18
York, Duke of, *see* Edward Augustus
York, theatre of, 406, 413
York Courant (1728–   ), 417
York Waggon, 203
Yorke, Philip, 1st Earl of Hardwicke (1690–1764), 74, 128–29
Yorke, Simon (d. 1767), 73–74
Young, Bernard, 505
Young, Edward (1683–1765), xiv, 7–8, 76–77, **116**, 228, 349, 504; Charles Hanbury Williams's satire on Young's *Night Thoughts, II*, 494–98; **Letters from**, 116, 205–6, *554,* **Letter to**, 244; **Works**: *Argument Drawn from the Circumstances of Christ's Death* (1758), 116; *Brothers,* 9, 34, 45, 116, 529; *Conjectures on Original Composition* (1759), 116; *The Centaur not Fabulous* (1755), 9, 31, 116, 195, 205–6, 529; *Complaint; or Night Thoughts* (1742–45), 3, 8–9, 29, 34, 41, 48, 71–72, 79–80, 82–83, 116, 166, 205, 529; *Infidel Reclaimed,* 529; *The Revenge* (1721), 226, 229, 272; *Sea-Piece* (1755), 116

Zuylestein, William Henry, 4th Earl of Rockford (1717–81), 154–55

THE DREAMING VOID

Also by Peter F. Hamilton

The Greg Mandel series

Mindstar Rising

A Quantum Murder

The Nano Flower

The Night's Dawn Trilogy

The Reality Dysfunction

The Neutronium Alchemist

The Naked God

In the same timeline

A Second Chance at Eden

The Confederation Handbook
(a vital guide to the Night's Dawn Trilogy)

Fallen Dragon

Misspent Youth

The Commonwealth Saga

Pandora's Star

Judas Unchained

Peter F. Hamilton

THE DREAMING VOID

PART ONE OF THE VOID TRILOGY

MACMILLAN

First published 2007 by Macmillan
an imprint of Pan Macmillan Ltd
Pan Macmillan, 20 New Wharf Road, London N1 9RR
Basingstoke and Oxford
Associated companies throughout the world
www.panmacmillan.com

ISBN 978-1-4050-8880-0 HB
ISBN 978-1-4050-8881-7 TPB

9 8 7 6 5 4 3 2 1

A CIP catalogue record for this book is available from
the British Library.

Typeset by SetSystems Ltd, Saffron Walden, Essex
Printed and bound in Australia by
Griffin Press

Visit **www.panmacmillan.com** to read more about all our books
and to buy them. You will also find features, author interviews and
news of any author events, and you can sign up for e-newsletters
so that you're always first to hear about our new releases.

THE DREAMING VOID

Prologue

The starship *CNE Caragana* slipped down out of a night sky, its grey and scarlet hull illuminated by the pale iridescence of the massive ion storms which beset space for lightyears in every direction. Beneath the deep space vessel, Centurion Station formed a twinkling crescent of light on the dusty rock surface of its never-named planet. Crew and passengers viewed the enclave of habitation with a shared sensation of relief. Even with the hyperdrive powering them along at fifteen lightyears an hour, it had taken eighty-three days to reach Centurion Station from the Greater Commonwealth. This was about as far as any human travelled in the mid-thirty-fourth century, certainly on a regular basis.

From his couch in the main lounge, Inigo studied the approaching alien landscape with a detached interest. What he was seeing was exactly as the briefing files projected months ago, a monotonous plain of ancient lava rippled with shallow gullies that led nowhere. The thin argon atmosphere stirred the sand in short-lived flurries, chasing wispy swirls from one dune to another. It was the station which claimed his real attention.

Now they were only twenty kilometres from the ground the lights began to resolve into distinct shapes. Inigo could easily pick out the big garden dome at the centre of the human section on the northernmost segment of the inhabited crescent. A lambent emerald circle, playing hub to a dozen black transport tubes that ran out to large accommodation blocks which could have been transplanted from any exotic environment resort in the Commonwealth. From those the tubes carried on across the lava to the cube-like observatory facilities and engineering support modules.

The pocked land to the south belonged to the alien habitats; shapes and structures of various geometries and sizes, most of them illuminated. Next to the humans were the silver bubbles of the hominoid Golant; followed by the enclosed grazing grounds where the Ticoth roamed amid their food herds; then came the mammoth interconnecting tanks of the Suline, an aquatic species. The featureless Ethox tower rose up ten kilometres past the end of the Suline's metal-encased lakes, dark in the visible spectrum but with a surface temperature of 180 degrees C. They were one of the species which didn't interact with their fellow observers on any level except for formal exchanges of data concerning the probes which orbited the Void. Equally taciturn were the For-leene, who occupied five big domes of murky crystal that glowed with a mild gentian light. And they were positively social compared to the Kandra, who lived in a simple metal cube thirty metres to a side. No Kandra ship had ever landed there since the humans joined the observation two hundred and eighty years ago; not even the exceptionally long-lived Jadradesh had seen one, and the Raiel had invited those boulder-like swamp-dwellers to join the project seven thousand years earlier.

A small smile flickered on Inigo's face as he took in all the diverse zones. It was impressive to see so many aliens physically gathered in one place, a collection which served to underline the importance of their mission. Though as his view strayed out to the shadows thrown by the station, he had to admit that the living were completely overshadowed by those who had passed on before them. Centurion Station's growth and age could be loosely measured in the same way as any humble terrestrial tree. It had developed in rings which had been added to over the centuries as new species had joined the project. The broad circle of land along the concave side of the crescent was studded with

4

ruins, crumbling skeletons of habitats abandoned millennia ago as their sponsoring civilizations fell, or moved on, or evolved away from mere astrophysical concerns. Right at the centre the ancient structures had decayed to simple mounds of compacted metal and crystal flakes, beyond the ability of any archaeologist to decipher. Dating expeditions had established that this ancient heart of the station had been constructed over four-hundred-thousand years ago. Of course, as far as the timescale of the Raiel observation was concerned, that was still short.

A ring of green light was flashing on the lava field which served as a spaceport for the human section, calling down the *CNE Caragana*. Several starships were sitting on the drab rock beside the active landing zone; two hefty deep-space vessels of the same class as the *Caragana*, and some smaller starships used for placing and servicing the remote probes that constantly monitored the Void.

There was a slight judder as the starship settled, then the internal gravity field switched off. Inigo felt himself rise slightly on the couch's cushioning as the planet's seventy per cent gravity took over. It was silent in the lounge as the passengers took stock, then a happy murmur of conversation broke out to celebrate arrival. The chief steward asked everyone to make their way down to the main airlock, where they would suit up and walk over to the station. Inigo waited until his more eager colleagues had left before climbing cautiously to his feet and making his way out of the lounge. Strictly speaking, he didn't need a spacesuit, his Higher biononics could cocoon his body in perfect safety, protecting it from the thin malignant atmosphere, and even from the cosmic radiation that sleeted in from the massive stars of the Wall five hundred lightyears away. But . . . he'd travelled all this way partly to escape his unwanted heritage, now was not the time to show it off. He started suiting up along with the rest.

The handover party was a long tradition at Centurion Station. Every time a Navy ship arrived bringing new observers there was a short overlap before the previous group departed. It was celebrated in the garden dome as a sunset gala with the best buffet the culinary unit programs could produce. Tables were laid out under ancient oaks that glittered with hundreds of magic lanterns, and the dome overhead wore a halo of gold twilight. A solido projection of a string quartet played classical mood music on a little stage surrounded by a brook.

Inigo arrived quite early on, still adjusting the sleeves of his ultra-black formal evening suit. He didn't really like the jacket's long square-cut tails, they were a bit voguish for his taste, but had to admit the tailor back on Anagaska had done a superb job. Even today, if you wanted true quality clothes you needed a human in the style and fitting loop. He knew he looked good in it; in fact good enough that he didn't feel even remotely self-conscious.

The station's director was greeting all the arrivals personally. Inigo joined the end of the short line and waited his turn. He could see several aliens milling round the tables. The Golant, looking odd in clothes that approximated to the ones worn by humans. With their grey-blue skin and tall narrow heads, the polite attempt to blend in only made them appear even more out of place. There were a couple of Ticoth curled up together on the grass, both the size of ponies, though there any further resemblance ended. These were very obviously predator carnivores, with dark-green hide stretched tight over powerful muscle bands. Alarmingly big and sharp teeth appeared every time they growled at each other and the group of humans they were conversing with. Inigo instinctively checked his integral force-field function, then felt shameful for having done so. Several Suline were also present, floating about in big hemispherical glass tanks like giant champagne saucers that were held up by small regrav units. Their translators babbled away while they looked out at the humans, their bulbous bodies distorted and magnified by the curving glass.

'Inigo, I presume,' the director's overloud voice proclaimed. 'Glad to meet you; and you're bright and early for the party, as well, most commendable, laddy.'

Inigo smiled with professional deference as he shook the tall man's hand. 'Director Eyre,' he acknowledged. The briefing file's

CV had told him very little about the director, other than claiming his age was over a thousand years. Inigo suspected corrupted data, although the director's clothing was certainly historical enough; a short jacket and matching kilt with a very loud amethyst and black tartan.

'Oh please, call me Walker.'

'Walker?' Inigo queried.

'Short for LionWalker. Long story. Not to worry, laddy. Won't bore you with it tonight.'

'Ah. Right.' Inigo held his gaze level. The director had a thick stock of brown hair, but something glittered underneath it, as if his scalp was crawling with gold flecks. For the second time in five minutes Inigo held off using biononics; a field scan would have revealed what kind of technology the director was enriched with, it certainly wasn't one he recognized. He had to admit, the hair made LionWalker Eyre look youthful; just like the majority of the human race these days, no matter what branch – Higher, Advancer, Natural – vanity was pretty much uniform. But the thin grey goatee lent him an air of distinction, and cultivating that was very deliberate.

LionWalker waved his whisky tumbler across the darkened parkland, ice cubes chittering at the movement. 'So what brings you to our celebrated outpost, then, young Inigo? Thinking of the glory? The riches? Lots of sex? After all, there's not much else to do here.'

Inigo's smile tightened slightly as he realized just how drunk the director was. 'I just wanted to help. I think it's important.'

'Why?' The question was snapped out, accompanied by narrowed eyes.

'Okay. The Void is a mystery that is beyond even ANA to unravel. If we can ever figure it out we will have advanced our understanding of the universe by a significant factor.'

'Huh. Do yourself a favour, laddy, forget ANA. Bunch of decadent aristos who've been mentally taxidermied. Like they care what happens to physical humans. It's the Raiel we're helping, a people who are worth a bit of investment. And even those galumphing masterminds are stumped. You know what the Navy engineers found when they were excavating the foundations for this very garden dome?'

'No.'

'More ruins.' LionWalker took a comfortable gulp of whisky.

'I see.'

'No you don't. They were practically fossilized, nothing more than dust strata, over three quarters of a million years old. And from what I've picked up, looking at the early records the Raiel deign to make available, the observation has been going on a lot longer than that. A million years pecking away at a problem. Now that's dedication for you. We'd no be able to manage that, far too petty.'

'Speak for yourself.'

'Ah, I might have known, a believer.'

'In what?'

'Humanity.'

'That must be pretty common among the staff here, surely?' Inigo was wondering how to disengage himself, the director was starting to irritate him.

'Damn right, laddy. One of the few things that keeps me all cheered up out here all by my wee lonesome. Och ... here we go.' LionWalker tipped his head back, and stared out across the dome where the low layer of hazy light faded away. Overhead, the crystal was completely transparent, revealing the vast antagonistic nebulas that washed across the sky. Hundreds of stars shone through the glowing veil, spikes of light so intense they burned towards violet and into indigo. They multiplied towards the horizon as the planet spun slowly to face the Wall, that vast barrier of massive stars which formed the outermost skin of the galactic core.

'We can't see the Void from here, can we?' Inigo asked. He knew it was a stupid question. The Void was obscured on the other side of the Wall, right at the very heart of the galaxy. Centuries ago, before anyone had even ventured out of Earth's solar system, human astronomers had thought it was a massive black hole, they'd even detected X-ray emissions from the vast loop of superheated particles spinning round the event horizon, which helped confirm their theories. It wasn't until Wilson Kime captained the Commonwealth Navy ship *Endeavour* in the first successful human circumnavigation of the galaxy in 2560 that the truth was discovered. There was indeed an impenetrable event horizon at the core, but it didn't surround anything as natural and mundane as a superdense mass of dead stars. The Void was an artificial boundary guarding a legacy billions of years old. The Raiel claimed there was an entire universe inside, one that had been fashioned by a race that lived during the dawn of the galaxy. They had retreated into it to consummate their journey to the absolute pinnacle of evolution. In their wake, the Void was now slowly consuming the remaining stars in the galaxy. In that it was no different from the natural black holes found anchoring the centre of many galaxies; but while they employed gravity and entropy to pull in mass, the Void actively devoured stars. It was a process that was slowly yet inexorably accelerating. Unless it was stopped, the galaxy would die young, maybe three or four billion years before its allotted time. Far enough in the future that Sol would be a cold ember and the human race not even a memory. But the Raiel cared. This was the galaxy they were born in, and they believed it should be given the chance to live its full life.

LionWalker gave a little snort of amusement. 'No, of course you can't see it. Don't panic, laddy, there's no visible nightmare in our skies. DF7 is rising, that's all.' He pointed.

Inigo waited, and after a minute an azure crescent drifted up over the horizon. It was half the size of Earth's moon, with a strangely regular black mottling. He let out a soft breath of admiration.

There were fifteen of the planet-sized machines orbiting within the Centurion Station star system. Nests of concentric lattice spheres, each one possessing a different mass property and quantum field intersection, with the outer shell roughly the same diameter as Saturn. They were Raiel-built; a 'defence system' in case a Void devourment phase broke through the Wall. No one had ever seen them in action, not even the Jadradesh.

'Okay. That is impressive,' Inigo said. The DFs were in the files, of course. But a machine on that scale and head-on real was awesome.

'You'll fit in,' LionWalker declared happily. He slapped a hand on Inigo's shoulder. 'Go find yourself a drink. I made sure we had the very best culinary programs for alcohol synthesis. You can take that as a challenge.' He moved on to the next arrival.

Keeping one eye on DF7, Inigo made his way over to the bar. LionWalker wasn't kidding, the drinks were top quality, even the vodka that fountained up through the mermaid ice sculpture.

Inigo stayed at the party longer than he expected to. There was something about being thrown together with a bunch of like-minded devoted people that instinctively triggered his normally dormant social traits. By the time he finally got back to his apartment his biononics had been deflecting alcohol infiltration of his neurones for several hours. Even so, he permitted some to percolate through his artificial defences, enough to generate a mild inebriation and all the associated merits. He was going to have to live with these people for another year. No advantage in appearing aloof.

As he crawled into bed he ordered a complete de-saturation. That was one superb benefit of biononics: no hangover.

And so Inigo dreamed his first dream at Centurion Station. It wasn't his.

1

Aaron spent the whole day mingling with the faithful of the Living Dream movement in Golden Park's vast plaza, eavesdropping on their restless talk about the succession, drinking water from the mobile catering stalls, trying to find some shade from the searing sun as the heat and coastal humidity rose relentlessly. He thought he remembered arriving at daybreak; certainly the expanse of marble cobbles had been virtually empty as he walked across it. The tips of the splendid white metal pillars surrounding the area had all been crowned with rose-gold light as the local star rose above the horizon. He'd smiled round appreciatively at the outline of the replica city, matching up the topography surrounding Golden Park with the dreams he'd gathered from the gaiafield over the last ... well, for quite some time. Golden Park had started to fill up rapidly after that, with the faithful arriving from the other districts of Makkathran2 across the canal bridges and ferried in by a fleet of gondolas. By midday there must have been close to a hundred thousand of them. They all faced the Orchard Palace which sprawled possessively over the Anemone district on the other side of the Outer Circle Canal like a huddle of high dunes. And there they waited and waited with badly disguised impatience for the Cleric Council to come to a decision. Any sort of decision. The Council had been in conclave for three days now, how long could they possibly take to elect a new Conservator?

At one point in the morning he'd edged his way right up beside the Outer Circle Canal, close to the central wire and wood bridge that arched over to Anemone. It was closed, of course, as were the other two bridges on that section; while in ordinary times anyone from ultra-devout to curious tourist could cross over and wander round the vast Orchard Palace, today it had been sealed off by fit-looking junior Clerics who had undergone a lot of muscle enrichment. Camped out to one side of the temporarily forbidden bridge were hundreds of journalists from all over the Greater Commonwealth, most of them outraged by the stubborn refusal of Living Dream to leak information their way. They were easily identifiable by their chic modern clothes, and faces which were obviously maintained at peak gloss by a membrane of cosmetic scales; not even Advancer DNA produced complexions that good.

Behind them the bulk of the crowd buzzed about discussing their favourite candidate. If Aaron was judging the mood correctly, then just about ninety-five per cent of them were rooting for Ethan. They wanted him because they were done with waiting, with patience, with the status quo preached by all the other lacklustre caretakers since the Dreamer himself, Inigo, had slipped away from public life. They wanted someone who would bring their whole movement to that blissful moment of fulfilment they'd been promised from the moment they'd tasted Inigo's first dream.

Some time in the afternoon Aaron realized the woman was watching him. Nothing obvious, she wasn't staring or following him about. Instinct smoothly clicked his awareness to her location – which was an interesting trait to know he had. From then on he was conscious of where she would casually wander in order to keep an easy distance between them, how she would never have her eyes in his direction when he glanced at her. She wore a simple short-sleeved rusty-orange top and knee-length blue trousers of some modern fabric. A little different from the faithful who tended to wear the more primitive rustic clothes of wool, cotton, and leather which were favoured by Makkathran's citizens, but not contemporary enough to be obvious. Nor did her looks make her stand out. She had a flattish face and a cute-ish button nose; some of the time her slim copper shades were across her eyes, while often she had them perched up in her short dark hair. Her age was unknowable, like everyone in the Greater Commonwealth her appearance was locked into biological mid-twenties. He was certain she was well past her first couple of centuries. Again, no tangible proof.

After they'd played the orbiting satellites game for forty minutes he walked over, keeping his smile pleasant. There were no pings coming off her that his macrocellular clusters could detect, no active links to the unisphere, nor any active sensor activity. Electronically, she was as Stone Age as the city.

'Hello,' he said.

She pushed her shades up with the tip of a finger and gave him a playful grin. 'Hello yourself. So what brings you here?'

'This is a historic event.'

'Quite.'

'Do I know you?' His instinct had been right, he saw; she was nothing like the placid faithful shuffling round them, her body language was all wrong; she could keep tight control of herself, enough to fool anyone without his training – *training?* – but he could sense the attitude coiled up inside.

'Should you know me?'

He hesitated. There was something familiar about her face, something he should know about her. He couldn't think what, for the simple reason that he didn't have any memories to pull up and examine. Not of anything, now he thought about it, certainly he didn't seem to have had a life prior to today. He knew that was all wrong, yet that didn't bother him either. 'I don't recall.'

'How curious. What's your name?'

'Aaron.'

Her laughter surprised him. 'What?' he asked.

'Number one, eh? How lovely.'

Aaron's answering grin was forced. 'I don't understand.'

'If you wanted to list terrestrial animals where would you start?'

'Now you've really lost me.'

'You'd start with the aardvark. Double A, it's top of the list.'

'Oh,' he mumbled. 'Yeah, I get it.'

'Aaron,' she chuckled. 'Someone had a sense of humour when they sent you here.'

'Nobody sent me.'

'Really?' She arched a thick eyebrow. 'So you just sort of found yourself at this historic event, did you?'

'That's about it, yes.'

She dropped the copper band back down over her eyes, and shook her head in mock-dismay. 'There are several of us here, you know. I don't believe that's an accident, do you?'

'Us?'

Her hand gestured round at the crowd. 'You don't count yourself as one of these sheep, do you? A believer? Someone who thinks they can find a life at the end of these dreams Inigo so generously gifted to the Commonwealth?'

'I suppose not, no.'

'There's a lot of people watching what happens here. It's important, after all, and not just for the Greater Commonwealth. If there's a Pilgrimage into the Void some species claim it could trigger a devourment phase which will bring about the end of the galaxy. Would you want that to happen, Aaron?'

She was giving him a very intent stare. 'That would be a bad thing,' he temporized. 'Obviously.' In truth he had no opinion. It wasn't something he thought about.

'Obvious to some, an opportunity to others.'

'If you say so.'

'I do.' She licked her lips with mischievous amusement. 'So, are you going to try for my unisphere code? Ask me out for a drink?'

'Not today.'

She pouted fulsomely. 'How about unconditional sex, then, any way you like it?'

'I'll bank that one, too, thanks,' he laughed.

'You do that.' Her shoulders moved up in a slight shrug. 'Goodbye, Aaron.'

'Wait,' he said as she turned away. 'What's your name?'

'You don't want to know me,' she called out. 'I'm bad news.'

'Goodbye, Bad News.'

There was a genuine smile on her face as she looked back at him. A finger wagged. 'That's what I remember best,' she said, and was gone.

He smiled at the rear of her rapidly departing head. She vanished quickly enough amid the throng; after a minute even he couldn't spot her. He'd seen her originally because she wanted him to, he realized.

Us, she'd said, *there are several of us here.* That didn't make a lot of sense. But then she'd stirred up a lot of questions. *Why am I here?* he wondered. There was no solid answer in his mind other than it was the right place for him to be, he wanted to see who was elected. *And the memories, why don't I have any memories of anything else?* It ought to bother him, he knew, memories were the fundamental core of human identity, yet even that emotion was lacking. Strange. Humans were emotionally complex entities, yet he didn't appear to be; but he could live with it, something deep inside him was sure he'd solve the mystery of himself eventually. There was no hurry.

Towards late afternoon the crowd began to thin out as the announcement remained obstinately unforthcoming. Aaron could see disappointment on the faces moving past him on their way home, a sentiment echoed by the whispers of emotion within the local gaiafield. He opened his mind to the thoughts surrounding him, allowing them to wash in through the gateway which the gaiamotes had germinated inside his cerebellum. It was like walking through a fine mist of spectres, bestowing the plaza with flickers of unreal colour, images of times long gone yet remembered fondly; sounds muffled, as experienced through fog. His recollection of when he'd joined the gaiafield community was as hazy as the rest of his time before today, it didn't seem like the

15

kind of thing he would do, too whimsical. Gaiafield was for adolescents who considered the multisharing of dreams and emotions to be deep and profound, or fanatics like Living Dream. But he was proficient enough with the concept of voluntarily shared thoughts and memories to grasp a coherent sensation from his exposure to the raw minds in the plaza. Of course, if it could be done anywhere it would be here in Makkathran2, which Living Dream had made the capital of the Greater Commonwealth's gaiafield – with all the contradictions that threw up. To the faithful, the gaiafield was almost identical to the genuine telepathy which the citizens of the real Makkathran possessed.

Aaron felt their sorrow first-hand as the day began to wind down, with several stronger undercurrents of anger directed at the Cleric Council. In a society where you shared thoughts and feelings, so the consensus went, an election really shouldn't be so difficult. He also perceived their subliminal wish slithering through the gaiafield: Pilgrimage. The one true hope of the whole movement.

Despite the regret now gusting around him, Aaron stayed where he was. He didn't have anything else to do. The sun had almost fallen to the horizon when there was some movement on the broad balcony along the front of the Orchard Palace. All across the plaza, people suddenly smiled and pointed. There was a gentle yet urgent movement towards the Outer Circle Canal. Security force fields along the side of the water expanded, cushioning those shoved up against the railings as the pressure of bodies increased behind them. Various news company camera pods zoomed through the air like glitter-black festival balloons, adding to the thrill. Within seconds the mood in the plaza had lifted to fiery anticipation; the gaiafield suddenly crackled with excitement, its intensity rising until Aaron had to withdraw slightly to avoid being deluged by the clashing storms of colour and ethereal shouts.

The Cleric Council marched solemnly out on to the balcony, fifteen figures wearing full length scarlet and black robes. And in their centre was a lone figure whose robe was a dazzling white, edged in gold, the hood pulled forward to obscure the face inside. The dying sun glowed against the soft cloth, creating a nimbus around him. A huge cheer went up from the crowd. Camera pods edged in as close to the balcony as their operators dared; Palace force fields rippled in warning, keeping them back. As one, the Cleric Council reached out into the gaiafield with their minds; unisphere access followed swiftly, making the grand announcement available right across the Greater Commonwealth to followers and nullifidians alike.

In the middle of the balcony, the white-robed figure reached up and slowly pushed back the hood. Ethan smiled beatifically out across the city and its adulating faithful. There was a kindness about his thin solemn face which suggested he was attuned to all their fears; he sympathized and understood. Everyone could see the dark bags under his eyes which could only come from the burden of accepting such a terrible high office, of carrying the expectations of every Dreamer. As his face was exposed to the rich sunlight so the cheering down in the plaza had increased. Now the other members of the Cleric Council turned towards the new Cleric Conservator, and applauded contentedly.

Without conscious intervention, the ancillary thought routines operating inside Aaron's macrocellular clusters animated his ocular zoom. He scanned along the faces of the Cleric Council, designating each image with an integral code as the ancillary routines slotted them into macrocellular storage lacunas ready for instant recall. Later he would study them for any betraying emotion, an indicator of how they had argued and voted.

He hadn't known he had the zoom function, which piqued his curiosity. At his request the secondary thought routines ran a systems check through the macrocellular clusters enriching his nervous system. Exoimages and mental icons unfolded from neutral status to standby in his peripheral vision, lines of shifting iridescence bracketing his natural sight. The exoimages were all default symbols generated by his u-shadow, the personal interface with the unisphere which would instantly connect him to any of its massive data, communication, entertainment, and commerce functions. All standard stuff.

However, the mental icons he examined represented a great deal more than the standard physiological enrichments which Advancer DNA placed at the disposal of a human body; if he was reading their summaries correctly he was enriched with some extremely lethal biononic field function weaponry.

I know something else about me, he thought, *I have an Advancer heritage.* It was hardly a revelation, eighty per cent of Greater Commonwealth citizens had similar modifications sequenced into their DNA thanks to the old fanatic genetic visionaries on Far Away. But having biononics as well narrowed the scope fractionally, putting Aaron closer to his true origin.

Ethan raised his hands in an appeal for silence. The plaza fell quiet as the faithful held their breath, even the babble from the media pack was stilled. A sensation of serenity coupled with steely resolution issued out of the new Cleric Conservator into the gaiafield. Ethan was a man who was sure of his purpose.

'I thank my fellow Councillors for this magnificent honour,' Ethan said. 'As I begin my tenure I will do what I believe our Dreamer wanted. He showed us the way – nobody can deny that. He showed us where life can be lived and changed until it is perfect however you chose to define that as an individual. I believe he showed us this for a reason. This city he built. The devotion he engendered. It was for one purpose. To *live the Dream*. That is what we will now do.'

There was cheering out on the plaza.

'The Second Dream has begun! We have known it in our hearts. You have known it. I have known it. We have been shown inside the Void again. We have soared with the Skylord.'

Aaron scanned the Council again. He no longer needed to review and analyse their faces for later. Five of them already looked deeply uncomfortable. Around him the cheering was building to an inevitable climax, as was the speech.

'The Skylord awaits us. It will guide us to our destiny. *We will Pilgrimage!*'

Cheering turned to a naked, violent roar of adulation. Inside the gaiafield, it was as though someone was setting off fireworks fuelled by pleasure narcotics. The burst of euphoria surging through the artificial neural universe was awesome in its brightness.

Ethan waved victoriously to the faithful, then gave a last smile and went back inside the Orchard Palace.

Aaron waited as the crowd wound down. So many cried with joy as they departed he had to shake his head in dismay at their simplicity. Happiness here was universal, obligatory. The sun crept down behind the horizon, revealing a city where every window glowed with warm tangerine light – just as they did in the real one. Songs drifted along the canals as the gondoliers gave voice to their delight in traditional fashion. Eventually even the reporters began to drift away, chattering among themselves; those with doubts were keeping their voices low. Out in the unisphere, news anchors and political commentators on hundreds of worlds were beginning their sombre doomsday predictions.

None of it bothered Aaron. He was still standing in the plaza as the civic bots emerged into the starlight and began clearing away the rubbish which the excitable crowd had left behind. He now knew what he had to do next; the certainty had struck him as soon as he heard Ethan speak. Find Inigo. That's why he was here.

Aaron smiled contentedly around the dark plaza, but there was no sign of the woman. 'Now who's bad news?' he asked, and walked back into the jubilant city.

*

Looking out from the balcony along the front of the Orchard Palace, Ethan watched the last rays of the sun slide over the crowd like a translucent gold veneer. Their cries of near-religious approval echoed off the thick walls of the Palace, he could even feel the vibration in the stone balustrade in front of him. Not that there had even been any inner doubts for him during his long difficult progress, but the response of the faithful was profoundly comforting. He knew he was right to push for his own vision, to haul the whole movement out of its slothful complacency. That was evolution's message: go forward or die. The reason for the Void's existence.

Ethan closed his mind to the gaiafield and strode off the balcony as the sun finally sank below the horizon. The others of the Council followed respectfully, their scarlet cloaks fluttering in agitation as they hurried to keep up.

His personal secretary, Chief Cleric Phelim, was waiting at the top of the broad ebony stairs which curved down to the cavernous Malfit Hall on the ground level. The man was in the grey and blue robes which indicated a rank just below that of a full Councillor – a status which Ethan was going to elevate in the next couple of days. His hood was hanging down his back, allowing the soft orange lighting to glimmer off the black skin of his shaven scalp. It gave him a formidable skeletal appearance unusual amid Living Dream members who followed the fashion of long hair that was prevalent in Makkathran. When he fell in beside Ethan he was almost a head taller. That height along with a face that could remain unnervingly impassive had been useful for unsettling a great many people; he could talk to anyone with his mind fully open to the gaiafield, and yet his emotional tone was completely beyond reach. Again, not something the politely passive community of Living Dream were accustomed to. To the Council hierarchy, Phelim and his mannerisms were an uncomfortable intruder. Privately, Ethan rather enjoyed the consternation his utterly loyal deputy generated.

The giant Malfit Hall was full of Clerics who began applauding as soon as Ethan reached the bottom of the stairs. He took the time to bow at them as he made his way across the sheer black floor, smiling thanks and occasionally nodding in recognition. The images on the arching ceiling overhead mimicked the sky of Querencia; Malfit Hall was perpetually locked in dawn, producing a clear turquoise vault, with the ochre globe of the solid world Nikran circling gently around the edge, magnified to an extent where mountain ranges and a few scudding clouds were visible. Ethan's procession moved on into the Liliala Hall, where the ceiling hosted a perpetual storm, with its seething mantle of glowing clouds haloed in vivid purple lightning. Intermittent gaps allowed glimpses of the Mars Twins belonging to the Gicon's Bracelet formation, small featureless planets with a deep, dense red atmosphere that guarded whatever surface they might have from any enquiry. Senior Clerics were gathered beneath the flashing clouds. Ethan took longer here, muttering several words of thanks to those he knew, allowing his mind to radiate a gentle pride into the gaiafield.

At the arching door into the suite of rooms which the Mayor of Makkathran used to hold office, Ethan turned to the Councillors. 'I thank you once more for you confidence in me. Those who were reluctant in their endorsement, I promise to double my efforts to gain your support and trust in the years ahead.'

If any of them were vexed with their dismissal they shielded such thoughts from the openness of the gaiafield. He and Phelim alone passed into the private quarters. Inside, there were a series of grand interconnecting chambers. The heavy wooden doors were as intrusive here as they were in Makkathran; whatever species designed and built the original city clearly didn't have the psychology for enclosing themselves. Through the gaiafield, he could sense his own staff moving about within the reception rooms around him. His predecessor's team were withdrawing, their frail emotions of disgruntlement leaking into the gaiafield. Handover was normally a leisurely good-spirited affair. Not this time. Ethan wanted his authority stamped on the Orchard Palace within hours. Before the conclave began, he'd prepared an inner circle of loyalists to take charge of the main administrative posts of Living Dream. And as Ellezelin was a hierocracy, he was also faced with endorsing a new cabinet for the planet's civil government as well.

His predecessor, Jalen, had furnished the Mayor's sanctum

in paoviool blocks, resembling chunks of stone that shaped itself as required, a state intuited from the gaiafield. Ethan settled into the seat that formed behind the long rectangular slab of desk. Dissatisfaction manifested itself in small emerald sparkles erupting like an optical rash on the paoviool surfaces around him.

'I want this modern rubbish out of here by tomorrow,' Ethan said.

'Of course,' Phelim said. 'Do you want Inigo's furnishings restored?'

'No. I want this as the Waterwalker showed us.'

Phelim actually smiled. 'Much better.'

Ethan glanced round the oval sanctum with its plain walls and high windows. Despite his familiarity with the chamber he felt as if he'd never seen it before. 'For Ozzie's sake, we did it!' he exclaimed, letting out a long breath of astonishment. 'I'm sweating. Actually sweating. Can you believe that?' When he brought his hand up to his brow, he realized he was trembling. For all the years he'd planned and worked and sacrificed for this moment, the reality of success had taken him completely by surprise. It had been a hundred and fifty years since he infused the gaiamotes in order to experience the gaiafield; and on his very first night of communion he'd witnessed Inigo's First Dream. A hundred and fifty years, and the reticent adolescent from the backwater External World of Oamaru had reached one of the most influential positions in the Greater Commonwealth still available to a simple Natural human.

'You were the one they all wanted,' Phelim said; he stood slightly to one side of the desk, ignoring the big cubes of paoviool where he could have sat.

'We did it together.'

'Let's not fool ourselves here. I would never be considered even for the Council.'

'Ordinarily, no.' Ethan looked round the sanctum again. The enormity was starting to sink in. He began to wonder what the Void would look like when he could see it with his own eyes.

22

Once, decades ago, he had met Inigo. He hadn't been disappointed, exactly, but the Dreamer hadn't quite been what he'd expected. Not that he was sure what the Dreamer should have been like – more forceful and dynamic, perhaps.

'You want to begin?' Phelim asked.

'I think that's best. The Ellezelin cabinet are all faithful Living Dream members, so they can remain more or less as they are, with one exception. I want you as the Treasury Secretary.'

'Me?'

'We're going to build the starships for Pilgrimage. That isn't going to be cheap, we'll need the full financial resources of the whole Free Market Zone to fund construction. I need someone in the Treasury I can depend on.'

'I thought I was going to join the Council.'

'You are. I will elevate you tomorrow.'

'Two senior posts. That should be interesting when it comes to juggling schedules. And the empty seat on the Council I shall be filling?'

'I'm going to ask Corrie-Lyn to consider her position.'

Phelim's face betrayed a hint of censure. 'She's hardly your greatest supporter on the Council, admittedly, but I think she'd actually welcome Pilgrimage. Perhaps one of our less progressive colleagues . . .?'

'It's to be Corrie-Lyn,' Ethan said firmly. 'The remaining Councillors who oppose Pilgrimage are in a minority, and we can deal with them at our leisure. Nobody will be challenging my mandate. The faithful wouldn't tolerate it.'

'Corrie-Lyn it is, then. Let's just hope Inigo doesn't come back before we launch the starships. You know they were lovers?'

'It's the only reason she's a Councillor.' Ethan narrowed his eyes. 'Are we still looking for Inigo?'

'Our friends are,' Phelim told him. 'We don't quite have those sort of resources. There's been no sign of him that they've reported. Realistically, if your succession to Conservator doesn't bring him back within the first month or so, I'd say we are in the clear.'

'Badly phrased. That makes it sound like we've done something wrong.'

'But we don't know why Inigo was reluctant to Pilgrimage.'

'Inigo is only human, he has flaws like the rest of us. Call it a failure of nerve at the last moment if you want to be charitable. My own belief is that he'll be watching events from somewhere, cheering us on.'

'I hope so.' Phelim paused as he reviewed the information accumulating in his exoimages, his u-shadow was balancing local data with a comprehensive overview of the election. 'Marius is here, requesting an audience.'

'That didn't take him long, did it?'

'No. There are a lot of formalities required of you tonight. The Greater Commonwealth President will be calling to congratulate you, as will the leaders of the Free Market planets, and dozens of our External World allies.'

'How is the unisphere coverage?'

'Early days.' Phelim checked the summaries his u-shadow was providing. 'Pretty much what we were expecting. Some hysterical anti-Pilgrimage hotheads saying you're going to kill all of us. Most of the serious anchors are trying to be balanced, and explain the difficulties involved. The majority seem to regard Pilgrimage as a politician's promise.'

'There are no difficulties in accomplishing Pilgrimage,' Ethan said in annoyance. 'I have seen the Skylord's dream. It is a noble creature, it will lead us inside the Void. We just have to locate the Second Dreamer. Any developments on that today?'

'None. Thousands are coming forward claiming to be dreaming the Skylord. They don't help our search.'

'You must find him.'

'Ethan . . . it took our best Dream Masters months to assemble the existing fragments into the small dream we have. We believe in this case there is no firm link such as Inigo had with the Void. These fragments, they could be entering the gaiafield in a number of ways. Unaware carriers. Directly from the Void? Perhaps it's Ozzie's galactic field. Then there's an overspill from the Silfen

Motherholme or some other post-physical sentient having fun at our expense. Even Inigo himself.'

'It's not Inigo. I know that. I know the feel of his dreams, we all do. This is something different. I was the one who was drawn to those first few fragments, remember. I realized what they were. There is a Second Dreamer.'

'Well, now you are Conservator you can authorize a more detailed monitoring of the gaiafield's confluence nests, track down the origin that way.'

'Is that possible? I thought the gaiafield was beyond our direct influence.'

'The Dream Masters claim they can do this, yes. Certain modifications can be made to the nests. It won't be cheap.'

Ethan sighed. The conclave had been mentally exhausting, and that had just been the beginning. 'So many things. All at once.'

'I'll help you. You know that.'

'I do. And I thank you, my friend. One day we'll stand in the real Makkathran. One day we will make our lives perfect.'

'Soon.'

'For Ozzie's sake I hope so. Now, ask Marius in, please.' Ethan stood courteously to receive his guest. That it should be the ANA Faction representative he saw first was a telling point. He didn't relish the way he and Phelim had relied on Marius during his campaign to be elected Conservator. In an ideal universe they would have needed no outside aid, certainly not one with so many potentially worrying strings attached. Not that there was ever any suggestion of *quid pro quo* from Marius. None of the Factions inside the near-post-physical intelligence of Earth's Advanced Neural Activity system would ever be so blunt.

The representative smiled courteously as he was shown in. Of average height, he had a round face with sharp green eyes emphasized by wide irises; nose and mouth were narrow, and his ears were large but flattened back so severely they could have been ridges in the skull. His thick auburn hair was flecked with gold, no doubt the outcome of some Advancer ancestor vanity. There was nothing to indicate his Higher functions. Ethan was using his internal enrichments to run a passive scan, and if any of the representative's field functions were active they were too sophisticated to perceive. He wouldn't be surprised by that, Marius would be enriched with the most advanced biononics in existence. The representative's long black toga suit generated its own surface haze which flowed about him like a slim layer of mist, the faintest tendrils slithered behind him as he walked.

'Your Eminence,' Marius said, and bowed formally. 'My most sincere congratulations on your election.'

Ethan smiled. It was all he could do not to shudder. Every deep-honed primitive instinct he possessed had picked up on how dangerous the representative was. 'Thank you.'

'I'm here to assure you we will continue our support of your goals.'

'You don't consider Pilgrimage will trigger the end of the galaxy, then?' What he desperately wanted to ask was: who is *we*? But there were so many Factions inside ANA constantly making and breaking alliances it was virtually a null question. It was enough the Faction Marius represented wanted the Pilgrimage to go ahead. Ethan no longer cared that their reasons were probably the antithesis of his own, or if they regarded him as a simple political tool. Not that he would ever know. Pilgrimage was what mattered, delivering the faithful to their promised universe. All that mattered, in fact. He didn't care if he assisted someone else's political goal as long as it didn't interfere with his own.

'Of course not.' Marius grinned in such a way it was as if they were sharing some private joke about how stupid the rest of humanity was compared to themselves. 'If that was the case, then those already in the Void would have triggered that event.'

'People need to be educated. I would appreciate your help with that.'

'We will do what we can, of course. However, we are both working against a considerable amount of mental inertia, not to mention prejudice.'

'I am very conscious of that. The Pilgrimage will polarize opinion across the Greater Commonwealth.'

26

'Not just those of humans. There are a number of species who are showing an interest in this development.'

'The Ocisen Empire.' Ethan spat it out with as much contempt as possible.

'Not to be entirely underestimated,' Marius said. It wasn't quite chiding.

'The only ones I concern myself with are the Raiel. They have publicly stated their opposition to anyone trying to enter the Void.'

'Which is of course where our assistance will be most beneficial to you. Our original offer still stands, we will supply ultradrives for your Pilgrimage ships.'

Ethan, a scholar of ancient history, guessed this was what the old religious icon Adam had felt when he was offered the apple. 'And in return?'

'The status quo which currently reigns in the Greater Commonwealth will be over.'

'And that benefits you, how?'

'Species survival. Evolution requires progression or extinction.'

'I thought you would be aiming for transcendence,' Phelim said flatly.

Marius didn't even look in his direction, his eyes remained fixed on Ethan. 'And that isn't evolution?'

'It's a very drastic evolution,' Ethan said.

'Not unlike your hopes of Pilgrimage.'

'So why not join us?'

Marius answered with a mirthless smile. 'Join us, Conservator.'

Ethan sighed. 'We've dreamed what awaits us.'

'Ah, so it boils down to the old human problem. Risk the unknown, or go with the comfortable.'

'I think the phrase you want is: better the devil you know.'

'Whatever. Your Eminence, we still offer you the ultradrive.'

'Which no one has ever really seen. You just hint at it.'

'ANA tends to be somewhat protective towards its advanced technologies. However, I assure you it is real. Ultradrive is at least equal to the drive used by the Raiel, if not superior.'

Ethan tried not to smile at the arrogance.

'Oh, I assure you, Conservator,' Marius said. 'ANA does not make that boast lightly.'

'I'm sure it doesn't. So when can you supply them?'

'When your Pilgrimage ships are ready, the drives will be here.'

'And the rest of ANA, the Factions which don't agree with you, they'll just stand by and quietly let you hand over this supertechnology?'

'Effectively, yes. Do not concern yourself with our internal debates.'

'Very well, I accept your most generous offer. Please don't be offended, but we will also be building our own more mundane drive units for the ships – just in case.'

'We expected nothing else.' Marius bowed again, and left the room.

Phelim let out a soft whistle of relief. 'So that's it, we're just a trigger factor in their political wars.'

Ethan tried to sound blasé. 'If it gets us what we want, I can live with it.'

'I think you are wise not to rely on them exclusively. We must include our own drives in the construction program.'

'Yes. The design teams have worked on that premise from the beginning.' His secondary routines started to pull files from the storage lacunas in his macrocellular clusters. 'In the meantime, let us begin with some simple appointments, shall we?'

*

Aaron walked across the red marble bridge that arched over Sisterhood Canal, linking Golden Park with the Low Moat district. A strip of simple paddock land which had no city buildings, only stockades for commercial animals, and a couple of archaic markets. He strode along the meandering paths illuminated by small oil lanterns hanging from posts and on into the Ogden district. This was also grassland, but contained the majority of the city's wooden-built stables where the aristocracy kept their horses and carriages. It was where the main city gate had been cut into the wall.

The gates were open wide when he went through, mingling with little groups of stragglers heading back to the urban expanse outside. Makkathran2 was surrounded by a two-mile-wide strip of parkland separating it from the vast modern metropolis which had sprung up around it over the last two centuries. Greater Makkathran2 now sprawled over four hundred square miles, an urban grid that contained sixteen million people, ninety-nine per cent of whom were devout Living Dream followers. It was now the capital of Ellezelin, taking over from the original capital city of Riasi after the 3379 election returned a Living Dream majority to the planetary senate.

There was no powered transport across the park; no ground taxis or underground train, or even pedwalk strips. And, of course, no capsule was allowed into Makkathran2's airspace. Inigo's thinking was simple enough: the faithful would never mind walking the distance; that was what everyone did on Querencia. He wanted authenticity to be the governing factor in his movement's citadel. Riding across the park, however, was permissible, after all, Querencia had horses. Aaron smiled at that notion as he set off past the gates. Then an elusive memory flickered like a dying hologram. There was a time when he had clung to the neck of some giant horse as they galloped across an undulating terrain. The movement was powerful and rhythmic, yet strangely leisurely. It was as if the horse was gliding rather than galloping; bounding forward. He knew exactly how to flow with it, grinning wildly as they raced onwards. Air blasting against his face, hair wild. Astonishingly deep sapphire sky bright and warm above. The horse had a small, tough-looking horn at the top of its forehead. Tipped with the traditional black metal spike.

Aaron grunted dismissively. It must have been some sensory immersion drama he'd accessed on the unisphere. Not real.

The midpoint of the park was a uniform ridge. When Aaron reached the crest it was as though he was stepping across a rift in time; behind him the quaintly archaic profile of Makkathran2

bathed in its alien orange glow; while in front were the modern-
istic block towers and neat district grids producing a multicoloured haze that stretched over the horizon. Regrav capsules
slipped effortlessly through the air above it in strictly maintained
traffic streams, long horizontals bands of fast motion winding up
into cycloidal junctions that knitted the city together in a pulsing
kinetic dance. In the south-eastern sky he could see the brighter
lights of starships as they slipped in and out of the atmosphere
directly above the spaceport. A never-ending procession of big
cargo craft providing the city with economic bonds to planets
outside the reach of the official Free Market Zone wormholes.

When he reached the outer rim of the park he told his u-
shadow to call a taxi. A glossy jade-coloured regrav capsule
dropped silently out of the traffic swarm above and dilated its
door. Aaron settled on the front bench, where he had a good
view through the one-way fuselage.

'Hotel Buckingham.'

He frowned as the capsule dived back up into the broad
stream circling round the dark expanse of park. Had that instruction come from him or his u-shadow?

At the first junction they whipped round and headed deeper
into the urban grid. The tree-lined boulevards a regulation
hundred metres below actually had a few ground cars driving
along the concrete. People rode horses among them. Bicycles
were popular. He shook his head in bemusement.

The Hotel Buckingham was a thirty-storey pentagon ribbed
with balconies, and sending sharp pinnacles soaring up out of
each corner. It glowed a lambent pearl-white, except for its
hundred of windows which were black recesses. The roof was a
small strip of lush jungle. Tiny lights glimmered among the
foliage as patrons dined and danced in the open air.

Aaron's taxi dropped him at the arrivals pad in the centre.
He had a credit coin in his pocket, which activated to his DNA
and paid for the ride. There was a credit code loaded in a macrocellular storage lacuna which he could have used, but the coin
made the ride harder to trace. Not impossible by any means, just

taking it out of reach of the ordinary citizen. As the taxi took off he glanced up at the tall monochromatic walls fencing him in, feeling unnervingly exposed.

'Am I registered here?' he asked his u-shadow.

'Yes. Room 3088. A penthouse suite.'

'I see.' He turned and looked directly at the penthouse's balcony. He'd known its location automatically. 'And can I afford that?'

'Yes. The penthouse costs 1500 Ellezelin pounds per night. Your credit coin has a limit of five million Ellezelin pounds a month.'

'A month?'

'Yes.'

'Paid by whom?'

'The coin is supported by a Central Augusta Bank account. The account details are secure.'

'And my personal credit code?'

'The same.'

Aaron walked into the lobby. 'Nice to be rich,' he told himself.

The penthouse was five rooms and a small private swimming pool. As soon as Aaron walked into the main lounge he checked himself out in the mirror. A face older than the norm, approaching thirty, possessing short black hair and (oddly) eyes with a hint of purple in their grey irises. Slightly oriental features, but with skin that was rough, and a dark stubble shadow.

Yep, that's me.

Which instinctive response was reassuring, but still didn't give any clues by way of identity.

He settled into a broad armchair which faced an external window, and turned up the opacity to stare out across the night-time city towards the invisible heart which Inigo had built. There was a lot of information in those mock-alien structures which would help him find his quarry. Not the kind of data stored in electronic files; if it was that easy Inigo would have been found by now. No, the information he needed was personal, which brought some unique access problems for someone like him, an unbeliever.

He ordered room service. The hotel was pretentious enough to employ human chefs. When the food arrived he could appreciate the subtleties of its preparation, there was a definite difference to culinary unit produce. He sat in the big chair, watching the city as he ate. Any route in to the senior Clerics and Councillors wouldn't be easy, he realized. But then, this Pilgrimage had presented him with a fairly unique opportunity. If they were going to fly into the Void, they'd need ships. It gave him an easy enough cover. That just left the problem of who to try and cultivate.

His u-shadow produced an extensive list of senior Clerics, providing him with gossip about who was allied with Ethan and who, post-election, was going to be scrubbing Council toilets for the next few decades.

It took him half the night, but the name was there. It was even featured on the city news web as Ethan began reorganizing Living Dream's hierarchy to suit his own policy. Not obvious, but it had a lot of potential: Corrie-Lyn.

*

The courier case arrived at Troblum's apartment an hour before he was due to make his presentation to the Navy review panel. He wrapped a cloak round himself and walked out to the glass lift in the lobby as the emerald fabric adjusted itself to his bulk. Ancient mechanical systems whirred and clanked as the lift slid smoothly downwards. They weren't totally original, of course, technically the whole building dated back over one thousand three hundred and fifty years. During that time there had been a lot of refurbishment and restoration work. Then five hundred years ago a stabilizer field generator was installed, which maintained the molecular bonds inside all the antique bricks, girders, and composite sheets comprising the main body of the building. Essentially, as long as there was power to the generator, entropy was held at arm's length.

Troblum had managed to acquire custodianship over a hundred years ago, following a somewhat obsessional twenty-seven year campaign. Nobody owned property on Arevalo any more, it was a Higher world, part of the Central Commonwealth – back when the building had been put up they called it phase one space. Persuading the previous tenants to leave had taken up all his Energy and Mass Allocation for years, as well as his meagre social skills. He had used mediator councillors, lawyers, historical restitution experts, and even had to launch an appeal against Daroca City Council who managed the stabilizer generator. During the campaign he'd acquired an unexpected ally which had probably helped swing the whole thing in his favour. Whatever the means, the outcome was that he now had undisputed occupancy rights for the whole building. No one else lived in it, and very few had ever been invited in.

The lift stopped at the entrance hall. Troblum walked past the empty concierge desk to the tall door of stained glass. Outside, the courier case was hovering a metre and a half above the pavement, a dull metal box with transport certificates glowing pink on one end, and shielded against field scans. His u-shadow confirmed the contents and directed it into the hall, where it landed on his trolley. The base opened and deposited the package, a fat silvered cylinder half a metre long. Troblum kept the door open until the case departed, then closed it. Privacy shielding came up around the entrance hall and he walked back into the lift. The trolley followed obediently.

Originally, the building had been a factory, which gave each of the five floors very tall ceilings. Then, as was the way of things in those early days of the Commonwealth, the city expanded and prospered, pushing industry out of the old centre. The factory had been converted into high-class apartments. One of the two penthouse loft apartments which took up the entire fifth floor had been purchased by the Halgarth Dynasty as part of their massive property portfolio on Arevalo. The other apartments had all been restored to a reasonable approximation of their layout and décor in 2380, but Troblum had concentrated his formidable energies on the Halgarth one, where he now lived.

In order to get it as near perfect as possible he had extracted both architect and interior designer plans from the city's deep archive. Those had been complemented by some equally ancient visual recordings from the Michelangelo news show of that era. But his main source of detail had been the forensic scans from the Serious Crimes Directorate which he'd obtained direct from ANA. After combining the data, he had spent five years painstakingly recrafting the extravagant vintage décor; the end result of which gave him three *en suite* bedrooms and a large open-plan lounge which was separated from a kitchen section by a marble-topped breakfast bar. A window wall had a balcony on the other side, providing a grand view out across the Caspe River

When the City Council's historical maintenance officer made her final review of the project she'd been delighted with the outcome, but the reason for Troblum's dedication completely eluded her. He'd expected nothing else, her field was the building itself. What had gone on inside at the time of the Starflyer War was his area of expertise. He would never use the word obsession, but that whole episode had become a lot more than just a hobby to him. One day he was determined he would publish the definitive history of the War.

The penthouse door opened for him. Solidos of the three girls were sitting on the blue-leather settee up by the window wall. Catriona Saleeb was dressed in a red and gold robe, its belt tied loosely so that her silk underwear was visible. Long curly black hair tumbled chaotically over her shoulders as she tossed her head. She was the smallest of the three, the solido's animation software holding her image as a bubbly twenty-one-year-old, carefree and eager. Leaning up against her, sipping tea from a big cup was Trisha Marina Halgarth. Her dark heart-shaped face had small dark-green butterfly wing OCtattoos flowing back from each hazel eye, the antique technology undulating slowly in response to each facial motion. Lastly, and sitting just apart from the other two, was Isabella Halgarth. She was a tall blonde, with long straight hair gathered into a single tail. The fluffy white sweater she wore was a great deal more tantalizing that it strictly ought to have been, riding high above her midriff, while her jeans were little more than an outer layer of blue skin running down long athletic legs. Her face had high cheekbones, giving her an aristocratic appearance that was backed up with an attitude of cool distain. While her two friends called out eager hellos to Troblum, she merely acknowledged him with a simple nod.

With a regretful sigh, Troblum told his u-shadow to isolate the girls. They'd been his companions for fifty years, he enjoyed their company a great deal more than any real human. And they helped anchor him in the era he so loved. Unfortunately, he couldn't afford distractions right now, however delightful. It had taken him decades to refine the animation programs and bestow valid I-sentient personalities to each solido. The three of them had shared the apartment during the Starflyer War, becoming involved in a famous disinformation sting by the Starflyer. Isabella herself had been one of the alien's most effective agents operating inside the Commonwealth, seducing high-ranking politicians and officials, and subtly manipulating them. For a while after the War, to be *Isabella-ed* was a Commonwealth-wide phrase meaning to be screwed over. But that infamy had faded eventually. Even among people who routinely lived for over five hundred years, events lost their potency and relevance. Today the Starflyer War was simply one of those formative incidents at the start of the Commonwealth, like Ozzie and Nigel, the Hive, the *Endeavour*'s circumnavigation, and cracking the Planters' nanotech. When he was younger, Troblum certainly hadn't been interested; then purely by chance he discovered he was descended from someone called Mark Vernon who apparently played a vital role in the War. He'd started to casually research his ancestor, wanting nothing more than a few details, to learn a little chunk of family background. That was a hundred and eighty years ago, and he was still as fascinated by the whole Starflyer War now as he had been when he opened those first files on the period.

The girls turned away from Troblum and the trolley that

followed him in, chattering away brightly among themselves. He looked down at the cylinder as it turned transparent. Inside it contained a strut of metal a hundred and fifteen centimetres long; at one end there was a node of plastic where the frayed ends of fibre-optic cable stuck out like a straggly tail. The surface was tarnished and pocked, it was also kinked in the middle, as if something had struck it. Troblum unlocked the end of the cylinder, ignoring the hiss of gas as the protective argon spilled out. There was nothing he could do to stop his hands trembling as he slid the strut out; nor was there anything to be done about his throat muscles tightening. Then he was holding the strut up, actually witnessing the texture of its worn surface against his own skin. He smiled down on it the way a Natural man would regard his newborn child. Subcutaneous sensors enriching his fingers combined with his Higher field-scan function to run a detailed analysis. The strut was an aluminium-titanium alloy, with a specific hydrocarbon chain reinforcement; it was also two thousand four hundred years old. He was holding *in his own hands* a piece of the *Marie Celeste*, the Starflyer's ship.

After a long moment he put the strut back into the cylinder, and ran the atmospheric purge, sealing it back in argon. He would never physically hold it again, it was too precious for that. It would go into the other apartment where he kept his collection of memorabilia; a small specialist stabilizer field generator would maintain its molecular structure down the centuries. As was fitting.

Troblum acknowledged the authenticity of the strut and authorized his quasi-legal bank account on Wessex to pay the final instalment to the black-market supplier on Far Away who had acquired the item for him. It wasn't that having cash funds was illegal for a Higher, but Higher culture was based on the tenet of individuals being mature and intelligent enough to accept responsibility for themselves and acting within the agreed parameters of societal norm. *I am government*, was the culture's fundamental political kernel. However there was a lot of flexibility within those strictures. Quiet methods of converting a Higher citizen's Energy and Mass Allocation, the so-called Central Dollar, to actual hard cash acceptable on the External Worlds were well established for those who felt they needed such an option. EMA didn't qualify as money in the traditional sense, it was simply a way of regulating Higher citizen activity, preventing excessive or unreasonable demands being placed on communal resources, of whatever nature, by an individual.

As the trolley headed back out of the apartment, Troblum hurried to his bedroom. He barely had time to shower and put on a toga suit before he was due to leave. The glass lift took him down to the basement garage where his regrav capsule was parked. It was an old model, dating back two centuries, a worn chrome-purple in colour and longer than modern versions, with the forward bodywork stretching out like the nose-cone of some External World aircraft. He clambered in, taking up over half of the front bench which was designed to hold three people. The capsule glided out of the garage and tipped up to join the traffic stream overhead. Ageing internal compensators could barely cope with such a steep angle, so Troblum was pressed back into the cushioning as they ascended.

The centre of Daroca was a pleasing blend of modern structures with their smooth pinnacle geometries, pretty or substantial historical buildings like Troblum's, and the original ample mosaic of parkland which the founding council had laid out. Airborne traffic streams broadly followed the pattern of ancient thoroughfares. Troblum's capsule flew northward under the planet's bronze sunlight, heading out over the newer districts where the buildings were spaced further apart and big individual houses were in the majority.

Low in the western sky he could just make out the bright star that was Air. It was the project which had attracted him to Arevalo in the first place. An attempt to construct an artificial space habitat the size of a gas giant planet. After two centuries of effort the project governors had built nearly eighty per cent of the spherical geodesic lattice which would act as both the conductor and generator of a single encapsulating force field. Once it was powered up (siphoning energy directly from the star via a zero-width wormhole) the interior would be filled with a standard oxygen-nitrogen atmosphere, harvested from the system's outer moons and gas giants. After that, various biological components both animal and botanical would be introduced, floating around inside to establish a biosphere lifecycle. The end result, a zero-gee environment with a diameter greater than Saturn, would give people the ultimate freedom to fly free, adding an extraordinary new dimension to the whole human experience.

Critics, of which there were many, claimed it was a poor – and pointless – copy of the Silfen Motherholme which Ozzie had discovered, where an entire star was wrapped by a breathable atmosphere. Proponents argued that this was just a stepping stone, an important, inspiring testament that would expand the ability and outlook of Higher culture. Their rationale won them a hard-fought Central Worlds referendum to obtain the EMAs they needed to complete the project.

Troblum, who was first and foremost a physicist, had been attracted to Air by just that rationalization. He had spent a constructive seventy years working to translate theoretical concepts into physical reality, helping to build the force-field generators which studded the geodesic lattice. At which point his preoccupation with the Starflyer War had taken over, and he'd gained the attention of people running an altogether more interesting construction project. They made him an offer he couldn't refuse. It often comforted him how that section of his life mirrored that of his illustrious ancestor, Mark.

His capsule descended into the compound of the Commonwealth Navy office. It consisted of a spaceport field lined by two rows of big hangars and maintenance bays. Arevalo was primarily a base for the Navy exploration division. The starships sitting on the field were either long-range research vessels or more standard passenger craft; while the three matt-black towers looming along the northern perimeter housed the astrophysics laboratories and scientific-crew-training facilities. Troblum's capsule drifted through the splayed arches which the main tower stood on, and landed directly underneath it. He walked over to the base of the nearest arch column, toga suit surrounding him in a garish ultraviolet aurora. There weren't many people about, a few officers on their way to regrav capsules. His appearance drew glances; for a Higher to be so big was very unusual. Biononics usually kept a body trim and healthy, it was their primary function. There were a few cases where a slightly unusual bio-chemical makeup presented operational difficulties for biononics, but that was normally remedied by a small chromosome modifi-cation. Troblum refused to consider it. He was what he was, and didn't see the need to apologize for it to anyone in any fashion.

Even the short distance from the capsule to the column made his heart race. He was sweating when he went into the empty vestibule at the base of the column. Deep sensors scanned him and he put his hand on a tester globe, allowing the security system to confirm his DNA. One of the lifts opened. It descended for an unnerving amount of time.

The heavily shielded conference room reserved for his presentation was unremarkable. An oval chamber with an oval rockwood table in the middle. Ten pearl-white shaper chairs with high backs were arranged round it. Troblum took the one opposite the door, and started running checks with the Navy office net to make sure all the files he needed were loaded properly.

Four Navy officers walked in, three of them in identical toga suits whose ebony surface effect rippled in subdued patterns. Their seniority was evidenced only in small red dots glowing on their shoulders. He recognized all of them without having to reference their u-shadows. Mykala, a third-level captain and the local ftl drive bureau director; Eoin, another captain who special-ized in alien activities, and Yehudi, the Arevalo office com-mander. Accompanying them was First Admiral Kazimir Burnelli. Troblum hadn't been expecting him. The shock of seeing the commander of the Commonwealth Navy in person made him stand up quickly. It wasn't just his position that was fascinating, the Admiral was the child of two very important figures of the Starflyer War, and famous for his age: one-thousand-two-hundred-and-six years old, seven or eight centuries past the time most Highers downloaded themselves into ANA.

The Admiral wore a black uniform of old-fashioned cloth, stylishly cut. It suited him perfectly, emphasizing broad shoulders and a lean torso, the classic authority figure. He was tall with an olive skin and a handsome face; Troblum recognized some of his father's characteristics, the blunt jaw and jet black hair, but his mother's finer features were there also, a nose that was almost dainty and pale friendly eyes.

'Admiral!' Troblum exclaimed.

'Pleased to meet you,' Kazimir Burnelli extended a hand.

It took Troblum a moment before he realized what to do, and put out his own hand to shake – suddenly very pleased his toga suit had a cooling web and he was no longer sweating. The social formality file his u-shadow had pushed into his exovision was abruptly withdrawn.

'I'll be representing ANA:Governance for this presentation,' Kazimir said. Troblum had guessed as much. Kazimir Burnelli was the essential human link in the chain between ANA: Governance and the ships of the Navy deterrent fleet, a position of trust and responsibility he'd held for over eight hundred years. Something in the way he carried himself was indicative of all those centuries he'd lived, an aura of weariness that anyone in his presence couldn't help be aware of.

There were so many things Troblum was desperate to ask, starting with: *Have you stayed in your body so long because your father's life was so short?* And possibly: *Can you get me access to your grandfather?* But instead he meekly said, 'Thank you for coming, Admiral.' Another privacy shield came on around the chamber, and the net confirmed they were grade-one secure.

'So what have you got for us?' the Admiral asked.

'A theory on the Dyson Pair generators,' Troblum said. He

activated the chamber's web node so the others could share the data and projections in his files, and began to explain.

The Dyson Pair were stars three lightyears apart that were confined within giant force fields. The barriers had been established in AD1200 by the Anomine for good reason. The Prime aliens who had already spread from their homeworld around Alpha to Beta were pathologically hostile to all biological life except their own. The Starflyer was one of them that had escaped imprisonment, and it had manipulated the Commonwealth into opening the force field around Dyson Alpha, resulting in a war which had killed in excess of fifty million humans. Eventually, the force field had been reactivated by Ozzie and Mark Vernon, ending the War, but it had been a shockingly close call. The Navy had kept an unbroken watch on the stars ever since.

Centuries later, when the Raiel invited the Commonwealth to join the Void observation project at Centurion Station, human scientists had been startled by the similarity of the planet-sized defence systems deployed throughout the Wall stars and the generators that produced the Dyson Pair force fields.

Until now, Troblum said, everyone assumed the Anomine had a technology base equal to the Raiel. He disputed that. His analysis of the Dyson Pair generators showed they were almost identical in concept to the Centurion Station DF machines.

'Which proves the point, surely?' Yehudi said.

'Quite the opposite,' Troblum replied smoothly.

The Anomine homeworld had been visited several times by the Navy exploration division. As a species they had divided two millennia ago; with the most technologically advanced group elevating to post-physical sentience, while the remainder retro-evolved to a simple pastoral culture. Although they had developed wormholes and sent exploration ships ranging across the galaxy, they had only ever settled a dozen or so nearby star systems, none of which had massive astroengineering facilities. The remaining pastoral societies had no knowledge of the Dyson Pair generators, and the post-physicals had long since withdrawn from contact with their distant cousins. An extensive search of the sector by successive Navy ships had failed to locate the assembly structure for the Dyson Pair generators. Until now, human astro-archaeologists had assumed the abandoned machinery had decayed away into the vacuum, or was simply lost.

Given the colossal scale involved, Troblum said, neither was truly believable. First off, however sophisticated they were, it would have taken the Anomine at least a century to build such a generator starting from scratch, let alone two of them – look how long it was taking Highers to construct Air, and that was with near unlimited EMAs. Secondly, the generators were needed quickly. The Prime aliens of Dyson Alpha were already building slower than light starships, which was why the Anomine sealed them in. If there had been a century gap while the Anomine beavered away at construction, the Primes would have expanded out to every star within a fifty lightyear radius before the generators were finished.

'The obvious conclusion,' Troblum said, 'is that the Anomine simply appropriated existing Raiel systems from the Wall. All they would need for that would be a scaled-up wormhole generator to transport them to the Dyson Pair, and we know they already possessed the basic technology. 'What I would like is for the Navy to start a detailed search of interstellar space around the Dyson Pair. The Anomine wormhole drive or drives could conceivably still be there. Especially if it was a "one shot" device.' He gave the Admiral an expectant look.

Kazimir Burnelli paused as the last of Troblum's files closed. 'The Primes built the largest wormhole ever known in order to invade the Commonwealth across five hundred lightyears,' he said.

'It was called Hell's Gateway,' Troblum said automatically.

'You do know your history. Good. Then you should also know it was only a couple of kilometres in diameter. Hardly enough to transport the barrier generators.'

'Yes, but I'm talking about a completely new manifestation of wormhole-drive technology. A wormhole that doesn't need a correspondingly large generator: you simply project the exotic matter effect to the size required.'

'I've never heard of anything like that.'

'It can be achieved easily within our understanding of wormhole theory, Admiral.'

'Easily?' Kazimir Burnelli turned to Mykala. 'Captain?'

'I suppose it may be possible,' Mykala said. 'I'd need to re-examine exotic matter theory before I could say one way or another.'

'I'm already working on a method,' Troblum blurted.

'Any success?' Mykala queried.

Troblum suspected she was being derisive, but lacked the skill to interpret her tone. 'I'm progressing, yes. There's certainly no theoretical block to diameter. It's all down to the amount of energy available.'

'To ship a Dyson barrier generator halfway across the galaxy you'd need a nova,' Mykala said.

Now Troblum was sure she was mocking him. 'It needs nothing like that much energy,' he said. 'In any case, if they built the generators on or near their home star they would still have needed a transport system, wouldn't they? If they built them in situ, which is very doubtful, where is the construction site? We'd have found something that big by now. Those generators were moved from wherever the Raiel had originally installed them.'

'Unless it was produced by their post-physicals,' she said. 'Who knows what abilities they have or had.'

'Sorry, I'm going to have to go with Troblum on that one,' Eoin said. 'We know the Anomine didn't elevate to post-physical status until after the Dyson barriers were established, that's approximately a hundred and fifty years later.'

'Exactly,' Troblum said triumphantly. 'They had to be using a level of technology effectively equal to ours. Somewhere out there in interstellar space is an abandoned drive system capable of moving objects the size of planets. We need to find it, Admiral. I've already compiled a search methodology using current Navy exploration craft which I'd like—'

'Let me just stop you there,' Kazimir Burnelli said. 'Troblum, what you've given us so far is a very convincing hypothesis. So much so that I'm going to immediately forward your data to a senior department review committee. If they give me a positive verdict you and I will discuss the Navy's investigation options. And believe me, for this day and age, that's being fast-tracked, okay?'

'But you can sanction the exploration division to begin the search right away, you have that authority.'

'I do, yes; but it don't exercise it without good reason. What you've shown us is more than sufficient to start a serious appraisal. We will follow due process. Then if you're right—'

'Of course I'm fucking right,' Troblum snapped. He knew in a remote fashion he was acting inappropriately, but his goal was so close. He'd assumed the Admiral's unexpected appearance today meant the search could begin right away. 'I don't have the EMAs for that many starships myself, that's why the Navy has to be involved.'

'There would never be an opportunity for an individual to perform a search,' Kazimir replied lightly. 'Space around the Dyson Pair remains restricted. This is a Navy project.'

'Yes, Admiral,' Troblum mumbled. 'I understand.' Which he did. But that didn't quell the resentment at the bureaucracy involved.

'I notice you haven't included your results on this "one shot" wormhole drive idea,' Mykala said. 'That's a big hole in the proposal.'

'It's at an early stage,' Troblum said, which wasn't quite true. He'd held back on his project precisely because he was so near to success. It was going to be the clinching argument if the presentation hadn't gone well. Which in a way it hadn't. But . . . 'I hope to be giving you some positive results soon.'

'That I will be very interested in,' Kazimir said, finally producing a smile that lifted centuries away from him. 'Thank you for bringing this to us. And I do genuinely appreciate the effort involved.'

'It's what I do,' Troblum said gruffly. He kept silent as the shielding switched off, and the others left the chamber. What he wanted to shout after the Admiral was: *Your mother made her decisions without any committee to hold her hand, and as for what your grandfather would say about getting a consensus* ... Instead he let out a disgruntled breath as he sealed the files back into his storage lacuna. Meeting an idol was always such a risk, so few of them ever really matched up to their own legend.

*

The Delivery Man was woken by his youngest daughter just as a chilly dawn light was rising outside. Little Rosa had once again decided that five hours' sleep was quite sufficient for her, now she was sitting up in her cot wailing for attention. And milk. Beside him, Lizzie was just starting to stir out of a deep sleep. Before she could wake, he swung himself out of bed and hurried along the landing to the nursery. If he wasn't quick enough Tilly and Elsie would be woken up, then nobody would get any peace.

The paediatric housebot floated through the nursery door after him, a simple ovoid just over a metre high. It extruded Rosa's milk bulb through its neutral grey skin. Both he and his wife Lizzie hated the idea of a machine, even one as sophisticated as the housebot, caring for the child, so he settled her on his lap in the big chair at the side of the cot and started feeding her out of the bulb. Rosa smiled adoringly round the nozzle, and squirmed deeper into his embrace. The housebot extended a hose which attached to the outlet patch on her sleepsuit's nappy, and siphoned away the night's wee. Rosa waved contentedly at the housebot as it glided out of the nursery.

'Goobi,' she cooed, and resumed drinking.

'Goodbye,' the Delivery Man corrected. At seventeen months, Rosa's vocabulary was just starting to develop. The biononic organelles in her cells were effectively inactive other than reproducing themselves to supplement her new cells as she grew. Extensive research had shown it was best for a Higher-born human to follow nature's original development schedule up

45

until about puberty. After that the biononics could be used as intended; one function of which was to modify the body however the host wanted. He still wasn't sure that was such a good idea, handing teenagers unrestrained power over their own physiology frequently led to some serious self-inflicted blunders. He always remembered the time when he was fourteen and had a terrible crush on a seventeen-year-old girl. He'd tried to *improve* his genitals. It had taken five hugely embarrassing trips to a biononic procedures doctor to sort out the painful abnormal growths.

When Rosa finished he carried her downstairs. He and Lizzie lived in a classic Georgian townhouse in London's Holland Park district. It had been restored three hundred years ago using modern techniques to preserve as much of the old fabric as possible without having to resort to stabilizer fields. Lizzie had overseen the interior when they moved in, blending a tasteful variety of furniture and utility systems that dated from the mid-twentieth century right up to the twenty-seventh, when ANA's replication facilities effectively halted human design on Earth. Two spacious sub-basements had been added, giving them an indoor swimming pool and a health spa, along with the tanks and ancillary systems that supplied the culinary cabinet and household replicator.

He took Rosa into the large iron-framed conservatory where her toys were stored in big wicker baskets. February had produced its usual icy morning outside, sending broad patterns of frost worming up the outside of the glass. For now, the only true splash of colour to enjoy in the garden came from the winter-flowering cherries on the curving bank behind the frozen fish pond.

When Lizzie came downstairs an hour later she found him and Rosa playing with glow blocks on the conservatory's heated flagstone floor. Tilly who was seven, and Elsie their five-year-old, followed their mother in, and shouted happily at their younger sister, who ran over to them with outstretched arms, babbling away in her own incomprehensible yet excited language. The

46

three girls started to build a tower out of the blocks, the higher they stacked the faster the colours swirled.

He gave Lizzie a quick kiss and ordered the culinary cabinet to produce some breakfast. Lizzie sat at the circular wooden table in their kitchen. An antiquities and culture specialist, she enjoyed the old-fashioned notion of a room specifically for cooking. Even though there was no need for it, she'd had a hefty iron range cooker installed when they moved in ten years ago. During winter its cosy warmth turned the kitchen into the house's engine room, they always gathered in here as a family. Sometimes she even used the range to cook things which she and the girls made out of ingredients produced by the culinary cabinet. Tilly's birthday cake had been the last.

'Swimming for Tilly this morning,' Lizzie said as she sipped at a big china cup of tea which a housebot delivered to her.

'Again?' he asked.

'She's getting a lot more confident. It's their new teacher. He's very good.'

'Good.' The Delivery Man picked up the croissant on his plate and started tearing it open. 'Girls,' he shouted. 'Come and sit down please. Bring Rosa.'

'She doesn't want to come,' Elsie shouted back immediately.

'Don't make me come and get you.' He avoided looking at Lizzie. 'I'm going to be away for a few days.'

'Anything interesting?'

'There've been allegations that some companies on Oronsay have got hold of level-three replicator tech,' he said. 'I'll need to run tests on their products.' His current vocation was to monitor the spread of Higher technology across the External Worlds. It was a process which the Externals got very sensitive about, with hardline Protectorate politicians citing it as the first act of cultural colonization, deserving retribution. However, industrialists on the External Worlds were constantly seeking to acquire ever-more sophisticated manufacturing systems to reduce their costs. Radical Highers were equally keen to supply it to them, seeing it precisely as that first important stage for a planet converting to Higher culture. What he had to do, on ANA:Governance's behalf, was to decide the intent behind supplying replicator systems. If Radical Highers were supporting the companies, then he would subtly disable the systems and collapse the operation. His main problem was making an objective decision; Higher technology inevitably crept out from the Central Worlds, in the same way that the External Worlds were always settling new planets around the edge of their domain. The boundary between Central and External was ambiguous to say the least, with some External Worlds openly welcoming the shift to Higher status. Location was always a huge factor in his decision. Oronsay was over a hundred lightyears out from the Central Worlds, which effectively negated the chance that this was simple technology seepage. If there were replicators there, it was either Radicals pushing them, or a very greedy company.

Lizzie's eyebrows lifted. 'Really? What sort of products?'

'Starship components.'

'Well, that should come in handy out there right now, very profitable I imagine.'

He appreciated her guarded amusement. The last few days had seen a rush of starship company officials to Ellezelin, eager to do deals with the new Cleric Conservator.

The girls scuttled in and settled at the table; Rosa clambered on to the twenty-fifth-century suede mushroom that was her tiny-tot seat. It morphed around her, gripping firmly enough to prevent her from falling out, and expanded upwards to bring her level with the table top. She clapped her hands delightedly to be up with her family. Elsie solemnly slid a bowl of honey pops across, which Rosa grabbed. 'Don't spill it today,' Elsie ordered imperiously.

Rosa just gurgled happily at her sister.

'Daddy, will you teleport us to school?' Tilly asked, her voice high and pleading.

'You know I'm not going to,' he told her. 'Don't ask.'

'Oh please, Daddy, *please*.'

'Yes, Daddy,' Elsie chipped in. 'Please t-port. I like it. Lots and lots.'

'I'm sure you do, but you're getting on the bus. Teleport is a serious business.'

'School is serious,' Tilly claimed immediately. 'You always say so.'

Lizzie was laughing quietly.

'That's diff—' he began. 'All right, I'll tell you what I'll do. If you behave yourselves while I'm gone, *and only if*, then I'll teleport you to school on Thursday.'

'Yes yes!' Tilly exclaimed. She was bouncing up and down on her chair.

'But you have to be exceptionally good. And I will find out, your mother will tell me.'

Both girls immediately directed huge smiles at Lizzie.

After breakfast the girls washed and brushed their hair in the bathroom; with Elsie having long red hair it always took her an age to untangle it. Parents checked homework files to make sure it had all been done. Housebots prepared school uniforms.

Half an hour later the bus slipped down out of the sky, a long turquoise regrav capsule that hovered just above the greenway outside the house where the road used to be centuries before. The Delivery Man walked his daughters out to it, both of them wearing cloaks over their red blazers, the protective grey shimmer warding off the cold damp air. He checked one last time that Tilly had her swimwear, kissed them both goodbye, and stood waving as the bus rose quickly. The whole idea of riding to school together was to enhance the children's sense of community, an extension of the school itself, which was little more than an organized play and activities centre. Their real education wouldn't begin until their biononics became active. But it still gave him an emotional jolt to see them vanishing into the gloomy horizon. There was only one school in London these days, south of the Thames in Dulwich Park. With a total population of barely a hundred and fifty thousand the city didn't need another. Even for Highers the number of children was low; but then Earth's natives were notoriously reserved. The first planet to become truly Higher, it had been steadily reducing its population ever since. Right at the beginning of Higher culture, when biononics became available and ANA went on line, the average citizen's age was already the highest in the Commonwealth. The elderly downloaded, while the younger ones who weren't ready for migration to a post-physical state emigrated out to the Central Worlds until they chose to conclude their biological life. The result was a small residual population with an exceptionally low birth-rate.

The Delivery Man and Lizzie were a notable exception in having three kids. But then they'd registered a marriage as well, and had a ceremony in an old church with their friends witnessing the event – a Christian priest had been brought in from an External World that still had a working religion. It was what Lizzie had wanted, she adored the old traditions and rituals. Not enough to actually get pregnant, of course, the girls had all been gestated in a womb vat.

'You be careful on Oronsay,' she told him as he examined his face in the bathroom mirror. It was, he acknowledged, rather flat with a broad jaw, and eyes that crinkled whenever he smiled or frowned no matter how many anti-ageing techniques were applied to the surrounding skin areas, Advancer or Higher. His Advancer genes had given his wiry muddy-red hair a luxuriant growth-rate which Elsie had inherited. He'd modified his facial follicles with biononics so that he no longer had to apply shaving gel twice a day; but the process wasn't perfect, every week he had to check his chin and dab gel on recalcitrant patches of five o'clock shadow. More like five o'clock puddles, Lizzie claimed.

'I always am,' he assured her. He pulled on a new toga suit and waited until it had wrapped around him. Its surface haze emerged, a dark emerald shot though with silver sparkles. Rather stylish, he felt.

Lizzie, who never wore any clothes designed later than the twenty-second century, produced a mildly disapproving look. 'If it's that far from the Central Worlds it's going to be deliberate.'

'I know. I will watch out, I promise.' He kissed Lizzie in reassurance, trying to ignore the guilt that was staining his thoughts like some slow poison. She studied his face, apparently satisfied with his sincerity, which only made the lie even worse. He hated these times when he couldn't tell her what he actually did.

'Missed a bit,' she announced spryly, and tapped her forefinger on the left side of his jaw.

He peered into the mirror and grunted in dismay. She was right, as always.

When he was ready, the Delivery Man stood in the lounge facing Lizzie, who held a squirming Rosa in her arms. He held a hand up to wave as he activated his field interface function. It immediately meshed with Earth's T-sphere, and he designated his exit coordinate. His integral force field sprang up to shield his skin. The awesome, intimidating emptiness of the translation continuum engulfed him, nullifying every sense. It was this infinite microsecond he despised. All his biononic enrichments told him he was surrounded by nothing, not even the residual quantum signature of his own universe. With his mind starved of any sensory input, time expanded excruciatingly.

Eagles Harbour flickered into reality around him. The giant station hung seventy kilometres above southern England; one of a hundred and fifty identical stations which between them generated the planetary T-sphere. ANA:Governance had fabricated them in the shape of mythological flying saucers three kilometres in diameter, a whimsy it wasn't usually associated with.

He'd emerged into a cavernous reception centre on the station's outer rim. There were only a couple of other people using it, and they paid him no attention. In front of him, a vast transparent hull section rose from the floor to curve away above, allowing him to look down on the entire southern half of the country. London was almost directly underneath, clad in slow-moving pockets of fog that oozed around rolling high ground like a white slick. The last time he and Lizzie had brought the

51

kids up here was a clear sunny day, when they'd all pressed up against the hull while Lizzie pointed out historical areas, and narrated the events that made them important. She'd explained that the ancient city was now back down to the same physical size it'd been in the mid-eighteenth century. With the planet's population shrinking, ANA:Governance had ruled there were simply too many buildings left to maintain. Just because they were old didn't necessarily make them relevant. The ancient public buildings in London's centre were preserved, along with others deemed architecturally or culturally significant. But as for the sprawl of suburb housing ... there were hundreds of thousands of examples of every kind from every era. Most of them were donated or sold off to various individuals and institutions across the Greater Commonwealth, while those that were left were simply erased.

The Delivery Man took a last wistful look down at the mist-draped city, feeling guilt swell to a near-painful level. But he could never tell Lizzie what he actually did; she wanted stability for their gorgeous little family. Rightly so.

Not that there was any risk involved, he told himself as each assignment began. Really. At least: not much. And if anything ever did go wrong his Faction could probably re-life him in a new body and return him home before she grew suspicious.

He turned away from London and made his way across the reception centre's deserted floor to one of the transit tubes opposite. It sucked him in like an old vacuum hose, propelling him towards the centre of Eagles Haven where the interstellar wormhole terminus was located. The scarcity of travellers surprised him, there were no more passengers than normal using the station. He'd expected to find more Highers on their inward migration to ANA. Living Dream was certainly stirring things up politically among the External Worlds. The Central Worlds regarded the whole Pilgrimage affair with their usual disdain. Even so, their political councils were worried, as demonstrated by the number of people joining them to offer their opinion.

It was a fact that with Ethan's ascension to Cleric Conservator, the ANA Factions were going to be manoeuvring frantically for advantage, trying to shape the Greater Commonwealth to their own vision. He couldn't work out which of them was going to benefit most from the recent election; there were so many, and their internal allegiances were all so fluid anyway, not to mention deceitful. It was an old saying that there were as many Factions as there were ex-physical humans inside ANA; and he'd never encountered any convincing evidence to the contrary. It resulted in groupings that ranged from those who wanted to isolate and ignore the physical humans (some anti-animal extremists wanted them exterminated altogether) to those who sought to elevate every human, ANA or physical, to a transcendent state.

The Delivery Man took his assignments from a broad alliance that was fundamentally conservative, following a philosophy that was keen to see things keep running along as they were – although opinions on how that should be achieved were subject to a constant and vigorous internal debate. He did it because it was a view he shared. When he eventually downloaded, in another couple of centuries or so, that would be the Faction he would associate himself with. In the meantime he was one of their unofficial representatives to the physical Commonwealth.

The station terminus was a simple spherical chamber containing a globe fifty metres in diameter whose surface glowed with the lambent violet of Cherenkov radiation, emanating from the exotic matter used to maintain the wormhole's stability. He slipped through the bland sheet of photons, and was immediately emerging from the exterior of a corresponding globe on St Lincoln. The old industrial planet was still a major manufacturing base for the Central Worlds, and had maintained its status as a hub for the local wormhole network. He took a transit tube to the wormhole for Lytham, which was one of the furthest Central Worlds from Earth; its wormhole terminus was secured at the main starport. Only the Central Worlds were linked together by a long-established wormhole network. The External Worlds valued their cultural and economic independence too much to be connected to the Central Worlds in such a direct fashion. With just a few exceptions travel between them was by starship.

A two-seater capsule ferried the Delivery Man out to the craft he'd been assigned. He glided between two long rows of pads where starships were parked. They ranged in size from sleek needle-like pleasure cruisers, up to hundred-metre passenger liners capable of flying commercial routes up to a hundred lightyears. The majority were fitted with hyperdrives; though some of the larger mercantile vessels used continuous wormhole generators, which were slower but more economic for short-range flights to neighbouring stars. There were no cargo ships anywhere on the field; Lytham was a Higher planet, it didn't manufacture or import consumer items.

The *Artful Dodger* was parked towards the end of the row. A surprisingly squat chrome-purple ovoid, twenty-five metres high, standing on five tumour-like bulbs which held its wide base three metres off the concrete. The fuselage surface was smooth and featureless, with no hint of what lay underneath. It looked like a typical private hyperdrive ship, belonging to some wealthy External World individual or company; or a Higher Council with diplomatic prerogative. An ungainly metal umbilical tower stood at the rear of the pad, with two slim hoses plugged into the ship's utility port, filling the synthesis tanks with baseline chemicals.

The Delivery Man sent the capsule back to the rank in the reception building and walked underneath the starship. His u-shadow called the ship's smartcore, and confirmed his identity, a complex process of code and DNA verification before the smart-core finally acknowledged he had the authority to take command. An airlock opened at the centre of the ship's base, a dint that distended upwards into a tunnel of darkness. Gravity eased off around him, then slowly inverted, pulling him up inside. He emerged into the single midsection cabin. Inert, it was a low hemisphere of dark fabric which felt spongy to the touch. Slim ribs on the upper surface glowed a dull blue, allowing him to see round. The airlock sealed up below his feet. He smiled round at the blank cabin, sensing the power contained behind the bulkheads. The starship plugged into him at some animal level, circumventing all the wisdom and cool of Higher behaviour. He relished the power that was available, the freedom to fly across the galaxy. This was liberation in the extreme.

How the girls would love to ride in this.

'Give me something to sit on,' he told the smartcore, 'turn the lights up, and activate flight control functions.'

An acceleration couch bloomed up out of the floor as the ribs brightened, revealing a complex pattern of black lines etched on the cabin walls. The Delivery Man sat down. Exoimages flipped up, showing him the ship's status. His u-shadow cleared him for flight with the spaceport governor, and he designated a flight path to Ellezelin, two hundred and fifteen lightyears away. The umbilical cables withdrew back into their tower.

'Let's go,' he told the smartcore.

Compensator generators maintained a level gravity inside the cabin as the *Artful Dodger* rose on regrav. At fifty kilometres altitude, the limit of regrav, the smartcore switched to ingrav, and the starship continued to accelerate away from the planet. The Delivery Man began to experiment with the internal layout, expanding walls and furniture out of the cabin bulkheads. The dark lines flowed and bloomed into a great variety of combinations, allowing up to six passengers to have tiny independent sleeping quarters which included a bathroom formation; but for all its malleability, the cabin was basically variations on a lounge. If you were travelling with anyone, he decided, let alone five others, you'd need to be very good friends.

A thousand kilometres above the spaceport, the *Artful Dodger* went ftl, vanishing inside a quantum field interstice with a photonic implosion that pulled in all the stray electromagnetic radiation within a kilometre of its fuselage. There were no differences perceptible to ordinary human senses, he might have been in an underground chamber for all he knew, and the gravity remained perfectly stable. Sensors provided him with a simplified image of their course as it related to large masses back in spacetime, plotting stars and planets by the way their quantum signature affected the intersecting fields through which they were flying. Their initial speed was a smooth fifteen lightyears per hour, near the limit for a hyperdrive, which the sophisticated Lytham planetary spacewatch network could track out to a couple of lightyears.

The Delivery Man waited until they were three lightyears beyond the network, and told the smartcore to accelerate again. The *Artful Dodger*'s ultradrive pushed them up to a phenomenal fifty-five lightyears per hour. It was enough to make the Delivery Man flinch. He had only been on an ultradrive ship twice before; there weren't many of them; ANA had never released the technology to the Central Worlds. Exactly how the Conservative Faction had got hold of it was something he studiously avoided asking.

Two hours later he reduced speed back down to fifteen lightyears an hour, and allowed the Ellezelin traffic network to pick up their hyperspacial approach. He used a TD channel to the planetary datasphere and requested landing permission for Riasi spaceport.

Ellezelin's original capital was situated on the northern coast of Sinkang, with the Camoa River running through it. He looked down on the city as the *Artful Dodger* sank down towards the main spaceport. It had been laid out in a spiderweb grid, with the planetary Parliament at the heart. The building was still there, a grandiose structure of towers and buttresses made from an attractive mixture of ancient and modern materials. But the planet's government was now centred in Makkathran2. The senior bureaucrats and their departments had moved with it, leading a migration of commerce and industry. Only the transport sector remained strong in Riasi now. The wormholes which linked the planets of the Ellezelin Free Trade Zone together were all located here, incorporated into the spaceport, making it the most important commercial hub in the sector.

The *Artful Dodger* landed on a pad little different to the one it had departed barely three hours before. The Delivery Man paid a parking fee for a month in advance with an untraceable credit coin, and declined an umbilical connection. His u-shadow called a taxi capsule to the pad. While he was waiting for it, the Conservative Faction called him.

'Marius has been seen on Ellezelin.'

It was the second time that day the Delivery Man flinched. 'I suppose that was inevitable. Do you know why he's here?'

'To support the Cleric Conservator. But as to the exact nature of that support, we remain uncertain.'

'I see. Is he here in the spaceport?' he asked reluctantly. He wasn't a front-line agent, but his biononics had very advanced field functions in case he ever stumbled into an aggressive situation. They ought to be a match for anything Marius could produce. Although any aggression would be most unusual. Faction agents simply didn't settle their scores physically. It wasn't done.

'We don't believe so. He visited the Cleric Conservator within an hour of the election. After that he dropped out of sight. We are telling you simply so that you can be careful. It would not do for the Accelerators to know our business any more than they want us to know theirs. Leave as quickly as possible.'

'Understood.'

The taxi capsule took him over to the spaceport's massive passenger terminal. He checked in for the next United Commonwealth Starlines flight back to Akimiski, the closest Central World. All the time he waited in the departure lounge overlooking the huge central concourse he kept his scan functions running, checking to see if Marius was in the terminal. When the passengers boarded forty minutes later, there had been no sign of him, nor any other Higher agent.

The Delivery Man settled into his first-class compartment on the passenger ship with a considerable sense of relief. It was a hyperdrive ship, which would take fifteen hours to get to Akimiski. From there he'd make a quick trip to Oronsay to maintain his cover. With any luck he'd be back on Earth in less than two

57

days. It would be the weekend, and they'd be able to take the girls to the southern sanctuary park in New Zealand. They'd enjoy that.

*

The Rakas bar occupied the whole third floor of a round tower in Makkathran2's Abad district. Inevitably, the same building back in Makkathran also had a bar on the third floor. From what he'd seen in Inigo's dreams, Aaron suspected the furniture here was better, as was the lighting, not to mention the lack of general dirt which seemed so pervasive within the original city. It was used by a lot of visiting faithful who were perhaps a little disappointed by how small the nucleus of their movement actually was in comparison to the prodigious metropolises of the Greater Commonwealth. There was also a much better selection of drinks than the archetype boasted.

Aaron presumed that was the reason why ex-Councillor the Honourable Corrie-Lyn kept returning here. This was the third night he'd sat at a small corner table and watched her up at the counter knocking back an impressive amount of alcohol. She wasn't a large woman, though at first glance her slender figure made her seem taller than she was. Ivory skin was stippled by a mass of freckles whose highest density was in a broad swathe across her eyes. Her hair was the darkest red he'd ever seen. Depending on how the light caught her, it varied from shiny ebony to gold-flecked maroon. It was cut short which, given how thick it was, made it curl heavily; the way it framed her dainty features made her appear like a particularly diabolic teenager. In reality she was three hundred and seventy. He knew she wasn't Higher, so she must have a superb Advancer metabolism; which presumably was how she could drink any badboy under the table.

For the fourth time that evening, one of the faithful but not terribly devout went over to try his luck. After all, the good citizens of Makkathran had very healthy active sex lives. Inigo showed that. The group of blokes he was with, sitting at the big window seat, watched with sly grins and minimal sniggering as

58

their friend claimed the empty stool beside her. Corrie-Lyn wasn't wearing her Cleric robes, otherwise he would never have dared to go within ten metres. A simple dark purple dress, slit under each arm to reveal alluring amounts of skin wound up the lad's courage. She listened without comment to his opening lines, nodded reasonably when he offered to buy a drink, and beckoned the barkeeper over.

Aaron wished he could go over and draw the lad away. It was painful to watch, he'd seen this exact scene play out many times over the last few nights. The barkeeper came over with two heavy shot glasses and a frosted bottle of golden Adlier 88Vodka. Brewed on Vitchan, it bore no real relation to original Earth vodka, except for the kick. This was refined from a seasonal vine, Adlier, producing a liqueur that was eighty per cent alcohol and eight per cent tricetholyn, a powerful narcotic. The barkeeper filled both glasses and left the bottle.

Corrie-Lyn lifted hers in salute, and downed it in one. The hopeful lad followed suit. As he winced a smile against the burn of the icy liquid Corrie-Lyn filled both glasses again. She lifted hers. Somewhat apprehensively, the lad did the same. She tossed it down straight away.

There was laughter coming from the group at the window now. Their friend slugged back the drink. There were tears in his eyes; an involuntary shudder ran along his chest as if he was suppressing a cough. Corrie-Lyn poured them both a third shot with mechanical precision. She downed hers in a single gulp. The lad gave a disgusted wave with one hand and backed away to jeering from his erstwhile pals. Aaron wasn't impressed; last night one of the would-be suitors had kept up for five shots before retreating, hurt and confused.

Corrie-Lyn slid the bottle back along the counter top, where the barkeeper caught it with an easy twist of his wrist and deposited it back on the shelf. She turned back to the tall beer she'd been drinking before the interruption, resting her elbows on either side of the glass, and resumed staring at nothing.

Watching her, Aaron acknowledged that cultivating Corrie-

Lyn was never going to be a subtle play of seduction. There was only going to be one chance, and if he blew that he'd have to waste days finding another angle. He got to his feet and walked over. As he approached he could sense her gaiafield emission, which was reduced to a minimum. It was like a breath of polar air, cold enough to make him shiver; her silhouette within the ethereal field was black, a rift into interstellar space. Most people would have hesitated at that alone, never mind the Adlier 88 humiliation. He sat on the stool which the lad had just vacated. She turned to give him a dismissive look, eyes running over his cheap suit with insulting apathy.

Aaron called the barkeeper over and asked for a beer. 'You'll excuse me if I don't go through the ritual degradation,' he said. 'I'm not actually here to get inside your panties.'

'Thong.' She took a long drink of her beer, not looking at him.

'I . . . what?' That wasn't quite the answer he was prepared for.

'Inside my thong.'

'I suddenly feel an urge to get ordained into your religion.'

She grinned to herself and swirled the remains of her beer round. 'You've had enough time, you've been hanging round here for a few days now.'

His beer arrived and Corrie-Lyn silently swapped it for her own.

Aaron raised his finger to the barkeeper. 'Another. Make that two.'

'And it's not a religion,' she said.

'Of course not, how silly of me. Priest robes. Worshipping a lost prophet. The promise of salvation. Giving money to the city temple. Going on Pilgrimage. I apologize, easy mistake to make.'

'Keep talking like that offworlder, you'll wind up head first in a canal before dawn.'

'Head first or head-less?'

Corrie-Lyn finally turned and gave him her full attention; her smile matched up to her impish allure. 'What in Ozzie's Great Universe do you want?'

'To make you very rich indeed.'

'Why would you want to do that?'

'So I can make myself even richer.'

'I'm not very good at bank heists.'

'Yeah, guess it doesn't come up much at Priest school.'

'Priests ask you to have faith. We can take you straight to heaven, we even give you a sneak preview so you know what you're getting.'

'And that's where we come in.'

'We?'

'FarFlight Charters. I believe your not-religion is currently in need of starships, Councillor Emeritus.'

Corrie-Lyn laughed. 'Oh, you are dangerous, aren't you?'

'No danger, just an aching to be rich.'

'But I'm on my way to our heaven in the Void. What do I need with Commonwealth money?'

'Even the Waterwalker used money. But I'm not going to argue that case with you; or any other for that matter. I'm just here to make the proposition. You have contacts I need, and it is my belief you're none too happy with your old friends on the Cleric Council right now. Might be willing to bend a few ethics here and there – especially here. Am I speaking the right of things, Councillor Emeritus?'

'Why use the formal mode of address? Be bold, go the whole way, call me shitlisted. Everyone else does.'

'The unisphere news clowns have many labels for all of us. That doesn't mean you haven't got the names I need up here.' He tapped the side of his head. 'And I suspect there's enough residual respect for you in the Orchard Palace to open a few doors for me. Isn't that the way of it?'

'Could be. So what's your name?'

'Aaron.'

Corrie-Lyn smiled into her beer. 'Top of the list, huh?'

'Number one, Councillor Emeritus. So how about I buy you dinner? And you either have fun stringing me along, or give me your private bank account code so I can fill it up. Take your time to decide.'

'I will.'

FarFlight Charters was a legitimately registered company on Falnox. Anyone searching its datacore would have found it brokered for several spacelines and cargo couriers on seven External planets, not a huge operation but profitable enough to employ thirty personnel. Luckily for Aaron it was a simple front which had been put in place should he need it. He didn't know by whom. Didn't care. But if it had been real, then his expenses would have had serious implications for this year's profitability. This was the third night he'd wined and dined Corrie-Lyn, with much emphasis on the wine. The meals had all been five-star gourmet, as well. She liked Bertrand's in Greater Makkathran; a restaurant which made the Hotel Buckingham look like a flop-house for yokels. He didn't know if she was testing his resolve or not. Given the state she was in most nights she probably didn't know herself.

She did dress well, though. Tonight she wore a simple little black cocktail dress whose short skirt produced a seductive hem of mist that swirled provocatively every time she crossed or uncrossed her legs. Their table was in a perfectly transparent overhanging alcove on the seventy-second floor, providing an unenhanced view out across the huge night-time city. Directly below Aaron's feet, capsules slid along their designated traffic routes in a thick glare of navigation strobes. Once he'd recovered from the creepy feeling of vertigo needling his legs the view was actually quite invigorating. The seven-course meal they were eating was a sensory delight. Each dish accompanied by a wine the chef had selected to complement it. The waiter had given up offering a single glass to Corrie-Lyn, now he just left the bottle each time.

'He was a remarkable man,' Corrie-Lyn said when she finished her gilcherry leaf chocolate torte. She was talking about her favourite topic again. It wasn't difficult to get her started on Inigo.

'Anyone who can create a movement like Living Dream in just a couple of centuries is bound to be out-of-the-ordinary.'

'No no,' Corrie-Lyn waved her glass dismissively. 'That's not the point. If you or I had been given those dreams, there would still be Living Dream. They inspire people. Everyone can see for themselves what a beautiful simple life can be lived in the Void, one you can perfect no matter how screwed up or stupid you are, no matter how long it takes. You can only do that inside the Void, so if you promise to make that ability available to everyone you can't *not* gather a whole load of followers, now can you? It's inevitable. What I'm talking about is the man himself. Mister Incorruptible. That's rare. Give most people that much power and they'll abuse it. I would. Ethan certainly fucking does.' She poured the last of a two-and-a-half century old Mithan port into an equally ancient crystal glass.

Aaron smiled tightly. The alcove was open to the main restaurant floor, and Corrie-Lyn had downed her usual amount.

'That's why Inigo set up the movement hierarchy like an order of monks. Not that you couldn't have lots of sex,' she sniggered. 'You just weren't supposed to take advantage of the desperate faithful; you just screw around among your own level.'

'So far, so pretty standard.'

'Course, I wasn't very pure. We had quite a thing going, me and Inigo. Did you know that?'

'I do believe you mentioned it once or twice.'

'Course you did, that's why you hit on me.'

'This isn't hitting on you, Corrie-Lyn.'

'Slim and fit.' She licked her lips. 'That's what I am, wouldn't you agree?'

'Very much so.' Actually, he didn't want to admit how

physically attractive she was. It helped that any sexual impulse he might have felt was effectively neutralized by her drinking. After the first hour of any evening, she wasn't a pleasant person to be around.

Corrie-Lyn smiled down at her dress. 'Yeah, that's me all right. So ... we had this thing, this fling. I mean, sure, he saw other women. For Ozzie's sake, the poor shit had a billion females willing and eager to rip their clothes off for him and have his babies. And I enjoyed it too, I mean, hell, Aaron, some of them made me look like I'd been hit hard by the ugly stick.'

'I thought you said he was incorruptible.'

'He was. He didn't take advantage is what I'm saying. But he's human. So am I. There were distractions, that's all. The cause. The vision. He stayed true to that, he gave us the dreams of the Void. He believed, Aaron, he believed utterly in what he was shown. The Void really is a better place for all of us. He made me believe, too. I'd always been a loyal follower. I had *faith*. Then I actually met him, I saw his belief, his devotion, and through that I became a true apostle.' She finished the port and slumped back in her chair. 'I'm a zealot, Aaron. A true zealot. That's why Ethan kicked me off the Council. He doesn't like the old guard, those of us who remain true. So you, mister, you just keep your snide patronizing bollocks to yourself, you bastard, I don't fucking care what you think, I hate your smartarse weasel words. You don't believe and that makes you evil. I bet you haven't even experienced one of the dreams. That's your mistake, because they're real. For humans the Void is heaven.'

'It could be heaven. You don't know for sure.'

'See!' She wagged a finger in his direction, barely able to focus. 'You do it every time. Smartarse words. Not stupid enough to agree with me, oh no, but enough to make me have a go at preaching to you. Setting it up so I can save you.'

'You're wrong. This is all about the money.'

'Ha!' She held up the empty bottle of port, and scowled at it.

Aaron hesitated, he could never quite tell how much control

she had. He took a risk and pushed. 'Anyway, if the Void is salvation, why did he leave?'

The result wasn't quite what he'd expected. Corrie-Lyn started sobbing.

'I don't know!' she wailed. 'He left us. Left all of us. Oh where are you, Inigo? Where did you go? I loved you so much.'

Aaron groaned in dismay. Their quiet meal was now a full-blown public spectacle. Her sobs were increasing in volume. He hurriedly called the waiter and shuffled round the seats to sit next to Corrie-Lyn, putting himself between her and the other curious patrons. 'Come on,' he murmured. 'Let's go.'

There was a landing platform on the thirtieth floor, but he wanted her to get some fresh air, so they took a lift straight down to the skyscraper's lobby. The boulevard outside was almost deserted. A slim road running down the middle was partially hidden behind a long row of tall bushy evergreen trees. The footpath alongside was illuminated by slender glowing arches.

'Do you think I'm attractive?' Corrie-Lyn slurred as he encouraged her to walk. Past the skyscraper there were a couple of blocks of apartments, all surrounded by raised gardens. Local nightbirds swooped and flittered silently through the arches. It was a warm air, with the smell of sea ozone accompanying the humid gusts coming in from the coast.

'Very attractive,' Aaron assured her. He wondered if he should insist she take the detox aerosol he'd brought along for this very eventuality. The trouble with drinkers of this stature was that they didn't want to sober up that quickly, especially not when they were burdened with as much grief as Corrie-Lyn.

'Then how come you don't try it on? Is it the drink? Do you not like me drinking?' She broke away to look at him, swaying slightly, her eyes blurred from tears, hauntingly miserable. With her light coat undone to show off the exclusive cocktail dress, she presented a profoundly unappealing sight.

'Business before pleasure,' Aaron said, hoping she'd accept that and just shut the hell up. He should have caught a taxi from the skyscraper's platform. As if she was finally picking up on his exasperation, she turned fast and started walking.

Someone appeared on the path barely five metres in front of them, a man in a one-piece suit that still had the remnants of its black stealth envelope swirling away like water in low gravity. Aaron scanned round with his full field functions. Two more people were shedding their envelopes as they walked up behind him. His combat routines moved smoothly to active status, accessing the situation. The first of the group to confront them was designated One. Eighty per cent probability he was the commander. The subordinates were tagged Two and Three. His close-range situation exoimage showed all three of them glowing with enrichments. He actually relaxed: by confronting him they'd taken away all choice. With that accepted, there would only be one outcome now. He simply waited for them to present him with the maximum target opportunity.

Corrie-Lyn blinked in mild bewilderment, peering forward at the first man as she clutched her small scarlet bag to her belly. 'I didn't see you. Where were you?'

'You don't look too good, Your Honour,' One replied. 'Why don't you come along with us?'

Corrie-Lyn pressed back into Aaron's side, degrading his strike ability by a third. 'No,' she moaned. 'No, I don't want to.'

'You're bringing the Living Dream into disrepute, Your Honour,' One said. 'Is that what Inigo would have wanted?'

'I know you,' she said wretchedly. 'I'm not going with you. Aaron, don't leave me. Please.'

'Nobody is going anywhere they don't want to.'

One didn't even look at him. 'You. Fuck off. If you ever want a sales meeting with a Councillor, be smart now.'

'Ah, well now, here's the thing,' Aaron said affably. 'I'm so stupid I can't afford an IQ boost come regeneration time. So I just stay this way for ever.' Behind him, Two and Three were standing very close now. They both drew small pistols. Aaron's routines identified their hardware as jelly guns. Developed a century and a half ago as a lethal short-range weapon, they did exactly as specified on human flesh. He could feel accelerants slipping through his neurones, quickening his mental reaction time. Biononic energy currents synchronized with them, upgrading his physical responses to match. The effect dragged out spoken words, so much so he could easily predict what was going to be said long before One finished his sentence.

'Then I'm sorry for you.' One sent a fast message to subordinates, which Aaron intercepted, it was nothing more than a simple code. He didn't even need to decrypt it. Both of them raised their weapons. Aaron's combat routines were already moving him smoothly. He twisted Corrie-Lyn out of the way as he bent down. The first shot from Two's jelly gun seared through the air where Aaron's head had been less than a second before. The beam struck the wall, producing a squirt of concrete dust. Aaron's foot came up fast, smashing into the knee of Three. Their force fields clashed with a screech, electrons flaring in a rosette of blue-white light. The velocity and power behind Aaron's kick was enough to distort his opponent's protection. Three's leg shattered as it was punched backwards, throwing the whole body sideways. Aaron's energy currents formatted a distortion pulse which slammed into One. He was flung back six metres into the garden wall, hitting it with a dull thud. His straining force field pushed out a dangerous bruised-purple nimbus as another of Aaron's distorter pulses pummelled him, trying to shove him clean through the wall. His back arched at the impact, force field close to outright failure.

Two was trying to swing his pistol round, tracking a target that was moving with inhuman speed. All his enriched senses revealed was a blurred shape as Aaron danced across the path. He never got a lock, Aaron's hand materialized out of a dim streak to chop across his throat, overloading the force field. His neck snapped instantly, and the corpse flew through the air. Aaron snatched the jelly gun from Two's hand at the same time, wrenching the fingers off with a liquid crunching sound. It took Aaron a fraction of a second to spin round again. His force field expanded into the ground, an anchor snatching away inertia, allowing him to stop instantly, the pistol aligned on One as the dazed man was clambering unsteadily to his feet. Blood from the severed fingers dripped down on to the path. One froze, sucking down air as he stared at the nozzle of the jelly gun. Aaron opened his grip, allowing the fingers to slither away. 'Who are they?' he yelled at Corrie-Lyn, who was lying on the sodden grass where she'd landed. She was giving One a bewildered look. '*Who?*' Aaron demanded.

'The . . . the police. That's Captain Manby, special protection division.'

'That's right,' Manby wheezed as he flinched against the pain. 'So you just put that fucking gun down. You're already drowning in shit so deep you'll never see the universe again.'

'Join me at the bottom.' Aaron pressed the trigger on the jelly gun, holding it down on continuous fire mode. He added his own distortion pulse to the barrage. Manby's force field held out for almost two seconds before collapsing. The jelly gun pulses struck the exposed body. Aaron turned and fired again, overloading Three's force field.

Corrie-Lyn threw up as waves of bloody sludge from both ruined corpses cascaded across the ground. She was wailing like a wounded kitten when Aaron hauled her to her feet. 'We have to go,' he shouted at her. She shrank back from his hold. 'Come on, now! Move!' His u-shadow was already calling down a taxi.

'No,' she whimpered. 'No, no. They didn't . . . you just killed them. You killed them.'

'Do you understand what this is?' he growled at her, his voice loud, aggressive; using belligerence to keep her off balance. 'Do you understand what just happened? Do you? They're an assassination squad. Ethan wants you dead. Permanently dead. You can't stay here. They'll keep coming after you. Corrie-Lyn! I can protect you.'

'Me?' she sobbed. 'They wanted me?'

'Yes. Now come on, we're not safe here.'

'Oh sweet Ozzie.'

He shook her. 'Do you understand?'

'Yes,' she whispered. By the way she was shaking Aaron thought she was going into mild shock. 'Good,' he started to walk towards the descending taxi, hauling her along, heedless of the way she stumbled to keep up. It was hard not to smile. He couldn't have delivered a better result to the evening if he'd planned it.

Inigo's first dream

When Edeard woke, his dream was already a confused fading memory. The same thing happened every morning. No matter how hard he tried he could never hold on to the images and sounds afflicting him every night. Akeem said not to worry; that his dreams were made up from the gentle spillage of other sleeping minds around him. Edeard didn't believe the things he dreamed of came from anywhere like their village, the fragments he occasionally did manage to cling to were too strange and fascinating for that.

Cool pre-dawn light was showing up the cracks in the window's wooden shutters. Edeard lay still for a while, cosy under the pile of blankets that covered his cot. It was a big room, with whitewashed plaster walls and bare floorboards. The rafters of the hammer-beam roof above were ancient martoz wood that had blackened and hardened over the decades until they resembled iron. There wasn't much by way of furniture, two thirds of the floor space was completely empty. Edeard had shoved what was left down to the end which had a broad window. At the foot of the cot was a crude chest where he kept his meagre collection of clothes; there was a long table covered in his enthusiastic sketches of possible genistar animals; several chairs; a dresser with a plain white bowl and pitcher of water. Over in the corner opposite the cot, the fire had burnt out sometime in the night, with a few embers left glimmering in the grate. It was difficult to heat such a large volume, especially in winter, and Edeard could see his breath as a fine white mist. Technically, he lived in the apprentice dormitory of Ashwell village's Eggshaper Guild, but he was the only occupant. He'd lived there for the past six years, ever since his parents died when he was eight years old. Master Akeem, the village's sole remaining shaper, had taken him in after the caravan they had joined in order to travel through the hills to the east was attacked by bandits.

Edeard wrapped a blanket round his shoulders and hurried over the cold floor to the small brick-arch fireplace. The embers were still giving off a little heat, warming the clothes he'd left on the back of a chair. He dressed hurriedly, pulling up badly worn leather trousers and tucking an equally worn shirt into the waist before struggling into a thick green sweater. As always the fabric smelled of the stables and their varied occupants, a melange of fur and food and cages; but after six years at the Guild he was so used to it he hardly noticed. He sat back on the cot to pull his boots on; they really were too small for him now. With the last eighteen months seeing more genistars in the stables and Edeard taking on official commission duties, their little branch of the Eggshaper Guild had seen a lot more money coming it. Hardly a fortune, but sufficient to pay for new clothes and boots, it was just that he never had time to visit the cobbler. He winced slightly as he stood up, trying to wriggle his toes which were squashed together. It was no good, he was definitely going to take an hour out of his busy day to visit the cobbler. He grinned. *But not today.*

Today was when the village's new well was finished. It was a project in which the Eggshaper Guild was playing an unusually large part. Better than that, for him, it was an innovative part. Edeard knew how many doubters there were in the village: basically everybody. But Master Akeem had quietly persuaded the elder council to give his young apprentice a chance. They said yes only because they had nothing to lose.

He made his way downstairs, then hurried across the narrow rear yard to the warmth of the Guild dining hall. Like the dormitory, it was a sharp reminder that the Eggshaper Guild had known better times. A lot better. There were still two rows of long bench tables in the big hall, enough to seat fifty shapers and their guests on feast nights. At the far end the huge fireplace had iron baking ovens built in to the stonework on either side, and the roasting spit was large enough to handle a whole pig. This morning, the fire was just a small blaze tended by a couple of ge-monkeys. Normally, people didn't let the genistars get anywhere near naked flames, they were as skittish as any terrestrial animal, but Edeard's orders were lucid and embedded deeply enough that the ge-monkeys could manage the routine without panicking.

Edeard sat at the table closest to the fire. His mind directed a batch of instructions to the ge-monkeys using simple telepathic longtalk. He used a pidgin version of Querencia's mental language, visualizing the sequence of events he wanted in conjunction with simple command phrases, making sure the emotional content was zero (so many people forgot that, and then couldn't understand why the genistars didn't obey properly). The ge-monkeys started scurrying round; they were big creatures, easily the weight of a full-grown human male, with six long legs along the lower half of their body, and six even longer arms on top, the first two pairs so close together they seemed to be sharing a shoulder joint, while the third pair were set further back along a very flexible spine. Their bodies were covered in a wiry white fur, with patches worn away on joints and palms to reveal a leathery cinder-coloured hide. The head profile was the same as all the genistar variants, a plain globe with a snout very close to a terrestrial dog; the ears were situated on the lower part of the head back towards the stumpy neck, each one sprouting three petals of long creased skin thin enough to be translucent.

A big mug of tea was placed in front of Edeard, swiftly followed by thick slices of toast, a bowl of fruit and a plate of scrambled eggs. He tucked in heartily enough, already running through the critical part of the day's operation at the bottom of the well. His farsight picked up Akeem when the old man was still in the lodge, the residence for senior shapers annexed to the hall. Edeard could already perceive through a couple of stone walls, sensing physical structures as if they were shadows, while minds buzzed with an iridescent glow. That vision was of a calibre which eluded a lot of adults; it made Akeem inordinately proud of his apprentice's ability, claiming his own training was the true key to developing Edeard's potential.

The old shaper came into the hall to find the ge-monkeys ready with his breakfast. He grunted favourably as he gave Edeard's shoulder a paternal squeeze. 'Did you sense me getting up in my bedroom, boy?' he asked, gesturing at his waiting plate of sausage and tomato.

'No sir,' Edeard said happily. 'Can't manage to get through four walls yet.'

'Won't be long,' Akeem said as he lifted up his tea. 'The way you're developing I'll be sleeping outside the village walls by midsummer. Everyone's entitled to some privacy.'

'I would never intrude,' Edeard protested. He mellowed and grinned sheepishly as he caught the amusement in the old shaper's mind. Master Akeem had passed his hundred and eightieth birthday several years back, so he claimed, though he was always vague about the precise year that happened. Life expectancy on Querencia was supposed to be around two hundred years, though Edeard didn't know of anyone in Ashwell or the surrounding villages who'd actually managed to live that long. However, Akeem's undeniable age had given him a rounded face with at least three chins rolling back into a thick neck, and a lacework of red and purple capillaries decorated the pale skin of his cheeks and nose, producing a terribly wan appearance. A thin stubble left behind after his perfunctory daily shave was now mostly grey, which didn't help the careworn impression everyone received when they saw him for the first time. Once a week the old man used the same razor on what was left of his silver hair.

Despite his declining years, he always insisted on dressing smartly. His personal ge-monkeys were well versed in laundry work. Today his tailored leather trousers were clean, boots polished; a pale yellow shirt washed and pressed. He wore a jacket woven from magenta and jade yarn, with the egg-in-a-twisted-circle crest of the Eggshaper Guild on the lapel. The jacket might not be as impressive as the robes worn by Guild members in Makkathran, but in Ashwell it was a symbol of prestige, earning him respect. None of the other village elders dressed as well.

Edeard sheepishly realized he was fingering his own junior apprentice badge, a simple metal button on his collar; the emblem similar to Akeem's, but with only a quarter circle. Half the time he forgot to pin it on in the morning. After all, nobody showed him any respect, ever. But if all went well today he'd be entitled to a badge with half a circle. Akeem said he could never remember anyone attempting a shaping so sophisticated for their senior apprentice assessment.

'Nervous?' the old man asked.

'No,' Edeard said immediately. Then he ducked his head. 'They work in the tank, anyway.'

'Of course they do. They always do. Our true skill comes in determining what works in real life. From what I've seen, I don't believe there will be a problem. That's not a guarantee, mind. Nothing in life is certain.'

'What did you shape for your senior apprentice assessment?' Edeard asked.

'Ah, now well, that was a long time ago. Things were different back then, more formal. They always are in the capital. I suspect they haven't changed much.'

'Akeem!' Edeard pleaded; he loved the old man dearly, but oh how his mind wandered these days.

'Yes yes. As I recall, the assessment required four ge-spiders; functional ones, mind. They had to spin drosilk at the Grand Master's presentation, so everyone wound up shaping at least six or seven to be safe. We also had to shape a wolf, a chimp, and an eagle. Ah,' he sighed. 'They were hard days. I remember my Master used to beat me continually. And the larks we used to get up to in the dormitory at night.'

Edeard was slightly disappointed. 'But I can do ge-spiders and all the rest.'

'I know,' Akeem said proudly, and patted the boy's hand. 'But we both know how gifted you are. A junior apprentice is normally seventeen before taking the kind of assessment you're getting today, and even then a lot of them fail the first time. This is why I've made your task all the harder. A reshaped form that works is the standard graduation from apprenticehood to practitioner.'

'It is?'

'Oh yes. Of course I've been dreadfully remiss in the rest of the Guild teachings. It was hard enough to make you sit down long enough to learn your letters. And you're really not old enough to take in the Guild ethics and all that boring old theory, no matter how precise they are when I gift them to you. Though you seem to grasp things at an instinctive level. That's why you're still only going to be an apprentice after this.'

Edeard frowned. 'What kind of ethics could be involved in shaping?'

'Can't you think?'

'No, not really. Genistars are such a boon. They help everyone. Now I'm helping you sculpt, we can produce more standard genera than before, the village will grow strong and rich again.'

'Well I suppose as you're due to become a senior apprentice we should start to consider these notions. We'd need more apprentices if that were to truly come about.'

'There's Sancia, and little Evox has a powerful longtalk.'

'We'll see. Who knows? We might prove a little more acceptable after today. Families are reluctant to offer their children for us to train. And your friend Obron doesn't help matters.'

Edeard blushed. Obron was the village's chief bully, a boy a couple of years older than him, who delighted in making Edeard's life a misery outside the walls of the Guild compound. He hadn't realized Akeem had known about that. 'I should sort him out properly.'

'The Lady knows you've had enough provocation of late. I'm

proud you haven't struck back. Eggshapers are always naturally strong telepaths, but part of that ethics course you're missing is how we shouldn't abuse our advantage.'

'I just haven't because . . .' He shrugged.

'It's not the right thing to do, and you know that,' Akeem concluded. 'You're a good boy, Edeard.' The old man looked at him, his thoughts a powerful mixture of pride and sadness.

Proximity to the emotional turmoil made Edeard blink away the water now unexpectedly springing into his eyes. He shook his head, as if to disentangle himself from the old man's mind. 'Did you ever have someone like Obron ragging you when you were an apprentice?'

'Let's just say one of the reasons I came to stay in Ashwell was because my interpretation of our Guild ethics differed from the Masters of the Blue Tower. And please remember, although I am your Master and tutor, I also require Guild standards to be fulfilled. If I judge you lacking you will not get your senior apprentice badge today. That includes taking care of your ordinary duties.'

Edeard pushed his empty plate away and downed the last of his tea. 'I'd better get to it, then, Master.'

'I also fail anyone who shows disrespect.'

Edeard pulled a woolly hat on against the chill air, and went out into the Guild compound's main courtyard. It was unusual in that it had nine sides. Seven were made up from stable blocks, then there was a large barn, and the hatchery. None of them were the same size or height. When he first moved in, Edeard had been impressed. The Eggshaper Guild compound was the largest collection of buildings in the village; to someone who'd been brought up in a small cottage with a leaky thatch roof it was a palatial castle. Back then he'd never noticed the deep cloak of kimoss staining every roof a vivid purple; nor how pervasive and tangled the gurkvine was, covering the dark stone walls of the courtyard with its ragged pale-yellow leaves, while its roots wormed their way into the mortar between the blocks, weakening the structure. This morning he just sighed at the sight, wondering if he'd ever get round to directing the ge-monkeys on a clean-up mission. Now would be a good time. The gurkvine leaves had all fallen to gather in the corners of the courtyard in great moulder-ing piles, while the moss was soaking up the season's moisture, turning into great spongy mats which would be easy to peel off. Like everything else in his life, it would have to wait. *If only Akeem could find another apprentice,* he thought wistfully. *We spend our whole lives running to catch up, just one extra person in the Guild would make so much difference.*

It would take a miracle granted by the Lady, he acknowledged grudgingly. The village families were reluctant to allow their children to train at the Eggshaper Guild. They appreciated how dependent they were on genistars, but even so they couldn't afford to lose able hands. The Guild was just like the rest of Ashwell, struggling to keep going.

Edeard hurried across the courtyard to the tanks where his new reshaped cats were kept, silently asking the Lady why he bothered to stay in this backward place on the edge of the wilds. To his right were the largest stables, where the defaults shuffled round their stalls. They were simple beasts, unshaped egg-laying genistars, the same size as terrestrial ponies, with six legs support-ing a bulbous body. The six upper limbs were vestigial, producing bumps along the creature's back, while in the female over thirty per cent of the internal organs were ovaries, producing an egg every fifteen days. Males, of which there were three, lumbered round in a big pen at one end, while the females were kept in a row of fifteen separate stalls. For the first time since Akeem had taken him in, the stalls were all occupied; a source of considerable satisfaction to Edeard. Not even a Master as accomplished as Akeem, and despite his age he was a singular talent, could manage fifteen defaults by himself. Shaping an egg took a long time, and Edeard had as many grotesque failures as he had successes. First of all, the timing had to be right. An egg needed to be shaped no earlier than ten hours after fertilization, and no later than twenty-five. How long it took depended on the nature of the genus required.

Edeard had often spent half the night sitting in a stall's deep-cushioned shaper chair with his mind focused on the egg. Eggshaping, as Akeem had so often described it, was like sculpting intangible clay with invisible hands. The ability was a gentle combination of farsight and telekinesis. His mind could see inside the egg, and only those who could do that with perfect clarity could become shapers. Not that he liked to boast, but Edeard's mental vision was the most acute in the village. What he saw within the shell was like a small exemplar of a default genistar made out of grey shadow substance. His telekinesis would reach out and begin to shape it into the form he wanted – but slowly, so frustratingly slowly. There were limits. He couldn't give a genistar anything extra: seven arms, two heads ... What the process did was activate the nascent structures inherent within the default physiology. He could also define size, though that was partially determined by what type of genus he was shaping. Then there were sub-families within each standard genus, chimps as well as monkeys, a multitude of horse types – big, small, power-ful, fast, slow. A long list which had to be memorized perfectly. Shaping was inordinately difficult, requiring immense concen-tration. A shaper had to have a lot more than eldritch vision and manipulation; he or she had to have the *feel* of what they were doing, to know instinctively if what they were doing was right, to see potential within the embryonic genistar. In the smaller crea-tures there would be no room for reproductive organs, so they had to be disengaged, other organs too had to be selected where appropriate. But which ones? Small wonder even a Grand Master produced a large percentage of invalid eggs.

Edeard walked past the default stables, his farsight flashing through the building, checking that the ge-monkeys were getting on with their jobs of mucking out and feeding. Several were becoming negligent and disorderly, so he refreshed their instruc-tions with a quick longtalk message. A slightly deeper scan with his farsight showed him the state of the gestating eggs inside the defaults. Of the eleven that had been shaped, three were showing signs that indicated problems were developing. He gave a resigned sigh. Two of them were his.

After the defaults came the horse stables. There were nine foals currently accommodated, seven of which were growing up into the large sturdy brutes which would pull ploughs and carts out on the surrounding farms. Most of the commissions placed on Ashwell's Eggshaper Guild were for genistars which could be used in agriculture. The custom of domestic ge-monkeys and chimps was in decline, which Edeard knew was just because people didn't take the time to learn how to instruct them properly. Not that they were going to come here and take lessons from a fourteen-year-old boy. It annoyed him immensely; he was certain the village economy could be improved fourfold at least if they just listened to him.

'Patience,' Akeem always counselled, when he raged against the short-sighted fools who made up their neighbours. 'Often to do what's right you first have to do what's wrong. There will come a time when your words will be heeded.'

Edeard didn't know when that would be. Even if today was successful he didn't expect a rush of people to congratulate him and seek out his advice. He was sure he was destined to forever remain the freaky boy who lived alone with batty old Akeem. A well matched pair, everyone said when they thought he couldn't farsight them.

The monkey and chimp pen was on the other side of the horses. It only had a couple of infant monkeys inside, curled up in their nest. The rest were all out and about, performing their duties around the Guild compound. They didn't have any commissions for ge-monkeys on their books; even the smithy who worked five didn't want any extras. *Perhaps I should bring people round the Guild buildings*, Edeard thought, *show them what the ge-monkeys can do if they're ordered correctly. Or Akeem could show them, at least. Just something that would break the cycle, make people more adventurous.* The freaky boy's daydream.

After the monkey pen came the kennels. Ge-dogs remained

in high demand, especially the kind used for herding cattle and sheep. Eight pups were nursing from the two milk-bitches which he'd shaped himself. They allowed the defaults to go straight back to egg production without an extended nursing period. It had taken twelve invalid eggs before he'd succeeded in shaping the first. The innovation was one he'd introduced after reading about the milk-bitch in an ancient Guild text, now he was keen to try and extend it across all the genistar types. Akeem had been supportive when the first had hatched, impressed as much by Edeard's tenacity as his shaping skill.

The compound's main gateway was wedged in between the dog kennels and the wolf kennels. There were six of the fierce creatures maturing. Always useful outside the village walls, the wolves were deployed as guards for Ashwell and all its outlying farmhouses; they were also taken on hunts through the forests, helping to clear out Querencia's native predators as well as the occasional bandit group. Edeard stopped and looked in. The ge-wolves were lean creatures with dark-grey fur that blended in with most landscapes, their long snouts equipped with sharp fangs which could bite clean through a medium-sized branch, let alone a limb of meat and bone. The large pups mewled excitedly as he hung over the door and patted at them. His hand was licked by hot serpentine tongues. Two of them had a pair of arms, another of his innovations. He wanted to see if they could carry knives or clubs. Something else he'd found in an old text. Another idea the villagers had shaken their heads in despair at.

Out of the whole courtyard, he liked the aviary best. A squat circular cote with arched openings twenty feet above the ground, just below the eaves. There was a single doorway at the base. Inside, the open space was criss-crossed by broad martoz beams. Over the years the wood had been heavily scarred by talons, so much so that the original square cut was now rounded on top. There was only a single ge-eagle left, as big as Edeard's torso. The bird had a double wing arrangement, with two limbs supporting the large front wing and giving it remarkable flexibility, while the rear wing was a simple triangle for stability. Its gold and emerald feathers cloaked a streamlined body, with a long slender jaw where the teeth had merged into a single serrated edge very similar to a beak.

Trisegment eyes blinked down at Edeard as he smiled up. He so envied the ge-eagle, how it could soar free and clear of the village with all its earthbound drudgery and irrelevance. It had an unusually strong telepathic ability, allowing Edeard to experience wings spread wide and the wind slipping past. Often, whole afternoons would pass with an enthralled Edeard twinned with the ge-eagle's mind as it swooped and glided over the forests and valleys outside, providing an intoxicating taste of the freedom that existed beyond the village.

It rustled its wings, enthused by Edeard's appearance and the prospect of flight. *Not yet*, Edeard had to tell it reluctantly. Its beak was shaken in disgust and the eyes shut, returning it to an aloof posture.

The hatchery came between the aviary and the cattery. It was a low circular building, like a half-size aviary. Its broad iron-bound wooden door was closed and bolted. The one place in the compound that ge-monkeys weren't permitted to go. Edeard had the task of keeping it clean and tidy. A sheltered stone shelf to the right of the door had nine thick candles alight, traditionally one for each egg inside. He swept his farsight across them all, happy to confirm the embryos were growing satisfactorily. After they'd been laid, the eggs took about ten days to hatch, cosseted in cradles that in winter months were warmed by slow-smouldering charcoal in a massive iron stove. He'd need to rake out the ashes and add some more lumps before midday. One of the eggs was due to hatch tomorrow, he judged, another horse.

Finally, he went into the cattery, the smallest of the buildings walling the courtyard. Standard genistar cats were small semi-aquatic creatures, with dark oily fur and broad webbed feet, devoid of upper limbs. Guild convention had them as one of the seven standard genera, though nobody outside the capital

Makkathran ever found much use for them. It was the gondoliers who kept a couple on each boat, using them to keep the city's canals clean of weed and rodents.

The cattery was a rectangular room taken up by big knee-high stone tables. Light came in through windows set into the roof. As a testament to how prolific the kimoss had become, Edeard now always supplemented his ordinary sight with farsight as he shuffled along the narrow aisles between the tables. From inside, the windows had been reduced to narrow slits that provided a meagre amethyst radiance.

Glass tanks sat along the tables. They were ancient, basins the size of bulky coffins, dating back to when the whole compound had been built. Half of them had cracked sides, and dried and dead algae stained the glass, while the bottoms were filled with gravel and desiccated flakes of mud. Edeard had refurbished five to hold his reshaped cats, with another three modified to act as crude reservoirs. The pipes he used to test their ability were strewn across the floor in a tangled mess. All five reshaped cats lay on the gravel bed of the tanks, with just a few inches of water rippling sluggishly round them. They resembled fat lozenges of glistening ebony flesh, half the size of a human. There were no limbs of any kind, just a row of six circular gills along their flanks dangling loose tubes of thick skin. The head was so small it looked completely undeveloped to the point of being misshapen; there were no eyes or ears. It was all Edeard's farsight could do to detect any sparkle of thought at all within the tiny brain.

He grinned down cheerily at the unmoving lumps, searching through them for any sign of malady. When he was satisfied their health was as good as possible, he stood perfectly still, taking calm measured breaths the way Akeem had taught him, and focused his telekinesis on the first cat, the third hand as most villagers called it. He could feel the black flesh within his incorporeal grip, and lifted it off the bed of mucky gravel.

Half an hour later, when Barakka the village cartwright drove his wagon into the courtyard he found Edeard and Akeem standing beside five tarpaulins with the reshaped cats lying on them. He wrinkled his face up in disgust at the bizarre creatures, and shot the old Guild Master a questioning look.

'Are you sure about this?' he asked as he swung himself off the bench. The cartwright was a squat man, made even broader by eight decades of hard physical labour. He had a thick, unruly ginger beard that served to make his grey eyes seem even more sunken. His hand scratched at his buried chin as he surveyed the ge-cats, doubt swirling openly in his mind, free for Edeard to see. Barakka didn't care much for the feelings of young apprentices.

'If they work they will bring a large benefit to Ashwell,' Akeem said smoothly. 'Surely it's worth a try?'

'Whatever you say,' Barakka conceded. He gave Edeard a sly grin. 'Are you aiming to be our Mayor, boy? If this works you'll get my blessing. I've been washing in horse muck these last three months. Course, old Geepalt will have his nose right out of joint.'

Geepalt, the village carpenter, was in charge of the existing well's pump, and by rights should have built a new pump for the freshly dug well. He was chief naysayer on allowing Edeard to try his innovation – it didn't help that Obron was his apprentice.

'There are worse things in life than an annoyed Geepalt,' Akeem said. 'Besides, when this works he'll have more time for profitable commissions.'

Barakka laughed. 'You old rogue! It is your tongue not your mind which shapes words against their true meaning.'

Akeem gave a small, pleased bow. 'Thank you. Shall we begin loading?'

'If Melzar's team is ready,' Barakka said.

Edeard's farsight flashed out, surveying the new well, with the crowd gathering around it. 'They are. Wedard has called the ge-monkey digging team out.'

Barakka gave him a calculating stare. The new well was being dug on the other side of the village from the Eggshaper Guild compound. His own farsight couldn't reach that far. 'Very well, we'll put them on the wagon. Can you manage a third of the weight, boy?'

Edeard was very pleased that he managed to stop any irony

from showing amid his surface thoughts. 'I think so, sir.' He caught Akeem's small private smile; the Master's mind remained calm and demure.

Barakka gave the reshaped cats another doubting look, and scratched his beard once more. 'All right then. On my call. Three. Two. One.'

Edeard exerted his third hand, careful not to boost more than he was supposed to. With the three of them lifting, the reshaped cat rose smoothly into the air and floated into the back of the open wagon.

'They're not small, are they?' Barakka said. His smile was somewhat forced. 'Good job you're helping, Akeem.'

Edeard didn't know if he should protest or laugh.

'We all play our part,' Akeem said. He was giving Edeard a warning stare.

'Second one, then,' Barakka said.

Ten minutes later they were rolling through the village, Barakka and Akeem sitting on the wagon's bench, while Edeard made do with the rear, one arm resting protectively over a cat. Ashwell was a clutter of buildings in the lee of a modest stone cliff that had sheered out of the side of a gentle slope. Almost impossible to climb, the cliff formed a good defence, with a semicircular walled rampart of earth and stone completing their protection from any malign forces that might ride in from the wild lands to the north-east. Most of the buildings were simple stone cottages with thatch roofs and slatted shutters. Some larger buildings had windows with glass panes that had been brought in from the western towns. Only the broad main street running parallel to the cliff was cobbled, the lanes running off it were little more than muddy ruts worn down to the stone by wheels and feet. Although the Eggshaper compound was the biggest collection of buildings, the tallest was the church of the Empyrean Lady, with its conical spire rising out of the north side of the low dome. Once upon a time the stone church had been a uniform white, but many seasons of neglect had seen the lightest sections

84

moulder down to a drab grey, with kimoss pullulating in the slim gaps between the big blocks.

The road down to the village gate branched off midway along main street. Edeard looked along it, seeing the short brick-lined tunnel which cut through the sloping rampart; at the far end the massive doors were open to the outside world. On the top of the wall, twin watchtowers stood on either side of the door, with big iron bells on top. They would be rung by the guards at any sign of trouble approaching. Edeard had never heard them. Some of the older villagers claimed to remember their sound when bandit gangs had been spotted crossing the farmlands bordering the village.

As Edeard looked at the top of the rampart wall with its uneven line and many different materials he wondered how hard it actually would be to overcome their fortifications. There were places where crumbling gaps had been plugged by thick timbers, which themselves were now rotting beneath swathes of kimoss; and even if every man and woman in the village carried arms they couldn't stretch along more than a third of the length. In reality, then, their safety depended on the illusion of strength.

A sharp prick of pain on his left shin made him wince. It was a telekinetic pinch, which he warded off with a strong shield over his flesh. Obron and two of his cronies were flanking the wagon, mingling with the other villagers who were heading up to the new well. There was a sense of carnival in the air as the wagon made its slow procession through Ashwell, with people abandoning their normal work to tag along and see the innovation.

Now Edeard had been jerked away from his mild daydreaming he picked up on the bustle of amusement and interest filling the aether through the village. Very few people were expecting his reshaped cats to work, but they were looking forward to witnessing the failure. *Typical*, he thought. *This village always expects the worst. It's exactly the attitude that's responsible for our decline; not everything can be blamed on bad weather, poor crops, and more bandits.*

'Hey, Egg-boy,' Obron jeered. 'What are those abortions? And where are your pump genistars?' He laughed derisively, a cackling that was quickly duplicated by his friends.

'These are—' Edeard began crossly. He stopped as their laughter rose, wishing the wagon could travel a lot faster. There were smiles on the faces of the adults walking alongside as they witnessed typical apprentice rivalry – remembering what it had been like when they were young. Obron's thoughts were vivid and mocking. Edeard managed to keep his own temper. Revenge would come as soon as the cats were in place. There would be respect for the Eggshaper Guild, with a corresponding loss of status for the carpenters.

He was still clinging smugly to that knowledge when the wagon rolled up beside the new well. It was four months ago when the village's old well had partially collapsed. Rubble and silt had been sucked up into the pump, a large contraption assembled by the Carpentry Guild, with big cogwheels and leather bladders that were compressed and expanded by three ge-horses harnessed to a broad axle wheel. They walked round and round in a circle all day long, producing gulps of water that slopped out of the pipe into a reservoir trough for everyone to use. As no one had noticed the sludge at first, the ge-horses just kept on walking until the pump started to creak and shudder. It had been badly damaged.

Once the extent of the damage to the well had been assessed, the elder council had decreed a new well should be dug. This time, it was at the top of the village, close to the cliff where the water percolating down from the slopes above should be plentiful enough. There were also ideas that a simple network of pipes could carry fresh water into each house. That would have required an even larger pump to be built. At which point Akeem had brought his apprentice's idea to the council.

The crowd which had gathered round the head of the new well was good-natured enough when the wagon stopped. Melzar, who listed Water Master among many other village titles, was standing beside the open hole, talking to Wedard, the stonemason who had overseen the team of ge-monkeys that performed the actual digging. They both gave the reshaped cats an intrigued look. Edeard wasn't really aware of them, he could hear a lot of sniggering. It mostly came from the gang of apprentices centred around Obron. His cheeks flushed red as he struggled to hold the anger from showing in his surface thoughts.

'Have faith in yourself,' someone whispered into his mind, a skilfully directed longtalk voice directed at him alone. The sentiment was threaded with a rosy glow of approval.

He looked round to see Salrana smiling warmly at him. She was only twelve, dressed in the blue and white robe of a Lady's novice. A sweet, good-natured child she had never wanted to do anything other than join the Church. The Lady's Mother of Ashwell, Lorellan, had been happy to start her instructions. Attendance was never high in the village church apart from the usual festival services. Like Edeard, Salrana never quite fitted into the mainstream of village life. It made them feel kindred. She was like a younger sister. He grinned back at her as he clambered down off the wagon. Lorellan, who was standing protectively to one side of her, gave him a bland smile.

Melzar came over to the back of the wagon. 'This should be interesting.'

'Why, thank you,' Akeem said. The cold air was turning the blood vessels on his nose and cheeks an even darker shade than normal.

Melzar inclined his head surreptitiously towards the surrounding crowd. Edeard didn't turn round, his farsight revealed Geepalt standing in the front row, feet apart and arms folded, a glower on his thin features. Contempt scudded across his surface thoughts, plain for everyone to sense. Edeard was adept enough to detect the currents of concern underneath.

'What's the water like?' Barakka asked.

'Cold, but very clear,' Melzar said contentedly. 'Digging the well this close to the cliff is a boon. There is a lot of water filtering through the rock from above us, and it's wonderfully pure. No need to boil it before we make beer, eh? Got to be good news.'

Edeard shuffled closer to the hole, half expecting Obron's third hand to shove at him. His feet squelched on the semi-frozen mud around the flagstones, and he peered over the rim. Wedard had done a good job of lining the circular shaft, the stones were perfectly cut, and fixed better than a lot of cottage walls. This well wouldn't crumble and collapse like the last one. Darkness lurked ten feet below the rim like an impenetrable mist. His farsight probed down, reaching the water over thirty feet below ground level.

'Are you ready?' Melzar asked. The voice was sympathetic. Without the Water Master's support, the council would never have allowed Edeard to try the cats.

'Yes, sir.'

Edeard, Akeem, Melzar, Barakka, and Wedard extended their third hands to lift the first cat off the wagon. Everyone in the crowd used their farsight to follow it into the gloomy shaft. Just as it reached the water, Edeard tensed. *Suppose it sinks?*

'And release,' Akeem said so smoothly and confidently that Edeard had no alternative but to let go. The cat bobbed about, completely unperturbed. Edeard realized he'd been holding his breath, anxiety scribbled right across his mind for everyone to sense, especially Obron. His relief was equally discernible to the villagers.

It wasn't long before all five cats were floating on the water. Melzar himself lowered the thick rubber hose, unwinding it slowly from the cylinder it was spooled round. The end was remarkably complicated, branching many times as if it had sprouted roots. Edeard lay flat on the flagstones around the rim, heedless of the freezing mud soaking into his sweater. Warm air gusted up from the shaft to tickle his face. He closed his eyes, allowing himself to concentrate solely on his third hand as it connected the hose ends to the cat gills. Simple muscle lips closed round the rubber tubes on his command, forming a tight seal.

A standard genistar cat had three big flotation bladders, giving them complete control over their own buoyancy as they swam, allowing them to float peacefully or dive down several yards. It was these bladders which Edeard had shaped the new cats around, expanding them to occupy eighty per cent of the total body volume, surrounding them with muscle so that they were crude pumps, like a heart for water. His longtalk ordered them to start the muscle squeeze sequence, building up an elementary rhythm.

Everyone fell silent as he stood up. Eyes and farsight were focused on the giant stone trough which had been set up next to the well. The hose end curved over it. For an achingly long minute nothing happened, then it emitted a gurgling sound. Droplets of water spat out, prelude to a foaming torrent that poured into the trough. It began to fill up remarkably quickly.

Edeard remembered the flow of water from the old well pump: this had several times the pressure. Melzar dipped a cup into the water and tasted it. 'Fresh and pure,' he announced in a loud voice. 'And better than that: abundant.' He stood in front of Edeard, and started clapping, his eyes ranging round the crowd, encouraging. Others joined in. Soon Edeard was at the centre of a storm of applause. His cheeks were burning again, but this time he didn't care. Akeem's arm went round his shoulder, mind aglow with pride. Even Geepalt was acknowledging the success, albeit grudgingly. Of Obron and his cronies there was no sign.

There was the tidying up, of course. Sacs of the oily vegetable mush which the cats digested were filled and positioned beside the well; valves adjusted so they dripped a steady supply down slender tubes. Edeard connected the far end of each tube to the mouth of a cat, instructing them to suckle slowly. Wedard and his apprentices fastened the hose to the side of the well. The ground was cleared. Finally, the huge stone capping slab was moved over the shaft, sealing the cats into their agreeable new milieu. By that time apprentices and household ge-monkeys were already queuing at the trough with large pitchers.

'You have a rare talent, my boy,' Melzar said as he watched the water lapping close to the top of the trough, 'I see we're going to have to dig a drain to cope with the overspill. Then no doubt the council will soon be demanding that mad pipe scheme to supply the houses. Quite a revolution, you've started. Akeem, I'd be honoured if you and your apprentice would join us for our evening meal.'

'I will be happy to liberate some of the wine you hold prisoner,' Akeem said. 'I've heard there are whole dungeons full under your Guild hall.'

'Ha!' Melzar turned to Edeard. 'Do you like wine, my boy?'

Edeard realized that the question was actually genuine, for once he wasn't simply being humoured. 'I'm not sure, sir.'

'Best find out, then.'

The crowd had departed, creating a rare atmosphere of satisfaction pervading the village. It was a good way to start the new spring season, ran the feeling, a good omen that times were getting better. Edeard stayed close to the trough as the apprentices filled their pitchers. He wasn't sure if he was imagining it, but they seemed to be treating him with a tad more approbation than before. Several even congratulated him.

'Haunting the site of your victory?'

It was Salrana. He grinned at her. 'Actually, just making sure the cats don't keel over from exhaustion, or the hoses don't tear free. Stuff like that. There's a lot that can go wrong yet.'

'Poor, Edeard, always the pessimist.'

'Not today. Today was . . .'

'Glorious.'

He eyed the low clouds that were blocking the sun from view. 'Helpful. For me and the village.'

'I'm really pleased for you,' she exclaimed. 'It takes so much courage to stand up for your own convictions, especially in a place like this. Melzar was right; this is a revolution.'

'You were eavesdropping! What would the Lady say?'

'She would say, Well done, young man. This will make everyone's life a little better. Ashwell has one thing less to worry about, now. The people need that. Life is so hard, here. From small foundations of hope, empires can be built.'

'That has to be a quote,' he teased.

'If you attended church, you'd know.'

'I'm sorry. I don't get much time.'

'The Lady knows and understands.'

'You're such a good person, Salrana. One day you'll be the Pythia.'

'And you'll be Mayor of Makkathran. What a grand time we'll have together, making all of Querencia a happy place.'

'No more bandits. No more drudgery – especially not for apprentices.'

'Or novices.'

'They'll talk about our reign until the Skylords return to carry us all into the heart.'

'Oh look,' she squealed and pointed excitedly at the trough. 'It's overflowing! You've given us too much water, Edeard.'

He watched as the water began to spill over the lip of the trough. Within seconds it had become a small stream frothing across the mud towards their feet. They both ran aside, laughing.

2

Justine Burnelli examined her body closely before she put it on again. After all, it had been over two centuries since the last time she'd worn it. During the intervening years it had been stored in an exotic matter cage that generated a temporal suspension zone so that barely half a second had passed inside.

The cage looked like a simple sphere of violet light in ANA's New York reception facility, a building that extended for a hundred and fifty storeys below Manhattan's streets. Her cage was housed on the ninety-fifth floor, along with several thousand identical radiant bubbles. ANA normally maintained a body for five years after the personality downloaded out of it, just in case there were compatibility problems. Such an issue was unusual, the average was one in eleven million who rejected a life inside ANA and returned to the physical realm. Once those five years were up, the body was discontinued. After all, if a personality *really* wanted to leave ANA after that, a simple clone could be grown – a process not dissimilar to the old-fashioned re-life procedure that was still available out among the External Worlds.

However, ANA:Governance considered it useful to have physical representatives walking the Greater Commonwealth in certain circumstances. Justine was one of them. It was partly her own fault. She'd been over eight hundred years old when Earth built its repository for Advanced Neural Activity, the ultimate virtual universe where everyone was supposedly equal in the end. After so much life she was very reluctant to see her body 'discontinued', in much the same way she'd never quite acknowledged that re-life was true continuation. For her, clones force-fed on a dead person's memories were not the same person, no matter there was no discernible difference. That early-twenty-first century upbringing of hers was just too hard to shake off, even for someone as mature and controlled as she had become.

The violet haze faded away to reveal a blonde girl in her biological mid-twenties. Rather attractive, Justine noted with a little tweak of pride, and very little of that had come from genetic manipulation down the centuries. The face she was looking at was still recognizable as the brattish party *it* girl of the early-twenty-first century who'd spent a decade on the gossip channels as she dated her way through East Coast society and soap actors. Her nose had been reduced, admittedly, and pointed slightly. Which, now she regarded it critically, was possibly a little too cutesy, especially with cheekbones that looked like they were made from avian bone they were so sharp yet delicate. Her eyes had been modified to a pale blue, matching Nordic white skin that tanned to honey gold, and hair that was thick white-blonde, falling down below her shoulders. Her height was greater than her friends from the twenty-first century would have remembered; she'd surreptitiously added four inches during various rejuvenation treatments; despite the temptation she hadn't gained all that length in her legs, she'd made sure her torso was in proportion with a nicely flat abdomen which was easy to maintain thanks to a slightly accelerated digestive tract. Happily she'd never gone for ridiculous boobs – well, except that one time when she was rejuving for her two hundredth birthday and did it just to find out what it was like having a Grand Canyon cleavage. And yes men did gape and come out with even more stupid opening lines, but as she could always have whoever she wanted anyway there was no real advantage and it wasn't really her so she'd got rid of them at the next rejuvenation session.

So there she was, in the flesh, and still in good shape, just lacking a mind. With the monitor program confirming her visual review she poured her consciousness back into her brain. The memory reduction was phenomenal, as was the loss of all the advanced thought routines which comprised her true personality these days. Her old biological neurone structure simply didn't have the capacity to hold what she had become in ANA. It was like being lobotomized, actually feeling your mind wither away to some primitive insect faculty. *But only temporary*, she told herself – so sluggishly!

Justine drew her first breath in two hundred years, chest jerking down air as if she was waking from a nightmare. Her heart started racing away. For a moment she did nothing – not actually remembering what to do – then the reliable old automatic reflexes kicked in. She drew another breath, getting a grip on her panic, overriding the old Neanderthal instincts with pure rationality. Another regular breath. Calming her heart. Exoimages flickered into her peripheral vision, bringing up rows of default symbols from her enrichments. She opened her eyes. Long ranks of violet bubbles stretched out in all directions around her like some bizarre artwork sculpture. Somehow her meat-based mind was convinced she could see the shapes of people inside. That was preposterous. Inside ANA she'd obviously allowed herself to discard the memory of how fallible and hormone susceptible a human brain was.

A slow smile revealed perfect white teeth. *At least I'll get to have some real sex before I download again.*

Justine teleported out of the New York reception facility right into the centre of the Tulip Mansion. Stabilizer fields had maintained the ancient Burnelli family home through the centuries, keeping the building's fabric in pristine condition. She gave a happy grin when she saw it again with her own eyes. If she was honest with herself it was a bit of a monstrosity; a mansion laid out in four 'petals' whose scarlet and black roofs curved up to a central tower 'stamen' which had an apex 'anther' made from a crown of carved stone coated in gold foil. It was as gaudy as it was striking, falling in and out of fashion over the decades.

94

Justine's father, Gore Burnelli, had bought the estate in Rye county just outside New York, establishing it as a base for the family's vast commercial and financial activities in the middle of the twenty-first century. It had remained a centre for them while the Commonwealth was established and expanded outwards until finally its social and economic uniformity was shattered by biononics, ANA, and the separation of Higher and Advancer cultures. Today the family still had a prodigious business empire spread across the External Worlds, but it was managed in a corporate structure by thousands of Burnellis, none of whom was over three hundred years old. Gore, along with his original clique of close relatives (including Justine) who used to orchestrate it all, had long since downloaded into ANA. Though Gore had never formally and legally handed over ownership to his impatient descendants. It was, he assured them, purely a quirk for their own benefit, ensuring the whole enterprise could never be broken up, thus giving the family a cohesion that so many others lacked. Except Justine knew damn well that even in his enlightened, expanded, semi-omnipotent state within ANA, Gore wasn't about to hand anything over he'd spent centuries building up. *Quirk, my ass.*

She'd materialized in the middle of the mansion's ballroom. Her bare feet pressed down on a polished oak floor that was nearly as shiny as the huge gilt-edged mirrors on the wall. A hundred reflections of her naked body grinned sheepishly back at her. Deep-purple velvet drapes curved around the tall window doors which opened out on a veranda dripping with white wisteria. Outside, a bright low February sun shone across the extensive wooded grounds with their massive swathes of rhodo-dendrons. There had been some fabulous parties held in here, she recalled. Fame, wealth, glamour, power, notoriety, and beauty mingling in a fashion that would have made Jane Austen green with envy.

The doors were open, leading out into the broad corridor. Justine walked through, taking in all the semi-familiar sights, welcoming the warm rush of recognition. Alcoves were filled with furniture that had been antique even before Ozzie and Nigel built their first wormhole generator; and as for the artwork, you could buy a small continent on an External World with just one of the paintings.

She padded up the staircase which curved its way through the entrance hall, and made her way down the north petal to her old bedroom. Everything was as she'd left it, maintained for centuries by the stabilizer fields and maidbots; a comforting illusion that she or any other Burnelli could walk in at any time and be given a perfect greeting in their ancestral home. The bed was freshly made, with linen taken out of the stabilizer field and freshened as soon as she and ANA had agreed to the reception. Several clothes were laid out. She ignored the modern toga suit, and went for a classical Indian-themed emerald dress with black boots.

'Very neutral.'

Justine jumped at the voice. Irritation quickly supplanted perturbation. She turned and glared at the solido standing in the doorway. 'Dad, I don't care how far past the physical you claim to be, you DO NOT come into a girl's bedroom without knocking. Especially mine.'

Gore Burnelli's image didn't show much contrition. He simply watched with interest as she sat on the bed and laced her boots up. He'd chosen the representation of his twenty-fourth-century self, which was undoubtedly the image for which he was most renowned: a body whose skin had been turned to gold. Over that he wore a black V-neck sweater and black trousers. The perfect reflective surface made it difficult to determine his features. Without the gold sheen he would have been a handsome twenty-five-year-old with short-cropped fair hair. His face, which at the time he had it done was nothing more than merged organic circuitry tattoos, was all the more disconcerting thanks to the perfectly ordinary grey eyes peering out of the gloss. That Gore looked out on the world from behind a mask of improvements was something of a metaphor. He was a pioneer of enhanced mental routines, and had been one of the founders of ANA.

'Like it matters,' he grunted.

'Politeness is always relevant,' she snapped back. Her temper wasn't improved by the way her fingers seemed to lack any real dexterity. She was having trouble tying the boot laces.

'You were a good choice to receive the Ambassador.'

She finally managed to finish the bow, and lifted a quizzical eyebrow. 'Are you jealous, Dad?'

'Of becoming some kind of turbo-version of a monkey again? Yeah, right. Thinking down at this level and this speed gives me a headache.'

'Turbo-monkey! You nearly said animal, didn't you?'

'Flesh and blood is animal.'

'Just how many Factions do you support?'

'I'm a Conservative, everyone knows that. Maybe a few campaign contributions to the Outwards.'

'Humm.' She gave him a suspicious look. Even in a body, she knew the rumours that ANA gave special dispensation to some of its internal personalities. ANA:Governance denied it, of course; but if anyone could manage to be more equal than others it would be Gore, who'd been in there right at the start as one of the founding fathers.

'The Ambassador is nearly here,' Gore said.

Justine checked her exoimages, and started to re-order her secondary thought routines. Her body's macrocellular clusters and biononics were centuries out of date, but still perfectly adequate for the simple tasks today would require. She called her son, Kazimir. 'I'm ready,' she told him.

As she walked out of her bedroom she experienced a brief chill that made her glance back over her shoulder. *That's the bed where we made love. The last time I saw him alive.* Kazimir McFoster was one memory she had never put into storage, never allowed to weaken. There had been others since, many others, both in the flesh and in ANA, wonderful, intense relationships, but none ever had the poignancy of dear Kazimir whose death was her responsibility.

Gore said nothing as his solido followed her down the grand staircase to the entrance hall. She suspected that he suspected.

97

Kazimir teleported into the marbled entrance hall; appearing dead centre on the big Burnelli crest. He was dressed in his Admiral's tunic. Justine had never seen him wear anything else in six hundred years. He smiled in genuine welcome and gave her a gentle embrace, his lips brushing her cheek.

'Mother. You look wonderful as always.'

She sighed. He did look *so* like his father. 'Thank you, darling.'

'Grandfather.' He gave Gore a shallow bow.

'Still holding up in that old receptacle, then,' Gore said. 'When are you going to join us here in civilization?'

'Not today, thank you, Grandfather.'

'Dad, pack it in,' Justine warned.

'It's goddamn creepy if you ask me,' Gore grumbled. 'No one stays in a body for a thousand years. What's left for you out there?'

'Life. People. Friends. True responsibility. A sense of wonder.'

'We got a ton of that in here.'

'And while you look inwards, the universe carries on around you.'

'Hey, we're very aware of extrinsic events.'

'Which is why we're having this happy family reunion today.' Kazimir gave a small victory smile.

Justine wasn't even listening to them any more, they always ran through this argument as if it was a greeting ritual. 'Shall we go, boys?'

The doors of the mansion swung open and she walked out on to the broad portico without waiting for the others. It was a cold air outside; frost was still cloaking the deeper hollows in the lawn where the long shadows prevailed. A few clouds scudded across the fresh blue sky. Pushing its way through them was the Ocisen Empire ship sliding in from the south-east. Roughly triangular, it measured nearly two hundred metres long. There was nothing remotely aerodynamic about it. The fuselage was a dark metal, mottled with aquamarine patches that resembled lichen. Its crinkled surface was cratered with indentations that sprouted black spindles at the centre, whilst long boxes looked as though they'd been welded on at random. A cluster of sharp radiator fins emerged from the rear section, glowing bright red.

Gore gave a derisive chuckle. 'What a monstrosity. You'd think they could do better now we've given them regrav.'

'We took five hundred years to get from the Wright brothers at Kitty Hawk to the *Second Chance*,' Justine pointed out.

Gore looked up as the alien starship slowed to a halt above the mansion's grounds. 'Do you think it'll have jets of dry ice gushing out when it lands, or maybe they've mounted a giant laser gun that'll blast the White House to smithereens?'

'Dad, be quiet.'

The ship descended. Two rows of hatches along its belly swung open.

'For fuck's sake, haven't they even heard of malmetal?' Gore complained.

Long fat landing legs telescoped out. The movement was accompanied by a sharp hissing sound as high pressure gas vented through grilles in the undercarriage bays.

Justine had to suck her lower lip in to stop herself giggling. The starship was ridiculous, the kind of contraption Isambard Kingdom Brunel would have built for Queen Victoria.

It touched down on the lawn, its landing pads sinking deep into the grass and soft soil. Several radiator fins sliced down into silver birch trees, their heat igniting the wood. Burning branches dropped to the ground.

'Wow, the damage it causes. How will our world survive? Quick, you kids flee to the woods, I'll hold them off with a shotgun.'

'Dad! And cancel your solido, you know what the Empire thinks of ANA personalities.'

'Stupid *and* superstitious.'

His solido vanished. Justine watched his icon appear in her exoimage. 'Now behave,' she told him.

'That ship is leaking radiation all over the place,' Gore commented. 'They haven't even shielded their fusion reactor properly. And who uses deuterium anyway?'

Justine reviewed the sensor data, scanning the ship's hotspots. 'It's hardly a harmful emission level.'

'The Ocisens aren't as susceptible to radioactivity as humans are,' Kazimir said. 'It's one reason they were able to industrialize space in their home system with what equates to our mid-twenty-first-century technology. They simply didn't require the shielding mass we would have needed.'

Halfway down the starship's fuselage a multi-segment airlock door unwound. The Ambassador for the Ocisen Empire floated out, sitting on top of a hemispherical regrav sled. Physically, the alien wasn't impressive; a small barrel shaped torso wrapped in layers of flaccid flesh that formed overlapping folds. Its four eyes were on serpent stalks curving out from the crest, while four limbs were folded up against the lower half of its body. They were encrusted in cybernetic systems, amplifying its strength and providing a number of manipulator attachments ranging from delicate pliers up to a big hydraulic crab pincer. Further support braces ran up its body, resembling a cage of chrome vertebrae that ended in a collar arrangement just below the base of the eye stalks. Patches of what looked like copper moss were growing across various sections of its flesh; they sprouted small rubbery stalks covered in minute sapphire flowers.

Justine bowed formally as the sled stopped in front of her, floating half a metre off the ground, which put the Ambassador's eye stalks above her. Even with the regrav unit and the physical support it was obvious the Ambassador had come from a low-gravity world. It sagged against the metal and composite structures holding it up. Two of the eye stalks bent round so they were aligned on her.

'Ambassador, thank you for visiting us,' Justine said.

'We are pleased to visit,' the Ambassador answered, its voice a whispery burble coming from a slender vocalizer gill between his eye stalks. Translated into English by the sled processors, a speaker on the rim boomed the reply to Justine.

'My home welcomes you,' she said, remembering the formality.

100

Another of the Ambassador's eye stalks curved round to stare at Kazimir. 'You are the human Navy commander.'

'That is correct,' Kazimir said. 'I am here as you requested.'

'Many of my nest ancestor cousins fought in the Fandola assault.' Thin droplets of spittle ran out of the Ambassador's gill, to be absorbed by drain holes in its support collar.

'I am sure they fought with honour.'

'Honour be damned. We would have enjoyed victory over the Hancher vermin if you had not intervened that day.'

'We are friends with the Hancher. Your attack was ill-advised; I warned you we would not abandon our friends. That is not our way.'

The fourth eye stalk turned on Kazimir. 'You in person warned the Empire, Navy commander?'

'That is correct.'

'You live so long. You are no longer natural.'

'Is this why you are here, Ambassador, to insult me?'

'You overreact. I state the obvious.'

'We do not hide from the obvious,' Justine said. 'But we are not here today to dwell upon what was. Please come in, Ambassador.'

'You are kind.'

Justine walked into the entrance hall with the Ambassador's sled gliding along behind her. Somehow it managed to keep a distance that wasn't too close as to be blatantly rude, but still close enough to be disconcerting.

Kazimir's icon blinked up beside Gore's in her peripheral vision. 'You know,' he said, 'the Ocisens only started painting their sleds black after they found out humans are unsettled by darkness.'

'If that's the best they can come up with it's a wonder their species ever survived the fission age,' she replied.

'We shouldn't be in too much of a hurry to mock them,' Gore replied. 'However much we sneer, they do have an empire, and they would have obliterated the Hancher if we hadn't stepped in.'

'I'd hardly consider that to be an indicator of their superiority,' Justine told them. 'And they're certainly not a threat to us. Their technology level is orders of magnitude below Higher culture, let alone ANA.'

'Yes, but right now they only have one policy, to acquire better technology, especially weapons technology. A sizeable percentage of the Emperor's expansion budget is diverted to building long-range exploration ships in the hope they'll come across a world whose inhabitants have gone post-physical, and they can help themselves to whatever's left behind.'

'Let's hope they never encounter a Prime immotile.'

'They've made seventeen attempts to reach the Dyson Pair,' Kazimir told her. 'And they currently have forty-two ships searching for an immotile civilization beyond the region of space we Firewalled.'

'I didn't know that. Is there any danger they'll find a rogue Prime planet?'

'If we can't find one, they certainly won't be able to.'

Justine led their little party into the McLeod room, and sat at the head of the large oak table running down the middle. Kazimir took the chair at his mother's side, while the Ambassador hovered at the other end. Its eye stalks bent round slowly, as if it was having trouble with what it saw as it scanned the walls. The room's décor was Scottish themed, which surrounded the alien with tartan drapes, ancient Celtic ceremonial swords, and solemn marble mannequins dressed in clan kilts. Several sets of bagpipes were displayed in glass cases. A fabulous pair of stag antlers hung above the stone mantelplace that had been imported from a Highland castle.

'Ambassador,' Justine said formally, 'I represent the human government of Earth. I am physical, as you asked, and I am empowered to negotiate on the government's behalf with the Ocisen Empire. What do you wish to discuss?'

Three of the Ambassador's eyes curved round to stare at her. 'Although we disapprove of living creatures placing themselves subordinate to the mechanical, we consider your planetary computer is the true ruler of the Commonwealth. That is why I required this direct meeting, rather than with the Senate as usual.'

Justine wasn't about to start arguing about political structures with an alien who saw everything in terms of black and white. 'ANA has considerable influence beyond this planet. That is so.'

'Then you must work with the Empire to avert a very real danger.'

'What danger is that, Ambassador?' *As if none of us know.*

'A human organization is threatening to send ships into the Void.'

'Yes, our Living Dream movement wants to send its followers on a Pilgrimage there.'

'I am familiar with human emotional states after being exposed to your kind for so long, so I am curious why you do not react to this event with any sense of distress or concern. It is through humans that we know of the Void, therefore you know what effect your Living Dream is proposing to trigger.'

'They do not propose anything, they simply wish to live the life of their idol.'

'You are deliberately denying the implication. Their entry to the Void will provoke a massive devourment phase. The galaxy will be ruined. Our Empire will be consumed. You will kill us and countless others.'

'That will not happen,' Justine said.

'We are reassured that you intend to stop the Living Dream.'

'That's not what I said. It is not our belief that their Pilgrimage will cause a devourment phase of any size. They simply do not possess the ability to pass through the event horizon which guards the Void. Even the Raiel have trouble doing that, and Living Dream does not have access to a Raiel ship.'

'Then why are they launching this Pilgrimage?'

'It is a simple political gesture, nothing more. The Ocisen Empire, nor any other species in the galaxy, does not have anything to worry about.'

103

'Do you guarantee that your Living Dream group cannot get through the event horizon? Other humans have crossed over into the Void. They are the cause of this desire to Pilgrimage, are they not?'

'Nothing is certain, Ambassador, you know that. But the likelihood—'

'If you cannot guarantee it, then you must prevent the ships from flying.'

'The Greater Commonwealth is a democratic institution, complicated in this case by Living Dream being both trans-stellar and the legitimate government of Ellezelin. The Commonwealth constitution is specifically designed to protect every member's right to self-determination on an individual and governmental level. In other words we don't actually have the legal right to prevent them from embarking on their Pilgrimage.'

'I am familiar with human lawyers; everything can be undone, nothing is final. You play with words, not reality. The Empire recognizes only power and ability. Your computer government has the physical power to prevent this Pilgrimage, am I not correct?'

'Ability does not automatically imply intent,' Justine said. 'ANA:Governance has the ability to do many things. We do not do them because of the laws which govern us, both legal and moral.'

'It is not part of your morality to destroy this galaxy. You can prevent this.'

'We can argue strongly against it,' she said, wishing she didn't agree quite so much with the Ocisen.

'The Empire requires a tangible commitment. The Pilgrimage ships must be neutralized.'

'Out of the question,' Justine said. 'We cannot interfere with the lawful activities of another sovereign state, it goes against everything we are.'

'If you do not prevent the launch of this atrocity, then the Empire will. Even your lawyers will agree we have the right to species self-preservation.'

'Is that a threat, Ambassador?' Kazimir asked quietly.

'It is the course of action you have forced upon us. Why do you not see this? Are you afraid of your primitive cousins? What can they threaten you with?'

'They do not threaten us, we respect each other. Can you make the leap to understand that?'

Justine tried to read the Ambassador's reaction to the jibe, but it seemed unperturbed. Spittle continued to dribble from its vocalizer gill, while its arms flopped round like landed fish inside their cybernetic casings. 'Your laws and their hypocrisy will always elude us,' the Ambassador said. 'The Empire knows you always include extraordinary powers within your constitutions to impose solutions in times of crisis. We require you to invoke them now.'

'ANA:Governance will be happy to introduce a motion in the Senate,' Justine said. 'We will ask that Living Dream desists from reckless action.'

'Will you back this by force if they refuse?'

'Unlikely,' Kazimir said. 'Our Navy exists to protect us from external enemies.'

'What is the Void devourment, if not an enemy? Ultimately it is everyone's enemy. The Raiel acknowledge this.'

'We do understand your unease, Ambassador,' Justine said. 'I would like to reassure you we will work wholly to prevent any catastrophe from engulfing the galaxy.'

'The Raiel could not prevent devourment. Are you greater than the Raiel?'

'Probably not,' she muttered. Did it understand sarcasm?

'Then we will prevent your ships from flying.'

'Ambassador, I have to advise the Ocisen Empire against such a course of action,' Kazimir said. 'The Navy will not permit you to attack humans.'

'Do not think you can intimidate us, Admiral Kazimir. We are not the helpless species you attacked at Fandola. We have allies now. I represent many powerful species who will not allow the Void to begin its final devourment phase. We do not stand alone. Do you think your Navy can defeat the whole galaxy?'

Kazimir seemed unperturbed. 'The Navy acts only in defence. I urge you to allow the Commonwealth to solve an internal problem in our own way. Humans will not trigger a large-scale devourment.'

'We will watch you,' the Ambassador boomed. 'If you do not prevent these Pilgrimage ships from being built and launched, then we and our new, powerful, allies will act in self-defence.'

'I do understand your concern,' Justine said. 'But I would ask you to trust us.'

'You have never given us a reason to,' the Ambassador said. 'I thank you for your time. I will return to my ship, I find your environment unpleasant.'

Which was quite subtle for an Ocisen, Justine thought. She stood and accompanied the Ambassador back out to its ship. Gore materialized beside her as the hulking machine rose into the sky.

'Allies, huh? You know anything about that?' he asked Kazimir.

'Not a thing,' Kazimir said. 'They could be bluffing. Then again, if they are serious about stopping the Pilgrimage, they will need allies. They certainly can't do it alone.'

'Could it be the Raiel?' Justine asked in surprise.

Kazimir shrugged. 'I doubt it. The Raiel don't go sneaking round doing deals to pitch one species against another. If the Empire had approached them, I feel confident they would have told us.'

'A post-physical, then?'

'Not impossible,' Gore conceded. 'Most of them regard us as vulgar little newcomers to an exclusive club. Those that talk to us, anyway. Most can't even be arsed to do that. But I'd be very surprised if one had. They'd probably be quite interested in observing the final devourment phase.'

'How about you?' Justine enquired lightly.

Gore smiled, snow-white teeth shining coldly between gold

lips. 'I admit, it would be a hell of a sight. From a distance. A very large distance.'

'So what do you recommend?' Justine asked.

'We certainly need to start the motion in the Senate,' Kazimir said. 'The Ambassador was quite right. I don't think we can allow the Pilgrimage to launch.'

'Can't stop 'em,' Gore said with indecent cheerfulness. 'It's in the constitution.'

'We do have to find a solution,' Justine said. 'A political one. And quickly.'

'That's my girl. Are you going to address the Senate yourself? You carry a lot of weight out there: history in the flesh.'

'And it would be helpful to get confirmation from the Raiel,' Kazimir said. 'You do have the personal connection.'

'What?' Justine's shoulders slumped. 'Oh hellfire. I wasn't planning on leaving Earth.'

'I expect the Hancher Ambassador would like some reassurance, as well,' Gore added maliciously.

Justine turned to give her father a level stare. 'Yes, there's a lot of people and Factions we need to keep an eye on.'

'I'm sure Governance knows what it's doing. After all, you were its first choice. Can't beat that.'

'Actually, I was second.'

'Who was first?' Kazimir asked curiously.

'Toniea Gall.'

'That bitch!' Gore spat. 'She couldn't get laid in a Silent World house the day after she rejuved. Everyone hates her.'

'Now Dad, history decided the resettlement period was a minor golden age.'

'Fucking minuscule, more like.'

Justine and Kazimir smiled at each other. 'She was a good President as I recall,' Kazimir said.

'Bullshit.'

'I'll go and visit the Hancher Embassy on my way to the Senate,' Justine said. 'It would be nice to know about the Empire's military movements.'

'I'll start reassigning our observation systems inside the Empire to see if we can get a clearer picture of what's going on,' Kazimir said.

As Justine's body teleported out of Tulip Mansion, Gore's primary consciousness retreated to his secure environment within the vastness of ANA. As perceptual reality locations went, it was modest. Some people had created entire universes for their own private playground, setting up self-governing parameters to maintain the configuration. The bodies, or cores, or focal points they occupied within their concepts were equally varied, with abilities defined purely by the individual milieu. Quite where such domains extended to was no longer apparent. ANA had ceased to be limited to the physical machinery which had birthed it. The operational medium was now tunnelled into the quantum structure of spacetime around Earth, fashioning a unique province in which its manifold post-human intelligences could function. The multiple interstices propagated through quantum fields with the tenacity and fragile beauty of a nebula, an edifice forever shifting in tandem with the whims of its creators. It was no longer machine, or even artificial life. It had become alive. What it might evolve into was the subject of considerable and obsessive internal debate.

The Factions were not openly at war over ANA's ultimate configuration, but it was a vicious battle of ideas. Gore hadn't been entirely truthful when he claimed to be a Conservative. He did support the idea of maintaining the status quo, but only because he felt the other more extreme factions were being far too hasty in offering their solutions. Apart from the Dividers, of course, who wanted ANA to fission into as many parts as there were Factions, allowing each to go their own way. He didn't agree with them either; what he wanted was more time and more information, that way he believed the direction they should take would become a lot more evident.

He appeared on a long beach, with a rocky headland a few hundred metres ahead of him. Perched on top was an old stone tower with crumbling walls and a white pavilion structure attached to the rear. The sun was hot on his head and hands; he was wearing a loose short-sleeve shirt and knee-length trousers. His skin was ordinary, without any enrichments. The self-image and surroundings were taken from the early twenty-first century, back when life was easier even without sentient machines. This was Hawksbill Bay, Antigua, where he used to come with his yacht, *Moonlight Madison*. There had been a resort clustered along the shore in those days, but in this representation the land behind the beach was nothing more than a tangle of palm trees and lush grass, with brightly coloured parrots zipping between the branches. It didn't have the wind that blew constantly through the real Caribbean, either; although the sea was an astonishingly clear turquoise where fish swam close to shore.

There was a simple dirt path up the headland, leading to the tower. The pavilion with its fabric roof covered a broad wooden deck and a small swimming pool. There was a big oval table at one end, with five heavily cushioned chairs around it. Nelson Sheldon was already sitting there, a tall drink resting on the table in front of him.

In the days before ANA, Nelson had been the security chief for the Sheldon Dynasty, the largest and most powerful economic empire that had ever existed. When the original Commonwealth society and economy split apart and reconfigured as the Greater Commonwealth, the Dynasty retained a great deal of its wealth and power, but things weren't the same. After Nigel Sheldon left, it lost cohesion and dispersed out among the External Worlds; still a force to be reckoned with, politically and economically, but lacking the true clout of before.

Over two centuries spent looking after the Dynasty's welfare had turned Nelson into a pragmatist of the first order. It meant he and Gore saw the whole ANA evolution outcome in more or less the same terms.

Gore sat at the table and poured himself an iced tea from the pitcher. 'You accessed all that?'

'Yeah. I'm interested who the Empire has as an ally, or even allies.'

'Probably just a bluff.'

'You're overestimating the Ocisens, they lack the imagination for a bluff. I'd say they've managed to dig up some ancient reactionary race with a hard-on for the good old days and a backyard full of obsolete weapons.'

'ANA:Governance is going to have to give that one some serious attention,' Gore said. 'We can't have alien warships invading the Commonwealth. Been there, done that. Ain't going to let it happen twice. It was one of the reasons we started building ANA, so that humanity is never at a technological disadvantage again. There's a lot of very nasty hardware lying round this galaxy.'

'Amongst other things,' Nelson agreed sagely. 'We are going to have to give the Void some serious attention soon – just as the Accelerators wanted.'

'I want us to give the Void serious attention,' Gore said. 'We can hardly claim to be masters of cosmological theory if we can't even figure it out. It's only the analysis timescale which everyone disagrees on.'

'And the method of analysis, but yes I'll grant you we do need to know how the damn thing is generated. It's one of the reasons I'm with you on our little conspiracy.'

'Think of us as a very small Faction.'

'Whatever. I stopped screwing round with semantics a long time ago. Purpose is absolute, and if you can't define it: tough. And our purpose is to undo the damage the Accelerators have caused.'

'To a degree, yes. The Conservatives will be most active on that front, we can trust them to do a decent job. I want to try and think a couple of steps ahead. After all we're not animal any more, we don't just react to a situation. We're supposed to be able to see it coming. Ultimately something has to be done about the Void problem. Understanding its internal mechanism is all very well, but it cannot be allowed to carry on threatening the galaxy.'

Nelson raised a glass to his lips, and smiled in salute. 'Way to go, tough guy. Where the Raiel failed . . .'

'Where the Raiel tell us they failed. We have no independent confirmation.'

'Nothing lasts long enough, apart from the Raiel themselves.'

'Bullshit. Half the post-physicals in the galaxy have been around for a lot longer.'

'Yeah, and those that were don't bother to communicate any more. They're all quiet, or dead, or transcended, or retroevolved. So unless you want to go around and poke them with a big stick, the Raiel are our source. Face it, ANA is good, great even, we're damn nearly proto-gods, but in terms of development we are still lacking behind the Raiel, and they plateaued millions of years ago. The Void defeated them. They converted entire star systems into defence machines, they *invaded* the fucking place with an armada, and they still couldn't switch it off, or kill it or blow it to hell.'

'They went at it the wrong way.'

Nelson laughed. 'And you know the right way?'

'We have an advantage they never did. We have insider knowledge, a mole.'

'The Waterwalker? In Ozzie's name, tell me you're joking.'

'You know who paid the most attention to Inigo's dreams right at the start? The Raiel. They didn't know what was inside. They built ships which could theoretically withstand any quantum environment, yet not one of them ever returned. We're the ones who showed them what's in there.'

'It's a very small glimpse, a single city on a standard H-congruous planet.'

'You're missing the point.' His arm swept round Hawksbill to point at the thick pillar of black rock protruding from the water several hundred metres out to sea. Small waves broke apart on it, churning up a ruck of spume. 'You bring any human prior to the twenty-fifth century into here, and they'd think they were in a physical reality. But if you or I were to observe the environment through them, we'd soon realize there were artificial factors involved. The Waterwalker gives us the same opportunity. His telepathic abilities have provided a very informative glimpse into the nature of the universe hiding inside that bastard event horizon. For all it looks like our universe with planets and stars, it most definitely is not. This Skylord of the Second Dream confirms that. The Void has a Heart which is most distinctive, even though we haven't been shown it yet.'

'Knowing it's different in there doesn't give us any real advantage.'

'Wrong. We know nothing can be achieved on a physical level; you can't use quantumbusters against it, you can't send an army in to wipe out the chief villain's control room. The Void is the ultimate post-physical in the galaxy, and probably all the other galaxies we can see. What we have to do is communicate with it if we ever want to achieve any resolution to the problem it presents to our stars. I don't believe the Firstlife ever intended it to be dangerous; they didn't know there was anything left outside it could ever threaten. That's our window. We know humans can get inside, even though we're not sure how they did it that first time. We know there are humans in there who are attuned to its fabric. Through them we may be able to affect change.'

'The Waterwalker is dead. He has been for millennia of internal time.'

'Even if he were unique, which I don't believe for a minute, time is not a problem, not in there. We all know that. What we have to do is get inside and forge that tenuous little link to the Heart. That's the key to this.'

'You want to visit the Void? To fly through the event horizon?'

'Not me. Much as my ego would love being the union point, there's no empirical evidence that I would have the telepathic ability inside. Even if we took ANA inside there's no certainty it could become the conduit. No. We have to employ a method that has a greater chance of success.'

Nelson shook his head in dismay and not a bit of disappointment. 'Which is?'

'I'm working on it.'

*

It wasn't an auspicious start to the day. Araminta hadn't overslept. Not exactly. She had an Advancer heritage which gave her a complete set of macrocellular clusters, all functioning efficiently; she could order her secondary thought routines competently. So naturally she'd woken up on time with a phantom bleeping in her ears and synchronized blue light flashing along her optic nerve. It was just after that wake-up spike she always had difficulty. Her flat only had two rooms, a bathroom cubicle and a combi main room; that was all she could afford on her waitress pay. For all that it was cheap, the expanded bed with its a-foam mattress was very comfortable. After the spike she lay curled up in her cotton pyjamas, cosy as a nesting frangle. Hazy morning sunlight stole round the curtains, not bright enough to be disturbing, the room maintained itself at a comfortable warmth. If she bothered to check the flat's management programs everything was ready and waiting; the day's clothes washed and aired, a quick light breakfast in the cuisine cabinet.

So I can afford to laze for a bit.

The second alarm spike jerked her awake again, vanquishing the weird dream. This spike was harsher than the first, deliberately so, as it was an urgent order to get the hell up – one she never needed. When she cancelled the noise and light she assumed she'd messed up the secondary routines, somehow switching the order of the spikes. Then she focused on the timer in her exoimages.

'Shit!'

So it became a struggle to pull on her clothes whilst drinking the Assam tea and chewing some toast. A leisurely shower was replaced by spraying on some travel-clean, which never worked like the ads promised, leaving busy glamorous people fresh and cleansed as they zipped between meetings and clubs. Instead she

113

hurried out of the flat with her mouse-brown hair badly brushed, her eyes red-rimmed and stinging slightly from the travel-clean, and her skin smelling of pine bleach.

Great. That should earn me some big tips, she thought grouchily as she hurried down to the big building's underground garage. Her trike pod purred its way out into Colwyn City's crowded streets and joined the morning rush of commuters. In theory the traffic should have been light, most people these days used regrav capsules, floating in serene comfort above the wheeled vehicles except when they touched down on dedicated parking slots along the side of the roads or rooftop pads. But at this early hour the city's not-so-well-off were all on their way to work, filling the concrete grid close to capacity with pods, cars, and bikes; and jamming the public rail cabs.

Araminta was half an hour late when her pod pulled up at the back of Nik's. She rushed in through the kitchen door, and got filthy looks from the rest of the staff. 'Sorry!' The restaurant was already full of the breakfast crowd, mid-level executives who liked their food natural, prepared by chefs rather than cuisine units, and served by humans not bots.

Tandra managed to lean in close as Araminta fastened her apron. She sniffed suspiciously and winked. 'Travel-clean, huh. I guess you didn't get home last night?'

Araminta hung her head, wishing she did have an excuse like that. 'I was up late last night, another design course.'

'Honey, you've got to start burning the candle at both ends. You're real young and a looker, get yourself out there again.'

'I know. I will.' Araminta took a deep breath. Went over to Matthew who was so disgusted he didn't even rebuke her. She lifted three plates from the ready counter, checked the table number, cranked her mouth open to a smile, and pushed through the doors.

The breakfast session at Nik's usually lasted for about ninety minutes. There wasn't a time limit, but by quarter to nine the last customers were heading for the office or store. Occasionally, a tourist or two would linger, or a business meeting would run over time. Today there weren't many lagging behind. Araminta did her penance by supervising the cleaning bots as the tables were changed ready to serve morning coffee to shoppers and visitors. Nik's had a good position in the commercial district, five blocks from the docks down on the river.

Tables started to fill up again after ten o'clock. The restaurant had a curving front wall, with a slim terrace running around it. Araminta went along the outside tables, adjusting the flowers in the small vases and taking orders for chocolettos and cappuccinos. It kept her out of Matthew's way. He still hadn't said anything to her, a bad sign.

Some time after eleven the woman appeared and started moving along the tables, talking to the customers. Araminta could see several of them were annoyed, waving her away. Since Ethan declared Pilgrimage ten days ago, Living Dream disciples from the local fane had been coming in and pestering people. It was starting to be a problem.

'Can I help you?' Araminta asked, keeping the tone sharp; this was a chance to earn more redemption points with Matthew. The woman was dressed in a charcoal-grey cashmere suit, old-fashioned but expensive with a long flowing skirt, the kind of thing Araminta might have worn before the separation, back in the days when she had money. 'We have several tables available.'

'I'm collecting signature certificates,' the woman said. She had a very determined look on her face. 'We're trying to get the council to stop ingrav capsule use above Colwyn City.'

'Why?' It came out before Araminta really thought about it.

The woman narrowed her eyes. 'Regrav is bad enough, but at least they're speed and altitude limited inside the city boundary. Have you ever thought what would happen if an ingrav drive failed? They fly semi-ballistic parabolas, that means they'd *plummet* down at half-orbital velocity.'

'Ah, yes, I see.' She could also see Matthew giving them a wary look.

'Suppose one crashed on to a school at that speed? Or a hospital? There's just no need for them. It's blatant consumerism without any form of responsibility. People are only buying them to show off. And there are studies that suggest the ingrav effect puts a strain on deep geological faults. We could have an earthquake.'

Araminta was proud she didn't laugh out loud. 'I see.'

'The city traffic network wasn't designed with those sort of speeds in mind, either. The number of near-miss incidents logged is rising steadily. Will you add your certificate? Help us keep our lives safe.'

A file was presented to Araminta's u-shadow. 'Yes, of course. But you'll have to order a tea or coffee, my boss is already cross with me this morning.' She flicked her gaze towards Matthew as she added her signature certificate to the petition, confirming she was a Colwyn City resident.

'Typical,' the woman grunted. 'They never think of anything but themselves and their profit.' But she sat down and ordered a peppermint tea.

'What's her problem?' Matthew asked as Araminta collected the tea.

'The universe is a bad place, she just needs to unwind a little.' She gave him a sunny smile. 'Which is why we're here.'

Before he could say anything else she skipped back to the terrace.

At half past eleven Araminta's u-shadow collated the morning's property search it had run through the city's estate agencies, and shunted the results into one of her storage lacunas. She was on her break in the little staff lounge beside the kitchen. It didn't take her long to review them all; she was looking for a suitable flat or even a small house somewhere in the city. There weren't many that fitted her criteria: cheap, in need of renovation, near the centre. She tagged three agency files as possibles, and checked on how yesterday's possibles were doing. Half of them had already been snapped up. You really had to be quick in today's market, she reflected wistfully. *And have money, or at least some decent credit.* A renovation was her dream project; buying a small property and refurbishing it in order to sell on at a profit. She knew she could be good at it. She'd taken five development and design courses in the last eight months since separating from Laril, as well as studying every interior decorating text her u-shadow could pull out of the unisphere. Property development was a risky proposition, but every case she'd accessed showed her that the true key was dedication and hard work, as well as a lot of market research. And from her point of view she could do it by herself. She wouldn't depend on anyone. But first, she needed money . . .

Araminta was back in the restaurant at twelve, getting the table settings changed ready for lunch, learning the specials the chef was working on. The anti-ingrav crusader had gone, leaving a three-Viotia-pound tip; and Matthew was treating her humanely again. Cressida walked in at ten past twelve. She was Araminta's cousin on her mother's side of the family, partner in a mid-sized law firm, a hundred and twenty-three years old, and spectacularly beautiful with flaming red hair and skin maintained to silky perfection by expensive cosmetic scales. She was wearing a two-thousand-Vpound emerald and platinum toga suit. Just by walking into Nik's she was raising the whole tone of the place. She was also Araminta's lawyer.

'Darling.' Cressida waved and came over for a big hug; air-kissing had never been part of her style. 'Well, have I got news for you,' she said breathlessly. 'Your boss won't mind if I steal you for a second, will he?' Without bothering to check she grabbed Araminta's hand and pulled her over to a corner table.

Araminta winced as she imagined Matthew's stare drilling laser holes in her back. 'What's happened?'

Cressida's grinned broadly, her liquid scarlet lip gloss flowing to accommodate the big stretch. 'Dear old Laril has skipped planet.'

'*What?*' Araminta couldn't quite believe that. Laril was her ex-husband. A marriage which had lasted eighteen utterly miserable months. Everyone in her immediate family had objected to Laril from the moment she met him. They had cause. She could admit that now; she'd been twenty-one while he was three hundred and seven. At the time she'd thought him suave, sophisticated, rich, and her ticket out of boring, small (minded), agricultural Langham, a town over on the Suvorov continent, seven thousand miles away. They thought he was just another filthy Punk Skunk; there were enough of them kicking around the Commonwealth especially on the relatively unsophisticated planets that made up the outer fringes of the External Worlds. Jaded old folks who had the money to look flawlessly adolescent, but still envied the genuinely youthful for their spirit and exuberance. Every partner they snagged was centuries younger in a futile hope that their brio would magically transfer over. That wasn't quite the case with Laril. Close, though.

Her branch of the family on her father's side had a business supplying and maintaining agricultural cybernetics, an enterprise which was the largest in the county, and one in which Araminta was expected to work in for at least the first fifty years of her life. After that apprenticeship, family members were then considered adult and wealthy enough to take off for pastures new (a depressing number set up subsidiaries of the main business across Suvorov), leaving gaps for the latest batch of youngsters to fill, turning the cycle. It was a prospect which Araminta considered so soul-crushing she would have hired out as a love slave to a Prime motile in order to escape. By contrast, Laril, an independent businessman with an Andribot franchise among other successful commercial concerns, was like being discovered by Prince Charming. And given that these days an individual's age wasn't a physical quantity, her family objection to the three century difference was *so* bourgeois. It certainly guaranteed the outcome of the affair.

The fact that they'd been more or less right about him using her only made her post-separation life even worse. She could never go back to Langham now. Fortunately, Cressida wasn't judgemental, considering Araminta's colossal mistake as part of life's rich experience. 'If you don't screw up,' she'd told a weeping Araminta at their first meeting, 'you haven't got a base to launch your improvement from. Now what does the separation clause in the marriage contract entitle you to?'

Araminta, who had overcome a mountain of shame even to go to a family member (however distant) for legal help at the start of the divorce had to admit theirs had been an old-fashioned wedding, of the till-death-do-us-part variety. They'd even sworn that to the licensed priest in Langham chapel. It was all very romantic at the time.

'No contract?' an amazed and horrified Cressida had asked. 'Gosh, darling, you are headed for a Mount Herculaneum of improvement aren't you?'

It was a mountain which Laril's lawyers were doing their very best to prevent her ever setting foot on; their counter-suit had frozen Araminta's own assets, all seven hundred and thirty-two pounds she had in her savings account. Even Cressida with all her firm's resources was finding it hard to break through Laril's legal protection, and as for his commercial activities they had proved even more elusive to pin down. All his early talk of being the centre of a Dynasty-like network of profitable companies was either a lie or a cover-up for some astonishing financial irregularities. Intriguingly, Viotia's National Revenue Service had no record of him paying tax at any time in the last hundred years, and were now showing a healthy interest in his activities.

'Skipped. Departed. Left this world. Gone vertical. Uprooted.' Cressida grasped Araminta's hands and gave them a near-painful squeeze. 'He didn't even pay his lawyers.' And her happiness at that eventuality was indecent. 'And now they're just another name on the list of fifty creditors after his arse.'

Araminta's brief moment of delight suddenly darkened. 'So I get nothing?'

'On the contrary. His remaining solid assets, that's his town-house, and the stadium food franchise, which we did manage to freeze right at the start are rightfully yours. Admittedly, they don't quite add up to the kind of assets that bragging about will sway a naive young girl's head.'

Araminta blushed furiously.

'But not to be sneered at. Unfortunately, there is the question of back taxes. Which I'm afraid amounts to three hundred and thirty-seven thousand Viotia pounds. And if the NRS could ever prove half of Laril's ventures that you told me about, they'd claim the rest too. Bloodsucking fiends. However, they can't prove a damn thing thanks to the excellent encryption and strange lack of records your slippery ex has muddled his life with. Then there's my fee, which is ten per cent seeing as how you're family and I admire your late-found pride. So, the rest is yours, clear and free.'

'How much?'

'Eighty-three thousand.'

Araminta couldn't speak. It was a fortune. Agreed, nothing like the corporate megastructure Laril had claimed he owned and controlled, but still more than she'd expected and asked for in the divorce petition. Ever since she walked into Cressida's office she'd allowed herself to dream she might, just might, come out of this with thirty or forty thousand, that Laril would pay just to be rid of her. 'Oh, great Ozzie, you are kidding,' she whispered.

'Not a bit of it. A judge friend of mine has allowed us to expedite matters, on account of the circumstances of truly tragic hardship I claimed you're suffering. Your savings are now unfrozen, and we'll transfer Laril's money into your account at four o'clock this afternoon. Congratulations. You're a free and single woman again.'

Araminta was horrified that she was crying, her hands seemed to flap about in front of her face of their own volition.

'Wow!' Cressida put her arm around Araminta's shoulder, rocking her playfully. 'How do you take bad news?'

'It's over? Really over?'

'Yep. Really. So what say you and I go celebrate. Tell your manager where to stick his menu, go pour soup over a customer's head, then we'll hit the coolest clubs in town and ruin half the male population. How about it?'

'Oh.' Araminta looked up, wiping tears with the back of her hand; the mention of Matthew made her realize she was supposed to be serving. 'I need to get back. Lunch is really busy. They rely on me.'

'Hey, calm down, take a minute. Think of what's happened here.'

Araminta nodded her head sheepishly, glancing round the restaurant. Her co-workers were all trying not to glance in her direction; Matthew was annoyed again. 'I know. I'm sorry. It's going to take a while to sink in. I can't believe it's all over. I've got to . . . Oh, Ozzie, there are so many things I want to do.'

'Great! Let's get you out of here and bring on the serious partying. We'll start with a decent meal.'

'No.' Araminta could see Tandra staring anxiously, and gave her a weak thumbs up in return. 'I can't just walk out, that's not fair on everyone else here. They'll need to get a replacement. I'll hand in my notice properly, and work the rest of the week for them.'

'Dammit, you are horrendously sweet. No wonder your filthy ex could take advantage so easily.'

'It won't happen again.'

'Too bloody true it won't.' Cressida stood up, smiling proudly. 'From now on I'm vetting anyone you date. At least come out for a drink tonight.'

'Um, I really do need to go home after this and work things out.'

'Friday night, then. Come on! Everyone goes out Friday night.'

Araminta couldn't help the grin on her face. 'All right. Friday night.'

'Thank Ozzie for that. And get yourself some serious bad girl clothes first. We're going to do this properly.'

'Okay. Yeah, okay, I will.' She could actually feel her mood changing, like some warm liquid invading her arteries. 'Uh, where do I go for clothes like that?'

'Oh, I'll show you, darling, don't you worry.'

*

Araminta did work the lunch shift, then told Matthew she was quitting, but was happy to stay on as long as he needed her. He completely surprised her by giving her a kiss and congratulating her on finally breaking free of Laril. Tandra got all teary and affectionate while the others gathered round to hear the news and cheer.

By half past three in the afternoon she'd put on a light coat and walked out. The cool late spring air outside sobered her up, allowing her to think clearly again. Even so, she walked the route she so often walked in the afternoon. Along Ware Street, take a left at the major junction and head down the slope along Daryad Avenue. The buildings on either side were five or six storeys tall, a typical mix of commercial properties. Regrav capsules slid silently overhead, while the metro track running down the centre of the avenue hummed with public cabs. Right now the roads had few vehicles, yet Araminta still waited at the crossings for the traffic solidos to change shape and colour. She barely noticed her fellow pedestrians.

The Glayfield was a bar and restaurant at the bottom of the slope, occupying two storeys of an old wood and composite building, part of the original planet landing camp. She made her way through the dark deserted bar to the stairs at the back, and went up to the restaurant. That too was virtually empty. Up at the front it boasted a sheltered balcony where in her opinion the tables were too close; waitresses would have trouble squeezing between them when they were full. She sat at one next to the rail which gave her an excellent view along Daryad Avenue. This was where she came most afternoons to wind down after her shift at Nik's, sitting with a hot orange chocolate watching the people and the ships. Over to her right the Avenue curved upwards into the bulk of the city, producing a wall of tall buildings expressing the many construction phases and styles that had come and gone in Colwyn's hundred and seventy year history. While to her left the River Cairns cut through the land in a gentle northward curve as it flowed out to the Great Cloud Ocean twenty miles away. The river was half a mile wide in the city, the top of a deep estuary which made an excellent natural harbour. Several marinas had been built on both sides, providing anchorage to thousands of private yachts, ranging from little sailing dinghies up to regrav-assisted pleasure cruisers. Two giant bridges spanned the water, one a single unsupported arch of nanotube carbon, the other a more traditional suspension bridge with pure white pillars a flamboyant three hundred metres tall. Capsules slid along beside them, but the ground traffic was almost nonexistent these days. They were mainly used by pedestrians. They led over to the exclusive districts on the south bank, where the city's wealthier residents flocked amid long green boulevards and extensive parks.

On the northern shore, barely half a mile from the Glayfield, the docks were built into the bank and out into the mudflats; two square miles of cargo-handling machinery and warehouses and quays and landing pads and caravan platforms. It was the hub from which the Izyum continent had been developed, the second starport on the planet. There was no heavy industry on Viotia; major engineering systems and advanced technology were all imported. With Ellezelin only seventy-five lightyears away, Viotia was on the fringe of the Free Trade Zone. A market which the local population grumbled was free for Ellezelin companies all right, but disadvantaged everyone else caught in their commercial web. There wasn't a wormhole linking Viotia to Ellezelin. Yet. But talk was that in another hundred years when Viotia's internal market had grown sufficiently, one would be opened allowing the full range of cheap Ellezelin products to flood through, turning them into an economic colony. In the meantime, starships from External Worlds came and went. She watched them as she sipped her orange chocolate; a line of huge freighters, their metal hulls as dull as lead, heavy and ungainly, drifting down vertically out of the sky. Behind them, the departing ships rose away from the planet, brushing through Viotia's legendary pink clouds, accelerating fast once they reached the stratosphere. Araminta gave them a mild grin, thinking of the anti-ingrav woman. If she was right what would the starships' field effect be doing to the geology beneath the city? Maybe a simple wormhole would be the answer; she rather liked the idea, a throwback to the First Commonwealth era of genteel and elegant train travel between star systems. It was a shame that the External Worlds rejected such links out of hand, but they valued their political freedom too much to risk a return to a monoculture, especially with the threat of Higher culture overwhelming their hard-won independence.

Araminta stayed at the table long after she usually packed up and went home. The sun began to fall, turning the clouds a genuine gold-pink as the planet's hazy mesosphere diffused the dying rays of the K-class star. Trans-ocean barges shone brightly out on the Cairns, regrav engines keeping their flat hulls just above the slow rippling water as they nosed out of the dock and headed for the open sea and the islands beyond. She was always soothed by the sight of the city like this, a huge edifice of human activity buzzing along efficiently; a reassurance that civilization did actually work, that nothing could kick the basics out from under her. And now, finally, she could begin to take an active part, to carve out a life for herself. The files from the property agencies floated gently through her exoimage display, allowing her to plan what she might do to them in more detail than she ever bothered before. Without money such reviews had been pointless daydreams, but this evening they took on a comfortable solidity. Part of her was scared by the notion. If she made a mistake now, she'd be back waitressing tables for the next few decades. She only had one shot. Eighty-three thousand was a tidy sum, but it had to be made to work for her. Despite the trepidation, she was looking forward to the challenge. It marked her life truly beginning.

The sun set amid a warm scarlet glow. It seemed to match Araminta's mood. By then, the first customers of the evening were starting to fill up the restaurant. She left a big tip, and went downstairs. Her usual routine had her walking back to Nik's, maybe do some shopping on the way, and taking the trike pod home. But there was nothing usual about today. There was music blasting through the bar. People were leaning on the counter, ordering drinks and aerosols. Araminta glanced down at her clothes. She was wearing a sensible skirt, navy blue, that came down below her knees, a white top with short sleeves was made from a fabric that was specifically wipe-clean so she could cope with spills. Around her, people had made an effort to smarten up for the evening and she felt slightly downmarket by comparison.

But then who are they to judge me?

It was a liberating thought, of the kind she hadn't entertained since leaving Langham. Back when the future was full of opportunity, at least in her imagination.

Araminta sidled her way up to the bar and studied the bottles and beer taps. 'Green Fog, please,' she told the barman. It earned her a slightly bemused smile, but he mixed it perfectly anyway. She drank it slowly, trying not to let the smouldering mist get up her nose. Sneezing would really blow away any remaining credibility.

'Haven't seen anybody drink one of those for a while,' a man's voice said.

She turned and looked at him. He was handsome in that precise way everyone was these days, with features aligned perfectly, which she guessed meant he'd been through at least a couple of rejuve treatments. Like the rest of the bar's clientele, he'd dressed up, a simple grey and purple toga jacket that cloaked him in a gentle shimmer.

And he's not Laril.

'Been a while since I was let out,' she retorted. Then smirked at her own answer, the fact she was bold enough to say it.

'Can I get you another? I'm Jaful, by the way.'

'Araminta. And no, not a Green Fog, that's a nostalgia thing for me. What's current?'

'They say Adlier 88Vodka is going down in all the wrong places.'

She finished her Green Fog in a single gulp. Tried not to grimace too hard. And pushed the empty glass across the bar. 'Best start there, then.'

*

'Are you awake?'

Araminta stirred when she heard the question. She wasn't awake exactly, more like dozing pleasantly, content in the after-glow of a night spent in busy lovemaking. Her mind was full of a strange vision, as if she was being chased through the dark sky by an angel. Her slight movement was enough for Jaful. His hands slid up her belly to cup her breasts. 'Uh,' she murmured, still drowsy as the angel dwindled. Jaful rolled her on to her front, which was confusing. Then his cock was sliding up inside her again, hard and insistent. It wasn't a comfortable position. Each thrust pushed her face down into the soft mattress. She wriggled to try and get into a more acceptable stance, which he interpreted as full acceptance. Heated panting became shouts of joy. Araminta cooperated as best she could but the pleasure was minimal at best. *Out of practice,* she thought, and tried not to laugh. He wouldn't understand if she did. At least she was doing her best to make up for lost time, though. They'd coupled three or four times after they got back to his place.

Jaful climaxed with a happy yell. Araminta matched him. *Yep, remember how to do that bit as well.* Eighteen months with Laril had made faking orgasms automatic.

Jaful flopped on to his back, and let out a long breath. He grinned at her. 'Fantastic. I haven't had a night like that for a long time, if ever.'

She dropped her voice a couple of octaves. 'You were good.' It was so funny, like they were reading from a script.

Picked up in a bar. Back to his place for a one night stand. Compliment each other. Both of them playing their part of the ritual to perfection.

But it has been fun.

'I'm going to grab a shower,' he said. 'Tell the culinary unit what you want. It's got some good synthesis routines.'

'I'll do that.' She watched him stroll across the room and into the en suite. Only then did she stare round in curiosity. It was chic city bachelor pad, that much was evident by the plain yet expensive furniture and contemporary art. The wall opposite the bed was a single window, covered with snow-white curtains.

Araminta started hunting round for her clothes as the spore shower came on. Underwear (practical rather than sexy, she acknowledged with a sigh) close to the bed. Skirt halfway between bed and door. Her white top in the lounge. She pulled it on, then looked back at the bedroom. The shower was still on. Did he always take so long, or was he sticking with the part of the script that gave her a polite opportunity to exit. She shrugged, and let herself out.

There wasn't anything wrong with Jaful. She'd certainly enjoyed herself in his bed for most of the time. It was just that she couldn't think what they could say to each other over breakfast. It would have been awkward. This way she kept the memory agreeable. 'More practice,' she told herself, and smiled wickedly. *And why not? This is real life again.*

The building had a big lobby. When she walked out into the street she blinked against the bright pink light, it was twelve minutes until she was supposed to start the morning shift at Nik's. Her u-shadow told her she was in the Spalding district, which was halfway across the city. So she called a taxi down. It took about thirty seconds until the yellow and purple capsule was resting a couple of centimetres above the concrete, three metres in front of her. She watched in bemusement as the door opened. In all her life she'd never called a taxi herself; it had always been Laril who ordered them. After the separation, of course, she couldn't afford them. *Another blow for freedom.*

As soon as she arrived at Nik's she rushed into the staff toilets.

Tandra gave her a leery look when she came out, tying her apron on. 'You know, those look like the very same clothes you wore when you left yesterday.' She sniffed elaborately. 'Yep, travel-clean again. Did something happen to your plumbing last night?'

'You know. I'm really going to miss you when I leave,' Araminta replied, trying not to laugh.

'What's his name? How long have you been dating?'

'Nobody. I'm not dating, you know that.'

'Oh, come on!'

'I need coffee.'

'Not much sleep, huh?'

'I was reviewing property files, that's all.'

Tandra gave her a malicious sneer. 'Sweetie, I ain't never heard it called that before.'

After the breakfast shift was over, Araminta ran her usual review. This time was different. This time her u-shadow contacted the agencies who gave her virtual tours of the five most promising properties using a full-sense relay bot. On that basis, she made an appointment to visit one that afternoon.

As soon as she walked through the door, she knew it was right for her. The flat was the second floor of a converted three-storey house in the Philburgh district. A mile and a half north of the dock and three blocks back from the river, with two bedrooms it was perfect for someone working in the city centre on a modest salary. There was even a balcony which you could just see the Cairns from, if you really leaned out over the railing.

She went through the official survey scan with the modern analysis programs recommended by half a dozen professional property development companies. It needed redecorating, the current vendor had lived there for thirty years and hadn't done much to it. The plumbing needed replacing, it would require new domestic units. But the structure was perfectly sound.

'I'll take it,' she told the agent.

An hour negotiating with the vendor gave her a price of fifty-eight thousand. More than she would have liked, but it did leave her with enough of a budget to give the place a decent refurbishment. There wouldn't be much left over to live on, but if she completed the work within three or four months she wouldn't need a bank loan. It would be tough, just looking round the lounge with its broken dust capillary flooring and ageing light-fabric walling, she could see the amount of work involved. That was when she experienced a little moment of doubt. *Come on,* she told herself, *you can do this. This is what you've waited for, this is what you've earned.*

She took a breath, and left the flat. She needed to get back to her place and grab a shower. Travel-clean could only cope for so long. Then, she might just get changed and go out again. There were a lot of bars in Colwyn City she'd heard about and never visited.

*

Troblum double woke in two of the penthouse's bedrooms. His actual self lay on a bed made from a special foam that supported his large body comfortably, providing him with a decent night's sleep. It had been Catriona's room, decorated in excessively pink fabrics and ornaments; a lot of the surfaces were fluffy, a very girly girl's room which he was now quite used to. His parallel sensorium was coming from a twinning link to the solido of Howard Liang, a Starflyer agent who had been part of the disinformation mission. Howard was in the penthouse's main bedroom, sharing a huge circular bed with the three girls. It was another aspect of the solidos which Troblum had spent years refining. Now, whenever he wanted sex the four characters would launch themselves eagerly into a mini-orgy. The permutations their supple young bodies could combine into were almost endless, and they could keep going for as long as Troblum wanted. He immersed himself for hours, his own body drinking down the pleasure which Howard's carefully formatted neural pathways experienced, as much the puppet as the puppeteer. The four of them together wasn't strictly speaking a historical reality. At least he'd never found any evidence for it. But it wasn't impossible, which sort of legitimized the extrapolation.

The image and feeling of the beautiful naked bodies draped across him faded away as his actual body reasserted itself, cancelling the twinning with Howard. After the shower had squirted dermal fresher spores over him, he walked through into the vast lounge, bronze sunlight washing warmly across his tingling skin.

His u-shadow reported there was still no message from Admiral Kazimir, which he chose to interpret as good news. The delay at least meant it was still being considered. Knowing the Navy bureaucracy, he suspected that the review committee still hadn't formally met. His theory was struggling against a lot of conventional beliefs. Briefly, he considered calling the Admiral direct in order to urge him along, but his personal protocol routines advised against.

He wrapped one of his cloaks round himself, then took the lift down to the lobby. It was only a short walk down to the Caspe River where his favourite café was situated on the edge of the quiet water. The building was made from white wood, and sculpted to resemble a Folgail, a bird even more sedate than a terrestrial swan. His usual table underneath a wing arch was free and he sat himself down. He gave his order to the café network, and waited while a servicebot brought him a freshly squeezed apple and gonberry juice. The chef, Rowury, spent several days every week in the café, cooking for his enthusiastic clientele of foodies. For a culture which prided itself on its egalitarian ethos, Highers could be real snobs about some traditions and crafts, and 'proper' food was well up on the list. There were several restaurants and cafés in Daroca set up as showcases for their gastronomic patrons.

The first dish to arrive was a shredded cereal with fruit and yogurt, all grown naturally (by agriculture enthusiasts), and brought in from five different planets. Troblum started spooning it up. Rowury had come up with a delicious combination, the taste was subtle yet distinctive. It was a shame he couldn't have a second dish, but apart from the delbread toast the quantities here were fixed. If you wanted repeats, seconds or giant portions then you visited a fully automated eatery.

Troblum had finished the cereal and started on his tea when someone sat down in front of him. He looked up in annoyance. The café was full – inevitably, but that was no excuse for rudeness. The rebuke never made it out of his lips.

'Hope you don't mind,' Marius said as he settled in the chair, his black toga suit trailing thin wisps of darkness behind him as if he was time-lapsed. 'I've heard good reports about this place.'

'Help yourself,' Troblum said grouchily. He knew he shouldn't show too much resentment at Marius's appearance, after all the Faction representative had channelled the kind of EMA funds to Troblum's private projects which were normally only available to huge public enterprises. It was the demands placed on him in return which he found annoying, not the challenges themselves, they were intriguing, but they always took so much time. 'Oh you already have.'

The servicebot delivered a second china cup for Marius. 'How are you keeping, Troblum?'

'Fine. As you know.' His field functions detected a subtle shielding unfurling round the table, originating from Marius. Not obvious, but enough to prevent anyone from hearing or scanning what they were saying. He'd never liked the representative, and it was unusual to meet in person. An unarranged meeting was unheard of, it made Troblum worry about the reason. *Something they consider very important.*

Marius sipped the tea. 'Excellent. Assam?'

'Something like that.'

'Those left on Earth do take a lot of pride in maintaining their ancient heritages. I doubt they actually go out and pick the leaves themselves, though. What do you think?'

'I couldn't give a fuck.'

'There are a lot of things that elude you, aren't there, my friend?'

'What do you want?'

Marius fixed his green eyes on Troblum, the faintest shiver of distaste manifesting in his expression. 'Of course, bluntness to the fore. Very well. The briefing you gave to the Navy concerning the Dyson pair.'

'What about it?'

'It's an interesting theory.'

'It's not a theory,' Troblum said in irritation. 'That has to be the explanation for the origin of the Dark Fortress.'

'The what?'

'Dark Fortress. It's what the Dyson Alpha generator was originally called. I think it was Jean Douvoir who named it that first, he was on the original *Second Chance* exploration mission, you know. It was meant ironically, but after the War it fell out of fashion, especially with the Firewall campaign, people just didn't—'

'Troblum.'

'Yeah?'

'I couldn't give a fuck.'

'I've got the unabridged logs from the *Second Chance* stored in my personal secure kube if you'd like to check.'

'No. But I believe your theory.'

'Oh for Ozz—'

'Listen,' Marius snapped. 'Seriously, I believe you. It was excellently argued. Admiral Kazimir thought well enough of your presentation to order a full review, and he is not easily won over. They are taking you seriously.'

'Well, that's good then. Isn't it?'

'In the greater scheme of things, I'm sure it is. However, you might like to consider where your comprehensive knowledge of the Dark Fortress came from.'

'Oh.' Now Troblum was really worried. 'I never mentioned I was there.'

'I know that. The point is, that we really don't want ANA:Governance to be aware of the detailed examination you and your team made of the Dark Fortress. Not right now. Understand?'

'Yes.' Troblum actually ducked his head, which was ridiculous, but he did feel contrite; maybe he should have realized his presentation would draw a little too much attention to him. 'Do you think the Navy will review my background?'

'No. They have no reason to right now. You're just a physicist petitioning for EMA funds. It happens all the time. And that's the way we'd like it to remain.'

'Yeah, I get it.'

'Good. So if the review committee advises the Admiral that no further action should be taken, we'd prefer you not to kick up a fuss.'

'But what if they favour a proper search?'

'We're confident they won't.'

Troblum sat back, trying to work out the politics. It was difficult for him to appreciate the motivation and psychology of other people. 'But if you have that much influence on the Navy, why worry?'

'We can't affect the Navy directly, not with Kazimir as the safeguard. But your advisory review committee is mostly external, some of them are sympathetic to us, as you are.'

'Right.' Troblum could feel despair starting to cloud his mind. 'Will I be able to put it forward again after the Pilgrimage?'

'We'll see. Probably, yes.'

It wasn't exactly good news but it was better than a flat refusal. 'And my drive project?'

'That can continue, providing you don't publicize what you're doing.' Marius smiled reassurance. It didn't belong on his face. 'We do appreciate your help, Troblum, and we want to keep our relationship mutually beneficial. It's just that events are entering a critical stage right now.'

'I know.'

'Thank you. I'll leave you alone to enjoy your food now.'

With suspicious timing, the servicebot arrived as Marius departed. Troblum stared at the plate it deposited in front of him, a tower of thick buttered pancakes was layered with bacon, yokcheese, scrambled garfoul eggs, black pudding, and topped with strawberries. Maple syrup and afton sauce ran down the sides like a volcanic eruption. The edges of the plate were artistically garnished with miniature hash browns, baked vine salfuds and roasted golden tomatoes.

For the first time in years, Troblum didn't feel remotely hungry.

Inigo's second dream

Edeard had been looking forward to the trip for months. Every year in late summer the village elders organized a caravan to trek over to Witham, the closest medium-sized town in Rulan province, to trade. By tradition, all the senior apprentices went with it. This was part of their landcraft training, of which they had to have a basic knowledge before they could qualify as practitioners. They were taught how to hunt small animals, to clear farmland ditches, which fruit to pick, how to handle a plough, what berries and roots were poisonous, along with the basics of how to make camp in the wild.

Even the fact that Obron would be a travelling companion for three weeks hadn't dented Edeard's enthusiasm. He was finally going to get out of Ashwell. Sure he'd been to all the local farms, but never further than half a day's travel away. The caravan meant he would see a lot more of Querencia, the mountains, people other than the villagers he'd lived among for fifteen years, forests. A chance to see how others did things, explore new ideas. There was so much waiting for him out there. He was convinced it was going to be fantastic.

The reality almost lived up to his expectations. Yes, Obron was a pain, but not too much. Ever since Edeard's success with the ge-cats, the constant hassle hadn't ended but it had certainly eased off. They didn't speak as friends, but on the journey out Obron had been almost civil. Edeard suspected that was partially down to Melzar, who was caravan master, and who had made it very clear before they left that he would not tolerate any trouble.

'It might seem like this is some kind of holiday,' Melzar told the assembled apprentices in the village hall the night before they departed. 'But remember this is part of your formal education. I expect you to work hard and learn. If any of you cause me *any* problems, you will be sent back to Ashwell right away. If any of you slack off or do not reach what I consider a satisfactory level of landcraft, I will inform your Master and you will be dropped back a year from qualification. Understood?'

'Yes, sir,' the apprentices muttered grudgingly. There were a lot of smirks hidden from Melzar as they filed out.

They had taken five days to reach Witham. There were seventeen apprentices and eight adults in the caravan. Three big carts carried goods and food; over thirty farm beasts were driven along with them. Everyone rode ge-horses; for some apprentices it was the first time they'd ever been up on the animals. Melzar quickly assigned Edeard to help tutor them. It allowed him to open up conversations with lads who'd ignored him before, after all he was the youngest senior apprentice in Ashwell. But out here on the road they began to accept him as an equal rather than the freaky boy Obron always complained about. Melzar also entrusted him with controlling the ge-wolves they used to keep guard.

'You're better than all of us at guiding those brutes, lad,' he'd said as they made camp that first night. 'Make sure they do their job properly. Keep three of them with us, and I want the other four patrolling round outside.'

'Yes, sir, I can do that.' It wasn't even a brag, those were simple orders.

Talk that night among the apprentices was of bandits and wild tribes, each of them doing their best to tell the most horrific stories. Alcie and Genril came top with the cannibal tribe that supposedly lived in the Talman Mountains. Edeard didn't mention that his own parents had been killed while on a caravan, but everyone knew that anyway. He was thrown a few glances to

135

check out how he was reacting. His nonchalance earned him quiet approval. Then Melzar came over and told them all not to be so gruesome, that bandits weren't half as bad as legend. 'They're basically nomad families, nothing more. They're not organized into gangs. How could they be? If they were a real threat we'd call the militia from the city, and go after them. It's just a few bad 'uns that give the rest a lousy rep. No different from us.'

Edeard wasn't so sure. He suspected Melzar was just trying to reassure them. But the conversation moved on, quietening down as they gossiped about their Guild Masters. Judging by their talk, Edeard was convinced he'd got a saint in Akeem. Obron even claimed Geepalt would beat the carpentry apprentices if they messed up.

Witham might have been five times the size of Ashwell, but it shared the same air of stagnation. It was set in rolling, heavily cultivated farmland, with a river running through the middle; unusually it had two churches for the Lady. Edeard bit back on any disappointment as they rode through the big gates. The buildings were stone or had thick timber frames supporting some kind of plaster panelling. Most of the windows were glass rather than the shutters used in Ashwell. And the streets were all stone cobble. He found out later that water was delivered into houses through buried clay pipes, and the drains worked.

They spent two days in the central market square, negotiating with merchants and locals, then stocking up with supplies (like glass) that weren't made in Ashwell. The apprentices had been allowed to bring examples of their own work to sell or trade. Edeard was surprised when Obron brought out a beautifully carved box made from martoz wood, polished to a ebony lustre. Who would have thought an arse like him could create something so charming? Yet a merchant gave him four pounds for it.

For himself, Edeard had brought along six ge-spiders. Always the trickiest of the standard genera to sculpt, they were highly valued for the drosilk they spun. And these had only just hatched, they'd live for another eight or nine months; during that time they would spin enough silk to make several garments, or armour jackets. Three ladies from the Weaver's Guild bid against each other for them. For the first time in his life Edeard's farsight couldn't quite discern how eager they were when they haggled with him; they covered their emotions with steely calm, the surface of their minds as smooth as a genistar egg. He just hoped he was doing the same when he agreed to sell for five pounds each. Surely they could sense his elation? It was more money than he'd seen in his life, let alone held in his hands. Somehow he didn't manage to hang on to it for very long. The market was huge, with so many fabulous items, as well as clothes of a quality rarely found in Ashwell. He felt almost disloyal buying there, but he did so need a decent full-length oilskin coat for the coming winter, and found one with a quilted lining. Further on there was a stall selling knee-high boots with sturdy silkresin soles that would surely last for years – a good investment, then. They also sold wide-brimmed leather hats. To keep the sun off in summer, and the rain in winter, the leatherworker apprentice explained. She was a lovely girl and seemed genuinely eager for him to have the right hat. He dragged out the haggling as long as he dared.

His fellow apprentices laughed when he returned dressed in his new finery. But they had spent their own money, too. And few had been as practical as him.

That evening Melzar allowed them to visit the town's taverns unchaperoned, threatening horrifying punishments if anyone caused trouble. Edeard joined up with Alcie, Genril, Janene and Fahin. He spent the evening hoping to catch sight of the leather-worker apprentice, but by the time they reached the third tavern the town's unfamiliar ales had rendered them incapable of just about anything other than drinking more ale. And singing. The rest of the evening was forever beyond recollection.

When he woke up, slumped under one of the Ashwell carts, Edeard knew he was dying. He'd obviously been poisoned then robbed. Too much of his remaining money was missing, he could barely stand, he couldn't eat, he stank worse than the stables. It was also the first night he couldn't remember being troubled by his strange dreams. Then he found out it was a mass poisoning. All the apprentices were in the same state. And all of the adults found it hilarious.

'Another lesson learned,' Melzar boomed. 'Well done. You lot should graduate in record time at this rate.'

'What a swine,' Fahin grunted as Melzar walked away. He was a tall boy, so thin he looked skeletal. As a doctor's apprentice he'd managed to get one of the few pairs of glasses in Ashwell to help his poor vision. They weren't quite right for him, magnifying his eyes to a quite disturbing degree for anyone standing in front of him. At sometime during the night he'd lost his jacket, now he was shivering, and not entirely from the cold morning air. Edeard had never seen him looking so pale before.

Fahin was searching through the leather physick satchel that he always carried. It was full of packets of dried herbs, small phials, and some rolled linen bandages. The satchel made him the butt of many jokes in the taverns all last night, yet he refused to abandon it.

'Do you think they'll let us ride in the carts?' Janene asked mournfully as she looked at the adults, who were huddled together chortling. 'I don't think I can take riding on a ge-horse this morning.'

'Not a chance,' Edeard said.

'How much money have you got left?' Fahin asked. 'All of you.'

The apprentices began a reluctant search through their pockets. Fahin managed to gather up two pounds in change, and hurried off to the herbalist stall. When he came back he started brewing up tea, emptying in several packets of dried leaves and adding the contents of a phial from the satchel.

'What is that?' Alcie asked as he sniffed the kettle and stepped back, his eyes watering. Edeard could smell it too, something like sweet tar.

'Growane, flon seed, duldul bird eyes, nanamint.' Fahin squeezed some limes into the boiling water, and started stirring.

'That's disgusting!' Obron exclaimed.

'It'll cure us, I promise on the Lady.'

'Please tell us you rub it on,' Edeard said.

Fahin wiped the condensation from his glasses, and poured himself a cup. 'Gulp it down in one, that's best.' He swallowed. His cheeks bulged as he grimaced. Edeard thought he was going to spew it up again.

The other apprentices gave the kettle a dubious look. Fahin poured the cup full again. Edeard could sense the doubt in their minds; he felt for Fahin who was trying to do his best to help and be accepted. He put his hand out and took the cup. 'One gulp?'

'Yes,' Fahin nodded.

'You're not going to . . .' Janene squealed.

Edeard tossed it back. A second later the taste registered, kind of what he imagined eating manure would be like. 'Oh Lady! That is . . . Urrgh.' His stomach muscles squeezed up, and he bent over, thinking he was going to be sick. A weird numbness was washing through him. He sat down as if to catch his breath after a winding blow.

'What's it like?' Genril asked.

Edeard was about to slag Fahin off something rotten. 'Actually, I can't feel anything. Still got a headache, though.'

'That takes longer,' Fahin wheezed. 'Give it fifteen minutes. The flon seed needs to get into your blood and circulate. And you need to drink about a pint of water to help.'

'So what was the lime for?'

'It helps mask the taste.'

Edeard started laughing.

'It actually works?' an incredulous Alcie asked.

Edeard gave him a shrug. Fahin poured another cup.

It turned into a ritual. Each of the apprentices gulped down the vile brew. They pulled faces and jeered and cheered each other. Edeard quietly went and fetched himself a bottle of water from the market's pump. Fahin was right, it did help clear his head. After about quarter of an hour he was feeling okay again. Not a hundred per cent, but the brew had definitely alleviated the worst symptoms. He could even consider some kind of breakfast.

'Thanks,' he told Fahin. The tall lad smiled in appreciation.

Afterwards, when they packed the carts and got the ge-horses ready, the apprentices were all a lot easier around each other, the joshing and pranks weren't so hard-edged as before. Edeard imagined that this was what it would be like from now on. They'd shared together, made connections. He often envied the casual friendships between the older people in the village, the way they got on with each other. It was outings like this that saw such seeds rooting. In a hundred years' time, maybe it would be he and Genril laughing at hung-over apprentices. Of course, that would be a much bigger caravan, and Ashwell would be the same size as Witham by then.

Melzar led the caravan on a slightly different route back, curving westward to take in the foothills of the Sardok mountain range. It was an area of low valleys with wide floors, mostly wooded, and home to a huge variety of native creatures. There were few paths other than those carved out by the herds of chamalans who grazed on the pastures between the forests. Farsight and the ge-wolves also sniffed out drakken pit traps which would have swallowed up a ge-horse and rider. The drakken were burrowing animals the size of cats, with five legs in the usual Querencia arrangement of two on each side and a thick highly flexible limb at the rear which helped them make their loping run. The front two limbs had evolved into ferociously sharp claws which could dig through soil at a phenomenal rate. They were hive animals, digging their vast warrens underground, with populations over a hundred strong. Singularly they were harmless, but they attacked in swarms which even a well-armed human had trouble fighting off. Their ability to excavate big caverns just below the surface provided them with the means to trap their prey; even the largest of native creatures were susceptible to the pit traps.

A bi-annual hunt had eliminated the drakken from the lands around Ashwell, but here in the wild they were prevalent.

Watching for them heightened Edeard's senses as they passed through the endless undulating countryside. On the third day out of Witham they reached the fringes of the foothills and entered one of the massive forests there, parts of which reached across to the base of the Sardoks themselves.

Edeard had never been in a forest this size before; according to Melzar it predated the arrival of humans on Querencia two thousand years ago. The sheer size of the trees seemed to back up his claim, tall and tightly clustered, their trunks dark and lifeless for the first fifty feet until they burst into a thick interlaced canopy where branches and leaves struggled against each other for light. Little grew on the floor beneath, and in summer when the leaves were in full bloom not much rain dripped through either. A huge blanket of dead, crisped leaves covered the ground, hiding hollows from sight, requiring the humans to use their farsight in order to guide the ge-horses safely round crevices and snags.

It was quiet in the gloom underneath the verdant living awning, the still air amplifying their mildest whisper to a shout that reverberated the length of the plodding caravan. The apprentices slowly abandoned their banter, becoming silent and nervy.

'We'll make camp in a valley I know,' Melzar announced after midday. 'It's an hour away, and the forest isn't as wretched as it is here. There's a river as well. We're well past the trilan egg season so we can swim.'

'We're stopping there?' Genril asked. 'Isn't that early?'

'Don't get your hopes up, my lad. This afternoon you're going galby hunting.'

The apprentices immediately brightened. They'd been promised hunting experience, but hadn't expected it to be galbys, which were large canine equivalents. Edeard had often heard experienced adults tell of how they thought they'd got a galby cornered only to have it jump to freedom. Their hind limb was oversized and extremely powerful, sometimes propelling them as much as fifteen feet in the air.

True to Melzar's word, the forest began to change as they

reached a gentle downhill slope. The trees were spread out, and shorter, allowing pillars of sunlight to swarm down. Grass grew again, swiftly becoming an unbroken stratum. Bushes grew in the long gaps between trees, their leaves ranging from vivid green to a dark amethyst. Edeard couldn't name more than a handful of the berries he could see, there must have been dozens of varieties.

As the light and humidity increased, so the yiflies and bite-wings began to appear; soon they were swirling overhead in huge clumps before zooming down to nip all the available human skin. Edeard was constantly using his third hand to ward them off.

They stopped the carts by a small river, and corralled the genistars. That was when Melzar finally distributed the five revolvers and two rifles he'd been carrying. The majority belonged to the village, though Genril had his own revolver, which he said had been in his family since the arrival. Its barrel was longer than the others, and made out of a whitish metal that was a lot lighter than the sturdy gun-grade steel produced by the Weapons Guild in Makkathran.

'Carved from the ship itself,' Genril said proudly as he checked the mechanism. Even that snicked and whirred with a smoothness which the city-made pistols lacked. 'My first ancestor salvaged some of the hull before the tides took the ship down into the belly of the sea. It's been in our family ever since.'

'Crap,' Obron snorted. 'That would mean it's over two thousand years old.'

'So?' Genril challenged as he squeezed some oil out of a small can, rubbing it on to the components with a soft linen cloth. 'The ship builders knew how to make really strong metal. Think about it, you morons, they *had* to have strong metal, the ship fell out of the sky and still survived, and in the universe they came from ships flew between planets.'

Edeard didn't say anything. He'd always been sceptical about the whole ship legend. Though he had to admit, it was a *great* legend.

Melzar slung one of the rifles over his shoulder and came

round with a box of ammunition. He handed out six of the brass bullets to each of the apprentices who had been given a revolver. 'That's quite enough,' he told them when there were complaints about needing more. 'If you can't hit a galby after six shots, it's either jumped back out of range or it's happily eating your liver. Either way, that's all you get.'

Only five apprentices had been given a gun (including Genril). Edeard wasn't one of them. He looked on rather enviously as they slid the bullets into the revolving chamber.

Melzar crouched down, and began to draw lines in the earth. 'Gather round,' he told them. 'We're going to split into two groups. The shooters will be lined up along the ridge back there.' His hand waved into the forest where the land rose sharply. 'The rest of us will act as the flushers. We form a long line with one end *there*, which will move forward in a big curve until we're level with the first shooter. That should force anything bigger than a drakken out in front of us, and hopefully into the firing line. *Under no circumstances* does anyone go past the first shooter. I don't care if you're best friends and using longtalk, you do not walk in front of the guns. Understood?'

'Yes, sir,' they all chorused.

'Okay then, after the first sweep we'll change over the guns and move to a new location.' He glanced up at the sky which was now starting to cloud over. 'There'll be enough light to do this three times this afternoon, which will give everyone a chance to use a pistol.'

'Sir, my father said only I can use our pistol,' Genril said.

'I know,' Melzar said. 'You get to hang on to it but not the ammunition when you're in the flusher line. Now: if you're a part of the flusher line, you must keep within farsight perception of the people on either side. So in reality that means I want you spaced no more than seventy yards apart. Orders to start, stop, and group together will be issued vocally and in longtalk. You will relay both along the line. You will obey them at all times. The flusher line will use three ge-wolves to help encourage the galbys to run. This time, Edeard and Alcie will control one each,

I will take the third. No one else is to order them, I don't want them confused. Any questions? No. Good. Let's go, and the Lady smile on us.'

Edeard called one of the ge-wolves over, and set off in the group following Melzar. Toran, one of the farmers, led the pistol carriers up towards the stony ridge.

'I don't see the point of this,' Fahin complained grimly as he hiked along beside Edeard. 'We've all done pistol shooting at the targets outside the walls, and galbys aren't eatable.'

'Don't you listen to anything?' Janene said. 'This is all about experience. There's a world of difference between firing at a target and being out here in the woods with dangerous animals charging round. The elder council needs to know they can rely on us to defend the village in an emergency.'

Except Melzar told us the nomad families aren't threatening, Edeard thought. *So what is the village wall actually for? I must ask Akeem when I get back.*

'So what if the galbys don't go towards the shooting line?' Fahin asked. 'What if they come at us?' He gripped his satchel tighter, as if it could shield him from the forest's animals.

'They won't,' Edeard said. 'They'll try and avoid us, because we're a group.'

'Yeah, in theory,' Fahin grumbled.

'Quit whinging, for the Lady's sake,' Obron said. 'Melzar knows what he's doing; he's done this with every caravan for the last fifty years. Besides, galbys aren't all that dangerous. They just look bad. If one comes at you, use your third hand to shield yourself.'

'What if we flush out a fastfox?'

The apprentices groaned.

'Fastfoxes live down on the plains,' an exasperated Alcie said. 'They're not mountain animals. You're more likely to get one in Ashwell than here.'

Fahin pulled a face, not convinced.

As they approached the edge of the forest again, Melzar used his longtalk to tell them, 'Start to spread out. Remember, keep the people on both sides within your farsight. If you lose contact, longtalk them.'

Edeard had Obron on one side and Fahin on the other. He wasn't too happy about that. If anyone was going to screw up it would be Fahin. The lanky boy really wasn't an outdoors type; and Obron wasn't likely to help either of them. *But the worst thing Fahin can do is fall behind. It's not like he's got a pistol. And he'll yell hard enough if he can't see us.* He sent the ge-wolf ranging from side to side. The mood of excitement was filling his farsight, the minds of everyone in the flusher line twinkling with anti-cipation.

They moved forwards, slowly spreading out as Melzar directed until they had formed the line. The trees were growing tall again, their dark-green canopy insulating the apprentices from the cloudy sky.

'Move forwards,' Obron ordered. Edeard smiled and repeated the instruction to Fahin, who grimaced.

Edeard was pleased he'd kept his new boots on. The forest floor here was littered with sticks among manky clumps of grass, uneven ground with plenty of sharp stones. His ankles were sore where the new leather pinched, yet they protected his feet well enough.

With his farsight scouring the land ahead he kept a slow pace, making sure the line stayed straight. Melzar told them to start making a racket. Obron was shouting loudly, while Fahin let out piercing whistles. For himself, Edeard picked up a thick stick and thwacked it against the tree trunks as he passed by.

There were more bushes in this part of the forest. Big zebrathorns with their monochrome patterned leaves and oozing (highly poisonous) white berries, coaleafs that were like impen-etrable black clouds squatting on the earth. Small creatures were exposed to his farsight, zipping out of the way of the humans. Nothing big enough to be a drakken, let alone a galby. The ground became soft under his feet, wet loam that leaked water from every footprint. The scent of mouldering leaf was strong in his nose. He was sure he could smell fungus spores.

Obron was out of eyesight now, somewhere behind the bushes. Edeard's farsight picked him up on the other side of dense trunks.

'Close up a little,' he longtalked.

'Sure sure,' Obron replied casually.

A ripple of excitement went down the line. Somewhere up towards Melzar's end a galby sped away, not quite in the direction of the shooting line. Edeard's heart started to beat quickly. He knew he was smiling and didn't care. This was the kind of thing he'd wanted ever since he learned he was going on the caravan. There were galbys here! He would get a chance to flush one, and if he was really lucky maybe take a shot later on.

Something squawked above him. Edeard flicked his farsight focus upwards in time to see a couple of birds dart up through the canopy. There was a thicket up ahead, a dense patch of zebrathorn, just the kind of place for a galby to nest in. His farsight swept through it, but there were dark zones and steep little gullies he couldn't be sure about. He sent the ge-wolf slinking in through the bushes as he skirted round the outside. Now he couldn't see Fahin either, but his farsight registered the boy's mind.

Apprehension hit him like a solid force, the mental equivalent of being doused in icy water. Suddenly all his delight deserted him. His fingers actually lost their grip on the stick as his legs seized up. Something *terrible* was happening. He knew it.

'What?' he gasped. He was frightened, and worse, frightened that he was frightened. *This makes no sense.*

In the middle of the thicket, the ge-wolf he was casually directing lifted its head and snarled, responding to the turmoil bubbling along his tenuous longtalk contact.

'Edeard?' Fahin called. 'What's wrong.'

'I don't . . .' Edeard pulled his arms in by his side as his knees bent, lowering him to a crouch. He instinctively closed his third hand around himself to form the strongest shield he was capable of. *Lady, what's the matter with me?* He pushed his farsight out as far as he could, and swept round as if it was some kind of illuminating beam. The tree trunks were too dense to get any kind of decent picture of anything beyond his immediate vicinity.

'What is the matter with you?' Obron asked. His mental tone was scathing.

Edeard could sense both apprentices hesitating. The ge-wolf was wriggling round, trying to get out of the thicket and back to him. Dry leaves rustled, and he whirled round, raising the stick protectively. 'I think someone's here.' He directed his farsight where he thought the sound had come from, pushing its focus as hard as he could. There were a few tiny rodent creatures scuttling along the forest floor. They could have made the noise—

'What do you mean: someone?' Fahin demanded. 'Who?'

Edeard was gritting his teeth with the effort of extending his farsight to the limit. 'I don't know, I can't sense them.'

'Hey, we're falling behind,' Obron longtalked impatiently. 'Come on, get moving.'

Edeard stared back into the forest. *This is stupid.* But he couldn't get rid of his dread. He took a last look at the forest behind, then turned. The arrow came out of the empty trees on his left, moving so fast he never saw it, only his farsight caught the slightest ripple of motion. His shield tightened up as he gasped, his mind clamouring its shock.

The arrow hit his left pectoral muscle. His telekinetic shield held. The force of impact was sufficient to knock him backwards. He landed on his arse. The arrow tumbled down in the loam and weeds beside him; a long blackened shaft with dark-green needlehawk feathers and a wicked barbed metal tip dripping some thick violet liquid. Edeard stared at it in horror.

'Edeard?'

His mind was swamped by the telepathic voices. It seemed as if the entire flusher line was mentally shouting at him, demanding an answer.

'Arrow!' he broadcast back at them as forcefully as he could. His eyes didn't move from the arrow lying beside him, showing everyone. 'Poison arrow!'

A mind materialized thirty yards away, sparkling vivid sapphire amid the cluttered grey shadows which comprised Edeard's ethereal vision of the forest.

'Huh?' Edeard jerked his head round. A man stepped out from behind a tree, dressed in a kind of ragged cloak that was almost the same colour as the forest's trunks. His hair was wild, long and braided, filthy with dark-red mud. More mud was smeared across his face and caked his beard. He was snarling, anger and puzzlement leaking out of his mind. One hand reached over his shoulder and pulled another arrow from his quiver. He notched it smoothly into the biggest bow Edeard had ever seen, levelling it as his arm pulled back.

Edeard screamed with voice and mind, a sound he could hear replicated along the flusher line. Even his assailant winced as he let fly.

Edeard thrust his hands out, a motion he followed with his third hand using his full strength. The arrow burst into splinters before it had covered half of the distance between them.

This time it was the forest man who radiated shock into the aether.

'Bandits.' Melzar's call echoed faintly round Edeard, spoken and telepathic. 'It's an ambush. Group together everyone, combine your strength. Shield yourselves. Toran, help us!'

Edeard was scrambling to his feet, vaguely aware of other shouts and adrenaline-boosted emotional pulses reverberating across the forest. More bandits were emerging from their concealment. Arrows were being fired. His mind reached for the ge-wolf, directing it with frenzied urgency. There wasn't going to be time. The forest man had slung his bow to the ground, and was charging. A knife glinted in his hand.

A telekinetic shove nearly knocked Edeard back to the ground. He countered it easily, feeling the force slither over his skin like icy fingers. The bandit was trying for a heartsqueeze, an attack method which apprentices talked about in nervous awe when they gathered together back in Ashwell. Using telekinesis inside someone else's body was the ultimate taboo. Anyone found to have committed the act was exiled. For ever.

Now a bandit was thundering towards Edeard. Knife ready. Death lust fevering his mind. Third hand scrabbling to assail vulnerable organs.

His earlier fear had left Edeard. He wasn't even thinking about the others. A maniac was seriously trying to kill him. That was the whole universe. And as Akeem had explained during their all-too-brief sessions on defensive telekinetic techniques, there is no such thing as a disabling blow.

Edeard stood up and let his arms drop to his side, closing his eyes. He shaped his third hand. Waiting. The pounding of the bandit's bare feet on the forest floor reached his ears. *Waiting.* The man's berserker cry began. The knife rose up, gripped by white knuckles. *Wait . . . judge the moment.* Edeard's farsight revealed the man in perfect profile, he even perceived the leg muscles exerting themselves to the limit as they began the leap. *Any second—*

The attempted heartsqueeze ended, telekinesis was channelled to assist the attack leap, to strengthen the knife thrust.

—now.

The bandit left the ground. Edeard pushed his third hand underneath the airborne figure and shoved, effort forcing a wild roar from his throat. He'd never exerted himself so much before, not even when Obron's torment was at its worst.

In an instant the bandit's semi-triumphant scream turned to pure horror. Edeard opened his eyes to see a pair of mud-encrusted feet sail over his head. 'FUCK YOU!' he bellowed, and added the slightest corrective sideways shove to the trajectory. The bandit's head smashed into a bulky tree four yards above the ground. It made a horrible *thud*. Edeard withdrew his third hand. The man dropped like a small boulder, emitting a slight moan as he struck the ground. The ge-wolf pounced.

Edeard turned away. All his emotions returned with tidal-wave power as the ge-wolf began tearing and clawing at the inert flesh. He'd forgotten just how fierce the creatures were. His legs were threatening to collapse under him they were shaking so bad, while his stomach heaved.

The loud crack of shots ripped across the forest. They made Edeard spin round in alarm. *That has to be us. Right?*

There were shouts and cries all around. Edeard didn't know what to do. One of the cries was high pitched: Janene.

'Lady please!' Obron wailed. His mind was pouring out dread like a small nova.

Edeard's farsight flashed out. Two fastfoxes were racing straight at the weeping apprentice. He'd never seen one before, but knew instantly what they were. Only just smaller than a ge-wolf, but faster, especially on the sprint, a streamlined predator with a short ebony fur stiff enough to act like armour. Head that was either fangs or horns, and way too many of both. Its hindlimb was thick and strong, allowing it a long sprint-jump motion as the ultimate lunge on its prey.

They had collars on.

Edeard started running towards them and reached out with his third hand. They were forty yards away, yet he still felt their metal-hard muscles flexing in furious rhythm. He didn't even know if they had hearts like humans and terrestrial beasts, let alone where they were. *So forget a heartsqueeze.* His telekinesis penetrated the brain of the leading one and simply *shredded* all the tissue he found there. It dropped in mid-bound; flaccid body ploughing a furrow through the carpet of dry leaves. The remaining fastfox lurched aside, its demon head swinging around to try and find the threat. It stopped, growling viciously as Edeard trotted up. Limbs bent as it readied itself to pounce.

'What are you doing?' Obron bawled.

Edeard knew he was acting crazy. Didn't care. Adrenaline was powering him on recklessly. He snarled back at the fastfox, almost laughing at it. Then before the creature could move he closed his third hand round it, and lifted it clean of the ground. The fastfox screeched in fury. Its limbs ran against nothing, pumping so fast they were a blur.

'Are you doing that?' an incredulous Obron asked.

'Yeah,' Edeard grinned.

'Oh crap. *Look out!*'

Three bandits were running towards them. They were dressed the same as the one who attacked Edeard, simple ragged camouflage cloaks, belts with several dagger sheaths. One of them carried a bow.

Edeard sent out a single longtalk command, summoning the ge-wolf.

The bandits were slowing. Consternation began to glimmer in their minds as they saw the furious fastfox scrabbling uselessly in mid-air. More gunshots rang through the forest.

'Protect yourself,' Edeard ordered sharply as the bandit with a bow notched an arrow. Obron's shield hardened.

The three bandits came to a halt, still staring disbelievingly at the writhing fastfox. Edeard rotated the predator slowly and deliberately until it was pointing directly at them. He was studying the animal's thoughts, noting the simple motivational currents. It was similar to a genistar mind, although the strongest impulses seemed to be fear-derived. *Some kind of punishment/ reward training, probably.* The bandit with the bow shot his arrow. Obron yipped as Edeard confidently swiped it aside.

There was another pause as the bandits watched it clatter against a tree. Telekinetic fingers skittered across Edeard's skin, easily warded off. All three bandits drew short swords. Edeard slammed an order into the fastfox's mind, sensing its original compulsions changing. It stopped trying to run and snarled at the bandits. One of them gave it a startled look. Edeard dropped it lightly on the ground.

'Kill,' he purred.

The fastfox moved with incredible speed. Then its hindlimb slapped the earth and powered it forward in a low arc. Telekinetic shields hardened round the bandits. Against one demented predator they might have stood a chance. The ge-wolf hit them from the side.

'Oh, Lady,' Obron shuddered as the screaming began. He paled at the carnage, yet couldn't pull his gaze away.

'Come on,' Edeard caught his arm. 'We have to find Fahin. Melzar said to join up.'

Obron stumbled forward. A burst of pistol fire reverberated through the trees. It must be from the shooting line, Edeard thought, they've come to help. The turbulent shouting was turning into distinct calls. Edeard heard several apprentice names yelled. Longtalk was hysterical snatches of thought mostly over-whelmed with emotional outpourings, a few raw visions threat-ened to overwhelm him. Pain, twinned with blood pumping out from a long gash in Alcie's thigh. Arrow sticking out of a tunic, numbness from its entry point spreading quickly. Mud-caked faces bobbing as punches were thrown. Impact pain. Camou-flaged bandit sprinting between trees as the rifle barrel tracked. Fastfox a streak of grey-black. Blood forming a huge puddle around a torn corpse.

Edeard ran round the side of the zebrathorn thicket. 'Fahin! Fahin, it's us. Where are you?' He couldn't see anyone. There was no revealing glimmer of thought in his farsight. 'Fahin!'

'He's gone,' Obron panted. 'Did they get him? Oh, Lady!'

'Is there any blood?' Edeard was scanning the leaves and soil.

'Nothing. Oh—'

Edeard followed Obron's gaze and caught sight of a bandit running through the woods. The man had a sword in his hand, dripping with blood. Anger surged through Edeard, and he reached out with his third hand, yanking at the man's ankle, then pushing him down hard. As the bandit fell, Edeard twisted the sword, bringing the blade vertical. The agonized bellow as he was impaled made Edeard recoil in shock. The bandit's dying mind wept with frustration and anguish. Then the glimmer of thoughts were extinguished.

'He was fifty yards away,' Obron whispered in astonishment and no small measure of apprehension.

'Fahin,' Edeard called. 'Fahin, can you hear me?' His farsight picked out a tiny iridescent glow that suddenly appeared inside the thicket. 'Fahin?'

'Edeard?' the lanky boy's longtalk asked fearfully.

'Yes! Yes, it's me and Obron. Come on, come out. It's safe. I think.'

They both watched as Fahin crawled out of the bushes. His face and hands had been scratched mercilessly, his loose woollen sweater was missing completely. Tacky berry juice was smeared into his hair, and over his glasses which hung from one ear. Amazingly, he was still clutching his physick satchel. Obron helped him up, and abruptly found himself being hugged. 'I was so frightened,' Fahin mumbled piteously. 'I fled. I'm sorry. I should have helped.'

'It's okay,' Obron said. 'I wasn't much use either.' He turned and gave Edeard a long thoughtful look, his mind tightening up pensively. 'Edeard saved me. He's killed a score of them.'

'No,' Edeard protested. 'Nothing like that—' then trailed off as he realized he really had killed people today. His guilty glance stole back to the bandit impaled on his own sword. A man was dead, and he'd done it. But the sword had been slick with blood. And the other bandits . . . they would have killed us. *I didn't have a choice.*

Sometimes you have to do what's wrong in order to do what's right.

'Can anyone still see or sense bandits?'

Edeard's head came up as he received Melzar's weak longtalk. Obron and Fahin were also looking round.

'Anyone?' Melzar asked. 'Okay, then please make your way towards me. If anyone is injured, please help bring them along. Fahin, are you here?'

Somehow, Melzar being alive made the world a little less intimidating for Edeard. He even managed a small grin. Obron let out a whistle of relief.

'Yes, sir, I'm here,' Fahin replied.

'Good lad, hurry up please, we have injured.'

'Oh, Lady,' Fahin groaned. 'I'm just an apprentice. The doctor won't even let me prepare some of her leaves.'

'Just do the best you can,' Edeard said.

'But—'

'You cured our hangovers,' Edeard said. 'Nobody will start mouthing off at you for helping the injured. We're not expecting you to be as good as old Doc Seneo. But Fahin, you have to do something. You can't turn your back on wounded people. You just can't. They need you.'

'He's right,' Obron said. 'I think I heard Janene scream. What would her parents say if you walked away?'

'Right, yes,' Fahin said. 'You're right, of course. Oh Lady, where are my glasses? I can't do everything by farsight.' He turned back to the thicket.

'They're here,' Edeard said. His third hand lifted them gently into place, at the same time wiping the berry goop from them.

'Thank you,' Fahin said.

They hurried through the forest towards Melzar. Other figures were moving with them in the same direction. Several apprentices sent panicky hellos via longtalk. Edeard remembered an image of Alcie, the wound in his thigh. It had looked bad.

Toran and the apprentices with pistols had gathered into a defensive group with Melzar. Edeard exchanged a relieved greeting with Genril, who was all jitters. He said he had one bullet left in his revolver, and he was sure he'd hit at least one bandit. 'I got really scared when the fastfoxes charged us. Toran killed one with his rifle. Lady! He's a good shot.'

'You should see what Edeard did,' Obron said flatly. 'He doesn't need guns.'

'What?' Genril asked. 'What did you do?'

'Nothing,' Edeard said. 'I know how to deal with animals, that's all. You know that.'

'Just how strong are you?' Obron asked.

'Yeah,' Genril said. 'We heard your longtalk right over on the ridge, it was like you were next to me screaming into my skull. Lady, I almost ducked when that arrow came at you.'

'Does it matter?' Edeard asked. He was looking round, wondering where the others were. Out of the twelve apprentices and four adults in the flusher line, only five had made it so far, including the three of them. Then Canan the carpenter arrived carrying an unconscious Alcie. Fahin gave his friend a worried look, seeing the crudely wrapped wound already soaked in blood. His mind started to get agitated.

'Go,' Edeard directed with a quiet longtalk. 'Do as much as you can.'

'P-p-put him down,' Fahin said. He knelt beside Alcie and started rummaging through his satchel.

Edeard turned back to the forest, sending his farsight ranging out. *Where are the others?* His heart quickened as he detected some movement. A couple of apprentices came running through the trees.

'It's all right,' Melzar said soothingly. 'You're safe now.'

'We left Janene,' one of them wailed. 'We tried to save her, but she took an arrow. I ran—' He collapsed on the ground, sobbing.

'Nine,' Edeard whispered as he kept his vigil. 'Nine out of twelve.'

Melzar's hand came down on his shoulder. 'It would have been none without you,' he said quietly. 'Your warning saved us. Saved me, in fact. I owe you my life, Edeard. We all do.'

'No,' Edeard shook his head sadly. 'I didn't warn you. I was terrified. That was all. You heard my fear.'

'I know. It was – powerful. What happened? What tipped you off?'

'I . . .' He frowned, remembering the sensation of fear that had gripped him. There was no reason for it. 'I heard something,' he said lamely.

'Whatever, I'm glad.'

'Why couldn't we sense them? I thought I had good farsight. They were closer to me than Obron and Fahin and I never knew.'

'There are ways you can eclipse your thoughts, bend them away from farsight. It's not a technique we're very familiar with in Ashwell, and I've never seen it practised so well as today. The Lady knows where they learned it from. And they tamed fastfoxes, too. That's astonishing. We'll have to send messengers out to the other towns and warn them of this new development.'

'Do you think there are more of them out there?' Edeard

could imagine whole armies of bandits converging on their little caravan.

'No. We put them to flight today. And even if there were others lurking about, they have pause for thought now. Their ambush failed. Thanks to you.'

'I bet Janene and the others don't think it failed,' Edeard said bitterly. He didn't care that he was being rude to Melzar. After this, nothing much seemed to matter.

'There's no answer I can give you to that, lad. I'm sorry.'

'Why do they do this?' Edeard asked. 'Why do these people live out here hurting others? Why don't they live in the villages, in a house? They're just savages.'

'I know, lad. But this is all they know. They're brought up in the wilds and they'll bring their children up the same way. It's not a cycle we can break. There are always going to be people living out beyond civilization.'

'I hate them. They killed my parents. Now they've killed my friends. We should wipe them out. All of them. It's the only way we'll ever be allowed to live in peace.'

'That's anger talking.'

'I don't care, that's what I feel. That's what I'll always feel.'

'It probably is. Right now I almost agree with you. But it's my job to get everyone home safely.' Melzar leaned in close, studying Edeard's expression and thoughts. 'Are you going to help me with that?'

'Yes, sir. I will.'

'Okay, now call back our ge-wolves.'

'Right. What about the fastfox?' Edeard was still aware of the animal prowling round at the limit of his farsight. It was confused, missing its original master.

'The fastfox?'

'Edeard tamed it,' Obron said. 'His third hand scooped it up, and he made it attack the bandits.'

The other apprentices turned to look at Edeard. Despite the exhaustion and apprehension dominating their thoughts a lot of them were registering surprise, and even some concern.

156

'I told you,' Edeard said sullenly. 'I know how to deal with animals. It's what my whole Guild does.'

'Nobody's ever tamed a fastfox,' Toran said. Melzar flashed him an annoyed glance.

'The bandits did,' Genril said. 'I saw the collars on them.'

'They'd already learned to obey,' Edeard explained. 'My orders were stronger, that's all.'

'All right,' Melzar said. 'Call the fastfox in. If you can control it, we'll use it to guard the caravan. If not, well . . .' He patted his rifle. 'But I'll warn you now, lad, the village elders won't allow you to keep it.'

3

In Aaron's opinion, Riasi had benefited from being stripped of its capital city status. It retained the grand structures intrinsic to any capital, as well as the expansive public parks, a well-financed transport grid, and excellent leisure facilities, yet with the ministries and their bureaucrats decamped across the ocean to Makkathran2 the stress and hassle had been purged from everyday life. So too had exorbitant housing costs. What was left was a rich city with every possible amenity; consequently, its population were kicking back and enjoying themselves.

It made things a lot easier for Aaron. The taxi flight from Makkathran2 had taken nine hours; they'd landed at the spaceport, one of hundreds of identical arrivals. Mercifully, Corrie-Lyn had spent most of the journey asleep. When she did wake she placidly did whatever he told her. So they moved through the vast passenger terminus on the ped walks, visiting just about every lounge there was. Only then did he go back out to the taxi rank and take a trip to the old Parliament building at the centre of the city. It was late morning by then, with a lot of activity in the surrounding district. They swapped taxis again. Then again. Three taxis later they finally touched down in a residential zone on the east bank of the Camoa River.

During the flight from Makkathran2, Aaron had rented a ground-floor apartment in a fifteen-storey tower. It was anonymous enough, a safe house he called it. To Corrie-Lyn it probably seemed secure. Aaron knew his multiple taxi journeys and untraceable coin payment for the apartment were strictly amateur stuff. Any half-decent police officer could track them down within a day.

For two days he did nothing. It took Corrie-Lyn the entire first day just to sober up. He allowed her to order anything she wanted by way of clothes and food, but forbade any alcohol or aerosols. For the second day she just sulked, a state exacerbated by a monster hangover. He knew there was plenty of trauma involved too as she reconciled what had happened with Captain Manby's squad. That night he heard her crying in her room.

Aaron decided to go all out with breakfast the next morning to try and reach through her mood. He combined the culinary unit's most sophisticated synthesis with items delivered fresh from a local delicatessen. The meal started with Olberon bluefruit, followed by French toast with caramelized banana; their main course was buckwheat crepes with fried duck eggs, grilled Uban mushroom, and smoked Ayrshire bacon, topped by a delicate omelette aux caviar. The tea was genuine Assam, which was all he could ever drink in the morning – it wasn't his best time of day.

'Wowie,' Corrie-Lyn said in admiration. She'd wandered in from her bedroom all bleary eyed, dressed in a fluffy blue towelling robe. When she saw what was being laid out she perked up immediately.

'There's sugar for the bluefruit,' he told her. 'It's refined from Dranscome tubers, best in the galaxy.'

Corrie-Lyn sprinkled some of the silvery powder over the bluefruit, and tried a segment. 'Umm, that is good.' She spooned out some more.

Aaron sat opposite her and took his first sip of tea. Their table was next to a window wall, giving them a view out across the river. Several big ocean-going barges were already coasting along just above the rippling water; smaller river traffic curved round them. He didn't see them, his eyes were on the loose front of her robe which revealed the slope of her breasts. Firm and excellently shaped, he admired cheerfully; she certainly had a great body, his gaze tracking down to her legs to confirm. There were no mental directives either way on having sex with her. So he suspected the hormonal admiration was all his own. It made him grin. *Normal after all.*

'You're not a starship-leasing agent,' Corrie-Lyn said abruptly, her face pulled up in a peeved expression.

He realized he was allowing some of his feelings to ooze out into the gaiafield. 'No.'

'So what are you?'

'Some kind of secret agent, I guess.'

'You *guess*?'

'Yeah.'

'Don't you know?'

'Not really.'

'What do you mean?'

'Simple enough. If I don't know anything I can't reveal anything. I just have things I know I have to do.'

'You mean you haven't got any memories of who you are?'

'Not really, no.'

'Do you know who you're working for?'

'No.'

'So how do you know you should be working for them?'

'Excuse me?'

'How do you know you're not working for the Ocisen Empire, that you're helping bring down the Greater Commonwealth? Or what if you're a left-over Starflyer agent? They say Paula Myo never did catch all of them.'

'Unlikely, but admittedly I don't know.'

'Then how can you live with yourself?'

'I think it's improbable that I'm doing something like that. If you asked me to do it now, I wouldn't. So I wouldn't have agreed to do it before my full memory was removed.'

'Your full memory.' Corrie-Lyn tasted the idea with the same care as she'd sampled the bluefruit. 'Anyone who agrees to have their memory taken out just to get an illegal contract has got to be pretty extreme. And you kill people, too. You're good at it.'

'My combat software was superior to theirs. And they'll be re-lifed. Your friend Captain Manby is probably already walking around looking for us. Think how much improved his motivation is now, thanks to me.'

'Without your memories you can't know what your true personality is.'

Aaron reached for his French toast. 'And your point is?'

'For Ozzie's sake, doesn't that trouble you?'

'No.'

She shook her head in amazement. 'That's got to be an artificial feeling.'

'Again, so what? It makes me efficient at what I do. Personality trait realignment is a useful procedure at re-life. If you want to be a management type, then have your neural structure altered to give yourself confidence and aggression.'

'Choose a vocation and mould yourself to fit. Great, that's so human.'

'Now then what's your definition of human these days? Higher? Advancer? Originals? How about the Hive? Huxley's Haven has kept a regulated society functioning for close to one and a half thousand years; every one of them proscribed by genetic determination, and they're still going strong, with a population that's healthy and happy. Now you go and tell me plain and clear: which of us won the human race?'

'I'm not arguing evolution with you. Besides it's just a distraction to what you are.'

'I thought we'd gone and agreed that neither of us knows what I am. Is that what fascinates you about me?'

'In your pervert dreams!'

Aaron grinned and crunched down on some toast.

'So what's your mission?' Corrie-Lyn asked. 'What do you *have to do*, kidnap Living Dream Councillors?'

'Ex-Councillors. But no, that's not the way of it.'

'So what do you want with me?'

'I need to find Inigo. I believe you can help.'

Corrie-Lyn dropped her spoon and stared at him in disbelief. 'You've got to be kidding.'

'No.'

'You expect me to help you? After what you've just said?'

'Yes. Why not?'

'But . . .' she spluttered.

'Living Dream is trying to kill you. Understand this: they're not going to stop. If anything, the other night will only make them more determined. The only person left in the galaxy who can put the brakes on your dear new Cleric Conservator is Inigo himself.'

'So that's who you're working for, the anti-Pilgrimage lobby.'

'There's no guarantee that Inigo will stop the Pilgrimage if he comes back. You know him better than anybody. Do I speak the right in that?'

She nodded forlornly. 'Yeah. I think you might.'

'So help me find him.'

'I can't do that,' she said in a low voice. 'How can you ask when even you don't know what you'll do to him if we find him.'

'Anyone who has hidden himself this well is never going to be taken by surprise even if we do manage to track him down. He knows there are a lot of serious people looking for him. Besides, if I wanted to kill him, why would I take the trouble of hunting him down. If he's off the stage he can't direct any of the actors, now can he? So if I want him back, I must want him back intact.'

'I don't know,' she said weakly.

'I saved your life.'

Corrie-Lyn gave him a sly smile. 'The software running you saved my life. It did it because you needed me. I'm your best hope, remember.'

'You're my number one choice.'

'Better get ready to schmooze number two.'

'Not even my liver could take another night in Rakas. I *do* need you, Corrie-Lyn. And what about you? What do you need?

Don't you want to find him? Don't you want to hear why he upped and left you and all the billions who believed in him? Did he lose faith? Was Living Dream just that all along, nothing more than a dream?'

'Low blow.'

'You can't do nothing. You're not that kind of person. You know Inigo must be found before the Pilgrimage leaves. Somebody *will* find him. Nobody can stay hidden for ever, not in this universe. Politics simply won't allow it. Who do you want to find him?'

'I . . . I can't,' Corrie-Lyn said.

'I understand. I can wait, at least for a little while longer.'

'Thanks.' She put her head down and started to eat her French toast, almost as if she was ashamed by the decision.

Aaron didn't see her for nearly three hours after breakfast. She went back into her bedroom and stayed there. His u-shadow monitored a small amount of unisphere use; she was running through standard information files from the Living Dream fanes in the city. He had a shrewd idea what she was looking for, a friend she could trust, which meant things could well be swinging his way. If they set foot outside it wouldn't be long before Manby or his replacement were racing up behind them, guns flaring.

When she came out she was wearing a loose-neck red sweater and tight black trousers; a silver necklace made a couple of long loops round her neck before wrapping round her hips. She'd fluffed her dark hair neatly, and infused it with purple and green sparks that glimmered on a long cycle. He gave her an appreciative smile. Which she ignored.

'I need to talk to someone,' she announced.

Aaron tried not to make his smirk too obvious. 'Sure thing. I hope you're not going to insist on going alone. There are bad people out there.'

'You can come with me, but the conversation is private.'

'Okay. Can I ask if you've already set up a meeting?'

'No.'

'Good. Don't call anyone. The Ellezelin cybersphere has government monitors in its nodes. Manby's team will fall on you
like a planet-killer asteroid.'

Her expression flickered with worry. 'I already accessed the
unisphere.'

'That's okay. They probably can't trace your u-shadow access,'
he lied. 'Do you know where this person is likely to be?'

'The Daeas fane, that's over on the south side of the city.'

'Right then, we'll take a taxi to that district and land a couple
of blocks away. Once we're at the fane we'll try and get a visual
on your friend.'

'He's not a friend,' she said automatically.

Aaron shrugged. 'Whoever the person is. If we find him then
you can have your chat in private, okay. Calling him is our last
resort; and please let me do that. My u-shadow has fixes available
that should circumvent the monitor systems.'

She nodded agreement, picked up her scarlet bag and wrapped
a long fawn-coloured scarf round her shoulders. 'Let's go.'

Aaron was perfectly relaxed in the taxi flight over the city. He
spent it looking down on the buildings, enjoying the vertical
perspective as the towers flipped past underneath. The inhabitants
certainly enjoyed their roof gardens, nearly half of them had
some kind of terrace fenced in by greenery; swimming pools were
everywhere.

He didn't know what the outcome of Corrie-Lyn's meeting
would be. Nor did he really care. His only certainty was that he'd
know exactly what to do when the time came. There was, he
reflected, a lot of comfort to be had in his unique level of
ignorance.

They landed on an intersection at the edge of the Daeas
district. It was a commercial area dominated by the monolithic
buildings that had been the Ellezelin Offworld Office, the ministry
which had masterminded the Free Market Zone and Ellezelin's
subsequent commercial and diplomatic domination of neighbouring star systems. Now the structures were given over to
hotels, casinos, and exclusive malls. They walked along the ornate

stone facades towards the fane, with Aaron making sure they didn't take a direct route. He wanted time to scan round and check for possible – make that probable – hostiles.

'Did you know he was leaving before he actually went?' Aaron asked.

Corrie-Lyn gave him an unsettled glance. 'No,' she sighed. 'But we'd cooled off quite a while back. I hadn't been excluded, exactly, but I wasn't in the inner circle any more.'

'Who was?'

'That's the thing. No one, really. Inigo had been getting more and more withdrawn for a long time. Years. Because we were so close, it took a time for me to notice how distant he was growing. You know what it's like.'

'I can imagine,' he said, which earned him a frown. 'So there was no one event, then?'

'Ah, you're talking about the fabled Last Dream, aren't you? No, not that I was aware. But then that rumour had to come from somewhere.'

Even before they won a majority in Parliament, the Living Dream's Chief Councillor of Riasi boasted that you could never travel more than a mile in the city without encountering a fane. The buildings didn't have a specific layout: anything which had a hall large enough to accommodate the faithful, along with office space and living quarters, would do. Given the inherent wealth of the Daeas district it was inevitable that the local fane should be impressive; a contemporary Berzaz cube, with horizontal stripes twisted at fifteen degrees to each other, their fluid-luminal surfaces shining with an intensity that automatically matched the sunlight, delineating each floor in a spectromatic waterfall. The overall effect was a city block that was trying to screw itself into the ground. It was surrounded by a broad plaza with a fountain at each point. Tall jets squirted out from the centre of inclined rings that were ticked out with ingrav to make the water flow upslope.

Aaron scanned round the bustling plaza, performing a meticulous assessment of the locale, allowing his combat software to plot escape routes. His u-shadow was busy extracting the civic plans for the neighbouring buildings, along with utility tunnels and traffic routes. Directly opposite the fane's main entrance was an arcade with a curving crystal roof sheltering fifty high-class shops and boutiques on three levels; it had multiple entrances on to three streets and five underground cargo depots, as well as seven cab platforms and ten rooftop landing pads. That would be difficult to cover even for a large surveillance team. Next to it was a staid old ministry building that now housed several financial institutions and a couple of export merchants. There weren't so many ways in and out, but it did have a large subterranean garage full of expensive regrav capsules. The boulevard running alongside was lined with shops and entertainment salons mixed in with bars and restaurants; tables outside played host to a vibrant café culture. Aaron's u-shadow called down three taxis and parked them on public pads nearby, paying for them to wait with three independent and genuinely untraceable coin accounts.

'Do you want me to go in and try and find him?' Corrie-Lyn asked.

Aaron studied the fane's main entrance, a truncated archway which the fluid-luminal flowed round on either side, presenting it as a dark passageway. Plenty of people were coming and going, the majority dressed in the kind of clothes found on Querencia. Brightly coloured Cleric robes were easy to spot.

'I'm assuming this somebody is a Living Dream Cleric, quite a senior one given your own rank.'

She gave him a short nod. 'Yves. He's still the deputy here. I've known him for fifty years. Completely devoted to Inigo's vision.'

'Old guard, then.'

'Yes.'

'Okay, not likely to bump into him running errands round the place then. He's going to stay put in his office.'

'That's on the fourth floor. I can probably get up there, I do have some clearance. I'm not sure I can take you with me.'

'Any clearance you had will be revoked by now. And if you interface with a Living Dream network it'll send up an alert they can see back on Old Earth.'

'So what do you want to do, then?'

'If honesty doesn't pay . . . I have a few tricks that should be able to get us up to his office without drawing attention to ourselves. All you have to do is pray he doesn't turn us in the minute we say "hello".'

'I say hello,' she emphasized.

'Whatever.' His software had now identified three probable hostiles amid the bustle of pedestrians across the plaza. Looking at the shimmering building he got the distinct sensation of a trap waiting to snap shut. His trouble was that pointing out the three suspects wouldn't be anything like enough to convince Corrie-Lyn that she should be doing her utmost to help him. That would require a genuine scare on the same scale as Captain Manby had provided back in Greater Makkathran. The difference being this time she would be awake, sober, and clean. She had to realize Living Dream was her enemy on every level.

'We'll go in by the front door,' he said. 'No sense drawing attention to ourselves trying to sneak in round the back.'

'Each side of the fane has an entrance which leads to the main reception hall. They're all open, we welcome everyone.'

'I was speaking metaphorically,' he said. 'Come on.' His u-shadow told him the Riasi metropolitan police had just received an alert that two political activists known to be aggressive had been seen in the city. 'Ladies and Gentlemen, Elvis is well and truly back in the building,' he muttered without really knowing why.

Corrie-Lyn let out a hiss of exasperation at his nonsense, and headed off towards the fane's entrance. Aaron followed behind, smiling at her attitude. The thoughts within the plaza's gaiafield were pleasurable and enticing, a melange of sensations that made the hair along his spine stand up. It was almost as if the inside of his skull was being caressed. Something wonderful resided inside the fane the gaiafield promised him. He just had to step inside . . .

Aaron grinned at the crudity of the allure, it was the mental equivalent of fresh baked bread on a winter's morning. He imagined it would be quite an attraction to any casual passer-by; the problem he had with that was the lack of any such specimen, the majority of Ellezelin's population were all Living Dream devotees. But this fane like all the others in the Greater Common-wealth housed a gaiafield confluence nest, it was inevitable the lure effect would be at its peak in the plaza.

No one even looked at them as they walked into the archway with its moiré curtain of luminescence. Aaron's level-one field scan showed him the three suspects outside had started to move towards the fane. Hopefully they couldn't detect such a low-power scan, they certainly didn't appear to be enriched with biononics.

There were sensors built into the entrance, standard systems recording their faces and signatures, making sure they had no concealed weapons. The kind every public building was equipped with. Aaron's biononics deflected them easily enough.

Inside, the siren call within the gaiafield slackened off to be replaced by a single note of harmony. Décor and aether blended to give a sense of peaceful refuge, even the air temperature was pleasantly cool. The reception hall was a replica of the main audience chamber in the Orchard Palace where the Mayor greeted honoured citizens. Here, Clerics talked quietly to small groups of people. Aaron and Corrie-Lyn walked through the hall and into the cloister which let to the eastern entrance. A corridor on the right had no visible barrier. Aaron's biononic fields manipulated the electronics guarding it, and the force field disengaged. He paused, checking the building network, but there was no alarm.

'In we go,' he told her quietly.

A lift took them up to the fourth floor, opening into a windowless corridor narrower than the one downstairs. As they stepped out, his u-shadow informed him that the three waiting taxis had all just had their management programs examined. Aaron was undecided at what point to tell her that they were being targeted again. The longer he left it, the more difficult it would be to extricate them from the fane. He needed her just rattled enough to sign up for his mission, but not too scared she lost all sense.

With activity in the fane still at a minimum he walked with her along several corridors until they reached Yves' office. The room had an active screen, but Aaron's field scan could cut right through it. There was just one person inside, no enrichments showing.

Corrie-Lyn put a hand lightly on Aaron's chest. 'Just me,' she said. Her voice had dropped to a husky tone. He couldn't tell if she was being playful or insistent. Either way, there didn't seem to be a threat in the office, so he smiled gracefully and gestured at the door.

Once she was inside, he walked down the rest of the corridor, checking the other rooms. A woman in plain brown and blue Cleric robes came out of one after he'd passed. She frowned and said: 'Can I help—'

Aaron shot her with a low-power stun pulse from the weapons enrichment in his left forearm. His scrambler field severed her connection with the unisphere as she crumpled on to the floor, blocking the automatic call for help to the police and city medical service emitted by her multicellular clusters. He didn't even bother scooping her up and shoving her inside an empty room. That simply wasn't the kind of timescale he was looking at.

When he started back to Yves' office, all the lifts began to descend to the ground floor. By expanding his level-one field scan to its limit he could just detect weapons powering up down there. He walked straight into Yves' office. 'We have to go—' he began, then cursed silently.

Corrie-Lyn was sitting on the edge of a long leather couch, with Yves slumped at the other end. Her red bag was open, an aerosol in her fist, moving hurriedly, guiltily, from her face. A blissful expression weighed down her eyelids and mouth. Aaron couldn't believe he hadn't checked her bag while she'd been sleeping. It was completely unprofessional.

'Oh hi,' she slurred. 'Yves, this is the guy I was telling you about, my saviour. Aaron, this is Yves, we were just catching up.'

Yves waved his hand at Aaron, producing a dreamy smile. 'Cool.'

'Fuck!' Aaron shot the man with a stun pulse. He was shifting the weapon on Corrie-Lyn when his tactical programs interrupted the action. In her current state it would be a lot easier for him to evacuate her if she was unconscious and inert, however she had to be aware of the danger she was in to make the right choice and confide in him.

Yves tumbled backwards over the end of the couch and landed on the floor with a soft thud. His legs were propped up by the end of the couch, shoes pointing at the ceiling. Corrie-Lyn stared at her old friend as his feet slowly slithered sideways.

'What are you *doing*?' she wailed.

'Putting my arse on the line to save yours. Can you walk?'

Corrie-Lyn hauled herself along the couch to peer down at the crumpled body. 'You killed him! Yves! Oh, Ozzie, what are you, you bastard?'

'He's stunned. Which gives him the perfect alibi. Now can you walk?'

She turned her head to peer at Aaron, which was clearly an action that required a lot of effort. 'He's all right?'

'Oh sod it!' He didn't have time to waste being her shrink. 'Yep, he's fine. Forget him, we have to get out of here right now.' He pulled her off the couch and slung her over his shoulder.

Corrie-Lyn wailed again. 'Put me down.'

'You can't even stand up, let alone walk. And we need to run.' The field medic sac in his thigh opened and ejected a drug pellet. Aaron slapped it against Corrie-Lyn's neck, above the carotid. 'That should straighten you out in a minute.'

'No no no,' she protested. 'Leave me alone.'

Aaron ignored her and went out into the corridor. She was hanging over his shoulder, arms beating ineffectually at his buttocks as she cursed him loudly. Several Clerics opened their

170

doors to see what the commotion was. Aaron stunned each one as they appeared.

'What's happening?' Corrie-Lyn slurred.

'Getting out of here. Your old friends have found us.'

Her arms stopped flailing and she started to weep. Aaron shook his head in dismay; he'd thought she was more capable than this. He reached the lift and his biononics produced a small disruptor effect. The lift doors cracked, their glossy surface darkening as if he was watching them age centuries in every second. They crumbled away into dust and flakes, pouring away down the shaft where they pattered on to the top of the lift as it stood waiting on the ground floor. Aaron tightened his grip on Corrie-Lyn and jumped down the shaft. She screamed as the darkness rushed past her, a genuine terrified-for-her-life bellow of fear.

His integral force field expanded, cushioning their landing. Another disruptor pulse flashed out from his biononics and the top of the lift disintegrated beneath his feet. Two very startled police officers were looking up as he fell through on top of them. Both of them had force field webbing, which protected them from the impact. The weapons enrichment in Aaron's forearm had to increase its power level by two orders of magnitude to puncture the webbing with a stun pulse. He walked out, still carrying a now-silent Corrie-Lyn. There were several police officers in the corridor between the lift and the welcome hall. They shouted at him to stop, which he ignored. A barrage of energy shots smacked across his force field, encasing him and Corrie-Lyn in a screeching purple nimbus. It didn't even slow him down. He emerged into the welcome hall to see Clerics and visitors running for cover, yelling for help vocally and digitally. Police were taking cover in the archways to three corridors, their weapons peppering him with shots. He fired several low-power disruptor pulses at the hall's ceiling. Thick clouds of composite fragments plummeted down, filling the air with cloying particles; steel and carbon girders sagged, emitting dangerous groans.

Police officers flinched, retreating away from the collapsing hall. Aaron walked on towards the main entrance while Corrie-Lyn gasped and moaned in martyred dismay at the chaos raging around them.

Outside, the city cybersphere was broadcasting distress and warning messages to anyone within two blocks of the fane. People were scurrying out of the plaza, an exodus which Aaron's tactical programs decided worked against him. Sentient police software was downloading into the district's cybersphere nodes, taking charge, safeguarding the local network from any subversion he might try and activate, suspending capsule and ground traffic, monitoring sensors, sealing him in.

Aaron's u-shadow went for the unguarded systems managing the plaza's fountains, changing the direction of the ingrav effect on the angled rings. The tall jets began to waver, then suddenly swung down until they were horizontal. They slashed from side to side, hosing everyone in the plaza like giant water cannon. People went tumbling across the stone floor, buffeted by thick waves of spray. Aaron reached the fane's entrance and began sprinting across the plaza, partially obscured from the police by the seething spume clouds. His biononics strengthened his leg muscles, the field effect amplifying and quickening every movement. He covered the first hundred metres in seven seconds. Flailing bodies washed past him as the jets continued to play back and forth. Police officers were singled out for merciless drubbing. Their force fields did little to protect them from the powerful deluge, and they toppled easily from the soaking punches. Those that did fire energy shots into the furious spray simply created crackling vortices of ions that spat out curlicues of scalding steam. Victims on the ground scrabbled desperately out of the way as the dangerous vapour stabbed out, screaming at them to stop shooting.

The fountains began to run out of water when Aaron was two thirds of the way across the plaza. Two energy shots hit his force field, throwing off a plume of sparks. The strike made him skid on the wet stone.

'Slow down,' Corrie-Lyn yelped as he regained his footing. 'Oh, Ozzie, NO!'

Aaron's sensory field scanned round. The fane was starting to collapse, folding in on itself and twisting gently, as if in mimicry of the pattern of its fluid-luminary surfaces. 'I must have damaged more than I realized,' he grunted. Dust and smoke was flaring out of the entrances like antique rocket engine plumes, billowing over the plaza.

He reached the entrance to the arcade. People had been crowded round, watching the spectacle in the plaza. When Aaron appeared out of the chaos and started charging towards them they'd backed away fast. Now they scattered like frightened birds; no one in the Commonwealth was accustomed to civil trouble, let alone Riasi's residents. As he paused on the threshold, at least five police officers were given a clear line of sight. Energy slammed into his force field, producing a fearsome starblast of photons, its screeching loud enough to overwhelm Corrie-Lyn's howls. Unprotected surfaces around him started to blister and smoulder. He fired three bolts of his own, hidden in the mêlée, targeting structural girders around the archway. The crystal ceiling began to sag, huge cracks ripped through the thick material. Behind them, the fane finally crumpled, the process accelerating. Chunks of debris went scything across the plaza to impact the surrounding buildings. Tens of thousands of glass fragments created a lethal shrapnel cloud racing outwards. The police officers stopped shooting as they sought cover.

Corrie-Lyn was sobbing hysterically at the sight, then the arcade's archway started to disintegrate. She froze as giant daggers of the crystal roof plunged down around them. Fire alarms were yammering, and bright-blue suppressor foam started to pour down from the remaining nozzles overhead. Aaron dived into the third store, which sold hand-made lingerie. A slush of foam rippled out across the floor as it slid off his force field. Two remaining assistants saw him and sprinted for a fire exit.

'Can you walk?' he asked Corrie-Lyn. His u-shadow was attacking the police programs in the arcade's nodes, interfering with the building's internal sensors, and trying to cut power lines directly. It sent out a call to one of the parked taxis, directing it to land at the back of the arcade.

When he pulled Corrie-Lyn off his shoulder all she could do was cross her arms and hug her chest. Her legs were trembling, unable to hold her weight.

'Shit!' He shunted her up over his shoulder again, and went into the back of the store. There was a door at the top of the stairs which led down into the basement stockroom, which he descended quickly. His field scan showed him a whole flock of police regrav capsules swooping low over the plaza, while a couple of hardy officers were making their way over the tangle of archway girders. They seemed to be carrying some very high-powered weaponry.

It was cooler in the stockroom, the air dry and still. Overhead lights came on to reveal a rectangular room with smooth concrete walls, filled with ranks of metal shelving. The far end was piled up with old advertising displays. His u-shadow reported that it was having some success in blocking the police software from nearby electronics. They would know he was there, but not what he was doing.

The big malmetal door to the loading bay furled aside, and he went out into the narrow underground delivery road which served all the stores. It was empty, the police prohibition on all traffic was preventing any cargo capsules from using it. Ten metres away on the other side was a hatchway into a utility tunnel. His u-shadow popped the lock and it swung open. He sprinted across the delivery road and clambered inside pushing an unresisting Corrie-Lyn ahead of him. The hatch snapped shut.

Aaron scanned round. There was no light in the tunnel other than a yellow circle glowing round the hatch's emergency handle. It wasn't high enough for him to walk along, he'd have to stoop. Corrie-Lyn was sitting slumped against the wall just beside the hatch.

'There are no visual sensors inside the tunnel,' his u-shadow reported. 'Only fire and water alarms.'

174

'Water?'

'In case of flooding. It is a city regulation.'

'Typical bureaucratic overkill,' he muttered. 'Corrie-Lyn we have to keep going.'

She didn't acknowledge. Her limbs were still trembling uncontrollably. But she moved when he pushed at her. Together they shuffled along the tunnel, hunched over like monkeys. There were hatches every fifty metres. He stopped at the sixth one and let his field scan function review the immediate vicinity outside. It didn't detect anyone nearby. His u-shadow unlocked it, and they crawled out into the base of a stairwell illuminated by blue-tinged polyphoto strips on the wall.

'The building network is functioning normally,' his u-shadow said. 'The police sentients are currently concentrating their monitor routines on the fane and the arcade.'

'That won't last,' he said, 'they'll expand outward soon enough. Crack one of the private capsules for me.'

He pulled Corrie-Lyn to her feet. With one arm under her shoulder, supporting her they went up a flight of stairs. The door opened into the underground car park of the old ministry building. His u-shadow had infiltrated the control net of a luxury capsule, and brought it right over to the stairwell.

The capsule slid up out of the park's chuteway at the back of the building, and zipped up into the nearby traffic stream. Police sentients queried it, and Aaron's u-shadow provided them with a genuine owner certificate code. Corrie-Lyn stared down at the sluggish mass of boiling dust behind them. Her limbs had stopped trembling. He wasn't sure if that was the mild suppressor drug he'd given her finally flushing the aerosol out of her system, or a deeper level of shock was setting in.

A small fleet of civic emergency capsules and ambulances were heading in to the fane.

'They just shot at us,' she said. 'They didn't warn us or tell us to stop first. They just opened fire.'

'I had jumped down a lift shaft to try and get out,' he pointed out. 'That's a reasonable admission of guilt.'

'For Ozzie's sake! If you didn't have a force-field web we'd be dead. That's not how the police are supposed to act. They were police, weren't they?'

'Yeah. They're the city police, all right.'

'But we did get out,' she sounded puzzled. 'There were how many . . . ten of them? Twenty?'

'Something like that, yeah.'

'You just walked out like nothing could stop you. It didn't matter what they did.'

'That's Higher biononics for you. The only way standard weaponry can gain an advantage is overwhelming firepower. They weren't carrying that much hardware.'

'You're Higher?'

'I have weapons-grade biononics. I'm not sure about the culture part of it. That way of life seems slightly pointless to me, sort of like the pre-Commonwealth aristocracy.'

'What's that?'

'Very rich people living a life of considerable ease and decadence while the common people slaved away into an early grave, with all their labour going to support the aristocrats and their way of life.'

'Oh. Right.' She didn't sound interested. 'Inigo was Higher.'

'No he wasn't.' Aaron said it automatically.

'Actually, he was. But he kept that extremely quiet. Only a couple of us ever knew. I don't think our new Cleric Conservator is aware of his idol's true nature.'

'Are you—'

'Sure? Yes, I'm sure.'

'That's remarkable. There's no record of it; that's a hell of an achievement these days.'

'Like I said, he kept it quiet. No one would have paid any attention to a Higher showing them his dreams, not out here on the External Worlds. He needed to appear as ordinary as possible. To be accepted as one of us.'

Aaron gave an amused grunt. 'Highers are people, too.'

'Some of them.' She gave him a meaningful glance.

'Was Yves the other Cleric who knew about Inigo?'

'No.' She drew a short gasp, and glanced back. 'Oh, Ozzie, Yves! He was unconscious when the fane collapsed.'

'He'll be all right.'

'All right?' she yelled, finally becoming animated. 'All right? He's dead!'

'Well, he'll probably need re-lifing, yeah. But that's only a couple of months' downtime these days.'

She gave him an incredulous snort, and leant against the capsule's transparent fuselage to gaze down on the city.

Shock, anger, and fright, he decided. Mostly fright. 'You need to decide what to do next,' he told her as sympathetically as he could. 'Team up with me, or . . .' He shrugged. 'I can give you some untraceable funds, that should help keep you hidden.'

'Bastard.' She wiped at her eyes, then looked down at herself. Her red sweater had large damp patches, and the lower half of her trousers were caked in blue foam. Her knees were grazed and filthy from the inside of the utility tunnel. Her shoulders slumped in resignation. 'He used to go somewhere,' she said in a quiet emotionless voice.

'Inigo?'

'Yes. This isn't the first time he took off on a sabbatical and left Living Dream covering up for his absence. But none of the other times were for so long. A year at most.'

'I see. Where did he go?'

'Anagaska.'

'That's his birthworld.'

'Yes.'

'An External World. One of the first. Advancer through and through,' he said significantly.

'I'm not arguing with you.'

'Did he ever take you?'

'No. He said he was visiting family. I don't know how true that was.'

Aaron reviewed the files on Inigo's family. There was very little information; they didn't seek publicity, especially after he founded Living Dream. 'His mother migrated inwards a long time ago. She downloaded into ANA in 3440, after first becoming . . .'

'Higher, yes I know.'

He didn't follow the point; but for someone to convert to Higher without leaving any record was essentially impossible. Corrie-Lyn must have been mistaken. 'There's no record of any brothers or sisters,' he said.

Corrie-Lyn closed her eyes and let out a long breath. 'His mother had a sister, a twin. There was something . . . I don't know what, but some incident long ago. Inigo hinted at it; the sisters went through this big trauma together. Whatever it was drove them apart, they never really reconciled.'

'There's nothing in the records about that, I didn't even know he had an aunt.'

'Well now you do. So what next?'

'Go to Anagaska. Try and find the aunt or her children.'

'How do we get there? I imagine the police will be watching the spaceports and wormholes.'

'They will eventually. But I have my own starship.' He stopped in surprise as knowledge of the starship emerged into his mind from some deep memory.

Corrie-Lyn's eyes opened in curiosity. 'You do?'

'I think so.'

'Sweet Ozzie, you are so strange.'

Seventeen minutes later the capsule slid down to land beside a pad in Riasi's spaceport. Aaron and Corrie-Lyn climbed out and looked up at the chrome-purple ovoid that stood on five bulbous legs.

She whistled in admiration. 'That looks deliciously expensive. Is it really yours?'

'Yeah.'

'Odd name,' she said as she walked under the curving underbelly of the fuselage. 'What's the reference?'

'I've no idea.' His u-shadow opened a link to the *Artful Dodger*'s smartcore, confirming his identity with a DNA verification along with a code he abruptly remembered. The smartcore acknowledged his command authority.

'Hang on,' Aaron told Corrie-Lyn, and grabbed her hand. The base of the starship bulged inwards, stretching into a dark tube. Gravity altered around them and they slid up inside the opening.

*

Sholapur was one of those Commonwealth planets that didn't quite work. All the ingredients for success and normality were there: a standard H-congruous biosphere, G-type star, oceans, big continents with great landscapes of deserts, mountains, plains, jungles, and vast deciduous forests, handsome coastlines and long meandering archipelagos. The local flora had several plants humans could eat; while the wildlife wasn't wild enough to pose much of a threat. Tectonically it was benign. The twin moons were small, orbiting seven hundred thousand kilometres out to produce the kind of tides and waves that satisfied every kind of marine sports enthusiast.

So physically, there was nothing wrong with it. That just left the people.

Settlement began in 3120, the year ANA officially became Earth's government. It was the kind of incentive which flushed a lot of the remaining political, cultural, and religious malcontents out of the Central Worlds. The greatest machine ever built was obviously taking over, and Higher culture was now so dominant it could never be revoked. They left in their millions to settle the then furthest External Worlds. At 470 lightyears from Earth, Sholapur was an attractive proposition for anyone looking for a distant haven. To begin with, everything went smoothly. There was commercial investment, the immigrants were experienced professionals; cities and industrial parks sprang up, farms were established. But the groups who arrived from the Central Worlds weren't just dissatisfied with Higher culture, they tended to be insular, intolerant of other ideologies and lifestyles. Petty local disputes had a way of swelling to encompass entire ethnic or ideological communities. Internal migration accelerated, transforming

179

urban areas into miniature city states; all with massively different laws and creeds. Cooperation between them was minimal. The planetary parliament was 'suspended' in 3180, after yet another debate ended in personal violence between Senators. And that more or less marked the end of Sholapur's economic and cultural development. It was regarded as hermitic by the rest of the Commonwealth. Even the External Worlds with all their attitude of forthright independence viewed it like a kind of embarrassing drop-out cousin. The nearest settled worlds called it Planet of the Hotheads, and had little contact. Despite that, a great many starships continued to visit. Some of the micro-nations had laws (or a lack of laws) which could be advantageous to certain types of merchant.

Five thousand kilometres above the planetary surface, the starship *Mellanie's Redemption* fell out of hyperspace amid a collapsing bubble of violet Cherenkov radiation. There was no single planetary traffic control Troblum could contact; instead he filed an approach request with Ikeo City, and received permission to land.

The *Mellanie's Redemption* measured thirty metres long, a sleek flared cone shape, with forward-curving tailfins that looked functionally aerodynamic. In fact they were thermal radiators added to handle the extensively customized power system. The cabin layout was a central circular lounge ringed by ten sleeping cubicles and a washroom. Hyperdrive ships didn't come much bigger, they simply weren't cost effective to build. Starline companies used them almost exclusively for passengers wealthy enough to pay for fast transport. Most starships used a continuous wormhole drive; they were slower but could be built to any size required, and carried the bulk of interstellar trade around the External Worlds. Originally, *Mellanie's Redemption* had been a specialist craft, built to carry priority cargo or passengers between the External Worlds. A risky proposition at the best of times. The company who commissioned her had lurched from one financial crisis to another until Troblum made them an offer for their superfast lame duck. He claimed she would be refitted as a big personal yacht, which was a white lie. It was her three large cargo holds which made her perfect for him; their volume was ideal for carrying the equipment he was working on to recreate the Anomine 'one shot' wormhole. Marius had agreed to the acquisition, and the additional EMAs materialized in Troblum's account. Although the ship was supposed to remain on Arevalo until Troblum was ready to move the project to its test stage he found it indispensable for some of the transactions he was involved in. The addition of a Navy-grade stealth field was especially beneficial when it came to slipping away from Arevalo without Marius being aware of anything untoward.

City was a somewhat overzealous description for Ikeo which comprised a fifty-mile stretch of rugged sub-tropical coastline with a small town in the middle and a lot of mansions spread along the cliff tops on either side. The province's ideology could best be described as a free trade area, with several individuals specializing in artefact salvage. It did have a resident-funded police force, which its poorer neighbouring states referred to as a strategic defence system.

Mellanie's Redemption descended at the focal point of several ground-based tracking sensors. She landed on pad 23 at the city's spaceport, a two-kilometre circle of mown grass with twenty-four concrete pads, a couple of black dome-shaped maintenance hangars, and a warehouse owned by an Intersolar service supply company. There were no arrival formalities. A capsule drew up beside the starship as Troblum walked down the short airstair, puffing heavily from the rush of heat and humidity that hit him as soon as the airlock opened.

The capsule took him several miles out of town to a Roman-esque villa atop a low cliff. Three sides of the single-storey building surrounded an elaborate pool and patio area festooned with colourful plants. Several waterfalls spilled down large strategically positioned boulders to splash into the pool. The view down on to the white beach was spectacular, with a needle-profile glide-boat anchored just offshore.

Stubsy Florac was waiting for him by the bar at the side of the pool. Not that anyone called him 'Stubsy' to his face; Florac was sensitive about his height. Sensitive to a degree that he didn't get it changed during rejuvenation therapy because to do that would be to admit that he was a head shorter than most adults and that it bothered him enough to do something about it. He wore knee-length sports trousers and a simple pale-blue shirt open to the waist to reveal a chest covered in hair and a stomach that was starting to bulge. When Troblum appeared he smiled broadly and pushed his oversize sunglasses on to his forehead. His hairline was a lot higher and thinner than Troblum was used to seeing even on External World citizens.

'Hey! My man,' Florac exclaimed loudly. He held his arms out and shifted his hips from side to side. 'You been dieting, or what?' He laughed loudly again at his own joke. All his companions smiled.

There were seven of them visible in the pool area, either lying on sunloungers, or sitting at the table in the shallow end of the pool sipping drinks that were mostly fruit and ice. Troblum was always slightly uncomfortable about the girls Stubsy kept at the villa. Not quite clones, but there were standard requirements. For a start they were all a lot taller than their boss, two were even taller than Troblum; naturally they were beautiful, with long silken hair, bodies toned as if they were part of some ancient Olympic athlete squad, and wearing tight bikinis – dressing for dinner here was putting on a pair of shorts and sandals. A low-level field scan revealed them to be enriched with several advanced weapons systems; half of the muscle ridges etched beneath their taut skin was actually force-field webbing. If they ganged up on Troblum they could probably overwhelm his biononic defences. They acted like a hybrid of floozies and executive assistants. Troblum knew the image which the whole stable arrangement was supposed to convey, but just didn't understand why. Stubsy must have a lot more insecurities than just his height.

Troblum's worn old toga suit rippled round his vast body as he raised his arms. 'Do I look smaller?'

'Hey, come on, I'm just fucking with you. What I got, it entitles me.'

'What you claim you've got.'

'Man, just shove that stake in a little further, I don't think it went right through my heart. How are you, man? It's been a while.' Stubsy gave Troblum a hug, arms reaching almost a third of the way round. Squeezing like he was being reunited with a parent.

'Too long,' Troblum suggested.

'Still got your ship. Sweet ship. You Higher guys, you live the life all right.'

Troblum looked down on Stubsy's head. 'So come and join us.'

'Wowa there! Not quite ready for that. Okay? Man, don't even joke about. I'd need to spend a decade wiping all my bad memories before they'd let me set foot on the Central Worlds. Hey, you want a drink. Couple of sandwiches, maybe. Alcinda, she knows how to boss a culinary unit around.' He lowered his voice and winked. 'Not the only thing she knows her way around, huh.'

Troblum tried not to grimace in dismay. 'Some beer maybe.'

'Sure sure.' Florac gestured to some chairs beside a table. They sat down while one of the girls brought a large mug of light beer over. 'Hey, Somonie, bring it out for my man, will you?'

A girl in a vivid-pink bikini gave a short nod and went inside.

'Where did you find it?' Troblum asked.

'A contact of mine. Hey, have I been retrofitted without a brain and somebody not tell me? If I tell you about my people what's left for me in this universe?'

'Quite.'

'You know I've got a network pumping away down there in the civilized Commonwealth. This week it's some guy, next it's another. Who knows where shit is going to appear. You want to stab me in the back, first you got to build yourself your own network.'

'I already have.'

Florac blinked, his best-friends smile fading. 'You have?'

'Sure. Hundreds of guys like you.'

'You kill me, you know that?' He laughed, too loud, and raised his glass. 'People like me. Ho man!'

'I meant, what planet was it recovered from? My record search confirmed Vic Russell handed it back in to the Serious Crimes Directorate when he returned from the Boongate relocation. It was obsolete by then. The SCD would have disposed of it.'

'Beats me,' Florac said with a shrug. 'Guess there were people like you and me around even back in those days.'

Troblum said nothing. The salvager could be right. For all his personality faults and distasteful lifestyle, he had always provided bona fide items. A large number of artefacts in Troblum's museum had come from Florac.

Somonie returned from the villa carrying a long stable-environment case. It was heavy, her arm muscles were standing proud. She put it the table in front of Troblum and Stubsy.

'Before we go any further,' Troblum said. 'I have the SCD serial code. The genuine one. So. Do you still want to open the case?'

'I don't give a shit what fucking number you think you got, man, this is for real. And *hey* guess what, you aren't the only asshole in the Commonwealth that creams himself over this shit. I come to you first because I figure we got a friendship going by now. You want to call me out, you want to crap all over my reputation, and you know what, fatboy, you can roll all the way back to your ship and fuck the hell off this world. My fucking world.'

'We'd better look at it then,' Troblum said. 'I'd hate to lose your friendship.' He didn't care about Stubsy Florac, there were dozens of scavengers just like him. But it was an interesting claim; he'd never really thought there were other collectors outside museums. He wondered idly if they could be persuaded to sell. Perhaps Florac could enquire . . .

Florac's u-shadow gave the case a key, and the top unfurled to reveal an antique ion rifle. A protective shield shimmered faintly around it, but Troblum could clearly see the metre-long barrel which ended in a stubby black metal handle that had several attachment points and an open induction socket on the bottom.

'Yeah well,' Stubsy said with a modest grimace, which could almost have been embarrassment. 'The other bit is missing. Obviously. But what the fuck, this is the business end, right? That's what counts.'

'There is no "other bit",' Troblum said. 'This is designed to be used by someone in an armour suit; it clips on to the lower arm.'

'No shit?'

It was an effort for Troblum to speak calmly. The weapon certainly looked genuine. 'Would you turn off the field, please.'

The shimmer vanished. Troblum's field function swept across the antique rifle. Deep in the barrel's casing were long chains of specifically arranged molecules, spelling out a unique code. He licked the sweat from his upper lip. 'It's real,' he whispered hoarsely.

'Yo!' Stubsy slapped his hands together in victory. 'Do I ever let you down?'

Troblum couldn't stop staring at the weapon. 'Only in the flesh. Would you like payment now?'

'Man, this is why I love you. Yes. Yes please. I would very much like payment now, please.'

Troblum told his u-shadow to transfer the funds.

'You want to stay for dinner?' Stubsy asked. 'Maybe party with some of the girls?'

'Put the protective field back on, please. This humidity is inimical.'

'Sure thing. So, which one do you like?'

'You don't have any idea how important this artefact is, do you?'

'I know it's value, man, that's what counts. The fact some policeman shot an alien with it a thousand years ago doesn't exactly ding my bell.'

'Vic Russell worked with Paula Myo. And I know you've heard of her.'

'Sure man, this planet's living nightmare. Didn't know she was around in those days, too.'

'Oh yes, she was around even before the Starflyer War. And it wasn't an alien Vic shot, it was Tarlo, a Directorate colleague who had been corrupted by the Starflyer, and betrayed Vic and his wife. Arguably, Tarlo is one of the most important Starflyer agents there was.'

'Ozzie, now I get it: this was the gun that killed him. That connects you.'

'Something like that.'

'So are you interested in genuine alien stuff as well?'

'Anything that is part of the Starflyer's legacy. Why, have you located another section of its ship?'

Stubsy shook his head. 'Fraid not, man. But one of my neighbours, she specializes in weird alien technology and other interesting little chunks. You know, the odd sample that crews on pathfinder missions pick up, stuff you never get to hear about in the unisphere, stuff ANA and the Navy like to keep quiet. You want I should put you in touch, I got a unisphere code, she's very discreet. I'll vouch for her.'

'Tell her if she ever comes across any Anomine relics I'll be happy to talk,' he said, knowing she wouldn't. 'Apart from that, I'm not interested.'

'Okay, just thought I'd ask.'

Troblum raised himself to his feet, quietly pleased he didn't need his biononics to generate a muscle reinforcement field; but then this world had a point-eight standard gravity. 'Could you call your capsule for me, please?'

'Money's in, so sure. This is another reason I like you, man, we don't have to screw around making up small talk.'

'Exactly.' Troblum picked up the stable-environment case. It was heavy; he could feel a mild sweat break out on his forehead and across his shoulders as he lifted it into the crook of his arm. Hadn't Stubsy ever heard of regrav?

'Hey, man, you're the only Higher I know, so I've got to like ask you this. What's ANA's take on this whole Pilgrimage thing?

Is it a bunch of crap, or are we all going to get cluster fucked by the Void?'

'ANA:Governance put out a clear statement on the unisphere. The Pilgrimage is regrettable, but it does not believe the actions of Living Dream pose any direct physical threat to the Greater Commonwealth.'

'I accessed that, sure. Usual government bullshit then, huh. But . . . what do you think, man? Should I be stocking up my starship and heading out?'

'Out where, exactly? If the anti-Pilgrimage faction is right, the whole galaxy is doomed.'

'You are just one giant lump of fun, aren't you? Come on, man, give it to me straight. Are we in the shit?'

'The contacts I have inside ANA aren't worried, so neither am I.'

Stubsy considered that seriously for a moment before reverting to his usual annoyingly breezy self. 'Thanks, man, I owe you one.'

'Not really. But if I find a way to collect, I'll let you know.'

Troblum puzzled over Stubsy's question in the capsule back to his ship. Perhaps he'd been unwise to admit to contacts inside ANA, but it was a very general reference. Besides, he didn't really consider Stubsy to be some kind of agent working for Marius's opponents – of which there were admittedly many. Of course the Starflyer had procured agents a lot more unlikely than Stubsy. But if Stubsy was an agent for some ANA Faction they were playing a long game, and from what Troblum understood, the Pilgrimage situation would be resolved sooner rather than later. Troblum shook his head and shifted the case slightly. It was an interesting theory, but he suspected he was overanalysing events. Paranoia was healthy, but he wouldn't like to report that particular suspicion to Marius. More likely it was a genuine concern on Stubsy's part, one born of ignorance and popular prejudice. That was a lot easier to believe.

The capsule arrived back at *Mellanie's Redemption* and Troblum carefully carried the stable-environment case into the starship.

He resisted the impulse to open it for one last check, but did stow it in his own sleeping cabin for the flight back to Arevalo.

*

The first thing Araminta knew about the failure was when a shower of sparks sizzled out of the bot's power arm, just above the wrist multi-socket where tools plugged in. At the time she was on her knees beside the Juliet balcony door, trying to dismantle its seized-up actuator. The unit hadn't been serviced for a decade at least. When she got the casing open every part of it was covered in grime. She wrinkled her nose up in dismay, and reached for the small all-function electrical toolkit she'd bought from Askahar's Infinite Systems, a company that specialized in recycled equipment for the construction trade. Her u-shadow grabbed the user instructions from the kit's memory and filtered them up through her macrocellular clusters into her brain; supposedly they gave her an instinctive ability to apply the little gizmos. She couldn't even work out which one would stand a chance of cleaning away so much gunk. The cleanser utensils were intended for delicate systems with a light coating of dust. Not this compost heap.

Then as she peered closer at the actuator components bright light flashed across them. She turned just in time to see the last cascade of sparks drizzle down on the pile of sealant sheets stacked up in the corner of the flat's lounge. Wisps of smoke began to wind upwards. The bot juddered to a halt, as the whole lower segment of its power arm darkened. As she watched, its pocked silvery casing tarnished rapidly from the heat inside.

'Ozzie's mother!' she yelped, and quickly started stamping on the sheets, trying to extinguish the glowing points which the sparks had kindled. Her u-shadow couldn't get any access to the bot at all, it was completely dead, and now there was a definite hot-oil smell in the air. Another bot slid away and retrieved an extinguisher bulb from the kitchen. It returned and sprayed blue foam on the defunct bot's arm. Araminta groaned in dismay as the bubbling fluid scabbed over and dripped on to the floor-boards, soaking in. The whole wood-look was coming back in vogue, which was why she'd ordered the bot to abrade the original old floorboards down to the grain. As soon as they were done she was going to spread the sealant sheets down while the rest of the room was decorated and fitted, then she'd finish the boards with a veneer polish to bring out the wavy gold and rouge pattern of the native antwood.

Araminta scratched at the damp stain with her fingernail, but it didn't seem too bad. She'd just have to get another bot to abrade the wood down still further. There were five of the versatile machines performing various tasks in the flat, all second or third hand; again bought from Askahar's Infinite Systems.

Now the immediate danger of fire was over her u-shadow called Burt Renik, proprietor of Askahar's Infinite Systems.

'Well there's nothing I can do,' he explained after she'd told him what had happened.

'I only bought it from you two days ago!'

'Yes, but why did you buy it?'

'Excuse me! You recommended it.'

'Yes, the Candel 8038; it's got the kind of power level you wanted for heavy duty attachments. But you came to me rather than a licensed dealer.'

'What are you talking about? I couldn't afford a new model. The unisphere evaluation library said it was dependable.'

'Exactly. And I sell a lot of refurbished units because of that. But the one you bought had a manufacturer's decade-warranty that expired over a decade ago. Now with all the goodwill in Ozzie's universe, I have to tell you: you get what you pay for. I have some newer models in stock if you need a replacement.'

Araminta wished she had the ability to trojan a sensorium package past his u-shadow filters, one that would produce the painburst he'd get from a good smack on the nose. 'Will you take part exchange?'

'I could make you an offer on any components I can salvage, but I'd have to bring the bot in to the workshop to analyse what's left. I can come out, oh . . . middle of next week, and there would have to be a collection charge.'

'For Ozzie's sake, you sold me a dud.'

'I sold you what you wanted. Look, I'm only offering to salvage parts as a goodwill gesture. I'm running a business, I want return customers.'

'Well you've lost this one.' She ended the call and told her u-shadow never to accept a call from Burt Renik again. 'Bloody hell!' Her u-shadow quickly revised her refurbishment schedule, adding on an extra three days to her expected completion date. That assumed she wouldn't buy a replacement for the 8038. It was a correct assumption. The budget wasn't working out like she'd originally planned. Not that she was overspending, but the time involved in stripping out all the old fittings and démodé decorations was taking a lot longer than her first estimate.

Araminta sat back on the floor and glared at the ruined bot. *I'm not going to cry. I'm not that pathetic.*

The loss of the 8038 was a blow, though. She'd just have to trust the remaining bots would hold out. Her u-shadow began to run diagnostic checks on them while she tried to detach the abrader mat from the 8038's foam-clogged multi-socket. The attachment was expensive and, unlike the bot, brand new. Her mood wasn't helped by the current state of the flat. She had been working on it for five days solid now, stripping it down to bare walls, and gutting the ancient domestic equipment. The whole place looked just terrible. Every surface was covered in fine particles, with sawdust enhancing the whole dilapidated appearance; also not helped by the way any sound echoed round the blank rooms. After tidying things up today, she could start the refurbishment stage. She was sure that would re-fire her enthusiasm. There had been times over the last week when she'd had moments of pure panic, wondering how she could have been so stupid to have gambled everything on this ancient cruddy flat.

The abrader attachment came free and she pulled it out. With her u-shadow controlling them directly, two of the remaining bots hauled their broken sibling out of the flat and dumped it in the commercial refuse casket parked outside. She winced every time it bumped on the stairs, but the other occupants were out, they'd never know how the dints got there.

With the abrader plugged in to another bot, a Braklef 34B – only eight years old – she turned her attention back to the balcony door actuator. She knew if she started moping over the broken bot she'd just wind up feeling sorry for herself and never get anything done. She simply couldn't afford that.

The simplest thing, she decided, was to break the actuator down and clean the grime off manually; after that she could use the specialist tools to get the systems up to required standard. Her other toolbox, the larger one, had a set of power keys. She set to with more determination she had any right to without resorting to aerosols.

As she worked, her u-shadow skimmed the news, local and Intersolar, and summarized topics she was interested in, feeding it to her in a quiet neural drizzle. Now she'd bought the flat, she'd cancelled the daily review of city property. It would be too distracting, especially if something really good appeared on the market. So instead she chortled quietly at the images in her peripheral vision as a city councillor's son was indicted on charges of land fraud. The investigators were rumoured to be closing in on Daddy, who sat on the city board for zoning management. Last night, Debbina, the first-born daughter of billionaire Shel-donite Likan had been arrested once again for lewd conduct in a public place. The image of her coming out of Colwyn Central police station flanked by her lawyers this morning showed her still wearing a black spray dress from the previous evening, and her blonde hair in disarray. Hansel Industries, one of Ellezelin's top 100 companies was discussing opening a manufacturing district just outside Colwyn; the details were accompanied by economic projections. She couldn't help scan the effect on property prices.

As far as Intersolar political news was concerned the only item was the new Senate motion introduced by Marian Kantil, Earth's Senator, that Living Dream desist from reckless action in respect to its Pilgrimage. Ellezelin's Senator responded to the motion by walking out. He was followed by the Senators from Tari, Idlib, Lirno, Quhood and Agra – the Free Trade Zone planets. Araminta wasn't surprised to find Viotia's Senator had abstained from the vote, as had seven other External Worlds, all on the fringe of the Zone, and all with a large percentage of Living Dream followers in their population. The report went on to show the huge manufacturing yard on the edge of Greater Makkathran, where the Pilgrimage ships would be assembled. Araminta stopped cleaning the actuator to watch. An armada of civic construction machinery was laying down the field, flattening fifteen square miles of countryside ready for its cladding of concrete. The first echelon of machines swept the ground with dispersant beams, chewing into the side of hillocks and escarpments; loosening any material that stood above the required level. All the resulting scree slides of pulverized soil and sand were elevated by regrav modules then channelled by force fields into thick solid streams that curved through the air and stretched back to the holds of vast ore barges hovering at the side of the estuary which made up one side of the yard. Following the levelling operation was a line of more basic machinery which drove deep support piles into the bedrock to support the weight of the starship cradles. The Pilgrimage fleet was to be made up of twelve cylindrical vessels, each a mile long, and capable of carrying two million pilgrims in suspension. Already Living Dream was talking about them being merely the 'first wave'.

Araminta shook her head in mild disbelief that so many people could be so stupid, and switched to local reports of business and celebrities.

Two hours later, Cressida arrived. She frowned down at the prints her shiny leather pumps with their diamond encrusted straps made in the thick layer of dirt coating the hall floor. Her cashmere fur dress contracted around her to save her skin from exposure to the dusty air. One hand was raised to cover her mouth, gold and purple nailprint friezes flowing in slow motion.

Araminta smiled up uncertainly at her cousin. She was suddenly very self-conscious standing there in her filthy overalls, hair wound up and tucked into a cap, hands streaked with black grease.

'There's a dead bot in your casket,' Cressida said. She sounded annoyed by it.

'I know,' Araminta sighed. 'Price of buying cheap.'

'It's one of yours?' Cressida's eyebrows lifted. 'Do you want me to call the supplier and have it replaced?'

'Tempting. Ozzie knows it wasn't actually that cheap relative to my budget, but no I'll fight my own battles from now on.'

'That's my family. Stupidly stubborn to the last.'

'Thanks.'

'I'm here for two reasons. One to look round. Okay, done that. Came a month too early, obviously. Two, I want all the frightful details of Thursday night. You and that rather attractive boy Keetch left very early together. And darling I do mean *all* the details.'

'Keetch is hardly a boy.'

'Pha! Younger than me by almost a century. So tell your best cousin. What happened?'

Araminta smiled bashfully. 'You know very well. We went back to his place.' She proffered a limp gesture at the dilapidated hallway. 'I could hardly bring him here.'

'Excellent. And?'

'And what?'

'What does he do? Is he single? What's he like in bed? How many times has he called? Is he yearning and desperate yet? Has he sent flowers or jewellery or is he all pathetic and gone the chocolates route? Which resort bedroom are you spending the weekend in?'

'Wow, just stop there.' Araminta's smile turned sour. In truth Keetch had been more than adequate in bed and he had even tried to call her several times since Thursday. Calls she had no intention of returning. The thrill of liberation, of playing the field, of experimenting, of answering to no one, of making and taking her own choices, of just plain having fun; it was all she wanted right now. A simple life without commitments or attachments. *Right now* was what she should have been doing instead of being married. 'Keetch was very nice, but I'm not seeing him again. I'm too busy here.'

'Now I am impressed. Hump 'em and dump 'em. There's quite a core of raw steel hidden inside that ingénue facade, isn't there?'

Araminta shrugged. 'Whatever.'

'If you ever want a career in law, I'll be happy to sponsor you. You'll probably make partner in under seventy years.'

'Gosh, now there's an enticement.'

Cressida dropped her hand long enough to laugh. 'Ah well, I tried. So are we on for Wednesday?'

'Yes, of course.' Araminta enjoyed their girls' nights out. Cressida seemed to know every exclusive club in Colwyn City, and she was on all their guest lists. 'So what happened to you after I left? Did you catch anyone?'

'At my age? I was safely tucked up in bed by midnight.'

'Who with?'

'I forget their names. You know you really must go up a level and join an orgy. They can be fantastic, especially if you have partners who know *exactly* what they're doing.'

Araminta giggled. 'No thanks. Don't think I'm quite ready for that yet. What I'm doing is pretty adventurous for me.'

'Well when you're ready . . .'

'I'll let you know.'

Cressida inhaled a breath of dust and started coughing. 'Ozzie, this place is bringing back too many memories of my early years. Look, I'll call later. Sorry I'm not much practical help, but truthfully, I'm crap with design programs.'

'I want to do this by myself. I'm *going* to do this by myself.'

'Hell, make that partner in fifty years. You've got what it takes.'

'Remind you of you?' Araminta asked sweetly.

'No. I think you're sharper, unfortunately. Bye, darling.'

Lunch was a sandwich in her carry capsule as she flew across the city to the first of three suppliers on her list. The carry capsule, like her bots, had seen better days; according to the log she was the fifth owner in thirty years. Perfectly serviceable, the sales manager had assured her. It didn't have the speed of a new model, and if the big rear cargo compartment was filled to the rated load then it wouldn't quite reach its maximum flight ceiling. But she had a lot more confidence in the capsule than the 8038 bot; because of its age it had to pass a strict Viotia Transport Agency flightworthiness test every year, and the last one had been two months before she bought it.

The capsule settled on the lot of Bovey's Bathing and Culinary-ware, one of eight macrostores that made up a small touchdown mall in the Groby district. She walked into the store, looking round the open display rooms that lined a broad aisle with many branches. Bathrooms and kitchens alternated, promoting a big range of size, styles, and price, though the ones by the door tended to be elaborate. She looked enviously at the larger luxury units, thinking about the kind of apartment she'd develop one day in which such extravagance was a necessity.

'Can I help you?'

Araminta turned round to see a man dressed in the store's blue and maroon uniform. He was quite tall with his biological age locked in around his late twenties, dark skin offset by sandy-blond hair. Nice regular features, she thought, without being too handsome. His eyes were light grey, revealing a lot of humour. If they were meeting in a club she'd definitely let him buy her a drink – she might even offer to buy him one first.

'I'm looking for a kitchen and a bathroom. Both have to look and feel high grade, yet cost practically nothing.'

'Ah, now that I can understand, and provide for. I'm Mr Bovey, by the way.'

She was quite flattered the owner himself would come down on the floor and single her out to help. 'Pleased to meet you. I'm Araminta.'

He shook her hand politely. She thought he was debating with himself if he should try for a platonic greeting kiss. It was one of those times when she wished she had a connection to the gaiafield, which would enable her to gauge his emotions, assuming he'd broadcast them. Which as the owner of the store and therefore a professional he wouldn't. *Damn. Come on girl, focus.*

'What sort of dimensions can you give me to play with?' he asked.

Araminta gave him a slightly cheeky grin, then stopped. Perhaps it wasn't a double-entendre. Certainly sounded like one, though. 'Here you go,' she told him as her u-shadow produced the blueprint file. 'I would appreciate some help on price. This is my first renovation project, I don't want it to be my last.'

'Ah.' His eyes strayed to her hands, which still had lines of grime etched on the skin. 'Boss and workforce, I can relate to that.'

'Depleted workforce today, I'm afraid. One of my bots blew up. I can't afford any more expensive mistakes.'

'I understand.' He hesitated. 'You didn't get it from Burt Renik, did you?'

'Yes,' she said cautiously. 'Why?'

'Okay, well for future reference – and I didn't tell you this – he's not the most reliable of suppliers.'

'I know he's not the gold standard, but I checked on the evaluation library for that model. It was okay.'

This time he did wince. 'Next time you buy something in the trade, including anything from me, I'd recommend some research on Dave's Coding.' His u-shadow handed over the address. 'The evaluation library is fine, all those "independent" reports on how the product worked – well, the library is financed and managed by corporations, that's why there's never really a bad review. Dave's Coding is truly autonomous.'

'Thank you,' she said meekly as she filed the address in one of her storage lacunas. 'I'll take an access sometime.'

'Glad to help. In the meantime, try aisle seven for a kitchen. I think we can supply your order from there.'

'Thanks.' She walked off to aisle seven, more than a little

disappointed he didn't accompany her. Perhaps he had a policy of not flirting with customers. *Shame.*

The man waiting in aisle seven had on an identical blue and maroon uniform. He was perhaps five years older than Mr Bovey, but even taller, with a slender marathon runner frame. His skin was Nordic pale with ginger hair cut short except for a slender ridge right at the crest of his skull. Strangely, his green eyes registered the same kind of general amusement at the world as Mr Bovey.

'I'd recommend these two kitchen styles,' he said in greeting, and gestured at a small display area. 'They're a good fit to your dimensions, and this one is an end of the line model. I've got two left in the warehouse, so I can give you a sweet deal.'

Araminta was slightly nonplussed. Mr Bovey had obviously passed on her file to this employee; but that was no reason for him to start off as if they were already on familiar terms. 'Let's take a look,' she said, lowering the temperature of her voice.

It turned out the end of the line model was quite satisfactory, and it was a good deal. As well as a mid-range culinary unit with a range of multichem storage tanks she got a breakfast bar and stools, ancillaries like a fridge, food prepper, maidbot, shelving and cupboards. The style was chaste white, with black and gold trim. 'If you throw in delivery, I'll take it,' she told him.

'Any time you want it, I'll get it to you.'

She ignored the flirty overture, and told her u-shadow to pay the deposit.

'Bathrooms: aisle eleven,' he told her with unabashed enthusiasm.

The salesman waiting for her in aisle eleven had allowed himself to age into his biological fifties, which was unusual even for Viotia. His ebony skin was just starting to crinkle, with his hair greying and thinning. 'I've got four that I think will suit your aesthetics,' was his opening gambit.

'Hello,' she snapped at him.

'Ah . . . yes?'

'I'm Araminta, pleased to meet you. And I'm looking for a bathroom for my flat. Can you help me?'

'What . . .?'

'This whole relay thing you've got going here really isn't polite. You could at least say hi to me first before you access the file you're all shooting around here. I am a person, you know.'

'I think . . . ah.' His surprised expression softened. Araminta found it a lot more disconcerting than his initial smug chumminess.

'You do know what I am, don't you?' he asked.

'What do you mean?'

'I am Mr Bovey. We are all Mr Bovey in this store. I am a multiple human.'

Araminta was certain she'd be turning bright red with embarrassment. She knew what a multiple was, of course; one personality shared between several bodies through an adaptation of the gaiafield technology. This way, its practitioners claimed, was the true evolutionary leap for humanity that everyone else was pursuing down futile dead ends. A multiple human could never die unless every body was killed, which was unlikely in the extreme. In a quiet non-evangelical way they believed that everyone would one day become multiple. Perhaps after that the personalities would start fusing, leaving one consciousness with a trillion bodies – a much better outcome than downloading into the artificial sanctity of ANA.

It was a human heresy, their detractors claimed, a long-term conspiracy to imitate the Prime aliens of Dyson Alpha. More vocal opponents accused the multiple lifestyle of being started by left-over Starflyer agents trying to continue their dead master's corrupting ideology.

'I'm sorry,' she said, shamefaced. 'I didn't know.'

'That's okay. Partly my fault in assuming you did. Most people in the trade know.'

Araminta gave a wry grin. 'I guess continuity of service is a big plus.'

'I've got to be better than Burt Renik.'

'Definitely!'

'All right then. So are you and I good to go and look at bathrooms?'

'Of course we are.'

Araminta wound up buying the third suite the older Mr Bovey showed her. It wasn't out of guilt, he was genuinely offering a good deal, and the plain gold and green style was perfect for the flat. And once she'd let her awkwardness subside, he was fun to talk to. She couldn't quite throw off the weird little feeling of disconnection talking to his older body and knowing he was exactly the same person who'd greeted her, and that body was probably smiling privately at her while dealing with another customer.

'Just let us know when you want it delivered,' he said when her u-shadow handed over the deposit.

'Do you . . . that is: some of you. Ones of you. Handle delivery as well?'

'Don't worry, tense hasn't caught up with us multiples yet. And yes, I'll be the one in the carry capsule and helping the bots when they get stuck on the stairs. Not necessarily this body given its age, but me.'

'I'll look forward to seeing the rest of you.'

'There's a couple of mes who are young and handsome. Call it vanity if you like, I'm not immune to all the usual human flaws. I'll try and schedule thems for the delivery.'

'As handsome as you?'

'Hey, there's no more discount. You've squeezed me dry already.'

She laughed. 'I'd better get back to work then.'

Araminta smiled the whole flight back to the flat. Mr Bovey really had been charming. All his versions. She suspected it was more than good client relations. And was he joking about the young and handsome bodies? Actually, even the last one she'd seen, the older one, was quite distinguished. And what if he did ask her out for a date? Would it be just her and twenty of him sitting at a table?

If he asks.

And if he did, what am I going to answer?

The whole idea was unusual, which made it very interesting.

And what if the evening went well? Do I ask twenty of him back to my place?

Oh stop it!

She was still smiling when she walked back up the stairs and opened the front door. Then her mood came down at the sight of the flat. The bots had made some progress cleaning up; but one with a vacuum attachment was all clogged up. None of the bots had self-maintenance capacity, so she'd have to clear that out manually. And she'd still not put the balcony door actuator back together. It could well be quite a while before Mr Bovey delivered her new kitchen and bathroom and she got round to finding out how well she'd read their encounter.

Late in the afternoon when the place was finally getting straightened out she'd started spreading the sealant sheets over the lounge's floorboards. That was when her u-shadow told her there was a call from Laril. 'Are you sure?' she asked it.

'Yes.'

She debated with herself if she should call Cressida, maybe the Revenue Service would pay a reward. 'Where's he calling from?'

'The routing identity originates on Oaktier.' A summary slid into her peripheral vision.

'A Central Commonwealth World,' she read. 'What's he doing there?'

'I do not know.'

'Right,' she sat on the cube that was her portable bed and took her gloves off. Wiped her forehead. Took a breath. 'Okay, accept the call.' His image appeared in her exovision's primary perspective, making it seem as if he was standing right in front of her. If he was providing a real representation he hadn't changed much. Thin brown hair cut short, round face with a chubby jaw and a wide neck, as always thick dark stubble longer than she liked. It was scratchy, she remembered. He never gelled it down smooth no matter how many times she asked.

'Thanks for taking the call,' he said. 'I wasn't sure you would.'

'Neither was I.'

'I hear you're doing okay; you got the money.'

'I was awarded the money by the court. Laril, what are you doing? Why are you on Oaktier?'

'Isn't it obvious?'

That took a few seconds to register, and even longer to accept. It must be some stunt, some scam. 'You're migrating inwards?' she asked, incredulous.

He smiled the same carefree smile he'd used when they first met. It was very appealing, warm and confident. She hadn't seen it much after they married.

'Happens to all of us in the end,' he said.

'No! I don't believe it. You are going Higher? You?'

'My first batch of biononics have been in a week. They're starting to integrate some basic fields. It's quite an experience.'

'But . . .' she spluttered. 'For Ozzie's sake. Higher culture would never take you. What did you do, erase half your memories?'

'That's a pretty common myth. Higher culture isn't the old Catholic Church, you know; you don't have to confess and recant your past sins. It's current attitude which counts.'

'I know they don't take criminals. There was that case centuries ago – Jollian thought that he could escape what he'd done with a memory wipe and a migration to the Inner Worlds. Paula Myo caught up with him and had his biononics removed so he could face trial on the External Worlds as the type of human he was when he committed his crime. I think he got a couple of hundred years' suspension.'

'That's what you think of me, that I qualify for the Jollian precedent? Well thanks a whole lot, Araminta. A couple of things you might want to consider. One, Paula Myo isn't after me. And she isn't after me because I haven't committed any crime.'

'Have you told the Viotia Revenue Service that?'

'My business economics were a mess, sure. I'm not hiding

201

from that. I even told my Higher initiator about my finances. You know what she said?'

'Go on.'

'Higher culture is about rejecting the evil of money.'

'How very convenient for you.'

'Look I just wanted to call and apologize. I'm not asking for anything. And I wanted to make sure you're all right.'

'A bit late for that, isn't it?' she bridled. 'I'm not part of some therapy session you have to complete before they'll take you.'

'You're misunderstanding this, perhaps with anger leading you away from what I'm actually saying.'

'Ozzie! This *is* your therapy session.'

'We don't need therapy to become Higher, it is inevitable. Even you will migrate eventually.'

'Never.'

His image produced a fond lopsided smile. 'I remember thinking that once. Probably when I was in my twenties. I know it probably doesn't make a lot of sense to someone your age when every day is fresh, but after a few centuries living on the External Worlds you begin to get bored and frustrated. Every day becomes this constant battle; politicians are corrupt and crap, projects never get finished on time or in budget, bureaucrats delight in thwarting you, and then there's the eternal fight for money.'

'Which you lost.'

'I fed myself and my families for over three centuries thank you very much. Even you came out ahead with the residue of that work. But face it, I didn't achieve much now did I? A few tens of thousands of dollars to show for three and a half centuries. That's not exactly leaving your mark on the universe, is it? And it's not just me, there are billions of humans that are the same. The External Worlds are fun and exciting with their market economy and clashing ideologies and outward urge. Youth thrives on that kind of environment. Then there comes a day when you have to look back and take stock. You did that for me.'

'Oh come on! You're blaming me for the dog's dinner you made of your affairs?'

'No. I'm not blaming you. Don't you get it? I'm thanking you. I was old, it took you to reveal that to me. The contrast between us was so great even I couldn't close my eyes to it for ever. There really is no fool like an old fool, and part of that foolishness came from deluding myself. I was tired of that life and didn't want to admit it. Turning Punk Skunk and taking a young wife was just another way of trying to ignore what I'd become. Even that didn't work, did it? I was making both of us miserable.'

'That's putting it mildly,' she muttered. In a way though, it was gratifying hearing him admit it was all his fault. 'I left my whole family behind because of you.'

He showed her a sly smile. 'And that was a bad thing?'

'Yeah, all right,' she grinned puckishly. 'You did me a favour there. I'm not really cut out for two centuries of selling agricultural cybernetics.'

'I knew that the minute I set eyes on you. So how's the world of property development coming on?'

'Harder than I thought,' she admitted. 'There are so many stupid little things that bug me.'

'I know. Well imagine today's frustration multiplied by three hundred years, that's how I wound up feeling.'

'And now you don't?'

'No.'

'I don't believe Higher culture is free of bureaucracy, or corruption, or idiots, or useless politicians. They might not be so blatant, but they're there.'

'No, they're not. Well . . . okay, but nothing like as bad as they are in the External Worlds. You see, there's no need for any of that. So many of the social problems the External Worlds suffer from is born out of markets, capital and materialism; that's what old-style economics produces, in fact trouble just is about all it produces. The cybernated manufacturing and resource allocation procedure which Higher culture is based on takes all those difficulties out of the equation. That and taking a mature sensible perspective. We don't struggle for the little things any more, we can afford to take the longer, intellectual view.'

'You talk like you're one of them already.'

'*Them.* That's perspective for you. Higher culture is mainly a state of mind, but backed up by physical affluence.'

'You are what the External Worlds strive to be: everyone's a millionaire.'

'No. Everyone has equal access to resources, that's what you lack. Though I'd point out that External Worlds always convert to Higher culture in the end. We are the apex of human social and technological achievement. In other words, this is what the human race has been aiming for since proto-humans picked up a club to give us an advantage against all the other predators competing for food out on the African plains. We improve ourselves at every opportunity.'

'So why didn't you go straight to ANA and download? That's how Highers improve themselves, isn't it?'

'Ultimately, I will, I suppose. But Higher is the next stage for me. I want a time in my body which isn't such an effort. A couple of centuries where I can just relax and learn. There are so many things I want to do and see which I never could before. The opportunities here are just astounding.'

Araminta laughed silently; that at least sounded like the old Laril. 'Then I suppose I wish you good luck.'

'Thank you. I really didn't want to leave things the way they were between us. If there's anything you ever need, please call, even if it's just a shoulder to cry on.'

'Sure. I'll do that,' she lied, knowing she never would. She felt indecently content when he ended the call. Closure obviously worked both ways.

*

The people had no faces. At least none that he was aware of. There were dozens of them, men, women, even children. They were in front of him. Running. Fleeing like cattle panicked by a carnivore. Their screams threatened to split his eardrums. Words rose struggling out of the soundwall. Mostly they were pleas for help, for pity, for sanctuary, for their lives. However hard they ran he kept up with them.

The bizarre mêlée was taking place in some kind of elaborate hall with crystal grooves running across its domed ceiling. Rows of curving chairs hindered the frantic crowd as they raced for the exit doors. He wouldn't or couldn't turn round. He didn't know what they were trying to escape from. Energy weapons screeched, and the people flung themselves down. For himself, he remained standing, looking down at their prone bodies. Somehow he was remote from the horror. He didn't know how that could be. He was there with them, he was a part of whatever terror was happening here. Then some kind of shadow slid across the floor like demon wings unfolding.

Aaron sat up in bed with a shocked gasp. His skin was cold, damp with sweat. Heart pounding. It took a moment for him to recognize where he was. The lights in the sleeping cabin were brightening, showing him the curving bulkhead walls. He blinked at them as the dream faded.

Somehow he knew the strange images were more than a dream. They must be some memory of his previous life, an event strong enough to cling on inside his neurones while the rest of his identity was wiped. He was curious and daunted at the same time.

What the hell did I get myself mixed up in?

Thinking about it, whatever the affray was, it didn't look any worse than anything this mission had generated so far. His heart had calmed without any help from his biononics. He took a deep breath and climbed off the cot.

'Where are we?' he asked the *Artful Dodger*'s smartcore.

'Six hours out from Anagaska.'

'Good.' He stretched and rolled his shoulders. 'Give me a shower,' he told the smartcore. 'Start with water; shift to spores when I tell you.'

The cabin began to change, cot flowing back into the

bulkhead, the floor hardening to a black and white marble finish. Gold nozzles extruded from each corner, and warm water gushed out.

Even given the ship's obvious Higher origin, it had come as a wondrous surprise to discover it was equipped with an ultradrive. Aaron had thought such a thing to be nothing more than rumour. That was when he realized he had to be working for some ANA Faction. It was an idea he found more intriguing than the drive. It also meant the Pilgrimage was being taken a lot more seriously than people generally realized.

After the spores cleaned and dried his skin he dressed in a simple dark purple one-piece suit and went out into the main lounge. His small cabin withdrew into the bulkhead, providing a larger floorspace. Corrie-Lyn's cabin was still engaged, a simple blister shape protruding into the hemispherical lounge. His suggestion yesterday that they share a bunk had been met by a cold stare and an instant: 'Good night.'

She probably wouldn't come out again until they touched down.

The culinary unit provided an excellent breakfast of fried benjiit eggs and Wiltshire drycure bacon, with toast and thick-cut English marmalade. Aaron was nothing if not a traditionalist. *So it would seem*, he mused.

Corrie-Lyn emerged from her cabin while he was munching away on his third slice of toast. She'd dressed in a demure (for her) turquoise and emerald knee-length cashmere sweater dress which the ship's synthesizer had produced. Her cabin sank back into the bulkhead, and she collected a large cup of tea from the culinary unit before sitting down opposite Aaron.

Recognizing a person's emotional state was an important part of Aaron's assessment routine. But this morning Corrie-Lyn was as unreadable as a muted solido.

She stared at him for a while as she sipped her tea, apparently unperturbed by the awkwardness of the situation.

'Something on your mind?' he asked mildly, breaking the

silence. That he was the one who broke it was a telling point. There weren't many people who could make him socially uncomfortable.

'Not *my* mind,' she said, a little too earnestly.

'Meaning? Oh come on, you're an attractive woman. I was bound to ask. You'd probably be more insulted if I didn't.'

'Not what I'm talking about.' She waved her hand dismissively. 'That was some dream you had.'

'I . . . Dream?'

'Did you forget? I didn't become a Living Dream Councillor just because I've got a great arse. I immerse myself in people's dreams, I explore their emotional state and try to help them come to terms with what they are. Dreams are very revealing.'

'Oh shit! I leaked that into the gaiafield.'

'You certainly did. I'd like to tell you that you are one very disturbed individual. But that would hardly be a revelation, now would it?'

'I've seen my fair share of combat. Hardly surprising my subconscious throws up crap like that.'

She gave a small victory smile. 'But you don't remember any combat, do you? Not previous to this particular incarnation. That means whatever event you participated in was truly epochal for it to have survived in your subconscious. Wipe techniques are generally pretty good these days, and I suspect you had access to the very best.'

'Come off it. That was too weird to be a memory.'

'Most dreams are engendered by memory, except Inigo's of course. They have their roots in reality, in experience. What you see is the event as your real personality recognizes it. Dreams are very truthful things, Aaron, they're not something you can ignore, or take an aerosol to ward off. Unless you face that which you dream you will never truly be at peace with yourself.'

'Do I cross your palm with silver now?'

'Sarcasm is a very pitiful social defence mechanism, especially in these circumstances. Both of us know how disturbed you were.

You cannot shield yourself and your emotions from someone as experienced as myself. The gaiafield will show you for what you are.'

Aaron made very sure the gaiamotes were completely closed up, allowing nothing to escape from inside his skull. 'Okay then,' he grumbled. 'What was I dreaming?'

'Something in your past.'

'Hey wow. Surely I am in the presence of a truly galactic master of the art.'

Unperturbed Corrie-Lyn took another drink of tea. 'More relevantly: a darkness from your past. In order to have survived erasure and to manifest so strongly, I would evaluate it as a crux in your psychological development. Those people were very frightened; terrified even. For so many to be running so fearfully the threat must have been lethal. That is rare in the Commonwealth today, even among the outermost External Worlds.'

'So I was running an evacuation mission out of some disaster. Rare but not unfeasible. There's a lot goes on among the External Worlds that the more developed planets turn a blind eye to.'

Corrie-Lyn gave him a sad smile. 'You were above them, Aaron. Remember? Not running with them. You were what they feared. You and what you represented.'

'That's bullshit.'

'Men. Women. Children. All fleeing you. All hysterical and horror-struck. What were you going to do to them, I wonder. We established back at the fane that you have no conscience.'

'Very clever,' he sneered. 'I pissed you off, and now you come gunning for a little psychological payback. Lady, I have to tell you, it takes a great deal more than anything you've got to spook me out, and that's Ozzie's honest truth.'

'I'm not trying to spook you anywhere, Aaron,' she said with quiet earnest. 'That's not what Living Dream, the true Living Dream, is about. We exist to guide human life to its fulfilment. The promise of the Void is a huge part of that, yes; but it is not the only component to understanding what you are, your basic nature. I want to liberate the potential inside you. There is more

208

than senseless violence lurking inside your mind, I can sense that. You can be so much more than what you are today, if you'd just let me help. We can explore your dreams together.'

'Call me old fashioned, but my dreams are my own.'

'The darkness you witnessed at the end interests me.'

'That shadow?' Despite himself, Aaron was curious she'd picked up on it.

'A *winged* shadow – which has a strong resonance for most humans no matter which cultural stream they come from. But it was more than a simple shadow. It held significant meaning to you. A representation of your subconscious, I think. After all, it didn't surprise you. If anything you felt almost comfortable with it.'

'Whatever. We have more important things to concentrate on right now. Touchdown is in five and a half hours.' Something in his mind was telling him to close this conversation down now. She was trying to distract him, to throw him off guard. He couldn't allow that, he had to remain completely focused on his mission to locate Inigo.

Corrie-Lyn raised an eyebrow. 'Are you seriously saying you're not interested? This is the real you we're talking about.'

'I keep telling you, I'm happy with what I am. Now, you said Inigo came to Anagaska to visit his family.'

She gave him a disheartened gaze. 'I said he visited his homeworld on occasion, when everything got too much for him. All I know was that he had family. Any further inference is all your own.'

'His mother migrated inwards then downloaded into ANA. What about the aunt?'

'I don't know.'

'Did the aunt have children? Cousins he would have grown up with?'

'I don't know.'

'Was there a family estate? A refuge he felt secure in?'

'I don't know.'

He sat back, and just about resisted glaring at her. 'His official biography says he grew up in Kuhmo. Please tell me that isn't a lie?'

'I'd assume it was correct. That is, I have no reason to doubt it. It's where Living Dream built his library.'

'Central worship point for your living god, huh?'

'I'm not surprised you don't want to know yourself. You're a real shit, you know that.'

The good ship *Artful Dodger* slipped back into real space a thousand kilometres above Anagaska. Aaron told the smartcore to register with the local spacewatch network and request landing permission at Kuhmo spaceport. The request was granted immediately, and the starship began its descent into the middle of the cloud-smeared eastern continent.

When it was first confirmed as H-congruous and assigned for settlement by CST back in 2375, Anagaska was an unremarkable world in what was then called phase three space, destined for a long slow development. Then the Starflyer plunged the Commonwealth into war against the Prime aliens and its future changed radically.

Hanko was one of the forty-seven planets wrecked during the Prime's last great assault against the Commonwealth, its sun pummelled by flare bombs and quantumbusters, saturating the defenceless planet's climate and biosphere with a torrent of lethal radiation for weeks on end. Its hundred and fifty million strong population was trapped under city force fields on a dying world whose very air was now deadly poison. Evacuation was the only possible option. And thanks to Nigel Sheldon and the CST company operating Hanko's wormhole link, its citizens were shunted across forty-two lightyears to Anagaska.

Unfortunately, Anagaska at the time was nothing more than wild forest, native prairie, and hostile jungle; with a grand total of five pre-settlement research stations housing a few hundred scientists. Nigel even had a solution to that. The interior of the wormhole transporting Hanko's population to their new home was given a different, very slow, temporal flow rate relative to the outside universe. With the War over, trillions of dollars were poured into creating an infrastructure on Anagaska and the other forty-six refuge worlds. It took over a century to complete the basic civic amenities and housing, producing cities and towns that were near-Stalinist in their layout and architecture. But when the wormhole from Hanko finally opened on Anagaska, everyone who came through was provided with a roof over their head and enough food to sustain them while they built up their new home's agriculture and industry.

It was perhaps inevitable that after such a trauma, the refuge worlds were slow to develop economically. Their major cities progressed sluggishly in an era when the rest of the Common-wealth was undergoing profound change. As to the outlying towns, they became near-stagnant backwaters. Nobody starved, nobody was particularly poor, but they lacked the dynamism that was sweeping the rest of humanity as biononics became available, ANA came online, and new political and cultural blocs were formed.

Kuhmo was such a town. Little had changed in the seven centuries between the day its new residents arrived, stumbling out of giant government transporters, and the time Inigo was born. When he was a child, the massive hexagonal arcology built to house his ancestors still dominated the centre of the civic zone, its uninhabited upper levels decaying alarmingly while its lower floors offered cheap accommodation to underprivileged families and third-rate businesses. In fact it was still there sixty years later when he left, a monstrous civic embarrassment to a town that didn't have the money to either refurbish or demolish it.

A hundred years later, the arcology's upper third had finally been dismantled with funds from Anagaska's federal government made available on public safety grounds. Then Living Dream made the town council a financial offer they couldn't really refuse. The arcology was finally razed, its denizens rehoused in plush new purpose-built suburbs. Where it had stood, a new building emerged, nothing like as big, but far more important. Living Dream was constructing what was to be Anagaska's primary fane, with a substantial library and free college attached. It attracted the devout from across the planet and a good many nearby star systems, many of them staying, changing the nature of Kuhmo for ever.

Aaron stood under the tall novik trees that dominated the fane's encircling park, and looked up at the tapering turrets with their bristling bracelets of stone sculptures, his nose wrinkling in dismay. 'The arcology couldn't have been worse than this,' he declared. 'This is your leader's ultimate temple, his statement to his birthplace that he's moved onwards and upwards? Damn! He must have really hated his old town to do this to it. All this says to me is beware of Kuhmoians bearing gifts.'

Corrie-Lyn sighed and shook her head. 'Ozzie, but you are such a philistine.'

'Know what I like, though. And, lady, this ain't it. Even the old Big15 worlds had better architecture than this.'

'So what are you going to do, hit it with a disruptor pulse?'

'Tempting, I have to admit. But no. We'll indulge in a little data mining first.'

The Inigo museum, in reality a shrine, was every bit as bad as Aaron expected it to be. For a start they couldn't just wander round. They had to join the queue of devout outside the main entrance and were assigned a 'guide'. The tour was official and structured. Each item was accompanied by a full sense recording and corresponding emotional content radiating out into the gaiafield.

So he gritted his teeth and put on a passive smile as they were led round Inigo's childhood home, diligently uprooted from its original location two kilometres away and lovingly restored using era-authentic methods and materials. Each room contained a boring yet worshipful account of childhood days. There were solidos of his mother Sabine. Cute dramas of his grandparents whose house it was. A sad section devoted to his father Erik Horovi who left Sabine a few short months after the birth. Cue reconstruction of the local hospital maternity ward.

Aaron gave the solido of Erik a thoughtful stare, and sent his u-shadow into its public datastore to extract useful information. Erik had been eighteen years old when Inigo was born. When Aaron checked back, Sabine was a month short of her eighteenth birthday when she gave birth.

'Didn't they have a contraception program here in those days?' he asked the guide abruptly.

Corrie-Lyn groaned and flushed a mild pink. The guide's pleasant smile flickered slightly, returning in a somewhat harder manifestation. 'Excuse me?'

'Contraception? It's pretty standard for teenagers no matter what cultural stream you grow up in.' He paused, reviewing the essentially non-existent information on Sabine's parents. 'Unless the family was old-style Catholics or initiated Taliban or Evangelical Orthodox. Were they?'

'They were not,' the guide said stiffly. 'Inigo was proud that he did not derive from any of Earth's appalling medieval religious sects. It means his goals remain untainted.'

'I see. So his birth was planned, then?'

'His birth was a blessing to humanity. He is the one chosen by the Waterwalker to show us what lies within the Void. Why do you ask? Are you some kind of unisphere journalist?'

'Certainly not. I'm a cultural anthropologist. Naturally I'm interested in procreation rituals.'

The guide gave him a suspicious stare, but let it pass. Aaron's u-shadow had been ready to block any query the man shot into the local net. They'd managed to get through the museum's entrance without any alarm, which meant Living Dream hadn't yet issued a Commonwealth-wide alert. But they'd certainly respond swiftly enough to any identity file matching himself and Corrie-Lyn, no matter what planet it originated from. And the fact it came from Anagaska barely two days after the Riasi incident would reveal exactly what type of starship they were using. He couldn't allow that.

'Hardly a ritual,' the guide sniffed.

'Anthropologists think everything we do is summed up in

terms of rituals,' Corrie-Lyn said smoothly. 'Now tell me, is this really Inigo's university dorm?' She waved her hand eagerly at the drab holographic room in front of them. Various shabby and decayed pieces of furniture that resembled those shown in full 3Dcolour were on display in transparent stasis chambers.

'Yes,' the guide said, returning to equilibrium. 'Yes it is. This is where he began his training as an astrophysicist; the first step on the path that took him to Centurion Station. As an environment, its significance cannot be overstated.'

'Gosh,' Corrie-Lyn cooed.

Aaron was impressed that she kept a straight face.

'What was that all about?' Corrie-Lyn asked when they were in a taxi capsule and heading back for the spaceport hotel.

'You didn't think it was odd?'

'So two horny teenagers decided to have a kid. It's not unheard of.'

'Yes it is. They were both still at school. Then Erik vanishes a few months after the birth. Plus you tell me Inigo had an aunt, who has been very effectively written out of his family. And you claim Inigo is Higher, which must have happened either at birth or early in his life; that is, prior to his Centurion mission.'

'What makes you say that?'

'Because, as you said, he took extreme care to hide it from his followers; it's not logical to assume he'd acquire biononics after he began Living Dream.'

'Granted, but where does all this theorizing get you?'

'It tells me just what a load of bullshit his official past is,' Aaron said, waving a hand back at the shrinking museum. 'That farce is a perfect way of covering up his true history, it provides a flawless alternative version with just enough true points touching verifiable reality as to go unquestioned. Unless of course you're like us and happen to know some awkward facts which don't fit. If he was born Higher, then one of his parents had to be Higher. Sabine almost certainly wasn't; and Erik conveniently walks out on his child a few months after the birth.'

214

'It was too much for the boy, that's all. If Inigo's birth was an accident like you think, that's hardly surprising.'

'No. That's not it. I don't think it was an accident. Quite the opposite.' He told his u-shadow to review local events for the year prior to Inigo's birth, using non-Living Dream archives. They'd almost reached the hotel when the answer came back. 'Ah ha, this is it.' He shared the file with her. 'Local news company archive. They were bought out by an Intersolar two hundred years ago and the town office downgraded to closure which is why the files were deep cached. The art block in Kuhmo's college burned down eight and a half months before Inigo was born.'

'It says the block was the centre of a gang fight,' Corrie-Lyn said as she speed-reviewed. 'A bunch of hothead kids duking out a turf war.'

'Yeah right. Now launch a search for Kuhmo gang-culture. Specifically for incidents with weapons usage. Go ahead. I'll give you thousand to one odds there aren't any other files, not for fifty years either side of that date. Look at the history of this place before Inigo built his monstrosity. There was nothing here *worth* fighting over; not even for kids on the bottom of the pile. The Council switched between three parties, and they were all virtually indistinguishable, their polices were certainly the same: low taxes, cut back on official wastage, attract business investment, and make sure the parks look pretty. Hell, they didn't even manage to get rid of the arcology by themselves. That thing stood there for nearly nine hundred years. Nine *hundred*, for Ozzie's sake! And they couldn't get their act together for all that time. Kuhmo is the ultimate middle-class dead-end, drifting along in the same rut for a thousand years. Bad boys don't want a part of that purgatory, it's like a suspension sentence but with sensory torture thrown in; they just want to leave.'

'All right, *all right*, I submit. Inigo has a dodgy family history. What's your point?'

'My theory is a radical infiltration; it's about the right time period. And that certainly won't be on any news file, deep cached or otherwise.'

'So how do we find out what really happened?'

'Only one way. We have to ask the Protectorate.'

Corrie-Lyn groaned in dismay, dropping her head into her hands.

*

The maintenance hangar was on the edge of Daroca's spaceport. One of twenty-three identical black-sheen cubes in a row; the last row in a block of ten. There were eighteen blocks in total. It was a big spaceport, much larger than the Navy compound on the other side of the city. Daroca's residents were a heavily starfaring folk, and the Air project had added considerably to the numbers of spaceships in recent centuries. Without any connection to the unisphere's guidance function a person could wander round the area all day and not be able to distinguish between any of the hangars. A subtle modification to the spaceport net management software provided a near identical disorientation function to any uninvited person who was using electronic navigation to find Troblum's hangar. While the other structures were always opening their doors to receive or disgorge starships, Troblum's was kept resolutely shut except for his very rare flights. When the doors did iris back, a security shield prevented any visual or electronic observation of the interior. Even the small workforce who loyally turned up day after day parked their capsules outside and used a little side door to enter. They then had to pass through another three shielded doors to enter the hangar's central section. Nearly two thirds of the big building was taken up by extremely sophisticated synthesis and fabrication machinery. All of the systems were custom-built; the current layout had taken Troblum over fifteen years to refine. That was why he needed other people to help him. Neumann cybernetics and biononic extrusion were magnificent systems for everyday life, but for anything beyond the ordinary you first had to design the machinery to build the machines which fabricated the device.

Troblum had no trouble producing the modified exotic matter theory behind an Anomine planet-shifting ftl engine, and even describing the basic generator technology he wanted. But turning those abstracts into physical reality was tough. For a start he needed information on novabomb technology, and even after nearly 1,200 years the Navy kept details of that horrendously powerful weapon classified. Which was where Emily Alm came in.

It was Marius who had put the two of them in touch. Emily used to work for the Navy weapons division on Augusta. After three hundred years she had simply grown bored.

'There's no point to it any more,' she told Troblum at their first meeting. 'We haven't made any truly new weapons for centuries. All the lab does is refine the systems we have. Any remotely new concept we come up with is closed down almost immediately by the top brass.'

'You mean ANA:Governance?' he'd asked.

'Who knows where the orders originate from? All I know is that they come down from Admiral Kazimir's office and we jump fast and high every time. It's crazy. I don't know why we bother having a weapons research division. As far as I know the deterrence fleet hasn't changed ships or armaments for five hundred years.'

The problem he'd outlined to her was interesting enough for her to postpone downloading into ANA. After Emily, others had slowly joined his motley team; Dan Massell whose expertise in functional molecular configuration was unrivalled, Ami Cowee to help with exotic matter formatting. Several technicians had come and gone over the years, contributing to the Neumann cybernetics array, then leaving as their appliance constructed its required successor. But those three had stuck with him since the early years. Their age and Higher-derived patience meant they were probably the only ones who could tolerate him for so long. That and their shared intrigue in the nature of the project.

When Troblum's ageing capsule landed on the pad outside the hangar he was puzzled to see just Emily's and Massell's capsules sitting on the concrete beside the glossy black wall. He'd been expecting Ami as well.

Then as soon as he was through the second little office he knew something was wrong. There was no quiet vibration of machinery. As soon as the shield over the third door cut off, his low level field could detect no electronic activity beyond. The hangar had been divided in half, with *Mellanie's Redemption* parked at one end, a dark bulky presence very much in the shade of the assembly section. Troblum stood under the prow of the ship, and looked round uncomprehendingly. The Neumann cybernetic modules in front of him were bigger than a house; joined into a lattice cube of what looked like translucent glass slabs the size of commercial capsules, each one glowing with its individual primary light. It was as if a rainbow had shattered only to be scooped up and shoved into a transparent box. At the centre, three metres above Troblum's head, was a scarlet and black cone, the ejector mechanism of the terminal extruder. It should have been wrapped in a fiercely complex web of quantum fields, intersecting feeder pressors, electron positioners, and molecular lock injectors. He couldn't detect a glimmer of power. If all had gone well over the last few days the planet-shift engine should have been two-thirds complete, assembled atom by atom in a stable matrix of superdense matter held together by its own integral coherent bonding field. By now the cylinder would be visible within the extruder, glimmering from realigned exotic radiation as if it contained its own galaxy.

Instead, Emily and Massell were sitting on a box-like atomic D-K phase junction casing at the base of the cybernetics, drinking tea. Both silent with mournful faces, they flashed him a guilty glance as he came in.

'What happened?' he demanded.

'Some kind of instability,' Emily said. 'I'm sorry, Troblum. The bonding field format wasn't right. Ami had to shut it down.'

'And she didn't tell me!'

'Couldn't face you,' Massell said. 'She knew how disappointed you'd be. Said she didn't want to be responsible for breaking your heart.'

'That's not— Arrrgh,' he groaned. Biononics released a flood of neural inhibitors as they detected his thoughts growing more and more agitated. He shivered as if he'd been caught by a blast of arctic air. But his focus was perfectly clear. A list of social priorities flipped up into his exovision. 'Thank you for waiting to tell me in person,' he said. 'I'll call Ami and tell her it wasn't her fault.'

Emily and Massell exchanged a blank look. 'That's kind of you,' she said.

'How big an instability?'

Massell winced. 'Not good. We need to re-examine the whole effect, I think.'

'Can we just strengthen it?'

'I hope so, but even that will be a domino on the internal structure.'

'Maybe not,' Emily said with a weak confidence. 'We included some big operating margins. There's a lot of flexibility within the basic parameters.'

Troblum fell silent with a dismay which even the inhibitors couldn't overcome. If Emily was wrong, if they needed a complete redesign, then the Neumann cybernetics would need to be rebuilt. It would take years. Again. And this drive generator had been his true hope, he'd genuinely thought he would have a functional device by the end of the week. It was the only way to get people to agree with his theory. Marius would see the Navy never backed a search, he was sure of that. This was all that was left to him, his remaining shred of proof.

'You can get the resource allocation, can't you?' Massell said in an encouraging voice. 'I mean, you've managed to push your theory to this level.' His gesture took in the silent hulk of Neumann cybernetics. 'You've got to have some powerful political allies on the committees. And this wasn't a setback as such; only one thing was out of alignment.'

Troblum deliberately avoided looking in Emily's direction. Massell hadn't been one of Marius's candidates. 'Yes, I can probably get the EMA for a rebuild.'

'Okay then! Do you want to get on it right away, or leave it a few days?'

'Give it a few days,' Troblum said, reading from his social priority list. 'We'll all need a while to recharge after this. I'll start going over the telemetry and give you a call when I think I know what the new bonding field format should be.'

'Okay.' Massell gave him an encouraging smile as he slid off the casing. 'There's a certain Air technician I've been promising a resort time-out with. I'll let her know I'm free.' He gave Emily a blank gaze, then left.

'Will there be the resources to carry on?' she asked.

'I don't know. Maybe not from our mutual friend.' At the back of his mind was a nasty little thought that this had been the result which benefited Marius best. Just how far would the Accelerator Faction representative go to achieve that? 'But I'll carry it on one way or another. I still have some personal EMA left.'

Her expression grew sceptical as she looked round the huge assemblage of ultra-sophisticated equipment. 'All right. If you need any help reviewing the data, let me know.'

'Thanks,' he said.

Troblum's office wasn't much. A corner in one of the annexe rooms big enough for a large wingback chair in the middle of a high-capacity solido projection array. He slumped down into the worn cushioning and stared through the narrow window into the hangar's assembly section. Now he was alone and the neural chemicals were wearing off, he didn't have the heart to begin a diagnostic review. The drive engine should have slid smoothly out of the extruder and into the modified forward cargo hold of *Mellanie's Redemption*. He would have been ready to show the Commonwealth he was right by the end of the week, to open up a whole new chapter in galactic history. Highers weren't supposed to become frustrated but right now he wanted to kick the shit out of the Neumann cybernetics.

*

Some time later that afternoon the hangar security net informed Troblum a capsule had landed on the pad outside. Frowning, he flipped the sensor image out of his peripheral vision, and watched as the capsule's door flowed open. Marius stepped out.

Troblum actually feared for his life. The warning at the restaurant had been awful enough. But Troblum had been so sure the design for the drive engine was valid he couldn't stop thinking that the whole manufacturing process had somehow been deliberately knocked out of kilter – sabotaged, in other words. There was only one person who could have that done. He gave the *Mellanie's Redemption* a calculating glance. Even with his Faction-supplied biononics, Marius wouldn't be able to shoot through the ship's force field.

It wasn't going to happen. Troblum didn't have anywhere to run to; he certainly didn't have a friend – not one, not anywhere. And if Marius was here to eliminate him, it was on orders from the Accelerators. Hiding inside the starship would only postpone the inevitable.

I must start thinking about this, about a way out.

Reluctantly, he ordered the hangar net to open the side door.

Marius came into the office, gliding along in his usual smooth imperturbable fashion. He glanced round, not bothering to hide his distaste. 'So this is where you spend your days.'

'Something wrong with that?'

'Not at all.' Marius gave a thin smile. 'Everyone should have a hobby.'

'Do you?'

'None you'd appreciate.'

'So what are you here for? I did as you asked, I haven't pressed the Navy.'

'I know. And that hasn't gone un-noted.' He studied the huge stack of Newman cybernetics through the office window. 'My commiserations. You put a lot of effort into today.'

'How did you know . . .'

The representative's eerie green eyes turned back to stare at

Troblum. 'Don't be childish. Now, I'm here because you need more funds and we have another little project which might interest you.'

'A project?' Since he didn't seem in danger of immediate slaughter, Troblum couldn't help the tweak of interest.

'One you'll find difficult to refuse once you know the details. Its an ftl drive which we're putting into production. Who knows? Perhaps there will be some overspill into this which you can take advantage of.'

Troblum really couldn't think what type of drive the ANA Faction might want, especially after the last ultra-classified project he'd worked on for Marius. 'And you'll help me acquire extra EMAs for a rebuild here?'

'Budgets are tight in these uncertain times, but a swift and successful conclusion to our drive programme would probably result in some unused allocation we can divert your way. However, we also have something else you might be interested in, a bonus if you like.'

'What's that?'

'Bradley Johansson's genome.'

'What? Impossible. There was nothing left of him.'

'Not quite. He rejuvenated several times at a clinic on an Isolated world. We had an access opportunity several centuries ago.'

'Are you serious?'

Marius simply raised an eyebrow.

'That sounds good,' Troblum said. 'Really good. I almost don't have to think about it.'

'I need an answer now.'

Once again Troblum was uncertain what would happen if he said no. He couldn't detect any active embedded weapons in the representative, but that didn't mean death wouldn't be sudden and irrevocable. Talk about carrot and stick. 'All right. But first I have to spend a couple of days analysing what happened here.'

'We would like you to fly to our assembly station immediately.'

'If I can't settle this problem to my own satisfaction I won't be any good to you. I think you know that.'

Marius hardened his stare, his eyes darkening from emerald to near-black. 'Very well, you can have forty-eight hours. No more. I expect you to be on your way by then.' He transferred a flightplan file over to Troblum's u-shadow.

'I will be.' It took a lot of biononic intervention to prevent Troblum from shaking as the representative left the office. There wasn't anything he could do to stop the sweat staining his suit right along his spine. When the sensors showed him the representative's capsule lifting off the pad, he turned to gaze back into the assembly section. It was all far too neat. The problem on the verge of success. The generous offer to help pay for a solution, plus the unbelievable promise of being able to clone Bradley Johansson. Troblum let his biononic field sweep out to flow through the inert cybernetics. 'What did that bastard do?' he murmured. Around him the solido projectors snapped on, filling the air with a multicoloured blizzard of fine equations, sparkling as they interacted. Somewhere there had to be a flaw in the blueprint that had taken him fifteen painstaking years to devise, a deliberate glitch. The only person who could put it there was Emily. He called up the sections she was directly involved with. There was an emotion tugging at him as he started to review the data. It took a while, but he eventually realized it was sadness.

*

From the office he was visiting in the hangar five down from Troblum's, the Delivery Man could just see Marius's capsule as it took to the air again. All he used was his eyes, there was no way the Accelerator representative could know he was under direct observation. 'He's gone,' he reported. 'And that hangar has distorted the spaceport's basic guidance protocols – you can't get there unless you're invited. It's definitely a nest for some bad boy activity. Do you want me to infiltrate?'

'No thank you,' the Conservative Faction replied. 'We'll use passive observation for the moment.'

'What about this Troblum character it's registered to?'

'Records indicate he's some kind of Starflyer War enthusiast. His starship flightplan logs are interesting, he visits some out of the way places.'

'Do you think he's another representative?'

'No. He's a physicist, with some high-level Navy contacts.'

'He's involved with the Navy?'

'Yes.'

'In what regard?'

'Left-over artefacts and actions from the Starflyer War. His interest verges on the fanatical.'

'So why would Marius pay him a personal visit?'

'Good question. We will research him further.'

'I can go home now?'

'Yes.'

'Excellent.' If he got to Arevalo's interstellar wormhole terminus in the next ten minutes, he could be back home in time for tea with the girls.

Inigo's third dream

It was a glorious summer evening, the bright sun tinting to copper over the Eggshaper Guild compound while Edeard walked across the main nine-sided courtyard. He took a contented breath as he watched the team of five ge-chimps cleaning the last patch of kimoss off the kennel roof. Their strong little claw hands were tearing up long dusty strips of the thick purple vegetation, exposing the pale slate. The kennels were the last of the courtyard buildings to be spruced up. Roofs and gutterings all around the other sides were clean and repaired. There were no more leaks down on to the young genistars, no more drains overflowing every time it rained. The walls had also benefited from the new chimp team renovating the Guild compound. The mass of gurk-vine had been pruned back to neat fluttering yellow rectangles between doors and windows, allowing the apprentice stone-masons to restore the mortar joints in the walls. An additional benefit of the long-neglected pruning was a bumper crop of fruit this year, with dangling clusters of succulent claret-coloured berries hanging almost to the ground.

Edeard stopped to allow Gonat and Evox herd the ge-horse foals into the stables for the night. 'All brushed down and ready?' he asked the two young apprentices. He cast his farsight over the animals, checking their short, rough fur for smears of dirt.

'Of course they are,' Evox exclaimed indignantly. 'I do know how to instruct a ge-monkey, Edeard.'

Edeard grinned good-naturedly, struck by the way he now sounded like Akeem in the way he presided over the Guild's three new apprentices. He could sense Sancia in a stall over in the default stables, sitting quietly in a chair as her third hand flowed around an egg, subtly sculpting the nature of the embryonic genistar. The youngsters were talented. Impatient, naturally, but eager to learn. Two of the new ge-horses had been sculpted by Evox, who was inordinately proud of the foals.

Taking on the apprentices had been a real turning point for Akeem and Edeard. Evox had joined them barely a week after the fateful Witham caravan last year. Sancia and Gonat had moved into the apprentice dormitory before winter set in; and now two more farmers were already discussing sending children to the Guild, at least for the coming winter months. After a hectic six months of initiation and adjustment, things had settled down in the compound. Edeard even found he had some of that most luxurious commodity: spare time. And that was on top of having the compound's ge-chimp team to start the desperately needed renovation. With the apprentices honing their instructional skills, the chimps had performed some internal restoration, whitewashing walls, cleaning floors and even preserving food in jars and casks. This coming winter season wouldn't be anything like as bleak as those of the past.

'How are the cats?' Gonat asked.

'Just going to inspect them,' Edeard said. So successful had the ge-cats been at extracting water, that the council had commissioned a second well to be dug at the other end of the cliff face behind the village. As well as producing replacements for the existing well, Edeard now had to supervise a whole new nest. In truth they didn't last as long as he'd hoped, barely two years. And they were still inordinately difficult to sculpt. 'Don't forget we have a delivery from Doddit farm in the morning. Make sure there's enough room in the stores.'

'Yes,' Gonat and Evox groaned. They mentally pushed and goaded the frisky foals into their stable before Edeard could heap any more tasks on them. The whole courtyard resonated to the hoots, snarls, bleating, and barks of various genera. With the apprentices now capable of basic sculpting, the Guild had suddenly doubled hatching rates. There were a full twenty defaults in the stables; Akeem had consulted with Wedard on building more. The majority of the animals still went out to the farms, but most houses in the village had cleaned out their disused nests and asked for a ge-chimp or a monkey. The demand for ge-wolves since the Witham caravan had increased dramatically. It was all kind of what Edeard had wanted, but he was still disheartened by the way the older villagers refused to let him give them a simple refresher course in instruction, gruffly informing him they'd been ordering genistars round since before his parents were born. True enough; but if you'd been doing it wrong since then nothing was going to change, and they'd wind up with a lot of badly behaved genistars cavort-ing round Ashwell annoying everyone. So Edeard surreptitiously tried to make sure that the village children had a decent grounding in the ability. The Lady's Mother, Lorellan, helped in her own quiet way by allowing Edeard to sit in on her own instructions to the village youth. Nobody dared protest about that.

Edeard reached the main hall, and sped up the stairs, pleased to be away from the courtyard. One further side effect of their Guild's rising fortune and greater genistar numbers was the stronger smell seeping out from the stables. He'd moved out of the apprentice dormitory the week Evox arrived, taking over a journeyman's room. 'I can't confirm you as a Master yet,' Akeem had said gravely, 'no matter what you did beyond these walls, or how proficient you are. Guild procedures must be followed. To be a Master you must have served at least five years as a journeyman.'

'I understand,' Edeard had replied, secretly laughing at the formality. *Lady help us from the way old people try to keep the world in order . . .*

'And I'll thank you to take the Guild a little more seriously, please,' Akeem had snapped.

Edeard rapidly wound down his amusement. Akeem seemed able to sense any emotion, however well-hidden.

His new room actually had some furniture in it. A decent desk he'd commissioned himself from the Carpentry Guild; a cupboard and a chest of drawers – needed to store his growing new wardrobe. His cot had a soft mattress of goose down. After some gruesome disasters, he'd eventually got the finer points of laundry ritual over to his personal ge-monkey; so once a week he had fresh sheets, scented with lavender from the herb bed in the compound's small kitchen garden – also now properly maintained.

He washed quickly, using the big china jug of water. The Guild compound wasn't yet connected up to the village's rudimentary water-pipe network, but Melzar had promised it would be done by the end of the month. Both he and the smithy were trying to design a domestic stove which would heat water for individual cottages, producing various ungainly contraptions with pipes coiled round them. So far the pipes had all burst or leaked, but they were making progress.

Edeard scraped Akeem's ancient spare razor over his straggly chin hairs, wincing at the little cuts the jagged blade made. A new razor was next on his list of commissions – and a decent mirror. The ge-chimps had left a pile of newly washed clothes from which he chose a loose white cotton shirt, wearing it with his smart drosilk trousers. He'd found several weaver women in the village who would willingly make clothes for him in return for ge-spiders. Akeem called the unregistered trade enterprising, cautioning that it must not interfere with their official commissions. He still had the boots he'd bought in Witham. A little worn now after a year, but they remained comfortable and intact; the only problem was how tight they were becoming. He'd put on nearly two inches of height in the last year, not that he'd bulked out at all. His horror was that he'd wind up looking like Fahin as he put on more height without the corresponding girth.

He opened the top of the small stone barrel in the corner

opposite the fire and removed the leather shoulder bag. It was one place relatively immune from casual farsight. He checked the bag's contents hadn't been discovered by the other apprentices, and slung its strap over his arm.

'Very dapper,' Akeem observed.

Edeard jumped, clutching the bag in an obviously guilty fashion. He hadn't noticed the old Master sitting in the main hall. Everyone had been trying to duplicate the way the bandits had shielded themselves, with varying degrees of success. Edeard wasn't sure how much mental effort Akeem put into the effect. He'd always had the ability to just sit quietly and blend naturally into the background.

'Thank you,' Edeard replied. He self-consciously tugged at the bottom of his shirt.

'Off out, are you?' Akeem asked with sly amusement, he gestured at the long table set for five. He'd made nothing of the bag.

'Er, yes. My tasks are complete. I'll start sculpting the new horses and dogs for Jibit's farm tomorrow. Three of the defaults are ovulating; the males are in their pens.'

'Some things are definitely easier for other species,' Akeem observed, and gave Edeard's clothes another meaningful look. 'So which of our town's fine establishments are you gracing tonight?'

'Um, I can't afford the tavern. It's just me and some of the other apprentices getting together, that's all.'

'How lovely. Are any of your fellow apprentices female by any chance?'

Edeard clamped down hard on his thoughts, but there was nothing he could do about his burning cheeks. 'I guess Zehar will be there. Possibly Calindy.' He shrugged his innocence in such matters.

For once Akeem appeared awkward, though he'd put a strong shield around his own thoughts. 'Lad . . . perhaps sometime we should talk about such things.'

'Things?' Edeard muttered in alarm.

'Girls, Edeard. After all, you are sixteen now. I'm sure you notice them these days. You do know what to ask Doc Seneo for if uh . . . *circumstances* become favourable.'

Edeard's expression was frozen into place as he prayed to the Lady for this horror to end. 'I . . . er, yes. Yes I do. Thank you.' *Go to Doc Seneo and ask for a phial of vinak juice? Oh dear Lady, I'd rather chop it off altogether.*

Akeem sat back in his chair and let his gaze rise to the ceiling. 'Ah, I remember my own youthful amorous adventures back in Makkathran. Oh those city girls in all their finery; the ones of good family would do nothing else all day long but pamper and groom themselves for the parties and balls that were thrown at night. Edeard I so wish you could see them. There isn't one you wouldn't fall in love with at first sight. Of course, they all had the devil in them when you got their bodice off, but what a vision they were.'

'I *have* to go or I'll be late,' Edeard blurted. Someone of Akeem's age shouldn't be allowed to use words like amorous and bodice.

'Of course,' the old Master seemed amused by something. 'I have been selfish keeping you here.'

'I'm not that late.'

'And I don't mean tonight.'

'Uh . . .'

'I'm not up to instructing you any more, Edeard. You have almost outgrown your Master. I think you should go to Makka-thran to study at the Guild in their Blue Tower. My name may still be remembered. At the very least my title demands some prerogatives; I can write you a letter of sponsorship.'

'I . . . No. No, I can't possibly go.'

'Why not?' Akeem asked mildly.

'To Makkathran? Me? It's, no. Anyway, it's . . . it's so far away I don't even know how far. How would I get there?'

'Same way everyone does, my boy, you travel in one of the caravans. This is not impossible or remote, Edeard. You must learn to lift your eyes above the horizon, especially in this province. I would not see you stifled by Ashwell. For that is what surely will happen if you remain. I do not want your talent wasted. There is more to this world, this life, than a single village alone on the edge of the wilderness. Why, just travelling to Makkathran will show you that.'

'I will hardly waste my talent by staying here. The village needs me. Look what has happened already with more genistars.'

'Ah really? This village is already nervous about you, Edeard. You are strong, you are smart. They are neither. Oh, don't get me wrong, this is a pleasant place for someone like me to live out my remaining days. But it is not for you. Ashwell has endured for centuries before you; it will endure for centuries yet. Trust me. A place and people this stubborn and rooted in what they are will not vanish into the black heart of Honious without you. I will write your letter this week. The Barkus caravan is due before the end of the month. I know Barkus of old, he owes me some favours. You can leave with them.'

'This month?' he whispered in astonishment. 'So soon?'

'Yes. There is no benefit in delay. My mind is clear on this matter.'

'The new ge-cats . . .'

'I can manage, Edeard. Please, don't make this any more difficult for me.'

Edeard walked over to the old Master. 'Thank you, sir. This is—' He grinned. 'Beyond imagination.'

'Ha. We'll see how much you thank me in a year's time. The Masters of the Blue Tower are not nearly as lax as I have grown. They will have a fine time beating obedience into you. Your bones will be black and blue before the first day is half-gone.'

'I will endure,' Edeard said. He laid a hand on the man's shoulder, for once allowing the love he felt to shine in his mind. 'I will prove you right to them. Whatever happens I will endure, for you. I will never give them cause to doubt your pupil. And I will make you proud.'

Akeem gripped the hand, squeezing strongly. 'I am already

proud. Now come. You are dallying while your friends carouse. Leave now, and I will have yet another fine meal with our three juvenile dunderwits, listening to their profound talk and answering their challenging questions.'

Edeard laughed. 'I am a bad apprentice deserting my Master thus.'

'Indeed you are. Now go, for the Lady's sake. Let me summon up what is left of my courage else I shall flee to the tavern.'

Edeard turned and walked out of the hall. He almost stopped, wanting to ask what Akeem had meant by *they are already nervous about you*. He would enquire tomorrow.

'Edeard,' Akeem called.

'Yes, Master?'

'A word of caution. Stay silent that you are leaving, even to your friends. Envy is not a pretty blossom, and it has a custom of breeding resentment.'

'Yes, Master.'

The sun had dropped to the top of the rampart wall by the time Edeard hurried up a lane off the main street, heading for the granite cliff at the back of the village. Already the glowing colours of the night sky were emerging through the day's blue like trees out of morning mist. Old Buluku was directly overhead. The vulpine serpent manifesting as a violet stream that slithered through the heavens in a fashion which none of Querencia's few astronomers could ever fathom. It certainly didn't shift with the seasons, nor even orbit round the sun. As Edeard watched, a sliver of electric-blue light rippled lazily along its length, a journey which would take several minutes, too weak to cast a shadow across the dry mud of the lane. Odin's Sea was already drifting towards the northern horizon. A roughly oval patch of glowing blue and green mist that visited the summer nights. The Lady's teachings were that it formed the Heart of the Void, where the souls of men and women were carried by the Skylords so they could dream away the rest of existence in quiet bliss. It was only the good and the worthy who were blessed with such a voyage, and the Skylords hadn't been seen in Querencia's skies for so long they were nothing but legend and a faith kept by the Lady's followers. Protruding from the ragged edges of Odin's Sea were the reefs, scarlet promontories upon which Skylords carrying the souls of those less worthy were wrecked and began their long fall into Honious and oblivion.

Edeard often wondered if so many unworthy humans had been carried aloft by the Skylords that there were simply no more of the great creatures left. It would be so typical that humans should bring such casual destruction to this universe. Thankfully, the Lady's teachings said that it was humans who had declined in spirit; that was why the Empyrean Lady had been anointed by the Firstlifes to guide humans back to the path which would once again lead them to the Heart of the Void. It was a sad fact that not many people listened to the Lady's kind words these days.

'Calling to the Skylords?' a voice asked.

Edeard smiled and turned. His farsight had kept watch on her since she stepped out of the church ten minutes ago. One of the reasons he'd chosen this particular route. Salrana emerged from the shadows of the market place. Behind the deserted stalls, the church curved up above the rest of the village buildings with quiet purpose. Its crystal roof glimmered in refraction from the altar lanterns.

'They didn't answer,' he said. 'They never do.'

'One day they will. Besides you're not quite ready to sail into the Heart yet.'

'No. I'm not.' Edeard couldn't quite match her humour. He might as well have been travelling into the Heart given the distance to Makkathran. *How will she cope with me leaving?*

He wasn't the only one growing up this summer. Salrana had also put on several inches over the last couple of years; her shoulders were broad as if she was growing into a typical sturdy farmer's girl, but whereas her contemporaries were thickening out ready for their century of toil on the land she remained slim and agile. Her plain blue and white novice robe had grown quite tight, which always made Edeard glance at her in a wholly inappropriate fashion. Not that there was any helping it, she was losing her puppy fat to reveal the sharpest cheekbones he'd ever seen. Everyone could see how beautiful she was going to be. Thankfully, she still suffered from spots and her auburn hair remained wild and girlish, otherwise being in her presence would be intolerable. As it was, he viewed her friendship with delight and dismay in equal measure. She was far too young to be wanting to bed, though he couldn't help wondering how long it would be before she was old enough. Such thoughts made him fearful that the Lady would strike him down with some giant lightning bolt roaring out from Honious itself. Though of course Her priestesses did marry.

Irrelevant now. Even if I do come back, it won't be for years. She'll be with some village oaf and have three children.

'You're in a funny mood,' Salrana said, all innocent and curious. 'Is everything all right?'

'Yeah. Actually it is. I've had some good news. Great news.' He held up a hand. 'And I will tell you later, I promise.'

'Gosh, a secret and in Ashwell. Bet I find out by noon tomorrow.'

'Bet you don't.'

'Bet me what?'

'No. I'm being unfair. It's a private thing.'

'Now you're just being cruel. I'll pray to the Lady for your redemption.'

'That's very kind.'

She stood right up close to him, still smiling sweetly. 'So are you off up to the caves?'

'Er, yeah, one or two of the others said they might go in. I thought I'd see.'

'So when do I get asked?'

'I don't think Mother Lorellan would want you in the caves at night.'

'Pha. There's a lot of things the good Mother doesn't know I do.' She shook her hair defiantly, squaring her shoulders. The aggressive pose lasted a couple of seconds before she started giggling.

'Well I'll pray she doesn't find out,' he told her.

'Thank you, Edeard.' Her hand rubbed playfully along his arm. 'Who'd have thought it just a few years ago. Both of us happy. And you: one of the lads now.'

'I was in a fight before they accepted me.' *I killed people.* Even now he could still see the face of the bandit before the man smashed into the tree, the astonishment and fear.

'Of course you were, that's a typical boy thing. That's why you're going into the caves again tonight. We all have to find a way to live here, Edeard. We're going to be in Ashwell for a long long time.'

He couldn't answer, just gave her a fixed smile.

'And watch out for that Zehar. She's already bragging how she intends to have you. She was very descriptive. For a baker's apprentice.'

'She. Is? She wants . . . ?'

Salrana's face was devilsome. 'Oh yes.' She blew him a kiss, giggling. 'Let me know the details. I'm dying to know if you can really do such wicked things.' Then her back was to him, her skirt held high by both hands, and she went racing off down the slope, giggling all the way.

Edeard let out a long breath. His emotions were as unsteady as his legs. If there was ever a reason to stay in Ashwell, he was looking at it. His farsight followed her long after she'd turned a corner on to main street, making sure she was safe as she ran along on her errand.

There were a number of caves burrowing into the cliffs behind Ashwell. A lot of them had been expanded over the decades, modified into storerooms for the long winter months, where the temperature and moisture hardly varied at all. Several of the larger were used as barns. Edeard wasn't interested in those. Instead, he headed for a small oddly angled fissure in the rock on the western end of the cliff, only thirty yards from where the encircling wall began. He had to scramble up a pile of smoothed boulders to reach it, then grip the upper lip and swing himself into the darkness. Anyone larger than him would have real trouble passing through the gap; he'd only be able to use it for another year or so himself. Once inside, the passage opened up, and the soft background babble of the village's longtalk cut off abruptly. His immediate world contracted to a dank gloomy blackness; even his farsight ability couldn't perceive through such a depth of rock. All he could sense was the open cavity around him. Only after he'd gone round a curve did he see a glint of yellow light ahead.

Seven apprentices were gathered in the narrow cave with its high crevice apex, sitting round a couple of battered old lamps whose wicks were chuffing out a lot of smoke. Their talk stopped as he entered, then their smiles bloomed in welcome. It was a gratifying sensation of belonging. Even Obron raised a cheery hand. Fahin beckoned him over. Edeard was very conscious of Zehar watching him with a near-feline intent, and gave her a nervous grin. Her answering smile was carnivorous.

'Didn't think you were coming,' Fahin said.

'I got delayed slightly,' Edeard explained. He opened his bag and pulled out the large wine bottle, which earned him some appreciative whistles as he held it up.

Fahin leaned in closer. 'Thought you were running scared of Zehar,' he murmured in a knowing whisper.

'Sweet Lady, has she told everyone but me?'

'I overheard it from Marilee. She was trying to get Kelina to take some vinak juice from Seneo's pharmacology store. I assumed you were party to it.'

'No,' Edeard growled.

'Okay. Well should the need arise, and I do mean *rise*, just ask me. I can get you a phial without anyone being any the wiser, especially Seneo.'

'I shall remember it well, thank you.'

Fahin nodded, as if unconcerned. An attitude confirmed by his passive surface thoughts. He unbuckled his ancient physick satchel and took out some dried kestric leaves. The pair of them became the centre of some not very subtle attention from the other apprentices in the cave.

Edeard shifted position and opened the wine. It was dark red, which Akeem always claimed was a sign of quality. Edeard was never certain. All the wine available in Ashwell had a strong taste which lingered well into the next day. He supposed he'd get used to it eventually, but as for actually liking it . . . 'Fahin, where do you see yourself in fifty years?'

The doctor's tall apprentice glanced up from the little slate pestle he was preparing. 'You're very serious tonight, my friend. Mind you, she does have that effect on people.'

For an instant Edeard thought he was talking about Salrana, then Fahin's eyes glanced over at Zehar, a movement amplified by his over-size lenses.

'No,' Edeard said irritably. 'Seriously, come on: fifty years' time. What are you working towards?'

'Why I'll be doctor, of course. Seneo is actually a lot older than most people realize. And she says I am her most promising apprentice in decades.' He began grinding the kestric leaves with smooth easy motions of the mortar.

'That's it? Village doctor?'

'Yes.' Fahin wasn't looking at Edeard any more, his thoughts took on an edge. 'I'm not like you, Edeard; Honious take me, I'm not even like Obron. I'm sure you're going to build our Eggshaper Guild to greatness over the next century. You'll probably be Mayor inside thirty years. Ashwell's name will spread, people will come, and this land will flourish once again. We all hope that from you. So, given the circumstances, village doctor and your friend in such times is no small goal after all.'

'You truly think I will do that?'

'You *can* do it.' Fahin mashed up the last flakes of leaf into a thin powder. 'Either that or you'll lead a barbarian army to sack

Makkathran and overthrow the old order. You have the strength to do either. I saw it. We all did. That sort of strength attracts people.'

'Don't say that,' Edeard said. 'Not even in jest.'

'Who's jesting?' Fahin poured the kestric powder into a small white clay pipe, adding some tobacco.

Edeard stared at his friend in some alarm. *Is this what people think? Is this why I make them nervous?*

'You know the gate guards say they still farsight your fastfoxes at night sometimes,' Fahin said. 'Do you keep them out there?'

'What? No! I sent it away when we got back; you were with me, you saw me do it. And how would the guards know that, the old fools. They're asleep most of the night anyway, and they can't tell one animal from another at any distance.'

'These fastfoxes have collars.'

'They're not mine!' he insisted. 'Wait, there's more than one? You know I only mastered one. When did they see them?' he asked in curiosity.

Fahin struck a match and sucked hard on his pipe stem, pulling the flame down into the bowl. 'I'm not sure,' he puffed out some smoke. 'A couple of months now.'

'Why did nobody tell me? I could find out if they are real.'

'Why indeed?' The match went out, and Fahin took a deep drag. Almost immediately, his eyes lost focus.

Edeard stared at his friend with growing dismay. They all gathered up here for a drink and a smoke and talk, just as apprentices had done since Ashwell was founded. But lately Fahin was smoking on a near-nightly basis. It was a habit which had grown steadily ever since they got back from the Witham caravan.

'Sweet Lady,' Edeard muttered as the other apprentices came over. *Maybe leaving this place is the right thing to do.* Fahin passed the pipe up to Genril. A smiling Zehar held out a hand for Edeard's wine. He deliberately took a huge swig before handing it over.

*

The first thing Edeard did when he woke up was retch horribly. When he tried to turn over he banged his temple hard on cold floorboards. It took a moment to realize, but he wasn't lying on his nice soft mattress. For some reason he was sprawled on the floor beside the cot, still fully dressed apart from one boot. And he stank!

He groaned again and felt the acid rising in his throat. Gave up all attempts at control and threw up spectacularly. As he did so the fear hit, squeezing cold sweat from every pore. He was shaking as he wiped pitifully at the fluid dribbling from his lips, nearly weeping with the misery. Hangovers he could take, even those from red wine, but this was more than just the payback for overindulgence. He'd felt like this before. The forest. The bandit ambush.

His body was reacting to the alcohol and a couple of puffs on the pipe. While his mind was yelling at some deep instinctive level of the mortal danger closing in out of the surrounding darkness. He forced himself to sit up. A thin pastel light from the night sky washed round the shutters revealing his small room. Nothing was amiss, apart from himself. He whimpered from the sheer intensity of fright pouring through him, expecting something terrible to envelop him at any second. The hangover made his head throb painfully. It was hard to concentrate, but he slowly managed to summon up some farsight and scan round.

The three apprentices were asleep in their dormitory. He forced the ability further, almost crying out from the pain sparking behind his eyes. Akeem, too, was asleep on his bed. Out in the courtyard, the young genistars dozed the night away, shuffling and shaking as was their style. A couple of cats trod delicately along the roofs as they tracked small rodents. By the gate, the ge-wolf in its traditional stone guardkennel lay curled up on its legs, big head swaying slowly as it obediently kept watch on the road outside.

Edeard groaned with the effort of searching so far, and let his farsight wither to nothing. He was still shaking and cold. The front of his shirt was disgustingly sticky, and the smell was getting worse. Nausea threatened to return. He struggled out of the shirt and lurched over to the nightstand where there was a glass of water and took several large gulps. In the drawer at the bottom of the little stand was a pouch of dried jewn petals soaked in an oil which Fahin had prepared. He opened it, closed his eyes and shoved one of the petals into his mouth. It tasted foul, but he took one final gulp from the glass, forcing it down.

In all his sixteen years he had never felt so wretched. And still the fear wouldn't abate. Tears threatened to clog his eyes as he shivered again, hugging his chest.

What is wrong with me?

He wobbled over to the window and pushed the shutters open. Cool night air flowed in. Odin's Sea had nearly fallen below the horizon, which meant it was no more than a couple of hours past midnight. The low thatched roofs of the village were spread out around him, pale in the wan flickering light of the nebulas. Nothing moved. But for whatever reason the sight of such serenity simply made the fear even worse. For an instant he heard screams, saw flames. His stomach churned and he bent over the window sill.

Lady, why do you do this to me?

When he straightened up he instinctively looked at the village gate with its twin watchtowers. There was no sign of the guards. But then they were nearly half a mile away and it was night. Edeard gathered his breath and gripped the side of the windows in grim determination. His farsight surged out. *If they're all right I'm going straight back to bed.*

The towers were built from smooth-faced stone; recent decades had seen them strengthened inside with thick timber bracing. Even so, there were no holes in the walls, just some alarmingly long cracks zigzagging up and down. Their parapets were large enough to hold ten guards who could fire a number of heavy weapons down on anyone foolish enough to storm the gate. Tonight the eastern tower was empty. A solitary man stood on the western parapet underneath the alarm bell. He was facing inwards, looking across the village. Three bodies lay on the flagstones at his feet.

Edeard lurched in shock, and tried to refocus his farsight. It swept in and out before centring back on the parapet. The lone man's thoughts shone with a hue of satisfaction; Edeard felt a filthy mental smile. 'Greetings,' the man longtalked.

Edeard's throat contracted, snagging his breath. 'Who are you?'

Mental laughter mocked him. 'We know who you are. We know all about you, tough boy. We know what you did to our friends. Because of that you're mine tonight. And I promise you won't die quickly.'

Edeard yelped in horror and dived away from the window. Even so he could still feel the tenuous touch of the other's farsight upon him. He put as much strength as he had behind his longtalk, and cried: 'Akeem! Akeem, wake up. The bandits are here. They're in the village.'

His mental shout was like some kind of signal. The soft glow of minds materialized in the alleyways and lanes that wound through the cottages and Guild compounds. Edeard screamed. They were everywhere!

So many! Every bandit in the wilderness must be here tonight.

'What in the Lady's name,' Akeem's fuzzy thoughts came questioning.

'Bandits,' Edeard called again, with voice and mind. 'Hundreds of them. They're already here.' He jabbed every ge-wolf in the compound with a mental goad, triggering their attack state. Loud, dangerous snarling rose from the courtyard.

Five bandits appeared in the street outside the Guild, strong and confident, making no further attempt at cover. They didn't have the muddy skin and wild hair of the ones in the forest; these wore simple dark tunics and sturdy boots. There were no bows and arrows, either. Strangely they wore two belts apiece, looped round their shoulders so they crossed over their chest. Little metal boxes were clipped on to the leather, along with a variety of knives. Whispers spilled out of the aether as they longtalked.

Then Edeard sensed the fastfoxes walking beside them; each had two of the tamed and trained beasts.

'Oh sweet Lady, no,' he gasped. His mind registered Akeem longtalking the other elders, fast and precise thoughts raising the alarm.

It was too late. Flames appeared among Ashwell's rooftops. Torches thick with oil-fire spun through the air, guided by telekinesis to land full square on thatch roofs. The fire spread quickly, encouraged by the dry months of a good summer. A dreadful orange glow began to cover the village.

The ge-wolves were racing across the Guild courtyard. Edeard extended his third hand with furious intent and slammed the gates open for them. That was when he heard the noise for the first time. An awful thunderous roar as if a hundred pistols were all firing at once. White light flashed across his open window, and his mind felt the dirty glee of the bandits' thoughts coming from the street below. Ge-wolves fell in torment, their minds radiating terrible flares of pain as their flesh was shredded. Some of them managed to survive the strange weapons to collide with fastfoxes. The metallic roaring abated as the animals fought, tearing at each other as they writhed and spun and jumped.

That was when Edeard heard a woman scream. There was too much turmoil, too much anguish storming across Ashwell, for his farsight to track her down, but he knew what the sound meant. What it would mean for every woman in the village caught alive. And girl.

He sent a single piercing thought at the church. 'Salrana!'

'Edeard,' her panicked longtalk barked back. 'They're here, they're in the church.'

His mind found her instantly, farsight zooming in as if he was illuminating her with a powerful beam of light. She was cowering in her room in the Mother's house which formed the back of the church. Inside the dome itself, three bandits were advancing along the empty aisles, radiating triumph and contempt as their fastfoxes stalked along beside them. Mother Lorellan was already out of bed and heading for the church to deal with the desecrators. For a devout woman her mind shone with inordinately strong aggression.

The bandits and their fastfoxes would cut her to ribbons, Edeard knew. 'Get out,' he told Salrana. 'Move now. Out of the window and into the garden. Stay ahead of them, keep moving. Head for the market, it's cobbled, there's no fire there. I'll meet you at the corn measure station.'

'Oh Edeard!'

'Do it. Do it now.'

He raced over to the window. It wasn't such a big jump to the street, and the carnage the fastfoxes were wreaking on the surviving ge-wolves was almost over. Whatever victors were left he could take care of them. Flames were racing across the thatch of the terraced cottages opposite. Doors were flung open, and men charged out, shields firm round their bodies, knives held high. The bandits raised their weapons, and the noise began again. Edeard watched numbly as the squat guns spat a blue-purple flame. Somehow they were firing dozens of bullets, reloading themselves impossibly fast. The villagers shook and flailed in agony as the bullets overwhelmed their shields.

'Bastards,' Edeard yelled, and jumped.

'No! Don't.' Akeem's longtalk was strong enough to make half the village pause. Even the guns were temporarily stilled.

Edeard landed, his bare heel shooting pain up his leg. He turned towards the nearest bandit, crouching as if he was about to go for a wrestling hold. Somehow he sensed both Akeem and the bandit in the guardtower both holding their breath. The bandit in front of him lifted the dark gun, snarling with delight. Edeard reached out with his third hand, closing it round the gun. He wasn't sure if even his shield could withstand quite so many bullets striking at him, but like every gun, you first had to pull the trigger. The bandit's eyes widened in surprise as his own shielding was unable to ward off Edeard's power. Then the street was subject to an unnerved screech as the bandit's fingers were snapped in quick succession. Edeard rotated the gun in front of the bandit's numb gaze until the man was staring right into the muzzle, then pulled back hard on the trigger. The discharge was awesome, even though it lasted barely a second before something snarled inside the gun's mechanism. It blew the bandit's head apart. Tatters of gore lashed down on the muddy street.

Three other bandits raised their guns. Edeard exerted himself, gripping their flesh tight with his third hand, preventing the slightest movement. 'Get them,' he told the surviving villagers stumbling out of the blazing cottages.

'Oh, your death will be exquisite,' the bandit in the watch-tower sent.

A gun roared behind Edeard. He turned, flinching, to see the fifth bandit falling on his own weapon, borne down by a swarm of ge-chimps which Akeem had instructed.

'I did say "don't",' Akeem's longtalk chided.

'Thank you,' Edeard replied. The villagers were dispatching the bandits with a ferocity that he found disturbing. Edeard let go of the bloody corpses. Then everyone was turning to him, awaiting guidance.

'Get into the Guild compound,' he told them, aware of how it became an eerie echo of Melzar's instructions back in the forest. 'Group together. That will give your shields real strength.'

'You, too, lad,' Akeem said as Edeard picked up one of the bandit's guns. It was a lot heavier than he was expecting. A sweep with his farsight revealed an internal mechanism that was inordinately complicated. He didn't understand anything about it other than the trigger. There didn't seem to be many bullets left in the metal box in front of the stock. 'I have to help Salrana.'

'No. All's lost here. Get out. Live, Edeard, please. Just survive tonight. Don't let them win.'

Edeard started running up the street, wincing every time his boot-less foot touched the ground. 'They won't destroy this village.'

'They already have, lad. Take cover. Get out.'

He sent his farsight flowing out ahead, alert for any bandits. Saw a fastfox loping along an alley. When it emerged Edeard was almost level with it; he pushed his third hand into the creature's skull and ripped its brain apart. It fell in the evil wavering light of burning thatch. The street was a gulley of leaping flame, as bright as any dawn. Screams, shouts and gunfire split the harsh, constant flame-growl.

'You are good, aren't you?' the watchtower bandit taunted.

Edeard pushed his farsight into the tower, but the man was no longer there. A quick scan of the surrounding area revealed nothing except the broken main gates and dead village guards. 'Where did he go?' Edeard asked fretfully. 'Akeem, help, I can't sense half of them.' He actually heard a gun mechanism snick smoothly, and hardened his shield. The blast of bullets came from a cottage he'd just passed. He got lucky, he decided afterwards, not all of the bullets hit him, the bandit's aim was off. That and his mind picked up a quiet longtalked, 'No, not him.' Even so, the force of the shots which did hit was enough to send him sprawling backwards, half dazed. He instinctively lashed out with his third hand to the source of the shots. A bandit went staggering across the road, shaking his head. Edeard reached up to the furnace of thatch above, and tugged hard. Dense waves of flame peeled off the disintegrating roof and splashed down over the bandit, driving him to his knees. His screams were thankfully muffled.

'Are you all right?' Akeem asked.

Edeard groaned as he rolled back to his feet, There were flames everywhere, their ferocity sending huge sparking balls of thatch high into the sky. Windows and doors were belching out twisting orange streamers. The heat was intense on his bare torso, he was sure he could feel his skin starting to crack and blister. 'I'm here,' he replied. 'But I can't sense them, I don't know where they are.' And he knew the watchtower bandit was coming, slipping stealthily through the swirling flames and sagging walls.

'Try this,' Akeem said. His longtalk voice became stretched as if rising to birdsong. It seemed to fill Edeard's skull. A knowledge gift, thoughts and sometimes memories that explained how to perform a specific mental task. Edeard had absorbed hundreds of basic explanations on the art of sculpting but this was far more complex. As the song ended he began to shape his farsight and third hand together into a symbiotic force that wove a darkness through the air around him. It was like standing in the middle of a thick patch of fog.

'Now please,' Akeem pleaded. 'Get out. Do not waste your life, Edeard, don't make some futile gesture. Please. Remember: the Blue Tower in Makkathran. Go there. Be someone.'

'I can't leave you!' he cried into the terrible night.

'The village is already lost. Now go. Go, Edeard. Don't let everything be wasted.'

Edeard wanted to shout out that his Master was wrong, that his valiant apprentice friends and strong Masters like Melzar and Wedard were leading the fight back. But looking at the fiery devastation around him he knew it wasn't true. The screams were still filling the air, along with the snarl of fastfoxes and the deadly clamour of guns. Resistance was contracting to a few Guild compounds and halls. The rest of the village was burning to ruin. There was nothing to be saved. Except Salrana.

Edeard forced himself to his feet and started running towards the market again. Once, a bandit hurried past him along the street, not five yards away. The man never knew how close they were. Edeard could so easily have killed him, extracted some vengeance. But that would have shown the watchtower bandit where he was, and even through his anger and desperation Edeard knew he had neither the skill nor strength to win that confrontation.

He sped past three more bandits before charging into the marketplace. The square was surrounded by a wall of flame, but it was cooler amid the stalls. Two bandits were holding down a woman, laughing while the third of their band raped her. Their fastfoxes prowled round the little group, keeping guard.

Edeard just couldn't ignore it. He even recognized the woman though he didn't know her name; she worked at the tannery, helping prepare the hides.

The first the bandits knew of anything amiss was when their fastfoxes suddenly stopped circling. All six beasts swung their heads round, huge jaws opening to ready fangs the size of human fingers.

'What—' one of the bandits managed to say. He brought his gun up, but it was too late. The fastfoxes leapt. More screams echoed out around the stalls.

'Ah, there you are,' a longtalk voice gloated. 'I was worried you'd run away from me.'

Edeard snarled into the smoke-wreathed sky. Try as he might, he couldn't track where the longtalk was originating.

'Now what are you doing there, apart from slaughtering my comrades? Oh yes, I see.'

Edeard was aware of Salrana hunched up behind the counter in the corn measure stall, glancing upwards with a puzzled expression. He started to sprint towards her.

'He's in the marketplace,' the bandit announced across the whole village. 'Close in.'

Edeard sensed bandits turning to head towards him.

'Oh she is lovely. The very young one from the church, isn't it? Yes, I recognize her. Well congratulations, my tough little friend. Good choice. She's certainly worth risking everything for.'

Edeard reached the corn measure stall, and dropped his concealment. Salrana gasped in astonishment as he appeared in front of her.

'Got you.'

Edeard was only too well aware of the urgent satisfaction in the bandit's longtalk. There was the tiniest flashover of pounding feet, leg muscles straining with effort *to get there, to capture the feared boy.*

'Right at the end I'm going to cut your eyelids off so you have no choice but to watch while I fuck her,' the bandit said, twining his longtalk with a burst of dark pleasure. 'It'll be the last thing you see before you die. But you'll go straight to Honious knowing this; I'll keep her for my own. She's coming with me, tough boy. And I'll put her to work every single night. Your girl is going to spend the next decade bearing my children.'

'Get up,' Edeard yelled, and tugged at Salrana's arm. She was

247

crying, her limbs limp and unresponsive. 'Don't let him get me,' she wept. 'Please, Edeard. Kill me. I couldn't stand that. I couldn't, I'd rather spend eternity in Honious.'

'Never,' he said; his arms went round her and he enfolded her within his concealment.

'Get the fastfoxes in the market,' the bandit ordered. 'Track him. Find his scent.'

'Come on,' Edeard whispered. He started for the main entrance, then stopped. Over ten bandits with their fastfoxes were heading up the street towards him. They ignored the frantic chickens and gibbering ge-chimps that were running away from the swirl of lethal flames consuming the buildings. 'Lady!' He searched round, not daring to use his farsight in case the diabolical bandit could detect that.

'I don't care if the fire's making it hard to track. Find him!'

The bandit's tone was angry, which was the first piece of good news Edeard had encountered all night. Now he glanced round, he saw just how awesome the fire had become. Every building was alight. A foul smoke tower billowed hundreds of feet over the village, blocking the constellations and nebulas. Below its dismal occlusion, walls were collapsing, sending avalanches of burning furniture and broken joists across the lanes. Even the bandits were becoming wary as the smaller alleys were blocked. Of course, the blazing destruction was also closing off Edeard's escape routes. What he needed was a distraction, and fast. His third hand shoved a pile of beer barrels, sending them toppling over. Several burst open. A wave of beer lapped across the cobbles, spreading wide. As the same time he grabbed the minds of as many genistars he could reach, and pulled them into the market, offering them sanctuary. The animals bounded over the stalls, stampeding down the narrow aisles. Flustered fastfoxes charged after them, shaking off their mental restraints to obey more basic hunter instincts.

'Almost clever,' the bandit announced. 'You think that'll cover your smell? Well why don't you avoid this, tough guy?'

The bandits in the market square formed a loose line, and

began firing, sweeping their blazing gun muzzles in wide arcs. Genistars howled and whimpered as the bullets chewed through their flesh. They jumped and sprinted for cover as lines of bullets swept after them. Fastfoxes snarled in hatred and distress as they too were hit. Dozens of animals tumbled lifeless on to the cobbles. Blood mingled with beer, washing down the slope.

Edeard and Salrana hunched down as bullets thudded into the stalls around them. Wood splinters whirled through the air. They started to crawl. It wasn't long before the guns stopped. Edeard waited for the next longtalk taunt, but it didn't come. 'Hurry,' he urged her. Holding hands, they ran for the alley which led round the back of the Carpentry Guild compound. Bandits and their fastfoxes were on patrol around the walls. The inside of the compound burned like a brazier as fire consumed the woodworking halls and timber stores, sending vast plumes of flame into the smoke-clotted sky. The slate roof of the main building had already collapsed. Edeard wondered if anyone was still alive inside, maybe sheltering in the cellars. Surely Obron would have found a way. He couldn't imagine a world without Obron.

They came to a crossroads, and Salrana made to turn right.

'Not that way,' he hissed.

'But that's down to the wall,' she whispered back.

'They'll be expecting that. The fastfoxes will scent us if we try to climb over the ramparts.'

'Where are we going then?'

'Up towards the cliff.'

'But . . . won't they search the caves?'

'We're not sheltering in the caves,' he assured her. He found a dozen genistars still alive nearby, mainly dogs, with a couple of chimps and even a foal; and ordered them to walk across and around the track they were leaving to lay false scents. Though he suspected not even fastfoxes would be able to track them with so much smoke and ash in the air.

It took a couple of minutes to reach the site where the new well was being dug. So far Wedard and his team had only excavated five yards down, with barely the top third lined in stone. 'In you go,' Edeard told her. There was a small ladder leading down to the wooden framework at the bottom of the hole where ge-monkeys spent their days digging into the stone and clay.

'They'll look in here,' Salrana said desperately.

'Only if it's open,' Edeard said grimly, and gestured at the big stone cap which would seal the shaft once it was complete.

'You can move that?' she asked incredulously.

'We'll find out in a minute. But I'm pretty sure no one can farsight through it.'

Salrana started down the crude ladder, her mind seething with fright. Edeard followed her, stopping when his head was level with the rim. This was the biggest gamble, the one on which both their lives now depended, but he couldn't think of any way out of the village, not past the fastfoxes and alert bandits. He fired a longtalk query directly at the Eggshaper Guild compound. 'Akeem?' he asked quietly. There was no reply. He still didn't dare use his farsight. With a last furious look at the raging firestorm which was his home, he reached out with his third hand and lifted the huge slab of stone. It skimmed silently through the air, keeping a couple of inches off the ground before settling on the top of the well shaft with a slow grinding sound. The orange glow of the flames, the sound of collapsing masonry and human anguish cut off abruptly.

Edeard waited for hours. He and Salrana clung to each other on the planking at the bottom of the pit, drawing what comfort they could from each other. Eventually, she fell into a troubled sleep, twitching and moaning. He wouldn't allow himself the luxury.

Is this all my fault? Were they seeking revenge for the ambush in the forest? But they started it. His worst guilt came from a single thought which nagged and nagged at his soul. *Could I have done more?* Now he was sober and the worst of the hangover had abated, he kept thinking about the sensation which had woken him so abruptly. It *was* the same as the alarm he'd felt in the forest, a foresight that something was wrong. Normally the senior priestesses of the Empyrean Lady claimed to have a modest timesense; granted of course by the Lady Herself. So such a thing was possible. *If I hadn't been so stupid. If I hadn't wasted the warning . . .*

He didn't want to open the stone cap. The scene which he knew would greet them was almost too much to contemplate. *My fault. All my fault.*

A few hours after they took refuge, some slices of pale light seeped in round the edge of the cap where the stone rim wasn't quite level. Still Edeard waited. The rise of the sun wasn't going to automatically make the bandits go away. There was nothing left for them to fear for tens of miles. It would be the villages now who would wait for the fall of each night with dread.

'We never suspected they were so well organized,' Edeard said bitterly. 'Me of all people, I should have realized.'

'Don't be silly,' she said. In the dark she reached out for him again, her slim arm going round his waist. 'How could you have known? This is something beyond even the Mother to see.'

'Did Mother Lorellan have a timesense?'

'Not much of one, no. Yesterday evening she was concerned about something, but she couldn't define it.'

'She couldn't see her own murder? What kind of timesense is that?'

Salrana started sobbing again.

'Oh, Lady, I'm so sorry,' he said, and hugged her tight. 'I didn't think. I'm so stupid.'

'No Edeard. You came to help me. Me, out of everybody in Ashwell; all your friends, your Master. Why? Why me?'

'I . . . All those years, it was like just me and you against the world. You were the only friend I had. I don't think I would have made it without you. The number of times I thought about running off into the wild.'

She shook her head in dismay. 'Then you'd have been a bandit, you would have been one of the invaders last night.'

'Don't say that. Not ever. I hate them. First my parents, now . . .' He couldn't help it, he hung his head and started weeping. 'Everything. Everything's gone. I couldn't help them. Everybody was scared of how strong I am, and when they really needed me I was useless.'

'Not useless,' she said. 'You helped me.'

They spent a long time just pressed together. Edeard's tears dried up after a while. He wiped at his face, feeling stupid and miserable. Salrana's hands came up to cup his face. 'Would you like me?' she whispered.

'Er . . . I. No.' It was a very difficult thing to say.

'No?' Her thoughts, already fragile, fountained a wave of bewildered hurt. 'I thought—'

'Not now,' he said, and gripped her hands. He knew what it was, the shattering grief, the loneliness and fright; all so evident in her thoughts. She needed comfort, and physical intimacy was the strongest comfort of all. Given his own shaky emotional state it would have been heartening for him, too. But he cared too much, and it would have felt too much like taking advantage. 'I really would, but you're young. Too young.'

'Linem had a child last year, she wasn't quite as old as I am today.'

He couldn't help but grin. 'What kind of example is that for a novice to set to her flock?'

'Flock of one.'

Edeard's humour faded. 'Yes: one.'

Salrana looked up at the stone cap. 'Do you think any of them are left?'

'Some, yes. Of course. Ashwell village is stubborn and resilient, that's what Akeem always said. That's how it's resisted change so effectively for the last few centuries.'

'You really wanted to?'

'I—' He found it disconcerting the way she could jump between topics so lightly, especially when *that* was one of the subjects in question. 'Yes,' he admitted cautiously. 'You must know how beautiful you're becoming.'

'Liar! I have to visit Doc Seneo three times a week to get ointment for my face.'

'You are growing up lovely,' he insisted quietly.

'Thank you, Edeard. You're really sweet, you know. I've never thought of any other boy. It's always been you.'

'Um. Right.'

'It would be terrible to die a virgin, wouldn't it?'

'Lady! You are the worst novice in the whole Void.'

'Don't be so silly. The Lady must have enjoyed a good love life. She was Rah's wife. Half of Makkathran claim to be descended from them. That's a lot of children.'

'This has to be blasphemy.'

'No. It's being human. That's why the Lady was anointed by the Firstlifes, to remind us how to discover our true nature again.'

'Well right now we need to think survival.'

'I know. So how old do I have to be? Your age?'

'Um, probably, yes. Yes, that's about right.'

'Can't wait. Did you go with Zehar last night?'

'Not— Hey, that is not your concern.' For some stupid reason, he suddenly wished he had given in to Zehar's advances. *She'll be dead now; quickly if she was lucky.*

'You're going to be my husband. I'm entitled to know all about your old lovers.'

'I'm not your husband.'

'Not yet,' she taunted. 'My timesense says you will be.'

He threw up his hands in defeat.

'How long are we going to stay in here?' she asked.

'I'm not sure. Even if there's nothing left to scare them off, they won't want to stay too long. The other villages will know what's happened by now. The smoke must have reached halfway to Odin's Sea, and the farms would have fled, longshouting all the way. I expect the province will raise the militia and give chase.'

'A militia? Can they do that?'

'Each province has the right to form a militia in times of crisis,' he said, trying to remember the details Akeem had imparted about Querencia's constitutional law. 'And this definitely qualifies. As to the practical details, I expect the bandits will be long gone before any decent force can get here, never mind chase them into the wilderness. And those guns they had.' He held up his trophy, frowning at the outlandish design. No doubting its power, though. 'I've never heard of anything like these before. It's like something humans owned from before the flight into the Void.'

'So that's it? There's no justice.'

'There will be, as long as I remain alive they will curse their boldness of this day. It is their own death they have brought to our village.'

She clutched at him. 'Don't go after them. Please, Edeard. They live out there, it's their wilderness, they know this kind of life, the killing and brutality, they know nothing else. I couldn't stand it if they caught you.'

'I had no notion to do it right away.'

'Thank you.'

'Okay, I think it's the afternoon now. Let's take a look.'

'All right. But if they're still there and they see us . . . I can't be his whore, Edeard.'

'Neither of us will be caught,' he promised, and meant it. For emphasis he patted his gun. 'Now let's see what's out there.' He started to apply his third hand to the cool stone. Lips touched his. His mouth opened in response and the kiss went on for a long time.

'Just in case,' Salrana murmured, pressed up against him. 'I wanted us both to know what it was like.'

'I . . . I'm glad,' he said sheepishly.

This time it was a lot harder to move the huge stone slab. It was only after he started he realized how exhausted he was, and hungry, and scared. But he shifted the stone a couple of inches until a slim crescent of mundane grey sky was visible. There were no excited shouts or farsight probes down into the pit. He couldn't send his own farsight across much distance given the tiny gap and the fact he was still below ground. Instead, his mind called out to the Guild's sole ge-eagle. His relief when the majestic bird replied was profound. It was perched up on the cliffs, distressed and bewildered. What it showed him when it took flight swiftly brought his mood back down again.

There was nothing left. Nothing. Every cottage was a pile of smouldering rubble; the Guild compounds with their sturdy stone walls had collapsed. He could barely make out the street pattern. A thin layer of grubby smog drifted slowly over the ruins.

When the eagle swooped in lower, he could see the bodies. Charred clothes flapped limply on blackened flesh. Worse still were the parts that stuck out of the debris. Motion caught the eagle's attention, and it pivoted neatly on a wingtip.

Old Fromal was sitting beside the ruins of his house, head in his hands, rocking back and forth, his filthy old face streaked by tears. There was a small boy, naked, running round and round the wrecked market stalls. He was bruised and bleeding, his face drawn into a fierce rictus of determination, not looking at anything in the physical world.

'They're gone,' Edeard said. 'Let's go out.' He dropped the hated gun and shoved the slab aside.

The stench was the worst of it; cloying smell of the smoking wood remnants saturated with burnt meat. Edeard almost vomited at the impact. It wasn't all genistars and domestic animals that were roasting. He tore a strip of cloth from his ragged trousers, damped it in a puddle, and tied it over his face.

They halted the running boy, who was in a shock too deep for reason to reach. Led old man Fromal away from the hot coals that had been his home for a hundred and twenty-two years. Found little Sagat cowering in the upturned barrels beside the working well.

Seven. That was how many they and the eagle found. Seven survivors out of a village numbering over four hundred souls.

They gathered together just outside the broken gates, in the shadow of the useless rampart walls, where the reek of the corpses wasn't so bad. Edeard went back in a couple of times, trying to find some clothes and food, though his heart was never in the search.

That was how the posse from Thorpe-By-Water village found them just before dusk. Over a hundred men riding horses and ge-horses, well armed, with ge-wolves loping along beside them. They could barely believe the sight which awaited them, nor did they want to accept it was organized bandits who were responsible. Instead of giving chase and delivering justice, they turned and rode back to Thorpe-By-Water in case their own loved ones were threatened. The survivors were taken with them. None of them ever returned.

*

Edeard used his longtalk to tell Salrana: 'The caravan is here.'

'Where?' she answered back. 'I can't sense them.'

'They've just reached Molby's farm, they should be at the village bridge in another hour or so.'

'That's a long way to farsee, even for you.'

'The ge-eagle helps,' he admitted.

'Cheat!'

Edeard laughed. 'I'll meet you in the square in half an hour.'

'All right.'

He finished instructing the flock of ge-chimps clearing out the stables and excused himself with Tonri, the senior apprentice. All he got for his courtesy was an indifferent grunt. Thorpe-By-Water's Eggshaper Guild hadn't exactly welcomed him with open arms. There was a huge question about his actual status. The Master hadn't yet confirmed him as a journeyman. Edeard's request that he should be recognized as such had generated a lot of resentment among the other apprentices, who believed he should be the junior. That his talent was so obviously greater than any of them, even the Master, didn't help the situation.

Salrana had been accepted a lot more readily into the Lady's Church by Thorpe-By-Water's Mother. But she wasn't happy, either. 'This will never be our home,' she told Edeard sadly after their first week. Thorpe-By-Water's residents didn't exactly shun the refugees from Ashwell, but they weren't made welcome. Rulan province now lived in fear of the bandits. If they could strike Ashwell, which was three days' ride from the edge of the wilderness, they could strike anywhere in the province. Life had changed irrevocably. There were patrols out in the farmlands and forests constantly now; and craftsmen were having to leave aside all non-urgent tasks to strengthen village walls. Everyone in the Rulan province was going to be poorer this winter.

Edeard walked into the market square to the same averted glances he'd been getting every day for the last three weeks. With its stalls and cobbled floor it was remarkably similar to the one in Ashwell. Larger, of course, Thorpe-By-Water was a bigger village, built in a fork of the River Gwash, providing it with natural protection along two sides. A canal moat had been dug between the two fast-flowing water courses, with a sturdy draw-bridge in the middle, completing the defences. Edeard thought that might make them safer than Ashwell. There really was only one real point of entry. Unless the bandits used boats. Where would bandits get enough boats from . . .

His farsight was casually aware of Salrana hurrying towards him. They greeted each other in front of one of the many fish stalls. She was dressed in the blue and white novice robe of the Lady, one which was slightly baggy this time.

'Almost like before,' Edeard said, looking her up and down. He was quietly aware of the glances she was drawing from the other young men in the market.

She wriggled inside it, pulling at the long flared sleeves. 'I'd forgotten how prickly this fabric is when it's new,' she said. 'I only ever had one new one before at Ashwell, for my initiation ceremony; the rest were all second-hand. But the Mother here has had five made for me.' She gave his clothes an assessment. 'Still not found a weaver?'

Edeard rubbed at his ancient shirt with its strange mis-coloured patches. His trousers were too short as well, and the boots were so old the leather was cracked along the top. 'You need money for a weaver to make a shirt. Apprentices are clothed by their Guild. And apprentices without status get the pick of everything the others don't want.'

'He still hasn't confirmed your journeyman status?'

'No. It's all politics. His own journeymen are totally inept, and that's mostly thanks to his poor training. They lose at least six out of every ten eggs. That's just pitiful. Even Akeem's apprentices didn't lose that many. They're also five years older than me, so putting me on their level would be an admission of how rubbish he actually is. I didn't appreciate what I'd got with Akeem.' He fell silent at the painful memory. They should have made time to recover the bodies, to give their village a proper funeral blessed by the Lady.

'You knew,' she said supportively.

'Yes. Thanks.' They wandered through the market, Edeard looking enviously at the various clothes on display. As an apprentice he wasn't allowed to trade any eggs he sculpted, they all belonged to the Guild. Akeem had been decently flexible about it, believing in a quiet rewards system. But now Edeard found himself with no money, no friends, and no respect. It was like being ten years old again.

'One of the patrols came in last night,' Salrana said as they walked. 'The Mother was at the meeting of village elders this morning; the patrol leader told them they'd found no sign of bandits, let alone a large group of them. Apparently there's talk about cutting down the patrols.'

'Idiots,' Edeard grunted. 'What were they expecting to find? We told them the bandits can conceal themselves.'

'I know.' Her expression turned awkward. 'Our word doesn't count for much.'

'What do they think destroyed Ashwell?'

'Give them some grace, Edeard; their whole world is being turned upside down right now. That's never easy.'

'Whereas we've had a cosy ride.'

'That's not nice.'

'Sorry.' He took a long breath. 'I just hate this: after all we went through, and we get treated as if we're the problem. I really should have kept that gun.' He'd left it at the bottom of the well shaft, not wanting any part of a bandit legacy. The gun was pure evil. Ever since, he'd been trying to draw the fidgety little components he'd sensed inside. Thorpe-By-Water's blacksmith had laughed when he'd taken the sketches to him, telling him no such thing could be made. Now people were becoming sceptical about the whole repeat-shooting-gun story.

'You did the right thing,' she said. 'How awful would life be if everyone had a weapon like that.'

'It's pretty awful that the bandits have it and we don't,' he snapped at her. 'What's to stop them sweeping through the whole province? Then further? How about the entire region?'

'That won't happen.'

'No, it won't, because the governor will raise an army. Thankfully, there are more of us than them, so we can win no matter how terrible their weapons are. But that will mean bloodshed on a scale we've never known.' He wanted to beat his fists against the nearest stall. 'How did they get that gun? Do you think they found one of the ships we came in?'

'Maybe they never left the ship they came in,' she said in a small voice.

'Perhaps. I don't know. Why will no one listen to us?'

'Because we're children.'

He turned to snarl at her, then saw the deep worry in her thoughts, her tired face dabbed with greenish ointment. She was so lovely. Somehow he knew Akeem would approve him risking everything to save her. 'I'm sorry. I don't know why I'm taking it out on you.'

'Because I'm the only one who listens,' she told him.

'Lady, it's worse here than at Ashwell in some ways. The elders are so . . . backward. They must inbreed like dogs.'

Salrana grinned. 'Keep your voice down,' she scolded.

'Okay,' he grinned back. 'Not much longer now, I hope.'

People were gathering along the side of the market square to watch the caravan arrive. Edeard counted thirty-two wagons rolling along the road and over the drawbridge. Most had terrestrial beasts tethered to them; horses, donkeys, oxen, cows; some had pens carrying huge pigs. Ge-wolves padded alongside. There were more outriders with pistols than Edeard remembered from before. The wagons were as large and impressive as he recalled, with their metal-rimmed wheels as tall as him. Most of them were covered by curving canopies of dark oiled cloth, though several were clad in tarred wood almost like tiny mobile cottages. Entire families sat on the driver's bench, waving and smiling as they wound their way into the market. Every summer the caravans would tour the district, trading animals, seeds, eggs, tools, food, drink, and fancy cloth from Makkathran itself. They didn't always visit Ashwell, but Edeard could remember the excitement when they did.

Even before the wagons had stopped, villagers were shouting up at the travelling families, asking what they'd brought. It was a good-natured crowd who had little time for the Mayor's welcoming speech to the caravan leader. Trading was already underway before the formalities were over. Samples of wine and beer were handed down, mostly to apprentices. Edeard chewed on some dried beef that had been flavoured with a spice he'd never tasted before. Salrana picked daintily at trays of fruit and pickled vegetables though she was less restrained when it came to exotic chocolates.

As the evening sky began to darken, Edeard was in considerably better spirits. A lot of the villagers were making for home and supper before returning for the night's traditional festivities. He and Salrana made their way to the lead caravan. The last remaining villagers were leaving, studiously ignoring the Ashwell pair as they did so.

Barkus, the caravan Master, was also as Edeard remembered. A man several decades into his second century, but still hale. He had the largest sideburns Edeard had ever seen, white whiskers bristling round the curve of his jawbone, framing ruddy cheeks. His barrel torso was clad in a red silk shirt and an extravagant blue and gold waistcoat. 'And what can I do for you two?' he chortled as Edeard and Salrana edged in close to his wagon; his large family glanced at them and kept about their work, extending the awning on a frame of martoz wood to form an extensive tent. 'I think we've run out of beer samples.' He winked at Edeard.

'I want to come with you to Makkathran, we both do.'

Barkus let out a booming laugh. Two of his sons sniggered as they pushed the awning pegs into the hard ground. 'Very romantic, I'm sure. I admire your pluck, young sir, and you my Lady's lady. But sadly we have no room for passengers. Now I'm sure that if the two of you are to be ah . . . how shall we say, *blessed* by an addition, your parents won't be as fearsome as you expect. Trust me. Go home and tell them what's happened.'

Salrana drew her shoulders back. 'I am not pregnant. I take my vows of devotion very seriously.'

Which blatant lie almost deflated Edeard's indignation. 'I am Edeard and this is Salrana; we're the survivors from Ashwell.' He was very aware of the silence his statement caused. Barkus's family were all looking at them. Several strands of farsight emanating from the other side of the wagon swept across them. 'I believe you knew my Master, Akeem.'

Barkus nodded sagely. 'You'd best come inside. And the rest of you, get back to work.'

The wagon was one of those boasting a wooden cabin. The inside was fitted with beautiful ancient golden wood, intricately carved with a quality which would have eluded Geepalt and his apprentices. Every section of the walls and ceiling were made of doors which came in sizes from some no bigger than Edeard's fist to those taller than he. Barkus opened a pair of horizontal ones, and they folded down into long cushioned benches. Two of the small doors along the apex slid aside to expose misty glass panels. Barkus struck a match and pushed it through a small hole at the end of the glass, lighting a wick. The familiar cosy glow of a jamolar oil flame filled the cabin.

Edeard smiled round, very impressed.

'I remember your Master with great fondness,' Barkus said, waving them on to the bench opposite himself. 'He travelled out here with us a long time ago. I was barely your age at the time. Your Mother, too, novice Salrana, always showed us kindness. Both will be missed and mourned. It was a terrible thing.'

'Thank you,' Edeard said. 'I don't wish to impose, but neither of us can stay in Thorpe-By-Water. We're not very welcome, and in any case it's too close to Ashwell.'

'I understand. The whole province is shaken by what happened, though I've heard a great many different versions already. Including, I have to say, a couple which cast you in a less than favourable light, young man. I held my tongue at the telling of such tales because I remember you from our last visit, four summers ago. I also remember what Akeem said about you. He was impressed with your talent, and old Akeem was not easily swayed especially by one so young.'

'Edeard risked his life to save me,' Salrana said.

'That also I have heard.'

'Before that night, Akeem said he wanted me to go to Makkathran to study at the Blue Tower of my Guild. I would – no, I *will*, see his wish come true.'

Barkus smiled softly. 'A worthy goal, young man.'

'We will work our passage,' Edeard said forcefully. 'I will not freeload.'

'Nor I,' said Salrana.

'I would expect nothing less,' Barkus said. He seemed troubled. 'However, it is a long way, we will not reach Makkathran until next spring, and that is if all goes well. Many caravans have already cut short their regular journey to leave this province. The stories of Ashwell's fate are many, but they have unnerved all of us. As I remember, Akeem said you have a strong third hand?'

'That's true. But my talent is in sculpting. There are many wild defaults in the woods and hills of this province. By the time winter falls I can sculpt you a pack of ge-wolves that no bandit gang will ever get past no matter how strong their concealment. I can sculpt them with a stronger sense of smell than any you've used hitherto. I can also sculpt eagles which will circle for miles on every side of the convoy searching out the slightest hint of treachery or ambush.'

'I'm sure you can.' Even now Barkus was unsure.

'I can also teach you and your families this,' Edeard said. He wove his concealment around himself. Barkus gasped, leaning forward blinking. Edeard felt the caravan Master's farsight whipping back and forth across the cabin. He quietly got up and sat next to the startled Barkus, then withdrew his concealment. 'How could the bandits attack you if they can't see you?'

'Dear Lady!' Barkus grunted. 'I never knew such a thing . . .'

'Akeem gifted this to me.'

Barkus regained his composure quickly. 'Did he now. Akeem was right about you, and so I think are half the tales. Very well my dear youngsters, I will accept you both as family tyros. You will come with us as far as Makkathran. And you will indeed work your passage. Let's see if you think such nobility is worthwhile when we reach the Ulfsen mountains. However, Edeard, this arrangement is conditional on you not teaching anyone your concealment trick, do you concur?'

'I do, sir. I don't understand why, though.'

'You haven't taught it to anyone in Thorpe-By-Water, have you?'

'No, sir.'

'That's a good political instinct you have there, my boy. Let's just keep it that way, shall we. There's enough trouble infecting our poor old world as it is without everyone sneaking around unseen. Though if you can find a way for farsight to uncover such trickery, I'd be grateful if you would inform me at once.'

'Yes, sir.'

'Good lad. We leave with the dawn light in three days' time. If you're not here that morning, we still leave. Though I don't suppose your Master will object to your exodus.'

'I don't believe he will, sir.'

'Makkathran!' Edeard said as they hurried away from the wagon. Now Barkus had said he'd take them, all his earlier worries and doubts had dried up. He'd thought that he was running away, that he was being a coward for putting all the provinces between himself and the bandits, for allowing them to deal with the problem and endure their blood being spilt to safeguard the land while he lived a safe comfortable life in the city. But now they were going and that was that. 'Imagine it.'

'I can't believe it.' Salrana's smile was wide and carefree. 'Do you think it will be as wonderful as the stories we've heard?'

'If it is only a tenth as fabulous as they say, it will be beyond anything I have dreamed.'

'And we'll be safe,' she sighed.

'Yes.' He put his arm round her shoulder. In a brotherly fashion! 'We'll be safe. And what splendid lives we'll live in the capital of the world.'

4

The glitch had been surprisingly easy to find. But then Troblum supposed Emily Alm didn't have a lot of time to insert it, nor would she suspect he'd come looking, at least not right away. She'd made several modifications to the blueprint; in itself each one was relatively innocuous which made them even harder to spot, but the cumulative effect was enough to throw the binding effect out of kilter. It was less than an hour's work for him to remove them. Then he restarted the production process.

With that underway, his u-shadow established a secure one-time link back to his apartment. Now he knew that Marius was trying to manipulate him, and would go to any lengths to achieve what he wanted, Troblum knew he needed an escape route. There was only one which would put him beyond even the representative's reach: the colonies. After the Starflyer War each of the old Dynasties had been left with a fleet of redundant lifeboats, starships capable of evacuating the entire senior strata of each Dynasty to the other side of the galaxy where they would have been safe had the Prime alien won. Given the phenomenal amount of money poured into their construction, the Dynasty leaders were never going to scrap them simply because the Commonwealth was victorious. Instead, the lifeboats set off to found new worlds and cultures completely independent of the Commonwealth. Over forty ships had launched, though even that figure was ambiguous; the Dynasty leaders were reluctant to admit how much money they'd poured into their own salvation at the expense of everyone else. In the following centuries, more colony ships had set forth. No longer exclusive to Dynasties, they had carried an even broader selection of beliefs, families and ideologies seeking to break free to a degree which even the External Worlds could never offer. The last major departure had been in AD 3000, when Nigel Sheldon himself led a fleet of ten starships, the largest craft ever built, to set up a 'new human experience' elsewhere. It was strongly rumoured at the time that the ships had a trans-galactic flight range.

With the ultra-secure link established to his apartment, Troblum used a similarly guarded connection for his u-shadow to trawl the unisphere for the possible destinations of the colony ships within this galaxy. There were over a hundred departures listed, and subsequently thousands of articles presented on each of them. A lot of those articles speculated on why not one colony had got back in touch, even if it was only for a 'so there' message. Certainly there were no records of any Navy starships stumbling across a human world anywhere else in the galaxy, not that they'd ever explored a fraction of a per cent of the available H-congruous stars. Of course, it was the core of Living Dream dogma that most, if not all, such voyages had wound up inside the Void. However, a lot of genuine academic work had gone into estimating probable locations, despite the best efforts of the dwindling Dynasties to suppress such work. Even assuming the studies were correct, the areas that needed to be searched were vast, measuring hundreds of lightyears across. But *Mellanie's Redemption* was a fine ship, she should be able to make the trip out to the Drasix cluster, fifty thousand lightyears away, where the Brandt Dynasty ships were said to have flown.

Troblum knew he wouldn't miss the Commonwealth, there was nobody he had any attachment to, and most of the colony worlds would have a decent level of civilization. If he did find the Brandt world, they would presumably be glad to accept his knowledge of biononics which had been developed long after their ships had departed. That just left the problem of what to do with his Starflyer War artefacts. He couldn't bear to be parted from them, yet if he transported them to the hangar, Marius might notice. He began instructing the apartment net on shipping arrangements, then made a painful call to Stubsy Florac.

The Neumann cybernetics took thirty-two hours to produce a planet-shifting ftl engine. Troblum stood underneath the sparkling cylinder as the terminal extruder finished, marvelling at its elegance. His field functions reported a dense knot of energies and hyperstressed matter all in perfect balance. So much exotic activity was present it almost qualified as a singularity in its own right.

If the colony doesn't want biononics, they'll surely want this.

He watched in perfect contentment as force fields manoeuvred the cylinder into *Mellanie's Redemption*. The modified forward cargo hold closed, and Troblum sent the device into standby mode. Nobody would be able to break the command authority encryption, not even ANA he suspected. The device was his and his alone.

Once it was safe and shielded he went back into the office and restored Emily Alm's glitches to the blueprint, then began adding some of his own, at a much deeper function level. Now the engine really was unique.

Marius called several hours later. 'Have you finished your analysis yet?'

'Just about. I think I'm going to have to initiate a complete redesign of the exotic stress channels.'

'That sounds bad and I don't even know what you're talking about.'

'It's not good, no.'

'I'm sure our funds will cover it. But for now I need a small favour.'

'Yes?'

'I want you to take a colleague to our station.'

'A passenger?' Troblum asked in alarm. If there was someone else on board, he would never be able to fly free. With a growing sense of dismay he realized that was probably the whole idea. Had Marius detected something? He would have sworn nothing could get through his encryption, but then ultimately he was dealing with an ANA Faction.

'Problem? Your ship can accommodate more than one person, and it's a relatively short flight. We're still inside the Commonwealth, after all.'

There was a definite implication in that. 'Not a problem. I'll need to flight prep.'

'That shouldn't take more than an hour. Bon voyage.'

There had been no polite enquiry as to whether he was ready, in fact it was more like an order. Annoyance warred with a slight curiosity. *What do they need me for so urgently?*

'Troblum?'

'Wha—?' Troblum twisted round as fast as his bulk would allow. There was a man standing in the office, a very tall man whose skeletal skull was frizzed by a stubble of ginger hair. He wore a simple grey suit that emphasized exceptionally long limbs. 'Who the fuck are you?' Troblum's bionomics had instantly cloaked him in a defensive force field, now his one weapons enrichment was active and targeting the intruder.

'I'm Lucken. I believe you're expecting me?'

'You're . . .'

'Your passenger, yes. Is the ship ready?'

'How did you get in?'

Lucken's face remained completely impassive. 'Do you require assistance to prepare for flight?'

'Ah, no.'

'Then please begin.'

Troblum adjusted the front of his old toga suit in angry reaction to the arrogant imposition. 'The umbilicals are already attached. We'll leave as soon as the tanks are full. Do you want to go to your cabin?'

'Are you embarking now?'

'No. I have important work here to complete.'

'I will wait. I will accompany you on board.'

'As you wish.' Troblum settled back in his chair, and reactivated the solido projectors. Just to show how indifferent he was.

Lucken didn't move. His eyes never left Troblum.

It was going to be a long flight.

The station was a real flight into nostalgia. It had been fifty years since Troblum saw it last, and he never thought he'd be back – in fact he was rather surprised it was still intact. *Mellanie's Redemption* took three days to fly from Arevalo to the unnamed red dwarf star. There were no planets, solid or gas, orbiting the weak speck of ruddy light, just a large disc of mushy hydrocarbon asteroids. There were less now than there had been when he first came to work here. He smiled when he remembered that test sequence. It was the last time he'd been genuinely drunk, and hadn't cared what a fool he was making of himself.

Mellanie's Redemption dropped out of hyperspace ten AUs away from the star and eight thousand kilometres directly above their destination. Troblum accelerated in at seven gees, heading straight for the centre of the dark torroid that measured five kilometres in diameter. A squadron of defence cruisers shed their stealth effect and soared around the starship in fast tight turns. They were over a hundred metres long, like quicksilver droplets frozen in mid-distortion to produce bodies of warped ripples sprouting odd pseudopod crowns. Their flight was so elegant and smooth they resembled a shoal of aquatic creatures cavorting with a newcomer. However, there was nothing playful about the quantum level probes directed at the *Mellanie's Redemption*. Troblum held his breath as he waited to see if the sophisticated shielding around the forward hold would deflect the scan. It did, but then he'd helped design the cruisers – seventy years ago now. He found it interesting that nothing new had been produced in the intervening decades. Human technology was edging ever closer to its plateau. Emily Alm was probably right about her time in the Navy; given their knowledge base there was nothing new in the universe, just innovative variants on that which already existed.

The cruisers escorted them into the station. *Mellanie's Redemption* fell below the rim of the torroid, and slid along the broad internal tube, which was almost as long as its diameter. Observing the structure through the starship's modest sensor net Troblum could see that vast sections had been reactivated. The titanium-black fuselage was covered in long slender spikes as if a sharp frost had settled across the whole station. The majority of spikes were translucent blue-white; though in among them, seemingly at random, several of the smaller ones were glowing with a low crimson light, as if they'd caged a few of the photons from the nearby sun.

Troblum piloted *Mellanie's Redemption* to the base of a red spike which measured nearly seven hundred metres long. A hangar door was open and waiting for them. When it closed, he couldn't help but think of the door to an antique jail cell slamming shut.

'Thank you for flying Troblum Lines, and have a pleasant day,' he said cheerily.

Lucken opened the airlock and went outside. The man hadn't spoken a single word since they'd embarked. Hadn't slept, either, just sat in the central cabin the whole time. He'd vanished by the time Troblum activated a small case and pulled his emerald cloak on. *Mellanie's Redemption* looked small and inadequate inside the giant shiny-white cavity. White tubes had wormed out of the floor to plug into her umbilical sockets. There was no sign of the external door or indeed a way into the station. As Troblum walked along the curving floor, gravity shifted to accommodate him so he was always standing vertical. The whole effect was quite disorientating on a visual level.

A woman was waiting for him under the starship's nose. She was his height, completely hairless, with large perfectly round eyes that dominated her flat face. Her neck was long, over twenty centimetres, but invisible behind a sheath of slim gold rings, as if it was some kind of segmented metallic limb. All of her skin had the surface shimmer of a toga suit tuned to steel-grey. Troblum assumed her skin had actually been biononically modified, the effect was so tight around her. A lot of Highers close to download chose to experiment with physiological modifications.

'Greetings,' she said in a pleasant, almost girlish voice. 'I've heard a lot about you.'

'Sadly I can't return the compliment,' he said, reading off the protocol behaviour program showing in his exovision.

'I'm Neskia, I run the station. My predecessor was most favourable in his assessment of your abilities. Our Faction would like to thank you for returning.'

As if I had a choice. 'All very well, but why exactly am I here? Is the swarm malfunctioning?'

'Not at all.' She gestured gracefully, her neck curving in a fluidly serpentine motion to keep her face aligned on him as she started walking. Troblum followed her along the curve, his case hovering just behind his head. Up above them, a circular door irised open. The station's internal nature had certainly changed in seventy years.

'Oh.'

'You sound disappointed,' she said and hesitated by the door.

Troblum wasn't sure if the circle had flipped out of the curve to stand upright or if the local gravity manipulation was even weirder than his ordinary senses told him. He refused to verify with a field scan. Disorientation attempts were really very childish. 'Not disappointed. I assume I'm here to inspect and validate the swarm, just in case the worst case Pilgrimage scenario proves true. There have been a few recent advances which could be used to upgrade.'

'The swarm has dispersed to its deployment point. It has been constantly upgraded. We don't anticipate the Void's expansion to pose any problem.'

'Really? So that's why you kept this station going.'

'Among other things.' She stepped through the door and into a corridor that had the old simple grey-blue layout which Troblum recognized. They hadn't changed everything.

'I've assigned you a suite in sector 7-B-5,' Neskia said. 'You can have it modified to your own tastes, just tell the station smartcore what you want.'

'Thank you. And the reason I'm here?'

'We are building twelve ultradrive engines to power the Pilgrimage fleet. Your experience in the assembly techniques we are using is unmatched.'

Troblum stopped abruptly, his case almost banging into the back of his head. 'Ultradrive?'

'Yes.'

'You mean it's real? I always assumed it was just a rumour.'

'It isn't. You'll be working with a small team, fifty or so experts have been recruited. The Neumann cybernetics that built the swarm will handle the actual fabrication.'

'Fascinating.' His bleak mood at being blackmailed and bullied actually began to lift. 'I'll need to see the theory behind the drive.'

'Of course.' Her huge eyes blinked once. 'We'll brief you as soon as you've settled in.'

'I'm settled right now.'

*

Araminta waited in the flat until Shelly arrived to take full legal possession. She didn't have to do it, Cressida's firm was tackling the sale registration – which meant nothing had gone wrong. But supervising the handover in person added that little professional touch; and in business, reputation was a commodity which couldn't be bought.

She watched from the balcony as Shelly's capsule landed on the designated pad outside, followed by a larger cargo capsule which used the public pad. The flat seemed strangely unattractive now Araminta had moved the dressing furniture out, all carefully chosen pieces that emphasized how spacious and contemporary the property was.

'Is everything all right?' Shelly asked as Araminta opened the door.

'Yes. I just wanted to check you were happy.'

'Oh yes. I can't wait to get in.' Shelly was already walking past her, smiling contentedly at the empty rooms. She was a tall, pretty girl who had her own salon business in the district. Araminta was slightly jealous about that, mainly because Shelly was a year younger than her and obviously successful. *But then, she's never made the Laril mistake.*

Shelly caught sight of the big bouquet of flowers resting on the kitchen worktop. 'Oh, thank you, that's so sweet.'

'My pleasure.' Araminta's u-shadow transferred the flat's activation codes over to Shelly. 'Now if there are any problems, please call me.' She had to flatten herself against the wall as she made her way downstairs. A regrav lifter was hauling a big scarlet and black sofa up to the flat. It wasn't quite what Araminta would have chosen, but . . . She shrugged and left the house.

Her old carry capsule flew her across Colwyn city to the Bodant district where it settled on a public parking pad. The morning was a dull one, with grubby-ginger clouds darkening towards rain as the wind blew in from the sea. Araminta climbed out and smiled up at the six-storey apartment block. It was a fairly standard layout, ribbed by white balconies that dripped with colourful vines and flowering creepers. The corners were black glass columns alive with purple and blue refraction stipples that swarmed up and down like rodent climbers. At night the effect was sharp and conspicuous, but under a dank daylight sky it lacked any kind of verve. There was a gold crystal dome on the roof, sheltering a communal pool and spa gym. A wide swathe of elegantly maintained gardens along the front were sitting on top of the private underground garage.

Cressida's sleek purple capsule slipped down out of the low clouds to land beside Araminta. 'Well, darling, what a coup.' The lawyer was wrapped in a furry black and white coat that snuggled cosily round her with every move. She glanced up at the front of the building, eyes narrowing as she saw three balconies piled high with junked fittings. 'I have the access codes and the owner certificates. So let's go up, shall we?'

Araminta had bought the entire fourth floor, with all five

apartments. The whole apartment block was undergoing redevelopment, presenting an opportunity she couldn't resist when Ikor, one of the original developers, had pulled out. Cressida walked into the first apartment and rolled her eyes. 'I can't believe you've done this.'

'Why not? It's a perfect opportunity for me.' Araminta grinned at her cousin's dismay and walked over to the balcony doors. The glass curtained wide for her and she stepped out. There was a faint sound of buzzing and drilling as the other developers prepared their floors for occupancy. 'It's ninety years old, it needs a makeover. And look at the view.'

Cressida pushed her sapphire-glossed lips together as she looked out across the Bodant district's park to the Cairns beyond. There was a marina along the embankment directly opposite them, its curving deco buildings radiant white, as if they had just been forged in some fusion furnace. 'You got the wrong side of the park, darling. Over there is where the action and the smart money is. Besides, here you're only a few streets from the Helie district. Really!'

'Stop being such a grump. I've proved I can do this, and you know it.'

'I also know how much you paid for these hovels. Honestly darling, a hundred K each. Were you kidnapped and held for ransom?'

'They have three bedrooms each. They need a lot less work than the flat. The two largest have this view. And I cleared a forty K profit on the flat.'

'I still can't believe the bank gave you the money for this.'

'Standard commercial loan. They liked my business model,' Araminta said proudly.

'And Ozzie's coming back to save us all. Go on, you can tell me. You slept with the entire staff of the local office, didn't you?'

'It's very simple economics.'

'Ha! That just proves you don't know what you're talking about. Economics is never simple.'

'I renovate one of them – this one probably – as the show apartment, and sell the rest off-plan based on people seeing the quality of the finish. The deposits will pay off the mortgage while I refurbish them.'

'This is the best one? Oh help me.'

'Yes, this one. And Helie is an up-and-coming area. Don't be so negative. It's annoying.' Her tone was more prickly than she'd intended.

Cressida was instantly apologetic. 'I'm sorry, darling. But my life is without risk now. Honestly, I admire you for taking this gamble. But you have to admit, it is a gamble.'

'Of course it's a gamble. You never get anywhere in life without taking a gamble.'

'Well well, whatever happened to the little farmgirl from Langham?'

'She died. Nobody came to the funeral.'

A perfectly shaped eyebrow rose in surprise. 'What have I unleashed on the world?'

'I thought you'd be happy to see me move forward like this.'

'I am. Are you going to do all the work yourself, again?'

'Most of it, yes. I've got some new bots, and I know where to go for all my supplies and fittings now. This is going to be a prestige development, you'll see, all the apartments will fetch a premium.'

'I'm sure they will. Did you know most of the hotels in town are fully booked?'

'Is that relevant?'

Cressida wiped the balcony rail with a hand then leant on it. 'There's a lot of Living Dream devotees flooding in. Rumour in the gaiafield is that the Second Dreamer is on Viotia.'

'Really, I didn't know that, but then I haven't accessed a news show in weeks. I'm a working gal these days.'

'Keep it quiet, but the government is worried about the pressure that's going to be put on housing, among other things – like public order.'

'Oh, come on!'

'Seriously. We've had over two million of the faithful arrive in the last seven weeks. Do you know how many have left again?'

'No.'

'None. And if they all apply for residency, that's going to shift the political demographic.'

'So we're receiving immigrants again. That's how planets develop. There's going to be a big demand for housing. I come out a winner.'

'All I'm saying is that in times of civil disturbance property values take a dive.'

'It's that serious?' Araminta asked in sudden alarm; after all, Cressida was very well connected.

'You know there's always been an undercurrent of resentment towards Ellezelin. If the Living Dream numbers keep rising at their current rate, then there could be trouble. Who wants to wind up living in a hierocracy?'

'Yes, but there's the Pilgrimage. That'll call them back to Ellezelin, won't it? And it's not like they're going to find this stupid Second Dreamer, least of all here. The whole thing's a political stunt by the new Cleric Conservator. Isn't it?'

'Who knows. But I'd respectfully suggest, darling, that you find a sucker who you can offload these apartments on to at very short notice.'

Araminta recalled how keen Ikor had been to sell to her. And it was a good deal, or so it seemed at the time. *Am I the sucker?* 'I suppose it wouldn't harm to look for one,' she said.

Mr Bovey let loose a small chorus of swearing as four of him tried to manoeuvre the old-fashioned stone bath along the hallway and through the bathroom door. It was an awkward angle, and the apartment's rear hallway wasn't particularly wide.

'Can I help?' Araminta sang out from the kitchen where she and three bots were making last-minute changes to the new utility connections ready for the units she'd ordered.

'I'm quite capable, thank you,' quadraphonic voices grunted back.

His hurtful insistence made her giggle. 'Okay.' It was another twenty minutes before one of him walked into the kitchen. He was the Bovey she'd first encountered in his macrostore's bathroom aisle, the one with ebony skin and an ageing body. In his biological late-middle-age he may have been, but he didn't shirk from hard work. His wrinkled forehead was smeared with sweat.

'I made some tea,' she said, gesturing at the kettle with its cluster of ancient cups. 'You look like you need a break.'

'I do, my others are younger.' He smiled in admiration at the steaming cups and the packet of tea cubes. 'You really did make it, too, didn't you?'

'Waiting for my culinary unit to arrive,' she said with a martyred sigh.

'It's in the next load, I promise,' he told her, and picked up a cup. His eyes took in the packets of folded food and the hydrator oven. 'Are you actually living here?'

'Yeah. Not renting saves me a bucket load of money. I mean, what's the point? I've got five apartments, and they're not that bad – the roofs don't leak and the rest is just aesthetics. I can stick it out for a few months.'

'You know I really admire your attitude. There's not many your age would take on a project like this.'

She batted her eyes. 'And what's my age?'

'Honestly? I've no idea. But you come across as a first life.'

'I'll own up to that.'

'Can I offer you an alternative to hydrated food tonight? There's a nice restaurant I know.'

She grinned, her hand curling round her own mug of tea. 'That would be lovely. Oh, I don't like curry!'

'That's okay, some mes don't, either.'

'Your tastes are different?'

'Sure. Taste is all down to biochemistry, which is subtly different in every human body. And, face it, I have quite a variety to chose from.'

'Okay,' she said, and dropped her gaze bashfully. 'I have to ask. I've never been on a date with a multiple before. Do you all come and sit at the table with me?'

'Nah, I think that would be a little full on for you, wouldn't it? Besides, I have the macrostore to run, deliveries to be made, installation, that kind of thing. My life goes on the whole time.'

'Oh. Yes.' It was a strange notion. Not an objectionable one, though.

'Now if you were another multiple, it might be different.'

'How?'

'We'd book the whole restaurant of romantic tables for two and take over the lot. Yous and mes everywhere having fifty different conversations simultaneously and trying out the entire menu and wine list all at once. It's like speed dating in fast forward.'

She laughed. 'Have you ever done that?'

'Tell you tonight.'

'Right. So which one of you do I get sitting at that romantic table for two?'

'You choose. How many mes and which ones.'

'One, and you'll do just fine.'

Araminta took a great deal of thought and care over what to wear and which cosmetic scales to apply. Dressed exactly to plan two hours early. Took one look at herself in the mirror and chucked the whole image. Fifty minutes later all the cases in her bedroom were hanging open. Every outfit she had bought in the last two months was draped over floor and furniture leaving little space to walk. She'd experimented with four different styles of scale membrane. Her hair had been sparkled then damped. Oiled then fluffed. Bejewelled with red scintillators, blue scintillators, green, blue-white . . .

In the end – with eleven minutes to go – she took an executive decision: go basic. Mr Bovey wasn't the kind to concern himselfs with surface image.

His capsule landed on the pad outside, and she took a lift down to the lobby. The doors opened to a dusty space piled with junk and newly delivered boxes. It was all illuminated by too-bright temporary lighting.

Mr Bovey was dressed in a simple pale-grey toga suit with minimal surface shimmer. He smiled as the doors opened, and said: 'A lady who is on time, now that's – oh, wow.'

She permitted the smallest nod of approval as he stared. In her mind was an image of his customers left unattended, installations stalled, delivery flights landing at the wrong addresses all over town.

'You look,' he swallowed as he tried to regain equilibrium, 'fantastic. Absolutely amazing.'

'Why thank you.' She held her hands behind her back, and presented the side of her face for a formal greeting kiss like some girly ingénue. It was the right choice then. A black sleeveless dress of plain silky fabric with a wide cleft down the front, barely held together by a couple of slim black emerald chains, making it look as if she was about to burst out. Hair glossed pale auburn, and brushed with just a couple of waves to hang below her shoulders. No scales other than lips slightly darker than her natural pigmentation, and emerald eyelash sparkles on low radiance. Most important was the sly half-smile guaranteed to totally befuddle the male brain – all of them.

Mr Bovey recovered. 'Shall we go?'

'Love to.'

The restaurant he'd booked was Richard's. Small but stylish, occupying two floors of an old white stone house in the Udno district. The owner was also the chef; and as Mr Bovey explained he had a small boat which he took out down the estuary a couple of times each week to catch fish for the specials.

'So do you date other multiples?' she asked once they'd ordered.

'Of course,' he told her. 'Not that there are a lot of us on Viotia yet.'

'What about marriage? Is that only with multiples?'

'I was married once. A multiple called Mrs Rion. It was,' he frowned, as if searching for a memory, 'pleasant.'

'That sounds pretty awful.'

'I'm being unfair to her. We had a good time while it lasted. Sex was great.' His smile was shameless. 'Think on it, thirty of her, thirty of me. All of us at it every night. You singles can't get that close to physical paradise even in an orgy.'

'You don't know how good I am in an orgy.' As soon as she said it she could feel her ears burning. But it was the second time she'd startled him this evening, and they weren't even an hour into the date. *Cressida would be proud of me.*

'Anyway . . .' he said. 'We called time on the marriage after seven years. No hostilities, we're still friends. Thankfully, we didn't merge our businesses as well. Always sign a pre-marriage contract, no matter what you are.'

'Yes. I found that out the hard way.'

'You've been married?'

'Yeah. It was a mistake, but you were right, I'm young. My cousin says mistakes are the only way to learn.'

'Your cousin is right.'

'So are you going to try and convert me tonight?'

'Convert you?'

'Sell the whole multiple idea. I thought you believed multiples are inevitable.'

'I do. But I'm not an evangelical. Some of us are,' he admitted.

'And you date – uh . . .'

'Outside the faith? Of course I do. People are interesting no matter what type they are.'

'Highers seem quite boring. If that sound bigoted, I should explain my ex is currently migrating inwards.'

'Not a wholly balanced opinion, then.'

Araminta raised a glass. 'Ozzie, I hope not.'

'Going Higher is wrong, it's a technocrat route. We're a humanist solution to immortality and evolution.'

'You still rely on technology, though.'

'It's a very small reliance. A few gaiamotes to homologize our thoughts. It's a simple procedure.'

'Ah hah! You *are* trying to convert me.'

He grinned. 'You're paranoid.'

'All divorcees are. So are any of you female?'

'No. Some multiples are multisexual, but that's not for me. Too much like masturbation I'd imagine.'

'I've just thought of something, and you have to answer because it's not fair.'

'What's not fair?'

'Well, you can see that I'm not with anyone else this evening—'

'Ah,' his smile turned devious. 'So in among all the hard work the rest of mes are doing back at the macrostore, is there another of me in a different restaurant chatting to another woman? Right?'

'Yeah,' she admitted.

'Why would it have to be a different restaurant?' he gestured round extravagantly. 'Be honest, how could you tell if one of them is me?'

The idea made her draw a breath and glance round.

Mr Bovey was laughing. 'But I'm not,' he assured her. 'All I'm interested in tonight is you and you alone.' His gaze dropped to the front of her dress. 'How could I not be?'

'That's,' she took another drink of the wine, 'very flattering, thank you.'

Which got the evening back on more or less standard lines.

The mighty creatures fly free amid glorious coloured streamers which glow strongly against the infinite dark of the outer reaches. They loop round the great scarlet promontories which extend for lightyears, curving and swooping above the mottled webbing of faint cold gas. As they fly, the notions of what was brush against their bodies to tingle their minds as if they are travelling through the memories of another entity. Such a notion is not far from the truth, especially this close to the nucleus of their universe.

This one she tenants turns lazily along its major axis, aware of its kindred surrounding it. The flock is spread across millions of kilometres. Over a planetary diameter away, another of its own is also rolling, mountain-sized elongated body throwing its vacuum wings wide, tenuous tissues of molecules as large as atmospheric clouds that shimmer delicately in the thin starlight. Somewhere out across the vast gulf it is aware of the whispers of thought arising once more from a solid world. Once more there are individual minds growing strong again, becoming attuned to the fabric of this universe. As it basks in the gentle radiance pouring out of the nebula, it wonders when the minds will have the strength to truly affect reality. Such a time, it agrees with its kindred, is sure to come. Then the flock will depart the great nebula to search out the newcomers, and carry their completed lives back to the nucleus, where all life eventually culminates.

It was a pleasurable notion which made Araminta sigh contentedly even though the creature was slipping away into the darkness where it dwelled. Misty starlight gave way to a row of flickering candles. The gossamer breath of nebula dust firmed up into strong fingers sliding along her legs; more hands began to stroke her belly, then another pair squeezed her breasts. Sweet oil was massaged into her skin with wicked insistence. Tongues licked with intimate sensuality.

'Time to wake up,' a voice murmured.

On the other side of her another voice encouraged, 'Time to indulge yourself again.'

Amid a delicious drowsiness Araminta bent herself in the way the hands were urging. She blinked lazily, seeing the Mr Bovey she'd had dinner with standing beside the vast bed. He smiled down. As she grinned back up at him she was impaled from behind. She gasped, startled and excited, seeing a look of rapture cross his face. A further set of hands started to explore her buttocks. She opened her mouth to receive the cock of a really young him. Which was extremely bad of her.

She didn't know how many hims she was accommodating this

time. She didn't know if it was nearly morning or still the middle of the night. She didn't care. Flesh and pleasure were her here and now, her whole universe.

After the meal at Richard's, his capsule had brought them back to his place, a large house set above the city's south bank with lawns that reached down to the river. It wasn't even midnight. Several hims were in the lounge, a couple were cooking, three were in the swimming pool. More were resting or sleeping upstairs, he told her.

It was like holding court. Her sitting on a broad leather sofa, hims on either side, and more sprawled on cushions at her feet as they chatted away. She took a long time to fight down her instinct that they were all separate people. He enjoyed teasing her, switching speaker mid-sentence, even arguing among himself. But the simultaneous laughter his bodies came out with was endearing. It was a wonderfully languid seduction.

Then the one she'd gone to dinner with leaned over and kissed her. By then the wine and the anticipation were making her heart pound and her skin burn.

'You choose,' he murmured silkily.

'Choose?'

'How many, and which ones.'

She'd glanced round, and seen identical expressions of delight and eagerness on each of him. For that long moment every one of him was completely indistinguishable; he could have been clones. That was when she accepted on a subconscious level that he truly was one.

'You, of course,' she told her dinner companion. 'You did all the hard work getting me back here, after all.' Then she pointed. 'You.' The handsome one. 'You.' Young and very well muscled – she'd seen that when he climbed out of the pool.

The chosen three led her upstairs. Araminta thought that was daring enough, but the night swiftly evolved into a strenuous sexual adventure as Mr Bovey began teaching her acts that could only be performed as a group. 'Trust me,' one of him said as he opened an aerosol in her face. 'It's a booster. It'll amplify your pleasure, sort of even things up between you and mes.' Araminta breathed it down. It was potent.

They gathered round, strong hands supporting her in different positions. She was made to climax with each of him in turn, with the booster increasing the sensation each time as it gradually saturated her bloodstream. After the third one she flopped back on the mattress in a lovely warm fugue. That was when she saw more hims had arrived to wait silent and naked around the bed. She didn't protest as they stared down excitedly. 'Yes,' she told them. In unison the fresh bodies closed in.

More than once that night Araminta swooned from a combination of exhaustion and aerosol-fuelled ecstasy. Each time he allowed her a small rest before rousing her again. Those were the occasions when she dreamed her strange dream.

She didn't wake up until mid-morning. When she did, the details of the night had merged together into a single strand of relentless animal behaviour. She'd surprised herself by yielding to everything he'd demanded from her.

The dinner-date Bovey was lying on the bed beside her. He was the only one left in the bedroom. 'Good morning,' he said with soft politeness.

'Yeah,' Araminta said. She still felt hopelessly tired, as well as unpleasantly sore. The aerosol had worn off, leaving her skin cool and slightly clammy.

'You look beautiful when you're sleeping, did you know that?'

'I . . . No one has told me that before.'

'How do you feel?'

'Uh, okay I suppose.'

'All right,' he said in an understanding tone, and stroked some dishevelled hair from her face. 'Let me put it this way; would you like another night like that?'

'Yes,' she whispered, and knew she was blushing. Despite the frequent outrages he'd committed it had been absolutely the best sex she'd ever had. Exactly the kind of multiple-partner athleticism Cressida always boasted about and she'd been too timid to try. But last night it had technically only been one man; this way she got the thrill without the emotional guilt – almost.

'I hoped you would. Not every single can cope with me like that. You're very special, Araminta.'

'I . . .' She hesitated, unsure how much to confide. *Which is stupid.* 'It was like I was becoming part of you. Is that silly?'

'No. With an experience that acute there's always a merger through the gaiafield with anyone nearby, though you mostly remained closed to me. Was that by choice?'

'I don't have gaiamotes.'

He gave her a curious look. 'Interesting. I was sure . . . nah, skip it. The house is running a bath for you.'

'Thank you. So where do we go from here?'

'There's a play on at the Broadway Empire, some kind of comedy, with real actors. I've booked for tonight.'

Which wasn't quite what she wanted qualifying. 'Lovely. And after?'

'I would like you to come back here, back to this bed. I'd really like that.'

Araminta nodded demurely. 'I will.' She didn't think it could ever be as exciting as last night had been. First times were always special, but if hes were just as randy tonight it would still be the hottest sex in town. She eased herself off the bed, drawing a sharp breath as she straightened up. 'Um, how many bodies have you got?'

It was his turn to seem reticent. 'Over thirty.'

'How many . . . last night?'

'Six,' he said with a very male grin of satisfaction.

'Ozzie!' *That's it, I'm now officially a complete trollop. Can't wait to see Cressida's face when I tell her that. Six! She'll be as jealous as hell.*

'What do you want for breakfast?' he asked as she opened the door to the en-suite bathroom.

285

'Orange juice, Bathsamie coffee strong, croissants with straw-berry and hijune jam.'

'It'll be ready when you are.'

*

The regrav capsule sped low over the scrub desert. Dead and desiccated bushes virtually the same colour as the crumbling jaundiced mud from which they'd grown merged to a speckled blur as Aaron looked down through the transparent fuselage. Their jumbled smear confused his visual perspective, making it difficult to tell if their altitude was one metre or a thousand. He often found himself searching for the capsule's jet-black shadow slithering fast across the low undulations to provide a clue.

A couple of minutes before they reached the ranch, he saw a fence; posts of bleached wood sticking up in a section of desert which appeared no different to the rest of the wretched expanse. Rusty spikewire sagged between them. More fences flashed past underneath as they drew closer. The fields they marked out were smaller, closer together. Eventually the clutter of buildings which comprised the ranch itself were visible, nestling at the centre of a vast web of spikewire.

'What does he raise out here?' Corrie-Lyn asked.

'Korrimues,' Aaron said.

'I can't see anything moving.'

'Wrong season, I think.'

She gave the vast desert a disapproving look. 'There are seasons out here?'

'Oh yes. It rains every ten years.'

'Gosh, how do the ranchers stand the excitement?'

The capsule began to circle the ranch. He counted eight large outlying barn sheds, all built from an ancient ginger-coloured composite, while the house in the middle was a white stone structure surrounded by a big emerald garden. An outdoor swimming pool shimmered deep turquoise. Terrestrial horses cantered around a broad paddock.

'Okay, that actually looks rather nice,' Corrie-Lyn said grudgingly.

His field functions reported the capsule was being given a broad-spectrum scan. 'Not quite paradise,' he muttered. His own passive scan was registering some dense power clumps in the ground. They were arranged in an even circle around the perimeter. A defence ring of some kind.

The capsule settled on a designated zone just outside the garden.

'Can you . . .' he started to say to Corrie-Lyn, then saw her disinterested expression. 'Just leave the talking to me, okay?'

'Of course I will. Shall I just stay in here? Or would you like to gag me? Perhaps you'd prefer me stuffed into a suspension pod?'

'Now there's true tempting,' he told her cheerfully, ignoring the scowl.

Paul Alkoff was leaning on the five bar gate which led to the paddock, dressed entirely in faded blue denim with a Stetson perched on his head. A tall man who was finally allowing his seven and a half centuries to show. His hair was snow white, worn long at the back but perfectly brushed. His movements were noticeably slow, as if each limb was stiff. With skin that was tanned dark brown his pale-blue eyes seemed to shine out of his thin face. A neatly trimmed goatee added to his palpable air of distinction. Even Aaron recognized he was in the presence of a formidable man; he immediately began to wonder just how much living had been crammed into those seven hundred and fifty years. A great deal, if he was any judge.

'Sir, thank you for agreeing to see me.'

Corrie-Lyn shot him a surprised look at the respectful tone.

Paul gave a small smile then lifted his Stetson an inch off his hair and inclined his head to Corrie-Lyn. 'Ma'am. Welcome.'

'Um, hello,' a thoroughly confused Corrie-Lyn managed.

'Don't normally allow your kind in my home,' Paul said directly to Aaron. 'So you'll understand if I don't ask you in and break bread with you.'

'My biononics are for combat, I'm not Higher.'

'Uh huh. Don't suppose it makes no difference these days, son. That battle was fought a long time ago.'

'Did you win?'

'Planet's still human, so I guess we did some good back then.'

'So you are Protectorate?'

'My old partners asked me to let you land. When I enquired, I heard they got leaned on by people high up in the movement, people we haven't heard from in a long time. You made that happen, son, so I'd appreciate it if you don't go all coy with me now.'

'Of course not.'

'What do you want?'

'Information.'

'Figured as much.' He turned and rested his elbows on the top of the gate. 'You see Georgia out there? She's the one with the dappled mane.'

Aaron and Corrie-Lyn walked over to the gate. 'Yes, sir,' Aaron said.

'Frisky little thing, ain't she? I can trace her blood-line right back to Arabians on Earth from the mid-nineteenth century. She's as pure as they come. Not an artificial sequence in her whole genome; conceived naturally and born from her mother's belly just as every one of her ancestors have been. To me, that is a thing of beauty. Sublime beauty. I do not wish to see that spoiled. No indeed, I don't want to see her foals *improved*. She and her kind have the right to exist in this universe just as she was intended to by the planet that created her.'

Aaron watched the horse as she cantered around, tossing her mane. 'I can understand that.'

'Can you now? And my hat.'

'Sir?'

Paul took his Stetson off, and examined it before returning it to his head. 'This is the real McCoy, I'll have you know. One of the very last to come out of Texas, over two hundred and fifty years ago in a factory that's manufactured them for damn near a millennia, before ANA finally shut down what it regarded as an inconsequential irrelevance. The once-humans who live on that poor ole world these days don't even make them as a hobby any more. I bought a whole batch and keep them in stasis so every time I wear one out I'll have another a fresh one. I have only two left now. That's a crying shame. But then I don't expect to be around long enough to use that last one. It'll sit right there on top of my coffin.'

'I'm sorry to hear that, sir.'

'So tell me, son, do you see what I am now?'

'Not quite, no.'

Paul fixed Aaron with a perturbingly intense stare. 'If I can get all hot under the collar about the purity of a hat, just think what I'm like when human heritage is threatened with extinction.'

'Ah.'

'Yes. I'm Protectorate, and proud of it. I've played my part in preventing those obscene perversions from spreading their sanctimonious bullshit supremacy across these glorious stars. Higher isn't like some old-fashioned religion or ideology. With them, fellas who hold two different beliefs can argue and cuss about such notions all night long over a bottle of whisky and laugh it off in the morning like gentlemen. But not Higher culture. I regard it as a physical virus to be exterminated. It will contaminate us and take away choice. If you are born with biononics infecting your cells, your choice is taken away from you. You *will* download your thoughts into ANA. That's it. No option, no alternative. Your essence has been stolen from you before you are born. Humans, true humans, have free will. Highers do not. No indeed.'

'And the life they live between birth and download?' Corrie-Lyn asked.

'Irrelevant. They're the same as pets, or more likely cattle, cosseted and protected by machines until the moment they're ready to submit to their metal god in a final sacrifice.'

'So what's the point in that god creating them?'

'Ultimately, there won't be one. Despite the years, this is early days yet. ANA believes it is our replacement. If it is allowed free rein it will see us extinct.'

'A lot of species continue after their post-physical plateau,' Aaron said. 'For most a singularity is a regeneration event, those that don't go post-physical diversify and spread across new stars.'

'Yes. But no longer what they were.' Paul gazed out at Georgia again. 'Unless she is protected, the universe will never see her like again. That is wrong. It cannot be allowed.'

'The radical Higher movement is almost extinct,' Aaron said. 'There are no more infiltrations. ANA saw to that.'

Paul smiled thinly. 'Yeah, and ain't that an irony. Maybe the Good Lord is having a joke on his metal pretender over morals.'

'I need to ask you about your time as an active Protectorate member.'

'Go right ahead, son. I don't know what you are, but I'm pretty sure what you're not, and that's the police or some version of them.'

'No, sir, I am not.'

'Glad to hear it.'

'I'm here about Inigo.'

'Ah. That was high up on my list. You two looking for him?'

'Did you know he was Higher?'

Paul's reaction startled Aaron. The old man slapped his hand on the gate, and produced a beaming smile. 'Son of a *bitch*! I knew it, I goddamn knew it. Hell, he was a wily one. Do you know how long we watched him?'

'So you suspected?'

'Of course we suspected.'

'That means Erik Horovi was Higher?'

'Erik? Hell no. Poor kid. He was used just like the sisters by that bastard angel.'

'Sisters? Are you talking about Inigo's aunt?'

'You don't know so much after all, do you, son?'

'No, sir. But I do need to learn. It is urgent.'

'Ha. Everything is urgent. The whole universe is in a hurry these days. I know it's that way because I'm older, but damn—'

'Erik,' Aaron prompted gently.

'We'll start with the angel. You know what they are?'

'I've heard of them.'

'The radical Highers wanted to convert entire worlds to their culture. They didn't want to give people a choice about it. Like I said, if you're born with biononics you don't have any options in life, in what you become. So back then these angels would land on a planet and do their dirty work; starting the infection which would spread across the entire population. Now the Protectorate watched the spaceports for anyone with biononics, and kept tabs on them while they were visiting. Still do, so I gather. So the angels would land out in the wilds somewhere. They'd jump offship while it was still in low orbit, and their force fields would protect them through aerobraking.' He gave Aaron a long look. 'Could you do that?'

'Yes, I suppose so. It's just a question of formatting. But back then it would have been cutting edge.'

'Oh the bastards were that, for sure. The force fields were what earned them their name. They were shaped like wings, and brought them down to the world amid a fiery splendour. A lot of them got through unnoticed. This time, though, we got lucky; a sympathizer out fishing saw the thermal trail it left over the ocean and called it in. Me and my team tracked the monster to Kuhmo. But we weren't quick enough. By the time we got there it had hooked up with Erik Horovi and Imelda Viatak, who were dating just like normal kids. Now the thing with angels is they're hermaphroditic, and they're beautiful. I mean really beautiful. This one was exceptional even by their standards, either a pretty boy or a real humdinger of a girl depending on your own gender. It was what you wanted it to be. So it made friends with Erik and Imelda and went to bed with both of them. Erik first. Now that's important. Its organs injected his sperm with biononics. Then it lay with Imelda and impregnated her with Erik's altered sperm.'

'Contraception?' Aaron queried.

'No use. Angels can neutralize it faster than any medic. So the kids find they're having a baby, and the DNA test proves it's theirs no question. Biononics are hellishly difficult to detect in an embryo even today. Back then it was near impossible. So, bang, you've got a changeling in the nest without ever knowing it. Biononics don't come active until puberty, so by then it's too late. Plant enough of them in a population, and a few generations later most of the births are Higher. But we intercepted this little love triangle in time.'

'The college art block,' Corrie-Lyn said.

'Yes, ma'am. You might say the angel put up something of a fight. But we got it. All you really need to defeat biononics is a heavier level of firepower. The art block got in the way.'

'What about the baby?'

'We took Erik and Imelda back to our field headquarters. She was pregnant, about two weeks gone as I recall, and it was infected.'

'I thought you couldn't tell.'

Paul looked straight ahead at the horizon. 'There are ways you can find out. You have to test the cells directly.'

'Oh, Ozzie,' Corrie-Lyn breathed, her face had paled.

'We took it out of her and checked. No kind of embryo can survive that kind of test. Fortunately we were right this time, it was one of them.'

'You're not human, no matter what you claim.'

Aaron gave her a furious look. She started to say something then threw her hands up in disgust and walked away.

'Sorry about that,' Aaron said. 'What happened?'

'Standard procedure in cases when the girl knows she's pregnant, which Imelda did. We can't wipe weeks from their memories, that would be detectable. So we took another ovum from her and fertilized it with Erik's contribution, and implanted. Then they both got a memory wipe for the evening they spent with us. Next morning they wake up with a bad hangover, and can't remember what they did. Typical teenage morning after.'

'Did it go wrong, then?'

'No, son, everything worked perfectly. Nine months later they had a lovely little girl. A normal one.'

'So how was Inigo conceived?'

'Imelda had a sister.'

'Sabine.'

'Yes. They were twins. Identical twins.'

'Ah. I think this is starting to make sense.'

'I should have realized. It's every teenage boy's ultimate fantasy; plenty of men, too.'

'He slept with both of them.'

'Yes. Him and the angel. You just confirmed that for me. Finally. Part of the Protectorate's whole clean-up procedure is to review the angel's memories, to find out who it has contaminated. Hacking into its brain is a terrible, terrible thing, one of the greatest abuses of medical technology possible. It takes days to break the protection which biononics provide for the neurones. I used to do it for the team, may God forgive me, but it was necessary. There's no other way of discovering what those devil-spawned monsters have been up to. It's not an exact science, now or then. Minds are not tidy little repositories like a memory kube. I had to merge my mind with its and endure its vile slippery thoughts inside my own skull. When I reviewed its recent memories I actually experienced coupling with Imelda.' He closed his eyes, clearly pained by the fraudulent memory. 'Her face was inches from me. She tasted so ... sweet. But, now, I don't suppose it was all her. Rather, the memories weren't just of her. I couldn't tell the difference between the girls. Dammit, at the time I didn't know there was a difference I should be searching for.'

'So Inigo was born as part of a radical Higher infiltration plan.'

'Yes. We were shocked when we found out Sabine was pregnant, but that was just before she was due. There were a lot of arguments within my team about what we should do.'

'Snatch the baby and test it.'

'That was one option. The mild one.' Paul looked over at Corrie-Lyn who was sitting on a low concrete wall outside one of the barns. 'But intervention becomes progressively difficult as time winds away, especially once the child is born. We're not ... There's a difference between abortion and infanticide – to me, anyway. And once it was born it has a legal right of residency. Even if we took it away from the mother and shipped it back to the Central Worlds, they'd just send it right back. Legally, it's a mess. Which is why the Protectorate was formed, to stop the whole nightmare scenario before it gets politically complicated.'

'So what did you do?'

'I never really believed the girls having a kid two weeks apart was coincidence. In the event, we settled for observation. If Inigo was infected he'd give himself away eventually, they all do.'

'But he didn't.'

'No. We monitored him off and on for over twenty-five years. He never put a foot wrong. He was a straight down the line normal human. School. University. Girlfriends. Not exceptionally sporting. Got injured when he played football. Had to get a job. Kept out of local politics. Signed up with a rejuve finance company. When he took aerosols he got high. Took a boring academic position in the state university cosmology department. There was nothing to indicate he had biononics. Right up until you arrived today I'd still have said he most probably didn't. I had come to accept that his birth maybe was coincidence after all. Believe me, son, if we'd confirmed it when he reached legal age we would have made a quiet ultimatum.'

'Leave or die.'

'Yes. There's no other way you can treat them.'

'Then he did leave, didn't he? All the way to Centurion Station.'

'Yes. And what a goddamned pitiful mess that's turned into. Half the aliens in the galaxy want to shoot us out of space. Who can blame them?'

'It's only the Ocisen Empire.'

'You mean they're the only ones who have declared themselves. Don't tell me you think the others are just going to sit back and let us wreck the very stars themselves.'

'Who knows? If I can find him maybe we can put a stop to the whole Pilgrimage.'

'I should have killed him in the womb when I had the chance.'

'Whatever he is, he's not Higher.'

'He might not be polluted with their culture, yet, but it will come to him eventually.'

'Apparently not. He found an alternative to a route you believed was set in stone. His destiny is inside the Void, not with ANA.'

Paul shrugged. 'Whichever one it is, it's not a human destiny.'

'Our destiny is what we decide to make it. Free choice, remember.'

'You're wrong, son. I see you believe in yourself, and I wish you well in that. But you're wrong.'

'Okay, we'll just differ on that one. What happened to Erik?'

'Bodyloss.' Paul caught Aaron's expression. 'Not us, it was a genuine accident. He was working hard to support both girls. A decent lad, I guess. The farmer he was helping out didn't do very good maintenance. The agribot chewed him up something bad. This was maybe six months after the kids were born. His insurance was all paid up, but he'd only just had his memorycell fitted. It's always the same in cases like that. The new body only has a few months of memories, which is never enough to install a decent level of personality. In his re-life state he was very childlike, ironically because his entire childhood was what he lacked. There was no real emotional connection with the sisters and his two children. Not immediately. Imelda worked hard at correcting that. She did well. They went off together. Sabine and little Inigo got left behind. It kicked off a huge family row. The sisters never really spoke after that.'

'Which is why Aunt Imelda got written out of his official history.'

'That's pretty much it. Yes.'

*

'I've never met a more despicable human,' Corrie-Lyn said as the regrav capsule lifted from the ranch. 'And I include our dear Cleric Conservator in that statement.'

'Did you ever meet a Higher angel?'

'No.'

'Well then.'

'That's it?' she shouted angrily. 'That's your justification?'

'I'm not trying to justify anything. All I'm doing is pointing out that for every action there is an equal and opposite reaction. What he used to do was part of the era.'

'He's a psychopath. Fuck knows how many babies he's killed. He belongs in suspension for the rest of eternity.'

'Dead, you mean.'

'Whatever!' she snapped, and slumped down into the cushioning. Her delicate features set in a furious sulk.

'I told you to leave the talking to me.'

'Shut the fuck up.'

'Well at least he helped us.'

'How?'

'There now you see, if you hadn't gone stomping off in a huff...'

'Screw you. I bet you were Protectorate before the memory wipe. It certainly fits.'

'No.'

'You can't be certain, though. And how come you have such highly placed contacts in their filthy organization?'

'I simply know who to ask in such circumstances, that's all. Information does not imply compliance; and I don't know where my data originates from.'

'Pah!' She turned to watch the desert skim past.

Aaron waited a minute for her to relent. When she didn't, he smiled quietly and said, 'Inigo bought a rejuvenation policy.'

'So?' She managed to spit it out with more petulance than a tantrumming five-year-old.

'It was part of his attempt to fit in with a normal existence,' Aaron continued passively. 'No one with biononics needs a rejuvenation treatment, that's strictly for Advancers and normals. Biononics maintain human cells at an optimum state; the body doesn't age biologically after you hit twenty-five. He did it to fool the Protectorate. After all, he knew what his heritage was, which means he knew what they would do to him if he made a slip.'

'And that helps us how?'

'It means he had a secure memory store. It probably dates right up to his assignment to Centurion Station.'

'I'm so sorry, I didn't realize you were deaf. *And that helps us how?*'

'Somewhere on Anagaska there's an electronic version of the young Inigo's personality. Alkoff gave me the name of the company he bought the policy from.'

'That's not going to— Oh dear Ozzie! You have got to be kidding.'

Aaron grinned cheerfully at her. 'About time this planet saw a little excitement.'

*

Prior to the Starflyer War, when the Commonwealth was essentially one society comprising predominantly physical citizens, the government created a very senior committee named the Exo-Protectorate Council whose brief was to evaluate the threat level presented by each new alien species as it was discovered. After ANA came on line and took over design, manufacture, and operation of the Commonwealth Navy's warships, threat became something of a non-term. If the old Commonwealth could defeat the Primes, ANA with its near post-physical technology was unlikely to be menaced by anything less than a malevolent post-physical. That wasn't to say that the remaining physical sector of the Commonwealth couldn't encounter a whole load of grief out among the stars. So the ExoProtectorate Council lived on in a modified form inside ANA, operating independently from ANA: Governance.

Its meetings were few and infrequent. Therefore, when Admiral Kazimir called for one, every delegate appeared, suspecting the reason. They met in a neutral perceptual reality in a secure location within ANA, comprising an old-fashioned conference room with rather extravagant white and orange furniture and a panoramic window showing them the Mollavian plains with their wall of hydrogen volcanoes. Sheets of ice-pebble meteorites sleeted downwards, burning crimson contrails with lightning forks rippling in their wake.

Kazimir activated the perceptual reality, and materialized in the seat at the head of the table. Gore flicked in a millisecond later, sitting directly to Kazimir's right. He was followed by Justine. Ilanthe was next to appear, a delicate-looking woman dressed in a blue and grey leotard. Her dark hair had been cropped short and coloured with purple streaks. They didn't represent any kind of enrichments, they were just highlights. It was a style which Kazimir thought he recognized, but couldn't quite place without running a check through his enhanced neural structure. Ilanthe wasn't worth the effort; she was the Accelerator Faction's appointment to the Council, and enjoyed making mischief where she could. The trick with her was not to rise to the bait.

Crispin Goldreich arrived in the seat next to Justine. Over a thousand years ago he'd been a Senator sitting on the original ExoProtectorate Council. It was an appointment he'd maintained ever since. Kazimir and ANA:Governance allowed him to remain because when it came to advising on the political angle of a crisis there were few better short of a full Governance convocation. Unfortunately, his usefulness was limited by a somewhat xenophobic view of aliens; several members of his family had been lost on Nattavaara during the Starflyer War, which had shaped his opinion ever since. As such he was a strong advocate of both the Isolationist and Internalist Factions.

The last two were Creewan and John Thelwell, who respectively put forward Custodian and Darwinist Faction positions.

'Thank you for attending,' Kazimir said. 'I have implemented this Council because the situation with regards to the Ocisen Empire has entered a new stage. The Navy squadron deployed in the Hancher domain have detected a massive Empire fleet now in flight. Its trajectory is aimed directly at the Commonwealth, specifically the sector containing Ellezelin.'

'How many ships?' Justine asked.

'Two thousand eight hundred and seventeen,' Kazimir replied. 'Of which nine hundred are their Starslayer class, the biggest, most expensive warships they've ever built. The Empire's economy has suffered a significant downturn over the last forty years in order to facilitate their production. They are armed with warheads similar to quantumbusters. They think we don't know about them, but we detected the trials they conducted forty-five years ago.'

'They have quantumbusters?' Crispin asked.

'A variant of, yes,' Kazimir said. 'Such a development was inevitable. They make our atom-bomb-era species look like a bunch of pacifists.'

'And the Navy hasn't bothered to share this with us?'

'The Empire believes their advantage is that we don't know. To make it public knowledge that the Empire possesses a device which the External Worlds would regard as a doomsday weapon would be to give away our advantage, not to mention damaging public confidence.'

'They must be insane,' Creewan muttered. 'The Emperor must realize how we'll react to an assault of that nature. They know how strong we are.'

'Actually, they don't,' Kazimir said. 'Nobody outside ANA: Governance and myself knows the exact capability of the deterrence fleet.'

'Please tell me it is strong enough to deal with the Ocisen Empire.'

'Don't concern yourself on that score. They do not pose any sort of threat.'

'Are they alone?' Gore asked. 'The Ambassador was quite adamant that they'd dug up some decent allies.'

'There were no non-Empire ships in the fleet which launched,' Kazimir said.

'We'll make a politician out of you yet, my boy. So do we know for sure that the Starslayer class are only armed with quantumbusters, or have they found some nasty leftovers from someone who went post-physical?'

'We'd have to intercept a Starslayer and scan it to be certain of the precise contents,' Kazimir said. 'I don't advise that. In Ocisen terms that provocation would be a declaration of war. Plus, we'd tip their hand about how powerful we are.'

'Well what the hell do you advise?' Crispin asked. 'They're going to find out eventually.'

'I'd like to avoid that. What I'd like to see applied to the Ocisens is something along the lines of intense diplomatic persuasion so that they turn the fleet round and go home.'

'Won't happen,' Creewan said. 'If the Empire has launched what is essentially their entire Navy at us, it will be politically impossible for them to return until the Pilgrimage has been halted. Asking them nicely just won't hack it. We'll have to use force.'

'What about another more immediate threat to the Empire?' Justine suggested. 'Some unknown ships approaching from another direction? We could deliver that, surely?'

'Yes,' said Kazimir. 'But it simply postpones the inevitable. We can manufacture what appears to be a threat, but if their fleet returns to challenge an intruder then our bluff will be called. I cannot blow up star systems simply to maintain an illusion. No matter the morality, there is a considerable physical problem with radiation. Our Firewall project showed that.'

'How long until they get here?' Ilanthe asked.

'Their flight-time to Ellezelin is seventy-nine days,' Kazimir said. 'A significant figure, because the Pilgrimage fleet will not be completed by then. It is reasonable to assume their aim is to hit the Pilgrimage ships while they're still on the ground. If the Living Dream were to get its ships into space, they would be a lot harder to intercept, especially for the Empire.'

'Then I don't understand your reluctance to create a diversion. Once the Pilgrimage ships are in space, the Empire fleet is effectively neutralized. You don't have to do anything as dramatic as blow up a star on the other side of the Empire. Launch a thousand drones with a phantom signature, so it appears a hostile fleet is heading to the Empire. Buy us some time for Living Dream.'

'They'd know,' Gore said. 'It's the timing again. They launch their fleet. We have to delay it and oh look, here's an unknown threat coming at them from the other side of space. How about that for coincidence? Even the Ocisens aren't that stupid.'

'Don't count on it,' John Thelwell muttered.

'It would have to be a credible threat to divert them,' Kazimir said.

'So skulk around the Empire's borders and wreck a couple of stars, or at least planets.'

'We employ the word *Empire* too glibly,' Justine said. 'The most literal translation of their planets is, *Worlds upon which we nest.* I'm ashamed this committee is prepared to demonize the Ocisens to justify force. We must concentrate on peaceful solutions.'

Ilanthe gave Gore a small victory smile as he glowered at his daughter.

'If they weren't sending a fleet towards us armed with enough quantumbusters to wipe out every Commonwealth planet I might not refer to them as a bunch of psychopathic fuckheads,' Gore snapped. 'As it is, we are here to advise the Navy on how to respond. You met the Ambassador. Exactly what sort of peaceful overture do you think the *Empire* will respond to?'

'We have to provide them with options,' Justine said. 'Preferably ones which allow them to save face.'

'Like pressuring Living Dream not to launch its ridiculous Pilgrimage,' Creewan said.

'Outside this committee's remit,' Ilanthe said swiftly. 'We advise the Navy on its response.' She didn't even turn to look at Creewan. 'You want to push for something like that, bring it up at a political meeting, or even Governance.'

'It is a valid option,' Justine said.

'Not here it isn't. Here we decide on how many of their suns we turn nova in order to convince them to turn back.'

'Nobody is turning Empire suns nova,' Kazimir said. 'As I said, their fleet does not pose a physical threat to any aspect of the Commonwealth. It can be effectively neutralized.'

'That's quite a big claim,' Ilanthe said. 'You sure about that?'

'Providing they do not possess an excess of stolen post-physical technology, yes.'

'Then do just that, neutralize them. Stop them cold in inter-stellar space. It's not like they have a back-up fleet to send if anything goes wrong.'

Kazimir glanced round the table. 'Is that the recommendation of this committee?'

'It certainly is not,' Justine said.

'And your plan is . . . ?' Ilanthe enquired archly.

'A warning,' John Thelwell said. 'In all likelihood, several warnings, considering who we're dealing with. Followed by a demonstration of our capability and intent.'

'Would that be several demonstrations?' Justine asked acidly. 'Just to get the point over how big and scary we are.'

'Once they see they cannot stop the Pilgrimage they will turn back.'

'That implies a governing factor of logic and reason,' Crispin said. 'This is the Ocisens we're talking about. They're committed to stopping us. Even if it meant the death of every starship in their fleet, they'll keep coming.'

'The warships will be disabled, not destroyed,' Kazimir said. 'I could not countenance such a loss of life.'

'Then I don't even see what you convened us for,' Crispin said.

'Because Governance and I don't want to reveal our true capability outside a genuine and serious threat, which this is not.'

'Rock and a hard place,' Gore grunted. 'The only way to deal with them without huge loss of life all round is by using ANA's technology, which in turn makes us frightening to all the physical aliens knocking around this section of the galaxy.'

'This is a morals debate?' Ilanthe mocked.

'It might even get the Raiel worried about us,' Justine said.

'Gets my vote,' Gore said. 'Supercilious little turds. It's about time someone gave their pedestal a good kicking.'

'Oh, stop it,' Justine told him.

Gore leaned forward. 'Deliver a warning to the command ship,' he said. 'If it is ignored, disable that ship. If they continue after that, take the lot of 'em down. Use the lowest-level of technology we've got that will do the job, but do it.'

'Seconded,' Crispin said.

'I would point out that it will be a nestling of the Emperor in charge of the fleet,' said Creewan. 'The political implications of the ruling nest being defeated are not good. The likelihood of subsequent instability are strong.'

'Which neither harms nor concerns us,' John Thelwell said. He gave the Custodian a dismissive glance. 'We've given the Empire a beating before; they never learn.'

'Our position gives us an obligation,' Justine said.

'Only according to human morals,' Ilanthe said. 'These are aliens.'

'I wish to remain true to myself, thank you,' Justine said primly.

'Of course you do.'

'I vote against any physical force being used against the Empire fleet, no matter how restrained. We need to seek an alternative.'

'Thank you, Mother,' Kazimir said. 'Anyone else against the motion?'

Creewan raised his hand.

Kazimir looked round the table. 'Then it is the majority vote that the Navy delivers a warning to the command ship, and subsequently disables it if that warning is ignored. I will initiate that immediately.'

'And what if they keep on coming after the command ship is taken out?' Justine asked. 'Which they will, and you all know it.'

'Then I will reconvene this committee,' Kazimir said.

She let out an exasperated hiss of breath, and against all

etiquette withdrew instantly. The others stared at the vacated space as the perceptual reality adjusted to her absence.

'That's what being in a real body does for you,' Ilanthe muttered archly.

'I will, of course, provide a secure link to the Navy ship delivering the ultimatum,' Kazimir said. 'All of you will be able to access the event.'

'How long until the demand is made?' John Thelwell asked.

'I'd like to bring in a ship which I know has the ability to disable a Starslayer without loss of life,' Kazimir said. 'We have that capability in the Hancher assistance squadron. Flight time will be within ten days. The warning will allow them one Earth day to turn round.'

'We'll be back here in a fortnight, then,' Gore predicted.

Less than a second after the meeting officially ended, Ilanthe requested access to Gore's personal perceptual reality. He'd been expecting it and permitted her entry as he ambled along the white-sand beach below the headland. She walked up out of the water, wearing a blue and white bikini.

'Very Ursula Andress,' he said appreciatively. Gone was the spiky Cat hairstyle of the meeting, she was shaking droplets out of long honey-coloured tresses.

'Thank you.' Ilanthe squinted up at the noon sun, holding a pale hand across her forehead. 'The governors you have configuring this place are very crude. Am I likely to get sunburn?'

'They're not crude, just strong. Prevents hostiles trojaning in nasty surprises. And no, you won't get sunburn, just increase your skin pigmentation factor.'

'Ah.' She blinked as her skin darkened to a rich bronze. 'It's still a very earthy environment to me. Will you get me drunk and seduce me?'

'Sex is common enough between enemies.'

'Oh, Gore,' she pouted. 'We're not enemies. Besides we both got what we wanted out of the meeting.'

'Did we?'

'We both voted for the same thing. Why? Is dear Justine still sulking?'

He started walking along the shoreline again. 'One word of genuine advice: don't ever underestimate my daughter. I still do occasionally. It's a mistake.'

'Point taken. Do you think Kazimir will delay because of her?'

'Fuck no. He's the most Right Stuff human you'll ever meet. Government gave him a clear order, so he clicks his boot heels, salutes, and presses the button.'

'You are so anachronistic. You really should update your references.'

'What? Haul myself all the way into the twenty-fifth century?'

'Well, one step at a time.'

'That's when you were born, wasn't it?'

She chuckled. 'They're right. You are pure evil.'

'Who's they?'

'Just about everybody.'

'They're probably right then. So what can I do for you?'

'Can we deal?'

'On the Pilgrimage? Sure.'

'Interesting capitulation. Why do I not believe you?'

'It's going to be a cusp event. Every Faction knows it. Hell, even some of the animals outside are waking up to what's going on. The Darwinists are wetting themselves with excitement. And your lot aren't much better, running round, pushing and prodding in places you shouldn't.'

'I don't know what you're talking about.'

'That arsehole Marius is clocking up a lot of lightyears.'

She pretended shock, her hand going to the base of her throat. 'As is your Delivery Man.'

'True Conservatives are paranoid little creatures. They have good cause.'

'You claim you're not one of them?'

'I have an affiliation.'

'Funny, according to our files you're the chairman of the board.'

'You really should update your references.'

She put her hands on her hips. 'Look, do you want to deal or not?'

'You're very hot in that pose, you know that?'

'Gore!'

'All right, what are you offering?'

'Some détente. A little less manipulation from both sides.'

'Let the animals decide, you mean. I don't think I can buy that coming from you. In any case, we've both spent so long moving our pawns into place that they'll just keep on going without us now.' He tilted his head to one side, and smiled. 'Or am I missing something?'

'No.'

'Really? Perhaps some critical event that you need to work smoothly?'

'Moments like that are made up by historians after the event to justify their own dreary existence. There's no one thing which will make or break the Pilgrimage.'

'Really? Have you ever tried telling Ozzie or Nigel that the actions of an individual are historically invalid?'

'Nobody manipulated them. And this is a distraction. We simply want both sides to cool down.'

'So the Accelerator Faction wants to let galactic events be decided by animals. Humm. No wonder you don't like my environment, it doesn't have any flying pigs.'

'Is that your answer?'

'No. But I am mildly curious. Unless either a Faction or ANA:Governance itself intervenes, the Pilgrimage ships will launch. So what the fuck exactly is the Accelerator line on the galaxy being devoured by the Void, exterminating all life including ourselves?'

'It won't happen. This is why I'm here, to tell you we have taken precautions in the event of the worst-case scenario.'

Gore stopped and turned to stare at her, genuinely surprised. 'What the fuck are you talking about?'

'If the Void's boundary sweeps through this sector of space, Earth and ANA will be perfectly safe.'

'You don't know that.'

'Oh yes we do.'

'I really, *really*, hope you're not basing your goals on some chunk of weapons technology you've managed to cobble together with a couple of old replicators. The Raiel can't defeat the boundary. Even ANA:Governance can't work out what will happen if and when the Void's boundary washes across itself.'

'That level of expansion is extremely unlikely, to the point of sheer impossibility. Firstly, the stars of the Wall have tremendous mass; enough to empower the will of every Living Dream pilgrim for centuries. It is an absolute fallacy that every star in the galaxy will be engulfed by the Void. Raiel propaganda shouted in tedious repetition by the Ocisens. The Raiel are an ancient failed race, as changeless as the Void itself, they have no right to dictate to us. Even if the entire galactic core gets devoured it doesn't matter. There's nothing alive in there, the planets are radiation-saturated husks of rock. You even believe it yourself, always accusing us of wanting the devourment. Have I ever said that?'

'No. I know exactly what Accelerators want: fusion. Right? You want to merge ANA with the fabric of the Void continuum. You think that's how we'll achieve post-physical status.'

'You have accessed Inigo's dreams, we know the Conservatives have analysed them as thoroughly as everyone else. Inside the Void, the mind directly affects the fabric of the universe, we can take charge of our own destiny.'

'No, no, no,' Gore shouted. 'The Void is not a fucking universe, it is a microverse, a tiny insignificant little speck of nothing. In cosmological terms, it doesn't even register. You can play God in there, for sure, the Waterwalker does it. But you're only God in there, nowhere else. It is an alien version of ANA, that's all. That's not transcendence, it's being so far up your own ass you can't see what's going on outside.'

'It is a huge opportunity for growth. The Void has stalled, it has been changeless for millions – billions – of years. We can reinvigorate it. Humans have already begun that process; ordinary pitiful animals that now have mental powers even we can only fantasize about. Imagine what will happen when ANA has full access to such a technology, and begins to manipulate it in new directions.'

'Sweet Ozzie, you are pitiful. I'd be contemptuous if I considered you sentient, but you're not even that.'

'We knew you would be opposed to the fusion, this is what our offer concerns.'

'Go on,' Gore said suspiciously.

'We will duplicate ANA. Those who wish to attain fusion with the Void can stay here, those who do not can transfer over and fly free.'

'That doesn't solve a fucking thing, girlie. The Void can't be allowed to fuse with a post-physical mind, or even ANA – which, face it, isn't there yet.'

Ilanthe's expression hardened. 'Your language betrays you. *Can't be allowed?* You don't have the right to make that judgement. Evolution will occur, either triggered by the Pilgrimage, or a more direct connection. For all you know the Waterwalker himself may bring about expansion.'

'He happened a thousand years ago, ten thousand for all we know.'

'Time is irrelevant in there.'

'Shit! You're not Accelerators, not any more, you've seen the light and converted to Living Dream.'

'We have seen an opportunity to advance ourselves, and taken it. We have never hidden our purpose from anyone.'

'Accelerators didn't start out lusting after the Void.'

'Now you are betraying your age, your own changeless nature.'

'I should just get out of the way then, should I? Maybe simply erase myself? Make it all nice and simple for the New Order.'

'You are responsible for your own destiny.' She shrugged an elegant shoulder. 'Your choice.'

'Okay, granted; and I will make it, believe me. But assuming you're right and the Void doesn't expand like a hyperspace tsunami when the Pilgrimage gets inside, how are you going to fuse ANA with it?'

'We don't have to. Highers will travel with the Pilgrimage ships. They will study the true nature of the Void fabric and the mechanism which generates it.'

'If it can be built once,' Gore said quietly, 'it can be built again.'

Ilanthe smiled. 'Now you understand. We can build a second Void here in this solar system and bring about the fusion right away. ANA will evolve and transcend.'

'Nice science experiment. What happens if it doesn't work? ANA is the core of Higher culture, Earth is the physical centre of the Commonwealth. If you take that away, two cultures will suffer.'

'I never thought I'd hear that: Gore Burnelli, whining liberal. Normal, Higher and Advancer humans will have to make their own way in the universe. That, too, is evolution.'

'In a galaxy that your arrogance will have given a very short future.'

'Our solution is one that will satisfy all Factions. Both of us can carry on almost as before.'

'You weren't even born on Earth. I was. It's my home. And I'm not letting anyone fuck with it.'

'Then you are even less developed that we gave you credit for. Our offer stands. I expect the other Factions will take us up on it when they see the inevitability of what is to come.'

'Are you planning to blow the Empire fleet out of space?'

Ilanthe looked genuinely indignant. 'Of course not. They are an irrelevance. Kazimir will deal with them, one way or another.' She smiled coldly. 'Please consider our offer, Gore. It is made in the spirit of reconciliation. After all, if anyone can be said to be ANA's father, it is you. Time perhaps to let go and allow your child to make its own way in life.' She trotted back into the waves and dived below the water.

Gore stared at the surf where she disappeared, his mind

tracing her withdrawal from his personal reality. 'Fuck me,' he grunted.

When he walked along the dirt track that curved up around the headland he found Nelson already sitting by the pool at the base of the tower. As usual, there was a tall drink on the table beside him.

'Did you get all that?' Gore asked as he sat down.

'I got it all. I just don't think I believe much of it. For a start she's being very glib about the Pilgrimage ships actually getting inside. What are you going to do?'

'I knew they wanted the kind of abilities the Void fabric has, that's a logical development on the way to becoming post-physical, but I'm concerned about their method of acquisition. I don't believe a damn word about some bunch of selfless academics going with the Pilgrimage to study how the thing is put together. We're going to have to root around a little harder to find out what they're really up to out there. Find out what you can about that guy Marius was visiting on Arevalo, that physicist: Troblum.'

'Will do. And what if ANA does finally become capable of ascending to post-physical status?'

'I've always known it would right from the start. That was the whole point of it – well, that and giving ourselves the ability to defend the Commonwealth.'

'Are you going to try and stop it?'

'Of course not. I just don't want the natural process hijacked. And that's what's going to happen if we're not careful.'

*

It was already night when Aaron's regrav capsule landed on the pad of St Mary's Clinic, just outside the reception block. He stepped out and looked round. The clinic was set in four square miles of thick forest, with individual buildings scattered across the landscape. Tall gistrel trees formed a dark wall around the pad, their long feathery branches blocking any view of the villas, medical blocks, spas, and leisure domes he knew were out there.

The only light came from the long windows of the reception block, thirty metres away, shining round the black trunks.

Corrie-Lyn stood beside him, straightening her blouse. Her face screwed up. 'Gosh, I love the whole gloomy jungle-with-wild-creatures look they've gone for. Very welcoming.'

'Perhaps we could get your manic depression eradicated while we're here.'

'Screw you.'

'Now remember, *darling*, happy faces.'

He gripped her hand and produced a big bright smile. She almost shook free, then remembered and drew a reluctant breath. 'Okay, but this better be quick.'

The reception doors opened as they walked towards the low building. It was a plush interior, which looked as if it had been carved out of pink and gold marble, with secluded grotto chambers recessed into the wall of the central hall. Most of the chambers had been utilized by exclusive retail outlets as display booths for their inordinately expensive designer clothes and products.

Their personal clinician was waiting to greet them; Ruth Stol, who was clearly designed to promote the clinic's expertise, with a body that resembled a teenage goddess draped in semi-translucent silver and pink fabric. Even Aaron who was perfectly mission-focused took a moment to admire and smile at the vision of vitality who extended her flawless hand in greeting. His field functions detected a discreet scan from the building security net, which he deflected easily enough, showing the sensors an image of a moderately overweight man. The additional volume around his torso was actually provided by a bandolier harness carrying an array of weapons.

Ruth Stol was devoid of all enrichments, though she had more macrocellular clusters than the average Advancer, and her nervous system shone with impulses operating at the kind of rate which normal humans could only achieve with a serious dose of accelerants.

'Thank you so much for choosing our clinic, Mr Telfer,' she

said. Her hand pressed against Aaron's palm, squeezing flirta-
tiously. His biononics ran a check for pheromone infiltration.
Paranoid! But her touch and voice were definitely arousing him,
his exovision grid showed his heart rate up, skin temperature
rising.

'No infiltration,' his u-shadow reported. So it was all natural,
then. *Hardly surprising.* 'You're welcome,' Corrie-Lyn said in a
voice so cold it should have produced ice droplets.

'Er, yeah,' Aaron mumbled belatedly. He reluctantly withdrew
his hand, enjoying the coy amusement in the clinician's limpid
green eyes. 'Thanks for seeing us at such short notice.'

'We're always happy to help couples achieve a more secure
relationship,' Ruth Stol said. 'I believe you said you wanted
twins?'

'Twins?' Corrie-Lyn repeated blankly.

'That's right.' Aaron put an arm round Corrie-Lyn's shoulders,
feeling the muscles locked rigid. 'The best we can have.'

'Of course,' Ruth Stol said. 'Boys or girls?'

'Darling?' Aaron enquired.

'Boys,' Corrie-Lyn said.

'Do you have an idea of their physiological status?'

'At least as good as you,' Aaron told her, which produced
another smile. 'And I'd like the pair of us to be advanced to that
level, too. It's about time I went cutting edge.' He patted his
bulky stomach ruefully. 'Perhaps a little metabolism tweaking to
thin me down.'

'I'd be very grateful for that,' Corrie-Lyn said. 'He's so
repugnant to look at right now. Never mind sex.'

'Oh, darling, you promised not to mention that,' Aaron said
tightly.

She smiled brightly.

'It's a wonderful step to acknowledge any problems right at
the start,' Ruth Stol said. 'You'll be an enviable family. We can
begin our appraisal tomorrow, and review what we can offer you.
Our premium service will fast-track your changes; I don't expect
this to take more than a couple of weeks. Were you intending to

carry the twins yourself?' she asked Corrie-Lyn. 'Or is it going to be a womb tank?'

'Haven't decided.' Corrie-Lyn smiled back. 'I love him enough to consider the physical burden, but you'll have to show me what you can do to make pregnancy easier before I commit.'

'How sweet. I'll have a simulated sensory package of the full pregnancy option ready for you to review in the morning, and remember we can always reverse the changes afterwards.'

'Lovely.'

'We've given you villa 163, which has its own pool, and it's not far from block three where you'll receive your treatments.'

'Excellent,' Aaron said. 'I think I'll go and check out the main pool and the restaurants first, especially that Singapore Grill I've heard about. What about you, dear?'

'It's been a long day. I'll go to the villa, and organize that.' Corrie-Lyn eyed the various displays around the hall. 'After some shopping. I really like some of these designs.'

'Don't spend too much.' He gave her a farewell peck on the cheek and headed out of the door. His u-shadow extracted the clinic map from the local net, which would give the appearance of normality for another few minutes. 'Can you get into the vault?' he asked it.

'No. There are no data channels into the vault.'

Aaron took a path away from the landing pad which would lead to the main pool building, a large blue-tinted dome that housed a lush tropical environment, with the pool itself fashioned to resemble a lagoon. The path lit up like a strip of glowing yellow fog under his feet. 'What about the security system?' he asked his u-shadow.

'I can only access the lower levels. All guests are under permanent surveillance of some kind, several are red-tagged.'

'Really? Are we red-tagged?'

'No.'

'Will they know if I leave the path?'

'Yes. Various passive sensors are feeding the smartcore.'

'Start some diversions, please. Trigger alerts and attack the security net in several places, well away from me. Nothing to warrant a police call-out.'

'Initiating.'

Aaron left the path and started to run through the trees. His suit spun a stealth effect around him. After a minute slipping unseen through the forest he arrived at the administration block. There were two storeys above ground, while his research had shown ten floors cut into the bedrock beneath the forest. The secure storage vault was on the bottom. His field function scan revealed a complex array of sensors guarding the walls and surrounding swathe of garden.

He began to sprint past the last trees, accelerating hard with field-reinforced muscles until he was at the edge of the lawn, then jumped, extending his force field wide, shaping it into two long swept-back petals. Suspended between his invisible wings he glided directly at a specific window on the upper floor like a silent missile. He grinned into the air that rushed against his face and rippled his suit. Excitement was starting to build, which his biononics could only suppress so much. Even though he knew what he was going to have to do, he was still enjoying himself; this was what he existed for.

Aaron let out an em pulse from his biononics, targeted to disable the sensors and power supply around the window. When he was five metres from the wall, he triggered a disruptor effect. Glass turned to white powder and blew inwards with the sound of damp cloth being ripped. He cancelled his force-field wings and dropped through the hole, hitting the floor with a roll.

Inside was a long finance department office. Deserted and dark. Door locked. He didn't use the disruptor effect, simply smashed it down with amplified muscle power. The corridor outside ran the length of the building. Orange emergency lighting produced strangely angled shadows across the walls. His scrambler effect knocked out the net across half of the building. He jogged to the emergency stairwell and burst through. Vaulted over the rail and landed with a loud thud on the concrete floor below, integral force field absorbing the impact. He scanned round.

Two security managers were sitting in the control centre, both heavily enriched. They were standing motionless as their u-shadows interfaced them with the clinic's security net and they struggled to make sense of what was happening across the forest.

The door broke apart as Aaron walked through it. Eight energy-dumps flew out from the bandolier straps under his suit, hand-sized black discs that zipped through the air like cybernetic hornets. They struck the security managers before either could fire a shot. Both of them were transformed into silhouettes of searing white light as their personal force fields were relentlessly overloaded; tendrils of electricity lashed out from the incandescent shapes, grounding through the desks and chairs next to them. Ribbons of smoke crept up from the carpet round their feet. They began to thrash about as the discharge of energy soared to an unbearable thunderclap screech. Light panels in the ceiling detonated into splinters of bubbling plastic.

Aaron drew a jelly gun from the bandolier harness as the nimbus of light on the first manager began to fade. The man's force field flickered erratically into a purple and orange shroud. Dark shadows infiltrated the dying luminescence, exposing swathes of smouldering uniform. Aaron fired. The manager disintegrated in a spherical wave of gore that splattered across the room. After that, Aaron simply waited a few seconds until the energy-dumps completed their work on the second manager, and her force field spluttered out. The room was plunged into darkness as she fell to the floor in a sobbing heap, barely conscious.

He knelt beside her and took the surgical cutter from his pocket. The little black and silver gadget extended its eight malmetal arms as he placed it carefully on her head. Unlike Ruth Stol, the clinic hadn't designed any beauty into the security manager. She had a plain round face with dark enriched eyes; the skin on her cheeks was red raw from the crackling electron currents. Tears were leaking across them as she gazed up at Aaron.

'Please,' she croaked.

'Don't worry,' he told her. 'You won't remember this night when you're re-lifed.'

The cutter settled on the crown of her head like some vampiric creature, the arms tightening to obtain a better grip on her singed flesh. Microsurgery energy blades slid out and began to cut. Aaron waited with only the sound of gooey blood droplets drizzling down from the soot-caked ceiling to break the dark silence of the room.

'Procedure complete,' his u-shadow reported.

Aaron reached down, and gently pulled the surgical cutter. It lifted upwards with a slimy sucking sound, taking the top of her skull with it. A small amount of blood welled up around the edges of the severed bone, dribbling down through the matted hair. Her exposed brain glistened a pale grey in the weak emergency lighting shining in from the corridor outside.

He poised his left hand a couple of centimetres above the gory naked flesh. The skin on his palm puckered up in seven little circles. Slender worm-like tendrils began to wriggle out of each apex. He brought the hand down on her brain, and manipulated his force field to bond the two together, preventing his hand from sliding, even fractionally. The tendrils insinuated themselves into her neurone structure, branching again and again like some plant root seeking moisture. These tips were hunting out distinct neural pathways, circumventing conscious control over not just her body but her thoughts.

Synapses were successfully violated and corrupted. His mentallic software began to pull coherent strands out of the chaotic impulses.

Her name was Viertz Accu. A hundred and seventeen years old. Advancer heritage. Currently married to Asher Lel. Two children. The youngest, Harry, was two years old. She was upset that she'd pulled another late shift; little Harry did so like her reading to him before bedtime.

Aaron's software moved the acquisition focus up towards the present.

All earlier emotional content was now superseded by sheer terror. Body's sensory input was minimal, sinking below waves of pain from the force field collapse. One memory rising above all the others, bright and loud: the surgical cutter descending. Starting to repeat. Thoughts becoming incoherent as the memory degenerates into a psychosis loop. Limbs shake as bodyshock commences.

Forget that, Aaron's thoughts instruct the brain he now rules. He has to concentrate, to exert his own thoughts to squash the terror memory. His influence is assisted by the flawless positioning of the neurone override tendrils, making it impossible for her to resist. A different kind of mental pressure is then exerted. Her conscious thoughts wither to insensate status, effectively sinking her into a coma.

Stand, he commands the puppet body.

It straightens up, and Aaron rises beside it. His hand remains locked in place on top of her ruined head by the mucilage force field.

Clinic security system review. Schematics flip up into their mutual exovision, showing alert points. His u-shadow ends its roguish electronic assaults as he accesses the clinic net through Viertz's private secure link. False signals are generated within the administration building to replace the equipment he neutralized during his entry.

Codes. Up from Viertz's own memory and her macrocellular clusters spill file after file of codes for every aspect of the clinic. He deploys them to damp down the security net, reducing it to a level-zero state. Another set of commands reset the smartcore's alertness, convincing it that it was receiving malfunction warnings and the security managers now have everything under control.

Several operatives across the forest are calling in.

It's all right, he mouths and Viertz sends on a secure link. *There's been a spate of glitches, those boogledammed glints have been getting into the cabling again. They were chewing on a node, little bastards.* Boogledammed is a phrase Viertz is fond of. Glints are tiny native rodents infesting the forest and always causing problems to the clinic and its machinery, despite two illegal attempts by the management to exterminate them.

Generally the explanation is accepted. Viertz exchanges a few more in-character comments with colleagues, and signs off.

Vault.

They walk along the ground-floor corridor, side by side, Aaron's hand still firmly in place on her head. Viertz's code opens the lift doors. Aaron extracts additional overrides which will clear him to accompany her down to the bottom.

The vault level poses more of a problem. It is covered in sensors, all of which are linked directly to the clinic smartcore through isolated, protected circuits. There are no overrides he can utilize to smooth his passage. If it sees him it will immediately query his identity.

The mission is now time-critical.

As the lift reaches the vault level, Aaron uses an em pulse to kill all power circuits and unguarded systems. His scrambler field disables the protected security network. The smartcore now knows something is wrong, but cannot detect what. The entire floor is an electronic dead zone.

Aaron slides the lift door open with his free hand. Metal provides considerable resistance. The activators emit a screech as they are buckled by the pressure he exerts. He steps into darkness. Field function scans and infrared imaging reveal the short, empty corridor ahead. He walks along it with the zombie Viertz marching beside him until they reach the large vault door of metabonded malmetal at the end. Both wall and door are guarded by a strong force field, powered independently from within. His free hand strokes across the undefended corridor wall until his fingers are resting over the armoured conduit carrying part of the security net's cabling. He presses down. A small disruptor pulse disintegrates the concrete. Dust pours out, and he pushes his hand deeper into the hole. He has to excavate up to his elbow until he reaches the conduit. There is a brief clash of energy fields and the conduit shatters, exposing the optical cables inside.

The fingertips of this hand extrude slender filaments which penetrate the optical cables, immersing themselves into the blaze of coherent light flashing along the interior. His enrichments are interfaced directly into the smartcore through an unprotected link. A torrent of destructive software is unleashed by his u-shadow, corroding the smartcore's primary routines like acid on skin. In the first eight milliseconds of the assault, the smartcore loses over half of its intellectual processing capacity. Its default preservation routines withdraw its connections to the vault security system, allowing it to retreat and lick its wounds in isolation.

Aaron's u-shadow turns its attention to the connections along the other end of the expropriated optical cable, and examines the security network inside the vault. It takes less than a second to map out the system's nodes and kubes allowing it to remove the smartcore's control and safeguard procedures. The force field switches off, and the thick door opens with a low swish of retracting malmetal.

Aaron removes his hand from the ragged hole. He and Viertz walk forward in tandem, passing through the air/dust shield with a gentle *buzzt*. Independent lighting panels click on, revealing a shiny oblong chamber filled with floor-to-ceiling racks of trans-lucent pink plastic kubes.

The registry is a simple slim pedestal of metal just inside.

Viertz accesses the dormant software within. She is asked for her DNA-based authority certificate.

As he passes the threshold, Aaron's field scans reveal two strange energy signatures emerging from the walls on either side of the vault. It is the final failsafe to protect the priceless half-million secure memorycells within the vault. Not listed anywhere in the security net inventory, and quietly imported from a Central World where such technology is unexceptional. Two guards with heavy weapons enrichments sealed within the temporal suspen-sion zone of exotic matter cages. Their enrichments were already fully powered up when they began their two-year duty period. They do not ask questions as they step back into real-time, they simply open fire.

Aaron's force field is immediately pushed close to overload as it struggles to protect him and Viertz. His disadvantage is terribly obvious as energy beams pummel into him and the woman. Dense waves of scarlet photons ignite with blinding ferocity around his chest and arms. He staggers back half a step.

Send authority certificate.

But the pedestal uses non-military grade hardware. It cannot receive and acknowledge any information in such a hostile electromagnetic environment.

'Shit!' His bandolier belts launch a flock of electronic counter-measure drones and five niling-sponges. The guards twist away from the threat, ducking behind the racks. Aaron reaches out with his free hand and manages to grip the top of the pedestal as the last of the energy barrage drains away from his force field. The filaments emerge from his fingertips and try to burrow into the nodes and cables underneath the metal.

Both guards spin out from behind the racks and open fire again. The niling-sponges cluster together and activate their absorption horizons. Energy beams from the weapons curve bizarrely through the hot air to sink harmlessly into the black-star blooms now drifting sedately in front of Aaron. Their horizons start to expand significantly. The guards shift to kinetic carbines. Their hypervelocity projectiles are unaffected by the niling-sponges and smash against Aaron and Viertz. The force field flares bright copper, shading up towards carmine. Aaron can feel the strain the impacts are punishing his body with, reinforcement fields are struggling to hold him upright.

On your knees.

Viertz sinks quickly to the shiny floor, presenting a smaller, more stable target. His filaments have penetrated the metal casing of the pedestal, and begin to affiliate themselves with the fine mesh of optical strands beneath.

A couple of energy-dumpers skim towards Aaron. He shoots

them with a simple ion shot from an enrichment in his forearm. His force field has to reformat momentarily to allow the ions through. It is a weakness which the guards exploit ruthlessly, concentrating their fire. He feels the kinetic projectiles lance into his shoulder and upper torso. Combat software reports five direct hits. Field scans reveal the nature of the foreign projectiles. Number one is a straight explosive, which is countered by a damping field, turning it to a lump of white hot metal. Two releases a pack of firewire tangles, which expand through his flesh, ripping it apart at a cellular level, incinerating as they go, wrecking biononic organelles. They can only be staved off by a specific frequency disruptor field to attack their molecular structure, which has a debilitating effect of the biononics still functional in the area. Three dispenses a nerve agent in sufficient quantity to exterminate five hundred humans. Biononics converge quickly to counteract the deadly toxin. Four is another explosive, neutralized along with one. Five is a cluster of microjanglers, microbe-sized generators that jam his nervous system, inhibiting biononic and enrichment operations; a secondary function is to induce pain impulses. They require a scrambler field to kill them.

Blood pumps out from the cratered flesh and torn suit, to be flattened back beneath the reformatted force field. The surrounding fabric of his suit is quickly saturated. Biononics congregate around the edge of the wounds, acting in concert to knit the damage back together, sealing up veins, arteries, and capillaries. Inside his body the firewire tangles halt their expansion as the disruptor sabotages their molecular cohesion. It is too slow, they are causing a massive amount of damage. Damage which is amplified by the microjanglers.

Aaron flings his head back to scream in agony as the microscopic technology war is fought within his muscles and blood vessels. But still he keeps hold of both Viertz and the pedestal.

His biononics shut off a whole series of nerves, eliminating the pain and all sensation in his shoulder and arm. A disconcertingly large section of the medical status display in his exovision is flashing red. Nausea plagues him. Shivers run along his limbs. The field medic sac in his thigh pushes a dose of suppressants into his bloodstream.

Another wave of kinetics pound him. He is in danger of falling backwards. His biononics and enrichments are reaching maximum capacity. Countermeasure drones do their best to confuse the enemy targeting sensors, but the narrow confines of the vault almost make such systems irrelevant.

His filaments interface with the registry kube in the pedestal. *Send authority certificate.*

The registry software acknowledges Viertz's authority. And the u-shadow runs a search for Inigo's secure store. It locates the memorycell. The physical coordinates are loaded into Aaron's combat routines. A volume of eight cubic centimetres to be held inviolate. The rest of the vault's structure is now expendable.

He lets go of the pedestal and Viertz. The woman slumps forward, a motion which jolts her unsecured brain. A fresh upwelling of blood bubbles out around the circle of cut bone. The protective swirl of niling-sponges deactivate, their black horizons folding in upon themselves. Aaron raises his head and smiles an animal snarl through the clear air at the guards. Their barrage has paused as they take stock.

'Payback time,' he growls enthusiastically.

The first disruptor pulse smashes out. Half of the precious racks rupture in a maelstrom of molten plastic. Both guards stagger backwards. Jelly gun shots hammer at their force fields. Energy-dumpers zip about, launched by both sides. Black niling horizons expand and contract like inverse novas. Kinetic projectiles chew into the vault's concrete and marble walls. More racks suffer, shattering like antique glass. The plastic catches fire, molten rivulets streaking across the floor, spitting feeble flames from their leading edges.

Aaron positions himself between the guards and Inigo's memorycell, shielding it from any possible damage. He manages to puncture the force field of one guard's leg and fires the jelly gun into the gap. The leg instantly transforms to a liquid pulp of ruined cells. The guard screams as he topples over. His force field reconfigures over the stump, allowing the blood and gore to splash across the ground where it starts to steam softly. Energy-dumpers attach themselves to him like predatory rodents. He thrashes about helplessly as his force field diminishes.

Now it is just Aaron and the remaining guard. They advance on each other, each trusting in his own weapons enrichments. This is no longer a battle of software or even human wits. It is brute strength only which will prevail now.

At the end they resemble two atomic fireballs colliding. A shockwave of incandescent energy flares out from the impact, vaporizing everything it touches. One fireball is abruptly extinguished.

Aaron stands over the clutter of charcoal which seconds before was his opponent. While still staring down he extends his good arm sideways. An x-ray laser muzzle emerges from his forearm. Its beam slices through the head of the legless guard. Curves up to annihilate the man's memorycell. Aaron lets out a long sigh, then winces at the dull pain throbbing deep in his shoulder. When he glances at it, the bloodstain has spread across most of his chest. The hole torn and burned through the suit fabric reveals nothing but a mangled patch of blackened skin seeping blood. His medical monitors report the firewire tangles have burrowed deep, the damage is extensive. Sharp stabs of pain from his left leg make him gasp. His knee almost gives way. Biononics act in concert to trace and eliminate the microjanglers that are cruising recklessly through his bloodstream. If they infiltrate his brain he will be in serious trouble. The medical sac is still pumping drugs into him to counter shock. Blood loss will become a problem very soon unless he can reach a medical facility. However, he remains functional, though he will have to undergo decontamination for the nerve agent. His biononics are not satisfied they have located all the toxin. The field scan function fine tunes itself, and scans again.

Aaron walks over to the rack containing Inigo's memory-cell. Niling sponges flutter through the air, and return to his bandolier, snuggling back into their pouches. His feet crunch on a scree of fragments before squelching on blood and plastic magma. Then the memorycell is in his hand, and the most difficult stage of the mission is over.

Flames are taking hold across Viertz's uniform as he walks out of the vault. She has not moved from her kneeling position. Aaron shoots her through the head with the x-ray laser, an act of mercy in case her memorycell is still recording impulses. It's not like him, but he can afford to be magnanimous in the face of success.

Three minutes later Aaron made it out on to the roof of the administration block. He walked over to the edge, drawing breath in short gasps. The numb shoulder wound had started to cold-burn, radiating out waves of dizziness which his medical enrichments could barely prevent from overwhelming him. A terrible burst of pain from his legs, stomach and spine drilled into him, blinding him as he convulsed. Unseen in his exovision displays, the biononics reported progress in their quest to trace and eliminate the remaining elusive microjanglers still contaminating his blood.

Slowly, stiffly, he straightened up again. Teetering close to a two-storey fall. His u-shadow reconnected to the unisphere as soon as he clambered up out of the lift shaft, and reported that the remnant of the smartcore was yelling for help on just about every link the clinic had with the unisphere.

'Police tactical troops are responding,' the u-shadow informed him. 'Clinic security officers are arming themselves. Perimeter is sealing.'

'We'd better leave then,' Aaron said with bravado. He winced again at a shiver of phantom pain from his collar bone, and called Corrie-Lyn. 'Let's go. I'm at designated position one-A.'

'Oh,' she replied. 'Are you finished already?'

For a moment he thought she was joking. 'What?'

'I didn't realize you'd be that quick.'

Anger swiftly turned him to ice. The schedule he'd given her

was utterly clear-cut. Not even the unexpected guards and subsequent fire fight had delayed him more than forty seconds.
'Where are you?' His exovision was showing him a local map
with the police cruisers closing on the clinic at mach eight.

'Er ... I'm still in the reception area. You know they have
some really nice clothes here, and Ruth Stol has actually been
quite useful with styling. Who'd have thought it? I've already
tried on a couple of these lovely wool—'

'Get the fuck into the capsule! Right fucking now!' he
screamed. Tactical software assessed the situation, corresponding
with his own instinct. The roof was far too exposed. Another
involuntary shudder ran up his legs, and he went with it,
tumbling over the edge, totally reliant on his combat software.
The program formatted his force field to cushion his landing.
Even so, the pain seemed to explode directly into his brain as he
thudded into the ground. He rolled over and stumbled to his
feet. Far too slowly.

'The doors won't open,' Corrie-Lyn said. 'I can't get to the
capsule. The alarm is going off. Wait ... Ruth is telling me not
to move.'

Aaron groaned as he staggered erratically across the band of
lawn surrounding the administration block. Not that the trees
would provide the slightest cover, not against the kind of forces
heading for him. Seeking darkness was a simple animal instinct.

'Take the bitch out,' he told Corrie-Lyn.

'What?'

'Hit her. Here's a combat program,' he said, as his u-shadow
shunted the appropriate file at her. 'Go for a disabling blow.
Don't hesitate.'

'I can't do that.'

'Hit her. And call the capsule over. It can smash through the
doors for you.'

'Aaron, can't I just get the capsule to break in? I'm really not
comfortable hitting someone without warning.'

Aaron reached the treeline. His legs gave way, sending him
sprawling in the dirt and spiky vines. Pain that was nothing to

do with the microjanglers pulsed out from his damaged shoulder. 'Help,' he croaked. 'Oh fuck it, Corrie-Lyn, get the capsule here.' He started crawling. His exoimages were a blurred scintillation coursing round his constricting vision.

'Hey, she's grabbed me.'

'Corrie-Lyn—'

'Cow!'

'I can't make it.' He pushed against the damp sandy soil with his good arm, trying to lever himself back on to his feet. Two police capsules flashed silently overhead. A second later their hypersonic boom smashed him back down into the ground. Tree branches splintered from the violence of the sound. Aaron whimpered as he rolled on to his back.

'Oh, Ozzie, there's blood everywhere. I think I've broken her nose. I didn't hit her hard, really.'

'Get me,' he whispered. He sent a single command thought to the niling-sponges in his bandolier harness. The little spheres soared away into the night, arching away over the waving trees. Violet laser beams sliced through the air, as bright as lightning forks. He grinned weakly. 'Wrong,' he told the unseen police capsules.

The niling-sponges sucked down the energy which the capsules pumped into them. Theoretically the niling effect could absorb billions of kilowatt hours before reaching saturation point. Aaron had programmed a limit in. When the police weapons pumped their internal levels to that limit, the absorption effect reversed.

Five huge explosions blossomed high over the forest, sending out massive clashing pressure waves. The police capsules couldn't be damaged by the blast, their force fields were far too strong for that. But the wavefronts sent them tumbling through the night sky, spinning and flailing out beyond the edge of the forest as the regrav drives fought to counter the force. Down below, trees tumbled before the bedlam as if they were no stronger than paper, crashing into each other to create a domino effect radiating out from the five blast centres.

A blizzard of splinters and gravel snatched Aaron off the ground and sent him twirling five metres to bounce badly. Amazingly he was still holding the memorycell as he found himself flat on his back gazing up into a sky beset with an intricate webbing of lambent ion streamers.

'Corrie-Lyn,' he called desperately.

Above him, the pretty sky was dimming to infinite black. There were no stars to be seen as the darkness engulfed him.

Inigo's fourth dream

After breaking camp just after dawn the caravan was on the road for three hours before it finally topped the last ridge and the coastal plain tipped into view. Edeard smiled down on it with an adrenaline burst of enthusiasm. With nearly a year spent travelling he was finally looking at his future. Riding on the ge-horse beside him, Salrana squealed happily and clapped her hands together. Several pigs in the back of O'lrany's cart grunted at the sudden noise.

Edeard ordered his ge-horse to stop. The caravan pushed on inexorably, wagon after wagon rolling down the stony road. Directly ahead of him the foothills of the Donsori Mountains fell away sharply to the awesome Iguru Plain below. It stretched away for mile after long mile. A flat expanse of rich farmland, almost all of which was under cultivation; its surface marked out in huge regular fields filled with verdant crops. A massive grid of ditches fed into wide, shallow rivers delineated by protective earthen embankments. Forests tended to sprawl around the lower slopes of the odd little volcanic cones which broke the plain's uniformity. As far as he could see there was no pattern to the steep knolls. They were dotted purely at random.

It was a strange geography, completely different to the rugged surrounding terrain. He shrugged at the oddity and squinted to the eastern horizon. Part imagination, part horizon-haze, the Lyot Sea was just visible as a grey line.

No need to imagine the city, though. Makkathran bestrode the horizon like a sunwashed pearl. At first he was disappointed by how small it was, then he began to appreciate the distance involved.

'Quite something, isn't it?' Barkus said as he rode his aged ge-horse level with Edeard.

'Yes, sir,' Edeard said. Additional comment seemed superfluous. 'How far away are we?'

'It'll take at least another half a day for us to get down to the plain; this last stretch of road down the mountains is tricky. We'll make camp at Clipsham, the first decent-sized town on the Iguru. Then it'll be near enough another day to reach Makkathran itself.' He nodded pleasantly and urged his ge-horse onward.

Almost two days away. Edeard stared entranced at the capital city. Allegedly, the only true city on Querencia. The caravan had visited some fabulous towns on their route, large conurbations with wealthy populations; several had parks bigger than Ashwell. At the time he'd thought them grand, sure that nothing could actually be larger. *Lady, what a bumpkin I am.*

'Doubts here, of all places?' Salrana asked. 'Those are some very melancholy thoughts you've got growing in your head there.'

'Just humbled,' he told her.

Her thoughts sparkled with amusement, producing a teasing smile. 'Thinking of Franlee?'

'Not for months,' he answered with high dignity.

Salrana laughed wickedly.

He'd met Franlee in Plax, a provincial capital on the other side of the Ulfsen Mountains. A spree of bad luck on the road, including broken wheels and sick animals, as well as unusually early autumn storms meant the caravan was late reaching Plax. As a consequence, they'd been snowed in for over six weeks. That was when he met Franlee, an Eggshaper Guild apprentice and his first real love affair. They'd spent most of the awful cold weather together, either in bed or exploring the town's cheaper taverns. The Eggshaper Guild's Master had recognized his talent, offering him a senior apprenticeship with the promise of journeyman status in a year. He'd been *this* close to staying.

But in the end his last promise to Akeem gave him a stronger direction. Leaving had been so painful he'd been sullen and withdrawn for weeks as the caravan lumbered slowly along the snowy Ulfsen valleys. A misery to live with, the rest of the caravan had grumbled. It took the remainder of winter and putting the Ulfsens between himself and Plax before he'd recovered. That and Roseillin, in one of the mountain villages. And Dalice. And . . . Well, several more girls between there and here.

'Look at it,' he said earnestly. 'We did the right thing.'

Salrana tipped her head back, half-closing her eyes against the bright morning light. 'Forget the city,' she said. 'I've never seen so much sky.'

When he glanced up he understood what she meant. Their high vantage point gave them a view into the azure infinity which roofed the plain. Small bright clouds scudded far overhead, wisps so tenuous they were almost sapphire themselves. They seemed to twist as they traced long arcs above the Iguru before hitting the mountain thermals where they expanded and darkened. *The wind above the city always blows in from the sea*, he remembered Akeem saying, *when it turns round, watch out*. 'What's that smell?' he asked, puzzled. The air was fresh, zingy almost, yet somehow tainted at the same time.

There was laughter from the wagon that rolled past. 'You backward village boy!' Olcus, the driver, mocked. 'That's the smell of the sea.'

Edeard dropped his gaze back down to the horizon. He'd never seen the sea before. In truth, from this distance it didn't look much: a grey-blue smudge line. He supposed it would become more interesting and impressive as they drew nearer.

'Thank you, old man,' he called back, and supplied a fast hand gesture. By now, he was on good terms with just about every family in the caravan. Abandoning them in Makkathran was going to be at least as hard as leaving Plax.

'Come on,' Salrana said. She ordered her ge-horse forward. After a moment, Edeard followed suit.

'I was talking to Magrith at breakfast,' Salrana said. 'She told me this road was the same one which Rah travelled on when he led his shipmates out of the strife which followed their landing on Querencia. He would have seen the city for the first time from this very same spot.'

'Wonder what he made of the Iguru,' Edeard muttered.

'There are times when I really don't understand you, Edeard. We've reached Makkathran, which I only ever half-believed in anyway. Us two, Ashwell villagers no less, are here at the centre of our whole world. And all you do is talk about the stupid farmland outside.'

'I'm sorry. It's . . . this place is odd, that's all. Look round, the mountains just end, like something cut them off.'

'I'm sure there's a Geography Guild if you're that interested,' she sniffed.

'Now that's an idea,' he said with sudden apparent interest. 'Do you think it would be hard to get into?'

'Oh!' she squealed in exasperation. Her third hand shoved against him, trying to push him off his saddle. He pushed right back, which sent her hunching down, tightening her grip on the reins. 'Edeard! Careful.'

'Sorry.' It was something of a standing joke along the caravan that he didn't know his own strength. He shook his head and concentrated on the phalanx of genistars walking alongside the caravan, making sure the ge-horses were pulling wagons in a straight line, ge-wolves kept close, and the ge-eagles spiralled wide. The surface of the road was excellent, laid with large flat stones, well maintained – it was almost like a town pavement. But then this was the main road through the mountains and led directly to the capital. Both eyes and farsight picked out several wagons and small convoys winding their way up and down the broad switchbacks ahead of them. He also saw a group of men on horseback accompanied by ge-wolves who were picking their way leisurely up the road. They'd reach the head of the caravan by noon, he reckoned.

With his senses open wide he slowly grew aware of the city's emanations. It was a quiet background burble, similar to the aura of any human settlement. Except this time he was too far away to be sensing Makkathran's population, no matter how talented and receptive he was. Besides, this had a different tempo to human minds; slower and so much more content. It was the essence of a lazy summer's afternoon distilled into a single long harmonic. Pleasant and relaxing. He yawned.

'Edeard!' Salrana called.

He blinked, the worry in her mind switching him to full alertness. His ge-horse was meandering close to the edge of the road. Not that it was dangerous, there was no sheer slope until further down the hill where the switchbacks began, here there was just uneven ground and the curving crest. A quick couple of instructions to the ge-horse's mind corrected his direction.

'Let's try and arrive intact,' she said scathingly. 'Lady, but your riding is still terrible.'

He was too disquieted to try and correct her with their usual banter. He could no longer sense the city's lumbering thoughts – too much adrenaline pumping through his veins. Now the city was in sight, he was getting genuinely excited. At last the dreadful past was well and truly behind them.

It was midday when the caravan drew to a gradual halt amid the groaning of wood and metal brakes, the snorting of animals and quiet grumbles of humans. They were strung out over half a mile, curving round one of the longer switchbacks which made it awkward for anyone else trying to use the road. The captain of the militia patrol who made them stop was mildly apologetic, but insistent none the less.

Edeard was only a couple of wagons behind the front as Barkus asked, 'Is there a problem, sir? This is our annual trip, we are well known to all the civic authorities.'

'I know you myself, Barkus,' the captain said as he eyed the caravan's ge-wolves. He was sitting on a midnight-black terrestrial horse, looking very splendid in a ceremonial blue and scarlet tunic with polished brass buttons gleaming down his jacket. Edeard used his farsight to examine the revolver in the man's white leather holster. It was remarkably similar to the one that had belonged to Genril's family. The rest of the militia were similarly armed; they certainly weren't carrying anything like the fast-firing gun of the bandits. Edeard didn't know if that was a good thing or not. If the city did possess such weapons, they probably wouldn't be put out on show with a patrol like this.

'However, I don't remember you having so many ge-wolves before,' the captain said.

'We were in the Rulan province last year; a village was sacked by bandits, farms suffered losses in raids. You can't be too careful.'

'Damned savages,' the captain spat. 'Probably just two tribes fighting over some whore. I don't know why you venture out there, Barkus, they're all bandits and ne'er-do-wells if you ask me.'

Edeard slowly sat up very straight, keeping his gaze fixed on the captain. He strengthened his shield around him.

'Do nothing,' Barkus shot at him with a longtalk whisper.

'Edeard,' Salrana hissed quietly. He could sense the rage in her own thoughts, barely contained. All around him, the minds of his friends were radiating dismay and sympathy.

'But profitable,' Barkus continued smoothly. 'We can buy very cheaply indeed out there.'

The captain laughed, unaware of the emotional storm gathering around him. 'For which my friends in the city will pay greatly, I suppose.'

'That's the essence of trade,' Barkus said. 'After all, we do travel at considerable risk.'

'Well good luck to you, Barkus. But I am responsible for the safety of Makkathran, so I must request that you keep your beasts on a leash within the city walls. They won't be used to civilization. We don't want any unfortunate accidents.'

'Of course.'

'You might want to get them accustomed to the idea as soon as you reach the plain.'

'I'll see to it.'

'Jolly good. And no trading to the denizens of the Sampalok district, eh?'

'Absolutely not.'

The captain and his men turned round and rode off down the road, their pack of ge-wolves chasing along behind.

Barkus saw the caravan start off again, then urged his ge-horse back to Edeard and Salrana. 'I'm sorry you had to hear that,' he said.

'They're not all like that in the city, are they?' Salrana asked anxiously.

'Sweet Lady, no. Officers in the militia are usually the younger sons of an old family; little idiots who know nothing of life. Their birth provides them with a great deal of arrogance, but no money. The militia allows them the illusion of continuing status, while all they actually do is search for a wealthy wife. Thankfully they can do no real harm patrolling out here.'

Edeard was almost shocked by the notion. 'If they need money, why don't they join a Guild and develop their psychic talent, or begin a new business?'

To his surprise, Barkus burst out laughing. 'Oh, Edeard, for all the distance you've travelled with us, you still have so much further to go. A nobleman's son *earn* a living!' He laughed again before ordering his ge-horse back to the next wagon.

After Clipsham, Edeard just wanted to take a horse and gallop across the Iguru until he reached Makkathran. Surely it would take no more than a few hours. However, he managed to keep his impatience in check, and dutifully plodded alongside the wagons helping to soothe the ge-wolves who were unused to being on a leash.

It was warm down on the plain, with the gentle constant wind blowing a sea-humid air which Edeard found strangely invigorating. Winter here was a lot shorter than he was used to in the Rulan province, Barkus explained, though those months could see some very sharp frosts and several snow blizzards. By contrast, summer in the city was very hot and lasted for more than five months. Most of the grand families kept villas in the Donsori Mountains where they spent the height of the hot season.

The Iguru's farmland reflected the climate, with luxuriant growth covering every field. The road was lined with tall slender palm trees cloaked in ribbons of cobalt moss and sprouting tufts of scarlet and emerald leaves right at the top. Crops were different to those Edeard was used to. There were few cereal fields here, but plenty of citrus groves and fruit plantations, with acre after acre of vines and fruiting bushes. Some cane fields were being burnt back, sending black smoke plumes churning up high into the clear sky. It was volcanic soil underfoot, which contributed as much to the healthy verdant hue of the vegetation as did the regular rain and sun-soaked sky. Armies of ge-chimps bustled about over the land, tending to the plants, with supervisors riding among them on horses. The farmhouses were grand white-washed buildings with red clay tile roofs, as big as the Guild compounds back in Ashwell.

For all they spent hours rolling forward that morning, the panorama on both sides of the straight road remained unnervingly similar. Only the volcanic cones offered landmarks by which to measure progress. Edeard could see veins of silver streams running down their slopes before vanishing into the dense skirts of dark-jade trees. But there were no caldera crowns; they rose to simple rounded crests.

Many of them had cottages built on narrow ledges, compact yet elaborate constructions which his friends explained were little more than pavilions for the city's wealthy to spend languid days enjoying the fabulous view; more common was to install a favoured mistress in one.

Traffic began to increase as they neared Makkathran. Terrestrial horses were now more common than ge-horses; their riders wearing expensive clothes. Wagons piled high with produce from the farms and estates of the plain lumbered towards the markets and merchant warehouses. Fancy carriages with curtained windows rattled past. Edeard was surprised to find them shielded from casual farsight by a mild variant of his own concealment ability; their footmen radiated sullen anger discouraging anyone from prying further.

The final approach to the city walls was home to an astonishing variety of trees. Ancient black and grey trunks sentried the road on either side, sending gnarled boughs overhead to form twined arches that were centuries old. At first Edeard thought there had been some kind of earthquake recently. All the trees, no matter their age and size, leaned one way, their branches bowing round in the same direction. Then it slowly dawned on him that the constant wind had shaped them, pushing their branches away from the shoreline.

For the last quarter of a mile, the ground was simple flat meadow, home to flocks of sheep. When they left the shelter of the trees, Edeard was awarded his first sight of the city since they'd descended out of the foothills. The crystal wall faced them, rising sheer out of the grass to a height of thirty yards. Although transparent, it possessed a gold hue, distorting the silhouettes of the buildings inside, making it impossible to gather a true impression of what lay within. It formed a perfect circle around the city, the same height all the way round except for the port on the eastern side where it dipped down to allow the sea to wash against the quays. Querencia's gentle tides had no visible effect on it; the stubborn crystal was as immune to erosion forces as it was to all other forms of assault. Neither bullets nor pickaxes could chip it, glue didn't stick to it. As a defensive barrier it was nearly perfect.

Its only known susceptibility was to telekinesis, which could gradually wear down its strength. That was how Rah opened the city to his people; a powerful telekinetic, he systematically cut through the crystal, shaping three gateways. Legend said each one took him two years to carve out. His followers fixed the huge detached segments to giant metal hinges, transforming them into tight-fitting gates. In the two millennia since, they had only ever been shut eight times. For the last seven hundred years they had remained open.

The caravan passed through the north gate. It was seven yards wide at the base, arching up ten yards above Edeard's head. The gate itself was hinged back flat against the wall on the inside. He found it hard to believe the huge thing could actually still move; the hinges seemed wondrously primitive contraptions, all bulbous iron joints and girders studded with rivets. Yet they hadn't corroded, and the pivots were kept oiled.

Directly inside, to the left of the road, was a broad swathe of paddock land named the High Moat, which followed the wall's curve round to the Upper Tail district next to the port. As horses were prohibited from the main districts many families maintained stables here, simple wooden buildings that had been added to over the centuries; there were also stockades for cattle and traveller pens, even a couple of cheap markets. On the opposite side of the road, the similar crescent of Low Moat led round to the Main Gate. Running along the inner edge of the Moats, was the North Curve Canal, lined with the same whitish material from which the majority of the city was fabricated, resembling icy marble yet stronger than any metal which humans could forge on Querencia.

Edeard stared enchanted at the gondolas as they slid along the canal. He'd seen boats before, Thorpe-By-Water had them in abundance, as did many other towns. Yet those were coarse workaday cousins compared to these elegant black craft. They had shallow keels, with tall prows rising out of the water carved into elegant figures. The cushioned benches of the midsection were covered from the hot sun by white awnings, while the gondolier stood on a platform at the stern, manipulating a long punt pole with easy grace. Each gondola was home to at least a couple of ge-cats. Edeard smiled happily at the traditional genistar forms, which were swarming in and out of the salty water. Unlike the bloated creatures he had shaped back in Ashwell these were streamlined aquatics, with webbed feet and a long sinuous tail.

The surface of the canal was alive with ripples as they continually chased after nimble fil-rats and chewed on strands of trilan weed to keep the canal clear.

'Oh my great Lady,' Salrana gasped, gawping out at the city.

'We did the right thing,' Edeard said with finality. 'Yes, we did.' Now he was inside the crystal wall, the true aura of the city was washing against him. He'd never sensed such vitality before, the kind of exhilarating emotional impact that could only come from so many people pursuing their hectic lives in close proximity. Individuality was impossible to distinguish, but the collective sensation was a powerhouse of animation. He felt uplifted simply by standing and drinking in the sights and sounds.

The caravan turned off the road. Barkus had a quick conversation with a city Travel Master who assigned them three pens on High Moat where they could set up to trade. The wagons rumbled along the narrow track to their final destination.

Edeard and Salrana walked their ge-horses over to Barkus's wagon. An act rich with association to that time back in Thorpe-By-Water when they'd come to the caravan master for help. The old man's family had been setting up the awnings on either side of the ancient wagon. They'd all been strangers back then, curious and suspicious. Now Edeard knew them all, and counted them as friends – which made this so very difficult. Salrana's thoughts were subdued and morose as Barkus turned to face them.

The old caravan master eyed the packs they were both carrying. 'You're really going to stay here, then?'

'Yes, sir.'

He hugged both of them. Salrana had to wipe some tears from her eyes. Edeard was fighting to make sure the same thing didn't happen to him.

'Have you got enough money?'

'Yes, sir, we're fine.' Edeard patted at the pocket inside his trousers. Along the route he'd sold enough ge-spiders to pay for weeks in a lavishly appointed tavern; and he was dressed respectably again.

'If it doesn't work out, we'll be here for a week. You're welcome to come with us. Both of you. You'll always have a home on the road with us.'

'I will never forget your kindness,' Edeard said.

'Nor I,' Salrana added.

'Go on then; be off with you.'

Edeard could see in the old man's agitated thoughts that this was just as painful for him. He gripped Barkus's arm and squeezed tightly before turning away. Salrana threw her hands round the caravan master's neck, and kissed him gratefully.

The road which had brought them into the city ended just short of the North Curve Canal. They walked beside the waterway for a little while until they found a bridge over. It was made from a tough ochre-coloured variety of the ubiquitous city material, a simple low arch to which wooden railings had been added on either side. Edeard had to clutch his shoulder bag tightly there were so many people using it, bustling against him. But no animals, he realized; not even ge-chimps. The bridge took them into the Ilongo district, which was made up of small box-like buildings, two or three storeys high with vaulting lierne roofs, and walls which often leaned away from perpendicular. Windows followed no pattern: there were angled slits, crescents, teardrops, circles, ovals, but never squares; they all had panes of a thick transparent crystal which grew, shaped, and replenished itself in the same slow fashion as the structures themselves. Entrances were simple arched oblongs or ovals cutting through ground-floor walls; it was the humans who'd added the wooden doors, fixing hinges into the structure with nails hammered into place with telekinesis. Over the years the pins would slowly be ejected by the city material as it repaired the puncture holes they'd made, necessitating re-fixing every decade or so. The constant sedate renewal of the city's fabric made the whole place look fresh, as if it had only just been completed.

The gap between the buildings was narrow. Sometimes, beside a canted corner, there was barely a couple of feet left between walls, forcing Edeard to turn sideways to squeeze through; while other passages were broad pavements allowing several people to walk side by side. They came across little squares and courtyards without warning, all of which were provided with fountains of fresh water bubbling up through the top of a thick pillar.

'Does nobody work?' Salrana asked in puzzlement after they'd been thoroughly jostled for ten minutes negotiating the narrow pavements. 'The whole city must be walking about.'

Edeard simply shrugged. The district was a confusing maze. It was also where he discovered the city material was almost opaque to farsight. He could only sense the murkiest of shapes on the other side of the walls; and he certainly couldn't perceive right through a building. He wasn't used to having his perception cut so short, it unnerved him slightly. Eventually he summoned his ge-eagle, and sent it soaring above the roofs, mapping a way for them.

He wanted to get to the Tosella district where the Eggshaper Guild had its Blue Tower. It was the district to the east of Ilongo, separated by the Hidden Canal. Despite it being so close, they took forty minutes to negotiate Ilongo before crossing the thin canal on a small wooden bridge.

Tosella's buildings were on a much larger scale than the ones they'd seen so far. Long rectangular mansions with tall slit windows stacked on top of each other up to six storeys high and topped with concentric ring domes that intersected each other like waves frozen in mid-swirl. The ground directly outside their walls was fenced off with high slender pillars, separating the public pavement from emblemata mosaics of glittering primary-colour flecks. Their ground floors were arched cloisters enclosing central quads where prim gardens grew in long troughs under the cool tinted light shining through the roof skylights high above. For the first time in the city, he sensed the minds of genistars. A ground floor in one of the mansions had been converted into stables for them. He even glimpsed apprentices and journeymen scurrying round the quads, their thoughts anxious and subdued as they tried to keep in their Master's good graces. It brought a smile to his face as he recalled some of Akeem's more outrageous stories of an apprentice's life in Makkathran.

'I know everyone asks this,' Salrana said as they tarried beside one of the huge mansions, admiring the subtle rainbow shades refracting off its glittering snow-white frontage. 'But I wonder who built this place?'

'I thought it was the Firstlifes. Isn't that what the Lady said?'

'It doesn't actually say that in any of her teachings. All she says is that the city was left by those who came before.'

'They couldn't have been humans, then.'

'What makes you say that?'

'Oh we can use it well enough, the concept of shelter is universal, I suppose. But nothing here is quite right for us. For a start, there were no gates until Rah arrived.'

'So the builders sailed in and out via the sea; that certainly ties in with all the canals,' she answered with a smile.

'No.' He couldn't match her light humour. His gaze swept along the length of the mansion. The root of architecture was species-based, from the basic functionality to the aesthetic; and Makkathran just didn't fit human sensibilities. He felt out of place here. 'Humans never built this place, we just adapted to it.'

'Aren't you the know-it-all; and we've only been here an hour.'

'Sorry,' he grinned. 'But it is intriguing, you have to admit that.'

'They say Eyrie district is the really weird one. That's where the Pythia has her church, which is the only building ever formed for humans. The city granted it to the Lady so her flock would be close to the towers when the Skylords finally return.'

'Towers?'

'Yes. That's where the Skylords alighted the last time they were here, the day they took Rah's spirit to its rest in Odin's Sea.'

'Oh. Hey wait, you mean humans designed the Lady's Church?'

She gave a mock sigh. 'See? If you'd ever bothered to turn up to church you'd have known that. It's right there in the Lady's scriptures.'

He gave the mansion another suspicious look. 'That's like shaping genistars but with buildings. I wonder if the city builders brought the defaults to Querencia.'

'If the Geography Guild turn you down you could always apply to the History Guild.'

'Cheeky!' He took a swipe at her.

Salrana danced away laughing, and stuck her tongue out. Several passers-by gave her a curious look, unused to seeing a Lady's novice behave in such a fashion. She pulled a contrite face and held her hands demurely behind her back, eyes and mind still sparkling with amusement.

'Come on,' he said. 'The quicker we get to the Blue Tower the quicker we get you locked up in the novice dormitory where you belong – out of harm's way and not causing any trouble.'

'Remember our promise? I'm going to be Pythia and you're going to be Mayor.'

'Yeah,' he grinned. 'It might take a couple of years, but we'll do it.'

Her smile faded away as her thoughts grew sober. 'Edeard, you won't forget me, will you?'

'Hey – of course not.'

'I mean it, Edeard. Promise. Promise we'll still talk each day, even if it's just a longtalk hello.'

He held up a hand, palm towards her. 'I swear on the Lady, I won't forget you. Such a thing is just not possible.'

'Thank you.' Her impish smile returned. 'Do you want to kiss me again before we both get locked up in separate dormitories each night?'

He groaned in dismay. 'Maybe I should just leave with the caravan.'

It was Salrana's turn to take a swipe at him.

*

The Blue Tower was in the middle of the Tosella district, standing at least twice the height of the biggest mansion they'd seen so far. For its walls, the city material had shaded down to a dark azure which seemed to soak up the sunlight, as if the facade possessed its own nimbus of shadow. Standing at the base between flying buttresses which resembled ancient tree roots Edeard felt quite intimidated by the heartland of his Guild. Surely such a structure had never been intended to house a profession which existed to lighten the load of people's lives. It was more like a fortress which bandits would dwell in.

'Are you sure you want to do this?' Salrana asked uncertainly. She was just as daunted by the overpowering structure as he was.

'Er. Yes. I'm sure.' He wished the vacillation in his thoughts wasn't quite so blatant.

They walked in through a wide door whose resemblance to a giant mouth was uncomfortably obvious. Inside, the walls and floor changed to the darkest red with a surface sheen to match polished wood. Strong beams of sunlight from the high lancet windows cut through the gloom of the broad entrance hall.

Edeard didn't know where to go, there didn't seem to be any kind of official to direct visitors to the appropriate room. His determination was fading fast, leaving him stalled in the middle of the wide open space.

'I somehow don't think this is where the apprentices have their dormitories,' Salrana said from the side of her mouth. There were several groups of men in the hall, all talking quietly together. They wore fine clothes under flowing fur-lined gowns with the egg-in-a-twisted-circle crest of the Guild embroidered in gold thread on both collars. Disapproving glances were cast at Salrana and Edeard, followed by a surprising number of people focusing their farsight on the youthful pair.

Edeard's own farsight alerted him to three guards armed with revolvers marching across the entrance hall. They wore light drosilk jackets over their immaculate white cotton tunics. The Guild crest was prominent on their helmets.

The sergeant glowered at Edeard, but was marginally less hostile to Salrana when he saw she was in her full novice dress. 'You two,' he grunted, 'what's your business here?'

So much for the warm welcome to a fellow Guild member from far away, Edeard thought dourly. Then he realized he wasn't at all intimidated by the guard. After bandits the sergeant and his little squad seemed faintly ludicrous. 'I am a journeyman of the Guild,' Edeard said, surprising himself by how level and authoritative his voice was. 'I've come from Rulan province to complete my training.'

The sergeant looked as if he'd bitten into a rotten fruit. 'You're very young to be calling yourself a journeyman. Where's your badge?'

'It's been a long journey,' Edeard said, suddenly not wanting to explain what happened to his village to someone who would never understand life beyond the city. 'I lost it.'

'I see. And your letter?'

'Letter?'

The sergeant spoke slowly, contempt colouring his thoughts. 'Your letter of introduction to the Guild from your Master?'

'I have none.'

'Are you trying to take the piss, sonny? Your pardon, miss,' he said grudgingly at Salrana. 'Leave now before we take you to the Courts of Justice for trespass and theft.'

'I have committed no theft,' Edeard protested loudly. 'My Master was Akeem; he died before writing a letter of introduction.'

'The only reason to trespass here is to thieve something from us you little country shite,' the sergeant snapped. 'Now you've gone and fucked me off, and that's not good for you.' He reached for Edeard, then blinked in surprise as his hand slithered off an extremely strong telekinetic shield. 'Oh ... you asked for this.' His third hand tried to grab.

Edeard warded him off easily, then hoisted the sergeant off the ground. The man yelled in shock as his feet kicked about.

'Take the little shite down,' he cried at his men. Their third hands closed round Edeard, to no avail. They went for their pistols, finding their arms moving slowly through impossibly thick air.

'Edeard!' Salrana squeaked.

Edeard couldn't quite comprehend how things had turned so crazy so fast.

'Enough,' a baritone voice commanded.

Edeard's farsight showed him an old man walking across the hall towards them. Long robes flowed behind him as he strode forwards. He'd taken to weight in his latter years, ochre trousers cut high so his curving belly didn't overhang, a baggy shirt to continue the discreet disguise, but his weight was still obvious from the podgy fingers to the rolling neck and heavy jowls. Yet he carried himself with the vitality of a man half his age. Even without sensing his regimented thoughts he was obviously a man of considerable authority.

'Put him down,' he ordered Edeard.

'Yes, sir,' Edeard said meekly. He just knew this was a Master equal to Akeem. 'I apologise. I was left little cho—'

'Be quiet.' The man turned to the sergeant, who was straightening his clothes, not making eye contact with anyone. 'And you, Sergeant, need to keep your temper in check. I am not prepared to have the Blue Tower guarded by petty-minded paranoia. You will learn a more rational attitude or you'll see your days out guarding a Guild estate on the other side of the Donsori Mountains. Do I make myself clear?'

'Sir.'

'Away with you while I determine how big a threat this boy presents.'

The sergeant led his men away, but not before managing a last look at Edeard which promised dire vengeance.

'Your name, boy?'

'Edeard, sir.'

'And I am Topar, a Master of the Guild Council, and deputy

to Grand Master Finitan. That should give you an idea of how deep you just dipped yourself in default crap. My Lady's novice, may I enquire your name?'

'Salrana.'

'I see. And I judge that both of you have only recently arrived in Makkathran. Correct?'

'Yes, sir,' Edeard said. 'I'm really sorry about . . .'

Topar waved an irritated hand. 'I should be annoyed, but the name Akeem hasn't been heard in our august Tower for a considerable time. I am intrigued. Did I hear you say he is dead?'

'Yes, sir. I'm afraid he is.'

For a moment the gusto vanished from Topar's stance. 'A shame. Yes, a very great shame.'

'Did you know him, sir?'

'Not I, no. But I will take you to someone who did. He will want the details, I'm sure. Follow me.'

He led them to an archway at the rear of the hall, and began to climb the broad stairs beyond. As he ascended, Edeard knew he'd been right about whoever created the city not being humans. The stairs were cumbrous, more like a slope of solidified ripples. They curved enough to provide an unsure footing, while their spacing was awkward for human legs. Edeard soon found himself sweating as they continued to climb round and round; his calf muscles weren't used to such strenuous exercise.

At one point, when they must have been four or five storeys above the hall, Topar turned round to smirk at the two youngsters. He grunted as if satisfied by their tribulation. 'Just imagine how much rounder I would be if I didn't have to negotiate these five times a day, eh.' He chuckled and carried on.

Edeard was panting heavily when they finally stopped in some kind of large anteroom. He had no idea how high they'd climbed, but the top of the tower could surely only be a couple of feet above them. That altitude would explain how light-headed he'd become.

'Wait here,' Topar said, and went through a wooden door bound with thick iron filigrees.

The walls of the anteroom were still red, but lighter than those of the lower floors. Overhead, the ceiling glowed a pale amber, turning Edeard's skin an unpleasant shade of grey. He dumped his shoulder bag on the floor and sank into a large chair of curving wooden ribs. Salrana sat on one next to him, looking thoroughly bewildered. 'Are we in trouble or not?' she asked.

'I don't think I care any more. That pig of a sergeant. He knew we were harmless.'

She smiled. 'You're not.'

He was too tired to argue. His farsight was all but blocked by the tower walls; but he could just sense two minds behind the wooden door. There was very little to discern about their emotional composition, but then walking through the districts he'd noticed how adept city people were in guarding their feelings.

Topar opened the door. 'You can come in now, Edeard. Novice Salrana, if you would be so kind as to indulge us for a moment longer. Someone will be here to take care of you momentarily.'

Even before he went into the room, Edeard guessed he was being taken to Grand Master Finitan. As he went in, he nearly faltered as a farsight swept through him like a gust of cold air. The hair on the back of his arms stood up in reaction. A little thought occurred to him that if anyone could see through a psychic concealment, it would be this man.

Grand Master Finitan sat in a high-back chair behind a large oak desk, facing the door. His office must have taken up nearly a quarter of the tower at this level. It was huge, but almost empty; there was no furniture other than the desk and chair. Two of the walls were covered by bookshelves containing hundreds of leather-bound tomes. Behind him, the wall was mostly crystal window with thin lierne ribs, providing a view clear across Makkathran. Edeard's jaw fell open. He only just managed to stop himself running over and gawping like a delighted child. From what he could see at this angle, the undulating rooftops swept away for miles, while the canals cut through them like blue-grey arteries. Looking at it like this, he knew for certain that the city was alive. Here, humans were nothing more than foreign bacteria living in a body they could never fully comprehend.

'Quite a sight, isn't it?' Grand Master Finitan said gently. In many respects he was the physical opposite to Topar. Slim and tall, with thick hair worn down to his shoulders, only just beginning to grey. Yet his age was evident in the lines creasing his face. Despite that, his thoughts were tranquil, he was curious and affable rather than dismissive.

Edeard shifted his gaze back to the Grand Master. 'Yes, sir. Er, I apologize again for what happened downstai—'

The Grand Master raised a finger to his lips, and Edeard fell silent. 'No more of that,' Finitan said. 'You've travelled a long way, yes?'

'From Rulan province, sir.'

Finitan and Topar exchanged a glance, smiling at some private joke. 'A long way,' Finitan said sagely. 'Some tea?' His mind sent out a fast longtalk instruction.

Edeard turned to see a door open at the base of one of the bookshelf walls; it was too small for a man, barely four feet high. Ge-chimps scampered out bringing a pair of chairs and a tray. The chairs were positioned in front of the Grand Master's desk, while the tray with its silver tea service was placed on the desk beside a cradle which held a genistar egg.

'Sit down, my boy,' Finitan said. 'Now, I understand you claim our colleague Akeem is dead. When did this happen?'

'Almost a year ago, sir.'

'Those are some very dark thoughts in your mind accompanying that memory. Please tell me the story in its entirety. I believe I'm old enough to endure the full truth.'

Embarrassed at his mind being so transparent, Edeard took a deep breath and began.

Both the Grand Master and Topar were silent when he finished. Eventually, Finitan rested his chin on steepled forefingers. 'Ah, my poor dear Akeem; for his life to end like that is an

348

unforgivable tragedy. An entire village slaughtered by bandits. I find that extraordinary.'

'It happened,' Edeard said with a flash of anger.

'I'm not questioning your tale, my boy. I find the whole concept deeply disturbing, that there is some kind of society out in the wilds different to our own; and one which is so implacably hostile.'

'They're animals,' Edeard growled.

'No. That's your instinctive reaction; and a healthy one it is, too. But to organize such a raid is quite an accomplishment.' He sat back and drank some tea. 'Could there really be a rival civilization somewhere out there beyond our maps? They have concealment techniques and fanciful weapons. I'd always believed such things were the provenance of this city alone.'

'You have the repeat-fire guns?' Edeard asked. In all his travels, no one had ever heard of such a thing. A year of constant dismissal had made him doubt his own memories of that terrible night.

Finitan and Topar exchanged another glance. 'No. And that is more worrying than knowing how to conceal yourself. But how lovely that Akeem knew the technique which is supposed to be practised only by Guild Masters.'

'He was a Master, sir.'

'Of course. I mean those of us who sit on the Council. Sadly, Akeem never achieved that. It was politics of course. I'm afraid to say, young Edeard, that you are going to learn life here in the city is all about politics.'

'Yes, sir. Did you know Akeem, sir?'

Finitan smiled. 'Have you not worked it out yet, my boy? Dear me, I thought you quicker. We share a bond, you and I. For he was my Master when I was a lowly young apprentice here.'

'Oh.'

'Which means you present me with a very unpleasant problem.'

'I do?' Edeard said anxiously.

'You have no formal letter of confirmation from your Master. Worse than that, with your village gone, we cannot ever confirm that you were taken in by the Guild.'

Edeard smiled uncertainly. 'But I know how to sculpt an egg.' His farsight swept through the egg on the Grand Master's desk, revealing the folded shadows of the embryo inside. 'You have sculpted a ge-dog; I don't recognize some of the traits, they're outside the traditional form, but it is a dog. Two days from hatching, I'd guess.'

Topar nodded in appreciation. 'Impressive.'

'Akeem was the best Master,' Edeard said hotly.

Finitan's sigh was heavier than before. 'You have obviously received Guild training, and you clearly have skill as well as strength. And that is the problem.'

'I don't understand, sir.'

'You say Akeem made you a journeyman?'

'Yes, sir.'

'I cannot accept you into the Guild at that level. I know this seems intolerably harsh, Edeard, but there are formalities which even I have to follow.'

Edeard was aware of his cheeks burning. It wasn't quite anger, but all he could think of was the pettiness of the Guild Master back in Thorpe-By-Water. Surely the Grand Master, the leader of the whole Eggshaper Guild, couldn't be so small-minded; what he said was law to the Guild. 'I see.'

'I doubt it, but I do sympathize with the exasperation you must feel. I will be delighted to accept you into the Guild here in Makkathran, Edeard, but it must be as a junior apprentice. I cannot make exceptions, especially not in your case.'

'What do you mean?'

'To acknowledge your journeymen status without a formal letter from your Master will lay me open to a charge of favouritism from others on the Guild Council.'

'Politics,' Topar said.

'I understand,' Edeard whispered. He was frightened he was

going to burst into tears in front of them. To get to Makkathran, to be in the presence of the Grand Master, then to be told all he had achieved was worthless because he lacked a piece of paper ... 'Pardon me, but that's stupid, sir,' he said sullenly.

'It's much worse than that. But I appreciate your politeness, my boy.'

Edeard sniffed and wiped his nose. 'How long would it take me to get back to being a journeyman?'

'Here at the Blue Tower, and assuming you have the appropriate talent: seven years. Appointing you a journeyman at your age was ... ambitious, even for Akeem. But at the same time so very typical of him.'

'Seven years,' Edeard repeated numbly. Seven years of repeating every lesson and knowledge gift he'd ever undergone. Seven years of having to hold himself back. Seven years of obedience to journeymen less able than himself. *Seven years!*

'I know what you're thinking, and I'm not even using farsight,' Finitan said gently. 'It is a terrible thing to ask you to undergo.'

'I'm not sure I can,' Edeard said. 'I thought when I came here I wanted nothing more than to be a part of the Guild, but now ... These formalities, Akeem always said I would find them so difficult. I thought he was teasing.'

'Listen to me, Edeard,' Finitan said. 'For I am about to say something which borders on the sacrilegious.'

'Sir?'

'The hierarchy we have in the Guilds, not just ours, but all Guilds, exists for those who seek to further themselves within our political system. Talent in your chosen field plays a part, but always it is down to money and politics. That is the way things are here in the capital. If you are not born into a grand family and have ambition then you join a Guild and fight your way to the top. Now consider that very carefully because this is a choice that will decide the rest of your life for you. Is the Eggshaper Guild what you truly want? It is what I wanted, and I have achieved my goal. I am Grand Master. But look at the battles I have to fight on every level. I am surrounded with so many people seeking the same thing, seeking this seat in this office, that I cannot make an exception for someone as gifted as yourself because a hundred years ago I had a Master that went on to teach you. Is that sanity, Edeard? Is that the life you want for yourself? To have a dozen such considerations every day, to be unable to put a foot wrong, to continue tradition no matter how dry and worthless it is because that is what supports you. To be unable to change, even though change was the one thing above all that used to drive you. That is what I am, Edeard, that is what Topar is. I despair of myself at times, of how helpless I have become, entrapped in the very system I once wanted to alter and improve.'

'But, sir, if you can't make changes, who can?'

'Nobody can, Edeard. Not now, not in these times. Our society is mature. Change is instability. That is why every institution we have resists change. To maintain the status quo is our sole objective in life.'

'That's wrong.'

'Yes, it is. But what do you want to do about it? Do you want to spend seven years working your arse off to become a journeyman, to make that first real step towards receiving Master status, at which point your talent is irrelevant and the politicking begins in earnest. You build allies and make enemies on every council upon which you sit in order to gain greater power and control. But it is only power and control over the councils. Ultimately it amounts to very little.'

'Are you saying I should go back and join the caravan?'

'No. My offer to admit you to the Guild is genuine and remains open while I am Grand Master. Who knows? Maybe you will make a difference if you make it to this office. I should tell you now that nobody under a hundred years old has ever sat here.'

'I don't know,' Edeard said helplessly.

'There is one alternative. You already know how to sculpt eggs, by joining the Guild you would be acknowledging your life is now orientated to a political goal. However, the city constables are always seeking recruits. It is a noble profession. My position on the Upper Council allows me to sponsor you into their ranks. They would delight in accepting someone with such a strong third hand. And this city desperately needs men of good stature to enforce the law. Without that we will all become nothing.'

'A constable?' He wasn't even sure what a constable was.

'Even a city as sophisticated as Makkathran has crime, Edeard. Decent people, especially those in the poorer districts, live in fear from gangs who roam the streets at night. Merchants suffer thefts and increase their prices accordingly, which injures everyone. You would be helping people directly. And immediately. Unlike the other Guilds, constable apprentices are not tucked away out of sight toiling to make their Master's life easy. The hierarchy of the constables is a lot less complex than any normal Guild. The prospect for advancement is good. You're smart and strong. I will not delude you that it is an easy life, for it is not. But you've even been in a real life or death fight, which is more than any other recruit. You should do well.'

'I'm not sure.'

'Of course not. I didn't expect you to give me an answer immediately. You need time to think about your future. What you decide now determines the rest of your life. Why don't you escort your friend to her church, then take a good look around. Get a feel for the city before you make your mind up. If you do want to give the constables a try, longtalk Topar here, and we will arrange for your admission.'

'Thank you, sir.'

'You are welcome. And Edeard.'

'Sir?'

'I'm glad Akeem had such a gifted pupil at the end. It wouldn't have been easy for him in Ashwell; you must have helped enrich his life considerably.'

'Thank you.' Edeard rose from the seat, knowing his time was up. 'Sir? Why did Akeem leave the Blue Tower?'

Finitan smiled fondly. 'He was like you, my boy. He wanted to make a difference, to help people. Here, he could do very little.

Outside our crystal wall, in Ashwell, I suspect he had a profound effect on the lives of the villagers.'

'Yes, sir; he did.'

'What happened in there?' Salrana demanded when Edeard reappeared in the anteroom. 'You don't seem very happy.'

'I'm not,' he admitted and picked up his shoulder bag. 'Come on, we need to get you to the church before nightfall. I'll tell you what happened on the way.'

'You can't give up,' Salrana said as they crossed a bridge over Grove Canal into the Eyrie district. Her voice was pleading. 'Not after so much.'

'Finitan was right, though. What's the point? I can already shape eggs as well as just about anyone. If I join the Guild I'll be doing it to climb up the hierarchy, nothing else. And what's there even if I do become Grand Master? Sitting at the top of a tower organizing the Guild while everyone else on the Council waits for me to make a mistake. I'd have a million enemies and no friends, and nothing will change. I won't be helping anyone. Remember Ashwell, what it was like before people accepted the genistars could improve their life? Well Makkathran is a thousand years along from that. You can't shape better genistars, you can't increase the amount in use here.'

'Then when you become Grand Master you must push genistars out on people next to the wild lands. The Eggshaper Guild can still make a difference to everyone beyond the Iguru Plain. You've seen what life's like in the distant provinces. Make it better for them, Edeard, make their life as easy as it is for everyone here.'

'It's too much,' he said. 'I can't do it, Salrana. Most of all, I can't stand seven years as an apprentice again. I just can't. I've learned the Guild teachings, I've been on the road fending for myself for a year. Any position less than journeyman would be a huge step backwards for me. I'm sorry.' He could just see Akeem shaking his head in that weary way of his. The guilt was terrible.

She stroked his cheek, which brought astonished glances from passers-by. 'I'm not going to give up on you. And I'm certainly not going to let you give up on your own dream. Not after what we've been through.'

'I don't know what I'd do without you.'

'You're welcome,' she said spryly.

He glanced up at the strangely twisted spires that jutted out of the ground like gigantic stalagmites. Even the smallest was higher than the Blue Tower. There were no windows or balconies, just a single entrance at ground level leading to a central spiral stair. Right at the tip, they flared out into broad platforms that looked terribly unstable, as if they would snap off at any second.

After the madcap bustle of the other districts they'd experienced, Eyrie was almost deserted by comparison. With night falling, the devout were making their way to the central church of the Empyrean Lady for the evening service of prayer and thanksgiving. Light was beginning to shine out of crevices in the crinkled towers around them, washing the hard ground in a pale tangerine illumination. Edeard regarded it curiously, realizing it was the same glow that had lit his way up the stairs of the Blue Tower, somehow the city material emitted it without heat.

'Where will you go tonight?' she asked.

'I don't know. Find a cheap tavern with a room, I suppose.'

'Oh Edeard, you'll be so lonely there. Why don't you go back to the caravan? Anyone there will be happy to lend you a cot.'

'No,' he said firmly. 'I won't go back.'

She pressed her teeth together in dismay. 'Your pride will be the end of you.'

He smiled. 'Probably.'

The Lady's central church was impressive. A large cloud-white dome with the top third made of the same crystal as the city wall. Three wings radiated out from the middle, lined with balconies.

'I'm here,' Salrana said in wonder. Tears glinted in her eyes and her mind shone with happiness. 'The Lady herself lived the last years of her life here. Can you feel how sacrosanct this ground is? It's all real, Edeard. The Lady's message to the word is real.'

'I know,' he said.

The main door to the church was wide open, shining a broad fan of rose-gold light across the broad plaza outside. Several Mothers dressed in splendid white and silver robes stood on the threshold to give a personal welcome to their congregation. Salrana straightened her shoulders and walked up to the first. There followed a long conversation which Edeard did his best not to eavesdrop on. It culminated with the Mother embracing Salrana. Another two Mothers hurried over at her longtalk call. They all began chattering excitedly around the suddenly overwhelmed girl.

Salrana turned, holding an arm out to Edeard. 'They'll take me in,' she said, her face suffused with delight.

'That's good,' he said softly.

'Come, child,' said the first Mother, and put her arm protectively around Salrana. 'Young man.'

'Yes, Mother.'

'We commend you for aiding our lost soul. May the Lady bless you for what you have done.'

He didn't know what to say, so he just ducked his head gracelessly.

'Will you stay for the service?'

'I, er, have to get to my lodgings, thank you.' He backed away and turned, walking quickly across the plaza.

'Don't forget,' Salrana's longtalk voice chided him. 'Talk to me first thing tomorrow. I want to know that you're all right.'

'I will.'

Even with the cold orange light shining down from the twisted towers, he was unnerved walking through the empty district. The dark upper sections of the towers formed black silhouettes against the glowing night sky. His mind kept firmly focused on the warm aura of human minds on the other side of the Grove Canal. Before he reached any bridge he came to a decision. His farsight strained to reach the Blue Tower. The sparks of minds were very hard to distinguish through its walls, but he persevered and eventually found one he recognized.

'Excuse me, sir?' he longtalked to Topar.

There was a small burst of surprise from the man, quickly smothered. 'Where are you, Edeard?'

'In Eyrie, sir.'

'And you farsighted me through the walls of the Blue Tower from there?'

'Er, yes, sir.'

'Of course you did. So what can I do for you?'

'I know this probably seems sudden to you, sir, but I have thought over what the Grand Master said to me. I'd like to join the constables. There's nothing else for me here.'

'Yes, we did make that promise to you, didn't we. Very well. Report to the main constable station in the Jeavons district. By the time you get there they will be expecting you. Your letter of sponsorship will be with the captain in the morning.'

'Yes, sir. Please thank the Grand Master for me, sir. I'll not let him down.'

'Somehow, Edeard, I don't think you will. One word of advice from a lifelong citizen of Makkathran.'

'Sir?'

'Don't let your fellow constables realize how strong you are, not at first. It may attract the wrong kind of interest. Politics, remember?'

'I remember, sir.'

.✱

'Get up, you little turds!'

Edeard groaned, immensely tired, blinking against the orange light flooding down into the dormitory. His thoughts were a confused whirl as reality intruded into the shrinking dream.

'Come on. Up! I haven't got the time to nurse you pathetic tits. If you can't even get up in the morning what use are you? None. Which doesn't surprise me in any respect. I want every one of you dressed and in the small hall in five minutes. Anyone who doesn't make it before I close the doors can piss off right back home to your mummy again. Now move it.'

'Whaa—?' Edeard managed. Someone walked past the end of his bed and whacked his feet with a truncheon. 'Ouch!'

'If you think that hurt, wait till I get to work on your feelings, farm boy.'

Edeard hurriedly pushed the blanket down and rolled out. There were six bed alcoves in the dorm room, only two were empty. He'd met the other constable recruits last night, a quick session before Chae, their squad's training sergeant, marched in and barked at them to shut up and get some sleep. 'Because you've got an early start in the morning.'

As he struggled into his shirt, Edeard suspected it was Chae who'd just woken them. The voice was familiar.

'He's got to be kidding,' said Boyd, a tall lad with lank blond hair and large ears. The fourth son of a baker in the Jeavons district not far from the station, he was in his early twenties and as he saw his elder brother take on more and more of the bakehouse he finally acknowledged he wasn't going to inherit any part of the family business. His sisters were married off, and his other brothers had all left the district to forge their own way forward. He lacked their entrepreneurial streak, so decided the only way out was the Guilds or signing up with either the militia or the constables. He didn't have the money to buy into the militia; and his psychic talents were limited.

'Oh no he's not,' Macsen said as he hurriedly pulled up his own trousers. His story was similar to Boyd's. He was the unrecognized son of a mistress to a grand family's patriarch. Usually such a father would quietly buy such an offspring a minor commission in the militia or smooth the way for entry to a professional Guild such as the lawyers or clerks. Unfortunately, this patriarch chose to travel on one of his trading ships voyaging south along the coast when one of the Lyot Sea's rare storms blew up. The wife and eldest son threw Macsen and his mother out of their estate cottage on the Iguru even before the memorial service had been held.

Edeard shoved his bare feet into his boots. 'We'd better do as he says, at least until we figure out how serious the officers are,' he said. He looked at the locker beside the cot where his shoulder bag was resting, and briefly wondered if it would be safe. Not that there was much of value inside. *And anyway, this is a constable station.*

'Chae's serious all right,' Dinlay said. Their final room mate was also a youngest son, but his father was a constable. As such, Dinlay was the only one to already have a uniform. He was doing up the silver buttons on the front of his dark-blue tunic. The little metal circles had been polished to a sheen, as had his black ankle-high boots. The trousers were pressed, showing a sharp crease down the front. It wasn't a new uniform, but you had to look carefully to see any wear. Dinlay had told them last night it used to belong to his father when he was a probationary constable. Out of the four of them, he seemed to be the only one enthusiastic about their new profession. He used a longtalk whisper to tell them, 'Father said Sergeant Chae is a heavy drinker. He was sent to this station because he's screwed up everywhere else in the city.'

'So they put him in charge of training recruits?' Macsen exclaimed.

Dinlay winced, glancing about uncomfortably. 'Not so loud. He doesn't like being reminded he threw his career away.'

Boyd chuckled. 'Career. In the constables. Aren't you the comedian.'

Dinlay gave him an angry look before putting his wire-rimmed glasses on. There was something about him which reminded Edeard of Fahin, not just his short-sight problem, but the way he was so dedicated to his life choice, yet at the same time so obviously wasn't cut out for it.

Edeard shivered despite pulling on a thick woollen jumper. He hadn't thought of Fahin in a long time. It was an unfortunate way to start his first morning.

Not that it was morning yet, he noticed as they scurried down the station's central stair to the small hall where they would spend the next six months learning their new craft. The glowing nebulas of Querencia's night sky were still visible through the feathery curtain of cloud drifting in from the sea. Dawn was at least another hour away.

Edeard still wasn't used to the way Makkathran buildings blocked his farsight. So he was surprised when they arrived in the hall that another probationary constable was already there along with Sergeant Chae. She was about his age, perhaps a little older, with dark hair cut shorter than he'd ever seen on a girl before. Her face was rounded with chubby cheeks and what looked like a permanent scowl. Even by Makkathran standards, her thoughts were heavily veiled, allowing no hint as to her true feelings. Edeard tried not to be too obvious in the way he checked her out, but when his eyes switched from her legs – long but thighs rather too plump – to her chest he suddenly realized she was watching him. She raised an eyebrow in scornful query. His cheeks reddened and he turned away.

Chae was standing at the head of the room, under one of the ceiling's circular light patches. Thankfully, his anger seemed to have vanished. 'Very good, boys and girls, almost on time. Now believe it or not, this early morning is not designed with the sole purpose to make your lives miserable, I'll have plenty of opportunity for that over the next few months. No. Today I want us to get acquainted. That means, we'll be starting with some simple tests to discover the level of your psychic abilities – or the lack of them. This way we can combine you into a squad which together will perform a great deal better than the sum of its parts. And believe me you will need to work together. There are gangs out there who will happily shred your flesh and feed you to the fil-rats if you try and interrupt their activities.'

Edeard wasn't quite sure he believed that, and hoped his thoughts didn't show his doubt. He concentrated on trying to achieve the same passivity that everyone else was displaying.

'Constable Kanseen, would you begin, please,' Chae said. He gestured at the bench in front of him. There were five metal balls resting on the ancient wood, the smallest was the size of a human fist, while the others were progressively larger. A sixth ball sat on the floor, a good eighteen inches in diameter.

'Which one?' Kanseen asked.

'You just show me what you can do, young lady,' Chae said. There was a strong note of contempt ringing through his voice. 'That way I can assess what duties to assign you. If any.'

Kanseen's face hardened into an even more disapproving scowl. She glared at the fourth ball. It slowly rose into the air.

Macsen whistled approvingly and clapped. The other probationary constables grinned appreciatively. Edeard took a moment, and joined in the acknowledgement. He assumed someone had given her the same advice as him about not revealing her full strength.

'That it?' Chae asked.

'Sir,' Kanseen grunted.

'Okay, thank you. Boyd, let's see what you're made of.'

A grinning Boyd stepped forward. The fourth ball quivered and rose a couple of inches above the wood. Boyd's brow glistened with perspiration.

Macsen managed to lift the fifth ball. Dinlay produced a confident grin and elevated the fifth and second balls, which drew him a heavy round of applause. Even Kanseen joined in.

'All right, Edeard, show them how the countryside is so much better than the city.'

Edeard nodded slowly and moved forward. The others were watching eagerly. He was sorely tempted to fling the sixth ball right at the sergeant, but Topar's caution was still fresh in his mind.

His third hand closed round the fifth ball and sent it bobbing up through the air until it was halfway to the ceiling. The others cheered. He lifted the second ball, then made a show of straining to lift the third, allowing it to hover a few inches above the wood.

The first ball shot off the table and streaked towards Edeard. His shield hardened, deflecting it easily enough. At the same time he dropped the three balls he was holding aloft.

All of the probationary constables fell silent, staring at him and Chae.

'Very good, Edeard,' Chae drawled. 'You almost convinced me. Little too much time between the hit and the drop, though. Work on that.'

Edeard gave the sergeant a sullen stare.

Chae leaned forward, in a stage whisper he said: 'I have friends in the Eggshaper Guild guard, lad.'

Edeard reddened.

'Constables should be honest above all else,' Chae continued. 'Especially with their own squad mates. Ultimately your lives may depend on each other. Now do you want to try again?'

Edeard pulled the sixth ball into the air. He heard Boyd gasp in surprise.

'Thank you, Edeard,' Chae said. 'Now then; farsight. I have placed some markers around the district. Let's see who can find what.'

Edeard let the sixth ball down gently. He wondered what Chae would have said if he'd known how much more he could lift.

The psychic tests went on for another hour, measuring their various talents until Chae declared he'd had enough of them. Edeard was interested in the results. Kanseen had a farsight almost as good as his own, while Dinlay could probably long-shout halfway across the Iguru Plain – a capability he was inordinately proud of. Macsen's shield seemed disproportionally stronger than his third hand – nothing Chae threw at him got through. Boyd was all round unexceptional. It left Edeard wondering if he was above average or if his squad mates were distinctly below average. Sergeant Chae's psychic ability was certainly powerful enough.

Chae told them to get some breakfast then report for uniform fitting. 'If any of you have money I'd advise you to spend it on your tunic. Those without money will have the cost taken out of their pay for the next six months, and I assure you it won't leave you with much at the end of the week.'

They trooped along to the station's main hall, a long chamber with an arching ceiling and a big crystal window at the far end. Some of the benches were already occupied. A sergeant told them the bench at the far end would be theirs for the duration of their probationary period. The rest of the constables ignored them.

Ge-monkeys hurried out of the kitchen bringing crockery. They were adept at receiving orders, Edeard found when he instructed one to bring tea and scrambled eggs. At least the station provided their food. He wondered if he should try to longtalk Salrana. The sun was just starting to rise outside.

'I've never seen anyone lift so much,' Boyd said. 'You've got a lot of talent, Edeard.'

Edeard shrugged.

'I claim first rights to stand behind him when the shit starts flying,' Macsen said. 'And the bullets.'

'You all look like you can handle yourselves if we get pushed into a corner,' Edeard said.

'Don't have a lot of choice, do we?' Macsen said. 'Not enough skill for a Guild, and not rich enough to buy into the militia. So here we are, all of us clinging to the arse end of life and we're only just starting out. One big long fall into the sewage from here on in, my fellow failures.'

'Ignore him,' Dinlay said. 'He's just bitter at the way he got treated by his father's family.'

'Not as bitter as they'll be when I'm through with them,' Macsen said with unexpected heat.

'Plans for revenge?' Kanseen asked.

'Don't have to plan. Those arrogant turds break the law a dozen times a week. One day I'll have the clout to have the whole lot of the bastards locked up and ruined.'

'Now that's what I like to see: ambition.'

'How come you didn't join a Guild, Edeard?' Macsen asked. 'You have more psychic talent than the rest of us put together.'

'I don't want to be ordered around for the next seven years,' he told them simply.

'Lady bless that,' Dinlay said. 'We just have to grit our teeth for six months and we've made it.'

'That's a curious definition of making it,' Kanseen said in a dismissive voice as a ge-monkey brought her a tray with a bowl of porridge and a tall glass of milk. 'Being allowed out on to the streets by ourselves to be shoved around by gangs and get beaten up trying to stop tavern fights.'

'Then why are you here?' Macsen asked.

She took a long drink of milk. 'Do you see me being a proper little wife to some oaf of a tradesman?'

'Not all tradesmen are oafs,' Boyd said defensively.

Macsen ignored him. 'Good for you,' he told Kanseen.

Her head turned ponderously to stare at him. 'Not interested, thanks.'

Edeard grinned while Dinlay and Boyd both laughed.

'Me neither,' Macsen insisted, but he'd lost the moment and sounded very insincere.

'So is Chae right about buying the uniform?' Edeard asked. He was conscious that he probably had more coinage in his pocket than the others.

'Depends,' Dinlay said. 'If you're definitely going to be a constable then it doesn't matter how you pay. But if you're uncertain then you're best off having them take it from your wages, that way when you leave after a couple of weeks you hand the uniform back and you haven't lost any of your own money.'

'Oh face facts,' Macsen said. 'If we're here, it's not because we're uncertain: we're plain desperate.'

'Speak for yourself,' Dinlay said. 'This is my family profession.'

'Then I apologize. I don't have the nicety of alternatives.'

'You could have joined the gangs,' Kanseen said lightly. 'It probably pays better.'

Macsen showed her a fast hand gesture.

'How bad are they?' Edeard asked. 'The gangs, I mean. I'd never heard of them before I reached town.'

'Lady, you really are from the countryside, aren't you,' Macsen said. 'When did you get here?'

'Yesterday.'

'*Yesterday!*' he said it in a voice so loud that several constables glanced curiously over at their table.

'Yesterday,' Edeard said firmly.

'Okay, well, too late now. The gangs are big in some districts and not in others; the majority are based in Sampalok. If you're rich they're not much of a problem, if you're poor then it's more difficult for you. They specialize in protection. Think of them as an alternative tax system to the Grand Council.'

'But with violence,' Dinlay said. 'They're murderous scum, and they should be wiped out.'

'After first being fairly found guilty in court,' Macsen said with a smile.

'They're a real problem and getting worse,' Boyd said. 'My brother is having to pay them to leave the bakery alone, and he's only ten minutes away from this station; which puts him about as far from Sampalok as you can be. It used to be safe there; my father never used to have such trouble.'

'Why doesn't he report them to the constables?' Edeard said.

Macsen gave a disrespectful snort. 'Take a look around you, Edeard. Would you ask us to protect you from an organized gang who think it's funny to throw your children or your mother into the canal with a rock tied to them? Are you going to stand outside a baker's shop for twenty-four hours a day for ten years just to save them? Do you think Chae would let you? And if he did, what about everyone else in the district? No. They're a fact of life in Makkathran now. The best the constables do is maintain an uneasy truce and stop us from falling into complete anarchy.'

'So young, so cynical,' Kanseen said. 'Ignore them, Edeard, it's nothing like as bad as they say.'

'I hope not,' he said in a subdued voice. Maybe he was still suffering from the shock of city life, but he had an uncomfortable feeling that Grand Master Finitan hadn't been entirely honest with him about life in Makkathran.

5

Investigator, second level, Halran stood in the vault's open
door and surveyed the chaos inside. Every surface – walls, floor,
ceiling, corpses – had been covered in a thick carpet of blue-
grey gossamer fibre, as if a million spiders had spent the night
spinning their webs together. The slender strands were actually
semi-organic filaments that had taken over three hours to neutralize the nerve toxin leaking from spent kinetic projectiles, and
also damp down several other lethal energy surges coming from
munitions left over from the firefight. Halran was mildly surprised that the St Mary's Clinic would use nerve agents, but then
important people did like reassurance that their secure memory
stores were truly *secure*. He'd told the clinic manager that he'd be
inspecting their toxic armaments user certificate at noon. A
timescale long enough for high-level calls to be placed and the
correct licence to be procured. It was that kind of flexible
interpretation of procedure which had earned Halran his last two
promotions. He figured what-the-hell, the big boys ran the world
anyway, there was little capital to be made from annoying them.
That was why the Police Commissioner handed him this assignment. And as soon as he got it, the Mayor's assistant was calling
him to explain certain political considerations. Foremost of which
was that the complete destruction of half a million memorycells
belonging to the wealthiest, most influential people living in the
state had not actually happened. If there was a temporary glitch

in kube data retrieval due to the unfortunate accident with the clinic's power generator it was regrettable, but not a cause for alarm, nor excessive media interest. Reporters could cover the damage to the forest, they were not to be permitted into the administration block and its sub-levels.

Halran's u-shadow completed its analysis of the gossamer and reported that decontamination was complete. 'All right,' he told the eight-strong forensic team standing behind him in the corridor, 'I want a full scene survey down to a molecular level. No budget limit; this is way way above our usual priority rating. Col, Angelo, you build the event sequence for me. Darval, see if you can get me the name of the memorycell that bastard Telfer was after.'

Darval peered over Halran's shoulder; the emergency lighting projector rigged up in the doorway produced a silver-blue holographic glow throughout the vault, eliminating shadows. It made the gossamer shimmer softly, resembling a rippled moonlit lake as its undulations smothered the congealed splinters of half a million kubes. 'How in Ozzie's name am I going to do that, Chief?'

Halran gave him an evil grin. 'There should be one missing. So all you have to do is reassemble the fragments of those that are still here, and tell me which one was taken.'

'Fuck me.'

'Good point. Plan B: go through the names on the registry and assign them a probability of someone wanting to steal their memories. Start with political, criminal, and financial categories.'

Darval gave a reluctant nod.

'Force fields on at all times, please,' Halran ordered. 'There were some very nasty munitions loose in here, I don't want to take any chances.'

The forensic team moved cautiously into the vault. Examiners scurried in with them, bots like lead cockroaches scuttling along on black electromuscle legs, bristling with sensory antenna that wiggled though the gossamer to stroke the surfaces beneath. Over two thousand were released, streaming over the floor and up the walls to build up a comprehensive molecular map of the vault.

Halran waited until the tiny bots had whirled round the corpse of Viertz Accu before he gave her a more detailed inspection. Her cocooned body was still in a kneeling position, spine curved forward as if she was at prayer. They'd found the top of her skull upstairs while they were waiting for the gossamer to run its decontamination procedure. Halran knew what that implied – this was turning into a bad case from every angle.

His exovision overlaid the results of the examiners, showing him the narrow burn lines on her exposed brain. A lot of energy had been applied in a fashion he recognized. He applied a deep scan module, tracking the depth of the beam penetration. Her memorycell had been destroyed.

'I hope she backed up recently,' he muttered.

'What do you make of these, Chief?' Angelo asked. He was standing in front of an exotic matter cage.

'Nice idea, I suppose. I haven't seen one before. Telfer obviously didn't know they were here.'

'Much good it did the clinic. Those guards didn't exactly slow him down, did they?'

'No. His enrichments were off the scale.' Halran called up the main case file again. Telfer appeared in his exoimage, a picture taken in the main reception area, showing a possible oriental ethnicity, but with odd grey eyes. Age locked into his thirties, which was unusual, and with a dense stubble shadow. Completely unexceptional. Which Halran knew to be deliberate. Not that visual features meant anything in this day and age; even DNA identification was inconclusive now – and they had enough of that from the blood trail back up to the roof. The picture showed him smiling as he greeted the beautiful young clinician. His accomplice, though, was a different matter, she certainly didn't qualify as unexceptional; a real beauty with a freckled face and thick dark-red hair. Cute nose, too, he thought admiringly. People would remember that face.

Everything about their arrival was perfectly normal, right up to the moment the clinic security net started glitching and Telfer vanished from the smartcore's passive surveillance. The raid, too, was extremely professional. Apart from the exit. The woman had seemed almost surprised, as if she was improvising the whole thing. Which didn't make a lot of sense.

'Chief,' Darval called.

'Yep.'

'The registry was hacked.'

Halran started to walk over to where Darval was stooped over the registry pillar. Several examiners were crawling over its gossamer cloak, prodding the top with their antennae. 'Has there been physical—' he began to say. The sentence was never finished. A woman walked into the vault. Halran gave her a surprised look, about to ask who the hell she was – suspecting another of the Mayor's staffers – because nobody else could get through the police cordon without his permission. Then her face registered and Halran didn't need to ask, he knew all about this living legend; everyone in law enforcement did. 'Oh sweet Ozzie,' he murmured – and an already bad case turned nightmare on him. She was shorter than most of the citizens of today's Commonwealth, but the confidence she exuded was so much greater than average. Harlan had encountered enough Highers in his time to recognize their slightly smug self-belief; she was on a level far above them, with a composure that rated glacial. Her face was enchanting, a combination of pre-Commonwealth Earth's Filipino and European features framed by thick raven hair brushed straight and devoid of any modern cosmetics, a beauty he could only describe as old-fashioned. Which was fair enough given she hadn't changed her appearance once in the last fourteen hundred years.

The whole forensic team had fallen into awed silence, staring at the woman.

Halran stepped forward, hoping he was concealing his nerves. She wore a conservative cream-coloured toga suit over a figure that was as ideal as any created by St Mary's specialists. When he attempted to scan her using the most subtle probes his enrichments could produce they were deflected perfectly. It was as if nothing was there; the only empirical proof he had that she existed was his own eyesight.

'Ma'am, I'm Investigator Halran, in charge of this case. I, er, that is we, are very flattered you're here.'

'Thank you,' said Paula Myo.

'Can I ask what your interest is?'

'It's not my interest; I am only ANA:Governance's representative.'

'In this universe,' Darval whispered to Angelo.

Paula gave him a sweet smile. 'The old jokes are always the best ones. And they don't come much older.'

Darvel's expression turned sickly.

'Okay,' Halran said. 'So what's ANA:Governance's interest?'

'Mr Telfer.'

'Is he Higher?'

'What do you think?'

'His weapons biononics are the most sophisticated we've ever seen on Anagaska. The vault guards were hired purely on the basis of their enrichments, and he took them both out in less than a minute. So if he's not Higher, he has access to the best the Central Worlds have to offer.'

'Very good,' Paula complimented. 'So?'

'He's probably working for one of your Factions.'

'Excellent rationale, Investigator. That's exactly why I'm here, to see if that particular conclusion is correct. Now I'd like first access to all your forensic results, please.'

'Er, I'll see you get copies, of course.'

'Your planetary government has granted ANA:Governance full cooperation on this case. I'm sure you appreciate the politics involved. Please feel free to check with your Commissioner, and even the city's Mayor; but that's not copies. I require first, and unrestricted, access to the raw data, thank you.'

Halran knew when he'd lost a battle. 'Yes, ma'am. First access. I'll set that up right away.'

'Thank you. Now who's analysing the registry?'

'That's me,' Darval said awkwardly.

'Who do you think Telfer was after?'

Darval glanced at Halran, who gave a tiny nod. 'Easy, actually. One of the secure stores belonged to Inigo.'

'Ah,' Paula smiled. She closed her eyes and drew a long breath through her nose. 'When was the last update?'

'3320.'

'The year he left on his Centurion Station mission,' she said. 'And he didn't return to Anagaska until 3415, correct?'

'Yes,' Halran said. 'Living Dream's central fane on Anagaska was built in Kuhmo; he was here to dedicate it.'

'Interesting,' Paula mused.

'You think someone's going to full-clone him?'

'Why else would you steal his mind?' Paula said. 'Thank you for your cooperation, Investigator. And I'd still like those results as they come in.' She turned and started to walk out of the vault.

'That's it?' Halran asked.

Paula halted, tipping her head to fix the investigator with a level stare. 'Unless you have something else to add.'

'What about Telfer?'

'Good luck hunting him down.'

'Are you going to help us?'

'I won't put any obstacles in your way, political or otherwise.' She left the vault, leaving Halran staring at his team in confusion and indignation.

Paula walked out of the administration block and glanced round at the forest. The air blasts had produced superficial damage, most of the clinic's buildings were still intact, and while the larger trees had been toppled there were still enough younger ones to maintain the forest once the dead trunks had been cleared away. A police cordon extended for several hundred yards, with uniformed officers reinforcing the patrolbots. Clinic ground staff were working with contractors and forestrybots to clear the worst of the damage. Little curls of smoke were drifting upward from the blackened ground where fires had burned for a couple of hours during the night before being extinguished.

She didn't pause as her field effect scanned round, but two of the contractor crew were red tagged by her u-shadow. Both of them were shielded, utilizing sophisticated deflection techniques only available to high-grade biononics. Hers, of course, were even more advanced. They were keeping their distance from the cordon, but her eyes managed to zoom in and snatch a facial image. Her u-shadow produced a cross reference for both of them in less than a second. Once upon a time, about a thousand years ago, Paula would have confronted them there and then. These days she liked to think she'd mellowed somewhat, although in truth it was more advantageous to let them think she hadn't spotted them.

Paula had been born on Huxley's Haven, a unique world funded by the Human Structure Foundation which genetically modified every citizen so they would fit into a simple social structure framed within a low-technology civilization. To the horror and dismay of the rest of the Commonwealth, what they condemned as genetic slavery actually worked, producing a population that was mostly happy with their predetermined lot. The few malcontents were kept in order by police officers who received specific psychoneural profiling. Among other traits was a variant on obsessive compulsive disorder to ensure they never gave up the chase. The Foundation had created Paula to be one of them, but she'd been stolen from a birthing ward by a group of radical liberals intent on liberating the poor slaves. She'd grown up in the Commonwealth at large, first becoming an investigator in the Serious Crimes Directorate, and then for the last seven hundred years acting as an agent for ANA:Governance.

Huxley's Haven still existed, its society chugging quietly along on its ordained course without changing or evolving. The Greater Commonwealth had very little contact with it these days; Paula herself hadn't been back for over three hundred years, and that had essentially been nostalgia tourism. There was no need to keep an eye on it. ANA:Governance was very protective of non-

Higher cultures. A policy which, ironically, gave Paula very little opportunity to return; her designated task of preventing the ANA Factions pursuing their illegal interference among the External Worlds kept her incredibly busy.

Her u-shadow established an ultra-secure link to Justine Burnelli. 'I'm at the Anagaska clinic,' she said.

'And?'

'We were right; the raid was organized by a Faction.'

'Any clues which one?'

'Well Marius and the Delivery Man are hanging round outside, which implies they are as interested as we are.'

'Ergo they didn't do it.'

'Don't be so sure. I've never known the Accelerators and the Conservatives to be so blatant before. More likely one of them did it, and the other is trying to expose or counter them. You know what they're like.'

'Whose memorycell were they after?'

'Now that's where it gets interesting: Inigo.'

'Oh my. Really?' Justine said. 'I'm surprised Inigo left himself open to that level of exposure.'

'To be exact, Inigo pre-Living Dream. This is an old store.'

'How does that help anyone?'

'I'm not sure. The Conservatives will benefit if he returns and stops the Cleric Conservator's Pilgrimage project. But there's no way of telling if he will. He might just applaud and join the Pilgrimage himself.'

'If one of the Factions full-clone him they'd be in possession of a puppet messiah. Very useful for endorsing your own agenda.'

'Except this won't be a full-clone,' Paula said. 'This is an early version.'

'I have a theory that might fit.'

'Go.'

'A full-clone early version would presumably be able to receive dreams from the Void just like the original, which would give its controllers a considerable advantage over their opposition.'

'You mean they'd be able to reach the supposed Last Dream?'

'More likely the new Skylord Dreams. Ethan still hasn't found the Second Dreamer, despite a phenomenal amount of effort. Did you know Living Dream is modifying every gaiafield confluence nest it sponsors? And that's about eighty per cent of the Greater Commonwealth. They're getting desperate; the new dreams are increasing. They're not just fragments any more. Whole sequences are seeping into the gaiafield.'

'I don't think Living Dream are behind the raid.'

'They'd benefit enormously,' Justine said.

'Yes, but, my u-shadow has identified the woman assisting Mr Telfer. It's Living Dream's ex-Councillor Corrie-Lyn. Now *persona non grata* to Living Dream, and wanted for several body-loss charges on Ellezelin. The Commonwealth warrants are quite extensive. They also list an accomplice called Aaron, who shares the facial features of Mr Telfer.'

'Now that is interesting. Any idea about Aaron alias Mr Telfer?'

'No. But the pair of them transferred to a starship immediately after the clinic raid. There's only one starship unaccounted for on Anagaska right now, the *Artful Dodger*.'

'What's the history?'

'Standard private yacht, registered on Sholapur.'

'Oh now we're getting somewhere. Sholapur: so in other words we don't know who it belongs to.'

'Indeed. There's no real background available; however the *Artful Dodger* was on Ellezelin until just after the ruckus at the Riasi fane.'

'Corrie-Lyn used to be Inigo's lover. Could she be pining for him? A full-clone would be one way of getting him back.'

'No. She's a pawn. Telfer is using her to get to Inigo.'

'How does an out-of-date memorycell help them get closer to him? Enough people have tried to find him. He's probably left the Commonwealth entirely. Either he set off to get into the Void by himself, or he's gone and joined Ozzie.'

'He hasn't joined Ozzie. I checked that fifteen years ago.'

'I was always envious of the life you lead,' Justine said. 'All that glamorous danger and travel, there's something intoxicating about it to a sheltered little rich girl like me. How was Ozzie?'

'Like me, essentially unchanged.'

'Who do you think this Aaron character is working for?'

'As you say, there are a lot of Factions and organizations who would benefit by finding Inigo. This raid simply tells us how urgent their pursuit is becoming. Nobody has been careless enough to show their hand until now.'

'So what's your next step?'

'This raid is only one aspect of a much larger process of political events. I think it's important to find the Second Dreamer before Living Dream do. That person will obviously play a huge part in determining the outcome of the Pilgrimage.'

'Wow, you still think big, don't you?'

'I always believed that solving a case is a holistic process. It's one of the few things I have remained true to in the last thousand years.'

'And what about Aaron and Corrie-Lyn?'

'That's the aspect I'll stay visible on. It won't take Investigator Halran long to identify Corrie-Lyn, and things will become quite public after that. If I start enquiring after the Second Dreamer it will create too much interest amid the Factions.'

'Would you like me to start looking for the Second Dreamer?'

'No. You're highly visible to the Factions. Almost as much as myself. I think it would be best if you could keep an eye on the Delivery Man and Marius.'

'I'll do that. Who gets to track down the Second Dreamer, then?'

Paula smiled broadly, knowing how the Faction agents out in the forest would focus on that and wonder. 'The last person anyone would suspect, of course.'

*

The condition of the utility feed pipes in the third apartment were a lot worse than Araminta had expected. She spent three unscheduled hours that morning tracing them through the walls and floor, supervising the bots as they ripped the corroded tubes out. It all made a great deal of mess, which meant more clean-up, which meant more time not spent on preparing the wall frames for the new fittings, which pushed completion back just that little bit further.

Her u-shadow told her when it was eleven o'clock, which barely gave her enough time for a spore shower in the fourth apartment, where she was living. Two of the old shower's five nozzles weren't working, and one of the remaining jets smelt funny. She just had time to apply some freshener and dress in smart trousers and jacket before the clients were due. The perfumed spray damping her skin gave her an unexpected flash-back to the day she found out Laril had left Viotia and her liberal use of travel-clean back in those days. All of which gave her a guilty prod that she hadn't been back to Nik's for ages.

She gritted her teeth against stupid sentiment and went out into the vestibule as the lift brought her new clients up from the lobby. Danal and Mareble were dressed strangely. Her in a long skirt of wide-weave ginger cotton, topped by a suede waistcoat with brass buttons that was worn over a plain white blouse. Sturdy brown boots were just visible below her swirling hem. Her thick raven hair was brushed back, its waves bound in simple elastic cloth bands. He wore leather trousers and boots similar to hers. A yellow jacket was almost hidden beneath a brown over-coat made of some oiled fabric.

Despite their historical appearance, Araminta couldn't help but smile as the lift doors opened. There was something irrepres-sibly enthusiastic about them. Youthful grins and the eager way they glanced around, the way they held hands the whole time.

'Welcome,' she said. The golden-wood door to the showcase apartment swung open.

She'd dressed the apartment with a simple two-tone colour scheme in each room, and kept the furniture minimalist. The floor of the open-plan living room was an expensive ebony-wood parquet. Artfully positioned tables and chairs and settee were all reproduction Herfal style, with sharp curves and metal-moiré legs

– a popular fad three centuries ago. The balcony was open, and it was a warm clear day outside, showing the park off to great effect.

Mareble drew a breath as they walked in. 'It's fabulous,' she exclaimed. 'Just what we're looking for.'

Danal chortled. 'Forgive my wife, she obviously doesn't believe in showing our hand before negotiations.'

'I did the same thing with the original vendor,' Araminta confessed. 'It's easy to become devoted to these apartments very quickly. I'm actually thinking about keeping one for myself.'

Mareble stood in front of the balcony door. 'Would the one we're considering have the same view?'

'Apartment three is on the corner,' Araminta gestured along the balcony. 'You get one aspect facing the park, as well as a view westward across the city. The suspension bridge is visible that way.'

'How lovely.'

'Can we see it?' Danal asked.

'Not just yet. City health and safety codes won't let me take people into an accredited construction site.' *And it's a complete shambles, which might put you off.*

'Construction site? Are there structural problems?'

'Absolutely not. The structure is perfectly sound. An independent deep scan survey file is registered at City Hall if you'd like to verify it. I'm just refurbishing and remodelling. Unfortunately, the city chooses to class that as construction because I'm replacing the electrics and utility feeds. It's just more filework for me, that's all.'

Danal gave a sympathetic sigh. 'That sounds just like Ellezelin. Dear Lady, the Waterwalker never had to put in requests to the Orchard Palace if he wanted to get things done. Try telling that to our government.'

'Now, darling,' Mareble squeezed his hand tighter. 'He has a thing about bureaucrats,' she explained.

'We all do,' Araminta assured them.

'Thank you,' Danal said.

'So are you moving here from Ellezelin?' Araminta asked.

'Oh yes,' they chorused happily.

'I'm a confluence nest technician,' Danal said. 'There's a lot of work going on upgrading the whole gaiafield right now. It's especially important on Viotia.'

'Why is that?' Araminta asked.

'The Second Dreamer is here,' Mareble said. 'We're sure of it. The last few dreams were so much more vivid than those first fragments. Don't you think?'

'I don't have gaiamotes,' Araminta said, keeping it light, as if it was some minor fault with an appliance she was going to get corrected, praying it wouldn't make any difference to the deal. She needed their deposit on apartment three; they hadn't been as easy to sell as she'd envisaged and her suppliers were submitting payment demands.

Mareble and Danal both wore the same compassionate expression, as if they felt sorry for her. A concord which instantly reminded her of Mr Bovey.

'The gaiafield is not something I could live without,' Mareble said quietly. 'I can always sense Danal no matter where we are, even when we're planets apart; that kind of permanent emotional connection is so satisfying and reassuring.'

'And of course we know Inigo's Dreams. Intimately,' Danal said. He smiled with the placid bliss only the truly devout could ever achieve.

Araminta tried to replicate that mien of joy. 'I didn't know you could tell where a dream came from,' she said, hoping that would divert them from her tragic defect. There was nothing the devout of any sect or ideology enjoyed more than making the benefits of their belief obvious to outsiders.

'That's the thing with the gaiafield,' Mareble explained earnestly. 'It's not all clear and precise like the unisphere. Human thoughts are not digital, they're emotion. I had the *feeling* with the last few dreams of the Skylord; they were close to me. Now the nests remember them they've lost that aspect, not that they aren't still wonderful. We're all hoping that we'll experience the Skylord flying to Makkathran to collect the Waterwalker's soul. After everything he's done for the people of Querencia, and us, he deserves to rest within Odin's Sea.'

Something about Mareble's evocation made Araminta pause, as if it connected with some old recollection. Which was stupid. 'I see,' Araminta said. Her knowledge of the whole Waterwalker epic was sketchy at best, she certainly didn't know any details. 'That's why you want to live here?'

Mareble nodded eagerly. 'I'm convinced the Second Dreamer is here. One day soon he'll reveal himself and the Pilgrimage can begin.'

'Will you join it?'

They smiled at each other, and clasped hands again. 'We hope so.'

'Well at the risk of being crass, you won't find anywhere better to wait than here.'

'I think we can consider putting in an offer,' Danal said. 'An uncomfortable number of our fellow followers are looking for property on Viotia. Living in a hotel is pleasant, but we'll be happy to move into a real home.'

'That I can fully appreciate.'

'We're prepared to offer you the full asking price, but we would need a guarantee that the apartment will be completed on time.'

'I can put my certificate on that file, yes.'

'And the virtual model we accessed, it was nice, but . . .'

'I want to make some changes,' Mareble said quickly. 'The technology needs to be de-emphasized, and the décor should be more naturalistic.'

'Naturalistic?'

'Less manufactured products, more wood. As it is on Querencia. We're not against technology, we use it all the time, but it shouldn't be featured. For instance, can you install a proper cooker in the kitchen? One with an oven and hob?'

'I'll check City regulations and get back to you on that one.'

*

'So can you supply me with a *proper* cooker?' she asked Mr Bovey that night over dinner. She was at his house, sitting at a small table on the balcony which overlooked the lawn. The River Cairns ran along the bottom edge where the mown grass gave way to shaggy reeds and a lengthy clump of coran twister trees that dangled chrome-blue fronds into the water. Bright lights in the buildings along the opposite bank glinted off the smooth black surface. It was a lovely relaxing ambience, with a delicious meal several hims had cooked, and three hims sitting with her. A pleasant end to an exasperating day.

'Actually, yes,' the handsome blond one said.

'You say that with such confidence.'

'Because I've already supplied three in the last ten days,' the shorter one with a dark complexion told her. 'Living Dream fanatics do like their primitive comforts. They prefer water baths to spore showers, too.'

'Dear Ozzie, my cousin was right, they are taking over. I ought to raise the price on the last two apartments.'

'I don't want to throw a damper on the evening, but I actually find that prospect quite disturbing. Mainly because it's rapidly becoming true. There are a lot of them here now, millions.'

'I'd have thought the rush for housing will benefit you as much as me, probably more so.'

'Financially yes,' the blond said, holding up a kebab of spiced torkal and pork, marinated in red honey. 'But multiples don't fit into the Living Dream ethos.' He bit into the meat and started chewing. 'We didn't exist in Makkathran,' the Oriental one explained.

'Surely they're not against your lifestyle, are they?' She had an unpleasant thought of how devoted Mareble and Danal were to their ideology, to the complete exclusion of just about everything else. That didn't make them hostile, just unaccepting.

'Oh never actively, no. Perish the thought. Their precious Waterwalker wanted everyone to live together and get along without conflict. But tell me this, how did your buyers react when they found out you weren't sharing the glory that exists only within the gaiafield?'

'Surprised,' she admitted. 'Then I think they wanted to convert me.'

'I bet they did.'

'It won't last long,' she assured him. 'As soon as the Pilgrimage starts, they'll all flock away to join it. My couple told me that. They're only here because they think this is where the Second Dreamer is hiding.'

'Which is equally disturbing.'

'Why?' she asked as she poured herself some more of the excellent rosé wine.

'If you're the next chosen one, why hide? And more than that, why keep releasing the dreams that let everyone know you exist and are in hiding?'

'I don't understand anything about Living Dream. The whole thing seems stupid to me.'

'The word you're looking for is dangerous,' the short one said. 'Too many impossible promises; too many people believing. Bad combination.'

'You're an old cynic.'

All three hims at the table lifted their wine glasses. 'Guilty and proud of it.'

'You have gaiamotes. Are these second dreams real?'

'Is a dream real?' three mouths grinned in unison. 'The dreams exist. Everything else is down to personal perspective. If you want to believe in them, then the Second Dreamer is somewhere out there receiving dreams from a Skylord somewhere inside the Void. If not . . .'

'I don't know what to believe. I'm almost tempted to get gaiamotes just to find out.'

'Take it from me,' said the blond. 'It's not worth it. The gaiafield is just another fad that got hijacked by a bunch of fanatics.'

'Why did Ozzie invent it?'

'He said so that people could understand each other better. If we had more empathy we would be more peaceful. Nice theory. Haven't seen it having much effect on human nature recently.'

'Yet you wouldn't exist without it. And you think you're the future.'

The Oriental Mr Bovey produced a modest smile. 'True. And I doubt Ozzie envisaged us, either.'

She held her wine glass close to her face, and dropped her gaze demurely. 'I never envisaged you.'

'There's a lot of things we don't know about until we encounter them.' The Oriental Mr Bovey pressed up against her and plucked the glass from her hands. She liked the warmth of him against her. On her other side, the blond one stroked her cheek and turned her unresisting head for a kiss.

She closed her eyes. Hands stroked her spine. Hands stroked her legs. The kiss went on and on.

'Come with me,' one him instructed.

The kiss ended, and she saw all three of him smiling in *that* way, gentle and knowing, not bothering to conceal his anticipation.

The three hims escorted her to a warm second-floor bedroom where the lighting was a cosy candle-flame orange. She stood at the end of the bed while they stripped off in front of her, just the way she liked, making her the centre of attention, the centre of desire. Then it was her turn, removing her clothes slowly, showing herself off, drinking in the admiration from hims, exultant with approval. When she was naked, hes began to explore her flesh with formidable intimacy. 'Yes,' she finally shuddered in delight, and they lifted her on to the bed.

Rushing headlong through space the creature could feel stray molecules kiss its broad vacuum wings as it stretched them wide. Scintillations from the tenuous impact dripped from its trailing edge, leaving a weak contrail of fluorescence through the empty gulf. Ahead, a star gleamed bright against the glorious background of an undulating turquoise nebula, creating a warm pressure of photons which so very slowly assuaged its physical nourishment. The creature spun leisurely in the rich torrent of light as it listened to the thoughts grow stronger on the solid planet that was still lightyears away.

One thought was exceptionally clear. 'You see, you have to rest now; if you were multiple another body could simply carry on. The ecstasy would continue for hours. More bodies could perform at the same time; imagine that pleasure you've just experienced doubled, quadrupled, increased tenfold. Wouldn't you like that? Wouldn't your life be so much better, so much greater . . .?' The thought dwindled away into the vastness as the solar wind cooled and dimmed.

There were only two hims asleep on the bed when Araminta woke. She checked the time in her exovision and groaned in dismay. Five past seven already. There was so much to do in the third apartment today. The bots should have spent the night stripping out the old tiles in the fifth apartment, but her u-shadow revealed they'd stopped work at three in the morning as they encountered a problem their semisentient software couldn't cope with. She had two prospective buyers for apartment four arriving before noon.

'Great Ozzie,' she complained as she heaved herself out of bed. No time for a shower. She grabbed the clothes she'd worn to dinner last night – which really weren't everyday garments. *Must bring a bag with some decent clothes for morning. Would he object to that?*

She escaped the bedroom without waking the Mr Boveys. Scuttled down the stairs, raking fingers through awful strings of tangled hair. The smell of coffee and toast was permeating out of the big kitchen. Which was sorely tempting given her body's chill. *I must ease off those booster aerosols.* Surely a single minute spent with one cup of tea wouldn't jeopardize the whole day?

She put her head round the archway to smile into the long open-plan kitchen diner. Five hims were sitting round the break-fast bar, with another three lounging in the big old settee. 'Hi—' The smiled faded from her face. A woman was perched on the sixth stool at the breakfast bar wearing a big fluffy towelling robe. One him had his arm round her, hand lovingly massaging the base of her neck. The woman glanced up from a big mug of steaming coffee, and pulled a delinquent face. 'Oh, hi there. I'm Josill. I guess I was being worn out by the half of hims you weren't with last night. He's good sex, huh. I managed four.' She grinned round proudly at her entourage of Mr Boveys.

Araminta managed to freeze her expression before she did anything petty like glare or pout or start shouting about what a useless pile of shit he was. 'Right,' she said in a croak. 'Got to go. People I'm honest with coming to see me.' She headed for the front door, as fast as she could without actually running. Even managed to get outside. Her old carry capsule was resting on the gravel pad. Fifteen metres away.

'Just hold on.'

She turned. It was the body she'd had that first dinner date with. He always used that one to talk to her with when it was something serious. Obviously working the whole age equals wisdom angle, with maybe a little trust mixed in. 'Drop dead,' she snapped. 'All of you.'

'You knew I would date other women.'

'I . . .' She spluttered with indignation. 'No! Actually, no I didn't! I thought we—' Some stubborn little part of her was desperately trying not to cry in front of him. What the point was with someone who knew her so completely eluded her – still she wasn't going to give him the satisfaction of seeing how much she cared.

'Listen to me.' He stood in front of her, taking a moment to compose himself. 'You are a lovely, fantastic person. I haven't met someone I was this attracted to in years. And I think you know that.'

'Well this is a—'

'Funny way of showing it? No. No. That's a single person's line, not mine.'

'How ridiculous,' she shouted.

'Maybe you've been trying to hide from this, I don't know.

Adjusting to multiple life does take time. It isn't easy, and you're upset.'

'I'm not upset,' she announced haughtily.

'I have a great time with you, every time no matter where we go and what we do, and that's the problem. Think on this. You are a wonderful, healthy, strapping girl with a huge sexual appetite. Every man's dream. And I'm always amazed and excited by how many mes you take on when we go to bed. But not even you can physically satisfy thirty-eight male bodies every night. We've been going out all this time and there are still some mes you haven't met, let alone had sex with yet. You get me all hot and randy, and every time you do that the majority of mes are left frustrated.'

'I . . . Oh. Really?' It was kind of obvious when he explained it like that. But he was right, it really wasn't something she wanted to think through.

'I can only take so much. Josill and the others help release the pressure you create.'

Others. Again, something she didn't want to consider. This whole multiple thing was turning out to be one giant complication. She took a breath and stared at the gravel round her feet. 'I'm sorry. You're right, I didn't consider that part of it. It's been so good for me I just assumed it was the same for you. Singles thinking, huh.'

'Yes.' He put a hand on her shoulder. It comforted her – that whole wise and sympathetic thing still. 'But I'm hoping, really hoping we can work through this.'

She gave the door a guilty glance. 'I'm not sure I can get round the idea of you having sex with her as well. Were you . . . no. I don't want to know.'

He raised an eyebrow. Waited patiently.

Araminta sighed. 'Last night, were you having sex with both of us at the same time?'

'Yes.'

A particularly malicious thought crept out of her mind. 'And she could only cope with four?'

'Fraid so.'

'Poor girl.' Her little spike of humour withered away. 'I don't know about this. I'm not sure I can cope. There would need to be so many women. That's not part of a long-term relation-ship.'

'Listen, I said you were special right at the start, and the more I get to know you the more I know that I don't want to lose you.'

'So what do you do? Get half of you neutered? I really can't . . . not thirty-eight.'

He grinned. 'That's my Araminta, considering it even now. But there's another option, isn't there?'

'What?'

He didn't answer straight away. Instead his hand touched her chin, tipping her head back until she couldn't avoid staring into his eyes. Eventually she gave a defeated little nod. 'I get myself some extra bodies,' she said in a quiet voice.

'I'm not going to browbeat. I couldn't do that to you, it would be wrong. The decision has to be you alone. I just want you to think about it. You've seen all the practical benefits first-hand. And I reminded you about the sexual advantages again last night.'

She fixed him with a firm stare. 'Tell me: if I do this, would you stop dating the other women? Would it be just you and me?'

'Yes, emphatically, just you. Yous in my life, yous in my bed. Cross my hearts. I want this, Araminta, I want this so much. I wish you had gaiamotes so I could show you just how serious I am. We'll just have to settle for registering it at City Hall instead.'

'Ozzie! A marriage proposal and a lifestyle change in one. And it's not even half past seven yet.'

'Sorry you had to run into it like this.'

'Not your fault. You're right, I should have thought about this. So I'll be a big girl and think about it properly now. Don't expect an answer right away. This is a hell of a lot more than I'm used to dealing with in a day.'

His arms went round her, hugging tight as if he was the one

seeking reassurance. 'It's momentous. I remember. So take all the time you need.'

*

He rode the gigantic horse for hour after hour, his young legs barely stretching over the saddle. In the distance were real mountains, their snow-capped peaks stabbing high into the glorious sapphire sky. He was leaving them behind, riding away from the forests that covered the foothills. It was wild veldt beneath the hooves now, lush tropical vegetation split by streams and small rivers. Trees from a dozen planets grew across the low slopes, their contrasting evolutions providing a marvellous clash of colour and shape. Hot air gusted against him, heavy with alien pollen.

His friends rode beside him, the six of them shouting encouragement to each other as they wove around the knolls and ridges. None of them yet adult, but now finally old enough to be trusted out on their own. It was days like this which made sense of his life, full of freedom and joy.

Then the cry went up. 'The king eagles, the king eagles are here.'

He scoured the brilliant sky, seeing the black dots above the rumpled horizon. Then he too was yelling in welcome, his heart pounding with excitement. The horse ran faster as the noble lords of this world's sky grew larger and larger.

Red lights flashed across the heavens. The king eagles elongated, black lines curving and twisting to form a grey rectangular shape. His horse had vanished, leaving him lying flat on his back. The red lights turned violet-blue and began to retreat as the top of the medical chamber opened. A face slid into view, peering down. He blinked it into focus. Very pretty and heavily freckled, with a mass of dark red hair tied back.

'You okay?' Corrie-Lyn asked.

'Urrgh,' Aaron told her.

'Here drink this.' A plastic straw was eased into his mouth. He sucked some welcoming cool liquid down his sore throat.

387

'What?' he mumbled.

'What?'

'What happened?'

'You've been in the ship's medical chamber for a couple of days.'

He winced as he tried to move his arms. His whole left side was stiff, as if the skin had shrunk. 'A moment,' he told her. His u-shadow flipped medical records into his exovision. He skipped the details, concentrating on the major repairs. The damage had been more extensive that he expected. The projectile entry wounds combined with firewire mutilation and toxin contamination meant the medical chamber had to cut and extract a lot of ruined tissue and bone from his chest. Foreign meat had been inserted, neutral-function cells which could have their pre-active DNA switched to mould the cell into whatever organ, bone, or muscle function they were replacing. He spotted a supplementary file, and opened it. The foreign meat stored in the chamber actually wasn't so foreign, the DNA was his; it also had full-complement biononic organelles.

The repairs had been woven into his body by the chamber and his existing biononics. They were still integrating which was why he felt so awful. Estimated time for the biononics to complete the binding and the cells to acclimatize to their new function was a further seventy-two hours.

'Could have been better, could have been worse,' he decided.

'I was worried,' she said. 'Your wound was huge. The blood . . .' Her face paled, even the freckles faded.

Aaron slowly shifted his arms back along the chamber padding, propping himself up. At which point he realized he didn't have any clothes on. 'Thank you.'

She gave him a blank look.

'I should be thanking you, shouldn't I? What happened? The last thing I remember was you hitting Ruth Stol.'

'That little princess bitch.'

'So? What came next?' Aaron swung his feet over the lip of the capsule; his inner ears seemed to take a lot longer to register the movement. Bulkheads spun round him, then twisted back. The starship's cabin was in its lounge mode, with long couches extending out from the bulkhead walls. He hobbled over to the closest one as the medical chamber withdrew into the floor. Sitting down he tentatively poked his chest with a forefinger. Half of his torso was a nasty salmon pink, covered with some glistening protective membrane.

'I did what you suggested,' Corrie-Lyn said. 'The capsule smashed its way into the reception hall. I just got inside when there was this almighty explosion over the forest. It knocked the capsule around quite a bit, but I was caught by the internal safety field. We zipped over to the administration block. You were . . . a mess, but I managed to pull you inside. Then we rendezvoused with the *Artful Dodger* outside the clinic, the way you set it up. The starship put its force field round the capsule while we transferred in. Good job. The police were going apeshit with me. They were shooting every weapon they had at us; there were craters all over the place when we took off. I told the smartcore to get us out of the system, but it followed your preloaded flightplan. We're just sitting in some kind of hyperspace hole a lightyear out from Anagaska. I can't make a unisphere connection. The smartcore won't obey me.'

'I loaded a few options in,' he said. His u-shadow gave the smartcore an instruction, and a storage locker opened. 'Do you think you could get me that robe, please?'

She frowned disapprovingly, but pulled the robe out. 'I was really worried, I thought I was going to be stuck here for ever if you died. It was horrible. The medical chamber would rejuvenate me every fifty years, and I'd just sit in the lounge plugged into the sensory drama library being drip fed by the culinary unit. That's not how I want to spent eternity, thank you.'

He grinned at her drama queen outrage as he slipped the robe on. 'If the chamber could rejuvenate you, it could certainly re-life me.'

'Oh.'

'In any case, if I die, the smartcore allows you full control.'

'Right.'

'But!' He caught hold of her hand. She jerked round, suddenly apprehensive. 'None of this would have happened if you'd been ready to pick me up when I told you.'

'I haven't seen any decent clothes in weeks,' she protested. 'I just lost track of time, that's all. I didn't *mean* to be late. Besides, I thought you got wounded before the scheduled rendezvous.'

He closed his eyes in despair. 'Corrie-Lyn, if you're on a combat mission, you don't call a fucking time-out to go shopping. Understand?'

'You never said combat. A quick raid sneaking into their vault, you said.'

'For future reference, a covert mission in which all sides are armed is a combat situation.'

She pulled a face. '*Nothing they have will be a match for my bionomics.*'

'I never said that.'

'Yes, you did.'

'I . . .' He let out a breath and made an effort to stay calm. *Yoga. She always made us do yoga. It was fucking stupid.*

Corrie-Lyn was frowning at him. 'You okay? You need to get back in the chamber?'

'I'm fine. Look, thank you for picking me up. I know this kind of thing is not what your life is about.'

'You're welcome,' she said gruffly.

'Please tell me we still have the memorycell.'

Corrie-Lyn produced a minx smile and held up the little plastic kube. 'We still have the memorycell.'

'Thank Ozzie for that.' His u-shadow told the smartcore to show him the ship's log; he wanted to check how much effort had been made to try and track them. Since they'd left Anagaska in a hurry, several starships had run sophisticated hysradar scans out to several lightyears – but nobody could spot an ultradrive ship in transdimensional suspension. The log also recorded that

Corrie-Lyn had managed to circumvent the lock-out he'd placed on the culinary unit to prevent it making alcoholic drinks. Now really wasn't the time to make an issue of it.

'Okay,' he told her. 'I don't think anyone's spotted us. Though there were some mighty interesting comings and goings just after our raid. Several ships with unusual quantum signatures popped out of hyperspace above Anagaska; the smartcore thinks they might be ultradrives in disguise.'

'Who would they be?'

'Don't know. And don't intend to hang around to ask. Let's get going.'

'Finally.'

He held his hand out, carefully maintaining a neutral expression.

Corrie-Lyn gave the kube a sentimental look, and took a while to drop it into his palm. 'I'm not sure I like the idea of you reading Inigo's mind.'

'I'm not going to. Memory assimilation isn't like accessing a sensory drama off the unisphere, nor accepting experiences through the gaiafield. A genuine memory takes a long time to absorb. You can compress it down from real time, but still this kube contains nearly forty years of his life. That would take months to shunt into a human brain; it's one of the governing factors in creating re-life clones. If we're going to find him before the Pilgrimage, we don't have that much time to spare.'

'So what are you going to do?'

'Take it to someone who can absorb it a lot quicker than I can, and ask nicely.'

'You just said human brains can't absorb stored memories that quickly.'

'So I did. Which is why we're setting course for the *High Angel*.'

Corrie-Lyn looked shocked. 'The Raiel starship?'

'Yes.'

'Why would the Raiel help you?'

He smiled at the kube. 'Let's just say that we now have an excellent bargaining point.'

Corrie-Lyn didn't have the kind of patience for extensive research. Aaron had to fill in the decades and centuries she skipped through when she started to access the files her u-shadow trawled up on the Raiel. Humans discovered the *High Angel* back in 2163, he explained, when a wormhole was opened in its star system to search for any H-congruous planets. CST's exploratory division quickly confirmed there were no worlds that humans could live on, but the astronomers did notice a microwave signal coming from the orbit of the gas-giant Icalanise.

'What's that got to do with angels?' she asked. 'Were they all religious?'

'Not astronomers, no.'

When they focused their sensors on the microwave source they saw a moonlet sixty-three kilometres long with what looked like wings of hazy pearl light. The wings of an angel.

'Sounds like they were religious to me, if that's the first thing they think of.'

Aaron groaned. With more sensors urgently brought on line, the true nature of the artefact was revealed. A core of rock sprouting twelve stems which supported vast domes, five of which had transparent cupolas. Cities and parkland were visible inside.

It was a starship; a living creature, or a machine which had evolved into sentience. Origin unknown, and it wasn't telling. Several species lived in the domes. Only the Raiel consented to talk to humanity, and they didn't say very much.

Several of the biggest astroengineering companies negotiated a lease on three of the domes, and the *High Angel* became a dormitory town for an archipelago of microgravity factory stations producing some of the Commonwealth's most advanced, and profitable, technology. The workforce and their families soon grew large enough to declare autonomy (with *High Angel*'s approval) qualifying for a seat in the Senate.

With the outbreak of the Starflyer War, *High Angel* became

the Commonwealth's premier Navy base while the astroengineering companies turned their industrial stations over to warship production. More domes were grown, or extruded, or magically manifested into existence to accommodate the Navy personnel. Still nobody understood the *High Angel*'s technology.

'Do we know more about it now?' she asked.

'Not really. ANA might; the Central Worlds can duplicate some functions with biononics; but the External Worlds haven't managed to produce anything like it.'

Humans, he told her, had to wait for two hundred years after the War before the massive alien starship's history became a little clearer. Wilson Kime's epic voyage in the *Endeavour* to circumnavigate the galaxy revealed the existence of the Void to the Commonwealth, complete with Centurion Station and the Raiel defence systems maintaining the Wall stars. Other Navy exploration ships discovered more *High Angel* class ships; the one species common to each of them was the Raiel.

Confronted with that evidence, the Raiel finally explained that they created the *High Angel*-class of ships over a million years ago while their species was at its apex. It was a golden age, when the Raiel civilization spread across thousands of planets; they mixed with hundreds of other sentients, guided and observed as dozens of species transcended to a post-physical state. They even knew the Silfen before their Motherholme dreamed its paths into existence.

Then the Void underwent one of its periodic expansion phases. Nothing the Raiel could do stopped the barrier from engulfing entire star clusters. Gravity shifted around the galactic core as stars were torn down into the event horizon. The effect on civilizations just outside the Wall stars was catastrophic. Stars shifted position as the core gravity field fluctuated; their planets changed orbits. Thousands of unique biospheres were lost before evolution had any real chance to flourish. Whole societies had to be evacuated before stormfronts of ultra-hard radiation that measured thousands of lightyears across came streaming out into the base of the galaxy's spiral arms.

After it was all over, after rescue and salvage operations that went on for millennia, the Raiel declared that the Void could no longer be tolerated. The Firstlife who had created it while the galaxy was still in its infancy clearly didn't recognize the horrendous consequences it would have on those who lived after their era. The Raiel created an armada of ships that could function in any quantum state which theoretically might exist within the Void. And they invaded. A hundred thousand ships surrounded the terrible barrier and flew inside, ready for anything.

None returned.

The Void remained unbroken.

What was left of the once colossal Raiel civilization launched a rearguard action. A defence system to reinforce the Wall stars was built in the small hope it might contain the next macroexpansion. More ships were created to act as arks for emergent species, carrying them away from the doomed galaxy across the greater gulf outside where they could re-establish themselves on new worlds in peaceful star clusters. It was the last act of beneficence from a race that had failed its ultimate challenge. If they couldn't save the galaxy, the Raiel swore they would endure to the bitter end, shepherding entities less capable than themselves to safety.

'That's not a version of history I can believe in,' Corrie-Lyn said softly as the file images shrank to the centre of the cabin and vanished. 'It's very hard for me to accept the Void as something hostile when I know the beauty which lies within.' She took a sip of her hot chocolate and brandy, curling up tighter on the couch.

'That version?' Aaron queried from the other side of the cabin.

'Well it's not as if we can ever verify it, is it?'

'Unless I've got a false memory, you've got nearly six hundred years of human observations from Centurion Station to confirm the very unnatural way in which the barrier consumes star systems. And who was it now that took some of them? Oh yes, that's right: Inigo himself.'

'Yes, but this whole crusading armada claim? Come on. A hundred thousand ships with weapons that can crunch up entire stars. Where are they? None of Inigo's Dreams showed the smallest relic.'

'Dead. Vaporized into component atoms and consumed like every other particle of matter that passes through the barrier.' He paused, slightly troubled. 'Except for the human ship which got through and landed on Querencia.'

'Pretty crappy tactics for a species of self-proclaimed masterminds. Didn't they think of sending a scout or two in first?'

'Maybe they did. You can ask when we get to the *High Angel*.'

She gave him a pitying look. 'If they even let us dock.'

'Oh ye of little faith.'

The *Artful Dodger* fell back into spacetime ten thousand kilometres from the *High Angel*. Icalanise was waxing behind the alien starship, a horned crescent of warring topaz and platinum stormbands. Four small black circles were strung out along the equator, the tip of the umbra cones projected by a conjunction cluster of its thirty-eight moons.

Several sensor sweeps flashed across the starship. *High Angel* still hosted a large Commonwealth Navy presence. The base Admiral took security seriously. A fresh identity complete with official certification was already loaded into the smartcore for examination. Aaron's u-shadow requested docking permission with the New Glasgow dome for the *Alini*. They received almost immediate approach authority.

The archipelago of industrial stations glided lazily along a thousand-kilometre orbit, forming a dense loop of silver specks round the *High Angel*. Service shuttles zipped between them and the human-inhabited domes, collecting advanced technology and materials for forward shipment to the External Worlds where such systems were still prized. 'How about that,' Aaron muttered appreciatively as he accessed the ship's sensor imagery. 'An angel with a halo.'

'You can take religious analogies too far,' Corrie-Lyn chided.

There were seventeen domes rising out of the core's rocky surface now. The six occupied by humans all had crystal cupolas, allowing them to see the cities and parkland inside. Four of the remainder were also transparent to a degree; the spectra of alien suns shone out of them, following their own diurnal cycles. Strange city silhouettes could be seen parked on the landscapes within. At night they would shine with enticing colourful light points. One of those belonged to the Raiel. The remaining domes were closed to external observation, and neither *High Angel* or the Raiel would discuss their residents.

Following Aaron's instruction, the starship's smartcore aimed a communication maser at the Raiel dome. 'I would like permission to dock at the Raiel dome, please,' Aaron said. 'There is a resident I wish to speak to.'

'That is an unusual request for a private individual,' the *High Angel* replied with the voice of a human male. 'I can speak on behalf of the Raiel.'

'Not good enough. You're aware of the nature of this ship?'

'I do recognize it. Very few of ANA's ultradrive vessels have ever come into my proximity; the technology is extremely sophisticated. You must be one of its representatives.'

'Something like that, and I need to speak with a specific Raiel.'

'Very well. I am sending you a new flight path, please follow it.'

'Thank you. The Raiel I'd like to meet is Qatux.'

'Of course.'

The *Artful Dodger* changed course slightly, curving round the massive dark rock of the *High Angel*'s core towards the stem of the Raiel dome. Large dark ovals were positioned at the base, just before the point where the pewter-coloured shaft fused with the rock crust. One of the ovals dematerialized, revealing a featureless white chamber beyond. The *Artful Dodger* nosed inside, and the outer wall rematerialized behind it.

'Please stand by for teleport,' the *High Angel* said.

Corrie-Lyn looked very startled.

'Once again,' Aaron said. 'And yet still without any hope of you paying the slightest attention: let me do the talking.'

Her mouth opened to answer.

The cabin vanished, immediately replaced by a broad circular space with a floor that glowed a pale emerald. If there was a ceiling it was invisible somewhere in the gloom far above. An adult Raiel was standing right in front of them. Corrie-Lyn gasped and almost stumbled. Aaron hurriedly reached out and caught her arm. He didn't have any memory of being on Earth and using the planetary T-sphere, but the abrupt translation was about what he'd expected.

'Dear Ozzie,' Corrie-Lyn grunted.

'I hope you are not too shocked,' the Raiel said in its mellow whisper.

Aaron bowed formally. The Raiel was as big as all the adults of its species, larger than a terrestrial elephant, with a grey-brown skin that bristled with thick hairs. Not that Aaron was an expert, but this one looked like an exceptionally healthy specimen. From the front its bulbous head was surrounded by a collar of tentacle limbs; with a thick pair at the bottom, four metres long and tipped with segmented paddles which were intended for heavy work. The remaining limbs were progressively smaller up to a clump of slender manipulators resembling particularly sinuous serpents. Each side of its head had a cluster of five small hemispherical eyes that swivelled in unison. Below them on the underside of the head, the skin creased up into a number of loose folds to form the mouth zone. When it spoke, Aaron could just glimpse deep wet crevices and even a row of sharp brown fangs.

'No, that's fine,' Corrie-Lyn stammered. She remembered her manners and dipped her head awkwardly.

'I have not met humans in the flesh for some time,' said Qatux in its sad-sounding whisper. 'I was curious. I didn't realize my name was still known to you.'

'I'm afraid I only know your name, nothing more,' said Aaron. 'But I thank you for agreeing to see us.'

'My part in your history was brief. I took part in a human expedition during the Starflyer War. I had friends. Human friends, which is unusual for a Raiel, then as now. Tell me, do you know of Paula Myo?'

Aaron was surprised when his heart did a little jump at the name. *Must be the medical treatment.* 'I've heard of her.'

'I liked Paula Myo,' Qatux said.

'She is an ANA:Governance representative these days.'

'And you are not?'

'Not at her level.' Aaron prayed Corrie-Lyn wouldn't start mouthing off.

'Why are you here?' Qatux asked.

'I have a request.' He held up the kube. 'This is the memorycell of a human. I would like you to receive the memories. There are questions about his personality I need answering.'

Qatux did not respond. Its eyes swivelled from Aaron to Corrie-Lyn, then back again.

'Can you do that?' Aaron asked. He was aware that something was wrong, but didn't know what. His mind kept telling him that Qatux was the Raiel who was most likely to help in this fashion. So far on this mission all that intuitive knowledge loaded into his subconscious had been correct.

'I used to do that,' Qatux whispered. 'At one time I was captivated by human emotional states. I married a human.'

'Married?' Corrie-Lyn blurted.

'A most nice lady by the name of Tiger Pansy. I had never known someone so emotionally reactive. We spent many happy years together on the planet you named Far Away. I shared her every thought, every feeling.'

'What happened?' Aaron asked, knowing this wasn't going to be good.

'She died.'

'I'm sorry.'

'She died most horribly. A woman called the Cat prolonged her death for many days. Deliberately. I shared that time with my wife. I experienced human death.'

'Shit,' Aaron mumbled.

'I have not known human thought or emotion since. At the end, my wife cured me of this strange weakness. It was her last

398

gift, however unwillingly given. I am Raiel again. I now hold high rank among my own kind.'

'We shouldn't have asked you to do this,' Corrie-Lyn said humbly. 'We didn't know. I'm so sorry.'

Aaron wanted to use a stunshot on her. 'It's Inigo,' he said, holding the kube up again. 'The human who dreams the lives of humans inside the Void.'

Once again Qatux was perfectly still. This time its eyes remained focused on Aaron alone.

'Aaron!' Corrie-Lyn hissed through clenched teeth.

He could feel the anger powering out of her through the gaiafield, and completely ignored it. 'I'm looking for him,' he told the huge silent alien, staring straight into its multiple eyes. 'He needs to be found before his Living Dream believers spark off another devourment phase with their Pilgrimage. Will you help?'

'Inigo?' Qatux asked, the whisper had softened to near inaudibility.

'Yes. The kube holds his personality right up until he left for his Centurion Station mission. His formative years. Everyone knows his life since he founded Living Dream, even the Raiel. Or perhaps especially the Raiel. If you combine that knowledge with his formative years, I thought you might be able to under-stand his motivations, that you could work out where he has gone for me.'

'The Raiel have wanted to know the inside of the Void for so long. It is all we exist for now. We are its nemesis as much as it is ours. For over a million years we were content with the role fate had given us. And then a human comes along, and simply dreams what is in there. None of us are. The strongest of our race fell into that evil place, and no trace remains. Nothing.'

'It's not evil,' Corrie-Lyn said sullenly.

'I would like to believe that. I cannot. We have known the Void from a time before your species achieved sentience. It is the destroyer of life, of hope. Nothing escapes it.'

'Millions of humans live inside the Void. They live lives full of hope and love and laughter, they live lives better than any of us out here.'

'To do so, to achieve their greater life you envy so much, they are killing you. They are killing this galaxy. And now you wish to join them, to increase the damage to a level you cannot imagine.'

'Will you stop the Pilgrimage?' Aaron asked.

'Not I. Not this arkship. That is not the purpose of this Raiel; we are custodians alone. However, there are other Raiel who serve a different purpose. They are the defenders of this galaxy. I do not know what they will do to your Pilgrimage.'

Aaron glanced at Corrie-Lyn. Her mouth was set into a purposeful line.

'Can you help us with Inigo's memories? If I can find him, talk to him, there may be a chance he'll stop the Pilgrimage.'

Qatux moved towards him. Eight stumpy legs on either side of its underbelly tilting forward to move it in a smooth undulation. Aaron held his ground, though he was aware of Corrie-Lyn taking a small shuffle backwards; her emotions seeping into the gaiafield turning from pride to concern.

'I will do what I can,' Qatux said. It extended a medium-sized tentacle.

Aaron exhaled in relief, and handed the memorycell over. The tentacle tip coiled round it and withdrew, curling backwards. Just behind the collar of tentacles, hanging off the equivalent of a Raiel neck, innumerable small protuberances of flesh dangled down, each one crowned by a small heavy bulb that was technological in origin. The kube sank through the dark surface of a bulb like a pebble falling into water.

A long shudder ran along Qatux's bulk, and the giant alien let out a sigh that seemed close to pain. 'I will tell you when I have finished,' Qatux said.

Aaron and Corrie-Lyn were unceremoniously teleported back into the *Artful Dodger*.

*

The Mars Twins were an unusual turgid red as their upper-atmosphere hurricanes swirled and battled along thousand kilometre fronts, obliterating the dark shadows which occasionally hinted at surface features. Their dour ambiance matched Cleric Conservator Ethan's mood as he strode through the Liliala Hall. Above him the storms rampaging across the visionary ceiling flashed purple lightning and pummelled away at each other like waves assaulting a beach. They swirled together, veiling the two small planets. The silent, vivid battle made for an impressive entrance as he swept through the arching door into the Mayor's suite.

Rincenso and Falven, two of his staunchest supporters on the Council, were waiting for him in the first anteroom; cautious expressions made more sinister by the amber lighting. All they allowed of themselves into the gaiafield was a polite radiance of expectation. Not even Ethan's easily sensed mood could make them waver.

He beckoned them to follow as he pushed through into the oval sanctum. Strong sunlight shone in through the high Rayonnant-style windows, illuminating the grand wooden desk identical to the one which the Waterwalker had sat behind when he was Mayor of Makkathran. Five simple chairs were arranged before it. Councillor Phelim stood at the side of one, waiting for Ethan to sit himself behind his desk. He wore the simple everyday blue and green robe of a Councillor. It was meant to testify to an open and approachable person who would take time to solve someone's problem. On Phelim it was off-putting, emphasizing his height and severe facial features.

'So the Skylord would seem to be on its way to Querencia,' Ethan said as he sat down.

Falven cleared his throat. 'It is heading for some kind of planet. We have to assume it is Querencia. The prospect of another planet housing humans in the Void would open many complications for us.'

'Not so,' Rincenso said. 'I don't care how many other H-congruous planets there are, nor who lives on them. We are concerned only with Querencia and the Waterwalker. It is his example we wish to follow.'

'Too many unknowns to pronounce on,' Falven said.

'Not that many, surely,' Ethan said. 'We cannot doubt the Second Dreamer is dreaming a Skylord. This creature is aware of the souls and minds of living sentient entities. It and its flock are flying towards a solid planet to collect those souls and carry them to Odin's Sea. This flight fulfils every teaching of the Lady.'

'I wonder what life in Makkathran is like now,' Rincenso mused. 'So much time has passed.'

'You'll find out soon enough,' Ethan said. 'The hulls of our Pilgrimage ships are being fabricated. We will be ready to launch soon. Phelim?'

'We should have the hulls and internal systems finished by September,' Phelim said. 'The cost is colossal, but the Free Market Zone has a considerable manufacturing capacity. Component construction is heavily cybernated: once the templates are loaded in, production is a simple process. And of course, no matter how much criticism we face, External World companies are always eager for our money.'

'September,' Rincenso said. 'Dear Ozzie, so close.'

Ethan did not look at Phelim. No one else had been told of the ultradrive engines Marius had promised to deliver. 'The physical aspect goes well,' he said. 'That just leaves us with our enigmatic Second Dreamer to deal with. We still don't know why he hasn't revealed himself, but it is significant that his dreams have become so much more substantial as the ships are built.'

'Why does he not come forward?' Falven said. The gaiafield revealed the flash of anger in his mind. 'Curse him, are we never to find him?'

'He is on Viotia,' Phelim said.

'Are you sure?'

'Yes. The gaiafield confluence nests on Viotia were the first to receive his last dream. They disseminated it across the Greater Commonwealth gaiafield.'

'Do you know where on Viotia he is?'

'Not yet. But now we have confirmed the planet, our efforts will be concentrated on determining the exact geographical location. Of course, people move about. And if he is actively seeking anonymity he will simply relocate after every dream.'

'Which must be prevented,' Ethan said simply.

'How?' Rincenso asked.

'This is why I have asked you two here today, my dearest friends and allies on the Council. The Second Dreamer is crucial to Pilgrimage. He is the one who must ask the Skylords for guidance through the barrier, and onward to Querencia. In the absence of Inigo, he is the one who will light our way.'

'So what do you want us to do?' Falven asked.

'There are several routes available to us,' Ethan said quietly. 'I believe the one we will end up travelling along is to bring Viotia into the Free Market Zone.'

The two Councillors gave each other a puzzled look.

'It *is* part of our Free Market Zone,' Falven said.

'By treaty, yes,' Ethan said. 'It is not one of our core planets. Yet. We must be prepared to complete the admission process, culminating with Ellezelin opening a wormhole between our two worlds. Following that, Viotia's government should adopt a more favourable stance towards Living Dream. Ultimately, I would like to welcome them into our hierocracy.'

Falven sat back, looking startled.

Rincenso merely smiled in appreciation. 'There are a great many of our followers there already. Enough to tilt the demographic?'

'Possibly,' Phelim said.

'In which case I would be happy to raise the proposal in the Council.'

'I, too,' Falven said slowly.

'There is a degree of hostility and resentment currently being shown to our followers on Viotia,' Ethan said. 'If a wormhole were to be opened, binding their economy to ours, that resentment will manifest itself in street violence. We would need to guarantee the security of all Living Dream adherents.'

'Do we have that ability?' Falven asked cautiously.

'There are enough national security forces spread across the core planets of the Free Market Zone to enforce the rule of law on Viotia,' Phelim said. 'We have been recruiting additional personnel since Ethan's ascension to Conservator.'

'Enough for this?'

'Yes.'

'Oh. I see.'

'I regret any inconvenience this may cause to Viotia's citizens,' Ethan said. 'But we cannot afford to lose the Second Dreamer.'

'If we just knew why he's refusing to reveal himself...' Rincenso said acrimoniously.

'Because he doesn't yet know,' Ethan said with a weary sadness.

'How can he *not know*?'

'It took several weeks for Inigo to realize what was happening. At first he believed his dreams to be some kind of overspill from a full-sense drama that was leaking into the Centurion Station gaiafield. I believe that confusion is repeating again. To begin with all we had were small fragments, glimpses of the Skylord which we edited together. Now the contact has been established, the length and strength of the dreams are increasing. As they did with Inigo. Soon they will reach a crescendo and the Second Dreamer will realize what he has been chosen to do.'

Falven gave the others in the oval sanctum an uncomfortable look. 'Then why do we need to incorporate Viotia?'

'What if the Second Dreamer isn't an adherent of Living Dream?' Ethan asked mildly.

'But—'

'There's a much worse scenario than that,' Phelim said. 'If one of our opponents were to reach him first and use him to sabotage the Pilgrimage.'

'They'll be looking,' Rincenso said.

'Of course they'll be looking,' Ethan said. 'But we have a huge advantage with our command of the gaiafield. Not even ANA's despicable Factions can intrude upon that. We must reach him first.'

'And if he refuses to help?' Falven enquired.

'Change his mind,' Phelim told them. 'In a very literal sense.'

'I suppose that's necessary,' Rincenso said uneasily.

'I would hope not,' Ethan said. 'But we must be prepared for all eventualities.'

'Yes. I understand.'

'What I would like to do first is make a simple appeal to both the Second Dreamer and the Skylord,' Ethan said.

Falven's thoughts rippled with surprise, which he made no effort to hide. 'A unisphere declaration?'

'No. A direct intervention into the next dream.'

'How?'

'The Second Dreamer is issuing his dream into the confluence nests in real time,' Phelim said. 'Right at the end of the last dream, as it fades away, there is an anomaly, a tiny one. It is extremely hard to spot, we believe it has escaped attention among the majority of our followers. But our Dream Masters have been reviewing those last moments. There is a human emotion intruding into the Skylord's stream of consciousness. A weak sense of pleasure, but one with considerable sexual connotations. In all probability we are witnessing post-coital satisfaction.'

'The Second Dreamer receives the Skylord's dream when he's having sex?' Rincenso asked incredulously.

'The human brain is most receptive when relaxed,' Ethan said. 'The period immediately after sex certainly generates that state.'

'Did this happen to Inigo?' Falven was almost indignant.

Ethan's lips twitched in amusement. 'Not that I'm aware of. But Inigo never issued his dreams in real time, so I don't suppose we'll ever know. But this anomaly is the strongest indicator we have that this is real-time dreaming. In which case we should be able to intervene, to converse with both the Second Dreamer and the Skylord. If we can successfully perform the latter intervention we may be able to establish a direct connection without the

Second Dreamer. In which case our problems will be solved. Viotia becomes an irrelevance, as does our elusive Second Dreamer. And we will be one step closer to the Void.'

'That would be . . . wonderful,' Falven said.

'Our Dream Masters are now monitoring Viotia's confluence nests for the time the Second Dreamer starts to dream. When it happens we will make the attempt.'

'And if that fails?'

'Then you will bring your proposal to Council.'

*

Fourteen hundred years was a long time alive by anyone's standards. However, there were Commonwealth citizens who had remained in their bodies for longer; Paula had even met a few of them. She didn't enjoy their company. Mostly they were Dynasty members who couldn't let go of the old times when their family empires used to run the Commonwealth. After biononics and ANA and Higher culture changed the Central Worlds for ever, they'd grabbed what they could of their ancient wealth and re-established themselves on External Worlds where they set about recreating their personal golden age.

They had the money and influence to be bold and build new experimental societies, something different, something exciting; but for all their extraordinarily long life, they'd never experienced another way to live. And the longer they managed to maintain their own little empire around them the more resistant to change they became. Nothing new was attempted, instead they mined history for stability. On one planet in particular their social engineering reached its nadir. Iaioud, where a ruling Halgarth collective had founded and maintained a society that was even less susceptible to change than Huxley's Haven by the simple expedient of prohibiting conception. At the end of a fifty-year life every citizen was rejuvenated and memory wiped – except the state knew who they were and what job they did best. On emerging fresh from their clinic treatment they would then be appointed to the same profession again, and spend the next fifty years working as they had done for the last fifty – hundred, three hundred years. It was the ultimate feudalism.

Three hundred years ago, Paula had led an undercover team of agents there, infiltrating the clinics which performed the rejuvenation treatment and slowly corrupting them. Over the next few years memory wipes became incomplete, allowing people to remember what had gone before. Thousands of women discovered that their revitalized bodies had a functional uterus again. Underground networks were established; first to help the criminal outcasts who had given birth to children, then assuming a greater role in offering political resistance to the Halgarth régime.

Forty years after Paula and her team finished their mission to sow dissent on Iaioud, a revolution overturned the Halgarth collective using minimal force. It took a further hundred and fifty years for the twisted world to regain its equilibrium and claw its way back up the socioeconomic index to something approaching the average for an External World.

At the time, Paula had worried she still wasn't ready for that kind of mission. Change was a long time coming within herself. It was one thing to realize intellectually that she had to adapt mentally to keep up with the ever-shifting cultures of the Greater Commonwealth. But unlike everyone else, she had to make a conscious decision to alter herself physically in order for that evolution to manifest. Her carefully designed DNA hardwired her neurones into specific personality traits. In order to survive any kind of phrenic progression she had to first destroy what was. An action which came perilously close to individuality suicide. And in her, as in every human, vanity wasn't something bound to DNA; she considered her existing personality to be more than adequate – in short, she liked being herself.

But in slow increments, every time she needed to undergo rejuvenation, she modified a little bit more of her psychoneural profiling. At the end of the three-century process, she was still obsessive about a great many things, but now it was through choice rather than a physically ordained compulsion. One time long ago, when she'd tried to mentally overcome her need to apprehend a criminal in order to achieve a greater goal, the effort had put her body into a severe type of shock. By removing the Foundation's physiological constraints her mind could now flourish in ways her long-departed designers never envisaged. She'd been born with the intention of tracking down individual criminals, the kind that might plague the society of Huxley's Haven; but now she had the freedom to take an overview. Yet none of the liberations she selected for herself ever touched the core of her identity, she always retained her intuitive understanding of what was right and wrong. Her soul was untainted.

Iaioud tested her new, versatile self to the extreme. She accepted that the way in which the Halgarth collective had set up the constitution was intrinsically wrong, oppressing an entire population. In fact she would have probably acknowledged that before. But the whole nature of Iaioud's rigid society was uncomfortably close to that of Huxley's Haven. After a while she decided that the difference was simple enough. On Iaioud, people were being kept in line by a brutally authoritarian regime misusing Commonwealth medical technology. While on Huxley's Haven, strictures and conformity came from within. Possibly there had been a crime, right back at the founding, when the Human Structure Foundation started birthing an entire population with DNA modified to their grand scheme. The old liberal groups might have been right – a thought which would have finally pleased the radicals who had stolen her as a baby. But however great the sin committed at its genesis, the constraints placed on the population of Huxley's Haven were internal. Its people now couldn't be changed without destroying what they were. By far the bigger crime.

So she convinced herself, anyway. These days she wrote it off as an argument between philosophies. Interesting, and completely disconnected from real life. The Commonwealth had enough real problems to keep her fully occupied. Though even she had to admit, the whole Pilgrimage issue was throwing up some unique complications.

408

For once she couldn't decide if Living Dream had the right to set off on Pilgrimage, and be damned to possible consequences. The dilemma came from the total lack of empirical evidence that the Void would consume the rest of the galaxy. She had to admit that a lot of pro-Pilgrimage Factions and commentators were right to be sceptical. The assumption that Living Dream were courting annihilation was all based on information which came from the Raiel. The immense timescale since the last catastrophic macro-expansion phase would distort any information no matter how well stored; throw in aliens with their own agenda and she simply couldn't accept the claim at face value.

ANA:Governance was also keen to acquire more information on the situation, which gave Paula a useful outlet for her energies, and thankfully little time to brood over the politics involved. Her assignment, as always, was to stop the Factions from engineering the physical citizens of the Commonwealth into actions they wouldn't otherwise have performed.

She'd left St Mary's Clinic and returned to her ship, the *Alexis Denken*, a sleek ultradrive vessel which ANA:Governance had supplied and armed to a degree which would alarm any Navy captain. She left the planet, then hung in transdimensional suspension twenty AUs out from the star. It was a position which allowed her to monitor the ftl traffic within the Anagaska system with astonishing accuracy. Unfortunately, the one thing her ship's sensors couldn't do was locate a cold trail. There was no trace of Aaron's ship. Given the time between the raid on the clinic and her arrival, she suspected he had an ultradrive ship. Marius certainly had one. Her u-shadow monitored him arriving back at the city starport and getting into a private yacht. *Alexis Denken*'s sensors tracked it slipping into hyperspace. For those in the know, the signature was indicative of an ultradrive.

An hour later, the Delivery Man took off in his own ship which had an equally suspicious drive signature. He flew away in almost exactly the opposite direction to Marius. Ten minutes later another starship dropped out of transdimensional suspension where it had been waiting in the system's cometary halo, and began to fly along the same course as the Delivery Man.

'Good luck,' Paula sent to Justine.

'Thanks.'

Paula opened an ultra-secure link to ANA:Governance. 'It appears your ultradrive technology is completely compromised,' she reported.

'To be expected,' ANA:Governance replied. 'It does not require my full capacity to derive the theory behind it. Most Factions would have the intellectual resources. Once the equations are available, any Higher replicator above level-five could produce the appropriate hardware.'

'I still think you should exert a little more authority. After all, the Factions are all part of you.'

'Factions are how I remain integral. I am plural.'

'The way you say it makes it sound like you have the electronic version of bi-polar disorder.'

'More like multi-billion-polar. But that is what I am. All individuals who join me do so by imprinting their personality routines upon me. I am the collective consciousness of all ANA inhabitants, that is the very basis of my authority. Once that essence is bequeathed they are free to become what they want. I do not take their memories, too, that would be an annexation of individuality.'

'You have to pass through the eye of the needle to live in the playground of the gods.'

'One of Inigo's better quotes,' ANA:Governance said with a cadence of amusement. 'Shame about the rest of that sermon.'

'You don't help make my job any easier.'

'Any and all of my resources are available to you.'

'But there's only one of me, and I feel like I'm battling the Hydra out here.'

'This lack of self-confidence is unlike you. What is the matter?'

'The Pilgrimage, of course. Should it be allowed?'

'The humans of Living Dream believe it to be both their right and their destiny. They are billions in number. How can that much belief be wrong?'

'Because they might be endangering trillions.'

'True. This is not a question which has an answer. Not in the absolute terms you are demanding.'

'What if they do trigger the Void's final devourment phase, or at least a bad one?'

'Ah, now that is the real question. It's also one which I doubt we can have prior knowledge of. Neither I nor any of the post-physicals I have interacted with are aware of what happens inside the Void.'

'Inigo showed you.'

'Inigo showed us the fate of humans in the Void. Which incidentally isn't too dissimilar to downloading yourself into me; though the Void has the advantage of quasi-mystical overtones to win over the technophobes among humanity. And you get to remain physical. What he did not show us is the nature of the Void itself.'

'So you're prepared to take the risk?'

'At this moment I am prepared to let the players strut the stage.'

'Yes. That's about as un-definitive as it gets.'

'If I were to forbid the Pilgrimage and enforce that decision, it would trigger a split within myself. Pro-Pilgrimage Factions such as the Advancers would likely attempt to create their own version of myself. And kindly remember I am not a virtual environment. I am fully established within the quantum field intersections around Earth.'

'You're scared of a rival?'

'The human race has never been so unified as it is today. It has taken our entire history to reach this congruity. People, all people, lead a good life filled with as much diversity as they wish to undergo. They migrate inwards until they download into me. Within me they are free to transcend in any way imagination and ability can combine. One day, as a whole, I will become post-physical. Humans who do not wish to travel along that path will begin afresh. That is the vision of evolution which awaits us. A "rival" focal point would distort that, possibly even damage or dilute the moment of singularity.'

'There can only be one god, huh?'

'There can be many. I simply wish to avoid engendering hostile ones. No one wants to see a war in heaven. Trust me, it would make a Void devourment seem trivial.'

'I thought diversity was our virtue.'

'It is one of them, and as such flourishes within me.'

'But . . .'

'It is also a danger that can lead to our destruction. Opposing forces have to be balanced. That is my function.'

'And this is one instance where you're going to fail if you're not careful.'

'Undoubtedly.'

'So we have to find other options.'

'As people have sought since civilization began on Earth. That, I think, is a greater virtue.'

'Okay then.' Paula took a moment to marshal her thoughts. 'I'm uncertain who is behind the raid on the clinic. It is puzzling why the Advancers and Conservatives should both have their representatives there after the fact. Do you think a third Faction is involved?'

'Very likely. I do not know which one. Many alliances are being formed and broken. However, you may soon be able to establish the identity. Admiral Kazimir is currently receiving a report from the base Admiral at the *High Angel*. He will probably ask you to tackle it.'

'Ah.'

'If you need anything.'

'I'll let you know.'

The link ended. Paula sat back on the deep curving chair which the starship's cabin had moulded for her. Given her own uncertainty about the mission, she was feeling vaguely troubled by the lack of reassurance ANA:Governance could offer. She supposed she should be grateful it was so honest with her.

Kazimir called less than a minute later. 'How did the Anagaska enquiry go?' he asked.

'Positive result. It was definitely someone with advanced biononics and possibly an ultradrive ship. The target was Inigo's old memorycell.'

'Interesting. And I've just had a report that the *Alini*, a private starship, docked at *High Angel*.'

'How is that relevant?'

'It docked at the Raiel dome. The Navy sensors detected a drive signature which could indicate an ultradrive.'

Paula was suddenly very interested. 'Did it now? There are very few humans the Raiel will allow into their dome. Who does the *Alini* belong to?'

'Unknown. It's registered to a company on Sholapur.'

'I'm on my way.'

*

The Delivery Man landed at Daroca's main starport, parking his ultradrive ship, the *Jomo*, on a pad connected to the third terminal building, which dealt with private yachts. Then he started walking across the field to the nearby hangar zone. Even knowing all about the diversion bug infiltrated into the ground navigation section of the starport's smartcore didn't help him. All the hangars were identical, the rows regimented. It was mildly confusing. Not that he would lose his way, not with all his enrichments and an instinctive sense of direction. But just to be on the safe side . . . His u-shadow snatched real-time images from a sensor satellite and guided him directly.

Eventually, he was standing at the base of a glossy black wall where the small side door was protected by an excellent security shield. Not even his full field function scan could determine what lay inside. He smiled. *This* was more like it.

His biononics began to modify their field function, pushing a variety of energy patterns against the security shield, introducing small instabilities which quickly began to amplify. His u-shadow reached through the fluctuating gaps and launched a flurry of smart trojans into the hangar net.

The door irised open.

Ninety-seven seconds. *Not bad.*

Inside, his field function scanned round looking for possible guard armaments, while his u-shadow rifled through the hangar's electronic systems. Troblum had set up a fairly standard defence network, with concentric shielding around the main section of the hangar. The physicist was clearly more interested in maintaining privacy than physical protection.

His scan didn't reveal any human presence in the hangar. The first office was clearly just a reception area, cover for anyone who did make it past the diversion system. Beyond that was a second office with one of the biggest smartcores the Delivery Man had ever seen. It wasn't connected to the hangar network, or the unisphere. His u-shadow established a link to its peripheral systems and began to probe the available files.

The Delivery Man went on into the main hangar. He whistled softly at the vast array of Neumann cybernetic modules occupying half of the space inside. The machine was powered down, but he was familiar enough with the technology to guess its sophistication probably put it beyond a level-six replicator. That was not something an individual Higher citizen normally possessed. No wonder Troblum needed such a large smartcore, nothing else could operate such a rig.

'Can you access the main memory?' he asked his u-shadow.

'Not possible for me. I will need high-order assistance.'

The Delivery Man cursed, and opened an ultra secure link to the Conservative Faction. There was a small risk it could be intercepted by another Faction or more likely ANA:Governance itself, but in light of what he'd stumbled across he considered it necessary. 'I need help to gain access to Troblum's smartcore. It should tell us what he's been building with this machine.'

'Very well,' the Conservative Faction replied. With his u-shadow providing a link, the Delivery Man could almost feel the Faction's presence shift into the hangar. It began to infiltrate the smartcore. While it was doing that, he began to look through the mundane files in the hangar's net to try and find delivery schedules. The individual components of the machine had to come from somewhere, and the EMA to obtain them went far beyond an individual's resources. There was no court the Conservatives could use to confront the Accelerators with, even if he established a datatrail back to their representatives; but if he could find the proxy supplying Troblum with additional EMA there was a chance he could find other illicit EMA transfers from the same source. A whole level of Accelerator operations would be uncovered.

'There is only one design stored in the smartcore,' the Conservative Faction announced. 'It would appear to be an ftl engine capable of transporting a planet.'

The Delivery Man swung round to stare at the dark machine looming above him, his gaze drawn to the circular extrusion mechanism in the centre. 'A whole planet?'

'Yes.'

'Would it work?'

'The design is an ingenious reworking of exotic matter theory. It could work if applied correctly.'

'And this built it?' he said, still staring at the machine.

'There have been two attempts at producing the engine. The first was aborted. The second appears to have been successful.'

'Why do they want to fly a planet round at ftl speeds? And which planet?'

'We don't know. Please destroy the machine and the smartcore.'

The Delivery Man put his hands on his hips to give the machine an appalled look. 'What technology level can I go up to here?'

'Unlimited. Nobody must know it ever existed, least of all Highers.'

'Okay. Your call.'

The Conservative Faction ended the link, leaving the Delivery Man feeling unusually alone. Now he knew the purpose of the machine the silent hangar had the feel of some ancient murder scene. It wasn't a pleasant place to be, putting him on edge.

He called the *Jomo*'s smartcore, and told it to fly over. The hangar's main doors were open when it arrived, and it nosed through the security screen to settle on the cradles inside. Its nose almost touched the wall of Neumann cybernetics.

The Delivery Man made sure the hangar security screen was at its highest rating before he stood underneath the *Jomo*'s open airlock to be drawn up by an inverted gravity effect. Once inside he used a tri-certificate authorization to activate the Hawking m-sink stored in one of the forward holds. The little device was contained inside a high-powered regrav sled, which slipped out to hover in front of the Neumann cybernetics. With that in place, the Delivery Man aimed a narrow disrupter effect at the machine, just above the Hawking m-sink. A half-metre section of equipment vaporized, producing a horizontal fountain of hot ionized gas. It bent slightly in mid-air to pour into the Hawking m-sink, which absorbed every molecule. The Delivery Man tracked the disruptor effect along the front of the machine, with the Hawking m-sink following.

It took forty minutes to vaporize the entire machine. When it was over, the quantum black hole at the centre of the Hawking m-sink had absorbed three hundred and twenty-seven tons of matter, putting the regrav sled close to its weight lift limit as it edged back into the starship's hold. The Delivery Man requested flight clearance from the starport, and the *Jomo* lifted into Arevalo's warm summer skies.

Justine watched it go from the safety of her own ship, parked on a pad eight hangars down the row.

*

Twilight was bathing Hawksbill Bay with a rich gold hue, mild enough so that strange constellations could twinkle merrily across the cloudless sky. The only sound around the pavilion's swimming pool came from the waves breaking around the rocks of the headland below.

'An ftl engine that shifts planets,' Nelson said. 'Got to admire them. They don't think small.'

'They don't think: period,' Gore grunted. 'ANA is embedded in the local quantum fields. You can't just rip it out and fling it across the galaxy on a blind date with the Void.'

'They obviously believe it. Troblum's EMA came through one of their front committees. He built the engine for the Accelerators.'

'Don't believe it,' Gore said, shaking his head. 'He even made a presentation to the Navy about the Anomine using something like this to haul the Dyson barrier generators into place. Asked Kazimir to fund a fucking search for them for Christ's sake. Why would Ilanthe allow him to go public with the idea? They'd atomize him before he even put in a call for a meeting with the Navy. No, we haven't got enough information yet.'

'Makes sense if it's a diversion,' Nelson said reluctantly. 'They wouldn't build anything so critical to their plans on a Higher world. We don't.'

'And he's taken years to get it built, on a fairly pitiful budget. Wrong priority level. We really need to find Troblum and ask nicely what he's really been doing for the Accelerators.'

'He left Arevalo a while back. Filed a flight plan to Lutain. Never showed up there, or any other Commonwealth World, Central or External.'

'We need to find him,' Gore repeated firmly.

'That's not going to happen. Either the Accelerators have him, or he's hiding, or more likely he's plain and simple dead.'

'Then we find out which one it is.'

*

Justine stood in the middle of the weirdly empty hangar and called Paula.

'There's something seriously wrong here.'

'In what way?' Paula asked.

'I think the Delivery Man just cleared the whole place out.' Justine slowly looked round the big empty space, opening her optical vision to Paula. 'See that? There was something in here. My field scan shows those power cables were cut by a disruption effect, same goes for the support girders. Whatever it was, it was sizeable and used up a great deal of power. But the *Jomo* is no bigger than my ship. Which only leaves one option how he did it.'

'I thought the Hawking m-sink was even more secure than ultradrive technology. It would seem I'm wrong, which is disturbing.'

'Kazimir will have to be told,' Justine said. 'If there are starships flying round the Commonwealth equipped with that kind of weapon the Navy should know about it. The Factions don't use the most principled people as their representatives.'

'I'll leave that to you.'

'Great. Thank you. He's still human enough to blame the messenger.'

'He's a professional. You'll be all right. Do you know where the Delivery Man is heading?'

'His direction indicated Earth when he left my sensor range. I imagine he'll want to dump the mass stored in the Hawking m-sink first, and he'll do that deep in interstellar space. Expelling it will produce a colossal gamma burst.'

'Leave him alone for now. The focus is shifting back to Living Dream.'

'Why?'

'Our sources in the movement are reporting an alarming development,' Paula said. 'Living Dream is readying all the civil security forces on all the core worlds of the Free Market Zone. Leave has been cancelled and they're undergoing martial law enforcement training.'

'Martial law? Where is that applied in the Free Market Zone?'

'It isn't. Yet. But if they were to annex Viotia they would probably need that many police troopers to keep the populace under control.'

'Jesus! Are they planning that?'

'Ethan is becoming desperate to gain control over the Second Dreamer. He's the one person who could still stop this whole Pilgrimage in its tracks.'

'And everyone believes he's on Viotia,' Justine said, appalled. 'Dear heavens, an interstellar invasion. In this day and age, it's unthinkable, it's left over from the Starflyer War.'

'Start thinking it. I made a mistake not giving this a higher priority. We really need to offer ANA:Governance's protection to the Second Dreamer. That way no one will be able to pressure him into either helping or hindering the Pilgrimage.'

'But first we have to find him. How long before you can get your agent working on this?'

'Very soon now. I'm on my way to see him with one slight detour.'

Justine eyed the hangar's inner office suspiciously. There was an empty space which three communications conduits led into, their ends cut off clean. 'Whatever they were building here was clearly important, and the Delivery Man took quite a risk covering it up. I don't think we have a lot of time left.'

'The Pilgrimage ships won't be ready to fly until September.'

'And the Ocisen Empire fleet will be here in late August, that's less than three months away. I'd like to suggest a lead no one else seems to be following.'

'What's that?'

'Inigo started to dream when he was at Centurion Station. Did anyone else?'

'If they did, we'd know about it.'

'That's the point: would we? Suppose the contact was a weak one that was never fully established. Or the recipient didn't want any part of Inigo's religion. A reluctant person just like the Second Dreamer has turned out to be.'

'I think I see where you're going with this, or rather intend to go.'

'I want to check out the confluence nest on Centurion Station, see if it has any memory of Void dreams, or fragments of them.

419

Maybe the Second Dreamer started his connection with the Skylord when he was there, just like Inigo.'

'You're right, no one else has covered that angle.'

'If I leave now, my ship can get me there in five hundred hours.'

'You're going to fly there? Why not use the Navy's relay link?'

'Too much chance of it being intercepted.'

'If you do find anything it'll take you another five hundred hours to get back. It'll probably all be over by then.'

'If I find anything important, I'll use the relay link to send you the name in the heaviest encryption we have.'

'Okay. Good luck.'

＊

Troblum woke up slumped in the chair he'd sat in all day reviewing various schematics. His exovision displays had paused at the point where he'd fallen asleep. Colourful profiles of exotic mass density modulators floated like mechanical ghosts around him, each one beleaguered by shoals of blue and green analytical displays. Supposedly these components would perform their designated function without any trouble; the designers had simply scaled up from existing ultradrives. Except, nobody had ever built them this size before, which left Troblum with a mountain of problems when it came to the kind of precise power control they needed. And they hadn't even got to the fabrication stage yet.

He stretched as best his thick limbs would allow and tried to get out of the chair. After two attempts which made him look like a overturned glagwi struggling to right itself his u-shadow ordered the station to reduce the local gravity field. Now when he pushed with his legs and back he gave his body an impetus which propelled him right out of the clingy cushions. Gravity returned slowly, giving him time to straighten his legs before his feet touched the decking. He let out a wet belch as the falling sensation ended. His stomach was still churning, and his legs felt weak and stiff. He had a headache, too. The medical display in his exovision showed him his sugar levels were all over the place.

There was a load of crap about toxins and blood oxygen levels too, which he cancelled just as the nutrition and exercise recommendations came up. *Stupid anachronism in the age of biononics.*

He set off to the saloon which the ultradrive team used as their social and business centre. It also had the best culinary units on the station. When he arrived several of the tables along the curving wall were occupied by groups of people discussing various aspects of the project. He saw Neskia with a couple of technicians he recognized from the team handling the drive's hyperspace fluidity systems. They all stared at him as he sat down in the spare seat, wincing as his knees creaked. Both technicians registered mild disapproval. Neskia's long metallized neck curved sinuously so her flat face was aligned perfectly on him. 'Thank you,' she said to the technicians. 'We'll go with that.'

They nodded thanks and left.

'Was there something you wanted?' she asked Troblum in a level voice.

'I need to change the design for the mass density modulator,' he said. A maidbot slid over with a tray of food his u-shadow had ordered from the culinary units. He started unloading the plates.

Neskia's face tipped down; her large circular eyes regarded the food without any trace of emotion. 'I see. Do you have the proposed new design?'

'No,' he mumbled round a mouthful of spaghetti. 'I want you to okay the change before I waste a week on it.'

'What's wrong with the existing modulator?'

'It's a pile of crap. Doesn't work. Your idiots didn't take the power control requirements into account.'

'Do you have an analysis of the problem?'

Troblum could only nod as he chewed his hot floratts bread with mozzarella and herbs. His u-shadow sent the file over.

'Thank you. The review team will examine this. You will have a reply in an hour. That is the procedure.'

'Sure. Good.' He sighed. Great that the tech problem was sorted, but the spaghetti with its balls of jolmeat and attrato sauce could have done with more black pepper. He reached for his tankard, only to find Neskia's hand on top of his, preventing him from lifting the beer. Her skin shimmered between white and silver. He couldn't sense any temperature from her fingers, hot or cold. 'What?'

Her eyes blinked slowly, turning the irises from black to deep indigo. 'In future. In public. While you are here in my station. Please ensure your social interaction program is running, and that you follow its advice.'

'Oh. Okay.' He dipped his head towards the tankard.

'Thank you, Troblum.' She lifted her hand away. 'Was there anything else? The project seems to be absorbing most of your time.'

'Yeah, it's interesting. I might get some crossover into one of my own projects. Ultradrive is a fascinating reworking of quantum dimensional theory. Who came up with it?'

'I believe it was ANA:Governance. Is it important?'

'No.' He pushed the spaghetti plate aside, and started on the rack of lamb.

Neskia still hadn't stopped looking at him. She was about to speak again when two people came over to stand beside their table. Troblum finished chewing before he glanced up – he knew that was the kind of thing the social program counselled. Marius was looking down at him with his usual rarefied contempt. But it was his companion who turned Troblum immobile. His limbs wouldn't move. Thankfully, neither did his mouth, which stopped him from opening his jaw and grunting in shock. He couldn't breathe either as something like frost ripped down through his lungs.

'I'd introduce you,' Marius said coldly. 'But of all the people on this station, Troblum, you are the one who doesn't need it. Now do you?'

'Really,' the Cat said, and grinned. 'Why's that?'

Troblum's very dark fascination kept his muscles locked up tight. She wasn't easy to recognize, she didn't have that trademark spiked hair out of all her history files. It was still short and dark, but today she wore it in a smooth swept-back style with a pair of slim copper shades perched up above her forehead. She was dressed in a chic modern suit rather than the leather trousers and tight vest she used to favour. But that darkish complexion and wide amused grin veering on the crazy . . . There was no mistake. She was so much smaller than he imagined, it was confusing, she barely came up to his shoulder height, yet he'd always visualized her as an Amazon.

'Troblum has a penchant for history,' Marius said. 'He knows all sorts of odd facts.'

'What's my favourite food?' the Cat asked.

'Lemon risotto with asparagus,' Troblum stammered. 'It was the specialty dish at the restaurant you waitressed in when you were fifteen.'

The Cat's grin sharpened. 'What the fuck is he?' She turned to Marius for an explanation.

'An idiot savant with a fetish about the Starflyer War. He's useful to us.'

'Whatever turns you on.'

'You're in suspension,' Troblum said flatly; he couldn't help the words coming out even though he was afraid of her. 'It was a five thousand year sentence.'

'Aww. He's quite sweet, actually,' the Cat told Marius. She gave Troblum a lewd wink. 'I'll finish it one day. Promise.'

'If you have a moment, please,' Marius asked Neskia. 'We need to sort a proper ship out for our guest.'

'Of course.' She stood up.

'Oh yes,' Marius added, as though it were of no consequence. 'Is Troblum behaving himself?'

Neskia looked from Marius to Troblum. 'So far so good. He's been quite helpful.'

'Keep it up,' Marius said. He wasn't smiling.

Troblum bowed his head, unable to look at any of them. Too many people. Too close. Too intrusive. *And one of them is the Cat!* He wasn't prepared for that kind of encounter today. Nor any day. But she was out of suspension – somehow, walking around. *She's in this station!*

His medical display flashed up blue symbols down the side of his exovision, telling him his biononics were engaging, re-animating his chest muscles, calming them into a steady rhythm. It hadn't registered with him the way he'd started to suck his breath down as if his throat was constricted. A small cocktail of drugs were flushed out of macrocellular glands, bringing down his heart rate.

Troblum risked a glance up, his face pulled into a horrendously guilty expression. The three of them were gone, out of sight, out of the saloon. He was gathering an excessive number of curious looks from his colleagues who were still seated. He wanted to tell them, to shout: *It's not me you should be staring at.*

Instead, he felt the trembling start deep in his torso. He stood up fast. Which made his head spin. Biononics reinforced his leg muscles, allowing him to hurry out of the saloon. In the corridor, his u-shadow diverted a trollybot for him sit on. It carried him all the way back to his quarters, where he flopped on to the bed. He loaded a nine-level certificate into the lock even though he knew how useless that was.

The Cat!

He lay on the bed with the cabin heating up, feeling the shock slowly ebbing away. Release from the physical symptoms did nothing to alleviate the dread. Of all the megalomaniacs and psychopaths in history, the Accelerators had chosen to bring her back. Troblum lay there in the warm darkness for hours wondering what they were facing which was so terrible they had no choice but to use her. He'd always been behind the whole Accelerator movement because it was such a logical one. They were nurturing an evolutionary lineage which had started with single cell amoebas and would end with elevation to post-physical status. A necessity that couldn't be disputed. The other Factions were wrong, it was that obvious. To him. Accelerator philosophy appealed to his physicist nature; because that hurtful vicious bastard Marius was right, there was very little else in the way of personality.

Forget that. It's not relevant.

Because anything that has to use the Cat to make it work can't be right. It just can't.

Inigo's fifth dream

'—thus because the city is deemed to be a sole entity in its own right no human can "own" their residence in the traditional legal sense. However, in the fifteenth year after Rah's arrival, the newly formed Upper Council passed the first Act of Registry. Essentially that means that any human can claim a residence within the city wall for their own usage. In order to register you simply have to find a house or maisonette or room which is unoccupied, stay in it for two days and two nights, then register your claim with the Board of Occupancy. This claim once notarized will allow you and your descendants to live there until such time as they choose to relinquish it. As there are no new buildings, and can never be, the most desirable and largest homes were claimed within ten years of Rah opening the first gate. These are now the palaces of our most ancient families, the District Masters, and as such can have up to five generations living in them, all of them first sons waiting to inherit the estate and seat on the Upper Council. The remaining available accommodation in the city today is small and badly configured for human occupation. Although even this is diminishing rapidly. Thus, while districts such as Eyrie are basically uninhabitable—'

Edeard hoped he hadn't just groaned out loud from the terrible boredom. He was now as adept as any Makkathran citizen at veiling his emotions from casual farsight, but if Master Solarin from the Guild of Lawyers used the word *thus* one more time ... It was a mystery how the old man could talk so long without a break. Rumour at the station was that Master Solarin was over two hundred and fifty years old. Edeard would be surprised if that were true. He certainly didn't look that young. His white hair had receded so far that the top of his skull was now completely bald, something Edeard had never seen before, though the remaining strands were long enough to reach down over his shoulders. And his limbs were horribly thin and frail, while his fingers had swollen to the point where he had trouble flexing them. His vocal chords, however, suffered no such malaise.

Along with his fellow probationary constables, Edeard was sitting at a bench in the small hall of the Jeavons station, listening to their weekly lecture on basic Makkathran law. In another two months they'd be facing a batch of exams on the subject, which they had to pass in order to graduate. Like all of them, he found Solarin a sore test of patience. A quick scan round showed Boyd was almost asleep. Macsen's eyes were unfocused as he longtalked the girls in the dressmaker's shop at the end of the street. Kanseen appeared to be paying polite attention but Edeard knew her well enough now to see she was as bored as him. Dinlay, though, was sitting up with rapt attention and even taking notes. Somehow Edeard couldn't quite laugh at that. Poor old Dinlay had so much to prove to his father and uncles he would undoubtedly pass his exams with high grades. That presented the rest of them with the very real danger that once they graduated, Dinlay would be appointed their squad leader. It would be something he took *very* seriously.

'—thus the precedence was set for the lower ancillary court to hear any application to evict when a civil malfeasance is suspected of taking place within the property itself. In practice a full hearing is unnecessary, and you may request a provisional eviction notice from the duty magistrate who acts as *de facto* high council to the lower court. And that I'm afraid brings this session to its successful conclusion. We will deal with the criteria for such application next week. In the meantime I'd like you all to read

Sampsols Common Law, Volume Three, chapters thirteen through twenty-seven by the time I return. It covers the main parameters of weapons usage within the city wall. I might even enliven our time together with a small test. How exciting that will be, eh? Until then, I thank you for your interest and bid you farewell.' Solarin gave them a vague smile and removed his gold-rimmed glasses before shutting the big book he'd covered with annotations. His ge-monkey placed it carefully in a leather shoulder bag along with the other books the lawyer used for his lecture.

Dinlay stuck his hand up. 'Sir?'

'Ah, my dear boy; sadly I am in something of a rush today. If you could possibly write your question down and submit it to my senior apprentice at the Guild, I'd be most grateful.'

'Yes, sir.' Dinlay's hand came down and his shoulders slumped with disappointment.

Edeard remained seated as the lawyer walked slowly out of the hall, assisted by two ge-monkeys, wondering what Solarin would actually look like *rushing* somewhere.

'Olovan's Eagle tonight?'

'Huh?' Edeard shook himself out of his absurd daydream.

Macsen was standing over his desk, a smug expression on his face. 'Clemensa will be going. Evala said she's been asking about you. A lot!'

'Clemensa?'

'The one with the dark hair always tied up in a long tail. Big chest. Big legs, too, sadly, but hey, nobody's perfect.'

Edeard sighed. It was another of the girls from the dressmaker's. Macsen spent most of his time sweet-talking them or trying to set them up with his friends. Once he even tried to match Kanseen with a carpentry apprentice – he wouldn't be doing that again. 'No. No. I can't. I am so far behind on my law texts, and you heard what Solarin said.'

'Remind me.'

'There's going to be a test,' Edeard said wearily.

'Oh right. It's only the exam at the end which counts. Don't worry. Listen, I've got a friend in the Lawyer's Guild. A couple of gold shillings and he'll gift us the whole *Sampsols*.'

'That's cheating,' Dinlay said hotly.

Macsen put on a suitably wounded expression. 'In what respect?'

'In all respects!'

'Dinlay, he's just winding you up,' Kanseen said as she got up to leave.

'I'm being perfectly serious,' Macsen said, his face as innocent as a newborn.

'Ignore him,' she said, and gave Dinlay's shoulder a gentle shove. 'Come on let's find some lunch before we go out.'

Dinlay managed one last scowl before hurrying after Kanseen. He started to ask her something about the residency laws.

'Must be true love,' Macsen warbled cheerfully as they turned out of sight.

'You're evil,' Edeard decided. 'Pure evil.'

'Only thanks to years of practice and dedication.'

'You know he's going to be our squad leader, don't you.'

'Yes. He'll get his appointment the day after the Eggshaper Guild announces its sculpted a ge-pig that can fly.'

'I'm serious. His grades will be way above ours, plus his father and a whole load of family are already constables. Senior ones at that.'

'Chae isn't stupid. He knows that'll never work.'

Edeard wanted to believe Macsen was right.

'Um, Edeard, are you really not interested in Clemensa?' Boyd asked.

'Ho, this is perfect,' Macsen said, rubbing his hands together. 'Why, do you fancy your chances?'

'Actually, yes,' Boyd said with more courage that Edeard had credited him with.

'Good for you. She's a lovely girl. As randy as a drakken in a bloodfrenzy, I just happen to know.'

Boyd frowned. 'How do you know?'

'Evala told me,' Macsen said smoothly. 'Her last boyfriend was dumped for not having enough stamina.'

Boyd gave Macsen a suddenly entranced look. 'I'll come with you tonight. But you have to get Evala to put in a good word for me.'

'Leave it with me, my fine friend. You're as good as shagged senseless already.'

Edeard rolled his eyes and promised the Lady he'd be good for evermore if she'd just stop Macsen from being ... well, Macsen. 'Come on, let's get something to eat before the constables grab it all again.'

'Oh yes,' Boyd said. 'Our helpful and welcoming colleagues. I hate the way they treat us.'

'Only for another two months, that's all,' Macsen said.

'You really think they'll show us any respect after we qualify. I don't.'

'No they won't,' Macsen agreed. 'But at least we can shovel shit on to the new probationees. I know it'll make me feel better.'

'We're not going to do that,' Edeard said. 'We're going to talk to them, help them with problems, and make them feel appreciated.'

'Why?'

'Because that's what I would have liked to happen with us. That way more people might just be encouraged to join up. Haven't you counted the numbers, not just at this station but citywide? There aren't enough constables in the city. People are starting to organize themselves into street associations to take on the gangs. That's going to undermine the rule of law.'

'Great Lady, you really mean it, don't you?' Macsen said.

'Yes,' Edeard said forcefully, and let them sense his mental tone so they knew he wasn't joking with them. 'I know what happens when civil government means nothing. I've seen the violence that the barbarians use when a society leaves itself open to any bastard who knows how weak it is. And that's not going to happen here. Makkathran can't be allowed to tear itself apart from within.'

'I don't know why you're worried about Dinlay being squad leader,' Macsen said, equally serious. 'You're the one. Sir!'

Edeard was still slightly self-conscious about wearing the constable uniform in public. Only the white epaulettes distinguished probationees from regular constables. The rest of it was *actually real* as Macsen put it. A smart dark-blue tunic with silver buttons up the front; matching trousers with a wide regulation leather belt containing a truncheon, two pepper-gas phials, a pair of iron handcuffs with a fiendishly tricky six-lever lock that was just about impossible to pick with telekinesis, and a small first aid pack. Under the tunic was a white shirt, that Sergeant Chae made very sure was indeed an unblemished white each morning. Boots were up to an individual, but they had to be black and at least ankle-high (but not over the knee); they also had to shine from polishing. The domed helmet was made from an epoxied drosilk mesh, with padding on the inside to protect the wearer's skull from a physical blow. Like the others, Edeard had bought his own drosilk waistcoat which was supposedly tough enough to resist a bullet. Macsen had gone one further, and bought drosilk shorts.

In theory the cost wasn't too bad. But in practice every constable needed two tunics, and at least three shirts. Then there was a constant supply of flaked soap for the dormitory's ge-chimps to wash everything. Edeard gained considerable kudos when the others found how good he was at instructing the ge-chimps with laundry tasks. After the first week Chae stopped trying to find fault when they turned out in immaculate uniforms each morning.

The daily routine hardly varied. In the morning they would have various physical and telepathic teamwork training sessions, followed by lectures. In the afternoon they would be taken out on patrol under the alarmingly vigilant eye of Chae. Sometimes their division captain, Ronark, would accompany them. Evenings were theoretically all their own. Study was advised at least during the week.

Edeard always hated it when Ronark did come out with them to 'check on progress'. The man was in his eighties, and was never going to rise any higher than his current position. His wife had left him decades ago, his children disowned him. That just left him the constables, which he believed in with a religious fervour. Everything was done according to regulation; variations were not permitted, and such infringements were subject to severe fines, restrictions and demotions. Jeavons station had one of the lowest recruitment rates in the city.

Nobody paid any attention to them when Chae led them out of the station at one o'clock precisely. Ronark was standing at his curving fish-eye window above the big double gate, observing the shift change, clocking the patrols in and out on his ancient pocket watch. Out on the narrow pavement, a squad was double-timing back to the station, its corporal red faced and panting as they tried to minimize their delay. Three ge-dogs scampered along beside them, happy at the run.

Probationary constables were not permitted genistar support. Thankfully, Chae kept a discreet silence about Edeard's ge-eagle, which now lived with two others in the station's rooftop aviary.

Jeavons was a pleasant enough district. It even had a small park in the centre which a team of city ge-monkeys kept in good horticultural order. There was a big freshwater pond in the middle, with exotic scarlet fish measuring a good two feet long – they always seemed sinister to Edeard who disliked their fangs and the way they looked up at everyone who stood by the rail watching them. But the park had a football pitch marked out, and he occasionally joined the games at weekends when the local lads ran a small league. He rather enjoyed the fact that Jeavons didn't house many grand families; its buildings were on a relatively modest scale, though the mansions along Marble Canal were regal enough. The carpenters, jewel smiths, and physicians all had their Guild headquarters there. It was also the home of the astronomical association, which had been fighting for Guild status for seven centuries, and was always blocked by the Pythia, who claimed the heavens were a supernatural realm, and astronomy verged on the heretical. Boyd, of course, was full of gossipy facts like that as they walked the winding streets; he probably knew the layout better than Chae.

Today Chae led them over Arrival Canal and into the smaller Silvarum district. The buildings here were oddly curved, as if they were once clusters of bubbles that had somehow been compressed. Squeezed-up insect hives, Boyd called them. None of them were large enough to be palaces, but they all belonged to wealthy families – the smaller merchants and senior Masters of professional Guilds. The shops all sold goods far beyond Edeard's dwindling coinage.

As they passed over the ornate wooden bridge Edeard found himself walking with Kanseen.

'So you're not going out tonight?' she enquired.

'Nah. I don't have much money left, and I really need to study.'

'You're serious then, about turning this into a career.'

'Ask me again in a year's time. In the meantime I'm not going to blow it by being stupid. I need to graduate.'

'All of us do,' she said.

'Humm.' Edeard eyed Macsen, who was lingering on the end of the bridge, exchanging some good-natured words with a gondolier passing by underneath. The gondola's benches had been removed, replaced by a simple slatted platform carrying a pile of wooden crates. 'For someone supposedly thrown penniless on the street, Macsen seems to have a lot of coinage.'

'Didn't you hear?' she said with a superior smile.

'What?'

'His mother has been taken up by a notorious Master in the Musician's Guild. She's living in a nice little maisonette in Cobara district. Apparently he's a hundred and ten years older than her.'

'No!' Edeard knew he shouldn't be interested in this gossip, but such talk was Makkathran's second currency. Everybody had some piece of hearsay or rumour about the District Master families that they couldn't wait to share. And scandal was the hugest currency of all.

'Oh yes. He used to be in one of the travelling bands which tour round the Iguru and villages in the Donsori Mountains.' She leant in closer to murmur. 'Apparently he had to stop touring some while ago because there were so many *offspring* in those villages. Now he just tutors apprentices at the Guild building and plays for the families.'

Some little memory surfaced in Edeard's thoughts; late night talk in a tavern several months ago that he wasn't supposed to hear, and she had said *notorious*. 'You're not talking about Dybal?'

Kanseen's smile was now victorious. 'I couldn't possibly say.'

'But ... wasn't he caught in bed with two of the Lady's novices?'

'That's part of his myth. If he wasn't so popular with his satire songs they'd have thrown him out of the Guild decades ago. Apparently they're very *upbeat*. The younger members of noble families idolize him, while the older ones want him to wind up in the bottom of a canal.'

'Yeah, but ... Macsen's mother?'

'Yes.'

Kanseen seemed disturbingly pleased with herself, mainly because of his incredulous reaction. That was the way with her, always coming on just that little bit superior. He didn't buy it, that was just her way of coping with the probationary period, establishing a reasonable barrier around herself. It couldn't be easy being a girl in the constables; there certainly weren't many.

Chae started off heading directly for the plaza where the Chemist Guild headquarters was situated. The pavements between the buildings were a reddish brown in colour, with a central row of thick cones rising to waist height. They were filled with soil and planted with big saffcherry trees whose branches created a verdant roof between the bowed walls on either side. Pink and blue blossom was just starting to fall, forming a delicate carpet of petals. Edeard tried to keep searching the pedestrians for signs of criminal activity the way Chae kept telling them. It was hard. Akeem's memory had remained crystal clear and true on one aspect of city life: the girls. They were beautiful. Especially those of the noble families, who seemed to use districts like Silvarum to hunt in packs. They took a great deal of care about how they appeared in public. Dresses which had plunging neck-lines, or skirts with surprising slits amid the ruffles; lace fabric which was translucent. Hair styled to look carefree. Makeup skilfully applied to emphasize smiles, cheekbones, huge innocent eyes. Sparkling jewellery.

He passed one gaggle of maidens in their mid-teens who wore more wealth with the rings on one hand than he would earn in a month. They giggled coyly when they caught him staring. Taunted:

'Can we help you, Officer?'

'Is that really your truncheon?'

'It's a long truncheon, isn't it, Gilliaen?'

'Will you use it to subdue bad people with?'

'Emylee is very bad, Officer, use it on her.'

'Hanna! She's indecent, Officer. Arrest her.'

'Does he have a dungeon to throw her in, do you think?'

Third hands performed indecent tweaks and prods on private areas of his body. Edeard jumped in shock before hastily shielding himself, and turning bright red. The girls shrieked in amusement at his behaviour and scuttled off.

'Little trollops,' Kanseen muttered.

'Er, absolutely,' Edeard said. He glanced back – just to make sure they were causing no trouble. Two of them were still checking him out. More wild giggles rang down the street. Edeard shuddered and faced front, hardening his expression.

'You weren't tempted, were you?' Kanseen asked.

'Certainly not.'

'Edeard, you're really a great bloke, and I'm glad to be in the same squad as you. But there's still a lot of the countryside in you. Which is good,' she hastened to add. 'But any family girl would eat you for breakfast and spit out the pips before lunch. They're not nice, Edeard, not really. They have no substance.'

Then how come they look so gorgeous? he thought wistfully.

'Besides,' Kanseen said. 'They all want District Master first sons for husbands, or guildsmen or, if they're desperate, militia officers. Constables don't come close, not in status or money.'

After the plaza they made their way along to the markets. There were three of them just a couple of streets away from the Great Major Canal which boarded Silvarum's northern side. Open areas not quite as big as the plaza, packed full with stalls. The first one concentrated on fresh food. A quilt of canvas awnings formed an undulating ceiling, stitching all the stalls together, whilst providing a strangely warm shade underneath. The still air was heavy with scents. Edeard stared at the piles of fruits and vegetables with mild envy as the stallholders called out their prices and promises of taste and quality. It had been a long time since he'd sat down to a truly decent meal like he used to eat at the Guild compound back in Ashwell. Everything at the station hall came wrapped in pastry; and none of the ge-chimps in the kitchen had ever been instructed in the art of making salad.

'Those are melancholy thoughts,' Kanseen said quietly.

'Sorry,' he said, and made an effort to be alert. Chae said markets were always rife with sneak thieves and pickpockets. He was probably right. Here, as always, the stallholders greeted them warmly, with smiles and the odd gift – apples, pears, a bottle or two; pledges of a good deal if they came back off duty. They liked the constables to be visible. It discouraged pilfering.

Edeard had been dismayed by the reception they received in some districts and streets as Chae led them right across the city. Sullen expressions and intimidating silences, unshielded emotions of enmity. People turning their backs on them. Third hands jostling when they were close to canal banks. Chae, of course, had walked on undaunted, but Edeard had been unnerved. He didn't understand why whole communities would be repelled by law and order.

They moved on to the second market, the one specializing in cloth and clothes. There was a dismaying number of young women strolling along, examining colourful fabrics, chattering happily among themselves. He kept a small shield up, and did his best not to make eye contact. Though there were some truly pretty girls who just begged for a second look. Macsen had no such inhibitions. He chatted happily to any girl who even glanced in his direction.

'You never said which district you come from,' Edeard said.

'I didn't, did I?' Kanseen agreed.

'Sorry.'

'You need to stop saying that, as well,' she said, and smiled.

'Yes. I know. It's just that all of you are used to this.' He gestured round. 'I'm not. There are more people here in this market than ever lived in Ashwell.' For a moment he was struck by real guilt. He thought about his home less and less these days. Some of the faces had faded from memory. Not Akeem, that never would; but Gonat now – did he have red hair or was it dark brown? He frowned from the effort of remembering, but no clear image came.

'Bellis,' Kanseen said. 'My family lives in Bellis.'

'Right,' he said. Bellis was on the eastern side of the city, close to the port, and directly over the Great Major Canal from Sampalok. They hadn't patrolled round there yet. 'You've never been back to see them.'

'No. Mother didn't approve of my becoming a constable.'

'Oh. I'm sor— Shame.'

'I think she would have preferred me to take the Lady's vows.'

'Nothing wrong with that.'

'You really are from the countryside, aren't you?'

'Is that bad?' he said stiffly.

'No. I guess that's where the values this city used to have are kept alive, out there beyond the Donsori Mountains. It just gives me a shock to hear someone with convictions, that's all. You're rare in Makkathran, Edeard. Especially in the constables. That's why you make people uncomfortable.'

'I do?' he asked, genuinely surprised.

'Yeah.'

'But . . . You must believe in values. Why else did you join?'

'Same as half of us. In a few years I'll shift over to bodyguard work for a District Master family. They're always desperate for people with a constable's training and experience. Particularly one like me; female constables are very thin on the ground. And the noble ladies need protection as much as their husbands and sons. I can just about name my own price.'

'Oh.' The notion surprised him, he'd never considered the constables as a route to anything else, let alone something better. 'Who do I make uncomfortable?'

'Well Dinlay for a start. He believes in truth and beauty just like you, and he's a lot noisier about it. But you're stronger and smarter. Chae's going to nominate you as squad leader.'

'You don't know that.'

She smiled. It made him realize how attractive she actually was; something the uniform normally made him overlook. But that smile was a match for any of the silly family girls swanning round the market.

'Put money on it?' she challenged.

'Of course not,' he said with mock indignation. 'That's bound to be illegal.'

They both laughed.

'You two need a room?' Macsen called over his shoulder. 'I know one that'll do cheap rates.'

Kanseen gave him a forceful hand gesture.

He pulled a face. 'Wow, it's true; you can take the girl out of Sampalok, but you can't take Sampalok out of the girl.'

'Arsehole,' she growled.

'We're on patrol,' Chae snapped. 'What does that mean?'

'Professionalism at all times,' the squad muttered dutifully.

'Then kindly remember that, and apply it.'

Macsen, Kanseen, and Edeard grinned at each other as they moved on to the third market, which featured crafts. Stalls displayed small items of furniture, ornaments, cheap jewellery, and alchemic potions. There was even a section selling rare animals as pets. The awnings here were all a uniform orange and white striped canvas arranged in hexagonal cones with centre poles swamped by eaglevine. It was warm underneath, but the full power of the sun was held back.

Edeard stretched his farsight out across the Great Major Canal that ran the length of the city from the Port district to the Circle canals where the Orchard Palace was situated. Ysidro district was on the other side from Silvarum, wedged between the back of Golden Park and the Low Moat. It was where the Lady's novistery was sited.

'This a good time?' his mind enquired.

'Hello,' Salrana replied with a burst of good cheer. 'Yes, I'm fine. We're in the garden, planting summer herbs. It's so lovely in here.' A gentle image gift came with her happiness. He saw a walled garden with conical yews marking out gravel paths. Vines and climbing roses painted the walls in bright colour. There was a broad lawn in the middle, which was unusual in Makkathran; it was trimmed so neatly Edeard wondered what kind of genistar they used to chew it down. A snow-white statue of the Lady stood at one end, almost as high as the walls. She was smiling down on the novices in their white and blue robes as they skittered about with wicker baskets full of plants.

'Nice. Why don't you use ge-chimps to plant the herbs?'

'Oh, Edeard, you have got to start reading more of the Lady's teachings. The purpose of life is to achieve harmony with your environment. If you use genistars for everything, you establish a barrier between yourself and the world.'

'Okay.' He thought that was stupid, but clamped down tight on the emotion for fear Salrana would sense it. She was developing quite an acute empathy these days.

'Where are you?' she asked.

'I'm patrolling Silvarum's markets.' He let her see the bustle surrounding him, showing the rich stall displays.

'Arrested anybody bad?'

'No. They all run in terror from us.'

'Oh, Edeard, you feel sad.'

'Sorry.' He caught himself and winced. 'I'm not. It's just

439

boring, that's all. You know I'm actually looking forward to my exams. This'll all be over after I take them. I can be a proper constable then.'

'I can't wait to see your graduation ceremony.'

'I don't think it's that grand. The Mayor hands us a pair of dark epaulettes, that's all.'

'Yes, but it's at the Orchard Palace, and all the probationary constables from the city are there, and their families are watching. It's a big event, Edeard, don't knock it.'

'I wasn't really. Do you think you'll manage to get to it?'

'Of course I will. Mother Gallian approves of formal functions like that. I've already told her you're graduating.'

'Hey, those exams aren't easy, you know.'

'You'll pass, Edeard. I'll ask the Lady to give you simple questions.'

'Thanks! Can you get out this weekend?'

'I'm not sure. It's difficult with the main service on—'

Angry shouts up ahead made Edeard look round. His farsight could sense several minds inflamed with fury. Around them were minds were blazing with sour determination; they began to move faster and faster.

Shouts reverberated under the awnings.

'Stop them!'

'Thieves. Thieves.'

'Kavine is hurt.'

'Thieves in the market!'

Identical longtalk cries flooded into the aether. Jerky image gifts of faces clashed in Edeard's mind. Too many, and too poor to make any sense.

His farsight swirled round the shifting commotion, contracting on the centre. Men were running, their arms flailing wide as people swarmed round. Hands gripped long metal blades, swiping wide, keeping everyone away. Overtones of fear bubbled into the clamour of longtalk.

'That's us!' Sergeant Chae shouted. 'Come on. Constables! Clear the way! Constables coming through.' His longtalk was directed to warn people sauntering between the stalls at the same time as he shouted. He began to run. Edeard immediately followed, as did Macsen and Kanseen.

'Move! Move aside!'

After a moment of shock, Boyd took off after them. Dinlay had frozen, his mind radiating dismay.

Edeard was running hard now, keeping close to Chae. People were jumping out of the way, pressing themselves against the stalls to open a path. Women were screaming. Children shouted, excited and fearful. The theft ahead was still kicking up a hurlyburly.

'Remember: act together,' Chae told them all with remarkably calm longtalk. 'Minimum of two at all times, don't get separated. Keep your shields up.'

Edeard sent his ge-eagle streaking through the sky, heading towards the edge of the market where the thieves must surely emerge. Every street beyond the rippled roof of canopies had a covering of pleasant saffcherry trees, their pink and blue blossom clotting any view of the pavement and people below. His farsight was still concentrating on the criminals as they sped from the scene of the robbery. There were four of them, three wielding the blades, while the fourth was lugging some kind of box. From what Edeard could sense it was full of metal. And plenty of the stalls around him were displaying jewellery.

Chae drew his truncheon as they burst through a group of people gathered round a couple of overturned stalls. A man lay on the floor groaning and thrashing about, blood pooling beside him.

'Lady!' Chae exclaimed. 'All right, stay back, give him air.' He scrambled for his medical pack and knelt beside the fallen stallholder.

'A doctor?' Chae's longtalk demanded, rising over the general clamour. 'Is there a doctor in the Silvarum craft market? Wounded man.'

Edeard's farsight was still following the criminals. 'Come on,' he yelled at Macsen and Kanseen.

'Where?' Macsen demanded. 'I've lost them.'

'They've just reached the edge of the market. Albaric Street. I can still sense them.' He ploughed on through the clutter of bystanders.

'Edeard, no!' Chae yelled after him.

Edeard almost stopped at the command, but he just couldn't ignore the fleeing thieves. *We can still catch them.* It would be their first real arrest. So far all they'd ever done in their four probationary months was clear drunks off the streets and break up fights. Never any real constable duty. He charged along a narrow passage between rows of stalls. Macsen and Kanseen were racing after him.

'Come back,' Chae bellowed.

Ignoring the sergeant sent a flash of wicked glee along Edeard's nerves.

Stall holders were cheering the three probationary constables as they sped on through the market. Edeard and Macsen were using their longtalk to order people aside. By and large it was working. They were closing the gap on the fleeing thieves.

Edeard's ge-eagle swooped low over the saffcherry trees of Albaric Street, its wings skimming inches above the waving blossom. The four thieves were pounding along the pavement underneath, heading straight for the Great Major Canal. Their blades had been sheathed so as not to draw attention. Even so, the minds of people around them pulsed with curiosity and alarm.

'Where are they going?' Kanseen demanded.

'Got to be the canal,' Macsen replied. There was a lot of exhilaration flooding along his longtalk voice.

Edeard finally saw the end of the market up ahead; the striped canvas roof gave way to the hazy radiance of blossom-filtered sunlight. 'Can you locate any other constables?' he demanded.

'Lady, it's all I can do to watch where I'm going,' Macsen complained.

'What are you planning on doing?' Kanseen asked, all apprehension and doubts.

'Stopping them,' Edeard said. *Wasn't that obvious? What was wrong with her?*

'There's more of them. And they've got blades.'

'I'll take them down,' he growled. Her uncertainty flowed away from him, as if it was another landmark he'd left behind.

They were closing fast now. Albaric Street was almost deserted compared to the busy market, allowing the constables to race onwards, weaving round the occasional recalcitrant pedestrian.

The ge-eagle flashed over the last saffcherry tree. It showed Edeard the street ending abruptly at the edge of the Great Major Canal. The big waterway stretched away on both sides, cutting the city in half. Away to the west was the Birmingham Pool, intersecting the Outer Circle Canal, while eastwards the High Pool formed a junction with Flight Canal and Market Canal. There were only two bridges between Silvarum and the Padua district on the other side, one beside each pool. Like every bridge over the Grand Major Canal they were narrow and steep; most people preferred to use a gondola to cross the hundred and fifty yard width of water. Several were bobbing at a mooring platform where the street ended.

'Got them,' Edeard exclaimed. 'They just ran out of street.' His jubilant mood suddenly dropped as the four criminals sped down the wooden steps to the platform and hopped on to a waiting gondola. It looked scruffy and badly maintained compared to the craft that normally slid along the city's waterways, with dull scratched paint and a drab awning. There were two gondoliers standing on the back, both holding a pole. 'Oh Honious!'

'What?' Kanseen demanded. She was red-faced and breathing heavily, but still keeping up.

'Boat,' he gasped back at her. 'Come on, we can still catch them.' Right in front of him a very grand-looking old lady in a billowing black and white dress and her entourage of younger handmaids were leaving one of Albaric Street's high-class restaurants. His longtalk demands to move didn't seem to be registering with any of them. He dodged round the old lady, cursing. A third hand swatted at him as one might an annoying insect. He flashed her an exasperated look.

The ge-eagle spiralled up, watching the shabby gondola ease out from the mooring platform and into the multitude of craft flocking along the big canal. Downbeat the gondoliers might have been, but they knew their watercraft. With two punts available, and working in harmony, they were soon moving a lot quicker than anything else on the water. The four thieves flopped down on the benches, and started laughing.

Edeard, Macsen, and Kanseen came hurtling up to the canal bank, coming dangerously close to toppling down into the water as they stopped at the top of the mooring's wooden steps.

'Bastards!' Macsen shouted at them.

One of the gondoliers raised his green and blue ribboned boater in mocking salute. They were already twenty yards downstream. Edeard knew with grim certainty they'd be going all the way down to Sampalok, and the wounded stall owner would be ruined. 'Help us,' he called down to the gondolier who was left moored below. 'Take us after them.' This gondola was a fancy craft, its black paintwork shining in the afternoon sun, the awning embroidered with a scarlet bird crest. Somehow Edeard just knew it belonged to the old woman behind.

'Not a chance, pal,' the gondolier called back. 'This is Mistress Florell's private gondola.'

For a moment Edeard considered shoving him into the canal, and commandeering the craft to set off in pursuit. Except he didn't have the first idea of how to use a punt pole.

'Somebody help,' he called with his voice and longtalk. It drew a few interested looks from the gondoliers out on the canal. But no one even asked what he wanted.

A chorus of jeering carried over the water. Thirty yards away, the criminals were leaning over the gunnels to wave and gesture. Edeard stared at his tormentors with a rage that chilled his blood. He smiled back savagely. Some hint of his fury must have flashed out. Macsen and Kanseen swayed back. The jeering stopped.

Edeard reached out with his third hand and plucked the box

from the man holding it. Hands grasped empty air in futility as he lifted it ten feet above the gondola. The thieves exerted their own third hands, trying to prise it back. 'Is that the best you can do?' Edeard taunted. They never even managed to unsettle his grip.

People on nearby gondolas watched in silence as the box drifted sedately through the air. Edeard's smile turned malicious as it landed softly at his feet. He crossed his arms and gloated. 'Don't come back to our district,' he longtalked to the departing gondola. 'Not ever.'

'You're fucking dead, you little shit,' came the answer.

Edeard pressed his third hand down against the bow of the gondola, causing it to rock alarmingly. But it was too far away now for him to capsize. And the six of them hurriedly erected a strong enough shield to deflect him.

Macsen started laughing. His hand came down hard on Edeard's shoulder. 'Oh Lady, you are the greatest, Edeard, the absolute greatest. Did you see their faces?'

'Yeah,' Edeard admitted with a malign grin.

'They won't forget today,' Kanseen said. 'Heavens, Edeard, you must have frightened the life out of them.'

'Let's hope, eh.' He smiled at his friends, very content with the way they'd bonded that little bit more from the shared event. A frilly parasol hit the side of his arm. 'Ow!'

It belonged to the old woman they'd pushed past. 'In future, young man, you will display the correct courtesy due to your elders and betters,' she snapped at him. 'You could have knocked me over the way you were charging about with complete disregard for anyone else. At my age, too; I would never have got up again.'

'Er, yes, madam. Sorry.'

'Mistress Florell!' she said, her wavery voice rising an octave with indignation. 'Don't you pretend you don't know who I am.'

Edeard could hear Macsen chortling behind him, it was muffled as if a hand was over his mouth. 'Yes, Mistress Florell.'

Her eyes narrowed with suspicion. Edeard thought she looked

at least as old as Master Solarin. 'I shall be reporting you to my nephew,' she said. 'There was a time in this city when the constabulary had decent people in its ranks. That time is clearly over. Now get out of my way.'

He wasn't actually *in* her way, but he took a step back anyway. She brushed past with a swirl of her tent-like skirt to descend the steps to the mooring platform. Her entourage followed with immaculately shielded minds. A couple of the handmaids flashed him amused grins. They all settled in the gondola.

'See,' Macsen said, sliding his arm round Edeard's shoulders. 'That's our true reward, the respect of a grateful populace.'

'Who *is* that?' Edeard whined.

Which set Macsen off laughing again.

'You really don't know, do you?' Kanseen said incredulously.

'No.'

'Among other family connections, Mistress Florell is the Mayor's aunt.'

'Oh. I suppose that's not good, then?'

'No. Every Mayor for the last century is some relative or other to her. She basically decides who the Grand Council will elect.'

Edeard shook his head and checked the gondola below. Mistress Florell had vanished under the awning. The gondolier gave him a wink, and cast off.

'Let's get back,' Edeard said.

A cheerful Macsen bent over to pick up the box. He shot Edeard another look as he felt the weight. 'I can sense a whole load of necklace chains in here. Must be gold.'

'I hope he's all right,' Edeard said.

'Chae?' Kanseen asked. She sounded slightly nervous.

'No. The stall holder.'

'Oh yeah. Right.'

High above the Grand Major Canal, the ge-eagle soared lazily on a thermal, keeping the shabby gondola in sight as it hastened towards Sampalok.

*

Most of the crowd had gone when Edeard and his companions returned to the scene of the crime. Several stall holders in their distinctive dark-green aprons were fussing round the stalls they'd righted, restoring the display of goods. Boyd and Dinlay were helping to fix the awning directly overhead, which had ripped free when the stalls were shoved over.

The wounded stall holder was still on the ground. A woman was tending to him, a doctor's satchel open at her feet as she knelt beside her patient. Two young apprentices were aiding her. Between them they'd bandaged the stall holder's chest, now the doctor was holding herself perfectly still, eyes closed, her hands pressed gently on the bandages as her telekinesis operated on the torn flesh underneath, manipulating blood vessels and tissue. Her distinguished face was puckered with intense concentration. Every now and then she would murmur some instruction to her apprentices, who would apply their telekinesis as she directed.

Edeard watched intently, trying to sense with his farsight as well. Old Doc Seneo had never used her third hand to operate with; though Fahin had always said the technique was in the Doctor's Guild tuition books.

'You three okay?' Boyd's longtalk asked.

'Of course,' Macsen retorted.

Boyd glanced over to where Sergeant Chae was talking to a group of stall holders. 'Careful,' he mouthed.

Chae marched over, his face set in a furious mask. Edeard thought his boots were going to leave imprints in the grey-brown market pavement he was stamping them down so heavily. By some process Edeard didn't quite understand, he was now standing ahead of Macsen and Kanseen.

'I believe I gave you a direct order,' Chae said in a menacingly level tone.

All Edeard's good humour at recovering the box faded away. He'd never thought Chae would be quite this angry. For once the sergeant was making no attempt to shield his feelings. 'But, Sergeant—'

'Did I or did I not tell you to stop?'

'Well . . . yes. But—'

'So you heard me?'

Edeard hung his head. 'Yes, Sergeant.'

'So you disobeyed me. Not only that but you put the safety of yourself and your colleagues in danger. Those men were gang members, and armed. Suppose they had pistols?'

'We got it,' Macsen announced defiantly.

'What?'

'We got it back from the bastards,' Macsen said loudly. He turned slightly so he was facing the gaggle of stall holders, and held up the box.

The burst of amazement emanating from the market folk surprised Edeard. It also silenced Sergeant Chae, though he continued to glare at the constables. Macsen walked over to the people closest to the wounded man. 'Here,' he said, and proffered the box. One of the younger men in a green apron stepped forward. 'I am Monrol; Kavine is my uncle. This is what they stole from him.' He turned the lock dial with several precise twists, and the lid popped open. 'It's all here,' he said with a smile. He showed the open box to the market. 'All of it. They brought it back. The constables brought it back.'

Someone started clapping. They were soon joined by the onlookers. Whistles of approval split the air, then the three constables were abruptly surrounded by the men and woman in green aprons. Their hands were shaken, their backs were pummelled. A beaming Monrol gave Macsen a hug, then moved on to Kanseen. Edeard, too, was swept up in his embrace. 'Thank you, thank you.'

'Sergeant Chae,' a deep voice boomed.

The stall holders fell quiet as Setersis came forward. Edeard had seen him a couple of times before, normally when he was complaining to Chae about the infrequency of constable patrols through the market. Setersis was the head of the Silvarum stall holders association, and through that had a seat on the city traders council; as such he had almost as much political influence as a Guild Council Master.

'Did I hear right?' Setersis asked. 'Did the constables finally come to our aid?'

For once Chae looked uncertain. 'We were able to assist.' He stopped glaring at Edeard, and produced an almost sympathetic expression. 'I was about to ask the more reckless members of my patrol to report what happened on the chase.'

'Reckless members, eh?' Setersis grinned at the three probationary constables. 'Yes, you are young, aren't you? Good for you. If we had more constables with balls we wouldn't be in the sorry state we are. Your pardon, my girl.'

'Granted,' Kanseen said graciously.

'Come then, so tell me what happened on the chase. Did you manage to accidentally drop the scum into the canal?'

'No, sir,' Edeard said. 'I'm afraid they got away on a gondola. They headed down towards the port.' Something made him hold back from mentioning that his ge-eagle was showing him the thieves had already passed through Forest Pool and were approaching Sampalok.

'None of the gondoliers would help us,' Macsen blurted. 'We asked them.'

'Ha! Fil-rats in human guise,' Setersis grunted. 'Still, you did a good job. I can't remember the last time a constable returned stolen goods.' He gave Chae a meaningful glance. The sergeant's lips tightened. 'You have my thanks. I'm sure my fellow stall-holders will show their appreciation next time your patrol ventures into the market.'

Edeard knew he was grinning like a fool. It didn't matter, so were Macsen and Kanseen. Then he finally caught sight of Dinlay, who looked like his closest family had just died.

Once the doctor announced Kavine would be all right, Chae declared that the patrol was over and they were going back to Jeavons station. He led them out of the market without another word. Edeard couldn't work out if they were in serious trouble or not; the sergeant's mind was perfectly shielded.

Macsen shot Boyd a direct longtalk query, which he shared with Edeard and Kanseen: 'What did Chae say?'

'Nothing much,' Boyd replied, equally furtive. 'He was yelling for you to stop. When none of you came back, he just concentrated on helping the stall holder. I had to hold the flesh together to slow the bleeding down. Lady! I thought I was going to faint there was so much blood. Monrol said they hacked him a couple of times with those blades to make him let go of the box. I wish I'd gone with you instead, but I just hesitated for that first second. I'm sorry.'

'Don't be,' Edeard said. 'The more I think about it, the more stupid I was. Chae was right.'

'What!' Macsen exclaimed out loud. He glanced at Chae, but the sergeant didn't seem to notice.

'There was four of them, and they had blades; six if you count the gondoliers. We could have been killed, and it would be my fault.'

'We got the box back.'

'Luck. That's all. Pure luck. The Lady smiled on us today. She won't tomorrow. We have to act like proper constables; stay together, work as a team.'

Macsen shook his head in dismay. Edeard gave Kanseen an apologetic shrug.

'I went with you,' she told him quietly. 'I got just as carried away. Don't try to claim this is all your fault.'

He nodded. Up ahead, Chae was still marching on, not looking round, his back rigid. Beside him, Dinlay was avoiding any communication with his friends. When they'd walked back to the market from the Great Major Canal, the three of them had been triumphant; now that whole mood was badly inverted. Right there, Edeard felt like turning round and heading off out of the city. It was going to be awful back at the station, he just knew it.

'That's not the kind of attitude the returning hero is supposed to wear,' Salrana told him, her longtalk conveying a lot of concern.

Edeard tipped his head up to give the sky a sheepish smile. 'I'm sorry. We did it, though, we actually chased off some thugs from a gang.'

'I know! I farsighted you the whole time. You were terrific, Edeard. I wish I'd chosen to be a constable.'

'Our sergeant doesn't share your opinion. And what's worse, he's right. We didn't behave properly.'

'Have you told the stall holder that?'

'That's not the point.'

'Yes it is, Edeard. You did good today. It doesn't matter how you did it. You helped someone. The Lady saw that, and she'll be pleased.'

'Sometimes you have to do the wrong thing—' he mouthed silently. Some good cheer returned as he tried to imagine what Akeem would have to say about all Chae's rules and procedures. It would be short and very succinct, he knew.

'What?' Salrana asked.

'Nothing. But thank you. I'm going to go back to the station now and do whatever it takes to put things right with my sergeant.'

'I'm always so proud of you, Edeard. Talk to me tonight, tell me what happens.'

'I will. Promise.'

When they got back to the station Chae's temper seemed to have vanished. Edeard was expecting to be shouted at as soon as they passed through the big gates. Instead Chae stood there with a genuinely weary expression on his worn face; for once his shielding had slipped enough for Edeard to sense just how tired his thoughts were. 'Small hall,' he told the squad.

The others dutifully trooped into the building. Edeard waited until they were through the doorway.

'It was my fault,' he told Chae. 'I encouraged the others to follow me. I didn't listen to you, and I ignored procedure.'

Chae studied him, his own mind becoming inscrutable again. 'I know. Now would you like to guess what will happen if Setersis hears I gave you all a bollocking?'

'Er, he'd probably take our side?'

'He would. Now grow up fast, lad; learn how things balance in this city. Come on, I need to talk to all of you.'

The other constables rose to their feet when Chae came into the small hall. Dinlay saluted smartly.

'Pack that in,' Chae said. His third hand shut the hall doors. 'Sit down.'

The squad exchanged mildly perplexed looks. Except for Dinlay who was still keeping himself apart.

'So how do you think we did?' Chae said.

'Wrong procedure,' Kanseen ventured.

'Yeah, wrong procedure. But we saved a stall holder's life. Some gang scum got a nasty surprise. And we recovered the stolen merchandise. Those are all the plus points. The constables will be popular in Silvarum's markets for a couple of weeks. That's good, there's nothing wrong with that. I'd even go so far as to say the rule of law was upheld. Edeard?'

'Sir?'

'Did your eagle follow them back home?'

'Er, yes, sir. I watched them go into Sampalok. It's a building not far from the Grand Major Canal. They haven't come out yet.'

'So we know which building they probably live in. What do we do about that? Do we put together a big squad and go in and arrest them?'

'Probably not.'

'Why? They've broken the law. Shouldn't they be brought before a court?'

'Too much effort for a minor crime,' Macsen said.

'That's right. So bring the eagle back, please.'

'Sir.' He sent a command through the sky above Makkathran, and felt the eagle soar round, dipping the wing vertically back to the ground. It began to flash back over the big canal.

Chae was giving him an odd smile. 'And you really can longtalk that far, can't you?'

'Sir?'

'All right. Now, I'm not mad at you, any of you. So just relax, and for the Lady's sake try to listen to what I'm about to tell you. What you did today was what you joined up for, preventing criminal activity and protecting the people of this city. That's good, it shows you have a sense of duty, and loyalty to each other. Technically, it's my duty to get you all through the next two months; then you're on your own, and I start with the next batch of hopeless youths. My responsibility to you ends then. But what I have got to try and instil in you before you go out by yourselves is a sense of proportion, and maybe even some political awareness. Let's think about this. Those gang members are going to be a little shaken by Edeard's strength, and furious that they came back empty-handed after taking so much risk. Next time they go out they'll want to make sure their crime produces some results. So they'll go the extra mile to make sure. Boyd, what would you do in their shoes? How would you make certain?'

'Take a pistol?'

'Very likely. So whatever constable patrol tackles them, is going to get shot at.'

'Hold on,' Edeard said. 'We can't let that stop us. If we become so afraid of cracking down on the gangs that we do nothing, they've won.'

'Correct. So?'

'Next time, we chase them out but that's it,' Macsen said.

'Good option. Though actually your response was about right. I didn't behave too well out there, myself – mainly because I was worried about you lot running off like that. There's an old natural law that says for every action there is an equal and opposite reaction. If those gang members come into a market in broad daylight and use a blade on a stall holder, then they must expect a reaction from the constables. They were the ones who overstepped the mark on this occasion. But that still doesn't mean three of you can go chasing off after four of them. With or without blades and pistols, you were outnumbered. That has "tragedy" written all over it. So that was wrong. It was also wrong to leave a member of the public injured and unattended. You didn't stop to assess, which is the most critical thing to do; you also let raw instinct override my orders, which is the greater crime no matter how much you thought yourselves in the right. I'm supposed to be training you to respond to situations in a professional manner, and I clearly haven't drilled it in hard enough. Now I'm quite prepared to write today's lapses off to first-time excitement and the general confusion. You need experience more than you do theory, so nobody's getting disciplined and there'll be no recriminations. But understand this, it *must not* happen again. Next time we encounter a criminal act in progress you follow procedure to the letter. Do I make myself clear?'

'Yes, Sergeant,' they chorused.

'Then we understand each other. So take tonight off, get yourselves down to the Olovan's Eagle for a drink or ten, and be back in this hall for another dose of theory first thing tomorrow morning. I'll also go against my own policy to tell you something: unless you completely screw up your graduation exams you will all pass your probation.'

'I was useless,' Dinlay complained. 'I just froze. I was just so useless.' He gulped down more of his beer.

Edeard looked over at Macsen, who simply shrugged. They'd been in the Olovan's Eagle for an hour, and Dinlay had said very little else. It was a small miracle they'd got him to join them in the first place. He hadn't said ten words since Chae dismissed them from the small hall.

'You froze for a couple of seconds, that's all,' Kanseen said. 'That means you were close to Chae when he ordered us all to stop and help the stall keeper. You couldn't do anything else.'

'I should have ignored him like you did. I didn't. I failed.'

'Oh sweet Lady,' Kanseen grumbled and sat back in her own chair. She was wearing a blue and white dress with orange flowers. It wasn't the most stylish garment Edeard had seen in Makkathran, nor the newest, but she looked good in it. Her short hair still set her apart from all the other girls, who wore theirs fashionably long. But he rather liked it this way, it suited her, setting off a flattish nose and thin dark-green eyes. Now he'd known her for a few months she wasn't quite as intimidating as she had been at the start. Not that he thought of her as anything other than a colleague and friend.

'Nobody failed,' Edeard said. 'This afternoon was chaos, that's all. And you helped Chae with the stall holder.'

'I froze,' Dinlay said wretchedly. 'I let you all down. I let my family down. They expect me to be the station captain within ten years, you know. My father was.'

'Let's have another drink,' Macsen said.

'Oh yes, that'll solve everything,' Kanseen said sourly.

Macsen gave her a wink, then shot a longtalk order to one of the tavern waitresses. Something else must have been said. Edeard caught her flash him a mock-indignant smile.

How does he do that? It's not what he says, it's his whole attitude. And why can't I do it? Edeard sat back to give his friend a critical examination. Macsen was sitting in the middle of a small couch with Evala on one side, and Nicolar on the other. Both girls were leaning in towards him. They laughed at his jokes, and gasped and giggled when he told them what happened in the market, an extravagant tale of thrills and bravery Edeard didn't quite recognize. He supposed Macsen was quite handsome, with his light brown hair and flat jaw. His brown eyes were constantly filled with amusement that bordered on nefarious, which was an additional attraction. It helped that he always dressed well whenever they went out. Tonight he'd pulled on fawn-coloured trousers cut from the softest suede, belted by woven black strands of leather. His sky-blue satin shirt just showed under a dark-emerald frock coat.

See, I'd never have the courage to wear a combination like that, but he carries it off perfectly. The epitome of a grand family's junior son.

In fact the rest of them looked quite drab in comparison. Edeard used to be quietly pleased with his own black jacket, tailored trousers, and knee-high boots. Now he'd been relegated to the poor friend who Macsen's girls felt sorry for and tried to pair up with their own charity case girlfriend. On which note . . . Edeard tried not to stare over at Boyd who was sitting on the opposite side of their table, his face bewitched. Clemensa was next to him, chattering away about her day. She was easily the same height as Boyd, and must have been close in weight, too. Edeard couldn't help the way his eyes always slipped down to the front of her very low-cut dress every time she bent over, which was suspiciously frequent.

The waitress brought over the tray of beer Macsen had ordered. Dinlay immediately reached for his tankard. Edeard fumbled with the money pouch in his pocket.

'Oh no, my round,' Macsen said. His third hand deposited some coins on the empty tray. 'Thank you,' he said sincerely. The waitress smiled. Evala and Nicolar pressed in closer.

Edeard sighed. *He's always so polite, as well. Is that what does it?*

'Boyd,' Macsen called out loudly. 'Close your mouth, man, you're drooling.'

Boyd snapped his jaw shut and glared at Macsen. A bright flush crept up his face.

'You pay him no heed,' Clemensa said. She brought a hand up to Boyd's cheek, turned his head and kissed him. 'A girl likes it when a man pays attention.'

Edeard thought Boyd might faint with happiness.

'Got to go,' Dinlay muttered. 'Back in a minute.' He stood up and swayed unsteadily, then headed for the archway at the back of the saloon where the washrooms were.

The fact that there were toilets on an upper floor was one of the many revelations about city buildings which had taken Edeard a time to get used to. But then a tavern which sprawled over many floors was also a novelty. As was the pale-orange light radiating out of the ceiling that was nearly as bright as daylight. The first night they'd visited the Olovan's Eagle he'd wondered why there was no straw on the floor. Life in the city was so *civilized*. Sitting here in the warmth, with a window showing him the lights outside stretching all the way to the Lyot Sea, good beer, comfortable with his friends, he found it hard to fit this with the crime and gangs who cast such a shadow over the streets outside.

'What are you doing?' Kanseen hissed at Macsen. 'He's had too much to drink, already.'

'Best thing for him. He's not a fighting drunk. Another couple of pints and he'll fall asleep. Next thing he'll know it's tomorrow and we'll be so busy he won't have time to brood. Tonight's what we need to get him through.'

Kanseen looked like she wanted to protest but couldn't think how. She looked at Edeard.

'Makes sense,' he admitted.

Macsen placed another order with the waitress.

'My liver has to sacrifice its life so we can get Dinlay through graduation,' Kanseen complained.

'In the constables we stick together,' Edeard said and raised his tankard. 'To the memory of our livers. Who needs 'em?'

They drank to that.

'Don't worry,' Macsen said. 'I've made arrangements. Our beer is watered. Dinlay's has two shots of vodka in each pint.'

Even Kanseen had to laugh. She tipped her tankard to Macsen. 'You're so . . .'

'Beautifully evil?' Edeard suggested, giving his tankard a mortified stare. *This is watered? I couldn't tell; it tastes the same.*

'Spot on,' she said.

'I thank you.' Macsen put his arms round the shoulders of the girls and pulled them in; kissing Evala first, then Nicolar.

'Not just tonight we've got to worry about,' Boyd said.

'Does our Boyd need to worry about tonight?' Macsen asked Clemensa.

She gave Boyd a hungry look. 'He certainly doesn't. After what

457

you did today, you're all heroes in my book. That needs a lot of rewarding.'

'He's going to want to prove himself,' Boyd said. 'Nothing the sergeant said is going to hold him back. Next time we come across a fight or a robbery, Dinlay will be at the front and aching to take on the bad guy.'

'I figured that too,' Edeard said.

'We'll have to be ready,' Kanseen said. 'We can't hold him back, that would make it worse. But we can be up there with him.'

'Everyone together,' Macsen said. He raised his tankard. 'No matter what.'

'No matter what,' they toasted with a roar.

Edeard still couldn't taste the water.

The four ge-monkeys from Jeavons constable station walked slowly along the street, looking like pallbearers as they carried a comatose Dinlay home to his dormitory bed.

Kanseen kept looking back to check. 'Do you think he'll be all right?'

'Not really,' Edeard said. 'If Macsen was serious about the vodka, he's going to have the hangover from Honious tomorrow morning.' He turned to inspect the ge-monkeys himself. Using them wasn't the ideal solution, but it was better than him and Kanseen hauling Dinlay along. Boyd and Macsen had stayed on at the tavern with the girls. There were private rooms upstairs which they'd no doubt be using that night. Edeard was trying to keep his envy in check.

'Macsen!' she exclaimed.

'He's not so bad. Actually, I'd rather have him by my side than Dinlay.'

'Some choice.'

'And you're preferable to all of them.' All that beer and now the balmy night air were making him light-headed. That must have been why he said it.

Kanseen said nothing for a while as they walked back along the long, nearly deserted street. 'I'm not looking for anyone right now,' she said solemnly. 'I just broke up with a man. We were engaged. It . . . ended badly. He wanted a nice traditional girl, one who knew her place.'

'I'm sorry. But I have to say it's his loss.'

'Thank you, Edeard.'

They walked on a while more, shadows shifting as they passed under the bright orange light patches on the outside of the buildings.

'I don't know what it is about you,' she said quietly. 'I'm not just talking about how strong your third hand is. You stand out. You're what I imagine the sons of noble families are supposed to be like, or were like before they got so rich and fat.'

'Nothing noble about me.'

'Nobility doesn't come from a bloodline, Edeard, it comes from within. Where was your village?'

'Ashwell, in the Rulan province.'

'Doesn't mean anything, I'm afraid. I don't know any geography beyond the Iguru Plain.'

'Ashwell was a long way past there, right on the edge of the wild lands. I'll show you on a map if I can find one. It took a year for us to travel here.'

'Gift me.'

'What? Oh.' Edeard concentrated, trying to find a recollection that would do his home justice. Spring, he decided, when the trees were bursting into life, and the sky was bright, and the winds warm. He and some other children had gone outside the rampart walls and taken the long route round to the top of the cliffs where they looked down on the cosy buildings sheltering below.

He heard a soft pull of breath, and realized how heavily involved in the memory he'd become, lacing it with melancholy.

'Oh, Edeard, it's so beautiful. What happened? Why did you leave?'

'It was attacked by bandits,' he said stiffly. In all the time he'd spent in the station dormitory he'd never told his new friends the truth about Ashwell. All they knew was that he'd lost his family to bandits.

'I'm sorry,' she said. For once she dropped the veil round her thoughts, allowing him to sense the sympathy. 'Was it very bad?'

'Salrana and I survived. And five others.'

'Oh, Lady! Edeard.' Her hand held his arm.

'Don't worry. I've come to terms with it. Except for losing my Master, Akeem. I still miss him.' The emotional currents welling up in his thoughts were both unexpected and alarmingly strong. He truly thought he'd put all this sentiment and mourning behind him. Now all he'd done was picture his old home, and the feelings were rushing back as strong as the day it had happened.

'You should talk to one of the Lady's Mothers. They give excellent council.'

'Yeah. Maybe.' He made his legs work again. 'Come on, I have a notion Chae isn't going to be too gentle with us tomorrow.'

The ge-monkeys laid Dinlay out on his mattress and pulled a thin blanket over him. He never woke, just groaned and shuffled round a bit. Edeard couldn't be bothered to take his friend's boots off, he was suddenly incredibly tired himself. He barely managed to remove his own boots and trousers. The dormitory's ge-chimps scampered about, collecting his clothes for the laundry.

Of course, now he was actually lying down, his mind was too restless to deliver the sleep his body craved. He sent a thought to the main ceiling's rosette pattern of illumination, and it dimmed to a nebula-glow. That was about the only reaction the city buildings ever did have to human thought. The ge-chimps quietened down. Faint sounds from downstairs whispered through the big empty room, the usual comings and goings of the night shift officers. Edeard had never really got used to the way walls in the city curved. Back in Ashwell, walls were laid out in straight lines; the nine sides of his old Guild courtyard were considered pretty adventurous architecture. Here in the dormitory, the oval bed alcoves were almost rooms in their own right, with arching entrances twice Edeard's height. He liked to imagine the dormitory was actually some kind of aristocratic bedroom, and that maybe the race which created Makkathran had more than two genders. Hence the six beds. That would make the station an important building. He couldn't quite assign a use for the honeycomb warren of little rooms below ground which were used as prisoner cells and store rooms. As he thought about it, he let his farsight drift down through the translucent grey panorama of the station's structure. The image was such that it seemed to surround him, engulf him. Gravity pulled at his mind, and he sank ghost-like through the floor of the basement. There were fissures in the ground beneath, smooth fissures that looped and bent as they wound deeper and deeper. Some were no wider than his fingers, while others were broad enough to walk through. They branched and intersected, forming a convoluted filigree that, to his quixotic thoughts, resembled the veins within a human body. He felt water pulsing through several of them, while strong winds blew along others. Several of the smaller fissures contained threads of violet light which appeared to burn without ever consuming the fissure walls. He tried to touch them with his third hand, only for it to slide through as if he were grasping at a mirage.

His farsight expanded, becoming tenuous. The fissures spread away from the station, burrowing under the street outside, knitting with other extensive hollow filigrees which supported the surrounding buildings. Edeard gasped in wonder as his farsight grew and grew; the more he relaxed the more he could perceive. Slivers of colour shone through his mind, as if this shadow world was growing in texture. He couldn't even sense the dormitory any more. The station was a small glowing jewel embedded in a vast whorl of similar multichromic sparks.

Makkathran.

Edeard experienced the wonder of its thoughts. Immersing himself in a melody where a single beat lasted for years, chords so grand they could shake the very ground apart if they ever gained substance. The city slept the long sleep of all giants;

untainted by the pitiful frantic tempo of parasitic humans crawling through its physical extremities.

It was content.

Edeard bathed in its ancient serenity, and slowly fell into a dreamless sleep.

6

'How long?' Corrie-Lyn asked.

Aaron growled again and ignored her. He was inside a gym cage that the starship's cabin had extruded; testing the flexibility and strength of his restored upper torso. Pulling weight, pushing weight, bending, twisting. Working up a sweat as endurance was evaluated, measuring the oxygen consumption of the new flesh, blood flow rate, nerve speed . . .

'You knew Qatux could do it,' she whined. 'So you must know how long it'll take.'

Aaron gritted his teeth as gravity shifted off vertical and increased, forcing him to pull the handle he was gripping while stretching at the same time. Biononics reported the tendons were approaching their tear limit.

His patience was also undergoing a strenuous work out. They'd been back in the *Artful Dodger* for fifteen hours, a time which Corrie-Lyn had devoted to drinking and moaning. She now considered handing over Inigo's memories to be a terrible betrayal, not to mention a bad idea. A really bad idea. Stupid actually. As she kept saying.

'So it'll have like a mini-Inigo hanging round inside its own brain?'

Aaron took a look at the oxygen usage in his shoulder muscles. The levels were only a couple of points off the original muscle. Not bad for a couple of days. Drugs and biononics had done what they could, the rest of it was down to good old-fashioned exercise. A decent callisthenics program should see the levels equalize over the next week or so. He shut the gym down.

'Something like that,' he said.

Corrie-Lyn blinked at the unexpected answer. She rolled over on the couch and reached for the pitcher of tasimion margarita. 'So you ask the mini-Inigo a question . . .'

'And Qatux answers it for us. Yes.'

'What a load of bullshit.'

'We'll see.' He slipped his T-shirt off, and examined his torso. The membrane was starting to peel off. Underneath, the new skin was tender, but at last the colour was deepening to the same shade as the rest of him. 'I'm going to take a shower,' he said.

'You're shaping up good,' she giggled. 'Need a hand in there?'

Aaron rolled his eyes. 'No thanks.' He now had a strong theory of his own why Inigo had run away from Living Dream, and it wasn't anything to do with Last Dreams or the pressure of being idolized by billions. *Maybe she only turned into this after he left?*

The gym sank into the wall, and there was a moment's pause before the shower cubicle extended out from the same section. He slipped his shorts off and stepped in as Corrie-Lyn let out a wolf-whistle. He must be recuperating, his cock was stirring. But if Qatux did come up with a notion of where the reluctant messiah was hiding out, she'd be more necessary than ever. So he turned the spore temperature down about as low as it would go, and thought of other things. Unfortunately, with a memory that didn't reach back past Ethan's appointment he didn't have much to mull over. Except his odd dreams. That horse ride . . . he'd been young. So it must have been his childhood. Seemed pleasant enough.

After he'd showered, they carried on their research into the odd Raiel who'd agreed to help them. Clued in by what it had said they'd sent their u-shadows out into the unisphere to search for files on the history of Far Away during the Starflyer War. The first surprise was to find just over a million files on the period available. It took eight hours for them to filter it down to relevant and useful information. Even then, there was no direct evidence Qatux had been there.

There were endless documents on Bradley Johansson's team of Guardians chasing the Starflyer back to its lair, and how they joined up with an odd security team that Nigel Sheldon assigned to help them. Admiral Kime was one of them, of course; that was a common history text. His audacious hyperglider flight over Mount Herculaneum, and subsequent rescue by Nigel himself. Anna the Judas. Oscar the martyr. Paula Myo and the Navy interdiction squad, Cat's Claws.

'I didn't know it was Nigel who originally sent the Cat to Far Away,' Corrie-Lyn exclaimed. 'What was he thinking of?' She was sober again after a meal and a couple of alcohol-binder aerosols. Aspects of the search seemed to genuinely interest her.

'Be fair, he couldn't see the future.'

There were some appendices that claimed the pursuit was aided by an alien. But the context was strange. The Bose motile was known to be part of Nigel's secret clique at the time. There were no references to a Raiel. One file said the Barsoomian group helped Johansson because he'd brought their genetic holy grail to Far Away. Again, nothing as to what that grail actually was.

'Let's try another angle,' Aaron said. He told his u-shadow to find all files relating to a Commonwealth citizen called Tiger Pansy around the time of the Starflyer War.

The cabin's portal projected a rather startling image.

'No way,' Corrie-Lyn said.

Aaron stared at the woman in equal disbelief. She was a complete mess. Terrible hair; bad facial reprofiling ruining the symmetry of her eyes, nose, and lips, appalling cosmetics making them appear worse; ridiculous breast enlargements; tight, short clothes that no girl over twenty could ever get away with wearing, let alone this one who must have been close to rejuvenation time again.

'Signed to the Wayside Production company on Oaktier,' Corrie-Lyn read off her exovision. 'Appeared in a large number of their, aha, *productions*. Left them in the last year of the Starflyer War. No subsequent information. Nothing; no residency listing on any planetary cybersphere, no records of rejuvenation treatment, no bodyloss certificate. She simply dropped out of sight.'

Aaron shook himself and cancelled the projection. 'Easy enough at the time. There was a mass migration from the Lost23 worlds which the Primes had invaded. After that, it got even more chaotic.'

'Coincidence?'

'The Raiel are not known for their lies. Maybe Qatux did marry her. She certainly looks the emotional type.'

'That's not quite how I'd describe her,' Corrie-Lyn muttered. 'And how did she get to Far Away? The planet was virtually cut off for decades until the starlines started flying there.'

'She must have been with the Johansson team. I don't think it's relevant.'

'No, but it's interesting. Why would a Raiel go there?'

'You want to ask?'

She shook her head. 'Naa, too intimidated.'

'I'll ask for you.'

'No. Let's just drop it.'

'You're right though. It is interesting. I was obviously given the correct information. Qatux helps humans.'

'He said he used to. Until Tiger Pansy was killed.'

'By the Cat, no less. That'd be enough to shock anyone out of their dependency routine, no matter how delightful and ingrained.'

'Yes, well, thank Ozzie, Paula Myo finally caught her.'

'Yeah. And in about another four thousand years we can all share the joy of her coming out of suspension.'

'Urrgh. I won't be around for that no matter what.'

'Qatux knew Paula Myo,' Aaron said. 'I wonder if that's relevant.'

'How could it be?'

He waited for a moment to see if his subconscious produced any clues. It didn't. 'No idea.'

The *Artful Dodger*'s smartcore told them the *High Angel* was calling. 'Please prepare for teleport,' the alien starship told them.

'Oh bollocks,' Corrie-Lyn said as she clambered to her feet. 'I really don't like this—'

The cabin vanished. Once again they were standing in the large circular chamber facing Qatux.

'—part.' She wrinkled her nose in distaste.

Aaron bowed to the Raiel. 'Thank you for obliging us.'

'You are welcome,' the big alien whispered.

'Were you successful?'

'I have lived through Inigo's early life. It was not that distinguished.'

Aaron looked straight at Qatux, avoiding Corrie-Lyn. His gaiamotes revealed the pique which that last remark had triggered in her mind. 'None the less, it must have provided you with an understanding of his behaviour patterns.'

'Guilt drives him.'

'Guilt?'

'He spent his whole life hiding what he was from everyone, his family, those he loved, and his enemies.'

'Are you talking about the Protectorate?'

'Yes. He was aware of their constant surveillance. Towards the end he took perverse enjoyment from maintaining the illusion that he was an ordinary Advancer. But such a lie weighed heavily on him. It was one of the main reasons he volunteered for duty at Centurion Station.'

'All right, I can buy into that scenario. Given the circumstances of his later life, where do you think he might have gone?'

'Hanko.'

Which wasn't the kind of answer Aaron was bracing himself for. Not even close. 'The Second47 world?'

'Yes.'

'I know that was where Anagaska's population originated from, but they were forced off because it became uninhabitable after the Prime attack. There's nothing there, not any more.'

'Inigo was always fascinated by what he considered his true

467

ancestral home,' Qatux said. 'Remember he did not belong in Anagaska's Advancer culture. Hanko gave him a psychological ground point, amplified by an ancestor obsession rooted in his psyche due to the loss of his father so soon after his birth. Such a trauma affects any child, Higher as much as Advancer, especially when the event is regarded with such bitterness by his mother.'

'A wound she kept open, unintentionally or otherwise.'

'Correct. Hanko provided the perfect solution to someone as displaced as Inigo. A real place, yet at the same time unattainable. The illusion which could not be broken. He often contributed to charities which supplemented the official government Restoration teams. A telling point. He was never a wealthy man on Anagaska.'

'And you think he's gone back there?'

'If he abandoned Living Dream due to his own uncertainty on the direction it was taking, I would assign it a very high possibility. He is Higher, the radiation and climate will have little physical effect on him.'

'There are a lot of unknowns in this assumption.'

'If you had certainties you would not be here.'

'I apologize. I was expecting you to say he had fled the Commonwealth, or there was some secret cabal devoted to helping him. But Hanko would certainly explain why no one has found him.'

'Will you go there?'

Aaron looked over at Corrie-Lyn, who looked very puzzled. 'Yes,' he said.

*

'Ambition and good intentions are always an excellent starting point,' Likan said. 'Then before you know it you come right smack up against reality. You either adapt, become realistic and respond in kind, or you flounder along until you sink under the weight of your own capitulations. Now I know those of you in this auditorium aren't quitters. Hell, quitters couldn't afford these ticket prices.' He grinned round at the murmur of dutiful amusement. 'In life, either you get pressured or you apply pressure. Same for business—'

Three rows back from the small podium, Araminta glanced round at her fellow entrepreneurs. It was like the gathering of a clone army. All eager young business people, smartly dressed and sharply styled; hanging on to every word the richest man on the planet had to say about acquiring that same wealth. Each one of them desperate for a tiny hint of which way the market would go, a quip about financial trends, what new law to watch out for, a state project that was worth trying to bandwagon.

If they thought the Sheldonite would give them that, they were in for a big disappointment. Basic research: Likan was a ruthless man. He was here in Colwyn City to give another of his How-I-Made-It lectures for publicity and prestige, not to help fledgling rivals. A high profile helped his business, and in addition he got a buzz out of being adulated. This whole evening exemplified his favourite catchphrase: win-win.

Bovey would hate all this, she knew, and smiled secretively at the knowledge. Sitting amidst the faithful, such thoughts were near-sacrilege. But then Bovey had a little bit of a hang-up about the genuinely rich and powerful. All politicians were worthless incompetents. All billionaires corrupt criminals. It was one of those quirks she was fond of. It could be quite funny hearing his youngest self, the biological fourteen-year-old, raging on about the cabinet secretary for social affairs. Mr Bovey had the true hatred of every self-employed person for bureaucracy, and the taxes it demanded to keep functioning; and, worse, expanding. In her mind, fourteen-year-olds didn't have adult concerns like that, it was all angst and impossible aspirations at that age. She recalled it well.

Araminta sighed warm-heartedly. Louder than she intended. She saw Likan's gaze flick in her direction, though his speech never faltered. Her lips pressed together in self-censure.

The speech was exactly what she was expecting. Plenty of motivational talk, a few anecdotes, a whole load of financial-services product-placement, and an excess of toothy smiles during the pauses for applause and laughter. Araminta even clapped along with the rest of them. It was all standard stuff, but there were some nuggets among the waffle. She was interested in his early years, how to make the jump from a small operation like hers up to a more corporate level. According to Likan, advancement was all down to risk, and how much of it you were prepared to take. He mentioned self-confidence a lot, along with determination and hard work. Araminta wondered if he'd ever met Laril. Now *that* would be an interesting conversation.

Likan finished, and was provided with a standing ovation. Araminta got to her feet with the rest of them, and applauded half-heartedly. She wished he'd been more specific, maybe given some case-study examples. The chairman of the Colwyn Small Business Association thanked their distinguished guest, and announced refreshments were available in the function room outside.

By the time Araminta made it out of the auditorium, her fellow small business owners were forming tight little groups to chatter away to each other while they gulped down the free drinks and canapés. From the snippets she overheard on her way to the bar the majority ran virtual companies. Talk was about expansion curves and cross-promotional market penetration and share options and when to merge. Men glanced at her as she walked past. There were welcoming smiles, even a few pings to her u-shadow, offering compliments and invitations. Her u-shadow didn't respond – pings were *so* adolescent. *If you want to take me out to dinner have the courage to ask me to my face.* She'd chosen a deep-turquoise dress that complemented her hair colour. Strictly speaking the neckline was low and the hem high for a business occasion; but she now had the confidence to buck convention – at least on a small level. Independence and all that exposure to Cressida had given her that.

'Pear water,' she told the barman.

'Interesting choice.'

She turned to find Likan standing behind her. For someone

so rich, his appearance was puzzling. The skin on his face was slightly puffy, with flushed cheeks as if he were permanently out of breath. His biological age was higher than usual, fixed in his late thirties rather than the mid-twenties everyone else favoured. The clothes he wore were always expensive, but never quite gelled, as if he got his dress sense from adverts. His jacket with a shark-skin shimmer was chic, but not with that particular purple shirt and green neck twister. And the brown shoes were best worn when gardening.

'I have to work later tonight,' she said. 'Can't afford lack of judgement from alcohol.'

'Good self-control. I like that.'

'Thank you,' she said levelly.

'I got the impression you weren't impressed tonight.'

People nearby were discreetly looking their way. Likan's voice was as forceful as it had been on the podium. That at least gave the impression of a strong personality.

Araminta sipped her pear water, wondering how to play this. 'I was hoping for more detail,' she told him.

'What kind of detail? Come on, you paid for your ticket, you're entitled.'

'Okay: small company, doing well. Needs to step up a level. Do you re-invest profits and ride a gradual expansion with each project slightly larger than the last, or do you take the bank loan and jump ten levels.'

'How small a company?'

'One woman band, supported by some bots.'

'Company product?'

'Property development.'

'Good choice for a start up. High profitability relative to scale. There is a ceiling, though, especially with one person. After the first three properties there should be enough profit to take on more staff. With that you move on from one property at a time, and start multiple developments. Timing for that has never been better, property is the hot item here today thanks to Living Dream.'

'Everything is relative. With that demand, a developer has to buy high.'

'Then this developer should buy a whole street that's in decline. It's a profit multiplier, the individual unit prices rise because you've taken the entire street upmarket and made it desirable.'

'That's a big step.'

'The level of risk you are prepared to undertake is proportional to your growth potential. If you don't take it you are declaring this far and no further. That will define your life. I don't think you want that.'

'Question: would you advise the staff expansion be accomplished by becoming multiple?'

'No.'

'Why not?'

'Going multiple only seems like a solution to a solo act. Ultimately it's a lifestyle choice rather than a business one. Ask yourself what you can accomplish by being multiple that you can't by good aggressive management. As you came to listen to me tonight I know you're already thinking ahead, thinking big. Property is a foundation stone for a corporate empire. A good one, I still have a vast property portfolio, but to achieve real market dominance you must diversify and interlock your interests. That's what Sheldon did. He used his interstellar transport monopoly as a cash source to fund industrial, commercial, and financial enterprises on a hundred worlds. At the time of the Starflyer War he was effectively Emperor of the Commonwealth.'

'Do you want to be our emperor?'

'Yes.'

Araminta was slightly shaken by his bluntness. She thought he was somehow calling her bluff. 'Why?'

'Because it's a position where you can do whatever you want. The ultimate freedom. Isn't that what we all strive for?'

'With power comes responsibility.'

'That's what politicians tell you when they want your vote. There's a difference between political power and financial power, especially out here in the External Worlds. I'd like to demonstrate that to you.'

'How would you do that?'

'Come and stay with me at my home for a weekend. See first hand what I've achieved. Decide if that's what you want for yourself.'

'What about your wives?' It was common knowledge just how staunchly committed he was to replicating his idol's ideology and life, including (or perhaps especially) the harem.

'What about them?'

'Won't they mind my visit?'

'No. They'll be joining us in bed.'

That'll teach me; you can't be more direct to my face than that. She was pleased with the way she kept her reaction in check, no startled expression, no give-away body language – squaring the shoulders, straightening the back. In effect telling him she could hold her own against him any day. 'I accept,' she said as if it was some kind of request to review finance statements.

'I knew I was right about you,' he said.

'In what way?'

'You know yourself, you know what you want. That's always dangerous.'

'To whom?'

'To everyone else. That's what makes you so desirable.'

'Win-win, then,' she mocked.

*

The *Alexis Denken* slid comfortably into the big airlock at the base of the Raiel dome stalk. Behind it, the stars vanished as the wall materialized again. Paula stood up, pulled wrinkles out of her suit jacket self-consciously, and straightened her spine. The *High Angel* teleported her into Qatux's private chamber. Raiel homes were traditionally split into three sections: public, residence, and private. You had to be a very good friend indeed to be invited beyond the public. The circular chamber had a pale-blue floor while, in keeping with tradition, the ceiling was invisible somewhere overhead. Around her, silver and grey walls rippled as if water was flowing down them, yet there was no sound, no dampness in the air. Beyond the cavorting surface, images of planetscapes and strange galaxies writhed insubstantially. However, one image remained firm and clear, a human face that Paula knew only too well.

She inclined her head to the big alien who occupied the centre of the chamber.

'Paula, I rejoice you are here.'

'It's been a long time, Qatux. How are you?'

'I am well. If I were a human, I would be fit.'

'I am glad.'

'I have risen to the *High Angel*'s fifth echelon.'

'How many are there?'

'Five.'

Paula laughed, she'd forgotten Qatux's sly humour. 'So you're the captain, then.'

'I have that honour.'

'Congratulations.'

'And you, Paula, do you continue to prosper?'

'I continue to be very busy. For me that's about the same thing.'

'That is to be expected. There are few of your species who remain in their bodies for as long as you have.'

'It's also why I'm here. I need information.'

'Just like the good old days. How intriguing.'

Paula cocked her head to one side as she regarded the big alien. That phrase was slightly out of kilter. Qatux's eye clusters remained steady on her. Long ago it would never have been so bold as to tease her. But then long ago it had been something of a wreck, until the Far Away mission came along. Of course, she'd been very different then, too. 'The starship *Alini* has just visited the Raiel dome. Can you tell me if these people were on board?' Her u-shadow retrieved image files for Aaron and Corrie-Lyn.

'They were,' Qatux whispered.

474

'What did they want?'

'I believe their mission was confidential.'

She gave her old friend a shrewd glance, not liking the conclusions she was drawing. 'It was you who saw them, wasn't it?'

'Yes.' The bottom set of tentacle limbs shivered slightly, the Raiel equivalent of a blush.

'Qatux, did you review Inigo's memories?'

'I did.'

'Why?' she asked, genuinely concerned. 'I thought that had stopped centuries ago. Tiger . . .' She couldn't finish. Her gaze was drawn to the face suspended behind the wall. Tiger Pansy's silly carefree grin looked hauntingly back at her, obviously captured at a moment when the woman was blissfully happy.

'I know,' the Raiel whispered. 'It is not a return to my addiction, I assure you. There would be few Raiel indeed who could refuse the opportunity of experiencing Inigo's mind. He dreams the Void, Paula. The Void! That evil enigma bedevils us to a degree which humans will never appreciate.'

'All right,' Paula ran her hand back through her hair, making an effort to ignore the uncomfortable personal side effects which the case was kicking up. 'Inigo's memorycell was stolen from a clinic on Anagaska. Why did you help Aaron?'

'I did not know the memories were stolen. He arrived in an ultradrive starship. It was intimated that he was a representative of ANA:Governance. In truth, he never confirmed that. I am sorry. I believe I was *had*. How stupid, me of all Raiel. The deception was quite simple.'

'Don't beat yourself up over it. Happens to the best of us. So what did he want to know?'

'He asked me to guess where Inigo might be.'

'Clever man. Which is curious in itself. There aren't many humans who knew of your little problem. One of them must have joined up to a Faction. So what did you tell him?'

'I guessed Inigo might be on Hanko.'

'Hanko? But it's just a radioactive ruin.' She stopped, examining the idea. 'But, Earth aside, it is his ethnic birthworld. Still, an odd choice.'

'Are you aware he was born Higher?'

'No I was not! That has never been on any file. Are you sure?'

Qatux's biggest tentacles waved in agitation. 'I am forty years of his early life, Paula. Through me you are talking to the young Inigo.'

'If ANA:Governance and I didn't know, then it's pretty certain very few other people did, either. That changes his whole profile. No wonder nobody could ever find him. As a Higher he has much greater personal resources.'

'Will you go after Aaron and Corrie-Lyn?'

'I'm not sure. I hadn't envisaged Aaron being so close to finding Inigo. But even if he is on Hanko it'll take Aaron a while to actually track him down. I need to consult with ANA: Governance on this. Thank you for helping, Qatux.'

'You are welcome, Paula. Always.'

She was on the verge of asking to be teleported back to her ship when she hesitated. 'What do the Raiel think of the Pilgrimage?'

'That it is incredibly foolish. Opening the Dyson Alpha barrier was one thing, but this takes your obduracy to a whole new level. Why does ANA:Governance allow it?'

Paula sighed. 'I have no idea. Humans always want to test their boundaries, it's an instinctive thing.'

'It is a stupid thing.'

'We're not as old as you. We don't have species-wide wisdom, let alone responsibility.'

'Higher humans do.'

'The tenet of universal responsibility is the root of their culture, but as individuals they have a long way to go. And as for ANA, it's like the intellectual equivalent of primordial ooze in there; who knows what's going to come wiggling out triumphantly at the end of the day. I'm beginning to doubt ANA: Governance's ability to keep order.'

'Are you serious?'

'I don't know,' she admitted. 'This whole event has me badly troubled. There are too many people playing with catastrophic unknowns. Part of me, the old part that worships order, wants to shut down the entire Pilgrimage project. It's obviously a monstrous folly. Yet the liberal side of me agrees that these people have a right to seek happiness, especially when nothing in the Commonwealth appeals to them. It's indicative of our cultural heritage that we cannot provide a home for everyone.'

'But Paula, their "right" to seek the solution of perfection in the Void will endanger the rest of the galaxy. That right cannot be permitted.'

'Quite. And yet, we don't have conclusive proof that the Void will respond the way you claim.'

Qatux was silent, as if startled. 'You doubt us, Paula?'

'Humans need to know things for themselves. It is our nature, Qatux.'

'I understand that. I am sorry for you.'

'We're being too melancholy. I give you my word I'm working to try and sort out this mess.'

'As always you are honourable. I hope you succeed. I would not like to see our two species fall into conflict.'

'We won't.'

The *High Angel* teleported Paula back into the cabin of the *Alexis Denken*. Like all modern starships the cabin could provide her with every physical necessity; like a hotel room with a particularly bad view. She ordered up a plain chair and took her guitar out of the storage locker. Music was something she'd come to late in life. As her genetically ordained compulsions were slowly erased, so she found her cultural horizons expanding. Art was a whole area she could never quite appreciate, she was always looking for rationalist explanation in every work. Literature was a lot more satisfactory, stories had a point, a resolution. Not that there were many books released into the unisphere these days, current writers tended to produce outlines and scripts for sensory dramas.

But the classics were enjoyable enough; the only genre she tended to shy away from was crime and thrillers. Poetry she ignored as an absurd irrelevance. Music, though, had something for every mood, every place. She took a great deal of pleasure from it, listening to everything from orchestral arrangements to singer-songwriters, jazz to gaianature tonality, choral to starsphere dance. The *Alexis Denken* would often streak between star systems reverberating to the sounds of Rachmaninoff or Pink Floyd or Deeley KTC.

Paula sat back and started to pluck a few chords at random, then gradually dropped into Johnny Cash's 'The Wanderer'. She didn't try to sing; there were some limits in life you just had to accept. Instead the smartcore projected the Man in Black into the cabin, and he started to croon along to her melody.

The song helped her think.

She knew she should be heading straight for Orakum or even Hanko, but she was feeling a lot more troubled by Qatux's last comment than she ought to have been. It seemed as though this whole Pilgrimage situation was designed to disrupt her judgement and objectivity.

That, or I'm just getting lonely and uncertain in my old age.

Paula finished strumming. The Man in Black gave her a forlorn look, and she waved her hand dismissively. The smartcore cancelled the projection.

Her u-shadow opened a link to Kazimir – someone who did have empathy for her position.

'What can I do for you?' he asked.

'I'm at the *High Angel*. Aaron gave Inigo's memorycell to Qatux. Someone knew about our friend's predilection.'

'Did Qatux review it?'

'Oh yes. Qatux told Aaron that Inigo was probably hiding out on Hanko.'

'Interesting. Presumably that's where the *Artful Dodger* aka the *Alini* is heading?'

'Yes.'

'Another ultradrive ship arrived in the system just before the

Artful Dodger departed. The Navy commander at *High Angel* said it stood off in the cometary belt, and left in hot pursuit.'

'Does every Faction have ultradrive ships?' she asked indignantly. 'Justine caught the Delivery Man using a Hawking m-sink on Arevalo.'

'So she told me. I consider it significant that the Factions are openly using such technology. This whole Pilgrimage event could well be the trigger for an irreversible culture split within the human race.'

'Whose side will you take?'

'The Navy was created by ANA to protect humans from stronger, hostile aliens. That is what it will continue to do until I am removed from my position. If ANA chooses to leave the physical universe, I will stay behind and ensure that whatever sections of us remain continue to receive that protection. Is that a side, do you think?'

'No. But it's certainly a plan.'

'Are you going after Aaron?'

'Not immediately. Can you provide some protection for Hanko and Inigo, if he's there?'

'I will observe and advise you of developments; but you know the Navy cannot intervene directly in the internal affairs of Commonwealth citizens. Despite the scale of the problem, that's what this is.'

Paula was thrown by the answer. She was expecting Kazimir to be a lot more helpful. 'A thousand years ago I stuck to the rules, too. No good comes of it. You need to bend a little, Kazimir.'

'You and other representatives exist so I don't have to. You handle the grey areas, while I deal in black and white.'

'There's no such thing.'

'Nonetheless, I operate within a set of rules that I will not break.'

'I understand. Just do what you can, please.'

'Of course.'

*

The *Artful Dodger* dropped out of hyperspace five thousand kilometres above Hanko's equator. Sensors examined the surrounding environment, bringing up several amber warning symbols, and even a couple of red ones. The local star had an abnormally large number of sunspots chasing across its surface, producing a dangerously thick solar wind. Below the starship's metallic purple hull, a global cloud blanket reflected the star's sharp white glow back into space, its uniform glare broken only by the vast aural streamers that lashed across the stratosphere. Above the atmosphere monstrous arches of violet fluorescence soared out far beyond geosynchronous orbit, engorged Van Allen radiation belts that choked the planet with a hurricane of high-energy particles. The *Artful Dodger*'s hull sparked with a corposant discharge as it slid across into a high inclination orbit.

'Welcome to hell,' Aaron muttered as he monitored the images from outside. The ship began to probe through the clouds with high-resolution hysradar sweeps, standard radar, magnoscan, quantum signature receptors, and electromagnetic sensors; revealing the lay of the frozen land underneath. Several com-beacon signals appeared on the emerging cartography, the only indication of activity on this bygone world. They broadcast the official channels of the Restoration team, asking all arriving ships to make contact.

Corrie-Lyn watched the images in the portal with a mournful face as the starship flew round and round the planet, building up a detailed survey of the surface. Twelve hundred years after the Prime attack, glaciers were still advancing out of the polar regions. 'I can't believe Inigo was ever attracted to this place,' she said.

'You heard Qatux; he enjoyed the *idea* of an ancestral homeworld.'

'Even if he came here, he'd take one look and leave. There's nothing here.'

'There are Restoration teams down there, even today,' Aaron said, waving at the little scarlet lights dotted across the map. The beacons acted as crude relays across continents, the only communication net on the planet.

'That's got to be the biggest lost cause in the galaxy,' she said.

'You're probably right. Seventeen of the Second47 worlds have officially closed their Restoration projects, and the remainder are winding down. Budgets get reduced every year. Nobody kicks up a fuss about it any more, not like the first couple of centuries after the War.'

After ten orbits, the smartcore had mapped all the exposed land lurking below the eternal cloud. Sensors had located twenty-three centres of dense electromagnetic activity. The largest was a force-field dome in the centre of Kajaani, the old capital city. All the others were little more than clumps of machinery and buildings scattered across the dead tundra of three continents. No thermal sensor could begin to penetrate the cloud, so he had no way of telling if any of the outposts were occupied. There didn't seem to be any capsules in flight. Electrical activity in the air was strong, interfering with several sensor fields.

'No way of telling if he's down there,' Aaron said. 'Not from up here. I can't even see what ships are parked under the force field.'

'What were you expecting?'

'Nothing more than this. I'm just scouting the territory before we go in to make sure there are no surprises.'

Corrie-Lyn rubbed her arms, as if the cold from the planet was seeping into the cabin. 'So what's our cover story this time?'

'No point in one. It's not like the teams are heavily armed.'

'So you just shoot them one at a time until they give him up to us?'

He gave her an annoyed stare. 'We'll tell them that you're searching for a former lover. He changed his name and profile to forget you, but you've tracked him down here. All very romantic.'

481

'That makes me look like a complete loser.'

'Oh dear,' he sneered, and told the smartcore to call the beacon at Kajaani.

It took several minutes to get a reply from the shielded base. Eventually a very startled Restoration project director called Ansan Purillar came on line to give them landing authority.

The *Artful Dodger* sank deftly through the three kilometres of the upper cloud layer. Two hundred kph winds buffeted the hull with near-solid clumps of grey mist while lightning clawed furiously at the force field. Eventually they cleared the base of the layer into a strata of super-clear air and the outside temperature plummeted. A gloomy panorama opened up beneath them. Black ice-locked land smeared with long dunes of snow. Denuded of vegetation, every geographical feature was shaded in stark monochrome. Long braids of grubby cloud chased across the dead features.

'It must have been terrifying,' Corrie-Lyn said sadly.

'The Primes dropped two flare bombs into the star,' Aaron told her. 'The only way the Navy could knock them out was by using quantumbusters on the corona. Between them, they produced enough radiation to slaughter every living cell a million times over. Hanko's atmosphere absorbed the energy until it reached saturation point, which triggered a superstorm, which in turn threw up enough cloud to cover the planet and kick off an ice age. And the star still hasn't stabilized. Even if it did, it wouldn't matter; the radiation has completely destroyed the biosphere. According to the files, there's some marine life that's still alive in the deepest parts of the oceans, but that's all. The land is as sterile as a surgical chamber. Check out those radiation levels – and we're still five kilometres high.'

'I didn't appreciate what a scale this War was fought on.'

'They were going to genocide us.' The words were almost painful to speak. It had been a fearful time. Aaron shuddered. *How do I know what the War was like?* A deeper instinct assured him he wasn't that old.

The *Artful Dodger* continued its descent through the rampaging lower clouds, blazing with solar brilliance as it sloughed off whip-like tendrils of electrical energy. At this altitude the wind speeds had dropped to a hundred and fifty kilometres per hour, but the air density meant the ship's ingrav units were straining to hold them stable against the pressure.

Corrie-Lyn tried not to look alarmed as the starship began to shake. High-velocity ice crystals shattered against the force field as an amok cloud braid hurtled around them. The crunch of disintegrating ice could be heard inside the cabin.

'Okay then, this is why there aren't any capsules flying down here,' Aaron muttered. His exovision was showing him the force field dome below altering its permeability index to allow them through. The wind speed was now less than a hundred kph.

Outside the dome, there was very little evidence of the city remaining. In its time, Kajaani had been home to three million people. Its force field had warded off the storms in the days following the Prime attack, protecting the wormhole station so that the planet's population could be evacuated to Anagaska. The process had taken over a month, with government vehicles transporting refugees from outlying countries on every continent as the storms grew worse and worse and vegetation withered and died. Seven weeks and three days after the planet's Premier Speaker led the way, CST closed the Hanko wormhole. If there was anybody left on the planet, they were beyond contact. Every effort had been made, every known habitation and isolated farmstead searched.

With the people gone, the force fields protecting cities and towns failed one by one, allowing the winds to pound against the buildings and floodwater to scour the ground around them. Not even modern superstrong materials could resist such pummelling for ever. The structures began to crumple and collapse. Eventually, with the climate spiralling down into its ice age the rains chilled to become snow, then ice. Mushy scree piled up against the frozen ruins, obliterating yet more evidence that this had once been an inhabited world.

The *Artful Dodger* passed through the force field and into the calm bubble of warm air that was the Restoration team's main base. It was centred on one of Kajaani's old parks. Under the protective auspice of the force field, the ground had been decontaminated and replanted. Grass grew once again, as did a short avenue of trees. Clusters of airborne polyphoto spheres shone an imitation sunlight on to the lush greenery; irrigation pipes provided clean water; there were even native birds and insects humming about, oblivious to the dark sky with its sub-zero winds outside.

They landed on a small patch of concrete on the edge of the park which held just one other starship, a thirty-year-old commercial combi-freighter with a continuous wormhole drive that could carry a mix of cargo and passengers. The difference between the two ships was patent, with the *Artful Dodger*'s smooth chrome-purple hull seeming almost organic compared to the Restoration team's workhorse with its carbon-bonded titanium fuselage and fading paintwork.

Aaron and Corrie-Lyn floated gently down out of the airlock to touch down between the five bulbous landing legs. Ten people had turned out to greet them, quite a crowd by the base's standards; and all curious to see the unscheduled arrivals. Ansan Purillar stood at the head of the delegation, a slightly rotund man with fair hair cut short, dressed in a simple dark-blue tunic with a Restoration logo on the arm.

'Greetings to both of you,' he said. 'I'd like to know why you're here. We're pleased to see you, of course, don't get me wrong. But we never have visitors. Ever.' His attitude was pleasant, but there was an underlying determination.

Aaron's biononics performed a fast low-level field scan. Director Purillar was an ordinary Advancer human; as were his co-workers, none were Higher. 'It's rather awkward,' he said with a twisted smile. 'Er, Corrie . . .'

'I'm looking for someone,' she said.

It was a low voice, hauntingly mournful. Aaron was quite impressed; she'd backed it up with a soft ache in the base's tiny gaiafield. The team were suddenly all attention and sympathy.

'A man. Yigo. We were in love. Then it went bad. My fault. I was so stupid. I shouldn't have . . . I don't want to say . . .'

Aaron put his arm comfortingly round her shoulder as she sniffed convincingly, head bowed. 'There there,' he assured her. 'They don't want details.'

Corrie-Lyn nodded bravely and continued. 'He left. It took me a long time before I realized what a mistake I'd made. But I'd hurt him, really badly. I've been looking for him for three years. He changed his name and his profile, but his sister let slip he'd come here.'

'Who is it?' Director Purillar asked.

'I don't know. All I know is what his sister said, that he'd joined the Restoration project. I just had to come. If there is *any* chance . . .'

'Um, yes, sure.' Purillar glanced round at his colleagues, who were busy checking each other out to see if any of them was going to own up to being The One. He waved an arm about. 'Anyone look familiar?'

Corrie-Lyn shook her head despondently. 'No. I probably won't recognize him.' She faced her little audience. 'Yigo, please, if it's you, please just tell me. I just want to talk, that's all. Please.'

Now nobody was meeting her gaze.

'You don't have to do it in front of your friends,' she said. 'Come to me later. I really *really* miss you.' That last was accompanied by a burst of sincere desperation into the gaiafield.

'All right then,' a now thoroughly embarrassed Purillar said to his team, 'I'll get this organized. We can meet up again at dinner.'

People broke off, heading back towards the main expanse of grass, keeping their smiles under tight control. As soon as they were a few paces away, couples went into deep intense conversations, heads pressed close together.

Aaron watched them go, keeping his own face impassive. The base would be talking about this for the next twenty years.

Ansan Purillar was left standing in front of his two uninvited guests, one hand scratching at his fuzz of hair in some perplexity. His gaiamotes were leaking an equal amount of disquiet. 'You're welcome to use the accommodation here. There are plenty of rooms spare, a legacy of when the project was conducted on a grander scale. But, quite frankly, I suspect your own ship would be more comfortable.' He eyed the *Artful Dodger* jealously. 'Our living quarters haven't been updated in a century.'

'That's very kind of you, and of course we'll use the ship,' Aaron said. 'We have no intention of imposing.'

'Quite the contrary,' Purillar said sheepishly. 'You are going to be excellent for morale. The only entertainment we get here is sensory dramas, and they tend to pale after a while. Whereas a quest like this . . . One of us dull old souls with a romantic past. Well!'

'How long have you been here?' Aaron asked.

'Myself? I will have notched up twenty-five years in the last hundred and thirty.'

Aaron whistled. 'That's devotion. Do you mind telling me why?'

Purillar beckoned to them, and set off across the grass. 'I'm nearly three hundred years old, so in fact it's a small portion of my life. I don't mind donating the time because I can extend my life as long as I want to make up for it.'

'That sounds almost like Higher philosophy.'

'I suppose it does. I'll probably migrate inwards once the Restoration project ends. Higher culture appeals to me.'

'But why that first donation?'

'Simple enough, I met one of the Restored. She died just after the Prime attack, caught outside a force field when the storm struck. Seven hundred years later one of our teams found her corpse and extracted her memorycell. She was re-lifed in a clone, and lived happily on Anagaska. It was her contentment which affected me; she had such a busy fulfilling life, there was a huge family, her involvement with the local community. I was struck by how much poorer the world, my world, would have been without her. So I signed up for a tour. Then when you're here you get to see first hand the people who you find, follow them from excavation through assessment and DNA extraction, memorycell rehabilitation, right up to re-life. You understand? I meet the living individual after I dig up their corpse. Innocent people who were struck down, people who didn't deserve to die; victims of a hideous war. Maybe it's self-serving, but do you have any idea how *good* that makes me feel?'

'I can't even imagine. I can see I'm going to have to make a financial contribution when I get back to Anagaska.'

They crossed the big grass field to the low buildings on the other side. Housing for the team members consisted of small individual cottages arranged in five neat circles, each with a central clump of community buildings. As they approached, Aaron saw an open-air swimming pool and several barbeque areas, even a sports pitch was marked out. Only two of the circles were in use now. It was impossible to see what the cottages were built out of; they were all covered by thick creepers with long brown leaves that dangled golden flowers from their tips. It was a pleasant arboreal contrast to the icy desolation outside the force field. A deliberate one he suspected; the vines were nicely shaggy, but pruned so as not to obstruct windows.

Behind the cottages were two modern functional blocks. One containing the project laboratories, Purillar explained, while the other housed their maintenance shops and garaged their equipment.

'We're heavily cybernated,' he told them, 'But even we need a few technicians to repair the bots now and again.'

'Could he be working as a technician?' Aaron asked Corrie-Lyn.

'Who knows?' she said lightly. 'I just know he's here. Probably. It is a long-shot, after all.'

Aaron didn't look at her. *That hell-damned mouth of hers!* He'd managed to get into the starship's culinary unit program, altering her patches on his original blocks so the drinks she ordered only had half the alcohol content she'd designated. Her attitude hadn't made any miraculous changes. 'Can we meet everyone?' Aaron asked.

'Sure. I suppose. This is a civil outpost after all. I'm not exactly a police commissioner, you know. I can't compel anyone who doesn't want to be introduced.' He gave Corrie-Lyn an apologetic shrug.

'Anyone who refuses is pretty likely to be him, don't you think?' said Aaron.

'Sounds about right,' the director said. 'You do realize that everyone on the planet will now know you're here, and especially why. This is a small operation.'

'How many people is that, exactly?'

'Four hundred and twenty-seven of us; of which a hundred and eighty are here in the base. Five hundred years ago, there were six thousand people involved.'

'How many people have you restored?'

'Two point one million in total,' Purillar said proudly.

Aaron whistled appreciatively. 'I had no idea.'

'The bulk of them were in the early years, of course. But our techniques have improved dramatically since then. Thankfully, because, even with the cold helping preservation, entropy is our real enemy. Come on in, I'll show you.' He stepped through the door of the laboratory block.

The assessment room was the first section they looked in. A big clean chamber with ten long medical tables surrounded by plyplastic limbs tipped with instruments and sensors. One of the tables had a recently discovered corpse on it. Aaron wrinkled his nose up at the sight. It was hard to tell the thing had been human. A dark lump wrapped in shrunken cloth and smeared with grime, its limbs were difficult to determine, showing as long ridges. Strings of hair at one end at least showed him where the head was located. After a minute he realized the corpse was curled up in foetal position.

Two of the Recovery team were standing beside the table in sealed white overalls, peering down through their bubble-helmets as they directed the wand-shape sensors sliding along various creases in the body's surface. Their movements dislodged grains of snow, which were carefully vacuumed up from the table top.

'We keep the temperature in there the same as outside,'

Purillar said. 'Any sudden change in environment could be catastrophic. As it is we have to keep the assessment room sterile, too.'

'Why?' Corrie-Lyn asked.

'The radiation has killed off Hanko's microbial life. It's another factor which helps the preservation process. If any bugs got in there, they'd have a feast day, and we'd be left with slush.'

'They must be very delicate by now,' Aaron said.

'Yes. This one is almost intact. We normally deal with broken segments.'

'Don't you use a stabilizer field?'

'Not if we can help it. We found the field actually has a detrimental effect on their memorycells. Don't forget, back then the Commonwealth was still using crystal matrices. In some early cases we scrambled ten per cent of the information.'

'Must be hard to remove the memorycell, then.'

'We don't even try. Once we've extracted enough DNA samples to sequence a full genome, we deploy infiltrator filaments into the crystal. Even that can be hazardous. Powering up a memorycell after this long is fatal. It has to be read cold, which is done a molecular layer at a time. Each one takes about nine months.'

'I'd have thought that crystal memorycells would last longer than this.'

'They built them pretty robust, even back then. But consider what they've endured for twelve hundred years. It doesn't help.'

'Who is he?' Corrie-Lyn asked.

'Her, actually. We think she's Aeva Sondlin. We'll know for certain when her genome has been read, but the location was right.'

'Location?'

'She was found four kilometres from her car. In itself that was hard to find. Washed downstream in a flash flood. We know from records that she lived in the house above the valley's flood level. We think she was making a dash for the nearest town during a break in the storm. There was an official evacuation point set up there, and she informed the authorities she was coming. Never arrived. Must have got caught by the winds, or the water. Maybe she'll be able to tell us.'

'You knew she was missing?'

'Yes. The records of the time aren't perfect, naturally, given the circumstances. But we have a full census, and of course everyone who arrived on Anagaska was fully documented. It's our job to try and determine what happened to those who got lost. We have to handle each case separately. In Aeva's case, we've been searching possible locations for seventy years.'

'You're bullshitting me,' Aaron said.

'I assure you I'm not.'

'Sorry, but seventy years?'

'We start with the route she must have taken, pick the obvious danger points, and seed them with sensor bots. They spread out in a circle, trying to find some trace. Like all our equipment, the bots have improved considerably during the centuries we've been here. The majority are tunnellers, burrowing through the snow and surface soil layers. So much topsoil was displaced during the storms that the continent's whole topology shifted, and now it's all locked into place by the permafrost. Ninety-nine per cent of the people we recover these days are buried. It means the bots operate in highly detrimental conditions even for this world. In total, the Restoration project has deployed four hundred and fifty million since it began. There are still eleven million active and searching. They're not fast moving, but they are thorough.'

'How many people are you still looking for?'

'A third of a million. I don't hold out much hope. Most of them will have been washed into the sea.' He gestured at the wrinkled lump on the table. 'Dear Aeva's car was forty-seven kilometres from the road she used, and that was the easy find; she was deep under sediment. Persistence pays off. We still find about twenty or so each year, even now.'

They moved on into DNA sequencing. To Aaron it was just an ordinary office with five large smartcores. Even in ordinary circumstances, human DNA decomposed quickly; after twelve hundred years on Hanko, only the smallest fragments remained. But there were a lot of cells in each body, each with its own fragments. Piecing them together was possible with the right techniques, and a vast amount of computing power. Once the main sequences had been established, the project could use family records to fill the gaps. In a lot of cases, there were full DNA records from clinics available. As soon as the body had been properly identified, a clone was grown for re-life.

'But not here,' Purillar said. 'Clinics back on Anagaska handle that part. After all, who would want to wake up here? People have enough trouble adjusting to the present – their future – as it is. Most need specialist counselling.'

'Is life that different?'

'Essentially no, and most died hoping for rescue in the form of re-life. It is the amount of time involved which shocks them. None of their immediate family and friends remain. They are very much alone when they wake.'

After DNA there was the memory rehabilitation section, which tried to reassemble the information read from memorycells. A process orders of magnitude more complex than DNA sequencing.

The history archive: for recovered people who couldn't be identified. All of Hanko's civic records, and memoirs of families with lost relatives, the logs and recollections of the evacuation teams. Lists of people who may have been visiting Hanko when the attack started. The Intersolar missing persons list of the time.

Laboratories specializing in analysis of molecular structures; identifying baroque, minute clues the bots had discovered as they wormed their way through Hanko's frozen earth. Trying to place flakes of paint with individual car models. Tying scraps of cloth to specific clothes, from that to manufacturer, to retail outlet, to customer lists, to bank statements. Items of jewellery. Even pets. A long register of unknown artefacts, each one potentially leading to another lost corpse.

The case room. With files on everyone still known to be missing.

Operations centre, which monitored the sensor bots and the outpost teams which were excavating in terrible conditions.

After two hours, they'd met everyone in the building. None reacted to Corrie-Lyn, and nobody tried to avoid her. Aaron quietly scanned all of them. No one was enriched with biononics.

'There are a few other people around,' Purillar said. 'You'll probably meet them tonight at the canteen. We tend to eat together.'

'And if he's not there?' Aaron asked.

'Then I'm sorry, but there's not much I can do,' the director said. He gave Corrie-Lyn an uncomfortable glance.

'Can we visit the outposts?' she asked.

'If he is here, he'll know about you by now. He would have used the beacon net to call in. I guess he doesn't want to get back with you.'

'Seeing me in the flesh might be the one thing he can't resist,' Corrie-Lyn said. 'Please.' Her outpouring of grief into the gaia-field was disturbing.

The director looked deeply unhappy. 'If you want to venture outside, there's nothing I can do to stop you, technically this is still a free Commonwealth world. You can go wherever you want. I'd have advise against it, though.'

'Why?' Aaron asked.

'You've got a good ship, but even that would be hard pressed to manoeuvre close to the ground. We can't use capsules here, the winds are too strong, and the atmospheric energy content too high. The two times we tried to use our ship for an emergency rescue nearly ended in disaster. We aborted both, and wound up having to re-life the team members.'

'My ship has an excellent force field.'

'I'm sure it does. But expanding the force field doesn't help, you just give the wind a bigger surface area to push at. Down here it actually makes you more susceptible to the storm. The only stability you have in the air is what your drive units can provide.'

Aaron didn't like it. The *Artful Dodger* was just about the best protection possible. *Under normal circumstances.* He couldn't forget the way the regrav units had approached their limits bringing them down to the base's force field dome, and that was a big target. 'How do your teams get about?' he asked.

'Ground crawlers. They weigh three tons apiece, and move on tracks. They're not fast, but they are dependable.'

'Can we borrow one? There must be some you're not using. You said there used to be a lot more personnel here at one time. Just an old one will do.'

'Look. Really. He's not here.'

'Whatever release document you want us to certify, we'll do it,' Corrie-Lyn said. 'Please. Give me this last chance.'

'I've got over twenty teams out there. Half of them aren't even on this continent. We use the polar caps as a bridge to get to the other landmasses. It would take you a year to get round them all.'

'At least we can make a start. If Yigo hears we're going round everyone, he'll know he'll have to face me eventually. That might make him get in contact.'

Purillar rubbed agitated fingers across his forehead. 'It will have to be the mother of all legal release claims. I can't have any come-back against the project.'

'I understand. And thank you.'

After dinner, Aaron and Corrie-Lyn made their way over to the second block to inspect the ground crawler Purillar was oh-so-reluctantly allowing them to use. Overhead, the airborne lights were dimming down to a gentle twilight. The effect was spoiled by constant flares of lightning outside the force field.

'He wasn't at the canteen then?' Corrie-Lyn asked.

'No. I've scanned everyone in the base now. None of them have biononics. Though quite a few have some interesting enrichments. It can't be as tame here as the good director claims.'

'You always judge people, don't you?'

'Quite the opposite. I don't care what they do to each other in the privacy of their own cottage. I just need to make a threat-assessment.'

The malmetal door of garage eleven rolled apart to show them the ground crawler. It was a simple wedge-shape of metal on four low caterpillar tracks. With the bodywork painted bright orange, its slit windows made empty black gashes in the sides. Force field projectors were lumpy bulbs on the upper edges, along with crab-like maintenance bots which clung to the surface like marsupial babies. When Aaron queried the vehicle's net he found it had a large self-repair function. A third of the cargo compartments were filled with spares.

'We should be all right in this,' he told her. 'The net will drive it. All we have to do is tell it where we want to go.'

'And that is, exactly? You know, Purillar was right. If Inigo is here, then he knows I'm here looking for him. He would have contacted us. Me, at least.'

'Would he?'

'Oh don't,' she said, her face furrowed in disgust. 'Just don't.'

'He obviously doesn't miss you as much as you miss him. He left, remember.'

'Screw you!' she screamed.

'Don't hide from this. Not now. I need you functional.'

'Functional,' she sneered. 'Well I'm not. And if we find him the first thing I'll tell him is not to help you, you psychofuck misfit.'

'I never expected anything else from you.'

She glowered, but didn't walk away. Aaron smiled behind her back.

'If he's here, the Pilgrimage will be long gone before we find him,' she said sulkily.

'Not quite. Remember we have an advantage that lets us reduce the search field. We know he's Higher.'

'How does that help?' There was distain in her voice still, but warring with curiosity now.

'The field scan effect would be very useful out there, helping

494

to track down bodies buried in the ground. I can use it to detect anomalies several hundred metres away. It's a little more difficult through a solid mass, but the pervasive function is still capable of reaching a reasonable distance.'

'If he's here, he'll have a better success rate than the others,' she said.

'There are other factors, such as getting the location of a lost person reasonably accurate. Which is all down to how well an individual case has been researched. But yes. It's a reasonable assumption to say the team with the best success rate will be Inigo's.'

'Is there one?'

'Yep. My u-shadow didn't even have to hack any files. They're all open to review. The team with the current highest Recovery rate is working up at Olhava province. That's on this continent, nine hundred kilometres south-west. If we start first thing tomorrow morning, we'll be there in forty-eight hours.'

*

Oscar Monroe had fallen in love with the house the first moment he saw it. It was a plain circle, with a high glass wall separating floor and ceiling, standing five metres off the ground on a central pillar that contained a spiral stair. Both the base and the roof were made from some smooth artificial rock similar to white granite, which shone like mountain-top snow in Orakum's blue-tinged sunlight. The sprawling grounds outside resembled some grand historical parkland that had fallen into disuse, with woolly grass overgrowing paths, lines of ornamental trees, and a couple of lakes with a little waterfall between them. There were even some brick Hellenic structures resting in deep nooks, swamped by moss and flowering creepers to add to the image of great age. That image was one which several dozen gardening bots worked hard at achieving.

He had lived there for nineteen years now. It was a wonderful home to return to every time his pilot shift was over, devoid of stress and the kind of bullshit politics that went in tandem with

495

any corporate job. Oscar flew commercial starships for Orakum's thriving national spaceline, which had routes to over twenty External planets. Piloting was the only job he'd sought since he'd been re-lifed.

Waking up in the clinic had been one hell of a surprise. The last thing he remembered was crashing his hyperglider into an identical one piloted by Anna Kime. Saving the Commonwealth – good. Killing the wife of his best friend – not so hot. Without Anna to wreck their flight, Wilson Kime should have managed to fly unimpeded on a mission that was pivotal in the Starflyer War. Oscar could remember the instant before the collision, a moment of complete serenity. He hadn't expected anyone to recover his memorycell. Not after his confession, that in his youth he'd been involved in an act of politically motivated terrorism that had killed four hundred and eight people, a third of them without memorycells, mostly children too young for the inserts. The fact that he'd never intended it, that the deaths were a mistake, that they'd missed their actual target – that should never have counted in his favour. But it seemed as though his service to the Commonwealth, and ultimate sacrifice, had meant something to the judge. He wanted to think Wilson had maybe paid for a decent lawyer. They'd been good friends.

'I guess this means we won, then,' were his first words. It even sounded like his own voice.

Above him, a youthful doctor's face smiled. 'Welcome back, Mr Yaohui,' he said.

'Call me Oscar. I was that longer than I was ever Yaohui.' His new identity when he went on the run for over forty years.

'As you wish.'

Oscar managed to prop himself up on his elbows. A movement which surprised him; he'd seen re-life clones several times; pitiful things with thin flesh stretched over bones and organs that had been force-grown to adolescence, unable to move for months while they painfully built up muscle mass. This body, though, seemed almost complete. Which meant the technique had improved. There had been a lot of bodyloss in the War – tens of millions at least. He'd probably been shoved down to the bottom of the list. 'How long?'

'Please understand, er, Oscar, you were put on trial for your, uh, previous crime. It set quite a few legal precedents, given your, uh, state at the time.'

'What trial? What do you mean, *state*? I was dead.'

'You suffered bodyloss. Your memorycell survived the crash intact – legally that is recognized by the Commonwealth as being your true self. It was recovered by one Paula Myo.'

'Uh—' Oscar was suddenly getting a very bad feeling about this. 'Paula recovered me?'

'Yes. You and Anna Kime. She brought both of you back to Earth.'

'But Anna was a Starflyer agent.'

'Yes. Under the terms of the Doi amnesty her Starflyer conditioning was edited out of her memories and she was re-lifed as a normal human. Apparently she went on to have a long life and a successful marriage to Wilson Kime. She was certainly on the *Discovery* with him when it flew round the galaxy.'

Oscar's shoulders weren't so strong after all; he sagged back on to the mattress. 'How long?' he repeated; there was an urgency in his growl.

'You were found guilty at the trial. Your Navy service record was a mitigating factor in sentencing of course, but it couldn't compensate for the number of people who were killed at Abadan Station. The judge gave you suspension. But as the Commonwealth clinics were unable to cope with the sheer quantity of, uh, non-criminals requiring re-life at the time, he allowed you to remain as a stored memory rather than be re-lifed before the sentence began.'

'How long?' Oscar whispered.

'You were sentenced to one thousand one hundred years.'

'Fuck me!'

He was all alone. That was probably a worse punishment than suspension. After all, he wasn't aware of time passing during that millennia, he couldn't reflect and repent on his wrongdoing. But

497

in this present, life was different. Everyone he'd known had either died or *migrated inwards* – ridiculous phrase, a politically correct way of saying they'd committed euthanasia with a safety net. Maybe that was the point of suspension after all. It certainly hurt.

So, with no friends, no family, knowledge and skills that even museums wouldn't be interested in, Oscar Monroe had to start afresh.

The Navy, rather understandably, didn't want him. He explained he didn't expect to be part of the deterrence fleet, and offered to retrain as a pilot for their exploration crews. They declined again.

Back before the Starflyer War he'd worked in the exploration division at CST. Opening new planets, giving people a fresh start, was kind of like a self-imposed penance. Except he'd really enjoyed it. So he did train as a starship pilot. Fortunately the modern continuous wormhole drive used principles and theories developed during his first life, and he brought himself up to speed on its current technology applications quite rapidly.

Orakum SolarStar was the third company he'd worked for since his re-life. It wasn't much different to any other External World starline. In fact it was smaller than most. Orakum was on the edge of the Greater Commonwealth, settled for a mere two hundred years. But that location made it a chief candidate from which to mount new exploration flights, opening up yet more worlds. They were rare events. The Navy had charted every star system directly outside the External Worlds. Expansion to new worlds was also at a historical low. The boundary between Central and External Worlds hadn't changed much for centuries. The old assumption that Higher culture would always be extending out-wards, and the ordinary humans would be an expanding wave in front of it was proving to be a fallacy. With inward migration, the number of Higher humans remained about constant; and the External Worlds provided just about every kind of society in terms of ethnicity, ideology, technology, and religion. Should any citizen feel disenfranchised on their own planet they just had to take a commercial flight to relocate. There was very little reason to found a new world these days.

In the nineteen years he'd been on Orakum, SolarStar had only launched three planetary survey flights. Two of these had been closer than the company's long-range commercial flights travelled. Hardly breaking through new frontiers. But he had seniority now. If another outward venture came along, he ought to be chosen. Like all pilots, he was an eternal optimist.

There was no hint of that elusive mission in the company offices when he filed his flight report. He'd just got back from a long-haul flight to Troyan, seventy lightyears away. A fifteen-hour trip with nothing to do other than talk to the smartcore and trawl the unisphere for anything interesting. One day soon, he was sure, people would finally chuck the notion that they had to have a fellow human in charge. He was only sitting up in the front of the starship for public relations. In fact there were probably people sitting in the passenger cabin who were better qualified than him if repairs were ever needed. Not that they ever were.

But at least he got to visit new planets. The same ones. Over and over again.

His regrav capsule sank out of the wispy clouds to curve sedately round the house and land on the grass beside the spinney of lofty rancata trees, nearly twenty metres tall with reddish-brown whip-leaves that swayed in the mild breeze. He climbed out and took a deep breath of the warm, plains-scented air. Out beyond the horizon, Orakum's untamed countryside was carpeted by spiky wildflowers that budded most of the year. Another reason to choose Orakum was its benign climate.

Jesaral was walking out from underneath the house. The splendidly handsome youth didn't quite have a welcoming smile on his face, but definitely looked relieved to see Oscar. He was only wearing a pair of knee-length white trousers, showing off a tanned body that always got Oscar's blood pumping a little faster. Jesaral was the youngest of his three life partners, barely twenty.

Which, Oscar suspected, probably qualified him as the worst Punk Skunk in the galaxy. A thousand-year-plus age gap: it was delightfully naughty.

The youth opened his arms wide and gave Oscar a big hug to accompany a long sultry kiss. Enthusiasm sprayed out heedlessly into the gaiafield.

'What's the matter?' Oscar asked.

'Them,' Jesaral said, stabbing a thumb dismissively back at the house.

Oscar refused to sigh. He and his other partners Dushiku and Anja had been a stable trio for over a decade. They were both over a hundred, and completely at ease with each other. At their age they understood perfectly the little accommodations necessary to make any relationship work. It was taking everyone longer than expected to accommodate and adjust to their newcomer – who didn't have anything like their experience and sophistication. Which was what made him so exciting in and out of bed.

'What have they done?'

'It's a surprise for you. And I know how you hate surprises.'

'Not always,' Oscar assured him. 'Depends if it's good or bad. What's this one?'

'Oh no. I'm just telling you there is a surprise for you. I don't want you to be upset that it's there, that's all.'

Oscar used a macrocellular cluster to connect to the house's net. Whatever was waiting inside had been skilfully blocked. That would be Anja, who developed commercial neural routines. She was one of the best on the planet.

'You have the strangest logic I've ever known,' Oscar said.

Jesaral smiled broadly. 'Come on! I can't wait.' He tugged at Oscar's arm, his outpouring of enthusiasm shining like sunrise.

They hurried to the base of the pillar and climbed the wide spiral stair. It brought them out into a small vestibule, planted with colourful bushes from several worlds, their flowers reaching for the open sky above. Ten doors opened off it. Jesaral led the way into their main lounge. In contrast to the exterior, the lounge was clad in caranwood, a local variety that was a rich gold-brown.

The grain of the planks had been blended so skilfully it looked as if they were inside a giant hollowed-out trunk. Its furniture was scarlet and gold, contributing to the sumptuous feel.

Dushiku was waiting in the middle of the big room, holding out a tumbler of malt whisky, three ice cubes. He had a mischievous smile on his broad face. 'Welcome home.'

'Thanks.' Oscar took the drink wearily.

'I see Jesaral's restraint is as strong as ever.'

'I didn't tell him,' Jesaral protested.

'So?' Oscar enquired.

Dushiku raised an eyebrow, and half turned, indicating the balcony beyond the glass wall at the far end of the lounge. Anja was standing out there, leaning on the rail as she spoke about some aspect of the gardens below. Her laughter-filled voice was just audible through the open door. Oscar knew the tone well, she was playing perfect hostess: marking her territory. Anja was astonishingly beautiful, a beauty which took a full third of her salary to maintain. Two visits to a clinic each year were considered an essential minimum, for beauty was fluid and fashions were treacherous ephemera even on Orakum. She'd returned three weeks ago from her last treatments, showing off her reduced height and dark satin-texture skin. Her face was all gentle curves veiled by a mane of thick chestnut hair swishing down past her shoulders. Huge fawn-coloured eyes peered innocently out of the shadows, projecting a girlish innocence complemented by a perpetual ingénue effervescence into the gaiafield. Her clothes were deceptively simple, a scarlet T-shirt and dark-blue swirling skirt demonstrating her compact figure's expensive femininity.

Yet for once, Anja wasn't impressing the person she was talking to. Oscar watched the other woman leaning on the rail. Easily half-a-head shorter than Anja, wearing a modern white dress with a slight surface shimmer, and a rust-red short-sleeved jacket. Stylish without Anja's feminine overload. She wasn't responding with the kind of attention Anja was used to extracting from everyone she came across. He could tell. After ten years, Anja's body language, the tone of her voice were an open book.

And the more she failed to impress, the more huffy she got. He even allowed some of his amusement to trickle out into the gaiafield.

Anja must have sensed it. Her full lips hardened into a rebuke as Oscar walked towards the balcony. 'Oscar, darling, I've been talking to an old friend of yours.'

The other person on the balcony turned round. Smiled shrewdly.

Oscar dropped the tumbler as his hands along with every other part of his body were shocked into loss of sensation. The crystal smashed, sending the ice cubes bouncing across the polished wood.

'Hello, Oscar,' Paula Myo said.

'Holy shit!'

'Long time no see.'

Oscar couldn't even grunt.

Alarm was starting to seep into the gaiafield as his life partners took in the tableau.

'You two . . .' Jesaral said, his finger rising to point accusingly at Paula. 'I thought—'

'It's all right,' Oscar managed to croak.

'What is this?' Jesaral said accusingly to Paula. 'You said you were friends.'

'We used to be. A long time ago.'

'That old excuse. Again! Everything happened before I was born.'

'Everything did,' Oscar said. His u-shadow summoned a maid-bot to clean up the broken tumbler. Only then did he finally manage a weak smile. 'How are you doing, Paula?'

'Same as usual.'

'Yeah.' She hadn't changed. Not physically. Nothing was different, except maybe her straight dark hair was a couple of centimetres longer. Unlike him, who'd been given a great new Advancer body, based on his own DNA then enriched with all the macrocellular clusters, and stronger bones, more efficient organs, and greater longevity. After eighty-six years, he still wasn't anywhere near needing rejuvenation, although his face was now starting to show signs of his newly lived years – as Anja never tired of pointing out. But her . . . He guessed she must be Higher now. Somehow he couldn't see her visiting clinics for vanity's sake.

'You do know each other, then?' Dushiku asked uncertainly.

'Yes.' Oscar cleared his throat. 'Could you give us a moment, please?'

His life partners exchanged troubled glances, flooding the gaiafield with concern and considerable irritation. 'We'll be outside,' Anja said, patting his arm as she went past. 'Just yell.'

The maidbot waddled into the lounge and started sucking up the malt. Oscar backed up to a settee and sat down hard. The numbness was dissipating, replaced by a growing anger. He glared at Paula. 'One thousand one hundred years. Thanks for that.'

'I recovered your memorycell.'

'You put it on trial!'

'You're as alive now as the day you flew the hyperglider. That's more than can be said for your victims at Abadan.'

'Jesus fucking wept! Will you stop persecuting me?'

'I can't make you feel guilty. You do that to yourself.'

'Yeah yeah.' He sank deeper into the cushioning. 'What the hell are you doing here?'

'You live well.' She turned her head, studying the lounge. 'Anja was quite proud of the house. I can see why.'

'My CST R&R pension fund was paid over into a trust the day the trial ended, courtesy of Wilson. You want to know what one thousand one hundred years' interest looks like? You're standing in it. Bloody inflation! I should have been able to buy a planet.'

'And your life partners; they're good people. Jesaral is rather young, isn't he?'

'Yeah,' Oscar growled at her. 'He's also got a very big cock.'

Paula smiled. 'Did you ever get in touch with Wilson when you were re-lifed?'

503

'He left a message. So did Anna. They both downloaded into ANA long ago. Which frankly I don't admire. Look, this is bullshit; what the fuck do you want?'

'I need you do a job for me.'

Oscar wouldn't have believed it possible. He was in the same room as Paula Myo, and laughing at her. 'Oh boy, did you ever lose it over the centuries. You want *me* to do a job for *you*? You've got to be fucking joking.'

Paula's answering smile veered towards immoral. 'Exactly.'

Oscar's humour vanished abruptly, leaving him with a very queasy sensation heating his stomach. 'Oh shit: you're not joking.'

'Of course not. It's a perfect arrangement. Who would ever suspect such a thing?'

'No. No chance. Go and blackmail someone else. I'd rather go back into suspension.'

'Come on, Oscar, you're not Jesaral so stop acting like him. I'm not here to threaten, I'm here to ask because I know you and I know what you want.'

'You do not know me, lady!'

Paula leaned in towards him, her eyes shining. 'Oh yes I do, Oscar. We spent the last few days of your life together. I nearly died, and you did. Don't tell me we don't understand each other. You martyred yourself so that the human race could survive. You are an honourable man, Oscar. Screwed up by guilt, but honourable.'

Oscar was doing his best not to be intimidated by her. 'That was a mad situation. It won't ever happen again.'

'Oh really? Who do you think I work for these days?'

'I'll take a wild guess and say ANA. You never change.'

'You're right about ANA, but wrong about change. I am different.'

'Yeah, it looks it. The same job for thirteen hundred years. I barely recognized you. Paula, you can't change, that is you.'

'Far Away altered me. It nearly killed me, but I understood I had to adapt. So I resequenced my DNA to edit out the compulsive-behaviour trait.'

'It shows.'

'Self-determination can overcome artificial nature.'

'I'm sure the old nature versus nurture philosophers will be delighted to hear it. Why don't you call them and let them know? Oh, yes, right. They're all *dead* for two thousand years.'

'You're trying to avoid answering me. Trying to justify your fright to yourself.'

'Wrong, lady. Utterly totally, wrong. The answer is no. No I will not help you. Would you like that clarifying? No.'

'How bad do you think it is, that I'm here to ask you?'

'Don't care. I won't help you.'

'It's the Pilgrimage. Oscar, I'm worried about it. Really worried.'

He stared up at her, not sure if he could take many more shocks. 'Look, I've followed the story closely enough, who hasn't? The Navy will stop the Ocisen Empire dead in its tracks. ANA will halt the Pilgrimage ships. It's not stupid. The Void will eat up half the galaxy if Inigo's dumb-ass sheep ever get inside.'

'And you think that's all there is to it? Oscar, you and I were there with Nigel before we travelled to Far Away. You know how complex that situation was, how many factors were at play. Well, this is worse, a lot worse. The Void is only a peripheral event, a convenient gadfly; this is the Factions finally marching out to fight. This is a battle for the destiny of humanity. Our *soul* will be decided by the outcome.'

'I can't help,' he said, mortified by the way it was nearly a wail. 'I'm a pilot for Christ's sake.'

'Oh, Oscar.' Her voice was rich with sympathy. She knelt down in front of him and grasped his hands. Her fingers were warm to the touch. 'Enough humility. It's your character I desperately need help from. I know that once you agree I don't have to worry about the problem any more. You won't quit on me, and that's what's important.'

'This is a nostalgia trip for you. I'm just a pilot.'

'You were just a Navy captain, but you saved us from the

Starflyer. I'm going to tell you what I'm asking you to do. And then I'm going to tell you why you'll do it. If you want to hate me for making you face reality then that's fine by me, too.'

He shook his hands loose from her grip. 'Say your piece, then go.'

'The Factions know me, they watch me as I watch their agents. So I can't have them knowing that I am desperate to locate the Second Dreamer.'

Oscar just laughed. It trailed off into a near-whimper. 'Find the Second Dreamer? Me?'

'Yes. And you know why that'll work?'

'Because no one will be expecting it.' He made it sound like a schoolkid reciting a useless fact.

'Correct. And do you know why you'll do it for me – and please don't shoot the messenger.'

He braced himself. Surely there was nothing else in his life she could threaten him with? *Did I erase a memory? My God, was there another Abadan?* 'What?'

'Because you're bored shitless with this dreary monotonous life you sleepwalk through.'

Oscar opened his mouth to shout at her. Tell her she'd finally flipped. That she was so fantastically wrong. That his life was rich. That he had people who loved him. That every day was a joy. That he never wanted to go back to the crazy days of the Starflyer War. That he'd already endured all the terror and wild exhilaration one life could possibly contain. That such things were best left to the new generation. But for some reason his head had fallen into his hands, and he was sighing heavily. He couldn't look at her. And he could certainly never look at his life partners. 'I can't tell them that,' he whispered painfully. 'How can I? They'll believe it's their fault.'

Paula stood up. A hand rested on his shoulder with gentle sympathy. 'You want me to do it?'

'No.' He shook his head. Wiped the back of his hand across his eyes to remove the annoying smears of moisture. 'No. I'm not that much of a coward.'

'Whatever cover story you need, you've got it. I can arrange ... anything, basically.'

'Uh huh.'

'There's a starship waiting for you at the local spaceport.' She smiled mischievously. 'An ultradrive.'

Oscar smiled faintly, feeling the joy stirring deep inside him. 'Ultradrive? Well, at least you don't think I'm a cheap whore.'

*

This wasn't how Araminta expected to be returning to the Suvorov continent, sitting in an ageing carry capsule as it flew across the Great Cloud Ocean, lower and slower than every other capsule on the planet. It didn't exactly smack of style. She'd always promised herself she'd only ever return to her birth continent when she could step out of some swank luxury capsule and smile condescendingly around at Langham and the family's business.

Not there just yet.

Unfortunately, Likan's estate was on Suvorov. Understandably, as that was where Viotia's capital, Ludor, was situated. Likan wasn't a provinces kind of person, he had to be near the action. So back across the ocean she went. With a baggage hold packed with her best clothes, and a deepening sense of anxiety.

She was genuinely interested in the Sheldonite's abilities. To get to his level in under a hundred and fifty years illustrated a phenomenal achievement. There was a lot she could learn from him, providing she could get him talking.

Then there was the whole Sheldonite culture thing. Thousands of people on hundreds of External Worlds trying to emulate their ancient hyper-capitalist idol. An emulation dangerously close to blind worship, she thought. But she was willing to suspend judgement until she experienced it first-hand. Maybe this was the route she should be taking. Even Bovey couldn't deny Sheldonism was the pinnacle of business culture. Successful Sheldonism, that was. There were enough failed adherents littered across the External Worlds.

And finally the harem. Typical male fantasy; a rich man making his dreams come true. Yet a lot more common than in Sheldon's day; group-life-partner relationships were growing in popularity among the External Worlds. And she was hardly in any position to criticize; what she'd enjoyed with Bovey was essentially the same arrangement. So here she was, technically free and single, and still interested in experimenting sexually to see what suited her. She didn't think this was going to be her, but she'd surprised herself before with Bovey.

A last wild fling, then. So whatever I discover, this weekend will be win-win.

With that delinquent thought warming her, the capsule finally made land and began to fly over Likan's estate. He owned an area of a hundred thousand square miles, taking in a long stretch of coastline – developed with resort complexes. Massive tracts of farmland with square-mile fields, growing every imaginable luxury crop, the kind nobody produced in a culinary unit, tended by over a million agribots; all processed in immaculately hygienic cybernated factories and sold under his own brands.

Then there was Albany, his industrial complex. Set on a flat plain, it was a square eight miles to a side; tall boxy buildings laid out in a perfect grid; every one a factory or processing plant. A spaceport spread out of one side, long rows of landing pads stretching across the green meadows to a nearby river. Ocean barges clotted the water, while fat cargo starships formed near-solid lines stretching up through the sky. No humans actually lived in Albany itself; the technicians who kept it running were all housed in dormitory towns twenty miles away. She flew over one of them, surprised by how nice it looked, with large houses and plenty of green space, ornate civic buildings providing every amenity.

He owns it all. And more: he created it. Now that is real vision.

Her capsule's net was queried by local traffic control. She supplied her identity certificate and received a descent vector.

Likan's home was actually three separate buildings. Two of them were on the shore of a lake ten miles long. One was a giant chateau made of stone which must have had five hundred rooms. Araminta had seen smaller villages. The second, almost opposite the first, was an ultramodern ovoid of shimmering opalescence that seemed to dip down into the water as it lay longside across the ground. The third was small by comparison, just a wooden lodge atop the cliffs of a rugged island.

The capsule landed outside the ovoid. Araminta was quietly grateful. She wanted to see what it was like inside, if there were any design concepts she could use.

Two of the harem were waiting to greet her when she stepped out. Clemance, a slim teenager, dressed in a simple white shirt and blue cotton shorts. She had a fresh face, freckled on her nose and brow, an eager smile, and fair hair that was barely styled. Not quite what Araminta had expected. While the other, Marakata, was tall and classically beautiful, with ebony skin that gleamed in the sunlight. Her scarlet gown probably cost more than every item Araminta had brought put together. *And that's what she wears in the middle of the afternoon?* Subtle cosmetic scales highlighted jade eyes and a wide mouth. She didn't smile, her whole attitude was one of cool amusement.

Clemance bounded forward, her smile growing even wider. She threw her arms around Araminta. 'Likan has told us all about you. It's so great to finally get to meet you.'

A mildly startled Araminta gave the girl a tentative hug back. 'What did he say?'

'To be careful,' Marakata said. She raised an elegant eyebrow, observing Araminta's response.

'He says you're really ambitious, and smart, and attractive, and your own boss—' Clemance seemed to run out of breath. 'Just all-round fabulous.'

Araminta finally managed to disentangle herself from the girl. 'I didn't realize I'd made such an impression.'

'Likan makes very fast assessments,' Marakata said.

'Do you?' Araminta asked, as cool as she could.

It actually drew a small smile from the imposing woman. 'I take my time and get it absolutely right.'

'Good to know.'

Clemance giggled. 'Come on, we'll show you your room.' She grabbed Araminta's hand and pulled like a five-year-old hauling her parent to the Christmas tree.

'The staff will get your bags,' Marakata said airily.

Araminta frowned, then saw she wasn't joking. A couple of women in identical smart grey toga suits were heading for her capsule, followed by a regrav sled. 'You have human staff?'

'Of course.'

'So Nigel Sheldon must have had them.'

'Humm, you are quite quick, aren't you?'

Clemance laughed, and pulled harder. 'Come on! I chose this one for you.'

They were right up against the scintillating surface. Araminta hadn't realized how big the ovoid was. Standing at the base it must have reached ten storeys above her, though the curvature made it hard to tell. There were no discernible features, certainly no door. The entire base was surrounded by a broad marble path, as if it were resting on a plinth. A couple of thin gold lines had materialized underfoot, which Clemance had followed. She slipped through the torrent of multicoloured light. Araminta followed. It was similar to walking through a pressure field, or a spore shower, a slight tingle on the skin, bright flash against the eye, and she was in a bubble-chamber with transparent furniture delineated by glowing emerald lines, like curving laser beams. Closets and drawers were all empty, chairs and couches contained a more diffuse glow inside their cushions, looking like faulty portal projections. The floor and cupola walls were a duller version of the external scintillations. Only the cream and gold sheets on the bed were what she thought of as tangible.

'The house smartnet is offering an operations program,' her u-shadow told her.

'Accept it.' Her exovision showed her the file opening into a storage lacuna.

Clemance was already sitting on the edge of the bed, bouncing up and down. 'Like it?'

'The house's main entrance opens into a guest bedroom?'

'Only when you need it to be,' the girl said sprightly. 'Tell your control program you want to see out.'

Araminta did, and the walls on one side lost their lustre to show the gardens outside, and her capsule with the regrav sled loading up cases.

'Now, if you need the bathroom . . .' Clemance said. The whole room started to slide upwards, following the curvature of the external wall. There must have been excellent gravity compensators hidden somewhere below the floor because Araminta didn't feel any movement. Then they were sliding horizontally into the centre of the ovoid. Other bubble rooms flowed past them.

Araminta imagined this was the perspective which corpuscles had as they raced through a vein. She smiled in delight. 'How brilliant, the whole thing is protean.'

Her bedroom touched a bathroom, and the wall rolled apart to give her access. The design beyond the new door was more conventional, with a huge pool-bath, showers, dryer chambers. It was bigger than the living rooms back in the apartments she was developing.

'You want to see someone, or go to the dining room for dinner, or just change the view – tell the house,' Marakata said.

'I will,' Araminta said positively.

A door opened opposite the bathroom, and Marakata stepped through. Araminta caught a glimpse of an all-white chamber with a long desk, and gym apparatus. 'I'll see you later,' Marakata said, and the door swept shut behind her.

'Was that a threat?' Araminta muttered.

'Oh ignore her,' Clemance said. 'She's always shy around new people. She's a lot more fun in bed, honest.'

'I'm sure.' Araminta turned round, giving the room a more thorough inspection. The drawers began to fill up with her clothes. The process was like watching water bubble up into a glass. 'Take me to Likan,' she told her u-shadow.

The room closed the door into the bathroom. Curving walls

slipped past; horizontally then curving to vertical. 'And opaque the walls.' Gravity might be perfectly stable, but the sight was strangely disorientating.

Likan's room was huge. Araminta suspected it didn't move often. Everything else in the house would be displaced. It was circular with a polished oak floor which appeared to be a single giant segment. Vat grown; she'd read a file on the process in one of her design courses. The walls were pale pink and blue, with a translucent eggshell texture. They slipped into transparency along a third of the length, providing a panorama out across the lake.

Likan was walking towards her, dressed in a simple mauve sweatshirt and long green shorts. Small coloured symbols were shrinking around him, then vanishing. The walls must be portals, she thought, which gave them a vast projection capacity. This was probably his office. He smiled warmly, paused in front of her and gave her a kiss. The kind of kiss that told her what he was expecting from her later.

'Great house,' she said.

'I knew you'd like it. The concept is an old one, but we've just got the manufacturing process down to an affordable level. Not easy without Higher replicators.'

'I'd like to have the Colwyn City franchise.'

He responded with a warm, admiring smile. 'Now see, most developers would have made a crack about me putting them out of business. But you . . . you see how to adapt and move onward. That's what makes you stand out.'

'Thank you.'

Clemance scampered over to a new door. 'Catch you later.'

Likan waved dismissively as he led Araminta over to the transparent wall. 'Drink? Food?' he asked.

'I'm good for a few hours.'

'Good. The Prime Minister and two cabinet ministers are coming for dinner.'

'Are you trying to impress me?'

'They were coming anyway. But hopefully it gives you an idea of the life I lead. To get this big you have to delve into politics.'

'Colwyn City Hall can be a beast issuing permits.'

'Take the development officer for dinner. Loan your local councillor a high-end capsule. They're all in it for what they can get. Wouldn't be feeding from the public trough otherwise.'

'Unless they're in it to clean up the corruption.'

'Yeah. Those ones are a problem. Fortunately, they don't tend to last long.'

'You're a cynic.'

'Pragmatist, if you don't mind. I'm also a lot more experienced than you in every field. So trust me when I say politicians all have their weakness.'

'What's yours?' she teased.

'One, I'm an easy lay. But you already know that. Two, risk. Risk is my weakness. The sensation when a risk pays off is like nothing else. I always take the risk. I enjoy the reward too much not to.'

'So what risk are you taking right now?'

'You're smart, you've researched me. The finance files, at least. Tell me.'

'I accessed some background on my way over. Opinion is you're dangerously overextended.'

'And those loans have grown significantly in the last couple of years. So why do you think that is?'

'You're going to wipe out property companies with houses like this one? Flood the market.'

He grinned. 'Small scale. I think big. Besides, it'll take a decade for something like this to first become fashionable then generally accepted. Think, what's the most pressing problem Viotia has today?'

'Living Dream?'

'Kind of. Ellezelin is always looming over us. Rightly so. The Free Trade Zone is a massive market; it's not going away and it's always growing. Anyone already operating in it has a huge financial and production capacity advantage over some poor little Viotia company. The worry is that when they eventually open a wormhole here all our companies will lose out to cheap imports. Trade will be one way.'

Her mind went back to Albany, the sheer scale of the place. 'You're going to undercut them.'

'Albany is as automated as anyone can be without replicators. I've spent a decade investing in the most advanced cybernated systems we can have to drive production costs down. To do that, to push each unit cost as low as it can physically go, you have to have massive volume production. That's what's killing me at the moment. The factories are barely ticking over. But when that wormhole finally opens . . .'

'It's not going to be the financial massacre they expect.'

'They import. I export. Only the quantity of those exports will be ten times greater than they assume.'

'You'd need a distribution network.'

His smile was triumphant as he turned out to face the lake. 'Certainly would.'

'Wow,' she said. And meant it. Likan's ambition was so great hers wouldn't even register on the same scale. 'Why tell me? You can't be trying to impress me into bed. You've already got that.'

'Although I have an egotistical opinion of my own ability, I can't actually manage every aspect by myself, even with an augmented mentality. Too many details. For an expansion phase on this level, I need people I can trust in senior management positions; especially offworld.'

'That's very flattering.'

'Yes and no. You'd be capable management, I think; you have the right kind of drive and mindset. You don't have the experience to be top rank, but that will come.'

She frowned. 'Why me?'

'How much research did you really do? On Sheldon himself?'

'None,' she admitted. 'Just what I picked up in school.'

'The old Dynasties were just that, family enterprises. The surest way humans have ever come up with to retain loyalty and control. Nigel used his own flesh and blood.'

514

'Ah.' It was as if the room was suddenly on the move: down-wards.

'All the senior positions were held by his own children,' Likan said. 'That's also what I do.'

A memory abruptly rushed to the fore of her mind. 'Debbina?' she said before she could stop it.

Likan actually winced. 'What did I ever do to you? No, okay, not my beloved little girl. But a lot of my other children are running sections of my company.'

'And how do I fit into this?'

'How do you think?'

'Spell it out for me.'

'You become one of my wives. You have my children. They take their place in the company.'

'You really know how to romance a girl.'

He flashed her a wry smile. 'Come on, we're grown-ups. Every marriage today is half business. We'll have a great time in bed. I can afford any lifestyle you want. Your children grow up being part of the most dynamic company in this section of the Commonwealth. They'll never want for anything, and they'll be presented with virtually unlimited challenges. I know you well enough to know that appeals. Who wants trust-fund brats, right? And the same goes for you. Stick with me for ten, fifteen years, then you can either continue with a post in the company, or you cut loose with a huge chunk of money and enough insider knowledge to run circles around everyone else.'

'Ozzie's mother! Are you serious?'

'Perfectly.'

'It's very flattering, but isn't it a bit sudden?'

'You think Sheldon hesitated when he saw something he wanted? No way. He went out and got it. And this isn't quite that sudden, now is it? We had a connection back at my symposium; you're not going to deny that, now are you?'

'No,' she admitted.

'So. There's physical attraction. Which just leaves your abilities. I did some research.'

'Your fifth assistant's coffee boy did some research.'

'Indeed,' he acknowledged wryly. 'You're the original kid from nowhere. Rejects the cosy family business route. Looking to get out. Failed marriage. Now on the bounce-back curve. You're hungry. And capable. With the experience my organization can provide you'll flourish.' He sidled up close, and put his arm round her, kissing again, more gently this time. 'I don't want an answer this instant. This is why you're here. Experience everything you can and you want, then take you time and decide.'

Wow, second time I've had that proposal in a month.

'Okay,' she said shakily. 'I'll do that.'

'You mean it? You're not just saying that?'

'No. I mean it.'

Araminta didn't wear her own clothes for dinner. That was the first thing she learned about what membership of the harem would be like. A stylist called Helenna was waiting in her bedroom when it collected her from Likan's airy office. A jovial woman, close to rejuvenation, whose age meant she'd piled on a lot of weight in recent years. Genuinely friendly, she was keen to confide household gossip, most of which made no sense to Araminta, although there was a lot of it. She'd been with Likan for fifty years. 'So I know it all, honey, seen even more. I don't judge anyone, and nothing you do here is going to surprise me. You want anything *special* for tonight, you just ask me for it.' Araminta wasn't sure what counted as that *special*. It was tempting to ask what other girls had requested. One thing Helenna was sure of was that, 'Likan likes his women elegant. So we've got to get you spruced up, ready to stand your own ground against the others.'

That took hours. Her bedroom bounded all over the ovoid house to link up with various other specialist rooms. The sauna to start with, clearing her pores. Massage, by a man called Nifran, who was as brutal as he was skilful; afterwards she just sort of poured herself off the table with loose floppy limbs. The fitting room. *A house that has a fitting room?* Where she was measured up for her evening dress.

Spiralling down to the salon, where Helenna was finally exposed as a sorceress. Layers of cosmetic membrane were applied, yet when Araminta looked in the mirror there was no sign of them. Instead her nineteen-year-old self looked back at her. A nineteen that she'd never known but always wanted, with sharp cheekbones, absolutely no excess flesh, soft long eyelashes, perfectly clear skin, eyes that sparkled. Another hour saw her hair *repaired*, as Helenna disapprovingly termed the first procedure. Then extended, thickened, softened, waved, and styled.

Clemance had the chair next to her as it was being done. Another member of the harem, Alsena, took the other side. They chatted comfortably enough, which was an insight into the kind of sisterhood the women had. She was given a rundown of Likan's genealogy with emphasis on the wayward children, a saga for which she needed to open a new file in a storage lacuna to keep track of.

For all their friendliness, the girls weren't quite *engaged* with the real world. Which was a pretty bitchy observation, but one Araminta felt applied. If Likan wanted women like her, what was he doing with the others? They certainly didn't aspire to run sections of his corporate empire.

'He likes variety,' Helenna told her as the salon rendezvoused back with the fitting room.

The classic *little black dress* had never fallen out of style. And looking at the one the fitting room's apprentice sorceresses had conjured up for her, Araminta could see why. She felt randy just slipping into it – so Ozzie alone knew what effect it would have on any male that crossed her path. It clung disgracefully, yet allowed her breasts complete freedom of movement. She blushed the first time she walked in it. Somehow the high hem and silk-gloss microfabric sprayed on her legs made her calves and thighs slim down to that same nineteen-year-old ideal Helenna's spell had blessed her face with for the night.

Pre-dinner cocktails were served to the household and Likan's guests in the music room, which had claimed his office's lake view. Araminta walked in with her head held high, knowing just how great she looked. Likan's double-take, and the smiles from the harem, Clemance's little bounce as she clapped her hands excitedly, were all the accolades she was simply due. It all helped buoy her confidence close to levels of arrogance. So when Likan introduced her to the Prime Minister and her husband, she was perfectly civil, and treated them as if they were almost her equal.

All the while as she made small talk and sampled weird-tasting canapés she kept wondering how Bovey would behave if he were here. He enjoyed his culture, and could be as snobbish about food and wine as anyone. But the company she mingled with; the world's powerful and wealthy, and a few merely famous – she just couldn't get away from the idea of how he'd turn his nose up at them.

Yet here I am, holding my own.

The evening did have a downside. The Prime Minister's husband, who she was seated next to at the dinner table, was fantastically boring. Thankfully, Eridal, one of Likan's older sons, sat on her other side. As smart and charming as Likan, he ran a finance house in Ludor; but he lacked that bullish determination which drove his father. She dutifully tried to not spend the whole evening chatting to him.

When it was all over, after the dining hall had descended to ground level so the guests could walk to their capsules, there were just Likan and eight of his harem left. The door contracted and the walls resumed their sparkle; everyone gave a spontaneous laugh of release which Araminta joined in wholeheartedly.

Likan gave her a congratulatory kiss. 'Dammit I'd forgotten how awful that dickhead was,' he told her. 'I wanted to smack him one, and he wasn't even talking to me. Thanks for putting up with him.'

Doors were opening into various bedrooms around the dining hall. The harem were vanishing through them. Out of all the women at the dinner, they were undeniably the most beautiful, most of them astonishingly so. Despite all Helenna's efforts, Araminta couldn't help but feel like the poor relation in their presence.

'Go and get ready,' Likan told her. 'We'll be waiting.'

He turned and left through a door into a small darkened room. Araminta stared after him for a moment, then summoned her own bedroom. That whole alpha male issuing orders thing just didn't do it for her. For one, he didn't have the charisma to pull it off, not with his dress sense and throwback physical appearance. On the other hand to have accomplished so much was darkly compelling. She grinned at her own inner argument. *What the hell, at least Clemance will be fun.*

'Dress me the way he'll enjoy,' she told the waiting Helenna. A process which turned out to be more elaborate than she anticipated. For a start it involved Nifran again, who chided her about lack of proper exercise, and how he couldn't relax her enough. What he did with her legs was virtually sex in itself.

Helenna applied some fabulously scented oil which acted in conjunction with Nifran's pummelling to make her flesh glow.

'He's not into sadism or anything, is he?' Araminta asked. These preparations were all very detailed. Her usual idea of getting ready for a hot night was wearing something a man could remove quickly.

'Not to worry, sweetie, he enjoys sex the way he enjoys his women; tasteful.'

Pondering that, Araminta allowed Helenna to dress her. The white negligee was mostly straps, yet perversely managed to cover more of her body than the black dress. She checked herself out in the mirror. *So his idea of tasteful is a Slut Princess? How very male.*

Her bedroom whisked her away to Likan's boudoir – no other word for it. Vast bed in the middle, naughty-shaped furniture, low rose-gold lighting. Harem in attendance, and yes, dressed *elegantly* in silk and satin, with open gowns swirling, lounging on couches sipping champagne as they watched two of their number make love on the bed.

Araminta strolled in, trying not to appear too apprehensive. Likan greeted her, wearing a black robe. 'Champagne?' he offered.

'Thank you.' She took a crystal flute from Marakata, who gave her a detailed appraisal. There was something alarmingly erotic about the way the aloof woman seemed able to look right through the negligee.

'You two should kiss,' Likan said.

Araminta pressed herself against the statuesque woman, enjoying the sensual touch. Marakata certainly knew how to kiss.

When they'd finished Araminta took a sip of the champagne as Likan took her hand and led her slowly over to the couch where Alsena was waiting. Araminta knelt down, and began the kiss.

As she went on to kiss all the other women as he instructed, Araminta decided the experience wasn't so much tasteful as formulaic. Likan had ritualized his lovemaking. Finally she kissed him. After that she was taken over to the bed. There was a specific way of kneeling he wanted her to assume, very sex kittenish. One of the harem helped arrange her hair decoratively over her shoulder.

Clemance removed Likan's gown. Araminta stared at his huge erection.

'I have a gift for you.'

'Yes,' she said emphatically. 'I see that.'

'A program.'

'Huh?'

'A melange I've composed myself over several years. It allows you deeper access to your own mind, opening levels that verge on the subconscious in the way the old yogis achieved through meditation.'

'Right,' she said dubiously. Talk about killing the mood.

He smiled fondly, and stroked her cheek. 'I use it myself to focus. It helps to clean your mind of extraneous thought. You can revert to the animal basics which form our core identity.' His face came close to hers. 'There are no inhibitions to be had in such a state. Whatever you pursue is unashamedly pure.'

'No inhibitions?'

'Clarity is a helpful tool for business. But also for lovemaking. You can concentrate on the sensations of your body to the exclusion of anything else. It helps to amplify even the smallest nerve signal.'

'You mean I can make a climax stronger?' It sounded like an electronic version of the sex aerosols she and Bovey used.

'Yes. There are also adapted biofeedback routines which can influence your physical self. Once you determine the origin of your body's pleasure, you can repeat it.' His voice became softer, tempting. 'As many times as you have the physical strength for.'

Her u-shadow told her he was offering the program. Suddenly, she was feeling very hot in the negligee. 'Scan it for infiltrators and trojans,' she told her u-shadow as she held his level gaze.

'It's clean.'

'Load and run.' Through her exovision she watched the program expand into one of her lacunas. It had many similarities with a learning program, which she allowed to mushroom into her grey matter. Instinctive knowledge bubbled away in her mind.

'Don't be afraid,' Likan said softly. 'I'll use it with you. It will make our first time spectacular.'

She nodded, not trusting herself to speak. Now she considered it, clearing her mind was a simple process; following the rising sleep cycles yet never accepting them. Her breathing steadied, and she grew aware of the body's rhythms, the flow of nervous energy. Heartbeat. Peripheral thoughts fell away, allowing her to centre herself in the boudoir, on the bed. Her awareness grew of the light touch of fabric against her skin. Tiny beads of perspiration clung to her. The sound of bubbles fizzing in the crystal flutes. Likan's breathing. She saw his arm move out, a finger beckon.

Marakata answered the summons, sliding sinuously over the mattress. Her fingers stroked Araminta's skin. The sensations her nerves experienced flowed like a tidal wave into her brain. She gasped at the impact, and pulled her attention to the sensations which were most pleasurable. Wallowing in them.

Under Likan's direction, Marakata plucked the negligee straps off Araminta's shoulders. Air flowed over her exposed breasts, followed by warm fingers. Araminta shuddered fiercely at the touch, smiling as she centred her mind on the feeling. Blood was loud and hot as it rushed into her nipples, swelling the buds.

'There,' she told the owner of the fingers.

The caress was repeated, the ecstasy replicated. Then many hands were gliding over her. Warm eager mouths kissed. She wailed with helpless delight at the symphony of sensation which the harem kindled. The negligee was removed completely. Instinctively she arched her back. Likan's cock slid inside her. The experience was close to unbearable, it was all there was. Still her mind remained steadfast on the torrent of physical joy. Araminta promised herself, no matter what, she would not faint away as she had done with Bovey. This time there were no chemicals fugging her mind, this time she was free to experience its incredible conclusion. She laughed and wept simultaneously as Likan started to move in a powerful rhythm. Then the harem recommenced their virtuoso performance.

The Skylord glided across the outer atmosphere of the solid planet; its vacuum wings long since retracted. Thick turbulent streams of the ionosphere swept across its forward section, creating lengthy vibrations across its giant bulk. Energy stirred in specific patterns within it, thoughts mingling with its body's elemental power, manipulating the fabric of the universe outside. Its speed began to slow, as it imposed its wishes on reality. Gently it started to lower itself into the atmosphere. Far below, the minds of the sentient entities sang out in welcome.

'Now!' Cleric Conservator Ethan commanded the obedient waiting minds of the Dream Masters.

Their thoughts flared out into the gaiafield in a single stream, pushing at the dream fabric, seeking entry. Tendrils of raw will prodded and poked at the stubbornly resistant image emanating from the Second Dreamer. As the Skylord began to focus its attention on the ancient coastal city beneath, they felt its perception turn outwards, towards them. It felt them! It knew they were there!

'My Lord,' Ethan called with profound respect. 'We need your help.'

The Skylord's descent halted. Those dreaming the Skylord felt the mass of the planet press against the magnificent creature's perception. In that way they *knew* the winds that blew across the Iguru Plain. Experienced the waves rolling lazily over the Lyot Sea towards the coast. And there, right underneath them, so tantalizingly close, the physical form of Makkathran's buildings brushed against their consciousness. Each one exactly as it was in Inigo's dreams.

Adoration and gratitude swelled out into the gaiafield, buoying Ethan's thoughts along. 'We seek to reach you. Show us the way to you, my Lord. Receive us.'

The dream shattered into a glorious pinnacle of agony. The Skylord's magisterial thoughts were wrenched away by a terrible power.

'NO!' the Second Dreamer commanded amid the ruined bliss. 'I am me.'

An infinite black surface swelled with malignant anger, sealing the gulf between the gaiafield and the Skylord.

Blinding pain seared deep into Ethan's mind as the blackness snapped at him. He screamed, every muscle contorting to fling him out of his chair and fall into merciful unconscious.

Araminta woke with a gasp, shooting upright on the bed; heart racing and breath coming in judders. She instinctively applied the program's knowledge again; settling her racing mind and quelling her body's distress. It worked a treat.

What the fuck is it with that dream?

It had been quite pleasant to start with, drifting gently above a strange planet; warm sun on her back, mysterious continents rolling by underneath. Then something happened, a smothering sensation that triggered an adrenaline rush, and she had to thrash about, trying to wake herself. Push herself clear from that oppressive constriction. It was as if someone was trying to steal her soul. She yelled defiance at the dark force, and finally managed to wake.

Kicking and writhing around as she shouted. Surely? Yet actually all she seemed to have done was shuffle round a bit and sit up.

She looked about her in confusion. Likan's boudoir was still illuminated by the same warm light. Nobody else was awake. Clemance was curled up beside her, one arm draped over her legs. The girl was stirring, blinking in confusion as Araminta moved. Araminta stroked her tangled hair and cheek, soothing her as she would a troubled child. A drowsy Clemance smiled worshipfully then closed her eyes again.

Araminta blew out an exasperated breath, and slowly sank back down. Despite the supple mattress her body was stressed tight – which would no doubt annoy Nifran. As she lay there rigid, she could hear two of the harem whimpering softly in their sleep. So she wasn't the only one suffering a bad dream. She wondered if she should creep across the room to wake them. But eventually they subsided into a deeper sleep. Yet she still couldn't relax and drop off. There was something scrabbling about in her subconscious that was unsettling her, an elusive memory she was trying to connect. Not the dream, something before that.

Once again, the program came to her aid. She cleared her mind and concentrated on her memories of the orgy. Physically, it had been hugely satisfying – no denying that. And the harem had delighted in teaching her a whole range of sensual acts which they and Likan enjoyed. But it was that ritual thing again; true passion had been missing, and with it the heat which came from abandoning herself the way she did with Bovey. This had been a little too much like mechanics, with all of them busy doing as Likan instructed.

Araminta sat up on the bed again, her skin cooling with shock. The memory of Likan and Marakata was perfectly clear in her mind, all thanks to his own wonderful program. *And how's that for irony.* She thought it through again, then reviewed some other suspicious recollections before finally dropping her head into her hands and groaning in dismay. 'Oh shit.'

True to her word, Helenna didn't judge. She made no comment as the house emptied the drawers and closets, the clothes slithering away through the interstices between the rooms to fill her cases in the butler's lodge. Araminta almost wanted to ask how many others she'd seen leave abruptly after a night with Likan. But that would have been unfair on both of them.

Her bedroom wound through the ovoid house, and opened a door on to the path which ran round the outside of the building. Dawn light was shining a murky grey off the placid lake. Two of the household's smartly suited staff were loading her cases back into her carry capsule.

'It's a shame, sweetie,' Helenna said. 'I had you down as one who'd fit in easily here.'

'Me too,' Araminta said. Gave the maid a quick hug. 'Thanks for everything.'

'Hey, it was nice meeting you.'

Araminta turned and walked out of the bedroom. The door unrolled behind her.

'Wait!' Clemance called out. 'You can't leave!' She was hurrying out of another door, ten metres away, trying to pull on a translucent wrap.

Likan walked behind her, considerably more composed in a thick dark-purple robe. 'Not even going to say goodbye?' he asked. There was a nasty frown on his puggish face.

'The house's net is active. You knew I was leaving. If you wanted to say anything before I left, you could,' Araminta told him. 'And here you are.'

'Yes, here I am. I would like to know why you're running out. I think I'm entitled after the offer I made you. I know you enjoyed yourself last night. So what is this?'

Araminta glanced at the distraught girl who was hovering between them, uncertain who to go to. 'Are you sure?'

Likan took a step forward and put his arm around Clemance's shoulder, helping to pull her wrap on. 'I don't keep anything from my wives.'

'Even that they're psychoneural profiled?'

His face remained impassive. 'It was helpful to begin with.'

'*Helpful?*' she cried. 'You had them bred to be your slaves. Profiling like that is illegal, it always has been. It's a vile, inhuman

525

thing to do. They don't have a choice. They don't have free will. It's obscene! Why, for Ozzie's sake? You don't need to force people into your bed. I would have probably joined you. And I know there are thousands of others who'd love the chance. Why did you do it?'

Likan glanced down at Clemance with an almost paternal expression. 'They were the first,' he said simply.

'First?'

'Of my harem. I had to start it somewhere. It was the bootstrap principle.'

'What are you talking about?'

'To start with, when you have nothing, you begin by pulling yourself up by your own bootstraps. I needed to be him, to be Nigel Sheldon. He had a harem, therefore I had one. You don't understand what that man was. He *ruled* hundreds of worlds, billions of people. I wasn't joking when I called him an emperor. He was the greatest human who ever lived. I need to know how to think like he did.' He almost ground the words out.

'So you created slaves to achieve that?'

'They're not slaves. All of us are predisposed to various personality traits. The way they combine: that's what makes us individuals. I just amplified a few of the behavioural attributes in the girls.'

'Yeah: submissiveness! I watched them last night, Likan. They obeyed you like they were bots.'

'The relationship is a lot more complex than that.'

'That's what it boils down to. Why didn't you profile yourself to think like Sheldon? If you have to wreck somebody, why not yourself?'

'I have incorporated his known neural characteristics into my DNA. But a neural structure is only a vessel for personality. You need the environment as well. As complete as you can make it.'

'Oh, for Ozzie's sake! You have deliberately, maliciously bred slaves. And you think that's an acceptable way to achieve what you are. That makes me sick. I don't want any part of you or your perverted family. You won't even let them go! Why don't you remove their profiling when they go for rejuvenation treatment?'

'I created them because of my belief, wrongly in your opinion; now you think they should be altered because of your belief. Does that strike you as slightly ironic? There's an old saying that two wrongs don't make a right. I take responsibility for my wives, especially the profiled ones – just as Sheldon would have done.'

Araminta glowered at him, then she switched her attention to Clemance, softening her expression to plead. 'Come with me. Come away from here. It's reversible. I can show you what it's like to be free, to be truly human. I know you don't believe me, but just please try. Try, Clemance.'

'You're such a fool,' the girl said. She pressed harder into Likan. 'I'm not profiled. I like this. I like being in the harem. I like the money. I like the life. I like that my children will rule whole planets. Without Likan, what will yours ever be?'

'Themselves,' Araminta said weakly.

Clemance gave her a genuinely pitying look. 'That's not good enough for me.'

Araminta raised an uncertain hand. 'Is she . . . ?'

'There were only ever three,' Likan said. 'Clemance is not one of them. Would you like to guess again?'

Araminta shook her head. She didn't trust herself to speak. *Marakata. Marakata is one, I know. Perhaps if I just . . .*

'Goodbye,' Likan said.

Araminta climbed into the carry capsule, and told it to take her home.

*

Oscar had never thought he'd return to the very place where he died. Of course, he hadn't expected to see Paula Myo again, either.

Just to make matters worse, enterprising Far Away natives had turned his last desperate hyperglide flight into a tourist attraction. Worse still, it was a failing attraction.

Still, at least Oscar had got to name the brand-new starship which ANA had delivered to Orakum for him, and without much thought went and called it the *Elvin's Payback*. There was a large briefing file sitting in its smartcore, which he zipped through and sent a few queries to Paula, who by then was back in her own starship and en route to somewhere. She wouldn't say where.

After he'd finished the file, one thing became very clear to him. Paula had severely overestimated his abilities. There were a lot of very powerful, very determined groups searching for the Second Dreamer. Now that might not have fazed Paula, but . . . 'I'm only a pilot,' he repeated to her when she called him on a secure TD channel and asked him why he was flying to Far Away. She hadn't said she could track the *Elvin's Payback*, but somehow he wasn't surprised.

'I'm going to need help. And as you trust me, so I trust someone else.' He got an evil little buzz out of not telling her who. Though he suspected she would know – it was hardly hyper-space science.

He landed at Armstrong City starport, which was a huge field to the north-east of the city itself with four big terminal buildings handling passenger flights and a grid of warehouses where the freighters came and went. He picked out a parking pad out near the fence, away from any real activity. As the starship descended he swept its visual sensors across the ancient city that spread back from the shore of the North Sea. Inevitably, there was a dense congregation of tall towers and pyramids above the coast; while broad estates of big houses swamped the land behind. It was all a lot more chaotic than the layout of most Commonwealth cities, which he rather enjoyed. He was looking for a glimpse of Highway One, the historic road where his friends had chased the Starflyer to its doom. All that remained now was a long, fat urban strip following the old route as it struck out for miles across the Great Iril Steppes, as if city buildings were seeking to escape from their historical anchor at the centre. Like every Commonwealth world, Far Away's ground traffic was now a shrinking minority. The sky above the city swarmed with regrav capsules.

Oscar floated down out of the airlock underneath the *Elvin's*

Payback, and stood once more on the ground of Far Away. For some ridiculous reason he was trembling. He took a long moment, breathing in the air, then moved away from the starship. His feet pushed gently on the short grass, sending his body gliding in a short arc in the low gravity. He'd forgotten how enjoyable that part of this world was, those soar-lope steps were a freedom like having teenage hormones again.

Once he'd cleared the starship he stopped and turned a full circle. There was the city skyline on one side, some distant mountains. Nothing he recognized. Apart from the glorious sapphire sky. Thankfully, that had remained the same, as the planet's biosphere slowly regenerated with the new plants and creatures which humans had brought to this world.

Warm sea air gusted constantly from the passage of starships using the terminals, ruffling his hair. It was all very different to Orakum's main starport which he flew from, and had barely fifty flights a day. But then Far Away was the self-proclaimed capital of the External Worlds; the planet which had refused political and economic integration with the Greater Commonwealth. Even today, it was technically only an affiliate member. Its staunch independence had inspired a whole generation of newly settled worlds after the Starflyer War. The political will, coupled with the end of CST's transport monopoly which the starships brought, allowed the first cultural division to open within Commonwealth society as a whole. As the Sheldon Dynasty made biononics available, starting Higher culture, so Far Away's Barsoomians introduced genetic improvements which took the human body far beyond its natural meridian, developing into the Advancer movement. After that, Far Away with its fierce libertarianist tradition declared itself the ideological counterweight to Earth and ANA. The Commonwealth's Senators might regard the notion with their ancient wise distain, but Far Away's citizens *believed* their own destiny.

Oscar smiled at the busy city as he experienced the emotional tide of the local gaiafield. Even that had a stridency which celebrated the stubbornness of the inhabitants. His u-shadow opened a channel to the planetary cybersphere, and called a one-time address code he'd been given eighty-six years earlier, on the day he emerged from the re-life clinic. To his surprise, it was answered immediately.

'Yes?'

'I need to see you,' Oscar said. 'I have a problem and I need help sorting it out.'

'Who the fuck are you, and how did you steal this code?'

'I am Oscar Monroe, and this code was given to me. Some time ago.'

There was a long pause, though the channel remained open.

'If you are an impostor, you have one chance to walk away, and that chance is now.'

'I know who I am,' Oscar said.

'We'll know if you are.'

'Good.'

'Very well. Be at the Kime Sanctuary on top of Mount Herculaneum in one hour. One of us will meet you.'

The channel went dead. Oscar grinned. He shouldn't be all fired up by this, he really shouldn't.

His u-shadow contacted a local hire company, and he rented a high-performance ingrav capsule. Given who he was going to meet, he didn't want to risk technology leakage by arriving in an ultradrive ship.

The capsule bounced him over to Mount Herculaneum in a semi-ballistic lob that took twenty-eight minutes. The last time he'd seen the colossal volcano was the day he died by crashing into its lower slopes. Today, his arrival was all a lot more comfortable. The capsule shot out of the upper atmosphere, and followed the planet's curvature south-west. He watched through the sensors as the Grand Triad rose up out of the horizon. They were still the biggest mountains to be found on an H-congruous world. On a planet with a standard gravity, they would have collapsed under their own weight, but here they had kept on growing as the magma pushed further and further upwards. Mount Herculaneum, the biggest, stood thirty-two kilometres high, its plateau summit rising high above Far Away's tropo-sphere. Northwards, Mount Zeus topped out at seventeen kilo-metres. While south of Herculaneum, Mount Titan reached twenty-three kilometres high; it was the only one of the Triad to remain active.

Oscar's capsule rode a tight curve above the sea-like grasslands of the Aldrin Plains before it began to sink back down again. The view was magnificent, with the vast cone of Herculaneum spread out below him. Its plateau of grubby brown regolith was broken by twin calderas. Around that, naked rock dropped down to the glacier ring far below, before the lower slopes were finally smothered in pine forests and low meadowland. Luckily for him, Titan, was semi-active today. He looked down almost vertically into its glowing red crater, watching the slow-motion ripples spreading out across the huge lake of lava. Radiant white boulders spat upwards out of the inferno to traverse lazy arcs through the vacuum, spitting off orange sparks. Some of them were flung far enough to clear the crater wall and begin their long fall to oblivion.

His sight was inevitably drawn to the long funnel canyon between Zeus and Titan which led to the base of Herculaneum. Stakeout canyon, where the storm winds coming off the Hondu Ocean were funnelled into a rampaging blast of air, which the insane thrill seekers of the early Commonwealth used to fly their hypergliders along, allowing them to sail on winds so strong they'd push them out of the atmosphere and over Herculaneum. He'd never got to attempt that last part, because he crashed his hyperglider into Anna, so Wilson might stand a chance to reach the summit.

Even though he'd braced himself for some emotional shock-wave at seeing the site of his death, he felt nothing more than a mild curiosity. *That must mean I'm perfectly adjusted to this new life. Right?*

As he looked along the long rocky cleft in the ground, his exovision pulled up meteorological data and a file telling him that the winds now were never as strong as they had been a thousand years ago. Terraforming had successfully calmed Far Away's atmosphere. Hypergliding was just a legend now.

The capsule took him down to a big dome situated right on the eastern edge of Mount Herculaneum's plateau, where the cliffs of Aphrodite's Seat began their sheer eight-kilometre fall. There was a pressure field over the entrance to the dome's landing chamber, a big metal cave with enough room for twenty passenger capsules. It only had two resting inside, with another five ordinary capsules parked nearby.

Oscar stepped through the airlock pressure curtains into the dome's main arena, and paid his 20 FA$ entrance fee from a credit coin which Paula had given him. There were three low buildings inside, lined up behind Aphrodite's Seat. He went over to the first, which the dome's net labelled 'Crash Site'. A whole bunch of tourists were just exiting it, heading for the café next door, chatting excitedly. They never registered him, which he found amusing. It wasn't as if his face was any different now.

It was dark inside, with one wall open to the side of the dome above the cliffs. A narrow winding walkway was suspended three metres over the ground, with a pressure field below it, maintaining a vacuum over the actual regolith. There was also a stabilizer field generator running to preserve the wreckage of the hyperglider. The once-elegant fuselage was crunched up into the side of a rock outcrop, with the plyplastic wings bent and snapped. Oscar remembered how elegant those wings had been fully extended, and sighed.

He walked slowly along the walkway until he was directly above the antique. His heart had slowed right down as he imagined his friend terrified and frantic as the craft skidded along the dusty plateau, slipping and twisting, completely out of control. The fate of an entire species dependent on the outcome, and the cliffs rushing towards him. Oscar frowned as he looked down. The hyperglider was actually upside down, which meant there had been an almighty flip at one point. He looked along the ground to the rim of Aphrodite's Seat, where someone in an ancient pressure suit was sitting.

It was a solido projection, Oscar realized as he came to the end of the walkway. Wilson Kime, his head visible in a not terribly authentic bubble helmet. Pressure suit rips repaired with some kind of epoxy, leaking blood into the regolith. The solido Wilson stared out over the Dessault Mountain Range to the east, where the snow-capped peaks diminished into the bright haze of the curving horizon. This was exactly what the real Wilson had seen, what so many people had died to give him; those which history knew, and still more unknown. Twelve hundred years ago this glorious panorama had provided the data to steer a giant storm into the Starflyer's ship, slaying the beast and liberating the Commonwealth. Today, here on that same spot, he could sit in the Saviour View café next door and buy doughnuts named after himself.

'Without you, we wouldn't be here.'

Oscar started. There was a man standing behind him on the walkway, wearing a very dark toga suit.

Great secret agent I make; anyone can creep up on me.

'Excuse me?' Oscar said.

The man smiled. He was very handsome, with a square jaw, dimpled chin, and a flattish nose. Brown eyes were surrounded by laughter lines. When he opened his wide mouth, startlingly white teeth smiled out. 'I nearly got blown away by that burst of melancholy disappointment you let loose into the gaiafield,' he said. 'It's understandable.' He waved a hand round the darkened chamber. 'This travesty is all that exists to celebrate what you and Wilson achieved. But I promise you, *we* know and appreciate what you did. It is taught to all of our children.'

'We?'

The man bowed his head formally. 'The Knights Guardian. Welcome back to Far Away, Oscar Monroe. How can we help you?'

His name was Tomansio, he said as they walked back to Oscar's capsule. 'In full, Tomansio McFoster Stewart. It was my father who provided you with our code eighty-six years ago.'

'I barely saw him. The government had a tight little cordon

around my room. They were anxious I should have my privacy. Yet he just walked right in. And out again, too.'

'We thought you'd forgotten us,' Tomansio said. 'Or worse.'

'I'm not what I used to be,' Oscar said. 'At least, that's what I thought.'

'And yet here you are. It's an interesting time to come and seek us out again, for both the Greater Commonwealth and the galaxy at large. Not the kind of time a man chooses to indulge in nostalgia.'

'No. This has nothing to do with nostalgia.'

They sat themselves in the capsule. 'Do you mind if I navigate?' Tomansio asked. 'You would find it difficult to reach our lands unaided.'

'Of course,' Oscar said. His curiosity rose as they slid out of the dome's landing chamber. 'Where are your lands?'

'Where they've always been. From the north-east corner of the Dessault Mountains all the way to the Oak Sea.' The capsule began to accelerate, streaking northward over the mountains as it gained altitude. For the first time, Oscar saw the High Desert around which the lofty peaks huddled protectively.

'And I couldn't find you? I think that peak is Mount St Omer, isn't it? The *Marie Celeste* crashed close by.'

'Knowing and reaching are two separate things.'

'I didn't know you all turned Buddhist and spoke in fortune cookies.'

Tomansio tilted his head to one side with avian precision. His attractive smile poised. 'Ah, I see. I'm not being deliberately enigmatic. Though perhaps I am guilty of overdramatizing. But you are very precious to us, Oscar. I'm hoping to impress you.'

Just for a moment, Oscar felt as if he'd lived through every one of those eleven hundred years. *He had to history mine to understand me. Jesus fuck.* He'd been far too sheltered with his life partners. Small wonder he always felt as if the house put up a cosy barrier between his little family and the outside world.

'We protect our lands with a T-sphere,' Tomansio said.

'Really? I thought only Earth had one.'

'We don't advertise. It's actually quite an elegant defence on so many levels, although it does require a colossal amount of energy to maintain. If you walk or drive or fly towards us, as you approach our border you're simply teleported to the other side. You can't knock on a door which you can never face. You have to be invited in.'

'Cool.'

The lands they fell towards seemed particularly lush. Thick greenery split by meandering rivers, forest and meadowland squabbling to dominate valleys and rolling hills. Away to the east, a glimpse of the Oak Sea. They re-entered the atmosphere. Strands of cloud rushed up past the capsule's transparent hull, thickening fast. Then they were through, and a forest canopy unfolded below them, leaves of every colour, trees of immense size. Far Away had always celebrated its unique genetic diversity. Starting with a near-sterile landscape, the terraforming teams had brought the seeds of a hundred planets with them to create the ultimate contrasting florascape.

'Here we go,' Tomansio said as their altitude approached three miles.

The view outside suddenly switched. Oscar jumped in his seat. They were now floating a hundred yards above the ground at the head of a long valley. Blue-green grass rippled away for miles on every side, lapping against woodlands that spilled out of the dips in the valley walls. There were houses all around them, built from wood and stone, blending nicely with the environment, like some medieval village back on Earth. Except this was on a much grander scale.

'You live here?' Oscar asked.

'Yes.'

'I'm envious.'

'Appearances can be deceiving.'

The capsule touched down outside one of the stone houses, a long building with age-blackened wood beams protruding from beneath a slate roof. A balcony ran along one side. Big windows were open, showing a glimpse of a very modern interior. The grass swept right up to the walls, emphasizing the impression of natural harmony.

Oscar stepped out wearily. The gaiafield was resonating with a warm subtle joy, wrapping him in a daydream of a child being swept up in its mother's arms; the comfort and security of being *home.*

It was a welcome emanating from the people hurrying across the land to greet him. They came out of nearby houses, or simply teleported in, popping into existence to enlarge the crowd. Then the horses appeared, a whole cavalry squad riding up over a nearby ridge, dressed in some dark uniform which trailed gold and scarlet heraldic streamers behind their shoulders. The horses themselves were clad in a metal mesh, with hems of gold tassels brushing the tips of the grass. He stared at the giant, fearsome beasts, with their metal-clad horns and sharp tusks, memories stirring.

'I've seen one of those before,' he exclaimed, excitedly. 'On our drive to the mountains. A Charlemagne. Somebody guided us.'

'Yes,' Tomansio said. 'We still train to fight on them. But we've never actually ridden them into battle since the Planet's Revenge. It's all ceremonial now, part of our skill set. The riders are here to honour your arrival. As do the king eagles.' He gestured upwards.

Oscar just managed not to flinch; he did gasp, though. A flock of giant avian creatures swirled overhead. Resembling the petrosaurs of Earth's dinosaur era, they had been created by the Barsoomians as part of their quest for genetic expansion. Each one had a rider, dressed in long flowing robes that fluttered behind them. They waved as they passed overhead, turning and twisting with amazing finesse. Oscar grinned unashamedly at their acrobatic antics. Surely those riders had to be strapped on?

Tomansio cleared his throat discreetly. 'Perhaps a few words,' he whispered into Oscar's ear.

Oscar had been so entranced by the king eagles he hadn't noticed just how many people were now gathered in front of him. He gazed across them, slightly unnerved by their appearance. It was as if some kind of athletics squad had turned out to

536

see him. Without fail they were tall; the men handsome, the women beautiful; and all of them hugely fit. Even the smiling, eager children were healthy specimens. He couldn't help but think of H. G. Wells's particular vision of the future from *The Time Machine*. Here in their protected edenistic garden, the Knights Guardians were like Eloi, but with muscles, and *attitude*. Heaven help the Morlock who wandered into this valley.

Oscar drew a breath, *really* trying not to think of the media briefings he had to give while he was in the Navy. 'I haven't been to Far Away for a very long time. Too long, actually. You have made it a thrilling world, a world respected across the Commonwealth. For that I thank you, as I do for this welcome.'

The applause was heartfelt enough. Oscar bobbed his head, smiling round the earnest faces. He was hugely relieved when Tomansio ushered him into the house.

The reception room was clad in what looked like translucent white fabric that emitted a mild glow. There were strange deep folds in the walls, which hinted at parallel compartments. Aspects of the T-sphere, Oscar guessed. The furniture was solid enough, as was the little shrine which rested on a broad ancient wood table at the far end. Oscar slowed to a halt as he stared at the black-shrouded holographic portrait with its single candle burning underneath. The Cat's prim face returned her best enigmatic smile.

'For every Yin, a Yang,' Oscar murmured grimly. He should have known. The valley really had been too idyllic.

Tomansio came up to stand beside him. 'You knew her, didn't you? You actually spoke to her as you travelled to Far Away.'

'We spent a day together on the Carbon Goose flying across Half Way. I wouldn't say I knew her well.'

'How I envy you that day. Did she frighten you?'

'I was weary of her. We all were. Perhaps you should be?'

'I would not be frightened. I would be honoured.'

'She is evil.'

'Of course she is. But she is also noble. She showed us the way, she gave the Guardians of Selfhood purpose once more. She was the one who brought us together with the Barsoomians. After the Starflyer was destroyed, after you helped kill it, Oscar, there was nothing left for our ancestors. Bradley Johansson originally built us out of the ruin of enslavement. He forged us into warrior tribes to fight the greatest battle humans had ever known. The battle to save our entire species. And when it was over, he was dead, and we were lost, doomed to wither away as a dwindling band of old soldiers without a cause. An anachronistic embarrassment as Far Away was *civilized* by the Commonwealth.'

'Soldiers always have to hang up their weapons in the end.'

'You don't understand. It was our ethos she rescued. She showed us that strength is a virtue, a blessing. It is our evolution and should not be denied the way the liberals of the Commonwealth do, treating it as if it were some ignominious part of us to be always denied. If we had not been strong, if Bradley had not remained steadfast, the Commonwealth would have died on that same day you did, Oscar. If the Barsoomians hadn't maintained their clarity, today's humans would be emaciated short-lived creatures.' He smiled at the portrait. 'One of us had strength, the other, purpose. She saw them both and combined them into a single bold principle, she gave us a vision we can remain forever true to. There is no shame in strength, Oscar.'

'I know,' Oscar said reluctantly. 'That's why I'm here.'

'I had hoped that. You said you needed help.'

'I do.' He paused. 'What if it goes against your ideology?'

Tomansio laughed. 'We don't have one, Oscar. That's the point of the Knights Guardian movement. We follow one creed: strength. That is what we want to impart to humanity as it grows and diversifies. It is the most basic evolutionary tenet. Those sections of humanity who embrace it will survive, it's as simple as that. We are nature as raw as it can get. The fact that we are perceived as nothing other than mercenaries is not our problem. When we are hired to perform a job we do it thoroughly.'

'I need subtlety for this. At least to begin with.'

'We can do subtle, Oscar. Covert operations are one of our specialties. We embrace all forms of human endeavour, apart

538

from the blatantly wicked, or stupid. For instance, we won't perform a heist for you. The Knights Guardians take their oath of honour very seriously. '

Oscar almost started to ask about the Cat and what she used to do. Decided against. 'I have to find someone, and then extend them an offer of protection.'

'That sounds very worthy. Who is it?'

'The Second Dreamer.'

For the first time since they'd met, Oscar witnessed Tomansio lose his reserve. 'No shit?' The Knight Guardian started to laugh. 'Twelve hundred years without you, and now you bring us this. Oscar, you were almost worth the wait. The Second Dreamer himself!' He suddenly sobered. 'I won't ask why. But thank you from the bottom of my simple heart for coming to us.'

'The why is actually very simple. There are too many people who wish to influence him. If he does choose to emerge from the shadows, he should be free to make his own choice.'

'To go to the Void or not, to possibly trigger the end of the Galaxy in pursuit of our race's fate – or not. What a grail to guard, Oscar. What a challenge.'

'I take it that's a yes?'

'My team will be ready to leave in less than an hour.'

'Will you be leading them?'

'What do you think?'

*

'I was *so* sure!' Araminta exclaimed. 'She was this mild scatty little thing. She did everything he told her to, and I do mean everything.'

'Face it, darling, at the time you weren't in any *position* to be the perfect observer,' Cressida said archly.

'But it was the way she did it. You don't understand. She was eager. Obedient. Like the other ones. I think. Shit. Do you think he was chossing me about? Maybe she is profiled and he told her to always give that answer.' Araminta made an effort to calm down. Alcohol was a good suppressant. She tipped the wine bottle over her glass. There was none left. 'Damn!'

Cressida signalled the smart-suited waiter. 'Quite an offer, though.'

'Yeah. What is it about men? Why are they all complete shits? I mean, what kind of mentality does that? Those women are slaves.'

'I know.'

The waiter brought another bottle over and flipped the seal. 'The gentleman over there has asked if he can pay for it.'

Araminta and Cressida looked across towards the giant floor-to-ceiling window, which gave them a stunning view out across the luminous glow of the night-time city. The bar was on the thirty-fifth floor of the Salamartin Hotel tower, and attracted a lot of tourist types who thought nothing of paying the absurd bar prices. Today every room in the hotel was taken by Living Dream followers, which was why the lobby was besieged by protesters. Araminta had forced her way through the angry chanting mob to plead with the doorman to let her in. She'd been frightened; there was a strong threat of violence building up on the street. Cressida of course had the authorization code to land her capsule on the executive rooftop pad.

The man smiling at them from a table in front of the window was dressed in natural fabric clothes styled as only a Makkathran resident would wear.

'No,' Araminta and Cressida chorused.

The waiter smiled understanding, and started pouring.

Araminta watched morosely as her glass was filled. 'Do you think I should go to the police?'

'No,' Cressida said emphatically. 'You do not go down that road, not ever. He sat you next to the Prime Minister at dinner for Ozzie's sake. You know how powerful he is. Besides which, no police force on the planet would investigate him, and even if they did they'd never be able to prove anything. Those girls – if you were right, and I'm not saying you're not – wouldn't ever be found, let alone analysed to see if their brain was wired up illegally. Forget it.'

540

'How about the Commonwealth Government? Don't they have some kind of crime agency?'

'The Intersolar Serious Crimes Directorate. So you take a trip to their local office, which is probably on Ellezelin, and you walk in and say you think some of his wives might be psychoneural profiled, because of how they behaved while you were all having sex together, an orgy during which incidentally your macrocellular clusters were running a sexual narcotic program.'

'It wasn't a narcotic,' Araminta said automatically.

'Point in your favour, then. That should do it.'

'All right! What if I told them about his commercial plans? The way he's built up Albany's capacity?'

'Tell whom?'

Araminta pouted. For a friend, Cressida wasn't being very helpful. 'I'm not sure. The industrial association of Ellezelin, or whatever it's called.'

'Do you think they don't know? Albany isn't something you can hide. And exactly what has that got to do with psychoneural profiling?'

'I dunno.'

'Sounds more like vengeance than justice to me.'

'He's a shit. He deserves it.'

'Was he good in bed?'

Araminta hoped she wasn't blushing as she concentrated on pouring out some more wine. 'He was adequate.'

'Listen, darling, I'm afraid this is one of those nasty times when you just have to forget him and move on. You learned a valuable lesson: just how ruthless you have to be to get on in this sad old universe of ours.'

Araminta's head collapsed down into her hands, sending her hair tumbling down around her glass. 'Oh, Great Ozzie, I went and had sex with him! How humiliating is that?' She wished she could get rid of the memory, at least the bit about how much she'd enjoyed herself. Actually, there were various commercially available routines and drugs capable of performing neat little memory edits. *Oh, stop being so self-pitying, girl.*

'There there.' Cressida reached over and patted Araminta's hand. 'By now he'll have had half a dozen more girls in his bed, and won't even remember your name. It never meant as much to him as it does to you.'

'And you're telling me this to cheer me up?'

'That was his deal, wasn't it? You would be the second Friday of months with an R in them?'

'Yeah, I know. Hell, I'm a big girl, I knew what I was doing.'

'With hindsight, yes, the view is always clear.'

Araminta brought her head up and grinned. 'Thank you for not judging.'

'You're still a work in progress. And I think you're improving under my tuition. This was a much smaller mistake than Laril.'

'When you want to cheer someone up, you really go for it, don't you?'

Cressida pushed her glass across the table, and *chinked* it to the rim of Araminta's. 'You're starting to understand life. That's good. So what are you going to do about Mr Bovey?'

Araminta grimaced. 'Mr Bovey's proposal, actually.'

'What! He didn't?'

'He did. Marriage with me once I've gone multiple.'

'And you think I'm pushy! Wait a minute, did he ask you this before you had your little visit to Likan?'

'Umm. Yes.'

'You go, my girl. So what was the Likan thing all about?'

'Trying out options while I consider what to do.'

'Wow.'

'Have you ever considered going multiple? Likan said it was purely a lifestyle choice, not a business one. I'm not so sure. Ten pairs of extra hands would be very useful in my line of work.'

'I haven't considered it, no. It's still only one mind, which is all a lawyer needs. But if you're serious about property development then I can see the practical advantages.'

'It's self-limiting, though, isn't it? It's saying I'll always be somebody stuck doing some kind of manual job.'

'Your pride seems to be a very fluid thing.'

'I just want—' She didn't know how to finish that sentence, not at all. 'I don't know. I was just shaken up by what happened at the weekend. And I had this really awful dream, too. I was like this really big creature flying over a planet when someone tried to smother me. Been having a few of those lately. Do you suppose it's stress?'

Cressida gave her a puzzled look. 'Darling, everyone had that dream. It was the Second Dreamer's dream of the Skylord over Querencia. And that wasn't someone trying to smother you, that was Ethan trying to talk to the Skylord direct. They say he's still in a coma in hospital with his minions trying to repair his burned-out brain.'

'I couldn't have dreamed that.'

'Why not?'

'I don't have gaiamotes. It always seemed a bit silly to me, like a weak version of the unisphere.'

Cressida became very still; she pushed her glass aside and took Araminta's hand. 'Are you being serious?'

'Serious about what?'

'Didn't your mother tell you?'

'Tell me what?' Araminta felt panicky. She wanted another drink, but Cressida's grasp was surprisingly strong.

'About our great-great-great-grandmother.'

'What about her?'

'It was Mellanie Rescorai.'

After all that work up, Araminta felt badly disappointed. She'd at least been expecting some Dynasty heir – maybe old Earth royalty. Not someone she'd never heard of. 'Oh. Who is she?'

'A friend of the Silfen. She was named their friend. You know what that means?'

'Not really, no.' Araminta's knowledge of the Silfen was a little vague. A weird humanoid race that everyone called elves. They sang gibberish and had a bizarre wormhole network that stretched across half the galaxy allowing them to literally walk between worlds. An ability which a depressing number of humans found incredibly romantic and so they tried to follow them down their twisting interstellar paths. Few returned, but those that did told fanciful tales of adventure on new worlds and the exotic creatures they found there.

'Okay,' Cressida said. 'It goes like this. The Silfen named Ozzie their friend too. They gave him a magic pendant which allowed him to understand their paths, and even join their communal mind, their Motherholme.'

'Ozzie? You mean our Ozzie? The one we—'

'Yes. Now Ozzie being Ozzie, he broke open the pendant and figured out how the magic worked. That it wasn't magic but quantum entanglement. So humans then started to produce gaiamotes. Our gaiafield is basically a poor copy of the Silfen communal mind.'

'Right. So where does our ancestor come into this?'

'Mellanie was also a Silfen friend. Which is actually a little more than just being given the pendant. Their Motherholme accepts your mind and shares its wisdom with you. The pendant only initiates the contact. After a while, the ability becomes natural – well, relatively speaking. And like all magic it's believed to be inherited.' Cressida let go of Araminta's hands and smiled softly.

'You just said it wasn't magic.'

'Of course not. But consider this. Mellanie and her husband, Orion, came back. They had a little girl, Sophie, while they were out there walking across the galaxy. One of very few humans ever born on the paths, and certainly the first of two Silfen friends. She was attuned to the Motherholme right from the start, and passed the magic on to her children. Thanks to her, most of our family can feel the gaiafield, though it's weaker now with our generation. But on a good night, you can sometimes sense the Motherholme itself. I even ventured down one of the Silfen paths myself when I was younger; it's just outside Colwyn City in Francola Wood. I was thirteen, I wanted adventure. Stupid, but . . .'

'There's a Silfen path on Viotia?'

'Yes. They don't use it much. They don't enjoy planets with civilizations like ours on them.'

'Where does it lead?' Araminta asked breathlessly.

'They don't lead to any one place, they join up and twist. Time is different along them as well. That's why humans who aren't Silfen friends are always lost along them. I was lucky, I managed to get back after a couple of days. Mother was furious with me.'

'So . . . my dreams. They're not actually mine?'

'That Skylord one the other night wasn't, no.'

'It felt so real.'

'Didn't it just.' She glanced pointedly round the bar packed with its Living Dream followers. 'Now you see why they're so devout. If you're offered that kind of temptation every time you go to sleep, well who would want to wake up? That's what the Void is to them. Their dreams, for ever.'

'I don't get it. So what if they're real? That city they always go on about: Makkathran, it's medieval isn't it? And their Water-walker fights all the time. That's awful. Even if you've got telepathic powers, they're not that special. Our technology is just as good. Who wants to live like that?'

'You seriously need to review Inigo's dreams before you make that sort of judgement. The Waterwalker transforms an entire human society.'

'So he's a talented politician?'

'Oh no, darling, he's much more than that. He revealed the true nature of the Void to us. He showed us what it can do. That kind of power scares me shitless. Which is precisely what so many find so attractive.' Cressida waved her elegant hand round at the Living Dream supporters. 'Ozzie help us if these dreadful little prats ever gain the same ability the Waterwalker discovered. Eating up the galaxy would be the least of our worries.'

Inigo's sixth dream

Nearly eighty probationary constables sat together in a block of seats on the ultra-black floor of the Malfit Hall, while the vast arching ceiling above played images of wispy clouds traversing the beautiful gold and pink dawn sky. Edeard had one of the seats on the second row, his head tipped back so he could watch the giant ceiling in astonishment. He was sure it must be the marvel of the world. His fellow squadmates were all amused by his reaction. Not that they'd actually been in the Orchard Palace before – except for Dinlay. But at least they'd known about the moving imagery. And they hadn't thought to warn him.

Edeard gasped as Nikran rose up into the replica sky. The ruddy-brown planet here was a lot larger than it ever appeared in Querencia's skies. He could see tiny features etched on the world's eternal deserts. For some reason it made him think of it as an actual place rather than an element of the celestial panorama.

'Does anyone live there?' he whispered to Kanseen, who was in the chair next to him.

She looked at him, frowning, then glanced up at the image of Nikran, and giggled.

'What?' Macsen hissed.

'Edeard wants to know if anyone lives on Nikran,' Kanseen announced solemnly.

The whole squad snickered; surrounding squads joined in.

Edeard felt his face heating up. 'Why not?' he protested. 'Rah's ship fell on to this world, why not another ship to Nikran?'

'Absolutely,' Macsen said. 'Perfectly valid question. In fact, there's a whole other Makkathran up there.'

Edeard ignored them, and simply looked straight ahead in a dignified manner. He resolved to never ever tell his friends of his dreams, and what they showed him.

The block of probationary constables settled down. Edeard started to concentrate on what he was seeing. They were facing the grand curving staircase that dominated one side of the Hall. Owain, the Mayor of Makkathran, had appeared at the top, followed by the Guild Masters and District Masters who made up the Upper Council. They were all wearing their full ceremonial robes, producing a splendid blaze of colour as they filed down to the floor of the Hall.

'Oh, Lady,' Dinlay groaned.

Edeard caught a sensation of queasiness emanating from his friend. 'Ten seconds maximum,' he told Dinlay using a tiny directed longtalk voice. 'Then it's all over. Just hold it together for ten seconds. You can do that.'

Dinlay nodded, whilst appearing completely unconvinced.

Edeard resisted looking round at the much bigger block of seating behind him, where the families and friends of the probationary constables were gathered to watch them receive their bronze epaulettes. Probably an exaggeration, but half of them were Dinlay's family, and all of them were in uniform.

'I bet there's a crime wave going on in every district,' Macsen had muttered while they were all taking their seats earlier. 'There aren't any constables left out there to patrol.'

Owain reached the platform that had been set up at the bottom of the stairs. He smiled round at the attentive audience. 'It is always an honour and a privilege for me to perform this ceremony,' he said. 'In my position I hear so many people complain about the state which not just the city is in, but of the chaos which supposedly reigns in the lands outside our crystal walls. I wish they were standing here now, to see so many young people coming forward to serve their city. I am heartened by the sense of duty you are displaying in taking this commitment to serve your fellow citizens. You give me confidence for the future.'

Now that's a real politician, Edeard thought uncharitably. The Mayor of all people must have known how inadequate the number of constables was. That the eighty of them here today wasn't enough; that at least an equal number of constables had left in the last few months to become private bodyguards or for a better paid and respected job as a sheriff in some provincial town. *Why doesn't he do something about it?*

The Mayor finished his inspirational speech. The probationary constables stood up as one, then the first row trooped up to the platform to be greeted by the Mayor. The Chief Constable read the probationer's name out to the Hall, while an assistant handed a pair of epaulettes to the Mayor to be presented with a hand-shake and a smile.

Edeard's row started to move forward. He'd thought this would be boring at the least, that it was stupid, an irritation he could have done without. Especially as the only person in the audience clapping for him was Salrana, who'd been given the day off from her duties. But now he was here, now he was walking up to the Mayor of the entire city, he actually began to feel a sense of occasion. Behind him, the audience were radiant with pride. They believed in the constables. In front, the Upper Council were registering their approval. None of the councillors had to be here, it was a ceremony repeated three times a year, every year. They'd been to dozens, and would have to come to dozens more. If they'd wanted to cry off, they could have done. But no, it was important enough for them to turn out every time.

And here he was himself, coming forward to make a public pledge to the citizens of Makkathran that he would do his best to protect them and implement the rule of law. This was why Rah and those who followed him into office had created this ceremony and others like it, to recognize and honour the commitment the constables made to their city and lives. It was neither silly nor a waste of time, it was a show of respect.

Edeard stood in front of the Mayor, who smiled politely, and shook his hand as the Chief Constable read out his name. A pair of bronze epaulettes were pressed into his hand. 'Thank you, sir,' Edeard said. There was a lump in his throat. 'I won't let you down.' *Ashwell will never happen here.*

If the Mayor was surprised, he didn't show it. Edeard caught sight of Finitan standing on the grand staircase. The Master of the Eggshaper Guild looked rather splendid in a gold and purple gown, with elaborate scarlet symbols embroidered down the front; his silver-tipped hood was arranged over the left shoulder. He caught Edeard's eye and winked. 'Well done, lad,' his longtalk whispered.

Edeard stepped off the platform. There was a burst of applause. He nearly laughed, it was as if the audience was rejoicing he was out of the way. In fact it was Dinlay's considerable family clapping loudly as their relative received his epaulettes. Dinlay managed to not trip, or throw up, or collapse from fright. He followed Edeard back to their seats with a glowing face, grinning back at his kin.

Afterwards there was a formal reception party, with the Mayor and the Upper Council mixing with the new constables and their families, while ge-monkeys circled the Malfit Hall with trays of drinks. It was scheduled to last an hour. Edeard might have warmed to the graduation ceremony itself, but he planned to be out of the party in under ten minutes.

'No you don't,' Salrana decreed. 'Just look at who's here.'

Edeard frowned round at the people babbling away; the families in their finery, the resplendent Upper Council members. 'Who?'

She gave him a withering look. 'The Pythia for a start. And she noticed me. I felt her farsight on me during the ceremony.'

Edeard took another look round. 'Fair enough, you're the only novice here. She probably thinks you ducked out of your assignments to pick up the free booze.'

Salrana drew herself up. It shifted the fabric of her white and blue robe in a way Edeard couldn't help but notice. If he kept doing that, and kept thinking those accompanying thoughts about how she was growing up, the Lady really would blast him out of existence one day.

'Edeard you can still be disappointingly childish at times. We are both citizens of Makkathran now; you especially today. Try and act in an appropriate fashion.'

Edeard's mouth dropped open.

'Now we are going over to thank Grand Master Finitan for sponsoring you, as is the right expression of gratitude, which you *do* feel; and see if we can be introduced to others in the Upper Council as well. If you're to become Chief Constable, you need to start paying attention to the city's political dynamics.'

'Uh. Yes,' Edeard admitted. 'Chief Constable?'

'That's your route on to the Upper Council now you've chosen the constables over a Guild.'

'I've been graduated eight minutes.'

'Those that hesitate, lose. The Lady's book, fifth chapter.'

His lips twitched. 'I knew that.'

'Did you now?' Salrana raised an eyebrow. 'I might have to test you later.'

'I've had quite enough of exams these last few weeks, thank you.'

'Poor Edeard. Come on.' She pulled at his hand, all girlish again.

Grand Master Finitan was talking to a pair of fellow Upper Council members as Edeard and Salrana approached him. He smiled and turned to them. 'Congratulations, my boy. A proud day for you.'

'Yes sir. Thank you again for sponsoring me.'

'Well, it seems to have put me in credit with the Chief Constable. You graduated third in your class. That's an astonishing result for someone unfamiliar with our city.'

'Thank you, sir.'

'Allow me to introduce Masters Graley of the Geography Guild and Imilan of the Chemistry Guild. This is Constable Edeard from the Rulan province; a friend of my old Master.'

'Masters.' Edeard bowed formally. Then he saw Salrana pluck at her skirt and hold the fabric up daintily on one side as she performed a peculiar little bow which involved bending her knees and keeping her back straight.

'And Novice Salrana,' Finitan said smoothly. 'Also from Rulan.'

'A pleasure,' Imilan said.

Edeard didn't care for the way the Master's eyes lingered on Salrana.

'You're a long way from home, Novice,' the Master said.

'No, sir,' she said in a polite tone. 'Makkathran is my home now.'

'Well said, Novice,' Finitan said. 'I wish all our citizens were as appreciative of their city as you are.'

'Now, Finitan,' Graley chided. 'This is not the day.'

'Apologies.' Finitan inclined his head at the youngsters. 'So, Edeard, have you had a run-in with our criminal element yet?'

'A few, sir, yes.'

'He's being very modest, sir,' Salrana said. 'He led his squad after some thieves in the Silvarum market. He recovered the stolen items, as well.'

Edeard shifted awkwardly under the scrutiny of all three Masters.

'And are these miscreants now labouring away at the Trampello mine to pay for their crime?' Imilan asked.

'No, sir,' Edeard admitted. 'They got away. That time. They won't again.'

'I imagine they won't,' Finitan said with an edge of amusement. 'Come along, Edeard, let me introduce you to the Mayor. It's about time he saw an honourable man again.'

'Sir?'

'Old joke. We often clash in Council.' He signalled them to follow him. 'Not over anything important to the lives of real people, of course.'

The Mayor of Makkathran was talking to the Pythia just beside the little platform where he'd handed out the epaulettes. If he was bored or annoyed to be introduced to a new constable he didn't show it; Edeard had never encountered a mind so perfectly shielded. Not that he paid much attention. He was entranced by the Pythia. He'd been expecting some ancient woman, full of grandmotherly warmth. Instead, he was disconcerted to find the Pythia retained the beauty of a woman still awaiting her half-century. A beauty only emphasized by her gold-trimmed white robe with its flowing hood which she wore forward, casting her face in a slight shadow.

Salrana did her strange bow again to the Pythia.

'The Lady's blessing upon you, my child,' the Pythia said. She sounded bored in that way Makkathran's aristocracy always did when they had to deal with those they considered to be of a lower order. Which wasn't what Edeard expected from a Pythia. Then she turned her attention to him. Startling light-blue eyes fixed on him, surrounded by a mass of thick bronze hair twined with gold and silver leaves. The eyes narrowed in judgement, which Edeard found heartbreaking. He felt like he'd disappointed her, which was a terrible thing. Then she smiled, banishing his worry. 'Now you *are* interesting, Constable,' she said.

'My Lady?' he stammered. He could somehow feel the Pythia's farsight upon him, as if she were picking through his mind. There was something disconcertingly intimate about the contact. And she was very beautiful. Merely a yard away. Her half-smile open and inviting.

Salrana made a groaning sound in her throat.

'I'm not quite that exalted,' the Pythia said lightly. 'There is only one true Lady. My usual form of address is Dear Mother.'

'I apologize, Dear Mother.'

'Think nothing of it. You've come a long way to get here, and you still have a long way to travel.'

'I do?'

But the Pythia had turned to face Finitan. 'What a fascinating young friend you have, Grand Master.'

'I'm pleased you think so, Pythia.'

'So young, yet so strong.'

The way she said it sent a shudder of felonious delight down Edeard's spine. He didn't dare glance in her direction; instead he fixed his gaze on the Mayor, who was frowning.

'Do you foresee great things for him?' Finitan asked jovially.

The Pythia turned to stare directly at Edeard, an act he couldn't ignore, not in a group like this, not without appearing extraordinarily rude. He tried to return the look, but found it incredibly difficult.

'Your potential is very strong,' she said. There was an almost teasing quality to her voice. 'Do you follow the Lady's teachings, Constable Edeard?'

'I try my best, Dear Mother.'

'I'm sure you do. May She bless your endeavours in your new duties.'

Edeard almost didn't hear her. A movement behind Finitan had caught his eye. In horror, he watched Mistress Florell heading towards them, all black chiffon and wide veils hanging from a tall hat. His dismay must have leaked out. As one, Finitan, the Mayor, and the Pythia turned to acknowledge the approaching *grande dame*.

'Aunt!' the Mayor exclaimed happily. 'How lovely of you to come.'

'He's the one,' Mistress Florell declared in her scratchy voice. 'The young hooligan who nearly knocked me to the ground.'

'Now, Aunt.'

'Take his epaulettes away,' she snapped imperiously. 'He's not fit to serve this city. Time was we used to have men of good character in the constables, the sons of noblemen.'

The Mayor gave Edeard a half-apologetic look. 'What happened, Constable?'

'I was pursuing some thieves, sir. Mistress Florell came out of a building. I went round . . .'

'Ha! Tried to run over me, more like.'

'Come, come, Aunt. The lad was obviously just doing his job, a conscientious chap like this is just what we need. Suppose the thieves had snatched your bag, wouldn't you want him to give chase?'

'Nobody would steal *my* bag,' she snapped.

'I *am* sorry for any distress,' Edeard said desperately. The horrible old woman just wouldn't *listen*.

The Mayor shuffled round to stand between Mistress Florell and Edeard, flicking his fingers in a *go away* motion. Edeard did a kind of half bow and backed away fast, accompanied by Salrana and Finitan.

'Aunt, you know it's bad for you to dwell on such trivia. Now some of these Mindalla estate fortified wines are really quite lovely, you must try—' There was a note of tired desperation in the Mayor's voice.

Finitan smiled broadly as they hurried off. 'Thank you, Edeard: these reception parties are normally quite tedious.'

'Er . . . Yes, sir.'

'Oh come now, this is your graduation day. Don't let that daft old bat spoil it for you. She's embarrassingly well connected, as would you be if you clung to life for so long. Wouldn't surprise me if she did drink the blood of virgins after all. Your pardon, Novice.'

'I've heard of Mistress Florell, sir,' Salrana said.

'Everyone in the city has,' Finitan said. 'That's why she thinks she's so important, instead of just old and obnoxious.' He put his hand on Edeard's shoulder. 'And I say that as her great-great-nephew, myself. Twice removed, thankfully.'

'Thank you, sir,' Edeard said.

'Now off you go and enjoy yourselves. And, Edeard, when the time comes for you to apply for promotion to officer rank, come and see me again. I'll be happy to sign the letter.'

'Sir?' Edeard asked incredulously.

'You heard. Now be off with the pair of you. It's a bold bad city out there. Have fun!'

Edeard didn't need telling again. He and Salrana made for the Hall's big archway which led out to the antechambers.

'Hey, Edeard,' Macsen called, hurrying to intercept. 'Where are you off to?'

'Just out,' Edeard said. He didn't even want to glance over his shoulder in case Mistress Florell was looking his way.

Macsen reached them, and skidded to a halt. 'Mother and Dybal are taking me to the Rakas restaurant to celebrate. It's an open invitation to my squadmates as well.' Macsen stopped, and smiled at Salrana. 'Novice, I had no idea Edeard kept such pleasant company.' He gave Edeard an expectant look, ever the injured party.

'This is Novice Salrana, from my home village,' Edeard said sulkily.

'That is one village I am definitely going to have to visit.' Macsen bowed deeply.

'Why is that, Constable?' she asked.

'To see if all the girls there are as beautiful as yourself.'

She laughed. Edeard groaned, glaring in warning at Macsen.

'The invitation to Rakas is of course extended to the friends of my squadmates, Novice.'

'The friends accept with thanks,' she said primly. 'But only if you stop calling me Novice.'

'It will be my delight, Salrana. And I will also beg you to tell of Edeard's early life. It would seem he's been keeping secrets from us. Those who entrust our lives to him, no less.'

'Shocking,' she agreed. 'I will entertain such a request if correctly made.'

'Salrana!' a horrified Edeard exclaimed.

'Excellent,' Macsen said. 'I'll arrange another gondola for our party. Now, Edeard, where is Kanseen?'

Edeard glowered at his so-called friend.

'Edeard?' Salrana prompted with a jab to his ribs.

'Over there.' Edeard said it without having to concentrate; through his farsight he was automatically aware of all his squadmates – a trait Chae was always trying to emphasize. He pointed to where Kanseen was chatting to a heavily pregnant woman and a man in a smart tunic with the crest of the

555

Shipwright's Guild. 'Her sister came to the ceremony. They're catching up.'

'No sign of her mother, then, poor thing,' Macsen said sadly. 'Ah well, I'll go and ask her.'

'Boyd's family are all here,' Edeard said.

'And we'll yet sink under the weight of Dinlay's relatives,' Macsen concluded. 'So it's just us precious few left. See you at the Outer Circle Canal mooring in ten minutes.'

'What did you say that for?' Edeard asked as Macsen walked over to Kanseen.

Salrana cocked her head to one side and gave him a very haughty look. 'It was a gesture of honest friendship. Why should I not accept?'

'He was flirting with you.'

She grinned. 'Wasn't he just.'

'You're a Novice!'

'We are not professional virgins, Edeard. I seem to remember us kissing. And more, wasn't there a discussion about my age and when you would be ready to bed me?'

Edeard turned bright red. His farsight tried to sense sparks of interest in those standing closest – either they could shield too well, or they hadn't overheard. One thing was sure, she wouldn't back down. *She never has.* Her voice would only grow louder if he persisted. 'I don't wish to recall that day too closely if you don't mind. However, if I've offended you I apologize. I still think of you as my charge, especially after all we have been through. Which is why I overreacted with Macsen. Truly, Salrana, he's had more girls than I have socks.'

Her smile was forgiving. 'I've seen your wardrobe. You only have two pairs of socks.'

'I do not!'

'And they have holes in them. So you just concentrate on worrying about yourself, Edeard. I know and understand all about Macsen and boys like him. That's why he's perfectly harmless.'

'He's perfectly charming.'

'It's not a crime, you know. Perhaps if you showed a little more charm, then you could boast more conquests.'

'Charm, eh?' He bent his arm, and extended it towards her. 'May I escort you to the mooring, Novice Salrana.'

'Why thank you, Constable Edeard. You may indeed.' She linked her arm through his, and allowed him to lead her out of the Hall.

The Rakas restaurant was in the Abad district; which meant a gondola ride down the Great Major Canal. It was the first time Edeard had ever been in one of the elegant black boats. He didn't have the coinage to travel in them ordinarily. Money clearly wasn't an issue with Dybal.

The errant musician was everything Edeard had expected. Wild black hair reaching halfway down his back, barely contained by red leather bands which gave it a peculiar ropy appearance. A long face with weather-beaten creases and sunken cheeks above a narrow jaw; but with brown-gold eyes that always seemed to be seeing the funny side of life as they peeped over narrow blue-lens glasses. His whole mental aura was agreeable, akin to that of a carefree adolescent rather than a man well over a hundred. Just being able to say hello and shake hands was enough to banish Edeard's lingering dismay over Mistress Florell. As their little group assembled at the moorings, Dybal made them all feel welcome, even though they'd never met him before. He instinctively knew the right note to take with each of them.

'Come on then,' he said loudly once they were all present, and led them down the steps. His clothes were large, even though he was improbably slender for his age. Edeard imagined they needed to be that big to contain his ebullience, he certainly achieved the whole larger than life image effortlessly enough. Strident voice, big arm gestures, fur-lined velvet jacket, paisley-pattern shirt and leather trousers, their colours mimicking those of the Musician's Guild – or, more likely, a deliberate mockery of them. Edeard was only slightly disappointed the musician wasn't carrying his guitar; he wanted to hear the songs of rebellion which stoked up Makkathran's youth.

Dybal took the first gondola along with Macsen, and Bijulee, Macsen's mother. Edeard watched him talk to the gondolier, holding the man's hand between his own two palms, squeezing intently. Both men laughed, the kind of low merriment which usually came from a dirty joke. Dybal took his seat beside Bijulee, while the still-smiling gondolier pushed off.

'*That* is Macsen's mother?' Kanseen asked as they settled on the middle bench in their own gondola.

'Yeah,' Edeard said. And to think, a few minutes earlier he'd believed the Pythia was an attractive older woman. 'Macsen introduced me just before you arrived.' Which had gone a long way to making his world a better place.

'Can't be,' Kanseen declared as their gondola slipped out on to the Great Major Canal. 'That would mean she had him when she was what . . . ten? She looks like she's my age, for the Lady's sake.'

Edeard sat back on the bench, smiling. He was so content he came *this* close to putting his arm round Salrana, who was sitting next to him. 'Do I hear the little voice of envy, there, Constable?'

'You hear the little voice of disbelief,' Kanseen muttered.

'Perhaps it's his sister, and I misheard.'

'How does she keep her skin so fresh? It's got to be some ointment only available to the rich.'

'Maybe she imports it direct from Nikran.'

Kanseen pulled a face.

'You two.' Salrana laughed. 'You're like an old married couple.'

Edeard and Kanseen carefully avoided each other's gaze. The gondola had already reached Birmingham Pool, the big junction at the top of the Grand Central Canal. From Edeard's position, the entire circle of water seemed to be full of gondolas, dodging round each other as they slipped in and out of the various canals emptying into the Pool. He did his best not to flinch. None of the gondoliers were slowing down, they just seemed to instinctively know where to go. Craft slipped past them, close enough to touch if he'd been brave enough to stretch out an arm. Then they arrived at the head of the Grand Central Canal, and their gondolier gave a hard push on his punt.

The first thing Edeard looked at was the mooring on his right where the thieves had escaped. He caught Kanseen looking at it too. She gave a tiny shrug. Then he forgot all about it, and really enjoyed the view. At the top end of the city, along the Silvarum, Haxpen and Padua districts, the canal was lined with some of the grandest buildings in Makkathran; palaces up to ten storeys high, with huge windows, facades a swirl of colour in weird patterns. Turrets, belvederes, and spires produced a serrated skyline. Ge-eagles bigger than any Edeard had ever sculpted flew in lazy circles around the pinnacles, keeping watch on the approaches to each magnificent family seat. Kanseen pointed out some of them: the palace that was home to the Mayor's family, the ziggurat where Rah and the Lady were supposed to have lived – now home to the Culverit family who claimed direct lineage. She whispered about one red-tinged facade where Macsen's father had lived. When Edeard glanced at the gondola in front, both Macsen and Bijulee were looking in the opposite direction.

All of the stately buildings had low water-level archways leading into the warren of cellars underneath, guarded by thick iron gates which the families maintained in excellent order. The walls of the Purdard family palace were at an angle, actually overhanging the water. When Edeard looked up, he saw a glassed-in mirador running the length of the upper storey, with several youngsters standing watching the gondolas. A fabulously rich trading family, Kanseen said, with a fleet of thirty ships.

They passed through the High Pool, which provided a junction with Flight Canal and Market Canal. There was a bridge on either side of the pool; the first one was the city's own, a simple high white arch to which carpenters attached a broad rail along both sides. Famously, the apex was a ten-yard stretch of crystal, providing a view directly past any pedestrian's shoes down on to the water and gondolas thirty yards below. Not everyone could walk across it, the sight was too much for some; as many as one in twenty, the Doctor's Guild claimed. At Chae's insistence, Edeard and the rest of the squad had used it several times on patrol. Edeard had to gird himself to walk those few invisible yards; the vertigo wasn't strong enough to stop him though it was unpleasant. All of the squad had forced themselves across it – surprisingly, Dinlay had been the least affected. The bridge on the other side of High Pool was constructed out of iron and wood, a bulky creaking thing in comparison to its cousin, yet with far more traffic. Past the Pool, the towers of Eyrie stabbed up into the clean azure sky as if ready to impale any passing Skylord. Fiacre district's cliff-like frontage swarmed with vine plants, with long strands of flowers bubbling out of the emerald and russet leaves. Only the windows remained clear of foliage, producing deep-set black holes in the lush living carpet.

The gondolas pulled up at a mooring just beyond Forest Pool, and everyone climbed out. Dybal paid the gondoliers, and they all set off to the round tower which housed the Rakas restaurant on its third floor. Hansalt, the owner and chief chef, had reserved Dybal a table beside a long window overlooking one of the district's colourful plazas.

'An auspicious day for us,' Dybal announced as a waitress brought over a tray of chilled white wine. 'First, a toast to your squad, Macsen. May you rid the city of crime.'

They drank to that. Edeard gave the glass a suspicious glance, he'd never seen wine with bubbles in it before, but when he sipped the taste was surprisingly light and fruity. He rather liked it.

'Secondly,' Dybal said. 'To Edeard, for being appointed squad leader.'

Edeard blushed.

'Speech!' Macsen demanded.

'Not a chance,' Edeard grunted.

They laughed and drank to that.

'Thirdly,' his voice softened and he looked down at Bijulee,

'I am very proud to announce that my beloved has agreed to marry me.'

The cheer that went up made all the other customers look over at them. Everyone saw it was Dybal, and smiled knowingly. Macsen was hugging his mother. Edeard and Salrana were astonished, but clinked glasses anyway and downed some more of the bubbling wine. Another two chilled bottles arrived and were quickly poured out.

Afterwards, Edeard always thought back to that meal as the first time he'd been truly happy since Ashwell. The food was like nothing he'd ever eaten before. It arrived on big white plates arranged with such artistry he almost didn't want to eat it, but when he did tuck in the combination of tastes was marvellous. And Dybal had gossip on the city's élite that was downright scandalous. That all started because of Salrana, who was answering Macsen's question about what Novices did all day long.

'I mean no disrespect to the Lady,' he said. 'But surely it must be boring just reading Her scriptures and singing in Her church.'

'Hey,' Dybal objected. 'Less mockery about singing if you don't mind.'

'I've been assigned to Millical House,' Salrana said. 'I love looking after the children. They're so sweet.'

'What's Millical House?' Edeard asked. 'A school?'

'You don't know?' Bijulee asked. She was uncertain if Edeard was having a joke.

'I told you, Mother,' Macsen said. 'He really is from a village on the edge of the wilds.'

'Millical is an orphanage,' Salrana said solemnly. 'I cannot understand why any mother would give up her baby, especially the ones as gorgeous as we get in the nursery. But they do. So the Lady takes care of them. It's a fantastic place, Edeard, the children lack for nothing. Makkathran really cares.'

Dybal gave a *certain* cough. 'Actually, that's a rather exceptional orphanage.'

'What do you mean?' Salrana asked.

'You sure you want to hear this?'

Salrana twirled the stem of her wine glass between her fingers, giving Dybal a level gaze. 'We do take in anyone.'

'Yes, I suppose so. But it helps that you're in the Lillylight district. Consider who your neighbours are. You see, Edeard, Millical House is where the noble families deliver those little unwanted embarrassments which happen when the younger sons are out enjoying themselves with the lower order girls at the more disreputable entertainment theatres that grace our fine city.'

'The kind you play at?' Bijulee asked mildly.

'Yes, my love, the kind I play at.' He eyed the three young constables. 'Been to any, yet?'

'Not yet,' Kanseen said. Macsen kept quiet.

'Just a matter of time. Anyway, the reason Millical is so well funded is the tradition that the family concerned makes a donation – anonymous, of course – each time a babe is left on the house's charity step for the Novices to take in.'

'Any money for children is distributed equally among all the Lady's orphanages,' Salrana said.

'I'm sure a great deal of the bequests filter down to the other orphanage houses. And the Lady performs invaluable work caring for such unfortunates, as I do know. But if you ever get to work in any of the other houses, you'll notice the difference.'

'And how do you know for sure?' Bijulee asked teasingly.

Dybal turned to face her with a sad smile. 'Because I grew up in one.'

'Really?' Macsen asked.

'That's right. Which is why I'm so impressed with you four youngsters. You came from nothing, especially Edeard and Salrana here, and you're all making a life for yourselves. I admire that. I truly do. You're not dependent on anyone, let alone a decadent family. I know I'm the first to complain about the city's hierarchy, the way democracy has been expropriated by the rich, but there are some institutions which are still worthwhile. People need the constables for the security you bring to the streets and canals, and the Lady for hope.'

562

'I thought that was what your music brought,' Salrana said with a cheeky gleam in her eye.

'It depends which class you belong to. If you're rich, I'm a deliciously wicked rebel, hot and dripping with sarcasm and irony. They have to pay me to perform – which I'm glad to do for them. But for the rest of the city, the people who toil their whole life to make things work, I'm a focal point for resentment, I articulate their feelings. For them, I sing for free. I don't want their coinage, I want them to spend it on themselves so they don't have to give away their children.'

'So you compete with the Lady?' Salrana said.

'I offer a mild alternative, that's all. Hopefully an enjoyable one.'

'I must try and get to one of your performances.'

'I'll be happy to escort you,' Macsen said.

'I'll hold you to that,' she retorted before Edeard could intervene. He didn't say anything, not there and then, that would spoil the meal.

'Do you know all the Grand Council?' Edeard asked Dybal.

'Oh yes, they think that by associating with me they gain credibility. What they're actually doing by inviting me to their homes is contributing generously to lyrics of irony and hypocrisy. Why do you ask, Edeard? Do you need to know about their mistresses? Their strange shared interest in taxing cotton production in Fondral province? The scandal over funds for the militia? The money wasted on official functions? The disease of corruption which infects the staff of the Orchard Palace who are supposed to be impartial? How our dear Mayor, Owain, is already buying votes for the next election – the one time he needs public support?'

'Actually no, I was wondering about Mistress Florell.'

'Edeard has met her,' Macsen said with a chortle.

'We all did, while we were on duty,' Edeard countered.

'She hit him with her umbrella,' Kanseen added dryly.

Dybal and Bijulee laughed at that.

'The old witch tried to get Edeard thrown out of the constables,' Salrana said, hot-cheeked. 'At the ceremony today, she told the Mayor to take his epaulettes back.'

'How typical,' Dybal said. 'Don't worry Edeard; she has no real power, not any more. She's a figurehead for the noble families, that's all. They like to make out she's a much loved grandmother to the whole city. Total bollocks, of course. She was a scheming little bitch when she was younger. Which admittedly is history to all of us now. But she had three husbands before her fiftieth birthday, all first sons of District Masters, which is just about unheard of even today. She gave each of them two sons – and some say there was witchery in that. And by strange coincidence, all three second children went on to marry noble daughters in families where the male lineage had faltered in favour of the girls. By the next generation she'd spread her brood through eleven District Master families. With that kind of power bloc in the Upper Council, she controlled the vote for decades. Our last so-called Golden Age; which saw the rise of the militia at the expense of all other arms of government. You see, she believes there's an actual physical difference between the nobility and those without their obscene wealth. In other words, her offspring are born to rule and bring order to the uncivilized masses such as thee and me. Needless to say, she doesn't believe that we should have anything to do with the city's government. That sort of thing is best left to those whom destiny has blessed with good blood.'

'No wonder she didn't like you, Edeard,' Macsen grinned. 'You're not even city born. She could probably smell the countryside on you.'

'Not everyone in the Upper Council believes in that, do they?' Edeard asked, thinking of Finitan. A nephew, he'd said.

'Hopefully not, There are still a few decent noblemen around today. And of course, District Masters' seats on the Upper Council are checked by the Guild Masters. And the Lower Council itself is still directly elected, not that you'd know it in some districts. That makes for a lot of genuine debate in the

Grand Council. Rah knew what he was doing when he crafted our constitution.'

'But your songs are still popular.'

'They are. Dissatisfaction with those who rule is always attractive to the majority; it's an obsession which humans brought with them on the ships which fell to Querencia. As a species we find it as easy as breathing. And it's never helped by old men like me who reminisce on how things were always better in our lost youth.'

'You're a rabble-rouser, you mean,' Bijulee said fondly as she ran her hand through his ragged braids of hair.

'And proud of it,' Dybal raised his glass again. 'To making our masters lives a misery.'

The whole table drank to that.

'So what's the story with you and Salrana?' Kanseen asked. It was late at night. The celebratory lunch had lasted all afternoon. Edeard hadn't wanted it to end. He was perfectly relaxed, thanks to that lovely wine with bubbles, the company of friends, eating fine food, making happy intelligent conversation. No, today was a day which, if the Lady were kind, should last and last.

But as was the way of all things, they finished the final bottle of wine, ate the last morsel of cheese and bid each other farewell. Dybal winced theatrically when the bill arrived. The sun had set outside, leaving the city's own cold orange lighting to bathe the streets, along with the faint haze of the nebulas overhead. Edeard announced he would walk Salrana back to Millical House in the Lillylight district. As it was directly between Abad and Jeavons, Kanseen offered to walk with them.

The orphanage house was a nice one, close to the Victoria Canal, with its own garden and play yard. Yet he couldn't help noticing, it was the smallest building on the street. Salrana had given him a light peck on the cheek before scooting off through the imposing doors which filled the entrance arch.

Edeard and Kanseen carried on together, using a bridge over Castoff Canal to put them in Drupe district, where the palaces matched anything along the Great Major Canal. It was quiet on the narrow streets and broad squares. Bodyguards stood imposingly outside the iron gates of the palaces. Edeard tried not to stare as they passed the alert figures in dark uniforms; he was sure that staying a constable was better than such monotonous duty night after night. That disapproval must have escaped his shielding.

'That's not what I'll be doing,' Kanseen said quietly as their footfalls echoed around them in a narrow street high enough to block out all the night sky except for the slim violet thread of Buluku's meandering tail. 'None of them are ex-constables. Estate workers and farm boys who've come to the city in search of a better life. They only last a couple of years before they make their way back home. That or migrate into Sampalok.'

'Could have been me, then,' Edeard said.

'Somehow I doubt that.'

They walked over the third bridge across the Marble Canal, back into the familiar territory of Jeavons. Gondolas slid past quietly underneath them, a small white lantern glowing on the front of each. Their passengers snuggled up under the canopy, enjoying the romance of the ride. By now Edeard could recognize the wind rising from the sea, the moisture it carried. Clouds were scudding overhead, starting to veil the nebulas. It would rain tonight. In another hour, he decided as he smelt the air.

The constables' tenement was two streets away from Jeavons station, a big ugly building from the outside, but wrapped around a central oval courtyard boasting a pool of warmish water large enough to swim in and overlooked by four levels of walkways. It contained the maisonettes reserved for the constables. Those with families had taken over one end, with the bachelors at the other. Not that it was a fixed divide. Edeard along with the rest of the squad had moved in a couple of days ago. Each morning he'd been woken by children shouting outside his door as they raced along the walkway, playing some exciting game of chase.

Now the children were long in bed as he and Kanseen walked

up a set of awkward rounded stairs to the third level where they both had maisonettes.

'No real story,' he told her. 'You know Salrana and I travelled here together. I'm sort of like her elder brother.'

'She's in love with you.'

'What?'

'I was watching her this afternoon. It's obvious to anyone with half a brain. Even Macsen fathomed that out. Didn't you notice he'd stopped trying to flirt with her by the time the fish course arrived? There's no point. She's only interested in you.'

'She's smart enough to realize how shallow he is. That's all. If they don't fall at his feet in the first five minutes, he moves on. You know what he's like.'

'I never thought I'd see you in denial.'

'It's not denial. You asked a question and I answered it.'

They stopped at the top of the stairs, and looked out over the extensive courtyard. The rim of the pool was a thin intense line of pale-orange. It made the water look very inviting. Edeard knew a lot of the constables went for a night-time dip. His stomach was too heavy from a whole afternoon bingeing, he decided reluctantly.

'Actually, you didn't answer,' Kanseen said. 'All you admitted to was knowing her, which doesn't shed any light on your relationship at all.'

'Lady save me, you really did take in all of Master Solarin's lectures, didn't you?'

'My grades were almost as high as yours, yes. So on that long trip through the mountains and across swamps filled with monsters, did you sleep with her?'

'No!'

'Why not? She's very pretty. And slim. I've seen what your eye lingers on when we're out on patrol.'

'She's far too young, for a start. And she's getting pretty. Doctors in Makkathran have better ointments than we had on the caravan.'

'Edeard!' Kanseen gave a small shocked laugh. 'I think that's the most evil thing I've ever heard you say about anyone, let alone your little sister.'

'Lady, you're cruel. I don't answer a question to your satisfaction and you say I'm in denial; then I give an honest answer and you brand me evil.'

She sucked contritely on her lower lip. 'Sorry. But you can understand why.'

'Not really.' Edeard was looking at her profile in the coppery shimmer thrown off by the surface of the pool. In such a light she looked almost aristocratic, with her strong chin and slight nose, skin painted enticingly dark. She turned to face him, cocking her head slightly to one side in that questioning way he enjoyed.

He leant forward and kissed her. She pressed in against him, hands sliding over his back. For once he dropped his mental guard, showing her how much he delighted in the touch of her, the closeness . . . After a long time they ended the kiss. Her nose rubbed against his cheek, and she let him sense how much that meant to her.

'Come to bed with me,' he murmured. His tongue darted out to lick the lobe of her ear. She shivered from the contact. Hot lines of pleasure flickered across her mind. He was delightfully aware of her breasts against his chest, and hugged her closer. *This is going to be the best ever.*

'No,' she said. Her shoulders dropped, and she rested her hands against his shoulders, moving them apart to end the embrace. 'I'm sorry, Edeard. I feel a lot for you I really do, you know that. That's the trouble.'

'What do you mean?'

'We could work, you and me. I really think we could. Lovers, then marriage, children. Everything. I'm not afraid of that. It's just the timing. It's wrong.'

'Timing?'

'I don't think you're ready for a long-term commitment yet. And I certainly don't need another fling, not with someone I care about.'

'It wouldn't have to be a fling. I'm ready to settle down with someone as important to me as you are.'

'Oh Lady, you're so sweet,' she sighed. 'No, Edeard. I can't compete against the ideal of Salrana. You're closer to her than you know, or will admit. How could you not be after all the two of you shared. I'm not jealous, well, not exactly. But she's always going to be there between us until you sort your feelings out.'

'She's just a kid from the same village, that's all.'

'Open your feelings to me, show me your naked mind and say you don't want to bed her, that you don't want to know the feel of her against you.'

'I . . . No, this is stupid. You're accusing me of . . . I don't know: having dreams. This world is full of opportunities. Some we grasp, others we pass by. It's not me who's scared of what might be. You need to look at your own feelings.'

They were standing apart now, voices not raised, but firm.

'I know my own feelings,' she said. 'And I want yours to match mine. That means I can wait. You're worth waiting for, Edeard, however long it takes. You mean that much to me.'

'Well that's got to be the craziest way of showing it. Ever,' he said, trying not to let the hurt affect his voice. His mind hardened against releasing any emotion, which was difficult given the turmoil she'd kindled.

'Tell her,' Kanseen said simply. She reached out to stroke his cheek, but he dodged back. 'Be true to yourself, Edeard. That's the you I want.'

'Goodnight,' he said stiffly.

Kanseen nodded then turned away. Edeard was sure he saw a tear on her cheek. He refused to use his farsight to check. Instead he went into his own maisonette, and threw himself on the too-high bed. Anger warred with frustration in his mind. He imagined Salrana and Kanseen fighting, an image which quickly took on a life outside his control. His fist thumped the pillow. He turned over. Sent his farsight swirling out across the city, observing the vast clutter of minds as they wrestled with their own demons. It felt good not to be suffering alone.

He took a long time to fall asleep.

*

'Rumour has it, the Pythia uses her concealment ability to twist her features. She is over a hundred and fifty, after all; she could give Mistress Florell a run for her money in the withered crone stakes. There has to be some kind of devilment involved to make her look the way she does.' Boyd put a lot of emphasis on that last sentence, dipping his head knowingly.

'Can you do that?' a startled Edeard asked.

'I don't know.' Boyd lowered his voice. 'They say the Grand Masters can completely conceal themselves from view. I've never seen it myself.'

Edeard paused on the threshold of pointing out the slight logical flaw in that admission. 'Right.' They were on patrol in Jeavons, walking alongside the Brotherhood Canal, which bordered the southern side of the district. Beyond the water was Tycho, not strictly a district, but a wide strip of meadow between the canal and the crystal wall. Wooden stables used by the militia squatted on the grass, the only buildings permitted on the common land. He could see stable boys cantering horses and ge-horses along sandy tracks, the morning exercise which they and their predecessors had performed for centuries. Several horses had ge-wolves running alongside.

It was their sixth patrol since graduation. Six days during which he and Kanseen had barely exchanged a word. They'd been perfectly civil to each other, but that was all. He didn't want that, he wanted them at least to go back to how it was before that messed-up evening. How they might arrive back at that comfortable old association was a complete mystery. One he was definitely not going to consult the others on. He got the impression they already guessed something had happened. Knowing them, they'd royally screw up that speculation.

For some reason he'd also held off saying anything to Salrana.

Grudgingly, he acknowledged that Kanseen did have a small point there. He really was going to have to face up to the whole 'friends become lovers' issue simmering away between him and Salrana. It wasn't fair on her. She was growing up into a beautiful adolescent, so much more vivacious than any of the city girls he encountered. All he had to do was get over his notion of protectiveness. That was stupid too. She was old enough to look out for herself, and make her own choices. The only person who'd appointed him her guardian was himself. Something he'd done out of obligation, and friendship. To do anything different, especially now, could be considered as taking advantage.

Sometimes you have to do what's wrong to do what's right.

And physically he knew they would be fantastic together. *That body, and as for those legs . . .* Altogether too much time of late was spent thinking about how her legs would feel wrapped round him, long athletic muscles flexing relentlessly. It would end with them both screaming in pleasure. *We wouldn't even get out of bed for the first year.*

Then after that, after the passion, they'd still enjoy each other's company. Salrana was the only person he could ever really talk to. They understood each other. Two hick kids against the city. Future Mayor. Future Pythia.

He smiled warmly.

'—of course, I could just talk to myself instead,' an irritated Macsen said.

'Sorry, what?' Edeard asked, banishing the smile.

Macsen glanced over at Kanseen, who was standing beside Dinlay, the pair of them looking down on a gondola full of crates, calling something to the gondolier. 'Boy, she really worked you over, didn't she?'

'Who? Oh, no. There's nothing wrong. Kanseen and I are fine.'

'I'd hate to see you un-fine.'

'Really, I'm good. What did you want?'

'The shopkeepers in Boltan Street keep saying strangers are walking along, checking out the buildings with a strong farsight.

They're obviously a gang taking a scouting trip. So if we pitch up there in these uniforms we'll scare them off and they'll just come back in a week or a month – whenever we move on. But if we were to loiter around in ordinary clothes they wouldn't know we were there, and we could catch them at it red-handed.'

'I don't know. You know what Ronark is like about wearing the uniform on duty.' As they were starting their third patrol, the captain had unexpectedly appeared and performed a snap inspection. Edeard had almost been demoted for the 'disgraceful lack of standards'. Since then, he'd made sure his squadmates were properly dressed before leaving the station.

'Exactly,' Macsen said. 'If you're a constable in Jeavons you have to be in a uniform, everyone knows that. So they won't be expecting us out of uniform.'

'Humm, maybe. Let me talk to Chae first, see what he thinks.'

'He'll say no,' Boyd told them. 'You know procedure. If a crime is suspected, then you use ge-eagles to observe the area while the squad waits out of farsight range.'

'We don't know how long we'll have to wait,' Macsen said. 'And Edeard only has one ge-eagle.'

'You can sculpt more, can't you?' Boyd said. 'You told us you used to be an Eggshaper apprentice.'

'He can't sculpt without a Guild licence, not in Makkathran,' Macsen said. 'It's the law; we'd wind up having to arrest him. You know how keen they are on maintaining their monopoly. In any case, this is going to happen soon. We don't have time to sculpt ge-eagles. That's why we have to go patrolling in disguise.'

'Ordinary clothes aren't a disguise,' Boyd protested.

'It doesn't matter what clothes we wear, as long as it's not the uniform,' Macsen said, his temper rising. 'Dress how you want. Maybe in a dress – you're certainly acting like an old woman.'

'Good one, smartarse. If this gang's as clever as you say, they'll know all our faces anyway.'

'Enough,' Edeard said, holding up his hands. 'I will speak to Chae as soon as we get in. Until then I'll keep my ge-eagle close to Boltan Street. I can't do anything more in the middle of a patrol, so drop it for now, please.'

'Just a suggestion,' Macsen grumbled as he started to walk away.

'Are you deliberately winding him up?' Edeard asked Boyd.

The lanky boy gave a sly grin. 'I don't have to answer that, I'm not under oath.'

Edeard laughed. The Boyd of six months ago would never have dared any mischief at another's expense, let alone a friend.

The squad set off along the canal again, following the gentle curve northwards. Edeard's plan was to stay on the side path until they reached its junction with the Outer Circle Canal, then turn back in to Jeavons. He sent his ge-eagle swooping low over the roof and towers of the district, guiding it towards Boltan Street. It was a damp grey morning, with the last of the night's rain clouds still clotting the sky as they slid slowly westwards. Every surface was slick with rain. However, the indomitable citizens of Makkathran were out in force as usual, thronging the streets and narrow alleyways.

Edeard's ge-eagle flashed silently above them, ignored by most. Then he caught a movement that was out of kilter. Halfway along Sonral Street, someone in a hooded jacket turned away from the eagle and adjusted their hood, pulling it fully over their head.

It could have been nothing, the ge-eagle was still over fifty yards away. And it was damp, the air chill. Perfectly legitimate for someone to pull their hood up in such circumstances. A lot of people in the same zigzagging street were sporting hats this morning. The man wasn't even alone in wearing a hooded jacket.

It's wrong though, I know it.

'Wait,' he told the squad. He swept the street with his farsight, searching for the one suspicious figure. The man's mind was shielded, though the tinge of uncertainty seeped out. Again, perfectly legitimate, he could be worrying about anything, from a bad quarrel with his wife to debts.

Edeard observed the direction he was taking and ordered the

ge-eagle round in a long curve. It settled on the eaves of a three-storey house at the end of Sonral Street out of sight from its target. As he waited, Edeard realized the man in the hooded jacket wasn't alone; he was walking with two others. Then the ge-eagle caught sight of him on the street as he came round one of the shallow turns. By now, the hood had slipped back slightly.

'Oh yes, Lady, thank you,' Edeard said.

'What's happening?' Dinlay demanded.

'He's back,' Edeard growled. 'The thief from Silvarum market, the one who was holding the box.'

'Where!' Kanseen demanded.

'Sonral Street. Top third.'

The squad registered annoyance. 'We can't farsight that far,' Boyd complained.

'Okay, here you go,' Edeard gifted them the ge-eagle's sight.

'Are you sure?' Macsen asked.

'He's right,' Kanseen said. 'It is him, the bastard. I can just farsight him.'

'There are two others with him,' Edeard told them. 'And he's nervous about the ge-eagle, so they're not here for anything legitimate. Let's spread out and surround them. Keep a street between yourself and them the whole time. I'll track them with farsight, I don't want to risk him seeing the ge-eagle again, that'll scare them off.'

They all smiled at each other, edgy with nerves and excitement.

'Go!' Macsen cried.

After five minutes' steady jogging Edeard wished he paid more attention to keeping fit. As before, Makkathran's citizens were reluctant to give ground to anyone in a hurry, least of all a red-faced, sweating, panting young constable. He dodged and shoved and wiggled his way along streets and through alleys, ignoring the whingers, and glaring down anyone who voiced a complaint. His uniform made it worse with its hot, heavy fabric restricting his movements.

Eventually he got himself into position a street to the west of the trio. His farsight showed him his squadmates taking up positions all around. 'Got them,' Dinlay's longtalk announced as he slowed to a walk.

'Me too,' Boyd reported.

'What do you think they're here to steal?' Macsen asked.

'Small enough to carry easily, valuable enough to be worth the risk,' Dinlay replied.

'Another one who's been paying attention during our lectures. But unfortunately that covers about ninety per cent of the shops around here.'

'Could be something in one of the storerooms, too,' Boyd suggested.

'Or a house,' Kanseen added.

'Let's just keep watch on them,' Edeard told them. 'When they go into a building, we close in. Remember to wait until the crime has been committed before arresting them.'

'Hey, never thought of that,' Macsen said.

Edeard let his farsight sweep through the buildings around the trio, trying to guess what they might be interested in. Hopeless task.

The suspects turned off Sonral Street into an alley so narrow one person could barely fit. Edeard hesitated, they were heading towards his street, but it was a blind alley, blocked by a house wall twenty feet high. His farsight probed around, revealing a series of underground storerooms beneath one of the jewellery shops on Sonral Street. There was a passage leading up to a thick metal door in the alley.

'At least they're consistent,' he remarked. 'That's a jeweller's shop on top.'

'On top of what?' Boyd asked.

'There's some kind of passage leading off the alley,' Kanseen told him. 'It leads downwards somewhere. Edeard, can you actually sense what's there?'

'A little bit,' he admitted reluctantly. 'Just some kind of open chamber. I think.' For a moment he wished everyone had his ability – life would be a lot easier.

'So now what do we do?' Macsen asked. 'We can't rush them, not down that alley.'

'Wait at the end,' Dinlay said. 'They can hardly escape.'

Edeard's farsight was showing him a whole network of interconnecting passages and rooms running under the row of shops. The passages all had locked doors, but once the thieves were inside, there was a chance they could elude his squad within the little underground maze.

'The rest of you get into Sonral Street,' he ordered. 'I'm going round the back to see if I can find another way down there.'

'You're not going in alone?' Kanseen asked. 'Edeard, there's three of them, and we know they carry blades.'

'I'm just going to make sure they don't have an escape route, that's all. Come on, move.'

He was faintly aware of his squadmates hurrying to the broad street beyond the alley. One of the thieves had bent down beside the small door, doing something to the first of its five locks. From what he could sense of the locks, Edeard knew he wouldn't like to try and pick them open. He concentrated hard, pushing his farsight through the city's fabric to map out the buried labyrinth of rooms and passages. In truth there were only three exits in addition to the one the trio were currently trying to break through.

Below that level, though, Edeard sensed the web of fissures which wove the city structures together. Several twisted their way up past the storerooms, branching into smaller clefts that laced the walls of the buildings above. He tracked back, finding a convoluted route that led to the street he was standing in. His third hand reached out, probing the fabric of the wall at the back of a tapering alcove between two shops. Nothing, it was as solid as granite.

Please, his longtalk whispered to the mind of the slumbering city. *Let me in.*

Something intangible stirred beneath him. A flock of ruugulls took flight from the roofs above.

Here, his mind pressed into the rear of the alcove. Something pushed back. Colourful shapes rose into his thoughts, swirling so much faster than the birds overhead. In his dazed state he thought they resembled numbers and mathematical symbols, but so much larger and more complex than any of the arithmetic Akeem had ever taught him. With these equations the universe could surely be explained away. They danced like sprites, rearranging themselves into a new order before twirling away.

Edeard gasped, struggling to stand up as his legs shook weakly. His heart was pounding far harder than it had been from his earlier run through the streets. He felt the structure of the wall change. When he peered forward it looked exactly the same as before, a dark-purple surface with flecks of grey stretching all the way up to where the curving roofs intersected three storeys above him. But it *gave* when his third hand touched it.

There were people on the street around him, strolling along. Edeard waited until a relatively clear moment, and stepped into the little alcove. Nobody could see him now. His hand touched the section of wall at the back, and slipped right through. The skin tingled round his fingers, as if he were immersing them in fine sand. He walked into the wall. It was a sensation his brain interpreted as a wave of dry water washing across him. Then he was inside. He opened his eyes to complete darkness. His farsight cast around, and showed him he was suspended in a vertical tube. Even without visual sight, Edeard instinctively looked down. Farsight confirmed his feet were standing on nothing.

'Oh, Lady!'

He started to descend. It was as though a very powerful third hand was gently lowering him to the bottom of the fissure which snaked away horizontally under the buildings. Yet he was convinced it wasn't a telekinetic hold. He couldn't sense anything like that; some other force was manipulating him. Oddly, his stomach felt as though he was plummeting even though he was moving relatively slowly.

His feet touched the ground. That was when whatever force had gripped him withdrew, leaving him free to sink into a crouch. When he touched the wall of the fissure, he felt a slick of water coating it. A rivulet was trickling over the toe of his boots – he could hear it gurgling softly.

'It's a drain,' he said out loud, astonished that anything so fantastical could actually exist to serve such a mundane purpose.

Despite perfectly clear farsight, he patted round with his hands. The drain fissure was slightly too small for him to walk along it upright. Its side walls were about five feet apart. He took a breath, none too happy at the claustrophobic feeling niggling the back of his mind, and started to move forwards at a stoop.

The thieves had got through the locked door at the top of the passage. An impressive feat in such a short space of time. Two of them were descending the curving stairs to the door which sealed off the bottom, while the third stood guard outside. Edeard moved faster, navigating several forks along the drain fissure. He observed the thieves manipulate the locks on the second door, and go through. Then he was directly underneath the storeroom they were ransacking. The layout was distinct, the wooden racks laid out in parallel. Small boxes piled up on the shelves. A large iron box in one corner, with a very complicated locking mechanism. They were ignoring that.

Edeard looked up as his farsight pervaded the city's substance above him, a solid mass of rock-like material five yards thick. He concentrated. Closed his eyes – stupid but, well . . . And applied his mind. Again the equations rose from nowhere to pirouette breezily around his thoughts. He began to rise up, slipping though the once-solid substance like some piece of cork bobbing to the surface of the sea. Once again his stomach was convinced he was falling, to a degree which brought on a lot of queasiness. He had almost reached the floor, when he realized the thieves would sense him the second he popped up. Quickly, he threw a concealment around himself. Then he was emerging into the storeroom, with a weak orange light shining all around. The floor hardened beneath his boots.

'What was that?' a voice asked.

Edeard was standing behind the rack at the back of the storeroom, out of direct sight. He held his breath.

578

'Nothing. Fucking stop panicking will you. There are only two doors, and the other one is locked. Now help me find the crap we came here for before someone senses us down here.'

Edeard slowly walked round the end of the rack. He could see the pair of them, moving along a rack, taking boxes off the shelf and prising them open with some kind of tool. A quick look inside, and the box would be tossed aside. Most of them seemed to contain little bottles. Dozens of them were clinking as they rolled about on the floor.

'Here we go,' the one in the hooded jacket announced. He'd just forced open a box full of tiny packets. One was opened to reveal a coil of metal thread. Edeard wasn't sure in the store-room's low orange light, but it might be gold.

'I'll check out the rest,' the other one said.

The one with the hooded jacked began stuffing the packets into an inside pocket.

Edeard dropped his concealment.

'What the fuck—' Both thieves swung round to face him.

'Hello again,' Edeard said. 'Remember me?'

'Edeard!' Kanseen's panicky longtalk reverberated in his skull. 'Sweet Lady, where've you been? We've been going frantic. How did you get in there?'

'It's the little shit from the market,' the thief in the hooded jacket spat. 'I fucking knew that ge-eagle was on the prowl.' He reached inside his jacket and pulled out a long blade. At the same time his third hand tried to push into Edeard's chest for a heartsqueeze.

Edeard laughed as he deflected the attack. Then his own third hand slipped out and crushed the blade the thief was holding. The metal rippled, then warped into a slim bent spike. Edeard twisted the tip round into a U-shape. 'You're under arrest for theft and the attempted assault on a constable.'

'Fuck!' the other one yelled, and raced for the door.

'One coming out,' Edeard's longtalk told his squadmates.

'Are you all right?' Dinlay demanded.

'Never better.' He hadn't taken his eyes off the hooded thief.

The man held up the ruined knife, and gave an admiring grin. 'Tough guy, huh. Are you smart with it? There's enough precious metal in here to make everyone happy.'

'You want attempted bribery added to the charges?'

'Idiot.' The thief turned his back on Edeard, and walked casually towards the doorway out to the passage.

'Stop right there,' Edeard ordered.

The thief's third hand lifted one of the small bottles into the air behind him. Edeard frowned uncertainly. Another bottle rose, accelerating to crash into the first. Glass shattered.

A fireball spewed out, dazzling white in the gloomy storeroom. Edeard twisted away instinctively, his shield hardening. Flaming globules splattered against it.

'Edeard!' the squad longtalked in unison.

'I'm all right.' He was blinking his eyes furiously, trying to get rid of the long purple glare-blotches. An acrid smell was growing strong, yet his farsight revealed just a few flickers of flame on the racks closest to the fireball. His third hand swatted them, snuffing the flames before they posed any real danger. Then he noticed the black holes in the boxes scattered across the floor, as if flames had burned through very quickly. The raw edges were still smouldering. When he looked closer, he saw they were coated in some kind of tar which was bubbling away. He shook his head in bewilderment.

'Got them,' Macsen announced victoriously. 'Lady, that last one's an arrogant bastard. You sure you're okay, Edeard?'

'Yeah, I'm fine.' He started to walk out of the storeroom. Some deep instinct made him tread carefully round the patches of hot liquid glistening on the floor. Thin wisps of vapour were layering the air close to the ceiling, producing a stench which made his eyes water. When he passed the bulky metal door he trod on some of the packets containing metal thread. The thief had thrown them all away. Edeard picked one up, frowning.

Why did he do that?

Mystified, he hurried up the passage and out into the alley where his squad was waiting with the subdued prisoners. Now he had time to think about what he'd done, and what the squad had achieved, his elation was rising with the potency of a dawn sun.

*

The court was convened in Makkathran's Parliament House which dominated the Majate district. Technically one building, its component structures had amalgamated into a village of huge halls, assembly rooms, auditoriums, and offices, with cloisters instead of streets. Right at the centre was the elaborate Democracy Chamber where the Grand Council met to debate policy and laws. Wrapped protectively around that were tiers of offices for the Guild of Clerks who worked to administer the city's regulations and collect taxes. A whole wing contained well-appointed offices for each district representative, where they could be lobbied by their constituents about every perceived and actual injustice. Somewhere inside (underground it was rumoured) were the Treasury vaults, containing mountains of gold and silver, where the coins were minted. The Chief Constable was also based in one of the five conical towers, along with a modest staff. For centuries, the outermost tower, closest to the City Gate, used to house the militia barracks; but they had long departed, the serving soldiers to several barracks within the city, while their General and senior officers had taken up residence in the Orchard Palace next door. The vacated barracks had been eagerly taken over by the ever-expanding Guild of Lawyers.

Although democratically open to anyone, it was the interconnecting domes which ran alongside the Centre Circle Canal which the average Makkathran citizen was most likely to be familiar with. They housed the Courts of Justice as well as the constabulary's main holding cells. Edeard and the rest of the squad had been shown round by Master Solarin who explained the history of every corridor and room at inordinate and boring length. Part of their training was to attend trials so they could accustom themselves to the procedures, and listen to the verbal sparring of the lawyers. Edeard had been looking forward to that part, but in all the trials they watched the lawyers had confined themselves

581

to simple questions to those in the witness stand. Though there had been an obscure argument about interpreting a precedent established four hundred years ago to settle a dispute between two fishmongers and their supplier about who got priority on the catch based on the length of the contract. Edeard barely understood the words they used, let alone followed the logic involved. The only criminal trial they'd seen was one where the constables had arrested a bunch of minor family sons during an altercation in a theatre late one night. The young men had all been sheepish, never challenged the senior squad sergeant's account, pleaded guilty to all charges, and accepted the fine without question.

As preparation and experience went, Edeard was beginning to realize how useless it had all been.

Two middle court judges and a Mayor's Counsel judge had been appointed to preside over the case against the trio of thieves they'd arrested. They sat together behind a raised wooden podium which ran along the back of the oval courtroom, clad in flowing scarlet and black robes, with fur-lined hoods hanging over their right shoulders. The Mayor's Counsel also wore a golden chain, signifying his high-ranking status.

Arrayed in the dock on their left the thieves stood with two court constables in dress uniform standing guard. They had finally given their names. Arminel, the hooded leader called himself. No more than forty, with a drawn pale face and thick sandy hair that he wore long to cover large ears. At no time did he ever look worried. If anything his expression indicated ennui. His accomplices were Omasis and Harri. Harri was still in his teens, the one they'd told to stand guard in the alley. He'd only been charged with complicity to steal. Arminel and Omasis were both charged with theft and aggravated trespass. While Arminel had to face the additional charge of assaulting a constable. The jewellery shop owner had swiftly identified the contents of the two bottles Arminel had smashed together as a highly volatile spirit-based cleaning fluid and acid. Edeard had shivered at the thought of what could have happened if his shield had not been strong enough to ward off the fireball. He'd wanted Arminel to be charged with the attack on Kavine in the Silvarum market, but Master Vosbol, the lawyer that Captain Ronark had retained to prosecute the case, had said no. It was too long ago for witnesses to be considered reliable. 'But I recognized him immediately,' Edeard had cried.

'You saw someone behaving suspiciously,' Master Vosbol said. 'You believed him to be the participant in the previous crime.'

'Kavine will identify him.'

'Kavine was stabbed, quite badly. The defence will argue that makes him unreliable. Let's just go with these charges, shall we?'

Edeard sighed and shook his head.

It really should have served a warning as to the methodology of Makkathran's legal affairs. Instead, the first inkling that their case wasn't as watertight as they imagined came when the defendants all entered a plea of not guilty.

'They can't be serious,' Edeard hissed as Master Cherix, the defence lawyer, stood before the judges and entered the plea. The squad was sitting along the rear wall, all in their dress uniforms, waiting to be called by the prosecution. Captain Ronark sat on one side of them, with Sergeant Chae on the other.

Just about all of the seating was empty. Edeard didn't know if he was pleased about that or not. He wanted the city's citizens to see his squad had helped bring a small part of their troubles to justice. Show them that the law hadn't deserted them.

Master Cherix raised a surprised eyebrow at the exclamation, and turned to look at the squad. Master Vosbol shot them a furious look. 'Be silent,' his longtalk ordered.

It was, Master Cherix explained, a terrible misunderstanding. His clients were honest citizens going about their business when they perceived the blast in the alley. It had blown open a small door, and full of the concern for human life they had ventured into the storeroom filled with smoke and flames – at great personal risk – to make sure there were no injured inside. At which point the constables had stumbled upon them, and received a totally false impression.

One by one the three accused took the stand and swore under

oath that they had been acting selflessly. As they did so their unshielded minds radiated sincerity, along with a modicum of injured innocence that their good deed had been so misinterpreted. Master Cherix shook his head in sympathy, woebegone that the constables had acted so wrongly. 'A sign of the times,' he told the judges. 'These constables are well-meaning young folk, rushed through their training by a city desperate to make up staffing targets for the sake of politics. But in truth they were far out of their depth on that sad day. They too need to make arrests to prove themselves to their notoriously harsh station captain. In such circumstances it is only understandable why they chose to interpret events in the way they did.'

Edeard met Arminel's stare. *He tried to kill me, and his lawyer's making out it was all a misunderstanding? That we're in the wrong.* It was so outrageous he almost laughed. Then Arminel's expression twitched, just for an instant. That condescending sneer burned itself into Edeard's memory. He knew then that this was not the end. Nowhere near.

After two hours of listening to the defendants, Edeard was finally called to the stand. *About time, I can soon set this straight.*

'Constable Edeard,' Cherix smiled warmly. He was nothing like Master Solarin. He was a young man who dressed like the son of a trading family. 'You're not from the city, are you?'

'What's that got to do with this?'

Master Cherix put on a pained expression, and turned to the judges. 'My Lords?'

'Answer the questions directly,' the Mayor's Counsel instructed.

'Sir,' Edeard reddened. 'No. I was born in the Rulan province.'

'And you've been here for what? Half a year?'

'A little over that, yes.'

'So it would be fair to say that you're not entirely familiar with the city.'

'I know my way around.'

'I was thinking more in terms of the way our citizens behave. So why don't you tell me what you believe happened?'

Edeard launched into his rehearsed explanation. How Arminel tried to avoid the ge-eagle. The squad tracking them along Sonral Street. Arranging themselves in an encircling formation, whilst standing back and observing through farsight. Sensing Arminel picking the locks.

'At which point we closed in, and I witnessed the accused stealing gold wire from the storeroom.'

'I'm curious about this aspect,' Master Cherix said. 'You told your squad to wait in Sonral Street by the entrance to the alley. Yet you went down into the storeroom. But I thought you said Harri had been left "on guard duty" in the alley. How did you get past him?'

'I was lucky, I found another entrance through the shop which backed on to the jewellers.'

Master Cherix nodded in admiration. 'So it was hardly a secure storeroom then? If you could just walk in.'

'It was difficult,' Edeard admitted, praying to the Lady to help him rein in his guilt. But this wasn't a lie, just a slight rearrangement of his true route into the storeroom. 'I just managed to get there in time.'

'In time for what?'

'To see Arminel stealing the gold wire. He was doing that before he flung flaming acid at me.'

'Indeed. I'd like you to clarify another point, Constable. When you emerged after this alleged event to join up with your squad, did Arminel have any of this supposed "gold wire" on him.'

'Well, no, he dumped it when I challenged him.'

'I see. And your squadmates can confirm that, can they?'

'They know . . . yes.'

'Yes, what? Constable.'

'We caught them doing it. I saw him!'

'By your own statement, you were deep underground in the poorly illuminated storeroom at the time of the alleged theft. Which of your squadmates can farsight through fifteen yards of solid city fabric?'

'Kanseen. She knew I was there.'

'Thank you, Constable. Defence would like to call Constable Kanseen.'

Kanseen passed Edeard on her way to the stand. They both had meticulously blank expressions, but he could tell how worried she was. When he sat down next to Dinlay the others all smiled sympathetically. 'Good job,' Chae whispered. Edeard wasn't convinced.

'You have a farsight almost as good as your squad leader?' Master Cherix asked.

'We came out about equal in our tests.'

'So you could sense what went on in the storeroom from your position in Sonral Street?'

'Yes.'

Edeard winced, she sounded so uncertain.

'How much gold wire was in there?'

'I . . . er, I'm not sure.'

'An ounce? A ton?'

'A few boxes.'

'Constable Kanseen,' Master Cherix smiled winningly. 'Was that a guess?'

'Not enough gold to be obvious to a casual farsight sweep.'

'I'll let that go for the moment. Constable Edeard claims you perceived him in there.'

'I did,' she replied confidently. 'I sensed him appear in the back. We'd been worried when we lost track of him.'

'You sensed his mind. There's a big difference between a radiant source of thoughts, and inert material is there not?'

'Yes, of course.'

Master Cherix patted the jacket he wore under his black robe. 'In one pocket I have a length of gold wire. In another pocket I have an equal length of steel wire. Which is which, Constable?'

Edeard concentrated his farsight on the lawyer. Sure enough, there was some kind of dense line of matter in his pockets, but there was no way to tell the nature of either.

Kanseen looked straight ahead. 'I don't know.'

'You don't know. Yet there is only five feet of clear air between us. So can you really say with certainty you perceived my client picking up gold wire when he was on the other side of fifteen yards of solid mass?'

'No.'

'Thank you, Constable, no more questions.'

It came down to an argument between two lawyers. Edeard found himself grinding his teeth together as it was presented as his word against Arminel's.

'Acting suspiciously,' Master Vosbol ticked off on his fingers. 'Gaining entry to a storeroom behind two locked doors. Seen by a constable of impeccable character stealing gold wire. Attacking that same constable. My Lords, the evidence is overwhelming. They came to the storeroom with the express intent of theft. A theft which was valiantly thwarted by these fine constables at great personal danger to themselves.'

'Circumstantial evidence only,' Master Cherix pronounced. 'Facts twisted by the prosecution to support a speculated sequence of events. A country boy alone in an underground city storeroom full of smoke and flame. Confused by the strange environment and regrettably unreliable; his claims unsupported by his own squadmates and friends. My clients do not deny being in the storeroom, responding to the fire as any responsible citizen would. The prosecution has offered no proof whatsoever that they ever touched the gold wire. I would draw my Lords' attention to the precedent of Makkathran versus Leaney, hearsay is inadmissible.'

'Objection,' Master Vosbol barked. 'This is testimony by a city official, not hearsay.'

'Unsubstantiated testimony,' Master Cherix countered. 'Must be accepted as having equal weight to my clients' account of events.'

The judges deliberated for eight minutes. 'Insufficient evidence,' the Mayor's Counsel announced. 'Case dismissed.' He banged his gavel on the bench.

Edeard's head dropped into his hands. He absolutely could not believe what he'd just heard. 'Lady, no,' he gasped.

The defendants were cheering, slapping each other jubilantly. Edeard was disgusted to see Masters Vosbol and Cherix shake hands.

'It happens,' Captain Ronark said gravely. 'You did a perfect job, nobody could do better. I'm proud of you. But this is the way it is in Makkathran these days.'

'Thank you sir,' Dinlay and Macsen murmured sullenly.

Ronark flashed them all an anxious expression, debating with himself if he should say more. 'This will be useful to you,' he said. 'I can imagine what you think of that right now, but next time you'll know what to do, how to be extra careful gathering evidence, and we'll nail that little bastard good and proper.' He nodded at Chae, and walked down to talk with Master Vosbol.

'Buy you all a drink,' Chae said. 'I know how bad this hurts, believe me. I've had smartarse lawyers get scum off on worse charges than this.'

'A double of something illegally strong,' Macsen said. The others nodded in grudging agreement. They looked at Edeard.

'Sure,' he said.

Arminel saluted him with two fingers to his forehead. His smile was gloating.

Edeard quashed his impulse to dive across the court and smash his fist into the man's face. Instead he winked back. 'Be seeing you,' he whispered.

7

The unisphere had never been a homogenous system, nor was it designed along logical principles, which was quite an irony considering the purely digital medium it dealt with. Instead it had grown and expanded in irregular spurts to accommodate the commercial and civil demands placed on it by a proliferating interstellar civilization. By definition the unisphere was nothing more than the interface protocols between every planetary cybersphere, and they were incredibly diverse. Just about every hardware technology the human race had developed was still in operation across the Greater Commonwealth Worlds, from old-fashioned macro-arrays running RI programs, to semi-organic cubes, quantum wire blocks, smartneural webs, and photonic crystals, all the way up to ANA which technically was just another routing junction. The interstellar linkages were equally varied, with the Central Commonwealth Worlds still using their original zero-width wormholes, while the External Worlds used a combination of zero-width and hyperspace modulation. Transdimensional channels were becoming more common especially among the latest generation of External Worlds. Starships were also able to link in providing they were in range of a star system's spacewatch network. The massive gulf between technologies and capacities within the unisphere meant the management software had swollen over the centuries to accommodate every new advance and application. With effectively infinite storage capacity, the upgrades, adaptors, retrocryptors, and interpreters had accumulated like binary onion layers around each node. They had the ability to communicate with every other chunk of hardware to come on line since the end of the twenty-first century; but with such a complex procedure dealing with every interface, the problem of security increased proportionally. It was relatively easy for a specialist e-head to quietly incorporate siphoning and echoclone routines amid centuries' worth of augmentation files. The problem was one which every user got round by using their own encryption. However, in order to decrypt a secure message, the receiver had to be in possession of the appropriate key. Ultra-secure keys were never sent via the unisphere, they were physically exchanged in advance, a common method for financial transactions. A less secure method was for a user's u-shadow to dispatch a key using one route, then call on another. Given the phenomenal number of (randomly designated) routes available within the unisphere, most people (who even considered it) regarded that as sufficient. It would, after all, require a colossal amount of computing power to monitor every route established to a specific address code for a key, then follow up by intercepting the message.

Of course, that assumption had been made in the early centuries, prior to ANA. For any individual downloaded into ANA, access to that quantity of processing capacity was an everyday occurrence. The Advancer Faction routinely ran a scan of all messages to ANA:Governance to check if any of its own activities had been noticed and reported.

When the Faction's monitor routine detected a starship TD connection established to Wohlen's spacewatch network downloading a key fragment to ANA:Governance's security division an alert was flagged. Over the next two point three seconds, the remaining seven key fragments arrived via routes from seven different planets, and the monitor acknowledged that someone was trying to establish a very secure link. Nothing too out of the ordinary in that, it was the security division after all. However, all eight planets were within twenty-five lightyears of the

Advancer Faction's secret manufacturing station. That bumped the alert up to grade one.

Three seconds later, Ilanthe's elevated mentality was observing the secure call itself, placed through the ninth planet, Loznica, seventeen lightyears from the station.

'Yes, Troblum?' ANA:Governance asked.

'I need to see someone. Someone special.'

'I will be happy to facilitate any request in relation to Commonwealth security. Could you please be more specific?'

'I work for the Advancer Faction. Make that "worked". I have information, very important information concerning their activities.'

'I will be happy to receive your data.'

'No. I don't trust you. Not any more. Parts of you are bad. I don't know how far the contamination has spread.'

'I can assure you, ANA:Governance retains its integrity, both in structural essence and morally.'

'Like you'd say different. I can't even be sure if I'm talking to ANA:Governance.'

'Scepticism is healthy providing it does not escalate into paranoia. So given you don't trust me, what can I do for you?'

'I'm entitled to be paranoid after what I've seen.'

'What have you seen?'

'Not you. I'll tell Paula Myo. She's the only person left that I trust. Route this call to her.'

'I will ask if she will be willing to listen to you.'

Fifteen seconds later, Paula Myo came on line. 'What do you want?' she asked.

'There's something you need to know. Something you'll understand.'

'Then tell me.'

'I need to be certain it's you. Where are you?'

'In space.'

'Can you get to Sholapur?'

'Why would I want to?'

'I'll tell you everything I know about their plans for fusion, all

591

the hardware they've built, all the people involved. All that, if you'll just listen to me. You have to listen, you're the only person left who'll deal with it.'

'With what?'

'Come to Sholapur.'

'Very well. I can be there in five days.'

'Don't stealth your starship. I'll contact you.'

The connection ended.

As ANA and its abilities were to the unisphere, so there were hierarchal levels within ANA. Discreet levels of ability surreptitiously established by a few of the humans who had founded ANA. Abilities only they could utilize. They couldn't corrupt ANA:Governance, or use the Navy warships for their own ends. That magnitude of intervention would be easily detectable. But there was a backdoor into several of ANA's communication sections, allowing them to watch the watchers without the kind of effort which the Advancers had to make for the same intelligence. And as they were there first, they had also observed the Advancers and other Factions spread their monitors into the unisphere nodes as their campaigns and reach grew. They knew which messages the Advancers intercepted.

'Ilanthe is going to go apeshit over that kind of betrayal,' Gore said.

'At least we know Troblum is still alive,' Nelson replied.

'Yeah, for the next five seconds.'

'Until he gets to Sholapur at the very least. And never ever underestimate Paula.'

'I don't. If anyone can collect him in once piece, she can.'

'So we might just be able to sit back and relax if Paula does bring back information on what the Advancers are up to. Hardware, Troblum said. That has to be the planet-shifting ftl engine.'

'Maybe so,' Gore said. 'But he was offering that as a bribe to make sure Paula listened to something else, something big and scary enough to get him really worried. Now what the fuck could that be?'

Marius sprinted down the corridor. It wasn't something the universe got to see very often. With his Higher field functions reinforcing his body, the speed was phenomenal. Malmetal doors had to roll aside very quickly or face complete disintegration. His dark toga suit flapped about in the slipstream, for once ruining the eerie gliding effect he always portrayed. Marius didn't care about appearance right now. He was *furious*.

Ilanthe's brief call had been very unsettling. He'd never failed her before. The implications were terrible, as she managed to explain in remarkably few words. He only wished he had time to make Troblum *suffer* for his crime.

He streaked through the three-way junction which put him into sector 7-B-5. Some idiot technician was walking down the middle of the corridor, going back to her suite after a long shift. Marius charged past her, clipping her arm which broke instantly from the impact. She was spun round, slamming into the wall. She screamed as she crumpled to the floor.

The door to Troblum's suite was dead ahead, locked as of two minutes ago with Marius's own nine-level certificate to prevent the little shit from leaving. The suite's internal sensors showed Troblum sitting at a table slurping his way disgustingly through a late-night 'snack'.

Marius began to slow as his u-shadow unlocked the door. It expanded as he arrived, and he coasted through. Troblum's head lifted, crumbs of burger bap dropping from the corner of his mouth. Despite bulging cheeks he still managed a startled expression.

A disruptor pulse slammed into him, producing a ghost-green phosphorescent flare in the suite's air. Marius followed it up immediately with a jelly gun shot. He would obliterate the memorycell in a few seconds, then that would just leave Trob-lum's secure store back on Arevalo.

Instead of disintegrating into a collapsing globule of gore,

Troblum simply popped like a soap bubble. A rivulet of metal dust spewed out from the wall behind the table where the jelly gun shot hit. Marius froze in shock, his field-scan functions sweeping round. It hadn't been Troblum. No biological matter was in the room. His eyes found a half-melted electronic module on the seat, ruined by the disruptor blast.

A solido projector.

Marius was perfectly still as he stared at it.

'What happened?' Neskia asked as she strode into the suite. Her long neck curved so her head could see round Marius.

'It would appear Troblum isn't quite the fat fool I'd taken him for.'

'We'll find him. It won't take long. This station isn't that big.'

Marius whipped round, the wide irises in his green eyes narrowing to minute intimidating slits. 'Where's his ship?' he demanded.

'Sitting in the airlock,' she replied calmly. 'Nobody enters or leaves without my authorization.'

'It better be,' Marius spat.

'Every centimetre of this station is covered by some sensor or other. We'll find him.'

Marius's u-shadow ordered the smartcore to show him the airlock. The *Mellanie's Redemption* was sitting passively at the centre of the large white chamber. Visually it was there, the airlock radar produced a return from the hull. The umbilical management programs reported a steady drain of housekeeping power through the cables plugged into its base. He queried the ship's smartcore. There was no response.

Marius and Neskia stared at each other. 'Shit!'

Four minutes later they walked into the airlock. Marius glowered at the long cone-shaped ship with its stupid curving tailfins. His field scan swept out. It was an illusion, produced by a small module on the airlock floor. He smashed a disruptor pulse into the solido projector, and the starship image shivered, shrinking down to a beautiful, naked young girl with blonde hair that hung halfway down her back. 'Oh, Howard,' she moaned sensually, running her hands up her body, 'do that again.'

Marius let out an incoherent cry, and shot the projector again. It burst into smouldering fragments, and the girl vanished.

'How in Ozzie's name did he do that?' Neskia said. There was a hint of admiration in her voice. 'He must have flown right past the defence cruisers as well. They never even saw him.'

Marius took a moment to compose himself. 'Troblum helped design and build the defence cruisers. Either he infiltrated their smartcores back then, or he knows a method of circumventing their sensor systems.'

'He compromised the station smartcore, too. It should never have let the *Mellanie's Redemption* out.'

'Indeed,' Marius said. 'You will find the corruption and purge it. This operation must not suffer any further compromise.'

'It was not me who compromised this station,' she said with equal chill. 'You brought him here.'

'You had twenty years to discover the bugs he planted. That you failed is unforgivable.'

'Don't try to play the blame game with me. This is your foul-up. And I will make that very clear to Ilanthe.'

Marius turned on a heel, and walked back to the airlock chamber's entrance. His dark toga suit adjusted itself around him, once more giving off a narrow black shimmer that concealed his feet. He glided with serpentine poise down the corridor towards the airlock chamber which contained his own starship.

His u-shadow opened a secure link to the Cat's ship.

'It's so nice to be popular again,' she said.

'We have a problem. I want you to find Troblum. Eliminate that shit from this universe. In fact, I want him erased from all of history.'

'That sounds personal, Marius dear. Always a bad thing. Messes with your judgement.'

'He's heading for Sholapur. In five days' time he will meet with an ANA representative there, and explain what we have been doing. His ship has some kind of advanced stealth ability we didn't know about.'

'Gave you the slip, huh?'

'I'm sure you'll be more than capable of rectifying our mistake.'

'What do you want me to do about Aaron? He's still down on the planet's surface.'

'Is there any sign of Inigo?'

'Darling, the sensors can barely make out continents. I've no idea what's going on down there.'

'Do as you see fit.'

'I thought this was all critical to your plans.'

'If Troblum exposes us to ANA there will be no plans, there probably won't be an Advancer Faction any more.'

'The strong always survive. That's evolution.'

'Paula Myo is the representative ANA is sending to collect Troblum.'

'Oh, Marius, you're too kind to me. Really.'

*

It should have been tempting. Alone in a small starship with three amazingly fit men, who would probably have been *honoured* to got to bed with him. Oscar had been delighted when Tomansio had introduced his team. Liatris McPeierl was his lieutenant, a lot quieter than Tomansio, with a broad mouth that could flash a smile that was wickedly attractive. He would handle the technical aspects of the mission, Tomansio said, including their armaments. Gazing at the pile of big cases on the regrav sled which followed Liatris about, Oscar had his first moment of doubt; he didn't want to resort to violence, though he was realistic enough to know that wasn't his decision. Cheriton McOnna had been brought in to help because of his experience with the gaiafield. There was nothing about confluence nest operations which he didn't know, Tomansio claimed. Oscar was slightly surprised by Cheriton's characteristics, they were almost Higher; he'd altered his ears to simple circle craters, his nose was wide and flat, while his eyes were sparkling purple globes, like multifaceted insect lenses. His bald skull had two low ridges reaching back from his eyebrows over his cranium to merge together at the nape of his neck.

'Multi-macrocellular enrichment,' he explained. 'And a hell of a lot of customized gaiamotes.' To prove it he spun out a vision of some concert. For a moment Oscar was transported to a natural amphitheatre, lost in a sea of people under a wild starry sky. On the stage far away, a pianist performed by himself, his soulful tune making Oscar sway in sympathy.

'Wow,' Oscar blinked, taking a half step back as the vision cleared. He'd almost been about to sing along, the song was familiar somehow – just not quite right.

'I composed it in your honour,' Cheriton said. 'I remember you told Wilson Kime you liked old movies.'

Now Oscar remembered. 'That's right. "Somewhere Over the Rainbow", yeah?' He took care to reduce his gaiamotes reception level. Cheriton had produced a very strong emission. It made Oscar wonder if the gaiafield could actually be used in a harmful way.

'Yes.'

The last member of the team was Beckia McKratz, whose gaiafield give-away made it very clear she'd like to bed him. An equal to Anja in the beauty stakes, and minus all the neurotic hang-ups. Oscar wasn't interested. Not even that first morning when he stumbled out of his tiny sleep cabin to find all four of them in the main lounge stripped to the waist and performing some strenuous ni-tng exercise. They moved in perfect syn-chronization, arms and legs rising gracefully to stick out in odd directions, limbs flexing. Eyes closed, breathing deeply. From their gaiafield emanations, their minds seemed to be hibernating.

Aliens teleported into human bodies, and carefully examining what they could do.

It was all very different to Oscar's wake-up routine, which normally involved a lot of coffee and accessing the most trashy unisphere gossip shows he could find. And that was the whole non-attraction problem. All this devotion to perfection and strength didn't seem to leave them much time to actually be human. It was a big turn-off.

So he crept round the edge of the lounge to the culinary unit, snagged a large cup of coffee and a plate of buttered croissants, and sat quietly in a corner munching away as he watched the strange slow-motion ballet.

They came to rest position, and took one last breath in unison before opening their eyes and smiling.

'Good morning, Oscar,' Tomansio said.

Oscar slurped some more coffee down. That morning routine also included no conversation until his third cup. The culinary unit was suddenly busy churning out plates with large portions of bacon and eggs, with toast.

'Something wrong?' Liatris asked.

Oscar realized he was staring at the man eat. 'Sorry. I assumed you'd all be vegetarians.'

They all exchanged an amused glance. 'Why?'

'When we were flying the Carbon Goose across Half Way I remember the Cat kicking up a big fuss about the on-board food. She refused to eat anything produced and processed on a Big15 planet.' His companions' amusement evaporated. To Oscar it was as though he'd been transformed into some kind of guru, steeped in wisdom.

'You did talk to her, then?' Beckia asked.

'Not much. It was almost as if she was bored with us. And I still don't get why you idolize her the way you do.'

'We're realistic about her,' Cheriton said. 'But she accomplished so much.'

'She killed a lot of people.'

'As did you, Oscar,' Tomansio chided.

'Not deliberately. Not for enjoyment.'

'The whole Starflyer War happened because humanity was weak. Our strength had been sapped away by centuries of liberalism. Not any more. The External Worlds have the self-belief to strike out for themselves against the Central Worlds. That's thanks to Far Away's leadership by example. And the

Knights Guardians are the political force behind Far Away. Politicians don't ignore strength any more. It is celebrated on hundreds of worlds in a myriad of forms.'

That was the trouble with history, Oscar thought. Once the distance has grown long enough any event can be seen favourably. The true horror fades with time, and ignorance replaces it. 'I lived through those times. The Commonwealth was strong enough to prevail. Without the strength we showed then, you wouldn't be alive today to complain about us and debate what might have been.'

'We don't want to offend, Oscar.' .

Oscar downed the last of his coffee, and told the culinary unit to produce another. 'So sensibilities aren't a weakness, then?'

Liatris laughed. 'No. Respect and civility are highpoints of civilization. As much as personal independence and kindness. Strength comes in many guises. Including laying down your life to give the human race its chance to survive. If the Knights Guardians have one regret, it is that your name is not as famous and revered as the others from your era.'

'Holy crap,' Oscar muttered and collected his coffee. He knew his face was red. *My era!* 'All right,' he said as he sank back on to the chair which the lounge extruded for him. 'I can see we're going to have fun times debating history and politics for the rest of the mission. In the meantime, we do have a very clear objective. My plan is quite a simple one, and I'd like some input from you as we shake it down into something workable. You guys are the experts in this field, and this *era*. So, for what it's worth: there are several ANA Factions extremely keen to find this poor old Second Dreamer, not to mention Living Dream, which has a very clear-cut agenda for him. Between them they have colossal resources which we can't hope to equal, so what I propose is to jump on their bandwagon, and let them do the hard work. We should position ourselves to snatch him as soon as they locate him.'

'I like it,' Tomansio said. 'The simpler it is, the better.'

'Which just leaves us with mere details,' Oscar said. 'Everyone seems to think the Second Dreamer is on Viotia. We'll be there in another seven hours.'

'Impressive flight time,' Cheriton said dryly. 'I've never been in an ultradrive ship before.'

Oscar ignored the jibe. Tomansio had never asked who was employing Oscar, but the ship was a huge give-away. 'Tomansio, how do we go about infiltrating the Living Dream operation there?'

'Direct insertion. We'll hack their smartcore's personnel files and assign Cheriton into the search operation. He's savvy enough to pass as a Dream Master, right?'

'No problem,' Cheriton said. He sighed. 'Reprofiling for me, then.' He ran a hand along one of his skull ridges.

'I'll make you look almost human,' Beckia assured him.

Cheriton blew her a kiss. 'Living Dream have been altering confluence nests all across the General Commonwealth to try and get a fix on his location,' he said. 'It must be costing them a fortune, which is a good indicator of how desperate they are. It's not a terribly accurate method, but once they narrow it down to a single nest, they'll know the district at least.'

'How does that help?' Beckia asked. 'A nest's gaiafield can cover a big area. If it's in a city it can include millions.'

'If it were me, I'd surround the area with specialist nests and Dream Masters, and try and triangulate the dream's origin.'

'So we can be in the general area just like them,' Oscar said. 'Then it's all down to speed.'

'The Factions will be running similar snatch operations,' Tomansio said. 'We'll be up against their agents as well as Living Dream.'

Oscar picked up on how enthused the Knights Guardians were by that prospect. 'The Faction agents will have biononics weapon enrichments, won't they?'

'I hope so,' Tomansio said.

'You can match that?' Oscar asked nervously.

'Only one way to find out.'

*

It was a gentle valley carpeted by long dark grass which rippled in giant waves as the breeze from the mountains gusted down. There was a house nestled in a shallow dip in the ground; a lovely old place whose walls were all crumbling stone quarried out of the nearby hills. An overhanging thatch roof gave it a delightful unity with nature. Its interior was a technology completely at odds with its outward appearance, with replicators providing him with any physical requirement. T-sphere interstices provided his family with an interesting internal topology, and any extra space they might want.

He stood facing it, holding his bamboo staff vertically in front of him. Torso bare to the air; legs clad in simple black cotton *dirukku* pants. Shutting down biononic field functions, attuning his perception to sight, sound, and sensation alone. Feeling his surroundings. Nesting cobra: the foundation of self. He moved into sharp eagle. Then twisted fast, assuming jumping cheetah. A breath. Opponent moving behind. Bring the bamboo down and sweep, the tiger's claw. Spin jump as a coiled dragon. One arm bent into spartan shield. Lunge: striking angel. Drop the staff and pull both curving daggers from their sheaths. Bend at the knees into woken phoenix.

A vibration in the air. Heavy feet crushing tender stalks of grass. He raised his head to see a line of black armoured figures marching towards him. Long flames billowed from vents in their helmets as they roared their battle call. His breathing quickened as he tightened his grip on the daggers. The smell of charred meat rolled across the grassland. Aaron gagged on the terrible stench. Coughing violently, he sat up on the couch in the ground crawler's cabin.

'Shit,' he spluttered, then coughed again, fighting for breath. Doubling up. Exovision medical displays showed him his biononics assuming command of his lungs and airway, overriding his body's struggling autonomic functions. He wheezed down a long breath and shook his head as the artificial organelles stabilized him.

Corrie-Lyn was gazing at him from her couch on the other

601

side of the cabin. She'd drawn her knees up under her chin, a blanket wrapped round her shoulders. For some reason she made him feel guilty. 'What?' he snapped, all caffeine-deprived bad temper.

'I don't know,' she said. 'Those warriors represent being trapped, I think. But they came to you outside your home. You were unable to escape what you are, what you had grown into.'

'Oh give me a break,' he growled, and tried to swing his feet off the couch. His blanket was wrapped round his legs. He pulled it off in an angry jerk.

Corrie-Lyn responded with a hurt scowl. 'They could also be a representation of paranoia,' she said with brittle dignity.

'Fuck off.' He told the culinary unit to brew some herbal tea. *To purge the soul.* 'Look,' he said with a sigh. 'Someone has seriously screwed with my brain. I'm bound to have nightmares. Just leave it, okay.'

'Doesn't that bother you?'

'I am what I am. And I like it.'

'But you don't know who you are.'

'I told you: drop this.' He settled into one of the two forward seats, and stared out of the thick windscreen slit. The ground crawler was lumbering forward, rocking about as if they were riding a ocean swell. Outside, the weather hadn't changed for the whole trip, a thin drizzle of ice particles blown along at high speed. High overhead, the dark underbelly of the cloud blanket seethed relentlessly, flickering with sheet lightning. They were traversing a drab landscape, where flood streams had gouged out deep sharp gullies. Broad headlight beams slithered over the dunes of filthy snow which migrated across the permafrost. Occasionally the surface of iron-hard soil was distended by some ruins, or stumps. Otherwise there was nothing to break the monotony.

Corrie-Lyn climbed off the couch without a word and went back to the little washroom compartment at the rear of the oblong cabin. She managed to slam the worn aluminium door.

Aaron rubbed his face, dismayed by how he'd handled the situation. Something in his dreams was eating away at his composure. He hated to think she was right, that his subconscious had somehow squirrelled away a few precious true memories. The personality he had now was simple and straightforward, uncluttered by extraneous attachments or sentimentality. He didn't want to lose that, not ever.

By way of apology, he started entering a whole load of instructions into the culinary unit. Thirty minutes later, when Corrie-Lyn emerged her breakfast was waiting for her on a small table. She pouted at it.

'The crawler's net reckons we're about ninety minutes from the camp,' he said. 'I thought you'd want to fortify yourself before we reached them.'

Corrie-Lyn was silent for a moment, then nodded in acknowledgement at the peace offering, and sat at the table. 'Has anyone been in contact?'

'From the camp? No.' They'd talked to someone called Ericilla last night, telling her their estimated arrival time. She'd seemed interested, though she laughed at the idea of any of her colleagues being an abandoned lover. 'If you knew any of my team mates you'd know you're wasting your time. Romantic they're not.'

'We're still connected to the beacon network,' Aaron said sipping another herbal tea. 'Nobody is owning up, yet.'

'What do we do if he's not there?'

Aaron resisted the impulse to look her up and down again. When she came out of the washroom she'd changed into a pair of black trousers and a light-green sweater with a V-neck. Her hair was washed and springy. No cosmetic scales on her face, but her complexion glowed. Clearly she was ready for her chance to reignite some of the old passion should *he* be there. She'd kept her gaiamotes closed up fairly tight since leaving Kajaani, but the occasional lapse had allowed Aaron to sense a lot of anticipation fermenting in her mind.

603

'I'm not sure,' he admitted. 'Time isn't in our favour.'

'And if he is there? What if he doesn't want to be hauled back to Ellezelin?'

Just for an instant something stirred Aaron's mind. Certainty. He did know what was going to happen afterwards. The knowledge was all there waiting for him. Ready for the moment. 'I'll just tell him what I have to. After that, it'll be up to him.'

Corrie-Lyn gave him a mildly doubtful stare before tucking in to her first bacon sandwich.

Camp, Aaron decided, was a rather grand description for the place where the team working in the Olhava province had set themselves up. A couple of ground crawlers were parked next to each other in the lee of some rugged foothills. Malmetal shelters had expanded out of their rear sections to provide the team with larger accommodation. But that was all.

Aaron parked a few metres away, and they both pulled on their bulky surface suits. Once his bubble helmet had sealed, Aaron went into the tiny airlock, and waited for the outside door to slide aside. He was immediately hit by the wind. Ice fragments swirled round him. He walked carefully down the ramp, holding the handrail tight. The wind was squally, but he could stand upright. There were enhancer systems built in to the suit for when the storms really hit. Its main purpose was to protect him from the radiation.

Although there wasn't too much physical effort involved, he wished he'd nudged their ground crawler closer to those of the team. He took nearly three minutes to cover the small gap and clamber into a decontamination airlock on the side of one of the shelters. Corrie-Lyn was grunting and cursing her way along behind him.

Ericilla was waiting for them in the closet-sized suit room. A short woman with a frizz of brown hair flecked with grey. She smirked as Corrie-Lyn wriggled out of her surface suit, licking her lips in merriment. 'No man is worth this,' she announced.

'He is,' Corrie-Lyn assured her.

Aaron had already extended his field-scan function, probing the whole camp. He'd detected four people including Ericilla. None of them were Higher.

Ericilla beckoned. 'Come and meet the boys.'

Vilitar and Cytus were waiting for them, standing in the middle of the shelter's cluttered lounge like an army of two on detention parade. Nerina, Vilitar's husband gave Corrie-Lyn a weary look.

'Oh shit,' Corrie-Lyn said despondently.

Nerina poked Vilitar in the chest. 'Well that lets you off.'

The two men relaxed, grinning sheepishly. Aaron sensed the tension drain away. Suddenly everyone was smiling and happy to see them.

'I thought there were five in your team,' Aaron said.

'Earl is down in the dig,' Ericilla said. 'The sensor bots picked up a promising signal last night. He said that was more important than, well—' The way she left it hanging told them she was on Earl's side.

'I'd like to see him, please,' Corrie-Lyn said.

'Why not?' Ericilla said. 'You've come this far.'

It was another trip outside. The entrance to the dig was on the other side of the shelters. A simple metal cube housing a small fusion generator and several power cells. An angled force field protected it from Hanko's venomous elements. There was a decontamination airlock to keep the radioactive air out so the team's equipment could work without suffering contamination and degradation. Big filter units filled the rest of the entrance cube, maintaining the clean atmosphere. The temperature inside was still cold enough to keep the permafrost frozen. Aaron and Corrie-Lyn kept their helmets on inside.

Excavation bots had dug a passage down at forty-five degrees, hacking crude steps into the rocky ground. Thick blue air hoses were strung along the roof, clustered round a half-metre extraction tube that buzzed as it propelled grains of frozen mud along to be dumped on a pile half a kilometre away. Polyphoto strips hanging off the cables cast a slightly greenish glow. Aaron trod carefully as they went down. The solid ground around him blocked any detailed field scan.

The bottom of the crude stairs must have been seven metres below ground level. Ericilla explained they'd cut into a lakebed which had filled with sediment during the post-attack monsoons. There were several people from the surrounding area who had never made it to Anagaska.

The passage opened out into a chamber ten metres wide, and three high, supported by force fields. Discarded arm-length bots were strewn over the floor with power cables snaking round them. A couple of hologram projectors filled it with a pervasive sparkly monochrome light. Ice crystals glinted in the sediment contained behind the force field.

There was an opening on the far side. Aaron's field scan showed him another cavern, with a great deal of electronic activity inside. Someone was in there. Someone who could shield his body from the scan.

'Holy Ozzie,' Aaron breathed.

Corrie-Lyn gave him a curious look and strode into the second chamber. It was larger than the first, a third of its wall surface was covered with excavator bots. They looked like a mass of giant maggots slowly wiggling their way forward into the gelid sediment. A huge lacework of tiny pipes emerging from their tails led back to the start of the extraction tube. Silver sensor discs floated through the air, bobbing about to take readings. Silhouetted by the retinue of cybernetic activity was a lone figure wearing a dark-green surface suit. Corrie-Lyn took a couple of hesitant steps forward.

The man turned, lifting his bubble helmet off. His face had a Latin shading rather than Inigo's North European pallor, and the hair was dark brown rather than ginger. But apart from that, the features hadn't been altered much. Aaron thought it a particularly inferior disguise, as if he was just wearing make up and a bad wig.

'Inigo!' Corrie-Lyn whispered.

'Of all the Restoration projects on all the dead worlds in the galaxy, you had to walk into mine.'

Corrie-Lyn sank to her knees, sobbing helplessly.

'Hey, girl,' Inigo said sympathetically. He knelt down beside her, and flipped the outer seals on her helmet.

'Where've you been, you bastard!' she screamed. Her fist smacked into her chest. 'Why did you leave me? Why did you leave us?'

He wiped some of the tears from her cheeks, then leant forward and kissed her. Corrie-Lyn almost fought against it, then suddenly she was wrapping her arms around him, kissing furiously. The fabric of their suits made scratching noises as they rubbed together.

Aaron waited a diplomatic minute, then unsealed his own helmet. The air was bitingly cold, and held the strangest smell of rancid mint. His breath emerged in grey streamers. 'You're a hard man to find.'

Inigo and Corrie-Lyn broke apart.

'Don't listen to him,' Corrie-Lyn said urgently. 'Whatever he wants, refuse. He's insane. He's killed hundreds of people to find you.'

'Slight exaggeration,' Aaron said. 'No more than twenty, surely.'

Inigo's steel-grey eyes narrowed. 'I can sense what you are. Who do you represent?'

'Ah.' Aaron gave a weak smile. 'I'm not sure.' *But we're about to find out.* He could feel the knowledge stirring in his mind again. He was about to know what to do next.

'I won't go back,' Inigo said simply.

'What happened?' Corrie-Lyn pleaded.

Aaron's u-shadow reported a call was coming in from Director Ansan Purillar. Transferred across the hundreds of desolate kilometres from Kajaani by the small sturdy beacons to enter the camp where it finally trickled down into the excavation through a single strand of fibre-optic cable.

607

'Yes, Director?' Aaron said.

Inigo and Corrie-Lyn gave each other a puzzled glance, then looked at Aaron.

'Do you have some colleagues following you?' Ansan Purillar asked.

'No.'

'Well there's a ship coming through the atmosphere above us, and it won't respond to any of our signals.'

Aaron felt his blood chill. His combat routines came on line as he instinctively shielded himself with the strongest force field his biononics could produce. 'Get out.'

'What?'

'Get out of the base. Everyone out. Now!'

'I think you'd better explain just exactly what is going on.'

'Shit!' His u-shadow used the tenuous link to the base to establish a tiny channel to the *Artful Dodger*'s smartcore. 'Tell them,' he yelled at Corrie-Lyn.

She flinched. 'Director, please leave. We haven't been honest with you.' She turned to Inigo. 'Please?' she hissed.

He gave a reluctant sigh. 'Ansan, this is Earl. Do as Aaron says. Get as many as you can into the starship. Everyone else will have to use the ground cruisers.'

'But—'

The *Artful Dodger*'s smartcore scanned the sky above Kajaani. Its sweep was hampered considerably by the protective force field over the base. But it showed Aaron a small mass thirty kilometres high, holding position above the thick outer cloud blanket. 'Come and get us,' he told the smartcore. 'Fast.' His exovision showed him the starship powering up. Flight systems took barely a second to come on line. Its force field hardened. Directly overhead, an enormously powerful gamma-ray laser struck the base's force field. A scarlet corona flared around the puncture point, and the beam sliced into the generator building.

Complete force-field failure was an emergency situation which had been incorporated into the base's design. Secondary force fields snapped on over the cottages and science blocks, almost in time to protect them from the first awesome pressure surge. Several sheets of ice crystals hammered against the walls, drilling holes in the grass. Staff caught outside screamed and flung themselves down as the impacts battered them. It was over in seconds as the re-trapped air stilled. When they looked up they could see the parkland being scoured of grass and bushes by the victorious wind. Their starship had been cut in two by the gamma-laser strike, uneven sections lying twisted on the pad as the cold storm buffeted it about.

Beside it, the *Artful Dodger* rose into the maelstrom of radioactive destruction which cascaded across the base the instant the main force field vanished. Sensors showed it a pinprick of dazzling white light searing its way downward, accelerating at fifty gees. The ship's smartcore blasted away at the weapon with neutron lasers and quantum distortion pulses. Nothing happened. The smartcore started to change course. It wasn't fast enough. The lightpoint struck the *Artful Dodger* amidships, unaffected by the force field. Enormous tidal forces tore at the ship's structure, destroying its integrity. Even spars reinforced by bonding fields were ripped out of alignment. Ordinary components were mangled beyond recognition. The entire hull buckled and imploded to a third of its original size. Then the Hawking m-sink punched through the other side of the ship and streaked onwards into the ground. Its intense spark of light vanished. The surrounding ground heaved as if Kajaani had been hit by a massive earthquake, annihilating the remaining buildings and structures. All the secondary force fields died, leaving the collapsing cottages and science blocks exposed to the planet's malignant atmosphere.

The wreckage of the *Artful Dodger* tumbled out of the hurricane to smash into the ruins of the base.

Aaron's contact with the starship was lost as soon as the Hawking m-sink penetrated the hull, when every microcircuit and kube physically distorted and ruptured.

A couple of Kajaani's sensors had caught the last moments of the star which had bolted out of the churning naked sky.

Its speed was such that human eyes registered it as a single line of light, like a perfectly straight lightning bolt. Radiation monitor records showed a swift peak which went off the scale.

'What the hell just happened?' Corrie-Lyn demanded.

Aaron was too stunned to reply immediately. His u-shadow confirmed the beacon relay now ended two kilometres short of the base's perimeter.

'They fired on the base,' Inigo said quietly. 'Lady, they were completely unarmed.' He glared at Aaron. 'Was that one of the Factions?'

'Could be. It might even have been the Cleric Conservator making sure of his tenure.'

'There's a place in the depths of Honious reserved for your kind. I hope you reach it quickly.'

'Where?' Aaron asked.

Inigo and Corrie-Lyn gave him an identical snort of disgust.

'We'd better get back up to the shelter,' Inigo said. 'I expect they'll want to get to Kajaani right away. We are one of the closest camps.'

As soon as they came through the cramped suit room, Ericilla pointed an accusing finger at Aaron. 'That was you,' she yelled in fury. 'You're responsible. You told them to get clear. You knew who that was. You brought them here.'

'I didn't bring them *here*. Those people were going to catch up with us eventually. The location was ... unfortunate.'

'Un-fucking-fortunate?' Vilitar spat. 'There were nearly two hundred people there. We don't know how many of them are still alive, but even if some of them survived the attack they'll be dying from the radiation. My friends. Slaughtered.'

'They'll be re-lifed,' Aaron said impassively.

'You bastard,' Cytus stepped forwards, his fist raised.

'Enough,' Inigo said. 'This won't help.'

Cytus paused for a moment, then turned away, his face contorted with disgust and anger.

'You knew, Earl,' Nerina said. 'You warned Ansan as well. What the hell is going on? Do you know these people?'

'I'm the one they're looking for. I didn't know about the attack.'

The rest of the team started at each other in mute bewilderment. 'We're going to Kajaani,' Ericilla said. 'We can help recover the bodies before the winds blow them too far.'

'How long before your organization sends another ship?' Aaron asked.

'Like you care!'

'How long? Please.'

'Too long,' Nerina said. 'Hanko isn't part of the unisphere. We can't just yell for help. Our only link to the Commonwealth was the hyperspace link in the starship, which was connected to our headquarters back on Anagaska. Without that we're completely cut off. Anagaska will assume there was some kind of equipment failure; then after we haven't repaired it in a week, they'll probably investigate. If I remember right, we're due a scheduled flight in a fortnight anyway. They'll probably wait until then. Budget considerations.' She snapped it out in contempt.

'By which time radiation poisoning will have killed everyone exposed to the atmosphere,' Vilitar said. 'We don't have enough medical facilities to help them all. Congratulations.' He stared challengingly at Aaron.

'We need to get moving,' Ericilla said. 'The medical systems on our ground crawlers can help a couple of them, maybe more. She pushed her way past Aaron, not looking at him. Cytus managed to knock Aaron's elbow as he went into the suit room.

'You coming, Earl?' Nerina asked.

'Yeah.'

'You've done enough already,' Vilitar said. 'Whoever the fuck you really are. I thought—' He snarled incoherently and hurried into the suit room.

'We'll come with you,' Corrie-Lyn said. 'We can help.'

'The Asiatic glacier is half a day from here,' Nerina said. 'The far end has mile-high cliffs. Why don't you *help* us by driving off them.' She went into the suit room and closed the door.

'Then there were three,' Aaron said.

'We'd better get going,' Inigo said. He faced Aaron. 'You know they'll probably close the Restoration project down because of this.'

'Do you think the next galaxy along will mount a Restoration project for all the species which the Void devourment phase exterminates?'

For a moment Aaron thought Inigo might actually activate his biononics in an aggressor mode. 'You know nothing,' the lost messiah whispered.

'I hope something, though.'

'What?'

'That you have a starship stashed away. Preferably close by.'

'I don't.'

'Really? I find that mighty curious. You took all this trouble to stay lost. Yet you have no escape route if someone came along to expose you.'

'Obviously not, otherwise I wouldn't have been here waiting for you.'

'You wouldn't have been waiting around here if it had just been me,' Aaron said. He gestured at Corrie-Lyn. 'But her? That's different. Seventy years is a long time to be alone. She stayed in love for that long. Did you?'

Corrie-Lyn moved up close to Inigo. 'Did you?' she asked in a quiet voice.

A mournful smile flickered over his lips. 'I'm glad it was you. Is that enough?'

'Yeah,' she rested her head on his shoulder.

'No ship,' Inigo told Aaron. 'And the only way I go anywhere with you, is in a bag as small lumps of charcoal.'

'That's a shame, because I know what weapon they used to take out my starship and the base.'

'Is that supposed to impress me? I expect you know a great deal about weapons and violence. Men like you always do.'

'It was a Hawking m-sink,' Aaron said. 'Do you know what that is? No? They're new and highly dangerous. Even ANA gets nervous around them. Basically, it's a very small black hole, but cranked up with an outsize event horizon to help absorption. It starts off as a little core of neutronium about the size of an atomic nucleus.'

Corrie-Lyn caught the emphasis. 'Starts off?'

'Yes. Its gravity field is strong enough to pull in any atoms it comes into contact with. They're then also compressed into neutronium and merge with its core. With each atom, it gets a little bit bigger. Not by much admittedly, not to begin with. But the larger the surface area, the more matter it can absorb. And after it tore through the *Artful Dodger* it hit the planet. Right now it is sinking through the mantle, eating every atom it encounters. It'll stop at the centre of the planet. Then it just sits there and grows.'

'How big will it get?' she asked anxiously.

Aaron shot Inigo a look. 'Black holes have no theoretical size limit. We used to think that was what the Void was.'

'But . . . Hanko?'

'It'll take about a fortnight to devour the entire mass of an H-congruous world. Except we'll be dead long before that. Hanko will start to disintegrate as it's consumed from within. The continents will collapse in three or four days' time. So, once more, with a awful lot of feeling, do you have a starship hidden nearby?'

*

Araminta kissed three hims as they sat at a table under a gazebo of flowering yisanthal in his garden. 'I missed that,' she told the rugged oriental one.

Mr Bovey smiled in unison. Hes raised his glasses. 'Cheers.'

'Cheers.' She sipped her white wine.

'So?' asked the one she'd had their first dinner with.

Araminta steeled herself. 'If your offer is still open, I'd like to accept.'

She even heard cheering coming from the big house as well as the racket which the three under the gazebo made.

'You've made some old men very happy.'

'Us young ones, too.'

Araminta laughed. 'And I have absolutely no idea how to go about this. The first three apartments will be ready in another week. I've accepted a deposit on the fourth.'

'Congratulations.'

'But until I've completed and the tenants are in, I won't see a profit. I need money to buy bodies.'

'Not as expensive as you might think. A friend, one of us, runs a clinic expressly for that purpose. She always gives discount to a first-expander.'

'Okay.' She took another drink to calm her shudders. It was momentous, sort of like accepting two proposals at once.

The young Celtic one squeezed her arm. 'You all right?' he asked, all full of sympathy.

'I guess so.' She knew she was smiling like an idiot. *But this does feel right.*

Two hims came hurrying out of the house. One of them who seemed about seventeen went down on his knee beside her. A slim athletic build, she saw, with a wild stock of blond hair. He proffered a small box which opened to show her an antique diamond engagement ring.

'I bought it just in case,' he told her.

Araminta slipped it on to her finger, then dashed away the tears.

'Oh, come here,' the youngster exclaimed.

His arms went round her, hugging tight; and she was laughing through the tears. 'I haven't seen you before.'

'I'm a slavedriver to me.'

She put her palms on his cheeks and kissed him thoroughly. 'I would like you to be one of tonight's.'

'My considerable pleasure.'

'I believe you said I still have several yous to get to know.'

'Oh trust me, you'll know all of mes before our wedding day.'

'And I don't mind, and won't complain about other women until I have enough bodies to cope. Just . . . I don't want to meet them.'

'I'll try and keep it to a minimum, I promise.'

'Thanks,' she whispered gratefully.

'Now what sort of bodies are you going to go for?'

'Gosh, I hadn't thought about that,' she admitted. 'What do you like?'

'Got to be a tall blonde Amazon type. Always popular.'

'Oh, and very black as well. Let's cover all the old ethnicities, I have – almost.'

'And one of you has to have huge breasts.'

'More than one!'

She slapped at him, feigning shocked dismay. 'You're appalling. I'm not doing anything like that.'

'That's not what you usually say in bed.'

Araminta laughed. She really had missed this. *I made the right decision.*

Araminta lay on the big bed, listening to three hims sleeping. Two on the bed with her, and one on the couch, curled up in a quilt, all breathing softly, not quite in synch. Tonight she'd refused any aerosols, wanting to try out Likan's program, to make sure it worked with other people, that he hadn't loaded in a hidden expiry key.

It worked.

And how.

Mr Bovey had been surprised, then very appreciative, at how much more responsive her body had become. As she'd suspected, a night in bed with hims had been a lot better than it had with Likan and the harem. *Always nice to have confirmation.*

Now she couldn't sleep. Not that she wasn't tired, she grinned to herself, but she couldn't stop thinking about the engagement, and embracing a multiple lifestyle. It was such an upheaval.

Everything was going to change for her. So much so, she was more than a little apprehensive. Her mind was churning over the same questions again and again. Unable to find answers, because she didn't actually *know* about being multiple. The only way to truly find out was to become one.

She turned her head to look at the young red-haired him who was nestled up cosily beside her. He'd help her through the transition, she knew. Mr Bovey loved her. That was enough to take her through the next few months. They hadn't set a date. He'd said he'd like at least two hers to register the marriage with him. Which was fair enough. She *really* needed to finish the apartments. Today had made that even more urgent.

Araminta settled back on to the soft mattress and closed her eyes. She used the program to still her whirling thoughts, emptying her mind. Her body started to calm as she found and slowed its natural rhythms, cycling down. Instead of sleep, the emptiness opening within made her aware of the images which lurked just below conscious thought. Not just one, but a whole range, all tasting and feeling very different. They twisted out of the infinite distance, a connection she now finally understood belonged to herself. Instinctively, she knew how to focus on whichever she wanted. Some were Mr Bovey's dreams, she was familiar enough with him to recognize his mental scent. She sighed fondly as she experienced his presence; part of his mind was so wound up, the poor man, while she also felt his happiness – her own face slithered in and out of his thoughts. One of the connections was completely alien, yet comfortably warm in that way a parent was with a child. Her lips lifted in a serene smile. The Silfen Motherholme. So Cressida had been telling the truth. In which case that oh-so-busy chorus of multicoloured shadows must be the gaiafield.

Araminta embraced the quiet one; the most tenuous connection of all. And found herself gliding through space far from any star. The Void's nebulas glimmered lush and glorious behind her as she rose to the darkness of the outer regions.

'Hello,' she said.

And the Skylord answered.

*

Justine had expected to feel a lot of excitement as her starship, the *Silverbird*, descended towards Centurion Station. Five hundred hours alone in a small cabin with no unisphere connection had left her unexpectedly strung out. Intellectually, she knew it was a nonsense, a quirk of her primitive body's biochemistry and neurological weakness. But it was still real.

Now here she was, at her destination, and all she could think about was the identical, boring trip back. *I must have been crazy to do this.*

The *Silverbird* touched down on the lava field which acted as a spaceport for the human section of the Centurion Station. Five other starships were sitting there, all of them bigger than hers. The smartcore reported several discreet sensor scans probing at the ship. The tall Ethox tower was the worst offender, using quite aggressive quantum signature detectors. More subtle scans came from the dour domes of the Forleene. There was even one quick burst of investigative activity from the observatory facilities in the human section. She smiled at that as her thin spacesuit squeezed up against her body, expelling all the air pockets to form an outer protective skin. She locked the helmet on.

It was a short walk over the sandy lava to the main airlock. Justine needed it for the sense of space and normality it gave her. She couldn't believe how much she felt reassured by the sight of a planetary horizon, even one as drab as this. When she stopped to look up, angry ion storms fluoresced the sky for lightyears in every direction. Pale mockeries of the nebulas inside the Void.

Director Lehr Trachtenberg was waiting for her in the reception hall beyond the airlock. A formidably sized man who reminded her of Ramon, one of her old husbands. Standing in front of him, shaking his hand in greeting, and tipping her head back just to see his face was another reminder of how negligible

617

her physical body was. Of course, that Ramon connection did shunt her mind back to the possibility of sex.

'This is a considerable honour,' Lehr Trachtenberg was saying. 'ANA has never sent a representative here before.'

'Given the political circumstances back in the Commonwealth, it was deemed appropriate to examine the data from the Void first-hand.'

The director licked his lips slowly. 'Distance makes no difference to data, Justine. We do send the entire range of our findings directly back to the Navy's exploration division, and the Raiel.'

'Nonetheless, I'd like the opportunity to review your operation.'

'I wasn't about to refuse you anything. Especially not after the trip you've just made. To my knowledge no one has ever travelled so far by themselves. How did you stand the isolation?'

She suspected that he suspected the *Silverbird* had an ultra-drive, but chose to gloss over the actual journey time. 'With difficulty and a lot of sensory dramas.'

'I can imagine.' He gestured at the five-seater cab which was waiting at the end of the reception hall. 'I've assigned you a suite in the Mexico accommodation block.'

'Thank you.'

'I'm also throwing a welcome party for you in three hours. Everyone is very keen to meet you.'

'I suppose they are,' she said. 'Fine, I'll be there. I could do with some company after that trip.'

They climbed into the little cab together, which immediately shot into the transport tunnel. 'I should warn you that nearly a third of our observation staff are Living Dream followers,' the director said.

'I reviewed personnel files before I came.'

'As long as you know.'

'Is it a problem?'

'Hopefully not. But, as you implied, it's a volatile situation right now.'

'Don't worry, I can do diplomatic when I have to.'

Her suite was equal to any luxury hotel she'd stayed in. The only thing missing was human staff, but the number of modern bots more than made up for it. The Navy had clearly spared no effort in making the station as cosy as possible for the scientists. The main room even had a long window looking out over the alien sections of the station. Justine stared at them for a while, then opaqued the glass. Her u-shadow established itself in the room's net. 'No visitors or calls,' she told it.

Justine settled back on the bed, and opened her mind to the local gaiafield. The darkened room filled with phantoms, colours glinted amid the deeper shadows. Voices whispered. There was laughter. She felt drawn to various emotional states which promised to immerse her in their enticing soulful sensations.

Resisting temptation, she focused her attention on the nucleus of the whimsy, the confluence nest itself. A quasi-biological neural module which simultaneously stored and emitted every thought released into its field. It had memories like a human brain, only with a much, much larger capacity. Justine formed her own images, offering them up to the nest. It responded with association. Naturally, it contained every one of Inigo's dreams; Living Dream had made sure of that. She ignored the vivid spectacle of the Waterwalker's life, brushing those memories aside as she refined her own fancy for a different recollection of life inside the Void. The nest was full of enigmas, the mental poetry left behind by observers baffled by the terrible dark heart of the galaxy. There were compositions of how a life might be lived for anyone fortunate to pass inside; wish fulfilment, easily discernible from the real thing. The promise-prayers which Living Dream's followers made every night to their mystic goal. All were imprinted on the nest. But nothing else. No other glimpse into another life lived on Querencia. No grand mellow thoughts originating from a Skylord.

The garden dome at the middle of the human section boasted trees over two hundred and fifty years old. Oaks with thick trunks sent out thick crinkled boughs, acting as lush canopies above the tables where the station staff were gathering. Up on a rustic tree-house platform, an enthusiastic amateur band were playing songs from different eras stretching back across several centuries, and were keen for requests. It was dusk inside, allowing the sharp violet light of the Wall stars to dominate the sky overhead.

Justine admired the broad patch of eye-searing scintillations with the kind of weariness she reserved for dangerous animals. Her arrival in the garden dome had created quite a ripple of interest. She liked to think that was at least partly due to the little black cocktail dress she'd chosen. It certainly seemed to have the required effect on Director Trachtenberg, who was becoming quite flirtatious as he fussed round, offering her various drinks and selections of the finger food.

Everyone she was introduced to was keen to know exactly what ANA's interest was in them at this time. She repeated the official line a dozen times that she was just visiting to ascertain the current status of the observation.

'Unchanged,' complained Graffal Ehasz, the observation department chief. 'We don't learn anything these days apart from ion storm patterns in the Gulf on the other side of the Wall stars. That tells us nothing about the nature of the beast. We should be trying to send probes inside.'

'I thought nothing could get through the barrier,' she said.

'Which is why we need a much more detailed study. You can't do that with remote probes fifty lightyears away.'

'The Raiel don't like us getting closer,' Trachtenberg said.

'When you get home, you might like to ask ANA why we still need their *permission* just to fart around here,' Ehasz said. 'It's fucking insulting.'

'I'll remember,' Justine said. The party was only twenty minutes old; she wondered how many aerosols Ehasz had already inhaled.

The director took her by the arm and politely guided her away.

'Sorry about that,' he said. 'There's not a lot of opportunity to blow off steam around here. I run a pretty tight schedule. This is

620

an expensive installation, and phenomenally important. We need to extract the best information we can with what we've got.'

'I understand.'

'It's Ehasz's third stint out here. He tends to get frustrated by the lack of progress. I've seen it before. First time, you're all swept along by the wonder of it all. Then when that fades away you begin to realize how passive the observation actually is.'

'How many times have you been here?'

He grinned. 'This is my seventh. But then I'm a lot older and wiser than Ehasz.'

'So would you like to join the Pilgrimage?'

'Not really. As far as three hundred years of direct observation has shown us, you touch the barrier, you die. Actually, you die a long time before you reach the barrier. I just don't see how they hope to get through.'

'Somebody did, once.'

'Yeah, that's the really annoying part.'

'So what do—' Justine stopped as the ground heaved, almost knocking her feet out from under her. She tensed, dropping to a crouch like just about everyone else. Her integral force field came on. The local net was shrieking out all sort of alarms. The huge oak boughs creaked dangerously; their leaves rustling as if tickled by a gust of wind.

'Hoshit,' Trachtenberg yelped.

Justine's u-shadow established a link to the *Silverbird*'s smart-core. 'Stand by,' she told it. 'Keep a fix on my position.' When she scanned round the dome it was still intact. Then she looked at the horizon, which appeared to be perfectly level. She'd been expecting big cracks to be splitting the lava plain open at the very least. The ground tilted again. *Nothing moved!* 'What is happening?' she demanded. Some kind of quake? But this planet was a dead husk, completely inactive in any respect.

'I'm not sure.' The director waved an annoyed hand to shush her.

The band were clambering down out of the tree-house as fast as they could go, jumping the last metre off the wooden steps.

They'd abandoned their instruments. Justine stared at the drink in her hand as the ground shifted again. The wine sloshed from one side of the glass to the other, yet she was holding it perfectly still.

'Holy Ozzie,' Trachtenberg exclaimed. 'It's gravity.'

'What?'

'Gravity waves. Fucking colossal ones.'

Ehasz hurried over to them, swaying badly as the ground seemed to tilt again. 'Are you accessing the long-range sensors?' he yelled at Trachtenberg.

'What have they got?'

'The boundary! There are distortion ripples lightyears long moving across it. And the damn thing is growing. The sensors in the Gulf can actually see it move. Do you realize what that means? The expansion is superluminal. This is an Ozziefucking devourment phase.'

The ground quivered badly. Water running along the little streams sloshed about, shooting up small jets of spray. For a moment, Justine actually felt her weight reduce. Then it came back, and the neat stacks of crockery and glasses on the tables crashed on to the grass. She stumbled away from the oak tree as it emitted a nasty splintering sound. Emergency force fields were coming on, reinforcing the dome. Around the rim, safety bunker doors rippled open.

'I want everyone to move to evacuation stage one,' Trachtenberg announced. 'Navy personnel report direct to your ships. Observation team, I need a precise picture of what is happening out there. We probably don't have much time, so we must do as much as we can before we're forced off.' He flinched as another gravity wave crossed the station. This time the upward force was so strong Justine felt as though she was going to lift off.

'Is that gravity coming from the Void?' she asked. The prospect was terrifying, they were hundreds of lightyears away.

'No,' Ehasz cried. 'This is something local.' He looked upwards, studying the intricate luminescent sky above the dome. 'There!'

Justine watched two azure moons traverse the sparkling smear of Wall stars. They were in very strange orbits. And moving impossibly fast – actually accelerating. 'Oh my God,' she gasped. The Raiel's planet-sized DF machines were flying into new positions.

'The Raiel are getting ready for the last fight,' Ehasz said numbly. 'If they lose, that monster will consume the whole galaxy.'

This can't be happening, Justine thought. *Living Dream hasn't even begun their Pilgrimage yet.* 'You can't!' she shouted up at the ancient invisible enemy as human hormones and feelings took complete control of her body and mind. 'This isn't fair. It's not *fair!*'

*

A mere five hours after the new dream had flooded into the gaiafield, over fifty thousand of the devout had already gathered in Golden Park, seeking guidance from the Cleric Conservator. They exerted their wish through their gaiamotes. The unanimous desire of fifty thousand people was an astonishing force.

Ethan was only too aware of it as Councillor Phelim supported him on the long painful walk out of the Mayor's offices where the doctors had set up an intensive care bay. He limped across the floor of Liliala Hall while the ceiling displayed surges of thick cumulus arrayed in mares' tails and clad in shimmering strands of lightning. Even though he'd closed himself to the gaiafield, the power of the crowd's craving was leaking into his bruised brain.

Phelim continued to support him as they crossed the smaller Toral Hall. Its midnight ceiling showed the Ku nebula with its twinkling gold sparks swimming within fat undulating jade and sapphire nimbi.

'You should have called them to your bed,' Phelim said.

'No,' Ethan grunted. For this occasion he would not, could not, show weakness.

They went through the carved doors to the Orchard Palace's Upper Council chamber. Its cross-vault ceiling was supported by broad fan pillars. Dominating the apex of the central segment a fuzzy copper star shone brightly, its light shimmering off a slowly rotating accretion disc. Moon-sized fireball comets circled the outer band in high-inclination orbits. None of Makkathran's enthusiastic astronomers had ever spied its location in the Void.

The Cleric Council waited for him in their scarlet and black robes, standing silently at the long table which ran across the middle of the chamber. Phelim stayed by Ethan's side until they reached the dais, then Ethan insisted on walking to his gold-embossed throne by himself. He eased himself on to the thin cushions with a grimace. The pain in his head nearly made him cry out as he sank down. He took a moment to recover as his body shuddered. Ever since he'd regained consciousness any sudden movement was agony.

The Councillors sat, trying to avert their eyes from the liver-like semi-organic nodules affixed to his skull, only half-hidden by his white robe's voluminous hood.

'Thank you for attending,' Ethan said to them.

'We are relieved to see you recovered, Cleric Conservator,' Rincenso said formally.

Ethan knew the contempt of the other Councillors towards his supporter without needing the gaiafield. He felt it himself. 'Not quite recovered yet,' he said, and tapped one of the glistening nodules. 'But my neural structure should be fully re-established in another week. Until then the auxiliaries will suffice.'

'How could such a thing happen?' Councillor DeLouis asked. 'Gaiamotes have been perfectly safe for centuries.'

'It wasn't the gaiamotes,' Phelim said. 'The Dream Masters who set up the interception believe the Second Dreamer's panic triggered a neural spasm within the Cleric Conservator's brain. They were attuned to a degree rarely achieved outside a couple's most intimate dreamsharing. The circumstances will not arise again.'

'The gaiafield and the unisphere are rife with rumours that the Second Dreamer is a genuine telepath, that he can kill with a single thought.'

'Rubbish,' Phelim said. His skeletal face turned to DeLouis. For an instant a dangerous anger could be glimpsed in his mind.

DeLouis couldn't meet his stare.

'In any case it is irrelevant,' Ethan said. 'The Dream Masters assure me that such a backlash can be nullified now they understand its nature. Any future contact with the Second Dreamer will be conducted with,' he smiled grimly, 'a safety cut-out, as they call it.'

'You're going to talk to him again?' Councillor Falven asked.

'I believe the situation requires it,' Ethan said. 'Don't you?'

'Well, yes, but . . .'

'I received his latest dream along with the rest of you. It was strong, at least as clear as those of the Dreamer Inigo himself. However, the crucial change within this dream was the conversation the Second Dreamer had with the Skylord.' The communication had shocked Ethan more than the pristine clarity of the new dream.

'I come to find you,' the Skylord had replied to the Second Dreamer's greetings.

'We are far beyond the edge of your universe.'

'Yet I felt your longing. You wish to join with us.'

'Not I. But other do, yes.'

'All are welcome.'

'We can't get in. It's very dangerous.'

'I can greet you. I can guide you. It is my purpose.'

'No.'

And with that finality the dream had ended. Before it faded completely, there was a hint of agitation from the Skylord's mind. It clearly hadn't expected rejection.

And it's hardly alone in that.

'The Skylord believes it can bring us to Querencia,' Ethan said. 'That is the final testimony we have been waiting and praying for. Our Pilgrimage will be blessed with success.'

'Not without the Second Dreamer,' Councillor Tosyne said. 'Your pardon, Conservator, but he is not willing to lead us into the Void. Without him there can be no Pilgrimage.'

'He is distressed,' Ethan replied. 'Until now he didn't even know he was the Second Dreamer. To discover you are the hope of billions is not an easy thing. Ultimately, Inigo himself found it too great to bear. So we can forgive the Second Dreamer his frailty, and offer support and guidance.'

'He might realize who and what he is now,' Councillor Tosyne said. 'But we don't even know where he is.'

'Actually, we do,' Phelim announced. 'Colwyn City on Viotia.'

'Excellent news,' Ethan said in a predatory fashion. He watched in amusement as the protest in Tosyne's mind withered away. 'We should welcome him, and thank Viotia for the gift it has brought us.' His gaze turned expectantly on Rincenso.

'I would like to propose bringing Viotia fully into the Free Trade Zone,' Rincenso said. 'And promote it to core planet status.'

'Seconded,' Falven said.

The rest of the Cleric Council responded with bemusement.

'You can't do that,' Tosyne said. 'They'll resist, the Commonwealth Senate will move to censure us. We'll lose every diplomatic advantage we have.' He glanced round the table, seeking support.

'It's not just our ambition,' Phelim said. He gestured at the empty end of the table, opposite Ethan's dais. His u-shadow established the ultra-secure link, and a portal projected an image of Likan standing just beyond the table.

Likan bowed politely. 'Conservator, I am honoured.'

'Thank you,' Ethan said. 'I believe you are acting as an unofficial emissary for your government.'

'Yes, sir. I have just finished talking with our Prime Minister. It is her wish to accept Ellezelin's generous offer to elevate us to core world status within the Free Trade Zone.'

'That's wonderful news. I will inform Ellezelin's cabinet of your decision.'

'The acceptance comes with the understanding that a zero tariff régime will be part of the accord,' Likan said.

'Of course. Full trade will commence as soon as the Second Dreamer joins us here in Makkathran2.'

'Understood. The Prime Minister will award the treaty her certificate of office as soon as it is sent.' Likan's image vanished.

'I believe,' Ethan said into the startled silence, 'that we were about to take a vote. Those in favour?' He watched the hands being raised. It was unanimous. In moments such as this he almost missed Corrie-Lyn's presence on the Council; she would never have left such a Soviet outcome go unchallenged. 'Thank you. I find your support of my policies to be humbling. There is no further business.'

Phelim remained seating as the others filed out. Flecks of light slid across his expressionless face as the comets orbited ceaselessly overhead.

'That was easy,' Ethan remarked.

'They don't know what to do,' Phelim said. 'They're just the same as the devout gathering outside: bewildered and hurt that the Second Dreamer would reject the Skylord. They're in need of strong, positive leadership. You provide that. You have the solution. Naturally they turn to you.'

'When can we open the wormhole?'

'I'll have your government office send the treaty to Viotia's Prime Minister immediately. If Likan doesn't let us down, it'll come straight back. The wormhole can be opened within two hours. We'd prepared a number of sites for it to emerge.'

'I hope Colwyn City was one of them.'

'Yes. It has a dock complex that will serve us very nicely.'

'And our police forces?'

'Forty thousand ready for immediate dispatch, along with transport and riot suppression equipment. We can push them through within six hours of opening the wormhole. Another quarter of a million will follow over the next four days.'

'Excellent.'

'I hoped you'd approve.' Phelim hesitated. 'We never planned on the Second Dreamer becoming aware of his ability in quite this fashion. It'll take us a day to get our Dream Masters into position across Colwyn.'

627

'But you can shut down all capsule and starship traffic before then?'

'Yes. That's our highest priority. We want to confine him within the city boundary.' Again the uncharacteristic hesitation. 'But in order to locate him, he has to dream again. After tonight, he might not.'

Ethan closed his eyes and sank down into the throne, enervated by his exertion. 'He will. He doesn't know what he's done yet.'

'What do you mean?'

'An hour ago I received a call from Director Trachtenberg at the Centurion Station. He considered it important enough to reveal his affiliation to us and use the Navy's relay posts. Just after the Second Dreamer ended his contact with the Skylord, the Void began a devourment phase. That is not coincidence. It would seem the Skylord doesn't take rejection lightly. Our reclusive friend will have to placate it, or we'll all wind up being consumed by the boundary. Quite an incentive, really.'

Inigo's seventh dream

Edeard woke with a mild hangover. Again. Last night was the third in a row he'd been out with Macsen and Boyd.

He sat up in bed and ordered the light on. The high curving ceiling started to shine with a low cream radiance. One of his three ge-chimps hurried over with a glass of water and a small compaction of powder he'd got from Doctor Murusa's apprentice. Edeard popped the little pellet on to his tongue, and took a drink to swallow. His mind drifted back to that morning years ago in Witham where Fahin had mixed his awful concoction of a hangover cure. It was still the most effective he'd ever had. Edeard was sure the pellets were little more than placebos, providing the apprentice with a small regular source of income. He finished the water quickly. Fahin had always said water helped flush away the toxins.

The circular bath pool in the maisonette's bathroom now had a series of small steps at one end so Edeard could walk down into it. He immersed himself up to his neck, settling into the seat shelf, and sighed in gratification. A ge-chimp poured in a soap liquid which produced a lot of bubbles. He closed his eyes again, waiting for the hangover to ebb away. The water temperature was perfect, exactly body warmth. It had taken him a couple of weeks experimenting to get that right; the bathing water in Makkathran was normally quite chilly for humans. He'd also remodelled the hole in the floor which served as a toilet. Now the ubiquitous wooden box employed by every Makkathran household had gone, replaced by a simple hollow pedestal which the room had grown for him. So much easier to sit on.

Various other little modifications had turned the maisonette into quite a cosy home. The standard too-high cube-shaped bed was now a lot lower, its spongy upper surface softer and more accommodating. Alcoves had shelves in them. One deep nook in the kitchen area was permanently chilly, allowing him to keep food fresh for days just like the larger city palaces did.

That was the greatest blessing of being in the constables' tenement rather than the station dormitory. Edeard could finally choose what he ate again. Half of his first monthly pay had gone on a new iron stove to cook on. He'd installed it himself, adapting the hole the previous tenant had hacked into the wall for the flue. It had pride of place in the kitchen, along with a growing collection of pans. There was even a small basin which could be used for washing up, rather than dumping everything into the bath pool as most people did. He liked that innovation enough to consider sculpting another one in the bathroom just for his hands and face. Although that really would let everyone know he had the ability to rearrange the city's fabric, sculpting it as easily as he once had genistar eggs.

Everyone who visited the maisonette.

So, no one, then.

Macsen had brought a girl back from the theatre last night. One of the dancers! As pretty as any of the grand family girls, but with an incredibly strong, supple body. He knew that because of the revealing clothes she wore when she danced on stage. Edeard gritted his teeth and tried not to be jealous. He and Boyd had struck out again. Though overall it had been a pleasant evening. Edeard enjoyed the theatres a lot more than just sitting round in taverns getting drunk. There were often several musicians up on the stage. Always Guild apprentices. Young and with passion. Just listening to some of their songs, so full of contempt for the city authorities, made him feel wickedly disloyal to the Grand Council. But he knew the words to many of the popular ones, of which several were Dybal's compositions. It was loud in the theatres, some of which were no more than underground storerooms. He'd been startled the first time he heard drums being played, it was as if the musicians had somehow tamed thunder.

One day they'd go and see Dybal playing, so Macsen promised. Edeard hoped it would be soon.

The bubbles started to disappear from the pool as the water cycled through the narrow slits around the bottom. Edeard groaned and climbed out. A ge-chimp had a robe waiting for him. He pulled it on as he walked though into the kitchen area and sat at the small table. It was right next to a cinquefoil window, giving him a view over the rooftops towards the centre of the city.

A ge-chimp placed a glass of apple and mango juice on the table, along with a bowl of mixed oats, nuts, and dried fruit. The juice was nicely chilled; the ge-chimps knew to leave it in the cold nook for an hour before serving it. He poured milk (also cold) into the bowl and started to eat, looking out across the city as it came to life under the rising sun.

It would have been a fine life indeed if he could just stop brooding about all the lawlessness haunting the streets and canals he could see. The squad had finally managed to get some convictions in the court over the last few weeks. But nothing important; some shop thieves in their early teens, a mugger who was drunk most of the time; once the Guild of Clerks sent them out to arrest a landlord defaulting on taxes. They had no impact whatsoever on the gangs who were at the heart of Makkathran's problems.

'You ready?' Kanseen longtalked as Edeard buttoned up his tunic.

He pulled his boots on. New, costing over three days' pay – but well worth it. 'Coming.'

She was waiting on the walkway outside, an oilskin cloak slung over her arm. 'Going to rain today,' she announced.

He eyed the wide clear sky. 'If you say so.'

She grinned as they started down the awkward stairs. Every morning he was *so* tempted to sculpt them into something less dangerous – write the miracle off to the Lady.

'This'll be your first winter in the city, won't it?' she asked.

'Yes.' Edeard couldn't quite imagine Makkathran being cold and icebound, the long summer had been gloriously hot. He'd become a good football player (he considered), with his team finishing third in Jeavons' little park league. Most taverns had seats and tables outside, where many pleasant evenings had been spent. There had even been a few days when he'd started sketching again, not that he showed anyone the results. After saving up some coinage, he and Salrana had finally taken a gondola ride around the city.

'It'll be fun,' Kanseen said. 'There's loads of parties leading up to New Year. Then the Mayor throws a huge free ox-roast in Golden Park for lunch on New Year's Day – except everyone is normally so hung-over they're late. And the parks and plazas all look so clean and fresh when they're covered in snow.'

'Sounds good.'

'You'll need a thick coat. And a hat.'

'On our pay?'

'I know some shops that sell quality for reasonable prices.'

'Thanks.'

'And don't forget to get in an early supply of coal for your stove; the buildings are never quite warm enough in midwinter and the price always go through the roof after the first snowfall. The Lady will damn those merchants, it's criminal what they get away with charging.'

'You're happy this morning.'

'My sister's having her boy's naming ceremony this Saturday. She's asked me to be a nominee for the Lady.'

'Nice. What's she going to call him?'

'Dium, after the third Mayor.'

'Ah, right.'

'And you haven't got a clue who that is, have you?'

He grinned broadly. 'Nope!'

She laughed.

That was the way it was between them these days. Best friends. Any discomfiture left over from that night after the graduation had long faded. Which he was sort of pleased about. He didn't want them to be awkward round each other, but on the other hand he couldn't quite forget about that kiss, nor the way both of them had felt. He'd never quite had the courage to bring up what they'd said. Neither had she.

Which had left him wrestling with his thoughts about Salrana, who was always so sunny and generally lovely. It was now incredibly hard to ignore how feminine she'd become. And he suspected she knew that. Of late her teasing had taken on quite an edge.

The rest of the squad were waiting in the main hall at Jeavons constable station, sitting around a table finishing off their breakfast. Unlike Edeard, few of them cooked for themselves. Macsen had on a pair of glasses with very dark lenses, not too dissimilar to those Dybal wore. Kanseen took one look at him and burst out laughing. 'Were you boys out in the theatres again last night?'

Macsen grunted, and scowled at her over his cup of strong black coffee.

Edeard desperately wanted to ask him what Nanitte, the dancer, was like. It must have been a fantastic night to leave him so wrecked. But friends though they were, Kanseen didn't have much tolerance for that kind of all-boys-together talk.

'Some news for you,' Boyd hissed, checking round the rest of the hall's bench tables to make sure no one was paying attention.

'Go on,' Edeard said as he drew up a chair. There was something almost comical about Boyd's behaviour.

'My brother Isoix is being leaned on again. They came round the shop yesterday evening as he was shutting up, and said they wanted twenty pounds to "put out the fire". They're coming back this morning to collect.'

Edeard didn't like it. Three times in the last few months Boyd had told them about gang members harassing his brother at the family bakery. There'd never been any specific threat, just warnings about falling into line. *Softening him up.* Well, now the demand had been made. 'That's very stupid of them,' he said slowly.

'What do you mean?' Dinlay asked.

'They must know Isoix's brother is a constable. Why would they risk it? There are hundreds of shops in Jeavons without that kind of connection.'

'They're gang members,' Dinlay said. 'Greedy and stupid. This time, too greedy and too stupid.'

'The ones that turn up won't be important,' Kanseen said. 'Thugs who're affiliated, that's all.'

'Are you saying we shouldn't help him?' Boyd asked hotly.

'No,' Edeard said. 'Of course not. We'll be there to make the arrest, you know that. What Kanseen is saying is that this arrest alone won't stop the problem.'

Macsen hooked a finger over his glasses and pulled them down to look out over the top of the rims. 'We've got to start somewhere,' he croaked.

'You make it sound like we're the ones who are going to break the gangs,' Kanseen said.

'Somebody has to. I don't see the Mayor or the Chief Constable doing it.'

'Oh, come on!'

He shrugged, and pushed his glasses back up. They all looked at Edeard.

'Let's go,' he said. 'And make sure you're all wearing your drosilk waistcoats. I don't want to have to explain casualties to Captain Ronark.'

Boyd's family bakery was at the northern end of Macoun Street, not far from the Outer Circle Canal. The street was narrow and twisty with baroque buildings lined up on either side, making direct observation difficult. At ground level, the sharp turns limited the squad's farsight. The three-storey bakery itself had a central square tower with a soft-ridged mansard-style roof. Tall crescent dormer windows protruded above a mid-storey balcony, while beneath that the lower floor was reached by several flowing steps from the street leading to a wide entrance arch between two curving bay windows. Each one was filled with racks of loafs and cakes. Three ugly metal chimney stacks from the coal-fired ovens rose out of holes hacked into the tower eves, blowing thin smoke into the dampening air.

Edeard positioned his squad carefully. The gang would want a fast exit route, so Macsen and Dinlay were in a shop between the bakery and the canal. Kanseen was covering the other end of Macoun Street, wandering round the stalls of a small arcade, her cloak covering her uniform; while Edeard himself settled down in the first-floor living room opposite. It belonged to a family who ran a clothing shop on the ground floor, and were close friends with Isoix. Boyd himself had returned home for the day, and was helping out in the bakery, dressing for the part in white apron and green cap. Edeard was uncertain if he should use the ge-eagle. In the end he settled for having it perch in a deep guttering furrow on the bakery's tower, almost invisible from ground level. It scared the ruugulls away, but no one else noticed it.

'At least we won't have to escort them far to the Courts of Injustice,' Macsen pointed out as they started their vigil. Edeard could actually see one of the conical towers of Parliament House through the living-room's balcony window.

They waited for two hours. Between them, they raised the alarm five times, only to be proved wrong on each occasion. 'So many citizens look so disreputable,' Kanseen declared after a couple of adolescents ran down the street after their third hands snatched up oranges from a grocery shop display. 'And act it.'

'We're all paranoid today, that's all,' Macsen longtalked back. 'We see the bad in everyone.'

'Is that a song title?' Dinlay asked.

Edeard smiled at the banter. There was a lot to be said for being squad leader. He was sitting in a comfortable arm chair, drinking tea which the wife of the shop owner kept bringing up for him. She brought a rather nice plate of biscuits each time, too. His good humour faded as the young hooligans turned a corner out of sight. Foreboding rose into his mind, strong enough to make his skin tingle. He knew that awful sensation from before. 'Oh, shit,' he whimpered.

'Edeard?' Kanseen queried.

'It's happening.'

'What is?' Macsen asked.

'They're here. It's about to start.'

'Where are they?' Boyd asked. 'Which ones?'

'I don't know,' Edeard said. 'Look, just trust me, please be careful. I *know* we have to be.' He could sense the uncertainty in their minds, they weren't used to him saying such things. It was difficult to get to his feet, his body was reacting so badly. When he did press up against the balcony window he found it hard to concentrate on the street below.

'I think I see them,' Boyd said.

Two youngish men were walking up the steps into the shop, while a third stood outside. Through Boyd's eyes, Edeard and the rest of the squad watched them swagger into the shop. Isoix straightened up from behind the counter. 'I told you before,' he said. 'I don't have that kind of money.'

'Yes, you do,' the first man said. His gaze kept darting nervously to Boyd, who was standing at the other end of the counter from Isoix.

Wrong, Edeard knew. Why would a gang member be worried about a shop assistant?

'Boyd, he knows what you are,' Edeard sent in the most direct longtalk he could manage, praying the gang members wouldn't pick it out of the general background of Makkathran's telepathic babble.

'Huh?' Boyd grunted.

The gang member glanced at him again, then turned back to Isoix. 'Give me twenty pounds, or we'll torch this place,' he said loudly.

'No,' Edeard said. The hairs on his neck were standing proud. 'No no no.' *Wrong!*

'You,' Boyd said. He pulled his apron aside to reveal a constable's badge pinned on his waistcoat. The two gang members turned to face him.

'I am a city constable, and I am placing you under arrest for threatening behaviour with intent to extort.'

'How do you like that, you bastards?' a gloating Isoix shouted.

'Everyone, close in,' Edeard ordered. He pushed through the narrow door on to the balcony. The gang member left on the street glanced up. And smiled.

'Oh shit,' Edeard growled.

'It's him,' the gang member declared in a powerful longtalk. Then he started running.

Inside the bakery, the first gang member pulled out a small knife. He flung it at Boyd, who swayed backwards. His third hand just managed to push the blade aside. Isoix snatched up a much larger knife, and threw it at the gang members as they fled through the doorway. It whirled out into the street, narrowly missing a woman who was walking by. She screamed.

Edeard vaulted over the balcony rail and dropped to the street below. Landed badly, rolling as his ankle gave way. His shoulder smacked into one of the steps leading up to the clothing shop door. He yelled at the bright pulse of pain, tears squeezing out of his eyes.

His farsight caught Boyd leaping over the bakery counter. Kanseen was sprinting up Macoun Street, her cloak abandoned on the ground by the stalls. Macsen and Dinlay were moving out of their shop, confident and eager. Their shields combined as they stood in the middle of the street, blocking the way. All three gang members were racing towards them.

'Let them go,' Edeard ordered.

Macsen's face registered bewilderment that came close to anger. 'What?'

Edeard had regained his feet, he started to totter down the street. 'Leave them.'

'You can't be serious.' The three gang members were barely twenty yards from Macsen and Dinlay.

'It's a set-up. They knew we were here.'

'Crap,' Dinlay sent. 'I can scan them completely, they've got a couple of small blades between them. That's all.'

'There'll be more, somewhere, waiting for us. Please, just let them go, I'll track them with the ge-eagle.'

Macsen hesitated. He took a step towards the side of the street.

'No!' Dinlay hissed fiercely. He opened his arms wide as the three gang members charged towards them.

'Dinlay, stop it,' Edeard yelled. He was running now, ignoring the pain in his ankle. Kanseen wasn't far behind, charging along like a warhorse, her teeth gritted in determination. Boyd came skidding down the steps from the bakery, and took off after them.

'Stop,' Dinlay proclaimed loudly, holding out a hand as if that alone would bring the whole city to a halt. 'You are under arrest.'

'Oh crap,' Macsen growled under his breath, and instinctively started to move back towards Dinlay. They came together as the three gang members ran into them. Fists swung, legs kicked out. Third hands scrabbled and pushed. Macsen went down with one of the gang members sprawling on top of him, his head cracked against the pavement. Dinlay was shoved hard against the wall of a hat shop, flailing wildly to regain balance. Then the gang member on top of Macsen was scrabbling to his feet, and fled with his companions. Dinlay started to chase after them.

'Come back!' Edeard howled in frustration. He reached Macsen who was struggling upright, hand clamped on the back of his head. A trickle of blood was running down his fingers.

'What do we do?' Macsen demanded, wincing against the pain.

Edeard's farsight could follow Dinlay easily enough as he ran towards the northern end of Macoun Street. The three gang members were ten yards ahead of him. 'Save him,' he growled out, furious with Dinlay. He sent a single clear thought to his ge-eagle, who immediately took flight.

Kanseen was slowing as she approached Edeard and Macsen.

Her face red. Boyd was charging up behind. 'Come on,' Edeard said, and took off again. Kanseen flashed a look of exasperation, and hurried along.

'You okay?' Boyd shouted as he ran past Macsen.

'Yeah.' Macsen took a breath, and started running.

The ge-eagle streaked along Macoun Street, swiftly overtaking Edeard and Kanseen. It shot forward, rising high above the roofs, looking down to see Dinlay racing on, his glasses askew. The three gang members had almost reached the end of the street. It came out just below Birmingham Pool, where a silver-blue bridge connected Jeavons with the lower point of Golden Park. As always, Birmingham Pool was thick with gondolas. A half-dozen moorings lined the edge beside the junction with the Outer Circle Canal all host to several waiting gondolas. The ge-eagle dipped down to the moorings as Edeard tried to work out which of the glossy black craft belonged to the gang. If this was a trap, they'd have their escape well planned.

Just before it happened, the ge-eagle was aware of two other birds, close and closing. It pivoted on a wing, looking up in time to see its attacker plummeting down towards it. Another ge-eagle, bigger, with talons clad in sharpened iron spikes. The impact punched it savagely. Gold and emerald feathers burst out of the collision point. Spikes sank into its front wing shoulder, slicing through skin and muscle, severing veins. Then the bigger ge-eagle twisted to try and snap the central wing bone. Edeard's ge-eagle fought back, writhing round to clamp its jaw on its attacker's rear wing. The two of them tumbled, falling fast. Then the second attacker hit, iron-blade talons ripping into flesh. Edeard and his ge-eagle screamed as one as its wing broke. Edeard saw talons rake towards his face, and ducked. His ge-eagle's mind abruptly vanished from perception, all that was left was a falling mass. The other two ge-eagles hurtled away over Birmingham pool. Edeard was sure he heard the splash as his bird's body hit the water.

'What happened?' Kanseen cried.

'Dear Lady, they *are* waiting for us.' Edeard pulled his perception down to find Dinlay emerging from the end of Macoun

Street. 'Stop! Dinlay, for the Lady's sake, I'm begging you.' He pushed his tired legs harder, sprinting for the end of the street. Thirty yards.

'I see them,' Dinlay replied gleefully. He gifted the squad, who saw the three gang members clustering above one of the moorings. They grinned barbarously. For the first time, there was a pulse of uncertainty in Dinlay's mind. He slowed to a halt, ten yards away, on the edge of the pool. Still the gang members did nothing but wait. 'Stay there,' Dinlay told them, taking big gulps of air after his helter-skelter dash, and waving a finger like an ancient schoolmaster dealing with a naughty class. They laughed at him.

Edeard burst out of Macoun Street. Directly to his left was the Outer Circle Canal, with the silver-blue bridge ahead, arching over the side of the pool directly into Golden Park. On his right, the buildings ended to provide a curving *alameda* round the side of Birmingham Pool. Neat stacks of crates were piled up above the various moorings, with shopkeepers and ge-monkeys sorting out their goods with the gondoliers. Tall weeping hasfol trees formed a long line between the edge of the pool and the *alameda*'s crescent facade, their blue and yellow tiger-stripe leaves starting to crisp with the end of summer. A lot of pedestrians were strolling around.

'Dinlay,' Edeard shouted as he ran as fast as he could towards his isolated squadmate.

Dinlay glanced round, a hand adjusting his glasses.

Arminel stepped out from behind one of the hasfol trees, fifteen yards from Dinlay. He had a revolver in his right hand. Edeard watched helplessly as Dinlay finally realized the danger, and began to turn. Arminel brought the pistol up.

'No!' Edeard bellowed at his adversary. 'It's me you want.'

Dinlay opened his mouth to cry out in horror.

Arminel fired. He was smiling as he pulled the trigger.

Dinlay's shield wasn't strong enough to ward off a pistol shot. Arminel's aim was excellent. The bullet struck Dinlay in the hip, just below his drosilk waistcoat. Half of the pedestrians around

Birmingham Pool yelped at the blast of pain flooding out from Dinlay. Then the vile heat of the bullet's penetration faded rapidly. Dinlay looked down disbelievingly at the blood pumping out of the wound. He collapsed.

Edeard was with him in seconds, falling to his knees, skidding into his limp friend. Dinlay's eyes were wide, he was panting in short gulps, one hand clasped over the bullet hole, skin covered in blood. 'I'm sorry,' he whimpered.

A mass of screaming had broken out along the *alameda*. People were racing for cover. Families hugged each other, cowering away from the gunman.

Right in the centre of all the commotion, Edeard heard the revolver's mechanism *snick*. He widened his shield to encompass Dinlay. The bullet smacked into his side, shunting them over the rough ground. But his shield held. He snapped his head round to snarl at a disconcerted Arminel. 'Not so fucking easy, is it?' he yelled defiantly. Arminel fired again. Edeard groaned in effort as the bullet hit his neck. The shield held. *Just.* Then someone else fired a shot.

Bastards. I knew this was an ambush.

Amazingly, his shield held. If anything it was easier to maintain now. His heart was pounding hard. Anger had washed every other sensation away, making it simple to concentrate on the shield, to see his mind's power, to channel it correctly.

Two more revolver shots thudded into his shield as he lay there, arms hugging Dinlay protectively. They shunted the pair of them a few inches over the ground, but that was all.

'Die, you little shit,' Arminel shouted.

Edeard felt the man's third hand shove against him. He wasn't nearly powerful enough to get through Edeard's shielding. Edeard laughed. Then another third hand was pushing, a third. The three gang members they'd chased joined in. Edeard gasped as he and Dinlay started to slither over the ground.

'Edeard,' Kanseen cried.

'Stay back,' he commanded.

The gang members gave a final push. Edeard and Dinlay were

propelled over the edge of the pool, and dropped three yards into the water. The impact broke Edeard's grip on Dinlay. He thrashed about just under the surface, trying to catch his friend again. Water occluded his farsight, making it difficult to perceive. He just made out Dinlay's wretched thoughts drifting down below him, close to extinction. His own clothes were saturated, weighing him down. It was relatively easy to swim downwards, following Dinlay's slow descent to the bottom of the pool.

'Edeard.' Dinlay's thoughts were weakening.

It was dark. Cold. Edeard could make out a shadowy mass, or maybe he was perceiving it. He pushed himself further down, kicking with boots as heavy as lead. His lungs were burning now, making every stroke painful. He would have called the city to help, but he knew it could do nothing. Water was pushing into his nostrils, scaring him.

His hand snagged something. Through the gloom he could see faint dots of light. Dinlay's polished tunic buttons! His fingers groped frantically and he got a grip on some fabric.

Now all I've got to do is get to the surface.

When he tilted his head up, he could see the silver-mirror surface. It seemed a long way above him. And his lungs didn't hurt quite so much any more. His vision was surrounded by red speckling, pulsing in time with his heart. When he kicked his legs they barely moved. His boots were pulling him down.

Oh, Lady, help.

Something knocked into his shoulder. His farsight perceived it as a slim black line.

'Edeard,' the combined longtalk of Kanseen, Macsen and Boyd shouted at him. 'Edeard, grab the pole.' They were a long way off.

The end of the punt pole thumped into his shoulder again. Edeard seized it. Abruptly he was moving upwards. It was a huge effort not to let go of Dinlay. Then the water was growing brighter.

He broke surface with an almighty gasp of air. Someone jumped in beside him, and held on to Dinlay. They were right beside a mooring platform. Hands clutched at his uniform, and he was hauled on to the planks, coughing and spluttering.

Kanseen's incredibly anxious face loomed large over him. 'Oh Lady. Edeard, are you okay?'

He nodded, which set off another bout of coughing. Hands slapped hard on his back as he rolled over on to his side, and vomited up a thin disgusting liquid.

Macsen and a couple of gondoliers were dragging Dinlay on to the platform, blood still pumping out of his hip wound. Boyd was in the water, his face pale.

'Dinlay,' Edeard called weakly.

'We've longshouted for a doctor,' Kanseen assured him. 'You just lie back.'

Edeard didn't. He watched Macsen start giving Dinlay the kiss of life. This was the third time his life had been struck by the force of anarchy and destruction. First the ambush in the forest on the way back from Witham. Then the death of Ashwell. Now this. And that was too many.

'No,' he spat. *Not again. I will not allow this to happen. People cannot live like this.*

'Edeard, sit back,' Kanseen ordered sternly.

'Where is he? Where's Arminel?'

'Stop it.'

He clambered to his feet, swaying slightly as he looked round, taking deep breaths. The edge of the pool was crowded with people, all looking down at the mooring platform. He turned towards Birmingham Pool itself. Most of the gondolas had come to a halt as the drama played out.

One was moving. Fast.

Edeard blinked the salty pool water from his eyes, sending his farsight lashing out.

Arminel was standing on the gondola's middle bench. He gave Edeard a rueful shrug, his thoughts glowing with a cheery regret. It was as if he'd lost a football game. Nothing more. Certainly nothing important. They'd play another game one day, and that time the result might be different.

Edeard's rage left him, dropping away like the water dripping off his soaking clothes. He felt eerily calm.

One of the gondoliers looking over Macsen's shoulder took a frightened step backwards.

'Edeard?' Kanseen said in a subdued voice.

He hadn't known such a thing was possible, he simply did it. There was no choice. As before, Arminel's gondola was moving too quickly. They'd never catch him, never bring him to justice. Edeard's third hand reached out to the water beside the mooring platform and steadied it.

'I'm finishing this,' he declared forcefully. 'One way or another.'

Edeard stepped on the patch of water he was controlling. An astonished gasp went up from the spectators around the edge of Birmingham Pool. Edeard grinned viciously, and took another step. Another. He moved his third hand's grip smoothly, always keeping the leading edge of the stabilized patch just ahead of himself.

Arminel's humour shattered. At the rear of the gondola, the two gondoliers stopped manoeuvring their punts and stared fearfully as Edeard walked across the pool towards them. There was absolute silence as he strode purposefully towards the craft. Every gondola in Birmingham Pool was now stationary. Gondoliers and passengers stared in awe and trepidation as Edeard walked past.

'Move!' Arminel yelled furiously at the gondoliers. 'Get us out of here.'

They didn't respond. The two gang members sitting on the bench with Arminel slowly put their hands up. They edged away from Arminel.

Edeard was ten yards away when Arminel dropped a hand to his waist where the revolver was tucked into his belt. He could sense the man's uncertainty, his fright. The animal backed into a corner. Nobody had any choices left now.

As he covered the last few yards to the gondola, Edeard opened his mind and longtalked with all his might. 'SO THAT

EVERYBODY KNOWS. SO THAT NO JUDGE OR LAWYER IS IN ANY DOUBT OF THIS DAY.' And he gifted them his sight.

Makkathran, from the Mayor in his Orchard Palace down to the sailors in the port district, saw a gondola with four men cowering, hands clamped over their ears. The fifth man stood straight, loathing on his face as his hand gripped the revolver sticking out of his belt. They felt Edeard's mouth move. 'Okay gang man, your time in this city is now over. If you think different, give it your best shot.'

Arminel brought the revolver up. Makkathran en masse flinched as the muzzle steadied not two feet from Edeard's eyes.

'Fuck you,' Arminel snarled. He pulled the trigger.

The single unified scream which rang out from the city was later said to be heard halfway across the Iguru Plain. When everyone gathered their breath, and realized they were still alive, they saw the bullet. It floated motionless six inches in front of Edeard's face.

Edeard's mouth moved again, this time into a thin smile. Arminel's expression was frozen in shock.

The last of the gifting allowed Makkathran's citizens to experience Edeard shaping his third hand into a fist. He slammed it forward into Arminel's face. Bone went *crunch* as the man's nose broke. Blood spurted out. His feet left the bench as he was thrown backwards. He landed with an almighty splash in the water, which closed over him.

'You're all under arrest,' Edeard announced.

It was pandemonium on the side of Birmingham Pool as the gondola made its steady way to the mooring platform where Kanseen, Boyd and Macsen waited. On the Jeavons side they were crammed fifteen deep around the edge. Frenzied kids were running over the blue and silver bridge from Golden Park, hanging over the railings, cheering and waving. Over a hundred constables stood behind the mooring platform waiting; half of them were Dinlay's family. People were still pouring out of the surrounding districts on to the *alameda* to see history as it unfolded. Bolder lads were shinning to the top of the hasfol trees to get a better view.

Edeard walked slowly behind the gondola, praying to the Lady that he wouldn't screw up now, that his telekinetic strength would hold out, and he didn't fall ignominiously back into the water. Out there in the crowd surrounding the pool he saw Setersis and Kavine standing in front of a big contingent of Silvarum market stall holders, leading the applause. A huge array of well-groomed family girls greeted him with shrill saucy laughter as they flashed their petticoats and bloomers. Isoix and his family were there. Evala, Nicolar, and all the girls from the dressmaker's, waving frantically and screaming to attract his attention. He even thought he saw Dybal and Bijulee laughing excitedly among the crowd, but by then he was definitely feeling tired.

The gondola's prow touched the mooring platform. Constables steadied it. Captain Ronark quickly took charge. Chae and several of the largest constables from Jeavons station handcuffed Arminel and his accomplices. A path was cleared across the *alameda*, and the prisoners marched back to the station.

Edeard finally stepped up on to the platform. His legs nearly gave out. He was trembling from exertion. Captain Ronark snapped to attention, and saluted him. Kanseen gave him a huge kiss to the delight of the crowd. 'You Lady-damned idiot,' she whispered into his ear. 'I'm so proud of you.' Macsen pounded his back. Boyd gave him a fierce hug.

'Dinlay?' Edeard asked.

'The doctors have him,' Macsen yelled about the thunderous sound of the crowd. 'He'll be okay. The bullet didn't hit anything vital. Not that he's got anything vital in that area.'

'You scared the living crap out of us,' Boyd said, wiping the tears from his eyes. 'What a stunt, you madman.'

'Look around you, Edeard,' Kanseen said. 'Make sure you see it all. This will be the day you tell your great-great-grandchildren about.'

'Wave to them, you dick,' Macsen ordered. He grabbed Edeard's hand, and held it high, waving and shouting wordlessly.

The cheer that erupted as Edeard grinned sheepishly up at the worshipful horde was scary in its power. The mental strength of so many people united in veneration was overwhelming, verging on a physical force. His grin broadened as Macsen swung him round so the other side of the *alameda* could see him.

'If there was an election today you'd be Mayor,' Boyd said.

'Listen to them,' Macsen said. 'They love you. They want you. You!' He laughed uproariously.

Edeard stared over at the blue and silver bridge, convinced the kids hanging over the railing would fall they were leaning out so far. They were chanting something. At each call, their fists punched the air in unison.

'What's that?' Edeard asked. 'What are they saying?'

'You,' Kanseen shouted back. 'They're calling for you.'

Then Edeard heard the cry in full, and laughed.

'Waterwalker,' the crowd chanted in adoration. 'Waterwalker. Waterwalker. Waterwalker.'

Timeline

1500 years between the Commonwealth Saga and the Void Trilogy

2384   First 'lifeboat' (a Brant Dynasty starship) leaves to found human colony outside Commonwealth

2384   Firewall project concluded, no further outposts of Prime aliens detected

2385   Barsoomians advocate Advancer genetic concept, declare Far Away politically independent from Commonwealth

2413   Last (23rd) original Dynasty lifeboat departs on colony founding flight

2403   Paula Myo wins final appeal in Senate Supreme Court to have Gene Yaohui serve a 1,100-year suspension sentence

2518   End of post-Starflyer War economic recession as new47 worlds approach completion, resettlement taxes reduced

2520   CST forms starship exploration division to scout new H-congruous worlds

2520–2532   Second47 populations emerge onto their new worlds

2545 onward	Use of large starships to establish Commonwealth 'External' worlds in phase 3–5 space, extending approximately 500 ly out from Earth
2547	The Cat establishes her Knights Guardian movement on Far Away
2550	Commonwealth Navy Exploration fleet founded to explore the galaxy beyond phase 5 space
2552–3450	Contact made with 47 sentient (physical stage) species across the galaxy
2560	Commonwealth Navy ship *Endeavour* circumnavigates galaxy, captained by Wilson Kime, discovery of the Void
2603	Navy discovers 7th High Angel type ship
2620	Raiel confirm their status as ancient galactic race who lost a war against the Void, builders of High Angel ships, which are trans-galactic arks
2652	Paula Myo arrests the Cat, riots on Far Away
2653	The Cat sentenced to 5,000 years in suspension
2833	Completion of ANA first stage on Earth. Grand Family members begin memory download into ANA rather than to SI.
2856	ANA begins to contact other post-physical entities in the galaxy
2867	Sheldon Dynasty gigalife project partially successful, first human body biononic supplements for regeneration and general iatrics
2872	Start of Higher humans, biononic supplements allowing a culture of slow-paced long life, rejection of commercial economics and old political ideologies
2880	Development of weapons biononics

2913	Earth begins absorption of 'mature' humans into ANA, the inward migration begins
2934	Knights Guardian adopt Higher biononic technology
2955	Phase one worlds now predominately Higher culture
2958	Contact with Hancher homeworld (Tochee-species) 8,640 light years away, on the other side of the Eagle Nebula (7,000 ly)
2967	First neoGuardian downloads memory into ANA
2973–3060	Commonwealth Navy helps defend Hancher homeworld against the Ocisen Empire expansion waves
2984	Formation of radical Highers who wish to convert the human race to Higher culture
2991	Establishment of the Protectorate, an anti-Higher movement, on External worlds
3001	Ozzie produces uniform neural entanglement effect, known as the gaiafield
3040	Commonwealth Navy Exploration Fleet joins Centurion Station, the Void observation project supervised by Raiel, a joint enterprise between over 30 alien species
3084	Non-incursion treaty agreed between Hancher homeworld and the Ocisen Empire
3088	Military assistance agreement inaugurated between Hancher homeworld and Commonwealth Navy, enforcing non-incursion
3120	ANA officially becomes Earth's government, planetary population fifty million (activated bodies) and falling

3150   Ellezelin settled, 420 ly from Earth, pro-cybernetic capitalist Advancer culture

3255   Radical Angel arrives on Anagaska, Inigo's conception

3290   Ellezelin opens wormhole to Tari 15 ly away, start of Ellezelin Free Market Zone

3320   Inigo goes to Centurion star system, his first dream

3324   Inigo settles on Ellezelin, founds Living Dream movement, begins construction of Makkathran2

3338   Ellezelin opens wormhole to Idlib

3340   Ellezelin opens wormhole to Lirno

3378   Ellezelin opens wormhole to Quhood

3407   Ozzie departs Commonwealth for The Spike to build a 'galactic dream'

3456   Living Dream movement has over 5 billion followers amid the External worlds, very strong across Ellezelin Free Market Zone.

3466   Ellezelin opens wormhole to Agra (last planet to be joined to the Core of the Free Market Zone)

3478   Living Dream becomes majority party in Ellezelin parliament (72 per cent), converts planet to theocracy, Makkathran2 becomes the planetary capital

3503   Gene Yaohui comes out of suspension, re-lifed in new Advancer/Higher body, settles on Tourakom at the boundary of External space, 520 ly from Earth

3520   Inigo 'rests' from public life, Cleric Council assumes guidance of Living Dream

3587   Fragments of Second Dream appear in the gaianet

3589   Ethan elected as Cleric Conservator, announces Pilgrimage